GLOBAL
MARKETING
MANAGEMENT

5th EDITION

A Casebook

John A. Quelch
Harvard Business School

•

Christopher A. Bartlett
Harvard Business School

THOMSON

SOUTH-WESTERN

Australia • Canada • Mexico • Singapore • Spain • United Kingdom • United States

Global Marketing Management:
A Casebook, 5e

John A. Quelch & Christopher A. Bartlett

VP/Editorial Director:
Jack W. Calhoun

VP/Editor-in-Chief:
Dave Shaut

Sr. Publisher:
Melissa S. Acuña

Executive Editor:
Neil Marquardt

Sr. Developmental Editor:
Susanna C. Smart

Marketing Manager:
Nicole C. Moore

Sr. Production Editor:
Elizabeth A. Shipp

Technology Project Editor:
Pam Wallace

Web Coordinator:
Karen L. Schaffer

Sr. Manufacturing Coordinator:
Diane Lohman

Production House:
GEX Publishing Services, Inc.

Art Director:
Stacy Jenkins Shirley

Printer:
Malloy, Inc.
Ann Arbor, Michigan

Internal Designer:
Design Matters

Cover Designer:
Design Matters

ISBN: 0-324-32284-4

Library of Congress Control Number: 2004118261

For more information about our products, contact us at:

Thomson Learning Academic Resource Center
1-800-423-0563

Thomson Higher Education
5191 Natorp Boulevard
Mason, OH 45040
USA

Asia (including India)
Thomson Learning
5 Shenton Way
#01-01 UIC Building
Singapore 068808

Australia/NewZealand
Thomson Learning Australia
102 Dodds Street
Southbank, Victoria 3006
Australia

Canada
Thomson Nelson
1120 Birchmount Road
Toronto, Ontario
M1K 5G4
Canada

UK/Europe/Middle East/Africa
Thomson Learning
High Holborn House
50/51 Bedford Row
London WC1R 4LR
United Kingdom

Latin America
Thomson Learning
Seneca, 53
Colonia Polanco
11560 Mexico
D.F.Mexico

Spain (including Portugal)
Thomson Paraninfo
Calle Magallanes, 25
28015 Madrid, Spain

Table of Contents

PREFACE

During the last quarter of the twentieth century, international business was shaken by a revolution in global competition unlike any previously experienced. As companies move through the twenty-first century, they need to be aware of the range of powerful, dynamic, and often conflicting forces shaping the emerging competitive environment. The globalization of markets, the increasing homogeneity of customer needs worldwide, and falling tariffs together mean that few companies can afford to remain focused on their domestic markets.

Managers responsible for marketing in a multinational or global enterprise must design appropriate marketing programs for each national market. To some extent, each country must be treated as a separate marketplace, because each has its own legal requirements, and business methods, and most have their own currencies. The dramatic changes in strategic thinking and organizational relationships has made the boom in alliances, consortia, and strategic partnerships a worldwide phenomenon.

Sensing, analyzing, and developing appropriate responses to the complex new demands of the expanded, global marketplace is difficult, and the greatest challenge comes in developing the organizational capabilities and managerial competencies to implement a clearly defined strategic intent. This book of cases provides real examples of these challenges.

SUPPLEMENTS

An Instructor's Resource Manual (ISBN 0-324-32364-6), which includes teaching notes for all the cases, is available. Please contact your Thomson sales representative to obtain a copy.

ACKNOWLEDGMENTS

We'd like to give our sincere thanks to those whose collaborations with us have made this fifth edition possible: Professors David Arnold, Ashish Nanda, and Das Narayandas of Harvard Business School, Dr. Christopher Lovelock and Professor Roderick White of the University of Western Ontario. Our research associates and MBA students—Michele Calpin, Claude Cohen, Barbara Feinberg, Yoshinori Fujikawa, Jamie Harper, Jean-Marie Ingea, Lisa Klein, Carin-Isabel Knoop, Nathalie Laidler, Diane Long, Afroze Mohammed, Takia Mahmood, Robin Root, and Kathleen Scharf—each aided in the field research of one or more cases and in the development of case drafts.

Thanks also to Dean Kim Clark and the Division of Research of Harvard Business School for the financial support that made possible the development of the materials included in this text. We also thank our Thomson editorial staff—Neil Marquardt, Melissa Acuña, Susan Smart, Libby Shipp, and Heather Churchman—for seeing the book through production.

Although many people have assisted us in preparing the book, we remain solely responsible for any inaccuracies or omissions. We wish our readers—whether they are managers, instructors, or students—success and enjoyment in grappling with the exciting challenges faced by the business protagonists in our cases, and we thank them for sharing their problems and experiences with us.

John A. Quelch
Harvard Business School

Christopher A. Bartlett
Harvard Business School

November 2004

John A. Quelch

John A. Quelch is senior associate dean for international development and Lincoln Filene Professor of Business Administration at Harvard Business School. Between 1998 and 2001 he was dean of London Business School. Before 1998, he was the Sebastian S. Kresge Professor of Marketing and co-chair of the marketing area at Harvard Business School.

Quelch is a long-standing student of global marketing and branding in emerging as well as developed markets. He is the author, co-author, or editor of twenty books, including The Global Market (2004), Global Marketing Management (4th edition, 1999), Cases in Advertising and Promotion Management (4th edition, 1996), and The Marketing Challenge of Europe 1992 (2nd edition, 1991). He has published more than fifty articles on marketing and public policy issues in leading management journals such as Harvard Business Review, McKinsey Quarterly, and Sloan Management Review.

Quelch serves as a nonexecutive director of WPP Group plc, the world's second-largest marketing services company. Since 2002, he has served pro bono as chairman of the Port Authority of Massachusetts. He serves as a nonexecutive director of Accion International, a leading microfinance lender, and is a member of the International Advisory Board of British-American Business Inc. He has been a consultant to more than fifty leading firms, including American Airlines, Apple Computer, AT&T, Coca-Cola, Colgate-Palmolive, Fidelity Investments, General Electric, Gillette, Hoffman LaRoche, Honeywell, IBM, Novartis, and Procter & Gamble.

Quelch was born in London, England, and was educated at Exeter College, Oxford University (BA and MA), the Wharton School of the University of Pennsylvania (MBA), the Harvard School of Public Health (MS), and Harvard Business School (DBA).

Christopher A. Bartlett

Christopher Bartlett is the Thomas D. Casserly, Jr. Professor of Business Administration at Harvard Graduate School of Business Administration. He received an economics degree from the University of Queensland, Australia (1964), and both the master's and doctorate degrees in business administration from Harvard University (1971 and 1979). Before joining the faculty of Harvard Business School, he was a marketing manager with Alcoa in Australia, a management consultant in McKinsey and Company's London office, and general manager at Baxter Laboratories' subsidiary company in France.

Since joining the faculty of Harvard Business School in 1979, Bartlett's interests have focused on the strategic and organizational challenges confronting managers in multinational corporations and on the effect of transformational change. He has published eight books, including (co-authored with Sumantra Ghoshal) Managing Across Borders: The Transnational Solution, reissued by Harvard Business School Press in a new edition in 1998 and named by the Financial Times as one of the fifty most influential business books of the century. It was also the winner of the Igor Ansoff Award for the best new work in strategic management and named one of the Best Business Books for the Millennium by Strategy + Business magazine. Both editions have been translated into more than ten languages. He has authored or co-authored more than fifty chapters and articles, which have appeared in journals such as Harvard Business Review, Sloan Management Review, Strategic Management Journal, Academy of Management Review, and Journal of International Business Studies. He has also researched and written more than 100 case studies and teaching notes.

Bartlett has been elected by his academic colleagues as a Fellow of both the Academy of Management and the Academy of International Business. In 2001, the International Management Division of the Academy of Management made him the recipient of its Distinguished Scholar Award. In addition to his academic responsibilities, he maintains ongoing consulting and board relationships with several large corporations.

Part 1

Designing Strategies for Global Competition

During the last quarter of the twentieth century, international business was shaken by a revolution in global competition unlike any previously experienced. The revolution rocked established multinationals such as Philips, Caterpillar, and ITT while providing the emerging basis for challengers such as Matsushita, Komatsu, and NEC to take them on. Yet even the forces of change that helped give birth to the Japanese competitive juggernaut of the 1980s are changing in dramatic ways. As companies head into the twenty-first century, they need to be aware of a range of powerful, dynamic, yet often conflicting forces shaping the emerging competitive environment.

FORCES FOR MULTIPLE-MARKET SCALE

Perhaps the most powerful force driving the globalization revolution has been the need for companies to capture economies at greater than national scale. One of the main triggers of this change was a technological revolution that swept across many industries, radically transforming both product designs and manufacturing processes. A classic example was the way in which the invention of the transistor and integrated circuit shook up all electronics-based businesses. In color TV set production, for example, minimum efficient scale jumped from 50,000 sets in the early 1970s to 500,000 sets a decade later. Around the world, scores of nationally focused companies that were unable to access new markets quickly enough were either swallowed up in acquisitions or forced to outsource their sets from global-scale competitors, or simply went out of business.

Having revolutionized plants worldwide, the forces of global scale next spread through the research and development laboratories. The technological revolution was putting equal pressure on companies' product development processes, forcing up the cost of new developments while simultaneously shortening product life cycles. In the telecommunications industry, for example, the arrival of powerful electronic switching technology forced companies to replace their old electromechanical designs with central network switches designed around the faster and cheaper digital technology. However, the cost of developing a digital switch exceeded $1 billion, and to recoup that investment, companies either had to dominate a huge market (like AT&T) or they had to have access to global markets. Among the latter, those that failed to leverage the global scale development investments, such as ITT, did not survive; those that did so, such as Ericsson, were able to develop new sources of competitive advantage.

CHANGING COMPETITIVE GAMES

It is important to note that these environmental forces did not trigger the radical change by themselves. They simply provided the potential for a company to capture a new source of competitive advantage, thereby changing the rules of the game. It was Matsushita's aggressive exploitation of the potential scale economies in color TVs that forced Philips, GE, and others to respond; and it was Ericsson's and NEC's ability to roll out their new digital switches around the world that challenged ITT's once-dominant position.

As competitors began taking the battle to the global marketplace, new competitive games emerged. Where once the overseas subsidiaries of multinational companies (MNCs) competed on a local-for-local basis with national companies and other MNC affiliates, some began playing a new, more sophisticated game. Leveraging the strong positions they developed in key markets (particularly at home), they began to increase their share of other major markets worldwide by pricing at or below cost. The strategy was particularly effective when they could force their main competitors with major market positions to follow their price lead, thereby draining the competitors' profit source. It was an approach strategists called "global chess" and economists called "cross-subsidization of markets." Politicians called it "dumping."

As many companies in large target markets learned at their cost, it was an extremely effective strategy. In the semiconductor industry, for example, Japanese exporters virtually eliminated U.S. manufacturers of memory chips in the pricing bloodbath that erupted in the mid-1980s. As became the standard response worldwide, such tactics were eventually checked by government-to-government negotiations, and occasional retaliations. Yet the new rules of the game had been established, and they still shape many global competitive battles today, albeit in less blatant form.

NEED FOR NATIONAL RESPONSIVENESS

The response of national governments to companies' competitive global strategies highlights another set of forces often overlooked in the current fascination with cross-market integration. Despite the emergence of regional economic and political entities such as ASEAN and the European Union, we are a long way from seeing the demise of the nation-state. And companies operating around the world still must recognize that it is the host government that frames the rules within which they must operate on a country-by-country basis. Frequently this requires them to make investments, transfer technology, or modify products in a way that is not consistent with their drive to achieve global scale or cross-border competitive advantage.

Beyond the political imperative, there are other powerful reasons why companies must adopt a flexible and responsive approach to local markets. Despite Professor Theodore Levitt's provocative 1983 statement that "the world's needs and desires have been irrevocably homogenized," wide national variances in consumer tastes and market structures still persist. Many behavioral differences, particularly those with strong ethnic, religious, or nationalistic roots, are deeply embedded and highly resistant to change. As the information age brought a network of electronic commerce to the most developed countries, market differences linked to a country's economic infrastructure have in many cases been diverging rather than converging. To compete effectively, truly global companies needed to develop the ability to sell products and services via the Internet in some markets, and through street bazaars in others.

THE RACE FOR WORLDWIDE INNOVATION

In the new game, developing cross-market scale, global chess positioning, and local flexibility are only the price of admission. In the knowledge-intensive, service-based information age, perhaps the most vital new skill a company must master is the ability to develop and diffuse innovations rapidly. This has led many companies to recognize that the key motivation for expanding abroad is no longer to access cheap labor or raw materials, to capture incremental scales, or even to build strategic positions on the global chessboard. Increasingly, the challenge is to tap into worldwide sources of information, knowledge, and expertise, the latest competitive intelligence, emerging technological trends, and scarce engineering skills, and use them to develop new products or capabilities that can be leveraged and adapted to market needs worldwide.

A classic example was provided by Procter and Gamble's development of its first truly global innovation, a liquid laundry detergent. Developed first in the United States in response to a competitive threat by Colgate's Wisk, the product was substantially improved by P&G Europe, where environmental legislation was challenging the use of phosphates. Then the Japanese sensed a market need for a liquid with cold-water washing power to respond to their market needs. And finally, another U.S. innovation to prevent redepositing of dirt was added. Coordinating all of these market inputs and technological capabilities, the company developed a new generation of products rolled out worldwide as Tide Liquid in the United States, Ariel Liquid in Europe, and Liquid Cheer in Japan. So successful was the process that P&G now sees its ability to develop and diffuse innovations globally as its prime source of competitive advantage.

BUILDING LAYERS OF COMPETITIVE ADVANTAGE

As these various environmental forces and competitive pressures interact, many companies are clinging to their old notions of developing a single dominant source of competitive advantage: low cost, differentiated, or niche. The reality in the emerging competitive environment is that such rules no longer apply. Recall how Toyota entered the U.S. market: first offering low-cost automobiles produced on a global scale in Toyota City, Japan; then developing the ability to play a sophisticated game of global chess, forcing U.S. manufacturers such as Chrysler into crisis; then complying with government pressures to build local plants and market pressures to develop products more adaptable to the U.S. market; and finally, picking off the top-end niches by developing and diffusing innovations on a global basis.

The global strategic challenge in the new millennium will be to continually develop new layers of competitive advantage. It is a challenge that one manager described as "learning how to walk, chew gum, and whistle at the same time."

Philips versus Matsushita: A New Century, a New Round

Throughout their long histories, N.V. Philips (Netherlands) and Matsushita Electric (Japan) had followed very different strategies and emerged with very different organizational capabilities. Philips built its success on a worldwide portfolio of responsive national organizations while Matsushita based its global competitiveness on its centralized, highly efficient operations in Japan.

During the 1990s, both companies experienced major challenges to their historic competitive positions and organizational models, and at the end of the decade, both companies were struggling to reestablish their competitiveness. At the turn of the millennium, new CEOs at both companies were implementing yet another round of strategic initiatives and organizational restructurings. Observers wondered how the changes would affect their long-running competitive battle.

PHILIPS: BACKGROUND

In 1892, Gerard Philips and his father opened a small light-bulb factory in Eindhoven, Holland. When their venture almost failed, they recruited Gerard's brother, Anton, an excellent salesman and manager. By 1900, Philips was the third largest light-bulb producer in Europe.

From its founding, Philips developed a tradition of caring for workers. In Eindhoven it built company houses, bolstered education, and paid its employees so well that other local employers complained. When Philips incorporated in 1912, it set aside 10% of profits for employees.

This case was prepared by Professor Christopher A. Bartlett.

Copyright © 2001 by the President and Fellows of Harvard College. Harvard Business School case 9-302-049.

Technological Competence and Geographic Expansion

While larger electrical products companies were racing to diversify, Philips made only light-bulbs. This one-product focus and Gerard's technological prowess enabled the company to create significant innovations. Company policy was to scrap old plants and use new machines or factories whenever advances were made in new production technology. Anton wrote down assets rapidly and set aside substantial reserves for replacing outdated equipment. Philips also became a leader in industrial research, creating physics and chemistry labs to address production problems as well as more abstract scientific ones. The labs developed a tungsten metal filament bulb that was a great commercial success and gave Philips the financial strength to compete against its giant rivals.

Holland's small size soon forced Philips to look beyond its Dutch borders for enough volume to mass produce. In 1899, Anton hired the company's first export manager, and soon the company was selling into such diverse markets as Japan, Australia, Canada, Brazil, and Russia. In 1912, as the electric lamp industry began to show signs of overcapacity, Philips started building sales organizations in the United States, Canada, and France. All other functions remained highly centralized in Eindhoven. In many foreign countries Philips created local joint ventures to gain market acceptance.

In 1919, Philips entered into the Principal Agreement with General Electric, giving each company the use of the other's patents. The agreement also divided the world into "three spheres of influence": General Electric would control North America; Philips would control Holland; but both companies agreed to compete freely in the rest of the world.

(General Electric also took a 20% stake in Philips.) After this time, Philips began evolving from a highly centralized company, whose sales were conducted through third parties, to a decentralized sales organization with autonomous marketing companies in 14 European countries, China, Brazil, and Australia.

During this period, the company also broadened its product line significantly. In 1918, it began producing electronic vacuum tubes; eight years later its first radios appeared, capturing a 20% world market share within a decade; and during the 1930s, Philips began producing X-ray tubes. The Great Depression brought with it trade barriers and high tariffs, and Philips was forced to build local production facilities to protect its foreign sales of these products.

PHILIPS: ORGANIZATIONAL DEVELOPMENT

One of the earliest traditions at Philips was a shared but competitive leadership by the commercial and technical functions. Gerard, an engineer, and Anton, a businessman, began a subtle competition where Gerard would try to produce more than Anton could sell and vice versa. Nevertheless, the two agreed that strong research was vital to Philips' survival.

During the late 1930s, in anticipation of the impending war, Philips transferred its overseas assets to two trusts, British Philips and the North American Philips Corporation; it also moved most of its vital research laboratories to Redhill in Surrey, England, and its top management to the United States. Supported by the assets and resources transferred abroad, and isolated from their parent, the individual country organizations became more independent during the war.

Because waves of Allied and German bombing had pummeled most of Philips' industrial plant in the Netherlands, the management board decided to build the postwar organization on the strengths of the national organizations (NOs). Their greatly increased self-sufficiency during the war had allowed most to become adept at responding to country-specific market conditions—a capability that became a valuable asset in the postwar era. For example, when international wrangling precluded any agreement on three competing television transmission standards (PAL, SECAM, and NTSC), each nation decided which to adopt. Furthermore, consumer preferences and economic conditions varied: in some countries, rich, furniture-encased TV sets were the norm; in others, sleek, contemporary models dominated the market. In the United Kingdom, the only way to penetrate the market was to establish a rental business; in richer countries, a major marketing challenge was overcoming elitist prejudice against television. In this environment, the independent NOs had a great advantage in being able to sense and respond to the differences.

Eventually, responsiveness extended beyond adaptive marketing. As NOs built their own technical capabilities, product development often became a function of local market conditions. For example, Philips of Canada created the company's first color TV; Philips of Australia created the first stereo TV; and Philips of the United Kingdom created the first TVs with teletext.

While NOs took major responsibility for financial, legal, and administrative matters, fourteen product divisions (PDs), located in Eindhoven, were formally responsible for development, production, and global distribution. (In reality, the NOs' control of assets and the PDs' distance from the operations often undercut this formal role.) The research function remained independent and, with continued strong funding, set up eight separate laboratories in Europe and the United States.

While the formal corporate-level structure was represented as a type of geographic/product matrix, it was clear that NOs had the real power. NOs reported directly to the management board, which Philips enlarged from 4 members to 10 to ensure that top management remained in contact with and control of the highly autonomous NOs. Each NO also regularly sent envoys to Eindhoven to represent its interests. Top management, most of whom had careers that included multiple foreign tours of duty, made frequent overseas visits to the NOs. In 1954, the board established the International Concern Council to formalize regular meetings with the heads of all major NOs.

Within the NOs, the management structure mimicked the legendary joint technical and commercial leadership of the two Philips brothers. Most were led by a technical manager and a commercial manager. In some locations, a finance manager filled out the top management triad that typically reached key decisions collectively. This cross-functional coordination capability was reflected down through the NOs in front-line product teams, product-group-level management teams, and at the senior management committee of the NOs' top commercial, technical, and financial managers.

The overwhelming importance of foreign operations to Philips, the commensurate status of the NOs within the corporate hierarchy, and even the cosmopolitan appeal of many of the offshore subsidiaries' locations encouraged many Philips managers to take extended foreign tours of duty, working in a series of two- or three-year posts. This elite group of expatriate managers identified strongly with each other and with the NOs as a group and had no difficulty representing their strong, country-oriented views to corporate management.

PHILIPS: ATTEMPTS AT REORGANIZATION

In the late 1960s, the creation of the Common Market eroded trade barriers within Europe and diluted the rationale for maintaining independent, country-level subsidiaries. New transistor- and printed-circuit-based technologies demanded larger production runs than most national plants could justify, and many of Philips' competitors were moving production of electronics to new facilities in low-wage areas in East Asia and Central and South America. Despite its many technological innovations, Philips' ability to bring products to market began to falter. In the 1960s, the company invented the audiocassette but let its Japanese competitors capture the mass market. A decade later, its R&D group developed the V2000 videocassette format—superior technically to Sony's Beta or Matsushita's VHS—but was forced to abandon it when North American Philips decided to outsource, brand, and sell a VHS product which it manufactured under license from Matsushita.

Over three decades, seven chairmen experimented with reorganizing the company to deal with its growing problems. Yet, entering the new millennium, Philips' financial performance remained poor and its global competitiveness was still in question. (See Exhibits 1 and 2.)

Van Riemsdijk and Rodenburg Reorganizations, 1970s

Concerned about what one magazine described as "continued profitless progress," newly appointed CEO Hendrick van Riemsdijk created an organization committee to prepare a policy paper on the division of responsibilities between the PDs and the NOs. Their report, dubbed the "Yellow Booklet," outlined the disadvantages of Philips' matrix organization in 1971:

> Without an agreement [defining the relationship between national organizations and product divisions], it is impossible to determine in any given situation which of the two parties is responsible. . . . As operations become increasingly complex, an organizational form of this type will only lower the speed of reaction of an enterprise.

On the basis of this report, van Riemsdijk proposed rebalancing the managerial relationships between PDs and NOs—"tilting the matrix" in his words—to allow Philips to decrease the number of products marketed, build scale by concentrating production, and increase the flow of goods among national organizations. He proposed closing the least efficient local plants and converting the best into International Production Centers (IPCs), each supplying many NOs. In so doing, van Riemsdijk hoped that PD managers would gain control over manufacturing operations. Due to the political and organizational difficulty of closing local plants, however, implementation was slow.

In the late 1970s, his successor CEO, Dr. Rodenburg, continued this thrust. Several IPCs were established, but the NOs seemed as powerful and independent as ever. He furthered matrix simplification by replacing the dual commercial and technical leadership with single management at both the corporate and national organizational levels. Yet the power struggles continued.

Wisse Dekker Reorganization, 1982

Unsatisfied with the company's slow response and concerned by its slumping financial performance, upon becoming CEO in 1982, Wisse Dekker outlined a new initiative. Aware of the cost advantage of Philips' Japanese counterparts, he closed inefficient operations—particularly in Europe where 40 of the company's more than 200 plants were shut. He focused on core operations by selling some businesses (for example, welding, energy cables, and furniture) while acquiring an interest in Grundig and Westinghouse's North American lamp activities. Dekker also supported technology-sharing agreements and entered alliances in offshore manufacturing.

To deal with the slow-moving bureaucracy, he continued his predecessor's initiative to replace dual leadership with

Exhibit 1   Philips Group Summary Financial Data, 1970–2000 (millions of guilders unless otherwise stated)

	2000	1995	1990	1985	1980	1975	1970
Net sales	F83,437	F64,462	F55,764	F60,045	F36,536	F27,115	F15,070
Income from operations (excluding restructuring)	NA	4,090	2,260	3,075	1,577	1,201	1,280
Income from operations (including restructuring)	9,434	4,044	-2,389	N/A	N/A	N/A	N/A
As a percentage of net sales	11.3%	6.3%	-4.3%	5.1%	4.3%	4.5%	8.5%
Income after taxes	12,559	2,889	F-4,447	F1,025	F532	F341	F446
Net income from normal business operations	NA	2,684	-4,526	n/a	328	347	435
Stockholders' equity (common)	49,473	14,055	11,165	16,151	12,996	10,047	6,324
Return on stockholders' equity	42.8%	20.2%	-30.2%	5.6%	2.7%	3.6%	7.3%
Distribution per common share, par value F10 (in guilders)	F2.64	F1.60	F0.0	F2.00	F1.80	F1.40	F1.70
Total assets	86,114	54,683	51,595	52,883	39,647	30,040	19,088
Inventories as a percentage of net sales	13.9%	18.2%	20.7%	23.2%	32.8%	32.9%	35.2%
Outstanding trade receivables in month's sales	1.5	1.6	1.6	2.0	3.0	3.0	2.8
Current ratio	1.2	1.6	1.4	1.6	1.7	1.8	1.7
Employees at year-end (in thousands)	219	265	273	346	373	397	359
Wages, salaries and other related costs	NA	NA	F17,582	F21,491	F15,339	F11,212	F5,890
Exchange rate (period end; guilder/$)	2.34	1.60	1.69	2.75	2.15	2.69	3.62
Selected data in millions of dollars:							
Sales	$35,253	$40,039	$33,018	$21,802	$16,993	$10,098	$4,163
Operating profit	3,986	2,512	1,247	988	734	464	NA
Pretax income	5,837	2,083	-2,380	658	364	256	NA
Net income	5,306	1,667	-2,510	334	153	95	120
Total assets	35,885	32,651	30,549	19,202	18,440	11,186	5,273
Shareholders' equity (common)	20,238	8,784	6,611	5,864	6,044	3,741	1,747

Source: Annual reports; Standard & Poors' *Compustat*; Moody's Industrial and International Manuals.
Note: Exchange rate 12/31/00 was Euro/US$: 1.074

	2000		1995		1990		1985	
Net Sales by Product Segment:								
Lighting	F 11,133	13%	F 8,353	13%	F 7,026	13%	F 7,976	12%
Consumer electronics	32,357	39	22,027	34	25,400	46	16,906	26
Domestic appliances	4,643	6	--	--	--	--	6,644	10
Professional products/Systems	--	--	11,562	18	13,059	23	17,850	28
Components/Semiconductors	23,009	28	10,714	17	8,161	15	11,620	18
Software/Services	--	--	9,425	15	--	--	--	--
Medical systems	6,679	8	--	--	--	--	--	--
Origin	1,580	2	--	--	--	--	--	--
Miscellaneous	4,035	5	2,381	4	2,118	4	3,272	5
Total	83,437	100%	64,462	100%	F 55,764	100%	F 64,266	100%
Operating Income by Sector:								
Lighting	1,472	16%	983	24%	419	18%	F 910	30%
Consumer electronics	824	9	167	4	1,499	66	34	1
Domestic appliances	632	7	--	--	--	--	397	13
Professional products/Systems	--	--	157	4	189	8	1,484	48
Components/Semiconductors	4,220	45	2,233	55	-43	-2	44	1
Software/Services	--	--	886	22	--	--	--	--
Medical systems	372	4	--	--	--	--	--	--
Origin	2,343	25	--	--	--	--	--	--
Miscellaneous	-249	-3	423	10	218	10	200	7
Increase not attributable to a sector	-181	-2	(805)	(20)	-22	-1	6	0
Total	9,434	100%	4,044	100%	2,260	100%	F 3,075	100%

Source: Annual reports

Notes:

Conversion rate (12/31/00): 1 Euro: 2.20371 Dutch Guilders

Totals may not add due to rounding.

Product sector sales after 1988 are external sales only; therefore, no eliminations are made; sector sales before 1988 include sales to other sectors; therefore, eliminations are made.

Data are not comparable to consolidated financial summary due to restating.

single general managers. He also continued to "tilt the matrix" by giving PDs formal product management responsibility, but leaving NOs responsible for local profits. And, he energized the management board by reducing its size, bringing on directors with strong operating experience, and creating subcommittees to deal with difficult issues. Finally, Dekker redefined the product planning process, incorporating input from the NOs, but giving global PDs the final decision on long-range direction. Still sales declined and profits stagnated.

Van der Klugt Reorganization, 1987

When Cor van der Klugt succeeded Dekker as chairman in 1987, Philips had lost its long-held consumer electronics leadership position to Matsushita, and was one of only two non-Japanese companies in the world's top ten. Its net profit margins of 1% to 2% not only lagged behind General Electric's 9%, but even its highly aggressive Japanese competitors' slim 4%. Van der Klugt set a profit objective of 3% to 4% and made beating the Japanese companies a top priority.

As van der Klugt reviewed Philips' strategy, he designated various businesses as core (those that shared related technologies, had strategic importance, or were technical leaders) and non-core (stand-alone businesses that were not targets for world leadership and could eventually be sold if required). Of the four businesses defined as core, three were strategically linked: components, consumer electronics, and telecommunications and data systems. The fourth, lighting, was regarded as strategically vital because its cash flow funded development. The non-core businesses included domestic appliances and medical systems which van der Klugt spun off into joint ventures with Whirlpool and GE, respectively.

In continuing efforts to strengthen the PDs relative to the NOs, van der Klugt restructured Philips around the four core global divisions rather than the former 14 PDs. This allowed him to trim the management board, appointing the displaced board members to a new policy-making Group Management Committee. Consisting primarily of PD heads and functional chiefs, this body replaced the old NO-dominated International Concern Council. Finally, he sharply reduced the 3,000-strong headquarters staff, reallocating many of them to the PDs.

To link PDs more directly to markets, van der Klugt dispatched many experienced product-line managers to Philips' most competitive markets. For example, management of the digital audio tape and electric-shaver product lines were relocated to Japan, while the medical technology and domestic appliances lines were moved to the United States.

Such moves, along with continued efforts at globalizing product development and production efforts, required that the parent company gain firmer control over NOs, especially the giant North American Philips Corp. (NAPC). Although Philips had obtained a majority equity interest after World War II, it was not always able to make the U.S. company respond to directives from the center, as the V2000 VCR incident showed. To prevent replays of such experiences, in 1987 van der Klugt repurchased publicly owned NAPC shares for $700 million.

Reflecting the growing sentiment among some managers that R&D was not market oriented enough, van der Klugt halved spending on basic research to about 10% of total R&D. To manage what he described as "R&D's tendency to ponder the fundamental laws of nature," he made R&D the direct responsibility of the businesses being supported by the research. This required that each research lab become focused on specific business areas (see Exhibit 3).

Finally, van der Klugt continued the effort to build efficient, specialized, multi-market production facilities by closing 75 of the company's 420 remaining plants worldwide. He also eliminated 38,000 of its 344,000 employees—21,000 through divesting businesses, shaking up the myth of lifetime employment at the company. He anticipated that all these restructurings would lead to a financial recovery by 1990. Unanticipated losses for that year, however—more than 4.5 billion Dutch guilders ($2.5 billion)—provoked a class-action law suit by angry American investors, who alleged that positive projections by the company had been misleading. In a surprise move, on May 14, 1990, van der Klugt and half of the management board were replaced.

Timmer Reorganization, 1990

The new president, Jan Timmer, had spent most of his 35-year Philips career turning around unprofitable businesses. With rumors of a takeover or a government bailout swirling, he met with his top 100 managers and distributed a hypothetical—but fact-based—press release announcing that Philips was bankrupt. "So what action can you take this weekend?" he challenged them.

Under "Operation Centurion," headcount was reduced by 68,000 or 22% over the next 18 months, earning Timmer the nickname "The Butcher of Eindhoven." Because European laws required substantial compensation for

Exhibit 3   Philips Research Labs by Location and Specialty, 1987

Location	Size (staff)	Specialty
Eindhoven, The Netherlands	2,000	Basic research, electronics, manufacturing technology
Redhill, Surrey, England	450	Microelectronics, television, defense
Hamburg, Germany	350	Communications, office equipment, medical imaging
Aachen, W. Germany	250	Fiber optics, X-ray systems
Paris, France	350	Microprocessors, chip materials, design
Brussels	50	Artificial intelligence
Briarcliff Manor, New York	35	Optical systems, television, superconductivity, defense
Sunnyvale, California	150	Integrated circuits

Source: Philips, in *Business Week*, March 21, 1988, p. 156.

layoffs—Eindhoven workers received 15 months' pay, for example—the first round of 10,000 layoffs alone cost Philips $700 million. To spread the burden around the globe and to speed the process, Timmer asked his PD managers to negotiate cuts with NO managers. According to one report, however, country managers were "digging in their heels to save local jobs." But the cuts came—many from overseas operations. In addition to the job cuts, Timmer vowed to "change the way we work." He established new performance rules and asked hundreds of top managers to sign contracts that committed them to specific financial goals. Those who broke those contracts were replaced—often with outsiders.

To focus resources further, Timmer sold off various businesses including integrated circuits to Matsushita, minicomputers to Digital, defense electronics to Thomson and the remaining 53% of appliances to Whirlpool. Yet profitability was still well below the modest 4% on sales he promised. In particular, consumer electronics lagged with slow growth in a price-competitive market. The core problem was identified by a 1994 McKinsey study that estimated that value added per hour in Japanese consumer electronic factories was still 68% above that of European plants. In this environment, most NO managers kept their heads down, using their distance from Eindhoven as their defense against the ongoing rationalization.

After three years of cost-cutting, in early 1994 Timmer finally presented a new growth strategy to the board. His plan was to expand software, services, and multimedia to become 40% of revenues by 2000. He was betting on Philips' legendary innovative capability to restart the growth engines. Earlier, he had recruited Frank Carrubba, Hewlett-Packard's director of research, and encouraged him to focus on developing 15 core technologies. The list, which included interactive compact disc (CD-i), digital compact cassettes (DCC), high definition television (HDTV), and multimedia software, was soon dubbed "the president's projects." But his earlier divestment of some of Philips' truly high-tech businesses and a 37% cut in R&D personnel left the company with few who understood the technology of the new priority businesses.

By 1996, it was clear that Philips' HDTV technology would not become industry standard, that its DCC gamble had lost out to Sony's Minidisc, and that CD-i was a marketing failure. While costs were lower, so too was morale, particularly among middle management. Critics claimed that the company's drive for cost-cutting and standardization had led it to ignore new worldwide market demands for more segmented products and higher consumer service.

Boonstra Reorganization, 1996

When Timmer stepped down in October 1996, the board replaced him with a radical choice for Philips—an outsider whose expertise was in marketing and Asia rather than technology and Europe. Cor Boonstra was a 58-year-old Dutchman whose years as CEO of Sara Lee, the U.S. consumer products firm, had earned him a reputation as a hard-driving marketing genius. Joining Philips in 1994, he headed the Asia Pacific region and the lighting division before being tapped as CEO.

Unencumbered by tradition, he immediately announced strategic sweeping changes designed to reach his target of increasing return on net assets from 17% to 24% by 1999. "There are no taboos, no sacred cows," he said. "The bleeders must be turned around, sold, or closed." Within three years, he had sold off 40 of Philips' 120 major businesses—including such well known units as Polygram and Grundig. He also initiated a major worldwide restructuring, promising to transform a structure he described as "a plate of spaghetti" into "a neat row of asparagus." He said:

> How can we compete with the Koreans? They don't have 350 companies all over the world. Their factory in Ireland covers Europe and their manufacturing facility in Mexico serves North America. We need a more structured and simpler manufacturing and marketing organization to achieve a cost pattern in line with those who do not have our heritage. This is still one of the biggest issues facing Philips.

Within a year, 3,100 jobs were eliminated in North America and 3,000 employees were added in Asia Pacific, emphasizing Boonstra's determination to shift production to low-wage countries and his broader commitment to Asia. And after three years, he had closed 100 of the company's 356 factories worldwide. At the same time, he replaced the company's 21 PDs with 7 divisions, but shifted day-to-day operating responsibility to 100 business units, each responsible for its profits worldwide. It was a move designed to finally eliminate the old PD/NO matrix. Finally, in a move that shocked most employees, he announced that the 100-year-old Eindhoven headquarters would be relocated to Amsterdam with only 400 of the 3,000 corporate positions remaining.

By early 1998, he was ready to announce his new strategy. Despite early speculation that he might abandon consumer electronics, he proclaimed it as the center of Philips' future. Betting on the "digital revolution," he planned to focus on established technologies such as cellular phones (through a joint venture with Lucent), digital TV, digital videodisc, and web TV. Furthermore, he committed major resources to marketing, including a 40% increase in advertising to raise awareness and image of the Philips brand and de-emphasize most of the 150 other brands it supported worldwide—from Magnavox TVs to Norelco shavers to Marantz stereos.

While not everything succeeded (the Lucent cell phone JV collapsed after nine months, for example), overall performance improved significantly in the late 1990s. By 1999, Boonstra was able to announce that he had achieved his objective of a 24% return on net assets.

Kleisterlee Reorganization, 2001

In May 2001, Boonstra passed the CEO's mantle to Gerard Kleisterlee, a 54-year-old engineer (and career Philips man) whose turnaround of the components business had earned him a board seat only a year earlier. Believing that Philips had finally turned around, the board challenged Kleisterlee to grow sales by 10% annually and earnings 15%, while increasing return on assets to 30%.

Despite its stock trading at a steep discount to its breakup value, Philips' governance structure and Dutch legislation made a hostile raid all but impossible. Nonetheless, Kleisterlee described the difference as "a management discount" and vowed to eliminate it. The first sign of restructuring came within weeks, when mobile phone production was outsourced to CEC of China. Then, in August, Kleisterlee announced an agreement with Japan's Funai Electric to take over production of its VCRs, resulting in the immediate closure of the European production center in Austria and the loss of 1,000 jobs. The CEO then acknowledged that he was seeking partners to take over the manufacturing of some of its other mass-produced items such as television sets.

In mid-2001, a slowing economy resulted in the company's first quarterly loss since 1996 and a reversal of the prior year's strong positive cash flow. Many felt that these growing financial pressures—and shareholders' growing impatience—were finally leading Philips to recognize that its best hope of survival was to outsource even more of its basic manufacturing and become a technology developer and global marketer. They believed it was time to recognize that its 30-year quest to build efficiency into its global operations had failed.

MATSUSHITA: BACKGROUND

In 1918, Konosuke Matsushita (or "KM" as he was affectionately known), a 23-year-old inspector with the Osaka Electric Light Company, invested ¥100 to start production of double-ended sockets in his modest home. The company grew rapidly, expanding into battery-powered lamps, electric irons, and radios. On May 5, 1932, Matsushita's 14th anniversary, KM announced to his 162 employees a 250-year corporate plan broken into 25-year sections, each to be carried out by successive generations. His plan was codified in a company creed and in the "Seven Spirits of Matsushita" (see Exhibit 4), which, along with the company song, continued to be woven into morning assemblies worldwide and provided the basis of the "cultural and spiritual training" all new employees received during their first seven months with the company.

In the post-war boom, Matsushita introduced a flood of new products: TV sets in 1952; transistor radios in 1958; color TVs, dishwashers, and electric ovens in 1960. Capitalizing on its broad line of 5,000 products (Sony produced 80), the company opened 25,000 domestic retail outlets. With more than six times the outlets of rival Sony, the ubiquitous "National Shops" represented 40% of

---

Exhibit 4   Matsushita Creed and Philosophy (Excerpts)

Creed

Through our industrial activities, we strive to foster progress, to promote the general welfare of society, and to devote ourselves to furthering the development of world culture.

Seven Spirits of Matsushita

Service through Industry
Fairness
Harmony and Cooperation
Struggle for Progress
Courtesy and Humility
Adjustment and Assimilation
Gratitude

KM's Business Philosophy (Selected Quotations)

"The purpose of an enterprise is to contribute to society by supplying goods of high quality at low prices in ample quantity."

"Profit comes in compensation for contribution to society. . . . [It] is a result rather than a goal."

"The responsibility of the manufacturer cannot be relieved until its product is disposed of by the end user."

"Unsuccessful business employs a wrong management. You should not find its causes in bad fortune, unfavorable surroundings or wrong timing."

"Business appetite has no self-restraining mechanism. . . . When you notice you have gone too far, you must have the courage to come back."

Source: "Matsushita Electric Industrial (MEI) in 1987," Harvard Business School Case No. 388-144.

appliance stores in Japan in the late 1960s. These not only provided assured sales volume, but also gave the company direct access to market trends and consumer reaction. When post-war growth slowed, however, Matsushita had to look beyond its expanding product line and excellent distribution system for growth. After trying many tactics to boost sales—even sending assembly line workers out as door-to-door salesmen—the company eventually focused on export markets.

The Organization's Foundation: Divisional Structure

Plagued by ill health, KM wished to delegate more authority than was typical in Japanese companies. In 1933, Matsushita became the first Japanese company to adopt the divisional structure, giving each division clearly defined profit responsibility for its product. In addition to creating a "small business" environment, the product division structure generated internal competition that spurred each business to drive growth by leveraging its technology to develop new products. After the innovating division had earned substantial profits on its new product, however, company policy was to spin it off as a new division to maintain the "hungry spirit."

Under the "one-product-one-division" system, corporate management provided each largely self-sufficient division with initial funds to establish its own development, production, and marketing capabilities. Corporate treasury operated like a commercial bank, reviewing divisions' loan requests for which it charged slightly higher-than-market interest, and accepting deposits on their excess funds. Divisional profitability was determined after deductions for central services such as corporate R&D and interest on internal borrowings. Each division paid 60% of earnings to headquarters and financed all additional working capital and fixed asset requirements from the retained 40%. Transfer prices were based on the market and settled through the treasury on normal commercial terms. KM expected uniform performance across the company's 36 divisions, and division managers whose operating profits fell below 4% of sales for two successive years were replaced.

While basic technology was developed in a central research laboratory (CRL), product development and engineering occurred in each of the product divisions. Matsushita intentionally under-funded the CRL, forcing it to compete for additional funding from the divisions. Annually, the CRL publicized its major research projects to the product divisions, which then provided funding in exchange for technology for marketable applications. While it was rarely the innovator, Matsushita was usually very fast to market—earning it the nickname "Manishita," or copycat.

MATSUSHITA: INTERNATIONALIZATION

Although the establishment of overseas markets was a major thrust of the second 25 years in the 250-year plan, in an overseas trip in 1951 KM had been unable to find any American company willing to collaborate with Matsushita. The best he could do was a technology exchange and licensing agreement with Philips. Nonetheless, the push to internationalize continued.

Expanding Through Color TV

In the 1950s and 1960s, trade liberalization and lower shipping rates made possible a healthy export business built on black and white TV sets. In 1953, the company opened its first overseas branch office—the Matsushita Electric Corporation of America (MECA). With neither a distribution network nor a strong brand, the company could not access traditional retailers, and had to resort to selling its products under their private brands through mass merchandisers and discounters.

During the 1960s, pressure from national governments in developing countries led Matsushita to open plants in several countries in Southeast Asia and Central and South America. As manufacturing costs in Japan rose, Matsushita shifted more basic production to these low-wage countries, but almost all high-value components and subassemblies were still made in its scale-intensive Japanese plants. By the 1970s, protectionist sentiments in the West forced the company to establish assembly operations in the Americas and Europe. In 1972, it opened a plant in Canada; in 1974, it bought Motorola's TV business and started manufacturing its Quasar brand in the United States; and in 1976, it built a plant in Cardiff, Wales, to supply the Common Market.

Building Global Leadership Through VCRs

The birth of the videocassette recorder (VCR) propelled Matsushita into first place in the consumer electronics industry during the 1980s. Recognizing the potential mass-market appeal of the VCR—developed by Californian broadcasting company, Ampex, in 1956—engineers at Matsushita began developing VCR technology. After six years of development work, Matsushita launched its commercial broadcast video recorder in 1964, and introduced a consumer version two years later.

In 1975, Sony introduced the technically superior "Betamax" format, and the next year JVC launched a competing "VHS" format. Under pressure from MITI, the government's industrial planning ministry, Matsushita agreed to give up its own format and adopt the established VHS standard. During Matsushita's 20 years of VCR product development, various members of the VCR research team spent most of their careers working together, moving from central labs to the product divisions' development labs and eventually to the plant.

The company quickly built production to meet its own needs as well as those of OEM customers like GE, RCA, and Zenith, who decided to forego self-manufacture and outsource to the low-cost Japanese. Between 1977 and 1985, capacity increased 33-fold to 6.8 million units. (In parallel,

the company aggressively licensed the VHS format to other manufacturers, including Hitachi, Sharp, Mitsubishi and, eventually, Philips.) Increased volume enabled Matsushita to slash prices 50% within five years of product launch, while simultaneously improving quality. By the mid-1980s, VCRs accounted for 30% of total sales—over 40% of overseas revenues—and provided 45% of profits.

Changing Systems and Controls

In the mid-1980s, Matsushita's growing number of overseas companies reported to the parent in one of two ways: wholly owned, single-product global plants reported directly to the appropriate product division, while overseas sales and marketing subsidiaries and overseas companies producing a broad product line for local markets reported to Matsushita Electric Trading Company (METC), a separate legal entity. (See Exhibit 5 for METC's organization.)

Exhibit 5   Organization of METC, 1985

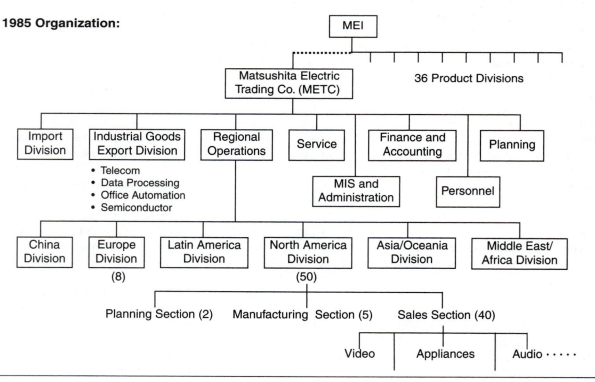

Source: Harvard Business School Case No. 388-144.

Note: ( ) = number of people.

Throughout the 1970s, the central product divisions maintained strong operating control over their offshore production units. Overseas operations used plant and equipment designed by the parent company, followed manufacturing procedures dictated by the center, and used materials from Matsushita's domestic plants. Growing trends toward local sourcing, however, gradually weakened the divisions' direct control. By the 1980s, instead of controlling inputs, they began to monitor measures of output (for example, quality, productivity, and inventory levels).

About the same time, product divisions began receiving the globally consolidated return on sales reports that had previously been consolidated in METC statements. By the mid-1980s, as worldwide planning was introduced for the first time, corporate management required all its product divisions to prepare global product strategies.

Headquarters-Subsidiary Relations

Although METC and the product divisions set detailed sales and profits targets for their overseas subsidiaries, local managers were told they had autonomy on how to achieve the targets. "Mike" Matsuoko, president of the company's largest European production subsidiary in Cardiff, Wales, however, emphasized that failure to meet targets forfeited freedom: "Losses show bad health and invite many doctors from Japan, who provide advice and support."

In the mid-1980s, Matsushita had over 700 expatriate Japanese managers and technicians on foreign assignment for four to eight years, but defended that high number by describing their pivotal role. "This vital communication role," said one manager, "almost always requires a manager from the parent company. Even if a local manager speaks Japanese, he would not have the long experience that is needed to build relationships and understand our management processes."

Expatriate managers were located throughout foreign subsidiaries, but there were a few positions that were almost always reserved for them. The most visible were subsidiary general managers whose main role was to translate Matsushita philosophy abroad. Expatriate accounting managers were expected to "mercilessly expose the truth" to corporate headquarters; and Japanese technical managers were sent to transfer product and process technologies and provide headquarters with local market information. These expatriates maintained relationships with senior colleagues at headquarters, who acted as career mentors, evaluated performance (with some input from local managers), and provided expatriates with information about parent company developments.

General managers of foreign subsidiaries visited Osaka headquarters at least two or three times each year—some as often as every month. Corporate managers reciprocated these visits, and on average, major operations hosted at least one headquarters manager each day of the year. Face-to-face meetings were considered vital: "Figures are important," said one manager, "but the meetings are necessary to develop judgment." Daily faxes and nightly phone calls between headquarters and expatriate colleagues were a vital management link.

Yamashita's Operation Localization

Although international sales kept rising, as early as 1982 growing host country pressures caused concern about the company's highly centralized operations. In that year, newly appointed company President Toshihiko Yamashita launched "Operation Localization" to boost offshore production from less than 10% of value-added to 25%, or half of overseas sales, by 1990. To support the target, he set out a program of four localizations—personnel, technology, material, and capital.

Over the next few years, Matsushita increased the number of local nationals in key positions. In the United States, for example, U.S. nationals became the presidents of three of the six local companies, while in Taiwan the majority of production divisions were replaced by Chinese managers. In each case, however, local national managers were still supported by senior Japanese advisors, who maintained a direct link with the parent company. To localize technology and materials, the company developed its national subsidiaries' expertise to source equipment locally, modify designs to meet local requirements, incorporate local components, and adapt corporate processes and technologies to accommodate these changes. And by the mid-1980s, offshore production subsidiaries were free to buy minor parts from local vendors as long as quality could be assured, but still had to buy key components from internal sources.

One of the most successful innovations was to give overseas sales subsidiaries more choice over the products they sold. Each year the company held a two-week internal merchandising show and product planning meeting where product divisions exhibited the new lines. Here, overseas sales subsidiary managers described their local market needs and negotiated for change in features, quantities, and even prices of the products they wanted to buy. Product division managers, however, could overrule the sales subsidiary if they thought introduction of a particular product was of strategic importance.

President Yamashita's hope was that Operation Localization would help Matsushita's overseas companies develop the innovative capability and entrepreneurial initiatives that he had long admired in the national organizations of rival Philips. (Past efforts to develop such capabilities abroad had failed. For example, when Matsushita acquired Motorola's TV business in the United States, its highly innovative technology group atrophied as American engineers resigned in response to what they felt to be excessive control from Japan's highly centralized R&D operations.) Yet despite his four localizations, overseas companies continued to act primarily as the implementation arms of central product divisions. In an unusual act for a Japanese CEO, Yamashita publicly expressed his unhappiness with the lack of initiative at the TV plant in Cardiff. Despite the transfer of substantial resources and the delegation of many responsibilities, he felt that the plant remained too dependent on the center.

Tanii's Integration and Expansion

Yamashita's successor, Akio Tanii, expanded on his predecessor's initiatives. In 1986, feeling that Matsushita's product divisions were not giving sufficient attention to international development—in part because they received only 3% royalties for foreign production against at least 10% return on sales for exports from Japan—he brought all foreign subsidiaries under the control of METC. Tanii then merged METC into the parent company in an effort to fully integrate domestic and overseas operations. Then, to shift operational control nearer to local markets, he relocated major regional headquarters functions from Japan to North America, Europe, and Southeast Asia. Yet still he was frustrated that the overseas subsidiary companies acted as little more than the implementing agents of the Osaka-based product divisions.

Through all these changes, however, Matsushita's worldwide growth continued generating huge reserves. With $17.5 billion in liquid financial assets at the end of 1989, the company was referred to as the "Matsushita Bank," and several top executives began proposing that if they could not develop innovative overseas companies, they should buy them. Flush with cash and international success, in early 1991 the company acquired MCA, the U.S.

entertainment giant, for $6.1 billion with the objective of obtaining a media software source for its hardware. Within a year, however, Japan's bubble economy had burst, plunging the economy into recession. Almost overnight, Tanii had to shift the company's focus from expansion to cost containment. Despite his best efforts to cut costs, the problems ran too deep. With 1992 profits less than half their 1991 level, the board took the unusual move of forcing Tanii to resign in February 1993.

Morishita's Challenge and Response

At 56, Yoichi Morishita was the most junior of the company's executive vice presidents when he was tapped as the new president. Under the slogan "simple, small, speedy and strategic," he committed to cutting headquarters staff and decentralizing responsibility. Over the next 18 months, he moved 6,000 staff to operating jobs. In a major strategic reversal, he also sold 80% of MCA to Seagram, booking a $1.2 billion loss on the transaction.

Yet the company continued to struggle. Japan's domestic market for consumer electronics collapsed—from $42 billion in 1989 to $21 billion in 1999. Excess capacity drove down prices and profits evaporated. And although offshore markets were growing, the rise of new competition—first from Korea, then China—created a global glut of consumer electronics, and prices collapsed.

With a strong yen making exports from Japan uncompetitive, Matsushita's product divisions rapidly shifted production offshore during the 1990s, mostly to low-cost Asian countries like China and Malaysia. By the end of the decade, its 160 factories outside Japan employed 140,000 people—about the same number of employees as in its 133 plants in Japan. Yet, despite the excess capacity and strong yen, management seemed unwilling to radically restructure its increasingly inefficient portfolio of production facilities.

In the closing years of the decade, Morishita began emphasizing the need to develop more of its technology and innovation offshore. Concerned that only 250 of the company's 3,000 R&D scientists and engineers were located outside Japan, he began investing in R&D partnerships and technical exchanges, particularly in fast emerging fields. For example, in 1998 he signed a joint R&D agreement with the Chinese Academy of Sciences, China's leading research organization. Later that year, he announced the establishment of the Panasonic Digital Concepts Center in California. Its mission was to act as a venture fund and an incubation center for the new ideas

Exhibit 6   Matsushita, Summary Financial Data, 1970-2000[a]

	2000	1995	1990	1985	1980	1975	1970
In billions of yen and percent:							
Sales	¥7,299	¥6,948	¥6,003	¥5,291	¥2,916	¥1,385	¥932
Income before tax	219	232	572	723	324	83	147
As % of sales	3.0%	3.3%	9.5%	13.7%	11.1%	6.0%	15.8%
Net income	¥100	¥90	¥236	¥216	¥125	¥32	¥70
As % of sales	1.4%	1.3%	3.9%	4.1%	4.3%	2.3%	7.6%
Cash dividends (per share)	¥14.00	¥13.50	¥10.00	¥9.52	¥7.51	¥6.82	¥6.21
Total assets	7,955	8,202	7,851	5,076	2,479	1,274	735
Stockholders' equity	3,684	3,255	3,201	2,084	1,092	573	324
Capital investment	355	316	355	288	NA	NA	NA
Depreciation	343	296	238	227	65	28	23
R&D	526	378	346	248	102	51	NA
Employees (units)	290,448	265,397	198,299	175,828	107,057	82,869	78,924
Overseas employees	143,773	112,314	59,216	38,380	NA	NA	NA
As % of total employees	50%	42%	30%	22%	NA	NA	NA
Exchange rate (fiscal period end; ¥/$)	103	89	159	213	213	303	360
In millions of dollars:							
Sales	$68,862	$78,069	$37,753	$24,890	$13,690	$4,572	$2,588
Operating income before depreciation	4,944	6,250	4,343	3,682	1,606	317	NA
Operating income after depreciation	1,501	2,609	2,847	2,764	1,301	224	NA
Pretax income	2,224	2,678	3,667	3,396	1,520	273	408
Net income	941	1,017	1,482	1,214	584	105	195
Total assets	77,233	92,159	49,379	21,499	11,636	4,206	2,042
Total equity	35,767	36,575	20,131	10,153	5,129	1,890	900

Source: Annual reports; Standard & Poors' *Compustat*; Moody's Industrial and International Manuals.
[a]Data prior to 1987 are for the fiscal year ending November 20; data 1988 and after are for the fiscal year ending March 31.

and technologies emerging in Silicon Valley. To some it was an indication that Matsushita had given up trying to generate new technology and business initiatives from its own overseas companies.

Nakamura's Initiatives

In April 2000, Morishita became chairman and Kunio Nakamura replaced him as president. Profitability was at 2.2% of sales, with consumer electronics at only 0.4%, including losses generated by one-time cash cows, the TV and VCR divisions. (Exhibits 6 and 7 provide the financial history for Matsushita and key product lines.) The new CEO vowed to raise this to 5% by 2004. Key to his plan was to move Matsushita beyond its roots as a "super manufacturer of products" and begin "to meet customer needs through systems and services." He planned to flatten the hierarchy and empower employees to respond to customer needs, and as part of the implementation, all key headquarters functions relating to international operations were transferred to overseas regional offices.

But the biggest shock came in November, when Nakamura announced a program of "destruction and creation," in which he disbanded the product division structure that KM had created as Matsushita's basic organizational building block 67 years earlier. Plants, previously controlled by individual product divisions, would now be integrated into multi-product production centers. In Japan alone 30 of the 133 factories were to be consolidated or closed. And marketing would shift to two corporate marketing entities, one for Panasonic brands (consumer electronics, information and communications products) and one for National branded products (mostly home appliances).

They were radical moves, but in a company that even in Japan was being talked about as a takeover target, observers wondered if they were sufficient to restore its global competitiveness.

Exhibit 7   Matsushita, Sales by Product and Geographic Segment, 1985-2000 (billion yen)

	2000		1995		FY 1990		FY 1985	
By Product Segment:								
Video and audio equipment	¥1,706	23%	¥1,827	26%	¥2,159	36%	¥2,517	48%
Home appliances and household equipment	1,306	18	--	--	--	--	--	--
Home appliances	--	--	916	13	802	13	763	14
Communication and industrial equipment	--	--	1,797	26	1,375	23	849	16
Electronic components	--	--	893	13	781	13	573	11
Batteries and kitchen-related equipment	--	--	374	4	312	5	217	4
Information and communications equipment	2,175	28	--	--	--	--	--	--
Industrial equipment	817	11	--	--	--	--	--	--
Components	1,618	21	--	--	--	--	--	--
Others	--	--	530	8	573	10	372	7
Total	¥7,682	100%	¥6,948	100%	¥6,003	100%	¥5,291	100%
By Geographic Segment:								
Domestic	¥3,698	51%	¥3,455	50%	¥3,382	56%	¥2,659	50%
Overseas	3,601	49	3,493	50	2,621	44	2,632	50

Source: Annual reports
Notes: Total may not add due to rounding.

Global Wine Wars: New World Challenges Old (A)

It's an art, not a science. We're creating products that are crafted, just as an artist or a chef would create.

Jean-Claude Boisset, CEO of a French wine company

We bring a total commitment to innovation . . . from vine to palate.

Mission Statement, Australia Wine Foundation

In early 2002, these two views reflected an honest difference of wine-making practice that had grown into a fierce competitive battle between traditional wine makers and some new industry players for the $90 billion global wine market. Many companies from the Old World wine producers—France, Italy, Germany, and Spain, for example—found themselves constrained by embedded traditions and practices, restrictive industry regulations, and complex national and European Community legislation. This provided opportunities for New World wine companies—from Australia, the United States, Chile, and South Africa, for instance—to challenge the more established Old World producers by introducing innovations at every stage of the value chain.

After decades of being dismissed and even ridiculed for their attempts to compete with exports from traditional wine countries, in the 1980s and 1990s the New World companies began winning international respect, and with it global market share. At the November 2000 annual charity wine auction in Beaune, Louis Trébuchet, head of the Burgundy Growers Association, told his French colleagues that they needed to be on guard against increasing challenges from Australian, South African, and South American wines.[1] The warning was underscored by a market forecast that in 2002 Australia would overtake France as the leading wine exporter to the United Kingdom, the world's highest-value import market and a bellwether for trends in other importing countries.

IN THE BEGINNING[2]

Grape growing and wine making have been human preoccupations for many thousands of years. Early archeological evidence of wine making has been found in Mesopotamia, and ancient Egyptians and Greeks offered wine as tributes to dead pharaohs and tempestuous gods. Under the Roman Empire, viticulture spread throughout the Mediterranean region, where almost every town had its local vineyards and wine maker.

In the Christian era, wine became part of liturgical services, and monasteries planted vines and built wineries. While today wine is often considered a sophisticated drink, during most of European history it was a peasant's beverage to accompany everyday meals. Eventually, the Benedictine monks raised viticulture to a new level, making wine not only for religious use but also to show hospitality to travelers requiring lodging. By the Middle Ages, the European nobility began planting vineyards as a mark of prestige, competing with one another in the quality of wine served at their tables. A niche market for premium wine was born.

Wine Production

Tending and harvesting grapes has always been labor intensive, and one worker could typically look after only

This case was prepared by Professor Christopher A. Bartlett with the assistance of Janet Cornebise and Andrew N. McLean.

1 "Le success des vins du nouveau monde inquite la filiere viticole [Burgundy Winegrowers Worried about Success of New World Wines]," La Tribune, October 24, 2000, p. 25.

2 Historical discussions are indebted to Harry W. Paul, *Science, Vine and Wine in Modern France* (Cambridge University Press, 1996), pp. 2–15; to Jancis Robinson, ed., *The Oxford Companion to Wine*, 2nd Ed. (Oxford University Press, 1999); and to James Wilson, *Terroir* (Berkeley: University of California Press, 1998), pp. 10–45.

a three-hectare lot (one hectare equals approximately 2.5 acres)—less for hillside vineyards. The introduction of vineyard horses in the early 19th century led to vines being planted in rows and to more efficient tending and harvesting. One person could now work a seven-hectare plot.

Yet despite these efficiencies, vineyards became smaller, not larger, over time. Over many centuries, small agricultural holdings were continually fragmented as land was parceled out by kings and emperors, taken through war, or broken up through inheritance. During the French Revolution, for example, many large estates were seized, divided, and sold at auction. After 1815, the Napoleonic inheritance code prescribed how land had to be passed on to all rightful heirs. By the mid-19th century, the average holding in France was 5.5 hectares and was still being subdivided. (In Italy, similar historical events left the average vineyard holding at 0.8 hectares.)

While the largest estates made their own wine, most small farmers sold their grapes to the local wine maker or *vintner*. Because payment was often based on weight, they had little incentive to adopt practices that reduced yield but intensified grape's flavor. Eventually, some small growers formed cooperatives, hoping to gain more control and to participate in wine making's downstream profit.

Distribution and Marketing

Traditionally, wine was sold in bulk to merchant traders— *négociants* in France—who often blended and bottled the product before distributing it. As *négociants* began shipping the product abroad, they soon found that poor roads and complex toll and tax systems made transportation extremely expensive. For example, in the early 19th century, shipments of wine from Strasbourg to the Dutch border had to pass through 31 toll stations.[3] Furthermore, wine often did not travel well, and much of it spoiled on long journeys. As a result, only the most sophisticated *négociants* could handle exports, and only the rich could afford the imported luxury.

In the late 18th and early 19th centuries, innovations such as the mass production of glass bottles, the introduction of the cork stopper, and the development of pasteurization revolutionized the industry. With greater wine stability and longevity, distribution to more distant markets and bottle aging of the best vintages became normal practice. Together, these factors led to increased vine plantings, expanded production, and the expansion of the market for fine wines.

Regulation and Classification

As the industry developed, it became increasingly important to the cultural and economic life of the producing countries. In France, wine was a staple item on every table, and in the mid-18th century it supported 1.5 million grower families and an equal number in related businesses. At one-sixth of France's total trading revenue, it became the country's second-largest export.

The industry's growing cultural and economic importance soon attracted a great deal of political attention. Over the years laws, regulations, and policies increasingly controlled almost every aspect of wine making. For example, Germany's 1644 wine classification scheme eventually expanded to encompass 65 classes of quality, with legislation prescribing ripeness required for harvesting, definitions of minimum sugar content, and penalties for those who added sugar. (Even as late as 1971, laws were passed in Germany requiring the registration of each vineyard and the appointment of a government panel to taste each vineyard's annual vintage and assign it a quality level.)[4] Similar laws and regulations prescribing wine-making practices also developed in France and Italy.

Rather than resisting, producers often supported and even augmented the classification schemes and regulatory controls as a way of differentiating their products and raising entry barriers. The venerable French classification system was created by a Bordeaux committee in preparation for the 1855 Exposition in Paris. To help consumers recognize their finest wines, they classified about 500 vineyards on one of five levels, from *premier cru* (first growth) to *cinquième cru* (fifth growth).

Because it helped consumers sort through the complexity of a highly fragmented market, this marketing tool immediately gained wide recognition, leading the government to codify much of it in the *Appellation d'Origin Controllée* (AOC) laws. These laws also defined the boundaries and set the standards for vineyards and wine makers in France's major wine-growing regions.[5] Eventually, almost 400 AOC designations were authorized, from the well known (St. Emilion or Beaujolais) to the obscure

3 Robinson, p. 308.

4 Ibid., p. 312.

5 Dewey Markham, *1855: A History of the Bordeaux Classification* (New York: Wiley, 1998), p. 177.

(Fitou or St. Péray). A similar classification scheme was later introduced in Italy defining 213 *denominazione di orgine controllate* (or DOC) regions, each with regulations prescribing area, grape varieties permitted, yields, and so on. These laws also prescribed almost all aspects of production, from permissible types of grape, to required growing practices, to acceptable alcohol content.[6]

Later, other wine regions of France were given official recognition with the classification of *Vins Delimités de Qualite Superieure* (VDQS), but these were usually regarded as of lower rank than AOC wines. Below VDQS were *Vins de Pays*, or country wine, primarily producing *vins ordinaires*. For example, the Languedoc, France's oldest wine region located in southern France, produced more than a third of the country's wine, yet remained largely unconstrained by AOC or VDQS regulation. It produced inexpensive but very drinkable wine for French tables—and increasingly, for export. There was almost no movement across the categories or within the hierarchies created by these classifications, since the French nurtured the concept of *terroir*, the almost mystical combination of soil, aspect, microclimate, rainfall, and cultivation they passionately believed was at the heart of the unique taste of each region's—and indeed, each vineyard's—grapes and wine.

But *terroir* could not always guarantee quality. As an agricultural product, wine was always subject to the vagaries of weather and disease. In the last quarter of the 19th century, a deadly New World insect, phylloxera, devastated the French vine stock. From a production level of over 5 million hectoliters in 1876, output dropped to just 2 million hectoliters by 1885. (A hectoliter is 100 liters, or about 25 gallons.) But a solution was found in an unexpected quarter: French vines were successfully grafted onto phylloxera-resistant vine roots native to the eastern United States and imported from the upstart Californian wine industry. It was the first time many in the Old World acknowledged the existence of a wine industry outside Europe. It would not be the last.

STIRRINGS IN THE NEW WORLD

Although insignificant in both size and reputation compared with the well-established industry in traditional wine-producing countries, vineyards and wine makers had been set up in many New World countries since the 18th century. In the United States, for example, Thomas Jefferson, an enthusiastic oenologist, became a leading voice for establishing vineyards in Virginia. And in Australia, vines were brought over along with the first fleet carrying convicts and settlers in 1788. At the same time, nascent wine industries were developing in Argentina, Chile, and South Africa, usually under the influence of immigrants from the Old World wine countries.

Opening New Markets

While climate and soil allowed grape growing to flourish in each of these new environments, the consumption of wine in local markets varied widely. Wine quickly became a central part of the national cultures of Argentina and Chile, and by the mid 1960s, per capita consumption was about 80 liters per annum in Argentina and 50 liters in Chile. While such rates were comparable with the 60 liter annual level in Spain, they were behind those of France and Italy, which boasted rates of 110–120 liters per person annually. (See Exhibit 1 for wine consumption figures over time.)

Other New World cultures were not so quick to embrace the new industry. In Australia, the hot climate and a dominant British heritage made beer the alcoholic beverage of preference, with wine being consumed mostly by Old World immigrants. The U.S. market developed in a more complex, schizophrenic way. Born of the country's role as a key player in the rum trade, one segment of the population followed a tradition of distilling and drinking hard liquor. But another large group, perhaps reflecting the country's Puritan heritage, espoused temperance. (As recently as 1994, a Gallup survey found that 45% of U.S. respondents did not drink at all, and 21% favored a renewal of the prohibition of the sale of alcohol.) As a result, until the post-World War II era, wine was largely made by and sold to European immigrant communities.

In the postwar era, however, demand for wine began to increase dramatically in the United States and Australia, as well as in other New World producers such as South Africa and New Zealand. In the United States, for example, consumption grew from a post-prohibition per capita level of 1 liter per annum to 8 liters by 1976.

---

6 Robinson, p. 235.

Exhibit 1   Wine Consumption Per Capita, Selected Countries, 1966–1998

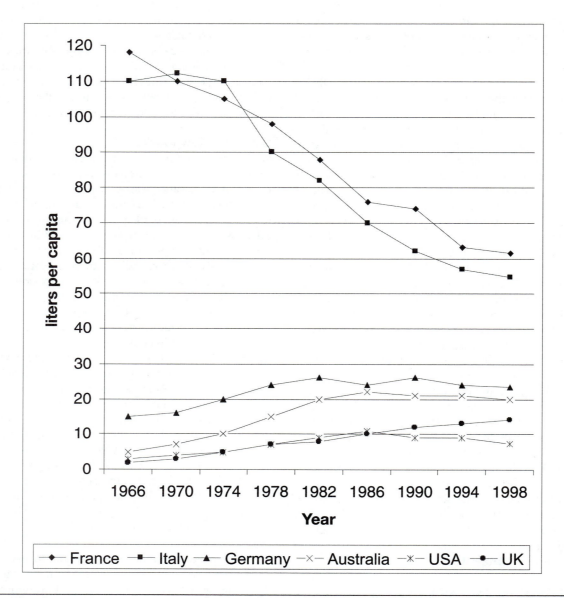

Source: Figures for 1966 through 1994 adapted by casewriters from Annemiek Geene, Arend Heijbroek, Anne Lagerwerf, and Rafi Wazir, "The World Wine Business,"   Market Study, May 1999, available from Rabobank International. Figures for 1998 from Wine Institute, "Wine Institute, the voice for California wine" Web site, <http://www.wineinstitute.org/communications/statistics/index.htm>, accessed September 10, 2002.

In Australia the increase was even more dramatic: from less than 2 liters in 1960 to 22 liters by 1986. Equally important, this growth in total consumption was coupled with a growing demand for higher-quality wines. It was this boom in domestic demand for both quality and quantity that established the young wine industry in these New World countries.

Challenging Production Norms

Expanding on the back of the postwar economic boom, New World wine producers developed in a very different industry environment than most of their European counterparts. First, suitable land was widely available and less expensive, allowing the growth of much more extensive vineyards. In the early 1990s, the average holding for a vineyard among New World producers was 158 hectares, compared with less than one hectare in the Old World countries.[7]

Unconstrained by either small size or tradition, New World producers began to experiment with new technology in both grape growing and wine making. In Australia, controlled drip irrigation reduced vintage variability and allowed expansion into new growing regions. (Predictably, irrigation was strictly forbidden in France under AOC regulations.) Larger New World vineyards also favored the use of specialized equipment. Mechanical harvesters, then mechanical pruners, became the industry standard. And night harvesting became the norm to maximize grape sugars. Trellis systems, developed in Australia, permitted vineyard planting at twice the traditional density, while other experiments with fertilizers and pruning methods increased yield and improved grape flavor. These bold experiments, when coupled with sunny climates, allowed the New World producers to make remarkably consistent wines year to year. In contrast, the rainy maritime climate in Bordeaux made late autumn harvests risky and held producers hostage to year-to-year vintage variations.

Experimentation also extended to wine making, where again the New World companies were more willing to break with industry traditions. Large estates usually had on-site labs to run tests and provide data helpful in making growing and harvest decisions. More controversially, by the 1990s many employed some form of a reverse osmosis technology to concentrate the juice (or *must*), thus ensuring a deeper-colored, richer-tasting wine. (Ironically, the technique was developed by a French desalination equipment maker, but most French producers publicly deplored the practice as "removing the poetry of wine.") The newer wine makers also developed processes that allowed much of the fermentation and even the aging to occur in huge, computer-controlled, stainless steel tanks rather than in the traditional small oak barrels. To provide oak flavor, some added oak chips—another practice strictly forbidden in most traditional-producing countries.

Reinventing the Marketing Model

Beyond their experiments in growing and wine making, New World producers also innovated in packaging and marketing. While following the European example of targeting the huge bulk wine market, the Americans and Australians did so in their own way. In the United States, the Old World standard liter bottle of *vin de table* was replaced by the half-gallon flagon, while the Australians developed the innovative "wine-in-a-box" package. Employing a collapsible plastic bag in a compact cardboard box with a dispensing spigot, the box's shape and weight not only saved shipping costs, it also made storage in the consumer's refrigerator more convenient. More recently, Australian producers had begun to use screw caps on premium wines—particularly the delicate whites susceptible to spoiling if corks are deficient.

In both countries, producers also began differentiating their products and making them more appealing to palates unaccustomed to wine. Several new products developed for unsophisticated palates were wildly successful—Ripple in the United States and Barossa Pearl in Australia, for example—but were held in great disdain by wine connoisseurs. These experiments led to forays into branding and marketing, skills that were rare in this industry prior to the 1970s.

When Coca-Cola acquired Taylor California Cellars in 1977—soon followed by other experienced consumer marketers such as Nestlé, Pillsbury, and Seagram—the conventional wisdom was that the application of sophisticated marketing techniques would finally crack the last major consumer product still largely unbranded. But forecasts of 25% annual demand growth proved wildly optimistic and within a decade almost all the outsiders had sold out. Yet their influence endured, and experiments with branding, labeling, and other market innovations continued.

---

7 Ibid., p. 391.

The other major change driven by New World companies occurred in distribution. Historically, fragmented producers and tight government regulations had created a long, multilevel value chain. (See Exhibit 2 for a representation.) In the Old World, the tasks of grape growing, wine making, distribution, and marketing were typically handled by different entities, with many of them lacking either the scale or the expertise to operate efficiently.[a] In contrast, the large wine companies from the New World typically controlled the full value chain, extracting margins at every level and retaining bargaining power with increasingly concentrated retailers. Because they retained responsibility for the final product, quality was ensured at every step.

To traditionalists, the New World's breaks with established grape-growing and wine-making ways were sacrilege. They argued that in the drive for efficiency and consistency, and in the desire to cater to less sophisticated palates, New World producers had lost the character and unpredictable differences that came with more variable vintages made in traditional ways. What piqued the critics even more was that, as part of their marketing approach, these upstart wineries were selling their more engineered products using appellation names— Chablis, Burgundy, Champagne, and so on. In the 1960s, the European Economic Community passed regulations making it illegal to use such names on wines other than those produced in the region.

While some New World producers continued their unauthorized labeling for decades, most New World wine makers responded to the EEC challenge by labeling their wines with the grape variety being used. Eventually consumers recognized and developed preferences defined by varietal type—cabernet sauvignon versus merlot, or chardonnay versus sauvignon blanc, for example. Indeed, many seemed to find this easier to understand than trying to penetrate the different regional designations that each of the traditional wine-producing countries had promoted.

---

[a] To overcome the competitive disadvantage of this long, compartmentalized chain, in the 1930s some small grape growers had formed cooperatives. The co-ops allowed them to integrate into wine making, or at least increase their bargaining power with *négociants* who had moved upstream into wine making and downstream into branding and marketing. But because they usually paid members based on weight rather than quality, growers' cooperatives rarely produced premium wines.

Exhibit 2 Wine Industry Value Chain

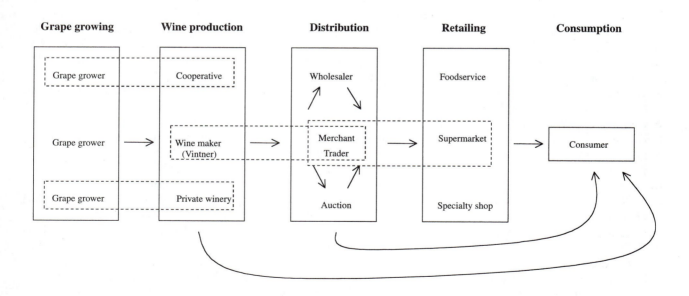

Source: Adapted by casewriters from Annemiek Geene, Arend Heijbroek, Anne Lagerwerf, and Rafi Wazir, "The World Wine Business," Market Study, May 1999, available from Rabobank International.

The Judgment of Paris: 1976

On May 24, 1976, in a publicity-seeking activity linked to America's Bicentenary, a British wine merchant set up a blind-tasting panel to rate top wines from France and California. In an event held in Paris with a judging panel of nine French wine critics, the French had an enormous "home field advantage." Against all odds, the American entries took top honors in both the red and white competitions. When French producers complained that the test that became known as "The Judgment of Paris" was rigged, a new judging was held two years later. Again, Californian wines triumphed.[8]

The event was a watershed in the industry for several reasons. The surrounding publicity raised public awareness of quality wines from New World sources and undermined the views of those who dismissed innovative approaches to wine making. It was a wake-up call to traditional producers, many of whom began taking their new challengers seriously for the first time. And finally, it gave confidence to New World producers that they had the quality to compete against the best in global markets. In short, it was the bell for the opening round in a fight for export sales.

MATURING MARKETS, CHANGING DEMAND

"The Judgment of Paris" was only one element of a series of disruptive changes the wine industry faced in the last quarter of the 20th century. More immediately alarming for most traditional producers was a pattern of declining demand that saw a 25% drop in worldwide consumption from 1976 to 1990. When coupled with some radical changes in consumer tastes and preferences, these trends presented industry participants with an important new set of opportunities and threats.

Country Demand Patterns

The most dramatic decline in demand occurred in the highest-consumption countries, France and Italy. In the mid-1960s, per capita consumption in both countries was around 120 liters annually; by the late 1980s it had fallen to half that level. Key causes of the decline were a younger generation's different drinking preferences, an older generation's concern about health issues, and stricter drunk-driving penalties. Similar steep declines occurred in other countries during the same two decades—Spain dropped from 60 liters to 30, Argentina from 80 to 40, and Chile from 50 to 15.

Although not fast enough to offset the losses in the traditional-producing countries, demand was growing in most wine-importing countries during the last two decades of the century, a change that served to escalate competition for export sales. (See Exhibit 3) From 1966 to 1998, per capita annual consumption in the United Kingdom rose from 3 liters to 14 liters, in Belgium from 10 liters to 25 liters, in Sweden from 5 liters to 15 liters, and in Canada from 3 liters to 8 liters. Even more promising was the more recent growth of new markets, particularly in Asia. Starting from a per capita consumption base of less than 1 liter per annum, Asia's largest wine-importing countries—China, Japan, Taiwan, Singapore, South Korea, and Thailand—grew imports at an average of 12% annually through the 1990s. In Japan, where wine emerged as the fashionable drink of the late 1990s, per capita consumption doubled in just three years—from 1.5 liters in 1996 to 3 liters in 1999.[9]

Shift to Quality

Another trend partly offsetting the overall volume decline was a growing demand for higher-quality wines. In terms of the five consumer segments defined by industry analyst Rabobank (see Exhibit 4), the major shift was from the basic segment to premium and super-premium wines. While the basic segment (less than $5 a bottle) still accounted for half the world market in volume, the premium ($5 to $7) and the super-premium ($7 to $14) now represented 40% of the total—and closer to 50% in younger markets such as the United States and Australia.

The trend was worldwide. Even in the 12 European Union (EU) countries, where overall demand was declining, consumption of premium wine kept rising. Despite government subsidies, per capita consumption of basic wine in the EU fell from 31 liters in 1985 to 20 liters in 1997, even as demand for quality wine increased from 10 liters to 14 liters. In the same 12-year period, jug wine sales in the United States declined from 800 million to 650 million liters, while consumption of premium wines increased from 150 million to 550 million liters.

Fluctuations in Fashion

With the declining importance of working families consuming locally produced table wine, the market was

---

[8] Gideon Rachman, "The Globe in a Glass," *The Economist*, December 18, 1999, p. 91.

[9] All statistics from Wine Institute, "Wine Institute, the voice for California wine" Web site, <http://www.wineinstitute.org/communications/statistics/index.htm>, accessed September 10, 2002.

Exhibit 3 **Consumption, Production, Export, and Import Figures for Selected Old World and New World Wine Producing and Consuming Countries, 2001**

Country	Consumption		Production	Exports		Imports	
	Liters Per Capita	Total hls 000s	Total hls (000s)	Total hls (000s)	Value ($Millions)	Total hls (000s)	Value ($Millions)
France	59.5	35,217	58,243	17,484	5,800.6	6,030	470.7
Italy	52.3	30,197	51,300	17,983	2,439.7	811	199.2
Argentina	34.0	12,743	15,796	1,041	155.5	134	13.2
Spain	38.5	15,199	31,127	11,662	1,346.1	309	82.6
Germany	24.1	19,825	9,662	2,488	368.1	13,453	1,975.3
Australia	20.6	3,990	9,080	3,750	901.0	140	54.7
United Kingdom	15.9	9,497	15	263	127.0	12,312	2,695.2
United States	7.9	22,401	23,800	2,839	511.2	5,657	2,155.2

Source: K. Anderson and D. Norman, *Global Wine Production, Consumption and Trade, 1961–2001: A Statistical Compendium* (Adelaide: Centre for International Economic Studies; 2003).
Note: In several European countries, production does not equal consumption (plus exports minus imports) due to excess production being subject to government purchase.

Exhibit 4 **Quality Segments in the Wine Industry**

	Icon	Ultra Premium	Super Premium	Premium	Basic
Price range (approx)	More than $50	$20–$50	$10–$20	$5–$10	Less than $5
Consumer profile	Connoisseur	Wine lover	Experimenting consumer	Experimenting consumer	Price-focused consumer
Purchase driver	Image, style	Quality, image	Brand, quality	Price, brand	Price
Retail outlets	Winery, boutique, food service	Specialty shop, food service	Better supermarket, specialty shop	Supermarket	Supermarket, discounter
Market trend	Little growth	Little growth	Growing	Growing	Decreasing
Competition	Limited, "closed" segment	Gradually increasing	Increasing, based on brand and quality/price ratio	Fierce, based on brand, price	Based on price
Volume market share	1%	5%	10%	34%	50%
Availability	Scarce	Scarce	Sufficient, year round	Large quantities, year round	Surplus

Source: Adapted by casewriters from Annemiek Geene, Arend Heijbroek, Anne Lagerwerf, and Rafi Wazir, "The World Wine Business," Market Study, May 1999, available from Rabobank International.

Global Wine Wars: New World Challenges Old (A)

increasingly driven by upscale urban consumers. The whole buying process changed dramatically, as educated consumers chose bottles on the basis of grape variety, vintage, and source. With the shift to quality came a greater fashion element that caused wider fluctuations in demand.

In the 1980s, an emphasis on light foods resulted in an increase in demand for white wines. In the U.S. market, the trend led to white-wine spritzers (wine with soda water and a lime) becoming a fashionable drink. By the late 1980s, white wine represented over 75% of U.S. sales. In the 1990s, however, the trend was reversed following the 1991 publication of a medical report identifying red-wine consumption as the major reason for the "French paradox"—the curious fact that the French enjoyed very low rates of heart disease, despite their well-known love for rich food. The report, widely covered in the press and featured on the television program *60 Minutes*, gave a huge boost to red-wine sales. In the United States, market share for red wine went from 27% in 1991 to 43% five years later, while in fashion-conscious Japan, red's share jumped from 25% to 65% in just two years.[10]

Even within this broad trend of red versus white preference, wine made from different grape varieties also moved with the fashions. The white-wine boom made chardonnay the grape of choice, with other white varietals falling in relative popularity. In red wine, a love affair with cabernet sauvignon was followed by a boom in demand for merlot, particularly in the United States.

Such swings in fashion posed a problem for growers. Although vines had a productive life of 60 to 70 years, they typically took 3 to 4 years to produce their first harvest, 5 to 7 years to reach full productive capacity, and up to 35 years to produce the best-quality grapes for wine. It was a cycle that did not respond well to rapid changes in demand. Nonetheless, New World wine regions still had capacity to plant new vineyards. For example, the California acreage planted with chardonnay grapes increased 36% in the 1990s, and merlot plantings increased 31%.

As these trends continued, the rankings of the world's top wine companies underwent radical change. Despite their relative newness and the comparative smallness of their home markets, U.S. and Australian wine companies took nine slots on the list of the world's top 20, which until recently had been dominated by French, German, and other Old World companies (see Exhibit 5).

The Government Solution

For producers in many Old World regions, however, the shifts in demand were more challenging. First, there was often no new land available to plant, particularly in controlled AOC regions. Equally restrictive were the numerous regulations prescribing grape varieties for a region's wines, affording no flexibility when consumer preferences shifted. One of the biggest victims of the fashion switch from sweeter white wines to drier reds was the German wine industry. Constrained by tight regulations on sugar content, German wine makers watched their exports drop from over 3 million hectoliters in 1992 to under 2 million just five years later.

Unable to respond as New World producers had, European growers sought government help. In France, growers regularly staged demonstrations and traffic blockages to pressure the government for higher price guarantees. EU agriculture supports and national agricultural subsidies were approved to support the overproduction of primarily low-quality, cheap wines. Most EU and national state aid was directed at the purchase of surplus wine—to be distilled into industrial alcohol—as well as for payments to reduce vineyard acreage.

By 2002, however, doubts were being voiced about this strategy in Brussels. After authorizing the purchase of 4 million hectoliters of excess European production, EU Agriculture Commissioner Franz Fischler challenged France on its frequent return to the EU commission for aid. "They are operating aids which do not bring about structural improvements in the sector," he said.[11] The EU commission was also attempting to reduce overproduction in Italy and Spain, with mixed results.[12] But the structural problem was not limited to low-quality, inexpensive wines. In 2002, over 13 million bottles of Beaujolais—10% of the region's production—went unsold. Beaujolais producers were compensated at 70 euros (€) per hectoliter, for a total payout of €7 million.[13]

10 Rachman, p. 100.

11 "Farm Council – Agriculture ministers approve wine aid, fail to agree to tobacco aid," *European Report*, February 20, 2002.

12 William F. Doering, "Production up, trade down in 2000," *Wines & Vines*, July 1, 2002, p. 36.

13 Carl Mortishead, "Beaujolais swallows hard and turns wine into vinegar," *The Times of London*, June 25, 2002.

Exhibit 5 World's 20 Largest Wine Companies, 1998

Company	Country	Wine Sales ($000s)	Major Brands
LVMH[a]	France	$1,462,000	Moet & Chandon, Krug, Dom Perignon, Veuve Cliquot, Pommery, Green Point (Australia), Domaine Chandon (Napa and Argentina); stakes in Chateau d'Yquem and Cloudy Bay (New Zealand)
E&J Gallo[b]	U.S.	1,428,000	Livingston Cellars, Carlo Rossi, Turning Leaf, Garnet Point, Ecco Domani (Italy), E&J Gallo
Seagram[c]	Canada	800,000	Wineries in 12 countries, including Sterling, Monterey, and Mumm Cuvee (United States)
Castel Frères[d]	France	700,000	Castelvins, Nicolas, Vieux Papes
Canandaigua[e]	U.S.	614,000	Inglenook, Almaden, Paul Masson, Arbor Mist, Franciscan Estate
Hengell & Sohnein Group[f]	Germany	521,000	Henkell Trocken (sparkling wine), Dienhard, Schloss Johannisberg
Reh Gruppe[f]	Germany	500,000	Kenderman, Black Tower
Diageo	U.K.	500,000	Le Piat d'Or (France), Blossom Hill, Glen Ellen, Beaulieu (United States), Croft Port, Navarro (Argentina)
Wein International Verw.[f]	Germany	480,000	Mainly generic wines for supermarkets
The Wine Group	U.S.	426,000	Franzia
Val d'Orbieu[g]	France	400,000	
Grands Chais de France[d]	France	390,000	Supermarket label wines in France
Southcorp[c]	Australia	376,000	Penfolds, Lindemans, Seppelt, Coldstream Hills, Rouge Homme (Australia), Lames Herrick (France), Seven Peaks (United States)
R. Mondavi[h]	U.S.	325,000	Woodbridge, Mondavi Coastal, Opus One (with Rothschild), Vichon (France), ventures in Chile and Italy
Freixenet[i]	Spain	318,000	Own-label sparkling wine
BRL Hardy Ltd.	Australia	292,000	Nottage Hill, Hardy's Stamp, D'Istinto (Italy)
Beringer Wine Estates	U.S.	279,000	Own-label varieties, Stag's Leap, Meridian
Mildara Blass	Australia	260,000	Wolf Blass, Rothbury, Mildara
Brown-Foreman Beverage[e]	U.S.	260,000	Fetzer
Pernod Ricard[e]	France	250,000	Jacob's Creek (Australia), Long Mountain (South Africa), Terra Andina (Chile), Alexis Lichine (France), Etechart (Argentina), Dragon Seal (China)

Source: Adapted by casewriters from Gideon Rachman, "The Globe in a Glass," *The Economist*, December 18, 1999, p. 102; and from Annemiek Geene, Arend Heijbroek, Anne Lagerwerf, and Rafi Wazir, "The World Wine Business," Market Study, May 1999, available from Rabobank International.

[a]Mainly champagne.
[b]Largest wine company in volume.
[c]Diversified company.
[d]Négociant.
[e]Beverage company.
[f]Includes *sekt*, a sparkling wine.
[g]Cooperative in Corbiéres and Minervois.
[h]All wine.
[i]World's largest sparkling wine producer.

THE BATTLE FOR BRITAIN

In the turmoil occurring in markets worldwide, nowhere were the stakes more important than in the bellwether U.K. wine market. It became the front line in the battle between Old World and New World producers, with France acting as the standard bearer of the traditional producers and Australia as the leader among the challengers.

The Prize: The Huge U.K. Market

Long before Napoleon derided the English as a nation of shopkeepers, England was a nation of importers. The preferences of the traditional upper crust were satisfied with French, German, and Italian wines, while the tastes of the rest of the nation ran to beer and pub fare. But by 2000, the burnished image of the upper class importing claret by the case was a thing of the past, as the British middle classes increasingly turned to wine as a mealtime beverage of choice. As the world's largest and most competitive import market, the United Kingdom represented not only a major market opportunity but also crucial territory in any quest for world wine domination (see Exhibit 6).

As their domestic markets shrank, many traditional European wine producers began looking at the U.K. market as more than a source of opportunistic or incremental sales. At the same time, however, newly confident companies

---

Exhibit 6   World Wine Imports and Exports: Share by Country

Imports as % of World Wine Imports by Value, 1989–2001

	1989	1992	1995	1998	2001
France	5%	5%	5%	4%	3%
Belgium-Luxembourg	6	8	7	6	6
Germany	16	19	17	16	14
Netherlands	5	6	6	6	5
United Kingdom	19	19	17	18	19
United States	14	13	10	12	15
Japan	4	4	4	8	6
Rest of World	30	27	34	30	31
Total (Millions of 1999 $US)	$8,765	$10,133	$11,606	$14,283	$13,345

Exports as % of World Wine Exports by Value, 1989–2001

	1989	1992	1995	1998	2001
France	51%	48%	42%	42%	41%
Italy	17	18	20	18	17
Spain	8	9	9	10	10
Germany	6	5	5	3	3
Australia	1	2	3	4	6
United States	1	2	2	4	4
Chile	1	1	2	4	5
South Africa	0	0	2	1	2
Rest of World	14	13	15	14	12
Total (Millions of 1999 $US)	$8,765	$10,133	$11,606	$14,283	$13,345

Source: Adapted by casewriters from K. Anderson and D. Norman, *Global Wine Production, Consumption and Trade, 1961–2001: A Statistical Compendium* (Adelaide: Centre for International Economic Studies, 2003).

from the emerging wine countries began expanding their export ambitions. The United Kingdom became a prime target, particularly for countries with old British Commonwealth ties. The battle lines were drawn for a serious engagement to which the contestants would bring different weapons—and an entirely different understanding of the rules.

Ascendancy of Brand Power

The extreme fragmentation of European producers gave few of them the volume to support a branding strategy. As a result, only the handful of producers whose wines achieved icon status—Lafite, Margaux, Veuve Cliquot, and Chateau d'Yquem, for example—became recognized brands. But these appealed to the elite, who represented only a tiny fraction of an exploding U.K. market.

Government efforts to compensate for lack of branding through classification schemes such as France's AOC had been only partially successful in ensuring consumer confidence. Their value had been eroded by their complexity and consumers' recognition that most classifications had been compromised[b]. For example, Burgundy's most famous vineyard, Chambertin, had its 32 acres divided among 23 different proprietors. While many produced the high-quality wine that had earned *grand cru* status, others rode on that reputation to sell—at $150 a bottle— legitimately labeled Chambertin that wine critic Robert Parker described as "thin, watery, and a complete rip-off."[14]

As wine consumption broadened well beyond educated connoisseurs, new consumers in the fast-growing premium wine segment were faced with hundreds of options on the shelf and insufficient knowledge to make an informed—or even a comfortable—choice. To make a good choice, they felt they had to learn the intricacies of region, vintage, and vineyard reputation. And even when they found a wine they liked, chances were that by their next purchase, the same producer was not stocked or the new vintage was much less appealing. Unsurprisingly, survey data showed 65% of shoppers had no idea what they would choose when they entered a wine store.

For years, the wine industry appeared ripe for branding. Compared to soft drinks, beer, and liquor, where global brands are dominant, in 1990 no wine brand had even 1% of the global wine market. Although European producers and their importing agents had succeeded in promoting a handful of brands on the basic segment in the 1960s and 1970s (e.g., Blue Nun, Mateus, Liebfraumilch, Hirondelle), it was the New World producers that made branding and labeling a routine part of wine marketing. A typical example was the red-wine offerings of Australian wine maker Penfolds. Over the years, it had built a hierarchy of brands with informative labels to help consumers move up each step from $9 to $185 wines as their tastes matured. (See Exhibit 7.) By sourcing grapes from various vineyards in multiple regions—even for its icon Grange brand— Penfolds ensured the vintage-to-vintage consistency that branding demanded.

After developing their marketing expertise in the 1960s and 1970s, producers in both the United States and Australia dominated their home markets with strong brands by the 1980s. By the mid-1990s, for example, 75% of sales on the Australian market were accounted for by 6% of the brands. It was also in their highly competitive home market that producers learned to respond to consumer preferences for the simpler, more fruit-driven wines that were easy to appreciate. With these lessons from their home market, particularly through the 1990s these producers took those wines and the marketing and branding skills that backed them into the export markets. In a bold statement of strategic intent, in 1996 Wine Australia announced Strategy 2025, by which it committed to a 300% increase in sales to $4.5 billion by 2025, with exports providing most of the growth. The 2025 target was achieved over the next five years, and by 2001, the Australians claimed 6 of the top 10 wine brands sold in the United Kingdom (see Exhibit 8 for top U.K. brands).

Apart from the high-value champagnes, the French had only one wine brand—LePiat, a *négociant's* label—among the top 10 brands in the United Kingdom. No other traditional-producing country made the list. Due to the fragmentation of Old World vineyards (Bordeaux alone had 20,000 producers),most had become accustomed to competing at the low end on price, the middle level on the umbrella reassurance of the AOC's reputation, and at the top end on the image of the icon brands. As a result, they lacked the skills, the resources, and even the interest to enter

---

b The same problem plagued wines from Italy, where DOC regulations were so often violated that the government introduced a DOCG classification in 1980 (the G stood for *guarantia*) to restore consumer confidence in notable wine regions. And in Germany, government standards were so diluted that, even in mediocre years, over 75% of wine produced was labeled *Qualitatswein*, while less than 5% earned the more modest Tatelwein (table wine) designation.

14 Robert M. Parker, Jr., *Parker Wine Buyer's Guide*, 5th Edition (New York: Fireside Press, 1999), p. 276.

Exhibit 7   Southcorp's Penfolds Red Wine U.S. Brand Structure, 2002

Label	Varietal Type	Years Before Release	Price Segment	Suggested U.S. Retail Price per Bottle ($US)
Rawson's Retreat	Varietal range[a]	1	Premium	$8.99
Koonunga Hill	Varietal range[a]	1-2	Premium	$10.99
Thomas Hyland	Varietal range[a]	1-2	Premium	$14.99
Bin 138	Shiraz Mourvedre Grenache		Super Premium	$19.00
Bin 128	Shiraz	3	Super Premium	$24.00
Bin 28	Shiraz	3	Super Premium	$24.00
Bin 389	Cabernet Shiraz	3	Super Premium	$26.00
Bin 407	Cabernet Sauvignon	3	Super Premium	$26.00
St. Henri	Shiraz	5	Ultra Premium	$39.00
Magill Estate	Shiraz	4	Ultra Premium	$50.00
RWT	Shiraz	4	Ultra Premium	$69.00
Bin 707	Cabernet Sauvignon	4	Ultra Premium	$80.00
Grange	Shiraz	6	Icon	$185.00

Source: Southcorp Wines, the Americas.

[a]Typical red varietal range included of these brands Merlot, Shiraz Cabernet, and Cabernet Sauvignon. (These brands also offer a range of white wines.)

Exhibit 8   Ten Largest Wine Brands in the United Kingdom, 1998

Brand	Company and Country of Origin	Sales ($000s)
E&J Gallo	Gallo (U.S.)	$55,600
Hardy's	BRL Hardy (Australia)	38,500
Jacob's Creek	Orlando (Australia)	38,400
Moet et Chandon	LVMH (France)	28,500
Le Piat[a]	Le Piat (France)	27,200
Sowells of Chelsea	Matthew Clark (U.K.)	26,400
Penfolds	Southcorp (Australia)	19,200
Lindemans	Southcorp (Australia)	15,200
Rosemount	Rosemount Estate (Australia)	13,000
Lanson	Lanson (France)	12,300

Source: Adapted by casewriters from Annemiek Geene, Arend Heijbroek, Anne Lagerwerf, and Rafi Wazir, "The World Wine Business,"
Market Study, May 1999, available from Rabobank International.

the battle developing for the increasingly branded middle market. "We are bottling history," said Paul Pontellier, chief winemaker at Chateau Margaux. "We must concentrate on our field of excellence and not spread ourselves too thin."

There were a few exceptions, however. As early as the 1930s, Baron Philipe de Rothschild had created a second label for "output deemed unworthy" of the icon level Mouton-Rothschild brand. Mouton Cadet grew to be a significant midprice brand. More recently, Baron Philipe's daughter, Baroness Philippine, had begun sourcing wines from the south of France and marketing them as Cadet Chardonnay, Cadet Merlot, and so on.

Lacking a response by growers, some intermediaries started filling the need for consistent quality and supply that branding ensured. Indeed, the names of *négociants* such as Georges Deboeuf and Louis Jardot became better known than the vast majority of Beaujolais and Burgundy producers they represented. And U.K. wine merchants such as Sowells of Chelsea and Oddbins developed their own brands to minimize buyer confusion while also capturing some of the value that branding provided in the fast-growing premium market segment.

A different approach was being followed by other traditional producers that felt they were too small and unskilled to mount their own marketing plans. They saw their best hope in linking up with the established marketing and distribution powerhouses such as the Australians and the Americans. For example, in 1997, Vinicola Caltrasi, a family-owned Sicilian company linked to local growers' cooperatives, entered into a joint venture with Australian producer BRL Hardy, a company that had already used its experience in branding and marketing to make a wine it imported from Chile the leading brand in its segment. Hardy developed the brand, label design, and marketing strategy for a line of Italian wines it called *D'Istinto* ("Instinctively"), which it launched on the U.K. market at prices from £3.49 to £6.99 per bottle (roughly $5.76 to $11.53).[15]

Increasing Distribution Power

Because branding and marketing had typically been handled by their *négociants*, most European producers were still very isolated from increasingly fast-changing consumer tastes and preferences—particularly in export markets like the United Kingdom. Equally problematic was their lack of bargaining power when dealing with retailers, particularly the rapidly concentrating supermarket chains such as Tesco and Sainsbury (see Exhibit 9). In contrast, New World wine companies tended to control operations from the vineyard to the retailer. They used their scale and integration to achieve market power in their domestic markets—in Australia, the largest five wine companies accounted for 85% of market share—thereby generating the resources and expertise to attack export markets. In contrast, the largest five French wine companies (excluding champagne specialists) accounted for only 8% of their market. The comparable number in Italy was 4%.

The large New World producers also developed significant distribution advantages from their scale and scope. By controlling the distribution chain, they added even more cost advantages to their lower production costs by avoiding more handling stages, holding less inventory, and capturing the intermediaries' markup. Even the transport and trade economics that once favored European suppliers selling into the United Kingdom had changed in the last decades of the century. Tariff barriers dropped under successive World Trade Organization negotiations, and transportation differentials shifted as trucking costs rose while containership costs fell. As a result, the cost of shipping wine from Australia to the United Kingdom was now about the same as trucking it from the south of France.

Size had also given the New World companies bargaining power in their dealings with the concentrating retail sector. For example, Australian giant Southcorp had 50 sales reps in Britain; CVBG, one of France's largest producers with sales of $150 million, could support only two. Because they could respond to retailers' need for consistent supplies of branded products, the Australians captured the high-volume sales.[16] As consumers became even more sensitive to pricing than brand, retailers reported that their sales trends followed whatever product offered the highest perceived quality-to-value ratio. With their cost advantage, Australian producers responded with aggressive pricing. In the face of this distribution-based, pricing-driven growth, French market share was maintained only with the aid of frequent promotions.[17] Even so, its share continued to slip.

---

15 For a full account of BRL Hardy's global strategy, including its Italian sourcing and branding decisions, see Christopher A. Bartlett, "BRL Hardy: Globalizing an Australian Wine Company," HBS Case No. 300-018 (Boston: Harvard Business School Publishing, 1999).

16 Rachman, p. 99.

17 Annemiek Geene, Arend Heijbroek, Anne Lagerwerf, and Rafi Wazir, "The World Wine Business," Market Study, May 1999, available from Rabobank International.

Exhibit 9   U.K. Off-License Wine Sales by Outlet, 1985–1995

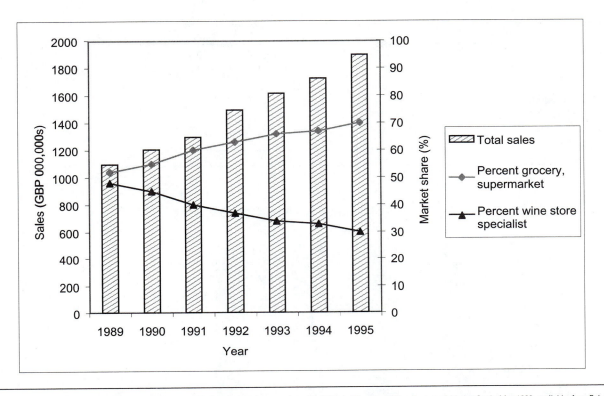

Source: Adapted by casewriters from Annemiek Geene, Arend Heijbroek, Anne Lagerwerf, and Rafi Wazir, "The World Wine Business," Market Study, May 1999, available from Rabobank International.

Reports from the Front: Victories, Defeats, and Responses

Results in the wine companies' Battle for Britain—and particularly in the contest between Australia and France for dominance in the U.K. market—were dramatic. During the 1990s French wine exports to the United Kingdom increased approximately 5% annually, while Australian imports grew seven times faster. So while French market share eroded from 39% in 1994 to 26% in 2000, the Australians' share increased from 8% to 17%. But of greater concern to the French was the forecast that the Australians would overtake them as market leaders some time during 2002. (See Exhibit 10 for source country market share in the United Kingdom.)

The Australian claim for dominance was even stronger than simple market share indicated. The bulk of French wine sales were in the less expensive (and less profitable) categories, which also were the market segments that expected little or no growth. Australian wines were largely positioned in the premium and super-premium segments, where trends indicated the greatest potential for growth. (See Exhibit 11 for distributions of price points of U.K. imports.) Moreover, for many historic and structural reasons discussed earlier, French producers faced greater

Exhibit 10   U.K. Retail Wine Sales: Market Share by Source, 1988–2002E

	1988	1994	2000	2002E
France	43%	39%	26%	22%
Germany	30	19	11	9
Italy	10	10	13	12
Other (including Chile and South Africa)	15	23	27	25
United States	1	2	7	10
Australia	2	8	17	22
	100%	100%	100%	100%

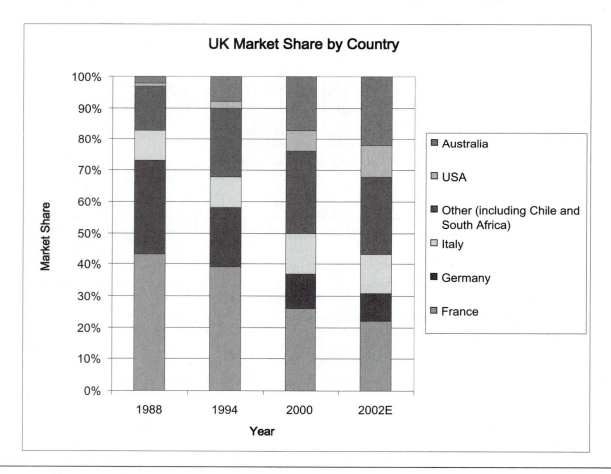

Source: Adapted by casewriters from Sheryle Bagwell, "The French Correction," *Business Review Weekly*, August 29, 2002, p. 34; and Paul Tranter and Christian van Tienhoven, "Why the New World is Winning in theWine Industry," unpublished manuscript, May 3, 2002.

Price range (£)	Australia	United States	France	Germany
>£4.51	41%	31%	18%	2%
£4.01 – £4.50	16	22	7	2
£3.01 – £4.00	41	44	43	28
£2.06 – £3.00	2	3	29	47
<£2.05	-	-	3	21
	100%	100%	100%	100%

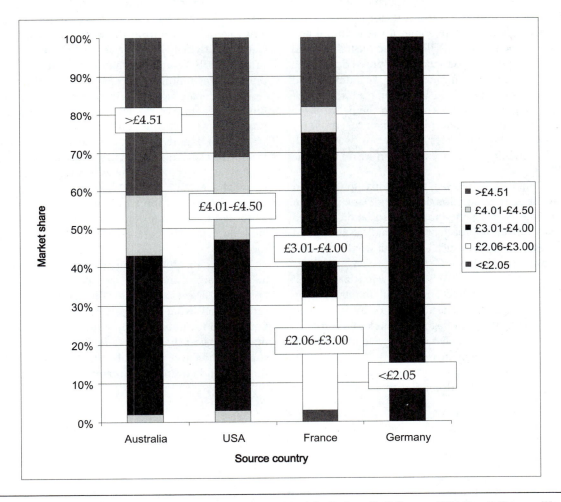

Source: Adapted by casewriters from Mike Gibbs, Steve Branley-Jackson, Claire Ross, Mark Lynch, Stephen Potter, Lisa Heffernan, and Girish Pamnani, "Beverages: Wines," Europe, February 11, 2002, available from Goldman Sachs Global Equity Research.

production costs in these segments than their New World rivals (see Exhibit 12).

In early 2002, many in the French wine industry were becoming concerned. Twelve months earlier, the French minister of agriculture had appointed his general controller, Jacques Berthomeau, as wine-crisis manager and asked him to prepare a report on the French industry. Released in July 2001, the report was frank in its evaluation and strong in its recommendations. "[The French wine industry] has lived too long on its past good name," it concluded. "It needs to come out of its haughty elitism and take the threat of the New World challenge seriously."[18] One of the report's main recommendations was that the French industry had to adopt some of the technical and marketing advances that had allowed the Australians and Americans to succeed. In particular, it proposed developing a much stronger commitment to branding. Said Berthomeau: "The French . . . have marketed wine based on heritage of growing regions, down to the fields of the chateaus where the vines are planted. France's rivals, by contrast, address the consumer the way you would with beer. . . . The question for us French is, can we do the same thing? The answer is yes."[19]

In the months that followed, the response to the report was as diverse as it was emotional. Jean-Luc Darien, director of *Onivins*, the French wine industry association, worried that a brand-driven approach was too radical and risked simplifying the product to such a degree it would "toss the baby out with the bathwater." After all, even though its share had declined from 50% in 1990, French wine still had 40% of the global market and was still the standard by which most consumers gauged other countries' wines. Rather than seeing the great fragmentation and diversity of French wine markets as a liability, he felt the industry should work to make them an asset.[20]

The *Federation des Exportateurs des Vins et Spiritueux*, which represented 2,000 companies that traded 80% of French exports, proposed a different solution. In its view, French AOC and VDQS wines should be produced and marketed as they had been historically. But wines for the lower half of the market should be grouped as "the country wines of France," sourced from multiple regions, and labeled based on grape variety, not region. In this way, France could produce more consistent wines with the fruit-driven taste that New World producers had made so popular.[21]

But Rene Renou, president of the *Institut National des Appellations D'Origine*, the body that administered the AOC rules, called this approach foolhardy. He proposed a renewed emphasis on *terroir* as the means to distinguish French wines from the worldwide glut. "We must claim the right to be unique, to be specific," he said. "There are thousands of Chardonnays, but there is only one wine from Bonnezeaux."[22]

As the debate raged, a new forecast from the Australian Bureau of Agricultural and Resource Economics saw Australia's wine exports growing 75% over the next five years. With exports eclipsing domestic sales for the first time in 2002—and expected to account for 67% of production by 2008—growers were aggressively expanding their vineyards. By 2007 180,000 hectares would be planted—almost three times the area planted in 1996.[23] Even M. Berthomeau took time out from his role as French critic to grumble that "[The Australians'] heads are getting a little too big."[24]

As French domestic consumption continued to fall and its share of the world market continued to decline by about 1% a year, there was little agreement within the industry on what strategy would reverse the trends. Equally concerning was the growing French realization that the biggest challenge would lie not so much in what strategic direction to take, but how to align the diverse industry and government interests to act on it.

18 Jacques Berthomeau, "Comment mieux positionner les vins français sur les marchés d'exportation?" Report to Jean Glavany, French minister of agriculture, July 31, 2001.

19 John Tagliabue, "For French Vintners, Lessons in Mass Marketing," *The New York Times*, April 14, 2002, Section 3, p. 4.

20 Ibid.

21 John Lichfield, "Our man in Paris," *The Independent*, October 12, 2002, p. 23.

22 Larry Walker, "Worldbeat," *Wines & Vines*, May 1, 2002, p. 86.

23 Daniel Lewis, "Fine time for wine as growers try to sate world thirst," *Sydney Morning Herald*, March 8, 2003, p. 3

Exhibit 12 Estimates of Nationally Variable Production Costs and Revenue by Market Segment for Selected Producer Countries[1]

($US per 9L case)	Australia				France				US			
	Basic	Premium	Super	Ultra	Basic	Premium	Super	Ultra	Basic	Premium	Super	Ultra
Grape costs[2]	$1.03	$6.43	$22.58	$45.45	$1.32	$6.43	$28.23	$104.55	$1.32	$5.71	$25.00	$63.64
Crush and capital costs	12.94	15.71	17.74	20.00	13.53	16.43	18.55	20.91	13.53	16.43	18.55	20.91
Barrel costs (corks, labels, etc.)[3]	0.00	0.00	0.94	2.25	0.00	0.00	0.94	2.25	0.00	0.00	0.94	2.25
Dry goods costs per case	0.06	0.08	0.09	0.10	0.08	0.10	0.12	0.13	0.07	0.09	0.10	0.11
Total winery costs	14.03	22.22	41.35	67.80	14.94	22.96	47.84	127.83	14.92	22.23	44.59	86.90
Ex-winery revenue[4]	16.00	25.00	50.00	155.00	16.00	25.00	50.00	155.00	16.00	25.00	50.00	155.00
winery margin	12%	11%	17%	56%	7%	8%	4%	18%	7%	11%	12%	44%

Source: Adepted by casewriters from Annemiek Geene, Arend Heijbroek, Anne Lagerwerf, and Rafi Wazir, "The World Wine Business," Market Study, May 1999, available from Rabobank International; "The Global Wine Industry," Apirl 23, 2001, available from Morgan Stanley Dean Witter Global Equity Research; and Mike Gibbs, Steve Branley-Jackson, Claire Ross, Mark Lynch, Stephen Potter, Lisa Heffernan, and Girish Pamnani, "Beverages: Wine Europe," Market Study, February 11, 2002, available from Goldman Sachs Global Equity Research.

Notes:

[1] All costs are best estimates from a wide range of available sources. Wide variations occur.

[2] Grape cost per case is median of price spread for grapes purchased on the open market in each country:

	Basic	Premium	Super Premium	Ultra Premium
Price for Grapes (US$ per metric ton)				
Australia	$75 to 100	$200 to 600	$800 to 2000	$2,000 to 3000
France	100 to 125	200 to 700	1,100 to 2500	3,000 to 7000
US	75 to 150	200 to 600	1,100 to 2000	2,500 to 4500
Metric tons per acre	8 to 20	5 to 7	3 to 5	2 to 3
Cases per metric ton	85	70	62	55
Cases per acre	680 to 1700	350 to 490	200 to 310	110 to 165
Grape prices reflect differences in mechanization, and particularly differences in land prices ($US per acre):				
Australia	$8,000	$15,000	$22,000	$30,000
France[a]	10,000	22,000	55,000	100,000
US	12,000	20,000	50,000	75,000

[3] Cost per vintage of barrel use assuming 7-year life of 300L American new oak barrel at $375.. Ultra premium is 20% of barrel cost ("new oak"). Super premium is 8% of barrel cost (not "new oak").

[4] Note that shipping and marketing costs as well as distribution and retailer margins of approx. 30% and 40% respectively must be added to bring price up to retail level.

Tesco Plc.

Our strategy is to take a successful U.K. company and make it a world leader in an industry we think will become an international industry. Neither of these things is proven yet: we haven't made the transition, and the industry hasn't yet become international.

Terry Leahy, Tesco CEO, 2002

We will have more space overseas than in the U.K. by 2003/04.

Tesco Interim Report, 2002

The 1990s had been a successful decade for Tesco, the British supermarket chain. The early 1990s found Tesco staggering under the effects of the recession that had hit the United Kingdom. Sainsbury's, Tesco's number one competitor and archrival, was announcing yet another record year. Marks and Spencer, another vaunted food rival, was still one of the world's most admired retailers. By the end of the decade, things were a bit different. Tesco was the number one food retailer in the United Kingdom, Sainsbury's was scrambling to recover and had been rumored as a takeover target, and Marks and Spencer had stumbled at home and internationally. So successful had Tesco been at almost everything it had touched, even Tesco.com, its Internet/home delivery service, was profitable, probably the only such example worldwide.

At the start of 2002, Terry Leahy, CEO since 1997, had reason to be pleased. Not only had the company's stock price more than doubled, from 89 pence[1] in April 1996 to 206 pence in October 2002, he had personally been recognized by the Queen for his services to food retailing and was now a knight, Sir Terence. At the tender age of 46, Leahy was not about to sail into the sunset. For one thing, at his accession to the role of CEO he had announced an aggressive 10-year growth plan for the company to (1) develop a strong core U.K. business, (2) be as much in the nonfood

business as in food, (3) develop a profitable retailing services business, and (4) be as strong internationally as domestically. For another, competition showed no signs of weakening. One of his main competitors, Asda, had been bought by Wal-Mart, the American retail giant. Asda, along with Morrisons and Tesco, occupied the value segment of U.K. supermarket retailing. With a recovering Sainsbury's together with another grocery competitor, Safeway, at a slightly higher price point and continuing vigorous competition from European discounters such as Aldi, Netto, and Lidl at lower price points, Tesco would not be number one for long if it grew complacent. What would the story be at the end of the next 10 years? Had Tesco deserved its success, or had it merely survived against inept competition? And if it had deserved its success, was that success transferable to Tesco's small but thriving international ventures?

COMPANY OVERVIEW

In 2002, Tesco operated 1,023 stores in 10 countries (750 in the United Kingdom), employed 260,000 people worldwide, and had access to a population of 280 million people. Since 1999, turnover had increased 38% and net profit 37%. (For more financial information see Exhibits 1 through 4 and Table A.) Tesco's main competitors included Sainsbury's, Safeway, Asda, and Morrisons supermarkets. Since the mid-1990s, Tesco's stock had outperformed those of its competitors as well as the industry index (see Exhibit 5).

In addition to its traditional supermarket format, Tesco operated Tesco Metro (urban convenience stores targeted

This case was prepared by David E. Bell with the assistance of Cate Reavis.

Copyright © 2002 by the President and Fellows of Harvard College. Harvard Business School case 9-503-036

[1] One pound (£1) was worth $1.57 in December 2002. One pound = 100 pence.

Exhibit 1   Tesco—Income Statement (millions of pounds)

Year to February	1999A	2000A	2001A	2002A	2003E	2004E	2005E
Sales—U.K.	15,835	16,958	18,372	20,052	21,461	23,049	24,708
—Europe	1,167	1,374	1,756	2,203	2,614	3,026	3,554
—Asia	156	464	860	1,398	2,343	3,573	4,955
Group sales	17,158	18,796	20,988	23,653	26,418	29,649	33,218
U.K. gross margin	25.4%	25.3%	25.3%	25.4%	25.4%	25.4%	25.4%
Operating profit—U.K.	919	993	1,100	1,213	1,308	1,409	1,516
—Europe	48	51	70	90	145	180	214
—Asia	(2)	(1)	4	29	70	125	190
Group operating profit	**965**	**1,043**	**1,174**	**1,332**	**1,523**	**1,714**	**1,920**
Group operating margin	5.6%	5.5%	5.6%	5.6%	5.8%	5.8%	5.8%
Income from associates	6	11	21	42	58	72	88
Net interest payable	(90)	(99)	(125)	(153)	(190)	(206)	(218)
Adjusted PBT	**881**	**955**	**1,070**	**1,221**	**1,390**	**1,580**	**1,790**
Exceptionals/amortization	(39)	(22)	(16)	(20)	(10)	(10)	(10)
Reported PBT	842	933	1054	1,201	1,380	1,570	1,780
Tax charge	(237)	(259)	(333)	(371)	(427)	(485)	(550)
Tax rate	28.1%	27.8%	31.6%	30.9%	30.9%	30.9%	30.9%
Net profit	605	674	721	830	954	1,085	1,230
Minority interest	1	0	1	0	(2)	(5)	(8)
Net attributable profit	**606**	**674**	**722**	**830**	**952**	**1,080**	**1,222**
Dividends	(277)	(302)	(340)	(390)	(435)	(491)	(551)
Retained profit	**329**	**372**	**382**	**440**	**517**	**589**	**671**
FRS3 EPS (p)	9.1	10.1	10.6	12.0	13.7	15.4	17.3
Adjusted, diluted EPS (p)	**9.4**	**10.2**	**10.7**	**12.1**	**13.6**	**15.3**	**17.2**
Total dividend (p)	4.12	4.48	4.98	5.60	6.25	7.00	7.80

Source: Company reports and Schroder Salomon Smith Barney estimates.

Tesco Plc.   39

Exhibit 2   Tesco—Balance Sheet (millions of pounds)

Year to February	1999A	2000A	2001A	2002A	2003E	2004E	2005E
Intangible fixed assets	11 2	136	154	154	134	124	11 4
Tangible fixed assets	7,441	8,391	9,884	11,349	12,774	14,117	15,381
Inventories	667	744	838	929	1,000	1,091	1,188
Debtors	151	252	322	454	477	521	570
Investments	201	258	255	225	225	225	225
Cash	127	88	279	445	445	445	445
Total assets	**8,699**	**9,869**	**11,732**	**13,556**	**15,054**	**16,523**	**17,923**
Shareholders' funds	4,382	4,769	4,978	5,530	6,097	6,735	7,457
Minority interest	(5)	29	36	36	36	36	36
Provisions	17	19	402	440	440	440	440
Long-term debt	1,218	1,559	1,925	2,741	3,320	3,753	3,991
Short-term debt	830	847	1,413	1,489	1,489	1,489	1,489
Trade creditors	1,100	1,248	1,538	1,830	2,053	2,304	2,580
Other short-term creditors	1,157	1,398	1,440	1,490	1,619	1,766	1,930
Total liabilities	**8,699**	**9,869**	**11,732**	**13,556**	**15,054**	**16,523**	**17,923**

Source: Company reports and Schroder Salomon Smith Barney estimates.

Exhibit 3 Tesco—Cash Flow Statement, 1999–2005E (millions of pounds)

Year to February	1999A	2000A	2001A	2002A	2003E	2004E	2005E
Operating profit (EBITA)	965	1,043	1,174	1,332	1,523	1,714	1,920
Depreciation	401	428	468	524	585	657	736
EBITDA	**1,366**	**1,471**	**1,642**	**1,856**	**2,108**	**2,371**	**2,656**
EBITDA margin	7.98%	7.83%	7.82%	7.84%	7.98%	8.00%	8.00%
Interest and taxes	(366)	(344)	(433)	(555)	(542)	(605)	(670)
Working capital	(19)	48	295	182	130	115	130
Net cash flow from operations	981	1,175	1,504	1,483	1,696	1,880	2,117
Dividends	(238)	(262)	(254)	(297)	(325)	(363)	(405)
Capital expenditure (net)	(1,005)	(1,211)	(1,910)	(1,835)	(2,000)	(2,000)	(2,000)
Exceptional items	(26)	(6)	0	0	0	0	0
Acquisitions/disposals	(274)	1	(76)	(96)	0	0	0
Other	0	(18)	(58)	(85)	0	0	0
Free cash flow	**(562)**	**(321)**	**(794)**	**(830)**	**(629)**	**(483)**	**(289)**
Shares issued	42	20	88	82	50	50	50
Noncash movements	(9)	(39)	(38)	(8)	0	0	0
Opening net debt	(1,191)	(1,720)	(2,060)	(2,804)	(3,560)	(4,13)	(4,573)
Closing net debt	**(1,720)**	**(2,060)**	**(2,804)**	**(3,560)**	**(4,139)**	**(4,572)**	**(4,810)**
Gearing	33.7%	37.3%	48.7%	56.4%	60.1%	60.6%	58.2%

Source: Company reports and Schroder Salomon Smith Barney estimates.

Exhibit 4   Tesco—Key Data, 1999–2005E

Year to February	1999A	2000A	2001A	2002A	2003E	2004E	2005E
Dividend cover	2.3	2.3	2.1	2.2	2.2	2.2	2.2
Interest cover	7.7	7.1	6.6	6.2	5.9	6.1	6.5
Book value per share (p)	77.0	82.6	84.7	91.7	99.0	107.5	117.1
ROCE	15.3%	14.5%	14.5%	14.4%	14.6%	14.8%	15.2%
Asset turnover	1.95	1.88	1.82	1.77	1.75	1.79	1.85
Payment period (days)	31.4	32.5	35.8	37.8	38.0	38.0	38.0
Collection period (days)	2.1	3.5	4.5	5.2	5.0	5.0	5.0
U.K. store numbers	639	659	691	728	792	827	882
U.K. sales area (000 sq. ft.)	15,975	16,895	17,949	18,822	20,076	21,106	22,136
Sales (ex VAT) per sq. ft. /wk. (£/wk.)	19.56	19.95	20.39	21.09	21.24	21.52	21.97
U.K. profit per sq. ft. (£)	1.14	1.17	1.22	1.28	1.29	1.32	1.35

Source: Company reports and Schroder Salomon Smith Barney estimates.

toward office workers who wanted ready-made meals), Tesco Express (a convenience store often near Esso gas stations), and Tesco Extra Hypermarkets. Tesco had achieved a 4% share of the nonfood market[2] in the United Kingdom and was well on its way to achieving its goal of a 6% share. Worldwide nonfood sales had increased to £7 billion. The company offered a number of retail services through the Tesco Personal Finance division.

In addition to the United Kingdom, Tesco had operations in Ireland, Hungary, Poland, the Czech Republic, Slovakia, Thailand, South Korea, Taiwan, and Malaysia. Tesco's international business accounted for 42% of the company's total floor space but only 10% of its net income.

Company History

In 1919, Jack Cohen invested his serviceman's gratuity worth £30 in a grocery stall in London. In 1924, he

Table A   First Six Months of 2002

	Sales	Operating Profit
United Kingdom	£10.5 billion	£537 million
International	£2.3 billion[a]	£59 million

Source: Company.
[a]One billion pounds in Asia, £1.3 billion in Europe.

introduced Tesco Tea, his first private-label product. (The name Tesco came from the initials of his tea supplier, T. E. Stockwell, and the first two letters of Cohen's name.) The first Tesco store opened in 1929 in London, and by the end of the 1930s there were over 100, mainly in London. After a visit to the United States in the mid-1930s, where he discovered the American self-serve supermarket model, Cohen decided to adopt the same "pile it high and sell it cheap" format. The first American-style Tesco was opened in 1947, the same year the company (Tesco Stores Holdings) went public. Cohen's emphasis on self-service led to his paying more attention to his suppliers and, in effect, ignoring his customers.

The fortunes of the once-thriving chain declined so much in this period that "doing a Tesco" became British jargon for snatching defeat from the jaws of victory. As a final insult, the Imperial Tobacco Company, Britain's major player in the tobacco industry, having considered an acquisition of Tesco as part of a diversification strategy, eventually declined on the ground that Tesco might damage Imperial's brand image.

RECOVERY—IMPROVING OPERATIONS

In the early 1980s, Ian MacLaurin became the first nonfamily CEO. MacLaurin reputedly had great charisma; he would lift the morale of any store just by entering it. But coming

---

2 Nonfood includes clothing, music, appliances and the like but not normal grocery items like shampoo and not automobiles.

Exhibit 5   U.K. Competitors' Stock Prices

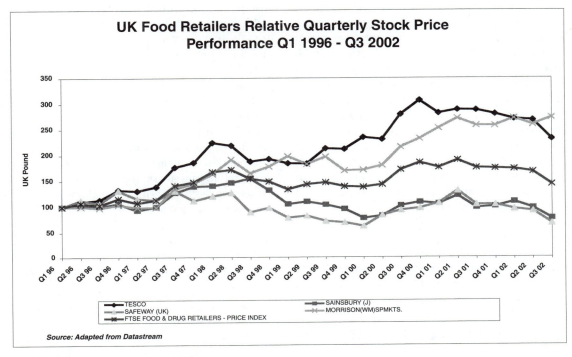

UK Food Retailers Relative Quarterly Stock Price Performance Q1 1996 - Q3 2002

Legend: TESCO • SAINSBURY (J) • SAFEWAY (UK) • MORRISON(WM)SPMKTS. • FTSE FOOD & DRUG RETAILERS - PRICE INDEX

Source: Adapted from Datastream

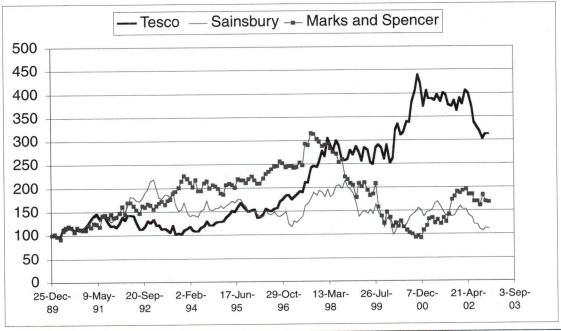

Legend: Tesco — Sainsbury — Marks and Spencer

Source: Graph based on data from Commodity Systems Inc. via Yahoo!

from the operations side of the business, he realized that the company needed to be streamlined to have any hope of survival. He closed many of Tesco's smaller stores and built larger, more economical 30,000-square-foot stores in the suburbs. His aggressive expansion into a core business of over 200 superstores and a centralized distribution system that left Sainsbury's trailing, as well as advances in fresh food and its own label, set Tesco up well strategically. As for the merchandising side of things, innovation was fairly straightforward—copy whatever Sainsbury's was doing.[3]

The economic boom of the 1980s provided some breathing space for Tesco, but it also permitted the company the (complacent) luxury of higher margins through higher prices. The recession of the 1990s exposed this copycat merchandising strategy; the lower-priced continental discounters attracted the value conscious, and Sainsbury's did a better job at attracting the quality conscious. Tesco had no differentiated offer to maintain the loyalty of its customers. Just at this time, as Tesco's fortunes again plummeted, the newspapers were rubbing it in with headlines announcing Sainsbury's most profitable year yet and the selection of Marks and Spencer as "Britain's most admired retailer."

RECOVERY—FOCUS ON THE CUSTOMER

In 1992 Leahy, by then director in charge of fresh foods, was elevated to the board with responsibility for marketing. He realized that if Tesco continued to lose 1% to 2% of share per year, the company would be in dire shape very quickly. As a good marketer should, he began to investigate a basic question: Why, exactly, were customers leaving? Based on focus groups, Leahy concluded that Tesco had squandered a lot of goodwill with its core customers. Their anger had less to do with a rational comparison of what the company had to offer but rather that Tesco had so obviously been chasing Sainsbury's, copying them on this, copying them on that, instead of trying to satisfy its own customers. By March 1993, Leahy was able to report to the board. He summarized what he thought Tesco needed to do:

1. Stop copying Sainsbury's as a merchandising strategy.
2. Institutionalize listening to customers.
3. Build a merchandising offer based on responding to what Tesco's own customers wanted.

Tim Mason, now marketing director, coined the phrase "bricks in the wall" to describe this incremental approach to merchandising: no sweeping innovation, just patient responses to customer needs. Describing the strategy internally, Leahy used the slogan "Tesco: The Natural Choice for Ordinary Shoppers," indicating that the chase for the upscale customer was over. Externally the slogan was "Every Little Helps," an expression that resonated with the people who had accused the company of deserting them.

In the fall of 1993 the first customer-driven innovation occurred with the introduction of a "value line," a low-priced, no-frills range of basic items. The investment community was aghast at the move. Critics said this would cheapen Tesco's image and no one would "lower" himself or herself to buy such things. But they were wrong. Some customers did buy them, but perhaps more importantly, the rest saw the value line as an indication that Tesco was trying to help. In the fall of 1994 Tesco introduced "One in Front," a commitment to keep lines short at the checkout counter. Cashiers were to signal for help if they saw more than one person waiting in line. As Leahy recalled:

In the busy days of the 1980s, stores were so crowded, long lines were the norm. Customers accepted that waiting was a necessary part of shopping, and management accepted that acceptance. But it didn't mean customers liked it. A consequence of "One in Front" was that we needed more cashiers, at least, more people who could be cashiers. So we progressed to have more staff—more multitasking staff—in our stores.

It wasn't long before I noticed a pattern in our focus groups. No matter what the focus group was talking about, whether being critical or not, there was always a point where somebody would stand up and praise the staff at Tesco. And the group would nod in agreement. So we made our staff the heroes of our "Every Little Helps" advertising campaign. We had a constant character, "Dotty," an elderly, difficult-to-please customer. Everyone in the U.K. got to know and love Dotty. And our staff were the heroes.

In February 1995 Tesco introduced the "Clubcard," which offered a penny back per pound spent (1%). Leahy thought of the rebate idea while sitting on a train. "I recalled shopping at the Co-op store when I was a boy. You gave your Co-op number when you bought something and at the end of the year got a dividend based on your purchases. The Co-op stopped doing it years ago, but in the '50s, when times

---

3 One of the young up-and-coming managers in charge of doing the copying was one Terry Leahy, hired in 1979.

were hard, it meant a lot to their customers." The Clubcard concept was tested in a few stores for a few months, with great success, and then rolled out nationally. The Clubcard was immediately productive in that it got a lot of people to try Tesco again. The Clubcard also offered an opportunity to use direct mail to target customers. The best customers, those spending in excess of £600 per quarter, were given special offers, such as flights not available to all or cash coupons.

Observers were not impressed with this innovation either, one critic referring to it scornfully as "electronic Green Shield stamps,"[4] but Tesco management credited the Clubcard, now with 10 million members, as a major contributor to the Tesco turnaround. One manager commented, "A loyalty card is a 'must have' these days for a retailer. Some have suggested that a loyalty card can be used as a device to merchandise to the best customers, but that's not how retail works. Once you've opened a store, you want everyone in your store, not just the big spenders. We don't think there is such a thing as a bad customer. Success in retailing comes from the last 3% of customers."

Telephone operators and the Tesco Web site together fielded over 100,000 customer queries per week, many relating to the Clubcard program (lost cards, enquiries about point accumulation) but also to the quality of products. All managers had online access to these customer comments. The company credited knowledge of customer needs derived from Clubcard data with adding three points to its in-stock percentage.

And the focus groups continued. Mason observed:

> We learn things all the time. We discovered that people didn't like our stainless steel refrigerators. They reminded people of a hospital. So now we install refrigerators that are colored. We also learned the importance of clean toilets. We all know they ought to be clean; what we didn't fully appreciate is that customers relate the hygiene of the toilets with the hygiene of the store as a whole.

RECOVERY—FOCUS ON EMPLOYEES

Tesco's focus on customers soon extended to employees. Leahy began meeting with "focus groups" of employees: "I would ask each group what Tesco stood for. A typical response would be 'caring for customers.' Then I asked what they would *like* Tesco to stand for, and they would

use words like teamwork, praise, and trust. These are part of our core values today. People want to enjoy being at work. The goodwill of the staff is the main productivity lever that you have."

Leahy knew that reenergizing the staff would require an attitude of respect, meaningful work, and training—throughout the organization. He said, "Too many people at high levels had vaguely defined roles; too many people in the stores were performing elementary tasks." From 1996 to 1998, all managers were put through a training program designed to teach fundamental aspects of management: how to run a meeting, how to identify the causes of a problem and, perhaps most importantly, how to spot resistance to change and to learn methods for dealing with that resistance. Treating employees with respect extended to job security. So far as possible, employees whose positions were eliminated were found jobs elsewhere in the company.

RECOVERY—FOCUS ON GROWTH

When Leahy became CEO in 1997 he was satisfied that Tesco had become a stable, competitive player in the U.K. supermarket business. But growth was only keeping up with inflation. The company he envisioned in 2007 would derive much of its revenue from nonfood products, and international business would be as important as the U.K. business. Leahy also announced the ambition of making Tesco an "essential part of the landscape" in the United Kingdom. He wanted the company to be a British institution, like the BBC or Marks and Spencer had been in their prime.[5]

Leahy's ambitious growth goals could be achieved in three ways:

- By increasing the effectiveness of the existing U.K. business
- By finding new ways to deliver value to U.K. customers
- By accelerating the pace of international expansion

But in order to be able to execute his strategy, Leahy knew that he would need an organization that would work hard, and effectively, in pursuit of the goals he had laid out. The organizational strategy was to communicate very clearly where the company was headed and empower everyone to make it happen. To make the empowerment succeed, Leahy ensured that each person had a set of

---

4 Green Shield stamps were a widely used "money-back" scheme, popular in the 1960s and 1970s, in which customers collected stamps at various participating retail stores and, after suitable accumulation, traded them in for gifts.

quantifiable objectives relevant to the employee's situation and a set of incentives for achieving them.

The approach, described as "the Tesco Way," was summarized in a widely distributed brochure (see Exhibit 6). One of the core values was "simplicity." Dido Harding, now a director of food procurement who joined Tesco after a stint at Woolworth's, noted that Tesco was run rather differently: "There was a clear message that bright people weren't supposed to use their intellect to make things more complicated, but rather to make things simpler." Tesco's corporate affairs director, Lucy Neville-Rolfe, said the notion of simplicity extended to communications:

> We have a message of the week that is sent by e-mail to our top 2,000 managers, any of whom can reply directly if they have a question. They in turn pass it on, perhaps translated appropriately. No one in management has a private secretary—even Terry sometimes picks up his own phone—which makes for good communication. It's the same on the outside. We don't use lobbyists because it is easier to communicate if we do it in person.

Another cornerstone of the Tesco Way was the "steering wheel," which laid out the objectives that managers would be judged by. Each quarter a manager would be shown the wheel and how his or her performance rated against those objectives, color-coded for impact: green indicated good progress, yellow a caution, and red declared a problem. A store manager's steering wheel included objectives such as shrinkage and the results of visits by mystery shoppers. The store manager was also measured on how well the store's employees understood the store's performance on key measures. As a result, employee back rooms were plastered with graphs on which key indicators were updated daily.

INCREASING THE EFFECTIVENESS OF U.K. STORES

Logistics

According to industry observers, Tesco's U.K. stores had one of the best distribution networks in the world. This was in spite of Tesco's reputation of being "obsessed with stores" rather than operations. Tesco spent £200 million to £300 million per year on its logistics systems, mostly on upgrading existing facilities.

The emphasis was on using existing resources more efficiently. For example, the distribution centers were increasingly using cross-docking, a system by which goods flow directly from inbound trucks to waiting store-bound trucks. Adoption of this technique was hampered by the lack of loading bays, which meant some doors needed to be used for loading and unloading. The critical bottleneck at the warehouses led to a number of creative initiatives designed to increase the ability to coordinate arrival and departures of trucks. One initiative was to use Tesco's own trucks to collect goods from suppliers, a technique known as primary distribution. Another initiative had store managers visiting the distribution centers to see firsthand the problems created if a truck was not unloaded at a store promptly.

Most stores currently received two deliveries per day: a "fill-up" delivery and a "top-up" delivery, though the goal was to move to two main deliveries per day, thus increasing turns and reducing out-of-stocks.

Procurement

The steering wheel for buyers included performance objectives such as delivered cost, product quality, and delivery reliability, but, said Harding, "We are mainly measured on gross margin because that's the only cost measure that is unique to the buying function. Even though we are held to account on gross margin, the attitude is to deliver for the customer: in our case, the store manager. That permeates everything. The customer really is king."

Negotiations with key suppliers usually occurred once per year. A pricing system would be agreed upon that laid out the price Tesco would pay as a function of the quantity it ultimately ordered and the reliability with which it was delivered. Tesco's goal was to hold as little inventory as possible, so flexibility was a key component of vendor selection.

Tesco had followed a trend in the industry by encouraging some vendors to dedicate themselves, or one of

---

5 This latter goal was accomplished not only through being an increasingly important part of customers' retail lives but also by touching their daily lives. Tesco had spent £77 million on a "Computers in Schools" program whereby customers could donate till receipts to a local school that in turn could trade those receipts for computer hardware and software. Tesco organized a running event, "Race for Life," which had attracted a quarter of a million women and had raised £12 million to support cancer research. Other programs integrated retail objectives as well as entering the fabric of peoples' lives. About 500,000 Tesco customers were members of a "baby club." A woman would be a member during pregnancy and until the baby was two years old. Every three months a member would receive a brochure appropriate to the age of the infant providing information about health and development of the child and tips about the concerns mothers typically faced. The brochure also contained coupons for relevant products.

Exhibit 6   The Tesco Way

Introduction

The Tesco Way

Over the years we've developed an approach to doing business and this has become known as the Tesco Way. We have drawn together the five elements of that approach and this booklet summarises them. They are:

- **Our Core Purpose**   the reason for all that we do
- **Our Goals**   what we have set out to achieve
- **Our Values**   the way we want to behave
- **Our Principles**   Better, Simpler and Cheaper
- **Our Steering Wheel**   which measures progress against our priorities and provides a visual reminder of our plans

This booklet is a reminder of the key messages, first delivered at the company conference in 1999. Understanding and managing the Tesco Way is a key ingredient for success at Tesco. The Tesco Way is a way of working which is:

BETTER, SIMPLER and CHEAPER

The Core Purpose

Our core purpose is all about customers:

To create value for customers to earn their lifetime loyalty

For us customers are at the heart of all that we do. The purpose, values and goals work together to create the culture and clarity of direction which enable us to achieve success.

Our strong UK core business has increased its market share and we are successfully expanding overseas because we understand better than others what our customers want - and how best to provide it. We create value for our customers because we understand them and improve our business for them.

The expansion of our non-food, e-commerce and Tesco Personal Finance businesses are all examples of our Core Purpose in action - delivering products, which delight customers and increase their loyalty to us.

---

their factories, exclusively to its needs. "In part, we were forced to do this by competitors, like Marks and Spencer and Sainsbury's, who were tying up suppliers," Harding said. Harding went on to describe Tesco's relationship with vendors:

> There are a lot of relatively small vendors who supply us with Tesco-branded merchandise. We are an important customer to them, so we have to make sure that our contracts are win-win. Dealing with larger vendors is a different story. With dedicated suppliers we need to think of cost in terms of total operations. With large vendors we like to concentrate on calculating their marginal cost. When a supplier has

many customers, some will be more profitable than others. We want to be their most demanding customer. But even though we may fight like cats and dogs over the price we need, we also cooperate about increasing sales in their category. This isn't an easy adjustment to make. Sometimes when we hire people from other companies they cannot understand the notion of cooperating with vendors.

The Tesco spirit of simplicity in communication extended to suppliers. They had access to the company's sales data, though not necessarily in real time. Twice a year, Leahy laid out to assembled vendors exactly what Tesco was up to in the coming months.

Exhibit 6   The Tesco Way (continued)

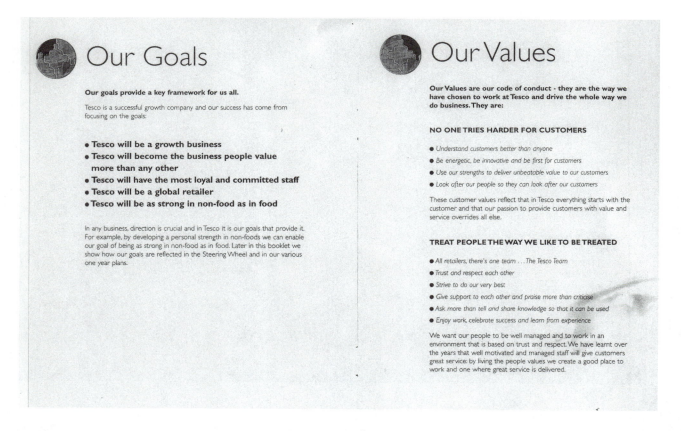

Our Goals

Our goals provide a key framework for us all.

Tesco is a successful growth company and our success has come from focusing on the goals:

- Tesco will be a growth business
- Tesco will become the business people value more than any other
- Tesco will have the most loyal and committed staff
- Tesco will be a global retailer
- Tesco will be as strong in non-food as in food

In any business, direction is crucial and in Tesco it is our goals that provide it. For example, by developing a personal strength in non-foods we can enable our goal of being as strong in non-food as in food. Later in this booklet we show how our goals are reflected in the Steering Wheel and in our various one year plans.

Our Values

Our Values are our code of conduct - they are the way we have chosen to work at Tesco and drive the whole way we do business. They are:

NO ONE TRIES HARDER FOR CUSTOMERS

- Understand customers better than anyone
- Be energetic, be innovative and be first for customers
- Use our strengths to deliver unbeatable value to our customers
- Look after our people so they can look after our customers

These customer values reflect that in Tesco everything starts with the customer and that our passion to provide customers with value and service overrides all else.

TREAT PEOPLE THE WAY WE LIKE TO BE TREATED

- All retailers, there's one team ... The Tesco Team
- Trust and respect each other
- Strive to do our very best
- Give support to each other and praise more than criticise
- Ask more than tell and share knowledge so that it can be used
- Enjoy work, celebrate success and learn from experience

We want our people to be well managed and to work in an environment that is based on trust and respect. We have learnt over the years that well motivated and managed staff will give customers great service: by living the people values we create a good place to work and one where great service is delivered.

The Stores

Though promotions were not unusual, the general pricing philosophy at Tesco was that of everyday low pricing (EDLP). There was a strong push to give more authority to store managers. A manager hot line was set up. A new program dubbed TWIST (Tesco Week in Store Together) required all corporate managers to spend a week in a store working on a specific store task. Phillip Clarke, the board member in charge of logistics and IT, spent a week stocking shelves, and Leahy had worked a cash register. Mason, the director of marketing, indicated that plans were afoot to use technology to permit store-specific plan-o-grams that would allow store managers to modify buyer-designed core offers. He continued:

> The Tesco brand has been transformed over time from being cheap, downmarket, and distressed to that of market leader and most admired. We did that by simply thinking of ourselves as being in "the shopping business." We aimed to provide the "best shopping trip for everybody." We recognize that Sainsbury's attempts to justify higher prices by being aspirational, but we find many customers with children are reluctant to shop there because they are afraid their children will misbehave. Asda is proud of its low prices, but they are perceived by many as a bit too cheap. We hope no one can complete the sentence, "I don't shop at Tesco because. . ."

EXTENDING THE RETAIL OFFER TO U.K. CUSTOMERS

Alternative Formats

Building on its core supermarket business, Tesco had three additional store formats. Metro stores were small

Exhibit 6   The Tesco Way (continued)

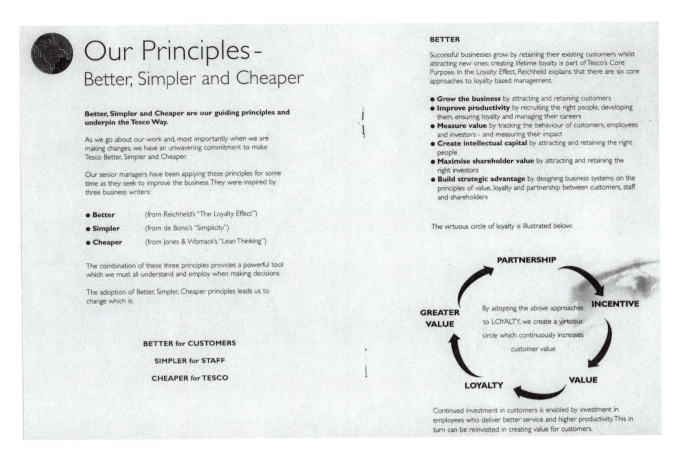

Our Principles –
Better, Simpler and Cheaper

Better, Simpler and Cheaper are our guiding principles and underpin the Tesco Way.

As we go about our work and, most importantly when we are making changes, we have an unwavering commitment to make Tesco Better, Simpler and Cheaper.

Our senior managers have been applying these principles for some time as they seek to improve the business. They were inspired by three business writers:

- **Better**   (from Reichheld's "The Loyalty Effect")
- **Simpler**   (from de Bono's "Simplicity")
- **Cheaper**   (from Jones & Womack's "Lean Thinking")

The combination of these three principles provides a powerful tool which we must all understand and employ when making decisions.

The adoption of Better, Simpler, Cheaper principles leads us to change which is:

BETTER for CUSTOMERS

SIMPLER for STAFF

CHEAPER for TESCO

BETTER

Successful businesses grow by retaining their existing customers whilst attracting new ones; creating lifetime loyalty is part of Tesco's Core Purpose. In the Loyalty Effect, Reichheld explains that there are six core approaches to loyalty based management.

- **Grow the business** by attracting and retaining customers
- **Improve productivity** by recruiting the right people, developing them, ensuring loyalty and managing their careers
- **Measure value** by tracking the behaviour of customers, employees and investors - and measuring their impact
- **Create intellectual capital** by attracting and retaining the right people
- **Maximise shareholder value** by attracting and retaining the right investors
- **Build strategic advantage** by designing business systems on the principles of value, loyalty and partnership between customers, staff and shareholders

The virtuous circle of loyalty is illustrated below:

PARTNERSHIP → INCENTIVE → VALUE → LOYALTY → GREATER VALUE → PARTNERSHIP

By adopting the above approaches to LOYALTY, we create a virtuous circle which continuously increases customer value

Continued investment in customers is enabled by investment in employees who deliver better service and higher productivity. This in turn can be reinvested in creating value for customers.

---

convenience supermarkets located in busy downtown areas, having a particular emphasis on sandwiches and casual food. Express stores were smaller convenience stores often located next to Esso gas stations. Finally, Tesco's hypermarket format, called Extra, was the major vehicle by which Tesco could fulfill Leahy's objective of growing rapidly in the nonfood area. Table B summarizes Tesco's store formats.

Retailing Services
In 1997 Tesco began offering financial services; by 2002 it had 3 million registered customer accounts. The goal was to provide customers with convenient financial products during their shopping trip. Customers could open a bank account enabling them to deposit checks as part of a register transaction; £6 million was deposited in a typical week. Money could be withdrawn from any ATM. Tesco also sold car insurance and by 2002 had 600,000 policies outstanding. Travel insurance could be bought as a routine register transaction, and loan applications could be filled out and handed in on the spot. Tesco's profits from these services were £20 million in the 2002 financial year.

Tesco.com
In December 1995 five people were assigned to study the idea of home shopping. Microsoft developed a Web site, and 12 stores were selected to act as shipment points. Orders were to be taken by phone, fax, or over the Internet. Launched in December 1996, the project

Exhibit 6   The Tesco Way (continued)

SIMPLER

In de Bono's book he says that as the world becomes increasingly more complex, so simplicity becomes a key value. Since the pace of change is not going to stop, we have to make a conscious effort to make things simpler.

Making things simple is, in itself, complex - and requires creativity and real effort. It can be achieved by knowing where to pay attention and what to ignore.

A **SIMPLE** approach can increase productivity through:

- **Reducing stress and anxiety**
- **Enabling us to work faster**
- **Increasing safety**
- **Reducing errors**
- **Different jobs being simpler to do**

Identifying simpler approaches is challenging; it requires exploration and lateral thinking! At Tesco we always look for improvements which are simpler for staff. It's an art!

CHEAPER

LEAN THINKING is a way of working which increases value through the elimination of waste. It has guided our supply chain thinking for over six years. Womack and Jones define waste as:

- **Errors**
- **Overproduction**
- **Waiting** for people, equipment or materials
- **Unnecessary transport** of goods
- **Unnecessary movement** of people
- **Excess stock**
- **Poor process design**
- **Dissatisfied customers**

.... and suggest an approach to reducing waste:

- Specifying **value** by defining the value a customer places on any good or service
- Lining up all the value-creating activities for a product along a **value stream** which reduces the eight wastes
- Making value **flow** smoothly, through the **pull** of the customer, in pursuit of **perfection**

APPLYING THE PRINCIPLES

At Tesco we improve the business for customers by living the Values - **no one tries harder for customers** and **treat people the way we like to be treated.**

Recently we have developed a framework which should be used for managing the changes which are required to make the business better for customers.

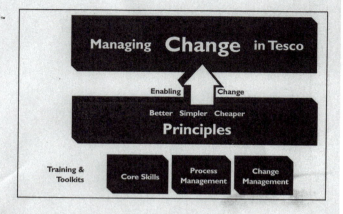

THE SKILLS DEVELOPMENT PLAN

Our **Core Skills** modules provide basic ways of working that are **Better, Simpler and Cheaper.** These are being built on with training modules on:

- Change Management
- Process Management (Project Process and Programme Management)

These training solutions are part of our Leadership Academy

Table B   Tesco Retail Formats, United Kingdom Only, 2002

Store Format	Number	Average Sq. Ft.
Express	100	2,000
Metro	180	10,000
Superstore	408	35,000
Extra	62	90,000

soon foundered. Taking orders by phone and fax proved prohibitively expensive. Moreover, as John Browett, CEO of Tesco.com (a legal subdivision of Tesco Plc.), observed, "We discovered that the 5% of the British population who had Internet access didn't buy groceries."

For a year the operation was held in a limited number of stores until it could be executed properly. Browett recalled the analysis that followed:

Around this time the belief spread that the best way to do home shopping was from a dedicated warehouse, but we studied the economics with great care and decided that was not correct. A lot of companies are afraid to do the numbers. They either don't want to or can't. But doing the numbers allows you to make the right call. For example, when we lower prices we know exactly how low we can go. Our analysis suggested that a given store would get no more than 500 orders per week. People argued that if we were

Exhibit 6   The Tesco Way (continued)

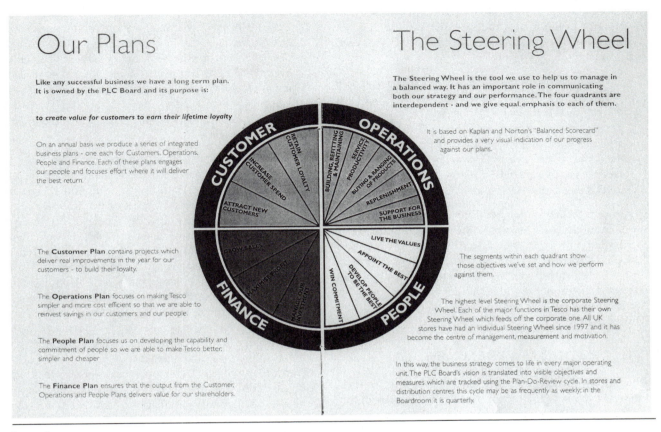

Our Plans

Like any successful business we have a long term plan. It is owned by the PLC Board and its purpose is:

to create value for customers to earn their lifetime loyalty

On an annual basis we produce a series of integrated business plans - one each for Customers, Operations, People and Finance. Each of these plans engages our people and focuses effort where it will deliver the best return.

The **Customer Plan** contains projects which deliver real improvements in the year for our customers - to build their loyalty.

The **Operations Plan** focuses on making Tesco simpler and more cost efficient so that we are able to reinvest savings in our customers and our people.

The **People Plan** focuses us on developing the capability and commitment of people so we are able to make Tesco better, simpler and cheaper

The **Finance Plan** ensures that the output from the Customer, Operations and People Plans delivers value for our shareholders.

The Steering Wheel

The Steering Wheel is the tool we use to help us to manage in a balanced way. It has an important role in communicating both our strategy and our performance. The four quadrants are interdependent - and we give equal emphasis to each of them.

It is based on Kaplan and Norton's "Balanced Scorecard" and provides a very visual indication of our progress against our plans.

The segments within each quadrant show those objectives we've set and how we perform against them.

The highest level Steering Wheel is the corporate Steering Wheel. Each of the major functions in Tesco has their own Steering Wheel which feeds off the corporate one. All UK stores have had an individual Steering Wheel since 1997 and it has become the centre of management, measurement and motivation.

In this way, the business strategy comes to life in every major operating unit. The PLC Board's vision is translated into visible objectives and measures which are tracked using the Plan-Do-Review cycle. In stores and distribution centres this cycle may be as frequently as weekly; in the Boardroom it is quarterly.

Source: Company.

filling online orders in the store we'd be crowding out our traditional customers. But our stores have an average of 40,000 customers per week. The online orders, which could be done at off-peak times, weren't going to bother anyone.

On the idea of dedicated warehouses, there is no way you could afford to stock all of the SKUs [stock-keeping units] you'd need to give a full assortment. The fact is, a lot of our early customers were shopping online precisely to find obscure items they couldn't find in their local store.

Tesco.com was relaunched with orders taken over the Web and fulfilled from the stores. Logistics were improved in two ways, one by reducing the flexibility of delivery windows and the second by improving the order-picking process. Customers could select one of two delivery windows, either 7–9 p.m. or 8–10 p.m. It was believed most people would be home on a weekday evening. The evening delivery times permitted more flexibility about when the orders could be picked and improved the delivery scheduling. Each store had several specially designed shopping carts with six containers to hold different orders. A touch screen on the cart informed the picker, who was a regular store associate and who followed a set path around the store, when to pick an item off the shelf and which container to put it in. In that way shopping for six took not much more time than shopping for one.

Store managers were happy with the presence of Tesco.com; the store was credited with the sales as if they had been made to a conventional shopper, the sales were largely made in off-peak periods, and, as an added bonus, the picker would notice irregularities such as out-of-stocks that could then be corrected.

As of 2002, Tesco.com covered 95% of the United Kingdom and was filling 100,000 orders per week worth nearly £10 million, or about 2% of Tesco total sales. Commenting on the kinds of customers that Tesco.com was attracting, Browett said:

> Tesco.com appeals to the cadre of people who have been doing it for a while and have become very adept; for them they can do an entire week's shopping in 10 minutes. Another group of regular users are people with small children at home for whom a trip to the supermarket can be a nightmare. A third group is the single professional for whom a trip to the store is a poor use of time. For them a £5 delivery fee is well worth it even if they buy only a few items.

Browett believed that in-store delivery would continue to be the most sensible system even if online sales became as much as 10% of store sales. Not only had Tesco.com reported a profit in 2001, as a further indication of the prospects for this channel, Tesco had exported the model to the Republic of Ireland, to South Korea and, via a joint venture with Safeway, Inc., to the United States.

INTERNATIONAL EXPANSION

Like many retailers facing a zero-sum game in their domestic markets, the lure of potentially fast-growth foreign markets was strong. In the mid-1990s, as its cash flow began to recover, Tesco made some decisions about what its international strategy should be. Leahy recalled:

> There were no texts on how to be successful at international retailing. It worked in our favor that we didn't start out believing we had all the answers. We thought about how we could add value for us and for customers. We needed countries where we would be early entrants, countries that were stable, and countries with sufficient spending power per capita and with growth potential. We also recognized that our skill set involved opening networks of stores rather than integrating preexisting chains. This thinking led us to identify the former Communist countries of Eastern Europe and a few emerging overlooked countries in Asia.

David Reid, vice chairman of Tesco and the person in charge of the international venture, described how Tesco selected the hypermarket as the correct vehicle for Tesco abroad:

> We knew that we did not have a ready-made international format. We had no hypermarkets in the U.K. at that time, but it became obvious that it was the right format. It was the only format that would help us achieve our goals for nonfood growth. It also helped that tastes are more international in nonfood than in food. It was also the right choice logistically. It didn't make sense to build distribution centers to service many small stores, at least not in the early stages. And finally, it seemed to us that no matter how we started, we'd end up opening hypermarkets, so it made sense to skip the first step and open hypermarkets to begin with.

Tesco recognized the advantages that local partnerships could provide. In Asia, Tesco found partners in the CP group (Thailand) and Samsung (South Korea), but in Eastern Europe there was a dearth of possibilities. Tesco instead identified small thriving retailers and bought them to obtain their managements, which were then given the task of building the number one retailer in their country. The first foreign country was Hungary, in 1994, quickly followed by Poland, the Czech Republic, and Slovakia. Later in the 1990s Tesco established a presence in Thailand, South Korea, Taiwan, and Malaysia.

Since Tesco had no experience with hypermarkets and no knowledge of the local customers, it gave great autonomy to the local management. According to Leahy: "Even today, with 65,000 employees overseas, there are only 70 of our U.K. managers living abroad. And they are trainers, not operating managers. We've told the local managers that they are to be the number one in their country, but we don't tell them how to do it. As a result, their enthusiasm is sky high."

The role of the trainers was to be sure the values of the local teams were in keeping with those of the parent. The Tesco Way, with its emphasis on simplicity, on the customer, and on steering wheels, was a constant, but not the retail solutions. Reid believed the Tesco Way had been absorbed and understood by senior management but less so as one went lower in the organization. Foreign managers had problems understanding the notions of empowerment and promotions based on merit; indeed, some actively resisted it.

The international strategy seemed to be working. By 2002, Tesco claimed market leadership in six out of the nine countries it had entered and profitability in eight, with a combined contribution to operating profit well in excess of £100 million. The company believed it was the most profitable international retailer in both Asia and Central Europe. Tesco had 150 hypermarkets overseas and had plans to start introducing other of its domestic formats, such as Express stores. As Tesco opened its 62nd hypermarket in the United Kingdom, it was clear that its overseas investments were paying off in more ways than simply providing operating profit.

Leahy reflected on the success of its strategy:

> You could say that we had pursued a "pull" strategy overseas by letting the local market dictate what we offer. A "push" strategy would have presumed we knew what could work and would have proceeded by rolling out store after store. I think there are very few economies of scale across countries in food retailing; what's important is not to lose any local economies of scale. That is why it is important to be number one within a country, rather than simply to build sales across countries. There are some cross-border synergies like IT and sourcing, but the main advantage we have is by exporting our culture. Global retail brands won't be the norm in my generation. After all, consumer goods companies have taken 100 years to achieve an 8% share. I doubt if it will be much different in retail. Most of our overseas customers think they are shopping in a local store.

THE NEXT FIVE YEARS

At the end of 2002 Tesco was on track to achieve the goals Leahy had set out in 1997. Tesco was nearing his goal of being 50% international, and perhaps most incredibly of all, it had become the most admired retailer in the United Kingdom, "an essential part of the landscape."

A lot had happened to Tesco since the early 1990s. But despite that success, it could be argued that Tesco faced stronger competitors in 2002 than it had in 1992. Domestically, Asda had become a formidable foe under the ownership of Wal-Mart and Sainsbury's had begun revitalizing its stores, and internationally Carrefour and Wal-Mart were being increasingly aggressive. Tesco International still benefited significantly from the strong financial condition of Tesco in the United Kingdom.

In the 1970s, "doing a Tesco" was a characterization of failure. In the 1990s, "the Tesco Way" was a symbol of retail revival. The new decade would reveal whether the Tesco Way was purely a local solution or a formula for international retail success.

Li & Fung: Beyond "Filling in the Mosaic," 1995–1998

In early 1998 Li & Fung Group Chairman Victor Fung and his brother Li & Fung Managing Director, William Fung reviewed the company's 1997 financial results: revenues of HK$13.3 billion ($1.7 billion) and an operating profit of HK$413 million ($53.4 million).[1] Pleased with the results, the two were confident that they were well on their way to achieving the goal of their three-year plan to double 1995 profits by the end of 1998 (see Exhibit 1 for consolidated financials). With 42 offices in over 20 countries in Asia, Europe and Africa, the company was emerging as one of the most important trading companies in the world.

In 1995 Li & Fung acquired the British trading company, Inchcape Buying Services (IBS)/Dodwell. Prior to the merger Li & Fung's suppliers had been largely centered in East Asia with the majority of its clients located in the United States. The merger with IBS almost doubled Li & Fung's headcount and brought with it new European clients and sourcing offices in other parts of Asia and the world. In their 1996-1998 three-year plan Victor and William focused on increasing profits by bringing IBS's less-than-1% margins in line with Li & Fung's margins of over 3%.

As the brothers planned for the next three years they focused on two major areas: the continued growth of their venture capital operation LF International (LFI) and the expansion of sourcing operations throughout the world. Customer demands for quick turnaround and reduced costs were forcing the brothers to consider developing operations in countries closer to their major customers in the United States and Europe. For their European customers, operations in Egypt and Tunisia had been established in late 1996 and early 1997 respectively. For the United States the company was contemplating establishing sourcing operations in Mexico. Victor and William wondered how they were going to support all this growth. They reviewed their current markets and operations and began to formulate their strategy for their next three-year plan.

COMPANY HISTORY

Founded in 1906 in Guangzhou, China, Li & Fung was the first Chinese-owned export firm to break the stranglehold on the China trade held by foreign commercial houses such as the English *hong*,[2] Jardine Matheson. Established by Fung Yiu-hing and Li To-ming, Li & Fung first consolidated its trading ventures in porcelainware, antiques, and handicrafts, later expanding to include silk, bamboo, jade, ivory, and firecrackers. The company was one of the first Chinese foreign trade houses to be financed solely by Chinese capital.

On December 28, 1937 the company was formally established as a limited company in Hong Kong. Trading was halted during World War II. After Fung Pak-liu passed away in 1943, his son Fung Hon-chu took over the company. The end of the war saw the retirement of silent partner Li To-ming, who sold his shares to the Fung family. Despite the absence of the Li family in the company, the name Li & Fung was kept because of the auspicious meaning associated with both of the characters in the company name (Li meaning "profit" and Fung meaning "abundance").

This case was prepared by Michael Y. Yoshino with the assistance of Anthony St. George and Carin-Isabel Knoop.

[1] In December 1997, $1=HK$7.74.

[2] *Hong* in Cantonese means "row" referring to the physical arrangement of the original English trading houses which were located in a row along the riverbank in Guangzhou.

Consolidated Profit and Loss Statement

(HK$ millions)	1993	1994	1995	1996	1997
Turnover	5,383	6,126	9,214	12,544	13,345
Operating profit	197	565[a]	258	326	413
Profit before tax and exceptional items	226	572	250	309	399
Taxation	-30	-19	-25	-22	-25
Profit after taxation	196	553	217	297	374

[a]Includes sale of Cyrk.

Consolidated Balance Sheet

(HK$ millions)	1993	1994	1995	1996	1997
Current assets	914	1,275	1,434	1,895	1,971
Fixed assets	383	754	795	899	1,113
Associated companies/investments	94	47	84	98	100
Total Assets	**1,391**	**2,076**	**2,313**	**2,892**	**3,184**
Current liabilities	750	1,035	1,287	1,715	1,814
Minority interests	0	-7	-15	-19	-21
Long-term loans	113	244	566	283	400
Deferred taxation	1	0	2	2	2
Total Liabilities	**864**	**1,272**	**1,840**	**1,981**	**2,196**
Share capital and premium	207	207	56	62	63
Capital reserve and retained profits	320	597	417	849	926
Shareholders' Equity	**527**	**804**	**473**	**911**	**989**
Total Liabilities and Equity	**1,391**	**2,076**	**2,313**	**2,892**	**3,184**

After the war, Li & Fung expanded its product trading range and sourcing network. New product sourcing services for garments, toys, electronics, and plastic flowers were added and the company's sourcing network was expanded to other countries in the Asia/Pacific region. During this same period, its client base began to globalize. The company became one of Hong Kong's largest exporters.

The Brothers' Return: 1973-1989

While post-war growth was stretching the company's managerial resources, Victor and William were studying in the United States, Victor completing his Ph.D. in Business Economics at Harvard University and William getting his MBA at the Harvard Business School. Observing the industry changes, the two decided that they needed to redefine the way the company was conducting its business. By 1970, as Victor pointed out, "both large foreign buyers and regional suppliers were becoming increasingly sophisticated, resulting in a serious decline in the company's margins." In 1972 William returned to run the trading business. Victor, at that time a professor at the Harvard Business School, helped his brother from overseas. He returned to Hong Kong in 1974. From 1972 to 1974 the brothers used their Western perspective and training to modernize the company and install professional management at all levels. As their father, Fung Hon-chu, recalled of that time:

> Victor and William started to review the company's organizational and administrative structure, as well as personnel problems. . . . It was the first time that the company had been reviewed in a systematic way with the application of professional management techniques. The study revealed areas to improve. The general quality of the staff of about 100 was found to be mediocre and with business expanding, there was a strong need for professional and experienced managers. Internal systems had to be formulated to ensure efficiency and control. Salary levels were uneven and there was no policy on salary systems. Staff turnover was high. No planning or budgeting existed. The accounting department did little more than tabulate sales and provide profit and loss figures.

"It was a classic case of a family company in transition," William commented about the business during that time. "Of my 30 cousins, most were not interested in the business." Victor and William decided that the best course to improve the business was to go public. The company was subsequently listed on the Hong Kong Stock Exchange in April 1973. The first applications for stock tranches not held within familial control were oversubscribed a record 113 times—a mark that remained for the next 14 years in the annals of the Hong Kong Stock Exchange.

In 1985 the company established a retail joint venture with the U.S. principals of Circle K convenience stores. In 1986 Li & Fung established another retail joint venture, a 50/50 partnership with Toys 'R Us. Stores were established throughout Hong Kong and the New Territories with subsequent stores opened in Taiwan. In 1989 Victor and William bought out the rest of the family and the company was taken private to facilitate restructuring the business into its two primary businesses, retail and export. With a 1992 relisting on the Hong Kong Stock Exchange, the export business was taken public while the retail operations remained private. In 1995 Li & Fung acquired IBS/Dodwell for HK$450 million ($58 million). At the time, Li & Fung and IBS had been roughly the same size.

In the 25 years that the brothers had managed the company they had built up strong relationships with government contacts in Hong Kong and Beijing and were recognized for their business talents in and outside of Hong Kong. In 1995 Victor was made chairman of Prudential Asia Investments Limited, the Hong Kong Trade Development Council, and the Li & Fung Group. That same year he was voted "Businessman of the Year" in the DHL/SCMP Hong Kong Business Awards and William was appointed chairman of the Hong Kong General Chamber of Commerce. The following year Victor was honored by the HBS Alumni Association. The two brothers worked as a team and felt that they complemented each other well, Victor as a visionary and strategist and William as an implementer. In 1996 the brothers were acknowledged by *Business Week* as two of the world's top 25 managers, listed along with such notables as: Stan Shih, chairman of Acer, Gerald Greenwald, chairman of United Airlines, and Scott McNealy, CEO of Sun Microsystems.

Company Culture

In 1998 Li & Fung was still, at heart, a Chinese family business. Victor noted: "Li & Fung is a company rooted in Chinese values. We do not retrench an employee. In fact, we retain some of the retirees as consultants. Furthermore, we do not believe in the ostensible trappings of titles and the attendant hierarchy; we treat employees of Li & Fung as family." As one overseas manager illustrated: "Whenever my wife goes to Hong Kong, Victor and William's mother invites her out to tea and to shop." The "Chineseness" of Li & Fung was important to Victor and William, yet they knew that the success formulas used at home had to be adapted to fit the local cultures of foreign offices. William commented:

> We may be a Hong Kong-based company with a Chinese view of life, but we do not ram notions best suited to Hong Kong down a Thai's throat, for example. Unlike an American firm that says that there is only one way to manage a foreign office, we tend to let our foreign operations run to the best local practices. All the formal structural elements (such as the incentive system) that make Li & Fung work, however, are kept the same.

The company's origins as a traditional Chinese family business had features that, as William described it, may have been difficult for some non-Chinese managers to accept:

> Li & Fung is a company based on three generations of a family in Hong Kong and has a strong sense of Chinese tradition, we expect loyalty and we reward diligence. Managers are rewarded strictly on a high profit-sharing model—their bonus is in direct relation to the success of their division. In an industry like fashion which is very cyclical this kind of reward can be very risky for those seeking greater stability. If managers don't succeed, however, we don't necessarily get rid of them right away. We understand the nature of the business and sometimes during a downturn a manager can do poorly for a few years. Our father taught us the value of loyalty, however, and we will keep a manager on or move them around if poor results are a consequence of something other than their efforts.

The ideal Li & Fung employees were, as William put it, "Entrepreneurs who wanted to run their own business. We give them the resources, opportunities and protection against the downside, making it more attractive for them to work for us." Bonuses were based solely on profit performance. "Some people are critical of our bonus system based on a formula using pretax profit as

the sole criterion," Victor explained. " They believe it is too cold or too narrow," he continued:

> But this was done by design. In a typical Chinese company it is a common practice for the head of the family to dispense a bonus to his key lieutenants whenever he felt like it. The amount was determined completely at his whim and based solely on his subjective judgment. We wanted to get away from such practice. We wanted to make it totally transparent. Everyone understands what net profit is before taxes. We may have gone overboard, but it has certainly been an effective way to motivate our managers.

William stressed:

> Compared to some of our larger competitors who limit the incentives to their employees within a salary plus a 15% to 20% bonus, we include our trading employees in a profit sharing scheme which can constitute upwards of 60% of their annual income. In other words, their bonus could be more than their annual income. And what is unique, we do not place a cap on the bonus for the top managers.

As one enthusiastic manager put it: "The incentive system is not based on something intangible like, 'train three managers.' If I raise turnover and contribution, my bonus increases, it's that simple. I like that." Nevertheless, in 1998 Victor and William were considering stock options and management by objective.

SOURCING SERVICES

By 1998 the company's trading operations encompassed a wide array of services, from assistance in the design of products, to materials sourcing for their manufacture, to the handling of logistics for delivery to the customer. Product expertise spanned from textiles to plastics, handicrafts, fashion accessories, sporting goods, and household merchandise. Li & Fung's clients were a carefully selected group of about 420 customers, primarily large retail chains in Europe and the United States. Some of their top customers included: The Limited, Inc (with sales of $8.6 billion from over 5,600 stores comprised of such retailers as Structure, Express, the Limited and Lane Bryant), Warner Brothers (with 185 stores and estimated sales of over $3 billion),[3] John Lewis Partnership (in the United Kingdom with group sales of $5.25 billion from 23 department stores and

---

3 De'Ann Weiner, "Hardly a Household Name," *Business Week*, December 22, 1997.

115 supermarkets) and Spain's El Corte Ingles (with over 60 department stores and sales of $7.88 billion).

The 4Cs

"To excel in this business," William explained, "you have to master the 4 Cs: Connections, Communications, Control of quality, and Consolidation of shipments." To ensure excellence in these four areas the brothers structured the company as a matrix, with divisions along product lines and countries of manufacture (see Exhibit 2 for the company organization chart). Each product group had its own profit and loss responsibility and was structured to function independently with all the functions of a trading company. Within each product group separate business units were dedicated either to a particular product or a specific client. Li & Fung senior managers worked closely with the clients, bringing to bear their knowledge of the client companies, their industries, and current market trends.

Negotiating price and conditions of delivery with customers required taking into account at least nine factors: raw materials selection, selection of the manufacturing site (in turn based on the reliability of manufacturers, the factory skill level, lead times, and quota availability), desired product quality standards, packaging, and costing. In addition, other 'soft' factors such as protectionist considerations or the financial integrity of the factories had to be considered.

Li & Fung managers benefited from the company's worldwide office network, working in an integrated manner with managers from other offices across the globe. In 1991 Li & Fung installed a PC-based intranet to link offices and facilitate access to pricing information. A top manager described its advantages:

> With the company e-mail system we can communicate with all our offices worldwide. For example, a buyer can ask us a question on sourcing dyed-cotton shirts and we can have an answer back from all our sourcing offices, be they in Thailand, Korea, or Indonesia, on any number of variables such as price and delivery. This increases our competitive edge because we can get back to our customers in the shortest possible time.

By 1998 the intranet had been upgraded twice. Victor noted:

> Our information technology really ties in our suppliers, our customers, and ourselves. We already have a deep knowledge of our suppliers. We have a history of working with several thousand factories throughout Asia and we know what each can and cannot do. Our detailed knowledge of our suppliers' capabilities allows us to maximize our response to customer needs.

The Mechanics of an Order

Li & Fung's sourcing services provided customers with what William called, "a virtual factory" or a "private label manufacturing program." According to Li & Fung managers, this was achieved by bringing together the lowest cost, highest quality final product components from various sources throughout the region for manufacture at one factory (see Exhibit 3 for a sample item and its component sources). The company had a network of about 3,000 independent manufacturers, 75%-80% of whom they would be working with at any one time.

Once a production agreement was signed with a client, the pre-production process began. Li & Fung's merchandising specialists in Hong Kong worked closely with the client on finalizing its design and manufacturing plans. The production process consisted of manufacturing and assembly work which was sub-contracted to independent factories in appropriate manufacturing sites. Li & Fung supervised the production process to ensure that product quality met specified standards. The finished products would then be brought back to Hong Kong for further testing, packaging, and shipping overseas. William noted:

> Fashion is a seasonal business with different styles and/or materials affecting the final product. What the retailer wants is to ride the fashion trend but these trends are not known far in advance. As a trader, we try to shorten the production cycle of garments so that the retailer can get in his order as soon as he knows what the consumer wants.

> Months before the production deadline, we work with the buyer on the design of the garment: possible fabric, color, and style. Next, we approach raw materials suppliers and place orders for the fabrics of choice. Then we approach four to five medium-sized manufacturers and reserve their capacity. We don't ask for 100% of their capacity for the order; rather, we ask for something like 30% capacity and will layer in another 70% of staple goods which can be given in advance and are not subject to the whims of style. This way, we have the raw materials and factories ready and just wait for the word from the buyer for the final specifications. Our buyers give the word

Exhibit 2   1998 Organizational Chart

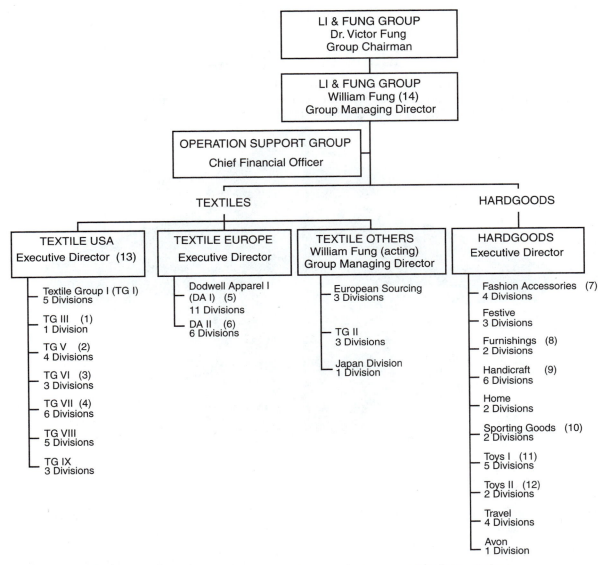

Individual Product Group managers were also responsible for the following countries or regions:

(1)   Philippines

(2)   Saipan

(3)   Indonesia

(4)   Pakistan; Honduras; Turkey; Portugal

(5)   Sri Lanka

(6)   Mauritius

(7)   Thailand

(8)   Malaysia; Singapore

(9)   Changsha; Liuyang; Zhangjian

(10)   Taiwan

(11)   Guangzhou; Shantou

(12)   Nanjing; Shanghai

(13)   Quingdao; Korea

(14)   India

Exhibit 3 "Borderless Manufacturing"

by
Made ~~in~~ Hong Kong

Hong Kong no longer makes much at home, but trading firm Li & Fung thrives by organizing production in the most cost-effective places. This parka, bound for the West, is a good example of what the company terms "borderless manufacturing."

Assembly
CHINA

Lining
TAIWAN

Shell
KOREA

Filler
CHINA

Label, elastic, studs, toggle and string
HONG KONG

Zipper
JAPAN

GREG GIRARD—CONTACT

---

and the manufacturers start the production. Upon completion of the order, we consolidate and ship the merchandise.

The logistics for hard goods was a variation on the soft goods example. William explained:

> Toys are typical of hard goods. We work with a designer from our buyer on the sketch of the final product. From the sketch, we basically do the mechanical drawings. We will have the details of the mechanism (its moving parts) and then we actually do the first hand sample. When that is approved, in some cases, we actually commission for the mold to be made ourselves. This way we

can then go out to assemblers and, depending upon their production, will make so many sets of molds and farm them out to different people. . . . As with soft goods, assembly is the part that we don't want to get into.

Clearing Hurdles

After an order was confirmed with a customer, it could take months for a Li & Fung supplier to receive the letter of credit. In certain circumstances, to accelerate turnaround time, once a buyer had confirmed an order, Li & Fung would themselves advance a letter of credit to the suppliers. "We charge interest," explained William, "but ultimately it speeds up the process. This way, we can expect more when push comes to shove."

Overall, the trading industry operated on extremely thin margins (~1%), but with their integrated services, Li & Fung had achieved historical margins of over 3.5% of annual turnover. These higher margins were achieved not by squeezing the margins of manufacturers, but by getting more of what Victor referred to as "the soft money"—the margin that came from consolidation of manufacturing and shipping. As he explained,

> If the ex-factory price is around $1, the final retail price might be between $4-$5. A good product manager might be able to squeeze 15 cents off the margin from the manufacturer, but we look to get the larger part of the margin from consolidating the rest of the process. There is a great deal of value to the customer in preventing stockouts, excess inventory, interest charges, ensuring quality and the like. This is where we can gain more value from the supply chain.

The company was also able to reduce the impact of quota limits placed on China and Hong Kong. In China, for example, 60% of the country's total quota was allocated to provincial factories by the state-owned China Textile Import Export Corporation, the remaining 40% was awarded to the highest bidder. Some agents would choose factories based on quota allotment rather than quality. Li & Fung got around this problem by backing chosen factories financially (once they had an order from a client) so that they could bid for additional quota allocation. In Hong Kong the quota system was less difficult: the central authority in charge of quota allocation could transfer a quota allotment directly to Li & Fung, enabling the company to use the quota through whichever factory it chose.

Attention to Detail

In addition to quota restrictions and margin issues, a sourcing manager always had to pay close attention to turnaround time and other details. William stressed, "This is an incredibly fast-paced business where the smallest detail can cause long delays and headaches for our customers. Emotions run high and every season is a lifetime. Our flexibility and quick decision-making directly impacts our customers' ability to succeed."

The brothers ran a tight ship and kept abreast of sourcing projects by involving themselves in some of the daily activities of the business and maintaining close personal contact with their client companies' senior management.

William illustrated:

> In the old days my father used to read every telex from customers, covering the range of complaints from wrong zipper color and short shipments to late deliveries and lost documents. Today the medium is slightly different but the issues are the same. When the fax machines replaced the telex system, we had to install many fax machines, which meant that we could no longer continue the old practice. We had a consultant develop simple but proprietary software so that all faxes come into one central location. This allows either Victor or myself to read a certain number of faxes every day. This is how we keep in touch with our operations on a day to day basis. Both of us pay close attention to details and how each transaction is carefully followed through. We make sure every fax is answered as we cannot afford to disregard a client's problems.

BEYOND LI & FUNG

If ensuring such personalized service was a challenge with a company with over 1,000 employees, extending such care to a company twice the size was even more formidable. Six months before the merger, the Fung brothers created a transition team to review organizational processes and implement a unit-by-unit transition. The team completed the integration in one year. One year later a follow-up review was carried out.

The merger with IBS had solved the major problem of diversifying Li & Fung's customer base. Not only did IBS bring with it a largely European customer base, but the addition of its sourcing offices in South Asia, Europe, the Mediterranean and Latin America increased Li & Fung's supply base as well (see Tables A and B for customer diversification and Exhibit 4 for map of global operations). In addition to the geographical growth, the addition of IBS managers with new product expertise (i.e. products not formerly covered by Li & Fung) had increased the company's product range, particularly in hardgoods.

Before the merger Li & Fung executives went to IBS's European customers to investigate their sourcing needs. The European retailing environment was 10 to 15 years behind that of the United States: traditional department stores were in decline, regional malls were beginning to be established, and discounters were getting stronger. With the shakeout in the retail industry, customers were looking anew at supply management and seeking "one-stop" sourcing and quick-turnaround manufacturing along the lines of Li & Fung's

Table A — Customer Base by Geography (as % of sales)

Customer Base by Geography	Pre-merger, 1994	Post-merger, 1997[a]
United States	84%	64%
Europe	13%	31%
Rest of World	3%	5%

[a] Company estimates.

Table B — Customer Base by Product (as % of sales)

Customer Base by Product	Pre-merger, 1994	Post-merger, 1997[a]
U.S. Textile Customers	68%	48%
Textile Clients, Rest of World	10%	30%
Hardgoods	22%	22%

[a] Company estimates.

Exhibit 4 Li & Fung Sourcing Network

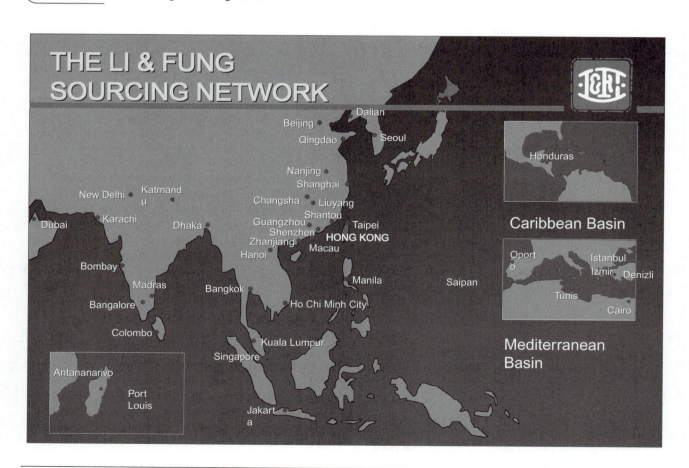

services. William recalled, "Once IBS's clients recognized the potential benefits of the Li & Fung sourcing system, they provided no resistance to the merger."

IBS's Istanbul, Turkey and Oporto, Portugal offices supported Li & Fung's growth in the European market. Customers realized that they would be willing to pay 20% to 30% more to have quick turnaround from Turkey rather than ordering six to nine months in advance from China (see Exhibit 5 for examples of production costs in different countries). William explained clients' needs:

> Customers have come to realize that the cost of the product is not just the cost paid to the factories and Li & Fung for production management. It's also the cost of buying the wrong merchandise, not getting the right assortment, having obsolete merchandise, having stockouts, etc. Ideally customers would like to do replenishment buying—if they sell five pieces, they want to replace those five pieces, and that is only possible if the manufacturing areas are a lot closer to their market.

> This is something we have worked on for a long time with The Limited Group, for example. We work with every division of The Limited. It was one of the pioneers in the Orient in terms of squeezing the production time down. We reduced turnaround from the Orient for them from around five months to 45 days. That was unheard of when I first started in this business.

William described IBS's original sourcing services:

"Before the merger IBS was a traditional trading company, acting as an introducing agent between clients and manufacturers. There is not much added value in this type of service so margins for IBS and similar companies are usually less than 1%. At Li & Fung we are able to get higher margins because of our regionally coordinated sourcing services." In 1994 IBS margins were 0.8%, while Li & Fung's had traditionally averaged over 3%. During the first two years of the integration, the combined average margin for the two companies reached 2.2%. By the time of the completion of the merger in 1997, margins had been raised to 3.1%. Li & Fung managers credited margin improvements at IBS operations to the introduction of the Li & Fung product sourcing matrix.

According to Li & Fung managers some IBS country managers had initially been somewhat resistant to altering their sourcing methods. Each country manager wanted to be in control of the entire process, sourcing and manufacturing within his or her own country. According to William:

> The top management was psychologically ready, but country managers needed to work in a regional team and they couldn't. It took an acquisition to really snap them out of it. When the merger came through we assigned IBS managers to customer groups and not countries, telling them to focus on the product but to work with our network to source from the region instead of just one country.

None of IBS's top executives left the company because of the merger. Similarly, despite projections of 20% to 30% customer attrition, Li & Fung lost no customers in the integration.

Across Cultures

When the merger was announced in 1994, analysts were particularly concerned about the differences between Li & Fung and IBS's company cultures: Li & Fung was a U.S.-style Chinese company with no experience in South Asia and IBS was a British company unaccustomed to Chinese-family business practices. IBS had been largely managed by British expatriates who had certain lifestyle and salary expectations that were not a part of Li & Fung's standard human resources practices or cost structure.

Communication and management style differed. Western managers tended to be more "outspoken" at meetings, different from Li & Fung managers' less confrontational, consensus approach to decision-making. With the arrival of IBS managers, however, this style of communication began to change and some former IBS managers felt that Chinese managers were learning from them and speaking out more.

With the addition of several non-Chinese speakers to the company, Victor and William established monthly English-only operational meetings between themselves, senior management, and product and country managers to facilitate communication. At these meetings participants presented product and country turnover updates and discussed tactics. In addition, twice-yearly corporate meetings were held to fashion global strategic responses to upcoming challenges. "We make sure that all the key managers can air their views. Although it is up to us to make the final decision, we must be able to justify our decisions. This is completely different from the traditional top-down Chinese family-run company," Victor stressed.

IBS's British expatriate culture introduced an unforeseen advantage to Li & Fung: IBS's managers were accustomed

Exhibit 5   Delivered Cost to USA Retailer (*circa* 1Q1997)

Men's Shirt 100% Combed Cotton

USD $/shirt	United States	%	Mexico	%	India	%	Thai	%
Fabric								
Manufacturing cost	2.37							
SG&A expenses	0.17							
Margin (10%)	0.25							
Fabric cost	$2.79	32.6%	$2.60	47.7%	$2.45	50.0%	$2.51	46.8%
Cut and Sew								
Manufacturing cost	4.73	55.4						
SG&A expenses	0.25	2.9						
Margin (10%)	0.78	9.1						
Shirt cost F.O.B.	$8.55	100%	$5.44	100%	$4.91	100%	$5.36	100%
Import cost[a]	0.00		1.23		2.18		2.21	
Delivered cost to retailer	$8.55		$6.67		$7.09		7.57	
Savings vs. USA			$1.88	22.0%	$1.46	17.1%	$0.98	11.5%

Source: Company documents.

[a]Freight, insurance, border fees and tariffs, keeping stock costs, pick and pack to USA retailer.

to being stationed in overseas positions and were largely willing to be stationed anywhere the company wanted to put them; Hong Kong managers were much less willing to leave Hong Kong.

Despite the success in retaining IBS managers and executives after the merger, turnover at the lower-end remained a problem. Recognizing that high turnover was a constant in the business, Victor and William had decided to focus on retaining their top-tier of management. Now that the company was the largest trading company in Hong Kong[4] they could no longer look to recruit managers from other companies. As Victor put it, "We can't recruit from the market because we are the market. Sometimes we even have to acquire a small local trading company just to gain experienced staff." The reverse was happening in fact, other companies were attempting to recruit managers from Li & Fung. In response Li & Fung sought to build a strong "cadet" corps by building allegiance to the company through internal training and a stronger corporate culture.

BEYOND SOURCING

In addition to its trading operations, in 1986 Li & Fung established a venture capital group, LF International (LFI), run by Harvard College and HBS MBA graduate, Mike Hsieh. According to Hsieh the textile and some hard goods industries (such as toys) were overlooked by most venture capitalists, leaving LFI with a wide field of opportunity.

LFI invested in companies that had a need for Li & Fung sourcing services. In the mid-1980s and again in 1995, LFI had established two venture capital funds. With the first fund $11 million was invested in 12 U.S. companies. The 1995 fund was a $15 million joint investment with Minorco (a European multinational with a minority stake in Li & Fung). By 1997 over $4 million of this fund had been invested in the United States, with just under $3 million invested in Europe (for a list of the two funds' investments, see Exhibit 6). As Hsieh explained, the strategy was to invest in "companies with at least $3 million in revenue, a need for

---

4 Li & Fung's biggest competitors—Swire Trading and AMC, were one-third and one-half the size of Li & Fung respectively.

Exhibit 6   LFI Investments to 1996

Company	Description	Gain/Loss
Fund 1		
Lewis Galoob	Promotional Toy Co	Gain
ACA Joe	Sportswear Retailer	Loss
Accuproducts	Computer Peripherals	Loss
Ansun (Lodge)	Sportswear Retailer	Gain
Cyrk	Promotional Products	Gain
Dechtar	Intimate Apparel Catalog	Gain
Albert Kessler	Gifts Wholesaler	Loss
Golden Gate	Fireworks Distributor	Loss
Millworks	Private Label Apparel	Loss
Toymakers	Toy Wholesaler	Loss
Wilke Rodriguez	Designer Menswear	Gain
Winco	Fireworks Wholesaler	Gain
Fund 2		
Zimbergs	Designer Menswear	Loss
Basic World	Sportswear Distributor	Gain
Body Fx	Teenage Cosmetics	Loss
Santana	Men's Shirt Wholesaler	Gain
Bartsons	Raincoats Distributor	Loss
Lloyd	Menswear Importer	Even

Source: Company documents.

overseas sourcing, and owners who want to continue with the business and maintain control." He continued, "We don't want control. We want the entrepreneurs who founded the company to continue to run it. After all they're the ones with the design and marketing talent."[5] LFI's strategy had been largely successful. As Hsieh pointed out, "Whereas the average venture capital investment in the United States might bring in around 30%, LFI's investments have averaged a 128% internal rate of return since 1986."

LFI's most notable home run was its 1990 $200,000 investment in the promotional company, Cyrk Inc. Originally a T-shirt printer, the company capitalized on its logo and promotional design capabilities and increased sales volume from $20 million to $400 million in three years by creating promotional programs for such companies as Philip Morris, Mars, and NationsBank. In 1994 LFI sold its stake in the company for over $65 million.

In 1997 LFI took a stake in a $15 million investment in the faltering U.S. dancewear and legwear company, Danskin Inc. Arranged by Danskin Investors, Inc., other investors included Onyx Partners, the Brener Group, and Alpine Associates. Danskin's market had been flat but seeing a potential for women's apparel in the active wear category, Danskin decided to reposition itself by introducing outdoor-oriented apparel such as fleece, jackets, jogging bras, etc. An influx of capital was required to reposition the brand and design and manufacture the company's new products. Li & Fung provided low-cost offshore manufacture for the new product lines.

LFI also invested in hard goods such as toys, computer peripherals, and Li & Fung's own historical specialty, fireworks. Because of the smaller size of the wholesale toy market (~$13 billion) finding companies to invest in required greater research on the part of LFI. In contrast, in

---

5 LFI information derived from Sidney Rutberg, "LF: Deep Pockets," *Women's Wear Daily*, October 13, 1997 and company documents.

the apparel market (with a wholesale market size of $80 billion and an overall market size of $160 billion) companies with investment opportunities often approached LFI directly.

Hsieh felt that a potential company's management was as important as the company's product or the industry it was in. "We pay close attention to a potential investment's managers," said Hsieh, "We want to know that they know how to adapt to market changes. A company that focuses only on the product doesn't necessarily have what it takes to maneuver with the market."

The Third Fund and Possibilities in Europe

By October 1997, LFI and two partners raised about $30 million for investment. 55% of this fund was to be invested in United States operations, with the remainder invested in European and other non-U.S. operations. Concerning LFI's European opportunities, Hsieh remarked:

> The United States is a large homogenous market where a product can be sold through retail chains all over the country. Europe, with its different languages and cultures, is more diversified and broken into niche markets. You can't get the same volume as you can in the United States. Finding larger companies with good growth potential will be more difficult.

In contrast to the earlier funds where project investments had been limited to $1 million or less for investment in start-up and early stage businesses, the new fund was going to expand investment into more established companies. Hsieh explained the strategy, "The first few years of a venture are often spent experimenting with product materials, pricing, and channels. The rapid changes required by start-ups make it difficult for Li & Fung Trading to help drive down the cost of goods by doing better and more consistent sourcing."

According to Hsieh, fund managers with greater experience and knowledge of the various markets were essential. European investments for the second fund had been managed by a two-man team in Brussels. For the third fund these two would continue to focus on possible investments in Italy, France, the Benelux countries and other countries in Southern Europe. At the same time a London-based manager would focus on opportunities in the United Kingdom, Germany, other Northern European countries and South Africa.

BEYOND BORDERS

With an increased customer and supply base, after the merger Victor and William wanted to expand the company's current Asian-based sourcing capabilities into regions closer to their target markets. For example, while the company might have a source for "knit tops" in the Far East it might be lacking such a product from a quick-turnaround manufacturer for its European clients and therefore would seek to find a source for such products in a neighboring Mediterranean country.

Accordingly, in 1996 Li & Fung established sourcing offices in Egypt to support its expansion into the European market. The Egyptian operation was a joint venture with an Egyptian company which had an annual turnover of around $10 million. "The deal looked promising," explained one manager, "they talked the talk . . . they had quality assurance." Li & Fung sent in a former country manager from India to oversee the integration. He spent six months hiring new workers, restructuring the organization and pulling together the joint venture. The terms of the joint venture were a 20% starting share with an option to increase the investment to 60%. The Istanbul office had helped in providing merchandising and bringing in clients. In late 1997, the venture had been proving challenging to manage. Different local accounting practices made financial review of the operation difficult and capacity still exceeded demand. Further attention to the operation would most certainly still be required.

Other recent investments had proven less problematic. In early 1997 the company established a sourcing office in Tunisia, hiring a former government employee who had relationships with the 15 major textile manufacturers in the country. By late 1997 the operation had filled a quick-turnaround trial order for a new European customer.

Trends in Trade

Despite the growth in 1996 and early 1997, in late 1997 changes in international trading had become apparent. In early 1997, the strong dollar had lessened demand from Li & Fung's European customers (all Li & Fung sourcing costs and services were paid for in U.S. dollars). In the second half of 1997 the Asian crisis resulted in drastic currency devaluations in such Southeast Asian countries as Thailand, the Philippines, and Indonesia. With the devaluations, demand rebounded: lowered exchange rates meant lower costs to Li & Fung and its customers and increased business for Li & Fung operations in the affected countries. The benefits were somewhat illusory, however, as the increased activity tended to be contracts shifted from Li & Fung offices in countries not as drastically affected by the crisis (e.g. India and Bangladesh).

William was aware that the cost benefits of the crisis would only hold until inflation began to rise. Of greater concern to him was the growing tendency towards regional trade protectionism. From 1993 to 1996 the volume of U.S. apparel imports from Asia to the United States fell from 70% to 53% while Mexico's share of imports increased from 4% to 11% in the same period. Imports from Central America and the Caribbean similarly increased from 12% to 17%.[6] In 1997 the trend had continued. See Table C.

William explained the shift:

> The protectionist barriers erected during the 1970s and 1980s are being strengthened rather than dismantled.

Table C	Top Five Foreign Suppliers of Apparel to the United States ($ millions)	
Supplier	January-June 1997	% Change from January-June 1996
Mexico	2,233	46.12
Caribbean	3,407	29.06
Bangladesh	636	28.29
China	1,394	-28.80
Hong Kong	1,432	-11.10

Source: *Daily News Record*, September 15, 1997.

> Whereas these barriers used to protect domestic industry now the scope has widened so that America wants to protect jobs in Mexico and the Caribbean. It's the same in Europe: they have political reasons why they are extending the protectionist umbrella to the surrounding countries. The world is shifting—due both to the demand for rapid turnaround and trade protectionism and Li & Fung will have to get into these neighboring markets in a very big way. That is the challenge that we are facing in the next two or three years.

The Effects of NAFTA[7]

Because of their proximity to the U.S. market, Mexico and the Caribbean Basin represented important expansion opportunities for Li & Fung. Attracted by cheap labor and rapid turnaround times, U.S. companies were looking for manufacturing opportunities in this region. Of particular appeal was 807 manufacturing: textile pieces were sent from the United States to Mexico or the Caribbean where complete apparel units were assembled and exported back into the United States. Duty for these finished pieces was only on the labor portion completed outside of the United States. Upon the signing of NAFTA, Mexican 807 apparel products became duty free. Duties on other apparel imports from Mexico were gradually being lowered. It was estimated that Mexico's 807 apparel exports to the United States in 1997 were 70% of total apparel exports; for the Caribbean Basin the figure was approximately 80%.

Textile manufacturers in Asia were concerned. In the first six months of 1997, exports from Mexico were up (from the same period the previous year) 43.9% with 807 and related exports up 42.7%. Exports from the Caribbean basin were not far behind, with 807 and related exports up 32.2% and 28.68% for textile and apparel exports overall. Leading exporters within the Caribbean were the Dominican Republic, Honduras, Costa Rica, Haiti, and Nicaragua.[8] In mid-1997 congressional lobbyists were pushing for textile export parity with Mexico for the Caribbean basin. With Caribbean wage rates at 60% to 70% of Mexico, Mexico's no-duty advantage was offset, although full-package manufacturing was still generally unavailable in the Caribbean region. Li & Fung was looking to provide sourcing through non-807 manufacturers in the region.

---

6 USITC, Industry & Trade Summary Data.

7 The North American Free Trade Agreement (NAFTA) was a free trade agreement between the United States, Canada, and Mexico.

8 "The Region: Central American Union to be Created," *Caribbean Update*, October 1, 1997.

Despite the time and cost advantages of Caribbean basin and Mexican manufacturing it was unclear how effectively the two regions would be able to compete with China and the Asia/Pacific region over the next few years. Although the infrastructure and technological capabilities of the Asia/Pacific region were still higher than those of Mexico, it was only a matter of time before Mexican manufacturers took advantage of the benefits of computer-aided design the way their Asian counterparts already had.[9] Finally, with China's plan to join the World Trade Organization came the promise of the cessation of textile export quotas in January 2005.

INTO THE SECOND CENTURY

Since the merger with IBS, Li & Fung revenue had increased almost 50% from its 1995 level of HK$9 billion ($1.2 billion). Victor and William were confident that growth could be maintained, but they were aware of the hurdles that remained. Staffing new operations with current Li & Fung managers who had no experience or understanding of the country or region they were to oversee was risky. The pool of higher level managers from which the company could pick was becoming sparse and the turnover of the lower ranks only exacerbated the problem.

Maintenance of standards could also prove challenging. The brothers needed to answer the following questions.

- Should Li & Fung expand to countries closer to their target markets? Was an operation in Mexico essential for future success or could the company rely on its expertise and network in Asia?
- What role would Asia play in the future? Although the Asian currency crisis of the second half of 1997 had resulted in increased business for Li & Fung operations in Southeast Asia, Victor and William did not expect such activity to continue indefinitely. Would the cost benefits of manufacturing in Asia only last until the devalued currencies rebounded?
- What of technological innovations at Li & Fung: would a proprietary information network which enabled clients to view the status of an order serve as a competitive advantage? What other steps could they take to improve their 'virtual factory' capabilities? Could Victor and William further reduce turnaround time from Asian manufacturers to compete with other countries?

Finally, "Filling in the Mosaic" had been the motto of the 1996-1998 plan. Victor and William wondered what slogan could propel Li & Fung into the twenty-first century.

---

9 "Caribbean Remains Competitive Even Without Parity," *Daily News Record,* September 15, 1997.

Hikma Pharmaceuticals

On May 19, 1996, Mr. Samih Darwazah, chairman of Hikma Investment, the holding company for Hikma Pharmaceuticals, proudly announced that the Jordanian company had begun exports of approved drugs to the United States:

> The shipment is of $100,000 worth of prescription drugs to four U.S. distributors. Hikma is the first Arab-owned drug company from the Middle East to obtain Food and Drug Administration (FDA) approval to sell to the U.S. market, following inspection of our plants in Jordan by an FDA team. This is a vote of confidence which will not only enable us to sell in the U.S. but also boost our sales in Jordan and the Arab world. It's the latest in a long series of marketing challenges that we've overcome.

Hikma was already selling drugs in the U.S. manufactured by its West-ward subsidiary, acquired in 1991 and run by Said, Mr. Darwazah's son. Hikma's top management team was keenly debating the appropriate strategy for the company's U.S. operations, how they should fit with Hikma's other operations in Jordan and Portugal, and how important a role they should play in the company's overall growth.

COMPANY BACKGROUND

Mr. Samih Darwazah, Hikma's founder, was born in Palestine. He came to the United States in the late 1960s on a scholarship to the St. Louis College of Pharmacology, earned a master's degree in industrial pharmacy and joined Eli Lilly on graduation. After fourteen years in a variety of international marketing positions in Europe and the

This case was prepared by Professor John A. Quelch with the assistance of Robin Root.
Copyright © 1997 by the President and Fellows of Harvard College. Harvard Business School case 9-598-019.

Middle East, Mr. Darwazah decided in 1977 to settle in Amman, Jordan. His objective, with the assistance of his two sons, was to create a pharmaceutical company to serve the Arab world. Mr. Darwazah explained:

> Jordan is a small country–only 4.3 million people. And a relatively poor country–with per capita income of only $1,650. Yet the multinational pharmaceutical companies were already selling here, so we had to think internationally from the outset.

First, Mr. Darwazah established a joint venture in Amman with an Italian firm. The joint venture negotiated a license from Fujisawa Pharmaceutical Corp. of Japan to manufacture in Jordan and market in the Middle East cefazolin[1], one of the world's top-selling injectable (rather than oral) cephalosporins (cephs).[2] In addition, the company manufactured and marketed its own formulation of another common, but less technically advanced, class of penicillin-based antibiotics called amoxicillin. However, because the Jordanian market was already well-served by multinational pharmaceutical firms, Mr. Darwazah knew he had to differentiate his new firm if he was to succeed. He built credibility among local physicians, who were skeptical of the quality of locally manufactured products, by emphasizing the company's commitment to research and new product development, by inviting them on plant tours and by stressing added value customer services delivered by highly trained salespeople, most of whom were former pharmacists. He identified three keys to the company's success: procure additional manufacturing licenses to expand the firm's product line; develop cutting-edge generics that were more than just "me-too" products; and market these product lines in ways that would make his firm an indispensable source to physicians in the Arab world.

---

1 Lederle held the license from Fujisawa to market cefazolin in Europe.

2 See page 6 [of the case] for a full description of cephalosporins.

Production began in 1978. Over time, manufacturing licenses were obtained from Fujisawa, Chugai and Dainippon of Japan for a range of additional drugs including anti-rheumatics, cardiovascular drugs, tranquilizers, anti-diabetics, anti-spasmodics, anti-ulcer medications and hormones. The factory was expanded in 1984 to include a sterile area for the production of injectables. To comply with best practices and avoid cross-contamination, a separate plant was set up in 1988 for production of cephalosporins and penicillins.

During the 1980s, Hikma supplemented the production of licensed products with branded generics to leverage further its sales and distribution organization.[3] Hikma became the first Arab drug company to perform bioequivalency studies. The company expanded the dosage forms for amoxicillin. First, Hikma developed a more convenient twice-a-day (as opposed to three times a day) dosage form of amoxicillin which resulted in higher patient compliance. Hikma also developed a chewable version of amoxicillin, previously unavailable even in the United States. As a result, Hikma enhanced its reputation as a quality company with a growing research and development capability.

Hikma gradually increased its focus on cephs. In 1985, the firm secured a second license from Fujisawa to manufacture Cefizox, another injectable ceph. Shortly thereafter, the company signed a manufacturing agreement with Smith, Kline and French Laboratories for a third injectable ceph (which needed to be administered to a patient only once a day). In return, Hikma furnished these multinationals with royalty payments on its sales.

As the focus on cephs increased, Mr. Darwazah decided that Hikma should backward integrate into the production of raw materials. Although supplies of the necessary raw materials were plentiful, he wanted to tighten quality control by backward integrating and to ensure Hikma's independence from outside sources. In 1990, a sterile plant was established with an initial annual production capacity of 24 tonnes of bulk cephs but with expansion potential to 48 tonnes. Only a few plants in India could produce bulk cephs at lower cost.

By 1995, Hikma was making 40 drug products in Jordan. The top five sellers accounted for 50% of sales. Oral cephalosporins accounted for 30% of sales, drugs manufactured under license for 30% and branded generics for 50%.[4]

INTERNATIONAL EXPANSION

By 1994, Hikma Investments included wholly-owned manufacturing operations in Portugal and the United States as well as four plants in Jordan. Exhibit 1 details Hikma's sources of revenues between 1990 and 1996, while Exhibit 2 breaks down Hikma Jordan's sales by drug class in 1990 and 1996. In 1996, the proportion of total company profits generated by Hikma Jordan was 45% and its capacity utilization rate was 70%. The corresponding figures for Hikma Portugal were 10% and 30%, and for West-ward (the United States operation) were 30% and 95%.

Hikma employed around 500 persons in Jordan, 70% of them college graduates; many managerial positions were held by women. Hikma also owned Arab Medical Containers, a health-care related plastics manufacturing company which supplied Hikma and other companies with containers, tamper resistant bottles and other drug packaging. A manufacturing joint venture had been established in Tunisia in 1992 to produce cephs and penicillins under the Hikma name for supply to the French-speaking countries of North and West Africa. Through a second joint venture, Hikma provided technical support for the manufacture and marketing of products in Egypt, the largest pharmaceutical market in the Middle East. A third joint venture had been signed to build a $35 million plant in Saudi Arabia, completion of which was expected at the end of 1997. Hikma had marketing offices in 20 countries, including Russia, Slovakia and China.

The pharmaceutical industry was the second most important exporter in Jordan. Hikma, as the largest pharmaceutical company in Jordan, was, therefore, one of the country's most significant exporters. In 1995, the Jordanian pharmaceutical industry produced $225 million worth of drugs of which $120 million worth were exported. Hikma exports in 1995 accounted for $50 million of the company's $60 million in sales. In contrast to exports, Hikma sales in Jordan were only $10 million in 1995. Despite Hikma's efforts, locally made drugs accounted for only 30% of Jordan's consumption. In 1996, Hikma was trying to persuade the Jordanian government to approve increases in local drug prices. Margins were so low that Hikma's ability to invest in research and development was limited. Hikma was contemplating curtailing the production of certain drugs, which would leave only the

---

3 In the United States, generic imitations of off-patent drugs did not usually carry brand names. In Europe and the Middle East, they often did and were, as a result, called branded generics.

4 Percentages do not total 100 because some of Hikma's oral cephs were made under license.

Exhibit 1 Sources of Hikma Sales ($000)[a]

	1990	1991	1992	1993	1994	1995	1996E
Jordan (domestic)	2.8	5.2	6.5	10.6	3.3	7.8	8.2
Jordan (exports)	21.9	19.5	30.8	41.2	34.2	30.9	27.9
Portugal (domestic)	--	--	0.6[b]	2.6[b]	4.9[b]	1.6	2.6
Portugal (exports)						4.6	4.1
USA (domestic)	N/A	3.5[c]	5.9	9.6	11.9	12.7	14.4

[a]Internal transfer sales have been excluded.
[b]Portugal domestic and export sales combined.
[c]United States 1991 reflects six months of sales only.

Exhibit 2   Sources of Hikma Jordan Sales by Drug Class: 1990 and 1996E

	Hikma Jordan	
	1990	1996E
Oral Cephs	2.7	5.7
Injectable Cephs	0.8	4.4[a]
Amoxicillins	4.0	4.2
Anti-inflammatories & Anti-Rheumatics	3.4	4.7
Cardiovasculars	2.0	1.0
Anti-diabetics	1.9	0.6
Anti-spasmodics	1.6	0.4
Anti-ulcer	1.1	0.5
Tranquilizers	0.1	0.4

Note: [a]Around 30 percent of Hikma Jordan's injectable cephs were exported.

more expensive imported substitutes available to the Jordanian consumer.

The Arab World

Mr. Darwazah's initial vision was to develop "an Arab company that serves the Arab world." In the early 1980s, he found markets for his joint venture's generic products in the Middle East and North Africa, winning government procurement contracts in Iraq, Syria and Tunisia. The firm's growth was restricted, however, as Saudi Arabia, a key market in the region, only allowed originator manufacturers to sell their drugs in the market. Hikma was the first company to secure permission from Saudi Arabia to market generic drugs, but then faced the further obstacle that Saudi Arabia only provided tax exemptions to 100% Arab-owned firms. To achieve this exemption, Mr. Darwazah bought out his Italian partner in 1984, and then obtained permission from his licensors to expand distribution into Saudi Arabia, Syria, and Iraq. In 1986, Hikma, an Arabic word denoting wisdom and reason, was selected as the company's new name.

Over time, Mr. Darwazah concluded that his initial vision for Hikma was too limiting and that the company should diversify further its sales base. He commented:

Increasingly Saudi Arabia, Syria and other countries in the region decided to promote their own pharmaceutical industries and protect them against imports, even from an Arab neighbor. Spimaco, a $100 million Saudi pharmaceutical manufacturer has, for example, pressured the Saudi government to protect the large domestic market for its benefit. In addition, the disruption to regional trade caused by the Gulf War in 1991 convinced us that we had to diversify further afield – though we cemented our relationships with Iraq's doctors by keeping supply lines open to them during the crisis.

In selecting countries for international expansion beyond the Middle East, Hikma's initial impulse was to explore opportunities in other Muslim markets, such as Malaysia and Indonesia, in order to gain experience that would equip the company to take on the more competitive

European and U.S. markets. Senior managers soon discovered, however, that the health services in these developing countries were not yet set up to accept imported generic drugs. Moreover, the predominantly European and North American (as opposed to Asian) experience of most of Hikma's senior managers justified an earlier-than-expected shift in the company's market focus towards Europe and the United States. Nevertheless, in 1996, 90% of Hikma exports from Jordan were still to the Middle East and North Africa.

Expansion Into Europe

Mr. Darwazah realized that the pharmaceutical industry was increasingly global, that there were no obvious reasons why generic drug manufacturers should not, like the research based companies, sell internationally, and that Hikma could not survive merely as a regional player. The Jordanian market was becoming cluttered as Hikma's success prompted half a dozen new pharmaceutical manufacturing companies to be established by 1987. Meanwhile, discussion of European economic integration attracted Mr. Darwazah's attention. For a small pharmaceutical firm, the prospect of a single new drug registration filing in Brussels to secure access to the 330 million consumers of the European Union was especially appealing. Finally, Mr. Darwazah had been able to recruit high caliber scientists and managers into Hikma's Jordanian operations, many of whom had European education and/or experience; their continued motivation depended in part on sustained corporate growth.

Mr. Darwazah therefore began to explore the possibilities of establishing a manufacturing plant in Europe. He focused on Ireland and Portugal, both members of the European Union with access to some 330 million consumers. The national governments of both countries along with the European Union in Brussels offered attractive investment and tax incentives to foreign companies interested in establishing high technology manufacturing plants. Mr. Darwazah explained why Hikma settled on Portugal:

There were three reasons. First, most of the major multinational pharmaceutical companies already had operations in Ireland. In Portugal, the pharmaceutical industry was less developed so we could offer something special by coming in. At the same time, our manufacturing processes were not that complicated so we didn't need a big pool of talented people to recruit from.

Second, the population of Portugal was 12 million versus 3 million in Ireland. Sales in the domestic market could justify the plant even if we didn't export that much.

Third, the multinational pharmaceutical companies were consolidating their Portuguese and Spanish operations in anticipation of the 1992 European Union market integration. This often resulted in the closure or downsizing of their Portuguese plants. As a result, there were many pharmaceutical managers and workers on the job market.

Jordanian banks which had already invested in Hikma's Jordanian operations were reluctant to loan Mr. Darwazah capital. However, the International Finance Corporation of the World Bank provided a $7 million loan commitment in 1988, and also purchased a 6% equity stake in Hikma Investments which owned 100% of Hikma Portugal.

The plant took three years to be completed. The fully automated 4,800-square-meter plant outside Lisbon was designed to incorporate two separate operations that both met Food and Drug Administration standards:

- A filling plant for injectable cephalosporins with an annual capacity of 30 million vials
- A liquid filling plant for other chemical entities with an annual capacity of 42 million vials and ampoules

By 1996, Hikma Farmaceutica, the Portuguese subsidiary, was generating sales of $10 million. All but 5% of these sales were of cephalosporins; 80% of the ceph sales were of injectables, 20% were of oral drugs. Sixty percent of ceph production was of cephs still under patent, manufacturing of which was licensed from Fujisawa, while 40% was of generic cephs. Certain of the raw materials for ceph production were imported from Jordan. The non-ceph 5% of revenues came from sales of branded drugs including oral antibiotics and tranquilizers which Hikma manufactured under license in Jordan and for which the company was able to obtain Portuguese marketing licenses. Marketing of these drugs occupied the firm's 25 salespeople and provided cash flow while production of injectable cephs was coming on line and the relevant manufacturing approvals were being obtained from the Portuguese health authorities.

Seventy percent of Hikma Portugal's sales were exported. Of the exports, 20% were of generic cephs shipped to Germany, 10% were sent to China and 70% were exported to the Middle East and North Africa. In effect, the role of the

Portuguese operation was to produce injectable cephs for Hikma's worldwide marketing network.

Mr. Darwazah was concerned about Hikma Farmaceutica's marketing efforts in Europe. While contracts with private hospital chains had been obtained, it was proving difficult to sell into the government agencies that dominated drug procurement for the national health care systems of many European countries. In particular, French manufacturers of injectable cephs defended their market shares vigorously. Another difficulty in Europe was that Brussels regulations (unlike U.S. regulations) precluded generic manufacturers from working on formulations of patented drugs until they actually came off patent. As a result, Mr. Darwazah was keenly waiting for FDA inspectors to visit the Portuguese plant in 1997 as part of the approval process that would permit Hikma to sell its generic injectable cephs in the United States. Mr. Darwazah believed U.S. demand could prompt a doubling of injectable ceph output within a year.

Entry Into The United States

In the late 1980s, Mr. Darwazah conceived a three-pronged geographical production strategy in the United States as well as in Europe and the Middle East. Mr. Darwazah explained:

> There were at least four reasons why I wanted to secure a foothold in the United States. First, the United States is the largest and most competitive pharmaceutical market in the world. If you can make it there, you can make it anywhere. Second, the prospects for generic drugs gaining a larger share of prescriptions were excellent as keeping health care costs under control became an ever more pressing political issue. Third, the U.S. is a well-organized and open market; the large Asian markets are not so straightforward. Fourth, I felt our manufacturing quality was up to U.S. standards. Finally I have to admit that cracking the U.S. market was an entrepreneurial challenge and, having studied in the States, I wanted the satisfaction of succeeding in the American market.

Hikma began, in 1989, to look for an acquisition candidate in the U.S. The pharmaceutical manufacturing sector in the U.S. was consolidating; the pressure to control health costs put many small companies under margin pressure. Cost concerns were also increasing the penetration of generics and many managed care health providers were mandating substitution of generics for their patients. Moreover, numerous drugs were scheduled to come off patent and thereby become available to generic competition. Hikma identified the West-ward company of New Jersey as one of several possible acquisition candidates and, after negotiations and due diligence, a deal was struck in June 1991.

West-ward's founders were manufacturing entrepreneurs with high quality standards. In the late 1980s, West-Ward had been an approved vendor to many large hospital chains. However, the West-ward manufacturing operation had been acquired by a large drug wholesaler in 1988, and within two years, the firm's quality control standards were challenged by the FDA. West-ward's 1990 sales of $12 million were primarily of off-patent drugs sold on contract. Convinced that Hikma technicians could bring West-ward's production facilities back into compliance with FDA standards, Mr. Darwazah decided to make an offer for the company. Following the acquisition, a team of managers and technicians from Jordan worked at the West-ward plant to secure FDA recertification.

As of 1996, West-ward had 83 tablet and capsule products in its line. Forty of these were based on Abbreviated New Drug Applications (ANDAs)[5] approved by the FDA, 35 of which had been approved since the Hikma acquisition. Forty percent of West-ward sales were private label products sold to several health maintenance organizations; 40% were tablets and caplets sold under the West-ward branded generic label to drug wholesalers; and 20% were products manufactured to the specifications of several major drug companies. Sales of $15 million in 1996 resulted in an $800,000 pretax profit. According to Said Darwazah, the West-ward operation had recovered to 80 percent of its peak performance in the 1980s.

HIKMA'S STRATEGIC FOCUS

By 1996, it was clear that Hikma's growth had stemmed from two key judgments Mr. Darwazah had made a decade earlier: the decision to focus on cephalosporins and the decision to focus on the manufacture of added value generics. Mr. Darwazah believed that continuation of these two strategies would enable Hikma to expand significantly its business in the United States. The proportions of Hikma sales that were cephs and generics in 1996 are shown in Table A.

---

5 Once the FDA approved an ANDA, the new drug could de facto be sold almost anywhere in the world except Canada, Japan and Western Europe which had their own approval procedures.

| Table A | Hikma Sales of Cephs and Generics: 1996E |

	% Cephs[a]	% Generics
Jordan (domestic)	25	50
Jordan (export)	20	50
Portugal (domestic)	50	30
Portugal (export)	100	60
United States	0	100

[a]Around 50% of ceph sales were of generics.

Cephalosporins

Cephalosporins were a class of anti-infective drugs with similar uses to penicillins. They were deployed against a broad array of bacteria-induced infections, especially those which occurred during or as a result of surgery. Most were used in hospitals rather than for out-patient treatment. In 1995, the value of all drugs sold worldwide at the dose form level was $270 billion. Of this, anti-infectives accounted for $23 billion, of which cephs, often described as "workhorse" antibiotics, accounted for 45% (or $10.2 billion), penicillins for 15% and quinolones for 11%. Cephs were the eighth most frequently prescribed category of drugs in the United States (60 million prescriptions in 1995).

Oral cephs accounted for around 70% of total doses taken but for only 50% of sales value. The best-known oral cephs were Eli Lilly's Ceclor and Ceflex with around 43% of the oral ceph market. Ceclor went off-patent in December 1994. Injectable cephs, accounting for 25% of total doses, were more effective than oral cephs and were used more heavily in hospitals to treat acutely sick patients.

By 1995, there were several generations of cephs on the market. The first and second generation cephs were largely off-patent, and therefore subject to competition from generics, while newer, third and fourth generation cephs had been developed, either to combat more virulent infections or to address more finely targeted indications. As shown in Exhibit 3, these cephs commanded higher margins than earlier generations. There were around 50 ceph products on the market; the cephalosporin molecule lent itself more readily than penicillin to line extensions because there were three places at which new chains could be attached. The frequency with which new versions of cephs were introduced led some physicians to refer semi-facetiously to the latest ceph discovery as the "ceph du jour."

The market share leaders in cephs were Eli Lilly (16% of doses worldwide in 1995), Glaxo Wellcome (15%) and Fujisawa (10%). Bristol Myers Squibb and Upjohn were developing and launching fourth generation cephs. Fujisawa had already licensed marketing of its fourth generation injectable ceph to Johnson & Johnson. Around one-third of cephs were sold in North America, one-third in Europe and one-third in Asia, principally Japan.

Bulk cephs, from which doses of cephs were made, were produced and marketed by a variety of companies, including companies in India and Taiwan. In 1995, 4,700 metric tons of bulk cephs were sold at prices ranging from $400 to $6,000 per kilo.

Generic Versions of Patented Products

Mr. Darwazah recognized in the 1980s that demand for generic drugs was increasing and was likely to continue. Generic drugs, called by their basic chemical names, had the same active ingredients, strength, dosage form and medical effects as their brand name counterparts. As patents on brand name drugs expired, there was an opportunity for lower priced generic manufacturers to capture market share.

In most Middle Eastern countries, drug patents were recognized for ten years (as opposed to twenty years in the United States) and slight variations in manufacturing processes permitted generic equivalents to be registered under new names. While generic versions of patented products could not be marketed in countries where the patents on the brand name drug were still in force, they could be sold in many developing countries where patent enforcement was not as tight. Hikma increasingly focused on the manufacture of generic cephs. Given the extra lead time and the opportunity to manufacture patented drugs under license, the company could perfect their production before they came off patent in the United States. Comparative cost and price structures for generic and branded injectable cephs are shown in Exhibit 4.

In the United States, where health care costs accounted for 15% of the gross national product, there was significant political pressure on the drug companies, even though pharmaceuticals represented only 7% of the total health care burden. Between 1985 and 1995, generics more than doubled their volume share of U.S. prescription drug sales to 43% but their share of the $50 billion U.S. prescription

Exhibit 3 Index of Cephalosporin Prices: 1996

Generation of Cephs	Middle East	Europe	USA
Generic:			
First	100	160	90
Second	200	250	N/A
Branded:			
First	150	200	120
Second	300	400	400
Third	500	500	600

Exhibit 4 Comparative Cost and Price Structures for Hikma Injectable Cephs: 1996[a]

	Generic	Branded
Raw Material Cost ($ per gram)[b]	$0.50	$2.00
Vial & Label	0.50	0.50
Quality Control	0.20	0.20
Variable Manufacturing Cost	1.20	2.20
Clinical Trials	--	0.20
Sales & Marketing	0.10	1.00
Total Cost	$1.30	$3.40
Avg. Manufacturer Selling Price	1.90	5.00
Profit Margin	0.60 (32%)	1.60 (32%)

Note: [a]Prices of injectable cephs (including those produced by Hikma) varied widely depending on the sophistication of the drug. Some third generation cephs sold for $36 or more per gram.
[b]A gram was a typical patient dosage.

market was only 12% in value terms. Sales of generics were boosted in 1991 by the so-called "drug product selection law" which permitted pharmacists to substitute cheaper generics in place of brand name drugs when filling prescriptions and required that health care providers charge the government-run Medicaid and Medicare the lowest possible drug prices.[6]

Price-sensitive consumers paying health care insurance through managed care companies and health maintenance organizations fueled demand for lower priced generics. The FDA set up a special office to handle ANDAS applications from generic drug manufacturers; these applications, of which 250 were approved in 1995 alone, could be filed before a brand name drug's patent expired, required bioequivalency studies and took, on average, eighteen months to process.

Adding further to the potential for generic drug sales to increase in the U.S. was the fact that, between 1995 and 2005, 60 major brand name drugs, representing $40 billion in annual sales, would come off patent. Between 1995 and 2000, five major cephs were due to come off patent; as a result, Hikma was especially keen to file ANDAs applications for its generic equivalents, and obtain approval for them as soon as possible.

The large, research-based drug companies reacted to the advent of generic competition in several ways. In some cases, successful generic manufacturers were acquired. In other cases, the research-based drug companies fought generic competition claiming that the generic differed in

some key way (for example, a binding or dispersing ingredient or chemical delivery variation). A third approach was to offer special long-term pricing contracts to the large managed care organizations while a drug was still covered by patent to insulate against share erosion when it expired. A fourth approach was to sign an agreement with a generic drug manufacturer ahead of patent expiration to try to influence the pricing of both the generic and the brand name versions. Eli Lilly signed such an agreement with Mylan Pharmaceuticals on Ceclor, its leading ceph, a year before the U.S. patent expired in 1994. By 1995, Ceclor's market share had, nevertheless, dropped from 36% to 14%.

Cephalexin was, in 1995, the tenth most frequently prescribed generic drug in the United States, accounting for 2.8% of generic prescriptions. Amoxicillin, which Hikma also produced in a generic version, accounted for 17% of generic prescriptions.

Because of the size of the ceph market, there were not so many generic competitors as in some of the more heavily prescribed drug categories. However, Hikma was far from being the only small pharmaceutical company interested in producing and marketing generic cephs. Marsam of the U.S. and Rambaxy of India were well-known in the field.

---

6 Although generic purchases by pharmacies represented 12% of total prescription dollars, the same generics accounted for 30% of pharmacy dispensing revenues, indicating higher markups than on brand name drugs.

Another competitor, Lupin Laboratories of India, signed an agreement with Merck Generics in 1995 to manufacture and market a line of injectable cephs.

U.S. GROWTH OPTIONS

Having established a U.S. foothold by purchasing West-ward, Said Darwazah was keen to grow Hikma's sales in the United States. His ambition was to achieve $30 million in sales of West-ward manufactured drugs by 2000 with another $70 million coming from sales of cutting-edge injectable cephs made in Portugal. These drugs would not be subject to import tariffs and transportation costs would be minimal. Hikma Portugal was not finding it easy to make sales in other European countries so capacity to supply the U.S. market was likely to be available. West-ward would continue to manufacture tablets and capsules; the plant could not be upgraded to produce injectable cephs. However, sales and distribution of these highly technical drugs from Portugal would add to West-ward's reputation and help boost sales of its branded generics.

Two large firms had approached Hikma offering quantity purchase deals on the firm's injectable cephs. The first option was to sell injectable cephs to Northaid[7], which was the fifth largest manufacturer of ethical pharmaceuticals in the United States in 1995 and a division of a giant consumer goods company. West-ward had manufactured orally administered drugs for Northaid for several years through a joint venture in which both parties shared the profits equally. Northaid purchases accounted for 10 percent of West-ward's sales in 1995. Said Darwazah commented on Northaid's proposal:

They have indicated an interest in buying $60 million worth of injectable cephs from us by 2000 plus $30 million worth of generic drugs manufactured by West-ward. Northaid wants a U.S. exclusive on our injectable cephs.

A second option was to supply Sanitas[7], a large managed care organization which had distribution contracts to supply drugs to over 1,000 hospitals throughout the U.S. Sanitas sales represented about 20% of 1995 hospital purchases of drugs through managed care organizations. Darwazah commented on the Sanitas opportunity:

Sanitas have told us they can take all the injectable cephs we can supply. They say they'll need to procure $200 million worth of injectable cephs by 2000. We would have to double the capacity of our plant in Portugal to supply them at this level. Of course, they want rock-bottom prices, guaranteed delivery dates and an exclusive on sales of our injectable cephs in the U.S. They would put the Sanitas name on the product label; West-ward would not be mentioned.

Sanitas would not normally be talking to a company of our size, but we have the range and quality of injectable cephs they need. They gave West-ward a one year contract to supply them with some generic drugs to check out our quality control and customer service. That worked well but, unlike Northaid, they really don't want West-ward's branded generics. But, like Northaid, they want to sign a deal with a supplier soon, and we're not the only game in town.

Said Darwazah was attracted by the high volume purchase commitments these companies were prepared to make. Agreeing to one of these deals would however, reduce Hikma's independence and practically turn it into a captive OEM supplier. Said wondered if he could develop a strong enough sales and distribution system in the United States with the necessary breadth and depth of hospital contacts to go it alone and promote the West-ward brand. Alternatively, a two- or three-year agreement with Northaid or Sanitas would give Hikma time and cash to establish its reputation in the U.S. market and then sell direct with branded generics.

---

7 Disguised name.

Part II

Global Expansion Strategies

The globalization of markets, the increasing homogeneity of customer needs worldwide, and falling tariffs together mean that few companies can continue to afford to remain focused on their domestic markets. The company that has profited for decades serving a single market—thanks perhaps to protectionist tariffs and government regulations—must now face the challenge of international expansion as competitors from other countries increasingly invade its home base. In the words of Professor Howard Stevenson of Harvard Business School, today's companies must "eat lunch or be lunch."

There are six main reasons why companies expand beyond the borders of their domestic markets:

- To capitalize on economies of scale and scope and to use additional capacity
- To leverage a specialist manufacturing or marketing capability, often to a customer niche that can be found in multiple markets worldwide
- To learn how to compete in foreign markets and thereby develop knowledge and skills that can improve competitiveness in the domestic market
- To challenge foreign competitors, who may be invading the domestic market, on their own home turf
- To diversify risk and stabilize sales when the economy in the domestic market is volatile
- To satisfy the vision or ambition of the chief executive officer and to make employees proud

Initially, most companies enter international markets opportunistically, responding to rather than developing overseas orders and filling them with products no different than those sold domestically. Over time, international sales may become more integral to success, and further penetration of international markets often warrants local adaptation.

This pattern of international sales gradually increasing as a percentage of total revenues is being challenged as a result of globalization. Many small companies marketing specialist-niche products or services are "born global." Using a fax machine, a site on the Internet, and an express delivery service, they are able to reach international customers on a modest sales base without building sales organizations and distribution systems in multiple country markets. Other small companies on the cutting edge of technology find that no matter where they are based, they have to enter the United States early on, because acceptance in this highly competitive market is key to customer acceptance worldwide.

In selecting which markets to enter, a variety of other criteria are relevant. These range from macroeconomic indicators, political stability and government regulations through industry structure, market size and growth, and competitive intensity to product-market fit and likely customer response. If companies screen markets first on the basis of macroeconomic indicators, fast-growing emerging markets will often be eliminated from further consideration. It is preferable that the market potential and value added for local customers take precedence in the sequence with which market entry criteria are admitted to the market selection decision process.

Sometimes there is a window of opportunity to enter a market ahead of competition that should be exploited. In other cases, it may be appropriate to enter a market to achieve a quick success that will, as a result of learning or increased credibility, facilitate entry into other markets.

Only the largest, wealthiest companies can enter all markets at once. Most must follow a sequential approach that often involves an evolving portfolio of both small and large countries in both emerging and developed markets in all geographic regions of the world.

Once it is decided which markets to enter, the mode and timing of entry must be considered. Many companies work initially through licensed agents, gradually increasing their commitment to establish a representative sales office, perhaps as a joint venture. Later, a wholly-owned subsidiary is often set up that may engage in local manufacturing as well as marketing. Throughout this process of progressive commitment, there is a simultaneous increase in the dollars invested and the degree of corporate control, as shown in Figure 2.1.

Regarding timing, there are clear prime-mover advantages to entering emerging markets early in their development. Brand reputation can be built cheaply because advertising is inexpensive. Contracts can be signed with the best local suppliers, distributors, and joint venture partners. Early entry often attracts host government goodwill along with favorable regulatory and tax treatment. Finally, early entrants such as Nestle and Coca-Cola gain experience and confidence and develop a pioneering image that enables them to enter other markets ahead of their competitors.

Figure 2.1   Entry Mode

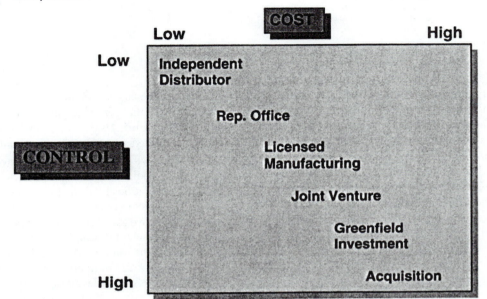

Bajaj Auto Ltd.

Rahul Bajaj, chairman and CEO of Bajaj Auto Ltd. (BAL), reflected on the changes that had taken place in the Indian market during the late 1980s and early 1990s and the challenges that his company faced early in 1993. BAL, an Indian manufacturer of two- and three-wheeler vehicles, faced a stagnant domestic market that had declined by 5% in 1991-92 and increasing competition from the major Japanese two-wheeler manufacturers. Bajaj wondered what strategy would both protect BAL's dominant share of the Indian market and permit exports to rise to 15% of total sales by 1998.

COMPANY BACKGROUND

The Bajaj family came from a trading community in Central India. The founder of the current Bajaj Group, Jamnalal Bajaj, set up a sugar factory and steel mill in the 1930s and his son, Kamalnayan Bajaj, established Bajaj Electricals in 1938 and Bajaj Auto in 1945. Between 1950 and 1956, Bajaj Auto imported scooters and three-wheelers from Piaggio (the Italian manufacturer of the Vespa brand). In 1959, the company was granted a license from the Indian government to produce 6,000 scooters and three-wheelers per annum. In 1960, BAL entered into a technical collaboration with Piaggio to manufacture its products in India, set up a manufacturing unit at Akurdi (near Pune), 170 km south of Bombay, and went public. In 1961, BAL began manufacturing.

During the 1960s, the company concentrated on indigenizing components and establishing a dealer network in India. Initially, local component content was only 26% but, due to the Indian government's emphasis on import substitution, this was gradually increased. By 1966, BAL had become the largest Indian producer of two-wheelers, and product demand exceeded supply. The Piaggio collaboration lasted until 1971, when new government regulations prohibited a continuation of the alliance.

The company's growth had been restricted by the Indian economic and political environment since its inception. In 1969, new regulations made it even more difficult for large private companies to obtain licenses to increase production capacity. Restrictive government import policies also created a protected market for BAL and other domestic two-wheeler manufacturers, permitting BAL to enjoy a high share of a sellers' market for 22 continuous years. During this period, waiting lists for BAL vehicles averaged 10 years.

During the 1970s, both government licensing and price controls remained in place. In 1975, BAL established a manufacturing joint venture with the state government of Maharashtra. BAL held a 24% stake and operating control. In 1982, the government permitted infusion of further foreign technology and expansion of capacity and, in 1985, BAL established a second plant at Waluj (near Aurangabad), 225 km north of the Akurdi plant. The 1980s were a period of explosive growth for BAL: production volumes increased from 172,000 in 1981 to 800,000 units a year by 1990. In addition, BAL entered both the motorcycle and moped segments of the two-wheeler market and established a technical collaboration with Kawasaki in 1984. This agreement centered on the development and production of 2-stroke and 4-stroke motorcycles and gave BAL access to Kawasaki motorcycle design and production expertise. The collaboration provided BAL with a full range of two-wheeler products and helped the company respond quickly to competition from other Japanese manufacturers.

Prior to 1993, BAL's business strategy had focused on four objectives: keeping costs and prices low; improving product quality; concentrating on two- and three-wheeler vehicles; and striving for economies of scale. BAL's goals in the 1980s had been to increase product demand and

This case was prepared by Professor John Quelch with the assistance of Nathalie Laidler and Afroze Mohammed.

Copyright © 1993 by the President and Fellows of Harvard College. Harvard Business School case 9-593-097.

build both volume and market share. As Bajaj described it: "The 1980s were a period of growth for the sake of growth."

BAL IN 1993

In 1993, BAL was the world's largest manufacturer of scooters and the world's third-largest manufacturer of two- and three-wheeler vehicles. Annual revenues placed it among the top 10 manufacturing companies in the Indian private sector and fourteenth in profits before tax. (Exhibit 1 reports past and projected income statements.) Bajaj himself was acclaimed as one of India's most successful entrepreneurs.

Products

In 1993, BAL manufactured 12 different models: 5 scooter models (Cub, Super, Super FE, Chetak, and Stride); 3 motorcycle models (M-80, Kawasaki RTZ, and Kawasaki 4S); 1 moped model (the Bajaj Sunny); and 3 three-wheeler models (rear-engine Autoriksha, front-engine Autoriksha, and a goods carrier). The two-wheeler

market included scooters, motorcycles, and mopeds. (Table A gives a brief description of these products, and Exhibit 2 depicts examples from each product category.) Two-wheeler products were relatively simple in technology, economically priced, and had average lifetimes between 10 to 15 years (scooters averaged 12 to 15 years, motorcycles 10 to 12 years, and mopeds 8 to 10 years). Ninety percent of three-wheeler vehicles were used as low-cost passenger taxis, known as Autorikshas; the remaining 10% were used as light commercial vehicles. (Examples of both are shown in Exhibit 3.) The average life of three-wheeler products was 10 years.

Manufacturing

By February 1993, BAL was the world's lowest-cost manufacturer of two-wheelers, capable of producing at a rate of over 3,000 vehicles a day in two (rather than three) shifts, six days a week. The Akurdi plant employed 5,800 direct workers and manufactured four scooter models, the M-80 motorcycle, and the front-engine Autoriksha goods carriers. The Waluj plant with 4,800 workers made three of the scooter models, the KB 100 and 4S motorcycles, the

---

| (Exhibit 1) | BAL Income Statements: 1986–1996 |

Year End 31 March	1986	1988	1990	1992	1994E	1996E
Sales (Rs. million)	4,202	4,997	10,095	12,108	17,391	23,362
Two-wheelers	3,308	3,780	7,849	9,396	14,022	18,990
Three-wheelers	742	1,023	1,929	2,181	2,800	3,734
Spare parts	152	194	31 7	531	569	638
Sales (000s units)	467	510	805	809	1,054	1,182
Two-wheelers	429	460	731	739	975	1,094
Scooters	387	405	641	587	678	748
Motorcycles	42	55	90	11 7	1 81	207
Mopeds	0	0	0	34	11 6	139
Three-wheelers	38	50	74	70	79	88
Average Sales Price (Rs.)						
Two-wheelers	7,709	8,212	10,745	12,721	14,388	17,367
Three-wheelers	19,405	20,645	26,036	31,200	35,232	42,630
Operating expenditures	3,415	4,562	8,766	10,788	15,878	21,176
Operating profit	787	435	1,329	1,320	1,513	2,186
Net profit after depreciation, interest and taxes	297	293	650	447	831	1,520

Source: Company records.

Average Product Profiles Within the Two-Wheeler Market

Product	Retail Price 1992 Rupees[a]	Mileage	Power/Engine Capacity
(50cc)Motorcycles	34,000	65 km/liter	7 HP
(100cc)Scooters	20,000	45 km/liter	6 HP (150cc)
Mopeds	12,000	55 km/liter	2.5 HP

[a]In April 1993, US$1 = 31.6 rupees.

rear-engine Autoriksha, and Sunny moped. Since 1990, both plants had been modernized and production efficiencies increased. Some stages of the manufacturing process such as stamping, welding, painting, and assembly were flexible and could accommodate line changes fairly easily. Machining however, required special-purpose equipment which was less flexible to line changes. Approximately 50% of components were sourced from outside vendors with whom BAL engineers worked hard to achieve consistently high quality. As Kamath, BAL's general manager of manufacturing, explained: "In India, it takes a long time to train and educate suppliers so that they can reliably deliver the right quality."

Recent production changes, influenced by the technical agreement with Kawasaki and outside consultants, were based on Japanese manufacturing models. Kamath described the production organization in 1993: "Our goal is continuous improvement." Throughout the Akurdi plant, large posters bearing the slogans "Zero Defects" and "Think Quality" were in evidence. "We have worker quality circles and pay our workers much higher than the average wage. We have practically no turnover and there's virtually life-time employment at BAL." Due to the large volumes, cost benefits were achieved by dedicating certain equipment, thereby reducing down-time from changeovers. The use of CAD/CAM (computer-aided design/computer-aided manufacturing) and CNC (computer numerically controlled) equipment was widespread.

INDUSTRY STRUCTURE

Between the 1950s and the 1980s, India's industrial development policy was characterized by excessive regulation. Initially set up to avoid overcapacity in a capital-scarce economy, it spawned a maze of regulations governing product, capacity, technology, and foreign exchange availability. In the 1980s, inflows of foreign technology and equity were permitted and manufacturing capacity constraints lifted. This gradual opening of the Indian economy resulted in the entry of foreign competitors and expanded production by domestic manufacturers. By the 1990s, the Indian economy was undergoing structural change, and imports were largely unregulated. Though in recession in the early 1990s, the economy was expected to recover and grow at 5% per year during the latter half of the decade. Since 1990, consumers had felt the pinch of recession; inflation had averaged 13%, interest rates had shot up, and consumer purchasing power had dropped considerably.

The Indian market for two- and three-wheelers was the second-largest in the world with 1.53 million new units sold in 1992 including 66,000 three-wheelers. (China was the largest market with 2.4 million unit sales in 1992.) Scooters represented 47% of these unit sales, motorcycles 24%, mopeds 27%, and three-wheelers 2%. (Table B summarizes key characteristics of the personal transport market in India in 1992.) Due to the economic recession and the increase in the range and volume of consumer goods available to Indian consumers (such as televisions, VCRs and washing machines), demand for two-wheelers had declined substantially, and in 1993, the Indian two-wheeler vehicle industry suffered from chronic overcapacity.

Consumers and Market Segments

Of 844 million Indians in 1991, 250 million lived below the poverty line (defined as 3,000 rupees per person per year), 52% were literate, and 74% lived in rural areas. Consumer research undertaken in 1990 segmented households by earnings and identified those groups more likely to purchase two-wheeler products. These data are summarized in Table C.

In India, two-wheelers were used for daily commuting as opposed to the leisure/fun use common in developed

Exhibit 2   Examples of BAL Two-Wheeler Vehicles

SUPER

CHETAK

SUNNY

M-80
MOTORCYCLE

KB100 RTZ

Exhibit 3   Examples of BAL Three-Wheeler Vehicles

The famous Bajaj Autoriksha

The Personal Transport Market in India, 1992 (figures in 000s)

Means of Personal Transport	Total Units in Use in 1992	Unit Purchases in 1992	Projected Unit Purchases in 1995
Cars	3,000	165	200
Motorcycles	3,900	380	500
Scooters	7,500	690	900
Mopeds	4,600	407	500
Bicycles	69,000	7,000	7,500

Table C Distribution of Indian Households by Income Groups and Related Purchases of Two-Wheelers in 1990

Annual Household Income (000 rupees)	Percentage of Households	Percentage of Scooters Owned by Income Group	Percentage of Motorcycles Owned by Income Group	Percentage of Mopeds Owned by Income Group
Up to 12.5	58%	8%	8%	10%
12.5-25	27	26	27	41
25-40	10	36	34	35
40-56	3	17	18	8
Above 56	2	13	13	6

countries. Public transport in India was inadequate and, as housing costs in the cities increased, larger numbers of people moved to the suburbs. A major priority for many individuals entering the work force after school or college was to obtain means of personal transport.

The early 1990s witnessed a saturation of the market, excess production capacity, and increased competition. BAL executives believed that pent-up demand for two-wheelers had subsided by 1993, and that the proportion of consumers replacing their current vehicles, as opposed to first-time buyers, would increase. Concurrently, the secondary or resale market for two-wheelers was increasingly strong. Although this cannibalized BAL new product sales, it also enabled existing BAL owners to change models regularly since they could recapture a good portion of their purchase costs by reselling in the secondary market. In 1992, the resale value of a five-year-old BAL scooter averaged 60% of the current retail price of a new BAL scooter. (By comparison, the resale value of a five-year-old Kinetic

Honda scooter averaged 40% of the current retail price.) By 1993, it was estimated that 6.5 million BAL two-wheelers were on the road and that all brands of two-wheelers combined had penetrated 20% of the potential Indian market.

In 1992, 40% of BAL's domestic sales (and 30% of its scooters, 45% of mopeds, and 55% of motorcycles) were made to rural consumers. Rural consumers were concerned primarily with value for money, whereas urban customers were driven by a concept of value that included the visual appeal of the product. Although rural consumers tended to have lower incomes than urban consumers, housing and food were less costly in rural areas and the rural consumer had a higher proportion of disposable income. Some BAL executives believed that, during the next decade, most domestic sales growth would come from the rural segment. Major regional differences existed within India. In the North and East, consumers were more traditional; women did not typically drive and men usually made the major household purchase decisions. In the major cities of the

South and West, women played a more active role in the economy and society, and many women could be seen driving scooters and mopeds.

BAL executives described the target consumer groups for each two-wheeler product as follows:

- *Scooters* targeted the "family man," aged between 27 and 38 years. The scooter was a family vehicle that could be used to transport a whole family. Word of mouth recommendations, brand name, and features such as mileage (fuel efficiency), low maintenance, and high resale value were important to these consumers.

- *Motorcycle* consumers either lived in the countryside, where the rough road conditions required a sturdy vehicle, or were young single men. Seventy percent of BAL's M-80 sales were made to rural consumers, concerned with fuel efficiency and product durability. Younger, single male consumers, between 21 and 30 years of age, looked for power and style, and the Kawasaki KB 100 appealed to them. 2-stroke motorcycles were more powerful and were often targeted at young males. 4-stroke motorcycles, regarded as workhorses, were more fuel efficient and gave the consumer better value for the money.

- *Mopeds* appealed to a broader customer segment because they were the cheapest two-wheelers available. In recent years, style and features had become more important to the urban moped customer who accounted for 55% of all moped sales. Products such as the Bajaj Sunny were targeted at teenagers and women who looked for style and trendy features. Secondary targets included consumers over 55 years who wanted a low-cost means of personal transport.

In 1993, consumers sought reliable and robust products, with low maintenance needs and a long life, at a low cost. Important product features included fuel efficiency, style, and riding comfort. Indian consumers were characterized by one of BAL's dealers as being traditional, seeking to buy proven products. Peer pressure and "keeping up with the neighbors" were increasingly important. Dealers believed that an additional key success factor for two-wheeler manufacturers was service reach, as defined by spare parts availability and number of service locations.

Competitors

Bajaj described the competitive environment in the Indian two-wheeler market in 1993: "The best of the world are here and they're here to stay." Six Indian groups dominated the domestic market, all with foreign collaborators. *BAL* was the only competitor manufacturing a full range of two-wheeler products and three-wheelers. It manufactured two of its motorcycles in technical collaboration with Kawasaki. *Kinetic* manufactured both scooters and mopeds and had an equity collaboration with Honda for scooters. *Hero* manufactured motorcycles and mopeds and had an equity collaboration with Honda for motorcycles. *LML* manufactured scooters in collaboration with Piaggio. *Escorts* manufactured motorcycles in a technical collaboration with Yamaha. *TVS* manufactured mopeds and motorcycles and had an equity collaboration with Suzuki for motorcycles. (Exhibit 4 summarizes these companies' shares of the two-wheeler market over time.)

The major Japanese brands had all been marketed in India since 1984. All production was domestic, with the percentage of imported parts varying with the number of years since local production began. Imported components could constitute up to 45% of a product's value during the first year of production, but had to fall to a maximum of 5% by the fifth year, according to local content requirements set by the Indian government. Tariffs on imported components were 30% in 1993. Japanese products were perceived by Indian consumers as being higher-tech, more modern, and better finished than domestic products. However, they also had a reputation for being less fuel efficient and more costly both to purchase and maintain, with limited spare parts availability. In contrast, BAL products were renowned for being rugged, reliable, and fuel efficient. Perceived as reasonably priced, BAL products were also known for their low maintenance cost, good spare parts availability, and good resale value.

Honda was BAL's most important competitor in 1993. Its scooter product, the Kinetic Honda, competed directly with BAL and held 14% of the scooter market in 1992. It had a technical advantage over the BAL scooters with features such as electric starter and a modern automatic drive which appealed particularly to women, and was priced at a 15% premium to BAL. It took Kinetic Honda five years to overcome initial consumer perceptions that it was less sturdy and safe than a Bajaj scooter. It was, however, positioned primarily as an urban product. In 1985, Honda had also launched the first 4-stroke motorcycle, the Hero Honda, which resulted in substantial fuel economies for the consumer. In 1992, Hero Honda was the market leader in the motorcycle market, with a 33% share.

Exhibit 4   Competitor Market Shares by Product Type in India: 1985–1992

	1985	1986	1987	1988	1989	1990	1991	1992
SCOOTERS								
Total Bajaj	78	83	69	73	73	73	77	74
Cub	8	11	13	9	7	6	5	2.5
Super	34	32	21	26	27	23	22	28
Super FE	NA	NA	NA	NA	NA	NA	1	
Chetak	21	25	21	27	28	36	36	41.5
Stride	NA	NA	NA	NA	NA	NA	0	2
MSL Priya	15	15	14	11	11	8	13	DIS
Total Others	22	17	31	27	27	27	23	25
Kinetic Honda	2	4	5	6	7	8	11	14
LML Vespa	17	10	21	17	17	17	11	11
Others	3	3	5	4	3	2	1	0
MOTORCYCLES								
Total Bajaj	14.5	15	20	20.5	21	26	27.5	28
M-80	14	8	12.5	12	12	16	19	19
Kawasaki RTZ	0.5	7	7.5	8.5	9	10	6	2
Kawasaki 4S	NA	NA	NA	NA	NA	NA	2.5	7
Total Others	85.5	85	79	79.5	79	74	72.5	72
Escorts RX 100	6.5	12	12	12	14	14.5	15	13
Escorts Radjoot	25	24	22	23	24	18.5	12.5	13
TVS Suzuki	20	15	14	13	9	8	8	8
Hero Honda	20	20	23	23	23	26	31	33
Enfield	8	9	6	6	6	6	6	4.5
Jawa-Yezdi	6	5	2	2.5	3	1	0	0.5
MOPEDS								
Bajaj								
Sunny	NA	NA	NA	NA	NA	NA	8	14
Total Others	100	100	100	100	100	100	92	86
Kinetic	46	41	51	55	50	45	35	32
TVS	33	38	44	41	31	28	33	31
Avanti	3	5	5	4	4	8	4	2
Hero	14	12	0	0	14	17	18	19
Enfield	4	4	0	0	1	2	2	2
BAJAJ TOTAL								
Two-wheeler	40	40	36	41	42	43	46	46.5
Three-wheeler	80	81	83	87	89	89	91	90

Source: Company records.

In 1993, Honda increased its equity in Kinetic to 51% and stated publicly that it aimed to capture 50% of the scooter market and a number one position in the Indian two-wheeler market overall. Honda's extensive line of two-wheeler products, both in scooters and motorcycles, allowed it to launch a regular stream of new products in the 50-150cc category. For example, Honda already had a proven 4-stroke 125cc scooter that could be adapted to the Indian market within two years. In addition, by 1993, Honda had gained significant experience of the Indian market through its two collaborations and had access to both Kinetic and Hero dealers throughout India. In 1993, Hero Honda was sold through 218 exclusive dealers and Kinetic Honda through 390 exclusive dealers.[1] Honda's strategy had been to increase its number of dealers and provide them with average margins of 4.5%.

Yamaha had a technical licensing agreement with Escorts, similar to the one between Kawasaki and BAL, and held 15% of the motorcycle market with the Escort RX 100. The product line was distributed through 490 exclusive Escort dealers. Although Yamaha had a good line of motorcycles and scooters that could be adapted to the Indian market, Escorts was losing market share and profitability. Yamaha and Escorts were thought likely to form an equity-based joint venture, and the Escorts group had sufficient financial resources to do so.

Suzuki had a joint venture with the TVS group and held 8% of the motorcycle market. Products were distributed through 337 exclusive dealers. Suzuki also had appropriate scooter and motorcycle products for the Indian market and had recently acquired a controlling interest in its four-wheeler joint venture in India. Although, in 1993, the TVS-Suzuki venture was not yet turning a profit, the TVS group as a whole had substantial financial resources.

Piaggio had recently acquired an increased stake in its Indian licensee, LML, and had taken complete management control. Piaggio's scooters were similar to BAL's products and held an 11% share of the scooter market. LML was in a relatively weak market position in 1992.

BAL MARKETING STRATEGY IN INDIA

For many years, BAL did not have a marketing department since demand outstripped capacity and BAL enjoyed a protected sellers' market. As competition increased in the mid-1980s and capacity constraints were lifted, a marketing department evolved from the existing distribution and service organization. In 1993, the marketing department's objectives were to increase annual sales to 1 million units (retaining at least a 50% domestic market share) and achieve share leadership in all three two-wheeler subcategories as well as in the three-wheeler segment.

Product Line Development

In 1993, BAL's product strategy was to provide consumers with a full line of competitively priced two- and three-wheeler products. The objectives governing product development were to protect market share by (1) providing consumers with what they wanted, (2) matching competitor product features by constantly improving existing products, and (3) periodically introducing new products. In 1993, 30% of product development resources were allocated to incremental improvements on current products and 70% to completely new product development. It was hoped that, eventually, these percentages would be reversed. Older scooter models were phased out—following a new model launch—when monthly sales volumes fell below 2,500 units and replaced by newer models that better fit customer preferences. In 1985, BAL had 9 two- and three-wheeler models on the market; by 1992 this number had increased to 12 and was expected to hold constant into 1995. Ranjit Gupta, general manager for product development, described the situation: "BAL is under pressure from competitors to continuously improve existing products. However, we want to lead with new product introductions, and hold share through quality and price."

Prior to the 1990s, marketing, manufacturing, and R&D were organized along functional lines. A 1992 reorganization aimed to achieve greater cross-functional coordination and to accelerate the product development cycle. Engineering thereafter worked closely with marketing to define consumer needs and to translate these into new product prototypes that were continuously tested by dealers and consumers. In 1992, BAL employed 346 staff and 124 workmen in R&D, and R&D expenditures totaled 1% of sales, compared with 0.5% of sales in 1990. BAL's new product development program was comprehensive and ambitious, comprising both substantial technical developments and new body designs, features and styling, for all product lines. R&D resources

---

1 Dealers were exclusive in the sense that they did not sell competitor products, with the exception of the Indian partner's products.

were allocated to each product line roughly in proportion to its sales. Gupta explained that it was not that easy to build BAL's R&D capability: "The issue is not just a question of throwing money at R&D; we need to develop the necessary human resources."

For many years, BAL products were based on Piaggio's designs for the 150cc scooter and three-wheelers. When the government curtailed BAL's technical collaboration with Piaggio in 1971, BAL continued to develop scooters along the same basic design. The 1970s saw the need for a bigger wheel in response to rougher roads and driving conditions, and the Bajaj Chetak was developed. Other needs, such as a higher number of gears for better fuel efficiency and flexibility, and a rear-engine three-wheeler for increased driver and taxi-passenger comfort, were also addressed during the 1970s. In the early 1980s, BAL entered the motorcycle segment with the launch of the first Indian motorcycle, the M-80, adapted from existing step-through motorcycle designs pioneered by the Japanese. The technical collaboration with Kawasaki resulted in the launch of a 2-stroke motorcycle in 1984, the Kawasaki RTZ in 1986, and a 4-stroke motorcycle, the Kawasaki 4S, in 1991. More recent product introductions included the Bajaj Sunny, a moped launched in 1991, that enabled BAL to enter this segment of the two-wheeler market; and the Super FE (Fuel Efficient) scooter launched in 1992, which increased fuel efficiency by 10%. Gupta described the current importance of product development for BAL: "In the past, product development was for fun; now it's for survival."

In 1993, product development efforts were focused on scooters. Fuel economy was an increasingly important consumer requirement due to a 30% increase in fuel prices in 1992. BAL was developing improvements in power and fuel efficiency, a new body styling, an improved electrical system, better lighting, an electronic ignition, and improved suspension system. The rationale behind this "scooter upgrade program" was to deliver increased value for money to the consumer with the objective of defending BAL's market share against competitor products that already offered many of these features. The retail price increase required for the "upgrade program" was estimated at 7%.

Future product development plans were influenced by further tightening of Indian emissions regulations between 1996 and 2001. These regulations would make it essential to change from 2-stroke engines to more fuel-efficient 4-stroke engines and/or to advanced fuel injection technology. The new 4-stroke scooters would be priced at a 15% premium over the existing 2-stroke models.

Despite being cost competitive, BAL lacked design capability and the ability to translate new products from concept to commercialization as fast as its Japanese competitors. BAL's average cycle time for a new model was four to five years, compared with two to three years for the Japanese manufacturers. BAL's main constraints were a lack of sufficient skilled R&D personnel and the slow response of suppliers. The main options for developing BAL's R&D capabilities were to build in-house experience by developing and testing more products with the aid of CAD/CAM technology and/or to establish specific collaboration agreements. Bajaj believed that there was little chance of further alliances with BAL's major competitors and that R&D capabilities would have to be developed in-house, supplemented by specific research agreements and technology acquisitions involving outside organizations such as Orbital. Orbital was an Australian company working on fuel injection technology for 2-stroke engines that would reduce both fuel consumption and emission levels. BAL's agreement with Orbital called for specific targets in fuel efficiency and emission levels to be reached at a predefined maximum unit cost. Some BAL executives however, believed that opportunities for technically upgrading two-wheeler vehicles were limited, that the rate of obsolescence was low, and that the technical performance gap between Honda and BAL was not large.

Distribution and Service

In February 1993, BAL had to ensure the effective distribution of its products to 330 exclusive dealers across the country. Physical distribution of BAL vehicles was subcontracted to 75 private transport companies who managed a total fleet of 1,400 trucks, each truck being capable of transporting 45 vehicles. Transport took between 3 and 21 days to reach a dealer. The distribution system was computerized with 30% of dealers connected by modem link, and orders were fed directly into BAL's production schedule. In 1992, 76 people were employed in marketing, sales, and distribution.

Forty BAL salespeople, organized geographically, helped the dealers plan product-specific sales targets, provided them with services and advertising support, and trained their staffs. BAL service engineers were deployed at dealerships to upgrade the technical capability of dealer service personnel, who were also trained at BAL factories. Spare parts sales had increased substantially through the service and dealer networks, and in 1990 an additional parts distributor channel was opened to serve the extensive independent retail parts network existing in the country. In 1992, 180 people were employed in service activities and 42 in spare parts. Pricing strategy for spare parts aimed to offer the consumer "readily available parts anywhere at reasonable prices." In 1992, 531 million rupees (at wholesale prices) of BAL spare parts were sold to service the 6.5 million BAL vehicles currently on the road. In 1992, it was estimated that 40% of all two-wheeler spare parts sold in India were made by BAL.

Dealer Network

By 1993, BAL had developed a network of 330 authorized dealerships in India, up from 184 in 1989, and 800 licensed service centers. BAL dealers sold only BAL two- and three-wheeler products and did not carry competitor brands; a few sold other automotive products, such as cars and trucks. All dealers maintained service centers and spare parts inventories in addition to vehicle inventories at their dealership locations. Dealerships were often family-run or partnerships that enjoyed a high status in their communities. Average sales were 150 vehicles a month with dealer inventories averaging 2.5 weeks of sales. On average, sales of new vehicles represented 80% of dealer revenues, while service and parts represented 20%. An average dealership would turn over its vehicle inventory 20 times a year and spare parts inventory 4 times a year. Unit margins were 3% of suggested retail prices; dealers supplemented their incomes with service and parts sales and the sale of used vehicles.

In 1993, BAL dealers were facing increasing competition, profitability pressures, more demanding and sophisticated consumers, and a drop in average sales volumes of around 20%. Dealers felt competition had intensified: the Kinetic Honda launched in 1987 had gained acceptance by 1990 in the Scooter segment; and Hero Honda's 4-stroke was strong in the motorcycle segment. They felt that BAL had not kept up with competitor product introductions and that recent BAL new product launches had experienced a number of technical problems. "Consumers need a problem-free product," explained one BAL dealer in Pune. BAL provided no credit to its dealers on vehicle purchases, and BAL dealers had to finance their inventories from their own working capital. Dealer interest rates on working capital loans were in the order of 22%, and the cost associated with sending funds to BAL could be as high as 25% of the dealer's absolute margin per vehicle. To improve dealer profitability and reduce transit time, BAL began, in 1991, to set up regional depots, management of which was subcontracted to carrying and forwarding agents. Effectively, a stock transfer was made to the depots from which dealers in the area sourced BAL vehicles, thereby cutting down their lead times to one or two days. By 1993, there were eight such depots, accounting for 40% of total vehicle sales to dealers. By 1994, it was expected that these and additional depots in high-volume markets a long way from the production plants would account for fully 50% of BAL's domestic sales. All major competitors had already established similar depot systems throughout the country.

BAL believed that its dealer network represented a key competitive advantage and that the company enjoyed considerable dealer loyalty. The key to dealer profitability and satisfaction, according to BAL, was a full range of two- and three-wheeler vehicles and rapid inventory turnover. BAL planned to expand its dealer network to 370 dealers over the next two years, particularly in rural areas. In all large towns, BAL had authorized more than one dealer. In recent years, many competitor dealers had switched to BAL but the reverse had never occurred. In 1993, BAL was also considering authorizing different dealers for sales of two- and three-wheelers.

Consumer Financing

The Indian government, which controlled the banking sector, did not encourage bank loans for two-wheeler purchases, and, in 1992, only 15% of two-wheeler purchases were financed in this way. To increase sales, BAL established Bajaj Auto Finance Ltd. (BAFL) in 1988 to provide consumer finance. By 1992, BAFL had financed over 100,000 vehicles through the BAL dealer network. Dealers were responsible for credit evaluations and collecting payments on loans and had to cover 50% of the cost of bad loans. This required substantial dealer personnel training. In February 1993, 160 of the 330 dealers operated BAFL consumer finance schemes, and BAFL executives believed that 10% of all future BAL sales could be financed in this way once all dealerships were properly trained and organized.

Advertising and Promotion

BAL's advertising expenditures had doubled in the 1990s from 54 million rupees in 1990 and 1991 to 110 million rupees in 1992, corresponding to 1% of total sales. In 1993, BAL was among the country's largest consumer durables advertisers, and Bajaj was a household name with many memorable television commercials. Advertising aimed to maintain Bajaj brand awareness and preference and also announce new product introductions. Advertising strategies were developed in collaboration with the dealers and focused on clarifying product positionings in response to consumer needs. (Exhibit 5 outlines the advertising objectives and copy strategies for selected BAL products. Table D summarizes advertising expenditures by product type and medium in 1992.)

In 1992, it was estimated that 20 million color televisions and 50 million black-and-white televisions were in use in India. Two channels existed: a national channel that broadcast in Hindi and English, and a local channel that broadcast in the language of the region. BAL television advertising represented 45% of total media costs, and each commercial focused on a single product, depicting a slice-of-life scene. A further 45% of advertising expenditures was dedicated to press advertising and the remaining 10% to magazine ads and radio commercials. Motorcycle print advertisements had a strong no-nonsense product focus and attempted to differentiate BAL products from the competition on the basis of technical features. The Kawasaki brand name was emphasized by BAL because of consumer perceptions that Japanese motorcycles were of better quality. Other print advertisements addressed the depressed economy with the slogan: "Times are bad, but, if you buy today, the high resale value of Bajaj is like a

---

Exhibit 5　　　Advertising Objectives and Television Commercial Copy Strategies for BAL Product Line: 1992

SCOOTERS

Objectives Increase awareness of dominant leadership position. Create demand in and expand rural/semi-urban markets.

Copy Strategies
1. Depict slice-of-life scenes throughout India, including all age groups, with the slogan: "This is my earth. The destiny of Bajaj and India are interwoven. Bajaj is India and India is Bajaj. Past and present."
2. A child asks his father, who comes to pick him up from school, why they don't have a scooter when all his friends' fathers do. The next day the father picks up his son from school on a Bajaj scooter.
3. The Bajaj Cub is positioned as a value-for-money product. A trader, renowned for being very careful with his money, explains his purchase of a Bajaj Cub: "I know what money means. I'm tight-fisted and Bajaj is value for money."
4. A wife scolds her husband for buying a Bajaj scooter without her advice. When the husband explains the benefits of the product, she tells him: "You've done the right thing, hand me the scooter keys."

MOTORCYCLES

Objectives Create strong product positions: M-80 as a rugged, low-cost vehicle for semi-urban/rural markets; Kawasaki 4S as highly fuel efficient with good driveability.

Copy Strategies M-80 commercials carry the slogan: "The tough one for the road." They use two characters from a popular television detective series in a variety of dangerous/criminal-chasing situations.

MOPEDS

Objectives Create a strong position for Sunny with teenagers as a stylish first-vehicle purchase.

Copy Strategies Commercials are based on youth love scenes and depict brief romantic stories.

Source:　Company records.

	Scooters	Sunny	Kawasaki 4S	M-80	Three Wheelers	BAL Corporate	BAFL	Dealer Coop	Total
TV	21	10.0	9.0	4.5	0	2.5	1	2	50
Press	15	7.0	12.0	0.5	2	2.5	3	7	49
Radio	1	0.0	0.0	0.0	0	0.0	1	1	3
Magazine	2	1.5	1.5	0.0	0	1.0	1	1	8
TOTAL	39	18.5	22.5	5.0	2	6.0	6	11	110

blank check. It's an investment." (Exhibit 6 reproduces a number of BAL print advertisements.)

In addition to national advertising, BAL cooperated with dealers locally, matching local advertising and promotion expenses incurred by dealers on a 1:1 basis. Dealers were broken down into four categories based on their sales volumes, and members of each group were allocated "matching" budgets for local press advertising. BAL would also match dealer expenses for approved promotions in conjunction with local festivals and special events. To maintain a consistent image across the country, all dealer point-of-sale posters and brochures were provided by BAL. However, the existence of 15 different languages in India meant that the same commercial could not always be used throughout India.

Advertising expenditures of 200 millon rupees were planned in 1993 to reinforce further the Bajaj brand equity. BAL planned to be more aggressive in its advertising, positioning its products more clearly, describing additional features and addressing competitor claims head on. New promotions planned for 1993 included two direct mail marketing campaigns: the first to companies, offering discounts for groups of employees; the second, to small businesses with transport requirements that could be met by three-wheelers.

Competitor advertising expenditures for 1992 were as follows: Hero-Honda spent 36 million rupees (corresponding to 1% of sales); TVS-Suzuki spent 23 million rupees (1% of sales); and Kinetic-Honda spent 35 million rupees (3% of sales).

Pricing

In the past, BAL had maintained a pricing strategy that ensured an average manufacturer's margin of 15%, gave dealers an adequate return, and created a reputation with consumers of "a company selling a good quality product at a reasonable price." In 1993, BAL was the industry's low-cost producer in India and aimed to maintain a price advantage in every market segment of two-wheelers. In scooters, BAL established price differences between models that reflected the value to consumers of incremental features. All BAL scooters were priced lower than comparable competitor products. The Bajaj M-80 was the only step-through motorcycle on the market and was positioned as a rugged, simple bike, priced at 50% of comparable Japanese motorcycles. However, on Kawasaki motorcycles, BAL's cost structure in 1993 did not allow for a similar lower price strategy and, in the moped category, the Bajaj Sunny was priced slightly higher than conventional mopeds because it offered consumers more features. (Exhibit 7 outlines 1992 retail prices and dealer margins by product for both BAL and competitors.)

In 1993, the majority of BAL's profits were generated by scooters and three-wheelers. These profits permitted the other products in the line to be priced lower in order to retain and/or gain market share. In 1993, the Kawasaki motorcycles, M-80, and Bajaj Sunny were all just about breaking even.

EXPORTS

Historical Perspective

For many years, due to high domestic demand and restricted production, BAL had not actively promoted exports. In 1975, for the first time, BAL exported 1,500 three-wheeler vehicles to Bangladesh and commenced talks in other South-East Asian countries. In the same year, the company concluded technical licensing agreements

Exhibit 6   BAL Print Advertisements

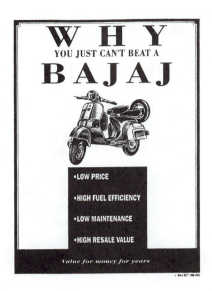

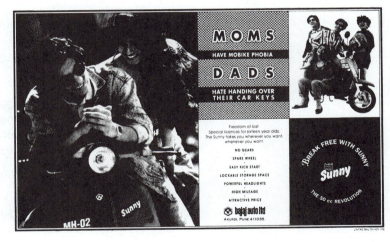

	Retail Price (Rs.)	Dealer Profit Margin
SCOOTERS		
Bajaj		
Chetak	20,720	650
Super FE	20,050	650
Stride	21,480	650
Cub	18,900	650
Kinetic-Honda	25,818	1,000
LML		
NV Special	22,349	775
T5 Special	24,027	850
MOTORCYCLES		
Bajaj		
Kawasaki RTZ	32,150	1,000
Kawasaki 4S	33,950	1,100
Bajaj M-80	16,200	550
Escorts		
Yamaha RX 100	35,058	1,055
Radjoot	25,157	835
Hero Honda		
Candy SS	34,354	1,130
Candy DLX	33,331	1,130
Sleek	34,821	1,130
TVS-Suzuki		
AX 100	32,800	1,400
Supra	24,061	1,400
Samurai	33,976	1,400
MOPEDS		
Bajaj Sunny	11,700	350
Kinetic		
Luna Super	10,232	650
Luna Magnum	11,335	650
Hero Puch	15,212	450
TVS		
XL	10,151	325
Champ	11,221	450

Source: Company records.

with private sector licensees in Indonesia and Taiwan. The license arrangement with the Indonesian collaborator covered assembly-cum-progressive manufacture of two scooter models, the Bajaj Chetak and the Bajaj Super, as well as a three-wheeler model.[2] The agreement with the Taiwanese licensee covered assembly-cum-progressive manufacture of Bajaj Chetak scooters. Between 1976 and 1982, over 60,000 units of CKD (completely knocked down) scooters and over 14,000 units of CKD three-wheelers were exported to Indonesia, resulting in similar unit margins to domestic product sales. Over the same period, 80,000 units of CKD Bajaj Chetak scooters were exported to Taiwan. In addition to CKD sales, BAL earned technical know-how fees for helping both licensees establish their assembly plants. The Indonesian licensee, unable to remain profitable due to the massive devaluation of the Indonesian currency, combined with government pressure for more local manufacturer content, was forced to stop production in 1982. The Taiwanese licensee, under pressure from the Taiwanese government, quickly developed its own component production capabilities. A similar licensee agreement was established in Bangladesh; this was BAL's only existing licensee agreement in 1993. BAL supplied this licensee with over 2,000 units of CKD three-wheelers in 1992.

BAL's Foreign Distributors

In 1979, the first BAL foreign distributorship was established in Sri Lanka and the export of complete vehicles was initiated. During the 1980s, distributorships were established on an opportunistic basis in the United States, Germany, Southeast Asia, and North Africa. However, BAL's attempts to export to developed countries in North America and Europe were cut short by a lawsuit instigated by Piaggio which threatened BAL dealers in those countries with legal action. Piaggio alleged that BAL was illegally copying unregistered trademarks of the exterior design and shape of the Vespa Scooter and using technology received from Piaggio before the cancellation of the technical agreement. The threat of litigation hindered the growth of exports to developed countries for a decade. Meanwhile, Japanese producers entered those markets and quickly established dominant shares. Ultimately, the lawsuits were settled to BAL's satisfaction but, until 1985, exports were limited.

When production capacity constraints in India were lifted in the mid-1980s, BAL once again turned to developing exports. Armed with a wider product range, BAL explored new export markets and, by 1992, sold vehicles to 52 countries through 34 nonexclusive and 17 exclusive distributorships. Nineteen of the distributor agreements had been signed within the previous year. Overseas distributor selection criteria were similar to those used in India, and BAL used the help of local Indian Embassies to establish short lists of potential distributors. BAL granted these distributors exclusive rights contingent on sales performance. To ensure motivation, BAL established agreements with one distributor per country at a time. Mexico was an exception with two distributors: one for two-wheeler vehicles and another for three-wheelers. BAL's foreign distributors operated essentially as wholesalers, redistributing to dealers that typically stocked a number of brands. Advertising in export markets was left up to distributors. (Exhibit 8 summarizes the main points of BAL's foreign distributorship agreements.) As Mr. Nulkar, head of BAL's export department, said: "Market development takes time; you need to go step-by-step and create a solid base." In 1992, export sales represented 2% of total sales, with recent export growth coming mostly from Latin America. (Exhibit 9 summarizes exports by product and geographical market in 1992.) One of BAL's corporate objectives was to increase exports to 15% of sales by 1998.

World Markets for Two- and Three-Wheelers

In 1992, the global three-wheeler market was broken down as follows: BAL held a 33% market share with 55,000 vehicles; Piaggio an 18% share; Tuck-Tuck (Thailand) a 3% share; and Chinese manufacturers a 38% share. In the three-wheeler market, BAL's exports were mostly to neighboring countries where the vehicles were used as taxis. In 1992, Bangladesh and Sri Lanka remained BAL's major export markets for three-wheelers, importing over 4,500 BAL units in 1992. In these markets, BAL held 90% and 95% market shares respectively. The concept of three-wheelers as passenger vehicles was not well developed outside Asia.

In 1982, the world market for two-wheeler vehicles was approximately 15 million units; by 1992, this had declined to 11 million units. Seventy-five percent of the global market was dominated by five manufacturers: Honda with 31% market share in 1992, up from 25% in 1982; Yamaha with 24% in 1992, up from 17.5%; Suzuki with 7% in 1992, down from 10.5%; BAL with 7%, up from 1.5%; and Piaggio with 6%, down slightly from 6.5%. (Exhibit 10

---

2 Assembly-cum-progressive manufacture agreements required BAL to initially supply all vehicle parts to be assembled, gradually reducing the number of parts supplied as the licensee became capable of manufacturing its own parts.

- The distributor may not carry competing products.

- BAL vehicles can be sold only within the distributor's specified territory/ country.

- All products must be sold under the Bajaj brand name.

- Marketing and advertising expenses are to be borne by the distributor.

- The distributor should establish showrooms and service stations conforming to BAL standards in the main towns within its territory.

- The distributor may appoint subdealers and authorized workshops for product repairs.

- Renewal of the appointment of the distributor is not automatic.

Source: Company records.

summarizes two-wheeler unit production and sales by country over time.) Experts believed that the decline of two-wheeler sales had stabilized in mature markets and that future sales growth would occur mostly in Asia, excluding Japan, which would account for 65% of global sales by the mid-1990s. Global import figures indicated that Europe as a whole accounted for 53% of all imports in 1992, North America 21%, and the rest of the world (including Asia, Africa, South America, and Oceania) 26%. Two distinct segments existed in the international market: the developed countries, comprising Europe, Japan, North America, and Australasia; and developing countries, divided further into three regions: Southeast Asia and China; Africa and the Middle East; and Latin America.

Developed countries In the United States, the 50cc market was dominated by Japanese competitors, and BAL had no products in the above-250cc category—the other large U.S. two-wheeler segment. In Japan, 71% of two-wheeler unit sales were of models of 50cc, characterized by fashionable, automatic, single-seater products with many plastic parts. The four main Japanese manufacturers held 80% of the Japanese market. Stringent Japanese product standards and the cost of freight made this market difficult to penetrate. In Europe, the 50cc market was also the largest segment, and recent trends in Europe showed that mopeds were being replaced by fashionable automatic scooters. In developed countries in general, product performance

requirements were exacting, and vehicles had to meet tough regulations on emissions, noise, braking, and electricals. In addition, distribution reach and after-sales service were critical. The market for three-wheelers in developed countries was virtually nonexistent; indeed, regulations often prevented their use on major roads.

Eastern European countries followed many of the product standards set in Western Europe but did not, in 1993, have adequate buying power, so their markets remained small. BAL executives believed that, with the right political and economic changes, these countries would emerge as important markets around 1997. In particular, Hungary, Poland, and the Southern CIS[3] countries might be targeted in the future.

Developing countries In Southeast Asia, imports of two-wheelers were restricted either by tariff barriers or import bans, and Japanese manufacturers had already established local joint-venture production facilities. China was the largest market in the world and all the major two-wheeler manufacturers, particularly the Japanese, had set up plants in China. Competition in China was already intense. The major problem with African countries was the difficulty of access to foreign exchange and low consumer purchasing power. Some potential, however, existed for exporting CKD units to the Middle East and North Africa, where GDP per capita was higher. Latin America was an attractive market, particularly for scooter products. In general, developing

---

3 Commonwealth of Independent States (the former U.S.S.R.)

Exhibit 9   BAL Unit Exports by Country and Product Line: 1992

	Scooters	Motorcycles	Three-Wheelers	Total Units	Total Revenues (Rs. 000s)
EUROPE					
Cyprus	2	0	0	2	17
France	0	0	0	0	0
Greece	30	29	36	95	1,775
Italy	18	0	0	18	261
Malta	18	8	0	26	342
Netherlands	3	0	1	4	55
Poland	20	3	34	57	1,667
Sweden	4	0	0	4	43
Turkey	1,100	0	0	1,100	14,072
United Kingdom	0	2	0	2	24
West Germany	666	0	0	666	6,540
Total	1,861	42	71	1,974	24,796
ASIA					
Bangladesh	136	200	1,858	2,194	37,608
Japan	6	0	1	7	94
Malaysia	0	0	1	1	37
Philippines	0	0	160	160	3,381
Sri Lanka	131	779	2,643	3,553	71,842
Singapore	6	44	0	50	1,074
Thailand	610	0	0	610	7,248
Vietnam	1	0	0	1	11
Total	890	1,023	4,663	6,576	121,295
MIDDLE EAST					
Bahrain	22	10	4	36	592
Dubai	5	70	0	75	1,166
Egypt	500	0	0	500	6,000
Iran	2	1	1	4	45
Saudi Arabia	0	0	1	1	32
Kuwait	48	14	69	131	3,251
Lebanon	18	6	0	24	330
Oman	26	15	8	49	855
Total	621	116	83	820	12,271

Exhibit 9   BAL Unit Exports by Country and Product Line: 1992 (continued)

	Scooters	Motorcycles	Three-Wheelers	Total Units	Total Revenues (Rs. 000s)
LATIN AMERICA					
Argentina	1,128	1,021	6	2,155	35,520
Belize	4	2	4	10	176
Chile	0	0	0	0	0
Colombia	6	4	0	10	134
Mexico	1,122	1,299	252	2,673	41,000
Paraguay	23	101	0	124	1,907
Peru	94	0	612	706	23,807
Venezuela	147	0	0	147	1,954
Total	2,524	2,427	874	5,825	104,498
AFRICA AND OTHER					
Angola	0	0	191	191	5,064
Benin	0	2	0	2	24
P.N. Guinea	8	0	3	11	212
Kenya	0	0	3	3	115
Mauritius	24	64	0	88	1,447
New Zealand	0	0	0	0	0
Nigeria	69	0	5	74	1,111
Rwanda	2	4	4	10	251
Sierra Leone	6	6	10	22	521
Sudan	108	0	0	108	1,448
Tanzania	0	0	1	1	33
Uganda	42	7	0	49	700
Zambia	0	46	42	88	1,924
Total	259	129	259	647	12,850
TOTAL (All Regions)	6,155	3,737	5,950	15,842	275,710

Source: Company records.

countries were more price sensitive, but product performance regulations were less stringent than in developed countries.

Table E provides a summary of the consumer and product characteristics for two-wheelers in both developed and developing countries in comparison to the Indian market.

Europe

In 1992, the total European market for two-wheelers was estimated at 2 million vehicles a year, with the under-50cc segment accounting for 60% of unit sales and the 125cc segment for 10%. Europe imported 500,000 two-wheelers a year, of which 65% were in the under-50cc moped segment. Indian vehicles imported into Western Europe benefited from the Generalized System of Preferences and did not pay import duties. Japanese vehicles, however, had to pay import duties of 9%. The 1992 regulatory harmonization of technical standards for two-wheelers in the European Community promised to reduce the need to meet diverse country

Exhibit 10   Two-Wheeler Unit Production and Sales by Country: 1981–1990

Units (000s)	1981 Production	Sales	1985 Production	Sales	1990 Production	%	Sales	%
Japan	7,413	3,062	4,536	2,096	2,807	27%	1,619	15%
India	499	476	1,126	1,107	1,891	18	1,868	18
Taiwan	669	692	656	685	1,062	10	997	10
China	14	N/A	1,035	N/A	965	9	N/A	N/A
Italy	1,240	857	808	569	910	9	576	6
Thailand	305	284	229	202	434	4	522	5
Indonesia	503	678	227	230	409	4	415	4
Spain	188	186	168	110	385	4	430	4
Korea	124	126	171	71	283	3	254	2
Malaysia	174	170	182	159	220	2	294	3
U.S.A.	125	828	130	722	120	1	294	3
West Germany	217	451	86	215	56	1	171	2
WORLD TOTAL[a]	14,368	14,368	12,761	12,761	10,467	100%	10,467	100%

Source: Company records.

[a] World total includes production and sales in countries in addition to those listed.

regulations. However, it was estimated that complete harmonization would not take effect until 1995 at the earliest.

In 1990, BAL adapted its moped product—the Bajaj Sunny, BAL's only product in the under-50cc-segment for the West European market. Product adaptation of the Bajaj Sunny, which consumed some 8% of total company R&D resources over the development period, included engine and silencer modifications, the usage of approved electricals, modification of components, and brake and clutch linings. BAL initially established dealerships in Germany, Sweden, and France. The Bajaj Sunny held a considerable price advantage in the moped segment, retailing at 2,000 DM in Germany, compared with Piaggio's "Sfera" which retailed at 4,000 DM.[4] However, the Sunny had fewer features and lacked the Sfera's auto-lube, electric start, and variomatic transmission (which provided better acceleration at lower speeds). (Exhibit 11 depicts the two products.) BAL had also developed a 125cc scooter, adapted from its traditional 150cc scooter, that appealed to a limited "nostalgia" niche market of consumers with a desire for an old-fashioned-style product. By 1992, BAL had sold a total of 1,500 vehicles in the under-50cc and 200 vehicles in the 125cc segment in Europe.

BAL's future strategy in Europe, which not everyone in the company agreed with, was to introduce the Sunny in as many European countries as possible, starting at the lower end of the moped and scooter markets and, over time, adding vehicles with more features and improved performance. However, the technical certifications necessary to export vehicles to Europe had taken BAL time and resources to understand and execute.

Latin America

In 1992, BAL exported 4,200 units to distributorships in Peru, Venezuela, Argentina, Mexico, Chile, Paraguay, and Colombia. Two-wheelers were shipped in semi-knocked down (SKD) condition to reduce freight costs. Re-assembly from SKD was simple and undertaken by distributor mechanics. Three-wheelers were shipped complete on special car carrier vessels. All shipments were made directly to individual distributors from India. Both two- and three-wheeler vehicles had been in demand, and BAL believed that these markets would continue to experience strong and steady growth. There was no competition in

---

4 US$1 = 1.6 DM, 1993.

Developed Countries: Europe/U.S./Japan	India/Bangladesh/Sri Lanka	Developing Countries: Latin America, Africa/Asia[a]
Mopeds, under 50cc. Teenager market.	Two-wheelers and three-wheelers. Scooters as the family vehicle.	Two-wheelers and three-wheelers. Vehicle is the work horse.
Peppy, good styling and performance.	Fuel efficient and reliable.	Low price, fuel efficient, durability of 10-15 years.
Quick model changes and latest features; auto-lube, electric start . . .	Up-to-date features for the same price.	Spare parts and service access critical. Model changes a negative.
Service and distribution extensive. Dealers have product liability.	Increasing product competition. Search to differentiate products.	Initial cost and ability to repair product cheaply critical.
Luxury/fun vehicle used for short distances within cities.	Personal transportation.	First and only vehicle. Essential for work and transportation.

[a]Developing countries more exposed to international products and consumer goods displayed consumer behaviors more similar to those found in developed countries.

three-wheelers, and BAL held a price advantage over Japanese two-wheeler products. (Exhibit 12 shows product-price comparisons in Mexico.) Japanese products appeared too sophisticated for these markets, requiring substantial servicing by the consumer. BAL was hoping to capture significant market shares in both Mexico and Argentina by 1995.

BAL was also evaluating the possibility of establishing technical licensing agreements and the exports of CKD units, similar to the arrangements that had been established in Taiwan and Indonesia. A licensing agreement became attractive for BAL when (1) a particular market's size and potential justified the investment required for a plant (that would follow an assembly-cum-progressive-manufacture strategy), (2) the difference in import duties on complete or SKD units and CKD units was large enough to make CKD imports substantially more competitive, and (3) when BAL desired to have a long-term manufacturing presence in a particular market. Possible licensee locations included Mexico.

STRATEGIC OPTIONS FOR GROWTH

Bajaj wondered how focused his company should remain in the future. Since the late 1960s many Indian companies with the financial resources to do so had diversified into other industries. A few BAL executives believed that, given the strength of competitors in the two-wheeler market, BAL would do better to invest in other Indian consumer goods markets and focus on the future economic and industrial development of India. Other BAL executives thought that the company should diversify geographically by developing its export markets further for both two- and three-wheeler products. A third group of executives cautioned that BAL would need to focus all its resources on protecting the company's current share of the Indian two- and three-wheeler market.

BAL executives were considering three options for international markets. First, BAL could remain focused on the domestic market and export only on an opportunistic basis. Second, BAL could pursue exports in developing countries that would require minimal adaptation of the current product line. Third, BAL could try to promote exports to developed countries, initially focusing on the lower end of the moped market in Europe.

Exhibit 11   The Bajaj Sunny and Piaggio Sfera

Manufacturer	Product	Retail Price
SCOOTERS		
Bajaj	Cub	$1,037
	Super	1,028
	Chetak	1,083
Honda	SA 50	1,282
	SA 50 2M	1,340
	AE R 100	1,544
	Elite 80	1,923
Suzuki	AX 100	1,784
	AG 100	2,131
	TS 185	2,268
Piaggio	STD 150	1,807
	LML 150	2,448
Yamaha	Axis 90	2,070
	Cygnus	2,800
MOTORCYCLES		
Bajaj	M-80	955
	Kawasaki RTZ	1,449
	Kawasaki 4S	1,632
Carabella[a]	Deluxe	1,555
	STD 175	1,747
Yamaha	RXZ 100	1,897
	RXZ 135	2,436
	DT 175	2,436
Kawasaki	KE 100	1,916
	KH 125	2,339
	KV 175	2,804
	GPZ 305	3,955
Honda	CG 125	2,272
	CT 125	2,535
	CB 250	3,088
	SR 250	3,321

Manufacturer	Product	Retail Price
MOPEDS		
Bajaj	Sunny	744
Carabella	Chispa-60	830
	City 60	830
	Runner 60	945
Yamaha	PW 50 CC	1,150
	MIN SH 50	1,174
Honda	SA 50	1,282
	SA 50 2 M	1,340
	C 90	1,515
Suzuki	AE 50 CC	1,418

Source: Company records.

[a]A local manufacturer of two-wheelers.

Mary Kay Cosmetics: Asian Market Entry

In February 1993, Curran Dandurand, senior vice president of Mary Kay Cosmetics Inc's (MKC) global marketing group, was reflecting on the company's international operations. MKC products had been sold outside the United States for over 15 years, but by 1992, international sales represented only 11% of the $1 billion total. In contrast, one of MKC's U.S. competitors, Avon Products Inc., derived over 55% of its $3.6 billion sales (at wholesale prices) from international markets in 1992.

Dandurand wondered how MKC could expand international operations and which elements of MKC's culture, philosophy, product line, and marketing programs were transferable. She wanted to define the critical success factors for MKC internationally and establish a marketing strategy for future international expansion. Specifically, she was currently evaluating two market entry opportunities: Japan and China. The first was a mature but lucrative market where cosmetics marketing and direct selling were well-known and accepted. The second was a rapidly growing and changing but relatively unknown market with substantially lower individual purchasing power.

THE COSMETICS AND DIRECT SELLING INDUSTRIES

In 1992, worldwide retail sales of facial treatments and color cosmetics products exceeded $50 billion, with the United States accounting for $16 billion. The top four companies in the U.S. cosmetics market in 1992 were Procter & Gamble with $4.3 billion cosmetics retail sales, Estee Lauder, Avon, and Revlon. L'Oreal, a subsidiary of Nestle, dominated the world market with $5.9 billion in retail sales, followed by Procter & Gamble, Avon, Unilever, Shiseido, Revlon, Colgate-Palmolive, Estee Lauder, SmithKline Beecham, and Gillette.

Retail sales by the U.S. direct selling cosmetics industry were estimated at $5 billion in 1992. Cosmetics companies used two approaches to direct selling: the repetitive person-to-person method, used by Avon, in which a salesperson regularly visited customers in their homes and sold products one to one; and the party plan method, in which a salesperson presented and sold products to a group of customers attending a "party" or "show" in one of the customers' homes. The party plan method was used by MKC.

Other large international direct selling organizations included Amway, which sold a variety of household and personal care products and recorded retail sales of over $3.5 billion in 1992, and Tupperware, which sold household products through the party plan method and had retail sales of over $1 billion. International sales for Amway and Tupperware accounted for 60% and 75% respectively.

MKC OPERATIONS AND PHILOSOPHY

Incorporated in Texas in 1963 by Mary Kay Ash, MKC was a direct selling cosmetics company with 1992 estimated retail sales of $1 billion, net company sales of $624 million,[1] cost of goods sold of $148 million, and earnings before interest and taxes of $110 million. (Exhibit 1 depicts the growth in MKC net revenues, operating cash flow, and number of consultants between 1986 and 1992.) MKC sold a range of skin care, personal care, and cosmetics products through approximately 275,000 independent salespeople worldwide, known as "beauty consultants," who purchased products from the company and resold them at skin care classes or facials held in homes that were attended by four to six, or one to two potential customers respectively.

This case was prepared by Professor John Quelch with the assistance of Nathalie Laidler.

Copyright © 1993 by the President and Fellows of Harvard College. Harvard Business School case 9-594-023.

[1] Net company sales were defined as sales of MKC products by the company to its sales consultants. Retail sales are defined as those sales made by consultants to consumers.

Net Revenues

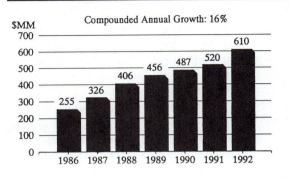

Operating Cash Flow

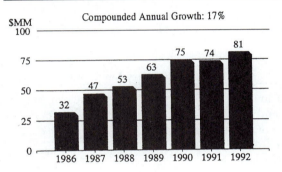

Beauty Consultants

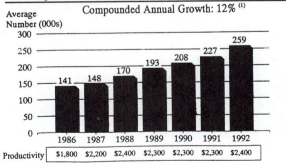

Note: (1) Based on year-end numbers of Beauty Consultants

The company's powerful culture was based on offering unlimited opportunities for women in business, coupled with a distinctive compensation and recognition plan. Mary Kay Ash's charismatic personality and drive had been central to the company's rapid growth and success, and, for many beauty consultants, she represented a caring and successful role model. In 1993, MKC defined its mission as promoting business opportunities for women, teaching women how to care for their skin and use cosmetics, offering skin care systems as opposed to individual products, and providing unsurpassed personal service to its customers. (Exhibit 2 outlines what the company considered to be its competitive advantages and points of difference with respect to both potential beauty consultants and cosmetics consumers.)

Product Line

In 1992, MKC manufactured a relatively narrow line of 225 SKUs (stockkeeping units), including different color shades.[2] Product policy emphasized skin care "systems" that included several related items formulated for specific skin types or skin conditions. (Table A reports the number of products—excluding different shades within color product categories—and percentage of 1992 sales for each of the eight product categories in which MKC competed.)

MKC regularly involved its sales force in product policy decisions, sending them samples of prospective new products for evaluation. Virtually all MKC products were manufactured in a single plant near Dallas, considered to be the most efficient cosmetics production facility in the world.

Sales Force

Four basic levels of independent contractors were included in the MKC sales force: beauty consultants, sales directors, senior sales directors, and national sales directors. Promotions were made from within and based entirely on performance, as defined by volume sales and recruitment of new salespeople. Virtually all MKC beauty consultants were

---

Exhibit 2   The Mary Kay Cosmetics Career and Consumer Program

The Mary Kay Career

- The Mary Kay career path allows a woman to advance into a management/training position if she so wishes. She cannot buy her way into these positions, but can earn them based on her proven ability to sell and build a team.

- The Mary Kay career path provides the opportunity to earn higher part-time and full-time compensation more quickly than other direct sales companies and most corporations.

- The company does not compete with its Consultants by offering products at retail locations, salons, or via "buying club" discounts.

- The company provides advanced training and the presentation and sales tools to allow a Consultant to offer her customers value-added services and information. "She is a teacher of skin care and glamour." In addition the Consultant receives training on leadership and aspects of running a successful business.

- The company supports a Consultant's business by offering business-building programs:

  - Direct Support (consumer direct mail program) to retain and increase current customer business.

  - Leads for new customers and recruits generated by company advertising, direct mail, and sampling programs.

- A Mary Kay Consultant is in business for herself, but never by herself. She receives ongoing training (product knowledge, business and leadership skills), recognition, and motivation from the company and her Director. The Director forms a mentorlike relationship and encourages ongoing involvement and success on the part of the Consultant.

- The unit concept of the sale force organization taps into the Japanese desire to belong to a group and compete with others based on team activities.

---

2 In 1992, Avon had an estimated 1,500 SKUs.

Exhibit 2　　　　The Mary Kay Cosmetics Career and Consumer Program (continued)

The Mary Kay Consumer Program

- Mary Kay Cosmetics offers women self-improvement and self-esteem enhancement through skin care and glamour education provided by a certified Beauty Consultant.

- Consumers are taught how to care for their skin and basic glamour application skills within a unique training class that provides:
  - Individualized analysis of their skin type.
  - Individual vanity tray and mirror that allows the customer to apply each product as it is explained and demonstrated.
  - The ability to try all products prior to purchase via hygienic, single-use samplers.
  - Hands-on glamour application training.
  - Fun, social interaction and entertainment aspect of a skin care class.

- Consumers are offered advanced training including the ColorLogic Glamour System, Advanced Glamour, Skin Wellness, Nail Care, etc.

- On-the-spot delivery of product is provided for most products.

- Enrollment in a unique gift-with-purchase program (Direct Support).

- 100% satisfaction guarantee or full refund.

- Products' packaging are designed to be as environmentally friendly as possible (refillable compacts, recycled/recyclable cartons).

- Ongoing advice and service from a trained expert.

- Skin care products designed for particular skin types and skin conditions.

- Unique glamour system designed to take the guess work out of selecting glamour shades.

- Customers have the opportunity to earn valuable product discounts or unique gifts by hostessing a skin care class.

- Value-added services and further education are provided through high-quality brochures, and newsletters given free of charge to customers.

Table A

	Number of Products	% Sales (1992)
Skin care (cleansers, creams, moisturizers, foundations)	27	46%
Glamour (lipsticks, eye colors)	24	30
Fragrances	9	10
Nail care	12	5
Body care	5	3
Sun care	7	2
Hair care	5	1
Men's skin care	6	1

female, and new consultants were recruited by existing salespeople whose compensation and advancement were partly dependent on their recruiting success.

A new MKC beauty consultant had to purchase a Beauty Consultant Showcase, which cost around $100. Consultants bought MKC products at a 40% to 50% discount off the retail selling price, depending on volume. A minimum wholesale order of $180 had to be placed once every three months for a consultant to remain active. If a consultant terminated her association with MKC, the company would, if requested, buy back all her MKC inventory at 90% of the price she had paid for it.

In addition to the margins made on product sales, salespeople received a 4% to 12% commission on the wholesale prices of products purchased by those beauty consultants they had recruited. This commission, which increased with the number of recruits achieved, encouraged consultants to devote time to recruiting and training other consultants. To be promoted to sales director, a consultant had to recruit 30 active consultants; to become a senior sales director one of the director's recruits had to become a sales director herself; and to become a national sales director, a director had to motivate at least 10 of the consultants in her group to become sales directors. Nonmonetary rewards and recognition incentives, for which MKC was renowned, included pink Cadillacs, diamonds, and furs.

Communications

MKC developed programs, manuals, and sales training aids for its sales force. Since the emphasis was on "teaching skin care and glamour" to consumers, beauty consultants had to be taught how to teach. A new recruit would attend three "classes" given by an experienced consultant, study the "Beauty Consultant's Guide," and sit through an orientation class organized by her unit director prior to her being enrolled as an MKC beauty consultant. Weekly training sessions covered product information, customer service, business organization, and money management. Each year, some 15% of the MKC sales force traveled to Dallas at their own expense for a three-day seminar where sales and recruiting achievements of top-performing consultants were recognized. Queens of Sales and Recruiting were crowned by Mary Kay Ash and well-known entertainers made guest appearances. Workshops on every aspect of building and managing the business were conducted by consultants and directors that had developed a particular expertise. In addition, many national directors held their own yearly "jamborees" patterned after the Dallas event.

MKC also supported its consultant sales force with consumer print advertising, placed in women's magazines. (Exhibit 3 reproduces some examples of recent MKC print advertisements in the United States.)

Challenges Facing MKC in 1993

In 1993, MKC was facing a mature U.S. cosmetics market, an increasing number of competing direct selling organizations, and potentially maximum historical penetration in some areas of the United States. At the same time, MKC's international subsidiaries' sales growth had been modest. Given that competitors such as Avon and Amway had been very successful internationally, MKC executives could see no reason why MKC could not do the same. They believed that the MKC culture could be transferred internationally and that Mary Kay Ash's charisma, motivation, and philosophy were likely to appeal to women throughout the world.

INTERNATIONAL OPERATIONS

In early 1993, MKC products were sold in 19 countries. The company had 100%-owned subsidiaries in nine countries: Argentina (which also served Uruguay and Chile), Australia (with additional sales to New Zealand), Canada, Germany, Mexico, Taiwan, Spain, Thailand, and Russia. MKC was also planning to enter Italy, Portugal, the United Kingdom, and Japan or China in the near future. In addition, distributors existed in Costa Rica, Singapore, Malaysia, Brunei, Bermuda, Guatemala, Sweden, Norway, and Iceland.

Historically, international expansion had been opportunistic, based largely on personal contacts. The first two markets entered, Australia and Argentina, were not chosen for strategic reasons but in response to approaches to the company from local entrepreneurs. An international division with separate back-room operations, based in Dallas, had evolved to support the international businesses; this ensured the latter received adequate attention but duplicated functions and resources at headquarters.

In 1992, MKC initiated an organizational change that resulted in the formation of global resource groups to support sales subsidiaries worldwide, thereby consolidating the human resource, legal, finance, manufacturing, and marketing functions. (Exhibit 4 depicts the new organizational structure.) The global marketing group, headed by Dandurand, provided subsidiaries with product development and marketing support, advertising, public relations and consumer promotion materials, and controlled the quality, consistency, and image of the Mary Kay brand around the world. Dandurand anticipated that marketing communication strategies would gradually become more locally driven. She explained:

> Once we have firmly established consistently high quality and clearly communicated the desired image for our company and brand, the local subsidiaries will be given more autonomy to develop their own marketing communication programs.

In addition, regional sales headquarters were established for Asia/Pacific, Europe, and the Americas (excluding the United States) to support the country subsidiaries within those regions more effectively and to facilitate MKC's future international expansion.

To illustrate the challenges MKC faced internationally, the evolution of each of four MKC subsidiaries is briefly described:

Canada The Canadian market was similar to the United States both in product requirements and organization, and U.S. sales directors were allowed to go to Canada to recruit and build sales areas. The Canadian subsidiary had been operating for 15 years. However, in 1993, market research indicated that MKC was perceived by some Canadian consumers as out of date. A salaried country manager with a marketing and sales staff ensured local contact with the Canadian consultants and the efficient order processing and delivery of MKC products.

Australia The Australian subsidiary began with the acquisition of an existing direct selling company in the early 1970s. In 1992, MKC had low brand awareness and a poor image. All products were imported from the United States and the U.S. pricing strategy had been replicated without much adaptation to local market conditions. Nutri-Metics, an Australian competitor, had successfully used a hybrid of party plan and door-to-door direct selling methods, backed by media advertising, catalog sales, and Buying Club sales.[3] Unlike MKC, Nutri-Metics did not hold skin care classes, and salespeople could buy in and

3 Buying Clubs enabled women to purchase products such as cosmetics at a discount for their personal consumption rather than for resale. Individuals were not required to purchase a minimum level of inventory to enroll in the club. The most successful clubs offered broad product lines.

Exhibit 4   Mary Kay Cosmetics Organization, 1992

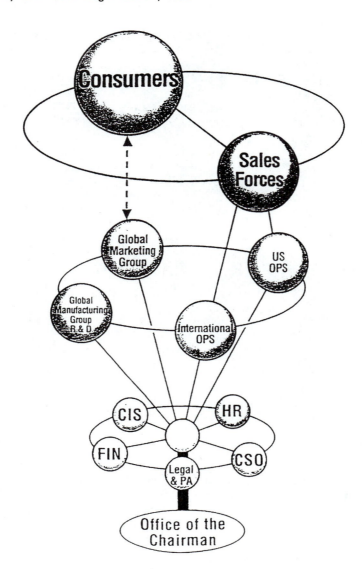

Note: CIS = Customer Information System
        CSO = Chief Scientific Officer
        OPS = Operations (incl. manufacturing)
        FIN = Finance
        HR = Human Resources

remain "active" with lower purchase commitments than were required of MKC consultants.

Mexico In 1988, MKC established a subsidiary in Mexico headed by a husband-and-wife team who had previously worked for the direct selling party-plan cosmetics company, Jafra. The couple became salaried employees with performance incentives. The new Mexican subsidiary also benefited initially from U.S. sales directors who went to Mexico to recruit consultants. Three thousand new consultants joined the company in the first three months. After four years, brand awareness was high, the brand image was positive, and sales force size exceeded 6,200.

Taiwan The Taiwan subsidiary, launched in July 1991, emphasized intensive training for new consultants. Chinese women were characterized as typically entrepreneurial, independent, and hardworking, with a strong drive to make money. The local country manager had previous experience in direct selling with both Avon and Tupperware. In 1992, rapid expansion had generated $3.3 million in sales through 1,800 consultants. Sales were expected to triple in 1993. All products were shipped from Dallas.

MKC also had established subsidiaries in Germany, with an estimated 1,500 consultants in 1993, and in Argentina which, despite periodic hyperinflation throughout the 1980s, was profitable in 1992. Poor results in the United Kingdom had resulted in the subsidiary being closed in 1985 after four years of operation, though there were plans to reopen in 1993. (Exhibit 5 presents data on MKC sales, number of directors, and number of consultants by subsidiary.)

Dandurand believed that MKC's limited international success was due partly to the direct application of the U.S.

marketing strategy, products, and communications to different subsidiaries without sufficient local modifications. Other factors constraining growth included low consumer brand awareness and insufficient marketing resources to develop it. Dandurand explained:

> In some countries, cultural barriers impede the use of the party plan and door-to-door selling. The size of a typical home may be smaller than in the United States, or a party for unfamiliar guests may be considered an invasion of privacy. In addition, the time required for a two-hour skin care class is sometimes an obstacle.

Future International Expansion

A strategic planning process in early 1993 identified a "great teachers" strategy to differentiate MKC worldwide from other retail and direct selling competitors and to build on the company's proven capabilities in this area. Greater emphasis would be placed on sales force training and on adapting MKC's positioning, the product range, and marketing communications mix to local market needs. A standard core product line would be supplemented with products developed specifically for each local market. Products would either be imported from the United States or manufacturing and/or final packaging would be subcontracted in individual country markets as was currently done in Mexico and Argentina. In particular, MKC was currently looking for a European manufacturing site to support its planned market entry into several European countries.

A country manager who wanted products adapted would have to seek the approval of the MKC regional president who, in turn, would meet with the international

| Exhibit 5 | Mary Kay Cosmetics Net Sales and Headcount, 1989 and 1992 |

	Net Sales ($000s)		Consultant Count		Director Count	
	1989	1992	1989	1992	1989	1992
United States	$404,990	$559,719	171,073	232,692	4,689	5,837
Argentina	3,638	12,450	5,142	6,675	152	152
Australia	9,494	7,812	4,161	4,143	122	116
Canada	24,811	25,386	9,866	10,597	167	283
Germany	1,210	5,131	583	1,306	9	26
Mexico	4,598	8,586	2,640	6,241	25	89
Taiwan	0	3,133	0	1,064	0	13
Distributors	3,333	4,690				

marketing and manufacturing managers. MKC regional presidents were all equity holders and therefore both advocates for the interests of the countries in their region as well as representatives of the headquarters' perspective.[4]

MKC executives believed that the company's values were transferable. Dandurand elaborated:

> Telling women they can achieve, making them believe in themselves and giving them caring and respect, is an international message. However, the message needs to be tailored to each market and communicated effectively and I'm not sure whether or not additional role models are needed in each foreign market for the company to be successful.

It was recognized that one or two charismatic leaders could generate massive growth in number of consultants and product sales.

Avon's International Strategy

Avon had become a successful international cosmetics company. Each country subsidiary was run by a country manager who had considerable decision-making authority so long as agreed-upon performance objectives were achieved. On average, 60% of the Avon products sold by a foreign subsidiary came from a common core line, while 40% were adapted to local markets. The company placed a heavy emphasis on merchandising with 18 three-week marketing campaigns used to promote specific consumer events such as Mother's Day, and 26 two-week drive periods supported by specific sales brochures each year. Avon sales consultants had to deal with the complexity of a product line of 1,500 SKUs. In contrast to MKC, Avon employed salaried sales managers who oversaw the company's independent salespeople.

In 1992, Avon eliminated its regional headquarters in favor of a single global support group based in New York. Many Avon subsidiaries were large enough to afford their own strong functional staffs and therefore no longer needed backup from regional headquarters. MKC executives believed that their lower product line turnover ought to permit a more streamlined and lower-cost central support group than Avon's.

Avon had been more willing than MKC to adapt its marketing programs internationally, adjusting prices according to the level of consumer buying power in individual countries. Avon hired strong local nationals as country managers, giving them specific strategic direction, generous resource allocations, and clear profit-and-loss responsibility. The Avon culture was considered "hard-nosed" and numbers-driven—return on equity and return on assets being especially important—but local country managers who delivered enjoyed considerable autonomy. According to some MKC executives, MKC had a more caring orientation and placed greater emphasis on support systems, mentoring, training, and recognition of consultants.

MKC IN ASIA

MKC's Taiwanese subsidiary had, by 1992, become profitable and promised good future sales growth. As part of the recent reorganization, an Asia/Pacific regional manager would shortly establish a base in Hong Kong from which to build MKC sales in Asia.

Asia was evolving as one of the fastest growing and most dynamic regions of the world. Its share of world GDP was scheduled to reach 32% by the year 2000, up from 24% in 1988. The choice between a Japanese or Chinese market entry would, Dandurand believed, impact MKC's long-term market position in Asia. She began to compare the two countries on some key characteristics to help make the decision (Table B). She wanted to build on MKC's past international experience and current competitive advantages to develop a market entry strategy that fit with the MKC culture and the local market environment and that would enable MKC to establish a firm base from which to build its Asian operations.

JAPAN

The Cosmetics Industry

In 1992, there were 1,100 cosmetics manufacturers in Japan but five companies accounted for 69% of domestic sales. Domestic production exceeded $9 billion in factory sales in 1991 and included local production by foreign firms, estimated at 18% of total domestic production. Imports represented 5% of total sales in 1991, up from 3% in 1989; over 45% of imports came from France, of which 27% consisted of fragrances and cologne. In addition, Japanese tourists purchased around $500 million of cosmetics at duty-free shops each year. Table C summarizes the size of the Japanese cosmetics market and the sources of product.

---

4 As a private company, MKC had a compensation plan for senior executives that worked like a partnership.

Key Characteristics of Japanese and Chinese Markets

	Japan	China
Population, 1992	124 million	1,139 million
Estimated population, 2020	137 million	1,541 million
Population distribution (0-24;25-49;50+):		
1993	32%; 37%; 31%	42%; 39%; 19%
2000	29%; 35%; 36%	40%; 39%; 21%
Urban population, 1992	77%	27%
Population/square mile	865	315
Gross domestic product (US$ billion)	3,370	371[a]
1993 GDP growth % (estimated)	2.3%	10.1%
1994 GDP growth % (estimated)	3.2%	9.5%
1990 per capita GNP	$14,311	$325
Average hourly compensation (US$)	$14.41	$0.24
Penetration of:		
Televisions	1 per 1.8 persons	1 per 8 persons
Radios	1 per 1.3	1 per 9
Telephones	1 per 2.3	1 per 66
1992 advertising expenditure per capita	$220	$0.86

[a]In early 1993, China's GDP was reestimated at $1,700 billion by the International Monetary Fund on the basis of purchasing power parity. This meant the Chinese economy was the third largest in the world.

The Japanese cosmetics market was mature, recording average annual value growth of 3% between 1988 and 1992, compared with a growth rate of 4.4% in the United States. Major consumers of cosmetics were women in their 20s and 30s. Foreign-made cosmetics were considered high-status products. Issues impacting the industry in 1992 included the end of manufacturers' control over the prices at which their products were resold by retailers and a continuing decrease in the number of independent cosmetics retailers. Strict Ministry of Health regulations governing imports and the manufacture of cosmetics involved lengthy approval processes. In many cases, common ingredients approved for use in cosmetics outside Japan were prohibited by the Ministry of Health, requiring reformulations of most products.

The Direct Selling Industry

In 1992, Japan was the largest direct selling market in the world with an estimated $19.2 billion in retail sales. Direct selling enabled consumers to bypass wholesale and retail distribution systems which some viewed as inefficient and non-price competitive. Japanese women who left business in order to have children came back into a company with no tenure and had to start up the corporate ladder from scratch. Consequently, direct selling, which could be done part time, was an attractive second career for mothers seeking to reenter the work force. According to the Japan Direct Selling Association, 1,120,000 women engaged in direct selling in 1992.[5]

Amway had been in Japan since 1977 and, by 1991, recorded sales of US$1.2 billion with a product line that included home care, personal care and food products, housewares, cosmetics, and gifts. The company had an extensive sales force of over 100,000 people, developed primarily through word-of-mouth. Training was conducted by direct distributors who sponsored new distributors. Compensation consisted of a 30% commission and a

5 In 1992, the total Japanese population was 124 million, of whom 41% were women over 15 years of age.

| Table C | Japanese Cosmetics Market Size and Sources of Shipments |

$ Millions (manufacturer shipments)	1989	1990	1991
Imports:	265	318	460
From the United States	41	57	89
Local production	8,983	8,433	9,072
Exports	128	147	214
Total market	9,119	8,603	9,319

bonus based on the sales of sponsored distributors. Conventions were held every year for training purposes and to recognize outstanding performance. In 1990, only seven other foreign companies generated more revenues in Japan than Amway. Reasons for this success were: an effective distribution system based on company-owned warehouses; high-quality, value-oriented products; good relations with dedicated distributors; and a philosophy that emphasized human relationships, fulfillment of dreams, and financial freedom.

Consumer Behavior

In the 1990s, an increasing percentage of Japanese women were going on to further education and working outside the home. In 1992, over 50% of the 51.8 million Japanese women aged over 15 years were employed, predominantly on a part-time basis. They earned lower salaries than men and preferred more flexible work schedules. Women's activities outside the home were increasing as were their expectations of equality. Many women were marrying later and having fewer children. (Exhibit 6 summarizes the results of a 1990 attitude study of 1,000 Japanese women.)

In 1992, Japanese women over 15 years old spent, on average, $400 on cosmetics (including skin care products and makeup). Forty percent of all cosmetics sales were to women in their 20s and 30s (26% of all Japanese women over the age of 15). The heaviest users were 8.8 million women aged between 20 and 29 (14% of all Japanese women over the age of 15). These heavy users were less price sensitive and more interested in high-quality cosmetics. Working women spent, on average, 25% more on cosmetic purchases than women who did not work outside the home. A fair complexion and fine-textured skin were considered hallmarks of beauty in Japan, so skin care

products accounted for 40% of all cosmetic sales. The growing sales of skin care products were also fueled by the increasing average age of the Japanese population; 23% of the population would be aged over 65 years by the year 2010, compared with 14% in 1992.

Fifty-four percent of facial skin care users and 40% of shaded makeup users purchased all or some of their products from direct sales companies. Corresponding figures in the United States were 25% and 22% respectively. Nineteen percent of Japanese skin care users and 20% of shaded makeup product users purchased only from direct salespeople. The average Japanese woman spent almost three times more on skin care than the average American woman. In the area of shaded makeup, Japanese women made half the number of purchases per year compared to women in the United States, but price differentials between the two countries resulted in almost equal annual expenditures. (Exhibit 7 summarizes Japanese consumer buying behavior for skin care and shaded makeup products.) In addition to functional product benefits, Japanese consumers placed a special emphasis on the visual appeal of product packaging.

Japanese consumers believed that they had sensitive skin as MKC confirmed when it ran extensive trials with Japanese women who had recently arrived in the United States. Pink was seen as a color more appropriate for children and teenagers so the classic MKC pink was muted on potential packaging and caps retooled to present a more upscale image. It was felt that redesigned packages might also appeal to U.S. consumers and that the potential existed for a global packaging redesign.

Products

Skin care products accounted for 40% of all cosmetics sales in Japan in 1992. (Exhibit 8 details sales of major cosmetics

Exhibit 6   1990 Survey of Japanese Woman

Age Group	Important Job Attributes	Points of Dissatisfaction at Work
19-24	Realize own potential and develop own capabilites.	Low bonus, too much overtime, inability to display or develop one's capabilities.
25-29	Able to continue after marriage and children, availability of nursery facilities, flexible time schedule to take care of children.	Feel job has no value.
30-39	Availability of nursery facilities, flexible time schedule, contributes to local community.	Low bonuses, too many trivial duties
40-43	Job encourages and promotes women.	Inadequate social benefits.
44-49	Close to home.	

Source: Adapted from a survey by *Pola Cultural Center*, 1990.
Note: Data based on a study of 1,000 Japanese women between 15 and 65 years of age.

product categories over time.) In the skin care category, sales of skin lotion increased by 12%, face wash and cleansing products by 4%, while cold cream, moisture cream, and milky lotion decreased by 1%. Makeup accounted for 23% of cosmetics sales but its share had been declining since 1986. Foundation products accounted for more than 50% of makeup sales.

In 1992, Kao and Shiseido dominated the Japanese skin care market. Foreign manufacturers were more successful selling makeup than skin care products while the reverse was true for domestic companies. Dandurand explained:

> In Japan, makeup products are associated with status, image, and dreams. Japanese women tend to aspire to look like the Western women on the cosmetics ads and so foreign brands, with the attached status, are more popular for color cosmetics. When it comes to skin care products, Japanese women tend to be more pragmatic. They believe that they have very delicate skins that require highly scientific products especially made for them by Japanese manufacturers who understand their needs better.

Distribution

Cosmetics were distributed in Japan through three main channels: franchise systems; general distributorships; and door-to-door sales.

Franchise systems were based on contracts between manufacturers and retailers, also known as chain stores, whereby a manufacturer's affiliated distribution company provided retailers with a full range of products, marketing support, and product promotions. In addition, trained beauty consultants were provided by manufacturers at each outlet. This enabled manufacturers to maintain control over the selling process and to provide consumers with individualized service. Franchise systems accounted for 40% of cosmetics sales in 1992 but were expected to decline. A variation of the franchise system was the direct selling franchise system whereby manufacturers dealt directly with retail accounts without going through a distribution company. This method was used by many foreign manufacturers who focused their marketing efforts, supported by face-to-face counseling, on a limited number of prestige shops and department stores.

General distributorships were the conventional channels whereby products flowed from manufacturer to wholesaler to retailer, and the manufacturer and retailer were not connected directly. The manufacturer provided full marketing support via advertising and promotion for products that tended to be lower-priced and less sophisticated. The volume share of cosmetics sold through this channel was estimated at 30% in 1992 and expected to increase.

Door-to-door sales or home visiting systems enabled manufacturers to bypass the costly, complex retailing network.

Exhibit 7 Japanese Cosmetics Consumer Buying Behavior

Product Category	Penetration: Percentage Purchasing	Market Share (Unit)	Market Share (Value)	Distribution Share Retail	Distribution Share Direct	Average $ Spent per Purchaser	Average Number of Purchases Per Year
Skin Care							
Cleansing	41.7	10.5	7.2	58.0	42.0	39.13	2.2
Cold and massage	19.1	3.2	3.1	43.1	56.9	36.40	1.6
Clear lotion	81.5	29.5	25.3	53.6	46.1	70.54	2.9
Milky lotion	52.9	10.9	9.9	57.4	42.6	42.29	1.7
Moisture cream	40.4	8.7	14.0	45.2	54.8	78.49	1.7
Mask	23.2	4.5	4.8	50.5	49.5	47.27	1.7
Whitening powder	2.1	0.4	0.6	73.4	26.6	64.72	NA
Essence	31.6	7.4	12.6	56.0	44.0	90.80	1.9
Foundation	78.9	24.8	22.5	66.1	33.9	64.59	2.5
Glamour							
Lipstick	68.9	38.8	47.3	65.5	34.5	33.93	1.7
Eye shadow	21.3	9.8	9.9	76.7	23.3	23.05	1.4
Eyeliner	11.6	4.9	3.9	65.3	34.7	16.58	1.7
Mascara	11.9	4.8	4.8	79.8	20.2	19.99	1.7
Eyebrow	20.6	8.7	6.3	70.7	29.3	20.00	1.5
Blusher	21.5	8.7	9.3	61.4	38.6	21.26	1.4
Manicure	25.9	16.0	6.1	75.6	24.4	11.72	1.9
Fragrance	16.8	8.3	12.4	63.2	36.8	36.38	1.8

Source: Adapted from *Cosmetics and Toiletries Marketing Strategies,* *Fuji Keizai,* 1992.

Exhibit 8   Japanese Cosmetics Market: Growth by Subcategory (billion yen)

Value of Factory Shipments	1986	1987	1988	1989	1990	1990/89
Skin Care Products	452.5	430.0	455.2	484.4	500.8	3.4%
Face wash cream/foam	41.4	42.7	46.8	51.0	53.0	
Cleansing cream/foam/gel	27.7	28.7	32.9	35.6	37.2	
Cold cream	22.5	18.2	18.4	16.8	16.7	
Moisture cream	87.9	68.7	79.0	75.9	75.3	
Milky lotion	64.6	60.6	63.0	64.6	62.1	
Skin lotion (freshener)	134.0	142.1	142.5	159.1	178.4	
Face mask	26.1	22.3	22.3	23.2	24.3	
Men's	10.2	10.2	11.6	11.8	10.7	
Other	38.1	36.5	38.7	46.4	43.1	
Makeup Products	306.8	308.8	300.3	301.9	295.8	(2.0)
Foundation	154.3	157.1	160.0	161.8	158.3	
Powder	19.6	18.2	18.9	18.8	18.5	
Lipstick	44.2	49.3	48.3	46.4	48.2	
Lip cream	9.7	9.2	10.0	8.6	9.1	
Blush	15.5	14.1	11.9	11.4	11.2	
Eye shadow	26.0	27.5	22.3	22.7	19.9	
Eyebrow/eyelash	15.2	15.0	15.1	16.9	15.8	
Nail care	17.8	15.4	11.8	13.5	13.0	
Other	4.5	3.0	2.0	1.8	1.8	
Hair Care Products	335.5	362.2	392.1	403.5	413.4	2.5
Fragrances	22.1	21.1	18.7	18.8	20.9	11.1
Special Use (Suncare, shaving, bath products)	27.3	27.9	30.2	31.1	33.7	8.6
Total	1,144.0	1,146.6	1,196.2	1,239.6	1,263.9	2.0

Source: Adapted from *The Complete Handbook of Cosmetics Marketing 1992, Shukan Shogyo.*

This direct selling system, which had worked well in the past, was facing problems in 1992: fewer women were staying at home, and direct selling companies were finding it increasingly difficult to attract sales personnel. In 1982, this channel had represented 25% of cosmetic sales; by 1992, it represented 19%. Some direct selling companies were diversifying into other ways of reaching the consumer. For example, Pola, a major Japanese direct selling cosmetics company, had started marketing its products in variety stores, aesthetic salons, and by mail order. Avon and Noevir,

also a large Japanese direct selling cosmetics company, and Menard, had opened retail stores and salons. Other channels included beauty parlors and hairdressers. (Shares of cosmetics sales in Japan by distribution channel and by consumer age group are given in Exhibit 9.)

Competitors

The top five domestic cosmetics manufacturers in 1992 were Shiseido with 27% of the market; Kao with 16%; Kanebo with 11%; Pola with 8%; and Kobayashi Kose

	Percentage Women 1985	Percentage Women 1990	Change 1985-1990	1990 Teens	1990 20s	1990 30s	1990 40s	1990 50s
Department store	22.8	25.2	2.4	37	30	19	19	24
Cosmetic store	44.6	37.5	(7.1)	26	48	33	37	43
Drug/pharmacy	12.7	22.3	9.6	25	20	29	18	18
Door-to-door	19.6	12.0	(7.6)	1	7	19	16	12
Supermarket	15.6	18.1	2.5	22	11	21	22	15
Beauty salon	3.7	6.1	2.4	3	7	4	7	9
Convenience store	NA	2.9		12	2	1	1	1
Variety shop	NA	1.7		5	2	2		
Others	NA	8.4		2	9	13	10	5

Source: Adapted from a survey by Marketing Intelligence Corp.

with 7%. These companies spent, on average, 4% of sales on research and development, double the level spent by the major foreign manufacturers. Shiseido, founded in 1872 as Shiseido Pharmacy, entered the cosmetics business in 1902. Ninety years later, Shiseido products were sold through 25,000 chain stores and 9,000 retail beauty consultants. Kao, Kanebo, and Kobayashi Kose also operated nationwide networks. Foreign companies such as Max Factor, Revlon, and Clinique entered the Japanese market in the early 1980s and pursued selective distribution through a limited number of prestigious department stores. (Exhibit 10 summarizes sales data for the major Japanese and foreign cosmetics manufacturers, and Table D profiles the major direct selling cosmetics companies.)

Pola was established in 1946 and had $740 million in sales in 1991. With 180,000 "Pola Ladies," 20,000 salespeople, and 6,500 retail outlets, Pola ranked third in cosmetics sales and first in direct sales of cosmetics in Japan. Originally targeted at older women, Pola had begun recently to focus on younger women with its moderately priced product line. Pola provided in-depth training for its staff, ranging from one month for a "Pola Lady" to over a year for sales research staff at company headquarters. The compensation structure for Pola Ladies had 21 levels: "Class 1" salespeople who sold up to $370 monthly made a 25% margin and no commission. A "Super Million Lady" salesperson, with monthly sales over $37,000, earned a 35% margin, a $400 jewel allowance, and $800 in bonus. In 1991, Pola spent $28.5 million on media advertising, of

which newspaper ads accounted for 9%, magazine ads for 28%, and television commercials for 63%.

Nippon Menard was established in 1959 and had $373 million in sales in 1990, of which 67% was derived from skin care products and 23% from makeup. Organized into 33 sales companies and sold through over 12,000 retail outlets and 160,000 beauty specialists, it ranked eighth among cosmetics companies and second among direct selling cosmetics companies. Main brands included Entals, Delphia, and Ires, positioned at lower price points and targeted at women in their 20s and 30s, and Eporea, positioned at a high price point and targeted at older women. Beauty specialists followed a series of four training classes and could advance through seven levels from "beginner" to "special" depending on their monthly sales. A beginner beauty specialist, who achieved monthly sales of $300 to $450, earned a commission of 30% but no bonus. At the other extreme, a "special" beauty specialist sold over $23,000 per month and earned a 38% commission plus between $350 and $1,000 in bonus. In 1991, Menard spent a total of $25 million on advertising, of which 6% was on newspaper ads, 11% on magazine advertising, and 83% on television commercials.

Noevir was established in 1978 and had $292 million in sales in 1990, of which 64% was derived from skin care products and 24% from makeup. It operated on a consignment basis with 580 sales companies selling to two levels of 109,000 agencies, through 200,000 salespeople. It ranked

Exhibit 10

Exhibit 10   Major Cosmetics Companies in Japan, 1990

Company	Total Sales $ Million Cosmetics	Skin Care	Makeup	Hair Care	Fragrances	Men's Cosmetics
Top 5 Cosmetics Companies						
Shiseido	$1,963.3	49%	31%	3%	3%	10%
Kanebo	1,331.2	39	36	5	3	12
Pola	704.1	54	28	2	3	2
Kose	553.8	51	36	5	1	3
Kao	470.8	46	42	2	0	10
Top 5 Foreign Cosmetics Companies						
Max Factor	440.8	37	54	1	2	1
Avon	303.8	35	30	4	0	0
Revlon	92.3	25	52	10	7	0
Clinique	80.7	72	25	1	0	0
Chanel	76.1	21	21	0	58	0

Source: Adapted from *Cosmetics and Toiletries Marketing Strategies, Fuji Keizai; 1992.*

Table D   Manufacturer Sales of Major Direct Selling Cosmetics Companies in Japan—1990

	Sales Growth 1989-90	Total Sales 1990 ($ million)[a]	Facial Skin Care (%)	Makeup (%)	Hair Care (%)	Fragrances (%)	Men's Cosmetics (%)
Pola	2.4%	$704	54%	28%	2%	3%	2%
Nippon Menard	(2.3)	373	67	23	1	1	2
Avon[b]	1.9	304	35	30	4		
Noevir	2.8	292	64	24	4	4	4
Oppen	0.0	213	64	24	3	1	1
Aistar	0.0	185	100				
Naris	12.0	110	58	26		1	2
Yakult	1.7	50	56	22	4	2	2

[a]Total company figures. Some companies were engaged in other businesses in addition to cosmetics; therefore, percentages of cosmetic sales do not add to 100%.
[b]Avon percentages total 69% because Avon also sold jewelry and lingerie.

ninth among cosmetics companies and third among direct selling cosmetics companies. In 1992, Noevir had two subsidiaries, Sana and Nov; Sana sold through 5,000 skin care retail outlets and 400 makeup retail outlets, and Nov sold through 2,000 pharmaceutical outlets. Sana targeted younger women while the Nov product line included hypoallergic cosmetics recommended by dermatologists. In 1991, Noevir spent $8 million on advertising—13% on magazine ads and the remainder on television commercials.

Avon was established in Japan in 1973 and had $325 million in sales in 1991, of which 69% was derived from cosmetics. Avon sold through mail-order catalogs and 350,000 Avon Ladies. In 1992, Avon had successfully floated 40% of the subsidiary's equity on the Tokyo stock exchange. It ranked thirteenth among cosmetics companies and fourth among direct selling cosmetics companies. The company targeted women in their 30s and 40s and, unlike other direct selling companies, Avon's products were not regularly demonstrated to consumers by Avon Ladies.

Avon, Menard, Pola, Noevir, and Amway also offered "buying club" programs. Most recruited salespeople on the basis of providing an opportunity to make extra income, but only Amway heavily stressed advancement into management based on recruiting and sales performance. Most competitors offered thorough product training at little or no cost; the training was more extensive than that provided by most U.S. direct selling organizations. Sales presentations typically were made one-to-one, but other than through catalogs and brochures, little instruction was provided to consumers. (Exhibit 11 profiles the characteristics of consumers using the principal brands, and Exhibit 12 reproduces competitor print advertisements.)

MKC in Japan

MKC began assessing the Japanese market in 1988 with a comparative study of products and competition. It was determined that the typical Japanese woman's skin care regimen involved a seven-stage process as opposed to three steps in the United States,[6] and that whitening products, not widely available in the United States, were very popular in Japan. In 1989, a comparative pricing study was undertaken and relationships established with an ingredient supplier and a private-label manufacturer who might produce an estimated 20% of the product line, tailored to the Japanese market, including whitening products and wet/dry foundation cake. In 1992, MKC proceeded with lengthy product approval processes involving the Japanese Ministry of Health. By year end, over $1 million had been invested in preparing to enter the Japanese market.

There was concern that MKC would be a late entrant in a mature, complex, fragmented, and highly competitive market. Dandurand believed that it would take three to five years before MKC would turn a profit and take share from competitors. On the other hand, 1993 might be an opportune time for MKC to launch in Japan since, increasingly, women wished both to raise children and be involved in activities outside the home, and an economic recession created more demand for part-time employment to supplement household incomes. Some MKC executives believed that success in Japan was essential to the company's future in the countries of the Pacific Rim.

CHINA

China covered 3.7 million square miles and was divided into 22 provinces, 3 municipalities (Beijing, Shanghai, and Tianjin), and 5 autonomous regions (Guangxi, Zhuang, Nei Mongol, Ningxia Hui, Xinjiang Uygur, and Tibet). The population was estimated at 1.1 billion in 1992 and was predicted to grow to 1.5 billion by the year 2020. Eighty percent lived in the eastern half of the country depicted in Exhibit 13. Thirty percent lived in urban areas. Thirty percent was under 15 years old. In the second half of the twentieth century, China experienced one of the fastest demographic transitions in history. Mortality rates decreased and average life expectancy rose from 42 years in 1950 to 70 in 1992. Fertility rates fell from an average of 6 children per woman in 1950 to 2.3 in 1992. Trends towards urbanization and a shift in population from the agricultural to the service sector were expected to continue in the 1990s.

In 1979, the "Open Door Policy" heralded a series of wide-ranging economic reforms: agriculture was decollectivized; the development of private and semiprivate enterprises to produce goods was permitted; free market pricing and more liberal foreign exchange conversion were introduced; and foreign investment became more acceptable. These economic reforms had the greatest impact on the coastal provinces where economic free zones were established to facilitate foreign investment. Guandong province, for example, had experienced the

---

6 In the United States a typical skin care regimen involved a cleanser, a toner, and a moisturizer. In Japan, several different cleansers and moisturizers were typically used in a single skin care regimen.

Exhibit 11

Exhibit 11 Customer Profiles of MKC's Principal Potential Competitors in Japan, 1992

	Menard	Pola	Noevir	Avon	Amway
Educational Background					
Current student	0.0	2.7	2.0	1.1	2.1
College	11.1	17.3	14.3	32.6	27.7
Senior high school	63.9	62.7	63.3	53.7	63.3
Junior high school	25.0	17.3	20.4	12.6	6.4
Marital and Employment Status					
Married—not working	27.8	32.9	22.9	44.2	39.1
Married—working	69.4	53.4	70.9	40.0	36.7
Unmarried	2.8	13.7	6.2	15.8	23.9
Age					
15-19	0.0	2.7	0.0	2.1	0.0
20-29	8.3	18.7	14.3	15.8	38.3
30-39	11.1	17.3	30.6	28.4	17.0
40-49	41.7	25.3	30.6	32.6	25.5
50-59	38.9	36.0	24.5	21.1	19.1
Occupation					
Not employed	27.8	32.0	22.4	43.2	38.3
Employed	72.2	65.3	75.5	55.8	59.6

Source: Company reports.

fastest growth in East Asia in the 1980s. Overall, China's GNP had increased by 9% annually during the 1980s, while consumption had increased by 6.6%. In 1990, 70% of industrial growth was attributed to private, cooperative, and foreign ventures.

Since 1988, a higher-income, urban middle class had emerged with household earnings over $125 a month and saving rates estimated at 35%. By the year 2000, it was estimated that 41 million households would have incomes of over $18,000 per annum. Retail sales had increased nearly fivefold since 1980 with the number of retail outlets increasing from 2 million in 1980 to 12 million in 1992, most being private enterprises. All types of goods were available in the major cities, and the adoption rate of new products was rapid. In 1992, China was viewed as a sellers' market but experts believed that more sophisticated marketing skills and product differentiation would become increasingly important.

In assessing the political and economic risks of investing in China, multinational companies had three main concerns. First, some thought political instability was likely to follow the retirement or death of China's long-standing Premier Deng Xiaoping. Political struggles between conservatives and reformers might delay further economic reforms. Second, the Chinese government was not granting its people political freedom commensurate

Exhibit 12   Competitor Print Advertisements: Japan 1993

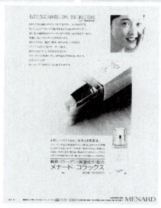

with their increasing economic freedom. Progress on human rights was essential to China maintaining most-favored nation status as a trading partner with the United States. Third, multinationals importing finished goods into China faced not only high tariffs but also the likely devaluation of the Chinese currency which would further increase the retail prices of their goods.

During the 1980s, cosmetics and toiletries became an important branch of China's light industry, and the number of cosmetics factories in China increased sixfold between 1982 and 1990. In 1992, the cosmetics market was estimated at $825 million (manufacturer sales), with skin care products dominant. There were approximately 3,000 cosmetics producers in China manufacturing limited product lines; about half were located in Shanghai.

Many local brands were available as import tariffs on cosmetics averaged 100%. In 1991, the Chinese Ministry of Commerce initiated a professional training program for two million cosmetics managers, purchasers, and sales clerks with the objective of teaching them how to appraise the quality of cosmetics and skin conditions of consumers.

Consumers

There was a growing difference in purchasing power and consumer behavior between the urban and rural populations in China, with the urban population becoming increasingly prosperous and demanding, and the rural consumer evolving less quickly. Eighty-seven percent of Chinese women worked and many held two jobs: one state job and

Exhibit 13   Map of Eastern China

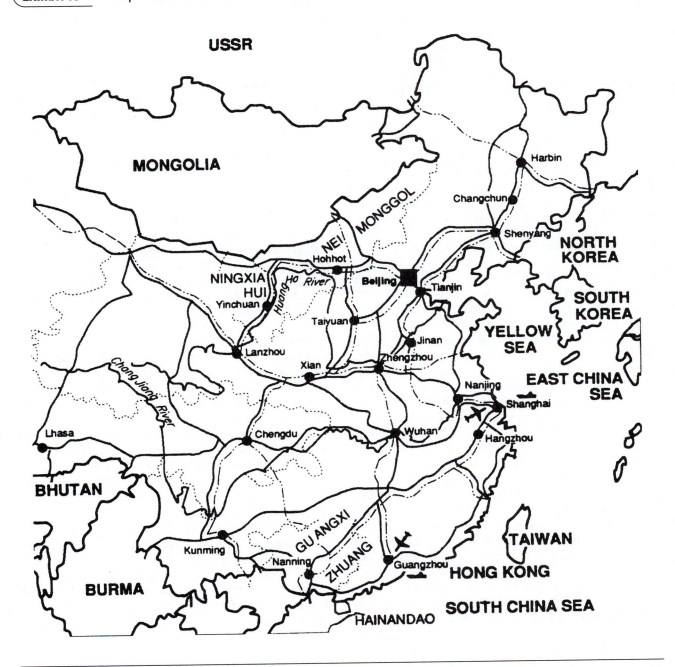

one independent job. Urban workers were generally employed in factories or workshops, employment assignments being allocated by local labor bureaus. Safety standards in factories were poor but compensation was adequate. The wage range from lowest grade to highest grade was a factor of three, and a sum equal to 10% of total wages was typically available for bonuses. Virtually all housing, medical, and transportation costs and midday meals were subsidized by Chinese government work units. Around 25% of the household income of a two-income urban household was typically spent on food and housing; the remainder was disposable income.

Government-subsidized housing units were small; 200 square feet was the typical size of a one-bedroom urban apartment. A workers' committee still managed each apartment building. A few apartments were also available for purchase; US$5,000 could purchase a two-bedroom apartment in Guangzhou in early 1993. Housing conditions were better in Guangzhou and Beijing than in Shanghai. Young workers, especially women, tended to live with their parents until they married. Once married, they would live with the husbands' parents or take their own apartments.

Female workers were entitled to 56 days of pregnancy leave and most factories had nurseries and kindergarten facilities. The Chinese government wished to encourage women to spend more time at home and therefore established the "Period Employment" system whereby women could elect to take three months maternity leave at 100% pay and/or up to seven years off at 70% of basic pay to aid in childraising. In 1992, an estimated 66% of Chinese women over the age of 25 were married.

A 1991 consumer study concluded that the average Chinese female urban consumer was 32 years old, married with one child, worked in a state factory, and earned the equivalent of $50 a month. She typically controlled the family budget and was concerned about the rising cost of living. Attracted to foreign brands, she considered skin care and cosmetics important, particularly those that prevented freckles and promoted cleanliness.

Chinese women were greatly interested in learning; education was held in very high esteem in Chinese culture. Chinese colleges and universities were increasingly asserting their independence; MKC might be able to sponsor skin care courses and sell products to the enrolled students and/or secure product endorsements from medical schools.

By 1992, differences in buying power and buyer behavior were evident across the various regions of China. The three most important regional markets were: Guangzhou, Beijing, and Shanghai. (Table E summarizes key characteristics of these three metropolitan markets.)

Guangzhou Hong Kong's influence was strongly felt in Guangzhou, whose economy was driven by the private sector. More interested in spending their disposable incomes on food, drink, eating out, and entertaining, Guangzhou consumers were wealthier but characterized as less cosmopolitan and sophisticated than other urban Chinese consumers. Described as flashy and ostentatious, Guangzhou consumers were also known as generous and free-spending. Many companies viewed the Guangzhou consumer market as very similar to Hong Kong's and believed that consumer characteristics of the two markets would continue to converge.

Beijing Beijing consumers were generally characterized as conservative and serious. Less concerned with appearances than Shanghai consumers, they spent less on clothing and personal care products. However, Beijing, being the home of senior government and Party officials, had an elite group of consumers interested in luxury goods and designer labels. Also characterized as straightforward and honest, advertisements based on fact and information were well-received. Before making a major purchase, Beijing consumers would be well-versed on the technical aspects of the product. On the other hand, these consumers also appeared to be more willing to try new products, and new brand launches were often initially more successful than in Shanghai.

Shanghai Being the largest city, Shanghai was the commercial and cultural center of China. Shanghai consumers were characterized as proud and very concerned about their appearances. While not the wealthiest consumers in China, they were known as the best dressed and smartest looking. Shanghai consumers spent a significantly greater proportion of their disposable income on clothing, jewelry, and personal care products than their counterparts elsewhere in China, and premium-priced products and brands moved better in Shanghai than anywhere else. Shanghainese acknowledged and even took pride in the historical European and Western influences on their city and personal habits. Housing conditions however, were distinctly worse in Shanghai than in most other cities in China.

Shanghai was also the manufacturing center of China, and Shanghai goods were recognized as among the best in China. As a result, Shanghai consumers were more loyal to their local brands than were other Chinese consumers. Considered the most influential market in China, it was

	Guangzhou	Bejing	Shanghai
Location	South (100 miles north of Hong Kong)	North (China's capital)	East Coast by Yangtze River
Population	6 million = city 25 million = province	4 million = city 11 million = province	13.5 million = city 60 million = province
Region characteristics	Low-cost manufacturing base for Hong Kong. Most flexible for business approvals and hiring.	Government ministries. Second-largest retail center and strong industrial base.	8.5% of China's industrial output. Cultural and commercial capita
Foreign companies	Avon, Colgate, P&G and Amway	Shiseido, L'Oreal	Johnson & Johnson, Unilever
Consumer characteristics	Unrefined. Main interest is food and family. But more interested in glamour.	Rigid, bureaucratic. More cerebral.	Elegant, vain, tough negotiators, seek quality.
Typical wage level	$200/month, highest consumer goods spending in China. Flooded by foreign consumer goods.	$80/month but rising level of affluence in the last two years.	Over $100/month. Highest spending on clothing, cosmetics, jewelry. (Estimates = 30% disposable income.)

believed that a successful launch in Shanghai was likely to be able to be extended to the rest of China, whereas a marketing program which worked in Beijing or Guangzhou would not necessarily work in Shanghai.

Products

Within the skin care category of the Chinese cosmetics market, the main product claims being made were prevention and removal of wrinkles; reduction of premature aging; absorption into and the effect upon functions of the skin; environmental protection; making skin snow-white, smooth and more elastic; healing acne; and purifying pores. Within the makeup category, Avon's Cake Foundation claimed to complement oily skins and give complexions a smooth, matte finish.

Packaging was much more basic than in the United States or Japan. Skin care products were mainly marketed in plastic or glass jars with decorated or colored caps. Labels were applied or jar screened (stamped directly onto the jar) and carried both English and Chinese copy. Outer packaging

was less common and varied widely in the quality of carton and liners used. Inserts ranged from instructions on thin paper in Chinese only to color brochures with pictures and illustrations in both English and Chinese.

Distribution

State-owned department stores with 280,000 outlets accounted for 40% of all consumer product retail sales. Collectively owned stores, of which there were 1.2 million, accounted for 32%, while 8 million individually owned stores accounted for 20% of retail sales. The remaining sales were made through 330 joint venture stores (5% of sales) and direct-selling companies (3%). Some observers argued that the Chinese distribution system was more accessible to U.S. companies than the Japanese system. However, it was even more fragmented.

Cosmetics displays in stores tended to be confusing and cluttered with many brands. In department stores however, imported brands were sold in separate cases from domestic products. Three price tiers existed: imported brands such as

Dior retailed at 8 times the retail prices of China-manufactured brands of Western/Chinese joint ventures and at 15 times those of local brands. Cosmetic companies rented cosmetic cases and shelf space from the department stores and paid the wages of the department store clerks.

Advertising

In 1992, per capita advertising spending in China was less than $1.00 but was expected to increase by 174% between 1992 and 1995. Newspapers were small and fragmented and rarely used for print advertising. Regional or provincial television channels were more popular than the single national channel, and advertising on the national television channel was more liable to censorship. A satellite television channel broadcast from Hong Kong, Star TV, could be accessed by 4.8 million households in China and advertising costs through this channel averaged $0.50 per 1,000 people.

The cost of television advertising varied according to the status of the advertiser. The cost of a 30-second prime time advertisement on provincial television in Guangzhou province in May 1993 was $200 for a local company, $500 for a joint venture partnership, and $2,000 for a foreign importer. In Guangzhou City, these costs were about 40% of those for advertising to the entire province. For a foreign importer, the cost of a 30-second prime time advertisement on Chinese national television was $4,000 compared to $9,000 on Hong Kong television.

Competitors

Foreign competitors in China in 1992 included Avon, Johnson & Johnson, Kao, Unilever, L'Oreal, Procter & Gamble, Revlon, and Shiseido. However, their combined sales accounted for only 3% of the market. (Exhibit 14 lists the main cosmetics products and brands available in China in 1992; Exhibit 15 provides comparative pricing data for the major cosmetics product segments.)

In 1992, Avon was the first and only direct selling cosmetics company in China. Avon had established a joint venture with the Guangzhou Cosmetics Factory (GCF) in which it owned 60% of the equity. GCF owned 35%, with the remaining 5% split between two Hong Kong business partners who had provided introductions to Chinese government officials. Avon operated only in the southern province of Guangdong. Sales in 1991 were about $4 million and rose to $8 million in 1992. Avon offered a full product line of 170 items (including a product that was a skin toner,

moisturizer, and cleanser all in one), selling for an average of $4.00 each. Sales of skin-whitening products were especially strong. It was estimated that half the items were imported.

In 1993, Avon used television advertising to promote product benefits and print advertising to recruit salespeople. Products were sold by about 15,000 Avon Ladies, mostly part-timers, who kept their regular state jobs to retain their housing subsidies, medical benefits, and pensions. Salespeople sold Avon products for whatever markup they could achieve. On average, they were believed to earn a 30% margin on product sales. Avon distributed its products through 10 branch depots located throughout Guangdong. Two hundred sales managers, who were salaried employees, oversaw 4,500 Franchise Dealers, who in turn managed the sales representatives. A training program for the Franchise Dealers included classes on product benefits, cosmetics and skin care, and general business management.

Avon positioned itself as offering consumers service, quality, reliability, and product guarantees; the latter, in particular, was a new concept for the Chinese consumer. Typical Avon consumers were urban women, aged between 20 and 35 years. Many were thought to live with their parents and spend their disposable incomes on Western goods. Compared with other imported brands, Avon was thought to be popular with younger women because Avon products were reasonably priced, and purchase—either at work or at home—was considered convenient. In addition, Avon Ladies gave their good customers a 10% to 20% discount on volume purchases and received "finders fees" for recruiting salespeople.

By 1993, Avon had achieved a beachhead in China, but several problems were evident. Inflation was forcing frequent pay increases for Avon's trained salaried employees, many of whom were receiving attractive job offers from other direct marketing firms. Avon's salaried employees were also demanding that the company provide housing as state-owned enterprises had traditionally done. In addition, Avon had not received the permanent discount off of the standard 30%-40% retail turnover tax and the temporary exclusivity for the direct marketing of cosmetics in Guangzhou that executives believed they had negotiated with the provincial government.[7]

Shiseido had established a joint venture company, Shiseido Liyuan Cosmetics Co., with Beijing Liyuan in 1987. Products were sold under the brand name Huazi and cumulative sales during the first five years after the launch

---

[7] "Avon Calling," *Business China*, Economist Intelligence Unit, July 12, 1993, pp. 1-2.

Brand/Product	Manufacturer
Avon Rich Moisture Face Cream	Avon (joint venture)
Avon Skinplicity	Avon (joint venture)
Ballet Pearl Beautifying Cream	Cosmetic Factory of Nanjing China
Ballet Pearl Cream	China Light Industrial Products Import and Export
Ballet Silk Peptide UV Defense Cream	Nanjing Golden Ballet Cosmetic Co. Ltd.
Bong Bao Maifanite Face-Beautifying Honey	Dongyang Mun Cosmetics Works, Zhejiang Provence
Bong Bao Maifanite Pearl Cream	Dongyang Mun Cosmetics Works, Zhejiang Provence
Dabao Instant Anti-Wrinkle Cream	Beijing Sanlu Factory
Lan Normolee Moisturizing Cream	International Gottin Cosmetics
Lorensa U.S.A. Retin-A Nourish Cream	Lorensa Cosmetics U.S.A.
Lychee Brand Pianzihuang Pearl Cream	Made in chemical factory for domestic use, Zhangzhou, Fujian, China Supervised by Pharmacy Industry Corporation, Fujian, China
Maxam Cleansing Lotion	Maxam Cosmetics (joint venture with S.C. Johnson)
Maxam	Maxam Cosmetics (joint venture with S.C. Johnson)
Meidi Beautiful Youth Nourish Cream	Grand Blom Co. Ltd., Hong Kong
Monica Beauty Skin Cleanser	Formulated in France
Montana Anti-Wrinkle Cream	Concord Group U.S.A. (joint venture)
Montana Bleaching Cream	Concord Group U.S.A. (joint venture)
Qinxiang Day Cream	Guangzhou Cosmetic Factory
Rhoure Ulan Cream	Guangzhou First Lab Cosmetics Industry Thailand First Lab Chemical Products Co. Ltd.
Ruby Nourishing Cream	S.C. Johnson (joint venture)
Swiss Natural Silk Cream	Wuxi Novel Daily Chemical Co. Ltd.
Ximi	—
Yue-Sai Protective Moisturizer	—
Ying Fong	Nan Yuan Ying Fong Group Co.

Source: Company research.

were estimated at $80 million. Shiseido positioned itself as offering high quality, technologically sophisticated products. The company offered 15 items at prices ranging from $4 to $6, in four product categories: eye makeup; hair care; nail care; and skin care.

MKC in China

In addition to choosing a location, MKC could choose to enter the Chinese market either by designating a licensed distributor or negotiating a joint venture agreement with a Chinese partner. Joint ventures were the most common structures Western companies used for entering China. Negotiations always involved government bodies and took an average of two years to complete. Successful joint ventures, such as those set up by Pepsi and Colgate-Palmolive, emphasized a careful search for the right partner, an in-depth market feasibility study, patience and a long-term commitment to the investment, and a strong focus on

Product	Domestic Joint Venture Products			Imported Products		
	Shanghai	Guangzhou	Beijing	Shanghai	Guangzhou	Beijing
Moisturizer	100	45	121	703	341	418
Cleanser	163	57	70	459	354	366
Toner	43	72	NA	340	368	NA
Mask	NA	104	NA	NA	400	NA
Day cream	48	55	76	345	351	373
Night cream	57	100	88	354	397	385
Pearl cream	45	84	NA	341	381	NA
Nourishing cream	55	58	83	352	354	380
Hand/body lotion/cream	37	43	68	333	340	364
Eye cream	NA	69	88	NA	366	385
Anti-aging cream	18	23	53	315	320	350
Whitening lotion	39	22	80	335	318	377
Lipstick	85	59	41	381	356	337
Cheek color	NA	72	NA	NA	368	NA
Foundation	71	128	NA	367	425	NA
Nail polish	40	72	32	337	368	328
Perfume	117	98	NA	413	394	NA

Source: Company reports.

training and developing local management. MKC could also choose to build a manufacturing facility as Gillette and Amway had, expand and upgrade an existing production facility as Avon had done, subcontract manufacturing, or simply import products from the United States. It was estimated that the construction of a one-million-square-foot manufacturing plant would take two years and cost over $20 million.

Timing was considered critical in the decision to enter the Chinese market: Avon was still marketing only in the South; the number of cosmetics competitors was increasing; and the retail infrastructure was expected to continue to improve.

MARKET ENTRY DECISION

One critical issue in deciding which markets to enter and in what order, was the acceptability and potential success of MKC's party plan approach to sales in the two markets. In Japan, Tupperware had pioneered the use of party plans, which were subsequently successfully used by a number of companies. By 1992, party plans had become an established and accepted sales technique in Japan. On the other hand, to date, no company had attempted the party plan approach in China. In 1992, MKC conducted a number of focus groups to help determine the acceptability and potential success of this sales approach. Initial findings suggested that the party plan method would be well-received in China. However, most homes were small, and in Shanghai living conditions were particularly difficult such that people did not, as a rule, entertain in their homes. In terms of consultant recruiting, results indicated that some Chinese women were entrepreneurial, placed an emphasis on learning and self-development, and were strongly attracted to a flexible financial opportunity that would enable them to supplement their state salaries. The focus group results indicated that Chinese women were interested in cosmetics and very eager to learn more about products and how best to use them. Dandurand believed that MKC could implement a successful party plan operation in China but that resources would be needed to explain and communicate the concept to both potential consultants and consumers.

Marketing Mix Options

Product line Dandurand believed that it was essential for MKC to enter any market with both skin care and makeup products. She explained: "The two product groups both depend on consumer education. First, we teach consumers how to care for their skin and demonstrate the available treatments, then how to use glamour products to enhance their natural beauty."

Individual products in both lines would require local adaptation. Developing a product line to meet the exacting government regulations and demanding consumers of Japan would require roughly three times as much time and resources as developing a line for the Chinese market. Some MKC executives argued that the product line should be adapted as little as necessary. They believed that, with the exception of certain shades of makeup, the current product line was already global in appeal.

Positioning Assuming MKC would be marketing both the skin care and makeup products, Dandurand had to decide whether the company should be positioned as a "glamour provider," offering makeup products and expertise combined with some skin care products, or as a "skin treatment" expert that also provided makeup products. Other decisions would include the level of emphasis to place in MKC communications on the career opportunities and consumer training aspects of the MKC organization, and what messages to use to communicate them. To help with the latter, MKC conducted recruitment research in Taiwan, Japan, and China in early 1993. The results of this study are given in Exhibit 16.

In Japan, Dandurand believed that competitive differentiation was key to success but was unsure what the basis of differentiation should be and which age group to target.

One suggested modification of MKC's U.S. strategy was a buying club, similar to those offered by Avon, Menard, and Noevir. This would accelerate the recruitment of consultants, would be more consistent with competition, and would offer women the discounts on products and purchase convenience that they wanted. However, some MKC executives argued that this approach was inconsistent with MKC's emphasis on offering consultants a career opportunity and professional consumer training, and that it would not differentiate MKC from other direct selling companies operating in Japan.

Pricing Even taking product development costs into account, it was estimated that unit margins obtained on products sold in Japan would be at least twice as high as for corresponding products sold in China. Dandurand, however, pointed out that start-up costs, office overheads, and advertising expenditures, could be somewhat lower in China and that a Chinese market entry was expected to break even within 24 months as opposed to three to five years for Japan.

Dandurand wondered how MKC products should be priced in relation to both domestic and foreign competitors, particularly Avon, to support her positioning decision, and whether to replicate the U.S. consultant compensation scheme or to adopt consultant compensation that matched competitors' programs and local economics.

Promotion In either market, consultant recruitment programs would have to be developed, backed by print advertising, public relations, and public service workshops on women's issues. In Japan, MKC was considering establishing a toll-free number, distributing videos, organizing career opportunity seminars, and/or developing a traveling showroom to target consumers in the suburbs. Dandurand wondered what the best ways to reach potential consultants and consumers in China might be.

To build the necessary level of MKC brand awareness among consumers in Japan would require at least $3 million per year in advertising. To create comparative brand awareness levels in one region of China might require $400,000 in advertising per year for the first three years.

In order to compare the economics of the two market entry options, Dandurand made the preliminary calculations summarized in Exhibit 17.

Exhibit 16   Recruitment Study in Taiwan, Japan, and China, 1993

	Taiwan	Japan	China
Ideal Life Aspirations	Would like to work as long as they can take care of family.	Key aspirations is to get marries and be a good mother/wife.	Most woman have government-sponsored jobs. Would like to reduce the number of nonproductive hours of work, expand their knowledge and feel more productive.
	Personal fulfillment and increased knowledge are important.	Lead fulfilling and satisfying personal lives and enjoy themselves.	
Jobs and Careers	Career: perceived as involving risk, long-term commitment and higher financial rewards.	Career: image of independence not positive.	Career: Sounded far fetched, an alien concept.
	Job: no risk, short-term way to make money.	Do not feel that it is possible to combine career and family.	Job: Only vehicle to earn money. Earning money perceived as a way to become independent, gain social acceptance and self-esteem.
	To work is to gain self-confidence	Job: Should be enjoyable and flexible, a hobby to pass time.	
		Interest was not in earning income.	
Role Model Images	Self-confident, independent but not tough. Good relationship with family. Nice environment and surroundings.	Good mother figure. Happy family. Children playing. Husband and wife.	Pretty, youthful, well-dressed. Romantic and relaxing life.
			Nice environment and surroundings.
			Career women type only prominent among younger, white-coller workers.

Source: Based on in-depth focus groups.

	Japan	China
Average retail unit price US$	$25.00	$9.00
Average MKC wholesale unit price	$12.50	$4.50
Cost of goods	$ 2.30	$1.20
Freight and duty	$ 0.75	$1.28
Gross margin	$ 9.45	$2.02
Product development costs/year	$ 0.9 million	$0.1 million
Promotion and advertising costs/year	$ 3.0 million	$0.4 million
Management overhead/year	$ 0.4 million	$0.25 million
Start-up investment costs	$10.0 million	$2.0 million

Real Madrid Club de Fútbol

In Spain it is easier to change spouses, political party or religion than it is to change soccer club. In soccer, a fan is a fan for life. The fan's relationship to Real Madrid is one of passion.

Real Madrid manager

In July 2003, Real Madrid, a 101-year-old member-owned soccer[1] club with an estimated 93 million fans worldwide, introduced its newest star player, David Beckham, a 28-year-old midfielder and international fashion icon. Over 1,000 journalists attended the 11 a.m. press conference in Madrid, Spain, which was timed to make the evening news broadcasts in Asia, where Beckham was particularly popular.[2] The event had the world's second-largest live TV audience ever, after Princess Diana's funeral. A Spanish journalist described Beckham's €35 million[3] transfer to Real Madrid from rival club U.K. Manchester United as "one of the most important things to have happened in Spain in a decade." The U.K.'s *Sun* newspaper set up a help line for distraught British fans.[4] The day of the press conference, Real Madrid sold 8,000 Beckham jerseys at €62 to €78 each.[5] A month later, Real Madrid capitalized on Beckham's popularity in Asia with a 17-day club tour featuring four matches through China, Hong Kong, Thailand, and Japan. The tour netted the club about €8 million.[6]

This case was prepared by Professor John Quelch and Professor José Luis Nueno with the assistance of Carin-Isabel Knoop.

Copyright © 2004 by the President and Fellows of Harvard College. Harvard Business School case 9-504-063.

The worldwide coverage and financial impact of Beckham's transfer symbolized Real Madrid's transformation and growing global reach. They grew out of the team's celebrated history as "the best soccer club of the 20th century"[7] and the actions taken by Florentino Pérez, a well-known Spanish businessman elected club president in June 2000, and his team of professional managers. Pérez had promised to turn around the club's finances, bring in world-class talent, and extend the club's brand around the world through multiple channels. Revenues, at €138 million in FY 2001, were forecast at €233 million for FY 2004 and €304 million for FY 2005.[8] In 2003, Real Madrid was the world's fourth-wealthiest professional soccer club by turnover (see Exhibit 1). The 29-time Spanish national and nine-time European champions[9] consistently appeared among top soccer clubs named in a worldwide survey.[10] Real Madrid also fielded seven soccer superstars: Raul, Figo, Zidane, Roberto Carlos, Ronaldo, Casillas, and Beckham. The June 2004 presidential election would amount to a referendum on the club's transformation as well as the sustainability of the business model Pérez and his management team had built.

---

1 The Americans called the game "soccer." In most other countries it was referred to as "football." The case uses the word "soccer."

2 Stefano Hatfield, "As Becks Suits Up for Spain, Real Action Happens in Stores," *Advertising Age*, July 21, 2003, p. 20, available from Proquest, accessed January 3, 2004. Five hundred journalists were allowed inside.

3 €1 = $0.85 at July 11, 2003.

4 Hatfield.

5 Emma Daly, "Real Madrid Learns to Win Off the Field," *International Herald Tribune*, August 15, 2003, available from Factiva.

6 <http://www1.chinadaily.com.cn/en/doc/2003-07/28/content_249783.htm>, accessed March 30, 2004.

7 As recognized in 2000 by soccer's governing body, the Fédération Internationale de Football Association.

8 The fiscal year in Spain ran from January 1 to December 31.

9 Real Madrid championship titles included the European Cup (1956-60, 1966, 1998, 2000); the Spanish Cup (1905–08, 1917, 1934, 1936, 1946–47, 1962, 1970, 1974–75, 1980, 1982, 1989, 1993); and the Spanish League (1932–33, 1954–55, 1957–58, 1961–65, 1967–69, 1972, 1975–76, 1978–80, 1986–90, 1995, 1997).

10 The survey was conducted by Landor, an international identity consulting and design firm.

Exhibit 1 Ranking of Top 15 Professional Soccer Clubs by 2003 Income

Position (prior-year position)	Club	Income (€ m)
1 (1)	Manchester United	251.4
2 (2)	Juventus	218.3
3 (4)	AC Milan	200.2
4 (6)	Real Madrid	192.6
5 (3)	Bayern Munich	162.7
6 (12)	Internazionale Milan	162.4
7 (8)	Arsenal	149.6
8 (5)	Liverpool	149.4
9 (13)	Newcastle United	138.9
10 (7)	Chelsea	133.8
11 (10)	AS Roma	132.4
12 (15)	Borussia Dortmund	124.0
13 (9)	Barcelona	123.4
14 (n/a)	Schalke 04	118.6
15 (16)	Tottenham Hotspur	95.6

Source: <http://www.presseportal.de>, accessed April 14, 2004.

THE BEAUTIFUL GAME

Soccer was the world's most popular sport. Simple rules and minimal equipment made it highly accessible. Over 240 million people played at least once a week.[11] Most children around the world kicked a soccer ball, even if it meant making balls out of rags. It was also a symbol of national pride. After the 2002 World Cup, the Mexican president wore a Mexican team T-shirt at a press conference.

The game, fielding 10 players at a time and a goalie, had two 45-minute halves of constant action, split by a 15-minute halftime. In elimination games, a tie led to overtime, lasting a maximum of two 15-minute periods, with a conditional sudden-death rule (the team that was scored upon still got a chance to tie the game). If no winner emerged after overtime, there was a penalty shoot-out. Referees could extend any half or period at their discretion to allow for interruptions in play due to injuries, for example. These extensions rarely exceeded five minutes. Playing time was more predictable than, say, that of American football games, which could last up to three hours (the usual TV schedule slot) due to stoppages.

A soccer club's reputation depended on its great games and players and the championships won. Its strength depended on its personnel and financial position. The health of a soccer club brand depended on

---

11 <http://images.fifa.com/images/pdf/IP-199_01E_big-count.pdf>, accessed January 8, 2004.

both dimensions. Like all brands, it could not be all things to all people and had to balance its ingredient brands (players) and the master brand (the club). Clubs had to reconcile the needs and expectations of grass-roots fans (who wanted competition) and brand advocates (who sought to affiliate with a certain lifestyle). The core promise behind a soccer brand was victory and/or a good show. Soccer's utility included excitement, a sensation of belonging, escapism, and competition. "We turn down the lights and people dream," said José Angel Sánchez, Real Madrid's marketing general manager.

Cities often lent their name and flair to local soccer teams. Madrid, as Spain's sunny capital and with over 3.5 million inhabitants (about 8% of the country's population), was a major cultural and business metropolis. Over 6 million tourists visited Madrid each year (some just to see Real Madrid play), and over 50 million tourists visited Spain each year (one of the world's three most visited countries).[12] In contrast, Manchester United hailed from a rainy, industrial British city with 390,000 inhabitants (in a country of over 59 million inhabitants).[13] The United Kingdom had 24 million tourists every year.[14]

In Europe, the big-five soccer countries were England, France, Germany, Italy, and Spain. In the Americas, the three majors were Argentina, Brazil, and Mexico, followed by the United States (1994 World Cup host), where soccer enjoyed a growing franchise with the Hispanic population and teenagers. About 75% of Latin Americans and 50% of all Europeans were interested in televised soccer. Only in the United States and Japan was soccer not the most watched televised sport. TV coverage of the 2002 World Cup (soccer's major international competition, held every four years) reached 213 countries, with over 41,000 hours of programming and a cumulative audience of 28.8 billion viewers over 25 match days.[15] (See Exhibit 2 for more data on the 2002 World Cup.) In comparison, the U.S. Super Bowl reached around 130 million U.S. viewers and 750 million worldwide. Worldwide TV viewership at the Athens Olympic Games in summer 2004 was expected to peak at 4 billion (437 hours of events).[16]

THE BUSINESS OF SOCCER

Organization

The Fédération Internationale de Football Association (FIFA), founded in Paris in 1904, established a unified set of rules regulating its 204-member national organizations. Six confederations enforced FIFA regulations and oversaw competition at the regional level. The Union of European Football Associations (UEFA) served as the governing body for Europe's 52 national associations. The Olympics-style FIFA World Cup competition, held every four years, was limited to "national selection" teams composed of the best players from each country.

European professional soccer focused on the UEFA's seasonal competitions, most importantly the European Champions League.[17] Top clubs from UEFA national associations participated in a series of elimination rounds, culminating at the end of the September–May season in the continent's most prestigious match, the European Cup Final.[18] Several other major international competitions, including the UEFA Cup and the UEFA European Cup, were

---

Exhibit 2	Data on the 2002 World Cup

Item	Volume
Official sponsors	15
FIFA revenues from sponsorship	€ 590 million
Cumulative TV audience	6 billion
Revenues from TV rights	€ 889 million
Impact in profits	2.2% GNP of Korea; 0.6% GNP of Japan

Source: Adapted from "El Mundial mas caro empieza a rodar," *Expansión Directo*, May 30, 2002.

---

12 <http://www.town-guides.unispain.com/Facts.htm>, accessed February 4, 2004.

13 <http://www.infoplease.com/ipa/A0108078.html>, accessed February 5, 2004.

14 <http://www.englandsnorthwest.com/englandsnorthwest_news/facts_and_figures/>, accessed February 3, 2004.

15 Defined as sum of total estimated viewers for each match. "FIFA World Cup and Television," *InfoPlus*, FIFA Web site, <http://images.fifa.com/images/pdf/IP-401_06E_TV.pdf>, accessed January 8, 2004.

16 Douglas S. Looney, *The Christian Science Monitor*, July 21, 2000.

17 The "European Cup," as it was commonly known, originated in 1955 as the European Champions Club's Cup and changed format and name to the UEFA Champions League in 1993. UEFA Web site, <http://www.uefa.com>, accessed January 9, 2004.

18 <http://www.uefa.com/competitions/ucl/CompetitionInfo/index.html>, accessed March 24, 2004.

open to lower-ranking national clubs. Some big soccer clubs lobbied for the creation of a European super league resembling major U.S. sports leagues such as the National Football League.[19]

In Europe, soccer clubs organized into leagues that often negotiated on behalf of their member clubs for marketing rights. The UEFA negotiated such rights for the European Champions League.[20] Most clubs were free to independently establish prices, market games, and adopt competitive strategies. Some of the bigger clubs, such as Real Madrid or Manchester United, negotiated marketing rights on their own behalf. Furthermore, European clubs (except the British soccer leagues) did not engage in the revenue sharing typical of U.S. sports. In U.S. soccer, for instance, TV revenues from national broadcasts were shared equally among teams, and gate receipts were split 60:40 between home and visiting teams. In Europe, the home team usually retained 100% of gate receipts.[21]

European soccer followed an open-league system: clubs could be promoted or demoted between the premier and secondary national leagues according to performance. Even within premier leagues, clubs often varied greatly in terms of wealth and prestige. Unlike the U.S. sports model generally characterized by some redistribution of economic resources and player talent to maintain competitive balance, European soccer had relatively few regulations to interfere with free market principles. In Europe, the handful of soccer clubs that could afford the star players easily dominated the sport on the playing field, in the media, and in the marketplace (see Exhibit 3). Players with strong scoring power dominated player rankings thanks to greater visibility and name recognition. This carried over to their clubs. In turn, player name recognition depended on clubs getting into the top competitions and winning championships. In 2004, players from Argentina and Brazil topped global player lists, but the most consistently cited player was Real Madrid's Zinedine Zidane, a French national.

Some observers worried that player imports suppressed the development of local talent. Player-exporting countries (such as Brazil and Argentina), in turn, complained that the globalization of the soccer labor market robbed their countries of talent. In 1961 Brazil even classified its soccer superstar Pelé as a national treasure so that he could not be sold to a foreign team.[22]

Professional Soccer Club Management

In the 1990s, European professional soccer had transitioned from the traditional business model emphasizing gate receipts and local corporate sponsorships to a strategy of maximizing merchandising and television revenues, and in some cases stock values, on an international basis.

Manchester United, master of the new globalization and commercialization model with 6 million U.K. supporters and 45 million supporters worldwide, was a club that Pérez openly emulated. Its commercial strategy involved brand recognition among supporter niches, segmented by age, and the development of subbrands and products targeted to each segment. "Fred the Red" (red was the team color) appealed mainly to children on the premise that fans chose team colors during childhood and usually remained loyal to this choice over their lifetime. Products included soccer balls, alarms, crayons, watches, sleepwear, T-shirts, and children's accessories. The "MUFC" brand appealed to teenagers with attributes of rebelliousness, friendship, nerve, and audacity. Products included backpacks, caps, binders, and stopwatches. The "Red Devil" line targeted adults with products that were to be perceived as unique and evoke status, leadership, and winning, such as elegant, quality shirts and sweaters.

These brands were featured on the team's Web site, manutd.com. The Web site was part of the club's value, with each unique user in 2000 ascribed an estimated lifetime value of €1,340 by a major bank. On this basis, the value of the manutd.com brand was estimated at €354.4 million. The value was based on the expectation that the site could create a unique content library that would generate high loyalty and repeated visits to the site.

19 Stefan Szymanski, "There must be losers for a thrilling contest," *The Financial Times*, August 1, 2003.

20 Sports leagues in the United States often negotiated national TV rights and market sponsorships for the "official" league soft drink or airline. Each club was separately owned and managed.

21 Waldimir Andreff and Paul D. Staudohar, "European and US Sports Business Models," in Carlos Pestana Barros, et al., *Transatlantic Sport: The Comparative Economics of North American and European Sports* (Cheltenham, UK: Edward Elgar Publishing, 2002), pp. 39–40.

22 Franklin Foer, "Soccer vs McSoccer," *Foreign Policy*, January–February 2004, p. 33.

Exhibit 3

Exhibit 3 — Leading Soccer Clubs as per Survey of Soccer Fans in Selected Countries

Rank	Argentina	Brazil	Mexico	Latin America	United States	Japan	England	France
1	Boca Juniors	Corinthians	Real Madrid	Real Madrid	Manchester United	Parma	Manchester United	Real Madrid
2	River Plate	São Paulo	América	Corinthians	Real Madrid	Milan	Liverpool	Manchester United
3	Manchester United	Flamengo	Cruz Azul	Barcelona	DC United	Real Madrid	Real Madrid	Juventus
4	Roma	Palmeiras	Boca Juniors	São Paulo	Milan	Roma	Barcelona	Paris Saint Germain
5	Real Madrid	Inter Milan	Guadalajara	Palmeiras	Barcelona	Juventus	Arsenal	Olympique Marseille

Source: Adapted from "Energizing the Brand through the ImagePower of Football: Scoring with Sponsorship." Landor Associates, July 2002, p. 18.

Exhibit 3 — Leading Soccer Clubs as per Survey of Soccer Fans in Selected Countries (continued)

Rank	Germany	Italy	Spain	Europe
1	Bayern München	Real Madrid	Real Madrid	Real Madrid
2	Real Madrid	Juventus	Barcelona	Manchester United
3	Manchester United	Manchester United	Manchester United	Bayern München
4	Barcelona	Milan	Bayern München	Juventus
5	Inter Milan	Inter Milan	Milan	Barcelona

Source: Adapted from "Energizing the Brand through the ImagePower of Football: Scoring with Sponsorship." Landor Associates, July 2002, p. 18.

In 1998, a subsidiary, Manchester United International, was launched to develop business in Asia and the United States. Activities in Asia included preseason tours and a shop and coffeehouse chain in southeastern Asia. It ran restaurants under the brand "Theater of Dreams" in the Middle East. "Theater of Dreams" was the club's most international brand, a reference to a former player's description of the club's Old Trafford stadium. In 1998 the club also opened its first international store, in Dublin Airport, catering to its numerous Irish fans. A Gatwick Airport store followed in 1999.

Expenses

Professional soccer clubs had to cover fixed costs and finance talent acquisition and retention. Professional soccer clubs often had to build and maintain their own stadiums, but stadium leasing, in which clubs paid a rental fee plus a cut of the gate receipts, was also common, more so on the continent than in the United Kingdom.

Players were developed and transferred in return for fees, with some clubs, particularly in France, specializing as player breeding grounds for the leading teams. In 2001, total player salary costs among leading clubs averaged 125% of revenue in Italy, 85% in Spain, and 75% in England.[23] Some annual salaries reached €15 million.[24] Skyrocketing transfer fees resulted from competition to lure the best players. Real Madrid paid a €59.8 million transfer fee to FC Barcelona for Luis Figo in July 2000 and a record €75.5 million to Juventus in Italy for Zidane in 2001. In the 1990s, player wages outpacing revenues bankrupted a fifth of the British National League clubs. In Germany, clubs reduced salaries and sold players. One even sold its stadium. Insolvency pushed Italy's Fiorentina, one of Europe's biggest clubs, to the lowest division.

A 1995 European Court of Justice ruling (the Bosman case) outlawed the payment-of-transfer fees for players whose contracts with their clubs had expired, turning players into free agents. It also lifted the limit of three foreign players per national league club (true for all EU-born players, but some limits remained on other nationalities),[25]

further heightening international competition among clubs for the best players. "It's all about money," said an observer. "Players have moved from being athletes to being brands."[26] Jorge Valdano, Real Madrid's general manager for sports and a former professional soccer player, noted, "They are an industry in and of themselves. In a team context, this requires careful management of each individual's prestige. In my time, soccer players were just soccer players." Player transfers were major news. Monthly references to Real Madrid in nonsports media spiked from 50–100 per month to over 250 during Ronaldo's transfer.

In late 2002, the G14—14 leading European soccer clubs from France, Germany, Italy, Portugal, Spain, the Netherlands, and the United Kingdom—struck a deal to control player wages. In what Pérez termed "a highly important gentlemen's agreement," G14 members vowed to limit their total staff costs to 70% of turnover and to try to link players' pay to performance.[27] Real Madrid came in at 72% in total staff costs per turnover in 2003, falling to 57% in 2004 and forecast at 46% in 2005.[28]

Revenues

For most top clubs, match-day income accounted for about a fourth of revenues, with sponsorship and merchandising revenues making up the balance. (Exhibit 4 shows Real Madrid's revenue sources.) Between 1996 and 2000, according to Real Madrid managers, revenues for the major European soccer leagues rose 22% in England and France, 24% in Italy, and 28% in Spain. These depended largely on a club's participation and performance in major competitive events such as the European Champions League. Manchester United, for example, drew 73% of its 2002 earnings before interest and taxes (EBIT) from Champions League-related income, including match sales, television rights, and prize money.

Match-day gate receipts continued to be an important but declining source of revenue.[29] Spanish soccer was less affected by this trend thanks to season ticket sales. In an 80,000-seat stadium, Real Madrid season ticket holders held 58,000 seats and a further 4,000 seats were reserved as

23 "Business: Players and Gentlemen: European football clubs," *The Economist*, November 9, 2002, p. 82, available from Proquest.

24 Mary Canniffe, "The Business of Soccer," *Accountancy Ireland*, August 2003, p. 17, available from Proquest.

25 The former quota system had limited national league teams to three foreign players, plus two more if the foreign players in question had played for five consecutive years in the host country.

26 Erin White and Maureen Tkacik, "Spend It Like Beckham," *The Wall Street Journal*, June 19, 2003, p. B1.

27 "Business: Players and gentlemen," *The Economist*, November 9, 2002, p. 82, available from Proquest.

28 Julian Easthope, "Man. Utd.," UBS Warburg Global Equity Research, May 30, 2002, from Investext.

29 Waldimir Andreff and Paul D. Staudohar, "European and US Sports Business Models," p. 29.

Real Madrid Revenue Sources and Net Profit (in € millions), 2000–2001 to 2004–2005 (forecast)

Season	2000–2001	2001–2002	2002–2003	2003–2004 (est.)	2004–2005 (forecast)
Match day	42	46	58	62	68
International competitions	12	13	25	19	29
Broadcast and pay-TV	45	47	47	69	65
Marketing	39	46	63	83	142
Total revenue	138	152	193	233	304
Earnings before interest, taxes, depreciation, and amortization	-23	-33	1	42	71

Source: Company documents.

Exhibit 4b Shifts in Real Madrid's Revenue Streams

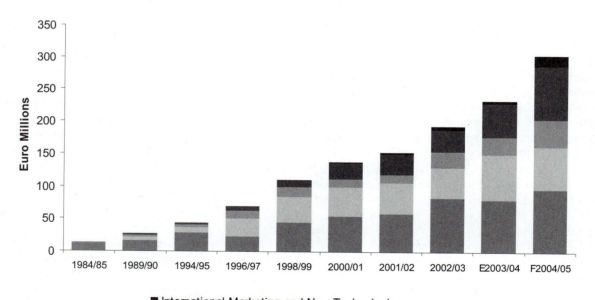

- International Marketing and New Technologies
- Merchandising
- Sponsorship
- Broadcast and Pay-TV
- Match Day/Competitions

Source: Company documents

Note: Yearly income distribution is representative and does not reflect precise data.

boxes and VIP seats. The balance was for sale each match. For some clubs, selling VIP packages coincided with the desire to optimize match-day revenues via the construction of more modern and comfortable stadiums. A VIP package could include champagne upon arrival, a four-course meal, official reserved seats in block, TV and video to watch other matches, and reserved parking.

Merchandising included the sales of branded goods such as soccer jerseys, mugs, caps, and watches. European clubs had long engaged in basic merchandising, but modern management teams brought in specialists to promote a larger variety of merchandise to a wider geographic market. In the 1970s and 1980s merchandising became seen as a stand-alone profitable business line instead of a somewhat haphazard way to increase team support.

Merchandising income ranged from 5% of total revenues for a typical national league team to over 20% for top merchandisers. Star players were crucial to generating merchandise sales. Real Madrid sold 480,000 Zidane soccer jerseys in the year following his 2001 transfer.[30] On the weekend of the Beckham transfer announcement, some 350,000 Real Madrid jerseys sold in Britain.[31] But licensing was complex. A branded item could not be too far removed from soccer (e.g., a tablecloth or wallet) or prohibitive for the fan base. Clubs had to strike the right balance between availability and scarcity and confront piracy. For example, during the 2003 Real Madrid Asia tour, counterfeit $4 T-shirts flooded China, cutting Real Madrid sales and disappointing sponsors such as Adidas.

Sponsorship from major corporations could account for up to 15% of a top club's revenue. In 2002, Nike, for example, signed a 13-year, €460 million contract to outfit Manchester United.[32] Vodafone paid the club €51.5 million to place its logo on player uniforms for four years. "With their partners' help," Manchester United's director of communication noted, "clubs can develop a better understanding of their fans. [And the fan base is] the key to growing existing business and developing new revenue streams."[33]

In choosing a player to support, sponsors had to find the right combination of attributes: age, playing position, nationality, career history, personality and reputation, and playing style (e.g., leadership, persistence, flair, aggressiveness). Some clubs received a portion of players' sponsorship earnings. For example, at Manchester United, Beckham was able to keep all of his personal endorsement earnings (estimated at over €8 million per year), but the deal with Real Madrid required him to turn 50% of these earnings over to the club.[34] Despite this constraint players felt that total earnings and prestige were enhanced by a Real Madrid affiliation.

TV rights displaced gate receipts as the single largest source of revenue for many clubs in the 1990s.[35] Deregulation of the media industry in Europe in the 1990s resulted in competitive bidding for TV rights, providing an important new revenue stream for most teams. (Exhibit 5 shows FIFA World Cup TV rights revenues from 1982 to 2002.) Before deregulation, soccer clubs had feared that the fees offered for live TV coverage by monopoly broadcasters would not offset the potential loss in stadium ticket revenue due to broadcasting. Unfortunately, high fees paid for match rights contributed to the financial collapse in March and April 2002 of two leading providers of soccer on European pay-TV, Germany's Kirch and the U.K.'s ITV Digital. Bankruptcies and media consolidation then led to declining television rights revenues for European clubs, prompting several leading national leagues to form their own television channels.[36] In 2004, EU regulation prohibited the collective selling of TV rights. No single company could own all of a country's soccer TV rights.

Public Share Offers

In 1999, shares of 33 soccer clubs in six countries were listed on stock exchanges.[37] By 2002, 24 British clubs were trading shares in England and Scotland and the largest, Manchester United, reached a market capitalization of over €576 million. The second-largest traded club, Italy's

30 Canniffe, p. 17.

31 Ibid.

32 Maureen Tkacik, "Shoe Strategy: Nike is Gambling Soccer Will Become Its New Basketball," *The Asian Wall Street Journal*, May 7, 2002, p. A1.

33 "Man U brand booming despite dip in form," *The Turkish Daily News*, September 22, 2002.

34 Adrian Curtis, "All-Star Cast Makes Real World's Richest Club," *The Evening Standard*, June 6, 2003, p. A83, available from Factiva.

35 Waldimir Andreff and Paul D. Staudohar, "European and US Sports Business Models," pp. 29–31.

36 "Business: Players and gentlemen," *The Economist*, November 9, 2002, p. 82, available from Proquest.

37 Waldimir Andreff and Paul D. Staudohar, "European and US Sports Business Models," p. 32.

Exhibit 5   FIFA Revenues from Selling TV Rights to the World Championships, 1982–2002

Year	Country	Revenues (millions €)
1982	Spain	24.04
1986	México	30.05
1990	Italy	54.09
1994	United States	66.11
1998	France	138.23
2002	Japan and South Korea	1,683.00[a]
2006	Germany	NA

Source: Adapted from "Fútbol y Televisión matrimonio en crises," El Pais, April 14, 2002.
[a]Includes rights for 2006 World Championship.

Exhibit 6   Market Values of Europe's Leading Publicly Traded Soccer Franchises, 2002

Company/Country	Market Cap ($ million)
Manchester United/England	466
Juventus/Italy	241
Rangers/Scotland	139
Arsenal/England	135
Lazio/Italy	111
Roma/Italy	93
Ajax/Netherlands	73
Borussia Dortmund/Germany	58
Newcastle United/England	50
Parken/Denmark	49

Source: <http://www.forbes.com/global/2002/0708/043.html>, accessed March 2, 2004. Originally published July 8, 2002 by *Forbes Global*.
Reprinted by permission of Forbes Magazine © 2004 Forbes Inc.

Juventus, sold 37% of its share capital for €164 million in a 2001 initial public offering (IPO).[38] (See Exhibit 6.)

Top clubs were initially attractive to investors because of high revenue forecasts and operating profits from gate receipts, sponsorship deals, and TV rights. But investors soon worried about club expenses skyrocketing.[39] Owners seemed more interested in league standings than shareholder value. "There are no profits and the team's money all goes toward new players," a financial analyst said. "Unfortunately, most owners spend more on players than what their clubs take in."[40] According to Manchester United's chief executive, clubs had not "changed their management structure. They have not demonstrated that they can manage their costs . . . [or] be anything other than a football club. [Investors don't] like great peaks and troughs and football as an industry gives you that."[41] Soccer, said an industry observer, was "a lot more volatile than for mainstream companies and the capitalization [could] drop like a stone after one bad season."[42]

Being listed added another dimension to player transfers. In deciding to transfer Beckham, for example, Manchester United ran the risk of alienating its shareholders and fans, many of whom were also shareholders, and possibly damaging the share price.[43] However, because Beckham's contract was due to expire in 2005, at which point he could have walked away free of charge,[44] selling him earlier provided Manchester United with a transfer fee that could be reinvested in the team.

Professional Soccer in Spain

Spain had over 10,000 soccer clubs (three professional national leagues with 20, 22, and 80 clubs each) with nearly 620,000 players. About 1,200 of them were professional players. The two largest clubs (Real Madrid and FC Barcelona) had won two-thirds of all the national championships of the league and 39% of all the cups.[45]

(Exhibit 7 shows the structure of soccer competitions in Europe and Spain.) Real Madrid's budget for the 2002–2003 season was €293 million, FC Barcelona's €171 million, and Valencia's €90.5 million.[46] Personnel costs accounted for 75% of professional club expenses in Spain. All in all (taxes, Social Security contributions, value-added taxes), soccer added €1 billion to Spain's government coffers every year.

Historically, soccer clubs were not-for-profit institutions backed by members and local authorities. Poor management and accountability bankrupted most of them. By 1990 the situation was unsustainable, and a new regulation was passed forcing all clubs without a solid balance sheet to become a *Sociedad Anónima Deportiva* (SAD), a legal structure similar to that of a U.K. public limited company. SAD shares did not have to be publicly traded. Out of 20 first-division clubs, only FC Barcelona, Real Madrid, Atlético de Bilbao, and Atlético de Osasuna escaped the requirement. No Spanish soccer club had gone public as of early 2004. The best candidates were clubs with strong brand identities and a wide international fan base. Financial analysts believed Real Madrid and FC Barcelona, each valued at over €450 million, to be the only Spanish clubs likely to interest investors.[47]

In 2003, over half of all Spaniards considered themselves soccer fans; nearly 80% of Spain's men were fans, versus 28% of the country's women. About 60% of soccer fans in Spain followed Real Madrid, and about 30% of Real Madrid spectators were women. Highest fan concentration occurred in the north and northwest of Spain and in cities with fewer than 50,000 inhabitants. Four soccer-focused daily newspapers in Spain reached a combined circulation of over 5.3 million. The top publication, *Marca*, owned by the international media company Pearson Plc, captured half of these readers. In addition, over 2 million people tuned in each day to sports radio

38 Mike Elkin, "IPO Dreams for Spain's Football Teams?" *The Daily Deal* (New York), January 22, 2002, available from Proquest.

39 In 2001, Manchester United's share price fell 38%, Arsenal's 33%, Lazio's 49%, and Roma's 51%. Mike Elkin, "IPO Dreams for Spain's Football Teams?" *The Daily Deal* (New York), January 22, 2002, available from Proquest.

40 Quoted in Mike Elkin, "IPO Dreams for Spain's Football Teams?" *The Daily Deal* (New York), January 22, 2002, available from Proquest.

41 Canniffe, p. 17.

42 Phil Minshull, Spanish football correspondent for *L'Agence France-Presse*, quoted in Mike Elkin, "IPO Dreams for Spain's Football Teams?" *The Daily Deal* (New York), January 22, 2002, available from Proquest.

43 Canniffe, p. 17.

44 Erin White and Maureen Tkacik, "Spend It Like Beckham—Competing Corporate Interests Complicated Madrid Move; 'It's All About the Money,'" *The Wall Street Journal*, June 19, 2003, p. B1.

45 Angel Agudo y Francisco Toyo, *Marketing de Fútbol*, Editorial Piramide, ESIC 2003.

46 Ibid.

47 Share prices of soccer clubs were influenced by the team's match performances. Canniffe, p. 17.

Exhibit 7   Structure of Soccer Competitions in Spain and Europe

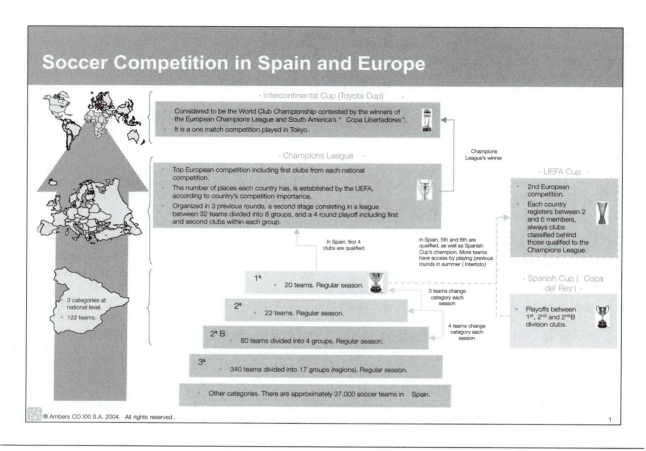

Soccer Competition in Spain and Europe

- Intercontinental Cup (Toyota Cup) -

Considered to be the World Club Championship contested by the winners of the European Champions League and South America's " Copa Libertadores".

It is a one match competition played in Tokyo.

- Champions League -

Top European competition including first clubs from each national competition.

The number of places each country has, is established by the UEFA, according to country's competition importance.

Organized in 3 previous rounds, a second stage consisting in a league between 32 teams divided into 8 groups, and a 4 round playoff including first and second clubs within each group.

Champions League's winner

- UEFA Cup -

2nd European competition.

Each country registers between 2 and 6 members, always clubs classified behind those qualified to the Champions League.

In Spain, first 4 clubs are qualified

In Spain, 5th and 6th are qualified, as well as Spanish Cup's champion. More teams have access by playing previous rounds in summer (Intertoto)

1ª   • 20 teams. Regular season.

3 teams change category each season

- Spanish Cup (Copa del Rey) -

Playoffs between 1st, 2nd and 2ndB division clubs.

2ª   • 22 teams. Regular season.

4 teams change category each season

2ª B   • 80 teams divided into 4 groups. Regular season.

3ª   • 340 teams divided into 17 groups (regions). Regular season.

• Other categories. There are approximately 37.000 soccer teams in Spain.

3 categories at national level.
• 122 teams.

1

Source: © Ambers & Co.

shows focused on soccer, and the top-rated broadcast on Spanish TV each year was the Real Madrid versus FC Barcelona match.

TV rights for Spain's professional soccer league were considered to be a matter of public interest, which made it illegal to sell all the matches to a single broadcaster, whether open or pay per view. The rights were therefore sold on an alternating basis to national TV stations (pay or open broadcast), regional TV stations, independently, or into a federation of regional broadcasters.

THE REAL MADRID STORY

In 1902, a group of Spanish soccer fans officially founded the Madrid Foot Ball Club. In October 1905, the team had its first international game, against Galia Sport from Paris. In 1920, the King of Spain granted the title of Royal ("Real") to the club. By 1927, the team was touring the United States, led by Santiago Bernabeu, one of its all-time top stars. In 1930, Ricardo Zamora, another star player, joined the team for 150,000 pesetas, then a fortune. His fame consolidated the team's reputation.

A major turning point in the club's history came with Bernabeu's 1943 unanimous appointment as its president. One year into his tenure, Bernabeu started building Spain's largest coliseum, in Chamartín, financed with bonds sold to fans. Upon its 1947 opening, the Santiago Bernabeu Stadium (capacity of 75,000) was rated by the international press as the best in Europe.

Willing to pay whatever was necessary for the best players, Bernabeu had by the early 1950s built a powerful team in search of challenges beyond the Spanish League. Real Madrid set the standard for championship soccer, winning the first five European Cup competitions from 1955 to 1960. By 1960, television coverage of the European Cup Final had made Real Madrid the world's best-known soccer team. A sixth European Cup win followed in 1966.

After Bernabeu died in 1978, the club declined for nearly two decades, on the field and financially. In 1995, Lorenzo Sanz took over as president. Under Sanz, players were regularly sold to cover operating losses. To reduce the club's significant debt, Sanz sold off several operating core assets, including stadium exploitation rights and media rights. The club gradually recovered on the field, winning a seventh European Cup in 1998. In 2000, Pérez defeated Sanz for the club presidency (after the club captured its eighth European Cup) and delivered on his campaign promise to woo superstar player Luis Figo from FC Barcelona. Pérez also announced his intentions to further sanitize the club's finances.

The Socios

Real Madrid's members were its owners. "The club is not the property of anyone," noted Manuel Sierra Redondo, presidential general manager, "but at the same time, it is the property of everyone." *Socios abonados*, cardholding members who paid their dues, had the right to go to the field every game. The *socios* got discounts on seats and a vote to elect club presidents for a four-year term.[48] For Spanish League games, season ticket holders held 58,000 seats, paying between €120 and €1,000 per year, with an average around €370 per year. A total of 31,000 out of the 58,000 league season ticket holders could attend UEFA and King's Cup games by paying a 30% premium over league game prices. *Socios non-abonados* benefited from some price discounts on available tickets and merchandise, attended two matches per year, and received the club's magazine.

A supporter could be defined as a nondues-paying member who attended matches whenever he or she could by purchasing admission tickets. A fan listed the team as his or her favorite, although they could be *socios* of another club. If their own team played against Real Madrid, they would support the local team but would support Real Madrid when it played UEFA games. Real Madrid also encouraged the organization of groups that brought together local Real Madrid fans. These fans would attend matches together and benefit from discounts on games. Real Madrid also had fan clubs all over the globe. "This system allows us to spread Madridismo all over the world and also serve as a marketing vehicle for Real Madrid," Redondo noted. "In general, the most important thing is getting information to the members. It is imperative that members feel involved with the business of the club. We're always creating new features to do that."

TRANSFORMING THE REAL

When they arrived in mid-2000, Pérez and his new management team felt that the club's operations and marketing approach did not match its reputation in sports. Carlos Martínez de Albornoz, corporate managing director responsible for finance, administration, control, legal affairs, and human resources, noted that the club's mission was not clear and not deemed important: "In soccer, there is a lot of passion. The biggest challenge is to be dispassionate in managing the organization. Today a modern soccer club needs to have a professional organization that makes decisions with the head, not the heart."

Pérez set out to build a professional organization. A successful entrepreneur with experience in politics, Pérez was running the ACS Construction Company upon his election to club president.[49] "We structured ourselves as a company and began to think of ourselves as content providers," Martínez de Albornoz noted. "This was an authentic revolution." Real Madrid's executive team comprised the corporate general director (Carlos Martínez de Albornoz), marketing (José Angel Sánchez), sport management (Jorge Valdano), and president's office (Manuel Redondo), all of whom worked with Pérez and reported to a board of directors. In early 2004, Real Madrid had 384 permanent staff, 230 players in all leagues (including youth leagues), 170 part-time staff, and 62 other associates, for a total staff of

---

48 Until 1988 all clubs in Spain were owned by their members.

49 In 2003, ACS merged with Dragados, making Pérez president and one of the main shareholders of the new ACS Dragados, Europe's second-largest construction company (about €10 billion in revenues).

about 850. Monthly nonplayer personnel costs reached €1.4 million.

"Our vision, which Pérez articulated very clearly," Martínez de Albornoz said, "is to be the best soccer club in the world. Our mission is to nurture and project the Real Madrid brand worldwide." To that end, Real Madrid managers identified four brand value drivers: (1) size of audience; (2) frequency with which the audience engaged with the brand, as a measure of commitment; (3) sociodemographic characteristics of the audience; and (4) bridges (usually in the form of local fan associations) that could be built to link the brand and the audience.

"To transform Real Madrid we went partly against what experts were used to," noted Sánchez.

> *Soccer is over 100 years old, and it takes a while to change the rules of the game. We are showing that our strategy works. Like all great revolutions, it is based on a few simple truths. First, the best players pay for themselves. The best will deliver the best performance and the best spectacle. It will allow us to play better and better soccer. Second, Real Madrid is a brand.*[50] *And third, the product—the players and the games—is the content. Everything we do flows from this.*

The team set three interrelated goals: (1) give Real Madrid the financial flexibility to acquire talent and expand its brand reach; (2) assemble a team of top players; and (3) leverage the Real Madrid brand and content across a variety of channels.

GAINING FINANCIAL BREATHING SPACE

Right after his election, Pérez worked to obtain approval for the rezoning of the club's old training pitches (*Ciudad Deportiva*) north of Madrid's financial district, covering 120,000 square meters at the very center of the Spanish capital. About 20% of the land was sold to private developers for office buildings. The remainder was ceded to local and regional governments to build a public park and a 20,000-seat sports pavilion, netting €500 million for the club. The process took about a year.

The second major initiative was recapturing exploitation rights sold off to various operators and licensees. "Everything that had value, like perimeter signage for example, had been sold," Sánchez explained. For example, the

VIP boxes had been sold off in a 10-year contract under which Real Madrid received an annual percentage fee. Real Madrid bought the boxes back for €16 million and, by 2003, Real Madrid had refurbished and doubled the number of boxes to 200, for which there was a long waiting list. Most major Spanish companies and some multinationals owned a box. They netted Real Madrid €16 million per year. Most of the nonperimeter in-ground signage, visible only to stadium visitors, featured local companies such as banks and hospitals. These seasonal contracts were priced on a per second basis.

A third way to bolster club finances was to set up a stand-alone legal entity (*Sociedad Mixta*) to own and manage, until the 2010–2011 season, some of Real Madrid's rights except audiovisual ones, but including merchandising and licensing, sponsorships and players-image rights, distribution business, online and new technology businesses, and international development. The Sociedad Mixta, managed by the club's marketing division, contacted, negotiated with, contracted with, and invoiced all current and potential partners. It paid a percentage of its income directly to Real Madrid and enjoyed a beneficial corporate tax rate of 25%, compared with the typical one of 35%.

In October 2000, Caja Madrid (a Spanish savings and loan) paid €78.1 million for a 20% share,[51] and in February 2001 Sogecable, the leading pay-TV group in Spain with over 2 million subscribers (part of Prisa, Spain's largest media group), signed a €39.05 million deal for a 10% share. Caja Madrid subsequently sold a 7.5% share to Media Pro.[52] Rafael Roldán, president of the Madrid-based merger and acquisitions firm Ambers & Co., who helped craft the Sociedad Mixta, recalled that finding the appropriate partners was not easy but that the process was "an exciting challenge to build a story of value upon simple concepts: brand and content."

In the licensing and sponsoring area, Real Madrid pursued opportunities for all types of products. For sportswear articles Adidas held rights until 2008. Real Madrid had licenses with more than 70 companies producing over 600 products. Adidas was considered a major sponsor as was Siemens. In July 2002, Real Madrid signed a three-year contract with Siemens Mobile IC (€12 million per year for the right to feature the Siemens name on player jerseys). Secondary sponsors included Audi, Pepsi, and Telefónica.

---

[50] Real Madrid managers defined brand as any entity that was in regular communication with an audience.

[51] "Real Madrid President Says Debt Will be Eliminated This Season," *El Pais*, October 19, 2000, available from Factiva.

[52] MediaPro was a media company focused on broadcasting rights, especially in sports. It also owned the assets (i.e., the mobile units or trucks) used to broadcast the signal from stadiums to TV stations.

In 2003 Audi made 30 vehicles available to the team and club management to promote itself inside the Bernabéu stadium and publicize its new partnership using images of the entire team. Official providers included Mahou (beer), Unilever, Sanitas (medical care), Solan (water), Kraft, Viceroy (watches), and Sánchez Romero (hams). (See Exhibits 8 and 9.) Furthermore, Pérez insisted that the club receive 50% of the image rights of every player it hired.

Marketing revenue was expected to rise from €39 million in 2000–2001 to €83 million in 2003–2004 (about 33% from sponsorship and image rights, 61% from merchandising, and 5% from new technologies and international development). The forecast for 2005 was €142 million. In 2003–2004, commercial and marketing activities were forecast to account for about 36% of turnover, competitions for 8%, match-day revenues for 27% (as opposed to 100% in 1970), and TV rights about 30%. Ticketing revenues had increased 55% since 2000, and the stadium had sold out for 24 matches in a row.

ASSEMBLING THE GALÁCTICOS

The 2000 transfer of Figo from rival club FC Barcelona was part of Pérez's electoral campaign. To finance the €60 million transfer, Pérez had personally secured a €78 million loan. Pérez and his team had subsequently engineered the transfer of at least one world-class player into the Real Madrid team each year. "We are buyers more than sellers," Sánchez noted. According to Martínez de Albornoz, "Most superstars are media figures because they are good in the pitch." "*Los galácticos*," as the galaxy of international and Spanish talents at Real Madrid were known,[53] included Zidane, Beckham, Figo, Brazilian striker Ronaldo, team captain Spanish forward Raúl, and Brazilian defender Roberto Carlos as well as goalkeeper Iker Casillas. All the *galácticos* had the same annual salary. A 2004 survey of the world's top-grossing soccer players featured five Real Madrid players in the top 10.[54]

Players saw advantages to being on a star-studded team. "The responsibility here is divided among multiple

---

Exhibit 8   Real Madrid's Merchandising and Licensing Business in 2003

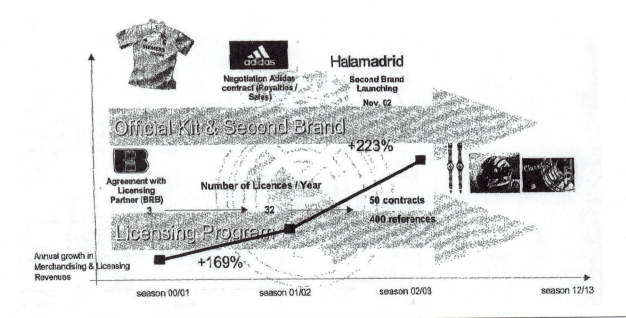

Source: Company documents.

---

53 "Beckham Blitz Sweeps Asia," *China Daily*, August 13, 2003, p. 8.
54 <http://www.forbes.com/lists/2004/03/26/cx_pm_0326playerintro.html>, accessed March 30, 2004.

Exhibit 9   Real Madrid Sponsorship and Image Rights in 2003

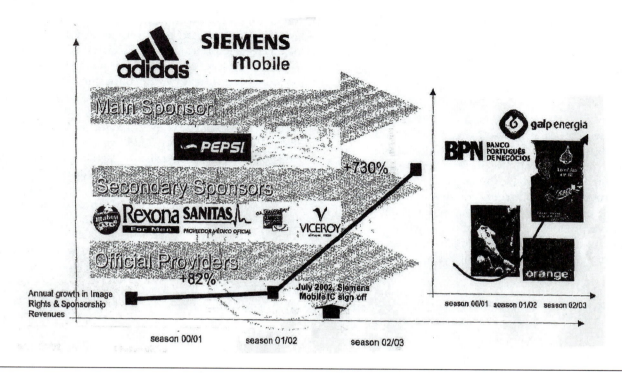

Source: Company documents.

players," Ronaldo explained. "Elsewhere it often rested entirely on my shoulders as the star of the team."[55] "The greatest players aspire to play with Real Madrid, with great talents like them," Valdano continued. "Players who join us know that they are taking a step forward, in prestige and in satisfaction as a soccer player."

MANAGING THE BRAND AND CONTENT

Some observers saw sports franchises like Real Madrid as generators of primary and premium content that offered the possibility of recurrent revenues across time, channels, and geographies. The content had value only if it generated demand that translated into revenues derived from exploitation. Real Madrid exploited various avenues to maximize revenues on its "content." Attracting and retaining star players was considered key

to this strategy. "The 'movie' we are selling," Sánchez noted, "is worth more if, say, Tom Cruise is in the lead." To understand models of successful content exploitation, Real Madrid studied Disney's leveraging of the movie *The Lion King*, which cost $50 million to make, grossed over $766 million at the box office worldwide in its first year of release, and generated over $1.5 billion in merchandising revenue within 18 months of its release. An analyst referred to such films as long-term entertainment brands, not just movies.[56]

Real Madrid saw opportunities in specialized publishing, audiovisual rights, video games and interactive applications, merchandising and official products, the Internet, video, and ticket and stadium development. (Exhibit 10 summarizes initiatives to date.) The key, Martínez de Albornoz said, "is to convert Real Madrid fans into Real Madrid customers wherever they are in the

---

55 Leslie Crawford and Jonathan Wilson, "Ronaldo's return to scoring for fun," *The Financial Times*, April 26, 2003, p. 16.

56 Quoted by Jeff Rayport and Carin-Isabel Knoop, "Disney's 'The Lion King' (A): The $2 Billion Movie," HBS Case No. 899-041 (Boston: Harvard Business School Publishing, October 14, 1998).

world." "We also want to control the content all the way to selling and distributing it," added Sánchez.

One way to do that was to expand the reach of Real Madrid Television. Real Madrid's own TV station, launched in 1999, provided 16 hours of daily coverage from the training grounds, including training, soccer and basketball matches, player interviews, and historical highlights. One of the leading thematic subscription channels in Europe, Real Madrid TV had 50,000 subscribers in 2001 (and annual revenues of €2.25 million) and 80,000 in 2004. Growth potential was enormous in Spain alone, with about 3.5 million pay-TV households. Real Madrid games were the most popular pay-per-view material in Spain.

Another channel was the club's Web site, RealMadrid.com, which had 1.5 million unique visitors each month in 2004 (28% of them in Spain, accounting for a quarter of online sales), up from 200,000 in 2001. During the 2000–2001 season 2 million pages were viewed every month; 18 million pages were forecast for the 2003–2004 season. Annual Web site revenues reached €1 million, 80% from shirt sales. The Web site featured interviews of players, live feed, and club news, usually of greatest interest to Web site visitors. Managers described the site as a community creator, also ideal for reaching more inaccessible fans. The typical Web site user was a 26-year-old single male. Advertising accounted for nearly 75% of sport Web site revenues, nearly half from sponsors. Real Madrid believed that the Internet would generate over €777 million for main European soccer clubs over 10 years. IDG estimated the cost of launching these sites at €4.75 million, with a further €10 million for annual promotion and operating expenses.

Real Madrid managers wanted the club to have a "one-on-one relationship" with each fan via mobile telephony, TV, wireless Internet, and so on. In November 2003, Real Madrid struck a significant four-year deal

Exhibit 10   Summary of Real Madrid Initiatives

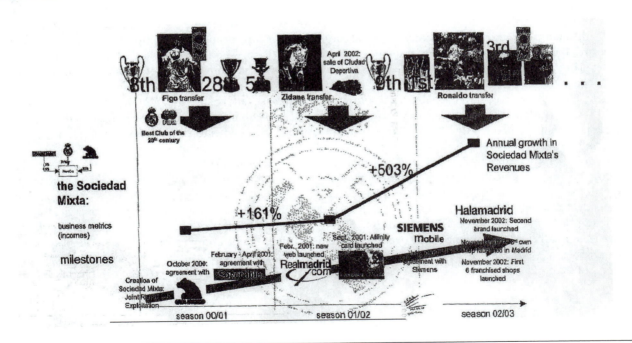

Source: Company documents.

with Spain's major telecom provider, Telefónica, to deliver Real Madrid content over Internet, broadband, and mobile services. Telefónica would provide hosting services to Real Madrid in Spain and 14 other countries. Internet game transmission was not possible. The visual rights contracts that Pérez inherited were concluded before the Internet was a significant potential distribution channel.

Fans could also keep connected and exposed to the Real Madrid brand and products through the Real Madrid stores, fan card, and magazine. As a complement to the Web site, Real Madrid managed four fully owned stores in Spain and aimed to develop a worldwide retail network, most likely through franchises. Retail revenues in 2001 reached nearly €4 million and were forecast to reach nearly €17 million for 2004. In November 2002, the club launched six franchise stores across Spain, including one in Barcelona, home of Real Madrid's main Spanish rival. Pérez also wanted to build the "Disney World of Madridismo" via a massive expansion of the club training grounds close to the Madrid Airport. Finally, under Pérez and his team, Real Madrid had invested about €100 million for the modernization of the Bernabeu.

The retail stores offered discounts to holders of the Real Madrid fan card, which was different from the core socio card, launched in October 2001 at a cost of €1.9 million. The card carried an annual fee of €19 in Spain and €38 abroad. Half of cardholders applied via the Web site. Holders received a free *Hala Madrid* subscription ("Let's Go Madrid," the club's official quarterly magazine, which reached nearly 300,0000 fans in 2004 and could also be purchased at newsstands), ticket preferences, a no-fee Visa credit card, and commercial discounts from partner companies, including financial institutions, restaurants, theme parks, and cinemas. Real Madrid had issued 190,000 cards by 2001 and was predicting 206,000 cards to be issued in 2004. "This allows Real Madrid to have members all over the world and gives the members a feeling of exclusivity," Redondo noted.

Real Madrid managers believed that these initiatives strengthened the Real Madrid brand, which in turn increased the value of Real Madrid "content." "Real Madrid is one of the best brands in the world," Pérez said. "Unlike most, it goes straight to the heart [and has] an endless list of positive values: prestige, effort, majesty, and leadership." Other values "transmitted from fathers to sons" mentioned by managers included "excellence," "fair play," "solidarity," and "sense of sacrifice."

EXPANDING INTERNATIONALLY

Expanding the brand internationally, Sánchez noted, was another key growth initiative. Like their European counterparts, Real Madrid managers saw great promise for soccer and their club in Asia, where soccer's appeal was growing fast and tours, especially by U.K. clubs, were becoming common. Newcastle United, for example, affiliated itself with the 2000–2001 Chinese league champions, a deal that included cross-promotions, some TV arrangements, and player exchanges. Clubs also gained exposure by getting their merchandise on shelves.[57] FIFA supported these developments, notably by holding the 2002 World Cup in Japan and South Korea. Soccer became the continent's most popular non-local sport, beating other imports such as baseball and basketball.[58] Pérez wanted Real Madrid to capture about 10% of the Chinese market for sports merchandise by 2013. During Real Madrid's summer 2003 Asia tour, Japanese fans spent $210,000 on club clothing at a practice session in the Tokyo Dome.[59] Real Madrid's plans in Asia included soccer academies, fan clubs, specialty shops, restaurants, and cafes.

Real Madrid's U.S. strategy was four-pronged: (1) take advantage of the club's increased global brand equity; (2) capitalize on the club's assets by generating returns in the U.S. market; (3) create a virtuous cycle in which economic returns strengthen the brand in the United States and vice versa; and (4) deploy assets in such a manner that the club establishes a foundation at the grass-roots level. Four major initiatives supported

---

57 "Europe's Soccer Clubs Make Asia Pitch," *The Wall Street Journal*, August 13, 2003.
58 Ibid.
59 "Beckham blitz sweeps Asia," *China Daily*, August 13, 2003, p. 8.

these strategic thrusts: (1) content development (training videos, cartoon series, and highlight packages), (2) fan loyalty (via local youth soccer organizations, co-sponsorships such as the U.S. McDonald's High School All Stars program, competitive domestic competitions), (3) development of intangible assets (lectures, soccer academies, Real Madrid youth teams), and (4) asset deployment (first-team tours, merchandising licensing and distribution). Alfredo Soriano, of Ambers & Co., saw great potential in the U.S. market for Real Madrid:

> Soccer is a growing segment in an entertainment-hungry market, with a solid Hispanic community as a starting fan base, where some first-mover advantages can yet be gained by European soccer teams. To fully exploit this opportunity, it would be no wonder if Real Madrid partners with a U.S. major [such as Disney and Viacom] with synergies in content exploitation [TV, video games, licensing, and merchandising]. In the years to come we could see a Real Madrid U.S. tour,[60] similar to the Asian tour, or the hiring of U.S.-born players.

Real Madrid's marketing department believed the U.S. market could be worth as much as 45% of global sports merchandise returns.[61] A U.S. tour was planned for August 2004.

REAL MADRID'S SECOND CENTURY

In spring 2004, Pérez and his team reflected on the quantum leap Real Madrid was making from a local brand with worldwide "awareness" to a real global brand with marketing capabilities, and they were looking ahead. "Today we are planning for 2008 and thinking 20 years ahead," Sánchez added, "when most clubs still do mostly cash management."

Planning for 2008 required worrying about the key anchor of Real Madrid's strategy—the talent. As with an entertainment company, Martínez de Albornoz said, "We worry about what could happen to the talent." Real Madrid players were aged 26½ on average. On a contractual basis,

Zidane had until 2007 with Real Madrid and Raul until 2010; Figo's contract expired in 2006. In March 2004 Ronaldo announced that he would extend his contract to June 2008. "Half a dozen superstars do not emerge each year," Valdano noted.

> Perhaps a dozen players appear per decade at the level we aspire to have on our team. We want people with amazing skill and people that can be converted into unique players. One challenge is the standardization of soccer. But we at Real Madrid aspire to be different and to play at a certain level of talent that is on the verge of extinction. We are always worried that great players will cease to exist, but then every year we seem to be faced with a miracle—a player that does not resemble any other and fascinates us.

In competing for talent, new market participants were at work. In July 2003, for example, Roman Abramovitch, 36-year-old Russian oil magnate and governor of a far-eastern Russian territory, purchased Chelsea, then a highly indebted soccer club.[62] By January 2004 he had spent the equivalent of $360 million on the venture, including $169 million on new players.[63] Chelsea was rumored to have offered a Real Madrid player twice his salary, but the player decided to stay in Madrid. Abramovitch was also said to have approached a former Real Madrid manager and had lured the former Manchester United chief executive to Chelsea.[64] The press had also reported that three billionaires from Russia, western Europe, and the Middle East had separately approached Manchester United. The problem with wealthy impresarios, Valdano noted, was that when the funding stopped, the clubs they once sponsored collapsed. They lacked the historical and institutional foundation of a club such as Real Madrid. But observers wondered what impact such deep-pocketed owners could have on player salaries and transfer prices.

Further, Real Madrid managers were wary of overexposure and excessive commercialization. Manchester United had been criticized for exploiting its fans by selling too many products and for constantly altering its strip design. According to the club's director of communications, the

---

60 This would involve playing the U.S. national team, the team that goes to the Olympics, as well as *ad hoc* teams composed of leading local players.

61 "Real Madrid Scores Marketing Link-up With Disney," *Associated Press*, November 18, 2003.

62 "Russian's £200m for Chelsea," *The Express*, July 3, 2003.

63 "Yellow card; The Kremlin warns Abramovitch and the oligarchs," *The Times*, January 31, 2004.

64 "Takeover Talk Kicks Manchester United Shares Higher," *National Post*, September 16, 2003.

club had stretched "the brand too far." He also noted that fans should always be considered fans and not customers. "The fans are part of the show and are part of the brand," he explained.[65]

Finally, all the planning and strategy could not lessen the fact that an element of uncertainty remained in soccer.

On March 9, Manchester United unexpectedly exited the Champions League after being scored upon in the 90th minute of a game that would have qualified it for the quarterfinals. That could mean up to £10 million ($18.23 million) in lost revenue, significant for a club with 2003 net revenues of £173 million.[66]

[65] "Man U brand booming despite dip in form," *The Turkish Daily News*, September 22, 2002.
[66] <http://uk.biz.yahoo.com/040310/80/eo5gs.html>, accessed March 10, 2004.

Brioni

In 1990, Umberto Angeloni became CEO of Brioni, an exclusive Italian manufacturer and retailer of men's suits. Brioni was known among the world's celebrities of businessmen, movie stars, and politicians as the brand for handmade suits. Angeloni had big plans. He thought the Brioni brand should be leveraged. Over the next decade he opened more stores; added accessories such as ties, shirts, belts, and sportswear; and initiated distribution through department stores such as Neiman Marcus and Saks. He also, and controversially, did a deal with the producers of the James Bond movies; since Pierce Brosnan took over the main role, Bond has been wearing Brioni suits. These moves had multiplied the company's manufacturing revenues alone by five, to more than $100 million, but Angeloni had even bigger plans for the second decade of his tenure.

On March 2, 2002, there was something approaching a media frenzy at No. 4 Via Gesù in Milan as Brioni opened its 20th store; an estimated 160 columnists from the top fashion magazines assembled to watch a floor show orchestrated by Brioni's new designer, Fabio Piras. But this was more than just another store: it was a women's store. As Angeloni watched the excitement unfold in his new 4,000 square foot, architect-designed, brightly decorated store, he wondered whether this might be just a little too bold; the Brioni men's store just across the street at No. 3, with its sober wood paneling still as sedate as the day the store was opened four years before, might as well have been a thousand miles away.

THE HISTORY OF BRIONI

In 1945, Nazareno Fonticoli, head cutter, and Gaetano Savini, manager of sales and public relations officer, were

This case was prepared by Professor David E. Bell.

Copyright © 2003 by the President and Fellows of Harvard College. Harvard Business School case 9-503-057.

both working at a men's store on the Via del Corso in Rome. Aspiring to be in their own business, they set up shop together on Via Barberini in Rome (a store still thriving nearly 60 years later). They wanted a name that was distinctly "non-English" and eventually settled on Brioni, after an island in the Adriatic well known to wealthy vacationers. From the beginning they emphasized high-quality, distinctive cloth and made not only suits but also coats and accessories to provide what became known as "The Total Look."

The Brioni style was greatly influenced by the arrival of the fashion show. In the early days, fashion shows were exclusively for women, and when men did finally play a role, it was as escorts for the women. The men's presence on stage, however, served to underline how unexciting their fashions were. Brioni set out to change that. It organized the first-ever men's fashion show in January 1952 (at the Palazzo Pitti in Florence); the buyer from B. Altman & Co. was sufficiently impressed to order tuxedos, not just in black but also in a range of colors and in a range of cloths, including silk. Soon B. Altman's main windows on Fifth Avenue in New York were devoted exclusively to Brioni, and a storm of interest followed. Films like *Roman Holiday* in 1953 featuring Gregory Peck and Audrey Hepburn made Rome a favorite of Hollywood, and soon stars such as John Wayne, Gary Cooper, Clark Gable, Henry Fonda, and Kirk Douglas were frequenting Via Veneto . . . and Via Barberini.

Demand, even at the exclusive levels of Brioni, was soon outstripping supply. Fonticoli decided that the solution was to open a factory in the region of Abruzzi, where many highly qualified tailors were to be found. In 1959 he selected his hometown of Penne as the site for this operation. The key to improving productivity was the novel solution of "serial production." Instead of one person making the whole suit, each person would specialize on a particular aspect. In 1973 Brioni launched its ready-to-wear line, "Roman Look."

MAKING THE BRIONI SUIT

Lucio Marcotullio joined Brioni in 1960 and moved to the factory at Penne just one year after it opened, when there were just six people. In 2002 he was the chief operating officer and ran a two-shift operation with 1,170 people. He said, "We make 75,000 garments [suits and jackets] a year, every one handmade down to the last stitch." We[1] began our tour in the warehouse, where a four-month supply of rolls of the finest cloth was stacked. One roll, when new, was long enough to make about 17 suits. In one corner a worker inspected each roll of cloth as it arrived, marking any imperfection so that it would not be incorporated in a garment. Marcotullio estimated that about 3% of their cloth was unusable, and about 20% was discarded for lack of demand. Fabric not used for off-the-rack suits might be selected by made-to-measure customers, who still comprised about 20% of Brioni's business. Cloth took about three to five months to arrive after being ordered, though women's only took one or two months. Although most cloth manufacturers supplied both men's and women's, Marcotullio put the difference in timeliness down to industry practice, women's being a more time-sensitive business. In a back room were stored paper patterns, each carrying a customer's name—many of them public figures and celebrities. When a customer was measured by one of Brioni's master tailors—three of them toured the world visiting customers in their homes or at their offices—a paper pattern was produced corresponding to the pieces of cloth from which the suit would be made. As long as the customer did not change weight, these could be used again and again.

We passed next into the cutting room. One worker was carefully arranging a paper pattern on a roll of cloth so as to minimize waste and, when satisfied, used chalk to transfer the desired shapes onto the cloth. A different worker then deftly cut around the pattern to create the pieces that would be passed on to another worker for stitching. "It takes one year to learn how to cut, and another year for those who will learn how to draw," Marcotullio explained. In the main hall hundreds of workers were quietly sewing cloth, each one repeating the same narrow task on a garment. One woman was patiently sewing some cloth stiffening into the front of a jacket. Marcotullio said, "It requires 2,000 stitches, and it's very careful work; the stitch is holding the suit cloth to the stiffening, and none of the stitches must show through the front, obviously. It would only take five minutes with a machine, but this customer specifically asked for the whole suit to be hand done, so that's what we are doing." In the corner we met a worker who had personally cut the buttonholes for every suit that had passed through the factory for the past 40 years. She had a rack of metal punches, each a different size. She waved one. "Mr. Angeloni's, he likes them longer, to accommodate a boutonnière," she said, smiling. Angeloni showed me his coat, with a noticeably longer buttonhole. "And he likes the buttons overlapping on the sleeve, and the buttons sewn in an X rather than as two parallel lines," added Marcotullio. "An advantage of a handmade suit is that it costs no more to incorporate personal touches," Angeloni explained.

Marcotullio continued:

> Our competitors do a lot of machine stitching, especially parts that are not seen. But hand stitching gives a garment body. The stitching shouldn't be perfect. A da Vinci painting isn't perfect. A computer-enhanced Mona Lisa doesn't make any sense. Designer suits are machine cut and machine sewn; they care about design, but not about manufacturing. We care about both. People notice the difference. We're not trying to be suit maker to the world. We don't want the customer who falls asleep at the opera. We are seeking people who need quality. Once a man tries on a Brioni suit he won't wear anything else. Many actors wear Armani these days because they aren't familiar with Brioni. We had [a very famous actor] come to our store recently. He had never worn Brioni. He said he only had 15 minutes for a fitting. He stayed five hours.

Marcotullio estimated that a suit jacket required up to 30 hours of labor but on average about 16 hours, from start to finish, with another five hours for the pants. For a made-to-measure suit, the elapsed time was about 21 days from order to completion. Shipment, usually from the factory to a store, then to a customer, took another 10 days. If a rush was really required, production could be done in three days, but this required someone to follow the garment around and push it to the front of the queue

---

1 Marcotullio, Angeloni, and the casewriter.

at each step. Asked if production cycle time could not be reduced, say by half, Marcotullio responded that the elapsed time was mostly to smooth out production. They could not afford downtime. Italian laws forbid casual work, unless the hours were carefully spelled out in advance. "You are permitted to have part-time labor but not flexible part-time labor," he said.

The final stop of the tour was the adjoining School of Tailoring ("Scuola Superiore di Sartoria"). Founded in 1986, the school trained master tailors during a full-time education that lasted four years. Graduation requirements included the preparation of the student's own graduation suit—prepared to the most exacting standards. This institution, unique in Italy, gave Brioni a formidable edge.

RETAIL DISTRIBUTION

Brioni suits were distributed through company-owned stores, through many high-end boutiques such as Louis in Boston and Wilkes Bashford in San Francisco, and through department store chains such as Saks and Neiman Marcus. (Exhibit 1 lists the locations of all Brioni stores as of 2002.) Fourteen Brioni stores were in major world cities such as Paris, London, and New York. Another nine were in resort locations such as Aspen and St. Moritz. In many cases the stores were as close as possible to a five-star luxury hotel. In New York, the men's store on 57th Street was next door to the Four Seasons; the new women's store planned for New York would open on the other side of the same hotel entrance. The Four Seasons Hotel in Milan was on Via Gesù; the new women's store had a partial glass ceiling that opened into the hotel lobby. The men's stores were elegantly appointed, with light cherry-wood paneling, separate areas for casual and formal wear, and a private "back room" luxuriously appointed with TV, bar, and phone for the customer who needed a little extra attention and privacy. Brioni stores had leases ranging from 12 to 25 years.

Despite the made-to-order possibilities, about 80% of Brioni suits were sold off the rack (see Exhibit 2) at retail prices starting at around $3,200 but averaging $3,500. Tailor-made suits cost about 15% more. Accessories such as shirts started at around $300, ties at $150. Due to the timeless styles that Brioni offered, store markdowns were held only twice per year. About 20% of Brioni sales were in Italy, 30% in the rest of Europe, 30% in the United States, 5% in Japan, and the remainder elsewhere. About 30% of factory sales were to Brioni's own stores; about 50% to Brioni-owned wholesalers in other countries (such as Brioni USA), which resold them to retail clients (such as Saks); and the remaining 20% were direct from the factory. Brioni's retail stores were charged the same prices as the wholesale channel and direct customers. Under this accounting, most of the company's operating profit was credited to the factory; the wholesale and retail channels each had their own markups but both broke even in terms of operating profit.

THE DESIGN AND SELLING CYCLE

Joseph Barrato, the CEO of Brioni USA, explained how the men's ordering cycle worked in the U.S. market. Barrato had been a vice president, general merchandising manager for Bergdorf Goodman and other retail stores during his career and had headed the U.S. distribution of Brioni since 1985. Brioni had about four core models (silhouettes) and at any time about 1,500 varieties of cloth. Each year would bring some new cloth designs in addition to the basics. "We order about 40% of our anticipated cloth needs before we actually work the collection with our wholesale customers. This represents a core purchase that our own stores carry and is then extended to our wholesale customers," said Barrato. The models changed infrequently; therefore, based on his knowledge of the market, Barrato would emphasize the purchase of cloth ordered:

> For fall/winter 2002, we showed our initial core purchase in early November 2001. The Neiman's buyers are familiar with our look, so each season it is a question of showing them the fabrics and developing a buying strategy for that season. Sometimes they will add their own touches to our suggested line, keeping a pattern that sold well last year, or asking for a different color for one of our styles. Fortunately, it is easy for us to be flexible.

Robert Ackerman, senior vice president and general merchandiser at Neiman Marcus, agreed that the interaction with Brioni was fairly simple:

> Since the cloths and styles change very slightly from year to year, the question of an appropriate order is simply a matter of looking at last year's sales figures. Brioni is one of our top three resources in the men's department and one of the top two in men's clothing [after Zegna]. At

Exhibit 1   Brioni Retail Locations

City	Address	Men's Opened	Men's Sq. M.	Ladies' Opened	Ladies' Sq. M.	Adjacent to:
Beverly Hills	337 North Rodeo Drive	Mar-01	428	Mar-01	75	
Florence	Via Calimala, 22 R	Nov-90	121			
Milan	Via Gesu, 4			Feb-02	186	Four Seasons
Milan	Via Gesu, 3	Nov-98	264			Four Seasons
New York	55 E 52 Street	Sep-82	116			
New York	57 E 57 Street	Mar-95	221			Four Seasons
New York	67 E 57 Street			Oct-02	151	Four Seasons
Paris	Avenue George V, 35	Sep-01	309	Sep-01	91	Four Seasons
Prague	Krizovnicka, 1048/3	Jul-01	125			Four Seasons
Rome	Via Barberini, 79	Dec-45	330	Sep-02	90	
Rome	Via Condotti, 21 A	Sep-95	109			
Rome	Via Veneto, 129	Sep-99	23			Hotel Excelsior
Tokyo	4-3-13 Ginza. Chuo-ku	Jul-02	170			
Aspen	212 South Mill Street	Dec-00	111	Dec-00	10	
Cala di Volpe	Hotel Cala di Volpe	Jun-75	44	Jun-75	30	Hotel Cala di Volpe
Capri	C. so V. Emanuele, 56	Apr-01	120	Apr-01	36	
Knokke	Kustlaan 146	Mar-02	96	Mar-02	36	
Marbella	Marbella Club Hotel	Mar-01	145	Mar-01	55	Marbella Club Hotel
Porto Cervo	La Passeggiata-Vicolo della Piazza	Mar-01	52			
Portofino	Calata Marconi, 26	Mar-01	29			
St. Moritz	Plazza da Scuola, 10	Dec-01	90			

Source: Company.

Note: Store areas are net selling space only. Total space was generally about twice that shown. One square meter is about 10.75 square feet.

Exhibit 2   Production Statistics Men's Line, 2001

Garment Type	Quantity	Value (Euro)	%
Suit	40,529	32,872,583	53.0
Suit with vest	857	900,016	1.4
Jacket	35,367	23,594,967	38.0
Pants	5,558	1,138,722	1.8
Overcoat	972	1,217,064	1.9
Tuxedo	1,517	1,399,342	2.2
Tuxedo jacket	98	68,512	1.1
Tailcoat	31	21,433	0.2
Morning coat	39	27,149	0.4
Total		**61,239,788**	**100**

Source: Company.

Note: One euro was approximately equal to one dollar at the time of the case.

their price level they are pretty much alone. All the buying is done centrally; if we allowed the stores to be involved, we'd have 32 different presentations in our 32 stores. There are three seasons: spring, fall, and cruise. We make a piece goods order in January for the cloth we will need for the fall season and finalize the size choices within the next month. Shipments start to arrive at the warehouse in July/August and continue through the fall. Sure we'd like them to arrive a little earlier than they do, and sure we wish Brioni could be more flexible about order modifications, but they are very easy to deal with. The last time we made a major change was about four years ago when we switched our basic model [from Traiano to Nomentano], but otherwise it's just a question of selecting the cloth and determining the sizes.

TWO CUSTOMERS

Richard Dorfman is a customer at the Brioni store on 52nd Street in New York City. He was introduced to Brioni at Bergdorf Goodman ("they gradually worked me up to Brioni over many years"). The suits, he found, were well cut, lightweight, and comfortable. "Clothes are not a substitute for competence, but there's an expectation in my job [as an international banker with ABN AMRO] that you'll be well dressed. It's even more important to look good outside the U.S. than here, much more important."

In part because the Brioni store was in the lobby of his office building, he began buying his suits there and on many occasions has ordered suits without a fitting ("they know my size to a T"). He has bought some Brioni ties and a few shirts, though he prefers to get his shirts in Paris. He said, "Despite the stratospheric prices they charge, Brioni is worth it. I get good advice, offered in an assertive but comfortable manner, and the quality of construction is outstanding."

Asked if people comment on his suits, he said that he prefers that that not happen: "Very occasionally someone will mention how well cut the suit is, and I acknowledge them, but I don't take it any further. I would never say where I get my suits. Clothing is contextual, it should be about you, not what you are wearing."

Another Brioni customer, the writer Gay Talese, had a tailor as a father and so was brought up to appreciate the virtues of hand-sewn suits: "I watched my father do a seam, stitch by stitch, never using a sewing machine

because he said the line was too straight and did not lend itself so perfectly to the shape of the body. I write by hand, and very slowly, just like my father used to sew. I stay away from the computer in the same way my father did from the sewing machine." Talese was asked why, having lived in London for so many years, he had not gravitated to wearing English suits. He said:

I don't own any Savile Row suits. English tailoring, world renowned as it may be, brings with it an atmosphere of the country. It is more casual, not elegant or sharply cut. It has sloped shoulders, rounded lapels and does not call attention to itself. It is understated, which is highly commendatory if one is interested in understatement. But I like tailoring that shows that masculinity can compete with femininity in terms of fashion.[2]

(Exhibit 3 shows the inside of a store and pictures of some other customers.)

BRIONI GOVERNANCE

The ownership of Brioni was quite complex. As Brioni expanded from its first store in Rome and the factory in Penne, the founders gave away some ownership in each new undertaking so the store in New York, or the tie factory, all had slightly different ownership. In addition, the main block of ownership once held by the two primary founders was now divided 10 ways among family members. Angeloni commented, "One of my challenges going forward is to consolidate the ownership so that decisions can be made without a lot of consultation and vetoing." Angeloni, whose wife was a member of one of the owner families, had been CEO of Brioni since 1990. With an economics degree from Rome University and an MBA from the University of Western Ontario, he had undertaken the task of turning Brioni from a neglected fashion curiosity into a global brand.

Angeloni's daring in marketing (the Bond deal), distribution (opening more stores and selling through U.S. department stores), and adding accessories (shirts, ties, knitwear, belts, etc.) caused controversy among the owners but had resulted in a fivefold increase in nonfactory sales during his tenure (see Exhibit 4). Since 1990 the number of factories had increased from one to nine, and employees from 500 to 2,000. (Company financials are shown in Exhibit 5.)

---

2 The remarks of Gay Talese are taken from Edizioni Octavo, *Brioni—Fifty Years of Style*, 1995. By permission of Brioni.

Exhibit 3   A Typical Men's Store, and Some "Typical" Brioni Customers

Source: Pictures are adapted from Edizioni Octavio, *Brioni—Fifty Years of Style*, 1995. By permission of Brioni.

THE MOTIVATION FOR A WOMEN'S LINE

Angeloni was satisfied with the growth of the company since he had been at the helm but realized that as a player in only the men's business, he was missing an opportunity. Brioni had had some experience making women's clothes, primarily special orders for wives of clients. He said:

The women's fashion market is twice the size of men's. We will never fully capture our potential without a women's line. For decades, the Brioni brand has been visible to the woman who accompanies our male customer. She is international and affluent, often does not work, and is in an age bracket just slightly younger (40–55) than the

Exhibit 4   Factory Sales Growth

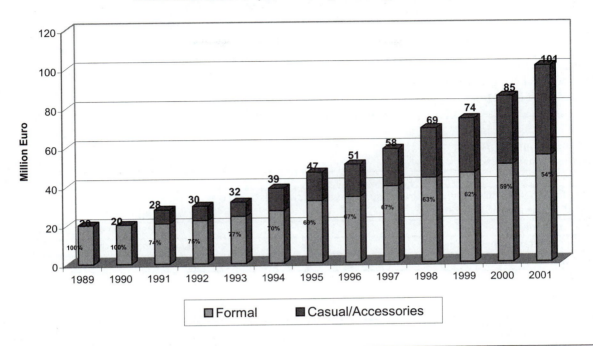

Consolidated Turnover (manufacturing sales only)* 1989-2001

Source: Company.

male consumer, who often has her at his side when he shops. She sometimes has experimented with certain masculine products [made-to-measure jackets, knitwear, robes, pajamas], and she appreciates high-quality materials and workmanship [generally lacking in women's lines]. She sees the jacket as Brioni's "core product." It is difficult to quantify the purchasing potential represented by this type of clientele, but early retail experiences seem to indicate that it could be as high as about one-third of men's sales. In any case, this target would be sufficient to sustain the project in its initial phase.

Then there is the female consumer who, while not familiar with the brand, is sensitive to its intrinsic characteristics [quality, perfect wearability, "timeless" elegance] and is willing to try both the jacket and other items. She falls into the same age bracket but is more independent [sometimes a career woman], and ideally she is a woman of above-average sophistication in the way she shops. That is, she looks for "style" more than fashion; chooses a product and not a brand; holds on to an item in her wardrobe for a long time, always keeping it "contemporary" through the skillful and creative use of accessories; and is interested in "custom-made" clothing.

Polo Ralph Lauren had launched a women's line in 1975, and now it comprised 25% of sales. But Angeloni also knew of other men's brands that had tried a women's line and stumbled. Hugo Boss was a recent example. He also was aware that Zegna had launched a women's line but had chosen to do so under a different name (Agnona). And last, but not least, he was fully aware that running a women's fashion line required some big changes at Brioni: "We may have to move our headquarters from Rome to Milan, to show we are a serious player." And a new cast of characters would be required. Angeloni began the task of assembling a free-lance team that would help him launch "Donna Brioni."

Exhibit 5   Brioni Consolidated Financials ('000 Euros)

COMBINED PROFIT AND LOSS ACCOUNT	2001	2000	1999	1998
Net Revenues	150,337	128,302	105,369	92,583
Cost of goods sold				
Labour costs (directly related to the production)	(24,860)	(23,705)	(21,960)	(19,590)
Depreciation of tangible and intangible assets employed in the production	(2,809)	(1,050)	(812)	(914)
Rentals or financial lease fees for assets employed in the production	(3,210)	(1,294)	(995)	(883)
General industrial expenses	(9,763)	(5,350)	(5,169)	(4,469)
Net change in inventories	5,385	2,013	890	4,835
Purchases of raw materials/goods	(49,519)	(37,453)	(30,030)	(28,278)
Gross profit	65,561	61,463	47,293	43,284
Selling, Commercial and Administrative costs (including related labour costs)	(45,875)	(36,196)	(27,774)	(23,472)
Goodwill and trademark amortization	(2,148)	(1,324)	(1,190)	(1,034)
Operating profit	17,538	23,943	18,329	18,778
Net income from side activities	1,478	830	1,176	629
Adjustments of financial assets	0	(297)	0	177
Other (costs) and income				
Net financial earnings and charges	(869)	2,038	1,636	(85)
Extraordinary revenue and expenses	(1,932)	376	512	(346)
Profit before income taxes	16,215	26,890	21,653	19,153
Income taxes	(6,376)	(11,628)	(8,644)	(9,123)
Net profit before minority interest	**9,839**	**15,262**	**13,009**	**10,030**
Minority Interest	705	(185)	28	124
Net Profit for year attributable to the group	**9,134**	**15,447**	**12,981**	**9,906**

THE LADIES' LINE DESIGNER: FABIO PIRAS

Fabio Piras had been a student, and later creative director, at St. Martins Fashion College in London. He said:

> Italian fashion in the 1960s was all about house couture, then in the 1970s and 1980s it was all about ready to wear: clothes made with machinery in mind. I knew of Brioni; Hollywood, Texas oil millionaires, well known in the 1950s for luxury, flamboyance, and above all, extravagant cloth. Brioni was unusual in that it tried to appeal to non-Italians and happened to hit it big with America. It seemed Brioni had invented industrialized tailoring: "supplying the world with handmade suits."

> You see, detail is important. The great movie director Luchino Visconti, he set up elaborate stage sets. He might have a chest of drawers as part of the set. In the drawers he would have period-correct clothes or silverware—even though the drawers were never opened by the actors. Brioni is like that; there are parts of the suit that are hand sewn that no one will ever see. It's not just a marketing ploy; there are advantages of hand sewing. Take the shoulder, for example. The seam across the top of the shoulder has more stitches on one side than the other. When it is pressed, the seam curves slightly, fitting the shoulder better. Try swinging your arms around; with a normal suit the jacket rides up and you feel awkward, with Brioni it's a natural activity. We take great pains on the cloth. For instance, there is a rare variety of sheep in Spain whose wool is lighter, curlier, and less prone to wrinkle. You take a Brioni suit out of a case and after a shake it will be wrinkle-free.

Exhibit 5   Brioni Consolidated Financials ('000 Euros) (continued)

COMBINED BALANCE SHEET				
	12/31/2001	12/31/2000	12/31/1999	12/31/1998
ASSETS				
Current assets				
Available funds				
- Till money and bank deposits	25,516	24,889	21,133	17,274
- Short-term financial receivable	1,582	1,137	941	780
- Short term financial receivable towards group companies	451	0	0	0
Financial assets other than fixed assets	289	1,112	3,511	1,520
Trade receivable	40,155	41,894	35,232	30,269
Trade receivable towards group companies	4,478	595	0	0
Other receivable	13,976	7,609	6,007	5,623
Inventories	37,551	28,335	25,425	22,633
Accrued income and deferred assets	3,618	2,332	2,290	1,769
Total current assets	**127,616**	**107,903**	**94,539**	**79,868**
Non- current assets				
Medium long-term receivable	1,546	253	611	790
Financial fixed assets:				
- Participations	2,652	3,117	1,269	1,252
- Other securities	2,092	1,944	1,822	1,656
- Financial receivable towards third parties	19	10	5	5
Tangible assets, net	33,002	21,933	15,055	13,320
Intangible assets	6,896	3,470	3,627	3,249
Total non-current assets	**46,207**	**30,727**	**22,389**	**20,272**
TOTAL ASSETS	**173,823**	**138,630**	**116,928**	**100,140**

Brioni is about slow-changing consumption. I don't like hurry, hurry, hurry fashion. I prefer something more substantial. When I think about Brioni I think about achieving a cohesive work for a brand which not only makes of tailoring its business, but a brand which kept its master-tailor identity and attitude. The world of Brioni is affected by seasonal fashion trends and at the same time, within that context, we must sell our private or wholesale customers the idea of complete exclusivity—individuality. The selection and offering of seasonal materials is exceptionally wide compared to usual fashion brands in order to respond to that concept.

Women's wear is really different. But we have to educate women about the brand. The brand is still going to have a tailor identity; she'll know it's a man's brand. So we go with that. Our icon will be the jacket, the blazer, everything else will revolve around it. Hermès is accessories, we are tailoring.

A man may buy all his suits from Brioni, but it's unrealistic to imagine that a woman will. But our tailored look works well, because our clothes look and feel good. Brioni will be a part of her life, relaxed, immaculate, not in-your-face fashion. There is a gap today in women's fashion: handmade,

COMBINED BALANCE SHEET				
LIABILITIES AND SHAREHOLDER'S EQUITY	12/31/2001	12/31/2000	12/31/1999	12/31/1998
Current liabilities				
Short-term financial payable	20,184	3,108	5,032	6,305
Trade payable	22,914	20,724	18,074	13,394
Short-term financial payables	379	0	0	0
Other short-term payable	11,625	10,529	8,358	8,459
Accrued expenses and deferred liabilities	2,554	3,376	1,033	843
Other short-term liabilities	1,207	543	289	1,378
Total current liabilities	**58,863**	**38,280**	**32,786**	**30,379**
Non-current liabilities				
Financial payable	4,327	5,527	3,909	4,992
Other medium long-term payable	1,443	671	302	961
Severance indemnities	10,502	9,708	8,829	8,119
Other non-current liabilites	1,687	1,315	1,129	1,059
Total medium/ long-term liabilities	**17,959**	**17,221**	**14,169**	**15,131**
Total liabilities	**76,822**	**55,501**	**46,955**	**45,510**
Shareholders' equity				
Share capital	5,296	5,296	602	602
Legal reserve	1,756	1,757	1,778	1,778
Other reserves	77,565	60,392	53,621	40,808
Profits (losses) carried forward	820	267	10	0
Net profit for the year	**9,134**	**15,447**	**12,981**	**9,906**
Minority interests and shareholders' equity	2,430	(30)	981	1,536
Total shareholders' equity	**97,001**	**83,129**	**69,973**	**54,630**
TOTAL LIABILITIES AND SHAREHOLDERS' EQUITY	173,823	138,630	116,928	100,140

Source: Company.

superior-quality, contemporary classics that will look good in, say, 20 years' time.

This is my fourth season. The first [spring/summer 2001] was just a few pieces. This season [fall/winter 2002] there are maybe 60 items/styles, with an average of three expressions [e.g., fabric or color type] for each. For example, there are about nine jackets this season. One style might be expressed in wool, leather, and knit. Then there are six coats, *two raincoats, six skirts, seven pants, four dresses, two tops, and two blouses, plus accessories.*

Piras explained how the design and sampling cycle would work for the women's fall line, sold from July to September 2002 (see Exhibit 6).

The Fashion Advisor: Anna Piaggi

Anna Piaggi is one of the world's most noted commentators on the fashion scene. As creative consultant to *Vogue*

End of July 2001	General discussion around trends, feeling for shapes, colors, textures
Early September	Establish a general color card, start research for materials: shirting, coating, leathers, furs
Early October	Commitment for cloth, trimmings accessories
October	Designs discussed with merchandisers, product and sales managers; designs given to pattern cutters and tailors to be developed
October to December	Fittings, finalizing designs to form a cohesive range
Mid December	Confirmation of samples and repeats to production factory
End of January 2002	Presentation of collection to the sales force, both in United States and Europe; taking Brioni retail orders
February to March	Selling season with wholesale clients; orders to be delivered end of June to August
Early March	Press presentation with 30-40 outfits presented statically to members of international press
March–April	Advertising campaign shoots
March–September	Samples available for use by stylist, photographers and journalists of magazines
July–January	Selling season

Source: Company.

Magazine (the bible of the fashion industry) and "inspiring muse" to a host of designers such as Pierre Cardin, Manolo Blahnik, Stephen Jones, and Karl Lagerfeld, she wielded enormous influence.[3] She commented:

> To a certain extent, fashion is a soap opera. Designers must understand the history of fashion. In the 1980s we were all so bold about brands, you were supposed to wear a brand. Now it's more about the person, the individual. The best designer is the one who gets the right balance between individualism and conformity. Brioni Women has an advantage in being a virgin operation, there's less baggage. Brioni could be a good basis for a woman's wardrobe. Women's bodies have changed over the years, more toned, more surgically enhanced. Fit becomes important. Brioni is a safe choice. It doesn't overwhelm your own personality. It doesn't detract from your accessories. She'll use other brands for their surprise value. Every woman's dream has been to find a jacket she can wear at work and then transform via accessories to evening wear. When I heard about the Brioni women's line I had mixed feelings; like others I wondered, does the world need another women's collection? Its success is to be seen. It's a long operation.

---

3 Following lunch with the casewriter, Piaggi was stopped by a young student designer who talked animatedly with her for a few minutes and then asked to have their photograph taken together. The casewriter took the picture.

THE IMAGE DIRECTOR: GIOVANNI SCIALPI

Scialpi was a communications consultant for luxury brands and cultural institutions, a professor at Urbino, and a lecturer at the Bocconi Business School in Milan. "We initially spent quite some time redesigning the logo and all of its applications, from labels to stationery; the logo [the name Brioni in red cursive] is a little sharper, more modern," he said.

We do not have a budget to advertise like the most famous brands, therefore our ads must stand out, and we must use our store windows to amplify and elaborate on the message. If the code of the year is color, the windows will be colorful and so forth. Everything moves around a theme, a precise idea true to the identity of the Brioni product.

The advertising campaigns for 2002 were done by two important fashion photographers: the first, for spring/summer, by David Bailey; while the autumn/winter, in black and white, was by Patrick Démarchelier. The Bailey campaign photographed Benedetta Barzini [a very famous model from 30 years ago] and her son Giacomo: a "couple," with a young man and a "glamorous" woman. The ad is not aimed at the consumer, though I will be glad if they see it. It is aimed at the fashion critics and the writers. It tells them something is different, it gives them something to write about. But it also wins them over. There are details the consumer would never know. My philosophy is to catch the eye with a detail, not aggressive; a piece of paper, some light, the idea is not to over-whelm the clothes.

(See Exhibit 7 for two of these ads, and a sample of two others, run in various magazines.)

THE BRAND CONSULTANT: ALESSANDRA ALLA

Alla was a specialist in marketing luxury brands, particularly in relating non-Italian brands, such as Mercedes and LVMH, to the Italian fashion scene. She would bring a global perspective about the market for luxury goods. She said:

Brioni is undertaking a process of transformation from a "product label"—a brand linked to a single product, men's suits—to a "lifestyle brand"—one linked to the way people live. The introduction of women's wear will generate more visibility for the brand and will bring it to the attention of a more glamorous media that generally overlooks masculine style.

But to be successful in women's wear will require a whole different sense of urgency about the brand. Brioni has to make an investment sufficient to trigger a drive to acquire *among women and to create an* aura of glamour *that can be consecrated by the press. That is the challenge for Brioni Women: to remain faithful to the brand's history while competing in a field that values other principles.*

Angeloni agreed: "Brioni must express its own stylistic identity within the universe of women's fashion. This should be discernible to the consumer and stimulating for the press, consonant with the brand concept, but at the same time occupying a position that is more advanced and developing more rapidly than Brioni Uomo."

THE STORE ROLLOUT

The women's store in Milan would be followed in September by a New York City store. At present, these were the only ladies-only stores. The two stores were designed by different architects with different approaches, to suggest innovation. In addition, the women's line would be offered in reduced form in some of Brioni's men's stores and by some wholesale customers. A suit at retail would start around $2,100 and average perhaps $2,500, again with a 15% premium if tailor-made. (Exhibit 1 shows the space allocated to the women's line by store.)

"Men and women buy clothes differently," said Angeloni. "A woman in Neiman's may ask the salesperson to see what's new from Chanel. A man is more likely to ask simply for a suit. Until Brioni is established as a brand that women follow, our belief is that when a woman accompanies the man to the store a salesperson will take her off, saying, 'Have you seen our Brioni collection for women?'"

Angeloni assembled a list of the expenses associated purely with the introduction of women's wear (see Exhibit 8). "As you can see," he noted, "the total investment so far is not as large as people might think. Even our advertising budget remains modest compared to our competition [see Exhibits 8 and 9]. Yet, given the size of the women's market, the potential impact for us is enormous." (Exhibit 10 shows the pro forma profitability projections for the Milan women's store and New York women's store, scheduled for opening in October 2002. Exhibit 11 shows the interior of the two stores. The plan called for the two stores to break even within two years.)

Exhibit 7   Brioni Fashion Shots

Spring/Summer 2001; Photo Bruno Barbazan

Fall/Winter 2001; Photo Bruno Barbazan

Spring/Summer 2002; Photo David Bailey
(Benedetta Barzini and her son)

Fall/Winter 2002; Photo Patrick Démarchelier

Source: All photos copyright Brioni: used with permission.

PRODUCTION IMPLICATIONS

Marcotullio commented:

Women's is different. But it's a natural extension of what we do. We have this vast reservoir of knowledge that we can use just as well for women. And women's is easier. It takes less time to make a typical woman's outfit. And the production cycles are different so there are opportunities to smooth out demand. We can handle the extra capacity that women's will bring, because, being hand sewn, it's just a question of hiring more people. We can't ramp up immediately because it takes at least a year of training before we let someone loose on a customer's suit.

Marcotullio thought that, for women, a suit jacket required about 10 hours of labor from start to finish, with another 1.5 hours for pants or a skirt. "But for women, even a three-day cycle time may be too long," he continued. The production differences had implications for the relative economics of the two lines (see Exhibit 12). A new factory would be dedicated to the women's line, with the intention that it would break even within five years, on sales of 18,000 items per year (see Exhibit 10 and Exhibit 13).

Exhibit 2 shows the breakdown of men's suit production in 2001 by model. The top three models comprised 85% of all orders. Marcotullio commented:

Here is a first key difference between men's and ladies'. The former is limited to a few models but with limitless

Exhibit 8

Exhibit 8   Investments Related to the Women's Line

	2001	2002
Incremental **Investments for the Women's Line ('000 Euros)**		
Factory (new, in Colle/Corvino)	1,440	1,300
Milan Store	2,250	
Milan Showroom	730	
Rome Store		350
New York Store		1,200
Shop-in-Shops	1,500	
Raw Materials (losses, initial collection)	1,250	250
Finished Goods (unsold initial collection)	500	100
Total (excludes store inventories)	**7,670**	**3,200**
Total **Brioni Advertising and Promotion ('000 Euros)**		
United States	225	550
Italy	94	285
France	84	180
Photo Production	150	150
Events	160	50
Total	**713**	**1,215**

Source: Company.

Exhibit 9   Comparative Advertising Expenditures

	Approximate Sales (million Euros)	Advertising as % Sales
Armani	1,270	5
Brioni	150	2
Chanel	730	4
Ferragamo	640	4
Gucci	2,300	11
Hermes	1,230	6
LVMH	12,230	11
Prada	1,730	6
Tod's	320	9
Versace	480	12
Zegna	690	3

Source: Advertising expenditures adapted from Studio Pambianco.

Exhibit 10   Pro Forma Projections for Ladies

Factory Pro Forma Ladies - Break even

	E
Clothing	3,753,000
Accessories	1,476,000
Total Sales	5,229,000
Labor	1,490,000
Outsourcing	170,000
Purchased cloth	972,000
Purchased accessories	1,080,000
Cost of Sales	3,712,000
Selling Costs	640,000
G&A	710,000
Milan Showroom	50,000
Publicity	117,000
Total Overhead	1,517,000
Net Operating Profit	0

Milan Ladies Store
Break Even Pro Forma

	E
Net Sales	2,424,000
Cost of Goods Sold	1,091,000
Gross Profit	1,333,000
Rent/Real Estate Taxes	500,000
Salaries & Benefits	299,000
Selling Expense	144,000
G&A	76,000
Depreciation	314,000
Operating Profit	0

New York Ladies Store
Break Even Pro Forma

	$
Net Sales	2,411,000
Cost of Goods Sold	867,960
Gross Profit	1,543,040
Rent/Real Estate Taxes	870,000
Salaries & Benefits	250,000
Selling Expense	186,040
G&A	126,000
Depreciation	111,000
Operating Profit	0

Source: Company.

Note: Pro formas reflect costs in start-up phase.

variations [open buttonholes, coat length], whereas the variety in women's stems from the number of lines. For example, the fall/winter 2002 collection includes 10 new models of jacket and 15 new overcoats, but very few will involve modifications for a customer. Most women don't want to wait even for a custom-made suit. They see it and want to wear it now.

CUSTOMER REACTIONS

Ackerman at Neiman Marcus said that the prospect of a Brioni women's line was attractive:

Anything that lifts our sales of Brioni is for the better, and a women's brand is bound to increase awareness and raise their whole profile. They'll have to adjust somewhat: women buy their clothes earlier in the season than men, they'll have to do some advertising, and they are not used to markdowns. But I'm confident they'll get the hang of it. We offered their first collections in two of our stores, Washington and Westchester, and got good sell-through in a difficult market.

Dorfman, the ABN AMRO banker, said his wife was excited about the Brioni women's offering because of the quality, the imported fabrics, and the design. He estimated that about half her wardrobe was Brioni: "With Brioni you don't see the same items on other people. At a restaurant you'll sometimes see three or four women wearing the same Chanel outfit."

Exhibit 11   The Milan Ladies Store

Source: Company.

Exhibit 11   The Milan Ladies Store (continued)

Source: Company.

Exhibit 11   The New York Ladies Store (continued)

Source: Company.

Exhibit 11   The New York Ladies Store (continued)

Source: Company.

Exhibit 12   Production Costs Compared for the Two Lines

	Men's	Ladies'
Direct Manufacturing Cost[a]	58	43
G & A	15	25
Selling Cost	14	15
Profit Margin	13	17
	100	100

Source: Company.

[a]This cost is the marginal labor and material cost for a garment. The Ladies' numbers assume a steady state of production.

Exhibit 13   Brioni Factories

Location	Production	Year of Foundation	Employees	Size (in sq. m.)
Penne (PE)	Men's Clothing	1959	1,170	12,220
Silvi (PE)	Ties	1991	133	5,496
Bergamo	Shirts	1991	79	3,245
Montebello (PE)	Sportswear	1993	173	5,313
Bologna	Leatherwear	1995	28	3,896
Milano	Haberdashery	1996	10	100
Modena	Belts	1998	19	500
Collecorvino (PE)	Ladies' Clothing	2000	47	1,400
Civitella (PE)	Knitwear	2001	30	4,430
Total			1,689	36,600

Source: Company.

THE CRISIS

Soon after the March 2 fashion presentation in Milan, Barrato met with the Neiman Marcus buyer to discuss what he would buy from the women's line. "Burton Tansky, the CEO of Neiman Marcus, was at the presentation and he thought the collection had potential," recalled Barrato. "However, their buyer took a conservative position and only wanted to buy a few items. Out of five swatches that they selected, four were in gray colors, and two were actually from the men's line. And they also wanted to repeat a jacket from the previous season that had been very successful."

Angeloni recalled:

> I was surprised that they had not stuck with the line we had at our presentation, after all that's the image we are trying to convey. There's no point having a designer if the customer is going to take charge of design. But Neiman's is a big account. They've got used to being able to choose the fabrics that they want in the men's line. I thought it over for a couple of nights before deciding that we had to stick to our guns. If we back down at the first sign of resistance, we'll never establish ourselves as a branded women's player. I called Joe and told him to go back to the buyer and insist.

Sitting in his office on Via Barberini, Angeloni saw that he had a new e-mail message. It read as follows:

> *From: Joe Barrato*
> *To: Umberto Angeloni*

Date: 20 March 2002
Subject: Neiman Marcus Ladies

Dear Umberto:

Neiman Marcus was very upset with your decision not to put in the additional swatches and models they requested. They are unhappy with our inflexibility and take it as a demonstration of our unwillingness to build a ladies' business with them. They reminded me that the two previous collections they purchased were a result of a relationship with Neiman Marcus and Brioni. And while the last two collections purchased had only fair retail results, they continued to show good faith and be willing partners. Many great design houses are inclined favorably to adjust items in their collection to accommodate the U.S. market. Why is it we couldn't accommodate them? They believe that their input will enhance the overall sell-through and help us build a successful ladies' business. We need to carefully reconsider our decision otherwise they will pass the Fall Ladies collection entirely.

Angeloni reflected that this might not be the last crisis he would have to face before Brioni Ladies was fully established. The economic aftermath of September 11 was not making the launch any easier. Even well-established luxury brands were experiencing double-digit drops in sales and a 50% drop in profits. He wondered what modifications to his strategy might be appropriate before things went too far.

BRL Hardy: Globalizing an Australian Wine Company

In January 1998, Christopher Carson smiled as he reviewed the Nielsen market survey results that showed Hardy was the top-selling Australian wine brand in Great Britain and held the overall number two position (to Gallo) among all wine brands sold in Britain's off-trade (retailers, excluding hotels and restaurants). As managing director of BRL Hardy Europe, Carson felt proud of this achievement that reflected a 10-fold increase in volume since his first year with Hardy in 1991.

But his mental celebration was short-lived. In front of him were two files, each involving major decisions that would not only shape the future success of the company in Europe but also have major implications for BRL Hardy's overall international strategy:

- The first file contained details of the proposed launch of *D'istinto*, a new line of Italian wines developed in collaboration with a Sicilian winery. Carson and his U.K. team were deeply committed to this project, but several questions had been raised by Australian management. Not least was their concern about *Mapocho*, another joint-venture sourcing agreement Carson had initiated that was now struggling to correct a disappointing market launch and deteriorating relations with the Chilean sourcing partner.
- The second issue he had to decide concerned two competing proposals for a new entry-level Australian wine. His U.K.-based management had developed considerable commitment to *Kelly's Revenge*, a brand they had created specifically in response to a U.K. market opportunity. But the parent company was promoting *Banrock*

Station, a product it had launched successfully in Australia which it now wanted to roll out as a global brand at the same price point.

Watching over these developments was Steve Millar, managing director of the South Australia-based parent company that had experienced a period of extraordinary growth, due in large part to BRL Hardy's successful overseas expansion (Exhibit 1). A great believer in decentralized responsibility, he wanted Carson to be deeply involved in the decisions. But he also wanted to ensure that the European unit's actions fit with the company's bold new strategy to become one of the world's first truly global wine companies. Neither did he want to jeopardize BRL Hardy's position in the critically important U.K. market that accounted for two-thirds of its export sales. For both Millar and Carson, these were crucial decisions.

INDUSTRY BACKGROUND[1]

Vines were first introduced into Australia in 1788 by Captain Arthur Phillip, leader of the group of convicts and settlers who comprised the first fleet of migrants to inhabit the new British colony. A wave of European settlers attracted by the gold rush of the mid-nineteenth century provided a boost to the young industry, both in upgrading the availability of vintner skills and in increasing primary demand for its output. Still, the industry grew slowly, and as late as 1969 annual per capita wine consumption in this beer-drinking country was only 8.2 liters—mostly ports and fortified wines—compared with over 100 liters per person per annum in France and Italy.

In the following 25 years, the Australian wine industry underwent a huge transformation. First, demand for fortified wines declined and vineyards were replanted with table

This case was prepared by Professor Christopher A. Bartlett.

Copyright © by the 1999 President and Fellows of Harvard College. Harvard Business School case 9-300-018.

[1] For a full account, see Christopher A. Bartlett, *Global Wine Wars: New World Challenges Old (A)*, HBS No. 303-056 (Boston: Harvard Business School Publishing, 2002) and (B), HBS. No. 304-016 (Boston: Harvard Business School Publishing, 2003).

	1992	1993	1994	1995	1996	1997
Sales revenue	151.5	238.3	256.4	287.0	309.0	375.6
Operating profit (before interest, tax)	16.7	26.6	30.2	34.0	39.3	49.2
Net after tax profit	8.8	13.3	15.8	17.4	21.2	28.4
Earnings per share	13.2¢	14.1¢	15.7¢	15.7¢	18.1¢	23.3¢
Total assets	216.8	234.6	280.7	329.0	380.6	455.5
Total liabilities	11 7.4	127.4	146.6	160.4	194.4	205.8
Shareholders' equity	99.4	107.2	134.1	168.6	186.2	249.7
Debt/equity ratio	70%	57%	57%	53%	58%	41%

Source: Company documents

wine varieties. Then, as consumers became more sophisticated, generic bulk wine sales—often sold in the two-liter "bag in a box" developed in Australia—were replaced by bottled varietals such as cabernet sauvignon, chardonnay, and shiraz, the classic grape type increasingly associated with Australia. By the mid-1990s, domestic consumption stood at 18½ liters per capita, eighteenth in the world.

Over this two-century history, more than 1,000 wineries were established in Australia. By 1996, however, the 10 largest accounted for 84% of the grape crush and 4 controlled over 75% of domestic branded sales. Most of these were public corporations, the largest of which was Southcorp whose brands included Penfolds, Lindeman, and Seppelt. The number two company was BRL Hardy Ltd. (BRLH), selling under the Hardy, Houghton, Leasingham, and other labels.

During the 1980s and 1990s changes in the global wine industry had a major impact on these emerging Australian companies. A rationalization and consolidation among wine wholesalers and retailers was increasing the power of historically fragmented distribution channels. At the same time, however, large-scale wine suppliers from New World countries such as the United States, South America, South Africa, and Australia were exploiting modern viticulture and more scientific wine-making practices to produce more consistent high-quality wine. These developments were occurring in an environment of rapidly growing demand from new consumers in nontraditional markets.

During this period of change, Australian wines began to find large markets abroad, and by 1995 exports accounted for more than 27% of production. But despite its rapid growth, the Australian industry accounted for less than 2% of the world wine production by volume and 2.5% by value. However, because only A$13 billion of the total A$65 billion global wine sales was traded product (80% of wine was consumed in the country of production), the Australian companies' A$450 million in 1995 exports represented 3.5% of the world export market. But in an industry that was becoming increasingly fashion-driven, Australian wine was becoming a "hot trend," and an ambitious industry association saw export potential growing to A$2.5 billion by 2025—a 16% share of the projected traded value.[2] Together with an increase in domestic consumption, this translated to A$4.5 billion in Australian wine sales and a doubling of production to 1.7 million tonnes by 2025.

The Australian industry association saw four export markets as key—the United Kingdom, the United States, Germany, and Japan. While the U.K. market would decrease in relative importance (in 1996 it was the world's largest non-producing wine importer and accounted for over 40% of Australian wine exports), over the next 25 years these four markets were expected to continue accounting for 60% of export sales. (See Exhibit 2.)

COMPANY BACKGROUND AND HISTORY

BRLH's roots could be traced back to 1853 when Thomas Hardy, a 23-year-old English vineyard laborer, acquired land near Adelaide, South Australia, and planted it with

---

2 All forecast values are in 1996 Australian dollars at wholesale prices. At 1996 year end, the exchange rate was A$1 = US$0.8.

Exhibit 2   Australian Wine Export Forecasts—Selected Markets 1996–2025

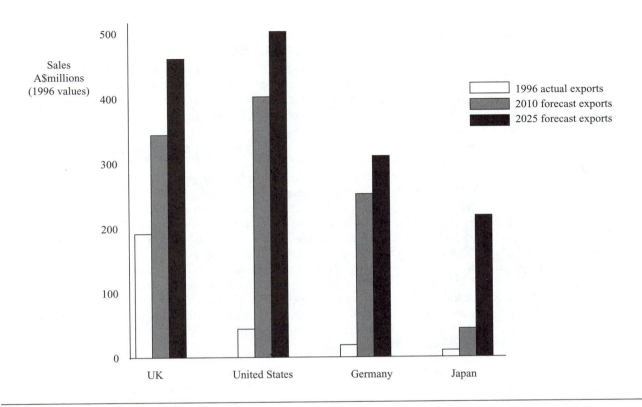

Source: Australian Wine Industry Association

vines. In 1857 he produced his first vintage, exporting two hogsheads to England, and by 1882 he had won his first international gold medal at Bordeaux. When Hardy died in 1912, his company was Australia's largest winemaker, but also one of the most respected.

Shortly after Hardy's death, in the Riverland region northeast of Adelaide, 130 Italian grape growers formed Australia's first cooperative winery in 1916, naming it the Renmano Wine Cooperative. In 1982 Renmano merged with the Riverland's largest winery and distillery, the Berri Cooperative to form Berri Renmano Limited (BRL). By the early 1990s, almost 500 member growers were delivering over 50,000 tonnes of grapes to BRL, giving it the second-largest crush in Australia. This huge-volume grape crush and its bulk-packaging operations led some to refer to BRL disparagingly as "the oil refinery of the wine industry."

Throughout their respective histories, Thomas Hardy & Sons and BRL followed quite different strategies and developed very different organizations. Hardy became known for award-winning quality wines, while the combined cooperatives specialized in fortified, bulk, and value wines—some sold under private labels. And in contrast to Hardy's "polite and traditional" values, BRL's culture was more "aggressive and commercial," according to one observer of both companies.

International Roots

Although BRL experienced considerable success when it began selling abroad in the late 1980s (particularly in

Scandinavia where it sold 6 million liters of bulk wines per annum), its efforts seemed quite modest when compared with Hardy's long history of exporting much higher-value-added bottled products and the huge additional commitments it was making in that same period. To expand on its U.K. sales base of 12,000 cases per annum, Hardy believed it needed to stop relying on importers, distributors, and agents who carried scores of brands from dozens of vineyards. After a long search, in 1989 it acquired Whiclar and Gordon, a respected U.K.-based wine importer-distributor, including its agency rights for a range of French, Chilean, and South African wines.

This move led management to begin talking about the possibility of buying European wineries that could provide their newly acquired distributors with the critical mass and credibility to give Hardy's wines greater access to Europe. Motivated by the looming 1992 target date for a unified European Community (EC) market, and stimulated by the notion that such alternative sources of supply could cushion the ever-present risk of a poor vintage in one region, Hardy's board felt this was an ideal time to invest. In contrast to the painstaking process of identifying acquisition targets for U.K. distribution, however, the vineyard purchasing decision seemed more opportunistic. In 1990, two Hardy directors visited the wine-growing regions in France and Italy, looking at properties on the market. Passing through southern France, they acquired the century-old Domaine de la Baume, a winery with extensive sources in the Languedoc region and several established domestic and export brands. Six months later, they took over Brolio de Ricasoli, a beautiful castle on a Tuscan hillside that made a well-known Chianti and was reputed to be Italy's oldest winery.

Almost immediately, however, problems surfaced in all three of the European acquisitions and soon they were bleeding the parent company of millions of dollars. Combined with a recession-driven market slowdown at home, these problems plunged Hardy into losses. Meanwhile, BRL was also struggling and was looking for ways to expand and upgrade its business. When one of Hardy's banks called in a loan and the company was forced to look for a financial partner, BRL was there. Despite its own marginal financial performance, BRL management decided to propose a merger. Said one ex-BRL manager, "We had access to fruit,

funds, and disciplined management; they brought marketing expertise, brands, and winemaking know-how. It was a great fit if we could learn to work together." Others, however, were less sanguine. Despite the fact that together the companies accounted for 22% of the Australian wine market and 17% of national wine exports, the dismissive industry view was, "When you put two dogs together, all you get is louder barking." Nonetheless, the companies merged in June 1992 and three months later became a publicly listed company.[3]

NEW MANAGEMENT, NEW STRATEGIES

Following the merger, ex-BRL executives assumed the majority of top jobs in BRLH: the newly merged company's deputy-chairman, CEO, operations and technical director, and the international trading director all came from BRL. From the other side, only Hardy's managing director (who became BRLH's business development director) and the Australian sales and marketing manager survived as members of the new top executive team. Steve Millar, formerly BRL's managing director and now CEO of the merged company, explained his early priorities:

> Our first task was to deal with the financial situation. Both companies had performed poorly the previous year, and although we thought our forecasts were conservative, the market was concerned we would not meet the promises made in our IPO [initial public offering]. . . . Then we had to integrate the two organizations. This meant selecting a management team that could both implement the necessary retrenchments and position us for growth. Since the Australian market accounted for the vast bulk of our profit, we initially concentrated our attention at home. . . . Only after getting these two priorities straight could we focus on our new strategy.

The Domestic Turnaround

The strategy that emerged was simple: the company would protect its share of the bulk cask business but concentrate on branded bottle sales for growth. This would require a commitment to quality that would support its brands. The initial management focus would be on the domestic market, first getting merger efficiencies, then implementing the new strategy.

---

3 The Italian Ricasoli operations were explicitly excluded from the merger due to their continued substantial losses and the likelihood they would continue.

As important as developing a clear strategy, in Millar's mind, was the need to change the company's culture and management style. His sense was that, although there was great potential in the company's middle management, much of it—particularly in the ex-Hardy team—had been held back by being resource constrained and excluded from major decisions. Millar's objective was to create a more decentralized approach, but to hold management accountable. He explained:

> It took time to get the message understood because Hardy management had tended to take a few big swings on high-risk decisions while keeping tight control over the small decisions. I wanted to delegate the small risks—to create a "have a go" mentality. The objective was to have us trying 20 things and getting 80% right rather than doing one or two big things that had to be 100% right.

The prerequisite to delegation, however, was that managers had to be willing to challenge the status quo, accept responsibility for the outcome of decisions that were delegated, and admit when they had made a mistake. David Woods, previously Hardy's national sales manager and now appointed to the same position in the merged company, recalled that the new management style was not easy for everyone to adopt: "Many of us from Hardy felt like outsiders, unsure if we would be allowed into meetings. It became easier after the first year or so when you had shown you could perform. But you definitely had to earn your stripes."

Woods "earned his stripes" by integrating the two sales forces, capturing the economies from the combination, and repositioning the product portfolio in line with the new strategy emphasizing quality branded bottle sales. The results were impressive with both domestic bottle market share and profitability increasing significantly in the first two years of BRLH's operation.

Relaunching International

Meanwhile, Millar had appointed Stephen Davies, an ex-BRL colleague who he regarded as a first-class strategic marketer, as group marketing and export manager for BRLH. A 12-year veteran of BRL, Davies had been responsible for establishing that company's export division in 1985 and had been credited with its successful expansion abroad. While the rest of top management's attention was focused on a major restructuring of the domestic operations, Davies began evaluating the company's international operations. What he found was a dispersed portfolio of marginal-to-weak market positions: a U.K. business selling a small volume of Hardy wines and just breaking even, a rapidly eroding BRL bulk business in Sweden, a weak Hardy-U.S. presence supported by a single representative, and a virtually nonexistent presence in Asia or the rest of Europe.

In Davies's mind, a few clear priorities began to emerge, many of which shadowed the domestic approach. The first priority had to be to clean up the operating problems that were the source of the financial problems. Only then would they focus on building on their strengths, starting with their position in the U.K. market. Making "Quality Wines for the World" the company's marketing slogan, Davies began to build the export strategy on the basis of a strong quality brand image. From the existing broad portfolio of exported products, he initiated a program to rationalize the line and reposition a few key brands in a stepstair hierarchy from simple entry-level products to fine wines for connoisseurs. At the mass market price points, for example, he focused the line on *Nottage Hill* and *Stamps* as the Hardy's "fighting brands," while at the top end he targeted the *Eileen Hardy* brand. (See Exhibit 3 for rationalized export portfolio of brands.)

BRL HARDY IN EUROPE

In the large, developed U.K. market, Davies found a turnaround had already begun under the leadership of Christopher Carson, managing director of Hardy's U.K. company. Carson was an experienced marketing manager with over 20 years in the wine business and particular expertise in Italian wines. He had been hired by Hardy in October 1990 to head the U.K. company's sales and marketing function, including the recently acquired distributor. Within a week of his joining, however, Carson realized that the financial situation in these companies was disastrous. He flew to Australia to tell Hardy's management that they would own a bankrupt U.K. organization unless drastic action was taken. He then proposed a series of cost-cutting steps.

In February 1991, Carson was appointed U.K. managing director and immediately began to implement his cost-cutting plan. Over the next 18 months, he pruned

Exhibit 3   Hardy Domestic versus Export Product Portfolio, 1993

SOFT PACK (CASK) WINE

- 2 litre   Benmano and Stanley range
- 3 litre   Berri fortified range
- 4 and 5 litre   Stanley, Berri and Buronga Ridge range
- 10, 15, and 20 litre   Stanley and Berri Range

BOTTLED TABLE WINE

less than $6.00	Brentwood range
	Brown Bin 60
	Hardy Traditional range
	* Hardy Stamp Series
	Spring Gully range
	* Nottage Hill
	Leasingham Hutt Creek
	McLaren Vale hermitage
• $6.00 to $10.00	* Houghton White Burgandy
	Hardy Siegersdorf range
	* Leasingham Domaine range
	* Houghton Wildflower Ridge range
	Hardy Bird Series range
	Hardy Tintara range
	Moondah Brook Estate range
	Renmano Chairman's Selection range
	Redman Claret and Cabernet Sanvignon
	Barossa Valley Estate range
	Chais Baumiere range
• $10.00 to $15.00	* Hardy Collection range
	* Houghton Gold Reserve range
	* Chateau Reynella Stony Hill range
• over $15.00	* Eileen Hardy range
	Lauriston range
	E&E Black Pepper Shiraz

SPARKLING WINE

- less than $6.00   Courier Brut
                                   Hardy Grand Reserve
                                   Chateau Reynella Brut
- $6.00 to $10.00   * Hardy's Sir James Cuvee Brut
- over $10.00   Hardy's Classique Cuvee
                                   Lauriston Methode Champenoise

FORTIFIED WINE

- less than $6.00   Brown Bin 60
                                   Cromwell
                                   * Tall Ships
                                   Stanley 2 litre port soft pack (cask)
- $6.00 to $10.00   Rumpole
                                   * Old Cave
- over $10.00   Lauriston Port & Muscat
                                   Hardy Show Port
                                   Vintage Port
                                   Chateau Reynella Vintage Port

BRANDY

                                   * Hardy Black Bottle
                                   Berri
                                   Renmano

All prices are based on the recommended retail price
* **Rationalized export line** (13 of 48 brands)

Source: Company documents

the product line from 870 items to 230 and reduced the headcount from 31 to 18 (including a separation with three of the six executive directors). He also installed strong systems, controls, and policies that put him firmly in charge of key decisions. As these actions were implemented, the 1990 losses became a breakeven operation in 1991, and by the time of the mid-1992 merger, it looked as if the European operations would be profitable again. (For BRLH Europe financials, see Exhibit 4.)

Developing the Headquarters Relationship

In his discussions with Davies in late 1992, Carson highlighted the key problems and priorities as he saw them. First was the need to build quickly on the 178,000 cases of Hardy-brand products that had represented less than a quarter of his total volume in 1991 (500,000 of his 700,000 case sales in 1991 were accounted for by a variety of low-margin French wines handled under agency agreements that had come with the purchase of Whiclar and Gordon). At the same time, if the company was going to restore the financial health of its French winemaker, Domaine de la Baume, he felt he would have to build substantially on the

10,000 cases of its product which he had sold in 1991. (He reported 1992 sales were on track to double their previous year's volume.) And finally, he wanted to protect an unstable imported Chilean product that had come as a Whiclar and Gordon agency. Carson told Davies of his plans to grow the high potential brand from 20,000 cases in 1991 to a forecast 60,000 cases for 1992.

Davies agreed with Carson's plans, particularly endorsing the focus on the Hardy brands. Yet the relationship was an uneasy one in the post-merger management uncertainties. The BRL-dominated headquarters management supported delegation—but only to those who had "earned their stripes." Within the Hardy-built European company, on the other hand, there were questions about whether their bulk-wine-oriented BRL colleagues understood international marketing. "There was a real tension," said one observer. "A real feeling of us versus them. I think Christopher and Stephen had some difficult conversations." The relationship was delicate enough that Steve Millar decided to have Carson report directly to him on the U.K. company's profit performance but through Davies for marketing and brand

---

Exhibit 4   BRL Hardy Europe Ltd.: Key Historical Data (£'000)

		1990	1991	1992	1993	1994	1995
Net sales turnover	In GB £	£10,788	£12,112	£12,434	£15,521	£18,813	£27,661
	In Australian $	A$22,243	A$24,973	A$29,965	A$33,830	A$37,946	A$57,734
Gross profit (after distribution expense)		£1,173	£1,429	£1,438	£1,595	£1,924	£2,592
GP %/sales		10.9%	11.8%	11.6%	10.3%	10.2%	9.4%
Administrative cost		£1,104	£1,261	£1,164	£1,172	£1,308	£1,896
	Admin %/sales	10.2%	10.4%	9.4%	7.6%	7.0%	6.9%
Profit after tax		-£26	£6	£157	£266	£395	£426
	PAT %/sales	-0.2%	0.0%	1.3%	1.7%	2.1%	1.5%
Average No. of employees		31	27	19	20	22	24
£ Sales per employee		£348	£449	£654	£776	£855	£1,153
Stock @ year end		£1,226	£1,043	£605	£897	£1,392	£1,265
	Stock turnover	7.8	10.2	18.2	15.5	12.1	19.8
Return on investment		-2.1%	0.5%	11.2%	17.9%	24.5%	23.5%

Exhibit 4 BRL Hardy Europe Ltd.: Key Historical Data (£'000) (continued)

| | | 1996 | Forecast per BRLH Europe Strategic Plan | | | | |
			1997	Plan 1998	Plan 1999	Plan 2000	Plan 2001
Net sales turnover	In GB £	£32,271	£40,100	£53,848	£66,012	£78,814	£91,606
	In Australian $	A$69,532	A$82,680	A$111,027	A$136,107	A$162,503	A$188,878
Gross profit (after distribution expense)		£3,202	£4,212	£5,453	£6,488	£7,630	£8,787
GP %/sales		9.9%	10.5%	10.1%	9.8%	9.7%	9.67%
Administrative cost		£2,118	£2,717	£3,649	£4,473	£5,340	£6,207
	Admin %/sales	6.8%	6.8%	6.8%	6.8%	6.8%	6.8%
Profit after tax		£723	£948	£1,087	£1,286	£1,460	£1,644
	PAT %/sales	2.2%	2.4%	2.0%	1.9%	1.9%	1.8%
Average No. of employees		28	34	48	62	76	91
£ Sales per employee		£1,153	£1,179	£1,122	£1,065	£1,037	£1,007
Stock @ year end		£1,504	£1,500	£2,100	£2,600	£3,300	£3,900
	Stock turnover	19.3	23.9	23.0	22.9	21.6	21.2
Return on investment		35.7%	39.7%	38.0%	37.8%	36.1%	37.2%

Source: Company documents

strategy. (For BRLH international organization, see Exhibit 5.) But Millar did not want the shared reporting relationship to pull him into a role of resolving disputes on operating issues. Instead, he hoped for negotiation:

> Christopher had a good reputation and knew the market well. I assumed he would be a key player and was willing to let him prove it. He and Stephen just clashed, but confrontation can be healthy as long as it is constructive. I just kept urging them to work with together—they could learn a lot from one another.

The biggest disputes seemed to emerge around marketing strategies, particularly branding and labeling issues. Although Hardy exported a dozen brands covering the full price range, its entry-level brands in the United Kingdom were Hardy's *Stamps*, blended red and white wines that then retailed for £2.99 and Hardy's *Nottage Hill*, a single varietal red and white at the £3.69 price point. Together, these two brands accounted for over 80% of Hardy brand sales by

value and even more by volume. Carson was concerned that the image of these brands had eroded in the United Kingdom, and that he wanted to relabel, reposition, and relaunch them. But it was difficult to convince the home office, and he expressed his frustration:

> Australia controlled all aspects of the brand and they kept me on a pretty tight leash. When I took my message to Reynella [BRLH's corporate office near Adelaide], they didn't want to hear. They expect you to get runs on the board before they give you much freedom. . . . But we were in the U.K. market and they weren't. Finally they agreed, and in 1993 we relabeled and relaunched Nottage Hill *and repositioned* Stamps. *By 1994 our volume of Hardy's brands quadrupled from 1992 and represented more than half our total sales. (See Exhibit 6.)*

Davies acknowledged that he yielded on the *Stamps* and *Nottage Hill* decisions, believing "it was better to let people follow a course they believe in—then the implementation

Exhibit 5   BRL Hardy's International Organization, 1993

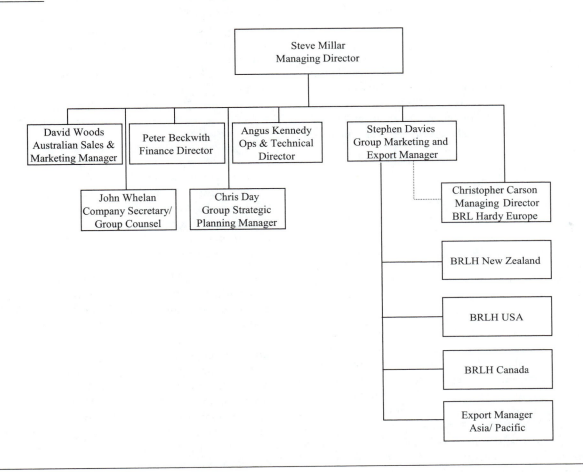

Source: Company documents

Exhibit 6   BRL Hardy Europe Ltd.: Case Summary History

In Std. 9 Liter Cases	1991	1992	1993	1994	1995	1996	1997
Hardy	178,500	194,303	411,084	856,876	1,031,071	1,383,772	1,763,698
Domaine de la Baume	10,000	19,564	49,698	63,540	89,256	155,608	158,587
Chile	20,000	58,848	24,855	76,775	112,954	120,540	50,537
French Agencies (AGW)	497,500	618,878	528,606	545,198	446,445	51,257	{186,180
French Projects					2,162	58,744	
Grand Total	706,000	891,593	1,014,243	1,542,389	1,681,888	1,769,921	2,159,002

Source: Company documents

will be better." But he became increasingly concerned about the demand for local control over branding, labeling, and pricing decisions, especially as the company's long-term strategy began to evolve.

The Evolving Strategy

In Reynella, by the mid-1990s, Millar and Davies began to conceive of BRL Hardy not as just a "quality exporter" but as an "international wine company" with worldwide product access backed by the marketing capability and distribution muscle to create global brands. As Millar explained:

> It was an important strategic shift. Most packaged goods businesses are dominated by multinational companies with global brands—like Coke or Kraft. We realized that there were no really established global wine companies and, despite our newness at the game, we had a real chance to be one. . . . I began describing BRL Hardy to our shareholders as a company based on three core strengths: our world-class production facilities, our global brands, and our international distribution. Controlling those assets allows us to control our destiny in any major market in the world.

Within the industry, the notion of building global wine brands ran counter to the established wisdom. For example, Jean-Louis Duneu, the head of the Paris office of Lander, a branding consulting firm, recognized the potential of global branding, but was skeptical about its applicability to wine. "The promise of a brand is that it will be the same quality every time," he said. "That means that branded wine probably has to be blended to ensure consistency. The result is never as satisfying." Jonathan Knowles, another corporate identity consultant warned of another potential problem. "Wine lovers look for something they haven't heard of," he claimed. "There's almost an anti-branding mentality. When people who are not in the know get to know the brand name, people in the know no longer want the product."

That view also seemed widespread among traditional wine producers. In the highly fragmented European industry—there were 12,000 producers in Bordeaux alone—only a few top-of-the-market names like Lafite, d'Yquem, and Veuve Clicquot had achieved global recognition, but these held minuscule market shares. Of those that had attempted to build mass market global brands over the years, only a handful—Mateus Rosé, Blue Nun, Mouton Cadet, and Hirondelle, for example—had succeeded. And of these, most had managed to capture only relatively small volumes and for brief periods of time.

After years of trying, Gallo, the world's biggest wine brand, accounted for considerably less than 1% of global wine sales, mostly in its home market.

Nonetheless, Millar and Davies believed that changes in wine-making, the opening of global markets, and the changing consumer profile would all support their objective to become a truly international wine company built on a global branding capability. To implement this strategic shift, Davies felt the Reynella headquarters had to be the "global brand owners." He explained:

> Although we believe in decentralization and want to listen to and support overseas ideas and proposals, we also have to be clear about Reynella's role. Everyone has opinions on label design, but we'll lose control of the brand if we decentralize too much. Our role should be as brand owners deciding issues relating to labeling, pricing, and branding, and overseas should be responsible for sales, distribution, and promotion strategy.

Carson and his U.K. management team had some difficulty with this concept, and disagreements between the two executives continued through the mid-1990s. Carson tried to convince Davies that, unlike the Australian market where branded products accounted for 90% of sales mostly through hotels and bottle shops, the United Kingdom was not yet a branded wine market. Retailers' own labels dominated, particularly in the supermarkets that accounted for more than 50% of retail wine sales. (Indeed, both BRL and Hardy had previously been sources for private labels, but had since discontinued the practice.) Proximity to Continental sources meant that another big segment was claimed by a proliferation of tiny vineyard or village labels with little or no brand recognition, leaving only 12% of sales to recognized proprietary branded wines in 1995. In such a market, Carson argued, it would be hard to support a brand-driven strategy. He elaborated:

> We have to manage a progression from commodity to commodity brand to soft brand to hard brand. And at the early stage of that progression, distribution is key. It's more push than pull, and you need retailers' support to get your product on their shelves. That's why labeling is so important. Women represent 60% of the supermarket wine buyers and the label has to appeal to them.

As the decade rolled on, the debate between Carson and Davies continued. But, as Steve Millar put it, "With 70% growth, we could support the tension."

THE 1997 WATERSHED DECISIONS

On the basis of the U.K. company's excellent performance, Carson was appointed chief executive of BRL Hardy Europe in 1995. He immediately began putting together some bold plans for the company's continued growth and, over the next couple of years, set in motion some initiatives that were to create a mixture of excitement and apprehension within the organization.

The Outsourcing Ventures

For the first five years following the merger, Carson had focused most of his attention on building sales of the Hardy brand wines. However, he remained acutely aware of the importance of the other non-Australian product lines he had inherited through the Whiclar and Gordon acquisition. Not only did the added volume bring scale economies to his sales and distribution operation, they also provided BRLH Europe with some other important strategic benefits.

As an agricultural product, every region's grape harvest was vulnerable to weather, disease, and other factors affecting the quality and quantity of a vintage. Carson recognized that sourcing from multiple regions was one way to minimize that risk. Furthermore, he became increasingly aware that major retailers—particularly grocery chains like Sainsburys—were trying to rationalize their suppliers. To simplify wine buying, they wanted to deal with only a few key suppliers who could provide them with a broad line of quality products. And finally, currency fluctuations exposed traded products like wine exports to currency-driven price variations that could substantially affect marketability, particularly for lower-priced products. (See Exhibit 7.)

For all these reasons, in 1997 Carson began to devote more of his time and attention to two non-Australian wine sources—a move that seemed to fit with Reynella's new emphasis on becoming "an international wine company." This shift was triggered by the unpleasant revelation in late 1996 that *Caliterra*, a brand he and his sales organization had built into the leading Chilean import in the United Kingdom, would not be renewing its distribution agreement. The supplier, Caliterra Limitade, had signed a joint venture agreement with U.S. winemaker Robert Mondavi.

Determined never again to invest in a brand he did not control, Carson initiated action on two fronts. In early 1997, he negotiated a 50/50 joint venture agreement with Jose Canopa y CIA Limitada under which the Chileans would provide the fruit and the winemaking facility while BRL Hardy would send in one of its winemakers to make several wines that it would sell in Europe under the *Mapocho* brand, using its marketing and distribution capabilities. Despite several mishaps, difficulties, and delays during the negotiations (including a near derailing when Carson's main contact left Canepa), by late 1997 the supply arrangements were in place.

At the same time he was finalizing the Chilean deal, Carson was also exploring alternative European sources, particularly for red wine. In March 1997, he made initial contact with Casa Vinicola Calatrasi, a family-owned winery in Sicily with links to a major grape grower's cooperative. After explaining his interest in developing a line of branded products to be sold through BRLH's distribution channels, he began analyzing product availability, volume forecasts, and prices.

Over the following months, he returned to Sicily a couple more times, meeting with the co-op farmers to explain

---

| Exhibit 7 | Key Currency Fluctuations Affecting BRLH Europe |

	$Aus/£	It Lira/£	Chilean Peso/£	$US/£
12/92	2.197	2239	NA	1.514
12/93	2.213	2516	NA	1.492
12/94	2.013	2546	NA	1.559
12/95	2.080	2455	630.8	1.541
12/96	2.088	2544	703.0	1.664
12/97	2.505	2892	727.1	1.659

Source: Company documents

how branding could give them security of demand and eventually better prices for their fruit. He told them of BRL Hardy's expertise in viticulture, and offered the help of the company's highly regarded technical experts to further enhance the value of their harvest through more productive vineyard techniques and new winemaking methods. Having experienced difficult negotiations with the Chilean joint venture, Carson wanted to avoid similar problems and emphasized that this would work only if it was a true partnership. He wanted the farmers' best fruit and their commitment to make the project work. At his first presentation, 60 farmers showed up. When the word spread, Carson found he had an audience of 135 receptive co-op members at his second presentation. "We all had a very good feeling about the relationship," said Carson. "It felt much more like a partnership than the Chilean JV where they were acting more like suppliers than part owners."

Returning to London, Carson engaged his organization in developing a strategy for the product code-named *Mata Hardy*. While detailed marketing plans were being developed internally, an external consultant began generating over 2,000 possible brand names. As Carson and his sales and marketing staff began narrowing the choices, they engaged a designer to develop labels and packaging that would capture the Mediterranean lifestyle they wanted the brand to reflect.

By July 1997, the marketing plans were developed to the point that Carson was ready to review his proposal with management in Reynella. He described how he wanted to offset projected Australian red wine shortages with alternative sources. Presenting his vision of sourcing from both the northern and southern hemispheres, he outlined his need for a full line to maximize his leverage as a distributor. He then described the broad objective of developing a brand that would respond to the average wine consumer who was interested in wine but not necessarily very knowledgeable about it. The new product was designed to give them the information they needed on appealing, easy-to-read labels with a pronounceable brand name. The objective was to give them a wine they would enjoy and a brand they would trust.

Carson then presented the portfolio of eight new Italian-sourced wines spread across the low and low-middle price points. At the baseline £3.49 price point would be wines made from less well known indigenous Sicilian grapes. At the next level would be blends of indigenous and premium varietals (a Catarrato-Chardonnay white and Nero d'Avola-Sangiovese red, for example)

priced at £3.99. At £4.99 he planned to offer pure premium varietals such as Syrah and Sangiovese, while to top out the line he wanted to offer blends of super-varietals such as Cabernet-Merlot at £5.99.

The highlight of the presentation was when Carson unveiled his idea about creating a strong branded product, revealing both the final name choice—*D'istinto*, which translated as "instinctively"—and the boldly distinctive labels and other packaging designs. (See Exhibit 8.) (He swore all who saw the branding materials to secrecy since his intention was to reveal the new name and label with great fanfare just before its planned launch in early 1998.) The plan was to give *D'istinto* a unique image built around the Mediterranean lifestyle—passionate, warm, romantic, and relaxed—and to link it strongly to food. Each bottle would have a small booklet hung on its neck, describing the wine and inviting the buyer to write for free recipes. The intention was to create a database of wine-and-food-loving consumers to whom future promotions could be mailed. "This line can help us build BRLH Europe in size, impact, and reputation," said Carson. "We need to become known as a first-class branding company—a company able to leverage great distribution and strong marketing into recognized consumer brands."

In the meanwhile, however, early signs were that the *Mapocho* project was not going well. For months, Canepa managers had been raising doubts and concerns about the JV. For example, they claimed their costs went up, and wanted to renegotiate the supply price. By the time things got back on track, the Chilean company had made other commitments and the new venture lost its opportunity to get early access to the pick of the 1997 grape harvest. As a result, first samples of *Mapocho* sent to London by BRL Hardy's winemaker were disappointing. The Chileans thought the problem was due to the winemaker sent from BRL Hardy being unfamiliar with Chilean wine, while he insisted they had not provided him with quality fruit. Early sales were disappointing and forecasts were that the first vintage would sell only 15,000 cases against the 80,000 originally planned. Unless there was a rapid turnaround, the company stood to lose up to £400,000. Despite this poor showing, however, the U.K. sales and marketing group was forecasting 1998 sales of 150,000 cases and the company was about to make a commitment to Canepa for this volume of their new vintage due in February. It was a forecast that made many in the Reynella headquarters very nervous.

Exhibit 8   *D'istinto* Proposed Packaging and Positioning

Capsule Product Position/Brand Image

- Value
- Quality
- Mass appeal

- Mediterranean lifestyle
- Food-friendly

- Relaxed
- Warm
- Romantic

Source: Company documents

As a consequence, while the Australians were impressed by Carson's ambitious ideas for *D'istinto*, many questions and doubts were raised and approval was slow in coming. Some senior management still had bad feelings about the Italian wine business left over from Hardy's earlier ill-fated Italian venture. Even those who had not lived through the Ricasoli losses had concerns about the troublesome ongoing experiment with the Chilean sourcing joint venture. And still others, including Stephen Davies, were concerned that the new Sicilian line could cannibalize Hardy's two fighting brands. *D'istinto* was initially proposed as a product to fill the price points that had been vacated as *Stamps*

and *Nottage Hill* had become more expensive. But, as the Australian management pointed out, the extended Sicilian line now clearly overlapped with Hardy's core offerings—not only *Stamps* at £4.49 but even with *Nottage Hill* now selling for £5.49 (see Exhibit 9).

Finally, Steve Millar raised a more organizational concern. He was worried about the possibility of Carson losing his focus and about the strength of the European sales organization to carry another brand when it was already struggling with *Mapocho*. In the context of the U.K.'s over-commitment to the *Mapocho* launch, he was even more concerned when he saw *D'istinto's* projected

Exhibit 9   U.K. Product Price Point Matrix

Recommended Retail Price Point (£)	Hardy	Leasingham Chateau Reynella	Houghton	Mapocho	D'istinto
27.99	Eileen Hardy Shiraz Thomas Hardy Cab Sauv		Jack Mann Red		
24.99		E&E Black Pepper			
19.99		Classic Clare Shiraz			
12.99	Eileen Hardy Chardonnay	Ebenezer Shiraz Ebenezer Cab Merlot	Crofters Cab Merlot		
11.99		Ch Reynella Shiraz Ch Rey Cab Merlot			
9.99	Coonawarra Cab Sauv	Leasingham Shiraz Leas Cab Malbec			
8.99		Ebenezer Chardonnay Ch Rey Chard Leas Chard	Crofters Chardonnay		
7.99	Pathway Chardonnay	Domain Grenache	Wildflower Shiraz		
6.99	Bankside Shiraz Nottage Hill Sparkling	Leas Chardonnay Leas Semillon			
6.49	Bankside Chardonnay				
5.99	Nottage Hill Shiraz Stamps Sparkling		Wildflower Chardonnay Wildflower Chenin Blanc	Merlot	Cabernet Merlot
5.49	Nottage Hill Cab Shiraz				
4.99	Nottage Hill Chardonnay Nottage Hill Reisling Stamp Shiraz Cabernet Stamp Grenche Shiraz			Cab. Sauv. Chardonnay	Syrah Sangiovese
4.49	Stamp Chardonnay Sem Stamp ReislingG/Traminer			Sauv. Blanc	
3.99					Cataratto/Chardonnay Sangiovese/Merlot
3.49					Trebiano/Insolia Nero d'Aviola

Source: Company documents

sales of 160,000 cases in the first year rising to 500,000 by year four. "You will never do those numbers," said Millar. Carson's response was that he thought *D'istinto* had global potential and could eventually reach a million cases. "By the next century, we'll even be exporting Italian wine to Australia!" he said.

Yet despite the lighthearted exchange with his boss, the widely expressed doubts he confronted in the Australian review meeting caused Carson to reflect. The financial investment in the branding, packaging, and launch expenses was relatively small—probably less than £100,000. But in a situation of continued difficulty with *Mapocho* sales, Carson understood that the real financial risk could come later in the form of contract commitments and excess inventory. Furthermore, he knew that the questions Steve Millar had raised about organizational capacity and his own risk of distraction were real. Would *D'istinto* overload human resources already stretched thin by the rapid expansion of the previous five years? And would it prove to be too big a competitor for management time, corporate funding, and eventually consumer sales? The questions were complicated by another decision Carson faced—one relating to the development of a new Australian product to extend the company's existing range of fighting brands.

The Australian Opportunity

As the *Stamps* and *Nottage Hill* brands gradually migrated upward to straddle the £4.49/£4.99/£5.49 price points, Carson believed there was an opening for a new low-end Australian brand to fill in the first rungs on the Hardy's price ladder. Because the price points below £4.49 represented more than 80% of the market, he felt it was an important gap to fill. Being fully occupied with the Chilean and Italian projects, however, he found himself unable to devote the time he wanted to developing a new Australian brand. To Steve Millar, this presented the ideal opportunity to push an agenda he had been urging on Carson for some time—the need to develop the senior levels of the U.K. organization, particularly on the marketing side. Said Millar:

> *Christopher had done an amazing job of building the U.K. But he had driven much of it himself. . . . For a couple of years I'd been telling him, "Get people even better than you below you." We'd even sent a few Australians to support him in marketing and help the communication back home. But most of them got chewed up pretty quickly.*

Finding himself stretched thin, and recognizing he had to stand back from controlling operations, Carson agreed to take on a new expat Australian marketing manager. The person he chose was Paul Browne, an eight-year company veteran whose career had taken him from public relations to brand management in Australia. Most recently, he had been responsible for export marketing for the United States and Oceania, reporting to the president of BRL Hardy USA. Carson explained his choice:

> *I wanted a driver. Someone who could take charge and get things done. As an Australian with an understanding of group level activities, Paul fit our need to fill the weakness in marketing. He roared into the business with great enthusiasm and linked up with our sales director and national accounts manager to understand the local market's needs.*

Browne concluded that there was an opportunity for a Hardy's brand positioned at the £3.99 price point, but able to be promoted at £3.49. He felt the market was ready for a fun brand—even slightly quirky—which would appeal to a younger consumer, perhaps a first-time wine drinker who would later trade up to *Stamps* and *Nottage Hill*. The brand he came up with was *Kelly's Revenge*, named for an important character in the history of the Australian wine industry, but also suggestive of Ned Kelly, the infamous Australian bushranger (outlaw) of the early nineteenth century. With backing and support of the U.K. sales management, they pursued the concept, designing a colorful label and preparing a detailed marketing plan. (See Exhibit 10.) As excitement and enthusiasm increased, Carson stood back and gave his new product team its head.

Meanwhile, in Reynella, BRLH in Australia was developing a major new product targeted at a similar price point. In 1995, the company had acquired Banrock Station, a 1,800-hectare cattle grazing property in South Australia's Riverland district, with the intention of converting a portion of it to viticulture. During the planting and development phase, visitors' universally positive reaction to BRLH's ongoing conservation efforts—planting only 400 hectares while returning the remaining land to its native state including the restoration of natural wetlands—convinced management that the property had brand potential. (See Exhibit 11.)

Positioned as an environmentally responsible product with part of its profits allocated to conservation groups, the *Banrock Station* brand was launched in Australia in 1996.

Exhibit 10   *Kelly's Revenge*: Label and Product Concept

Proposed Promotion Material/Back Label

It has taken 130 years for Dr. Alexander Kelly to have his revenge. Kelly was the first to recognize the wine growing potential to Australia's McLaren Vale region. His vision, however, was ahead of its time, and his eventual bankruptcy enabled the acquisition of the original Tintara Winery by Thomas Hardy. Hardy's wines eventually established the reputation of the McLaren Vale, winning tremendous praise at the Colonial and Indian Wine Exhibition in 1885. Kelly's descendents have continued to forge Hardy's winemaking tradition, and to this day Tintara Cellars are the home of Hardy's Wines, one of Australia's finest and most highly awarded winemakers. This wine is dedicated to the spirit of our pioneers.

Source: Company documents

The brand's image was reflected in its earth-tone labels and its positioning as an unpretentious, down-to-earth wine was captured by the motto "Good Earth, Fine Wine." Blended Banrock Station wines started at A$4.95, but the line extended up to premium varietals at A$7.95. In the United Kingdom, it would be positioned at the same price points as the proposed *Kelly's Revenge*. The product was an immediate success in Australia, and soon thereafter became the largest-selling imported brand in New Zealand.

Convinced of *Banrock Station's* potential as a global brand, Davies and Millar urged BRLH companies in Europe and North America to put their best efforts behind it. Canadian management agreed to launch immediately, while in the United States, the decision was made to withdraw the *Stamps* product, which local management felt was devaluing the Hardy's image, and replace it with *Banrock Station*. But in Europe, where the *Kelly's Revenge* project was in its final development stages, the management team

Proposed Product Promotion Material

Banrock Station's precious soil is treated with respect and in return it nurtures the premium grape varieties that create our value-for-money, easy drinking wines of great character. Situated in the heart of South Australia's Riverland region, directly opposite the historic Cobb & Co. stage coach station, Banrock Station is a 4,500 acre property featuring some of the world's most picturesque scenery. In its midst lie 400 acres of premium sun-soaked vineyard.

Because we understand that good earth is the starting point for most of nature's bounty, we are working with like minded organizations to ensure this natural haven which surrounds the vineyards of Banrock Station is preserved for future generations to appreciate and enjoy. Every sip of Banrock Station fine wine gives a little back to the good earth from whence it came.

Banrock Station: Good Earth, Fine Wine

Source: Company documents

expressed grave doubts about *Banrock Station*. They argued that the label design was too dull and colorless to stand out on supermarket shelves, and that the product's environmental positioning would have limited appeal to U.K. consumers half a world away.

Steve Millar described the conflict that emerged around the competing concepts:

I accept it as my mistake. I'd been pushing Christopher to delegate more and trying to get more Australians on his staff to help build links back to Australia. But Paul Browne became our biggest problem. He just didn't have the skills for the job but he wanted to control everything. Then on top of that he started playing politics to block Banrock Station. *When we asked him to give the new concept a try, he kept insisting it would never work. We got the feeling he had even organized customers to tell us how bad the label was. Instead of helping communications between Australia and Europe he became a major barrier.*

Meanwhile, Browne presented his new *Kelly's Revenge* concept to the Australian management to a very skeptical reception. Davies's reaction was immediate, strong, and negative, seeing it as "kitsch, downmarket, and gimmicky." He and his Reynella-based staff felt they knew more about marketing Australian wines than the European management. In Davies's words, "By decentralizing too much responsibility, we realized we risked losing control of brand issues. We wanted to take back more control as the brand owners."

Steve Millar recalled his reaction to the *Kelly's Revenge* proposal:

I told them I thought it was terrible, but that it really didn't matter what I thought. I suggested we get the customers' reaction. When we took Kelly's Revenge *to ASDA, the UK grocery chain, they were not enthralled. So I took that as an opportunity to suggest we give* Banrock Station *a try.*

Although Christopher Carson had been backing his new marketing manager to this point, with *Banrock Station* succeeding elsewhere and senior management behind it as a global brand, the issue was becoming very complex. He knew the organization could not support both brands and felt the time had come when he would have to commit to one project or the other. For Steve Millar, the situation was equally complex. Given the U.K.'s strong performance, he wanted to give Carson as much freedom as possible, but also felt responsible for the implementation of the company's global strategy. Running through his mind was how he would respond if Carson and his U.K. organization remained firm in its commitment to *Kelly's Revenge* over *Banrock Station.*

Part III

Global Marketing Programs

Managers responsible for marketing in a multinational or global enterprise must design appropriate marketing programs for each national market. To some extent, each country must be treated as a separate marketplace, because each has its own currency, legal requirements, and business methods. However, by coordinating operations on a regional or global scale, multinationals can gain important advantages.

The most important issue in the development of multinational marketing programs is the extent to which elements of the marketing mix are standardized regionally or globally, as opposed to being customized to each country market. The degree of customization typically varies from one mix element to another, and often varies from product to product and from country to country within the same multinational. Three generalizations may be made in this regard.

- Strategic elements of the marketing mix (see Figure 3.1), such as brand name and positioning, are more likely to be standardized than execution-intensive elements, such as distribution, sales promotion, and customer service.
- Marketing program standardization is more feasible in the case of higher technology and non-culture-bound products marketed to a younger customer base (such as personal computers and software) than in the case of traditional, culture-bound products used in the home (such as soups).
- Standardized programs are more readily accepted in smaller country markets, in which the local organization has fewer skills and resources, than in larger, older operating subsidiaries, which can assert their independence against headquarters more easily.

Customization of the marketing mix should be guided by a simple principle. The additional costs of adapting the marketing program to meet the needs of a national segment should be exceeded by the resulting extra margin generated through higher unit sales and/or higher unit margins.

When customization occurs, it is essential that the country-specific programs, although different, be in harmony. Given increased consumer mobility, global communications, and the cross-border spillover of media advertising, it may be unwise for a multinational to permit radically different positionings of the same brand. To do so may underleverage the advantages that being a multinational affords, including the cross-border transfer of best marketing practices. On the other hand, it is often argued that a customer in Paris does not obtain any added value from knowing that the exact

Figure 3.1   Marketing Mix: Standardization versus Customization

	Standardization		Adaptation	
	Full	Partial	Partial	Full
Product				
Positioning				
Branding				
Advertising				
Distribution				
Pricing				
Sales Promotion				
Customer Service				

same marketing program is being deployed in New York—and that marketing mix adaptation does not, therefore, detract from the appeal of global brands.

It happens that relatively few global brands are deploying the same marketing programs worldwide. Different country markets are invariably at different stages of category and/or brand development, even for global brands. For example, Heineken deploys one marketing mix in high-share markets with well-developed beer consumption and another mix in low-share markets with low per capita consumption. However, there are commonalities: outside the Netherlands, where Heineken is a mass-market beer, the brand is positioned worldwide as a premium beer consumed in social settings by good friends.

Like many other global brands, the Heineken brand name is the same as the company name. The mere fact that the brand is recognized worldwide enables Heineken to command a price premium and superior distribution. A segment of consumers in every country wants to enjoy the perceived status associated with using global brands. In addition, the commonalities in a global brand's marketing mix permit marketing investments to be amortized over a worldwide base of sales. Moreover, only global brands have the marketing muscle to participate in global sports sponsorships that are an increasingly important component of the marketing communications mix. Finally, global brands can attract and retain outstanding managers, instill pride among employees, and facilitate greater headquarters' control of far-flung subsidiaries.

Indeed, the issue of marketing program standardization versus customization cannot be separated from the management process issue of centralization versus decentralization. Although it is conceivable that an enlightened headquarters might decide in favor of customization, there is an ongoing tension in most multinationals between headquarters' advocacy of standardization, motivated primarily by cost and control considerations, and the field operations that respond to differences in customer behavior from one market to another. On the one hand, a weak headquarters will permit an excessive proliferation of country-specific adaptations; after all, if country managers cannot identify differences requiring adaptations, they might as well resign. On the other hand, an excessively controlling headquarters will leave money on the table by not permitting low-cost, yet potentially highly profitable, customization.

Sony Corporation: Car Navigation Systems

In April 1996, Masao Morita, President of the Sony Personal and Mobile Communication Company, a division of the Sony Corporation, pondered how to recover Sony's initial leadership in car navigation systems in Japan. As the first company to launch a reasonably priced (around $2,000) after-market model in 1993, Sony could claim to have created the world's largest car navigation systems market in Japan. Since the late 1980s, Sony had led a group of 40 companies in establishing an industry standard (called NaviKen) which enabled consumers to benefit from mutually compatible digital map software while manufacturers reduced their risk by sharing development costs. Sony's efforts grew the Japanese market from 58,000 units in 1992 to 160,000 in 1993. Sony held a 60% market share in 1993. Exhibit 1 reports unit sales of car navigation systems in Japan through 1995 and forecasts from 1996 through 2005.

Market growth fueled intense competition in Japan, leading to many new product launches and lower prices. The average retail price per unit decreased from $4,000 in 1990 to $2,500 in 1995.[1] Ironically, competitors not in the NaviKen group were able to introduce new and improved products more often and more rapidly by developing or acquiring proprietary digital map technologies. Increasingly sophisticated consumers sought out differentiated products with the latest features. In contrast, NaviKen member companies, including Sony, lost time while trying to agree on standard software upgrades. Sony's unit sales increased but at a slower growth rate than the market: Sony's market share fell from 60% in 1993 to 23% in 1994 and 17% in 1995, and was estimated to drop to 15% in 1996. Exhibit 2 summarizes the major competitors' market shares. Exhibit 3 compares sales performance of NaviKen and non-NaviKen companies.

In Europe and the United States, Sony was also the first to launch car navigation systems in the automobile after-market. Fewer than 1,000 units had sold in test markets to gather information in each region by the summer of 1996. In Europe, local manufacturers such as Philips and Bosch started to market competing products aggressively. Other Japanese competitors such as Alpine, Matsushita, and Pioneer were expected to enter Europe and the United States by 1997. Exhibit 4 summarizes market forecasts for car navigation systems by geographic region.

SONY CORPORATION: COMPANY BACKGROUND

The Sony Corporation was founded in 1946 in the remains of a bombed department store as the Tokyo Tsushin Kogyo (Tokyo Telecommunications Engineering) by Akio Morita (Masao's father) and Masaru Ibuka. As a young company, Sony did not have a keiretsu of affiliated companies and lacked the strong domestic sales base and the distribution networks that supported the other companies.

With only $500 in capital, the founders realized they would have to differentiate themselves from their larger competitors by developing more innovative products. And from the failure of their first new product—a tape recorder that customers deemed expensive and flimsy—they learned the importance of paying close attention to consumer needs. Throughout its history, Sony pursued the innovation of commercially appealing products, maintaining a large research organization and vesting unusual decision-making authority in its engineers. The company's first breakthrough occurred after Ibuka acquired a patent license for transistors. Morita and Ibuka began mass production of transistor radios in 1954, and dubbed their new product Sony, after

This case was prepared by Professor John A. Quelch with the assistance of Yoshinori Fujikawa. Copyright © 1996 by the President and Fellows of Harvard College. Harvard Business School case 9-597-032.

[1] $2,500 was the retail price with a monitor. A system retailed at around $1,500 in 1995 if a monitor was sold separately as shown in Exhibit 1.

Exhibit 1   Market Development and Forecasts in Japan

	Actual --> 1990	1991	1992	1993	1994	1995	Estimate 1996E
ENTIRE MARKET							
<1> Unit Sales	16,400	27,600	57,800	160,400	343,500	578,500	850,000
Growth Rate Year-on-Year (%)		168%	209%	278%	214%	168%	147%
<2> Retail Sales (¥ million)	6,430	10,290	15,470	25,020	51,530	83,880	114,080
Growth Rate Year-on-Year (%)		160%	150%	162%	206%	163%	136%
<3> Retail Price / Unit (¥)	392,073	372,826	267,647	155,985	150,015	144,996	134,212
<4> % Penetration of New Cars	0.27%	0.46%	0.96%	2.67%	5.73%	9.64%	14.17%
<5> Cumulative Number of Car Navigation System Installed	16,400	44,000	101,800	262,200	605,700	1,167,800	1,990,200
<6> % Penetration of All Cars	0.03%	0.07%	0.17%	0.44%	1.01%	1.95%	3.32%
AFTER MARKET							
<7> Unit Sales			39,000	139,016	297,900	462,500	550,000
Growth Rate Year-on-Year (%)				356%	214%	155%	119%
% of Entire Market (%)			67%	87%	87%	80%	65%
OEM MARKET							
<8> Unit Sales			18,800	21,350	45,600	116,000	300,000
Growth Rate Year-on-Year (%)				114%	214%	254%	259%
% of Entire Market (%)			33%	13%	13%	20%	35%

Exhibit 1   Market Development and Forecasts in Japan (continued)

	Forecast ---> 1997E	1998E	1999E	2000E	2005E
ENTIRE MARKET					
<1> Unit Sales	1,200,000	1,500,000	1,800,000	2,000,000	2,800,000
Growth Rate Year-on-Year (%)	141%	125%	120%	111%	107%
<2> Retail Sales (¥ million)	150,000	170,000	190,000	200,000	230,000
Growth Rate Year-on-Year (%)	131%	113%	112%	105%	103%
<3> Retail Price / Unit (¥)	125,000	113,333	105,556	100,000	82,143
<4> % Penetration of New Cars	20.00%	25.00%	30.00%	33.33%	46.67%
<5> Cumulative Number of Car Navigation System Installed	3,132,400	4,472,000	5,928,500	7,350,000	12,385,000
<6> % Penetration of All Cars	5.22%	7.45%	9.88%	12.25%	20.64%
AFTER MARKET					
<7> Unit Sales	700,000	800,000	850,000	900,000	1,100,000
Growth Rate Year-on-Year (%)	127%	114%	106%	106%	104%
% of Entire Market (%)	58%	53%	47%	45%	39%
OEM MARKET					
<8> Unit Sales	500,000	700,000	950,000	1,100,000	1,700,000
Growth Rate Year-on-Year (%)	167%	140%	136%	116%	109%
% of Entire Market (%)	42%	47%	53%	55%	61%

Notes:

<1> Manufacturer unit sales.

<2> Retail sales level do not include monitors, adapters, software, sold separately from the navigation systems.

<3> = <2>/<1>

<4> Assuming that annual new car sales in Japan were approximately 6 million. (i.e., <4>=<1>/6 million)

<5> Assuming that the car navigation system will be renewed every five years. (i.e., 1992 figure = 90-92 total, 1997 figure = 93-97 total, etc.)

<6> Assuming that there were approximately 60 million cars in Japan. (i.e., <6>=<5> / 60 million)

Source: 1990-1995 figures are actuals drawn from Yano Keizai Kenkyusho, *1996 Car Navigation Systems: Market Forecast and Corporate Strategy* (Tokyo, Japan) 1996-2005 figures are forecasts of the case writers, based on research interviews.

Exhibit 2 — Major Competitors' Unit Sales and Market Shares in Japan: 1994–1996E

Company/Brand		Unit Sales, Total Market (% Market Share) 1995		1996E		Three Years	
Pioneer	(24%)	######	(19%)	157,000	(19%)	351,000	(20%)
Sony	(23%)	98,000	(17%)	124,000	(15%)	302,000	(17%)
Matsushita	(15%)	90,000	(16%)	149,000	(18%)	289,000	(16%)
Alpine	(10%)	87,000	(15%)	127,000	(15%)	250,000	(14%)
Mitsubishi	(1%)	30,000	(5%)	41,000	(5%)	75,600	(4%)
Kenwood	(6%)	27,000	(5%)	38,000	(4%)	84,000	(5%)
Zanavi	(0%)	24,000	(4%)	45,000	(5%)	69,000	(4%)
Clarion	(5%)	24,000	(4%)	39,000	(5%)	80,000	(5%)
Fujitsu Ten	(5%)	20,000	(3%)	37,000	(4%)	75,000	(4%)
Nippon Denso	(2%)	15,000	(3%)	26,000	(3%)	47,500	(3%)
Sharp	(2%)	11,000	(2%)	13,000	(2%)	31,000	(2%)
Casio	(1%)	10,500	(2%)	11,000	(1%)	26,500	(1%)
Sumitomo Denko	(3%)	7,800	(1%)	10,000	(1%)	29,700	(2%)
Toshiba	(1%)	6,000	(1%)	8,000	(1%)	17,500	(1%)
Citizen	(0%)	6,000	(1%)	8,000	(1%)	14,000	(1%)
Calsonic	(0%)	2,800	(0%)	4,000	(0%)	7,300	(0%)
NEC	(0%)	2,000	(0%)	3,000	(0%)	6,500	(0%)
Chuo Jidosha	(0%)	2,000	(0%)	2,000	(0%)	4,000	(0%)
Maspro	(0%)	1,500	(0%)	1,000	(0%)	3,200	(0%)
Sanyo	(0%)	1,200	(0%)	2,000	(0%)	3,500	(0%)
Nakamichi	(0%)	700	(0%)	-(0%)		700	(0%) (0%)
TOTAL	(100%)	#####	(100%)	#####	(100%)	########	(100%)

sonus, the Latin word for sound. Soon thereafter, the pair renamed the company.

Internationally as well as in Japan, Sony was often first to market with technological innovations that set industry standards. In 1968, Sony's sophisticated Trinitron technology expanded the color television market. In 1979, it launched the legendary Walkman, a lightweight portable tape player with headphones. In the mid-1980s, Sony developed a compact size camcorder video camera. Such innovations turned Sony into a leader in consumer electronics with FY 1995 worldwide sales over $43 billion.

Sony's only significant failure came in the early 1980s, when its Betamax format VCR lost out to VHS. Sony had developed the video cassette recorder as early as 1975, but motion picture studios protested that the new machine would encourage widespread copyright infringement of movies and television programs. Discussions of this matter gave Sony's competitors such as Matsushita and JVC time to develop a different VCR format, VHS, which permitted an additional three hours of playing time and was incompatible with Sony's Betamax. Although Betamax was generally considered technically superior, VHS soon became the industry standard, and Sony lost its early lead in the lucrative VCR market.

The Betamax VCR experience in the early 1980s convinced Sony that technological innovation alone could not insure market dominance, and that the match between hardware and software was critical. Subsequently, Sony began to cooperate more with competitors to develop industry standards. In the 1980s, for example, Sony joined the Dutch electronic firm Philips to pioneer compact disc (CD) technology.

Company/Brand	1996E Unit Sales (% Market Share)			1996E Unit Sales (% Sales Composition)	
	After-Market	OEM		After-Market	OEM
Pioneer	(21%)	17,000	(9%)	89%	11%
Sony	(19%)	3,000	(2%)	98%	2%
Matsushita	(18%)	30,000	(16%)	80%	20%
Alpine	(11%)	57,000	(30%)	55%	45%
Mitsubishi	(4%)	16,000	(8%)	61%	39%
Kenwood	(6%)	-	(0%)	100%	0%
Zanavi	(1%)	36,000	(19%)	20%	80%
Clarion	(5%)	7,000	(4%)	82%	18%
Fujitsu Ten	(6%)	-	(0%)	100%	0%
Nippon Denso	(1%)	22,000	(12%)	15%	85%
Sharp	(2%)	-	(0%)	100%	0%
Casio	(2%)	-	(0%)	100%	0%
Sumitomo Denko	(1%)	3,000	(2%)	70%	30%
Toshiba	(1%)	-	(0%)	100%	0%
Citizen	(1%)	-	(0%)	100%	0%
Calsonic	(1%)	-	(0%)	100%	0%
NEC	(0%)	-	(0%)	100%	0%
Chuo Jidosha	(0%)	-	(0%)	100%	0%
Maspro	(0%)	-	(0%)	100%	0%
Sanyo	(0%)	-	(0%)	100%	0%
Nakamichi	(0%)	-	(0%)	-	-
TOTAL	(100%)	#####	(100%)	77%	23%

Source: Adapted from Yano Keizai Kenkyusho, op cit.

In the mid-1990s, Sony Corporation reorganized to keep the company market-driven and to increase autonomy. Sony organized its businesses into ten divisions, including Display, Home AV, Information Technology, Personal AV, Personal & Mobile Communications, Broadcast Products, Image & Sound Communication, Semiconductors, Components & Computer Peripherals, and Recording Media & Energy. To develop future top managers, Sony appointed promising young executives as presidents of each company with substantial autonomy. Masao Morita was appointed president of the Personal & Mobile Communication Company.

CAR NAVIGATION SYSTEMS

Evolving Products

A car navigation system plotted a driver's current location on a dashboard-mounted LCD monitor by calculating signals received from satellites and/or utilizing a dead reckoning system fed by speed and gyro sensors. The system also told the driver the best way to his or her destination by employing a digital map database stored on either a CD-ROM, a computer hard disk, or an IC-card. Unlike VCRs and personal computers, car navigation systems hardware and software were not standardized as of 1995, but a typical model consisted of hardware such as a satellite

Companies	NaviKen Format Group	Proprietary Format (Can Read NaviKen)[a]	Proprietary Format (Cannot Read NaviKen)[a]
	Sony	Matsushita	Pioneer
	Mitsubishi	Alpine	Clarion
	Zanavi	Kenwood	Nippon Denso
	Sharp	Fujitsu	Sumitomo Denko
	Casio		Nakamichi
	Toshiba		
	Citizen		
	Calsonic		
	NEC		
	Chuo Jidosha		
	Maspro		
	Sanyo		

Group Unit Sales (% Share)	NaviKen Format Group		Proprietary Format (Can Read NaviKen)[a]		Proprietary Format (Cannot Read NaviKen)[a]	
1994	103,100	(30%)	123,000	(36%)	117,400	(34%)
1995	200,000	(35%)	216,000	(37%)	162,500	(28%)
1996E	262,000	(31%)	361,000	(43%)	222,000	(26%)

1996E Group Unit Sales (% Composition)	NaviKen Format Group		Proprietary Format (Can Read NaviKen)[a]		Proprietary Format (Cannot Read NaviKen)[a]	
After-Market	246,000	(78%)	225,000	(73%)	173,000	(78%)
OEM	70,000	(22%)	82,000	(27%)	49,000	(22%)

Note: [a]The second group's car navigation systems can read both proprietary and NaviKen software, while the first group's systems can only read NaviKen CD-ROMs. The third group's systems can only read their respective original software.

Source: Calculation of the case writers, based on the figures in Exhibit 2.

signal receiver, a CD-ROM player, an LCD monitor mounted on/in a car dashboard, and digital map software in the form of a CD-ROM. See Exhibit 5 for a picture of a typical car navigation system. Exhibit 6 summarizes the cost and margin structure of the system.

In the late 1980s, the earliest car navigation systems could only report where a driver was, his/her desired destination, and whether or not the car was headed in the right direction. By the mid-1990s, however, the systems had become more intelligent. Recent models could inform a driver of his/her current location at all times and deduce the best route to a destination automatically by taking into account current traffic conditions. Some systems could even communicate verbally with the driver and provide turn-by-turn instructions on the LCD map or through voice.

Enabling Hardware

Car navigation systems were facilitated by the Global Positioning Satellite (GPS) system, a constellation of 24 satellites operated by the U.S. Department of Defense. GPS was originally developed at a cost of $10 billion for military applications during the Cold War, but became available for civilian use at no charge in the late 1980s.

The central concept behind GPS was triangulation. If a car's exact distance from a satellite was known, the car's

Exhibit 4   Market Forecasts for Japan, Europe, and the United States

	Estimate	Forecast --->				
	1996E	1997E	1998E	1999E	2000E	2005E
Japan						
<1> After Market (Unit)	550,000	700,000	800,000	850,000	900,000	1,100,000
<2> OEM Market (Unit)	300,000	500,000	700,000	950,000	1,100,000	1,700,000
<3> Entire Market (Unit)	850,000	1,200,000	1,500,000	1,800,000	2,000,000	2,800,000
<4> Entire Market (Retail ¥ mil.)	¥114,080	¥150,000	¥170,000	¥190,000	¥200,000	¥230,000
<5> Entire Market (Retail $ mil.)	$1,141	$1,500	$1,700	$1,900	$2,000	$2,300
<6> Retail Price / Unit ($)	$1,342	$1,250	$1,133	$1,056	$1,000	$821
<7> % Penetration of New Cars	14.17%	20.00%	25.00%	30.00%	33.33%	46.67%
<8> Cumulative Number of Installed Units	1,990,200	3,132,400	4,472,000	5,928,500	7,350,000	12,385,000
<9> % Penetration of All Cars	3.32%	5.22%	7.45%	9.88%	12.25%	20.64%
Europe[a]						
<1> After Market (Unit)	10,000	50,000	100,000	200,000	400,000	900,000
<2> OEM Market (Unit)	20,000	50,000	100,000	150,000	200,000	900,000
<3> Entire Market (Unit)	30,000	100,000	200,000	350,000	600,000	1,800,000
<4> Entire Market (Retail ¥ million)	-	-	-	-	-	-
<5> Entire Market (Retail $ million)	$60	$170	$300	$455	$600	$1,440
<6> Retail Price / Unit ($)	$2,000	$1,700	$1,500	$1,300	$1,000	$800
<7> % Penetration of New Cars	0.33%	1.11%	2.22%	3.89%	6.67%	20.00%
<8> Cumulative Number of Installed Units	30,000	130,000	330,000	680,000	1,280,000	3,752,000
<9> % Penetration of All Cars	0.02%	0.10%	0.25%	0.52%	0.98%	2.89%
US						
<1> After Market (Unit)	10,000	50,000	100,000	250,000	400,000	1,000,000
<2> OEM Market (Unit)	10,000	50,000	100,000	300,000	500,000	1,400,000
<3> Entire Market (Unit)	20,000	100,000	200,000	550,000	900,000	2,400,000
<4> Entire Market (Retail ¥ million)	-	-	-	-	-	-
<5> Entire Market (Retail $ million)	$34	$150	$260	$550	$720	$1,200
<6> Retail Price / Unit ($)	$1,700	$1,500	$1,300	$1,000	$800	$500
<7> % Penetration of New Cars	0.13%	0.67%	1.33%	3.67%	6.00%	16.00%
<8> Cumulative Number of Installed Units	20,000	120,000	320,000	870,000	1,770,000	4,720,000
<9> % Penetration of All Cars	0.01%	0.06%	0.16%	0.44%	0.89%	2.36%

	Estimate	Forecast --->				
	1996E	**1997E**	**1998E**	**1999E**	**2000E**	**2005E**
TOTAL (Japan, Europe, US)						
<1> After Market (Unit)	570,000	800,000	1,000,000	1,300,000	1,700,000	3,000,000
<2> OEM Market (Unit)	330,000	600,000	900,000	1,400,000	1,800,000	4,000,000
<3> Entire Market (Unit)	900,000	1,400,000	1,900,000	2,700,000	3,500,000	7,000,000
<4> Entire Market (Retail ¥ million)	-		-			-
<5> Entire Market (Retail $ million)	$1,235	$1,820	$2,260	$2,905	$3,320	$4,940
<6> Retail Price / Unit ($)	$1,372	$1,300	$1,189	$1,076	$949	$706

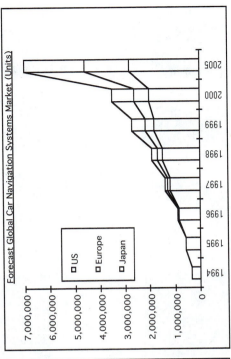

Forecast Global Car Navigation Systems Market (Units)

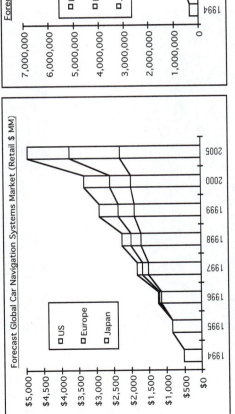

Forecast Global Car Navigation Systems Market (Retail $ MM)

Notes: [a]Europe figures include France, Germany, Italy, and UK.

<1>, <2>, <3> Manufacturer unit sales.

<3> = <1> + <2>

<4> The figures are for the value of retail sales.

<5> Assuming an exchange rate = ¥100 / $1 from 1996 throughout the year 2005.

<6> = <5> / <3>

<7> Assuming that annual new car sales in Japan, Europe and the US were approximately 6 million, 9 million, and 15 million, respectively. (i.e., <7> = <3> / 6 million)

<8> Assuming that the car navigation system will be renewed every five years. (i.e., 1992 figure = 1990-1992 total, 2000 figure = 1996-2000 total, etc.)

<9> Assuming that there were approximately 60 million cars in Japan, 130 million in Europe, and 200 million in the US. (i.e., <9> = <8> / 60 million)

Source: Forecasts of the case writers, based on research interviews.

Exhibit 5

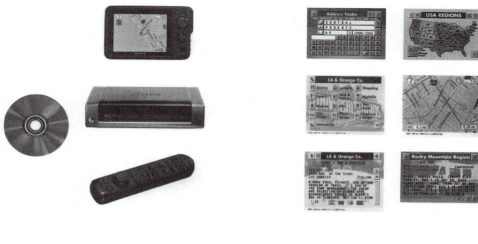

You Drive.

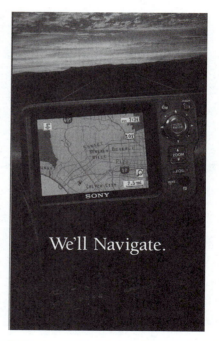

We'll Navigate.

location had to lie somewhere on the sphere defined by that radius. If the driver's distance from a second satellite were also known, the car's position had to lie along the circumference of the circle where the two spheres intersected. Knowing the distance from a third satellite would result in two points where all three spheres intersected. GPS in fact used four signals from four different satellites to locate the position of the antenna.

Exhibit 6   Typical Cost and Margin Structure for Car Navigation Systems

a. Typical Cost and Margin Structure for Car Navigation Systems:

Retail Price	100%
less **Dealer Margin**	35%
Manufacturer Selling Price	65%
less **Manufacturer Margin**	5%
Manufacturer Total Cost	60%
Indirect Cost (SGA)	10%
Direct Cost	50%
(LCD Monitor	30%)
(CD-ROM Player	8%)
(CPU	7%)
(GPS Receiver	3%)
(Other Components	2%)

b. Japanese Model (e.g., Sony NVX-F16):

Retail selling price	$2,000
less Dealer margin[a]	$700
Manufacturer selling price	$1,300
less Manufacturer total costs	$1,200
Manufacturer margin	$100

c. Overseas Model (e.g., Sony NVX-F160):

Overseas retail selling price	$3,000
less Overseas dealer margin[a]	$1,000
Manufacturer selling price	$2,000
less Manufacturer total costs[b]	$1,800
Manufacturer margin	$200

Notes: [a]Dealer charged separate fee for product installation. Japanese dealers charged around $200. US and European dealers charged around $300.

[b]Manufacturer total costs of overseas model included applicable transportation costs and import duties.

Source: Estimation of the case writers, based on research interviews.

Triangulation on GPS could result in accuracy as close as thirty meters. Worrying that GPS could be used by an enemy to guide missiles or smart bombs, Department of Defense engineers intentionally built errors into the system for civilian use. The civilian signal could deliver 95% accuracy within 100 meters of the actual location. The GPS signal could also be blocked by tall buildings, trees, or overpasses, a common problem in large cities.

In order to improve the precision in identifying the car's location on the earth, the car navigation systems were equipped with a few supporting technologies. When GPS did not function accurately, a back-up dead-reckoning system of speed and gyro sensors typically installed in the car trunk could take over seamlessly and relay the car's speed and direction to the navigation system. Aided by the dead-reckoning system, map matching technologies enabled the car navigation system to pinpoint the car's position on the digital map.

In car navigation hardware, there was no dominant product standard. Some products utilized both GPS signals and dead-reckoning systems, but others employed only one of the two. Product interfaces were also diverse. Some displayed a colorful digital map on an LCD monitor. On a typical LCD screen, a small red circle sign, representing the car, moved along a highlighted street leading the driver to his/her desired destination. Some other models' monitors showed only right or left arrow signs and the street name to signal the next appropriate turn. Others did not have display devices but provided directions verbally.

Diverse Software Formats

The software database technology used in car navigation systems was the offspring of GIS, or Geographic Information Systems. GIS was originally developed by the U.S. Department of Defense for guiding missiles. In essence, GIS software turned a conventional map into a digital database.

For accurate navigation, a digital map had to contain correct details of every street. Every sign, every painted line, every relevant piece of information along the road had to be included. For example, the database had to note whether there was a concrete divider along a highway, whether two streets intersect or one was on an overpass, and so forth. Consequently, each street corner required three to four dozen items of data.

As many data layers as desired could be added to the digitized map. Postal zip codes and phone numbers could be stored in the database so that a driver could find a destination by entering an address and/or phone number. Information on "points of interest," such as banks, restaurants and gas stations, could also be digitized on the map. One could analyze these data in hundreds of different ways and, in conjunction with a GPS receiver, could interact with the data on a real time basis. In real life, for instance, a stranger was not likely to know the ATM closest to any given spot. However, with a points of interest database, a car navigation system could sort through ATMs by distance, find the nearest one operated by the driver's preferred bank, and provide route guidance to this ATM.

Collecting and digitizing all the road related information and the point of interest data were labor intensive. Government geological surveys and commercially published maps were often old and inaccurate. Hence, digital map companies had to send out research teams to take aerial and ground photos to fill in gaps and update the old information. Collecting and digitizing the necessary information on the city of Boston, for example, required twenty engineers to work for one year. Given continuous change due to road construction and store openings and closings, digital map companies had to retain local staff to update the data.

The cost of digitizing the cartography of the United States was estimated at $1 billion with an additional $100 million a year for updating. A single company starting this task in 1995 could not achieve payback before 2005. There were two major digital map companies in the U.S. competing independently. As of early 1996, Etak, a Silicon Valley division of Rupert Murdoch's News Corporation, had covered cities representing 80% of the U.S. population. NavTech, another Silicon Valley startup, had covered 90% of the U.S. population.

There were three digital map companies working in Europe. Etak had focused its European operation on the United Kingdom and had so far covered cities accounting for 80% of the population. EGT, NavTech's European subsidiary, had covered 80% of Germany and 70% of France. A third company, TeleAtlas, was digitizing Italian maps. These companies had developed independently non-compatible digital map software.

In Japan, 40 companies, including car companies, electronic firms, and digital map developers, had formed the Japan Navigation Research Association, known as NaviKen, in the early 1980s, and completed 100% digitization of the entire country by 1988. The NaviKen format was consistently applied in the navigation systems produced by the NaviKen member companies such as Sony and Mitsubishi. However, other incompatible formats had been developed independently by Pioneer and Matsushita respectively, which did not join NaviKen. Exhibit 7 compares the number of CD-ROMs available for different competitors' car navigation systems.

The data storage media also varied. Some devices used the digital map stored on a CD-ROM, while others on computer hard disk or IC card. CD-ROM based navigation systems were popular in Japan and Europe, but hard disk and IC card were believed equally acceptable in the United States, especially for low-end products.

Distribution Channels

Car navigation systems could be sold either on an OEM basis or through after-market retail channels. Exhibit 8 summarizes the distribution alternatives.

In the OEM channel, car navigation system producers contracted with car assemblers to supply car navigation systems to the automaker's specifications. The systems were either pre-installed by the car manufacturers or installed later by dealers as a purchase option on new cars.

After-market models were usually designed and marketed by car navigation system makers and distributed through wholesalers to auto parts retailers and electronics outlets. Sales to end consumers were either made on a cash

Company Software Format	Sony NaviKen	Alpine Proprietary + NaviKen[a]		Matsushita Proprietary + NaviKen[a]		Pioneer Proprietary
General Road Maps	5	7	(2)	6	(1)	2
Sports (golf, ski, camping, etc.)	6	6	(0)	6	(0)	3
Travel (hotels, parks, etc.)	4	4	(0)	4	(0)	1
Shops/Restaurants	1	1	(0)	1	(0)	1
Radar Detection	0	0	(0)	0	(0)	1
Games/Quizzes	4	4	(0)	4	(0)	6
Karaoke	0	0	(0)	0	(0)	56
TOTAL	20	22	(2)	21	(1)	70

Note: [a]Numbers include both original and NaviKen CD-ROMs, since Alpine and Matsushita's systems can read NaviKen software.

Numbers in parentheses are proprietary CD-ROMs developed by Alpine and Matsushita.

Source: Adapted from various product catalogues.

Exhibit 8   Channels for Car Navigation Systems

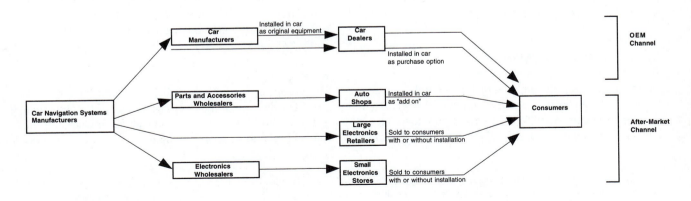

Source: Analysis of the case writers, based on research interviews.

and carry basis or involved dealer installation and other after sales services.

All components of OEM models including LCD monitors were neatly installed together with audio equipment such as radio, cassette and CD players in the car dashboard. In contrast, after-market systems usually had to be installed as "add ons" to the dashboard. Exhibit 9 compares OEM and after-market car navigation systems. Volume contracts with the car manufacturers meant that Japanese OEM products were technically one to two years behind and more expensive than after-market models.

In the Japanese market, 80% of the systems were sold through after-market channels while 20% were sold on an OEM basis. However, as the technological innovation diffused and products became more standardized, the percentages were forecast to be even by 2000 and to be reversed by 2005. The fledgling European markets mainly involved OEM sales in 1995, but the proportion of after-market sales was expected to increase. The U.S. market was still undeveloped, but OEM models were expected to exceed after-market sales, especially if the price decreased substantially.

In Japan, major auto parts chains, such as AUTOBACS and Yellow Hat, accounted for 60% of after-market unit sales. Hybrid models based on both GPS and dead-reckoning sensor were distributed though these auto parts retailers since they required professional installation and maintenance. These auto parts retailers carried at most five brands on their shelves. GPS-based systems which did not require complicated installation were channeled mainly through large electronics discount chains and more subject to price competition.

MULTINATIONAL MARKETS

Advanced Japanese Market

The Japanese market for car navigation systems was the world's largest in 1995 with sales of 580,000 units and $840 million.[2] Car navigation systems were installed in 10% of new Japanese cars in 1995. The penetration rate for all cars registered in Japan was 2%. With competition among 30 companies, the average retail price per unit decreased dramatically from $4,000 in 1990 to $2,500 in 1995. As competitors vied to introduce new models with the latest technological features, market shares fluctuated wildly.

The popularity of car navigation systems reflected the uniqueness of the Japanese car driving environment. First, the Japanese road system was more complicated than its European and U.S. counterparts. Since not all the streets had names and road signs were few and far between, people relied heavily on maps and landmarks for finding their way. Caught on narrow roads without the benefit of a highly developed highway system, drivers were always looking for a way to bypass heavily congested arteries, especially in major metropolitan areas.

Given serious traffic jams and well-developed train systems, most Japanese used their cars for weekend joy-riding rather than daily commuting.[3] Many therefore welcomed car navigation systems as a means of finding their way around in unfamiliar cities and towns.

Japanese car drivers, especially young people, were willing to spend heavily on cars and electronic accessories. Many drivers would readily invest over $2,000; few U.S. drivers would invest more than $1,000. Outside Japan, higher auto theft rates discouraged heavy investment in expensive electronic options. Exhibit 10 summarizes results of Japanese consumer and dealer research.

The Japanese car navigation market was boosted further by Japanese government investment in improving the efficiency of the Japanese road system. A real-time traffic information system called VICS (Vehicle Information and Communication System), would be launched in Tokyo and Osaka in 1996.[4] With VICS information, the next generation of navigation systems would be able to incorporate real-time traffic and weather alerts so that drivers could avoid gridlock, accidents or washed out roads.

Emerging European Market

The European market lagged behind Japan by some five years. However, once major electronics manufacturers such as Bosch and Philips introduced products in Germany, the market began to develop. The market was expected to grow

---

2 The concept of the car navigation system had been around in Japan since the early 1980s. Honda claimed to be the first company to put a navigation system on the road. However, the dead-reckoning system, which required a driver to replace a slide-like map at each town boundary, did not attract consumers. The Japanese market remained small during the 1980s although electronic car component producers such as Alpine and Nippon Denso did supply car navigation systems on an OEM basis to the automobile assemblers. They offered the navigation systems as optional accessories on a limited number of their luxury models, such as the Honda Legend and the Toyota Crown. The navigation systems at that time were priced at around $6,000.

3 If all the cars registered in Japan were to be on the road at the same time, the distance between each would be only four feet.

4 The ATIS (Advanced Traffic Information System) was launched earlier in 1995. The system allowed a driver to retrieve real-time traffic information by using a car cellular phone.

Exhibit 9

Exhibit 9   (continued)

Exhibit 10   Results of Japanese Consumer and Dealer Surveys: 1992–1995

1992 Consumer Survey[a]

- Forty-five percent expressed their interest in buying a car navigation system in one or two years; two percent had already purchased one.

- Those who would buy a system were willing to spend $500-$1,000 (50%), $1,000-$2,000 (40%) and $2,000+(10%).

- Seventy-five percent of those who would buy a system rated "accuracy of road map" as an important factor for their purchase decision, followed by "detailed traffic information" (56%), "number of CD-ROMs" (52%) and "up-to-date point-of-interest information" (43%).

- Benefits mentioned in order of frequency: can enjoy weekend drive better (90%); can drive in unfamiliar area (80%); can use landmarks for finding a route (75%).

1994 Dealer Survey[b]

- Eighty percent of respondents stated that the price of car navigation systems was too high. Among these, 80% believed $1,500 was appropriate and 20% said $1,000.

- The most frequently asked question by customers to retailers was: "Can I use NaviKen format CD-ROMs?"

- Ninety-two percent of dealer salespeople preferred selling systems with NaviKen compatible software.

1995 Customer Survey[c]

- Customer demographics was as follows: were as follows:
  - 20-24 years (15%), 25-29 years (30%), 30-39 years (40%), and 40 years and older (15%);
  - married (44%) and not-married (56%);
  - male (95%) and female (5%).
  - 75% owned new cars and 25% used cars
  - Average price of their cars was $33,000.

- Respondents used car navigation systems: when driving in unfamiliar areas (95%); when enjoying weekend drives (85%); not during regular commute (70%); all the time (15%).

- Ninety percent stated that a map display was essential for route guidance while 10% said arrow signs and voice guidance were sufficient.

- Important factors influencing the purchase decision in order of frequency of mention: accuracy of map and map-matching; automatic route calculation; easy-to-set-up destination; speed of route calculation.

- Respondents wished to have the following information: "real time traffic jam" (100%), "one-ways" (85%), "real-time parking space" (80%), "alternative bypass route" (80%), "expected arrival time to the destination" (75%).

Source: Compiled from the following surveys conducted by one of the car navigation systems producers:
[a]Survey of 550 high potential purchasers, sampled from car audio magazine readers in October 1992.
[b]Survey of dealer salespeople in 20 largest auto parts chain stores, conducted in May 1994.
[c]Survey of 600 owners of car navigation systems, sampled from car audio magazine readers in October 1995.

from annual sales of 30,000 units and $ 60 million in 1995 to 600,000 units and $600 million by 2000 (see Exhibit 4).

European road systems were complex, especially in historic inner cities. However, most streets had names and road signage was good. As a result, opinions differed on whether a car navigation system needed to show a digital map on an LCD monitor or if right/left arrow signs and voice guidance were sufficient.

European drivers frequently drove across borders. Car navigation systems therefore needed to provide multilingual guidance. Digital map software also had to correspond to different traffic rules and road regulations from country to country.

European governments collaborated on efforts to improve the highway system. For example, the European Union's DRIVE program analyzed how the car should relate to the road infrastructure, while the PROMETHEUS project involving all major European manufacturers examined how cars could communicate with each other. The technologies developed through these projects contributed to Philips' and Bosch's development of navigation technologies such as route calculation and guidance.[5]

Untapped U.S. Market

The U.S. market lagged both Europe and Japan. Car navigation systems were not widely known. However, one forecast expect the U.S. market would surpass the European market by 2000, with annual sales of 900,000 units and $720 million, and approach the size of the Japanese market by 2005, with sales of 2.4 million units valued at $1.2 billion a year (see Exhibit 4).

The United States was well-organized with street names, traffic signs, and highly developed highway systems. The value of car navigation systems which pinpointed a car's current location was not so obvious to the U.S. driver. For car navigation systems to be attractive, they had to provide turn-by-turn route guidance and other more sophisticated functions.

As of 1995, few U.S. consumers were familiar with car navigation systems. A manager at one digital map maker explained:

> If it were described to you before you experienced it, you might not understand. But after testing the system, most drivers come around. All it takes, after all, is the admission that a map database knows more about the road than you do.[6]

Consumer research studies indicated rising interest among U.S. consumers. One study reported that 58% of car owners had heard about vehicle navigation systems, primarily through television (37%) or published material (36%). Among those aware, most could recall the system's purpose and basic features, but relatively few understood what "GPS" meant, knew about voice prompts, or about systems being available in rental cars.

The same research reported that 70% of respondents were interested in purchasing a car navigation system. Among those, 26% were interested in buying an OEM, pre-installed, in-dash model with display, 57% voted for an after-market, on-dash model with a monitor, while 17% indicated preference for a lower-end, voice-navigation model with no display. Respondents were willing to pay $700 to $1,000 for a pre-installed OEM model, $600 to $700 for the second type, and $500 to $600 for the third type. Exhibit 11 summarizes the detailed research results.

Another survey conducted by J.D. Power and Associates focused on potential purchasers. The study involved 170 consumers taking two-day test drives of navigation system-equipped automobiles, and completing three questionnaires: prior to driving the system-equipped cars (to assess awareness and image of the navigation systems); following a ten-minute test drive (to simulate consumer impressions after a dealership test drive); and after driving the car for two days (to simulate impressions following an experience driving a system-equipped rental car). Exhibit 12 summarizes the research results.

The survey revealed that both the ten-minute and the two-day test drives enhanced respondents' understanding of the system's features, benefits, and ease of use. After the initial test drive, participants noted several key advantages including convenience, the ability to save time and money, the ability to replace maps, and less of a need to ask for directions. The extended two-day test led to lower stress and improved driving confidence. The longer test drive increased the likelihood of respondents recommending the system to family and friends.

In 1992, five years after Japan, the federal U.S. government began a six-year program of investing in smart highway technologies, including sensors, television

---

5 "Smart Cars," *TelecomWorld*, Aug. 1992, p.44-45
6 *Wired*, Winter 1995

Exhibit 11   Survey of California Car Renters: January 1996

- Drivers were willing to pay, on average, $5 more per day to rent a car with a navigation system.

- Drivers who would purchase or lease a car with a navigation system (70% of the sample) were willing to spend, on average, an extra $550. Eleven drivers were willing to spend over $1,000.

- Drivers who would buy navigation systems and install them in their current cars (35% of the sample) were willing to spend, on average, $1,100.

- Twenty percent said they would buy the navigation system if it cost $1,200.

- Twenty percent stated they used the system "all the time." Another 30% used it "a lot."

- Benefits mentioned in order of frequency: prevents you from getting lost in a new city; helps you find your destination; eliminates the need for maps; increases driving safety; you don't have to stop and ask directions; takes you via best route; gives feeling of confidence when driving.

- Problems mentioned in order of frequency: took time to figure out how to use it; destination not in computer; not able to calibrate alternate route; out of range error; directions unclear and/or hard to hear; monitor hard to read.

- Sixty percent found the navigation system worked better than they expected.

- Sixty percent used the system for guidance in getting to a destination. Twenty percent used it for finding points of interest, for experimenting with different routes and for determining current location.

- Two-thirds of respondents stated the device was easier to use when the car was parked. Forty percent believed it was distracting to use while driving.

Source: Compiled from survey of 53 frequent Avis car renters in California, conducted by Center for Strategy Research, January 1996.

cameras and radars to monitor city traffic and relay traffic conditions to central computers. From workstations at command headquarters, technicians would be able to alter freeway signals and stoplights to reroute traffic, and relay advisories to cars equipped with more sophisticated navigation systems. On the other hand, safety regulations in thirteen major states including California and New York prohibited any in-car visual devices, except for security purposes.

SONY IN INTERNATIONAL COMPETITION

Competition in Japan

In November 1990, the first GPS-based after-market car navigation system was introduced by Pioneer Electronic Corporation, a Japanese leader in car stereo and laser disc players. Since the GPS signal was not yet available around the clock and was easily interrupted by high-rise buildings in Tokyo, Pioneer defined the product as a "Satellite Cruising System," emphasizing the innovative

Exhibit 12   Results of J.D. Power Consumer Survey: August 1995

- Using a ten-point scale for satisfaction, where ten is "extremely satisfied," eighty percent of respondents rated their overall satisfaction as a "nine" or "ten," resulting in a mean of 8.43.

- Sixty percent were "very likely" to recommend the system to family and friends after the ten-minute test drive. The percentage increased to 70% after the two-day test drive.

- Respondents preferred an in-dash OEM system to an on-dash after-market model by a margin of four to one, due to perceived better quality and system reliability resulting from more professional installation and better integration with the vehicle's electrical system.

- Those who would buy an after-market system mentioned perceived transferability/portability and lower price as reasons for their preference. The average expected price for an after-market model was $900, versus $1,000 for an OEM system.

- Those preferring an after-market model expected to purchase it at "specialty store" (41%), "electronic store" (17%), "discount store" (13%) and "department store" (6%). "Specialty store" included outlets specializing in selling and installing alarms, audio systems, and vehicle cellular phones.

- Over eighty percent said that availability of a car navigation system would be an important factor in deciding which vehicle to purchase next time.

- Regarding the value of different point-of-interest information, "emergency assistance/hospital/police" was rated highest (9.03), followed by "auto care/gas" (8.23), "travel points" (8.13), "entertainment/tourist attractions" (8.04), "business facilities" (7.50) and "ATMs/banks" (7.39).

- Focus group discussions revealed high interest in point-of-interest listings of new and different entertainment and dining options, particularly in unfamiliar areas. Said one New York participant:

    "We went to Connecticut to visit relatives and arrived early and decided to get something to eat We just looked through point-of-interest listings and selected a restaurant."

A participant from Los Angeles noted:
    "The system opens up your world; it lists theaters and restaurants and places you haven't heard of."

Notes: Survey of 170 high potential purchasers by J.D. Power and Associates, July and August 1995.

Respondents participated in a two-day test drive of a vehicle equipped with an Avis car navigation system.

They were screened for the following criteria:

- Household income of at least $50,000
- Cellular phone ownership and monthly cellular phone bill of $50 or more
- Average of 2 or more hours per day in vehicle on business travel (excluding normal commute)
- Ages 25 to 59

Source: Adapted from J.D. Power and Associates, *The Power Report*, November 1995.

and entertainment aspects of the product rather than its practical capabilities as a navigation device.[7] Pioneer had developed its own digital map software and stressed the variety of point-of-interest information its system could provide, ranging from hotels to restaurants. In addition, to distract drivers from Japan's endless traffic jams, Pioneer included entertainment software containing games, quizzes, horoscopes and karaoke. Pioneer distributed the products through the same channels used for conventional car stereos, principally auto parts shops, since the product required professional installation. Despite a high retail price over $5,000, Pioneer sold 20,000 units annually in the early 1990s.

The market changed dramatically in June 1993, when Sony entered the after-market segment with the NVX-F10 including a 4-inch LCD monitor at a low-price of $2,000. Six months later, Sony introduced NVX-15 with a larger 5-inch display at $2,500. Unlike Pioneer, Sony emphasized the product's practical benefits and named it "Digital Map Car Navigation System." Sony advertised the product as a problem-solving device for drivers, who did not want to face traffic jams, get lost in unfamiliar towns, or be late for appointments. These GPS-based products showed only the driver's current position on the digital map screen, but did not provide route guidance toward the destination. However, sharply lower prices attracted many consumers. Aiming at rapid market expansion, Sony distributed almost 50% of its units through consumer electronics channels. Sony sold some 10,000 units monthly through 1993, achieving a 60% market share.

To develop the market further, Sony set out to establish an industry standard for digital map software. Sony was the most active member of the Navigation Research Association to set the NaviKen format for CD-ROM-based digital maps. The standard setting effort lowered entry barriers, resulting in 10 new entrants in 1994 and another 5 in 1995. Competition fueled market growth from 160,000 units in 1993, to 340,000 units in 1994, and to 580,000 units in 1995.

Market growth encouraged intense competition and faster new product development. Exhibit 13 reports the timing of product introductions by different competitors. Once every six months during 1994 and 1995, competitors introduced progressively more advanced products. In April 1994, Matsushita, which had not joined NaviKen, was the first to develop a hybrid system employing both GPS and dead-reckoning sensor. The Matsushita model was also the first to be able to calculate and communicate the best route to a destination. In October 1994, Alpine, which was originally a NaviKen member but later became an independent developer, introduced the first hybrid model that could provide turn-by-turn route guidance. In early 1995, Pioneer introduced a new hybrid model with a flash memory chip in its CPU; this enabled the entire system to be upgraded by just installing a new CD-ROM. As shown in Exhibit 14, these more sophisticated hybrid models began to outsell the simpler GPS-based products by 1995.

NaviKen member companies, including Sony, did not respond quickly enough. It took the 40 NaviKen members more than a year to agree on a standardized software upgrade. In addition, NaviKen members saw little room to differentiate their products from each other. As shown in Exhibit 15, Sony introduced new products almost every six months, but all were modified versions of the original GPS-based products, which did not provide automatic route calculation or turn-by-turn route guidance. In May 1994, Sony introduced NVX-F16, an extended version of the NVX-F15, but sold only 15,000 units by April 1996. In October 1994, Sony introduced NVX-B50 which employed a CD-ROM changer in which a driver could place six different CD-ROMs. The product sold only 9,000 units by April 1996. Sony had perhaps introduced the product too early because the average navigation system owner had only 1.5 CD-ROMs as of 1995.

In July 1995, Sony finally introduced NVX-S1, a hybrid system with a route guidance function. However, the market did not respond well to this late entry. According to a trade magazine, NVX-S1, which still employed the NaviKen standard in its digital map database, calculated a route too slowly and provided turn-by-turn guidance too infrequently, compared to competitive products. See Exhibit 16 for a summary of the magazine's product comparison.

By 1995, competition focused on the richness of the digital map databases. In October 1995, Alpine introduced another new product with a database of 11 million phone numbers built into its digital map software which a driver could use to identify his/her destination. The product sold well, giving Alpine to the market share leadership, as shown in Exhibit 17. Other competitors followed suit, building more advanced databases filled with large numbers of phone numbers, landmarks, and other point-of-interest information.

---

7 With only 12 satellites until 1992, GPS did not provide the signals necessary for 24-hour coverage. The system became complete with 24 satellites in 1993.

Company/Brand	1990	1991	1992	1993	1994	1995	TOTAL	1995 Product Line[a]
Pioneer	2	0	1	4	4	3	14	7
Sony	0	0	1	3	5	5	14	8
Matsushita	0	0	0	1	3	3	7	4
Alpine	0	0	0	3	2	2	7	2
Mitsubishi	0	0	1	1	3	4	9	6
Kenwood	0	0	1	0	3	2	6	3
Zanavi	0	0	0	0	0	4	4	4
Clarion	0	0	0	2	1	2	5	3
Fujitsu Ten	0	0	0	0	1	3	4	3
Nippon Denso	0	0	0	0	0	2	2	2
Sharp	0	0	0	0	3	0	3	2
Casio	0	0	0	0	1	1	2	2
Sumitomo Denko	0	0	0	1	3	1	5	3
Toshiba	0	0	0	2	2	3	7	5
Citizen	0	0	0	0	0	3	3	3
Calsonic	0	0	0	0	2	3	5	4
NEC	0	0	0	0	1	1	2	1
Chuo Jidosha	0	0	0	0	1	1	2	1
Maspro	0	0	1	0	1	1	3	2
Sanyo	0	0	0	1	0	3	4	3
Nakamichi	0	0	0	0	1	0	1	1
TOTAL	2	0	5	18	37	47	109	69

Note: [a]After adjusting for discontinued products.

Source: Analysis of the case writers, based on research interviews.

Fighting against heavy odds in the main models, Sony turned its product strategy back to the GPS-based model, by introducing portable navigation systems. In December 1995, Sony introduced Handy Navigation System GPX-5, the world's first detachable model. It could be used both inside and outside an automobile, targeting customers who wanted to use the system for outdoor camping, bike touring, and marine sports. The GPS-based device alone retailed for $2,000, with an option to purchase a gyroscopic sensor to convert the system into a hybrid for an additional $300. A customer could also add a home station kit for $200; this could connect a navigation system to a home television and enable a consumer to plan a route before going out to drive. See Exhibit 18 for pictures of Sony's portable navigation system.

European Competition

In Europe, car navigation systems were first installed on an OEM basis in luxury automobiles in late 1994. Philips developed its first system as an optional accessory to BMW's 7- and 5-Series models in October 1994. Philips' model employed a hybrid system with GPS and dead-reckoning sensors, provided route guidance by either map, arrows, or voice, and used the CD-ROM based digital map software developed by EGT, a subsidiary of NavTech of the United States. Retailing for DM6,900 ($4,600), the first model sold 10,000 units in 1995. In September 1995, Philips started marketing the same product at the same price through after-market channels in Germany and France, but sold only 400 units in the last three months of 1995.

Exhibit 14　　　Unit Market Shares of Advanced Models in Japan: 1993–1995

Turn-by-Turn Route Guidance

	No (GPS)	Yes (Hybrid)
1993	98%	2%
1994	56%	44%
1995	20%	80%

Automatic Route Calculation

	No (Manual)	Yes (Automatic)
1993	97%	3%
1994	50%	50%
1995	30%	70%

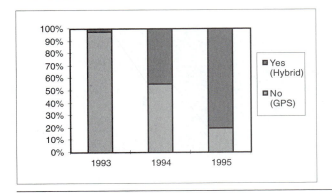

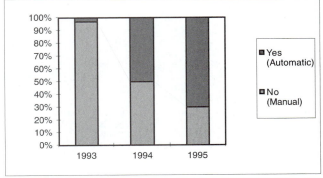

Source:　Analysis of the case writers, based on research interviews.

In October 1994, Bosch began supplying car navigation systems for Mercedes S-Class models. Bosch's product was similar to Philips' except that it provided route guidance only with arrow signs and voice direction, with no map on the display. Bosch employed the CD-ROM-based map database developed by Etak. Retailing for DM 4,000 ($2,700), the product sold 8,000 units in 1995. Bosch also developed a model with a map on the monitor for the after-market segment in Germany and France, introducing it in June 1995, three months earlier than Philips. Retailing for DM6,500 ($4,300), the after-market model sold 1,800 units by December 1995.

Besides the two European companies, only Sony competed in the after-market segment. Sony started test marketing its GPS-based model in France in late 1995, but sold only 300 units by April 1996. The product specification was similar to Sony's NVX-F16 and used Etak software. The GPS system pinpointed the car's current position on an LCD monitor, but did not give route guidance to the destination. It showed a driver where the destination was located, but the driver had to plan the route.

It was unclear whether Sony would continue marketing the tested model in Europe.

Some other companies including Alpine, Matsushita, and Pioneer were said to be planning to enter the European market in 1997-98. Luxury car manufacturers such as Jaguar and Volvo were reportedly considering OEM installation of car navigation systems. Volkswagen, Audi, and Opel were rumored to be seeking OEM suppliers of low-end models offering voice navigation with no monitor for around DM 600 ($400). Exhibit 19 summarizes current and prospective competitors in Europe and the characteristics of their products.

U.S. Competition

As shown in Exhibit 4, sales of 1 million units per year were expected in the United States by 2000. On the other hand, none of the models introduced to date had sold more than a few thousand units as of 1995. Car navigation systems were not yet widely known among U.S. consumers.

Industry observers believed price reductions would be critical before demand for car navigation systems would

Exhibit 15   Sony Product Introduction Chronology: 1992–1995

General Information

Product	Retail Price	Launch Date	Cumulative Unit Sales[a]	(%)	1995 Unit Sales[a]	(%)	Hardware GPS or Hybrid	w/ or w/o Monitor b
NVX-1	$4,700	92/06	7,000	(3%)	-	(0%)	GPS	w/
NVX-F10	$2,100	93/06	100,000	(41%)	-	(0%)	GPS	w/
NVX-F15	$2,800	93/10	15,000	(6%)	-	(0%)	GPS	w/
NVX-F1	$1,600	93/10	4,000	(2%)	-	(0%)	GPS	w/
NVX-2	open price	94/02	3,000	(1%)	-	(0%)	GPS	w/o
NVX-F16	$2,500	94/06	15,000	(6%)	7,000	(7%)	GPS	w/
NVX-3	$1,400	94/06	4,000	(2%)	-	(0%)	GPS	w/o
NVX-B50	$1,800	94/10	9,000	(4%)	4,000	(4%)	Hybrid	w/o
NVX-4	$1,500	94/10	9,000	(4%)	4,000	(4%)	Hybrid	w/o
NVX-F16MK2	$2,500	95/02	10,000	(4%)	10,000	(10%)	GPS (w/ Hybrid Option)	w/
NVX-A1	$1,300	95/04	4,000	(2%)	10,000	(10%)	GPS	w/o
NVX-S1	$1,500	95/07	40,000	(16%)	40,000	(41%)	Hybrid	w/o
NVX-F30	$2,300	95/07	20,000	(8%)	20,000	(20%)	GPS	w/
GPX-5	$2,100	95/12	3,000	(1%)	3,000	(3%)	GPS (w/ Hybrid Option)	w/
TOTAL			243,000	(100%)	98,000	(100%)		

Exhibit 15   Sony Product Introduction Chronology: 1992–1995 (continued)

| Product | Functions | | | |
	Route Guidance	Route Calculation	Auto Route Re-Calculation	Voice Recognition
NVX-1	No	No	No	No
NVX-F10	No	No	No	No
NVX-F15	No	No	No	No
NVX-F1	No	No	No	No
NVX-2	No	No	No	No
NVX-F16	No	No	No	No
NVX-3	No	No	No	No
NVX-B50	No	No	No	No
NVX-4	No	No	No	No
NVX-F16MK2	No	No	No	No
NVX-A1	No	Yes	No	Optional
NVX-S1	Yes	Yes	No	Optional
NVX-F30	Yes	Yes	No	Optional
GPX-5	Yes	Yes	No	Optional

Notes:

[a]All sales were made in Japan in the after-market. All products used the NaviKen format.

[b]"w/o monitor" means that the product was sold without a monitor. A customer needed to buy a monitor (which cost $500-$1,000) to complete the system.

Source: Analysis of the case writers, based on research interviews.

Exhibit 16   Top 10 Brand Product Comparisons: 1995

Company	Product[a]	Retail Price	Launch Date	1995 Unit Sales[a]	Hardware GPS or Hybrid	w/ or w/o Monitor[b]	Software Functions Digital Map Format	Route Guidance	Route Calculation	Auto Route Re-Calculation	Voice Recognition
Pioneer	AVIC-XA1	$2,630	95/11	30,000	Hybrid	w/	Original Only	Yes	Yes	No	No
Sony	NVX-S1	$1,500	95/07	40,000	Hybrid	w/o	NaviKen Only	Yes	Yes	No	Optional
Matsushita	CN-V700	$1,570	95/07	50,000	Hybrid	w/o	Both	Yes	Yes	Yes	No
Alpine	NTV-W055V	$2,480	95/11	40,000	Hybrid	w/	Both	Yes	Yes	Yes	No
Mitsubishi	CU-9510	$1,490	95/05	15,000	Hybrid	w/o	NaviKen Only	Yes	Yes	No	No
Kenwood	GPR-03EX	$1,450	95/10	15,000	Hybrid	w/o	Both	Yes	Yes	No	Yes
Zanavi	XA-N1	$1,480	95/06	5,000	Hybrid	w/o	NaviKen Only	Yes	Yes	No	No
Clarion	NAX9100	$1,470	95/11	10,000	Hybrid	w/o	Original Only	Yes	Yes	No	No
Fujitsu Ten	E500NCU	$1,650	95/11	10,000	Hybrid	w/o	Both	Yes	Yes	Yes	No
Nippon Denso	MV-1000S	$2,580	95/01	3,000	Hybrid	w/	Original Only	Yes	Yes	No	No

Company	Product[a]	User Test Result (5=excellent, 1=poor) Easy To Command	Easy To Use Read Monitor	Easy To Find Destination	Speed of Route Calculation (Seconds)	Accuracy of Route Guidance	Total Score
Pioneer	AVIC-XA1	2	3	3	2 (141)	3	13
Sony	NVX-S1	2	3	3	2 (121)	2	12
Matsushita	CN-V700	5	5	4	3 (58)	5	22
Alpine	NTV-W055V	4	4	5	5 (16)	5	23
Mitsubishi	CU-9510	3	3	2	2 (110)	4	14
Kenwood	GPR-03EX	3	3	2	3 (57)	2	13
Zanavi	XA-N1	4	3	4	4 (43)	3	18
Clarion	NAX9100	3	5	3	4 (46)	4	19
Fujitsu Ten	E500NCU	3	4	2	2 (110)	3	14
Nippon Denso	MV-1000S	5	4	5	4 (42)	4	22
	Average	3.4	3.7	3.3	3.1 (74)	3.5	17

Notes: [a]For each brand, this exhibit reports sales of the best selling after-market model in 1995.
[b]"w/o monitor" means that the product sold without a monitor. A customer needed to buy a monitor (which cost $500-$1,000) to complete the system.

Source: Adapted from *1996 New and Improved Car Navigation Systems* , Naigai Shuppan Publishing, 1995

1994 January-June		1994 July-December		1995 January-June		1995 July-December	
Pioneer	24%	Pioneer	29%	Alpine	24%	Alpine	29%
Sony	24%	Alpine	16%	Pioneer	21%	Pioneer	20%
Matsushita	15%	Sony	13%	Matsushita	14%	Matsushita	15%
Kenwood	9%	Matsushita	11%	Sony	8%	Clarion	10%
Fujitsu	7%	Fujitsu	8%	Clarion	7%	Kenwood	9%
Clarion	6%	Kenwood	7%	Kenwood	6%	Sony	7%
Alpine	5%	Clarion	6%	Fujitsu	6%	Fujitsu	4%
Sumitomo Denko	4%	Sumitomo Denko	6%	Sumitomo Denko	3%	Sumitomo Denko	3%
Others	4%	Others	4%	Others	10%	Others	3%

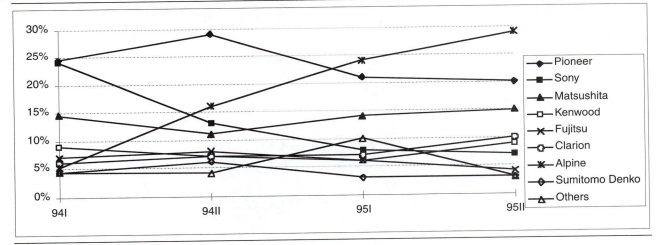

Note: This exhibit reports unit market shares in the auto parts chain channel, which represented 60% of after-market unit sales in Japan.

Source: Analysis of the case writers, based on research interviews.

take off in the United States. Market research revealed that few U.S. consumers would pay over $1,000 for car navigation systems. Auto manufacturers had told the car navigation makers that they needed prices to drop to as low as $500, which was not expected until 2005 after further investments in mapping, data storage, and route guidance were completed.

Zexel, a Japanese auto parts supplier, was the first to bring car navigation systems to the United States.[8] As an OEM, Zexel began supplying systems for GM's Oldsmobile Eighty Eight in summer 1994. Zexel's navigation products employed hybrid systems with GPS and dead-reckoning sensors and provided route guidance by either map, arrows, or voice. The digital map database was stored in a 170MB hard disk drive located in a car trunk. With the price tag of $1,995, however, the product was expensive. In 1994, the most expensive car accessory in the United States was a European branded premium hi-fi speaker system for $1,200. Due to a lack of marketing expertise at Zexel and Oldsmobile and due to the fact that digital maps were only available for a few major cities, only 2,500 units were sold by the end of 1995.

---

[8] Zexel did not sell car navigation systems either on an OEM basis or through after-market channels in Japan as of 1996.

Exhibit 18

車で Car Navigation

外で Field Navigation

家で Home Navigation

Exhibit 19 Current and Prospective Competitors in Europe

Current Competitors

OEM
General Information

Company	Auto Maker	Retail Price	Launch Date	Cumulative Unit Sales	Hardware GPS or Hybrid	Interface: map, arrow, voice	Software Digital Map Format	Software Media
Bosch	Mercedes	DM 4,025	10/94	8,000	Hybrid	arrow, voice	Etak	CD-ROM
Philips	BMW	DM 6,900	10/94	10,000	Hybrid	map, arrow, voice	NavTech	CD-ROM

After-Market
General Information

Company	Product	Retail Price	Launch Date	Cumulative Unit Sales	Hardware GPS or Hybrid	Interface: map, arrow, voice	Software Digital Map Format	Software Media
Bosch	Travel Pilot	DM 6,500	06/95	1,800	Hybrid	map,arrow,voice	Etak	CD-ROM
Philips	Carin	DM 6,900	09/95	400	Hybrid	map, arrow, voice	NavTech	CD-ROM
Sony	NVX-160	DM 5,500	10/95	300	GPS	map	Etak	CD-ROM

Prospective Competitors

OEM
General Information

Company	Auto Maker	Retail Price	Launch Date	Expected Unit Sales	Hardware GPS or Hybrid	Interface: map, arrow, voice	Software Digital Map Format	Software Media
Mitsubishi	Volvo	-	Early 97	-	Hybrid	map, arrow, voice	TeleAtlas	CD-ROM
Bosch	VW	DM 600	Early 97	-	GPS	voice	Etak	CD-ROM
Bosch	Audi	DM 600	Early 97	-	GPS	voice	Etak	CD-ROM

After-Market
General Information

Company	Product	Retail Price	Launch Date	Expected Unit Sales	Hardware GPS or Hybrid	Interface: map, arrow, voice	Software Digital Map Format	Software Media
Alpine	NTV-W055V	DM 6,000	Mid 96	-	Hybrid	map, arrow, voice	NavTech	CD-ROM
Matsushita	-	-	Early 97	-	Hybrid	map, arrow, voice	-	-
Pioneer	-	-	Early 97	-	Hybrid	map, arrow, voice	-	-

Source: Analysis of the case writers, based on research interviews.

Exhibit 20   Current and Prospective Competitors in the US

Current Competitors

OEM
General Information

					Hardware		Software	
Company	Auto Maker	Retail Price	Launch Date	Cumulative Unit Sales	GPS or Hybrid	Interface: map, arrow, voice	Digital Map Format	Software Media
Zexel	GM/Oldsmobile	$1,995	08/94	2,500	Hybrid	map, arrow, voice	NavTech	Hard Disk (170MB)

After-Market
General Information

					Hardware		Software	
Company	Product	Retail Price	Launch Date	Cumulative Unit Sales	GPS or Hybrid	Interface: map, arrow, voice	Digital Map Format	Software Media
Sony	NVX-160	$2,995	10/94	800	GPS	map	Etak	CD-ROM
Rockwell	GuideStar	$1,995	01/95	7,000	Hybrid	map, arrow, voice	NavTech	Hard Disk (170MB)
Amerigon	AudioNav	$600	12/95	-	Dead Reckoning No GPS	voice	NavTech	CD-ROM

Exhibit 20   Current and Prospective Competitors in the US (continued)

Prospective Competitors

OEM

General Information				Hardware		Software	
Company	Auto Maker	Retail Price	Launch Date	Cumulative Unit Sales	GPS or Hybrid	Interface: map, arrow, voice	Digital Map Format	Software Media
Alpine	Honda	$2,000	Mid 96	-	Hybrid	map, arrow, voice	NavTech	Hard Disk (170MB)
Nippon Denso	Toyota	-	Late 96	-	Hybrid	map, arrow, voice	NavTech	Hard Disk (170MB)
Bosch	Mercedes	-	Early 99	-	Hybrid	map, arrow, voice	Etak	CD-ROM

(Note: header rows shown above carry merged-column labels: General Information | Hardware | Software; columns are Company, Auto Maker, Retail Price, Launch Date, Cumulative Unit Sales, GPS or Hybrid, Interface: map, arrow, voice, Digital Map Format, Software Media.)

After-Market

General Information				Hardware		Software	
Company	Product	Retail Price	Launch Date	Cumulative Unit Sales	GPS or Hybrid	Interface: map, arrow, voice	Digital Map Format	Software Media
Delco (US)	Telepath 100	$500	Mid 96	-	Dead Reckoning No GPS	voice	NavTech	CD-ROM
Pioneer	-	-	Early 97	-	Hybrid	map, arrow, voice	NavTech	CD-ROM
Matsushita	-	-	Early 97	-	Hybrid	map, arrow, voice	-	CD-ROM
Clarion	-	-	Early 97	-	Hybrid	map, arrow, voice	NavTech	CD-ROM
Kenwood	-	-	Early 97	-	Hybrid	map, arrow, voice	NavTech	CD-ROM

Source: Analysis of the case writers, based on research interviews.

Zexel licensed its product technology to Rockwell for after-market sales. Rockwell sold the product to rental car companies such as Avis and Hertz. The rental car companies purchased a few thousand units in total and rented the systems for a $5 to $7 daily upcharge. However, neither Rockwell nor the rental car companies had aggressively marketed the product.

Sony began marketing the NVX-F160, the U.S. version of the Japanese model NVX-F16, in California and Florida in late 1994. Despite its lack of route guidance capability, Sony launched the NVX-160, the most advanced model in Sony's product line as of 1994, in order to be the first to market an after-market model. At a price of $2,995, only 800 units were sold by the end of 1995.

A low-end product priced under $1,000 was introduced in December 1995 by Amerigon, a Silicon Valley startup known for its voice recognition technology. The system was bundled with car stereos and sold under car audio brand names by manufacturers such as Alpine, Clarion, and Kenwood. The price was about $600, although when the stereo and installation were included, the price was more like $1,000 to $1,500. This CD-ROM-based system, named AudioNav, did not employ GPS, relying instead on a dead-reckoning sensor alone. There was no monitor; only a voice system that used a microphone similar to one used in a cellular phone. The driver had to spell out the destination for route calculation. It was hands free, but the driver had to find a street sign or local landmark if he/she became lost. Unit sales to date were unknown.

Within a year or two, Alpine and Nippon Denso were expected to supply OEM models to Honda and Toyota factories in the United States. Pioneer, Alpine, and Matsushita were expected to enter the U.S. after-market segment, introducing modified versions of their latest domestic market models. Exhibit 20 lists current and prospective competitors in the United States and characteristics of their products.

SUMMER 1996: RECONSTRUCT THE GLOBAL STRATEGY

Masao Morita, the son of the legendary founder Akio Morita, contemplated how to formulate its multinational marketing strategy for the fast changing car navigation systems market for the next five years. Given the different market conditions from one region to another and Sony's unsatisfactory position in each market, Morita resolved to reevaluate the company's marketing strategy for car navigation systems and the benefits Sony could and should provide drivers around the world. Morita needed to resolve the conflicting views within his company regarding several key issues.

Geographical Focus Issue

Some managers believed it was time to focus much more effort on markets outside Japan. One international marketing manager said:

> Both the European and United States markets are expected to grow as large as the Japanese market within 10 years. We should preempt competitors with our own after-market models. We will be too late if we wait until these overseas markets take off. We should be the company that creates these markets as we did at home.

In contrast, a marketing manager in Tokyo insisted that Sony should focus on reestablishing its competitive position in Japan:

> Our share is down because we have lagged behind our competitors in developing more accurate hybrid models and more sophisticated route guidance technology. The fact is, in 1996, 98% of our car navigation sales come from Japan. The growth forecasts for markets overseas are totally speculative.

The allocation of R&D resources depended in part on Sony's geographical priorities. In 1996, Sony employed 200 highly skilled engineers dedicated to car navigation systems development, all of whom were stationed in Japan, except for only one each in Europe and the United States.

Product Choice

Given the poor performance of the current overseas model NVX-F160, it seemed that a simple GPS-based model at a price of $3,000 was unlikely to appeal to drivers in Europe and the United States. There were at least three product options for Sony: (1) launch the Handy Navigation System GPX-5, the portable GPS model most recently introduced in Japan, as a global product; (2) modify the hybrid NVX-S1 for Europe and/or the United States; and (3) develop a new low-priced model for overseas markets.

A marketing manager in Tokyo emphasized the advantage of the GPX-5 as a global product:

> The portable nature of the GPX-5 should appeal to a much broader population including consumers interested in outdoor camping, bike touring and marine sports. Users can also use it to enjoy regular TV channels while traveling. Since

the product is detachable, it is not strictly an automobile device so auto safety regulation and product liability issues may not apply. Portability also reduces the risk of theft.

The U.S. country manager, however, questioned the product's potential:

> For the product to succeed in the United States, we need software with geocoded information specifically for camping sites, fishing locations, mountain skiing routes, and the like, all of which currently do not exist. It will cost at least $1 million and take 9 months to develop software for each recreation activity. By the time we have a variety of CD-ROMs, competition could be on different basis. In addition, if the product is priced around $3,000 again, it will flop. Finally, modifying the GPX-5 for the United States would require 5 engineers working for six months.

Another manager in Tokyo proposed to modify the NVX-S1, the hybrid model with turn-by-turn route guidance capability, for overseas markets:

> In the countries where street names are clearly signed and road systems are straightforward, the current GPS-based model which only shows the driver's position on the map adds little value to drivers. We need a more sophisticated hybrid model, which can be upgraded to accommodate future advances such as a real-time traffic information service and a traffic emergency warning system.

However, there were also pessimistic views regarding this product modification:

> In turn-by-turn route guidance technology, Sony lags far behind its competitors overseas. The product modification option requires Sony to reinvent its digital map software for the U.S. and European markets. When competitors launch more sophisticated route guidance systems, the present system will quickly become obsolete. Moreover, this option will incur substantial time and cost. It will take two years for our software vendor Etak to digitize U.S. and European maps for turn-by-turn route guidance. This will cost $100 million in initial development costs and $30 million for annual maintenance and content upgrades. This option will require 50 engineers to work with Etak in the United States and Europe. NavTech, Etak's competitor, will have soon digitized 100% of the U.S. and European maps for turn-by-turn guidance. We can switch from Etak to NavTech, but we are not sure how much competitive advantage we will lose by using the same database as our main competitors.

Rejecting the above product modification options, some sales managers in the United States argued for developing low-end models from scratch, solely for the overseas market:

> As consumer research has shown, it is obvious nobody here will buy a $3,000 gadget for his/her car. If we want to create a market here, we need a product designed to meet local needs. European and U.S. drivers don't need a fancy digital map nor an expensive LCD monitor and will be happy with some simple arrow and voice guidance at a price of $1,000 or less.

The international marketing manager in Tokyo, however, strongly opposed this low-end product strategy:

> Even if a low-end stripped-down product stimulates the market in the short run, Sony will gain little in the long run. It will precipitate price competition and may shrink the market, at least in value terms. The product will not be adaptable to future developments in road infrastructure. It will diminish Sony's leadership image in car navigation systems. Furthermore, this option will need 60 of our engineers to work for a year on developing this new product. Given the competition we face at home, we can not afford to divert them.

Standard Setting Issue

There was wide debate over continuation of the NaviKen consortium. Some managers contended that Sony should leave NaviKen or at least develop proprietary digital map technology in parallel in order to compete head-to-head with other companies. A young manager in charge of product development stated:

> The NaviKen format was helpful early on. However, product introductions are now so frequent that we need our own digital map technology to respond quickly to the market's evolving needs. Customers appreciate a differentiated database to standardized ones. As one survey says, an average consumer owns only 1.5 CD-ROMs, and most do not use CD-ROM maps across different hardware anyway. Car navigation systems are not the same as personal computers.

In contrast, several of the digital map engineers who were heavily involved in establishing NaviKen format in the 1980s opposed such a radical move. As one senior engineer stated:

> Such a myopic and opportunistic action may bring some market share in the short run, but hinder market

development for the future. Standardized software will always benefit the consumer as well as the industry, as has been shown in the cases of CD players and VCRs. Our market research shows 80% of our customers care about software compatibility. As a market leader, Sony always tries to grow the market pie. Sony does not pursue a larger share of a shrinking market. After all we've put into establishing the NaviKen standard, why should we quit now? Now it is time for us to extend our effort overseas and to stimulate consumer demand as we have done in Japan.

Other managers took a compromise view. While supporting NaviKen in Japan, they proposed to establish different digital map formats for Europe and the United States. One manager explained:

To boost the market overseas, especially early on, we need a variety of compatible software. However, the NaviKen standard was developed for the unique Japanese road system, and is not extendible to other markets. Since the traffic infrastructures are very different from country to country, we should try to establish new product standards region by region.

Planet Reebok (A)

In March 1993, David Ropes, Reebok's vice president of worldwide marketing services, was about to meet with the director of marketing communications for Europe to discuss the international rollout of *Planet Reebok* (PR), the company's first global advertising campaign. The campaign had been launched in the United States in January 1993 where initial reactions were positive. As part of the international rollout and at the explicit direction of corporate headquarters, PR was scheduled to be introduced soon in Reebok's three most important international markets: France, Germany, and the United Kingdom. Existing national television advertising campaigns in these three markets would have to be phased out as a result.

Prior to the meeting, Ropes reviewed PR copy research results from the three European countries. He wished to reassure himself that the PR campaign would be effective. He also wanted to determine whether he should encourage, permit, or initiate any further adjustments to the PR executions prior to the European rollout.

COMPANY AND INDUSTRY BACKGROUND

Reebok International Ltd., headquartered in Stoughton, Massachusetts, was a leading worldwide designer, marketer, and distributor of sports, fitness, and lifestyle products, principally footwear and apparel. Reebok's United Kingdom ancestor company was founded in the 1890s by Joseph William Foster, who made the first running shoes with spikes for top runners. In 1958, two of the founders' grandsons started a companion company that came to be known as Reebok, named for an African gazelle. In 1979, Paul Fireman negotiated for the North American distribution license for Reebok U.S.A. In 1984, in a reverse acquisition, Fireman and his backers, principally Pentland Industries Plc, acquired the U.K. licensor.

This case was prepared by Professor John A. Quelch with the assistance of Jamie Harper.
Copyright © 1994 by the President and Fellows of Harvard College. Harvard Business School case 9-594-074.

In 1981, Reebok introduced the first athletic shoe designed for women. With the Freestyle aerobic shoe, Reebok supported three trends that transformed the athletic industry: the aerobic exercise movement, the influx of women into sports, and the acceptance of well-designed athletic footwear by adults for street and casual wear. By 1992, the Freestyle had become the best-selling athletic shoe of all time. Reebok sales soared from $13 million in 1983 to over $3 billion by 1992. After-tax profits in 1992, before restructuring charges, were $232 million. Gross margins were 42% in 1992; selling expenses were 18% of sales. Around 80% of the company's sales and profits were generated by Reebok-branded footwear; the remainder were accounted for by the Avia and Rockport brands and by sales of branded apparel. Reebok employed 4,600 people in 1992, 21% of whom worked at company headquarters. Three hundred employees managed relations and ensured quality control with independent manufacturers of Reebok shoes in 50 factories located in six Far East countries.

In 1992, Reebok held a 20% unit share and a 24% dollar share of the U.S. branded athletic sports shoe market. Its primary competitor, Nike, held a 20% unit share and a 28% dollar share. Both companies held a 15% dollar share and a 13% unit share of the non-U.S. branded athletic shoe market. Adidas, a long-standing German manufacturer of athletic footwear, was thought to hold only a 3% unit share in the United States but held a 16% unit share outside the United States.

Reebok's rapid growth was driven by its introduction in 1982 of the first aerobic/dance shoe specifically targeted at women. The aerobics shoe established Reebok as a fitness brand. Even though Reebok soon produced shoes for men and women, the brand always remained particularly strong among women buyers and developed a more fashion-oriented image than Nike, which continued to emphasize performance sports and to appeal primarily to male athletes. In 1991, Reebok management consciously set out to broaden the brand image to establish its leadership in sports as well as fitness. Reebok's new goal was to become the number one performance sports and fitness brand in the world by the end of 1995.

To achieve this goal, Reebok first reorganized in early 1992 around three product groups:

- **Sports** (44% of 1992 sales) included running, basketball, tennis, football, baseball, soccer, rugby, lacrosse, volleyball, and indoor court shoes.
- **Fitness** (52%) included aerobics, cross training, walking and Preseason™ shoes; Step Reebok™ equipment; Reebok's Classic shoe lines; and Weebok™ shoes for infants.
- **Casual** (4%) included the Boks™ line of casual footwear and Reebok's line of golf shoes.

Second, Reebok placed renewed emphasis on research and development to bring to market new, performance-driven, shoe technologies such as Graphlite, a lightweight and high-strength composite material that created a lightweight shoe without any sacrifice in stability or strength. Reebok also continued to leverage the success of The Pump technology, an integrated system of one or more inflatable chambers that could be adjusted to provide custom fit and support in footwear. New product lines were also established for a variety of sports, such as cleated footwear for soccer and baseball. Introduced in 1992, Reebok's Outdoor line of hiking, mountain biking, and surfing shoe wear promised to become one of the company's fastest-growing shoe categories in 1993. The company also launched new athletic concepts such as Preseason footwear, a special line of training shoes for athletes who played competitive sports.

Third, Reebok invested a higher proportion of its marketing budget in securing individual athlete and team endorsements. Most notable among Reebok's new signings was Shaquille O'Neal (SHAQ), a basketball player who later signed with the Orlando Magic.

Fourth, Reebok developed a distinctive logo to reinforce the brand's performance orientation in the sports arena and compete against Nike's "swoosh" and Adidas's three stripes logo. In January 1993, Reebok launched its new "Vector" logo to replace the company's Union Jack flag logo. By fall 1993, all Reebok performance athletic footwear products, except its Classic product lines, were scheduled to carry the Vector logo.

International Development

Reebok's entry into international markets began in earnest in 1987. The company first established distributors and later, as the distributors reached critical mass, sought to acquire controlling interests in them. By 1993, the company was seeking to develop a global identity for the Reebok brand. Between 1988 and 1992, Reebok's international sales of footwear grew from $180 million to $1 billion. Reebok held the number one market share position in the United Kingdom, Canada, Australia, New Zealand, Denmark, Sweden, Hong Kong, and Singapore. The international branded athletic footwear market outside the United States was estimated at $7.2 billion and 221 million pairs of shoes in 1992.

The company's International Operations group, headquartered in London, England, was responsible for Reebok sales outside of the United States and Canada. A regional office in Hong Kong managed all operations in Asia Pacific, while another in Chile oversaw Latin American operations. The group marketed Reebok products in 140 countries worldwide through a network of wholly owned subsidiaries,[1] joint ventures, and independent distributors[2] (see Table A):

Europe was Reebok's largest regional market outside North America, representing 65% of 1992 international sales. Reebok's subsidiaries in France, Germany, and the United Kingdom were the company's largest in sales and profitability. (See Exhibit 1 for selected sales data by region and 2 for information on the European market.) An assessment of Reebok's overall competitive position in 1992 revealed the following:

- Worldwide market share was concentrated in the Big Three (Reebok, Nike and Adidas), although Adidas's share was in decline due to changes in ownership;
- Reebok was growing faster than Nike;
- Nike was increasing its advertising spending;[3]
- Overall market growth was sluggish due to the economic recession;
- Demand for casual shoes was increasing faster than for athletic shoes;

---

[1] Reebok's wholly owned subsidiaries were located in Austria, Chile, France, Germany, the Netherlands, Italy, Russia, and the United Kingdom; its majority-owned subsidiaries were located in Japan and Spain.

[2] Many of Reebok's 45 subsidiaries, joint ventures, and distributors also handled sales in smaller, neighboring countries.

[3] Outside of the United States, Reebok's 1992 media expenditures were about $35 million and Nike's were about $45 million, up 10% and 51%, respectively, from 1991.

Table A — Reebok's International Distribution Network

	Latin America	Europe	Asia/Pacific	Total
Subsidiaries	1	8	1	10
Joint Ventures	3	2	6	11
Distributors	1	18	5	<u>24</u>
Total	5	28	12	45

Exhibit 1 — Branded Athletic Footwear Sales by Region, 1992 ($ millions)

	Europe	North America[a]	Latin America	Asia/Pacific
Athletic footwear market				
Sales (at wholesale prices)	$4,300	$6,500	$1,200	$1,700
Pairs of shoes (millions)	124	391	44	53
Reebok sales (at wholesale prices)	$643[b]	$1,558	$137	$192

Source: Company records

Note: Numbers for all international markets are approximations only, and include estimates of the wholesale value of products sold by unowned distributors.

[a]United States and Canada only.

[b]Includes "other," such as Africa, Middle East, etc.

Exhibit 2 — Reebok Data on Selected European Markets, 1992

	France	Germany	United Kingdom
Reebok sales[a] ($MM)	171	116	186
Advertising expenditures ($MM)	9.8	6.7	7.4
Other marketing expenditures[b] ($MM)	8.4	6.7	7.0
Brand unit share (%)			
Reebok	19%	11%	25%
Nike	22	16	18
Adidas	28	40	12
Unaided brand awareness (%)			
Reebok	73%	56%	75%
Nike	76	80	71
Adidas	95	97	75

Source: Company records

[a]At factory prices.

[b]Includes sales promotion, merchandising, public relations, sponsorships, market research.

- New market opportunities were evident in Eastern/Central Europe.

Reebok established the following six strategic objectives for its European markets in 1993:

1. Prevent Nike from taking ownership of the 15- to 25-year-old consumer
2. Replace Adidas as the European performance brand
3. Win in Germany
4. Strengthen management support systems
5. Take "ownership" of the retail shelf
6. Lead, not follow, the market

Competitive Position

Nike, founded in 1964, was an Oregon-based manufacturer and distributor of performance athletic footwear and apparel and was Reebok's principal competitor. In the mid-1980s, Nike temporarily lost share leadership in the United States to Reebok, as it was late responding to the aerobics movement and the increased interest of women in fitness and sports. However, Nike recovered U.S. share leadership, aided by the endorsement of Michael Jordan, a highly successful basketball player with the Chicago Bulls, who endorsed Nike products in advertising. Nike dominated the basketball, football, and baseball shoe categories because the Air Jordan line of basketball shoes and apparel cast a performance halo over the rest of Nike's product lines. Beginning in 1991, Nike attempted to broaden its appeal to women, increase its share of the fitness shoe category, and displace Reebok as the leading brand in tennis footwear.

Throughout its history, Nike advertising consistently targeted athletic performance messages primarily at teens and young men active in sports. Since 1987, Nike's highly successful "Just Do It" campaign served as an umbrella for a variety of performance-based messages. Beginning in 1991, Nike softened its hard-driving performance message with more emphasis on humor and entertainment. For example, Nike's "Air/Hare Jordan" television ad featured Michael Jordan and Bugs Bunny working together in outer space to rescue millions of Nike shoes that had been stolen by Martians.

In the United States, Nike's relative brand position was stronger than in overseas markets. Nike had tended to control its international subsidiaries more tightly than Reebok. Advertisements developed in the United States were typically run in overseas markets with minimal adaptation.

REEBOK ADVERTISING STRATEGY

Reebok Campaigns 1986-1992

In the early 1980s, Reebok advertising appeared primarily in print media. Ads targeted at serious athletes and "weekend warriors" emphasized functional product attributes in sports contexts. The company also retained famous athletes to endorse its products. Beginning in 1986, however, Reebok started to introduce new advertising themes. *Because Life Is Not A Spectator Sport* was an 18-month-long umbrella campaign[4] that associated the Reebok brand with an active lifestyle. The campaign highlighted everyday sports participants rather than shoes, technical features, or high-profile athletes.

In 1987, as its brand franchise and product line expanded, Reebok marketing managers developed television, radio, and print ads for each athletic footwear category. These ads focused on one or more of the following four themes: performance; new technology; "classic" styling; and fashion. The proportion of the budget allocated to Reebok umbrella brand advertising diminished in favor of product category specific advertising.

In 1988, Reebok, lacking exciting new products to launch, commissioned a fresh and provocative umbrella to revitalize the Reebok name. The campaign, *Reeboks Let U.B.U.*, focused on the freedom of expression and individuality that one could achieve by wearing a pair of Reebok shoes. Television and print ads, targeted primarily at young women, showcased everyday people performing humorous and wacky acts. One television ad, for example, featured a bride emerging from a subway escalator wearing Reebok shoes, and showed a group of pregnant women aerobic dancing.[5]

During the two years that followed the *Reeboks Let U.B.U.* campaign, Reebok advertising struggled to achieve the appropriate balance between a serious performance and a lifestyle/fashion orientation. The 1989 *Physics Behind the Physiques* campaign was based on the

---

4 An umbrella advertising campaign aimed to establish a common brand image across all product categories within the brand franchise and was often tied together by a common tag line and logo.

5 For further information on Reebok's advertising through 1988, see Tammy Bunn Hiller and John A. Quelch, "Reebok International Ltd.," HBS Case No. 589-027.

premise that men and women work out in sports to look good as well as to stay fit. This theme was replaced in 1990 by the less-performance-driven *It's Time To Play* campaign, which stressed that the pursuit of sports and fitness should be "fun," not just a competitive battle.

Early in 1991, Reebok launched The Pump technology, which permitted athletes to inflate chambers built into Reebok shoes to achieve a customized fit. Reebok placed most of its advertising dollars into the *Pump Up and Air Out* campaign to launch the line head-on-head with Nike's Air technology.

The *Life Is Short. Play Hard.* (LISPH) umbrella campaign, introduced in the second half of 1991, reflected Reebok's new effort to position itself as the number one sports and fitness brand worldwide. The copy themes were "be the best you can be," "compete with yourself," "get the most out of life," and "in the striving lies the achievement." The campaign targeted 15- to 44- year-old branded athletic shoe buyers. Executions included:

- "Sky Surfer." A sky diver wearing The Pump Cross Trainers attached to a surfboard performing stunt maneuvers at 10,000 feet.
- "Talking Tennis Balls." A woman wearing The Pump Tennis shoes aggressively hit tennis balls with animated faces of an angry boss, a yapping poodle, and a slick pickup guy.
- "STEP." A couple wearing Reebok Step Aerobic shoes raced up an Aztec pyramid, interspersed with shots of men and women doing step aerobics in a gym.
- "Fence." A tennis player wearing The Pump Tennis shoes hit tennis balls into a wire fence until the fence was covered with yellow balls that spelled the word "Pump."

These executions were developed to meet the following criteria: originality, impact, correct brand/product balance, and performance with a human face. Copy tests in the United States indicated very high unaided and aided brand and copy recall.

The Dan and Dave campaign was developed under the LISPH umbrella. It was created to challenge Nike's sponsorship of the 1992 Olympics basketball "Dream Team" and high-profile athletes. The "Dan and Dave" executions, which included humorous interactions between two leading United States decathletes, ran for eight months. Reebok was the exclusive athletic footwear and apparel sponsor of the NBC Network telecast of the 1992 Summer Olympic Games.

Also running in 1992 was a Reebok campaign specifically targeting women under the tag line *I Believe*. This campaign focused on the self-esteem that women could achieve through pursuit of sports and fitness. It was designed to counter Nike's increasing efforts to penetrate the women's market.

Advertising Challenges in 1993

The company's 1993 marketing strategy was to position Reebok as the number one sports and fitness brand worldwide. Nike's recent move to softer advertising messages created an opening for Reebok to emphasize pure athletics but with a tone of humanity. According to one Reebok manager, "Sports are won with skill and not with an attitude." All Reebok executions were developed to communicate the message: "Pure athletics plus humanity."

This theme was reflected in the 1993 *SHAQ* campaign that featured Shaquille O'Neal, aged 21, of the Orlando Magic, a highly rated young basketball star whom Reebok executives hoped would assume the mantle of Michael Jordan, who endorsed Nike. The campaign was targeted at males, aged 12 to 34. The television executions portrayed a young superstar in the making, emphasizing O'Neal's basketball prowess and agility, his passion and commitment to the game, and youthful zest for life.

A continuing advertising challenge at Reebok was the lack of internal support for umbrella campaigns. Although they all shared a single brand name, Reebok's product categories operated as independent business units. Category managers were judged on the sales and profits of their product lines; they were not specifically responsible for building the Reebok brand. Because each of the category managers faced a different set of competitors, and because Reebok's market share differed across categories, they all wanted to develop their own category-specific advertising. Category managers were habitually concerned about the percentage of the total advertising budget that was siphoned off to fund umbrella campaigns that promoted the Reebok image.

International Advertising

Due to the speed of Reebok's international expansion, headquarters had not developed guidelines for the advertising used by international subsidiaries and distributorships. During the 1980s, individual country managers had appointed their own agencies and developed their own advertising copy and tag lines, while occasionally borrowing executions made for the United States and other country markets. For example, "Sky Surfer" was the principal Reebok television ad running in France and Germany but without the LISPH tag line. In fact, this tag line was not used in any advertisements in Europe (except in print ads in Switzerland) because it was variously regarded by local managers as too harsh or too hard to understand.

By 1991, international sales accounted for a third of Reebok's total revenues. Several headquarters executives believed that greater message consistency around the world would help develop the brand image and improve the cost effectiveness of Reebok advertising. The company selected a single advertising agency to work with each of Reebok's three regional offices covering Asia/Pacific, the Americas, and Europe. In Europe, the Euro RSCG agency was appointed to work with Reebok's European headquarters in London to establish advertising and brand image guidelines; to approve local adaptations of standard ad copy; to ensure the efficiency of Reebok's media purchases throughout Europe; and to place advertising on European satellite television networks, such as EuroSport and MTV, which reached countries where the Reebok subsidiaries were too small to afford their own television advertising.

After 1991, the marketing directors of Reebok's European country subsidiaries began to meet more often to exchange ideas and to provide input to regional and worldwide headquarters as new campaigns were developed. However, achieving agreement on a single pan-European campaign proved difficult because Reebok's advertising and positioning had evolved differently in each country. As one European country manager said:

> We have had to go to our own way on advertising. Even if Reebok's U.S. advertising were applicable in our market, which it usually is not, the campaigns change so often that to follow the United States would leave us and our customers confused about what the brand stands for.

Advertising objectives in foreign markets were often different from those in the United States because the Reebok brand was at an earlier stage of development overseas, the company's market shares were usually lower, and the product line was typically narrower. Because the Reebok advertising budget in each international market was much smaller than in the United States, country managers typically allocated 80% to umbrella campaigns that built Reebok's image. In the United States, where Reebok brand recognition was already high, category managers argued for spending at least 80% of the budget on product category-specific advertising and the remainder on umbrella campaigns.

Reebok's 1992 and 1993 advertising budgets for the United States and for international markets are summarized in Exhibit 3. Advertising accounted for 60% of Reebok's U.S. marketing budget in 1992, followed by public relations (5%), promotions (10%), merchandising (10%), and sponsorships (20%). Reebok marketing budgets in its larger international subsidiaries were allocated similarly.

PLANET REEBOK

Planet Reebok (PR) was conceived as a global brand campaign that would help define Reebok as the number one sports and fitness brand worldwide. It was believed that PR could finesse the divergent perceptions of Reebok that existed internationally by tapping into the universal values of sports and fitness. Perhaps an American spin could be added to the extent that the United States was widely perceived as the world leader in athletic culture.

PR advertising would hopefully ensure that Reebok was the desired brand badge—something that was worn not just because it worked functionally but because it evoked the following strong and appealing image:

> Reebok is the brand for individuals all over the world who play at the peak of their potential and live life to the fullest.

People who lived on or visited PR would not only excel physically but would also become mentally able to achieve a broader set of goals. As a result, the PR campaign platform, described in Exhibit 4, was highly versatile. The style, tone, and feel of PR advertising executions would convey a Reebok personality that was athletic, human, honest, self-confident, aspirational, occasionally outrageous, and one that could range from being soul-stirring to thrilling and aggressive.

	1992		1993 (Proposed)	
	United States	International	United States	International
By Category Type				
Product category specific	$30	$35	$30	$15
Planet Reebok	-	-	30	30
SHAQ	-	-	15	-
Dan and Dave	18	-	-	-
Dan and Dave (Olympics)	12	-	-	-
I Believe	25	-	-	-
	$85	$35	$75	$45.0
By Media Vehicle				
Television	$60	$10	$52	$22.5
Print	25	25	23	22.5
	$85	$35	$75	$45.0
By Geographic Area				
Asia	-	$25	-	$13
Europe	-	10	-	30
Latin America	-	-	-	2
		$35		$45

Source: Company records

The PR campaign's broad target would be men and women aged 18 to 49 who participated in sports and fitness activities. The core target, however, would be men and women aged 18 to 29 who worked out or played sports two or more times a week. The PR umbrella campaign was intended to work in all media from television and print to outdoor and cinema. Advocates believed it could also be the basis for exciting point-of-sale merchandising materials.

Creative Development

PR was developed originally as a creative concept for Reebok's Outdoor shoe category. In spring 1992, John Andreliunas, the Outdoor brand manager, recognized the trend toward action sports that was best reflected in Reebok's "Sky Surfer" ad. The fast cuts and provocative, daring outdoor shots suggested a world of sports and fitness where there were no limits to what could be attempted or achieved. Planet Reebok would be a place where such novel sports could be born and grow and where Reebok's outdoor shoes would be totally appropriate.

Ropes quickly realized the potential of PR as a broader global campaign and asked Reebok's U.S. agency,

Chiat/Day/Mojo, to explore PR as a single-brand identity for Reebok worldwide. Four challenges soon became evident. First, PR had to be integrated with the overall strategy of positioning Reebok as the number one sports and fitness brand worldwide. Second, the use of the word *planet* generated debate. Some executives were wary of its close connection with the environmental movement. Others believed it had no association with health, fitness, and sports. A third group objected that PR was not sufficiently innovative, given the existence of the Planet Hollywood chain of restaurants. Third, the U.S. category managers expressed their customary concerns about siphoning off funds from category-specific advertising. Fourth, by mid-1992, the *Life Is Short. Play Hard.* campaign had earned a loyal following among several marketing managers, country managers, and the trade.

Ropes presented preliminary PR television ads (known as "rip-o-matics") to all Reebok country managers at an off-site meeting in Scotland in August 1992. These executions, prepared in the United States without input from overseas managers, featured teenagers playing extreme sports, and heavy metal music played in the background. Throughout

Exhibit 4   Planet Reebok Campaign Platform

In Sport	In Life
Freedom	Losing the negative controls or limitations in life from parents, to school, to bad legislation, to too many lawyers.
No Drugs/Stimulants	Environmentalism, better air, less waste, no more products or services that we don't need and can no longer afford. No more false vanities or implants.
Pain	Suffering for the things in which you believe. Caring enough to endure discomfort.
Determination	Desire for a better, freer, more equal society; the ability to speak out against anything from racism to pollution.
Learning	Being open-minded, having freedom of action and spirit, not caring about race or creed. Having a cross-cultural view.
Confidence	Feeling empowered to change and achieve things that you desire, feeling that there are others like you, politically, emotionally, sexually—any way.
Training	Making yourself a better, stronger, more positive and valuable human being for the Planet to nurture.
Self-respect	Looking and feeling better, respecting the desires, rights and freedom of others.
Competition	Achieving what you want, not what others tell you that you can have.
Mental Agility	Better education for you and all. Being smart and able to cope.
Camaraderie	Feeling connected in a world intent upon finding differences and alienation.
Success/Winning	Achieving what you want and enabling others to have what they need.
Losing	Being capable of understanding your own weaknesses and those of others.

Source: Company records

the television commercials, "negative" captions such as "No Slogans," "No Meetings," "No Faxes" and "No Phones" flashed on the screen. Many of the country managers expressed concern that the preliminary PR commercials were too youth oriented. The quick cuts and action sports would be less appealing to audiences over 24 years old. The marketing directors from countries where Reebok was a relatively new brand and/or in close competition with Nike for market share leadership wanted Reebok to be more broadly positioned. However, Reebok managers from the United States, where Nike held a clear lead over Reebok in market share, especially among teenage males, welcomed the brand being positioned against a younger audience.

After the offsite meeting, the PR creative was reworked to have a broader appeal, particularly among women, by blending more everyday sports such as women's aerobics with the action sports. International settings and outdoor sports specific to foreign countries were also incorporated, based on input from country managers. At the same time, a new copy approach was considered for the PR campaign. Instead of the original negative positioning ("No Slogans," "No Meetings" etc.), Chiat/Day/Mojo proposed an approach that emphasized the positive attributes of life on Planet Reebok. The "No" captions were eventually adopted after the two versions were tested internationally in November 1992.

The final PR creative was completed by early 1993. Chiat/Day/Mojo prepared creative briefs that outlined the campaign's advertising objectives, target audiences, and intended consumer take-aways.

United States Executions

Five television commercials (summarized in Table B) formed the core of the U.S. PR campaign. Each began with an image of the Earth moving toward the viewer and the caption: "What is life like on Planet Reebok?" Quick cuts of exhilarating sports and fitness action followed, accompanied by fast-paced music and the "negative" captions. Exhibit 5 presents a storyboard of the "Planet Brand" television advertisement. Exhibit 6 shows a PR print ad for Reebok's Outdoor line of footwear.

PR was launched in the United States at the end of January 1993 during the football Super Bowl. Reebok purchased two minutes of commercial time for $3.4 million. One 60-second execution from both the SHAQ and PR campaigns was shown during the second and third quarters of the game.

The PR campaign in the United States included only a modest level of print advertising and point-of-sale materials. The U.S. sales force was preoccupied with placing point-of-sale materials that supported the new SHAQ product line and Reebok's new Vector logo.

Of the $75 million Reebok planned to spend in 1993 in the United States on media advertising, around $30 million would be devoted to PR, $15 million to SHAQ (which focused on basketball), and $30 million to other category-specific-advertising.

Communications Tests

After launch, Reebok management was interested in measuring consumer awareness, understanding, and perceptions of the PR and SHAQ campaigns. In March 1993, the company conducted communications tests of PR and SHAQ executions that targeted men and women against two Nike campaigns that also targeted men and women. The test structure was as follows:

Campaign and Executions	Gender and Age of Respondents
SHAQ ("Legends," "Elders")	Men aged 12 to 34
PR ("Women's Sports and Fitness)	Women aged 12 to 34
PR ("Planet Sports," "Planet Outdoor")	Men aged 12 to 34
Nike Women's ("Stretcher," "Runner")	Women aged 12 to 34
Nike Men's ("Barkley," "Majerle")	Men aged 12 to 34

Table B		Planet Reebok Executions	

Execution	Length (seconds)	Target Audience	Content
"Planet Brand"	60	Men 12-24	Professional athletes and "real" people playing a variety of sports
"Planet Sports"	30	Men 12-24	Professional athletes playing a variety of sports
"Women's Sports"	30	Women 12-24	Female professional athletes excelling at their individual sports
"Women's Fitness"	30	Women 12-24	"Real" women walking and doing step aerobics
"Planet Outdoor"	30	All 12-24	"Real" people playing action sports

Source: Company records

Around 1,000 respondents were interviewed in 30 U.S. markets. Respondents were divided into five groups of 200. Each was exposed to two representative executions from one of the five advertising campaigns included in the test. Each respondent, therefore, viewed only one campaign. Qualified respondents were female and male athletic shoe consumers, between the ages of 12 and 34, who spent at least $25 on a pair of athletic shoes.

Both the PR and SHAQ campaigns were received positively by respondents. Positive reactions to SHAQ were especially strong among young males, thanks to the charismatic personality of Shaquille O'Neal who was becoming an increasingly prominent role model for this group. Positive reactions to PR were also strong, particularly among women. However, PR's message seemed more diffuse and less tangible. Exhibit 7 summarizes the research findings.

INTERNATIONAL ROLLOUT OF PLANET REEBOK

PR was scheduled to be rolled out internationally in March 1993. Prior to PR, Reebok subsidiaries and their advertising agencies had developed separate campaigns with different themes. In France, Germany, and the United Kingdom, for example, the tag lines for their 1992 umbrella campaigns were *Break The Rules, Get The Feeling!*, and *The Edge*, respectively. Examples of print ads from each campaign are shown in Exhibits 8 through 10.

PR represented the first effort of Reebok headquarters to require worldwide adoption of an advertising campaign. As a result, the introduction of PR would require the phasing out of the existing individual country campaigns, no matter how successful. In the first quarter of 1993, Reebok

Exhibit 6 PR Print Ad for United States

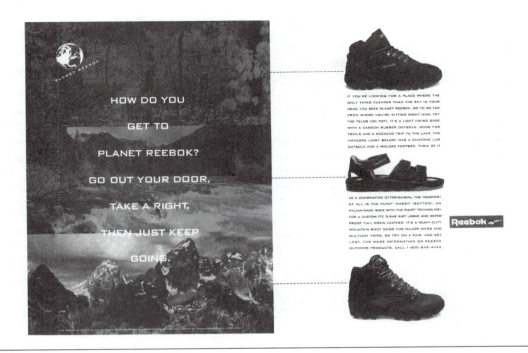

Source: Company records

marketing directors in the European subsidiaries had spent little on television advertising in anticipation of the arrival of finished PR commercials from the United States. While some Reebok country managers resented losing control over their advertising, others welcomed the flexibility PR allowed to show different sports under one campaign umbrella. The 1993 advertising media budget for PR outside the United States was $30 million, two-thirds of which would be spent in the United Kingdom, France and Germany. Some Reebok country managers argued that European headquarters should contribute to the launch expenditures of PR in European markets. Executives at Reebok's European headquarters were willing to explore spending an additional $3 million to advertise PR on MTV, EuroSport, and other satellite-based networks that delivered programming across Europe.

Both television and print advertising were included in the European PR budget in a 70:30 ratio. International television and print adaptations of the PR executions had to follow the guidelines summarized in Exhibit 11. The adaptations were paid for by Reebok's three regional organizations that covered Latin America, Europe, and Asia/Pacific. Reebok subsidiaries could modify PR print ads but only at their expense and subject to the approval of the communications director at Reebok's European headquarters. For example, they could choose the athletes, shots, and shoes they wanted to feature and write their own headlines and body/copy. Exhibits 12 through 14 present proposed PR print ads for France, Germany, and the United Kingdom. In the case of PR television ads, Reebok subsidiaries could translate the supers (captions) and voice-overs and suggest rough edits (e.g., the substitution of locally popular sports) to regional headquarters.

European Sports Shoe Market

Research on sports shoe markets outside the United States was limited to individual country-specific studies that included noncomparable data. Reebok therefore commissioned two multicountry studies to provide more comprehensive market research.

- Among men, *Planet* and *SHAQ* were well-received (top-two box likability scores of 83% and 80%, respectively), more so (in general) than the Nike ads tested (75%). *SHAQ* likability among younger men was higher than that of *Planet* (64% to 41% top-box likability).
- *Planet* far exceeded the Nike women's ads on top-box likability ("like them a lot") among women, although women awarded *Planet* and *Nike* similar top-two box scores (77% and 79%, respectively). A higher percentage of women than men reacted positively to *Planet*.
- Consumers believed that both *Planet* and *SHAQ* fit well with their overall image of the Reebok brand; the Nike commercials tested did not fit as well in consumers' minds with their overall image of Nike, particularly among women.
- *Planet Reebok* was most often described as exciting, fun, upbeat, fast-paced, and different/unique; women tended to feed back health and energy associations, while men focused on excitement/fun descriptors. Consumers appeared to be entertained by viewing the experiences on Planet, but were in some cases overwhelmed by the visuals and so less likely to translate these into a strong performance message. Athletics and performance-type messages appeared to be secondary to "fun," although consumers *did* tend to describe people living on *Planet Reebok* as "athletes/those who like athletics" while women described them as "fit/in good shape." In addition, performance enhancement (among women) and performance edge (among men) were communicated more often by *Planet* than by either *SHAQ* or the Nike ads.
- Unaided recall of Shaquille O'Neal as the spokesperson in the *SHAQ* series was nearly perfect, as was also the case for the Barkley execution; Majerle's recognition was much lower. Kareem Abdul-Jabbar also received 56% recognition in the *SHAQ* spot, followed distantly by Wilt Chamberlain, John Wooden, and Bill Walton in that order.
- Shaquille O'Neal was extremely well liked by the 12- to 34-year-old male audience who viewed the spots, particularly in comparison to Barkley and Majerle. He was widely viewed as an appropriate spokesperson for Reebok, top in his field, and an interesting person; additionally, he received higher scores for "someone I like" and "a good role model" than either of the two Nike athletes.
- The *SHAQ* campaign did a better job communicating performance to its male viewers than *Planet*, and registered high recall of "using a rookie to sell shoes" as the perceived main point of the commercial. The *SHAQ* ads were received more favorably among the younger male audience (12-18) than the older (19-34).
- However, *SHAQ* generated some confusion among viewers (27%), particularly the "Elders" execution. Many respondents could not understand the words (and/or meaning of the words) being spoken; however, this did not detract from the likability of the ad or its performance message. Additionally, the Nike Barkley/Majerle ads generated substantial confusion; questioning the executions' relevance to shoes.
- Notably, the Nike ads generated stronger brand imagery for Nike among men than the Reebok ads (*SHAQ* and *Planet*) did for Reebok, particularly for
  - best brand for sports,
  - comfortable shoes,
  - "in" with me and my friends,
  - more technologically advanced, and
  - appropriate for me.

  These results were more a function of the images cumulatively resulting from previous campaigns than the executions tested. Among women, the Reebok and Nike images were equally strong for most attributes.

- **The Nike ads appeared to appeal to a broader user profile than the Reebok ads.** All ads were successful at communicating a "competitive," "serious sports" profile; however, Nike also communicated dimensions such as "winner," "attractive," and "street smart."
- **Of concern was the relatively low top-two box (excellent, extremely good) overall brand rating for *Planet* (26%) compared with *SHAQ* (57%) or the Nike ads (50%).** The overall Reebok brand rating for those women exposed to *Planet* (52%) was comparable to the rating for Nike (55%) among those women exposed to Nike ads.

Source: Company records

Note: Based on a five-cell (200 respondents per cell) exposure test of five advertising campaigns (three Reebok and two Nike) conducted in 30 U.S. markets. Respondents were female and male athletic shoe wearers, aged 12 to 34.

In 1992, 1,000 consumers in France, Germany, and the United Kingdom were interviewed to profile sports shoe purchasers in each country. Respondents were 15 to 55 years of age and had purchased a pair of sports shoes within the previous six months for themselves or other members of their households. Selected results of the study are presented in Exhibit 15.

In January and February 1993, focus group interviews were conducted in France, Germany, and the United Kingdom. The study was sponsored by Euro RSCG, in advance of the PR campaign rollout, to understand the factors that influenced consumer attitudes, needs, and motivations for athletic footwear purchases and brand selections. Ten focus groups with 8 to 10 respondents in each group, segmented by gender, age, and level of athletic participation, were conducted in each country. Participants played a variety of sports, had purchased a pair of sports shoes in the past six months, and owned more than one brand. The most important findings addressed consumer perceptions of the Reebok and Nike brands across the three countries. These results are provided in Exhibit 16.

Pre-Launch Research Studies

Qualitative research to pretest consumer responses to PR advertising executions in Reebok's three principal European markets was conducted in two rounds. In November 1992, the first study researched PR rip-o-matics. In February 1993, a second research project elicited consumers' responses to three completed executions.

The November 1992 study was based on four focus groups conducted in France, Germany, and the United Kingdom. Qualified group members were males and females, aged 15 to 35, who participated in sports and/or fitness activities at least once a week, had purchased branded sports footwear in the previous 6 months, and intended to make their next purchase within 12 months. Two rip-o-matics were tested—one with the positive PR copy and the other with the negative copy. The objectives of the focus groups were:

- To assess what consumers understood PR to represent from the advertising
- To evaluate how well the advertising built the desired brand "badge" or image
- To gauge interest, identification with, and liking for the advertising
- To establish how the advertising could be made to work even harder

Reactions to the advertising executions in each of the three countries are presented in Exhibit 17. The results indicated consistently positive findings regarding the notion of "planet," the positioning of Reebok, product and user imagery, and the motivational impact of the ads. However, respondents in the three countries differed in their identification with and emotional connection to PR. Reebok executives explained these cross-border variations in terms of differences in cultural background, attitudes toward and participation in sports and fitness, and current brand perceptions. The most positive response appeared to be in the United Kingdom, but some executives thought this was due to Reebok's higher brand share in this market and/or to the fact that the commercials were tested in English in all three countries.

The second study also involved focus group discussions in France, Germany, and the United Kingdom. Four focus

Exhibit 8 1992 Print Ad from Break The Rules Campaign in France

Source: Company records

groups were conducted in each country with males and females, aged 16 to 24. In each group there were three Reebok owners, two Nike owners, and three owners of major local brands. Half the members of each group were serious athletes who played sports at least two times a week and selected their shoes based on their sports needs. The remainder were casual users who wore athletic footwear in non-sport situations. Respondents were exposed to three PR executions, one of which had been recently introduced in the United States and two of which were new executions developed just for Europe that included softer sport and lifestyle cues. Translations of the English captions were given in the French and German focus groups. Translations of the campaign platform concept were also provided to ensure comprehension of the PR strategy.

The study revealed that the appeal of the PR executions depended on the level of understanding achieved. Comprehension of the PR concept was strongest in the United Kingdom, followed by France and then Germany. Respondents in all countries were consistent in their views of the pace and visual appeal of the PR advertising. However, interest in the use of "planet" as a creative concept was modest. While some respondents found the PR philosophy to be interesting, the majority could not understand it. The researchers explored further the following three issues:

1. *The complexity of the advertising message delivered.* The PR campaign attempted to express Reebok's vision of life through a series of sports metaphors. Respondents

Exhibit 9   1992 Print Ad from Get The Feeling! Campaign in Germany

Source: Company records

had difficulty understanding how an individual's approach to sports was necessarily a metaphor for his or her approach to life. They were used to seeing sports and high performance in sports as a signal of product quality and technical features. The PR executions covered a lot of ground and did not clearly communicate the central concept. So, while they were exciting to watch, although too aggressive in tone for some respondents, they did not convey the complete message to many viewers.

2. *The inability of the creative vehicle to deliver the intended message.* Usually, advertising messages were thought to work as follows:

Creative vehicle → comprehension of the central creative idea → take-away of the intended message.

The PR executions, however, were assimilated differently:

Secondary cues → estimate of central creative idea → received message take-away different from what was intended

In the case of the PR ads, the sports activity depicted, rather than sports as a metaphor for life, was regarded as the central creative idea. Viewers played back observations on how sports were performed to achieve a winning competitive advantage. Only Reebok's attitude toward sports—not its approach to life—was communicated by the advertising, and this attitude was frequently interpreted as hard-edged and aggressive. Serious athletes tended to relate best to PR whereas casual athletes felt alienated and less comfortable. Viewers who played sports primarily for personal satisfaction also had trouble relating to PR. Although they might be committed athletes, PR showed an attitude they did not all want to be associated with.

3. *The dissonance between the PR advertising and existing brand perceptions.* In the United Kingdom, PR advertising was seen as positioning Reebok as American and similar to Nike; this contradicted current perceptions of the brand as British. In Germany, respondents were confused when the brand was presented

Exhibit 10   1992 Print Ad from The Edge Campaign in United Kingdom

BEST OF LUCK IF YOU'RE RUNNING FOR PARLIAMENT THIS SUNDAY.

Reebok
THE EDGE

Source: Company records

as performance-oriented as they associated it with a softer and more feminine image. There was a risk that those consumers unable to relate to the advertising would be distanced from the brand, and might then see Reebok as just another global sports shoe company. The researchers were concerned that the brand personality depicted by the current PR advertising would not be credible or motivating or differentiate Reebok. Exhibit 18 summarizes the conclusions of the research.

CONCLUSION

Following the campaign's March 1993 launch in Europe, Planet Reebok would be introduced in Asia/Pacific and Latin America. On his way to the staff meeting, Ropes considered the challenges that he and his colleagues faced with the European launch just a few weeks away. How much emphasis, he wondered, could Reebok management at world headquarters expect the three subsidiaries in Europe to place on Planet Reebok in 1993 and in the future? What more, if anything, could Ropes and his staff do to ensure the success of the global PR campaign in Europe?

Exhibit 11   Reebok Guidelines for International Television and Print Adaptations

	Global Agency	Regional Agency	Local Agency
TELEVISION			
Initial Cuts	To supply		
Footage Shot	To supply		
European Adaptation		Adapt and present to markets	
Local Market Interpretation			Review footage shot; supply rough edit to Regional Agency; supply translated supers
Local Market Adaptation		Approve supers Edit films	
Local Market Material		Supply to format required	
Local Market Broadcast			Send to TV stations
Pan-European Material		Supply to satellite stations.	
Billing	Negotiate global usage costs	Editing/film costs to RIL; courier costs to local agency	
Review	Review European reel with regional agency	Compile European reel	

	Global Agency	Regional Agency	Local Agency
PRINT			
Initial Executions	To present		
European Adaptation a) Photography			Decide local market requirements Source material from regional agency or locally
b) Copy	Supply copy briefs	Agree on European copy briefs; supply to local agency	Write copy; supply translated copy to regional agency for approval
c) Production			Develop mechanicals
European Implementation *Billing*	Negotiate usage for stock		Negotiate usage for local shots; fund all production costs
Review		Review with global agency	Supply proofs to regional agency

Source: Company records

Exhibit 12 Proposed PR Print Ad for France

Exhibit 13   Proposed PR Print Ad for Germany

Exhibit 14 Proposed PR Print Ad for United Kingdom

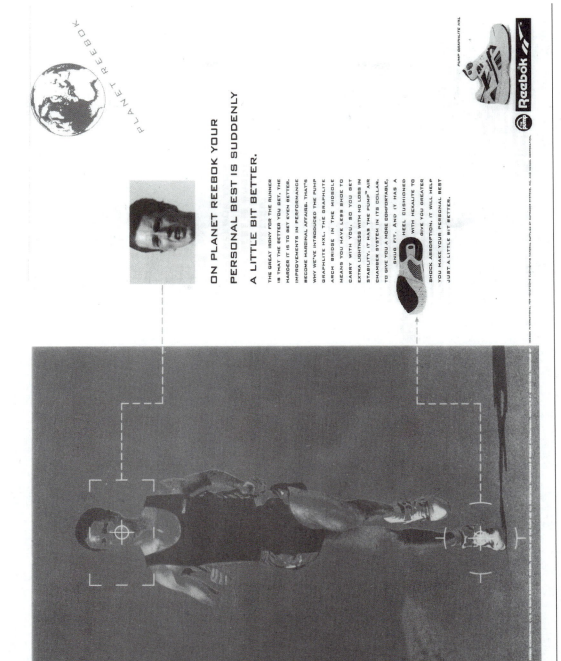

ON PLANET REEBOK YOUR
PERSONAL BEST IS SUDDENLY
A LITTLE BIT BETTER.

THE GREAT IRONY FOR THE RUNNER
IS THAT THE BETTER YOU GET, THE
HARDER IT IS TO GET EVEN BETTER.
IMPROVEMENTS IN PERFORMANCE
BECOME MARGINAL AFFAIRS. THAT'S
WHY WE'VE INTRODUCED THE PUMP
GRAPHLITE HXL. THE GRAPHLITE
ARCH BRIDGE IN THE MIDSOLE
MEANS YOU HAVE LESS SHOE TO
CARRY WITH YOU. SO YOU GET
EXTRA LIGHTNESS WITH NO LOSS IN
STABILITY. IT HAS THE PUMP™ AIR
CHAMBER SYSTEM IN ITS DOLLAR,
TO GIVE YOU A MORE COMFORTABLE,
SNUG FIT. AND IT HAS A
HEEL CUSHIONED
WITH HEXALITE TO
GIVE YOU GREATER
SHOCK ABSORPTION. IT WILL HELP
YOU MAKE YOUR PERSONAL BEST
JUST A LITTLE BIT BETTER.

PLANET REEBOK

PUMP GRAPHLITE HXL

Reebok

Source: Company records

Exhibit 15 Selected Findings of 1992 Sports Shoe Tracking Study in France, Germany, and United Kingdom

	France			West Germany			East Germany	United Kingdom		
	1990	1991	1992	1990	1991	1992	1992	1990	1991	1992
Profile of Sports Shoe Purchaser										
Male	50%	50%	55%	51%	50%	54%	50%	52%	50%	52%
Female	50	50	45	49	49	46	50	48	50	48
15-24	32	31	28	27	26	28	27	34	31	31
24-34	30	29	29	27	27	25	24	25	28	28
35-44	21	26	28	25	24	28	26	27	28	27
45-55	18	14	15	21	23	19	23	14	13	13
Profile of Reebok Brand Purchaser										
Male	53%	55%	54%	48%	54%	59%	NA	47%	43%	50%
Female	47	45	45	52	46	41	NA	53	57	50
15-24	36	38	36	33	33	37	25	40	36	29
24-34	27	21	29	30	27	22	--	26	24	28
35-44	18	27	23	19	18	24	25	21	26	31
45-55	18	14	13	16	23	17	50	13	15	12
Brand Share										
Reebok	12%	13%	19%	6%	8%	11%	2%	18%	19%	25%
Nike	18	22	22	14	16	16	12	13	13	18
Adidas	38	35	28	49	42	40	41	15	12	12
Puma	--	--	--	21	21	20	19	6	5	4
Brand Loyalty (% of owners likely to buy same brand next time)										
Reebok	48%	65%	58%	75%	81%	75%	75%	81%	76%	68%
Nike	54	50	48	81	75	73	67	71	54	59
Adidas	59	55	54	85	78	80	55	67	61	66
Puma	--	--	--	79	73	62	49	64	58	43
Brand Awareness—Unaided										
Reebok	49%	63%	73%	35%	49%	56%	33%	64%	75%	75%
Nike	61	78	76	68	69	80	65	64	66	71
Adidas	96	96	95	98	91	97	97	77	76	75
Puma	--	--	--	92	85	89	84	48	44	47
Brand Awareness—Aided										
Reebok	67%	82%	88%	63%	77%	85%	50%	94%	98%	99%
Nike	81	91	91	89	90	95	86	95	98	99
Adidas	95	98	98	100	100	100	100	98	99	100
Puma	--	--	--	99	99	98	96	93	97	97

	France			West Germany			East Germany	United Kingdom		
	1990	1991	1992	1990	1991	1992	1992	1990	1991	1992
Advertising Awareness—Unaided										
Reebok	27%	31%	46%	9%	20%	23%	15%	22%	46%	45%
Nike	42	48	50	33	34	41	40	26	33	41
Adidas	45	35	38	28	30	23	34	19	19	12
Puma	--	--	--	22	26	25	31	7	5	8
Advertising Awareness—Aided										
Reebok	34%	37%	54%	10%	20%	28%	17%	32%	60%	60%
Nike	47	55	61	36	34	44	45	36	47	55
Adidas	51	48	52	29	32	29	40	30	32	25
Puma	--	--	--	23	27	30	38	12	13	19
Sports Shoe Usage										
Only sport	23%	19%	23%	27%	21%	23%	10%	9%	9%	8%
Mainly sport, casual too	24	27	25	25	24	25	16	14	13	14
Mainly casual, sport too	17	16	13	24	24	22	35	19	19	20
Only casual	11	14	10	13	16	17	25	36	42	43
Work and casual	22	18	24	10	14	11	11	21	15	13
Other	3	4	5	--	1	1	1	1	2	2
Association of Brands with Technical Benefits										
Reebok Hexalite	3%	10%	11%	1%	5%	6%	2%	7%	13%	16%
Reebok Pump	8	25	42	2	23	29	15	19	42	45
Reebok ERS	12	17	15	4	11	9	2	20	21	23
Nike Air System	31	42	41	20	30	30	24	29	45	51
Adidas Torsion	30	38	38	27	31	29	18	16	28	29
Puma Disc	--	--	7	--	--	24	16	--	--	25

Source: Adapted from *1992 Sports Shoe Tracking Study*, prepared by Marketing Focus U.K. Ltd, January 1993.

Note: Responses based upon interviews with approximately 1,000 respondents in each country in each year

Exhibit 16 Perceived Brand Personalities of Reebok and Nike in France, Germany, and United Kingdom

	Gender	Commitment	Appearance	Technology	Nationality	Disposition
Reebok:						
France	• Feminine		• Subtle • Elegant	• Precise • Technological[a] • Leading edge[a]	• British • Cosmopolitan • American[a]	• Extrovert[a] • Sporty • Trendy • Exciting[a]
Germany	• Feminine	• Passive	• Plain • Discreet		• British • American(?)	• Sociable • Harmless • Serious
United Kingdom	• Feminine	• Passive • Safe	• Discreet • Subtle • Crafted	• Broad	• British • American(?)	• Inoffensive • Acceptable • Defendable • Down to earth
European Synthesis	• Feminine	• Passive	• Stylish • Classic • Elegant • Discreet • Subtle		• British • American(?)	• Serious • Sociable • Inoffensive
Nike:						
European Synthesis	• Masculine • Muscular	• Vigorous • Competitive • Aggressive • Performer • Player • Professional	• Complicated • Gaudy • Bulky	• Innovative • Technological • Specialist • Gimmicky	• American	• Exciting[a] • Young • Energetic • Hyped • Extrovert[a]

Source: Adapted from *Project Genesis: European Qualitative Research on Reebok and the Sport Shoe Market*, prepared for Reebok by Euro RSCG, March 1993.
[a]In France, there was overlap in the attributes associated with the two brands.

Exhibit 17	Selected Findings of Focus Group Research to Pretest Planet Reebok Concept and Execution, November 1992		
	France	Germany	United Kingdom
First Impressions	Dynamic, showed wide range of sports	Showed diversity of brand	Made you sit up and watch
	Visually rich	Difficult to understand, exposures too short	Liked fast change to different sports
	Violent & macho	Imitation of Nike	No everyday people, just sports professionals
	Spoke to everyone wanting to play sports	PR idea was unique and fast	Recalled "no" declarations
PR Perceptions: -PR Is...	An exclusive atmosphere	Stage for success-oriented, athletic people	World of sports
	Where one landed almost inadvertently	Place for people who loved sports	Land of opportunity
		Place for people who sought personal goals	America
			A place to escape to
-People On PR	Like machines	Young	Physically fit individuals into many sports
	Soulless	Conscious about body	False and competitive
	Only played sports	Sensation-seeking	Perfect, figure glamorous
	Didn't even eat	Risk-takers	The elite
-Life On PR	Sports	The American way of life	Not easy, had to do things for yourself
	Where being in shape was valued	Sports were everything	Where you could achieve the impossible
	Where men and women never met	Sports were fun as long as you were successful	Where everything was wonderful (not reality)
	Only sports and action mattered		
Attitudes Toward PR: -Motivation	NA	NA	Most males were highly motivated by ads
			Most females felt intimidated
-Appeal	Disliked focus on individualistic values in sports	Disliked watching ads too fast, music unpleasant	Most females felt on the outside looking in
	Overall absence of humanism	Unclear intended meaning, captions confusing	They disliked youth and sports professional focus
-Relevance	Relate better if more brotherhood, team focus	Couldn't relate played sports for fun, not danger	Most males related well & became really involved
	Relate better with more humanist sporting values	Couldn't identify with 'struggle' in ads	

Exhibit 17	Selected Findings of Focus Group Research to Pretest Planet Reebok Concept and Execution, November 1992 (continued)		
	France	Germany	United Kingdom
PR Brand Positioning:			
-Reebok	Performance & technology oriented Accessible Modern	Performance brand, but low credibility Reebok seen as leisure/casual oriented	Performance brand, not for casual wear Brand for the 1990s Reebok covered the world
-User	Serious & young athletes that were hand- picked Combative Superhuman	Individuals Pushing, testing limits Achiever of personal goals	Individuals that were young and athletic The elite Achievers, competitive
-Product	Broad range of shoes Sturdy Resistant	NA	Shoes for multiple sports, ages, & fitness levels Durable
-Other	Didn't believe Reebok had so many products	Didn't communicate fun, human factor, empathy	
Execution:			
-Music	Disliked change in music type & rhythm in ads	Similar to Nike's ads Reinforced restless feel	Intriguing, catchy, and inspiring Caught attention, but too slow
-Captions	Fairly well understood by all Preferred "No" version because it was funny	English words cool, but crucial meaning missed Too much information	Liked captions, but flashed by too quickly Many difficult to read
-Pace	Aggressive Breathless	Short exposures provoked curiosity and fear	Liked fast and exciting rhythm Too fast for older females
-Sports Shots	Liked diversity of sports But too many geared to performance Superhuman sports	Liked soccer most Also football, free-climbing, basketball, & rafting	Liked all sports But wanted more English-specific sports

	France	Germany	United Kingdom
-Product Shots	Barely noticed shoes	Didn't even notice shoes initially Wanted more technical information	Wanted more on shoes so could study them More information would make shopping easier
-Suggestions	Alternate violent with calm sports More women, less violence Inject enjoyment, comaraderie	Shots of tennis, volleyball, outdoor soccer	Shorter, bigger-sized captions on screen longer More "nos"[a] with better phrases
-"No" Version	Preferred by most for humor and humanism	Couldn't relate, play sports for fun, not danger Couldn't identify with 'struggle' in ads	Preferred by males about sports and competition Women felt intimidated
-Positive Version	Less preferred and understood Too complicated, philosophical, demanding	NA	Females really understood what PR life was like Males found less relevant and too philosophical

Source: Adapted from *Planet Reebok TV Advertising Test (France)*, prepared by Research International, November 1992; *Project No. 02384 (Germany)*, October 1992; and *Presentation on Planet Reebok (U.K.)*, prepared by Marketing Focus Ltd, November 1992.

[a]Executions that included the "no" captions, such as "No Meetings," "No Faxes," "No Phones."

I.   Of the three executions, the ad developed in the United States was the most appealing in all three countries, although it had less appeal among women over 20 years old and among casual athletes.

II.   The PR ads communicated effectively that Reebok was "the brand for all people all over the world," but the attitude that Reebok desired to have associated with the brand name were not nearly as well communicated:

- the brand personality that emerged was not "empathetic" or "human";
- the advertising message was interpreted in a confusing way, particularly in France and Germany, and was not seen to differentiate Reebok from Nike in either style or content.

III.   The advertising appealed strongly to sports and/or fitness enthusiasts, both male and female, aged 18 to 30 years old. However, the large portion of the market that purchased sports shoes for casual rather than sports use was not so motivated.

IV.   The effects of the ads, especially the ad developed in the United States, if run in the United Kingdom, could include

- reduced affinity of women toward Reebok;
- weak motivation toward purchase of Reebok;
- presentation of Reebok as a me-too to Nike which was neither credible currently nor desirable for Reebok in the longer term;
- building stronger empathy toward the brand among 14- to 17-year-olds.

V.   In Germany and France—and probably in other non-English speaking countries—PR was not expected to have a strong effect. It might be ignored by some due to comprehension problems or it might encourage perceptions of Reebok as a copycat of Nike.

Source: Adapted from *Planet Reebok: Advertising Creative Development Research,* prepared by Strategic Research Group, February 1993.

Heineken N.V.: Global Branding and Advertising

In January 1994, senior managers at Heineken headquarters in Amsterdam were reviewing two research projects commissioned to clarify Heineken's brand identity and the implications for television advertising. Project Comet defined five components of Heineken's global brand identity and explored how they should be expressed in Heineken brand communications. Project Mosa, which involved a different team of executives, identified the expressions of taste and friendship that had the most appeal and explored how they should be expressed in Heineken television advertising worldwide.

Heineken's senior managers were interested in assessing whether or not the conclusions of the two studies were mutually consistent. They also wished to determine how far they should or could standardize Heineken's brand image and advertising worldwide.

COMPANY BACKGROUND

The Heineken brewery was founded in Amsterdam in 1863 by Gerard Adriaan Heineken. He was quoted as saying: "I will leave no stone unturned in attempting to continuously supply beer of the highest quality." The strain of yeast which continued through the 1990s to give Heineken beer its special taste was developed in 1886. Heineken beer won a gold medal at the 1889 Paris World's Fair and, by 1893, was one of the largest selling beers in the Netherlands.

One hundred years later, in 1993, Heineken N.V. recorded net sales of 9,049 million guilders and a trading profit of 798 million guilders. Beer accounted for 82% of sales, the remainder being derived from soft drinks, spirits and wine. The geographical breakdowns of

This case was prepared by Professor John A. Quelch.

Copyright © 1995 by the President and Fellows of Harvard College. Harvard Business School case 9-596-015.

sales (in litres) for Heinekin and the worldwide beer industry were as follows:

	Heineken 1993 Sales %	% Change vs. 1992	Total 1993 Beer Sales %
Netherlands	24 }	(1.6) }	38
Rest of Europe	47 }		38
America	13	5.3	38
Asia/Australasia	8	23.7	19
Africa	6	(1.5)	5

In 1993, sales of beer brewed under Heineken's supervision reached 5.6 billion litres, second in the world only to Anheuser-Busch with 10 billion litres. World beer production in 1993 totaled 120 billion litres.

Sales of the Heineken brand were 1.52 billion litres in 1993. The company's other brands with some international distribution were Amstel (formerly made by the second-largest Dutch brewery, acquired by Heineken in 1968) which sold 630 million litres; Buckler, a nonalcoholic beer, which sold 90 million litres; and Murphy's Stout, recently acquired and sold principally in Ireland and the United Kingdom. As a result of acquisitions, Heineken also oversaw the brewing of many local and regional beer brands marketed by its subsidiaries, such as Bir Bintang, the leading Indonesian brand.

INTERNATIONAL PRESENCE

The Heineken brand had long been available in markets outside the Netherlands. In 1937, Heineken granted its first license to a foreign brewer to produce Heineken beer according to the original formula. While licensing agreements also aimed to specify how the Heineken brand should be marketed, Heineken could not influence how a licensee marketed its own brands. In management's view, some licensees did not maintain a sufficient price premium for the Heineken brand over their own national brands. By the 1980s, Heineken was seeking majority equity stakes in its existing and prospective partners to ensure tighter control over production and marketing. The ideal national brewer partner, from Heineken's point of view, was one that did not have international ambitions for its domestic brands.

By 1993, Heineken's worldwide brewing interests were as follows:

	Wholly Owned Subsidiaries	Majority Equity Stakes	Minority Equity Stakes	Licensees
Europe	3	5	0	2
American	0	4	10	2
Asia/ Australasia	0	2	8	2
Africa	0	4	10	2

In Europe, for example, Heineken owned outright its operations in the Netherlands, France, and Ireland. It held majority interests in breweries in Greece, Hungary, Italy, Spain, and Switzerland and licensed production to breweries in Norway and the United Kingdom (Whitbread). Heineken was not bottled in the large United States market, but was the number one imported beer. In Germany, the heaviest beer-consuming country in Europe (144 litres per capita), national brands still dominated the market and Heineken was available only through imports.

In the early 1990s, the brewing industry was becoming increasingly global as the leading brewers scrambled to acquire equity stakes and sign joint ventures with national breweries. This trend was especially evident in the emerging markets where population expansion and increased per-capita consumption promised faster growth than in the developed world. In Europe, in particular, overcapacity and minimal population growth resulted in price competition, margin pressures, and efforts to segment further the market with no- or low-alcohol beers, specialty flavored beers, and "dry" beers.

Despite the increasing globalization of the industry, there remained substantial differences in per-capita beer consumption, consumer preferences and behaviors, and the mix of competitors from one market to another. For example, annual per capita consumption ranged from 132 liters in Ireland and 88 liters in the U.S.A. to 56 liters in Japan and 30 liters in Argentina. Heineken executives believed that the beer market in each country followed an evolutionary cycle and that, at any time, different countries were at different stages of market development. Exhibit 1 depicts the beer market development cycle while Exhibit 2 notes Heineken's principal marketing objectives in selected markets.

At the end of 1993, the Heineken brand held a 24% volume share in the Netherlands, several share points ahead of its main competitor, Grolsch. As the market leader, Heineken was viewed as a mainstream brand. Sales volume was declining and the brand image needed some revitalization. Outside the Netherlands, however, Heineken had consistently been marketed as a premium brand. In some markets, such as the United States and Hong Kong, Heineken had successfully established a distinct image for the brand. The image was sometimes narrowly drawn such that Heineken was seen as appropriate solely for special occasions when making a social statement was important rather than for daily consumption. In other markets, such as in Latin America, Heineken was viewed as just one among many European imported beers. But across all markets, the Heineken brand was acknowledged as a lighter beer of superior quality presented in attractive packaging.

Comparative data on the Heineken brand's market position in seven European countries are presented in Exhibit 3. Premium brands accounted for around 25% of beer volume in 1993 and around 30% of measured media beer advertising. Heineken was the most heavily advertised premium brand in Europe and worldwide. Over 90% of Heineken advertising took the form of television commercials.

PROJECT COMET

Managers at Heineken headquarters were concerned that Heineken's brand image was not being consistently projected in the brand's communications around the world. Two television advertising executions were used in multiple country markets in 1991, but, particularly in the larger markets, local Heineken managers had the resources to develop their own commercials and justified their decisions to do so on grounds of unique competitive conditions, industry structures, and/or consumption behaviors.

Exhibit 1   Beer Market Evolution for Selected Counties and Regions

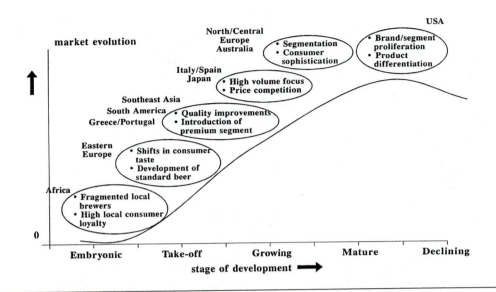

Exhibit 2   Key Heineken Marketing Objectives in Eight Countries

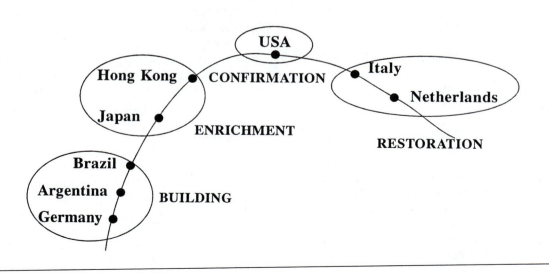

Exhibit 3 Comparative Heineken Usage Data for Seven European Markets

	Netherlands	France	Greece	Ireland	Italy	Spain	United Kingdom
Main brand usage[a]	17	14	44	25	7	5	11
Trial/awareness ratio	92	89	99	91	86	66	90
Regular/total usage ratio	46	40	54	42	28	25	41
Monthly brand penetration[b]	60	48	79	57	53	63	60
Market share position[c]	1	2	1	2	3	7	7
Advertising share of voice position[d]	1	2	4	5	4	6	6
Per capita beer consumption (litres)[e]	90	41	40	123	24	71	103

[a]Percentage of beer drinkers naming Heineken as their main brand.

[b]Percentage of beer drinkers who had consumed a Heineken in the previous month.

[c]Overall market share position. In most markets, Heineken was the largest-selling brand in the premium segment.

[d]Overall SOV position among beer brands advertised. In all markets except the United Kingdom, Heineken SOV ranked first or second in the premium segment.

[e]Based on consumption of *all* beer, not just Heineken.

Project Comet was established in 1991 by Heineken's international marketing manager to recommend how to enhance Heineken's competitive advantage by more consistently projecting the brand as "the world's leading premium beer." The project team concluded that Heineken's desired brand image was "good taste":

- Because of Heineken's flavor, its roots, commitment to and pride in brewing a high-quality lager.
- Because Heineken is a symbol of premiumness, taste, and tradition around the world.

The team believed that no other brand in the world could claim superior good taste with as much credibility as Heineken.

The brand's good taste image would be built on five core brand values:

- Taste
- Premiumness
- Tradition
- Winning spirit
- Friendship

Taste and premiumness were regarded as the price of entry. They had to be communicated in advertising messages but would not, in themselves, be enough to differentiate Heineken from its competition. A unique, differentiated image would depend on effective communication of the other three core brand values. Project team members acknowledge the challenge of communicating all five values in each advertisement. However, they thought that all five could be reflected in one way or another through the locations, situations, relationships, casting, lighting, style, and tone used in each commercial.

The team detailed how each of the core brand values should be portrayed in Heineken brand commercials:

Taste The product should be shown in slow-pouring shots where its golden color, sparkling texture and refreshing coolness would celebrate its taste. Actors should be portrayed genuinely enjoying Heineken with no gulps or "knocking it back." The slogan used should be competitive but not comparative.

Premiumness The production quality of every execution should be at the level of excellence to be expected of a premium brand. In some geographies, Heineken's premiumness might be a unique reason for purchase; in such cases, this attribute could be presented as part of the brand promise.

Tradition The genuine aura of the brand should be especially evident in the casting and tone of voice of each commercial. Heineken should be the preferred brand of people who believed in true values and whose brand choices reflected their personal value set.

Winning spirit Tone of voice was thought to be especially important in conveying this value "because winners are confident and relaxed, take a quiet pride in everything they do and do not shout."

Friendship Heineken should not be portrayed as a solitary beer or a "mass-gathering" drink. The Heineken group should be a few (even two) people who clearly enjoy their relationship. The "Heineken moment" should show people as themselves, content, relaxed with each other and confident. Interactions should be sincere, self-confident, warm and balanced, displaying mutual respect and free from game-playing.

The project team next tried to develop guidelines for the visual images—the people, the relationships and the settings—to be included in Heineken commercials.

The Project Comet report concluded as follows:

> All of our advertising must be consistent with these guidelines. We also need impactful advertising. Heineken advertising is therefore never safe. It should always be leading edge and state of the art, taking calculated risks and initiatives to achieve the desired effects.

PROJECT MOSA

In late 1993, Heineken's international advertising manager commissioned focus groups in eight countries[1] to understand (a) what male beer drinkers meant by taste and friendship in relation to premium beer drinking and (b) which expressions of taste and friendship could be used by the Heineken brand in advertising. The project team identified in advance the following expressions of taste which "appealed to the head" and expressions of friendship which "appealed to the heart":

Taste (Head)	Friendship (Heart)
Brand vision	Trust
Quality	Sports
Brewing skills	True friends
Tradition	You can count on
	Heineken as a friend
Availability	Respect

Exhibit 4   Sample Project Mosa Concept Boards: Taste Expressions

Alfred H. Heineken.
Chairman

---

[1]The countries were Netherlands, Italy, and Germany in Europe; USA, Argentina and Brazil in the Americas; and Japan and Hong Kong in Asia.

Exhibit 5   Sample Project Mosa Concept Boards: Friendship Expressions

Nevada, USA.   Yorkshire, UK.

Cameroon, West Africa.   Papeete, Tahiti.

Wherever you are, you can always count on Heineken

Heineken. When true friends get together.

Boards with visual and message stimuli depicting each of these expressions were used in the focus groups to elicit reactions. Examples of these boards are presented in Exhibits 4 and 5. Eight focus groups were run in each country, four with 21-27 year olds and four with 28-35 year olds. Four groups in each country explored taste cues, four explored friendship cues.

Members of the focus groups dealing with taste were asked to identify which of several factors they perceived as strong or weak indicators of beer taste. These responses are summarized in Exhibit 6. Members of the other four focus groups dealing with friendship discussed the different social occasions when a standard versus a premium beer would be appropriate. On this issue, there was substantial agreement across national markets. The conclusions are summarized in Exhibit 7.

Participants in the focus groups were then exposed to a variety of advertising boards for Heineken, each of them highlighting a particular attribute. Those in the focus groups dealing with taste were exposed to twelve boards while those in the friendship focus groups were exposed to ten. The objective was to elicit consumer reactions to both the visual and message claims presented on each board and to establish each claim's relevance to and overall suitability for promoting the Heineken brand. The overall suitability rankings, first for the four focus groups concentrating on taste cues and, second, for the focus groups concentrating on friendship cues, are presented in Exhibits 8 and 9.

Exhibit 6   Indications of Beer Taste: Summary of Focus Group Responses

	Netherlands	Germany	Italy	USA	Average 8 Countries
Manufacturing					
Ingredients	-	+	-	-	-
Water quality	+	+	-	-	0
Scale of plant	+	+	-	+	+
Product					
Taste experience	+	+	+	+	+
Balanced taste	+	+	+	+	+
Aftertaste	-	-	+	+	0
Freshness	+	-	-	+	0
Foam	+	+	0	+	+
Drinkability	+	+	-	-	+
Day After	+	+	-	-	0
Marketing					
Price	-	+	-	+	0
Advertising	+	-	+	+	+
Packaging	-	+	+	+	+

Note: A minus sign (-) indicates the factor is an unimportant or negative indicator of quality.

Exhibit 7   Standard vs. Premium Beer: Summary of Focus Group Responses

	Standard	Premium
Company	• nuclear family • large groups • your wife • colleagues	• intimate friends • smaller groups • girlfriend • boss
Occasions and Moments	• after work • at meals • at home • watching TV • thirst-quenching • (popular) bars • beach • to party • daytime • after sports • sport events	• meeting people • fancy meals • away from home • new encounters • savouring • traveling • intimate moments and places • elegant parties • nighttime • entertaining • disco/nightclub
Role of Beer	• social participation • thirst-quencher • alcohol effect • problem solver	• ego enhancement/self-esteem • a treat • a communication tool • signal function

Exhibit 8   Taste Expressions: Overall Heineken Suitability

	Netherlands	Germany	Italy	USA	Average 8 Countries
Brand Vision	-	+	+	-	-
Quality					
Two years Amsterdam training	+	+	+	+	+
24 quality checks	+	+	+	+	+
Bottles returned to Amsterdam	+	+	+	+	+
Brewing Skills					
100% malt	0	+	0	+	0
Smooth taste	-	+	+	+	0
Pure taste	+	-	+	+	0
Matured longer	-	0	-	-	-
Tradition					
Family since 1863	-	+	-	+	0
Original recipe	+	+	0	+	+
Where beer was born	+	+	+	+	+
Availability					
More bars/more countries	+	0	-	0	0

Exhibit 9   Friendship Expressions: Overall Heineken Suitability

	Netherlands	Germany	Italy	USA	Average 8 Countries
Friendship					
Cat and dog	0	0	+	-	0
Rugby (sport)	+	0	+	-	0
True friends	+	+	0	+	+
Always count on Heineken	+	+	+	+	+
Respect	-	-	-	-	-

DHL Worldwide Express

In July 1991, in Jakarta, Indonesia, the shouts of the kaki lima (street vendors) outside did little to soothe Ali Sarrafzadeh's concerns. Sarrafzadeh, DHL's Worldwide sales and marketing manager, had spent the previous three days chairing the Worldwide Pricing Committee workshop at DHL's annual directors' meeting. On the following day, he was to present his recommendations on pricing to the conference's 300 attendees.

Some of the statements made during the workshop meetings were still ringing in his head:

> If I have P&L [profit and loss] responsibility for my region, then I better be able to set my own prices. If not, how am I supposed to impact profits? By managing my travel and entertainment account?
>
> Jurgsen Beckenbauer
> Regional Director, Central Europe

> Many of our large multinational customers have come to us and told us that they want a consistent worldwide pricing structure. . . . If we don't offer worldwide prices and our competitors do, are we going to lose some of our largest accounts?
>
> Christine Platine
> Account Manager, Brussels headquarters

> If our pricing structures were consistent across regions, it would be much easier to consolidate regional reports. With better reporting, we could gain valuable information about our costs. . . . The simpler our pricing structure, the easier it is to manage hardware and software around the world.
>
> Adelina Rossi
> VP Systems, Brussels headquarters

> We are the only company which services some regions of Africa. Thus, we charge premium prices in these markets. If we are forced to charge the same rates as in other regions, we will only lose profits. Sales will not grow with lower prices.
>
> Aziz Milla
> Country Manager, Cameroon, Africa

> Our prices have always been 20%-40% higher than the competition's prices. We can command these premium prices by continuing to give more value to our customers. . . . Our pricing must not encourage "cherry picking." We don't want customers to just ship with us on routes that are difficult to serve, such as those to and from Africa.
>
> Bobby Jones
> Regional Director, USA

Sarrafzadeh wanted to make recommendations on pricing strategy, structure, and decision making. On strategy, he viewed his options as recommending either a price leadership strategy or a market response strategy. The former meant DHL would charge premium prices and aim to deliver superior value-added services in all markets. The latter meant DHL would set prices independently in each country, according to customer usage patterns and competitive pressures.

If the principle of standardized worldwide pricing was pursued, what were the pricing structure implications? For example, should DHL charge a weekly or monthly handling fee (a set fee in return for automatically visiting a customer each business day) in all countries? Should the same price be charged for shipments between any two cities, regardless of which was the origin and which the destination?

Regarding pricing structure, Sarrafzadeh had to address several additional questions. Should DHL have different pricing schedules for documents and parcels? Should DHL set different prices for different industries? For example, should prices be different for banking and manufacturing customers? Should DHL offer special prices to multinational corporations seeking to cut deals with individual shippers to handle all their express document and parcel delivery needs worldwide?

Another issue was the DHL discount program. Sarrafzadeh had to decide whether DHL should continue to offer volume discounts. If so, should they be based on units, weight, or revenue?

In addition, Sarrafzadeh wanted to recommend who should hold primary price setting responsibility. He considered his three options to be a centralized, decentralized, or hybrid approach. A decentralized approach would continue the present policy in which country/region managers set all prices and headquarters offered counsel and support. Under a centralized approach, a headquarters management committee would set all prices around the world. Country managers would be responsible for collecting data and making suggestions to headquarters. A third option was to establish multiple pricing committees, each including managers from both headquarters and the regions and each responsible for setting prices for one or more specific industries.

COMPANY BACKGROUND AND ORGANIZATION

DHL legally comprised two companies: DHL Airways and DHL International. DHL Airways was based in San Francisco and managed all U.S. operations. DHL International was based in Brussels and managed all operations outside the United States. Each company was the exclusive delivery agent of the other. Revenues for 1990 were split: $600 million for DHL Airways, and

$1,400 million for DHL International. One DHL executive commented, "The main reason DHL is involved in domestic shipping within the United States is to lower the costs and increase the reliability of our international shipments. If not for our domestic business, we would be at the mercy of the domestic airlines bringing our packages to the international gateways." In 1990, DHL accounted for only 3% of intra-U.S. air express shipments but 20% of overseas shipments from the United States.

DHL was the world's leading international express delivery network. It was privately held and headquartered in Brussels, Belgium. The company was formed in San Francisco in September 1969 by Adrian Dalsey, Larry Hillblom, and Robert Lynn. The three were involved in shipping and discovered that, by forwarding the shipping documents by air with an on-board courier, they could significantly reduce the turnaround time of ships in port. DHL grew rapidly and, by 1990, serviced 189 countries. In 1990, revenues were approximately $2 billion. Profits before taxes were 4%-6% of revenues. (Exhibit 1 summarizes the growth of DHL operations from 1973 to 1990; Exhibit 2 displays DHL's revenues by industry.)

DHL used a hub system to transport shipments around the world. In 1991, the company operated 12 hubs (as shown in Exhibit 3). Within Europe, the United States, and the Middle East, DHL generally used owned or leased aircraft to carry its shipments, while on most intercontinental routes it used scheduled airlines. In 1991, approximately 65% of DHL shipments were sent via scheduled airlines and 35% via owned or leased aircraft. The other leading shippers also utilized

---

Exhibit 1 DHL Operations Statistics, 1973–1990

	1973	1978	1983	1990
Shipments	2,000,000	5,400,000	12,400,000	60,000,000
Customers	30,500	35,000	250,000	900,000
Personnel	400	6,500	11,300	25,000
Countries served	20	65	120	189
Hubs	0	2	5	12
Flights/day	14	303	792	1,466
Aircraft	0	5	27	150
Vehicles	300	2,235	5,940	7,209

Note: Shipments included both documents and parcels. Hubs were major shipment sorting centers. Aircraft and vehicle data included both owned and leased equipment.

Exhibit 2 — DHL Worldwide Revenues by Industry, January–June 1991

Conglomerates	10%
High technology	8
Import-export	8
Banking	7
Transport	7
Heavy engineering	6
Chemicals	5
Precision manufacturing	5
Professional services	4
Foodstuffs	4
Textiles/leather	4
Other	32

scheduled airlines but to a lesser extent than DHL. Federal Express relied on its own fleet of planes to transport all its shipments. Pierre Madec, DHL's operations director, noted:

FedEx has a dedicated airfleet which ties up capital and limits the flexibility of its operation: express packages are forced to wait until the FedEx plane's takeoff slot, which at major international airports frequently does not tie in with the end-of-the-day courier pickups. By using a variety of scheduled international carriers, DHL is able to optimize its transport network to minimize delivery times.

DHL was organized into nine geographic regions. Region managers oversaw the relevant country managers and/or DHL agents in their regions and held profit and loss responsibility for performance within their territories. Revenues and profits were recognized at the location where a shipment originated. Only 70 people worked at DHL's world headquarters in Brussels. The main functions of the worldwide marketing services group, of which Sarrafzadeh was a member, were business development, information transfer, communication of best practice ideas, and sales coordination among the country operating units.

Of DHL's 60 million shipments in 1990, 50 million were cross-border shipments. DHL's worldwide mission statement, included in its 1990 annual report, read:

DHL will become the acknowledged global leader in the express delivery of documents and packages. Leadership will be achieved by establishing the industry standards of excellence for quality of service and by maintaining the lowest cost position relative to our service commitment in all markets of the world.

DHL management believed that achievement of this mission required the following:

- Absolute dedication to understanding and fulfilling DHL's customers' needs with the appropriate mix of service, products, and price for each customer.
- Ensuring the long-term success of the business through profitable growth and reinvestment of earnings.
- An environment that rewards achievement, enthusiasm, and team spirit, and which offers each person in DHL superior opportunities for personal development and growth.
- A state-of-the-art worldwide information network for customer billing, tracking, tracing and management information/communications.
- Allocation of resources consistent with the recognition that DHL is one worldwide business.
- A professional organization able to maintain local initiative and local decision making while working together within a centrally managed network.

DHL's annual report also stated: "The evolution of our business into new services, markets or products will be completely driven by our single-minded commitment to anticipating and meeting the changing needs of our customers."

THE INTERNATIONAL AIR EXPRESS INDUSTRY

Total revenues for the international air express industry were approximately $3.4 billion in 1989 and $4.3 billion in 1990. The air express industry offered two main products: document delivery and parcel delivery. Industry revenues were split roughly 75:25 between parcels and documents. In 1989, the parcel sector grew 40%, while the document sector grew 15%. The growth of parcel and document express delivery was at the expense of the air cargo market and other traditional modes of shipping.

The growth of the air express industry was expected to continue. One optimistic forecast for 1992 is presented in Table A. Other observers were concerned that shipping capacity would expand faster than shipments, particularly if economic growth slowed.

Acknowledging continuing progress toward completion of the European market integration program by the end of

Exhibit 3   DHL Hub System

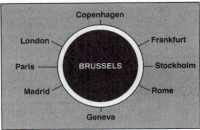

The word "Hub" derives from the image of a wheel with the spokes, the Hub is a sorting and redistribution centre and the spokes are flights in and out.

DHL routes material via Hubs, we do not use direct flights to every destination around the world. There are Hubs in every area of the world:

USA (Cincinnati, New York);   **AFRICA** (Johannesburg, Nairobi);

MIDDLE EAST (Bahrain);   **FAR EAST** (Hong Kong, Singapore);

AUSTRALIA (Sydney);   **EUROPE** (London, Brussels);

The routing of material through the Hubs passes on a saving of both time and cost for the customer.

Table A   Worldwide International (Cross-Border) Air Express 1992 Estimated Revenue Growth Rates

Market	1992 Estimated Growth Rate
Europe	28%
Asia/Pacific	30
United States	25
Rest of the world	9
Total	25%

Note: Growth rates are for time-sensitive documents/packages under 30 kilograms.

1992, an article on the air express industry in Europe in *Forbes* (April, 1991) noted:

> *The express-delivery business in Europe is booming. . . . Measured by revenues, the European express-delivery business is growing at a 28% compound annual rate. Big European companies are stocking products and parts in central locations and moving them by overnight express, instead of running warehouses in each country.*

COMPETITORS

Air express companies serviced a geographic region either by using their own personnel or by hiring agents. Building a comprehensive international network of owned operations and/or reliable agents required considerable time and investment and, therefore, acted as a significant barrier to entry.

DHL's principal competitors in door-to-door international air express delivery were Federal Express, TNT, and UPS. (Exhibit 4 provides operational data for the top four competitors; Table B summarizes their 1988 market shares.)

Founded in 1973, FedEx focused for many years on the U.S. domestic market. During the late 1980s, the company began to expand internationally through acquisitions and competitive pricing, sometimes undercutting DHL published prices by as much as 50%. Between 1987 and 1991, FedEx invested over $1 billion in 14 acquisitions in nine countries: the United Kingdom, Holland, West Germany, Italy, Japan, Australia, United Arab Emirates, Canada, and the United States. FedEx also entered the international air freight business through the acquisition of Tiger International (Flying Tigers), which expanded further FedEx's global reach in document as well as parcel delivery, particularly in Asia. However, the challenge of integrating so many acquisitions meant that FedEx's international operations lost $43 million in 1989 and $194 million in 1990. Nevertheless, with 45% of the U.S. air express market, 7% of the European market, and leadership in value-added services based on information systems technology, FedEx remained a formidable competitor.

Thomas Nationwide Transport (TNT) was a publicly owned Australian transport group which had historically concentrated on air express delivery of documents. TNT

Table B — International Air Express Market Shares by $ Revenue (1988)

Company	Market Share (%)
DHL	44%
FedEx	7
TNT	18
UPS	4
Others	27
Total	100%

focused mainly on Europe and had a low profile in North America. To participate in the North American market, TNT held a 15% stake in an American shipper—Airborne Freight Corporation. This stake could be increased to a maximum holding of only 25% under U.S. aviation laws. During the late 1980s, TNT began to target heavier shipments and bulk consolidations to fuel its growth.

United Parcel Service (UPS) was a privately held U.S. company, most of whose equity was owned by its employees. UPS had traditionally been known as a parcel shipper that emphasized everyday low prices rather than the fastest delivery. Unlike DHL, UPS sometimes held a package back to consolidate several shipments to the same destination in the interest of saving on costs.

Exhibit 4 — Major Air Express Competitors, 1988

	DHL	FedEx	TNT	UPS
International Air Express revenues (in $ millions)	$1,200	$200	$500	$100
International Air Express employees	23,000	5,000	10,000	3,000
Countries covered	184	118	184	175
Total service outlets	1,427	1,135	800	1,700
Service outlets outside United States	1,207	278	750	465
Ratio of Owned: Agent country operations	2.00:1	0.53:1	0.77:1	0.36:1
Owned aircraft	49	38	17	3
Years of international experience	20	5	17	3
Document: Parcel revenues	65:35	20:80[a]	50:50	20:80

[a]After FedEx's 1989 acquisition of Tiger International, Inc., its document:parcel revenue ratio remained relatively unchanged as Tiger concentrated on heavy air freight. However, post-acquisition, document and parcel combined revenues represented a smaller portion of total revenues.

UPS had historically tried to avoid offering discounts from its published prices.

UPS's 1990 annual report proclaimed the company's strategy as follows:

> UPS will achieve worldwide leadership in package distribution by developing and delivering solutions that best meet our customers' distribution needs at competitive rates. To do so, we will build upon our extensive and efficient distribution network, the legacy and dedication of our people to operational and service excellence and our commitment to anticipate and respond rapidly to changing market conditions and requirements.

In addition to the industry giants, there were many small shipping forwarders which concentrated on a specific geographic area or industry sector. In the late 1980s, many of these small companies were acquired by larger firms trying to increase their market shares. National post offices were also competitors in air express, but they could not offer the same service and reliability because they were not integrated across borders (that is, no national post office could control the shipment of a package from one country to another). One industry executive commented: "When we have internal competitive discussions on international business, the post offices just don't come up."

Finally, the regular airlines were minor competitors in door-to-door express delivery. British Airways operated a wholesale airport-to-door courier service called Speedbird in cooperation with smaller couriers that did not have international networks. Swissair serviced 50 countries through its Skyracer service in cooperation with local agents. In the heavy cargo sector, most airlines were allied with freight forwarders who consolidated cargo from different sources and booked space in aircraft. These alliances represented significant competition as DHL expanded into delivery of heavier shipments. Some airlines were reluctant to upset their freight forwarder customers by dealing with integrated shippers such as DHL.

Competition in the air express industry, aggravated by excess capacity, had resulted in intense price competition during the late 1980s.[1] DHL's chairman and CEO L. Patrick Lupo estimated that prices had dropped, on average, 5% each year from 1985 to 1990, with extreme price drops in some markets. For example, in Great Britain, DHL's list prices for shipments to the United States fell approximately 40% from 1987 to 1990. Some of the price reductions were offset, in part, by rising volume and productivity, yet Lupo noted, "There's no question that margins have been squeezed."

DHL SERVICES

DHL offered two services: Worldwide Document Express (DOX) and Worldwide Parcel Express (WPX). DOX offered document delivery to locations around the world within the DHL network. DOX was DHL's first product and featured door-to-door service at an all-inclusive price for nondutiable/nondeclarable items. Typical items handled by DOX included interoffice correspondence, computer printouts, and contracts. The number of documents sent to and from each DHL location was, in most cases, evenly balanced.

WPX was a parcel transport service for nondocument items that had a commercial value or needed to be declared to customs authorities. Like DOX, WPX offered door-to-door service at an all-inclusive price that covered DHL's handling of both the exporting and importing of the shipment. Typical items handled by WPX included prototype samples, spare parts, diskettes, and videotapes.

DHL imposed size, weight, and content restrictions for all parcels. The size of a package could not exceed 175 centimeters in exterior dimensions (length + width + height), and the gross weight could not exceed 50 kilograms. Further, DHL would not ship various items such as firearms, hazardous material, jewelry, and pornographic material.

Table C compares DHL's parcel and document businesses for 1990.

DHL offered numerous value-added services, including computerized tracking (LASERNET), 24-hour customer service every day of the year, and proof of delivery service. Customers could also tap the assistance of specialized industry consultants based in DHL regional offices. Such value added services could enhance customer loyalty and increase DHL's share of a customer's international shipping requirements. However, such services were expensive to provide and customers using them were often not always charged extra, particularly since those services were also offered by key competitors such as FedEx.

DHL had 20 years of experience in dealing with customs procedures and, by 1990, was electronically linked

---

1 DHL planes flew, on average, 85% full in 1990. FedEx and UPS planes on international routes were thought to be achieving only 60% capacity utilization.

Table C

DHL's Document and Parcel Businesses, 1990

	Total Revenues	Revenues Growth (1989–90)	Total Shipments	Total Weight	Gross Profits
Document	60%	+14%	70%	50%	53%
Parcel	40%	+28%	30%	50%	47%

into an international customs network. All shipments were bar coded, which facilitated computerized sorting and tracking. Thanks to a direct computer link between DHL and customs authorities in 5 European countries, customs clearance could occur while shipments were en route. In addition, DHL's staff included licensed customs brokers in 80 countries.

DHL had been cautious about differentiating itself on the basis of speed of service, and arrival times were not guaranteed. However, DHL executives believed that their extensive network meant that they could deliver packages faster than their competitors. Hence, in 1991, DHL commissioned an independent research company to send on the same day five documents and five dutiable packages from three U.S. origin cities via each of five air express companies to 21 international destinations (three cities in each of seven regions). Exhibit 5 reports the percentages of first place deliveries (i.e., fastest deliveries) achieved by each competitor in

each region. DHL had the highest percentage of first place results in six of the seven regions. The research also indicated that DHL was consistently able to deliver more dutiable items through customs in time for earliest business district delivery (before 10:30 a.m.) than any of its rivals. A similar intra-European study found that DHL also achieved the highest percentage of first place deliveries on packages shipped between cities within Europe.

DHL also commissioned the independent research company to ascertain how it was rated by customers against its key competitors. Table D reports the ratings on the two attributes considered by customers to be the most important in choosing an international air express service.

The study also asked the customer sample which air express carrier they would turn to first when sending both a document and a parcel to destinations in each of four geographic regions. Results are presented in Exhibit 6. The results of a comparative study of unaided brand awareness

Exhibit 5 — Shipment Delivery Speed Tracking Study: Fastest Delivery, 1991

	DHL	TNT	FedEx	UPS	Airborne
Western Europe	39%	34%	4%	26%	NA
Eastern Europe	42	16	14	28	1%
Southeast Asia	34	16	18	6	27
Far East	56	11	21	3	9
Middle East	70	6	16	2	7
South America	28	10	32	9	21
Africa	62	9	13	10	7
All documents	55	15	13	13	6
All parcels	40	14	21	11	14

Notes: To be read, for example: Of the packages shipped on the five carriers to Western Europe, 39% of the packages that arrived first at their destination were shipped by DHL. Some rows do not sum to 100% due to ties.

Ratings of Air Express Carriers

	DHL	TNT	FedEx	UPS
Reliability	8.4	7.7	7.8	8.1
Value for money	8.0	7.3	7.5	8.0

Source: Triangle Management Services Ltd. and IRB International Research, 1991.
Note: Respondents rated each carrier on a ten point scale (10 = high).

Exhibit 6

Sample Customers' First Choice of Air Express Carrier by Final Destination, 1991

	DHL	TNT	FedEx	UPS
Documents				
Europe	32%	7%	8%	5%
North America	38	10	10	4
Middle East	35	14	6	5
Australia	38	10	7	5
Other	40	14	6	6
Parcels				
Europe	28%	5%	7%	7%
North America	32	7	12	8
Middle East	33	13	6	7
Australia	27	9	10	9
Other	32	10	4	9

Source: Triangle Management Services Ltd., and IRB International Research, 1991.

for the major international air express companies are summarized in Exhibit 7.

CUSTOMERS

In the early years of air express, banks and finance houses were the major customers. For financial institutions, delays in delivery of checks and promissory notes could cause considerable financial losses. During the 1970s, most air express shipments were "emergency" in nature. Examples included an urgent contract, a check or note that sealed a financial transaction, a computer tape, a replacement part, and a mining sample which had to be studied before drilling could begin. During the 1980s, many customers began to use air express more systematically. For example, companies which operated "just-in-time" inventory systems began to use express delivery services to deliver components.

In 1990, DHL had 900,000 accounts, of which the top 250 accounts represented 10% of revenues and 15% of shipments. DHL had only about 10 global contracts with customers (representing 1% of revenues), as few multinational corporation (MNC) headquarters had expressed interest in negotiating such agreements. Like DHL, most MNCs were decentralized. However, DHL did have many regional agreements with MNCs as well as contracts in individual country markets.

Exhibit 8 shows how DHL segmented its U.S. customers in 1990 by level of monthly billings and provides

Exhibit 7 Sample Customers' Unaided Brand Awareness for International Carriers of Documents and Parcels, 1991

	DHL	TNT	FedEx	UPS
Documents				
All countries	87%	50%	23%	16%
France	77	27	20	20
Germany	90	71	25	20
Italy	91	45	19	15
United Kingdom	85	67	37	22
Parcels				
All countries	72%	58%	28%	29%
France	58	40	14	10
Germany	67	76	28	46
Italy	75	62	23	27
United Kingdom	72	58	43	35

Source: Company records

Exhibit 8 Profile of DHL's U.S.A. Customer Base (1990)

Customer Segment: Level of Monthly Billing, International	Percent of Total Accounts	Percent Typical Sales	Percent DHL Profits	Percent Using Discount[a]	Penetration[b]	Only DHL[c]
$ 0 - $ 2,000	15%	5%	45%	10-35%	70%	95%
$ 2,001 - $ 5,000	40	15	20	30-40	70	80
$ 5,001 - $15,000	35	30	25	40-50	60	60
$ 15,001 +	10	50	10	45-60	35	35
		100%	100%	100%		

Source: Company records

[a]The exact discount was negotiated between DHL and the account. Percentages represent discounts off the published DHL tariff.

[b]Penetration means the percentage of all accounts in the segment that used DHL for at least some of their international shipping needs.

[c]To be read, percent of DHL customers who use only DHL for international shipping.

profile information on each segment. Tony Messuri, DHL New England area sales manager, noted:

There are two principal types of customers. First, there are the people who know where they're shipping. They know where their international offices are located and will ask overseas offices for feedback about shippers. These customers select a carrier that's well-received and well-respected by their own customers, both internal and external.

Second, there are customers who cannot forecast where their future shipments will be going. They are more price sensitive but they can't give us enough information to enable us to set their discounts properly on the basis of anticipated volume. We are at more risk here of making a poor pricing decision. Sometimes a few months after we and the customer agree on a price and discount, the customer will conclude that it's overpaying, then seek more discounts from us or switch shippers.

Customers are very service sensitive. The small customers tend to switch shippers more readily. Often it only depends on which company's sales rep visited most recently.

The parcel market was typically more price sensitive than the document market. For most companies, the total cost of shipping parcels was a much larger line item than the total cost of shipping documents. Further, the decision-making unit was often different for the two services. The decision on how to ship a document was frequently made by an individual manager or secretary. As one shipper stated, "Documents go out the front door, whereas parcels go out the back door." Parcels were shipped from the loading dock by the traffic manager who could typically select from a list of carriers approved by the purchasing department. In some companies, parcel shipment decisions were being consolidated, often under the vice president of logistics. As one European auto parts supplier stated: "We view parts delivery as a key component of our customer service."

As a result, many customers split their air express business among several firms. For example, all documents might be shipped via DHL, while parcels might be assigned to another carrier. Alternatively, the customer's business might be split by geographic region; a multinational company might assign its North American business to Federal Express and its intercontinental shipments to DHL. For the sake of convenience and price leverage, most large customers were increasingly inclined to concentrate their air express shipments worldwide with two or three preferred suppliers.

Pricing

Evolution of pricing policy As DHL expanded service into new countries throughout the 1970s and 1980s, it developed many different pricing strategies and structures. DHL country managers had almost total control of pricing. They typically set prices based on four factors: what the market could bear, prices charged by competition (which was often initially the national post office), DHL's initial entry pricing in other countries, and DHL's then-current pricing around the world.

DHL's prices were historically 20% to 40% higher than those of competitors. (Exhibit 9 provides sample prices for DHL, TNT, FedEx, and UPS.) In most countries, DHL

Exhibit 9	Sample Published List Prices on Selected Routes (1990)			
Service	DHL	TNT	FedEx	UPS
1 kilogram document London – New York	$51	$47	$50	$44
2 kilogram document Brussels – Hong Kong	131	143	118	97
2 kilogram parcel Singapore – Sydney	120	120	39	34

published a tariff book which was updated yearly. Competitors who followed DHL into new markets often patterned their pricing structures after DHL's.

DHL had developed a sophisticated, proprietary software package called PRISM to analyze profitability. A PRISM staff officer at each regional office advised and trained country operating units on use of the software. The program could calculate profitability by route or by customer in a given country. However, PRISM could not consolidate the profits of a given customer across countries. (Exhibit 10 provides a fuller description of PRISM.) All profitability analyses had to be based on average costs due to the variability in costs associated with transporting a shipment. For example, a package from Perth, Australia, to Tucson, Arizona, might be consolidated seven to eight times in transit and travel on five to six planes. Further, every package from Perth to Tucson did not necessarily travel the same route. (Exhibit 11 shows the revenues and costs associated with two sample lanes to illustrate the significant impact of geographical differences on costs and profitability.)

PRISM was not used extensively by all DHL offices. As one country manager put it: "We and the customer both want a simple pricing structure. PRISM just provides more information, adds to complexity, and takes time away from selling."

Base prices and options DHL's base prices were calculated according to product (service), weight, origin, and destination. Prices were often higher for parcels than for documents of equivalent weight due to extra costs for customs clearance, handling, packaging, and

Exhibit 10   Development and Description of PRISM

DHL local management was judged on revenue and controllable costs. The contribution of each local operation was calculated by subtracting local costs from revenue. This measure of performance did not, however, consider the costs to other country operations of delivery and whether the selling price was sufficient to cover the cost of pickup, line haul, hub transfer, delivery, and headquarters overhead and management costs.

In 1987, all countries and regions analyzed their costs and provided DHL headquarters with detailed delivery, pickup, hub, and line haul costs. Using these data, headquarters developed the PRISM (Pricing Implementation Strategy Model) software package. The inputs to the model were cost data along with competitive price information. PRISM costs were based on historical data which had been consolidated and averaged.

Country organizations were provided with the PRISM software which enabled them to analyze their profitability at the country, customer segment, and individual customer levels. The methodology was refined further to take into account the scale economies large shippers provided to DHL.

PRISM was used for the following purposes:

- The distributor may not carry competing products.

- Analyzing the profit impacts of possible tariff adjustments, taking into account the competitive intensity of the route.

- Identifying low- or negative-margin customers whose yields should be managed upwards.

- Settling price strategy for different customer segments.

Country and regional managers were still measured on local contribution (local revenues minus local costs). They were, however, encouraged to analyze profitability by account when developing their annual budgets and use PRISM when considering price revisions. The level of use of PRISM varied by region and country.

Source: Company records.

additional paperwork. FedEx charged the same for parcels and documents. Shipment weights were computed in pounds in the United States and in kilograms in all other countries. Moreover, weight breaks varied among countries. For example, in Hong Kong breaks were every half kilogram, and in Spain, every two kilograms. Some DHL executives believed that, for the sake of simplicity, DHL's weight breaks should be the same worldwide. (Table E gives examples of base prices on routes from London.)

Pricing structures In all country markets served, DHL followed one of three pricing approaches: monthly handling fee, frequency discount, and loaded half-kilo.

Under the first approach, DHL charged a flat monthly fee to customers who wanted to be included on its regular pickup route. DHL automatically visited such customers once each business day without the customer having to contact DHL for pickup. The purpose was to motivate customer usage of DHL's services and encourage customers to process all their shipments through DHL. Customers who elected not to be on DHL's regular route could either call for shipment pickup or drop off a shipment at a DHL office. Customers who called for pickup were charged a nominal pickup fee. Under the monthly fee structure, customers did not receive volume discounts.

Exhibit 11   Revenue and Cost Lane Examples: DOX and WPX

	DOX (Document)	WPX (Parcel)
U.K. to United States (1990)		
Revenue	$5,723,000	$2,342,000
Outbound cost	2,392,915	667,712
Hub cost	596,608	490,436
Line haul[a]	1,121,882	647,915
Delivery	1,376,953	386,049
Margin	234,642	149,888
Margin %	4.1	6.4
Shipments	231,139	68,580
Revenue/shipment	$24.76	$34.15
Belgium to Hong Kong (1990)		
Revenue	$13,800,000	$6,660,000
Outbound cost	6,341,100	1,837,733
Hub cost	1,138,146	1,181,400
Line haul	2,926,662	1,767,733
Delivery	2,276,292	1,180,134
Margin	1,117,800	693,000
Margin %	8.1	10.5
Shipments	456,802	109,544
Revenue/shipment	$30.21	$60.25

[a]Line haul refers to the air segment of the shipment.

Sarrafzadeh summarized his views on the problems with this approach:

> The monthly fee can work but only if it is properly marketed. Because it does not relate to a unit of value, customers resent it and salespeople can't defend it. As a result, it has often proved hard to raise the monthly fees as fast as the per-shipment charges.

In some markets, including Great Britain, DHL offered a frequency discount structure under which a discount was provided based on number of units shipped. The more often a customer used DHL during a given month, the cheaper the unit shipment cost.

The frequency discount was based on the total number of documents and parcels shipped. For example, if a customer purchased 10 document and 20 parcel shipments in a given month, it received a discount of £10 per shipment.

Under the frequency discount structure, a customer did not pay a standard monthly route fee and DHL visited the account only upon request.

The per-shipment frequency discount was retroactive and was computed for each customer at the end of the calendar month. Conversely, FedEx's discounts were based on forecast demand rather than past performance and on revenues rather than unit shipments. FedEx monitored a new account's actual shipments for six months before the account qualified for a discount and then adjusted the discount upward or downward based on quarterly shipment data and shipment density.[2]

Sarrafzadeh noted:

> Once you publish your frequency discounts, they're no longer discounts. They're expected. Though they may sometimes attract the small routine shipper, it's easy for competitors

---

2 Shipment density referred to the number of items picked up per stop. The more items collected per stop, the lower the pickup cost per unit. DHL's information systems did not permit it to award discounts based on shipment density.

DHL Sample Prices, 1990

From London	First $1/2$ Kilo	Each Additional $1/2$ Kilo
Document:		
to New York	£24.50	£1.60
to Switzerland	£26.00	£2.20
to Japan	£26.50	£2.50
Parcel:		
to New York	£27.00	£1.60
to Switzerland	£32.00	£2.20
to Japan	£34.00	£2.50

to discover what the discounts are and undercut them. Better to publish only the book prices and apply discounts as needed on a case-by-case basis.

The loaded half-kilo structure used in the United States resembled the frequency discount structure, except that discounts were based on total weight shipped during a given month rather than on the number of shipments.

Price negotiations The largest customers sought one- or two-year deals with shippers to handle their transport needs. Typically, when a current agreement was nearing its end, the customer put its business up for bid and solicited proposals from interested shippers. Proposals incorporated the following information: transit times, overhead rate structures, rates for specified countries, tracking capabilities, sample tracking reports, sample annual activity report, and a list of international stations (indicating which were company-owned versus run by agents). Most bid requests were made by the purchasing manager, yet the decision-making unit was often a committee comprising managers from the traffic, sales and marketing, customer service, and purchasing departments. The decision was complicated because the major shippers were organized into different regions and lanes, thereby hindering direct comparisons among proposals. Sophisticated accounts typically calculated the bottom-line cost of each proposal, while unsophisticated accounts based their decisions on comparisons on a few "reference prices" (e.g., New York-London).

The average term of shipping agreements was two years, with almost all ranging between one and three years. Fifteen percent of DHL agreements involved formal contracts, while the other 85% were "handshake" agreements. Some customers tried to renegotiate prices in the middle of an agreement, though most *Fortune* 2000 companies abided by their deals.

DHL sales reps had significant flexibility when negotiating proposals. For example, the rep could tailor discount rates by lane such that an account would obtain large discounts on its most frequently used routes. DHL senior management typically gave only general direction to sales reps on negotiating discounts. For example, senior management might advise, "Hold price on Asia, yet you can give some on the United States and Europe." Most proposals associated a monthly minimum level of billings (adjusted, if necessary, for seasonality of the business) with the offer of any discounts.

DHL sales reps could negotiate discounts from book prices up to 35%. District sales managers could approve discounts up to 50%, while discounts above 50% required the approval of a regional sales director. Further, discounts over 60% required approval from the vice president of sales. For all discounts over 35%, a sales rep had to submit a Preferred Status Account (PSA) report, which included a detailed analysis of the profitability of the account. As shown in Exhibit 12, the PSA used a computer model to calculate fixed and variable costs, net profits by geographic lane and product line, and overall contribution margins. When deciding on the discount, management considered not only the financial implications of the discount but also competitive and capacity factors.

Tony Messuri, DHL New England area sales manager, stated:

> *It is good to have pricing flexibility. Managers at most companies are just looking for justification to use us. But they and DHL upper managers both know that we're not the only game in town. . . . We can sit down with a customer and build our own rate table leaving the book prices aside. We can customize the table to the customer's needs. This customization really helps negotiations.*

SALES AND ADVERTISING

DHL had a single sales force which sold both document and parcel services. Sales reps were organized geographically and

Exhibit 12   Sample DHL Preferred Status Account Report

PSA Analysis for: Plasmo Systems
No. of Pickup Sites: 1
Stops per Month: 20
Origin Station: Boston
Model Date: 1/31/90
Costs Date: 4/7/89

Margin by Lane (Note: not all lanes included)

Service	Lane	Revenue	Pickup Costs	Ship Costs	Weight Costs	Net Profit	% Profit
DOC	A Europe	45.89	3.12	24.02	7.62	11.13	24.3%
DOC	B Europe	48.02	3.12	28.72	7.66	8.70	18.0
DOC	C Europe	31.99	3.12	24.59	4.94	−0.66	−2.1
DOC	D Europe	23.17	3.12	20.46	2.34	−2.75	−11.9
DOC	E Latin Am	38.01	3.12	20.92	4.32	9.65	25.4
DOC	F MidEast	40.79	3.12	22.08	7.26	8.33	20.4
DOC	G Caribbn	31.32	3.12	21.29	3.76	3.15	10.1
WPX	A Europe	44.95	3.12	38.61	4.44	−1.22	−2.7
WPX	B Europe	73.25	3.12	47.36	5.49	17.28	23.6
WPX	D Canada	25.49	3.12	29.24	3.51	−10.38	−40.7

Margin by Product Line

Service	Revenue	Pickup Cost	Ship Cost	Weight Cost	Net Profit	% Profit
DOC	743	46	535	90	72	9.7%
WPX	214	12	196	21	−15	−7.0

Fixed/Variable Cost Report

Service	Revenue	Variable Cost	Gross Margin	Fixed Cost	U.S. Cost	Int'l Cost	Net Profit	% Profit
DOC	743	476	267	195	494	177	72	9.7%
WPX	214	173	41	56	180	49	−15	−7.0

were evaluated primarily on monthly sales. Typically, sales reps had separate monthly sales objectives for international, domestic, and total sales and received a bonus whenever they exceeded any one of the three. Sales managers were evaluated against profit as well as revenue objectives.

When a new account called for a pickup, that account was assigned an account number the next day and was called upon by a DHL sales rep within a week.[3] At large companies, sales reps targeted the traffic, shipping and receiving, and purchasing departments, while at small

3 In the United States, prospective accounts with less than $500 in annual express shipment expenditures were handled by DHL's telemarketing center in Phoenix.

companies, they focused their efforts on line managers such as the vice president of marketing or vice president of International.

Prior to 1984, DHL headquarters developed global advertising campaigns which the regions and countries could adopt or not as they saw fit. After 1984, each country operation could contract with its own local advertising agency. Headquarters approval of locally developed commercials was not required, though standard guidelines on presentation of the DHL name and logo had to be followed worldwide. In addition, headquarters marketing staff disseminated to all DHL offices commercials that had worked especially well in a particular market that might be worth extending to others.

DHL spent roughly 4% of worldwide sales on advertising. In 1990, DHL launched a new advertising campaign in the United States based on the slogan: "Faster to More of the World." This campaign, inspired by the fighter pilot movie "Top Gun," featured flying DHL delivery vans. (See Exhibit 13.) In the United States, the objectives of DHL's advertising campaign were three-fold. First, DHL wanted to raise brand awareness. Second, DHL aimed to explain that shipping overseas required different capabilities from shipping within the

Exhibit 13   Portion of a Sample U.S.A. Advertising Flying Van

Our business took off 21 years ago, and we're flying higher than ever.

It's significant that the letters DHL stand for the names of three people (Dalsey, Hillblom and Lynn).

Significant, because it took their personal entrepreneurial vision to recognise a business need, and their personal energy to get the solution off the ground.

Today, however, it's even more significant that the letters DHL stand for over 23,700 names: the highly trained, highly motivated employees.

DHL is as international as the United Nations. Our network spans 186 countries, states, territories and protectorates.

And from Ouagadougou to Wagga Wagga, Jakarta to Jeddah, there is not likely to be any city or town that you might wish to send something to, that does not feature on our list of 70,000 destinations served.

Most of all, however, the letters DHL have come to stand for two key words which mean so

If you're a major company you cannot afford anything less than total reliability when you air express your important documents and packages.

And as the world's largest international air express company, it is DHL's mission to provide it. Which we do.

It may be that your own company has an equally impressive growth story to tell. But old or new, large or small, please consider this.

and wouldn't you be better able to concentrate on your own job, if you allowed DHL to apply its expertise to your international air express needs?

continental United States. Third, DHL sought to convince consumers that DHL was the best at shipping overseas because of its experience, network, worldwide scope, and people.

DHL advertising in Europe used the slogan: "You know it's arrived the moment it's sent." (See Exhibit 14.)

CONCLUSION

As he pondered DHL's pricing options, Sarrafzadeh recalled the old adage: "The value of a thing is the price it will bring." Perhaps DHL's profits would be maximized if each country manager simply charged each customer "whatever the market could bear." However, from a headquarter's perspective, Sarrafzadeh believed a degree of order and consistency was necessary in DHL's pricing strategy, structure, and decision-making process. In particular, he wondered how pricing policy could enhance customer relationships, help to retain customers, and minimize their tendency to split their shipments among several air express carriers. Further penetration of existing accounts where DHL carriers were already making pickups and deliveries would, he was convinced, result in increased profits.

Exhibit 14   Part of a Sample Advertisement: Europe

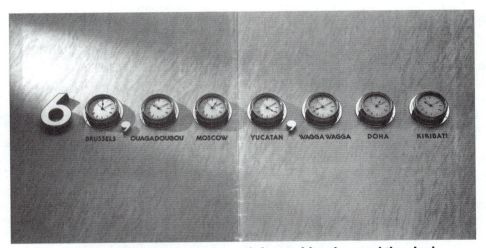

Sixty million deliveries a year around the world and around the clock.

London to Ouagadougou, Wagga Wagga, Yucatan, Kiribati — wherever. Take it from us that, with 70,000 cities and towns on our list, your air express destination is not likely to faze us.

Every 58 seconds, a plane takes off somewhere in the world carrying some of those 60,000,000 shipments.

190 of those planes are our own. Plus over 7,200 vehicles. Plus more owned-and-operated service centres in more countries than any of

Plus, above all, over 25,000 DHL employees. Trained in over 100 languages. But trained in the same company philosophy.

To think globally and act locally. To apply our global and group resources to each customer's advantage. To go that further mile which shows a customer that we're not just going through the motions — we care.

That care is demonstrated by the fact that we never use agents. We believe that if you want a

So if your concern is on-time delivery of your important documents and packages, you are unlikely to do better with any other operator.

But where you *definitely* will not be able to do better is with the total reliability which DHL provides.

From oil wells in Alaska, to clinics in Africa, farms in South America to factories in China, people turn to DHL when they have to be sure.

In some places, indeed, DHL is just about the

So please consider the implications of this for you and your business.

After all, such total reliability is hard to find these days.

Acer America: Development of the Aspire

In early 1998, Stan Shih, CEO of Taiwan-based personal computer (PC) manufacturer Acer, Inc., was reviewing the first estimates of 1997 year-end results. With revenue of $6.5 billion from own brand and sales to original equipment manufacturers (OEMs) such as IBM, the company was now acknowledged to be the third largest PC manufacturer in the world. Although the performance was respectable in the wake of a dramatic drop in memory chip prices that had plunged the company's semiconductor joint venture into losses, Acer's extraordinary growth period of the mid-1990s was clearly over. (See Exhibit 1.) The ever-restless CEO was wondering how to re-ignite the fire.

Shih was convinced that Acer's mid-1990s successes were due at least in part to the revolutionary "client-server" organizational structure he had introduced in 1992. The concept was inspired by the network computer model, where "client" computers—the strategic business units (SBUs) and regional business units (RBUs) in Acer's organizational metaphor—were capable of complete independence but could also take on the "server" role, adding value for the entire network. To Shih, proof of the client-server structure's potential had come with the 1995 introduction of the Aspire multimedia home PC. Created by Acer America Corporation (AAC), Acer's U.S. marketing subsidiary and one of Acer's five RBUs, this new product confirmed Shih's belief that major initiatives with global potential could be led from any part of the organization without centralized headquarters control.

But Aspire's difficult development experience and its less-than-successful global rollout had also highlighted some of the deficiencies in the client-server model.

Business unit independence had resulted in problems in communication, project ownership, product proliferation, and transfer pricing—and, in the end, had led to Aspire's $100 million of losses in the U.S. alone. Shih realized he had to find a way to balance independence with control, but did not want to sacrifice the employee initiative and entrepreneurial spirit he believed the client-server organization had released. Reviewing the lessons from the Aspire, he wondered what changes might be necessary to Acer's radically different strategic and organizational concepts if the company was to grow the Acer brand from its current position as number eight to one of the world's top five PC brands.

ACER'S GROWTH AND EXPANSION[1]

In 1976, with capital of $25,000, Stan Shih, his wife, and three friends established a company they called Multitech to commercialize microprocessor technology in Taiwan. The culture Shih established within the young company was built on three strong foundations—a commitment to entrepreneurial initiative (which translated in mistakes being viewed as tuition for learning, for example), a cost consciousness and financial conservatism that Shih described as a "poor man's philosophy" (financing was largely through employees, for example, who typically took equity instead of market salaries), and a sense of family that was based more on delegation to responsible sons and daughters than on the traditional Chinese company's nepotism and paternalism.

In the mid-1980s, with a product strategy that had finally focused on personal computers, the company (known as Acer after 1987) began expanding internationally pursuing a strategy Stan Shih described as the "Dragon Dream." Determined to take on the large established PC companies—"the nobility"—he co-opted his employee-owners, supplier-partners, distributors and mass-market

This case was prepared by Professor Christopher A. Bartlett with the assistance of Anthony St. George.

Copyright © 1998 by the President and Fellows of Harvard College. Harvard Business School case 9-399-011.

---

1 For a detailed history, see "Acer, Inc: Taiwan's Rampaging Dragon," HBS. No. 399-010.

Exhibit 1 — Acer Selected Financials, 1993–1997[a]

December 16, 1998
For the Year

	1993		1994		1995		1996		1997	
	Combined	Excluding TI-Acer[a]	Combined	Excluding TI-Acer[a]	Combined	Excluding TI-Acer[a]	Combined	Excluding TI-Acer[a]	Combined	Excluding TI-Acer[a]
Total Revenue	1,833	1,651	3,220	2,901	5,825	5,262	5,893	5,346	6,509	6,132
Revenue Growth (%)	49.4%	38.4%	71.0%	75.7%	80.9%	81.4%	1.2%	1.6%	10.5%	14.7%
Net Earnings	86	22	205	103	413	163	188	150	89	262
Net Earnings (%)	4.6%	1.3%	6.4%	3.6%	7.1%	3.1%	3.2%	2.8%	1.4%	4.3%
Total Equity	497	316	703	420	1,450	939	2,008	1,321	2,065	1,638
Return on Equity	18.5%	7.0%	34.2%	28.1%	38.4%	23.9%	10.9%	13.3%	4.4%	17.7%
Total Assets	1,584	1,143	2,082	1,520	3,645	2,340	4,192	3,156	4,758	3,608
Return on Assets	5.7%	2.0%	11.2%	7.8%	14.4%	8.4%	4.8%	5.5%	2.0%	7.7%
Net investment in property, plant, and equipment	497	181	538	197	963	284	1,347	418	1,470	616
Working Capital	173	149	288	280	767	758	996	995	875	974
Number of Stockholders	70,000	44,000	70,000	69,000	90,000	89,000	123,000	122,000	155,000	154,000
Number of Employees	7,200	6,348	9,700	8,612	15,352	13,942	16,778	15,272	22,948	21,307

[a]Due to the drastic drop in the market price of DRAM during 1996-97, the Acer Group reported its financial results excluding TI-Acer operations to allow evaluations of non-DRAM Acer Group operations.

customers into a partnership he described as a "commoners' culture." This loose alliance not only allowed Acer to reduce its own capital investment and risk, but also obtain committed partners with knowledge of their local market. To sidestep "the nobility," Acer pursued a strategy based on the Asian board game, Go. Using its limited resources to build strength in the corners, the company initially entered smaller developing markets before finally building positions in Europe and the U.S.

In the late 1980s, however, intense competition caused industry prices to drop about 30%, and Acer's gross margins fell from about 35% in 1988 to about 25% the following year. A public stock offering supported its continued aggressive expansion, but unfortunately, several costly acquisitions caused the company to become overextended. To bring discipline to the company, the loosely organized entrepreneurial organization was restructured into strategic business units (SBUs) responsible for product development and manufacturing, and regional business units (RBUs), responsible for marketing and distribution (see Exhibits 2a and 2b). But losses continued, totaling $26 million on sales of $1 billion in 1991.

As price wars continued to erode Acer's margins to around 20% in 1992, Shih realized that Acer's business model had to change. Shipping from centralized manufacturing in Taiwan not only delayed new product time-to-market and increased inventory, it also exposed Acer to widespread import duties on hi-tech products. A team of engineers solved the problem by creating the "Uniload" assembly system whereby carefully configured palettes of snap-together parts and components were shipped from Taiwan by air or sea depending on weight, value added, and price volatility, to assembly centers around the world. Lower value-added and less critical components were sourced locally. Shih labeled this new way of doing business the "fast food" model because of its similarity to McDonald's hamburger assembly approach of delivering products "hot and fresh" close to the customer. The radical business model change reflected Shih's belief that value added in the PC industry was rapidly migrating away from assembly, upstream to component design and software development, and downstream to branding and distribution. It was a concept he captured his "Smiling Curve" diagram (Exhibit 3).

Exhibit 2a   Acer, Inc. Organization Structure, c. 1997

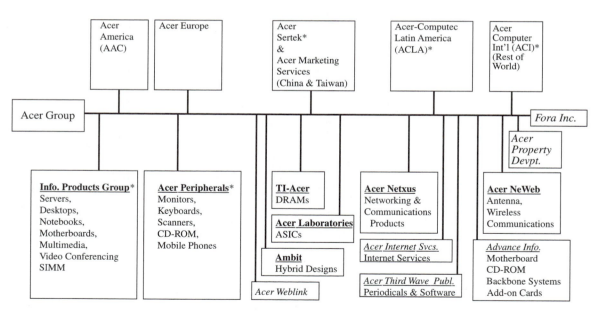

Names in plain text are RBUs, names in **bold** are SBUs, and names in *italics* are classified as "Other."   * Indicates a publicly listed company

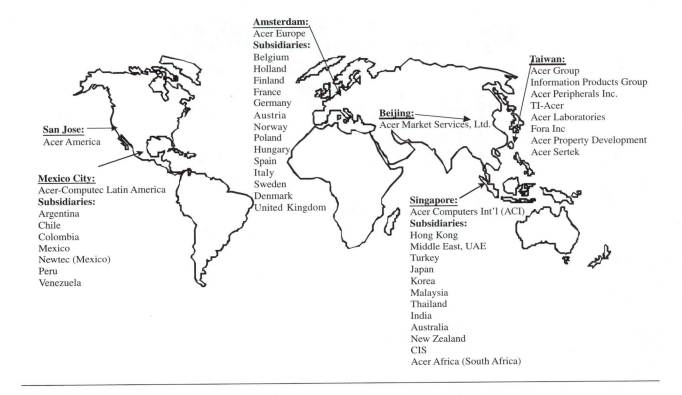

Amsterdam:
Acer Europe
Subsidiaries:
Belgium
Holland
Finland
France
Germany
Austria
Norway
Poland
Hungary
Spain
Italy
Sweden
Denmark
United Kingdom

Taiwan:
Acer Group
Information Products Group
Acer Peripherals Inc.
TI-Acer
Acer Laboratories
Fora Inc
Acer Property Development
Acer Sertek

Beijing:
Acer Market Services, Ltd.

San Jose:
Acer America

Mexico City:
Acer-Computec Latin America
Subsidiaries:
Argentina
Chile
Colombia
Mexico
Newtec (Mexico)
Peru
Venezuela

Singapore:
Acer Computers Int'l (ACI)
Subsidiaries:
Hong Kong
Middle East, UAE
Turkey
Japan
Korea
Malaysia
Thailand
India
Australia
New Zealand
CIS
Acer Africa (South Africa)

Concurrent with the establishment of dozens of offshore assembly centers, Shih continued to delegate greater decision-making authority. Under an organizational concept he described as the "client-server" model, RBUs were given greater freedom to configure the products to fit their local markets. Coupled with the long-established norm of delegation and the more recent emphasis on profit responsibility, this concept operated under the slogan "every man is lord of his castle." The change was not tension-free, however. As RBUs established a greater degree of independence, SBUs felt their role was shifting from product designers and manufacturers to components suppliers.

As the company evolved towards a federation of locally responsive units close to their markets yet linked by the emerging Acer brand, Shih dubbed the emerging management philosophy "Global brand, local touch." By encouraging business units to enhance "local touch" through local public listing, Shih's hope was to achieve "21 in 21,"—21 locally owned subsidiaries by the twenty-first century. By

early 1998, two RBUs and three SBUs were publicly listed companies.

By 1998 Acer had grown to 23,000 employees in 129 companies with 17 manufacturing plants and 30 assembly facilities in 24 countries. Through the client-server structure, Acer sales units were located in 44 countries, with particular strength in the developing country markets. Although Acer was only the eighth largest brand for PCs in the world overall (more than half its sales were still to OEM customers), it was the number one brand in 12 countries in Asia/Pacific, South America, and the Middle East, and in the top five in over 30 countries (see Exhibits 4a and 4b).

AAC AND THE BIRTH OF THE ASPIRE

Established in 1977 as a U.S.-based sourcing company, Acer America (AAC) was converted into a sales office in 1986. Acquisitions of two network computer manufacturers (Counterpoint and Altos) and a customer service

Exhibit 3   Stan Shih's PC Industry Conceptualization

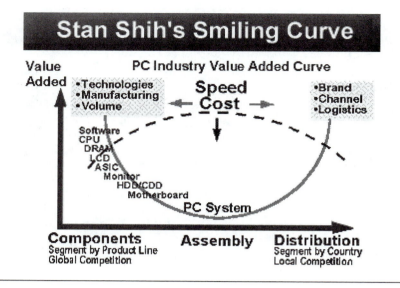

Source: Company document

organization (Service Intelligence) plunged the subsidiary into losses beginning in 1988. Losses continued in the early 1990s as industry-wide price cuts severely reduced margins. But through cost controls and the inventory reductions made possible by the Uniload process, AAC recovered. In 1994, AAC recorded its first profit in six years. (See Exhibit 5.) Hopes for further recovery were pinned to a new multimedia home PC named Aspire, a product local management believed could help implement Shih's desire to build a strong global brand.

Local Inspiration: Creating the Concept

In 1994, as the world began to take note of developments in the Internet, the World Wide Web, and new audio, telecom, video, and computing technologies, several companies saw the potential for an advanced multimedia home PC. Among those sensing this opportunity was Michael Culver, AAC's Director of Product Management. Although the company had been selling the Acer Acros, a slightly reconfigured version of its commercial desktop PC, through retail channels since 1990, its share of the huge U.S. home PC market was miniscule. With the newly granted authority to create local products, the 29-year-old MBA who had joined Acer 2½ years earlier leaped into

action with his vision to create "the first Wintel-based PC that could compete with Apple in external design, ease-of-use features, and multimedia capabilities."

To test his ideas, Culver put together a project team which began running focus groups to examine market needs. One clear finding of this research was that, in addition to enhanced multimedia capabilities, consumers wanted a home PC that had a different look and feel than the standard putty-colored, boxy PCs that sat in offices throughout the world. The team also discovered it would have to move fast: product cycle time for PCs was 6 to 9 months and shortening.

Not having local design capabilities (AAC had a staff of 20 engineers, mainly focused on software design and product testing) and believing that Acer's SBU staff did not have the appropriate skills, Culver and his team looked to external design firms for help. Frog Design, a local Silicon Valley firm that had designed everything from bicycles to consumer electronics appealed to the Acer team because of its reputation for "thinking outside of the box." At this point, Culver went to AAC President Ronald Chwang for $200,000 to fund the design phase and approval to go ahead with the project. "Especially since this was a decision to let an RBU design its own

Exhibit 4a   1997 Acer Brand Ranking and Market Share by Product

Product	Worldwide		United States		Latin America		Asia/Pacific		Europe	
	Rank	Market Share	Rank	Market Share	Rank	Market Share	Rank	Market Share	Rank	Market Share
Overall	8	3.6%	9	3.3%	3	9.1%	5	5.8%	10	2.8%
Desktop PCs	8	3.2%	8	3.0%	3	8.6%	6	5.3%	10	2.1%
Portables	6	5.1%	5	5.6%	2	21.5%	3	9.6%	4	7.8%
Servers	6	3.0%	7	2.8%	4	6.8%	4	8.9%	7	3.1%

Source: Company documents

Rank	Country
#1	Taiwan, Malaysia, Indonesia, Philippines, Bangladesh, Mexico, Chile, Panama, Uruguay, South Africa, Oman, Morocco.
Top 3	Bolivia, Venezuela, Colombia, Peru, Ecuador, Brazil, Singapore, Thailand, Bahrain, Jordan, Syria, Cyprus, Sri Lanka, United Arab Emirates, Tunisia
Top 5	Hong Kong, Israel, Turkey, Greece, Norway, Finland, Saudi Arabia
Top 10	Australia (6), Holland (7), Italy (7), Germany (7), Austria (9), USA (9), China (9), France (10)

Source: Company documents

Exhibit 5   AAC Simplified Financials: 1990–1997[a]

(Million US$)	1990	1991	1992	1993	1994	1995	1996	1997
Revenue	161	235	304	434	858	1437	1268	1141
Cost of Sales	133	190	283	399	764	1303	1225	1125
Selling and Marketing	27	61	25	23	55	103	84	72
General Administration	20	16	17	19	20	22	26	29
Research and Development	5	8	6	4	4	4	6	4
Operating Profit/(Loss)	(24)	(40)	(26)	(11)	15	6	(74)	(89)
Non-operating Profit/(Loss)	(1)	(7)	(3)	(5)	(3)	(4)	(7)	3
Profit/(Loss) Before Tax	(25)	(47)	(29)	(16)	12	2	(81)	(86)
Tax	1	(2)	0	0	1	1	0	0
Net Income/(Loss)	(26)	(45)	(29)	(16)	11	1	(81)	(86)
Current Assets	155	153	123	144	242	449	236	304
Fixed Assets (net)	39	43	28	25	25	26	32	33
Other Assets (net)	37	37	31	19	11	9	9	8
TOTAL Assets	231	233	182	188	278	484	276	345
Current Liabilities	155	169	154	136	218	423	243	365
Long-term debt	17	15	18	58	47	10	14	10
Stockholder Equity (including additional capital)	58	50	10	(6)	12	51	19	(30)
Total liabilities	231	233	182	188	278	484	276	345

[a]Totals may not add due to rounding.

product for the first time, the process was incredibly informal," related Culver. "It literally took place in one 20-minute discussion in the hallway in late November."

The Aspire product management team and the designers visited computer retail stores and brainstormed the product's external design. In two months Frog Design developed six foam model prototypes. In January 1995, the AAC team chose the final design: a sleek low-profile shape with rounded edges presented in a choice of colors—charcoal grey or emerald green. (See Exhibit 6.)

Meanwhile, the team had been defining the multimedia capabilities built into the computer. One significant innovation was to be voice-recognition software that would enable users to manipulate programs by voice commands. But the innovations presented significant design challenges. In addition to the microphone and speakers built into the monitor, the PC would also have fax and telephone capabilities with a built-in modem and answering machine. Finally, the Aspire was designed for ease of use from set-up to start-up to operation. Color coded cables, graphic icons, simple exploration and navigation software were all part of the design.

Global Aspirations: Developing the Product

In the early stages, the design of the product had been top secret, and even Shih viewed it for the first time only in February 1995. His immediate reaction was positive and enthusiastic: "This product will make Acer a household consumer electronics brand." He immediately asked Culver to present the concept at the next meeting of RBU heads. By May a consensus had emerged to aim for a global launch of Aspire in September.

With RBU heads' support and Shih's commitment to provide significant funds for "global" advertising, Culver and Chwang set out to present Aspire to SBU executives in Taiwan. Although the SBU heads liked the idea, their engineers felt they could be of only limited help at this stage of the development process. As one SBU executive recalled:

> Because the project was owned by AAC, our engineers did not have much influence during the integration phase. Most of the product design was dictated and decided by AAC and Frog Design, so when the SBU engineers came in it was a little too late. This was the first time that the product had been designed from the outside in and the

---

Exhibit 6   Aspire Design and Characteristics

Source: Company documents

radical housing created many challenges in getting our standard components to fit. When we designed products in Taiwan we worked from the inside out, so we had never run into this kind of problem before.

Because AAC lacked product development experience, four Taiwanese engineers from the Information Products Group (IPG) and Acer Peripherals (API) were sent to the United States in March to aid in the mechanical design. As the project team continued to develop the cosmetic design behind closed doors, the SBU engineers working in parallel on component design realized they had no control over product design. "At first there was a little of the 'not invented here' syndrome," Culver recalled, "and we had to work to make the SBU engineers feel a part of the process." In May, the top-secret development room was finally opened and the design and integration of key components proceeded more easily.

The computer's complex multimedia system was broken down into sub-assembly systems, each of which was assigned to a manager and a design team. But the greatest challenge came in integrating the components and subassemblies into the final product. Culver explained:

Different product managers across the globe were responsible for different sub-assemblies. One might be in charge of the speakers, another in charge of the voice-recognition software. I was in charge of overseeing the entire product development and had to coordinate over 70 different contacts. The biggest problems occurred when we ran into a delay with one of the sub-assemblies. For example, after we had selected a microphone for the monitor we found that the software didn't recognize the input. We then had to isolate whether it was a problem with the microphone, which would mean resourcing, or the software, which meant re-developing the application. When a delay threatened to throw off the schedule for the next part of the system we had to make snap decisions and go with them.

Similar problems occurred with many other components. With the answering machine, for example, the unit received the audio input signal but did not play back the message satisfactorily. Engineers had to decide whether the problem was in the software, the microphone input or the speakers, each of which was the responsibility of a different person. Aspire's innovative design also led to complications. For instance, the unique shape of the computer casing created a problem with the opening and closing of the CD-ROM tray, while the challenge of

matching designer colors on components caused additional headaches. In the end, no standard Acer parts were used in Aspire, and Culver estimated that specialized components added 10%-15% to the cost of items such as the CD-ROM units and monitor.

The RBU-SBU coordination challenges were further complicated by the fact that most of Acer's qualified suppliers were in Taiwan. As a result, the Taiwan-based SBU product managers had to source components and send them to AAC for approval and integration into the prototype. One engineer responsible for much of the sourcing described some of the challenges in Taiwan:

AAC did not have the engineering capabilities that we had in the SBUs, but they didn't trust us to do any of the integration. And it didn't matter if we had an opinion on the quality because Acer America insisted on doing their own review. For example, somebody from the SBU had flagged the CD-ROM tray problem early on, but he wasn't listened to. If AAC encountered a problem with a component, it took almost a week before I heard back from them. Several times an engineer from Taiwan had to get on a plane and hand-carry components to AAC to meet the sub-assembly deadline. In the end, we gave up questioning and just implemented what they told us.

As a result, production dates kept getting pushed back and costs kept escalating. The large projected U.S. demand and the constrained supply forced the SBUs in Taiwan to allocate all component units to AAC, abandoning the original plan for a global launch in order to keep the September 1995 U.S. introduction on target to catch the Christmas season. Culver explained:

The delays in integration caused us to delay manufacturing. Because the monitors were the last to be finalized, we had to ship them by air to get them to the United States in time. This cost almost $70 a monitor instead of the usual $10 by sea and added another $3 million to $5 million to our costs.

Despite the difficulties, the product was designed and manufactured in record time, and shipping began on September 5th—just nine months after concept definition. As Shih commented:

I believe that if the origins of the Aspire were to have gone through the traditional communications channels—to file reports at headquarters with SBUs and to go through the process of argument, revision, and approval—

it would have taken at least one-and-a-half to two years to see the final product. By that time, the daring creativity of the product may have already been diminished.

Planning Implementation: Creating the Marketing

Parallel to the product development activities, Culver was working on a marketing program for the product launch. Having decided that many of the targeted home users would be first-time buyers, the team created a marketing concept they described as "OOBE"—the "out of box experience" of being able to set up and use the PC immediately. Priced from $1,199 for the basic product to $2,999 for the high end system with monitor, the Aspire was positioned in the middle of the 15 to 20 percent price gap between the top-tier PC brands like IBM and Compaq and the low-end products like Packard Bell. Distribution would be through specialist computer electronics stores that had previously carried Acer's Acros PC. They would take their standard retail markup of 10-12% plus an additional 5% marketing allowance. To build confidence in this largely unknown brand, the one year warranty Acros had offered would become three years for Aspire.

Keen to build Aspire as Acer's flagship brand in the U.S., Culver budgeted $25 million in advertising for four months following the launch. In addition, an intensive public relations program targeted computer trade publications like *PC Magazine*, the general business press like *Business Week*, and even lifestyle magazines like *Architectural Digest*. He also planned to support the launch with extensive merchandising and point of purchase materials. In all, this would be the most ambitious new product launch in AAC's history—and even for the company as a whole.

THE LAUNCH

In September 1995, the first month of its introduction, Aspire sold 40,000 units at retail, double AAC's normal monthly sales of the Acer Acros after 3 years on the market. When October sales leaped to 80,000 units, Shih, Chwang, and Culver were ecstatic. Early reviews in the technical magazines were also positive, reinforcing the euphoria in AAC. Caught up in the excitement, Chwang and Culver forecast retail sales into 1996 at around 100,000 units per month, triggering orders on Taiwan for components and subassemblies to meet this expected demand.

Supernova Burnout?

Then the unexpected happened: sales fell to less than 60,000 units in November and 35,000 in December. The first clue to the reason for the decline came from customer service, where telephone representatives were being swamped. As product return rates approaching 15% confirmed, the Aspire still had several minor technical problems that had not been completely resolved before the September deadline—the problem opening and closing the CD-ROM tray was typical. This situation was exacerbated by the fact that Aspire had been targeted to first-time computer buyers and many of the calls to customer service reflected their inexperience. "Customer service was getting killed," explained Culver. "We couldn't keep up with the calls. Some lasted as long as 30 minutes!"

By the end of December, the AAC team finally acknowledged the need to cut dramatically their forecasts. By that stage, however, the company had already accumulated two to three months of excess inventory of a product that needed design changes. Although Culver and his team paused briefly to celebrate when Aspire was featured in *Business Week's* annual awards for new product design in 1995, they were more concerned that sales had showed no rebound in early 1996. (See Exhibit 7 for AAC's next month forecast and actual sales into channels.)

While other RBU heads had all committed to launch of the Aspire, nobody was clear how this global rollout would be coordinated. Shih was very active behind-the-scenes urging the organization to support Aspire, but also encouraging Culver to take on an informal leadership role—presenting the product plans to top management meetings, hosting visits of other RBU teams to AAC, and updating all RBUs on progress and performance. Despite early tension over the decision that only AAC would be able to launch in September, the other RBU heads mostly deferred to Culver and his team as the product experts. Yet they were looking for advice rather than directives and remained highly protective of their right to adapt the Aspire strategy to local markets—particularly as they watched the problems emerging with the U.S. launch.

By early 1996, Taiwan had developed sufficient production capacity to begin a worldwide phased rollout of Aspire during the spring. However, each RBU argued that the U.S. product would have to be adapted to suit its local markets. Typical was Michael Mak, Managing

Month	1995 Forecast	1995 Actual	1996 Forecast	1996 Actual
	(000 units)		(000 units)	
January			15	0
February			50	20
March			35	50
April			25	5
May			25	15
June			30	25
July			25	20
August	30	10	50	20
September	50	55	65	45
October	80	70	80	20
November	100	70	80	15
December	40	15	55	5

Source: Company documents

Director of Acer Hong Kong, who described the process he adopted:

> From the first time I saw Aspire, I knew we had to have this product. Originally, we brought in the unaltered U.S. product for a "soft-launch." Although the unadapted product generated some sales, most consumers were concerned by the $3,000 price tag we had to charge. At this stage, we realized we had to make some local modifications. We simplified the user interface and changed the language from English to Chinese, we included a card that allowed the use of a video-CD, we adjusted the phone software for the local telephone system, and we changed the modem. We also created a poster and videotape in Chinese and English showing the user how to get started.

The Hong Kong office had few local technical staff to make these changes. Of 200 people in the Hong Kong organization, only three or four were in product engineering and these individuals coordinated most of the software modifications. The hardware changes were largely handled by ACI, Acer's Asian RBU headquarters in Singapore. ACI negotiated directly with the SBUs, but some components (e.g., the video CD card) were directly sourced locally in Hong Kong.

By the time the Aspire had been launched in more than thirty countries, local adaptations had created over 100 different configurations. As one marketing manager pointed out, "Sometimes even a product of the same model number would have a completely different configuration in another market. For example, what sold in Singapore under one model number was completely different from the same model number sold across the bridge in Malaysia."

While local designs differed, most of the configuration problems—the CD-ROM tray jam, for example—remained the same from region to region. As local sales companies with newly created Uniload lines began assembling components and subassemblies, they experienced many of the same problems AAC had confronted. When the RBU contacted Taiwan, the SBUs often were unaware of the problem. Typically, they explained that they had simply supplied components and that the integration expertise was in AAC. But because AAC's earlier experience had not been documented or disseminated, each unit had to find its own solutions.

Marketing Coordination: A Global Brand?

Similar coordination difficulties hounded the plans to make Aspire the company's first global brand. Acting in his informal global champion role, in September 1995, Culver invited marketing teams form RBUs worldwide to the United States to review their marketing program. "They were all very interested," said Culver, "but when they got back home they pretty much developed their own programs. As a result, Aspire had a very different look and feel from country to country."

The different look began with the cost-driven decision to sell only the emerald green version outside the United States. The local differentiation of product features—Hong Kong's decision to add a video CD card, for example—further emphasized the divergence. But it was in product positioning that the marketing differences were most evident. While Australia largely followed the U.S. positioning of an innovative multimedia PC for home, Singapore positioned it as a "fashion" product emphasizing its color and design, and Taiwan chose to sell it in a stripped down version (e.g., no voice recognition or user interface) as a basic entry-level computer.

Pricing strategies also varied widely. In contrast to AAC's mid-range, value-pricing, Taiwan offered its stripped-down version at a low end price. Meanwhile, the Europeans began by listing Aspire at the top end of the market, then lowered price to build volume. And in Asia, ACI listed Aspire at a $200 premium to mainstream home PCs.

ACI's premium pricing strategy allowed companies in Asia to support a heavy advertising campaign, albeit one very different from Aspire's U.S. approach. Culver explained, "ACI worked with an advertising agency in New Zealand and came up with some pretty interesting ads they ran in Asia. I say 'interesting' because they had a slightly sexual overtones that I don't think would have worked in the States." In contrast, Acer Europe invested comparatively little in advertising, arguing that their PC retail channels (e.g, Dixons in the United Kingdom and Carrefour in France) were still fairly small in relation to Acer's other markets.

Promotions were also very localized. In Hong Kong, for example, Mak and his team developed a special promotion and marketing program for their adapted model. In an unusual move, they teamed with Chase Manhattan Bank to allow the computer to be purchased on a credit card with payments made over 18 months interest-free. With the price set around $2,000, the Aspire was finally launched in the fourth quarter of 1996 with locally produced advertisements featuring a popular Hong Kong singer. The credit card-linked program proved to be one of the most successful PC sales campaigns in Hong Kong. Within the first six weeks, the company received 20,000 orders, making it the number one PC product in a market of 300,000 units per year.

The success of these various approaches was mixed. While Hong Kong, Singapore and Australia had considerable success, the Aspire struggled in Europe. Furthermore, the diverse design and marketing approaches created problems for Acer's first globally advertised product. Following his commitment to fund a global branding campaign, Shih allocated significant corporate funds to advertising in international periodicals and in-flight magazines, a first for Acer. But because local subsidiaries had modified the design and product positioning, the global ads were not very effective. For example, a Taiwanese businessman might see an advertisement for a sophisticated prestige product in an international airline's in-flight magazine only to find that the Aspire available in his home country was a stripped down version that did not have the features he sought.

RBU/SBU Negotiations: Growing Tensions
Local independence also presented problems during the internal price negotiation process. After developing its market-tailored configurations, each RBU headquarters generally took tender bids for component parts in their local markets, using that data to negotiate prices with the SBUs in Taiwan. According to client-server organization policies, RBUs were not required to purchase components from an SBU if its quote was more expensive, and SBUs were not required to sell to RBUs if they could obtain better local distribution by selling directly to other customers in that market. In practice, however, the threat of either the RBU or SBU sourcing or selling outside of the company—the "nuclear option" in Acer parlance—was usually enough to keep the two units in line.

Nonetheless, the principle that "every manager was lord of his castle" could lead to unending negotiations. Instead of exercising the nuclear option, price negotiations often ended in stalemates: rather responding to a renegotiation request, the business units would simply sit on the request for weeks. As Simon Lin, CEO of IPG, pointed out, "In a time-sensitive industry with rapid price fluctuations you can't afford to do this; it delays production and reduces profit margins."

Pricing was not the only area in which negotiations became bogged down. Similar problems surfaced in inventory control, a problem area that had begun with Aspire's unique components and colored sub-assembly and had ballooned with the proliferation of models and component sources. The RBUs' unique local configurations made it difficult to re-distribute excess inventory of products or parts to markets where demand was outstripping supply. As a result, there was constant tension between RBUs and SBUs regarding the need for new models that involved only minor changes from an existing model.

NEXT GENERATIONS' ADJUSTMENTS

From the September 1995 launch on, competition in the United States was intense since other well-known brand companies like Hewlett Packard had also introduced their own multimedia home PCs. At AAC, design teams continued to work on the various problems—component integration, monitor problems, color matching—that continued to plague the manufacturing teams. With the release of each new generation, the sales organization's optimism surged, only to be deflated when it recognized that the product's quality problems continued.

New Product Generations

The design for the second generation, released in February 1996, was reviewed by SBU managers who gave their input, but Frog Design didn't want to compromise the styling to make the product more manufacturable. "After the first generation," remarked one manager, "Mike [Culver] recognized that AAC had limited experience in development and manufacturing, and tried to share more decision making and coordination with the SBUs. Unfortunately, we were not very successful." As a result, technical problems such as the CD tray fit continued. This led to key managers in Taiwan and the United States deciding that direct coordination between AAC and the SBUs had to become an immediate priority. They named Arthur Pai, a senior engineering manager from Information Products Group (IPG was the key supplying SBU in Taiwan) the project coordinator with responsibility to gain internal agreement and implementation of their urgent changes.

The third generation, launched in August 1996, sought to resolve continuing technical problems and to capture scale economies by increasing the number of common parts in the product. Under Pai's leadership, the CD-ROM

tray problem was fixed, the ambient noise of the machine was dampened, and a quick start-up feature was added. Simultaneously, Culver changed the marketing strategy and segmented the product into three different categories: business, family, and game-enthusiasts. Each was sold through its own channel—the business version through office superstores, the family version through mass merchants, and the gaming-enthusiast version through consumer electronics superstores. Expansion and reengineering customer service eventually reduced the 20-minute average wait time to less than two minutes. The customer satisfaction index doubled, but service costs rose to 8% of sales.

Then, in October 1996, Compaq again cut its PC prices. Culver recalled:

> They narrowed the price gap between top brand PCs and the secondary brands to about 5%. Basically they priced right on top of us. We didn't create enough perceived value to get a premium like Compaq, but our cost structure for our additional features was too high to match Packard Bell [in the lower tier]. So it took us about 12 months where we lost market share and money, until we got our fifth generation Aspire to market. It was completely redesigned for quality and cost.

For the fifth generation Arthur Pai asked Frog Design to design a new housing permitting Aspire to be made entirely of standard rather than custom parts. To reduce inventory problems and respond to dealers' requests, he replaced Aspire's emerald green version with the industry standard off-white that retailers could more easily bundle with other peripherals. In August 1997, an entirely revitalized Aspire product line was introduced, including two models priced below the important new $1,000 price point. Simultaneously, the company announced new distribution partnership with Sears and WalMart to capture consumers at the low-level entry point and provide them with an ability to upgrade easily within Aspire's wider product line.

Shifting Economics, Evolving Controls

As the substantial losses recorded on Aspire's 1996 sales continued into 1997, Culver and his team came under growing pressure. (See Exhibit 8.) Culver explained the problem:

> The industry rule of thumb is that PC prices come down 20% a year, but in reality they go through more dramatic, less orderly drops driven by price wars. We were

Millions US$	1995 (part year)		1996		1997	
	Budget	**Actual**	**Budget**	**Actual**	**Budget**	**Actual**
Sales	570	446	1015	454	540	268
Profit	17	(2)	9	(51)	(19)	(38)

Source: Company documents

not getting our costs down fast enough so our gross margins dropped from more than 20% in 1995 to about 15% in 1996 and headed for 12% by 1997. That's not much in a consumer business. On top of continuing SG&A expenses of 2-3% and our ongoing advertising and marketing cost of 1% of sales, customer service costs had risen from 2% of sales to 8% by 1997, and product returns were taking another 5% of our margin. Worst of all, retail inventory write-offs were running at 10% of sales in 1996 and 1997. There was no way we could be profitable.

The problem was in part created by accounting practices that made no provisions for future service costs, returns and inventory write-offs but instead charged them against same period sales. With a three-year warranty, this resulted in all the first and second generations' problems pulling down subsequent years' profitability and disguising real current performance.

Still, Stan Shih was concerned enough about AAC's deteriorating profit situation that he initiated a series of quarterly meetings between himself, AAC's Chwang and Simon Lin, head of IPG, the SBU supplying the Aspire. In July 1997, they dispatched Arthur Pai and another engineer from IPG in Taiwan to the United States to coordinate Aspire sourcing and logistics in AAC, both of which had become expensive problems. Pai commented, "AAC didn't understand Taiwan operations very well so we had to send over some individuals who could keep in contact with Taiwan and help with the communication with the component sources." IPG engineers were now tightly integrated into the design process and again felt responsible for the success of the product rather than simply for the supply of component parts.

As AAC's losses continued through 1997, more support was sent. A three person advisory committee of experienced Taiwan-based managers was assigned to work U.S.

top management to develop new strategies and tighten operations. One member was assigned to work on AAC's customer service programs, a second was to concentrate on manufacturing improvements, while the third was to team up with Culver to strengthen the U.S. consumer business. As Pai commented, "Acer America learned that it couldn't work without the SBUs, and we learned that Acer America was better off not being so totally independent. It was like bringing a runaway teenager back home."

By late 1997, inventories were being cleaned up, customer service reengineered, and logistics streamlined. Aspire's sales volume had returned to the levels reached in the second half of 1995, and its monthly losses had shrunk from $6 million to $2 million. Culver, now promoted to vice president of AAC's consumer products division, seemed relieved. "Now we have a second chance," he said.

RETHINKING THE MODEL

While pleased with the turnaround following the mid-year shakeup, Stan Shih was less sanguine about Aspire's long-term prospects. Over the previous two and a half years, the once-promising new product had generated losses of almost $100 million in AAC while its share of the home PC market had fallen from almost 14% at its introduction to less than 5% by the end of 1997. (See Exhibit 9 for U.S. market share figures.) Primarily due to Aspire's problems, AAC was expected to report losses of $80 million on sales of about $1 billion in 1997.

Once again, many were urging Shih to give up on his goal of building a global brand, arguing that the company could make much better profits on its component business selling CD-ROM drives, monitors, etc., and on OEM contracts to supply PCs to major players like IBM. (In 1997, the company manufactured 6.2 million computers. It was the

Exhibit 9   Acer Market Share

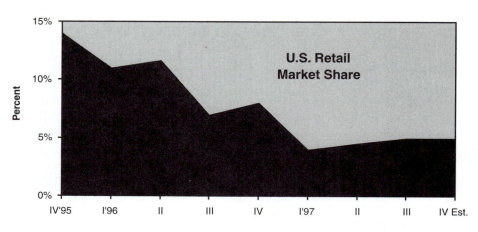

Acer's Home-PC

Source: "A New Attack Plan for Acer America," *Business Week*, December 8, 1997, p. 82.

number three PC maker in the world, with about half its output being branded and the other half sold under OEM contracts.) But the determined CEO remained firm in his commitment to elevate Acer's own branded PCs from their 1997 ranking as number eight to one of the top five brands in the world. At the same time, however, he felt there were some important lessons to be learned from the Aspire experience and he began to think through some key strategic and organizational issues.

Strategic Questions

Although the development of the Aspire was exciting because it had emerged in response to opportunities detected in a leading market, its global implementation had been hampered by the subsequent need to adapt the product to different market requirements around the world. Always trying to think ahead, Stan Shih began to look for opportunities not yet defined by the market but with global potential. Shih began to describe a vision for low-cost, limited task devices—he used the term "machines" or "appliances" rather than "computers"—that Acer would sell as "XCs." ("X" represented the individual applications these appliances could support; "C" stood for computer.) Costing less than $200, these devices would be designed for focused tasks such as playing computer

games, supporting home-use applications such as banking or stock tracking, sending and receiving email, or surfing the Internet.

Shih believed his new concept had an annual potential of a billion units by 2010 (ten times the current level of PC sales), expanding computer use in less affluent markets worldwide. He hoped Acer would supply 10%. Should this become the company's primary thrust in the consumer market? What continuing role, if any, should Aspire have in Acer's product line? And, most important, how should these issues be decided?

Organizational Options

While AAC had provided a textbook example of how an RBU could become a valuable source of entrepreneurial initiative, it had done so at considerable cost to Acer's traditionally efficient Taiwan-based operations. Was it time to rethink the networked organization model Shih had rolled out as his innovative "client server" concept? If so, how should he redefined the roles, responsibilities and operating relationships of Acer's SBUs and RBUs? What implications did any such changes have for the "Global Brand, Local Touch" philosophy of locally tailored products? And how could any proposal for greater centralization be implemented through the numerous independent companies spun out as independently listed public companies as part of the "21 in 21" program? (See Exhibits 10a and 10b for subsidiary ownership information.)

As Shih reflected: "In the mid- and late-1980s, we experienced the difficulties that come with heavily centralized systems and we don't want this to occur again. We have always striven to empower our employees at every level, but it is difficult to strike a balance between our principles in this arena and the need for greater cost efficiency."

Exhibit 10a — Acer, Inc. % Stake in Acer Subsidiaries, 1996

Subsidiary	% Stake
Acer America (AAC)	100.0
Acer Europe	100.0
Acer Laboratories	65.7
Acer Computer International	63.4
AMBIT Microsystems	50.0
TI-Acer	48.8
Acer Peripherals	40.9
Acer Sertek	36.2
Information Products Group (IPG)	100.0
Acer Computec Latino America (ACLA)	23.4

Source: Morgan Stanley Analyst Report, 1996

Exhibit 10b — Estimated Subsidiary Contributions to Acer, 1996–1997

NT$ millions	1996	1997
TI-Acer	229	-217
Acer Sertek	109	134
Acer Peripherals	525	593
Acer America	-1,365	41
Acer Computer International	406	442
Acer Laboratories	22	20
AMBIT	12	16
Acer Europe	-175	17

Source: Morgan Stanley Analyst Report, 1996

Part IV

Marketing in Emerging Markets

Before the fall of the Berlin Wall in 1989, emerging markets were a mere asterisk in the revenue base of most multinational corporations. Capital budgeting and marketing investment discussions at world headquarters focused invariably on the so-called Triad: Western Europe, North America, and Japan. The rest of the world was an afterthought. More than fifteen years later, resource allocation decisions in the boardroom are increasingly complicated. The countries of the so-called Triad still account for approximately 70 percent of world trade flows and equity market capitalization, so they can hardly be ignored, but future growth appears to lie in the emerging—yet more volatile—markets of Asia, Latin America, and Central Europe.

Paradoxically, in the era of globalization, more new nations have achieved independence in the 1990s than in any other decade of modern human history, as a result of the breakup of the USSR, Yugoslavia, and Czechoslovakia. The nomenclature has shifted from "Third World countries" that did little more than supply cheap raw materials to better-off nations, to "emerging markets," implying a demand as well as a supply role.

Emerging markets are attractive for two reasons. First, population and economic growth are outstripping population and economic growth of the so-called developed world (which will soon represent no more than 15 percent of the world's population). Second, serving the developed markets is more complicated, often requiring clever segmentation. Needs in the emerging markets are more basic. In many cases, the simple mass market that existed in the United States in the 1960s was mirrored in the emerging markets of the 1990s and beyond.

Not all emerging markets are created equal. Some, such as Hong Kong and Singapore, enjoy per capita incomes higher than many countries in the developed world. At the other extreme are so-called trailing markets, many in Africa, and are characterized by pervasive poverty.

Conventional wisdom in international marketing would have emerging markets follow—with an appropriate time lag—the patterns of market evolution established earlier in the developed world. Where per capita income constraints heavily influence a product's market penetration, this may be so. However, there are many examples of leapfrogging, whereby emerging markets move swiftly to adopt the latest technology, skipping over intermediate technologies used previously in the developed world; cellular and wireless communications are an example. In addition, the speed with which urban consumers in emerging markets have embraced "Western" brands of low-priced consumables has surprised many marketers. In some cases, steady-state market penetration rates comparable to those in developed countries have been reached within three years after launch.

Astute multinationals understand that marketing innovations in emerging markets can often inform and improve marketing practices in the developed world. Traditionally, idea transfers have involved one-way traffic from developed to emerging markets, with little emphasis on reverse learning. Recently, however, Motorola has uncovered important insights into the future of cellular telephones from consumer research in China. Similarly, Kentucky Fried Chicken (KFC) has learned how to design and operate large eat-in restaurants in China, where a visit to a KFC outlet is a special treat, as opposed to the convenient fast-food experience it is in the United States.

Although marketing programs often need to be adapted to emerging market cultures, the level of customization required is often surprisingly modest. For example, the functional benefits addressed by Gillette razor blades are the same worldwide, though the frequency of shaving and the areas shaved vary considerably across cultures. Gillette's sales mix also varies, with more expensive sensor systems accounting for a higher percentage of sales in developed markets, whereas basic double-edge blades, often sold singly, account for the bulk of sales in poorer emerging markets. The brand name and the product quality remain consistent worldwide. Prices of some Gillette products may be lower in emerging markets to encourage brand trial, but not to the point of encouraging widespread diversion of products from higher-to-lower-priced markets.

Consumers in emerging markets are as savvy as those in developed markets when evaluating product quality. The notion that obsolete product or surplus inventory can be dumped in emerging markets is naive. Indeed, in some trailing markets, harsh climatic conditions may require more robust product formulations and packaging, and narrower product lines may be appropriate when distribution is fragmented among many undercapitalized vendors.

Distribution systems are modernizing in the cities of emerging markets with surprising speed. For example, in Sao Paulo, Buenos Aires, and Mexico City, retail distribution has consolidated to the point that multinational marketers are having to deal with supermarket chains as powerful as any in the developed world. Falling tariff barriers and the arrival of Carrefour and Wal-Mart have prompted local retailers to consolidate and/or enter into strategic alliances with their global counterparts.

Beyond the cities, however, distribution in emerging markets remains uneven and fragmented. Bicycle vendors and mobile-delivery vans are often necessary to reach rural communities in India, for example. Multinationals entering emerging markets with poor transportation infrastructures are often surprised at how much they have to invest (for example, in their own delivery trucks) to achieve widespread distribution. Such investments must be calibrated against the long-term potential of these markets.

Zucamor S.A.: Global Competition in Argentina

"Oh, please, don't get Gustavo started," pleaded Norm Nelson to the group gathered at the bar. "This Harvard-educated economist will give us a long lecture," he joked, as Gustavo Herrero, Osvaldo Zucchini, and others responded with laughter. There was a lot of mirth at Union Camp's "International Senior Managers" meeting in Wayne, New Jersey, called for by Norm Nelson, division vice president.

Gustavo Herrero, the object of the joke, was the managing director of Zucamor in Argentina. Zucamor was the only overseas venture of Union Camp, a $4.0 billion (in sales) integrated U.S.-based paper and container producer, in which Union Camp had only a minority stake (30%); normally it fully owned or had a majority stake in its foreign holdings. But Zucamor's three local shareholding families retained 70% of the equity. Zucamor was unique in other respects, too. For example, its marketing director, Osvaldo Zucchini, was one of the principals, in fact, the chairman of the board of directors. In his role as marketing director, he reported to Gustavo Herrero, who was a professional manager with no equity.

With the collapse of worldwide paper prices in 1996, accompanied by aggressive foreign entry, Zucamor's operating profits had taken a dramatic tumble. But it remained one of the few paper companies in Argentina that even made a profit. By the middle of 1997, there were several strategic questions facing Herrero and his team of managers. They had to decide how much to push the "value-enhancement" concept as a way of serving customers. This had to be balanced, however, by persuasive internal data, which showed that Zucamor's sales volumes had gained when prices were lowered. No matter which option Zucamor's management took, the fundamental goal was to improve the profitability of its operations, which had slumped from $7.6 million in 1995 to $2.24 million in 1996.

"Don't believe it," said Gustavo Herrero, in a measured and well-moderated voice, "when economists tell you that businesses will prosper in open economies with free inflows and outflows of capital. Don't believe a word of it. Take it from me—globalization is a nanosecond phenomenon and when it happens, it is painful for local companies that are not quick on their feet." He paused. With Gustavo's gesticulating right hand frozen in mid-air, his international colleagues around him all raised their cocktail glasses in unison to loud chantings of "Sí! Sí! Gustavo. Speech, we want a speech."

BACKGROUND

Zucamor was founded in 1951 by four friends, Dante Zucchini, Bautista and Marceliano Campo,[1] and Luis Morra. In 1990, the first-generation owners and founders decided to retire simultaneously and make way for the next generation, represented by Osvaldo and Nestor Zucchini, Alberto Morra, Marcelo Campo, and his brother-in-law Hugo Anitori, all in the 35- to 45-year age group.

Each of the new generation owners had held significant functional responsibility for an aspect of the company's operations, but decided that under their new regime it would be best to remove themselves from the day-to-day operations and govern the company from their position on the Board. Their first attempt to professionalize the company got off to a moderate start and, yet, the experience did not prove to be totally successful. Two years later, they decided to hire Gustavo Herrero, 43-year-old managing director of a woolen textile mill, as their chief executive. About 10 years before coming to

This case was prepared by Professor V. Kasturi Rangan.

Copyright © 1999 by the President and Fellows of Harvard College. Harvard Business School case 9-599-096.

---

[1] Marceliano Campo sold his share to the other partners in the late 1980s.

Zucamor, Herrero had managed an integrated packaging company, and he and Osvaldo Zucchini had met each other then. Herrero was known to Osvaldo as someone who would not hesitate to make tough decisions and controlling costs was a priority concern for Zucamor.

In 1992, at the time of the transition to the new management, the company's sales were about $36 million, with a reported operating loss of about $1.4 million. The change in leadership and management at Zucamor coincided with a new political and economic climate in the country. See Exhibit 1 for a brief history.

The new administration under President Carlos Menem (elected in 1989 and re-elected in 1995 as well) broke with the past. Restrictive trade and investment barriers were lifted and nonproductive and non-self-sustaining public sector companies were privatized. Financial accounts were placed on a current basis by linking the Argentine peso to the U.S. dollar under the Convertibility Law. The intransigent Argentine system of 50 years was replaced by a largely open regime. Carlos Menem's government, anchored by Harvard Ph.D. Finance Minister Domingo Cavallo, engineered a three-pronged reform program for the economy.

The first pillar of the program was state reform. A fiscal equilibrium program forced through an all-inclusive privatization program, a sharp cutback in public employment and expenditure, the elimination of nearly all subsidies to public enterprises, a comprehensive pension reform, and improved tax collection coupled with the elimination of taxes that distorted economic incentives. Balanced budgets were submitted to Congress for timely review.

The second pillar of the program was the re-creation of a market economy through the elimination of controls on

---

Exhibit 1   Argentina—A Brief History[a]

With an estimated population of 34 million people in 1994, and a per-capita income of $8,159 (GDP: $280 billion), Argentina was considered an upper-middle-income country. Some 87 percent of Argentines lived in urban areas; more than 12 million lived in the Buenos Aires metropolitan area.

Argentina developed an economy based on the exchange of agricultural commodities for foreign capital and manufactured goods. At the beginning of the century, it was run primarily by and for the land owning aristocracy and porteño (Buenos Aires) business interests. However, this commodity-based economy was at the mercy of volatile international market prices and dependent on the nations which bought Argentina's low-value produce and in return sold Argentina expensive, value-added products.

In 1946, following 15 years of military influenced or direct military governments, free elections were held, resulting in the election of Juan Domingo Perón as president. Under Perón, labor took on a significant role in society, many industries were nationalized, and foreign investment and participation in the economy was restricted in an effort to allow Argentina to develop a self-sufficient industry. However, development was inefficient and Argentine goods became uncompetitive in world markets. The country incurred massive debt to support its various projects.

By 1955, deteriorating economic conditions led to a backlash among the middle class, students, and elements of the clergy, business, and military. Perón fled the country following a military coup. If Perón had erred by catering too much to the demands of labor, the military pushed the pendulum too far in the opposite direction, offending not only leftists but also students, business interests, and Argentina's large middle class. Greater military repression triggered more intense public discontent and gave rise to armed guerrilla opposition movements during the late 1960s. It was not until 17 years later that Democracy returned to Argentina. Perón returned from exile, and was re-elected in 1973, but passed away before his term ran out. His wife/vice president Isabel was ousted, by the military, in 1976. Finally, the Christian Democrats, under Raul Alfonsin, won the elections in 1983 and then in 1989, Peronists won power again with Carlos Menem at the helm.

---

[a]Much of this section has been taken from *Argentina Business: The Portable Encyclopedia For Doing Business with Argentina* (San Rafael, Calif.: World Trade Press, 1996).

prices, wages, interest rates, foreign exchange rates, and capital flows, as well as the removal of hidden subsidies. A broad deregulation effort swept away numerous regulations that impeded the operations of free markets.

The third pillar of the program was investment and trade liberalization. The regulations on foreign direct investment were liberalized: First, registration requirements were eliminated; second, foreign investors had full access to local credit markets; third, prior approval was required only in cases where special laws applied (such as defense); and fourth, there was no waiting period for the repatriation of profits and capital.

Few countries have had a worse experience with inflation than Argentina. Between 1980 and 1988, consumer price rises were in the triple-digit range every year except 1986, when they fell to 86%. Argentine inflation reached a high of 4,924% in 1989, dropped to 1,344% in 1990, and then fell precipitously to 3.9% in 1994. Despite the financial turmoil caused by the liquidity crisis in Mexico

and the devaluation of its peso, in late 1994, Argentina showed no change in inflation. Financial stability was there to stay, and inflation firmly in control.

Zucamor Takes a New Direction

One of Herrero's first decisions after taking over in November 1992 was to persuade each of the owners to accept a significant line responsibility within the operation. Thus, Osvaldo Zucchini became its marketing chief, Marcelo Campo took on the finance and administrative functions, Alberto Morra became its technical director, Nestor Zucchini agreed to oversee the company's business development effort, and Hugo Anitori became purchasing director (see Exhibit 2 for organization chart).

Shortly thereafter, Herrero began to streamline and regularize many business practices to be in tune with the new regulatory and economic environment. For example, he eliminated the procedure of paying labor out-of-contract. They were all brought in as regular employees and their

---

Exhibit 2   Zucamor Organization Chart

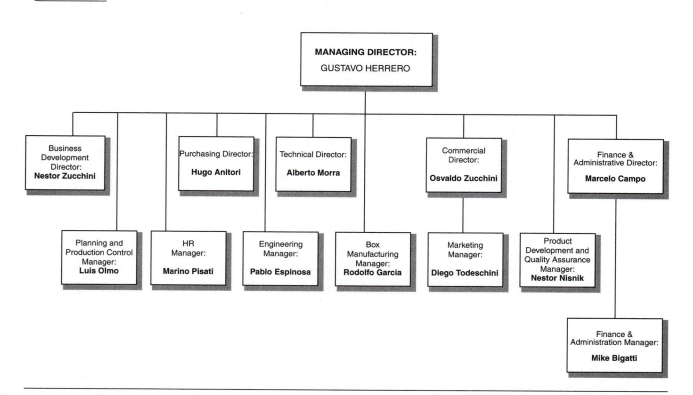

wages were paid "on the books." Zucamor, like many companies in Argentina at that time, paid a considerable portion (20% of wages) outside the books. Because the social security and pension benefits were often more than 100% of the basic wages, paying "off the books" saved the company a significant amount of labor costs. But in order to manage the payments, the company also had to generate an equivalent amount of revenue outside the books.

All in all, this ended up in lower reported earnings and tax payments. Herrero put a stop to this practice because he thought it was morally wrong to evade social costs, particularly when the government, conscious of this widespread behavior in the economy, had come out with a regularization program (*Blanqueo Laboral*), which allowed firms to straighten out their practices.

Herrero knew that all this would increase the costs of production by close to $1 million a year, so he set in motion a program to improve quality, productivity, and plant utilization. Managers and workers were provided bonuses and incentives linked to productivity gains. The managers' bonus, SBG (*Sistema de Bonus Gerencial*—Management Bonus System), was a group quarterly incentive based on achieving objectives, and the workers' bonus, PCP (*Programa de Calidad Productiva*—Productive Quality Program), was based on qualitative and quantitative productivity parameters and was paid out monthly, based on a bi-monthly moving average. By April 1993, these schemes were fully in place and Zucamor's productivity was beginning to pick up.

Notwithstanding the production improvements, Herrero and the shareholders were all convinced that the only way to survive and grow in the newly liberalized market environment would be to become a world-class manufacturer, and that would involve seeking partnerships with global players. Herrero recalled:

> Once I had the owners' blessings, I simply picked up the phone and dialed the directory assistance operator in New Jersey asking for the Union Camp number. Why Union Camp? Why not International Paper or Inland or Stone? Only because rumors were floating that Union Camp was actively looking around for a partner in Argentina. Well, I made contact with their vice president for international operations and that's how I first met Norm Nelson.

But Union Camp had already signed a "letter of intent" with another local company, and so Zucamor looked for an alternate suitor and signed a similar "letter of intent" agreement with a South African paper company. Herrero recalled the early days of the partnership.

> Norm and I had really hit it off very well and I struck a similar chord with Union Camp's Chairman and CEO, Craig McClelland. Both of us were educated at the Harvard Business School and had memories to share. But Union Camp was committed elsewhere. Fortunately for us at Zucamor, Union Camp's agreement with the other company started coming apart at the due diligence stage. When Norm Nelson called me to say they wanted to talk to us, we, in turn, were deep into assessing another potential partner's interest. In the end, it all worked out because the South African company's parent was not that interested in our idea.

> Marcelo Campo and I visited three U.S. paper companies—Union Camp and two others that had shown interest. We asked each of them five questions:

> - What was their expectation regarding equity control and management of their investment?
>
> - What was the ballpark figure for investment they had in mind?
>
> - Was the fact that Zucamor owned its own recycled paper mill an obstacle?
>
> - What was their strategy? Was it low cost? Valued-added?
>
> - Were they thinking of making the investment "in kind" or was it to be a cash transaction?

> It became clear that Union Camp was the right partner. We began exchanging information in mid-December 1993, signed a letter of intent on March 15, 1994, and closed the deal on August 22, 1994. It was lightning fast.

Union Camp was a leading manufacturer of paper, packaging, chemicals, and wood products. With annual sales of nearly $3.0 billion in 1993, and nearly 19,000 employees, Union Camp ranked among the top 200 U.S. industrial companies. See Exhibit 3 for Union Camp's revenue and balance sheet information. In 1993, the company's four paper and paper board plants produced a total of 1.92 million tons of paper products of which its 29 converting plants used 1.0 million tons for making corrugated containers and folding cartons. In addition, the company also produced another 265,000 tons of kraft paper for conversion in nine flexible packaging plants. The 1993 paper mill capacity in the United States

Exhibit 3   Union Camp: Key Financial Information

	1987	1988	1989	1990	1991	1992	1993	1994	1995	1996
Net sales	$2,361,684	$2,660,918	$2,761,337	$2,839,704	$2,967,138	$3,064,358	$3,120,421	$3,395,825	$4,211,709	$4,013,197
Income from operations	398,053	504,630	500,684	388,217	285,420	192,278	230,926	284,286	841,389	252,539
Net income	207,483	295,146	299,400	229,591	124,790	76,233	50,043	113,510	451,073	85,308
Working capital	458,065	443,244	354,233	216,756	145,074	124,002	1,346	67,209	413,704	354,241
Total assets	2,919,115	3,094,414	3,413,862	4,403,354	4,697,714	4,745,197	4,685,033	4,776,578	4,838,343	5,096,307
Long-term debt	632,706	627,928	690,149	1,221,597	1,348,157	1,289,706	1,244,907	1,252,249	1,151,536	1,252,475
Stockholders' equity	1,452,017	1,559,327	1,754,524	1,910,643	1,936,256	1,881,878	1,815,848	1,836,321	2,121,692	2,093,594

Source: Annual Report.

Note: 1996 includes a $46.9 million special charge relating to restructuring costs and asset writedowns.

was about 90 million tons, of which approximately 15 million tons was used for making medium and liner, the type of paper used in corrugated box making. The box market was about 30 billion square meters. The company's $23 million investment in Zucamor was split: a small part went to the owners, but most of it to Zucamor as new capital for effecting manufacturing improvements and paying off expensive local debt.

Union Camp had long been a leading exporter of kraft linerboard to world markets and by the mid-1980s had undertaken a strategy to expand its corrugated box manufacturing investments in select world markets. The strategy to grow packaging operations in international markets was consistent with Union Camp's overall strategy, which was based on the belief that its cash flow should be focused first on generating higher returns followed by investment for growth, and without necessarily serving as an outlet for linerboard from Union Camp mills. The U.S. consumption of corrugated paper was 96 kgs per capita in comparison to Argentine consumption at 12 kgs per capita. Moreover, with U.S. paper and box-making capacity usually outstripping demand, the industry was subject to pricing cycles and corresponding fluctuations in profitability.

According to division VP Norm Nelson:

> We had been in Europe for a long time; over 25 years in Spain, but we had not entered Latin America and Asia, where the opportunities for growth were attractive. In Latin America, Chile stabilized first and reformed its economy, so we entered there. Brazil was saturated with many strong local players, so we sought Argentina next. It was a systematic market entry process.

Craig McClelland in his chairman's report (1994 Union Camp Annual Report) explained the company's globalization strategy:

> A key strategic element is to build on our international presence especially in Latin America and the Pacific rim.

> We've been a major linerboard exporter for 40 years. We also have long experience in operating offshore container plants, with six facilities in Ireland, Spain, Chile, the Canary Islands and Puerto Rico, plus recent equity investment in an Argentine containerboard and corrugated box manufacturer. We intend to expand linerboard exports and add more corrugated plants outside the U.S. to strengthen this growing and profitable segment of our packaging group.

> In the Far East, we're setting up a business development office in Hong Kong to help us further penetrate the markets in Asia. Our aim is to expand our foothold through greater market presence in high-end reprographic paper and packaging—servicing the expanding needs of those high growth markets.

ZUCAMOR, CAPACITY AND PERFORMANCE

Zucamor was a vertically integrated corrugated box manufacturer. It made its own paper from recycled raw material (wastepaper); it then converted the paper to corrugated sheets by sandwiching a wavy middle layer called "medium" or "fluting" in between external layers called "liners." This operation was done by a corrugating machine. Finally, the corrugated sheets were converted to boxes. Depending on customers' specific needs (such as, where to have the handling slots in the box), customized die-cuts were used in slotting machines, which customized the box types. Similarly, depending upon the customers' desired printing requirements on the box, customized printing plates were used in the final printing (see Exhibit 4 for a process flow diagram).

The two distinctive aspects of the operation, papermaking and box making, were characterized by very different scale economies. Paper output was usually measured in "weight"—in this case, metric tons; and box output in "area"—square meters. A papermaking plant was capital intensive, while box making was labor intensive. A 300,000 metric ton/year paper mill cost about $500 million to set up—in comparison to a $25 million investment for a 60 million square meter/year box plant. Plant sizes below this threshold were increasingly uneconomical.[2] An approximate rule of thumb equated 1 metric ton (i.e., 2,200 lbs.) with 2,000 square meters of corrugated box. Ultimately, of course, the conversion was based on the grade of medium and liner used for box making.

Zucamor had an integrated paper and box-making capability at Ranelagh, just 20 miles south of Buenos Aires. It had two more box-making plants, one at Cuyo near the Chilean border at the heart of Argentina's wine country, and the other at Hurlingham, 20 miles west of Buenos Aires (see Exhibit 5 for Zucamor's paper and box shipment volumes). All three factories combined, Zucamor had

---

2 1 metric ton= 1,000 kilos. Given Zucamor's product mix, .58 kilos of pulp made 1 square meter of linerboard.

Exhibit 4   Paper-and Box-making Process: Line Diagram

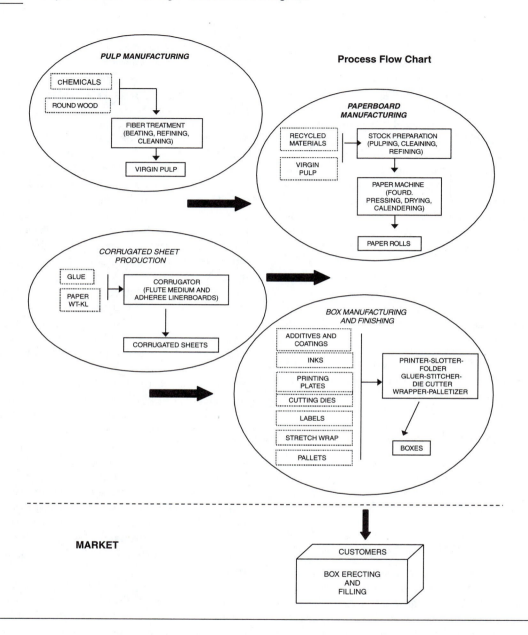

about 120 million square meters of box-making capacity. The Ranelagh mill was unique in that it used 100% recycled fiber as raw material. In the highly inflationary shortage environment (pre-1989), the strategy of owning a factory making paper based on recycled material was very helpful in keeping the prices of linerboard and medium at a predictable lower level. After Argentina's economic liberalization in 1990, however, many local box plants were

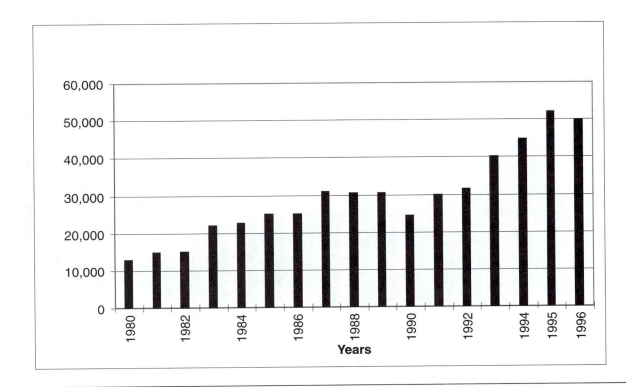

able to import virgin fiber kraft linerboard from paper-rich Brazil and from the United States for about the same price as (or even less than) Zucamor's recycled liner. Compared to recycled paper, virgin paper had longer fiber length and therefore displayed higher strength for an equivalent gauge of liner.

Argentina consumed about 421,275 metric tons of medium and liners in 1995, of which Zucamor supplied 60,000 metric tons for a 15% market share in the country. Of the domestic paper producers, Zucamor's share was even higher because about 100,000 tons of consumption were from imported sources. The bulk of Zucamor's paper production (about 50,000 metric tons) was consumed by its own box plants. It sold about 10,000 tons to other box manufacturers. Zucamor also bought about 10,000 tons of kraft linerboard for making special grades of boxes, mainly from Papel Misionero, a government owned paper plant. Of the six

paper companies in Argentina, only the government-owned Papel Misionero produced kraft liner (i.e., from virgin fiber); the other five, like Zucamor, produced test liner (i.e., from recycled fiber).

Herrero explained the transition to higher productivity:

We systematically and ruthlessly approached our operating task with the dual objective of increasing throughput and quality at the same time. This led to a series of initiatives that were pursued with key support from Union Camp's resources. By June 1995, all three of our box plants were certified under ISO 9001. The next two years brought achievements in other areas of operations. Product quality and service claims were brought down from nearly 10% of shipments to 1%. We cut machine set-up time by more than half, from 25 minutes to 10 minutes, even as we compressed the average run size from 10,000 square meters to 5,000 square meters. On-time delivery performance increased from 70% to 90%.

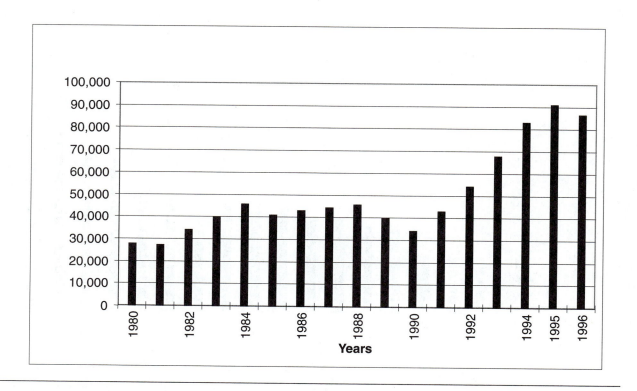

Absenteeism went down, productivity went up and labor cost per square meter produced was halved.

These tremendous gains in productivity led to impressive gains in market share and operating income (see Exhibits 6A and 6B for Zucamor financials).

GLOBALIZATION WITH A VENGEANCE

The largest corrugated boxmaker in Argentina was Cartocor with about 21% market share. Cartocor was wholly owned by Arcor, a local producer of packaged food (such as candies, crackers, and preserves.) Cartocor was the broadest player and served a complete range of markets in the industrial and agricultural segments. Zucamor, on the other hand, only catered to the industrial segment which comprised 80% of the market. Zucamor considered the agricultural segment too seasonal and risky to play in. Zucamor was second with 12% market share in box sales

(this was less than its 15% share of paper because it sold some paper in the open market), followed by Inland Argentina, Stone-Cartonex, FACCA, and Asindus-Smurfit, each with a 3% to 7% share. Inland Argentina was 100% owned by Inland Container, a $3.4 billion integrated U.S. paper- and boxmaker (entered in 1994); Stone-Cartonex was 51% owned by another large U.S. box manufacturer, Stone Container (entered in 1996); and Asindus-Smurfit was 80% owned by a large Irish box manufacturer, Jefferson Smurfit, a $3.6 billion global paper and box manufacturer (entered in 1996).

The top six players served about 44% of the market. The other 56% plus was catered to by nearly a hundred small boxmakers, many with sales as low as $1 million. Only four box manufacturers were integrated (i.e., produced their own paper) in Argentina—Zucamor, Stone-Cartonex, Asindus Smurfit and, to a much lesser extent, Cartocor.

"Given the competitive nature of the container business in North America, we should have expected this foreign

Exhibit 6A Zucamor: Financial History

Balance Sheet (in US$)

ASSETS

	12/31/96	12/31/95	12/31/94
Current			
Cash & bank	2,147,936	2,098,939	2,663,778
Investments	311,320	3,012,345	139,138
Accounts receivable	12,599,660	14,082,967	15,042,873
Other credits	6,844,294	6,269,534	5,539,314
Inventories	10,151,113	11,869,930	9,289,767
Other assets	2,176,560	2,231,880	0
Total current assets	34,230,886	39,563,598	32,674,872
Noncurrent			
Investments	65,137	57,119	175,446
Other assets	0	0	2,867,033
Fixed assets	72,318,146	69,542,102	68,827,694
Intangible assets	516	516	516
Total noncurrent assets	72,383,800	69,599,738	71,870,691
Total assets	106,614,686	109,163,337	104,545,563

LIABILITIES

	12/31/96	12/31/95	12/31/94
Current			
Accounts payable	4,742,504	6,226,974	7,044,897
Financial debt	4,807,054	1,216,718	2,118,104
Payroll and social security benefits	1,264,208	1,527,580	1,298,498
Taxes payable	1,015,355	3,823,751	2,094,668
Total current liabilities	11,829,122	12,795,025	12,556,169
Noncurrent			
Taxes payable	734,214	700,953	3,809,035
Other liabilities	0	0	0
Long-term debt	6,006,775	1,494,158	1,571,946
Total noncurrent liabilities	6,740,989	2,195,111	5,380,982
Total liabilities	18,570,111	14,990,137	17,937,151
Minority interest	111	103	86
Net worth	88,044,463	94,173,097	86,608,324
Total liabilities and net worth	106,614,686	109,163,337	104,545,563

	12/31/96	12/31/95	12/31/94
DIVIDEND DISTRIBUTION	8,363,810	0	0

Zucamor S.A.: Global Competition in Argentina

Exhibit 6B   Zucamor Income Statement (in US$)

	1996	1995	1994	1993
Net sales	60,813,737	75,076,430	66,166,231	47,395,423
Cost of goods sold	(46,200,534)	(52,750,752)	(49,823,922)	(37,692,034)
Gross income	14,613,202	22,325,677	16,342,309	9,703,388
Selling expenses	(7,076,347)	(6,696,067)	(5,273,457)	(3,593,517)
Administrative expenses	(4,224,026)	(4,587,622)	(4,487,455)	(2,254,11)
Other expenses	(722,129)	(987,308)	(722,155)	(1,491,634)
Total SG&A/other	(12,022,503)	(12,270,997)	(10,483,069)	(7,339,364)
Operating profit	2,590,698	10,054,679	5,859,239	2,364,024
Permanent investments result	0	0	0	0
Other income	787,513	931,408	893,807	1,298,552
Extraordinary income	88,278	1,569,553	11,611	59,811
Financial expenses & holding gains	(241,839)	(1,256,418)	(1,930,271)	(1,240,929)
(includes results from exposure				
to inflation)				
Minority interest income	(241,839)	(1,256,418)	(1,930,271)	(1,240,929)
	(11)	(9)	(3)	21
Profit before income tax	3,224,640	11,299,214	4,834,383	2,481,479
Income tax provision	(989,463)	(3,706,414)	(1,177,241)	0
Net income	2,235,176	7,592,799	3,657,142	2,481,479

invasion," offered Marcelo Campo, "but we were very surprised by its speed and intensity," he added. As shown in Exhibit 7, U.S. paper and container prices had started to climb up in 1994, and the larger players now had the cash for making offshore investments. Unlike the previous boom periods when domestic capacity expansion fueled excessive supply over demand in the down cycle, this time around manufacturers looked for offshore expansions. Gustavo explained, "Sheltered markets like Argentina became attractive because of the price umbrella they offered. But unlike previous price expansions, the U.S. recovery was short lived, soon putting even more pressure on overseas investments to outperform domestic operations."

Even as the Argentine economy opened up to post steady GNP gains, competition among the box manufacturers was quite intensive, especially for the larger, growth-oriented accounts. Meanwhile, in 1997, Cartocor had completed a state-of-the-art 100-million-square-meter capacity corrugated container plant near Buenos Aires, creating additional corrugated capacity in an industry that was already in an overcapacity situation. Zucamor's managers

considered Cartocor as the most formidable competitor. First of all, because it was only partially integrated it was able to buy paper in the open market for box conversion. Good quality paper from Brazil at cheap prices was abundantly available. Moreover, Cartocor's box-making lines were considered very modern and efficient, with good product development and design capability. It operated with a very lean marketing and sales overhead structure. For example, the company covered the entire Buenos Aires market with three sales people. All this combined with captive consumption at its own packaged food operations gave Cartocor clear cost leadership in the Argentine market. In contrast, Inland Argentina and Stone-Cartonex were rumored to be encountering some difficulties. Even though their equipment and the quality of the boxes they made were considered quite good, both these competitors resorted to aggressive competitive pricing and provided only moderate service levels.

According to a Zucamor executive:

For some reason, two of our multi-national competitors concentrated on the sale of produce boxes (fruits and

---

U.S. Linerboard (Paper) Price vs. Fibre Box Price (quarterly prices in $US per metric ton)

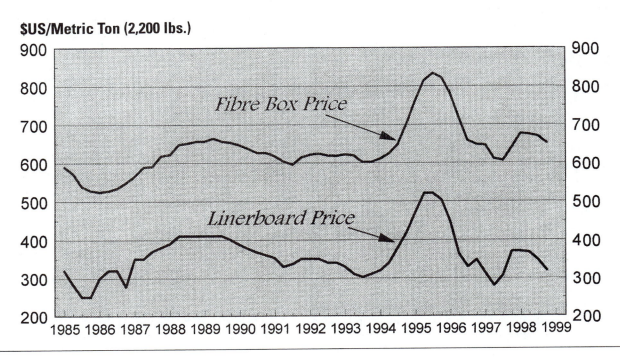

Source: Zucamor records.

vegetables), and on Tetrapack trays for the wine industry, which are two of the most competitive segments in our business. Both are fairly standard, so they are actually tradable across borders. The little business they captured in the regular consumer market was opportunistic; long runs, low margins, with price being the main buying attribute.

After Cartocor, Zucamor managers thought that Smurfit could turn out to be the most formidable competitor. One of them explained:

> *Jefferson Smurfit entered the market in 1997. They acquired a small, integrated local company that made paper and boxes. Even though the plant was poorly equipped, it had cornered the business of a couple of large customers, from which it made its living with probably handsome profits, given their low overhead. Smurfit has been re-equipping the firm since they bought it, and can be a fearsome contender. It will depend on whether they can develop the service skills that the more sophisticated markets require.*

As compared to the top-tier players, the small and medium boxmakers provided their customers with fast response and short runs. Even though their equipment and efficiency was not exactly top class, they managed to retain customer loyalty, and according to Herrero, "they are not subject to the same accounting principles and business standards that larger national players are used to."

CUSTOMERS

From Zucamor's viewpoint, the market could generally be divided into three types of customers by their buying behavior. Category 1 and 2 customers, who were the larger customers, accounted for about 47% of the market volume, and the small customers for the rest. Large suppliers like Zucamor supplied 44% of the market's requirements.

Among the large customers, some were very professional in their purchasing practices and strongly emphasized quality, often supplying custom specifications for their box design. A number of the multinational companies such as P&G and Unilever and domestic manufacturers like Molinos would fall into this category. They expected high service levels and would not tolerate overruns or underruns. Zucamor's sales division labeled them Category 1 customers. Other medium to large customers with similar requirements but at a slightly lower intensity were classified as Category 2 customers. Many of these customers along with almost all the Category 1 customers supplied to the aggressive retail industry in Argentina,

characterized by the likes of global giants like Carrefour and Wal-mart. Finally, the smaller customers who were somewhat less professional in their purchasing patterns were classified as Category 3 customers. They were known to buy on relationship.

Table A provides an estimate of how sales volume was distributed among the large, and medium and small boxmakers.

Table A	Corrugated Box Suppliers		
	Large Suppliers	Medium and Small Suppliers	Total
Category 1	14%	4%	18%
Category 2	22%	7%	29%
Category 3	8%	45%	53%
Total	44%	56%	100%

Of Zucamor's sales volume, 41% went to Category 1 customers, 32% to Category 2 customers, and 27% to Category 3 customers.

Zucamor's customer list had about 484 accounts, of which the top 5 (with annual purchases exceeding $3 million) accounted for 25% of sales, the top 16 (with purchases exceeding $1 million) for 50% of sales, and the top 51 (with purchases exceeding $.5 million) for 75% of sales. An internal survey of customers' buying preferences revealed that about half its customers bought on quality and service; another 40% included price as one of the buying attributes; only about 10% bought purely on price.

Exhibit 8 provides an analysis of the company's top 51 customers and their volume and purchasing characteristics.

Value-Enhancement

The senior management of the company, with leadership from Union Camp, was then engaged in a major cycle time reduction (CTR) program in the factory, and again with Union Camp's support, was adopting similar principles to reengineer the customer value chain. According to Marketing Director Osvaldo Zucchini:

> *With the technical help of Union Camp, we were squeezing out all these costs in the plant, so we attempted to extend those ideas to customers as well. After two days of intense brainstorming we arrived at the Paquete Zucamor*

	Segment	Category	Sq. Meters	Quality	Service	Price	Percent Share of Total	Customer Share (%)	Cartocor	Inland	Other Large Competitors	Small Competitors	Import
1.	Food Oils	I	5,521,250	X	X	X	7.45	60%	X			X	
2.	Beverages	II	3,864,715	X	X		4.64	80	X				
3.	Cleaning products	I	2,675,677	X	X		4.45	70	X			X	
4.	Beverages	I	3,272,197		X	X	4.40	25		X			
5.	Beverages	I	2,738,431	X	X		3.35	75	X				
6.	Foods	I	1,197,014	X	X		3.03	100				X	
7.	Foods	I	2,222,440	X	X	X	3.00	60	X			X	
8.	Glass/ceramics	II	1,993,759		X		2.75	80		X	X		
9.	Beverages	I	1,467,806	X	X		2.63	70				X	
10.	Beverages	II	1,902,484	X	X		2.14	80	X			X	
11.	Beverages	II	1,036,870			X	1.94	0	X			X	
12.	Meat packers	II	1,028,587	X	X		1.91	60					X
13.	Cleaning products	I	1,207,456	X	X		1.82	70				X	
14.	Tobacco	I	1,181,681	X	X		1.64	80				X	
15.	Beverages	II	696,690	X	X	X	1.28	60		X	X	X	
16.	Food oils	II	774,531	X		X	1.28	20	X				
17.	Meat packers	II	654,831		X		1.26	70					
18.	Foods	II	832,337	X		X	1.21	50		X		X	
19.	Milk Ind.	II	792,620	X	X		1.20	75		X	X	X	
20.	Foods	I	725,519	X	X		1.20	75	X	X	X		
21.	Cleaning products	I	862,741	X		X	1.08	5	X			X	X
22.	Cleaning products	I	757,381			X	1.06	20		X			X
23.	Beverages	II	657,363			X	0.94	25	X	X	X		X
24.	Meat packers	II	641,177	X	X		0.91	50				X	X
25.	Foods	III	675,889		X	X	0.90	20		X	X	X	X

Exhibit 8   Customer Analysis by Buying Attribute (1996) (continued)

No.	Segment	Category I	Category II	Category III	Sq. Meters	Quality	Service	Price	Percent Share of Total	Customer Share (%)	Cartocor	Inland	Other Large Competitors	Small Competitors	Import
26.	Beverages		II		665,948	X	X		0.82	100					
27.	Milk Ind.	I			435,179	X	X		0.80	10				X	
28.	Cleaning products	I			430,579	X	X		0.79	75	X			X	
29.	Foods	I			799,446			X	0.75	50	X			X	
30.	Beverages		II		578,240	X	X		0.73	100					
31.	Foods		II		500,160	X		X	0.73	50	X			X	
32.	Foods		II		384,069	X	X	X	0.72	80				X	
33.	Cosmetics		II		492,447	X	X		0.67	100					
34.	Beverages		II		440,029	X	X		0.66	100					
35.	Iron & Steel			III	332,434	X	X		0.65	80				X	
36.	Foods	I			500,963	X	X	X	0.65	50	X			X	
37.	Beverages		II		394,209	X	X	X	0.57	60	X				
38.	Foods		II		345,823	X	X		0.45	25	X				
39.	Beverages			III	341,275	X	X	X	0.43	90				X	
40.	Beverages		II		426,223	X	X	X	0.41	40	X	X			
41.	Iron & Steel			III	191,557	X	X		0.39	100					
42.	Beverages			III	441,296	X	X		0.39	100					
43.	Food oils			III	287,095		4	X	0.37	50	X	X			
44.	Chemicals/Refinery	I			182,736	X	X	X	0.33	100					
45.	Beverages			III	259,318			X	0.33	100					
46.	Beverages			III	209,414			X	0.31	50					
47.	Meat packers		II		181,042			X	0.30	20				X	
48.	Foods			III	207,327		X	X	0.30	90		X			
49.	Foods	I			189,104	X		X	0.27	5	X				
50.	Beverages		II		169,896	X	X	X	0.24	60	X			X	
51.	Chemicals/Refinery	I			94,883	X	X	X	0.19	0	X				
	Total	19	23	9	49,115,348	38	36	28	71.10		20	13	3	27	4

Source: Zucamor records.

(Zucamor Package). The Paquete *identified our sources of differentiable advantage along three dimensions—quantitative, qualitative and general (See Table B below.)*

We started by writing down the various elements that we felt entailed value to our customers (the "what"). We then qualified them in two categories: those that translated into specific cost reductions, and those that entailed intentions of goodwill on our part. Within those that implied reductions of cost (or addition of value), we identified "quantitative" attributes and "qualitative" ones. Finally, we covered the entire list, and we decided to leave out from our immediate value proposition certain elements where we felt we were not sufficiently equipped to deliver value to our customers. It was agreed that we should interpret the list of "ingredients," but the "recipe" should be custom-made for each account, depending on their needs and on their perception of value.

The two-day meeting also considered the question of which accounts to go after with the Zucamor package. According to Herrero:

We started by identifying those that had already expressed interest in the concept. We then matched their fit with our strategic objectives, their receptivity to letting us explore the value chain and the incidence of packaging costs in their overall product cost.

The team made a list of criteria to drive account selection for the value package:

1. Strategic long-term accounts
   a. Growth potential of firm and the business segment it participates in
   b. Their segment leadership and financial performance
   c. Our contribution margin
   d. Credit risk
   e. Professionalism in their management
   f. Competitive presence in their supply
2. Receptivity to our value proposition
3. Incidence of packaging cost on end product

In choosing which accounts to go after, Herrero highlighted the need for customers' top management commitment and assurance that the customer would not shift allegiance after the development work was completed. He recalled:

It was horrible at a Canadian food manufacturer. We worked through their packaging line and spotted many interesting ways to redesign their box so that it would lead to productivity gains at their end. Finally, after all the work was done, they simply turned around and placed the box order with one of our competitors who was willing to come in at a lower price.

Since then, Zucamor had been considerably more careful in its relationship building efforts with strategic accounts. At Avon, for instance, a study of their packaging line revealed significant scope for productivity improvements; there was also room for improving the integrity of the box. Following Zucamor's recommendations, Avon agreed to invest half a million dollars to revamp the picking

| Table B | Development of the Value Proposition |

Quantitative Attributes	Qualitative Attributes	General
Replenishment	Vertical integration	Teamwork
On-time delivery	Packaging training	ISO exposure
Space reduction		CTR experience
Waste reduction (elimination?)		UCC know-how
Administrative cost reduction		Global network
Less claims/less downtime		Value analysis
Faster/better response		Environmental
Practices		
Quality certification		Customer satisfaction program
Logistics skills		
Design capability		

line; Zucamor staffed and managed its operations. One full-time supervisor and four operators (two per shift) were hired and paid by Zucamor to operate Avon's final packaging step.

According to Avon's purchasing team (consisting of the purchasing manager and the engineering manager, both of whom had been on the job for over 10 years):

> This is a true partnership. We don't order boxes anymore. Once the parameters of the size and price have been established, Zucamor's supervisor on our shopfloor gets the needed quantity of boxes in, or stores them here, or does whatever it takes to operate a smooth finishing line. We simply pay for the actual quantity of boxes used. We don't pay for any defect, any inventories, or any transportation.

Nestor Nisnik, Zucamor's product development manager, commented on the evolution of this partnership:

> We were told by Avon of persistent pilferage problems of rather expensive cosmetics en route to their salesforce. We took a look at their box design and packing line and were able to come up with recommendations that will perhaps save them $300,000 in packaging and labor costs per year. This is a considerable savings on Avon's nearly $300 million turnover in Argentina. In turn, we were rewarded with a sole-source contract. We beat out Cartocor, who was a second source for Avon. Of course, Cartocor cannot offer our level of value engineering.

Diego Todeschini offered this note of caution:

> Zucamor has only recently rolled out its value analysis concept. The initial success is varied. For every successful account like Avon, we have corresponding accounts like Nabisco that are tough to crack. We need to understand why. Sometimes we don't even have to go all the way to demonstrate shopfloor productivity gains. At YPF (Argentina's recently privatized oil company), we have been able to get a sole-source arrangement for their motor oil shipments [in boxes] to retailers because they have faith in our logistics and JIT systems. But we have to get more customers on board to our value concept. We have the largest salesforce in the industry; they are most experienced with good relationships with their customers. We need to tap into this unique strength.

Besides, we must thoroughly review our cost structure. In spite of our progress, we continue to have higher overhead than all our competitors. Even if we choose not to be the low cost producers, we cannot afford to run with steeper costs. Prices may continue to drop, and our break-even point is too high.

Zucamor's marketing and sales organization had 10 salespeople, of whom 7 were direct employees and 3 were agents who carried nothing but the Zucamor line. The agents were paid on a straight commission basis. Because of the concentration of customers, nearly 60% to 70% of the salesforce was located in the Buenos Aires province. They had been with the organization an average of seven years and were considered knowledgeable and had good relationships with their customers. Each salesperson on average called on about 50 accounts. Three customer service representatives handled customer complaints and followed up on order status. The product development and quality assurance function with another three supporting staff usually handled customers' specific requests for design and customization.

But even as Zucamor's marketing team attempted to refine its Value Engineering Concept, internal analysis revealed a strong correlation between price and volume (see Exhibit 9). Some Zucamor managers wondered if they might be better served by simply attempting to gain share by keeping prices and costs at lower levels. This might involve product line rationalization, and an internal analysis revealed that the bulk of sales and contributions came from only 13 grades (see Table C).

Exhibits 10A and 10B provide further details on the margin contribution of Zucamor's product portfolio. In general, the thinking in the company was that much gain would not be achieved by tinkering with product mix and grades, especially when major strategic directions remained unresolved.

ACTIONS

Gustavo Herrero pondered his options: value enhancement versus volume gain (through competitive pricing). At times, he was convinced that the two were interrelated and intertwined and that the only way to sustain a competitive advantage in the marketplace was to pursue both. At other times, the two options seemed incompatible. At the end of the day, the only thing that mattered was to restore Zucamor's historical earnings performance. As an integrated producer of corrugated boxes, would mill production requirements and expected efficiencies be a dominant factor? Would value enhancement and cost cutting efforts be compatible?

Exhibit 9   Zucamor: Fibre Box Volume and Prices

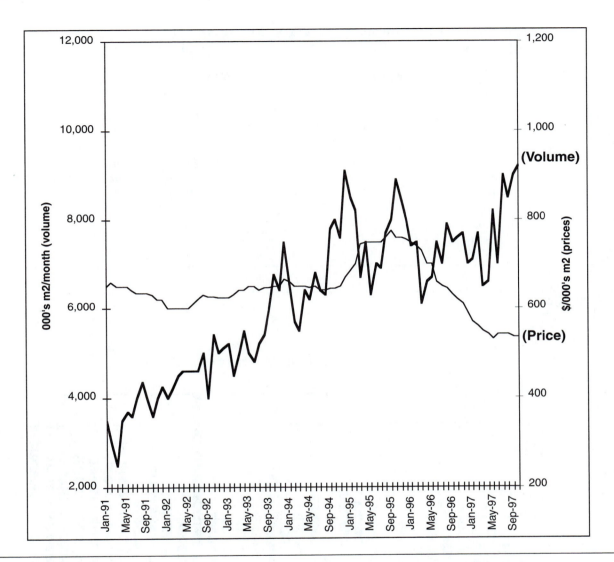

Source: Zucamor records.

Table C   Contribution and Volume of the Top 13 Grades

	Grades of Paper Used in Box	$ Contribution (% of total)	Volume (square meter) (% of total)
1	Z-6	13%	30%
2	Z-4	12%	24%
3	B-5	12%	21%
4	Z-5	6%	6%
5	Z-8	7%	5%
6	Z-7	7%	3%
7	Z-6/6	6%	2%
8	Z-4/6	5%	1%
9	B-4	5%	1%
10	E-8	6%	1%
11	B-5/6	6%	1%
12	B-4/6	3%	1%
13	Z-7/6	3%	<1%

Exhibit 10A

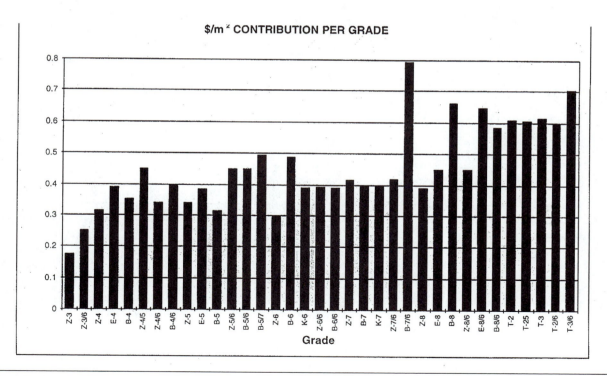

$/m² CONTRIBUTION PER GRADE

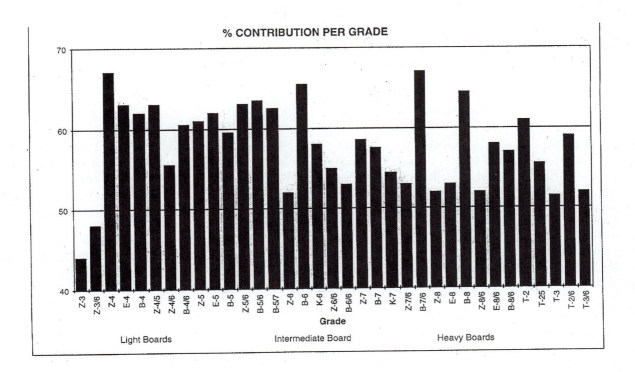

% CONTRIBUTION PER GRADE

Source: Zucamor documents.

Jollibee Foods Corporation (A): International Expansion

Protected by his office air conditioner from Manila's humid August air, in mid-1997, Manolo P. ("Noli") Tingzon pondered an analysis of demographic trends in California. As the new head of Jollibee's International Division, he wondered if a Philippine hamburger chain could appeal to mainstream American consumers or whether the chain's proposed U.S. operations could succeed by focusing on recent immigrants and Philippine expatriates. On the other side of the Pacific, a possible store opening in the Kowloon district of Hong Kong raised other issues for Tingzon. While Jollibee was established in the region, local managers were urging the company to adjust its menu, change its operations, and refocus its marketing on ethnic Chinese customers. Finally, he wondered whether entering the nearly virgin fast food territory of Papua New Guinea would position Jollibee to dominate an emerging market—or simply stretch his recently-slimmed division's resources too far.

With only a few weeks of experience in his new company, Noli Tingzon knew that he would have to weigh these decisions carefully. Not only would they shape the direction of Jollibee's future internalization strategy, they would also help him establish his own authority and credibility within the organization.

COMPANY HISTORY

Started in 1975 as an ice cream parlor owned and run by the Chinese-Filipino Tan family, Jollibee had diversified into sandwiches after company President Tony Tan Caktiong (better known as TTC) realized that events

This case was prepared by Professor Christopher A. Bartlett with the assistance of Jamie O'Connell.

Copyright © 1998 by the President and Fellows of Harvard College. Harvard Business School case 9-399-007.

triggered by the 1977 oil crisis would double the price of ice cream. The Tans' hamburger, made to a home-style Philippine recipe developed by Tony's chef father, quickly became a customer favorite. A year later, with five stores in metropolitan Manila, the family incorporated as Jollibee Foods Corporation.

The company's name came from TTC's vision of employees working happily and efficiently, like bees in a hive. Reflecting a pervasive courtesy in the company, everyone addressed each other by first names prefaced by the honorific "Sir" or "Ma'am," whether addressing a superior or subordinate. Friendliness pervaded the organization and become one of the "Five Fs" that summed up Jollibee's philosophy. The others were flavorful food, a fun atmosphere, flexibility in catering to customer needs, and a focus on families (children flocked to the company's bee mascot whenever it appeared in public). Key to Jollibee's ability to offer all of these to customers at an affordable price was a well developed operations management capability. A senior manager explained:

> It is not easy to deliver quality food and service consistently and efficiently. Behind all that fun and friendly environment that the customer experiences is a well oiled machine that keeps close tabs on our day-to-day operations. It's one of our key success factors.

Jollibee expanded quickly throughout the Philippines, financing all growth internally until 1993. (Exhibit 1 shows growth in sales and outlets.) Tan family members occupied several key positions particularly in the vital operations functions, but brought in professional managers to supplement their expertise. "The heads of marketing and finance have always been outsiders," TTC noted. (Exhibit 2 shows a 1997 organization chart.) Many franchisees were also members or friends of the Tan family.

In 1993, Jollibee went public and in an initial public offering raised 216 million pesos (approximately

Exhibit 1   Jollibee Philippines Growth, 1975–1997

Year	Total Sales (millions of pesos)	Total Stores at End of Year	Company-Owned Stores	Franchises
1975	NA	2	2	0
1980	NA	7	4	3
1985	174	28	10	18
1990	1,229	65	12	54
1991	1,744	99	21	80
1992	2,644	112	25	89
1993	3,386	124	30	96
1994	4,044	148	44	106
1995	5,118	166	55	113
1996	6,588	205	84	124
1997 (projected)	7,778	223	96	134

NA = Not available

Exhibit 2   Jollibee Corporation Organization Chart, 1997 (members of Tan family shaded)

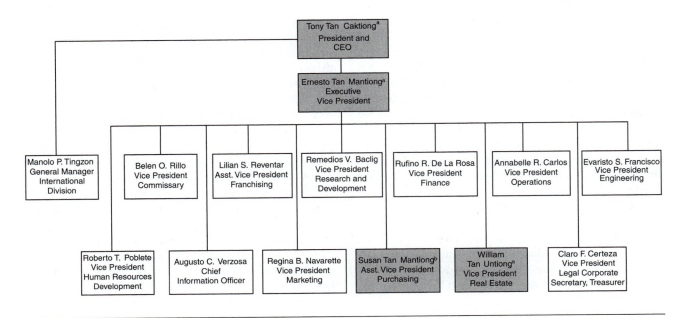

[a]Brothers
[b]Spouse of Ernesto Tan Mantiong

US $8 million). The Tan family, however, retained the majority ownership and clearly controlled Jollibee. Although the acquisition of Greenwich Pizza Corporation in 1994 and the formation of a joint venture with Deli France in 1995 diversified the company's fast food offerings, in 1996 the chain of Jollibee stores still generated about 85% of the parent company's revenues. (Exhibits 3 and 4 present Jollibee's consolidated financial statements from 1992 through 1996.)

McDonald's: Going Burger to Burger

The company's first serious challenge arose in 1981, when McDonald's entered the Philippines. Although Jollibee already had 11 stores, many saw McDonald's as a juggernaut and urged TTC to concentrate on building a strong second-place position in the market. A special meeting of senior management concluded that although McDonald's had more money and highly developed operating systems, Jollibee had one major asset: Philippine consumers preferred the taste of Jollibee's hamburger by a wide margin. The group decided to go head to head with McDonald's. "Maybe we were very young, but we felt we could do anything," TTC recalled. "We felt no fear."

McDonald's moved briskly at first, opening six restaurants within two years and spending large sums on advertising. Per store sales quickly surpassed Jollibee's and, by 1983, McDonald's had grabbed a 27% share of the fast food market, within striking range of Jollibee's 32%. The impressive performance of the Big Mac, McDonald's largest and best-known sandwich, led Jollibee to respond with a large hamburger of its own, called the Champ. Jollibee executives bet that the Champ's one wide hamburger patty, rather than the Big Mac's smaller two, would appeal more to Filipinos' large appetites. Market research indicated that Filipinos still preferred Jollibee burgers' spicy taste to McDonald's plain beef patty, so the Champ's promotions focused on its taste, as well as its size.

But the Champ's intended knockout punch was eclipsed by larger events. In August 1983, political opposition leader Benigno Aquino was assassinated as he returned from exile. The economic and political crisis that followed led most foreign investors, including McDonald's, to slow their investment in the Philippines. Riding a wave of national pride, Jollibee pressed ahead, broadening its core menu with taste-tested offerings of chicken, spaghetti and a unique peach-mango dessert pie, all developed to local consumer tastes. By 1984, McDonald's foreign brand appeal was fading.

In 1986, dictator Ferdinand Marcos fled the Philippines in the face of mass demonstrations of "people power" led by Aquino's widow, Corazon. After she took office as president, optimism returned to the country, encouraging foreign companies to reinvest. As the local McDonald's franchisee once again moved to expand, however, its management found that Jollibee now had 31 stores and was clearly the dominant presence in the market.

INDUSTRY BACKGROUND

In the 1960s, fast food industry pioneers, such as Ray Kroc of McDonald's and Colonel Sanders of Kentucky Fried Chicken, had developed a value proposition that became the standard for the industry in the United States and abroad. Major fast food outlets in the United States, which provided a model for the rest of the world, aimed to serve time-constrained customers by providing good-quality food in a clean dining environment and at a low price.

Managing a Store

At the store level, profitability in the fast food business depended on high customer traffic and tight operations management. Opening an outlet required large investments in equipment and store fittings, and keeping it open imposed high fixed costs for rent, utilities, and labor. This meant attracting large numbers of customers ("traffic") and, when possible, increasing the size of the average order (or "ticket"). The need for high volume put a premium on convenience and made store location critical. In choosing a site, attention had to be paid not only to the potential of a city or neighborhood but also to the traffic patterns and competition on particular streets or even blocks.

Yet even an excellent location could not make a store viable in the absence of good operations management, the critical ingredient in reducing waste, ensuring quality service and increasing staff productivity. Store managers were the key to motivating and controlling crew members responsible for taking orders, preparing food, and keeping the restaurant clean. Efficient use of their time—preparing raw materials and ingredients in advance, for example—not only enabled faster service, but could also reduce the number of crew members needed.

Exhibit 3   Jollibee Foods Corporation Consolidated Balance Sheets (in Philippine pesos)

	Years Ended December 31				
	1996	**1995**	**1994**	**1993**	**1992**
ASSETS					
Current assets					
Cash and cash equivalents	480,822,919	355,577,847	474,480,298	327,298,749	116,716,643
Accounts receivable:					
Trade	579,089,680	206,045,303	135,663,597	107,680,327	86,885,668
Advances and others	105,836,646	70,731,546	66,224,534	35,838,295	15,091,648
Inventories	323,019,198	201,239,667	183,154,582	135,263,988	116,828,086
Prepaid expenses and other current assets	223,680,221	132,077,935	88,995,824	41,462,780	66,028,987
Total current assets	1,712,448,664	965,672,298	948,518,835	647,544,139	401,551,032
Investments and advances	283,758,590	274,878,713	132,277,028	67,000,362	60,780,936
Property and equipment	2,177,944,193	1,181,184,783	753,876,765	568,904,831	478,857,474
Refundable deposits and other assets—net	363,648,234	224,052,247	91,575,543	92,035,464	72,310,079
Total assets	4,537,799,681	2,645,788,041	1,926,248,171	1,375,484,796	1,013,499,521
LIABILITIES AND STOCKHOLDERS' EQUITY					
Current liabilities:					
Bank loans	771,690,724	-	-	-	-
Accounts payable and accrued expenses	1,274,801,219	715,474,384	497,238,433	323,029,967	297,029,436
Income tax payable	58,803,916	28,103,867	17,205,603	23,206,109	19,851,315
Notes payable	-	-	-	-	133,000,000
Current portion of long-term debt	6,707,027	7,524,098	-	-	22,034,635
Dividends payable	16,810,812	-	-	-	-
Total current liabilities	2,128,813,698	751,102,349	514,444,036	346,236,076	471,915,386
Long-term debt	28,936,769	33,725,902	-	-	21,127,827
Minority interest	45,204,131	1,479,723	1,331,529	-	-
Stockholders' equity					
Capital stock—P par value	880,781,250	704,625,000	563,315,000	372,000,000	66,000,000
Additional paid-in capital	190,503,244	190,503,244	190,503,244	190,503,244	-
Retained earnings	1,263,560,589	964,351,823	656,654,362	466,745,476	454,456,308
Total stockholders' equity	2,334,845,083	1,859,480,067	1,410,472,606	1,029,248,720	520,456,308
Total liabilities	4,537,799,681	2,645,788,041	1,926,248,171	1,375,484,796	1,013,499,521
Average exchange rate during year: pesos per US$	26.22	25.71	26.42	27.12	25.51

	Years Ended December 31				
	1996	1995	1994	1993	1992
Systemwide Sales (incl. franchisees)	8,577,067,000	6,894,670,000	5,277,640,000	4,102,270,000	NA
Company sales	6,393,092,135	4,403,272,755	3,277,383,084	2,446,866,690	2,074,153,386
Royalties and franchise fees	511,510,191	448,200,271	328,824,566	255,325,825	221,884,104
	6,904,602,326	4,851,473,026	3,606,207,650	2,702,192,515	2,296,037,490
Cost and Expenses					
Cost of sales	4,180,809,230	2,858,056,701	2,133,240,206	1,663,600,632	1,469,449,458
Operating expenses	1,943,536,384	1,403,151,840	1,013,999,640	674,288,268	545,749,275
Operating income	780,256,712	590,264,485	458,967,804	364,303,615	280,838,757
Interest and other income—net	44,670,811	102,134,296	83,342,805	32,716,223	(13,599,219)
Minority share in net earnings of a subsidiary	-	-	499,770	-	-
Provision for income tax	219,900,353	168,589,520	138,001,953	104,230,670	66,172,056
Income before minority interest and cumulative effect of accounting change	605,027,170	523,809,261	403,808,886	292,789,168	201,067,482
Minority interest	2,829,654	137,694	-	-	-
Cumulative effect of accounting change		13,733,644			
Net income	602,197,516	537,405,211	403,808,886	292,789,168	201,067,482
Earnings per share	0.68	0.61	0.81	0.59	0.58
Average exchange rate (pesos per $US)	26.22	25.71	26.42	27.12	25.51

Managing a Chain

The high capital investment required to open new stores led to the growth of franchising which enabled chains to stake out new territory by rapidly acquiring market share and building brand recognition in an area. Such expansion created the critical mass needed to achieve economies of scale in both advertising and purchasing.

Fast food executives generally believed that chain-wide consistency and reliability was a key driver of success. Customers patronized chains because they knew, after eating at one restaurant in a chain, what they could expect at any other restaurant. This not only required standardization of the menu, raw material quality, and food preparation, but also the assurance of uniform standards of cleanliness and service. Particularly among the U.S. chains that dominated the industry, there also was agreement that uniformity of image also differentiated the chain from competitors: beyond selling hamburger or chicken, they believed they were selling an image of American pop culture. Consequently, most major fast food chains pushed their international subsidiaries to maintain or impose standardized menus, recipes, advertising themes, and store designs.

MOVING OFFSHORE: 1986–1997

Jollibee's success in the Philippines brought opportunities in other Asian countries. Foreign businesspeople, some of them friends of the Tan family, heard about the chain's success against McDonald's and began approaching TTC for franchise rights in their countries. While most of his family and other executives were caught up in the thriving Philippine business, TTC was curious to see how Jollibee would fare abroad.

Early Forays: Early Lessons

Singapore Jollibee's first venture abroad began in 1985, when a friend of a Philippine franchisee persuaded TTC to let him open and manage Jollibee stores in Singapore. The franchise was owned by a partnership consisting of Jollibee, the local manager, and five Philippine-Chinese investors, each with a one-seventh stake. Soon after the first store opened, however, relations between Jollibee and the local manager began to deteriorate. When corporate inspectors visited to check quality, cleanliness, and efficiency in operations, the franchisee would not let them into his offices to verify the local records. In 1986, Jollibee

revoked the franchise agreement and shut down the Singapore store. "When we were closing down the store, we found that all the local company funds were gone, but some suppliers had not been paid," said TTC. "We had no hard evidence that something was wrong, but we had lost each other's trust."

Taiwan Soon after the closure in Singapore, Jollibee formed a 50/50 joint venture with a Tan family friend in Taiwan. Although sales boomed immediately after opening, low pedestrian traffic by the site eventually led to disappointing revenues. Over time, conflict arose over day-to-day management issues between the Jollibee operations staff assigned to maintain local oversight and the Taiwanese partner. "Because the business demands excellent operations, we felt we had to back our experienced Jollibee operations guy, but the partner was saying, 'I'm your partner, I've put in equity. Who do you trust?'" When the property market in Taiwan took off and store rent increased dramatically, Jollibee decided to dissolve the joint venture and pulled out of Taiwan in 1988.

Brunei Meanwhile, another joint venture opened in August 1987 in the small sultanate of Brunei, located on the northern side of the island of Borneo. (Exhibit 5 shows the locations of Jollibee International stores as of mid-1997.) The CEO of Shoemart, one of the Philippines' largest department stores, proposed that Jollibee form a joint-venture with a Shoemart partner in Brunei. By the end of 1993, with four successful stores in Brunei, TTC identified a key difference in the Brunei entry strategy: "In Singapore and Taiwan, the local partners ran the operation, and resented our operating control. In Brunei, the local investor was a silent partner. We sent managers from the Philippines to run the operations and the local partner supported us."

Indonesia An opportunity to enter southeast Asia's largest market came through a family friend. In 1989, Jollibee opened its first store, in Jakarta. Initially, the operation struggled, facing competition from street vendors and cheap local fast food chains. When conflict between the local partners and the manager they had hired paralyzed the operation, in late 1994, Jollibee dissolved the partnership and sold the operation to a new franchisee. Nevertheless, the company viewed the market as promising.

TTC summed up the lessons Jollibee had learned from its first international ventures:

> *McDonald's succeeded everywhere because they were very good at selecting the right partners. They can get*

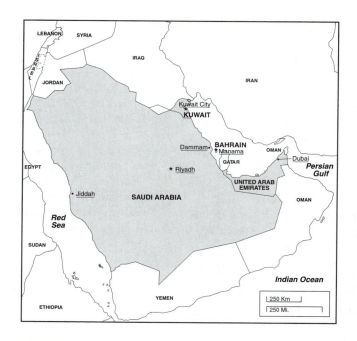

100 candidates and choose the best—we don't have the name to generate that choice yet.

Another key factor in this business is location. If you're an unknown brand entering a new country or city, you have trouble getting access to prime locations. McDonald's name gets it the best sites. People were telling us not to go international until we had solved these two issues: location and partner.

Building an Organization

In 1993, TTC decided that Jollibee's international operations required greater structure and more resources. Because most of his management team was more interested in the fast-growing domestic side of the business, in January 1994, he decided to hire an experienced outsider as Vice President for International Operations. He selected Tony Kitchner, a native of Australia, who had spent 14 years in Pizza Hut's Asia-Pacific regional office in Hong Kong. Reporting directly to TTC, Kitchner asked for the resources and autonomy to create an International Division.

Kitchner felt that his new division needed to be separate from Jollibee's Philippine side, with a different identity and capabilities. He agreed with TTC that attracting partners with good connections in their markets should be a priority, but worried that Jollibee's simple image and basic management approach would hamper these efforts. To project an image of a world-class company, he remodeled his division's offices on the seventh floor of Jollibee's Manila headquarters and instituted the company's first dress code, requiring his managers to wear ties. As one manager explained, "We had to look and act like a multinational, not like a local chain. You can't have someone in a short-sleeved open-neck shirt asking a wealthy businessman to invest millions."

Within weeks of his arrival, Kitchner began recruiting experienced internationalists from inside and outside Jollibee. To his inherited three-person staff, he quickly added seven more professionals, including new managers of marketing, finance, and quality control and product development that he brought in from outside Jollibee. The addition of two secretaries rounded out his staff. He claimed that greater internal recruiting had been constrained by two factors—Philippine management's resistance to having their staff "poached," and employees' lack of interest in joining this upstart division.

Strategic Thrust

While endeavoring to improve the performance of existing stores in Indonesia and Brunei, Kitchner decided to increase the pace of international expansion with the objective of making Jollibee one of the world's top ten fast food brands by 2000. Kitchner's strategy rested on two main themes formulated during a planning session in the fall of 1994—"targeting expats" and "planting the flag."

The Division's new chief saw the hundreds of thousands of expatriate Filipinos working in the Middle East, Hong Kong, Guam, and other Asian territories as a latent market for Jollibee and as a good initial base to support entry. Looking for a new market to test this concept, he focused on the concentrations of Filipino guest-workers in the Middle East. After opening stores in Dubai, Kuwait, and Dammam, however, he found that this market was limited on the lower end by restrictions on poorer workers' freedom of movement, and on the upper end by wealthier expatriates' preference for hotel dining, where they could consume alcohol. Not all overseas Filipinos were potential customers, it seemed.

The other strategic criterion for choosing markets rested on Kitchner's belief in first-mover advantages in the fast food industry. Jay Visco, International's Marketing manager, explained:

We saw that in Brunei, where we were the pioneers in fast food, we were able to set the pace and standards. Now, we have six stores there, while McDonald's has only one and KFC has three. . . . That was a key learning: even if your foreign counterparts come in later, you already have set the pace and are at top of the heap.

The International Division therefore began to "plant the Jollibee flag" in countries where competitors had little or no presence. The expectation was that by expanding the number of stores, the franchise could build brand awareness which in turn would positively impact sales. One problem with this approach proved to be its circularity: only after achieving a certain level of sales could most franchisees afford the advertising and promotion needed to build brand awareness. The other challenge was that rapid expansion led to resource constraints—especially in the availability of International Division staff to support multiple simultaneous startups.

Nonetheless, Kitchner expanded rapidly. Due to Jollibee's success in the Philippines and the Tan family's network of contacts, he found he could choose from many franchising inquiries from various countries. Some were far from Jollibee's home base—like the subsequently abandoned plan to enter Romania ("our gateway to Europe" according to one manager). In an enormous burst of energy, between November 1994 and December 1996, the company entered 8 new national markets and opened 18 new stores. The flag was being planted. (See Exhibit 6.)

Operational Management

Market entry Once Jollibee had decided to enter a new market, Tony Kitchner negotiated the franchise agreement, often with an investment by the parent company, to create a partnership with the franchisee. At that point he handed responsibility for the opening to one of the division's Franchise Services Managers (FSM). These were the key contacts between the company and its franchisees, and Kitchner was rapidly building a substantial support group in Manila to provide them with the resources and expertise they needed to start up and manage an offshore franchise. (See Exhibit 7.)

About a month before the opening, the FSM hired a project manager, typically a native of the new market who normally would go on to manage the first store. The

---

Exhibit 6   Jollibee International Store Openings

Location	Date Opened	
Bandar Seri Begawan, *Brunei*	August 1987	
Bandar Seri Begawan, Brunei (second store)	June 1989	
Seria, Brunei	August 1992	
Jakarta, *Indonesia*	August 1992	
Jakarta, Indonesia (second store)	March 1993	
Bandar Seri Begawan, Brunei (third store)	November 1993	International Division created
Kuala Belait, Brunei	November 1994	
Dubai, *United Arab Emirates*	April 1995	
Kuwait City, *Kuwait*	December 1995	
Dammam, *Saudi Arabia*	December 1995	
Guam	December 1995	
Jiddah, Saudi Arabia	January 1996	
Bahrain	January 1996	
Kota Kinabalu, *Malaysia*	February 1996	
Dubai (second store)	June 1996	
Riyadh, Saudi Arabia	July 1996	
Kuwait City, Kuwait (second store)	August 1996	
Kuwait City, Kuwait (third store)	August 1996	
Jiddah, Saudi Arabia (second store)	August 1996	
Hong Kong	September 1996	
Bandar Seri Begawan, Brunei (fourth store)	October 1996	
Ho Chi Minh City, *Vietnam*	October 1996	
Medan, Indonesia	December 1996	
Hong Kong (second store)	December 1996	
Dammam, Saudi Arabia	April 1997	
Hong Kong (third store)	June 1997	
Jakarta, Indonesia (third store)	July 1997	
Jakarta, Indonesia (fourth store)	September 1997	

Italics represent new market entry.

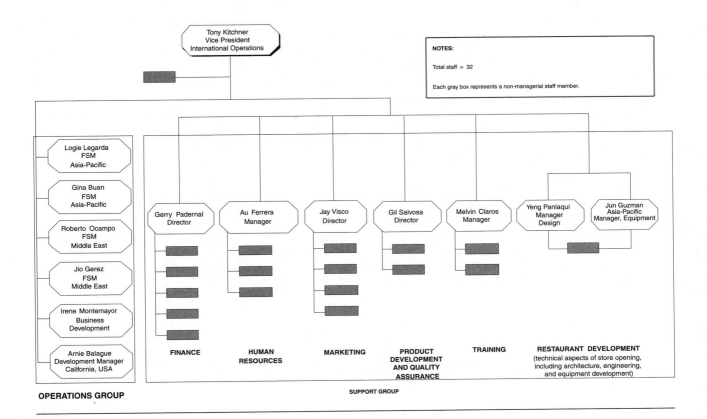

FSM and project manager made most of the important decisions during the startup process, with the franchisees' level of involvement varying from country to country. However, one responsibility in which franchisee was deeply involved was the key first step of selecting and securing the site of the first store, often with advice from International Division staff, who visited the country several times to direct market research. (Sometimes the franchisee had been chosen partly for access to particularly good sites.) Once the franchisee had negotiated the lease or purchase, the project manager began recruiting local store managers.

The FSM was responsible for engaging local architects to plan the store. The kitchen followed a standard Jollibee design that ensured proper production flow, but Kitchner encouraged FSMs to adapt the counter and dining areas to the demands of the space and the preferences of the franchisee. A design manager in the International Division provided support

During the planning phase, the project manager worked with International Division finance staff to develop a budget for raw materials, labor, and other major items in the operation's cost structure. He or she also identified local suppliers, and—once International Division quality assurance staff had accredited their standards—negotiated prices. (Some raw materials and paper goods were sourced centrally and distributed to franchisees throughout Asia.)

Once architectural and engineering plans were approved, construction began. As it often did in other offshore activities, the International Division staff had to develop skills very different from those of their Jollibee colleagues working in the Philippines. For example, high rents in Hong Kong forced them to learn how to manage highly compacted construction schedules: construction there could take one-third to one-half the time required for similar work in the Philippines.

Under FSM leadership, the International Division staff prepared marketing plans for the opening and first year's operation. They included positioning and communications strategies and were based on their advance consumer surveys, aggregate market data, and analysis of major competitors. Division staff also trained the local marketing manager and the local store manager and assistant managers who typically spent three months in Philippine stores. (Where appropriate local managers had not been found, the store managers were sometimes drawn from Jollibee's Philippine operations.) Just before opening, the project manager hired crew members, and International Division trainers from Manila instructed them for two weeks on cooking, serving customers, and maintaining the store. (See Exhibit 8 for a typical franchise's organization.)

Oversight and continuing support After a store opened, the FSM remained its key contact with Jollibee, monitoring financial and operational performance and working to support and develop the store manager. For approximately two months after opening, FSMs required stores in their jurisdictions to fax them every day their figures for sales by product, customer traffic, and average ticket. As operations stabilized and the store manager started to see patterns in sales and operational needs, FSMs allowed stores to report the same data weekly and provide a monthly summary.

FSMs used this information not only to project and track royalty income for corporate purposes, but also to identify ways they could support the local franchisee. When the data suggested problems, the FSM would contact the store manager, highlight the issue, and ask for an appropriate plan of action. For example, if FSM Gina Buan saw a decline in sales for two consecutive weeks, she

Exhibit 8   Organization of Typical Jollibee International Franchise

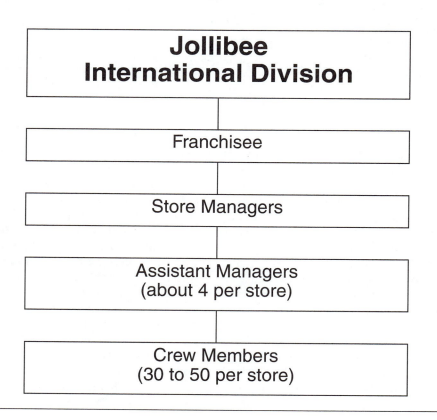

demanded specific plans within 24 hours of her call. If managers could not come up with solutions themselves, she would coach them to help them generate answers. "My aim," she remarked with a smile, "is to turn them into clones of me—or at least teach them my expertise."

In addition to the required sales reports, many stores voluntarily reported on their costs, because they found their FSM's analysis so helpful. This open partnership fit with TTC's view of franchise relations. "We get data from franchisees more to help us provide consulting assistance than for control," he said. Ernesto Tan, TTC's brother, explained that although Jollibee's royalty was a percentage of franchisees' sales, and local operations were focused more on profits, both interests were similar: "We want sales to grow, so that our royalty grows. But this will not happen if stores are not profitable, because our franchisees will not push to expand."

As well as support, however, the International Division was also concerned with control—especially in quality. Unannounced on-site inspections every quarter were Jollibee's primary tool. Over two days, the FSM evaluated every aspect of operations in detail, including product quality and preparation (taste, temperature, freshness, availability, and appearance), cleanliness, restaurant appearance, service speed, and friendliness. The manual for intensive checks was several inches thick. All international staff had been trained in Jollibee's quality standards and conducted less detailed "quick checks" whenever they traveled. Based on a 15-page questionnaire, a quick check took roughly two hours to complete and covered all of the areas that intensive ones did, although with less rigor and detail. Each store received an average of two quick checks per quarter.

In addition to FSMs' own rich industry experiences— Gina Buan, for example, had managed stores, districts, and countries for Jollibee and another chain—these field managers engaged the expertise of International Division functional staff. While they tried to shift responsibility gradually to the franchisee, division support staff often bore much of the responsibility long after startup. For example, the marketing staff tried to limit their franchise support role to creating initial marketing plans for new openings and reviewing new store plans. However, often they were drawn into the planning of more routine campaigns for particular stores, work they felt should be handled by the franchisee and store managers.

International vs. domestic practice As operations grew, Kitchner and his staff discovered that international

expansion was not quite as simple as the metaphor of "planting flags" might suggest. It sometimes felt more like struggling up an unconquered, hostile mountain. After numerous market entry battles, the international team decided that a number of elements of Jollibee's Philippine business model needed to be modified overseas. For example, the company's experience in Indonesia led Visco to criticize the transplantation of Jollibee's "mass-based positioning":

> When Jollibee arrived in Indonesia, they assumed that the market would be similar to the Philippines. But the Indonesian masses are not willing to spend as much on fast food as the Philippine working and lower-middle class consumers, and there were lots of cheap alternatives available. We decided that we needed to reposition ourselves to target a more up-market clientele.

Kitchner and Visco also felt that Jollibee needed to present itself as "world class," not "local" or "regional." In particular, they disliked the Philippine store design— a "trellis" theme with a garden motif—which had been transferred unchanged as Jollibee exported internationally. Working with an outside architect, a five-person panel from the International Division developed three new store decors, with better lighting and higher quality furniture. After Kitchner got TTC's approval, the Division remodeled the Indonesian stores and used the designs for all subsequent openings.

International also redesigned the Jollibee logo. While retaining the bee mascot, it changed the red background to orange and added the slogan, "great burgers, great chicken." Visco pointed out that the orange background differentiated the chain's logo from those of other major brands, such as KFC, Coca-Cola, and Marlboro, which all had red-and-white logos. The slogan was added to link the Jollibee name and logo with its products in people's minds. Visco also noted that, unlike Wendy's Old Fashioned Hamburgers, Kentucky Fried Chicken, and Pizza Hut, Jollibee did not incorporate its product in its name and market tests had found that consumers outside the Philippines guessed the logo signified a toy chain or candy store.

Kitchner and his staff made numerous other changes to Jollibee's Philippine business operating model. For example, rather than preparing new advertising materials for each new promotion as they did in the Philippines, the international marketing group created a library of promotional photographs of each food product that could be assembled, in-house, into collages illustrating new promotions (e.g., a discounted price for buying a burger, fries, and soda). And purchasing changed from styrofoam to paper packaging to appeal to foreign consumers' greater environmental consciousness.

Customizing for local tastes While such changes provoked grumbling from many in the large domestic business who saw the upstart international group as newcomers fiddling with proven concepts, nothing triggered more controversy than the experiments with menu items. Arguing that the "flexibility" aspect of Jollibee's "Five Fs" corporate creed stood for a willingness to accommodate differences in customer tastes, managers in the International Division believed that menus should be adjusted to local preferences.

The practice had started in 1992 when a manager was dispatched from the Philippines to respond to the Indonesian franchisee's request to create a fast food version of the local favorite *nasi lema*, a mixture of rice and coconut milk. Building on this precedent, Kitchner's team created an international menu item they called the Jollimeal. This was typically a rice-based meal with a topping that could vary by country—in Hong Kong, for example, the rice was covered with hot and sour chicken, while in Vietnam it was chicken curry. Although it accounted for only 5% of international sales, Kitchner saw Jollimeals as an important way to "localize" the Jollibee image.

But the International Division expanded beyond the Jollimeal concept. On a trip to Dubai, in response to the local franchisee's request to create a salad for the menu, product development manager Gil Salvosa spent a night chopping vegetables in his hotel room to create a standard recipe. That same trip, he acquired a recipe for chicken masala from the franchisee's cook, later adapting it to fast food production methods for the Dubai store. The International Division also added idio-syncratic items to menus, such as dried fish, a Malaysian favorite. Since other menu items were seldom removed, these additions generally increased the size of menus abroad.

Although increased menu diversity almost always came at the cost of some operating efficiency (and, by implication, complicated the task of store level operating control), Kitchner was convinced that such concessions to local tastes were necessary. In Guam, for example, to accommodate extra-large local appetites, division staff added a fried egg and two strips of bacon to the Champ's standard large beef patty. And franchisees in the Middle East asked the Division's R&D staff to come up with a spicier version of Jollibee's fried chicken. Although Kentucky Fried Chicken (KFC) was captivating customers with their spicy recipe, R&D staff on the Philippine side objected strenuously. As a compromise, International developed a spicy sauce that customers could add to the standard Jollibee chicken.

Overall, the International Division's modification of menus and products caused considerable tension with the Philippine side of Jollibee. While there was no controversy about reformulating hamburgers for Muslim countries to eliminate traces of pork, for example, adding new products or changing existing ones led to major arguments. As a result, International received little cooperation from the larger Philippine research and development staff and customization remained a source of disagreement and friction.

Strained International-Domestic Relations

As the International Division expanded, its relations with the Philippine-based operations seemed to deteriorate. Tensions over menu modifications reflected more serious issues that had surfaced soon after Kitchner began building his international group. Philippine staff saw International as newcomers who, despite their lack of experience in Jollibee, "discarded practices built over 16 years." On the other side, International Division staff reported that they found the Philippine organization bureaucratic and slow-moving. They felt stymied by requirements to follow certain procedures and go through proper channels to obtain assistance.

The two parts of Jollibee continued to operate largely independently, but strained relations gradually eroded any sense of cooperation and reduced already limited exchanges to a minimum. Some International Division staff felt that the Philippine side, which controlled most of Jollibee's resources, should do more to help their efforts to improve and adapt existing products and practices. Visco recalled that when he wanted assistance designing new packaging, the Philippine marketing manager took the attitude that international could fend for itself. Similarly, Salvosa wanted more cooperation on product development from Philippine R&D, but was frustrated by the lengthy discussions and approvals that seemed to be required.

However, the domestic side viewed things differently. Executive Vice President Ernesto Tan, who was in charge of Jollibee in the Philippines, recalled:

> *The strains came from several things. It started when International tried to recruit people directly from the*

Philippine side, without consulting with their superiors. There also was some jealousy on a personal level because the people recruited were immediately promoted to the next level, with better pay and benefits.

The international people also seemed to develop a superiority complex. They wanted to do everything differently, so that if their stores did well, they could take all the credit. At one point, they proposed running a store in the Philippines as a training facility, but we thought they also wanted to show us that they could do it better than us. We saw them as lavish spenders while we paid very close attention to costs. Our people were saying, "We are earning the money, and they are spending it!" There was essentially no communication to work out these problems. So we spoke to TTC, because Kitchner reported to him.

Matters grew worse throughout 1996. One of the first signs of serious trouble came during a project to redesign the Jollibee logo, which TTC initiated in mid-1995. Triggered by International's modification of the old logo, the redesign project committee had representatives from across the company. Having overseen International's redesign, Kitchner was included. During the committee's deliberations, some domestic managers felt that the International vice-president's strong opinions were obstructive, and early in 1996 Kitchner stopped attending the meetings.

During this time, TTC was growing increasingly concerned about the International Division's continuing struggles.. Around November 1996, he decided that he could no longer support Kitchner's strategy of rapid expansion due to the financial problems it was creating. Many of the International stores were losing money, but the cost of supporting these widespread unprofitable activities was increasing. Despite the fact that even unprofitable stores generated franchise fees calculated as a percentage of sales, TTC was uncomfortable:

Kitchner wanted to put up lots of stores, maximizing revenue for Jollibee. Initially, I had supported this approach, thinking we could learn from an experienced outsider, but I came to believe that was not viable in the long term. We preferred to go slower, making sure that each store was profitable so that it would generate money for the franchisee, as well as for us. In general, we believe that whoever we do business with—suppliers and especially franchisees—should make money. This creates a good, long-term relationship.

In February 1997, Kitchner left Jollibee to return to Australia. A restructuring supervised directly by TTC shrank the International Division's staff from 32 to 14, merging the finance, MIS and human resources functions with their bigger Philippine counterparts. (See Exhibit 9.) Jay Visco became interim head of International while TTC searched for a new Division leader.

A NEW INTERNATIONAL ERA: 1997

In the wake of Kitchner's departure, TTC consulted intensively with Jollibee's suppliers and other contacts in fast food in the Philippines regarding a replacement. The name that kept recurring was Manolo P. ("Noli") Tingzon, one of the industry's most experienced managers. Although based in the Philippines his entire career, Tingzon had spent much of this time helping foreign chains crack the Philippine market. In 1981 he joined McDonald's as a management trainee and spent the next 10 years in frustrating combat with Jollibee. After a brief experience with a food packaging company, in 1994 he took on the challenge to launch Texas Chicken, another U.S. fast food chain, in its Philippines entry. When TTC contacted him in late 1996, he was intrigued by the opportunity offered by his old nemesis and joined the company in July 1997 as general manager, International Division.

A Fresh Look at Strategy

Upon his arrival, Tingzon reviewed International's current and historical performance. (See Exhibit 10.) He concluded that because of the scale economies of fast food franchising, an "acceptable" return on investment in international operations would require 60 Jollibee restaurants abroad with annual sales of US$800,000 each, the approximate store level sales at McDonald's smaller Asian outlets. Feeling that Jollibee's international expansion had sometimes been driven less by business considerations than by a pride in developing overseas operations, Tingzon thought that a fresh examination of existing international strategies might reveal opportunities for improvement. As he consulted colleagues at Jollibee, however, he heard differing opinions.

Many of his own staff felt that the rapid expansion of the "plant-the-flag" approach had served Jollibee well and should be continued. For example, Visco argued that establishing a presence in each market before competitors

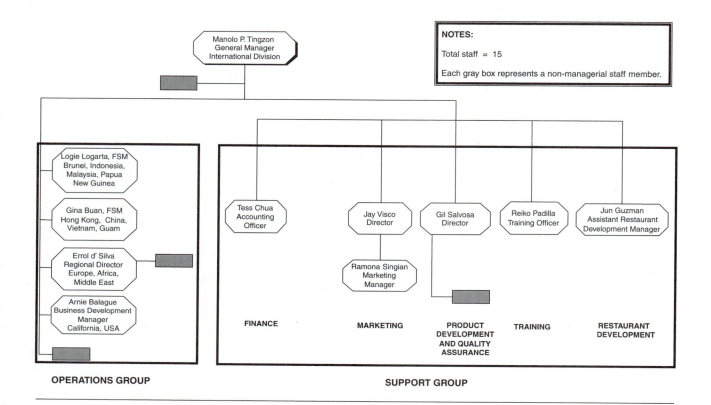

NOTES:

Total staff = 15

Each gray box represents a non-managerial staff member.

Manolo P. Tingzon
General Manager
International Division

Logie Logarta, FSM
Brunei, Indonesia,
Malaysia, Papua
New Guinea

Gina Buan, FSM
Hong Kong, China,
Vietnam, Guam

Errol d' Silva
Regional Director
Europe, Africa,
Middle East

Arnie Balague
Business Development
Manager
California, USA

Tess Chua
Accounting
Officer

Jay Visco
Director

Gil Salvosa
Director

Reiko Padilla
Training Officer

Jun Guzman
Assistant Restaurant
Development Manager

Ramona Singian
Marketing
Manager

FINANCE   MARKETING   PRODUCT   TRAINING   RESTAURANT
                                  DEVELOPMENT   DEVELOPMENT
                                  AND QUALITY
                                  ASSURANCE

OPERATIONS GROUP   **SUPPORT GROUP**

conferred important first-mover advantages in setting customer expectations, influencing tastes and building brand. He and others felt that Jollibee's success in the Philippines and Brunei illustrated this point especially well.

Others, particularly on Jollibee's domestic side, felt the flag-planting strategy was ill-conceived, leading the company into what they saw as rash market choices such as the Middle East, where outlets continued to have difficulty attracting either expatriates or locals. For example, Ernesto Tan advised Tingzon to "focus on expanding share in a few countries while making sure each store does well." He urged Tingzon to consolidate and build on existing Jollibee markets that had either high profit potential, such as Hong Kong, or relatively mild competition, such as Malaysia and Indonesia.

With respect to the strategy of initially focusing on Filipino expatriates in new markets, Tingzon appreciated that this approach had eased Jollibee's entry into Guam and Hong Kong, but wondered whether it might trap the chain. "Might we risk boxing ourselves into a Filipino niche that prevents us from growing enough to support operations in each country?" he asked. Again opinion was divided between those favoring the expatriate-led strategy and those who felt it was time for Jollibee to shake its Philippine identity and target the mainstream market wherever it went.

Strategy in Action: Three Decisions

Although he eventually wanted to resolve these issues at the level of policy, Tingzon faced three immediate growth opportunities that he knew would shape the emergence of the future strategy.

Papua New Guinea: Raising the standard In early 1996, at the recommendation of Quality Assurance Manager Gil Salvosa, a local New Guinea entrepreneur in the poultry business approached Tony Kitchner about a

Exhibit 10

Exhibit 10	International Store Sales by Country: 1996 (in U.S. dollars at contemporary exchange rates)

	1996 Sales	Number of Stores
Bahrain	262,361	1
Brunei	2,439,538	6
Guam	1,771,202	1
Hong Kong	1,142,240	2
Indonesia	854,259	3
Kuwait	864,531	3
Malaysia	391,328	1
Saudi Arabia	976,748	4
United Arab Emirates	487,438	2
Vietnam	112,578	1
Total	US$ 9,302,223	24

Jollibee franchise. He described a country of 5 million people served by only one poorly managed, three-store fast-food chain, that had recently broken ties with its Australian chicken restaurant franchise. "Port Moresby does not have a single decent place to eat," he told Kitchner. He believed Jollibee could raise the quality of service and food enough to take much of the Australian chain's market share while discouraging further entrants.

Although the original plan had been to open just one store in the foreseeable future—in the capital, Port Moresby—Tingzon was certain that the franchisee could only cover the costs of developing the market if he put in at least three or four stores soon after. But he was uncertain whether Papua New Guinea could support the 20 stores that he saw as the target critical mass for new markets. (For comparison, in the Philippines, approximately 1,200 fast food outlets competed for the business of 75 million people. GNP per capita in both countries was almost at US$2,500.)

When Tingzon explained his concerns, the would-be franchisee's response was that he would negotiate with a major petroleum retailer and try to open stores in five of their service stations around the country. Furthermore, he emphasized that he was willing to build more stores if necessary and would put up all the capital so that Jollibee would risk no equity in the venture.

Hong Kong: Expanding the base Also on Tingzon's plate was a proposal to expand to a fourth store in Hong Kong. The franchise, owned by Jollibee in partnership with local businessmen and managed by Tommy King, TTC's brother-in-law, opened its first store in September 1996 to instant, overwhelming success. Located near a major transit hub in the Central district, it became a gathering place for Filipino expatriates, primarily domestic workers. However, appealing to the locals had proven more difficult. While volume was high on weekends, when the Filipinos came to Central to socialize, it fell off during the week, when business was primarily from local office workers.

Although two more stores in Central had attracted many Filipinos, they both relied extensively on Chinese customers and generated sales of only about one-third of the first outlet. One problem was that, despite strenuous efforts, Jollibee had been unable to hire many local Chinese as crew members. According to one manager, Chinese customers who did not speak English well were worried that they would be embarrassed if they were not understood by the predominantly Philippine and Nepalese counter staff. Another problem was that in a city dominated by McDonald's, Jollibee's brand recognition among locals was weak. Working with Henry Shih, the sub-franchisee who owned the second store, Jollibee staff were trying to help launch a thematic advertising campaign, but due to the Hong Kong operation's small size, the franchise could not inject sufficient funds.

Shih also blamed rigidity over menu offerings for Jollibee's difficulties appealing to Chinese customers. In early 1997, his Chinese managers had suggested serving tea the Hong Kong way—using tea dust (powdered tea leaves) rather than tea bags and adding evaporated milk. More than six months later, he had still not received a go-ahead. His proposal to develop a less-fatty recipe for Chicken Joy, one of Jollibee's core menu items, had met more direct resistance. "The Chinese say that if you eat lots of deep-fried food you become hot inside and will develop health problems," said Shih who believed that the domestic side had pressured the International Division to reject any experimentation with this "core" menu item.

Meanwhile, staffing problems were worsening. The four locally-recruited Chinese managers clashed with the five Filipinos imported from Tommy King's Philippine franchise, with the Chinese calling the Filipinos' discipline lax and their style arrogant, while the Filipinos saw the Chinese managers as uncommitted. By August 1997, all of the Chinese managers had resigned, leaving Jollibee with only Filipinos in store-level management positions. Shih was afraid this would further undermine Jollibee's ability to hire local crews, as Chinese preferred to work for Chinese.

Partly due to staff turnover, store managers were focused on dealing with day-to-day operations issues such as uneven product quality and had little time to design even short-term marketing strategies. King's focus on his Philippine stores slowed decision-making. And while Gina Buan, the FSM, had visited Hong Kong more often than any other markets she supervised (including for an extraordinary month-long stay), she had been unable to resolve the management problems. In June, King appointed Shih General Manager to oversee the entire Hong Kong venture.

In this context, Shih and King proposed to open a fourth store. The site in the Kowloon district was one of the busiest in Hong Kong, located at one of just two intersections of the subway and the rail line that was the only public transport from the New Territories, where much of the city's workforce resided. However, the area saw far fewer Filipinos than Central and the store would have to depend on locals. Acknowledging that the fourth store would test Jollibee's ability to appeal to Hong Kong people, Shih argued that the menu would have to be customized more radically. However, Tingzon wondered whether expansion was even viable at this time, given the Hong Kong venture's managerial problems. Even if he were to approve the store, he wondered if he should support the menu variations that might complicate quality control. On the other hand, expansion into such a busy site might enhance Jollibee's visibility and brand recognition among locals, helping increase business even without changing the menu. It was another tough call.

California: Supporting the settlers Soon after signing his contract, Tingzon had learned of a year-old plan to open one Jollibee store per quarter in California starting in the first quarter of 1998. Supporting TTC's long-held belief that Jollibee could win enormous prestige and publicity by gaining a foothold in the birthplace of fast food, Kitchner had drawn up plans with a group of Manila-based businessmen as 40% partners in the venture. Once the company stores were established, they hoped to franchise in California and beyond in 1999.

Much of the confidence for this bold expansion plan came from Jollibee's success in Guam, a territory of the United States. Although they initially targeted the 25% of the population of Filipino extraction, management

discovered that their menu appealed to other groups of Americans based there. They also found they could adapt the labor-intensive Philippine operating methods by developing different equipment and cooking processes more in keeping with a high labor cost environment. In the words of one International Division veteran, "In Guam, we learned how to do business in the United States. After succeeding there, we felt we were ready for the mainland."

The plan called for the first store to be located in Daly City, a community with a large Filipino population but relatively low concentration of fast-food competitors in the San Francisco area. (With more than a million immigrants from the Philippines living in California, most relatively affluent, this state had one of the highest concentrations of Filipino expatriates in the world.) The menu would be transplanted from the Philippines without changes. After initially targeting Filipinos, the plan was to branch out geographically to the San Francisco and San Diego regions, and demographically to appeal to other Asian-American and, eventually, Hispanic-American consumers. The hope was that Jollibee would then expand to all consumers throughout the United States.

Like the expansion strategies in PNG and Hong Kong, this project had momentum behind it, including visible support from Filipino-Americans, strong interest of local investors, and, not least, TTC's great interest in succeeding in McDonald's back-yard. Yet Tingzon realized that he would be the one held accountable for its final success and wanted to bring an objective outsider's perspective to this plan before it became accepted wisdom. Could Jollibee hope to succeed in the world's most competitive fast-food market? Could they provide the necessary support and control to operations located 12 hours by plane and eight time zones away? And was the Filipino-to-Asian-to-Hispanic-to-mainstream entry strategy viable or did it risk boxing them into an economically unviable niche?

Looking Forward

Noli Tingzon had only been in his job a few weeks, but already it was clear that his predecessor's plan to open 1,000 Jollibee stores abroad before the turn of the century was a pipe dream. "It took McDonald's 20 years for its international operations to count for more than 50% of total sales," he said. "I'll be happy if I can do it in 10." But even this was an ambitious goal. And the decisions he made on the three entry options would have a significant impact on the strategic direction his international division took and on the organizational capabilities it needed to get there.

Harlequin Romances – Poland (A)

Nina Kowalewska, managing director of Arlekin Wydawnictwo (Arlekin), the wholly owned Polish subsidiary of Harlequin Enterprises Limited, sat at her Warsaw office in September 1992, reviewing the first year of operations. She was preparing for a meeting at Harlequin's European headquarters with Heinz Wermelinger, international executive vice president, and with Coen Abbenhuis and Ernst Boesch, regional directors for Europe. At the meeting, she intended to present a 1993 marketing plan and pro-forma income statement for Arlekin.

Harlequin Enterprises published romance fiction novels targeted at women. The novels were love stories in a wide variety of "girl meets boy" settings that aimed to offer women escape and entertainment. Launched in Poland in October 1991, Harlequin novels had, in just six months, captured 90% of the Polish romance series market and achieved market penetration levels comparable to those in North America. Kowalewska had played a key role in building Harlequin's popularity in Poland and now had to determine how best to maintain and develop further this success.

COMPANY BACKGROUND

Founded in 1949, Harlequin Enterprises Limited had evolved from a small Canadian printing house into the largest romance fiction publisher in the world. In 1991, Harlequin sold 193 million books, on six continents, in 20 languages. Harlequin held a 13% share of U.S. mass-market paperback sales and an even higher share in overseas markets. Harlequin had introduced and developed the mass-market romance series concept and pioneered the use of packaged consumer goods marketing techniques,

including branding, in book-selling. (Exhibit 1 summarizes key events in the company's development.)

The acquisition of the British publisher, Mills & Boon, in 1971 spurred Harlequin's international expansion. By 1991, 56% of unit sales came from outside North America, of which 86% came from Western Europe. The pace of Harlequin's new product launches had increased from eight new titles published each month in 1970 to 67 new titles each month in 1991. These new titles were published under 12 different series umbrellas, each with a distinct positioning and target audience.

Harlequin's parent company, Torstar Corporation, a large Canadian communications company with operating revenues of C\$ 895 million[1] in 1991, had experienced both revenue and profit declines since 1989. In 1991, Harlequin Enterprises Limited represented 40% of Torstar's revenues and 58% of its profits, with international sales, particularly in Japan, Australia, and Eastern Europe, fueling revenue and profit growth.

INDUSTRY CHARACTERISTICS AND PRODUCT LINE

The U.S. Book Publishing Industry[2]

Although 60% of the 91 million U.S. households did not buy a single book in 1991, an estimated 2 billion books were purchased by the other 40%; 62% of these were adult books, of which 66% were popular fiction books. Mass-market paperback books accounted for 63% of all adult books sold, and romance novels accounted for 46% of mass-market paperback sales. Bookstores accounted for 29.5% of romance novel sales, grocery and food stores for 23%, discount stores for 19%, drug stores for 11.5%, and department stores and direct mail for 8.5% each. Retail spending on romance novels in 1991 totaled $700 million,

This case was prepared by Professor John A. Quelch with the assistance Nathalie Laidler.

Copyright © 1993 by the President and Fellows of Harvard College. Harvard Business School case 9-594-017.

---

1 C\$1.14 = US \$1.

2 Some of the material in this section is adapted from the 1990/1991 Consumer Research Report on Book Purchasing prepared by the NPD Group, Inc., for The American Booksellers Association, The Association of American Publishers, and The Book Industry Study Group, Inc.

1949	Harlequin, a Canadian company, starts printing a wide variety of American and British books, ranging from mysteries and westerns to classics and cookbooks, written by authors such as Agatha Christie and Edgar Wallace.
1957	Harlequin begins buying the rights to romance novels from an English firm, Mills & Boon, the largest romance fiction publisher in the English-speaking world.
1964	Mills & Boon romances dominate Harlequin's product line.
1968	Harlequin issues a public stock offering in Canada.
1971	Harlequin purchases Mills & Boon and starts expanding internationally.
1972	Overseas acquisitions, partnerships, English-language export editions, and foreign licensee deals enhance Harlequin's international presence.
1973	Harlequin launches its North American direct mail operation, later expanded into the U.K., Australia, the Netherlands, France, and Scandinavia.
1981	Harlequin is purchased by Torstar Corporation, a large Canadian communications company.
1984	Harlequin purchases one of its major competitors, Silhouette, owned by Simon & Schuster.
1989	Harlequin celebrates its 40th anniversary by launching a novel in 18 languages in 100 countries on the same day.

27% more than in 1990, and was expected to increase by 37% in 1992. Although romance novels were often purchased on impulse, some devoted romance novel customers at Barnes and Noble (a large U.S. bookstore chain) were estimated to have spent $1,200 each on romance novels in 1991. For many publishers, the resilience of the romance segment provided much-needed cash during the 1991 recession.

Most publishers promoted books individually. Sales were hard to predict and returns to publishers of unsold books were permitted. While Harlequin had to compete with all mass-market paperback publishers, two forms of sales and marketing existed in the romance novel market:

publishing of individual "best-seller" romances, where success was dependent on the output and reputation of a particular author; and publishing and marketing series of romance novels as Harlequin did. Competitors included Zebra Books, Avon, Dell, and Berkley, which published both series and single titles, and combined, held a 20% share of the U.S. romance series market. Between 1990 and 1992, romance series sales stabilized while single-title, best-seller romances, such as novels by Danielle Steel, gained ground. Many U.S. publishers believed that this trend in favor of single titles that emphasized the author's name rather than the brand name of the publisher would continue.

Product Line

In 1991, Harlequin was one of the world's foremost publishers of paperback novels; 800 new titles were released and more than 6,600 foreign editions were published. The company attributed its success to its focus on romance fiction and the application of consumer packaged goods marketing principles to publishing. Marketing emphasized the Harlequin, Mills & Boon, or Silhouette brand names rather than each individual author or book title. By standardizing production and distribution methods across all titles, Harlequin achieved economies that translated into lower retail prices. Most titles retailed at US $2.95. In 1992, a Harlequin book was cheaper than many women's magazines.

Harlequin sold only paperbacks and published its books in 12 different series. Every month, each series published between two and eight new titles. The consumer could identify with the heroine, meet the hero of her dreams, travel the world, and revel in romance, all in two to four hours. Plots allowed many twists and surprises, but a satisfying ending was assured. In North America, eight series were published under the Harlequin brand: Superromance; American Romance; Temptation; Intrigue; Historicals; Regency; Romance; and Presents. Four series were published under the Silhouette brand:[3] Romance; Desire; Intimate Moments, and Special Editions. Harlequin U.K published three series under the Mills & Boon brand: Romance; Doctor/Nurse; and Masquerade/Historical. In addition to romances, Harlequin also offered an action adventure series, targeted at male consumers, and a mystery series, targeted at women who enjoyed clue/detective-oriented mysteries.

Each romance series targeted a specific type of reader. For example, Harlequin Temptation, a more sensual line, was aimed at younger women. Books within each series were all similar in appearance. For instance, Harlequin Presents books were classical romance stories that all had the same white cover, prominent logo and cover design with a circular inset. (Exhibit 2 illustrates some of Harlequin's North American book covers.) Regular monthly titles were complemented by special seasonal collections (for example, Christmas, Valentine, and Mother's Day editions), in-line promotions, and single titles.

Harlequin editors played an important role in segmenting the romance fiction market by differentiating each series according to length, level of sensuality, degree of realism, and setting. Editorial offices in London, New York, and Toronto worked with more than 1,200 established authors and, in addition, screened 14,000 unsolicited manuscripts received every year, about 30 of which were accepted for publication.

A new Harlequin book had a shelf life similar to a magazine. It might receive one month's shelf exposure before having to make room for one of the following month's releases. Unsold copies were returned by retailers. Harlequin return rates worldwide averaged 35% a month. While some returns were resold, most were shredded and destroyed. Returns were "a necessary evil"; a lower return rate would mean many retail outlets stocking a book would run out of it, resulting in lost sales for Harlequin.

Consumers

Harlequin defined its target segment as all women over the age of 15 years. In North America, this represented a market of 105 million consumers. In 1991, 11 million women in North America bought at least one Harlequin and/or Silhouette novel. A 1989 study found that 56% of women had purchased a paperback book in the previous three months, 27% had purchased a romance novel, 13% had purchased a Harlequin, and 9% had purchased a Silhouette. In a similar 1985 study, the corresponding figures were 60%, 28%, 13%, and 10%. (Exhibit 3 reports other findings of this study.) Respondents to the 1989 survey were found to be reading less than in 1985, but a higher proportion of them were reading romance fiction.

The average romance novel reader was aged 39 years, with a household income of $40,000. Forty-five percent were college graduates, and over 50% worked outside the home. Harlequin and Silhouette readers stated that relaxation, entertainment, and escape were the main reasons for purchase. Research indicated that women, many of whom worked both inside and outside the home, had less leisure time and that the "escape" offered by romance novels helped counteract the pressures they felt.

HARLEQUIN'S NORTH AMERICAN MARKETING PROGRAM

Distribution

Harlequin novels were sold in over 100,000 retail outlets in the U.S and 10,000 outlets in Canada. Harlequin

---

3 Harlequin had purchased Silhouette, its major North American competitor, in 1984.

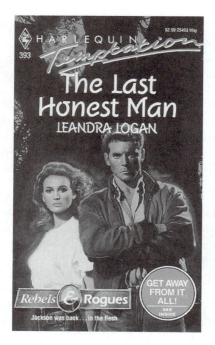

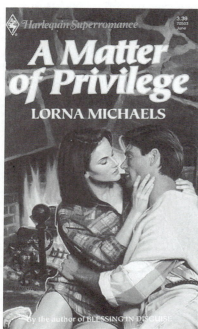

- In 1989, 69% of women had read a paperback in the preceding year compared with 73% in 1985. Of these readers, 58% in 1989 reported having read a romance paperback compared to 56% in 1985.

- The Harlequin brand had a 77% aided brand awareness in 1989 compared to a 90% aided brand awareness in 1985. Silhouette aided brand awareness was 45% in 1989 and 56% in 1985. Corresponding unaided brand awareness figures were 27% in 1989 and 35% in 1985 for Harlequin and 5% in 1989 and 9% in 1985 for Silhouette.

- In 1989, 64% of respondents had read at least one Harlequin novel and 31% had read at least one Silhouette novel.

- Among women who read Harlequin and Silhouette books, 85% and 79%, respectively, had been reading them for over two years.

- Among women who had purchased a romance novel in the previous three months, 28% had purchased from bookstores, 27% from grocery and food stores, 22% from discount and general merchandise stores, 15% from drug stores, 12% from department stores, and 12% through direct mail. For purchasers of Harlequin and Silhouette books, the channel mix was slightly different: 31% had purchased them from grocery and food stores, 26% from bookstores, 19% from discount and general merchandise stores, 19% from drug stores, and 15% through direct mail.

- Among Harlequin purchasers, 37% bought "what looked interesting, regardless of series or publisher," 21% planned the purchase as part of the weekly shopping trip, and 20% bought a Harlequin because the product "caught my eye."

- Women read Harlequin and Silhouette novels for the following reasons, in order of importance: good, relaxing read; good entertainment value; "leaves you feeling happy and uplifted"; exciting to read; for escape reading; "for someone like me."

- Harlequin readers spent relatively more time than nonreaders reading books in general, browsing in shopping malls, and watching videos and television movies, and relatively less time participating in active sports, attending plays and cultural events.

Source: Company records

Note: The 1989 survey was based on telephone interviews with 1,500 women aged over 15 years.

maintained its own sales force in Canada and was represented by Simon & Schuster Consumer Group in the United States. Harlequin placed wholesalers (accounting for approximately two-thirds of sales) and direct retail accounts on a monthly standing order system, whereby they received previously agreed-upon volumes of the 12 series each month. This reduced the need for the continuous selling of single titles.

The distribution process was constantly streamlined. Books were shrink-wrapped in various combinations of pre-packs, with dates on front covers to help consumers and retailers identify new titles at a glance. Books also carried bar codes that enabled books to be scanned at the point-of-sale for specific title and price information. In the 1970s, Harlequin North America began distributing its books through food, drug, and discount stores. By 1991, these channels accounted for the majority of Harlequin's retail sales, as they did for mass-market paperbacks in general.

Harlequin operated a direct mail system, distributing titles under the Harlequin, Silhouette, Worldwide Mystery, and Gold Eagle names. It provided advance home delivery sales of new titles to an estimated 250,000 readers.

Harlequin executives believed that, as consumers became more familiar with the Harlequin product line, they tended to settle on one or two specific series, and the added convenience of receiving books by mail became increasingly attractive.

Advertising and Promotion

Harlequin enjoyed high name recognition and a consistent image. However, in 1989, unaided brand awareness for Harlequin in the U.S. was 77%, down from 90% in 1985. Harlequin in North America planned a major advertising campaign to combat the decline in awareness.

In 1991, Harlequin spent US $8 million on advertising and promotion in North America. Harlequin's campaigns promoted an entire line rather than a single title.

In 1991, Harlequin focused its marketing budget on print advertising, consumer promotions, retail displays, and point-of-sale merchandising materials.

In 1975, Harlequin became the first publisher to use television advertising in North America. In 1991, television and radio advertising were not used, but extensive women's press advertising was employed to build awareness and encourage trial. (Exhibit 4 shows a two-page Harlequin advertisement from *People* magazine in 1992.) In addition, trade press advertising was used to keep booksellers up to date on new titles and series.

Consumer promotions focused on sampling non-readers. Sixteen-page samplers were inserted in women's magazines and complemented by money-off coupons. Best-selling authors held media tours and autographing

---

Exhibit 4   Two-Page North American Harlequin Print Advertisement from People Magazine, 1992

events, and the most dedicated readers were thanked for their support at lavish parties. Sales promotions, used to increase awareness and trial of Harlequin books, included (1) in-book and in-store promotions that encouraged cross-series sampling by offering gifts in return for multiple proofs-of-purchase; (2) in-line promotions with mini-series featuring special themes;[4] and (3) joint promotions with other firms selling perfume, cosmetics, lingerie, and confectionery. In 1991, a consumer sweepstakes under the banner "Fashion A Whole New You" offered prizes such as cars, trips, and fashion wardrobes. In addition, consumer competitions with books as prizes often ran in local media.

Harlequin offered retailers display racks to accompany standing orders. These ranged from spinners, wire racks, and wooden shelf systems, to cardboard bins in which promotional titles were displayed.[5] Colorful shelf stickers and window posters were also distributed to retailers. Trade promotions were usually linked to consumer promotions and often included prize drawings for store personnel.

Challenges

In North America, Harlequin faced several challenges in 1992. Unit sales of "best-sellers" were growing faster than expected, eroding Harlequin's share of the mass-market paperback category. Price increases to offset cost increases could protect profit margins but at the expense of demand. Management was concerned that Harlequin's image among consumers and retailers as the clear innovator in the series romance sub-category might be eroding. In response, Harlequin planned several new product launches along with changes in advertising and packaging.

INTERNATIONAL OPERATIONS

In 1991, Harlequin's international sales outside North America, including sales by licensees, exceeded 108 million units and generated net revenues of US $140 million. Overseas operations consisted of wholly owned subsidiaries in the United Kingdom, Australia and the Far East, Holland, Scandinavia, Japan, Spain, and Poland; joint ventures in Germany, France, Greece, Italy, and Hungary; and licensing of local publishers to publish in their native languages, in return for royalty payments, in Denmark,

Iceland, South America, and Korea. Harlequin subsidiaries and joint ventures were delineated primarily on a linguistic rather than geographical basis. For example, Axel Springer, Harlequin's German joint venture partner, had the rights to sell to the German-speaking populations of Switzerland and Austria as well as in Germany.

Once a book had been published in the U.K. or North America, it became available to the entire Harlequin network. Finished books were distributed to overseas editors who chose which titles to reprint, often combining editorial products from two or more series to create ideal blends for their particular markets. Their selections were then locally translated, edited, and printed. Cover illustrations were commissioned in Toronto and London for all titles and held on file at Harlequin's European headquarters for local editors to access as needed. Series names were decided locally, and editors either borrowed from existing series or created entirely new titles to suit their local markets. For example, the Mills & Boon Romance series was known in different countries as Sabrina, Julia, Romantikkaa, Azur, Jazmin, Bianca, and Safir. Most overseas operations released a given month's title between eight months and a year after North America or the United Kingdom. To illustrate the level of local adaptation, Exhibit 5 shows the North American, Polish, and Hungarian front covers of the same title.

Eastern Europe

In 1990, Harlequin's European Headquarters were established in Baar, Switzerland, by Heinz Wermelinger, who had previously managed European operations from Toronto, Canada. The need for a European office was fueled by flattening demand in Western Europe, management's interest in adding better direct mail operations, and the opening of the Eastern European economies, which greatly expanded the potential market for Harlequin novels. Harlequin was flooded by requests for licenses and joint ventures from publishers and private entrepreneurs in Eastern and Central Europe.

Within four months of the fall of the Berlin Wall in October 1989, Harlequin books, under the brand name Cora, were for sale on newsstands throughout the former East Germany. Harlequin's German joint venture partner, Axel Springer, simply increased production runs to meet the new demand from the former East Germany. In

---

4 In 1992, for example, a 12-title series was launched in the European Community with one title set in each member country.
5 Spinners were stand-alone rotating display racks.

April 1990, a Hungarian licensee launched Harlequin and, by September 1992, Harlequin was firmly established in both Hungary and Poland, with plans to launch in Czechoslovakia and Bulgaria later that year. Harlequin executives estimated that in 1995, they would sell 35 million books in Eastern Europe.

Decision making was shared between the local managing directors of these country subsidiaries and the Baar executives. The local knowledge and contacts of the former combined with the operational, technical, and historical experience of the latter, made these working relationships particularly effective. Back room operations, including standardized financial control systems, were run from Baar, which also shared experience, information, and ideas among subsidiaries.

Hungary

After initially licensing a local entrepreneur, Harlequin established a joint venture in Hungary in July 1991 to further penetrate the market. Harlequin expanded elsewhere in Eastern Europe through wholly owned subsidiaries.

In 1992, Hungary had a population of 11 million, a gross domestic product (GDP) per capita of $4,186, and an inflation rate of 25%. A Harlequin novel retailed for $0.85. Although Harlequin dominated the romance series market in September 1992, new competitors continued to appear. Cumulative sales had reached 8 million books by September 1992, with six titles issued per month and average book returns of 25%.

Distribution of Harlequin books in Hungary was carried out by the Post Office. Three thousand of the country's kiosks, the traditional retail outlets for newspapers and magazines, were privatized in 1992, while 6,000 remained under Post Office control. To use Post Office distribution, the Harlequin product had to be 8 inches by 5.8 inches in size—larger than a standard paperback and more like a magazine. This magazine format precluded Harlequin novels from being distributed in bookstores. Harlequin executives wanted to convert the product line to a standard paperback format but this might jeopardize Post Office distribution.

Despite frequent television commercials that explained the product and informed viewers of new titles, brand awareness remained modest. *Julia*, however, the main series name, had unaided brand awareness of 75% among adult women. The Harlequin brand name was placed on book covers after July 1992.

Harlequin executives believed that further growth depended on more intensive distribution. Two supermarket chains, with 830 stores, could be supplied by the current Post Office distribution system. The challenge was to convince them to stock the Harlequin line.

POLAND

Country Background

In 1992, Poland had a GDP per capita of $2,945 and an inflation rate of 45%. The population was 38 million, of whom 55% were women and 62% lived in urban areas.

Prior to 1989, Poland had suffered from persistent shortages of goods. A centrally planned economy, accompanied by price controls and limited hard currency convertibility, resulted in a market where goods were affordable but in short supply. As a result, even goods of inferior quality could find a market. In 1989, dramatic economic reforms, including the elimination of price controls, reductions in state subsidies, and free convertibility of the Polish zloty, were implemented to stimulate the private sector.[6] The country began moving rapidly toward a market economy, and a large market for foreign goods opened up. However, the transition was painful and characterized by high inflation, lack of financial resources, frustration and a "black-market" mentality. A common complaint was, "Before, there was nothing to buy. Now you can buy anything but nobody has the money to do so."

The Book Industry

Prior to 1989, under the Communist regime, all production and distribution of printed matter in Poland was centrally controlled. Every stage of book publishing and retailing was managed by a state monopoly. All 60 publishing houses, printing plants, and distributors were subsidized by the state, and only one advertising agency, also state-owned, existed.

Poland was a country with a strong literary tradition. However, censorship meant most people read "safe," classical literature. For 40 years, no new romance novels had been published legally in Poland. Due to subsidies, books were cheap and public libraries were supplied free-of-charge by all publishers. Authorized publishers (as opposed

---

6 In September 1992, U.S.$1 = 13,800 zlotys.

to black-market operators) would send their print runs to Skladnica Ksiegarska, the state controlled book distributor, which would, in turn, sell the books to 18 wholesalers who supplied all retail bookstores. However, by 1992, two of every five books published in Poland were shipped directly from publisher to retailer. Dozens of sidewalk vendors emerged as a growing retail channel, particularly for best-sellers. As the industry fragmented, distribution became a key challenge; publishers had to somehow inform the myriad of wholesalers and retailers about the publication and availability of each new title.

Economic restructuring in Poland impacted the book industry. Between 1989 and 1992, average book prices increased three to five times. With monthly interest rates of 12% in mid-1992, booksellers wanted to stock only books that sold out quickly. One result was an increase in the distribution of pornography and scandal stories at the expense of serious literature. As one industry expert said: "Poland no longer has money for culture." The demise of Communism created a strong demand for new books from the West, especially political fiction novels, followed by suspense novels, romances, and general-interest titles such as cookery books. For some Poles, Western novels held an appeal for that reason alone. However, Polish intellectuals dismissed many of these books as "Western trash." In addition, many Polish consumers associated reading with learning and perceived popular literature as a waste of time. "We still have to convince people that reading can be fun," stated Arlekin's editor-in-chief. "Reading is increasingly competing with watching videos and cable television."

Consumers

In 1992, there were 15 million women in Poland over the age of 15 years; 8.4% of them had college degrees, and a majority of the rest had completed high school. Eighty-five percent of adult Polish women worked outside the home and were responsible for a second source of household income as well as for household management. Given an average salary in mid-1992 of only 2.7 million zlotys a month, few women could afford modern household appliances to help them with their chores. At the same time, benefits such as day care and maternity leave had declined since the fall of Communism.

HARLEQUIN IN POLAND

In preparing to enter the Polish market, Harlequin Baar executives sought to appoint a strong local manager who could develop a team that would work in tandem with the European headquarters. Kowalewska was appointed managing director of Arlekin in August 1991. Previously, she had managed distribution of *The Financial Times* in Poland. Kowalewska then chose her own team of four editors and operating staff.

By September 1992, Arlekin was the largest foreign publishing company in Poland. Arlekin's cumulative sales in Poland had exceeded 10 million units, and 168 titles had been released. (Average monthly sales by product line are reported in Exhibit 6.) Kowalewska attributed Arlekin's success in part to a common message in every novel: "The heroines are always active women who succeed and win. They offer positive role models to our readers." The impact was evident in consumer correspondence. In the first eight months of 1992, Arlekin received over 20,000 letters, all of which were answered. To many Polish consumers, Arlekin was already more than just another company.

Exhibit 6   Arlekin Average Monthly Unit Sales: January–August 1992

Product Line	Average Monthly Gross Unit Sales
Romance	550,000
Desire	400,000
Temptation	95,000
Superromance	75,000
Valentine special[a]	90,000
Best-sellers	100,000
Summer specials[a]	45,000

Source: Company records

[a]Sales of these two categories are annual volume sales since they are published only once a year.

Note: These figures are not net of returns. During its first three months in distribution, Arlekin had no returns. In 1992, returns increased substantially to almost 30%.

In the fourth quarter of 1991, Arlekin generated a margin of 5% after marketing expenses. This margin rose to 11% during 1992. (Exhibit 7 summarizes Arlekin's income statements for the last three months of 1991 and for 1992, estimated as of September.)

Exhibit 7   Arlekin Pro Forma Income Statements: 1991 and 1992

	1991	1992E
Net units shipped ('000s)	2,500	10,200
Average retail cover price (zlotys)	10,000	15,000
Net revenue (millions zlotys)	15,600	95,000
Cost of goods[a]	10,200	53,000
Gross margin	5,400	42,000
Advertising and promotion	3,500	25,000
Selling, general & administrative overhead[b]	1,100	6,500
Operating margin	800	10,500

[a]Includes printing costs (75%), distribution costs (17%) and royalties (8%).

[b]Includes translation costs.

Source: Company records

The Product Line

Initial print runs were 50,000 copies per title per month, increasing, by September 1992, to between 75,000 and 150,000 copies per title per month, depending on series popularity. Arlekin had no warehouse capacity of its own; books were shipped from the printer directly to distributors' warehouses.

The initial product line was selected by the New York and Toronto editorial staffs who chose classical, successful, and representative titles. In October 1991, Harlequin entered the Polish market with a highly publicized launch of eight titles—four from the Romance and Presents lines, and four from Silhouette's Desire line, a somewhat more sensual series. This launch represented a "critical mass" of titles that permitted the promotion of multiple unit purchases and established a base on which to later build direct sales. Translation and editing were done by Arlekin.

A Polish cover design, promoting the Harlequin brand name and logo, was created to stimulate impulse purchases. Each series had a different background cover color: Romance was white, and Desire was red. The covers included the Joey Harlequin logo; the Harlequin brand name (the largest element on the cover); the name of the series; the title; and the author's name. Standard Harlequin artwork, featuring a realistic painting, also appeared on each cover, whereas Harlequin's Polish competitors used photographs on their covers. The English series names were retained to capitalize on the product's Western origin. Titles were translated.

Following the launch, additional product series were chosen by Baar executives and individual titles selected by Arlekin. Fifteen Polish volunteer readers rated existing Harlequin novels and determined which should be translated for the Polish market. Translations were subcontracted, took approximately two months, and cost 25 million zlotys per book. Four Arlekin editors and eight proofreaders checked translations for language and style. Kowalewska was determined that the product be of the highest possible quality and stated: "You may not like the genre, but, within this market, we are the best. Our books contain no mistakes; they are perfect."

In May 1992, Harlequin moved from 8 to 14 titles per month and from two to four series. (Exhibit 8 shows sample covers for a novel in each of the four series.) The Romance line was extended to six titles, while the Superromance series was introduced with one title and the Temptation series with two titles. The basic product line was also supplemented each month by best-seller and seasonal publications (for Christmas and Valentine's Day, for example). Best-sellers, such as Penny Jordan's *Power Play*, carried the Harlequin name only on the back cover. Book cover color coding was retained, and consumers often referred to their preferred series by color rather then by name. The cover artwork further distinguished each series. For example, the Romance novels' artwork was always placed in a circle, while the Superromance novels' artwork was always in an oval. Superromance novels were twice as long as the other series and double the price.

Exhibit 8 Sample Covers for Novels in Each of the Four Polish Series

Arlekin planned to introduce three new series in 1993: (1) an upscale Silhouette line; (2) an Intrigue line that would be a combination of mystery/paranormal with romance; and (3) a medical setting series. Existing lines would be expanded further to include each month eight titles in the Romance series, four in the Temptation series, six in the Desire series, and one best-seller title. As the product line expanded, Arlekin believed that many women would start choosing a single series rather than reading titles from multiple series as they still did in September 1992. The best-sellers had been especially successful; they were purchased by a broader audience beyond committed Harlequin readers and were not, therefore, thought to cannibalize sales of Harlequin series novels.

Distribution

Initially, Harlequin decided to distribute its novels through two channels: the formerly state-controlled magazine and press distribution channel, run by Ruch; and the book distribution channel, dominated by Skladnica Ksiegarska. During 1991, each accounted for 50% of Harlequin sales. By September 1992, Arlekin also sold to private distributors and directly to the largest Polish bookstore chain. Kowalewska believed that high visibility and availability were necessary to stimulate purchases of Harlequin novels. Distributors and retailers had to be educated on the importance of timely display of monthly publications and on the management of returns.

Ruch, the established distributor for newspapers and magazines in Poland, operated 49 regional warehouses and, by September 1992, distributed 80% of all Harlequin novels sold in Poland to a network of 22,000 kiosks. About 12,000 of these had recently been privatized, and the new owners were seeking to increase profits by expanding the range of goods they carried. Ruch earned a retail margin of 30% on Harlequin novels, of which 2% went to the company-owned kiosk operators. To motivate the privatized kiosk operators required an extra 5% margin. However, many independent, privatized kiosks obtained Harlequin novels not from Ruch but from independent distributors, earned higher margins, and then returned unsold Harlequin product through Ruch.

Because Skladnica Ksiegarska, Poland's largest state-owned wholesale book distributor, went bankrupt in 1992, Arlekin decided to sell direct to Poland's largest bookstore chain, Dom Skiazki (The House of the Book) with 660 stores throughout the country. This chain represented 5% of Arlekin's sales and earned a retail margin of 35%.

Fifteen percent of Harlequin sales were made through five private distributors that, together, served 3,000 to 5,000 private bookstores. The distributors earned a margin of 10% to 15%, while the bookstores earned 20% to 25%. These distributors did not yet fully understand the rationale for Harlequin's returns policy and therefore did not always comply with it.[7] In addition, they were thought likely to shift quickly to distributing other products if they became more profitable than books. Other "serious" book distributors regarded Harlequin products as frivolous and declined to carry them.

Arlekin enjoyed a competitive advantage due to its strong retail distribution. "We have an image of a solid, reliable company and we can get our books stocked by the trade because we do not request cash up front," explained Kowalewska. Arlekin believed that distribution costs would increase as more publishers sought to push their products through the established channels. Arlekin was therefore exploring two other distribution options in September 1992:

Post Office The Post Office served as a savings bank for many Polish consumers due to the underdevelopment of the banking sector. In September 1992, Arlekin began testing the use of post offices as retail outlets on a six-month trial basis. The central Post Office warehouse would be supplied each month with 16,000 copies of each title. After one month, Harlequin novels were available in 2,000 out of 8,000 post offices. The Post Office earned a retail margin of 30% on Arlekin sales.

Subscription Arlekin was considering offering consumers quarterly pay-in-advance subscriptions to receive Harlequin novels. The subscription plan would target rural consumers who had difficulty finding the product and current Harlequin readers. Subscription applications would be placed in magazines and inside the back covers of Harlequin novels. In addition, invitations to join the subscription service would be mailed to 60,000 consumers that had responded to Arlekin promotional competitions and questionnaires. Administration of the subscription program could be subcontracted to a large Polish magazine publisher who serviced 1 million subscribers each month. Arlekin was hoping to register 30,000 to 40,000 subscribers by the end of 1992, increasing to 100,000 by the end of 1993. After the costs

---

7 Returns were supposed to be destroyed but some found their way back to retail outlets, especially independent kiosk operators.

of postage and handling, Kowalewska expected initial margins to be comparable or slightly lower than on retail sales. She wanted to establish the direct sales channel as soon as possible since she believed that sales through this channel would eventually improve margins for the company.

Competition

In October 1991, Arlekin's two main competitors were Amber and Phantom Press. Both were private Polish companies publishing a variety of paperback best-sellers in the areas of suspense, crime, and romance. Phantom Press published two titles per month in four romance series, including translations of the Bantam series, Loveswept. Amber concentrated on best-sellers, but Kowalewska considered its translations to be of poorer quality. Both companies were, by origin, printers rather than publishers and their print runs averaged 150,000 copies per title in October 1991.

Alfa, a Polish company which had published unauthorized translations of Harlequin novels prior to Harlequin's entry, was sued in 1992 and exited the market. Another local company, Aramis, which entered the market in March 1992 with the same "Garden of Love" slogan that Arlekin used and similar book covers and typeface, was threatened with litigation and subsequently changed its marketing approach. (Table A summarizes competitor market shares between September 1991 and September 1992.) Competitors' average print runs for new titles had declined significantly and their return rates were reportedly as high as 85%.

In September 1992, the market was still growing and more new entrants were rumored. Some publishers regarded romance novels as an easy market in which to score quick sales because Arlekin had promoted the genre so successfully through its own heavy advertising.

After three months, Arlekin ceased its special promotion, allowing a retail price per unit of 15,000 zlotys to take effect on January 1, 1992. By September 1992, the principal competitive products were all retailing at 15,000 to 16,000 zlotys. Arlekin intended to hold its price at 15,000 zlotys until at least the end of the year despite increases in production costs. Kowalewska explained her pricing policy: "Our consumers need to feel that they can depend on Harlequin. Prices on everything else are so volatile that holding the price of a Harlequin novel constant goes a long way to creating loyalty among our consumers."

Promotion and Advertising

Prior to 1989, advertising in Poland was rare, and many consumers suspected that an advertised product was inferior to one selling without advertising. However, by 1992, television and radio commercials and print advertisements were widespread and accepted.

The Harlequin product line was launched as offering escape for women, with the slogan "Escape into the world of Dreams . . . Harlequin books are a garden of love." Harlequin consumer research indicated that romance novels were read most often in three situations: during travel; before going to sleep; and during vacations. Thus, three television commercials were created for the launch, one for each usage situation. The commercials opened with a monochromatic picture of a young woman, on a tram, lying next to a sleeping husband, or sitting alone at a cafe table. The woman's expression was slightly melancholic, a man's voice whispered, "Escape into the world of dreams. . . ." At this point the scene changed and full color was restored; the woman was seen traveling in a limousine, in a luxury bedroom, or on a yacht, each time accompanied by a handsome man. The commercial ended with the man's voice stating, "Harlequin is a garden of love." Kowalewska explained the objective of the commercials: "We wanted to show an average woman, tired and grey, who was transformed by the books into a happy, beautiful woman, adored by a wonderful man." During the launch the television commercials were aired three times a day in 10-day cycles with 10 days off between cycles. The television campaign cost 2.3 billion zlotys in the first three months.

In addition to the television commercials, Arlekin held press receptions and ran advertisements, based on

Table A	Arlekin and Competitor Market Shares		
	Sept. 1991	Jan. 1992	Sept. 1992
Harlequin	0%	50%	90%
Phantom Press	50%	30%	5%
Alfa	30%	0%	0%
Amber	10%	5%	3%
Others (including Aramis)	10%	15%	2%

the television commercials and book cover art work, both on radio stations (six exposures a day in 10-day cycles with 10 days off between cycles) and in all major women's magazines. Exhibit 9 reproduces a print advertisement, based on one of the television commercials used during the launch. Exhibit 10 reproduces a later print advertisement, based on book-cover art work, used in response to competition from Aramis. During the first three months following the launch, magazine advertising expenditures were 300 million zlotys.

Trade promotions during the first three months following the launch included free display racks to retail outlets to increase the product's accessibility and visibility. (Display racks used in bookstores and street kiosks are illustrated in Exhibit 11.)

Arlekin quickly achieved high brand awareness. Kowalewska believed the appeal of Western products for their own sake would be short-lived so she was determined that consumers perceive Arlekin as a Polish company, selling an international product. In 1992, Arlekin budgeted 25 billion zlotys for advertising and promotion, allocated as shown in Exhibit 12.

Following the launch, Arlekin developed eleven 10-second television spots to serve as "reminders." During 1992, Arlekin aired 50 spots per month on the two national television channels and sponsored Polish reruns of American television programs such as *Dynasty* and *Bill Cosby*, as well as local programs and talk shows. As a result of media price increases, Kowalewska planned to reduce the frequency of television spots. Radio commercials were also run three times a day, for two ten-day periods a month, on both Polish national radio and three private local radio stations. In addition, a Harlequin Club radio talk show was aired twice a month, during which women discussed their personal problems.

Full-page Harlequin advertisements appeared on the back covers of women's magazines. After Aramis attempted to use the slogan "Garden of Love," Arlekin responded with "There are many romances but only one true love, Harlequin." In September 1992, Arlekin was planning its first test of outdoor advertising, placing posters of book cover artwork in bus shelters throughout central Warsaw. Arlekin also planned to publish a "letter to consumers" in a print advertisement that would describe Arlekin's charitable donations to a children's hospital. Arlekin gave to charity, sponsoring cultural events, donating to hospitals and financing student scholarships. As a result, Arlekin enjoyed excellent media coverage.

Special events were an increasingly important element in Arlekin's communication strategy, especially as media advertising costs escalated. These included the creation and celebration of Valentine's Day in Poland in 1992, accompanied by special commercials and publicity stunts, such as the hanging of a huge heart from the top of the Palace of Culture (the largest and oldest building in central Warsaw) and Kowalewska's televised "speech to the nation," an infomercial in which she described both Harlequin products and the Arlekin company. In 1992, Arlekin also held its first "Readers Party," at which 100 randomly selected readers were invited to draw prizes, and a celebrity cocktail party when Arlekin's cumulative sales in Poland passed 1 million units. Kowalewska explained her strategy for deciding which special events to promote: "We want to be the experts on love. We want to be called upon to judge the best love songs and the beauty contests."

In developing her proposed 1993 communication plan, Kowalewska was especially concerned about how to overcome the prejudices of some Polish consumers against the romance genre and convince them to reach for a Harlequin novel. Some executives felt that the artwork in Arlekin advertising was incompatible with the images found in the more sophisticated, fashion magazines that appealed to some non-Harlequin readers. A new series of magazine print advertisements was developed to reach these consumers. (See Exhibit 13 for a sample proposed print advertisement.) The first ad showed a black-and-white modern photograph of a young boy with the headline "I can't recognize my mother." This would be followed the next month by a similar photograph of a middle-aged man with the caption "I can't recognize my wife." The third ad in the series would show a photograph of the same woman with a dreamy expression, holding a Harlequin novel in her arms. Kowalewska wondered whether the proposed advertising would, in fact, appeal to current nonreaders and whether it would confuse or alienate current readers.

Consumer Research

Three months after the launch, a questionnaire was placed inside the back covers of Harlequin books. The resulting 10,000 responses gave Arlekin the following consumer profile information:

- 39% of readers were younger than 19, 30% were between 19 and 26 years, 25% were 27 to 40 years, and 6% were older than 40.

Exhibit 9

Arlekin Print Advertisement: "Don't waste time! Every month, Harlequin offers you 8 new, fascinating stories about great love! With two series. Ask for them in bookstores and Ruch kiosks."

Exhibit 11   Harlequin Retail Display Racks In Poland

1. A Harlequin free-standing book display rack in the corner of a Polish bookstore. The rack displays only Harlequin novels.
2. A Harlequin flat shelf book display rack in a street vendor book-stall. The rack displays a variety of non-Harlequin books.

	1991 (3 months)	1992 (8 months)
Advertising:		
Television commercials	60%	50%
Radio commercials	4%	8%
Women's magazine advertising	7%	4%
Production costs	15%	4%
Promotions:		
Point-of-sale displays	8%	2%
-racks, plastic bags, stickers		
Promotional incentives	5%	5%
-cocktail parties, competitions		
Market research	1%	2%
Other/Reserve[a]		25%

Source: Company records

[a]Includes percentage of the budget that had not, as of September 1992, been used. The mix of expenditures would be similar to that during the first eight months.

- 67% lived in cities and towns.
- 52% purchased Harlequin novels in bookstores and 56% from "Ruch" kiosks.

A further market research study was conducted in June 1992 with 660 Polish women aged 15 and above. The purpose was to explore familiarity with and readership patterns for Harlequin books. Results are summarized in Exhibit 14.

Consumer panels were conducted in September 1992 to profile Harlequin readers and Harlequin nonreaders. Nonreaders expressed contempt for the romance genre and described Harlequin television commercials as unrealistic, difficult to relate to, and targeted at teenagers. Some nonreaders suggested that Harlequin novels should include suspense and horror series, others that the commercials should be more humorous. Many of these nonreaders had, however, either read or were interested in reading best-sellers such as novels by the author Penny Jordan. Harlequin novels were read as time fillers and as a means of escape. Committed users were emotionally attached to Harlequin and did not want the product changed in any way. There was, however, little attachment to a particular series; avid readers not only read all Harlequin novels but also read competitors' books. What nonreaders considered unrealistic and in poor taste, readers considered beautiful, particularly the book cover artwork. Readers could be divided into three categories: those that bought and collected the product; those that read the product but borrowed it rather than bought it; those that bought some but not all of the products they read and exchanged these with friends. A majority of readers stated that 10 titles published each month was sufficient and that they would purchase more books more often if the unit price was lower.

Challenges for 1993

By September 1992, Harlequin had sold over 10 million books but to fewer than 2 million consumers. To increase sales revenues in 1993, Kowalewska could raise unit prices, sell more books to current purchasers, and/or attract new purchasers and readers. As she prepared a 1993 marketing plan to present to Harlequin Baar executives, Kowalewska was considering how to adjust to the evolving distribution channels in Poland, whether to proceed with a subscription service, and whether to launch a new advertising campaign. She also wondered what additional consumer research and marketplace information she should gather to decide these issues.

Exhibit 14   Harlequin Market Research in Poland: June 1992

- 37% of respondents were not familiar with Harlequin books (but more than half of these were over 58 years); 39% were familiar with them but had never read them; 8% had read one or a few Harlequin books but no longer did so; 11% claimed to read Harlequin books; 69% of Harlequin readers had been reading the novels for over six months.

- 40% of respondents did not read books at all. Reasons given included lack of time (28%); inability to afford books (20%); lack of interest in reading (15%); and poor health/eyesight (9%).

- Among respondents who did not read Harlequin books, 46% did not read romance novels; 22% could not afford the books; 22% did not have the time; and 10% read competitive products.

- Among Harlequin readers, 35% bought the books themselves; 46% borrowed them from friends; 13% received them from relatives; and 7% borrowed them from the library.

- Respondents who read Harlequin books were influenced by family and friends (38%); bookstores and newsstand displays (15%); and television commercials (29%).

- 64% of Harlequin readers passed their books on to others once they had read them, while 26% collected them.

Source: Company records

Gillette Indonesia

In October 1995, Chester Allan, Gillette's country manager in Indonesia, was developing his unit's 1996 marketing plan. Once completed, it would be forwarded to Rigoberto Effio, business director in Gillette's Asia-Pacific group based in Singapore. Each year Effio received and approved marketing plans for the 12 countries in his region, which reached from Australia to China. Once approved by Ian Jackson, Asia-Pacific group vice president, the overall marketing plan for the region would be reviewed subsequently, along with other regional plans, by Robert King, executive vice president of Gillette's International Group.

Allan's plan projected a 19% increase in blade sales in Indonesia in 1996 from 115 million to 136 million. This seemed reasonable given a 17% increase in 1995 over the previous year. With a population of almost 200 million, Indonesia represented an important country in the portfolio of markets for which Effio and Jackson were responsible. Effio wondered whether investment spending in marketing beyond the 1995 level of 12% of sales might further accelerate market development. Given the growth rates of Gillette's business in other Asia-Pacific countries, Effio believed that a 25%-30% increase in blade sales could be achieved in Indonesia in 1996.

The Company

Founded in 1901, Boston-based Gillette was the world leader in blades and razors and in nine other consumer product categories—writing instruments (Paper Mate, Parker, and Waterman), correction products (Liquid Paper), men's electric razors (Braun), toothbrushes (Oral-B), shaving preparations, oral care appliances (Braun, Oral-B plaque remover), pistol-grip hair dryers (Braun), hair epilators (Braun), and hand blenders (Braun).

Gillette manufacturing operations were conducted at 50 facilities in 24 countries. A London office had been opened

This case was prepared by Professor John A. Quelch with the assistance of Diane E. Long. Copyright © 1996 by the President and Fellows of Harvard College. Harvard Business School case 9-597-009.

in 1905, and a blade factory opened in Paris the following year. The company's products were distributed through wholesalers, retailers, and agents in over 200 countries and territories.

Gillette managed its worldwide business through a combination of business and regional operational units. The North Atlantic Group manufactured and marketed Gillette's shaving and personal care products in North America and Western Europe. The Stationery Products Group, part of the Diversified Group, produced and sold Gillette's stationery products in North America and Western Europe. The Diversified Group also included Braun, Oral-B, and Jafra, each managed by a worldwide unit. The International Group, headed by Robert King, produced and marketed the shaving, stationery, and personal care products everywhere, except for North America and Western Europe. The International Group comprised three geographic divisions: Latin America; Africa, Middle East and Eastern Europe; and Asia-Pacific. Ian Jackson, group vice president based in Singapore, oversaw operations in 12 Asia-Pacific countries.

Of Gillette's 1995 sales of $6.8 billion, blades and razors accounted for $2.6 billion (40%). Blade and razor sales in the Asia-Pacific region were more than $600 million. The company had consistently maintained profitable growth over the previous five years. Between 1990 and 1995, sales grew by 9% annually, net income by 17%, and earnings per share by 18%. Gillette's mission was to achieve worldwide leadership in its core product categories. In 1995, three-quarters of sales came from product categories in which Gillette held worldwide share leadership. The company emphasized geographic expansion along with research and development, advertising, and capital spending as drivers of growth. New-product activity and entry into and development of new markets were considered essential.

Geographic expansion required the company management to "think global, act local." Eduardo Kello, International Group business manager, explained:

> Headquarters develops new products. They are usually launched first in the U.S. or Western European markets, but quickly introduced in every market world-wide. We start in a new emerging market with simple blades, we introduce the shaving concept. Later, we upgrade the market to higher value products and shaving systems. The country management in each market usually decides the mix of products to push and how to allocate marketing resources against them.

Robert King further emphasized the importance of persuading Gillette's country managers to take initiative:

> Trying to drive new product activity from headquarters is like pushing on a string. The string moves much more easily if a country manager is pulling on it than if headquarters is pushing on it.

While headquarters in Boston emphasized increasing worldwide sales and distribution of higher-margin shaving systems such as Sensor, this was not feasible in many Asian markets. Only a few consumers were sophisticated and wealthy enough to be potential customers for the Sensor. In Indonesia, for example, the focus was still on introducing the concept of shaving with basic Gillette products.

Indonesia in 1996

The Republic of Indonesia was an archipelago of more than 15,000 islands and 196 million people who spoke over 250 regional languages and dialects. (See Exhibit 1 for a map of the country.) Approximately 3,000 miles separated Sigli on Sumatra to the west from Sarmi on Irian Jaya to the east. President Suharto had led the country since 1965 and provided continuity and stability. Major economic development programs, legal reforms, and changes in domestic policies could be enacted only if supported by the president. Although rumors of his pending retirement circulated, there was no sign of any change in the political power structure in 1996.

By 1995, Indonesia's population had reached 196 million, with 35% living in towns and 65% in rural areas. Indonesia had averaged annual gross domestic product (GDP) growth of over 7% for more than 20 years. The country traditionally exported agricultural and oil petroleum products, but economic development plans since the oil crisis of 1988 had encouraged growth in nonoil-related industries. Economic policy was laid out in five-year plans known as Replita.[1] The goals of Replita VI, applicable in 1996, were to maintain annual GDP growth of 6.2%, expand the manufacturing sector by 9.4% a year, and expand the nonoil/gas component of manufacturing by 10.3% a year. Inflation in 1996 was expected to be 12%. Over the years, the liberalization of foreign investment policy had increased private sector involvement in the economy; the central government focused on developing infrastructure in the poorer regions and on human resources.

Economic progress was manifested in increased per-capita incomes and improved standards of living for most of the population. The government stressed export-oriented industrialization to fuel growth and a demand for labor that would keep pace with population growth. During Replita VI, it was expected that more than 2 million Indonesians would enter the workforce each year. The rupiah[2] had depreciated in order to maintain Indonesia's export competitiveness. The value of committed foreign investment reportedly increased from $826 million in 1986 to $10.3 billion in 1992 and to $23.7 billion by June 1994.[3] In 1996, Indonesia was expected to have the highest foreign direct investment/export ratio (74%) of any major emerging market. However, only around one-half of approved foreign direct investment projects had been implemented.

Economic growth had not been consistent throughout the archipelago. Java and Bali had grown much faster than poorer regions such as Irian Jaya and East Timor; contribution of these poorer regions to the country's economy was minimal. Java and Bali accounted for 7% of the land, 60% of the population, and 75% of the gross domestic product. Four of the five major urban centers (Jakarta, Bandung, Surabaya, and Semarang) were on Java.

The average standard of living on Java and Bali was much higher than in the rest of Indonesia. An improving education system ensured that foreign companies would be attracted to the major urban areas, fueling further growth. Market research showed that consumer marketers launched their campaigns in and expected most of their sales from the top five cities (the four in Java plus Medan on Sumatra)

---

1 *Replita* was the shortened form for the Indonesian name *Rencana pembangunan lima tahun*, which meant five-year development plans.

2 Rupiah exchange rate in 1995 was 1US$ = 2,200 rupiah.

3 *EIU Country Profile 1995*, p. 19.

Exhibit 1   Map of Indonesia

Total Population: 196.6 million		
Java:	96,389	49%
Sumatra:	20,533	10%
Sulawesi:	12,519	6%
Kalimatan:	9,111	5%
Total:	70% of the population on 4 islands	

Note: Numbers in parentheses indicate number of Gillette distributors in a particular region.

which together accounted for 35 million of the population. About 60% of Gillette's 1995 sales were made in these five metropolitan areas.

Table A shows the percentages of households falling into each of several income classes in 1995 and projections for 2000. Also shown is the percentage of each income group who shopped regularly in supermarkets in 1995.

INDONESIAN SHAVING PRACTICES

Gillette traditionally entered a market with the basic double-edge blade. Effio explained, "We lead with our strength—the shaving business. Later we leverage the distribution established for our blades on behalf of our other product lines."

Shaving was still underdeveloped in Indonesia, but the incidence of shaving was increasing. A 1995 survey of urban men over 18 years (of whom there were 40 million) indicated that 80% shaved. Those who did, shaved on average 5.5 times per month, compared with 12 times per month in Hong Kong and 26 times per month in the United States. Tracking data indicated that, in 1993, 66% of urban adult men had been shaving with an average incidence of 4.5 times per month.

Shaving incidence was influenced by several factors. There was increasing awareness of Western grooming practices, especially in urban areas, as a result of exposure to foreign media and the increasing presence of multinational companies and their overseas personnel. College students and graduates entering the workforce were especially important trendsetters. On the other hand, grooming products were still regarded as luxury items by many. In addition, Asian beards did not grow as fast as Caucasian or Latino beards, so shaving incidence would be lower, even in a fully developed market.

Forty percent of men who shaved used store-bought blades all or part of the time. The remainder used dry or wet knives. The average number of blades used in a year by the 20% of shavers who always used blades was fifteen. The average number of blades used by occasional users was four. Only 4% of men used shaving foam or lotion; 25% used soap and water, 12% used water alone, and 58% shaved dry.

Gillette's Operation

Gillette entered Indonesia in 1971 with majority ownership of a joint venture with a local company. Gillette's razor blade plant, built in 1972, was located about one hour from Jakarta. Gillette manufactured 75 stockkeeping units in the factory, of which 65 were shaving items. The major product was the double-edge blade for razors and cartridges. Double-edge blades accounted for 60% of the value of products manufactured. Oral-B products were a small portion of the plant's operations; the plant had just begun to "tuft" or put the bristles on the brush handles. The plant was highly automated and run by 68 full-time employees. In addition, 75 casual workers were employed on one- to two-year contracts. In 1995, the plant produced 150 million blades, of which 46 million were exported. The 1996 production plan called for output of 168 million blades, of which 50 million would be exported. Production manager Eko Margo Suhartono said:

> We are looking to import new equipment and expand the line capacity to 230 million double-edge blades per year which we hope will be sufficient to meet demand for the next five years. We needed this extra capacity by 1996 but implementation has been delayed to 1997. This means, in 1996 we will have more overtime and must continue to improve plant productivity.

| Table A | | Percentages of Households by Income Sector and Supermarket Shopping Incidence: 1995 and 2000E | |

	Percentage of Population		Percentage Shopping in Supermarkets: 1995
Income Segment	1995	2000	
> $10,000	15.9%	20.6%	40%
$5,000–$10,000	17.0%	19.6%	25%
$2,000–$ 5,000	32.7%	33.8%	10%
< $ 2,000	34.4%	25.9%	2%

Table B	Shaving Incidence per Month

Shaving Incidence per Month	Percentage of Surveyed
10 times or more	15%
5-9 times	34%
4 times	26%
3 times	10%
2 times	7%
1 time	8%

The manufacturing team had improved business processes as well as production efficiencies. They cut the cycle time from placement of order to product out the door from 50 to 43 days. Effio explained, "Before it would take us 7 days to make almost 3 million blades; now we only need 3 days on the floor. This is an incredible response to sales demand." Due to the demand of other MNCs for experienced workers, there was a need for continuous staff recruiting and training and increasingly upward pressure on worker wages.

In addition, the production team carefully planned the timing of materials inputs. Due to distribution and transportation inefficiencies, the need for buffer inventories was substantial. Cartridges and handles for the razors were imported. Gillette's women's razor was launched in 1995. The razor was imported, but packaged in the country. Problems with customs clearances could impact the entire manufacturing cycle.

The plant obtained electricity from the local grid, supplemented by two backup generators. Water was drawn from a well on the property. Gillette purchased ammonia and other basic raw materials from local suppliers.

Gillette and Competitive Product Lines

The Gillette brand name was synonymous with high-quality double-edge blades. In fact, the Bahasa Indonesian word for blade sounded similar to the name *Gillette*. In 1993 Gillette held 28% of the blade market by volume. By 1995 Gillette's unit share had grown to 48% and was expected to increase to 50% in 1996.

Gillette's policy was to make all of its products available to all of its country subsidiaries. Headquarters persuasion and successful launches of new products in other countries were often helpful in motivating country managers to adopt new products.

Gillette's product line in Indonesia included the following:

- Three types of double-edge blades: the basic Gillette blue stainless blade, a premium double-edge blade (Gillette Goal Red), and an improved blue blade (Gillette Goal Blue).
- Disposables. In the United States and Europe, Bic dominated the market for disposable razors with plastic handles as a result of aggressive pricing. In other markets, Gillette had been able to position its disposable as a system, rather than a low-priced convenience product. In Indonesia, Gillette sold two types of disposables, the Goal II and the more advanced Blue II.
- The GII (named Trac II in the United States) was the earliest shaving system from Gillette to incorporate twin blade technology, whereby the first blade lifted the hair out of the follicle for the second blade to then cut it off.
- The Contour system (named Atra in the United States) added a pivoting head (as opposed to the fixed head on the GII), which enabled the twin blades to stay on the face more consistently.
- The Sensor system added an improved pivoting action and independently sprung twin blades.

Exhibit 2 provides a detailed breakdown of Gillette sales by product. Information on Gillette's gross margin as well as manufacturer, distributor, and retailer selling prices by product line is also provided. Gillette sold 115 million blades in Indonesia in 1995, of which 100 million (87%) were double-edge. In contrast, double-edge blades accounted for 70% of sales in Malaysia and only 20% in Australia. Sales of systems and disposables accounted for 30% and 50% of units sold in Australia and 25% and 5% of units sold in Malaysia. The share of Gillette Indonesia sales accounted for by the higher-margin disposables and systems was projected to increase in 1996 to around 20% of units.

As indicated in Exhibit 3, Gillette Indonesia's 1995 sales from shaving products were valued at $19.6 million. Through a combination of volume increases (19%) and price increases (20%), Gillette Indonesia management projected that this number would increase to $27.6 million in 1996. Gillette's overall gross margin on shaving products was 46% of gross revenues (or 55% of net revenues after discounts). An income statement for Gillette Indonesia's shaving products business is presented in Exhibit 4.

Exhibit 2   Gillette Indonesia Product Line and Margin Structure: 1995

Products	Unit Sales (millions) 1995	Unit Sales (millions) 1996E	% of Units Sold Made Locally	Manufacturer Selling Price/Unit[a]	Manufacturer Gross Margin %	Distributor Selling Price/Unit[b]	Retail Selling Price/Unit
A. Double-edge Blades	**100**	**108**					
Gillette Blue Blade	5	5	100	0.06	47	0.08	0.11
Gillette Goal Red	80	90	100	0.11	50	0.15	0.20
Gillette Goal Blue	15	13	100	0.08	48	0.11	0.15
B. Disposables	**5**	**10**					
Goal II	4	8	100	0.21	32	0.31	0.40
Blue II	1	2	0	0.35	52[c]	0.49	0.64
C. Systems Blades	**10**	**18**					
Gillette GII	2	3	20	0.45	52	0.68	0.82
Gillette Contour	5	7	20	0.55	52	0.77	1.00
Gillette Sensor	3	8	0	0.65	40[c]	0.91	1.19

Notes:

[a] In U.S. dollar equivalent.

[b] Distributors often sold (at an average 8% markup) to subdistributors or wholesalers who in turn (at an average 12% markup) sold on to mom-and-pop retailers who took, on average, a further 20% markup.

[c] Represents, in the case of imported products, the difference between Gillette Indonesia's selling price and the landed transfer price.

Exhibit 3   Gillette Indonesia Sales Breakdowns: 1995 and 1996

Sales Revenues in 1995	1995	1996E
1995 Total Revenues	$23.0	$32.2
Revenues from export sales	1.4	2.3
Revenues from in-country sales	21.6	29.9
In-country Sales:		
a. Shaving products total sales	$19.6	$27.6
Blades	10.3	11.2
Disposables	1.2	2.5
Sensor	5.6	10.4
Razors	2.0	3.0
Prep products	0.5	0.5
b. Nonshave products	$2.0	$2.3

Exhibit 4   Gillette Indonesia: Percentage Income Statement for Shaving Products, 1995

Gross revenues from shaving products	100%
Less: Trade discounts	10
= Net revenues	90%
Less: Variable manufacturing costs	36%
Variable selling costs (sales commissions)	2
Variable distribution costs	6
= Gross margin	46%
Less: Advertising	9%
Consumer promotions and merchandising	3
General sales and administrative costs	14
= Profit from operations	20%

Gillette's main competitors were imported, low-end, double-edge blades from Eastern Europe and China. Based on market research conducted in the four major cities, Tatra, Super Nacet, and Tiger were the most often mentioned competing brands on the market. Gillette's retail prices were sometimes four times those of competitive products. Chester Allan in Jakarta explained, "Currently most of the poorer rural shavers cannot afford Gillette products and buy low-price, low-quality brands such as Tiger and Tatra.

However, with rising incomes and improved Gillette distribution and display, consumers are moving to Gillette. "

Gillette's disposables faced two competitors: Bic, from the United States, and Bagus, a locally manufactured brand. Neither of these sold in high volumes, so the competition was not keen. The Schick division of Warner Lambert imported its higher-end products, but sales were minimal. According to Allan, "Gillette has 90% of the premium-priced segment of the market which we developed."

Exhibit 5   Indonesian Male Consumer Awareness and Usage of Blades: 1995

Products in Survey	Brand Awareness	Ever Used	Brand Used Most Often
A. Double-Edge			
Gillette:			
Gillette Goal Red	97	85	55
Gillette Goal Blue	49	18	5
Gillette Blue Blade	14	5	1
Competitors:			
Tatra	42	21	4
Super Nacet	16	4	--
Tiger/Cap Macan	59	44	11
B. Disposable			
Goal II	41	16	4
Blue II	9	3	--
C. System Blades			
Gillette GII	12	4	1
Gillette Contour	9	4	3
Gillette Sensor	12	4	1

Source: Company records.

Note: Based on a sample of 300 male adult consumers.

Gillette-brand blades commanded high awareness in the Indonesian market. Market research conducted in 1995 among Indonesian male shavers, reported in Exhibit 5, showed 97% brand awareness and 55% brand used most often ratings for Gillette's Goal Red blade.

Distribution and Sales

Indonesian regulations prohibited a foreign company from directly importing or distributing its products. These regulations protected Indonesian distributors and resulted in inefficiencies. The American Chamber of Commerce in Jakarta estimated that 45% of retail prices in Indonesia covered distribution services.

To ensure distribution of products in the face of weak communications, poor traffic conditions, and lack of distribution service technology, Gillette managers and those in other MNCs had to focus on the basics of distribution over which they had little control and from which they extracted no direct profit.

Gillette had originally appointed a single national distributor, but by 1993 it was apparent the arrangement was not working satisfactorily. No single distributor could provide an even depth of coverage in every district throughout the entire country. Mohammad Slamet, Gillette's national sales manager in the early 1990s, explained:

> There are many distribution issues which require on-the-spot responses. A distributor who is headquartered hundreds of miles away cannot provide a quick enough response. In addition, there often arise sensitive, purely local, issues which can only be resolved by someone familiar with the relationships, customs, and dialects of each area.

In 1993, Gillette appointed 23 distributors dispersed across the country. The new distributors were previously known to Slamet or were identified through referrals. In the year following implementation of the new system, sales rose by 60%.

A good distributor had the working capital and/or bank credit line to stock sufficient inventory and to bridge the time gap between paying Gillette and receiving payments from its customers. Second, a good distributor also had sufficient salespeople, warehouses, and reliable transportation equipment. Third, strong local connections with government officials and the trade were critical to success.

A typical distributor represented different manufacturers and product lines. Gillette's distributors were encouraged to hire people to handle only the Gillette business in the belief that such focus would result in the greater push. Gillette itself expanded its internal sales and trade relations staff to work with the new distributors.

In 1995, Nyoman Samsu Prabata was Gillette's national sales manager. Nyoman's organization comprised three regional managers (covering Western, Central, and Eastern Indonesia) who supervised a total of 12 area managers and supervisors. These managers were well compensated but were often tempted away by better offers from other multinationals, such was the shortage of general management talent in Indonesia. Nyoman's group coordinated the efforts of 23 geographically based independent distributors and their 260 salespeople. While Gillette's distributors hired many of the sales staff and paid their base salaries, Gillette covered their commissions and other incentives for reaching targets, which averaged 20% of their total compensation.

Nyoman explained:

> The number one job of the Gillette sales team is educating the distributors and their salespeople. We have to train them how our products work, so they can demonstrate the products on their own. We have to educate them on the benefits of our products compared to both traditional shaving methods and to competitive products. We also educate them on warehousing and handling methods to reduce damage to the product.

For example, one distributor's warehouse was located in an area of Jakarta with poor transportation and prone to flooding. "A few days ago, the warehouse roof fell in under pressure from the rain. The actual damage was minimal but the operation had to stop for a day. He just would not listen to us," explained Nyoman.

In Indonesia, direct verbal confrontation was socially unacceptable. This sometimes resulted in strained relations between a distributor and an area manager festering for months without being solved. Another challenge was the different degree to which employees and consumers observed Muslim religious practices. Nyoman commented:

> In Jakarta, while people are faithful followers, the attitude is a bit more casual and there is an understanding that not everyone is practicing to the same degree. However, outside Jakarta, religious practices are more closely observed. In Aceh on Sumatra it would be an insult to wave good-bye with your left hand. In Bali, the Hindu religion is dominant so, for the "Galungan" holiday, Hindus fast for two days. For Nyepi, complete silence must be observed for one day, so any devout Hindu stays home and does not even turn on the electricity. Not only does this affect our business but I must plan ahead for holiday staffing.

Gillette gave its distributors 45 days' credit. In return, the distributors would give their customers anywhere from 30 to 60 days credit. Nyoman said:

> While we try to insist on timely payments via bank transfer, there are many times when receivables are overdue. Though the sales staff and area mangers are responsible for receivables, I often have to get involved and it is important to be tough on the issue. As you move further away from Jakarta, the legal system does not provide much support, so ensuring distributors have the working capital to cover the spread between payables and receivables is critical to their selection.

In addition to the distributors who supplied wholesalers and, in turn, the extensive network of small retailers in Indonesia, Nyoman also supervised a national accounts team who negotiated sales to the major Indonesian supermarket chains, often shipping to them direct. Supermarket chains included Hero which had 54 outlets, Metro with 5 outlets, and others located in the large urban centers. These chains purchased directly from manufacturers and could handle products efficiently. In 1995, supermarkets accounted for 5% of Gillette's shaving products sales in units and 8% in value; corresponding 1993 figures were 2% and 4%. Market research showed that higher-income, urban consumers were increasingly shopping in supermarkets. Most sales of Gillette's higher-priced shaving products were through these outlets. Competition for shelf space was intensifying. Some supermarkets were imposing slotting allowances on suppliers of up to 80% of a new product's cost to provide shelf space.

Traditional wholesalers and distributors came under pressure as a result of these trends. Many wholesalers had poor facilities, traditional goods-handling methods, and antiquated accounting—some still used an abacus to track the business. They tended to focus on turnover alone rather than in conjunction with profit margin. They were also slow to see the potential of upgrading their customers to higher unit margin products.

Distribution coverage in Indonesia required consumer goods manufacturers like Gillette to reach more than 60,000 small kiosks and mom-and-pop shops. Gillette did not distribute through the many itinerant salespeople who traveled with their wares on bicycles from village to village. The entrepreneurial owners of the small retail outlets would respond to requests from consumers and, in turn, demand the product from their wholesalers. "Pull marketing can be effective," Slamet said. "Once the mom-and-pops start getting requests for a new product, they are willing to stock it. This is how market testing takes place," Effio explained.

Communications

As indicated in Exhibit 4, Gillette Indonesia spent 9% of gross sales on advertising and 3% on consumer promotions and merchandising. Ten percent of gross sales was accounted for by off-invoice allowances to the trade and other forms of trade deals. The advertising budget for shaving products in 1995 was around $2 million.

Media advertising was targeted principally at urban male consumers. About half the advertising budget was spent on television (there were five private channels and one government-owned) and half on print. Television advertising included some program sponsorships. The adult literacy rate in Indonesia was 77%, and half of Indonesian adult males read a newspaper at least once a week. The allocation of Gillette advertising was weighted towards systems and disposables to encourage consumers to trade up.

Gillette headquarters developed television advertisements for use worldwide, with the intent that local voiceovers and local package shots would be superimposed. (A sample Gillette print leaflet, with translation, is shown in Exhibit 6). Gillette Indonesia's marketing manager explained:

> We are still in the early stages of educating consumers about shaving. An ad made in Boston for the U.S. market may not have sufficient details about the basics. Nothing can be taken for granted here, especially when it comes to advertising the entry-level products, the double-edge blades.

Gillette Indonesia managers differed over the relative emphasis that advertising should place on persuading consumers to shave for the first time, increasing the incidence of shaving among existing shavers, and trading existing shavers up to higher-margin, more sophisticated shaving systems. As a compromise, the 1995 advertising budget was split equally among these three objectives. One-third of the total budget was allocated to advertising Sensor.

Special promotions were run in 1995 on the Sensor and Contour systems. Gift-with-purchase promotions (involving an Oral-B travel toothbrush, a toilet bag, or a trial sample of Foamy shaving cream) were targeted at upper- to middle-income urban males. Promotional efforts were sometimes focused on the members of executive clubs, attendees at golf tournaments, or workers in specific office buildings.

Coupons were not used in Indonesia; redemption systems through retailers were not yet in place. However, Gillette found that lucky draws with entry forms inside product packages worked well; consumers had to mail in entry forms to be included in the draws.

Gillette used similar packaging in Indonesia as in the United States for its more expensive systems products. The Goal II, the cheaper of Gillette's disposables, was advertised on radio. The number of blades per pack varied by outlet; twice as many were included in the pack for supermarkets as in the pack for mom-and-pop stores.

Setting the Course

As Allan reviewed his initial projections for 1996 (see Exhibit 3), he wondered how rapidly the Indonesian market for blades and razors could or would expand. Should the Indonesian market be allowed to just move along at its own pace? If so, what would that pace be? Alternatively, should Gillette Indonesia invest additional resources either in advertising and promotion or in sales and distribution, to accelerate the process of market development? If so, which products should be emphasized? Would further investment be wasted if it were on concepts and products that were beyond consumers' understanding or willingness to pay?

Allan resolved to set out his objectives for Gillette Indonesia in 1996 and to develop a detailed marketing plan including an income statement projection. He knew his plan would have to satisfy Effio's objectives for Gillette's growth in the Asia-Pacific region.

Exhibit 6   Gillette Indonesia Print Leaflet

ENAM LANGKAH MENCUKUR LEBIH LICIN, LEBIH LEMBUT DAN LEBIH NYAMAN

1. Bersihkan Wajah

Cucilah muka dengan air hangat dan sabun, lalu bilas hingga bersih. Tak perlu dikeringkan, biarkan kulit wajah dan rambut dalam keadaan basah.

2. Usapkan Gillette Foamy

Usapkan Gillette Foamy secara merata di atas permukaan yang akan dicukur.

Mencegah penguapan air dan mengurangi gesekan antara kulit dengan mata pisau. Sekaligus melembutkan kumis atau janggut yang akan dicukur.

3. Mulailah dari tempat yang Tepat.

Cukur rambut cambang, pipi, dan leher terlebih dulu. Rambut yang paling kaku tumbuh di dagu dan sekeliling bibir dan memerlukan waktu lebih lama untuk menyerap air untuk menjadi lembut.

4. Bercukurlah Secara Benar.

Bercukurlah dengan tarikan yang lembut dan ringan. Usahakan untuk sesedikit mungkin melakukan tarikan.Pisau cukur Gillette dirancang untuk menghasilkan cukuran yang lebih licin, lebih lembut dan nyaman.

5. Bilaslah Mata Pisau

Di tengah kegiatan mencukur, sesekali bilaslah mata pisau cukur dengan air yang deras (misalnya dari keran) guna membuang limbah cukuran. Usai bercukur, mata pisau harus langsung dibilas dan dihentak - hentakkan sampai airnya kering.

6. Jangan Mengusap Mata Pisau.

Jangan sekali kali mengusap mata pisau dengan apa pun, karena akan merusak ketajamannya.

<u>Gunakan cartridge yang sesuai</u> dengan pisau cukur Gillette Anda.

Tahukah Anda ?

- Jumlah rambut yang tumbuh di wajah pria bisa mencapai 30.000 helai.
- Pertumbuhan rambut tersebut per hari rata-rala 0,38 milimeter.
- Panjang maksimum yang bisa dicapai seumur hidup sekitar 80 sentimeter.
- Dalam keadaan kering, janggut sama kakunya dengan serat tembaga yang berdiameter sama.

- **18.000 SEBELUM MASEHI** Manusia primitif mengerik rambut pada wajah mereka dengan batu dan tulang yang dipertajam, sebagaimana tergambar pada lukisan lukisan di gua purba.

- **336 SEBELUM MASEHI** Iskandar Zulkarnaen meminta para prajuritnya untuk bercukur, sehingga tentara Persia tak dapat menjambak janggut mereka dalam pertempuran.

- **1698.** Kaisar Rusia, Peter Yang Agung, mengenakan Pajak atas janggut, untuk membiasakan rakyatnya mengikuti tradisi bercukur yang dilakukan masyarakat Barat.

- **1895.** King C. Gillette, asal Amerika, menemukan pisau cukur moderen yang mengubah total kebiasaan bercukur pria di seluruh dunia. Dimana-mana orang meninggalkan pisau cukur tradisional dan menggantinya dengan pisau cukur bermata ganda yang dapat diganti-ganti.

Do you know?

- Up to 30,000 hairs can grow on a man's face.
- The hairs grow at an average rate of 0.38 millimeters per day.
- They can reach a maximum length of approximately 80 centimeters (32") over a lifetime.
- When it is dry, a beard is as stiff as copper fibers of the same diameter.

- **18,000** B.C. Primitive men scraped the hair off their faces with sharpened stones and bones, as depicted in drawings in ancient caves.

- **336** B.C. Alexander the Great ordered his soldiers to shave so that the Persian army would not be able to grab their beards in battle.

- **1698.** Peter the Great, Czar of Russia, imposed a tax on beards to get his people used to following the shaving practices of Western societies.

- **King C. Gillette,** an American, invented the modern razor, which totally changed men's shaving habits all over the world. People everywhere gave up traditional razors and replaced them with replaceable double-edged razors.

SIX STEPS TO A SMOOTHER, GENTLER AND MORE COMFORTABLE SHAVE

1. *Clean your face*

Wash your face with hot water and soap, then rinse it until it is clean. You don't have to dry it, leave your face and hair wet.

2. *Apply Gillette Foamy*

Apply Gillette Foamy evenly over the surface to be shaved. It prevents water evaporation and reduces friction between the skin and the razor blade. At the same time it softens the mustache or beard which you are going to shave.

3. *Start at the Right Place*

First shave the sidebums, cheeks and neck. The stiffest hairs grow on the chin and around the lips and need more time to absorb water in order to become soft.

4. *Shave Correctly*

Shave with gentle and light strokes. Try to make as few strokes as possible. The Gillette razor is designed to produce a smoother, gentler, more comfortable shave.

5. *Rinse the Razor Blade*

While shaving, rinse the razor blade once in a while under running water (for example from the tap) to get rid of the whiskers. After shaving, the razor blade must be rinsed right away and shaken until dry.

6. *Don't Wipe the Razor Blade*

Don't ever wipe the razor blade with anything, because it will destroy its sharpness. *Use the cartridge that is right for your Gillette razor.*

Koç Holding: Arçelik White Goods

In February 1997, the top management team of Arçelik, the major appliance subsidiary of Koç Holding, Turkey's largest industrial conglomerate, assembled in Cologne, Germany, for the biannual Domotechnica, the world's largest major appliances trade show. The team was led by Hasan Subasi, president of Koç Holding's durables business unit, and Mehmet Ali Berkman, general manager of the Arçelik white goods operation, which accounted for two-thirds of the durables business unit's turnover[1].

The Arçelik stand was in a prime location in Building 14; nearby were the booths of Bosch, Siemens and Whirlpool. The Arçelik stand displayed 236 products carrying the Beko brand name, 35% of them refrigerators and freezers, 25% washing machines, 20% ovens and 15% dishwashers[2]. Several innovative products were on display including washing machines that were more water and energy efficient than competitive products, as well as refrigerators made from materials that were 80% recyclable and incorporating special insulation panels for greater operational efficiency. In 1996, Arçelik's Beko brand had received a Green Dove award from the European Community (EC) for attention to the environment in design and production[3].

The trade show exhibit, costing $1 million to organize, reflected Arçelik's determination to become a major player in the global white goods industry. Yet there was still debate in the company regarding how much emphasis to place on international sales; which geographical markets to concentrate on; and whether to focus on supplying appliances on an OEM basis, building the company's own Beko brand, or both[4].

COUNTRY AND COMPANY BACKGROUND

Turkey

In 1997, Turkey, a country of 63 million people, was positioned at the historical crossroads between East and West, communism and capitalism, Islam and Christianity. Turkey bordered Eastern Europe, the Caucasus, the Balkans, North Africa and Middle East—all regions in various states of political and economic flux in the 1990s. In this context, successive Turkish governments promoted domestic and foreign policies that would nurture its still modest private sector yet promote the pursuit of global competitiveness so that Turkey would be a credible candidate for entry into the EC.

The establishment of the Republic of Turkey by Mustafa Kemal Ataturk as a secular nation state in 1923 marked the end of 600 years of sultan rule. Ataturk aimed to move Turkey quickly into the ranks of industrialized Western nations by anchoring the republic's constitution in a parliamentary democracy. From the start, a strict division between religion (Islam) and government was constitutionally guaranteed and backed by the Turkish military. To build the economy, Ataturk set up temporary state-run enterprises that would later be turned over to private sector management. Privatization, however, did not get fully underway until the mid-1980s, when the government also formally established the Istanbul Stock Exchange.

During the 1980s, the Turkish government established the convertibility of the Turkish lira, and promoted

This case was prepared by Professor John A. Quelch with the assistance of Robin Root.
Copyright © 1997 by the President and Fellows of Harvard College. Harvard Business School case 9-598-033.

---

1 "White goods" was a term used to describe major kitchen appliances. The corresponding term, "brown goods," described major household appliances used outside the kitchen, such as televisions and stereo systems.

2 Most Arçelik products sold outside Turkey carried the Beko brand name.

3 The European Community comprised, in 1997, 15 member countries with a combined population of around 350 million.

4 An OEM (original equipment manufacturer) sold products to other manufacturers, distributors or retailers; these products typically carried brand names specified by the purchasing companies.

exports to improve its balance of payments. Turkey's rapid growth and relative economic stability, while the envy of other developing countries, was long overlooked by Western governments who focused instead on its strategic role as a NATO firewall against Soviet expansion. The possibility of membership in the EC changed the business mentality within Turkey. Large family-run industrial conglomerates, the engines of Turkish modernization, started to emphasize professional management and to apply global manufacturing standards.

In 1990, the growth in Turkey's gross national product reached an all-time high of 9.2 percent, sparking the interest of investors from Europe and North America. After a slowdown to 0.9% growth in 1991, the Turkish government stimulated consumer demand and increased public investment; the economy grew 5.9% in 1992 and 7.5% in 1993. A major recession in 1994 which saw 5.0% negative growth was followed by 7.3% growth in 1995 and 7.1% in 1996. Despite the political uncertainties that accompanied Turkey's first Islamist government, sustained GNP growth of 8% was forecast for 1997. The country was, however, afflicted by high inflation (80% in 1996 and 75% forecast for 1997), high interest rates, depreciation of the lira, and a deepening budget deficit. Data on the Turkish economy between 1992 and 1996 are presented in Exhibit 1.

Koç Holding

Vehbi Koç began his business in 1917 with a $100 investment from his father, who was a shopkeeper. Seven decades later, he left behind one of the world's largest private fortunes and the most advanced industrial conglomerate in Turkey, Koç Holding, which was established in 1963. Until the death of Vehbi Koç in early 1996, at age 95, Koç Holding had been the only company on the Fortune 500 list of international businesses to still be owned and operated by its founder.

The legacy bequeathed by Vehbi Koç was as philosophical as it was financial. Shortly after Ataturk established the Republic of Turkey in 1923, Mr. Koç became the first Turk to challenge the trading power of the Republic's Greek, Armenian and Jewish minorities. By age 22, he had discerned that the higher living standard enjoyed by these groups was a function of their dominance in commerce—a vocation which most Turks had been discouraged from entering. Mr. Koç went on to become one of the first Turkish businessmen to realize the benefits of foreign partnerships. In the late 1930s, he became a sales agent for companies such as Burroughs, Mobil Oil and Ford, and in 1948 he built his first factory to manufacture light bulbs with General Electric. Half a century later, Koç Holding controlled close to 100 companies in nearly every sector of the Turkish economy, the total output of which accounted for approximately one-tenth of the country's GNP.

As a testament to the passions and principles he cultivated over his seven-decade reign, the Koç patriarch circulated a letter among his three grandsons just three months before he passed away in 1996. In it, he exhorted them to rise to the challenge faced by most third-generation managers in family businesses, namely, to single-mindedly focus on enhancing further the company's financial and social value.

In 1996, the 36,000 employees of Koç Holding generated $12 billion in revenues. Koç was a major player in the automotive industry, household appliances, consumer

---

(**Exhibit 1**)   Turkish Economic Data: 1992–1996

	1992	1993	1994	1995	1996
GDP growth rate (%)	6.4	8.1	-5.4	7.3	7.1
GDP per capita (US$ at PPP[1] rates)	4,991	5,562	5,271	5,411	5,634
Inflation	70%	66%	106%	94%	80%
Exchange rate (lira/US$)	8,555	14,458	38,418	59,501	81,995

Sources: Bank of America WIS Country Outlooks, November 1996; Union Bank of Switzerland New Horizon Economies, August 1995; Union Bank of Switzerland New Horizon Economies, April 1997; Statistical Yearbook of Turkey, 1996.

[1]Purchasing Power Parity (PPP) refers to the rates of currency conversion that equalize the purchasing power of different currencies. The GDP and PPP per capita in Istanbul were thought to be double the national average.

goods, energy, mining, construction, international trade, finance, tourism, and services sectors. The company grew three times faster than the Turkish economy between 1985-1995. Its corporate logo, a red ram's head (Koç means ram in Turkish), was visible on street corners, shops and office buildings throughout Turkey. Koç Holding had a nationwide distribution network of 9,400 dealers, and 23 overseas offices responsible for achieving $884 million in foreign exchange earnings. As the leading taxpayer in Turkey, Koç Holding initiated and underwrote numerous philanthropic projects in the areas of education, health, cultural heritage, and environmental conservation.

Arçelik

Arçelik was established in 1955 to produce metal office furniture.[5] In 1959, the company began manufacturing washing machines. Arçelik subsequently began manufacturing refrigerators, dishwashers, air conditioners and vacuum cleaners in five Turkish factories. Unit sales across these five categories reached 2,110,000 in 1995, making Arçelik the sixth largest European manufacturer of household appliances and the only significant white goods manufacturer between Italy and India. In addition, Arçelik sourced other appliances including ovens, televisions, water heaters and space heaters from affiliated Koç companies. Unit sales of these products reached 900,000 in 1995. Arçelik owned 63% of Ardem, a Koç company that made cooking appliances, and 23% of Bekoteknik, which made televisions and other consumer electronic products. To round out its product line, Arçelik sourced small household appliances such as irons from other companies outside the Koç Group. By 1996, Arçelik was the largest company within Koç Holding. Sales and earnings data for 1990-1996 are

reported in Exhibit 2. Key dates in Arçelik's history are summarized in Exhibit 3.

Arçelik manufacturing capacity, actual production and unit sales for 1992-1996 in the three most important white goods categories are summarized in Exhibit 4. Arçelik's unit market shares in Turkey in 1996 were 57% in refrigerators, 60% in washing machines and 70% in dishwashers. Competitive market share and market size data for each category of white goods are presented in Exhibits 5 and 6. Refrigerators accounted for 38% of Arçelik sales (by value), washing machines for 32%, dishwashers for 10%, and ovens for 15%.

In 1988, the Turkish government agreed to a phased program of tariff reductions with the European Community. With respect to white goods, Turkish tariffs on imports from the EC, which ranged between 40% and 55%, would be reduced to zero between 1992 and January 1996, according to the schedule shown in Exhibit 7. A 5% Turkish tariff on imported components from the EC would also be removed. As a result, exports into Turkey of Western European appliances would become progressively more price competitive (not least because white goods plants in Europe were operating at only 65% capacity utilization) and possibly challenge Arçelik's dominance of the Turkish market.

In preparation for the removal of import tariffs, Arçelik invested heavily in upgrading its manufacturing quality and productivity to world class standards. Between 1991 and 1996, capital expenditures totaled $247 million, approximately 6% of sales. By 1995, all Arçelik plants had received ISO 9001 quality certification. Through the incorporation of just-in-time and flexible manufacturing systems, Arçelik reduced raw material and labor costs, thereby increasing the productivity of its refrigerator production by 43% between 1990 and 1995. The corresponding increases for washing machines and dishwashers were 50%

| Exhibit 2 | Arçelik's Sales and Earnings: 1990–1996 | | | | | | |

$U.S. million	1990	1991	1992	1993	1994	1995	1996
Sales	765	1,001	1,060	1,150	859	982	1,241
EBIT	98	134	159	148	147	144	172
Net Earnings	72	91	86	97	39	60	84

Source: Company records.

5 Arçelik (pronounced arch-e-lick) is a Turkish word meaning clean steel.

Exhibit 3   Key Dates in Arçelik's History

Year	Event
1955	Arçelik is founded.
1959	Arçelik produces Turkey's first washing machine.
1960	Arçelik produces Turkey's first refrigerator.
1965	JV with General Electric to produce electric motors and compressors. Bekoteknik is founded to operate in the "brown goods" electronics industry.
1966	Arçelik produces vacuum cleaners.
1974	Bekoteknik manufactures TV sets. Arçelik produces Turkey's first automatic washing machine.
1975	Arçelik receives General Electric technology licenses for white goods.
1977	Ardem joins the Koç group to produce kitchen ranges.
1980	Arçelik exports refrigerators.
1985	Arçelik licenses washing machine technology (2 models) from Bosch-Siemens. (Production ceased in 1994.)
1986	Arçelik licenses dishwasher technology (1 model) from Bosch-Siemens. No exports are permitted. (Still in production in 1996.)
1989	Arçelik establishes its Beko sales office in the United Kingdom.
1991	Bekoteknik and Arçelik receive ISO 9001 certification. Research and development center is established. Arçelik launches first toll-free customer call center in Turkey.
1993	Arçelik opens a new dishwasher plant in Ankara.
1994	Bekoteknik receives the EU Green Dove Award.
1996	Arçelik agrees to supply 100,000 OEM dishwashers to Whirlpool each year for five years. Çayirova, Eskirsehir and Ankara plants receive ISO 14000 certification.

Source: Company records.

and 20%. Arçelik had no manufacturing plants outside of Turkey.

In addition, Arçelik also invested heavily in R&D. During the 1970s and 1980s, Arçelik licensed technology from General Electric and Bosch-Siemens. Arçelik paid unit royalties but was only permitted to sell its production in Turkey. Over time, Arçelik developed its own appliance designs, often at lower cost than the licensed technologies. Starting in 1989, Arçelik transformed itself from a manufacturer that used licensed technologies to one of the leaders in white goods research and development. The company sponsored master's theses at Turkish engineering schools on subjects relevant to its research agenda, and secured World Bank funding to research how to eliminate CFCs from

Exhibit 4

Arçelik Capacity, Production and Sales by Major Appliance: 1992–1996 ('000)

	Capacity	Production	Change	Capacity Utilization
Refrigerators				
1992	1,050	569.2	2.7%	54%
1993	1,050	709.6	24.6	67
1994	1,050	630.4	-11.1	60
1995	1,050	900.6	42.8	85
1996	1,050	990.8	10.1	94
Washing Machines				
1992	760	551.8	-7.2	72
1993	800	653.7	18.4	81
1994	800	500.4	-23.4	62
1995	900	625.6	25.0	70
1996	1,100	750.8	20.0	68
Dishwashers				
1992	200	180.0	36.9	90
1993	300	244.5	35.8	81
1994	300	217.3	-11.1	72
1995	300	205.3	-5.5	68
1996	500	301.6	46.9	60

Source: Company records.

Exhibit 5   Turkish Market Share and Unit Sales for White Goods[1]

	Refrigerators		Washing Machines		Dishwashers		Ovens	
	1995	1996	1995	1996	1995	1996	1995	1996
Koç	54.6%	56.5%	64.2%	59.7%	75.8%	70.4%	68.0%	67.6%
Peg	38.2	30.9	23.5	23.5	17.0	20.5	25.9	23.0
Merloni	4.3	4.1	4.0	5.5	1.9	2.6	-	-
Others	2.9	8.5	8.3	11.3	5.3	6.5	6.1	9.4
Unit Sales[1]	868,197	1,039,519	856,890	1,135,669	263,570	331,030	446,591	509,493

Source: Company records.

[1]Unit sales include imports so Arçelik market shares reported here are lower than the company's share of domestic production.

refrigerators. Between 1990 and 1995, $69 million or 1.5% of sales was allocated by Arçelik to R&D. The fruits of these investments were evident in the innovative technology-based features on display in the Arçelik booth at Domotechnica in 1997.

In the area of human resources, Arçelik prided itself on lean management with only four levels in the organization. The work force was highly educated and many Arçelik managers had attended business schools in North America and Europe.

	Refrigerators	Washing Machines	Dishwashers	Ovens
Koç Group				
Arçelik	39.2%	39.9%	53.7%	44.4%
Beko	17.3	19.8	16.7	22.9
Peg Group				
AEG	8.3	5.6	2.4	5.1
Profilo	18.9	10.6	2.8	13.1
Bosch	3.3	6.1	13.7	4.5
Siemens	0.4	1.2	1.6	0.4

Source: Company records.

Exhibit 7   Turkish Tariff Reduction Program for White Goods Imports from the European Community: 1992–1996

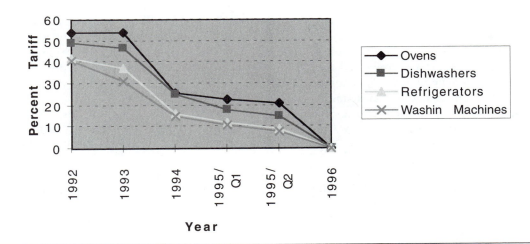

Source: Company records.

WHITE GOODS MARKETING IN TURKEY

Demand

As of 1996, 99% of Turkey's 13 million households owned refrigerators, the same percentage as in the EC. The corresponding percentages for other major appliances were 47% for automatic washing machines (90%), 15% for dishwashers (31%) and 56% for ovens (70%).

Demand for white goods in Turkey was influenced by the pace of household formations and urbanization, interest rates, retail price levels and the rate of economic growth. Sensitivity analyses estimating the effects of changes in some of these variables on unit sales of appliances in

Turkey are presented in Exhibit 8. Consumer purchases of appliances increased dramatically in the first half of 1996 as shown in Exhibit 9. Arçelik sales increased 21% in this period. Mr. Berkman commented:

> Domestic demand is strong and will remain so. Annual population growth is 1.7% and the number of households increases by 2.5% each year. Around 50% of the population is under 30 and an increasing percentage (currently 63%) live in cities and towns which makes it easier for us to reach them.

Imports satisfied some of the increase in domestic demand, reaching 3% of white goods sales in Turkey in 1993. When, in 1994, the Turkish lira devalued sharply and the economy went into recession, imports of white goods declined while exports increased. In January 1996, with the import tariffs cut to zero and the economy strengthening, imports increased. For example, between January and July of 1996, 20% of dishwashers sold in Turkey were imported. Analysts estimated the sustainable import penetration rate at 5% for refrigerators, 10% for washing machines and 15% for dishwashers.

Competition

Arçelik's principal white goods competitor was Peg Profilo. Facing increasing competition, Peg Profilo had been sold to Bosch-Siemens of Germany in 1995. Peg Profilo sold its products under the Profilo and AEG brand names[6]. Imports of premium-priced Bosch and Siemens appliances began in 1996. Although penetration was limited to date, Arçelik managers noted heavy advertising behind the Bosch name

aimed at challenging Arçelik's dominance of the premium end of the white goods market. Several Bosch shops were opened to supplement the existing network of Peg Profilo dealers. There was some evidence of strained relations as Bosch-Siemens tried to impose formal contracts on dealers used to the handshake-style agreements of Peg Profilo.

Profilo's market shares in 1996 were 31% in refrigerators, 24% in washing machines, 23% in ovens, and 20% in dishwashers. Profilo capacity utilization was only 60%. Arçelik managers expected that Profilo would become more competitive in washing machines and dishwashers (in which the firm had not invested in new production technology) as a result of the acquisition. Units carrying the Profilo name could be imported from Bosch-Siemens' efficient German or low-cost Spanish plants. In addition, Profilo refrigerators, which were more up-to-date, were expected to be exported through Bosch-Siemens' overseas network.

The number three competitor, Merloni, was a joint venture between the Italian consumer durables producer and Pekel, the Turkish white goods company owned by Vestel, which was originally owned by Polly Peck International. Merloni had obtained majority control of the refrigerator factory in 1993. Arçelik managers believed that Merloni competed for market share with Peg Profilo's brand more than with the Arçelik and Beko brands.

Consumer Behavior

Relative to per capita income, the penetration of white goods in Turkish households was high. This was attributed to the desire of Turkish consumers to buy prestigious

---

Exhibit 8   Impact of Changes in Interest Rates, Consumer Prices and GNP Per Capita on Arçelik Sales and Profits

Change in Arçelik's	Interest rates increase by 10%	Consumer prices increase by 10%	GNP per capita increase by 10%
Refrigerator unit sales	-12.5%	-12.7%	+1.3%
Washing machine unit sales	-8.1%	-7.1%	+4.3%
Dishwasher unit sales	-10.4%	-10.1%	+21.6%
Total sales revenues	-6.9%	-8.1%	+3.7%
Total profits	-13.3%	-14.1%	+11.5%

Source: Adapted from a Schroeders investment report, 1996.

---

6 AEG was an Electrolux brand sold under license in Turkey by Peg Profilo. After the Bosch-Siemens acquisition, little effort was put into promoting the AEG brand.

Exhibit 9

Change in White Goods Retail Unit Sales in Turkey

	January–April 1995	January–April 1996
Refrigerators	-8.6%	+17.8%
Washing machines	-36%	+68%
Dishwashers	-40%	+56%
Ovens	-15%	+4.5%

Source: Adapted from a Schroeders investment report, 1996.

durables for their homes and to sustained marketing efforts on behalf of the Arçelik and Beko brands.

When buying a new or replacement appliance, 50% of consumers were believed to shop only one store; the remainder shopped around. Replacement purchasers were invariably triggered by the breakdown of an existing appliance and were therefore especially unlikely to shop around. High inflation also encouraged consumers to shorten their decision making processes. In 1996, wage increases were outpacing inflation so demand for white goods was especially strong.

A consumer's perceived risk and brand sensitivity varied according to the white goods being purchased. As explained by Arçelik's marketing manager:

> *Refrigerators are nothing more than boxes and consumers are familiar with them. There's little that can go wrong. Dishwashers, on the other hand, are more complex appliances and first-time dishwasher purchasers are more risk averse.*

ARÇELIK MARKETING IN TURKEY

Brand Building

Arçelik sold white goods under two brand names, Arçelik and Beko. A third brand, Aygaz, that Arçelik had inherited through the acquisition of an oven manufacturer, was discontinued in 1995 and its product line absorbed into the Beko brand family.

In 1996, there were 33 million Koç white goods appliances in use in 13 million Turkish households. Arçelik was a trusted brand. However, some older consumers did not remember fondly the product quality of Arçelik's early appliances sold in the 1960s; to them, the quality of Turkish-made products was still doubtful. Though the product lines of both brands were similar, except for external design differences, Beko brand managers claimed their brand had a more "high tech" image that appealed to younger consumers. The strong penetration of Beko in brown goods (25% market share) was believed to reinforce this perception. Beko was also marketed in Turkey as a "world brand"; Beko retailers capitalized on the brand's penetration of export markets as a signal of quality to Turkish consumers.

In 1996, Arçelik and Beko advertising and promotion budgets accounted for 2% and 4%, respectively, of both brands' sales. Advertising included both television and print advertising. The print component included some cooperative advertising with the cost shared between Arçelik and its retailers on a 50/50 basis. Promotions included "trade-in" offers designed to accelerate consumers' repurchase cycles.

Pricing

Arçelik's product lines covered a full range of price points; the most expensive, fully featured item in a product line was typically double the price of the least expensive. With an inflation rate of 80% in 1996, Arçelik prices were increased that year by 9% every two months. Reductions in unit manufacturing costs, stemming from improved productivity and declines in world plastic and stainless steel prices, enabled Arçelik to take price increases below the rate of inflation. Doing so helped Arçelik retain market share.

Arçelik white goods were priced consistently nationwide. They were the highest priced among domestically manufactured white goods but retailed at prices lower than imported models. Exhibit 10 compares white goods retail prices (including 23% value added tax) across a variety of brands.

As shown in Exhibit 11, Arçelik's average operating profit before interest and taxes was 13%. Arçelik's operating profit on exports was considerably lower. While registering strong profits on refrigerators, Arçelik unit margins on washing machines and dishwashers in 1996 were lower than competitors' margins due to depreciation charges associated with Arçelik's heavy investments in plant modernization and the fact that several lines were still ramping up to efficient volumes of production.

Exhibit 10

Comparative Index of Retail Prices for Turkish White Goods Brands: 1996

Brand Name	Refrigerators	Washing machines	Dishwashers	Ovens
Arçelik (Arçelik)	100	94	58	42
AEG (Peg)	91	89	64	38
Bosch (Peg)	112.5	102	87	-
Miele (import)	123	-	-	-
G.E. (import)	320	-	-	-
Westinghouse (import)	147.5	-	-	-
Electrolux (import)	116	127	90	-

Source: Company records.

Exhibit 11   Arçelik Cost and Price Structure in Turkey

Cost Structure

Retail Selling Price[1]	125
Wholesale Price[2]	112
Advertising and Promotion	3
Selling and Distribution	5
Factory Price	100
Variable Costs	58
Direct Materials	51
Direct Labor	4
Variable Overhead	3
Research and Development	4
Depreciation	10
General and Administrative Expenses	15
Operating Profit	13
(Before Interest and Taxes)	

Source: Company records.

[1]The price at which exclusive Arçelik retailers sold to the end consumer excluding value added tax.
Retailers generally made 5-6% pretax profit.

[2]The price at which Atilim, Koç's captive marketing company, sold the product to the exclusive retail network in Turkey.

Distribution and Sales

Ninety-five percent of white goods were sold to individual consumers through retail stores; only 5% were sold by manufacturers direct to building contractors. Single brand retailers accounted for 60% of retail unit sales of white goods in Turkey; the remaining 40% were sold through multibrand outlets. In addition to traditional appliance specialty stores, new channels such as Carrefour and Metro hypermarkets were opening in greater Istanbul. Selected Beko products (but no Arçelik products) were sold through these outlets. Around 28% of Turkish white goods were sold in Istanbul.

Arçelik delivered products to the Turkish market through exclusive retailers. There were 1,650 outlets carrying only the Arçelik brand, of which 700 accounted for 70% of sales. Another 1,050 outlets carried only Beko products. Beko also reached consumers through a further 2,500 to 3,000 non-exclusive outlets, which accounted for 30% of Beko sales. Arçelik was not available in any multibrand outlets. Arçelik typically added 100 new outlets per year and discontinued 30. New outlets included existing multibrand appliance dealers who applied to become Arçelik dealers, stores established by the sons of existing Arçelik dealers, and stores started by sufficiently well-capitalized entrepreneurs. New outlets had to be established in new residential areas and in areas where appliance demand increased with disposable income. According to Arçelik's national sales manager:

Being the Arçelik dealer in a community is a much sought after position of importance. We have many applicants to choose from. Our dealers are loyal because our brand pull results in inventory turns three times faster than

for our nearest competitor. As a result, our unit margins at retail can be narrower.

The product mix varied according to the size of each store and the demographics of the neighborhood in which it was located. An Arçelik store manager commented:

Consumer demand for appliances is strong. People are switching from semiautomatic to automatic washing machines. First-time purchases of dishwashers are strong. Consumers living in apartments often have big families and need large refrigerators.

One hundred salespeople visited the Arçelik dealers, typically once every two weeks. Beko sold through 150 salespeople. Salesforce turnover was a modest 5% per year.

A strong Arçelik retailer might carry $100,000 worth of inventory in the store and $500,000 in a warehouse, all on 100 day payment terms from the manufacturer. Typically, 15 sales would be made each day including 6 washing machines, 4 refrigerators and 2 dishwashers. An average dealer might make 5 sales per day and hold $50,000 in floor inventory.

Ninety percent of Arçelik white goods were sold to consumers on credit installment plans of between three and fifteen months. In addition to factory-sourced finance, a newly established Koç finance company also offered credit, often at interest rates slightly below the rate of inflation[7]. Each Arçelik dealer was liable for payment on the units sold on installment. The bad debt rate was less than 1%. Arçelik's competitors such as Bosch were obliged to offer the same terms. Carrefour stores in the major cities could only offer their consumers bank credit at rates significantly higher than Arçelik.

Service

With the average white goods appliance in use for 12 years, the quality and availability of after-sales service was important to Turkish consumers in influencing other brand purchase decisions. Service for Arçelik and Beko white goods was provided by 500 authorized dealers who serviced only these two brands. Another 450 dealers serviced the brown goods of the two brands. There was no joint ownership of sales outlets and service dealers, though informal ties were common. Forty percent of service dealer revenues was generated by installations of newly-purchased appliances; delivery and installment

costs were included in the retail prices. The service organization was especially challenged when there was a surge in consumer sales, as in 1996.

INTERNATIONAL EXPANSION

Opportunistic exports of Arçelik white goods began in the 1980s through Koç Holding's export company, principally to the geographically neighboring markets of the Middle East and North Africa. Arçelik models did not have to be adapted to local requirements. In 1983, an export department was established within Arçelik. One of its tasks was to develop bid proposals on foreign government tenders and for foreign contract builders of low income housing. In 1988, Arçelik's export department contracted to supply refrigerators on an OEM basis to Sears Roebuck for distribution in the Caribbean and Latin America under the Kenmore name. Though Arçelik's exports were a modest percentage of total sales during the 1980s, Arçelik was the largest exporter among Koç Holding companies.

In 1988, the Turkish government's tariff reduction agreement with the European Community prompted an increased interest in exports. Mr. Berkman explained:

We needed to find out more about our likely future competitors. One way to do so was to sell Arçelik products in the tough developed markets. The Americas were too far away, in terms of both transportation costs, product adaptation requirements (for 110 volt current), and our ability to understand consumers. Western Europe was much closer. We thought we would learn a great deal by competing against the best in the world on their home turf and better prepare ourselves to defend our domestic market share against the likes of Bosch and Siemens.

As of 1996, almost half of the 990,000 Arçelik and Beko refrigerators produced were exported. In that year, 7.6% of Arçelik's total sales (by value) were exports, up from 2.4% in 1991. A breakdown of exports by destination is presented in Table A. Arçelik exported to the countries listed in Exhibit 12, which reports 1996 unit sales of refrigerators and washing machines by market. Arçelik's most successful European market was the U.K., where it had achieved 8% market penetration. In the Middle East and North Africa, Arçelik had achieved almost 20% market share in Tunisia. The firm held between 1% and 4% market share in most of the other product-markets listed in Exhibit 12.

---

7 Securitizing receivables and installment loans through Koç Finans reduced Arçelik's working capital needs and, therefore, its average cost of capital.

Destination	Percentage
United Kingdom	28%
France	18%
Other European Union	14%
North Africa	17%
Eastern Europe and Central Asia	6%
Other	17%

In 1996, Arçelik exports of white goods were principally refrigerators and washing machines, as shown in Table B. Technology licensing agreements precluded exports of most dishwashers. In 1996, Arçelik's refrigerator plants were operating at full capacity. By 1998, an extra 350,000 units of capacity was expected to come on stream. Management expected to double exports of washing machines in 1997 without any addition of capacity. Dishwasher exports were expected to increase to 110,000 units in 1997 when Arçelik was to supply the first of five annual installments of at least 100,000 OEM units to Whirlpool for distribution in Europe. This was the first time Arçelik had agreed to an OEM contract with a global competitor; Arçelik was not permitted to sell similar models in Europe under its own brand names.

Arçelik in Western Europe
Starting in 1989, Arçelik opened sales offices in the United Kingdom, then France, then Germany, reasoning that, in these larger European markets, there might be more opportunity for a new brand to establish a sufficient volume of sales to be viable. At the same time, the export effort to other markets continued. In all export markets, Arçelik focused on building the Beko name (since it was easier to pronounce than Arçelik in a wide variety of languages).

United Kingdom
A sales office was established in the U.K. in 1989. The U.K. market was selected for this initial effort because it was price sensitive and not dominated by domestic brands. By 1997, there were 1 million Beko appliances in use in the U.K., two-thirds of which were refrigerators and one-third televisions. Sales of 300,000 Beko refrigerators were expected in 1997, of which two-thirds would be tabletop height refrigerators and one-third full-size refrigerators[8].

In addition to refrigerators, Beko was beginning to sell dishwashers, washing machines and ovens. Management had focused from the outset on building the Beko brand; only 10,000 of the units sold in 1996 were marketed on an OEM basis.

Melvyn Goodship, managing director, explained Beko's success in the U.K.:

> We exploited an underserved niche for tabletop refrigerators. Our factories in Turkey had spare capacity in the early nineties, so could promptly fill our orders and deliver consistent product quality. At first, we were accused of dumping but lower priced brands from Eastern and Central European countries are now criticized for that. Through patience and persistence, we have built our brand reputation and distribution.

By 1996, Beko had penetrated the three principal specialty appliance chains in the U.K.—Curry's, Comet and Iceland. Beko appliances were also sold through the principal mail order catalogs—Empire and Littlewoods. Management believed Beko appliances were available through 65% of selling points in the U.K. Beko maintained a warehouse in the U.K. to serve its retail accounts.

In 1996, the Beko brand was supported by £600,000 of advertising, including £100,000 to launch Beko washing machines and £150,000 of cooperative advertising.[9]

The retail price of a typical Beko tabletop refrigerator was £150 including 17.5% value added tax and a 25% distribution margin. Comparable refrigerators of other brands would retail at £300 for Bosch, £200 for Hotpoint (the U.K. market share leader) and £160 for Indesit (an Italian manufacturer). Cheap brands of inconsistent quality from Eastern and Central European countries could be found for £120. Manufacturer prices of branded products were so competitive that large retailers saw no need to assume the inventory risk of contracting for OEM production.

---

[8] In contrast, the market as a whole comprised 60% full-size refrigerators and 40% tabletop height refrigerators.

[9] In 1996, one U.S. dollar was equivalent to 80,000 Turkish lira (June, 1996); one British pound was equivalent to $U.S. 1.60; and one German mark was equivalent to $U.S. 0.65.

	Refrigerators 1996 Unit Sales	Automatic Washing Machines 1996 Unit Sales
EUROPEAN COMMUNITY		
France	2,500,000	1,600,000
Germany	3,600,000	2,600,000
United Kingdom	2,500,000	1,400,000
Benelux	1,200,000	600,000
Denmark	200,000	130,000
Spain/Portugal	2,000,000	1,300,000
Greece	NA	NA
MIDDLE EAST & NORTH AFRICA (MENA)		
Egypt	500,000	250,000
Lebanon	100,000	40,000
Syria	200,000	100,000
Iraq	400,000	200,000
Iran	1,000,000	250,000
Tunisia	120,000	25,000
Algeria	250,000	30,000
Morocco	110,000	20,000
EASTERN & CENTRAL EUROPE, & CENTRAL ASIA		
Albania	NA	NA
Romania	300,000	150,000
Bulgaria	130,000	70,000
Russia	2,200,000	600,000
Malta	NA	NA
Turkmenistan	100,000	15,000
Uzbekistan	100,000	15,000
Kazakstan	100,000	15,000
Azerbaijan	NA	NA
Ukraine	300,000	50,000

Source: Company records.

France

Arçelik opened a French sales office in 1993. By 1996, annual sales were up to 75,000 units. However, according to the French sales manager:

The French market is in a recession and is cluttered with competitors. It is hard for us to break into new accounts. 1997 will be a crucial year.

The French white goods market was highly competitive. Fifteen trade accounts controlled 75% of consumer sales. Thirty percent of white goods unit sales carried store brand names. Appliance specialty stores accounted for 45% of unit sales, hypermarkets for 30%, and mail order companies and department stores for 25%. There were no dominant national brands. The long-standing French brands, Thomson and Brandt, each accounting for 20% of unit sales were, by 1997, owned by Italian manufacturers.

Table B	Arçelik White Goods Exports and Mix: 1996		

	Export Units	% Beko	% OEM
Refrigerators	430,000	70	30
Washing Machines	55,000	50	50

Arçelik pursued a two brand strategy in France. Management believed that, if the Beko brand was launched at a low price, it would be impossible to raise it later. The Beko brand was therefore positioned and priced similarly to the mainstream Candy brand from Italy. The Beko brand accounted for 25% of the company's unit sales in France in 1996. Other Koç or OEM brands were priced lower than Beko to attract volume orders.

Of 75,000 units sold in France in 1996, 68,000 were refrigerators and 7,000 were washing machines and ovens. Of the 75,000, 15% were sold to kitchenette manufacturers and 15% were sold on an OEM basis to Frigidaire. Seventy percent of the remaining units were shipped to hypermarkets, notably LeClerc (the third largest hypermarket chain in France), and 30% to appliance specialty stores. The French sales office had not yet been able to break into any department stores or mail order accounts. A two-year test, involving telemarketing Beko white goods to high street retailers, was currently underway. The only advertising for Beko in France appeared in the LeClerc catalog.

Germany

Arçelik opened a German sales office within an existing company called Interbrucke GmbH in 1994 under a general manager who had previously been an importer of Beko televisions.

Well-known, premium-priced German brands such as Bosch, Siemens, AEG and Miele held a 60% unit market share of white goods. The remaining 40% was divided among numerous lower-priced Italian and East European manufacturers, none of whom held more than a 4% share.

About 60% of white goods were sold through traditional appliance retailers, almost all of whom were members of retail buying groups or served through regional wholesalers. Twenty percent of white goods were sold through mail order firms like Quelle, usually at prices below those in the specialty retailers. Of the remaining units, 10% were sold through mass merchandisers, 5% through hypermarkets, and 5% through traditional department stores.

In 1996, Beko sold 30,000 refrigerators in Germany, up from 10,000 in 1995, and 20,000 washing machines, up from 5,000 in the preceding year. Unit sales of refrigerators and washing machines in Germany in 1996 were 3,600,000 and 2,600,000 respectively. Management predicted sales of 70,000 and 30,000 for the two Beko lines in 1997. To date, 80% of Beko sales had been made to retail buying groups and regional wholesalers; the remaining 20% had been made to the manufacturers of prepackaged kitchenettes which were sold to home builders. By the end of 1996, Beko white goods were being bought by 12 accounts, in all cases on an OEM basis.

Beko white goods were imported from Turkey and stored in a rented warehouse in Germany. The average retail price of a Beko refrigerator was DM 399. Comparable Bosch and Siemens refrigerators sold for DM 499 to DM 599.

Beko had no resources for a consumer advertising campaign, though some funds were available to buy advertising space in retailer catalogs.

The general manager commented on Beko's prospects in Germany as follows:

> The German economy is weak right now and population growth is flat. Demand for appliances is soft but fairly predictable. Consumers and, therefore, distributors are more price sensitive, especially in the former East Germany. This plays to our strength as a value brand. More retailers than ever before are scrambling to sell appliances, so that's putting further pressure on margins.

> In this price sensitive climate, I believe Beko's prospects are good. Germany is Turkey's largest trading partner. The challenge is to develop relationships with the big customers and persuade them to switch to Beko. If we can build unit volume by supplying OEM (or private label) product to these customers, we may be able to make enough money to invest in building the Beko brand.

Assessing Progress

Progress in Western Europe was slower than some executives expected, leading them to question the strategy. A senior manager at headquarters in Istanbul commented:

> We should not focus on breaking into Western Europe where growth is limited and where five companies control

75% of unit sales of white goods. Instead, we should focus on the emerging markets of Russia and Central Asia where foreign brand names are not yet entrenched in consumers' minds. We are geographically well-positioned to supply these markets. The fact that our products are made in Turkey will be a plus in those markets whereas, in Western Europe, we have to avoid mentioning it.

However, others supported the emphasis on Western Europe:

The former communist markets of East and Central Europe will be important but, right now, they are too volatile. Tariff rates change overnight and we have no tariff advantage over Japanese and Korean competitors in these markets like we do in Western Europe. We would have to make risky investments in local manufacturing and distribution; finding the right local partners and sufficiently skilled workers would be difficult. I would rather focus on Western Europe for the moment. The markets are tough to crack and our unit margins are lower than in Turkey but at least our goods enter duty free and demand is predictable.

CONCLUSION

In between hosting visitors to their Domotechnica booth in Cologne, Arçelik's managers continued to discuss informally whether or not they were placing the correct emphasis on international markets, and whether their brand-building and market selection strategies were appropriate. Some of the comments at the booth included:

In 1996, we showed we could hold our own in the Turkish market against the top brands in the world. In fact, our market share in refrigerators actually increased. This means we can now push our international exports more aggressively.

Wait a minute. Capacity is tight. If the Turkish market continues to grow at the current rate, we'll need most of our planned capacity for 1997 to meet domestic demand. And we know that we make at least twice as much unit margin if we sell an appliance in Turkey than if we export it.

The current rate of economic growth is not sustainable. The government, in anticipation of a general election, is pumping money into the economy. The economy will probably slow down, maybe even go into recession in 1997. I don't think we'll have a capacity problem.

We've got to emphasize building the Beko brand worldwide. We'll never make big money on OEM business, whether we are making to order for other manufacturers—who are, in fact, our competitors—or for retail chains. Special orders add to complexity costs in our plants and we lose our R&D edge when we simply follow the customers' blueprints. Occasionally, you can build up a long-term relationship with an OEM customer through consistent on-time deliveries but, more often than not, OEM orders are one-shot deals through which the customer is trying to exert leverage on his or her other suppliers or cover against a strike threat.

I'm not so sure. Selling OEM production is more profitable than selling the equivalent number of Beko branded units. Marketing costs per unit are lower and we don't have to invest in pull advertising support through our national distributors.

You don't understand. We're making products of outstanding quality these days. Because Turkey's reputation for quality manufactures is not well-established, we've had to work doubly hard to achieve recognition. We shouldn't be wasting any more time doing OEM production of lower-priced, simple models when we have the quality to take on the best in the world at the premium end of the white goods market.

Part V

Managing International Partners and Alliances

In the early 1980s, Professor Michael Porter's "five forces" analysis depicted companies in a value appropriation battle with their customers, suppliers, and competitors. Today we see them focused more on value creation by working in mutually advantageous partnerships with these same groups. Similarly, Professor Raymond Vernon's seminal analysis of business-government relationships described multinational corporations (MNCs) holding "sovereignty at bay," but today we see the same companies pursuing cooperative relationships with host governments worldwide, often becoming partners in ventures with them.

This dramatic change in strategic thinking and organizational relationships has made the boom in alliances, consortia, and strategic partnerships a worldwide phenomenon. It has been driven by some new market forces, has led to some new business forms, and has created some new strategic costs and risks.

NEW FORCES AND MOTIVATIONS

International business has long been characterized by joint ventures, but these were typically opportunistic, localized, and short-lived relationships established by companies to gain access to unfamiliar foreign markets. The more recent explosion in global alliances is much different: they typically involve much larger partners, are global in scale, and are strategic in nature.

The biggest driver of this change is the shift occurring in the critical scarce resources constraining companies' growth. Where once the constraints were imposed by the availability of capital, today the limiting resources increasingly are information, knowledge, and expertise. Although not restricted to research and development, this intellectual capital constraint is often seen earliest and most clearly in a company's research labs: efficient scale of R&D is rising, the scope of relevant technologies is broadening, and the product life cycles are shrinking. Together, these forces have created a situation in which the cost of product and process development has skyrocketed. Equally problematic is the reality that few companies by themselves have all the technology and expertise they need to become (or remain) leading-edge competitors in a competitive game increasingly played on the field of innovation. More than anything else, this has become the engine driving the scramble for alliance partners.

PARTNERSHIP MOTIVATIONS AND FORMS

The motivations for forming strategic partnerships are many and varied, and their legal forms and administrative frameworks are too numerous to catalog. Among the newest alliance relationships, however, four clearly interlinked categories deserve to be highlighted:

- **Partnership for technological exchange.** The huge advances made in various scientific and technological fronts have often led to the transformation of whole industries. (Think, for example, of the effect of the transistor and the semiconductor on the consumer electronics industry.) At one level, these forces drive industry consolidation through massive mergers and acquisitions such as the ones that have swept through the pharmaceutical, banking, and professional services industries. But even such consolidation has often proved insufficient to provide the critical mass necessary to gain global-scale efficiencies, and even newly merged pharmaceutical behemoths—such as SmithKline Beecham or Novartis—still are frantically expanding their huge portfolios of distribution agreements, cross-licenses, and other strategic partnership arrangements.
- **Partnership for global competitiveness.** In the face of such industry restructuring and the emergence of dominant players, a flurry of activity has occurred, creating partnerships and alliances among smaller players uniting to gain some competitive defense against the industry giants. This is the motivation that led to Fujitsu's various worldwide partnerships to combat IBM. It also is the driving force behind the numerous initiatives among the small players in the software industry to unite in strength against Microsoft. For many companies in smaller countries, the chance of partnering with a dominant global player represents the most effective way in which they can gain access to the benefits of the global competitive game. It is this motivation that has driven many companies to enter into joint-venture partnerships with Corning as that company expands into markets worldwide.
- **Partnerships for industry convergence.** The technological turmoil has no respect for industry boundaries, and one of the major forces driving the growth of the cross-border partnerships and alliances has been the convergence of once-separate industries and groups of competitors. Among the clearest examples of this has been the blurring of

the boundary between the computer and telecommunications industries, and more recently, software, media, and the whole field of entertainment. Another classic example has been the pharmaceutical companies' links to biotechnology. But perhaps the most interesting partnership arrangements have emerged in the field of high-definition TV (HDTV). Because HDTV involves a wide range of technologies, huge investments, and enormous risks, this development has led to the creation of several global consortia, many of which have primarily been nationally based. As a result, groups of companies in Japan are facing off against others in the United States, with a third epicenter in this emerging global battle developing in Europe.

- **Partnerships to create industry standards.** The HDTV battle is largely motivated by the recognition that a single set of global industry standards probably will emerge and the company (or, more likely, the consortium) that can establish the dominant format will have an enormous competitive advantage. When global markets were more fragmented, the world was able to develop multiple standards, attested to by the existence today of NTSC, PAL, and SECAM TV transmission standards. However, by the time of the videocassette recorder, global markets were converging and competitive rules were changing. Despite the technological superiority of Philips's V 2000 system and Sony's Betamax technology, the clear winner in the VCR battle was the VHS standard sponsored by Matsushita. Supported by a vast number of partners and licensees, this format quickly emerged as the dominant world standard. Its success became a powerful lesson for many companies, and has made developing industry standards a driving force for partnerships and alliances ever since.

PARTNERSHIP COSTS AND RISKS

Though there are numerous benefits to creating global partnerships, there are at least as many costs. Among the greatest risks is what has become known as the problem of the "obsoleting bargain." Although most partnerships are established on the basis of mutual interdependence and joint gains, that initial balance can easily be disrupted through the deliberate subversion of one of the partners. The critical interdependence is maintained only as long as both sides need each other, but if one partner develops the skill of the other, the basis for the partnership may be eroded. This has been the fate of many joint-venture relationships for market entry, particularly in Japan. When General Foods created a partnership with Ajinomoto, it was based on exchanging the company's technology in instant coffee manufacturing for the Japanese company's market access and management capability in that very different culture. Over several years, however, Ajinomoto learned most of General Foods' technology, whereas the American company learned very little about the Japanese market. Unsurprisingly, the balance that once held the partnership together began eroding and the problem of the obsoleting bargain became clear. Similar problems led to the breakup of the technology agreements between Komatsu on one side and International Harvester and Cummins on the other.

If the obsoleting bargain is the main strategic risk in most partnerships, then boundary management is the main organizational cost. Most companies entering into alliances of various kinds focus primarily on the strategic logic and spend very little of their negotiating efforts trying to understand the organizational logic of the new partnership. Yet research continually shows that it is in the organization and management of the partnerships that most of the difficulty arises. For managers in the partnership, the requirement is the ability to take responsibility for matters over which they do not have complete control. This classic partnership problem requires both partners to commit to careful selection of boundary-spanning managers, major integration of information systems, a realignment of incentives and rewards, and constant monitoring by top management.

If such intensive management attention comes at a cost, it is only because these alliances offer such substantial potential benefit. For many companies, they have become the linchpin of their global competitiveness.

Loctite Corporation—International Distribution

In December 1992, the senior management of Loctite Corporation was reviewing the company's international distribution policies in the light of a recent decision to acquire an equity interest in their Hong Kong distributor. Worldwide distribution capability had been a key element in the corporation's achievement of global leadership in the chemical adhesives industry. Loctite had a range of relationships through which it accessed international markets, including export agents, distributors, joint ventures, and wholly owned subsidiaries.

Chairman and CEO Ken Butterworth, a 17-year Loctite veteran who had once worked for Loctite's Australian distributor, was continually looking to open up new markets with potential. With economic recession limiting growth in Loctite's core North American and European markets, expansion in the Asia/Pacific region was a key strategic goal. Butterworth was discussing the company's Hong Kong options with David Freeman, president and COO, an Englishman with an 18-year Loctite career, and Martin Wiley, an American who had worked for the company for 30 years and was now regional manager for the southern half of Loctite's Asia/Pacific operations.

Company Background

Founded in 1956, Loctite Corporation, headquartered in Hartford, Connecticut, had grown to become the world's leading manufacturer and marketer of adhesives, sealants, and related products. During the 1980s, it had enjoyed impressive growth; net sales had increased from $228 million in 1983 to $608 million in 1992, and net earnings had grown during the same period from $22 million to

This case was prepared by Professor John A. Quelch with the assistance of David J. Arnold. Copyright © 1993 by the President and Fellows of Harvard College. Harvard Business School case 9-594-021.

$72 million. The 1992 balance sheet showed total assets of $557 million, stockholders' equity of $383 million, and long-term liabilities of $36 million. The company had achieved *Fortune* 500 status in 1990, and in 1991 was ranked 477 in revenue, 190 in profits, 24 in profit as a percentage of sales, and 18 in per share annual growth over the previous decade. (Exhibit 1 summarizes Loctite's income statements from 1990 to 1992.) By 1992, the company estimated its worldwide market share in industrial adhesives at 70%-80%.

As stated in the 1992 annual report, Loctite's growth had been based upon a "strategy of promoting diversity in end use markets and geographies for our core business; diversification into new businesses in which senior management has little expertise is not part of our strategy." This core business remained the sale of chemical adhesives to industrial users who had previously used mechanical fasteners such as screws and bolts; industrial chemical adhesives and sealants accounted for 50% of corporate revenues in 1992. From this base, Loctite had expanded into related markets in the 1970s, such as the automotive aftermarket, an entry built upon the acquisition of Permatex. In the mid-1970s, Loctite had also entered the consumer adhesives market and grew this business through acquisitions, principally the purchase of Woodhill Chemicals. More recently, Loctite had also expanded its technology base through the acquisition of silicone and polyurethane companies, and in 1990 had acquired a U.S. company selling hand-cleaning products, seen as a natural complement to adhesives and sealants.

Geographical expansion had begun early in the company's history. By 1992 Loctite had equity positions in operations in 33 countries outside the United States—with third-party distributors in other countries—and almost 60% of sales and 70% of earnings were derived from operations outside the United States.

| | Year Ended December 31 | | |
	1990	1991	1992
Net sales	$555,185	$561,218	$607,967
Cost of sales	215,132	21 7,501	229,175
Gross margin	340,053	343,717	378,792
R&D expense	21,731	22,498	26,152
Selling, general, and administration expenses	222,884	222,240	239,640
Restructuring charges	0	4,434	12,740
Earnings from operations	95,438	94,545	100,260
Investment income	11 ,010	13,365	9,173
Interest expense	(6,790)	(5,477)	(5,593)
Other expense	(934)	(346)	(94)
Foreign exchange loss	(7,440)	(6,202)	(8,601)
Earnings before income taxes	91 ,284	95,885	95,145
Provision for income taxes	23,861	23,971	22,834
Net earnings	$67,423	$71,914	$72,311
Earnings per share	$1.86	$1.98	$1.99

Source: Loctite Corporation annual reports

Organization

Loctite was organized into four regional groups: North America, consisting of the United States, Canada, and Mexico; Latin America, consisting of all countries south of Mexico; Europe, which included the former Communist bloc countries and was also responsible for operations in the Middle East and Africa; and Asia/Pacific, stretching from Korea to Australasia and as far west as India. Within these regions, operations were organized into three business groups: the industrial market, including original equipment manufacture (OEM) and maintenance, repair, and overhaul (MRO) customers;[1] the retail and consumer markets; and the automotive aftermarket.

Organization structures varied by region. The president of North America headed a functional organization with no country managers, as the United States, Mexico, and Canada were viewed as a single market and divided into 12 sales regions (one of which, for example, spanned the U.S.-Canada border). These regional sales managers reported to a vice president of sales in Hartford. In the three other regions, country managers with profit responsibility reported to regional management, who also sometimes had regionwide responsibility for a line of business. For example, the vice presidents of northern and southern Europe, based in Munich and Milan, were also responsible, respectively, for development of Loctite's industrial products and consumer products throughout the entire European region. On a more informal basis, Loctite's two vice presidents of Asia/Pacific, based in Hong Kong and Tokyo, had complementary sales and technical backgrounds that helped them jointly develop business in the region. A limited number of functional managers also had regional responsibilities, such as the vice president of manufacturing in Europe, based in Dublin near the major Irish plant, and regional marketing managers, who provided guidance to and transferred best practices among marketing managers in

---

1 Original equipment manufacturers (OEM) made products for sale as new items, either under their own brand name or those of third parties. Maintenance, repair, and overhaul (MRO) organizations were service businesses offering after-sales support to maximize the performance of the products. The automotive aftermarket, an industry built around the service and maintenance of motor vehicles, was an MRO market, although it was of sufficient importance to Loctite to merit its own business group.

Loctite's subsidiaries and distributors. (Exhibit 2 depicts Loctite's organization structure as in 1992, and Exhibit 3 gives a breakdown of employees by region.)

The corporation was run in a decentralized fashion, with only 56 people in the Hartford headquarters office. Direct reports to Butterworth and Freeman, besides the regional managers, included the heads of various corporate staff groups and New Business Development (NBD). The primary role of NBD was research and development, from basic chemical research through product development. There were no corporate marketing managers, as Butterworth believed that "marketing belongs at the coal face." Planning was a bottom-up process, which required national units to present their detailed plans annually to visiting corporate staff, usually either Butterworth and/or Freeman. Drawing on their years of experience at Loctite and their knowledge of other markets, they were able to challenge and refine the plans. Butterworth acknowledged that these sessions could be "brutal," but he always ensured that his visits incorporated customer meetings and social functions which ensured a strong enough relationship between headquarters and the field that the latter could accept his challenging management style.

Product Line

Loctite's strategy was to offer a full range of adhesive and sealant products to meet the different needs of a broad range of customers: as stated in the 1991 annual report, "Loctite generally does not rely on blockbuster products. . . . We tend to have more application-sensitive products, each of which requires specific marketing focus to introduce." Technical leadership in product development was key to Loctite's success. In 1992, the company spent 4% of its revenue on R&D at facilities in Connecticut, Ireland, and Japan. Loctite sought to derive a minimum of 25% of its annual revenues from products launched within the previous five years.

Loctite sold three principal product lines: anaerobic adhesives, which accounted for 28% of corporate sales in 1992 and were sold exclusively in industrial markets; cyanoacrylates (CAs), which sold in both industrial markets (15% of sales) and consumer markets (18% of sales); and

---

Exhibit 2   Loctite Corporation: Organization Structure, 1992

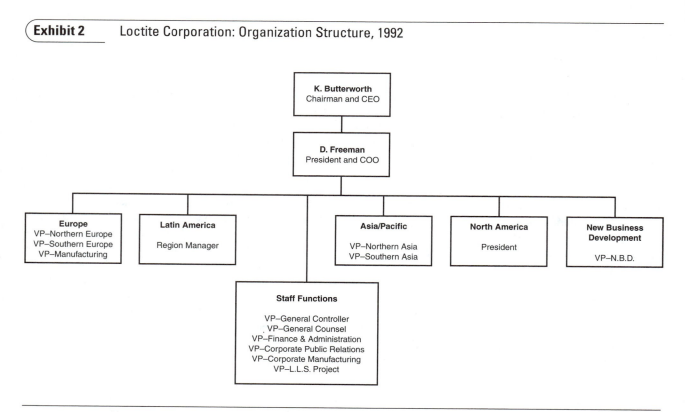

Source: Loctite Corporation

Exhibit 3   Employees by Region, December 1992

	Total		Regional Management
North America	1,792	(48.6%)	2
Europe	1,095	(29.7%)	4
Asia/Pacific	278	(7.5%)	4
Latin America	524	(14.2%)	2
	3,689		
Corporate headquarters	56		

Source: Loctite Corporation

silicones (12% of sales). Loctite also sold adhesives and sealants based on other technologies, such as the epoxies used to bond microchips to circuit boards. Other revenues were derived from hand-cleaning products, which Loctite had recently introduced in several countries under the Fast Orange brand name, and a variety of dispensing equipment which Loctite had developed for its products, ranging from simple hand-held guns or rollers to complex assemblies such as screen-printing devices which could fit into computer-controlled assembly lines.

Anaerobic adhesives were the "family crown jewels," the technology on which the company had been founded in 1956. They were stored and dispensed in liquid form, but self-hardened into tough plastics as soon as they were deprived of air. Originally developed to bond cylindrical metal parts (such as a bolt to a nut), they were later employed in a wide range of applications such as engine housings and bearings. The benefits of anaerobics compared to mechanical fixings were fourfold:

1. *Cost savings.* Unlike mechanical fixings, aerobic retention was not dependent upon the precision with which the parts were engineered, and so allowed manufacturers to achieve savings on components.

2. *Speed of assembly.* The application of the adhesive was simple and fast compared to mechanical fixings. By switching from mechanical fastenings to chemical adhesives, Westland, the U.K. helicopter manufacturer, reduced assembly time for each of the 200 bearings in its Lynx aircraft from 10-15 minutes to 2 minutes without any modification of the parts involved.

3. *Strength in service.* However fine the tolerance to which they were engineered, the two or more parts of a mechanical fixture could be in contact only at their high points, typically 25% of the surface, leaving what Loctite referred to as "inner space." The liquid anaerobic adhesive, by filling all this space, provided 100% surface contact, resulting in a stronger fitting, less wear in use, and lower maintenance requirements.

4. *Leakproofing.* Since total surface fit eliminated the leakage of liquids or gas, an anaerobic could act as a sealant and improve the performance of an assembly. Vibration and other wear caused by leakage of liquids or gas could also be eliminated, reducing maintenance requirements.

CAs set faster than anaerobics but were less tough and durable. Suitable for a wider range of applications and materials beyond metal-to-metal fixtures, they were also sold to consumers as instant general-purpose adhesives. The first CA had been introduced by a division of Eastman Kodak in 1958, and during the 1960s Eastman sold CAs to Loctite for repackaging. Loctite developed its own manufacturing technology in 1971 and, by 1978, was believed to have exceeded Eastman's share of the North American industrial CA market. Loctite's consumer CA brand, Super Glue, had grown to become a major player in selected markets around the world, although it faced tough competition from several international brands such as the world leader, Krazy Glue, manufactured by Toagosei of Japan.

Silicone products had been added to the product line in the late 1980s as part of Loctite's strategy of broadening its technology base. Sold exclusively in industrial markets, they were used for a range of applications complementary to the rigid plate fixings for which anaerobics were best suited, such as coating, sealing, lubricity, thermal conductivity, and electrical insulation. They were particularly important in "formed-in-place" gaskets (where their leakproofing qualities outperformed traditional materials such as metal or rubber) and in electronic manufacturing (for example, in the protection of electronic components on a printed circuit board).

Product formulations were, with few exceptions, identical in all markets and countries. Packaging was more variable and was customized to individual markets, with the Irish packaging plant able to print packages in 62 languages with low changeover costs. In line with Loctite's strategy of focus in product range and diversity in markets and geography, local salespeople were encouraged to adapt their communications messages to individual customers.

Sales Mix

The sales mix of Loctite products varied from one country to another, although Loctite's business was always based upon the core industrial product lines of anaerobics and industrial CAs. Freeman commented, "We will only enter the automotive aftermarket and/or consumer markets when a base of business has been established and profitability achieved in the industrial market." In Loctite's more mature American and European operations, the sales mix covered the entire Loctite product range. A typical distributor in these mature markets carried approximately 100 stock-keeping units (SKUs), consisting of various sizes of some 30 Loctite products. Around 25% of SKUs were common to virtually all distributors and these typically generated at least 50% of a distributor's sales. Having built its business on these core products, a mature market distributor then expanded its range of Loctite products according to the type of customer industries it served. In many less-developed markets, by contrast, Loctite was still building its core industrial business.

Loctite's sales mix was also broadly based in terms of customers, with no one end user in the United States accounting for more than 1% of corporate sales, and no North American distributor accounting for more than 10%. While some of the sales mix variation was due to inherent differences in market potential and stage of economic development, Butterworth also believed it was due to the differing skills, experience, or contacts of distributors which resulted in their focusing on one or two of Loctite's product lines at the expense of others. Experience gained in industrial markets, for instance, had seldom proved transferable to the building of a consumer business. In total, 18% of Loctite worldwide revenues in 1992 were from nonowned operations outside North America, consisting of 12.5% from joint ventures and 5.5% from independent distributors. Ten years earlier, independent distributors had contributed approximately one-third of revenues.

The greatest variation in sales performance was in consumer markets. In 1992, for instance, consumer product sales represented only 6% of revenues in North America, where Super Glue ranked second in market share, but were considerably higher in Europe, which accounted for over 60% of worldwide sales of Super Glue. Loctite's worldwide market share in consumer instant adhesives was 20%-25%. In markets where Loctite had been the first to launch consumer instant adhesives, or where a distributor had invested substantially in building a consumer business, Loctite was the market leader; Brazil and France were the primary examples. In many other countries, Loctite faced more intense competition for consumer product sales and could not easily afford the investment required to build a consumer brand franchise through advertising.

Despite its dominant worldwide share in industrial adhesives, Loctite believed its products had achieved only limited penetration of the available market. Mechanical engineers were generally untrained in the chemistry of adhesive technology and relied by a three-to-one margin on the traditional mechanical fastening approaches in which they had been educated. These prospective customers often rejected an initial Loctite sales approach by declaring that they had no need for chemical adhesives. Loctite's marketing and sales efforts, therefore, focused on educating both distributors and end users in the properties of its products through seminars, product videos, and product demonstrations at end user premises. Another problem was that prospective customers often regarded adhesives or fastenings as the least important components of their products. Wiley commented, "Selling industrial adhesives is like selling salt to restaurants." Butterworth believed that Loctite had to work hard on changing its image from a glue company to that of a high-technology company; in 1992 he had approved a partial three-year sponsorship of a Lotus Formula 1 racing car, which incorporated some Loctite products in its assembly.

Loctite faced few direct competitors, and none held more than a 5% share of the world market for industrial adhesives. Major competitors were National Starch, a Unilever subsidiary, which marketed under the Permabond brand name; the German chemical company Henkel; and, more recently, the Japanese Three Bond Corporation, which competed in both retail and industrial markets in Japan but in only industrial markets in North America. 3M had entered the CA market but had withdrawn in 1983. These competitors invested only a fraction of what Loctite invested in R&D. Each offered a narrower product line than Loctite, focusing either on a single adhesive technology or on products for a specific vertical market such as electronics. Most competitors simply copied Loctite products and sought to recruit employees of Loctite and its distributors.

Distribution in North America

By 1992, Loctite products were available through approximately 1,600 outlets across North America. Distributors ranged from single-outlet distributors to Loctite's largest customer, Bearings Inc., with some 260 outlets. The value of Loctite ex-factory sales to these distributors approximated $70 million in 1992. The average distributor margin was 30%-35%.

Loctite was represented in only a small proportion of the 50,000 potential outlets for its products in North America. Loctite believed that selective distribution allowed it to provide a superior level of service to its end customers while still achieving sufficient market coverage. Loctite devoted considerable effort to the selection of distributors. The process began with Loctite surveying the number of manufacturing plants, their sizes and lines of business in a given region, and calculating the sales potential. Selected potential end users of Loctite products were often researched as to their preferred suppliers, and a number of potential distributors was identified. The criteria for appointment as a Loctite distributor included the mix and type of the distributor's existing customers, other lines carried, creditworthiness, and any previous contacts with Loctite. It was Loctite's policy to have two or three distributors covering any market, so that end users had a choice of suppliers.

The low level of knowledge of adhesive technology among many end users was reflected at the distributor level, and in its early years Loctite had to persuade potential distributors to carry its line. Although the company's success in the 1980s meant more distributors applied to carry the Loctite line than the company needed, Loctite continued to provide more support to distributors than that offered by any other competing supplier. Support included training of the distributor's inside and outside salespeople, demonstrations of new products in Loctite seminars, and extensive merchandising aids such as item selection charts and case histories

of applications in different industries. A typical distributor employed one or two outside salespeople and four or five counter staff; Loctite usually targeted two of them for intensive product training. Loctite also undertook joint sales efforts with each distributor and ran seminars at end users' premises, hoping that, eventually, the distributor would learn enough to be able to run such seminars independently.

Distributors could expect attractive returns. Although Loctite products represented only 2%-5% of turnover for most distributors, their distributor margin of 30%-35% was 50%-100% higher than the average margin for the other products they carried. In addition, inventories of Loctite products turned over two to three times faster than most other distributors' product lines. While some of these distributors carried competitor adhesives in product lines which Loctite no longer covered—such as epoxy resins—they rarely carried directly competitive products in Loctite's categories.

These factors had resulted in a stable network of distributors. Of the 1,600 outlets, some 1,400 had been Loctite distributors for at least 10 years, with most of the growth in the 1980s coming either from additional appointments in areas that were insufficiently covered, or from the acquisition of new outlets by existing Loctite distributors. It was rare for a distributor to choose to leave the Loctite network, and only occasionally did Loctite have to dismiss a distributor. The company anticipated some broadening of its distribution in North America to approximately 1,800 outlets by 1996, while maintaining its selective distribution strategy.

The two largest categories of distributors were bearing distributors, serving engineering and equipment manufacturers, and general mill suppliers which offered a wide range of product lines to factories, from industrial clothing to nuts and bolts. Both served a broad base of customers. A few distributors served only specific vertical markets, such as automotive, oil, or electronics firms (although electronics customers were increasingly served by general distributors).

The Loctite North American sales force which served these industrial distributors was organized into 12 regions. Given the differences in buying patterns across Loctite's three product-market sectors, some salespeople within each region specialized in areas such as OEM when justified by the volume of business. Direct sales to large end users were managed by specialist sales representatives who reported to a national sales manager. In 1992, direct sales represented 40% of the industrial business in North America. This figure included some drop shipments, whereby Loctite delivered large orders direct to end users who were established customers of a distributor and paid the relevant distributor 10% of the end user price.

Working alongside the sales organization were six market managers, based in Connecticut and reporting to the vice president of marketing. The six markets were automotive, electronics, other OEM, maintenance, automotive aftermarket, and consumer retail. There were plans to consolidate the North American business into a single organization in Connecticut rather than continue to have efforts directed at the consumer retail market and automotive aftermarket run separately from Cleveland, Ohio—the preacquisition base of Woodhill.

A more intensive distribution strategy was adopted for the maintenance market, in which applications were less complex. For this market, Loctite products were available through some 5,500 outlets under a separate brand name, Permatex. When distributors applied to represent Loctite products in geographical areas that Loctite already covered sufficiently, they were often encouraged to take on the Permatex line instead. There was minimal overlap between the two sets of distributors: the 1,600 industrial distributors could stock the more widely available Permatex products, but the 5,500 maintenance outlets could not carry Loctite-branded products. Cannibalization between the two lines was minimal.

Loctite's International Development

In the late 1950s, Loctite began its international growth with opportunistic export sales to Canada, Australia, and the United Kingdom. Some shipments were also made to Japan under licensing agreements. This international business soon grew to the point where Loctite had to appoint national distributors who, as principals, bought product from Loctite for resale. During the 1960s, expansion continued into Europe: a French distributor was appointed, along with two in Germany—one for anaerobics and one for CAs. All overseas sales were of exported products, until the establishment of manufacturing plants in Ireland and the Netherlands in the late 1960s. International expansion was also accelerated by acquisitions; for example, joint ventures in Australia, Chile, and Venezuela came with the Permatex acquisition.

In the early 1970s, Loctite began acquiring equity interests in its distributors. This process began in Europe, with the establishment of the corporation's first joint venture in Belgium and the acquisition of distributor companies in the United Kingdom, Spain, and Italy. By 1992, Loctite's international operations consisted of a portfolio of wholly owned subsidiaries, joint ventures, and distributorships (see Exhibit 4). In most cases, Loctite's penetration of a country market began with a relationship with a distributor, followed by an increasing stake in the business and eventual Loctite ownership. All joint ventures and wholly owned subsidiaries had evolved from Loctite's relationships with third-party national distributors. (Exhibit 5 shows Loctite's equity transactions in international operations for 1985-1992.)

In 1992, the North America and Europe regions each accounted for approximately 40% of sales, but Europe contributed 50% of earnings. (Exhibit 6 summarizes financial data by region.) In 1992, an economic recession across much of Europe meant that slower growth was anticipated than in the 1980s. Wholly owned Loctite subsidiaries generated 97% of the company's European sales, the balance coming from distributors and joint ventures. Asia/Pacific sales depended heavily on automotive and electronics manufacturers in Japan, where sales had declined sharply in 1992. Growth in newer markets had offset this downturn, and these were expected to be the basis for the growing importance of the region in Loctite's global strategy. In 1992, 85% of Asia/Pacific sales were derived from wholly owned Loctite companies. In Latin America, 82% of sales were from wholly owned companies, 68% of sales were made in Brazil, and economic development and market conditions varied widely among countries.

The decision to enter a country typically began with an assessment by Loctite management of the market potential. There were several ways to identify potential distributors or partners. The most important, as in North America, was discussion with potential end users of Loctite products—typically, 10 or more manufacturers were approached and questioned about their preferred distributors for factory supplies. A second method was to obtain recommendations from Loctite distributors in neighboring countries, who often knew the major regional distributors of imported industrial supplies. Third, the distributors of complementary product lines, such as Borg Warner products, were identified. This three-pronged initial search would typically surface three

	Loctite Equity Holding (%)	Loctite Manufac- turing Plant (M)	Loctite Internal Packaging Plant (P)
North America:			
Canada	100		
Mexico	100	M	P
Puerto Rico	100	M	P
United States	100	M	P
Europe:			
Austria	100		
Belgium	100		
Czech Republic	100		
Denmark	0		
France	100		
Finland	0		
Germany	100		P
Hungary	100		
Ireland	100	M	P
Italy	100	M	P
Netherlands	100		
Norway	51		
Poland	100		
Portugal	0		
Slovenia	100		
South Africa	100	M	P
Spain	100		
Sweden	0		
Switzerland	0		
United Kingdom	100		
Asia/Pacific:			
Australia	100		
Hong Kong	0		
India	40	M	P
Indonesia	100		
Japan	100	M	P
Malaysia	100		
New Zealand	0		
People's Republic of China	50	M	P
Philippines	0		
Singapore	100		
South Korea	100		
Taiwan	51		
Thailand	51		

	Loctite Equity Holding (%)	Loctite Manufac- turing Plant (M)	Loctite Internal Packaging Plant (P)
Latin America:			
Argentina	100		
Brazil	100	M	P
Chile	100	M	P
Colombia	100		
Costa Rica	100	M	P
Ecuador	0		
Peru	0		
Venezuela	51	M	P

Source: Loctite Corporation

to six potential distributors, with whom discussions would then ensue. The whole selection process from assessing a country's market potential through to appointment of a distribution partner typically took one to two years. Although Loctite preferred distributors who had previous experience of distributing imported products, there were few other criteria regarding the most suitable type of business. In Taiwan, for instance, the appointed distributor was a large conglomerate operating many businesses besides distribution, whereas the distributor in Indonesia was a smaller, family-owned business.

Loctite usually granted a new distributor exclusive rights in its territory and provided extensive support. After initial product and sales training, Loctite sales personnel continued to visit a distributorship at least monthly, while senior regional officers visited at least quarterly. Butterworth and/or Freeman also visited every international distributorship and subsidiary for a business review at least once a year. This review would also be the basis for deciding whether a distribution contract would be renewed. Typically, contracts were open-ended rather than for fixed terms, with Loctite reserving the right to give six months' notice of severance if performance was significantly below agreed-upon sales and/or profit projections. (Exceptions could be made for extraneous factors such as a recession in the national market.) The right to terminate a distribution contract had rarely been exercised. Freeman believed that, in the past, Loctite had sometimes been too supportive of underperforming distributorships but that

many of the problems encountered might have been avoided with earlier and preventive intervention by Loctite management. Freeman commented:

> *The prime message we convey to distributors is the importance of pricing to value. It's difficult for many international distributors to understand what they regard as high Loctite prices. Instead of assessing the value of our products to the customer, they are tempted to set margins and prices low, as they do for the other products they carry, such as bearings, where price competition is fierce. We've learned that our support is necessary early in the relationship to help them adapt to this way of selling.*

Loctite regarded sales growth as the most important performance measure in evaluating distributors. Freeman explained:

> *In most international markets the business potential is not a constraint to growth, as chemical adhesives and sealants have little or no penetration, and mechanical fixtures are still dominant. A good distributor in Asia/Pacific, for instance, might be able to grow the business by 35%-40% annually, and we would expect a minimum of 10%-15%. The main reason why France is our second-largest market is not because it has greater potential, but because over a long period the distributor reinvested a large proportion of his profits back into growing the business.*

Once a distributor had established a profitable business in the industrial market, Loctite regional managers

	1985	1986	1987	1988
Mexico			Acquired 100% of manufacturing joint venture	
United States				
Belgium			Bought out remaining 49% of joint venture	
Czech Republic				
France		Acquired 51% of 20-year distributor		
Hungary				
Italy				
Netherlands				
Poland				
Slovenia				
Australia			Acquired 100% of joint venture partner in automotive aftermarket venture	
India				
People's Republic of China		Formed 50/50 joint venture with Loctite Technical Institute		
Singapore/ Malaysia				
South Korea	Formed subsidiary alongside national distributor to provide technical support			
Taiwan				
Thailand				
Argentina				Cancelled distribution contract and formed subsidiary
Chile	Bought out joint venture partner to form subsidiary			
Colombia	Bought out 20% balance of joint venture to form subsidiary			
Venezuela				Increased joint venture holding from 49% to 51%

	1989	1990	1991	1992
Mexico				
United States	Acquired specialty silicone company	Acquired hand cleaner company		
Belgium				
Czech Republic		Opened representative office		
France				
Hungary		Opened representative office		
Italy	Acquired polyurethane company			
Netherlands		Bought out national distribution rights and formed subsidiary		
Poland		Opened representative office		
Slovenia		Opened representative office		
Australia			Merged automotive aftermarket venture into Loctite Australia subsidiary	
India		Formed 51% joint venture with seven-year national distributor		
People's Republic of China				
Singapore/ Malaysia				Bought out national distribution rights from 23-year distributor and formed subsidiary
South Korea		Cancelled distribution contract to activate subsidiary as full marketing company		
Taiwan			Formed 51% joint venture with six-year distributor	
Thailand		Formed 51% joint venture with five-year distributor		
Argentina				
Chile				
Colombia				
Venezuela				

Source: Loctite Corporation

Exhibit 6

Loctite Corporation: Financial Data by Region (US$'000s)

	1990		1991		1992	
Sales Revenues:						
North America	242.4	43.7%	248.6	44.3%	266.7	43.9%
Europe	222.7	40.1%	220.0	39.2%	244.2	40.2%
Asia/Pacific	41.7	7.5%	47.0	8.4%	47.2	7.8%
Latin America	48.4	8.7%	45.6	8.1%	49.9	8.2%
	555.2		561.2		608.0	
Operating Profit:						
North America	39.8	30.0%	45.8	33.5%	56.8	36.8%
Europe	70.1	53.0%	67.9	49.7%	78.1	50.6%
Asia/Pacific	9.1	6.9%	9.6	7.0%	5.8	3.8%
Latin America	13.4	10.1%	13.3	9.7%	13.5	8.8%
New business development	-20.4		-21.7		-25.8	
Corporate headquarters	-16.5		-15.9		-15.4	
Restructuring change	0.0		-4.4		-12.7	
	95.5		94.6		100.3	

Source: Loctite Corporation

Note: Operating profit by region determined based on allocations of Sales and Expenses to units which generated or are responsible for the sales or expense.

would help the firm identify opportunities for growth by reviewing the range of applications for which Loctite products had been successfully employed in other countries. These case studies of vertical industry marketing programs would be introduced by regional sales management and by distributors from one country visiting another and reporting directly on successful initiatives they had undertaken. From surveys of the potential customers for these new applications and experience in other markets, Loctite managers were able to advise the distributor on potential sales volumes.

In many cases, slowing sales growth had stimulated Loctite's acquisition of equity stakes in international distributors. "Once a core business is established, it's tempting for a distributor to sit on the higher margins which Loctite products give him," commented Butterworth. Loctite also believed that many distributors found it difficult to execute the complex sales approach required for its products. In a country where double-digit sales growth was maintained, Loctite was content to continue to serve the market through an independent distributor. Historically, however, Loctite always managed to accelerate sales growth after taking an equity interest in a distributor.

Loctite had recently introduced two mechanisms for global management. The first was the appointment of multinational account coordinators for international customers. Based in the home country of a multinational, these managers were responsible for keeping distributors worldwide informed of their customer companies' plans and operations, and coordinating prices across country markets. A national distributor would be given a price range for a multinational customer by the account coordinator. This ensured that the subsidiaries of a company such as Seagate Technology, with R&D in California and manufacturing in Singapore and Malaysia, would be able to receive roughly equivalent prices no matter where Loctite products were procured, as well as a uniform worldwide service. In turn, each multinational account's profitability could be assessed worldwide. By 1992, about 25 accounts were managed in this way, representing approximately 5% of corporate sales, although the percentage was as high as 25% in markets such as Singapore and Malaysia. (Exhibit 7 shows a brochure produced by Loctite's Japanese multinational account coordinators describing their role.)

A second Loctite coordination initiative was the establishment of three global task forces, one for each business

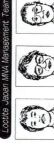

Exhibit 7

LOCTITE®

We are

Multi-National Account

Managers in Japan.

If you need our help,

contact us at.....

FAX No. 81-45(785)0747

Phone No. 81-45(784)2500

Loctite Japan MNA Management Team

Y. MAEDA
NISSAN
14 YEARS SERVICE AND 10 YEARS IN CHARGE OF NISSAN ACCOUNTS. LIVES IN YOKOHAMA.

N. FUJIWARA
MATSUSHITA
14 YEARS SERVICE AND 12 YEARS IN CHARGE OF MATSUSHITA ACCOUNTS. LIVES IN OSAKA.

H. KATO
HONDA
8 YEARS SERVICE AND 5 YEARS IN CHARGE OF HONDA ACCOUNTS. LIVES IN YOKOHAMA.

I. TSURUWAKA
SONY
11 YEARS SERVICE AND 9 YEARS IN CHARGE OF SONY ACCOUNTS. LIVES IN YOKOHAMA.

S. KASAMAKI
TOYOTA
ONE OF STARTING MEMBERS OF LOCTITE JAPAN AND 11 YEARS IN CHARGE OF TOYOTA ACCOUNTS. LIVES IN NAGOYA.

N. KOMATSU
MAZDA
8 YEARS SALES EXPERIENCE AT MAZDA ACCOUNTS. LIVES IN HIROSHIMA.

K. Fuji
Communications Coordinator

How to communicate ...

If you would like to know anything about Multi-National Accounts in Japan. Please fax to MNAMs and copy to K.Fuji, who will intercept your English message for MNAMs and vice versa.

Loctite (Japan) Corporation

Applications....

Electronics

FDD	Gimbal/Carriage	326 LVUV
HDD	Shaft/Bearing	648
LCD	Terminal sealing	350

Speaker	Magnet bonding	392/792
	Speaker assembly for phone	403, 411, 424
PCB	Tacking jumper wire to PCB	Tak Pak AD
Chip	SMT(one by one, pin transfer)	348, 3607

Automotive

Engine	Core Plugs sealing	962T
ATX	Flange sealing	518, FMD-127
Bolt	Precoating	Dri Loc
LIS	Power stearing case	PMS-10E

A.B.C. for communication with Japanese key staff at customers ---.

A — Provide Japanese catalogs and data.
B — Request a Japanese language letter of introduction from MNAM and bring it on the first call.
C — Introduce Japanese ACHs of the MNA in Japan.
D — Learn a few Japanese words and use them, for instance.

- KON-NICHIWA (HELLO)
- ARIGATO-GOZAIMAS (THANK YOU)
- YOROSHIKU-ONEGAISHIMAS. (WE HOPE FOR YOUR POSITIVE REPLY IN THE NEAR FUTURE)
- SHITSUREI-SHIMAS (GOOD-BY NOW)

For our timely support, what we need to know from you are ---.

A — Current business status and/or relationship between you and MNAs.
B — Applications you are developing at MNAs and ACHs.

Loctite Products Specified/used in Japan

(TOYOTA) Loctite products are listed in the following specifications.

Spec. NO	PRODUCT
TSK6706	962T
TSK6708	572, 575
TSK6709 CLASS 1	200
" " CLASS 2	204
TSH7910	PMS-10E

(NISSAN) A lot of Loctite products are specified in Nissan Engineering Standard (NES) as Anaerobic Adhesive M6514. Please contact us for details.

(MAZDA) D/Loc is specified in MAZDA Engineering Standard (MES) CF S10R as follows.

CLASS 1	202
CLASS 2	200

(HONDA) There is no specification for anaerobic adhesives, but their needs for pre-applied threadlockers, 200 and 204, have been growing. Design manual for Dri-Loc and liquid threadlockers will be compiled soon.

(MATSUSHITA) Our products are mainly applied for Audio-Visual Appliances and office automation equipment.
Try to develop all potential applications in parts assembly for VCR, HDD, FDD, LCD and telephone.

(SONY) UV products, such as 326UV Blue, 326LVUV etc., are mainly applied to motor assembly, optical devices, VCR, FDD and Audio parts assembly.
Since 348 was specified in Sony's chipbonder spec. No. 7-432-910-74 in 1992, this business is one of our most promising applications. Please try!

Profile of Accounts

TOYOTA
Date of Establishment: Aug. 1937
Sales* 8.941 Bill. Yen
Net profit* 201 Bill. Yen
Number of employees*: 75,300
Number of offshore manufacturing plants 34

NISSAN
Date of Establishment: Dec. 1933
Sales* 4.271 Bill. Yen
Net profit* 54 Bill. Yen
Number of employees*: 55,600
Number of offshore manufacturing plants 19

HONDA
Date of Establishment: Sept. 1948
Sales* 2.911 Bill. Yen
Net profit* 33 Bill. Yen
Number of offshore manufacturing plants 26

MAZDA
Date of Establishment: Jan. 1920
Sales* 2.304 Bill. Yen
Net profit* 9.2 Bill. Yen
Number of offshore manufacturing plants 13

MATSUSHITA
Date of Establishment: Dec. 1935
Sales* 4.995 Bill. Yen
Net profit* 110 Bill. Yen
Number of employees*: 47,600
Number of offshore manufacturing plants 44

SONY
Date of Establishment: May. 1946
Sales* 1.979 Bill. Yen
Net profit* 21 Bill. Yen
Number of employees*: 19,800
Number of offshore manufacturing plants 21

* : Annual business term(April 1991 – March 1992)

Loctite(Japan)Corporation
1-15-13, Fukuura, Kanazawa-ku,
Yokohama, Japan 236

Sales Headquarters
Phone No. 81-45(784)0747
Telefax No. 81-45(784)2500

area. Each task force included vice presidents from each of the four regions and met four times a year. Their main function was idea transfer across regions; the Industrial task force, for instance, was helping Loctite's European operations develop its electronics business, which had not grown as fast as in other regions. The task forces were also a vehicle for improving worldwide coordination of branding, packaging, and pricing of Loctite products.

Europe

Loctite gained most of its early experience of joint ventures and subsidiaries in Europe. Butterworth had managed Loctite's European operations in the 1970s out of a regional office in Paris which had been closed during the recession of the early 1980s. By 1992, the corporation had acquired all of its European operations except those in Switzerland, Portugal, Sweden, Denmark, and Finland, which continued as independent distributors, and in Norway, where Loctite owned 51% of a joint venture.

The evolution of the French business was typical. The French distributor had learned about Loctite products in the early 1960s as a result of an existing relationship with the company that served as Loctite's U.K. distributor. By 1979, the French distributor had grown the Loctite business to a point where it was established as a company in its own right. This opened the door for Loctite to buy the whole business, not just the franchise, but during the early 1980s the franchise plunged into loss as it attempted to develop the consumer market for instant adhesives, despite the fact that its key managers had experience serving only industrial markets. In 1986, Loctite acquired a 50% stake with an agreement to purchase the remaining 50% five years later, which it duly did according to a pre-agreed-upon formula. By 1992, France was the second-biggest market after the United States, with a strong consumer business. The original French manager, and most of the employees, were still in place two years after the change of ownership.

The distributor relationship had a less happy ending in the Netherlands, where the local distributor of 20 to 30 years standing refused to sell Loctite any stake in its business. Loctite wanted to establish a single company covering the three Benelux countries (Belgium, the Netherlands, and Luxembourg). The original contract imposed stiff penalties on Loctite for withdrawing its franchise. In addition, the Loctite distributor successfully contested a noncompete clause in the Dutch courts and

had it reduced from five to two years. By 1992, the former distributor was carrying a competitor's product line.

Loctite was seeking to establish itself early in the former Communist bloc countries of Eastern Europe, but was following a different approach to achieving distribution. In the 1980s, Loctite had developed export sales to these countries, working through a network of contacts ranging from the government agents who administered hard foreign currency purchases, to engineering academics involved in manufacturing process development. Following the collapse of Communism, the countries assessed as having the greatest potential were Poland, Hungary, and Czechoslovakia, since their economies relied to a greater extent on conversion or assembly technologies, whereas the economies of the former Soviet republics were based more on natural resources and raw materials. In each of these three countries, representative offices were established in 1990, headed by one of Loctite's previous contacts and typically supported by two local Loctite-trained sales engineers. All were full-time Loctite employees, able to supplement their salaries with bonuses based on sales performance. These representative offices carried minimal inventories; their orders were processed through Loctite's Vienna warehouse. Loctite planned to form full subsidiaries in these countries as soon as possible.

Latin America

Loctite attempted to minimize its capital investment in Latin America, serving all Central American countries from its subsidiary in Costa Rica and concentrating its South American regional management staff at its Brazilian subsidiary in São Paolo. The Latin American business had been strongest in the automotive aftermarket, with more recent success in consumer markets—the same number of tubes of Loctite Super Glue were sold to consumers in Brazil as in the United States. By 1992, corporate and regional managers were pushing local distributors to develop the factory maintenance market.

Loctite's experience in Argentina reflected a problem common to more regulated, emerging economies. Though small in annual sales, the Argentinean distributor had access to Loctite's technology as a result of the establishment of a local manufacturing plant in 1975, which government regulations at that time required Loctite setup to enter the market. When Loctite bought out the distributorship in 1988, the head of the company left and set up a plant in direct competition with his former partner.

Asia/Pacific

Although Loctite had long been active in Asia/Pacific, acquiring its joint venture distributors in Japan and Australia in the mid-1970s, penetration was still low in this region, partly because most of Loctite's investment in international expansion to date had concentrated on building business in Europe. Historically, Loctite had appointed agents in Asia/Pacific countries for whom Loctite's business typically represented a third or more of sales and a higher proportion of profit. In recent years, with more attention focused on the region, Loctite had reconsidered its approach to distribution.

In the 1980s, Thailand, Taiwan, and Korea had been identified by Loctite as especially attractive markets. After extensive search processes, distributors were appointed in each of the three countries, but sales growth over the first two years proved disappointing in all three cases. After several visits to the distributors, Butterworth concluded that the problem lay in a lack of familiarity with the sales approaches required for Loctite products and the operating policies of the company. "In North America, Europe, and Australia, we were able to appoint real Loctite veterans to build our businesses. There simply were no Asian *Loctite Charlies.*" Loctite's customary policy of relying entirely on local principals was therefore changed in two ways: Loctite began taking equity interests in its Asian distributors earlier in the relationships and began placing its own employees in the distributorships to provide the technical and sales education required to build their businesses.

Loctite formed 51% joint ventures with the Thai distributor in 1990 and the Taiwanese distributor in 1991, basing the business valuations upon current profitability, with agreements that the remaining 49% would be purchased five years later according to an agreed-upon formula. In the intervening five years, the formula guaranteed the distributor that Loctite would grow the business by an average of 10%-15% annually, and also guaranteed that Loctite would pay a pro rata share of any profits on sales growth above this level. In most cases, profits for the first two years were below the guaranteed minimums, as Loctite invested in business development. The "sunset" buyout price at the end of the five-year period was based upon profit levels in the fourth and fifth years.

In the years preceding the formation of the joint ventures, Loctite personnel had been appointed to work in the distributor companies, primarily to provide technical support. Wiley commented that this had met with mixed success:

> There were often control issues beneath the surface, and attempts to isolate the Loctite representative because he wasn't "family." While joint ventures seemed the obvious way to run the business in Asia/Pacific—combining Loctite product expertise with local culture—it was often difficult. We certainly need local managers to front the sales effort and to cope with the idiosyncrasies of local government and distribution systems, but it always takes several years before they really become Loctite people.

Soon after the Thai joint venture had been formed, the distributor was being run almost entirely by Loctite personnel. In Taiwan, where the joint venture partner, FTF Trading, was a large conglomerate with businesses ranging from supermarkets to the automotive aftermarket, Loctite employees again largely ran the business, with FTF contributing to management of the complex administrative requirements of doing business in Taiwan.

In Korea, the distributor resisted what he saw as Loctite's infiltration into his business and sought to retain all the cash flows generated by his Loctite distributorship. Loctite's appointment of a sales engineer only strained the relationship further. As the distributor's cooperation could not be obtained, Butterworth and Freeman decided that the market potential warranted establishing a wholly owned subsidiary alongside the distributor in 1985. Initial profitability was low, aggravated by the need to let the distributor's existing inventory sell through or be bought out by Loctite to avoid dumping of stock at low prices, but, by 1988, Loctite's Korean sales had tripled. Eventually, in 1992, Loctite canceled the distributor's contract.

Wiley believed some expatriate management was necessary to grow businesses in Asia/Pacific at the rate it now required:

> Our agents in this region used to be able to make gross margins as high as 70%-80% on our products. We are now considering cutting this margin, maybe by as much as half, and insisting on employing some local engineers, training them in Connecticut, and supporting them inside the distributorships.

He also considered it important that, in Asia/Pacific, Loctite maintain its approach of initially restricting each distributor to a few core products:

> In Asia/Pacific I start a distributor on a range of six to eight machinery adhesives. These are our bread-and-butter

products, offering good margins to the distributor, and they are also the perfect way for him to learn the Loctite approach. The ideas of selling the customer something which they didn't know they needed, and of pricing to value rather than cost, are new to many of these distributors, partly because of cultural background and partly because of the nature of the other products they carry. Only when the distributor has established this core business, which takes a year or two, do I encourage him to move into other markets and broaden his product line.

The trend toward greater Loctite involvement in its distribution operations had resulted in the number of Loctite employees in the Asia/Pacific region rising rapidly to 278 in 1992. Of these, only six were in the regional offices, the remainder being attached to Loctite's joint ventures or wholly owned subsidiaries in the region. At that time, only one Loctite employee, in Indonesia, was working inside an independent distributor company. Nevertheless, Loctite still believed in the need for local management; in cases where expatriate managers headed national distributors, they were required by Butterworth and Freeman to identify and develop local national successors within five years.

Despite this trend toward greater control of its distribution, Loctite had recently enjoyed a successful and cooperative relationship with a new independent distributor in Indonesia. Until 1991, Indonesian sales had been managed by the Singapore distributor. Loctite was unhappy with both the level and growth of sales, attributed to lack of attention by the domestically focused Singapore distributor, and decided that a separate national distributor was needed for Indonesia. The Indonesian distribution rights were reacquired with no payment to the Singapore distributor, and an initial survey of potential manufacturing customers produced a list of four potential distributors. In 1990, however, Loctite was introduced to a fifth candidate—a general mill supplier—by a former Loctite employee of 20 years standing, who now headed up international distribution for a spray gun manufacturer. After the head of this family-run business had attended a Loctite regional distributors' conference where he had impressed regional management with his knowledge of the region and its network of manufacturing supplies distribution, the firm was appointed as Loctite's exclusive distributor in Indonesia, without a formal contract and with an understanding that Loctite would eventually want to buy out the business for about twice the annual gross margin.

Wiley commented that Loctite was impressed by the management policies of Kawan Lama, the Indonesian appointee, which were unusual for a manufacturing supplies distributor in Asia:

The company has a very modern approach to human resource management, with extensive training and high levels of pay. They are also prepared to invest in growing our business, even appointing about a dozen subdistributors to cover specific regions and industries better than they could themselves.

Loctite had reciprocated with extensive training support:

Two weeks after we appointed Kawan Lama as distributor, at a time when they had only about $500 worth of Loctite products on their shelves, I ran a full-day training seminar on their premises and was impressed by the high number of staff who attended, including the head of the company. Since they were appointed, we have invested almost 100 man-days in training seminars for the company's staff, customers, and subdistributors.

In India, Loctite encountered problems which it attributed to the distributor's lack of familiarity with Loctite. Indian government regulations in the 1970s dictated that Loctite could initially take only a 40% stake in the business, and that the company had to establish manufacturing operations in the country. Disagreements soon emerged over pricing levels, with the local distributor cutting them below what Loctite regarded as appropriate in order to boost sales volume. Although the original principal of the distributorship had left the business when Loctite acquired the remaining equity, the corporation was still not confident that the new manager was enough of a "Loctite man." By 1992, Loctite was moving toward its goals of acquiring the balance of the business and launching, for the first time in Asia/Pacific, a product line targeting the consumer market.

The People's Republic of China (P.R.C.) had also long been regarded as a market with huge potential. A joint venture was required by local law, and Loctite had, in 1985, taken a 50% stake in such a business. This business was run by a Chinese manager with U.S. citizenship and extensive knowledge of Loctite. In 1992, Loctite was negotiating to increase its stake in the business, although 100% ownership was not legally feasible and not necessarily desirable. An assessment of the emerging Vietnamese market was also being conducted, so that Loctite would be able to act swiftly if and when the U.S. trade sanctions on doing business there were lifted.

Hong Kong

Loctite's distribution in Hong Kong had been managed for 10 years by a Hong Kong Chinese who had been Loctite's Asia/Pacific region manager. He had left the company to set up his own business with some modest financial assistance from Loctite. By 1990, the distributor had developed a sizable business, but was still almost entirely dependent upon Loctite products. Loctite sales to the Hong Kong distributor were $1,183,000 in 1992, and the distributor was estimated to achieve a gross margin around 50%. However, Loctite had become increasingly dissatisfied with the distributor's willingness to reinvest profits in the business and to expand its customer base. Loctite had therefore taken back the distribution rights to several product lines outside the core of industrial adhesive products. The relationship had been further strained by the refusal of the Hong Kong distributor to accept anything other than technical support from Loctite; this insistence on independence extended to a refusal to share accounts and business plans, which Loctite expected to receive from all its distributors.

Having decided that some form of Loctite control was necessary to boost sales growth in Hong Kong, Butterworth, Freeman, and Wiley were considering their options. The trend toward acquiring 100% of a Loctite distributorship and establishing a wholly owned subsidiary was exemplified by the recent acquisition of Singapore/Malaysia rights from Asia Radio, the Singapore-based firm that had distributed Loctite products for 23 years. The benefits of working with local companies, however, were exemplified by the early success of the relationship with Kawan Lama in Indonesia. Also prominent in their thoughts was the concept of a Greater China subsidiary formed from the operations in Hong Kong, the P.R.C., and Taiwan. The Greater China concept was fueled by the fact that control of Hong Kong was scheduled to revert to the P.R.C. from the United Kingdom in 1997. Wiley reported that Loctite's P.R.C. joint venture was already competing with the Hong Kong distributor to supply factories in the booming southern Chinese province of Guandong and offering prices substantially lower than those offered by Loctite's Hong Kong distributor. He estimated that P.R.C. customers accounted for 25% of the Hong Kong distributor's sales. Sales revenues in 1992 for the Taiwan and P.R.C. joint venture operations were $1,613,000 and $2,277,000 respectively. Wiley estimated that, as in Hong Kong, Loctite commanded 75%-80% of the established market in these countries. In terms of market penetration, however, the joint ventures lagged Hong Kong; penetration of market opportunity was estimated at less than 20% in Taiwan and less than 5% in the P.R.C., compared with less than 50% in Hong Kong.

Butterworth, Freeman, and Wiley concluded that Loctite had three options regarding the Hong Kong operation:

1. Buy 51% or more of the existing Hong Kong distributorship, and grow the business from its existing base.
2. Find a new distribution partner, probably an established local business, and form a second joint venture in Hong Kong.
3. Buy out 100% of the Hong Kong business and attempt to build a Greater China subsidiary.

There were no major legal issues or constraints shaping the decision.

Pechazur

Saliou N'Dione, founder, CEO, and 42-year-old majority shareholder of Pechazur, sat at his desk in Abidjan, Ivory Coast, considering alternative strategies to further the growth of his company. Pechazur had been marketing frozen fish to the Ivorian market for 12 years and had been exporting frozen wild shrimp and fish fillets to France for 10 years.[1] In early 1993, N'Dione was planning to open a new processing plant in the neighboring country of Benin, effectively doubling Pechazur's production capacity of frozen shrimp and fish fillets for the export market, and expand Pechazur's fishing fleet to supply fresh fish to the local Ivorian market.

The increased competition from farm-raised shrimp in the late 1980s and early 1990s had caused world prices for wild shrimp to fall steadily. N'Dione wondered what marketing strategy would enable him to expand his shrimp exports and ensure the continued growth and profitability of his company.

COMPANY BACKGROUND

N'Dione founded Pechazur in 1980 to import and distribute frozen fish in the RCI (Republique de la Cote D'Ivoire). N'Dione, Senegalese by birth, had previously worked in three large fish and seafood processing companies in Senegal during the 1970s. His decision to found a company in RCI rather than Senegal had been based not only on the large RCI market demand but also on the reduced social and family obligations he would face in the RCI. In West African society, individuals faced strong social pressures to share with extended family and friends. Although positive from a social welfare perspective, these pressures often made it difficult for individuals to reinvest business profits since they were expected to use surplus funds to provide financial assistance to their extended families.

In 1982, a decline in the purchasing power of Ivorian households due to an economic recession prompted N'Dione to seek export markets, and Pechazur began purchasing, processing, and exporting frozen shrimp and frozen fish fillets to France. In 1987, increasing demand for these export products led to the construction of a modern processing plant—80% financed by Pechazur's retained earnings—located at Dabou, 30 miles from the capital, Abidjan. At this time, Pechazur assisted local shrimp fishermen in forming cooperatives, providing them with nets and technical assistance. In 1988, Pechazur established its own fishing subsidiary, Sari-Fish, once again largely financed by retained earnings. Sari-Fish comprised five industrial sea fishing vessels, four of which were fully equipped with on-board freezers. In 1989, N'Dione purchased a majority shareholding of ICA, a French shrimp importer, thereby establishing a distribution and marketing subsidiary in France. In 1992, with the financial participation of the IFC (International Finance Corporation),[2] Pechazur was constructing a new processing plant in Benin, where shrimp were abundant and production costs lower, and developing a new fleet of fishing vessels to provide the local RCI market with fresh fish.

Pechazur was a family-run business: Mrs. N'Dione was the company's finance director; N'Dione's brother was the Dabou plant manager; his brother-in-law the director of Sari-Fish; and his cousin, a captain on one of Sari-Fish's fishing vessels. N'Dione had a very strong work ethic and paid particular attention to the training and development of his executive staff. N'Dione both inspired and required hard work and dedication from his colleagues and

This case was prepared by Professor John A. Quelch with the assistance of Nathalie Laidler.
Copyright © 1993 by the President and Fellows of Harvard College. Harvard Business School case 9-593-077.

1 Wild shrimp were fished from the sea and/or saltwater lagoons. They were distinct from farm-raised or aquaculture shrimp grown in controlled farm environments.
2 The IFC was part of the World Bank organization.

employees, and an attention to excellence was evident at every level of the organization. N'Dione commented, "In Africa, ideas are not as important as who one works with."

In January 1993, Pechazur was an integrated fish and shrimp producer and marketer, fishing, purchasing, importing, processing, packaging, distributing, and marketing frozen fish to the RCI market and exporting frozen shrimp and fish fillets, principally to France. (Table A reports volume sales from 1987 to 1992; Exhibit 1 presents Pechazur's income statements from 1989 to 1992.)

REPUBLIQUE DE LA COTE D'IVOIRE (RCI)

RCI, located on the coast of West Africa, flanked by Liberia and Ghana, and bordered by Guinea, Mali, and Burkina Faso, was a French protectorate between 1842 and 1960, when it became independent. From 1965 to 1975, RCI achieved real average GDP (gross domestic product) growth of 7.7% per annum based on exports of coffee, cocoa, and timber. Massive foreign-bank lending occurred from 1975 to 1977, and when the price of coffee and cocoa fell dramatically in 1979, the government's current account and budget deficits grew quickly. From 1980, the country fell into economic decline, and in 1987, the fall of the U.S. dollar, declining coffee and cocoa prices, large devaluations in neighboring Ghana and Nigeria, and inadequate controls on government spending threw the country into recession. Anticipating a recovery in commodity prices, RCI increased foreign borrowing to cover revenue shortfalls. However, commodity prices remained depressed; foreign debt rose from 37% of GDP in 1979 to 130% in 1991, and real GDP per capita fell by an average of 5% per annum during 1987-1990. Nevertheless, RCI's overall post-independence record of economic development was one of the best in Africa, and in 1991 the country's GDP per capita was US$770. (Exhibit 2 provides key data on RCI in 1991.)

Under Prime Minister Ouattara, appointed in 1990 by President Houphouet-Boigny, a program of stabilization and structural adjustment was implemented, aimed at reducing the fiscal deficit, privatizing public sector firms, and liberalizing the marketing of principal export crops. The RCI government also worked with foreign lenders to clear up public debt arrears and revitalize the illiquid banking system. Despite these measures, RCI in 1992 still suffered from relatively high production costs and a lack of competitiveness in international markets, due in large part to the overvaluation of the FCFA.[3] Diversification of exports and the development of import-substituting industries were hindered by high production costs and the domination of the public sector in the economy. In 1991, government investment accounted for 61% of total investment. The business sector operated under rigid job security and wage regulations and faced unfavorable fixed prices on a number of import and export commodities. In addition, as government revenues fell after 1980, taxes on established businesses rose sharply. In 1991, 94% of tax receipts came from business income taxes, payroll taxes, sales taxes, and taxes on imports and exports.

On the other hand, the RCI had invested heavily in infrastructure and education during the boom years and the land was fertile with many well-established plantations. In addition, the trade balance was generally positive.

The ownership and management of the industrial sector was largely foreign and included many Lebanese

| Table A | Pechazur Volume Sales, 1987–1991 |

Tons[a]	1987	1988	1989	1990	1991	1992
Frozen fish imports sold to the RCI market	1,500	780	800	757	350	101
Pechazur fish (frozen) sold to the RCI market	0	0	283	264	1,234	1,027
Export shrimp	320	430	398	406	352	434
Export processed fish	21 2	98	97	108	124	221
Total volume sales	2,032	1,308	1,578	1,535	2,060	1,783

[a]1 ton = 1,000 kg = 2,222 lbs.

---

3 RCI, along with 13 other African countries, ex-French colonies and protectorates, shared a common currency—the FCFA—that was tied to the French franc. In 1992 1 US$ = 248 FCFA.

Exhibit 1   Pechazur Income Statements, 1989 to 1992

	1989	1990	1991	1992
Sales revenues (FCFA millions):	1,659	1,656	1,753	1,837
Export subsidy	123	218	144	238
Total revenues	1,782	1,874	1,897	2,075
Production costs:				
Purchases and raw material	1,057	780	954	1,137
Water and energy	95	139	163	165
Maintenance	52	87	97	109
Other direct costs	58	20	39	14
Personnel	129	96	127	153
Depreciation	57	69	66	67
Total production costs	1,448	1,191	1,446	1,645
Operating margin	334	683	451	430
Overhead and fixed costs	199	396	246	206
Profit before interest and taxes	135	287	205	224
Interest	52	57	27	25
Tax	8	10	21	17
Net profit	75	220	157	182

Exhibit 2   Ivory Coast—Demographic and Economic Data, 1991

Population	12.4 million; 47% urban; 20% of workers come from poorer neighboring countries
Age distribution: 0-14; 15-59; 60+	45%; 50%; 5%
Ethnic and religious groups	Over 60 tribes and 5 main languages. 30% Moslem; 20% Christian, 60% indigenous
GDP per capita	US$770
Real GDP and consumer prices (% change 1990-1991)	-0.5% and 1.0%
GDP breakdown: primary, secondary, and tertiary sectors[a]	35%; 20%; 45%
Central government spending (% GDP)	30%
Chief crops, minerals, and other resources	Coffee and cocoa; diamonds and manganese; timber, rubber, and petroleum
Fish catch	93,000 tons
Exports: value and main partners	US$2.9 billion: Netherlands = 19%; France = 14%; United States = 11%; Italy = 8%
Imports: value and main partners	US$1.6 billion: France = 31%; Japan = 5%; United States = 5%
Communications: television sets, radios, telephones, newspaper circulation	1 per 19 persons; 1 per 8 persons; 1 per 97 persons; 12 per 1,000 population

[a]Primary sector = agricultural production; secondary sector = industrial production; tertiary sector = services.

immigrants; only 17% of managing directors were Ivorian in 1992, and privatized, formerly state-run enterprises were being purchased primarily by foreign companies. The strongest sectors of industry were those with some export potential. Frozen shrimp were, in 1991, among RCI's major exports and Pechazur was often cited by members of the local business community as one of the most successful companies in the RCI. In 1992, Pechazur was the only significant private company operating profitably in RCI that was owned and managed entirely by indigenous Africans.

The Ivorian Fish Industry

Fish was a staple of the Ivorian diet. Per capita consumption of fish in the RCI in 1991 was 18 kg, resulting in a total demand of 216,000 tons. Domestic fishing was carried out by both industrial fishing vessels, accounting for 48,000 tons in 1991, and small independent fishermen, accounting for an additional 45,000 tons. Imports of frozen fish were estimated at 115,000 tons in 1991, and smoked fish from Ghana and Mali at 8,000 tons.

The variety of fresh fish marketed in the RCI was impressive, ranging from "surface" fish such as mackerel and sardines to other fish such as carp. Fresh fish, landed daily by industrial vessels at the port, were purchased in bulk by wholesalers at the "Criee"[4] and sold to distributors who, in turn, ensured the link to retailers. Independent fishermen had well-established networks of intermediaries that enabled their products to quickly reach the market stands. Imports and distribution of frozen fish were dominated by a half-dozen companies that possessed the necessary refrigeration trucks and warehouses. Wholesalers would regularly collect product from these warehouses to supply their retail customers.

Although distribution was highly fragmented, relationships were well-established and long-standing. Fish wholesaling and retailing operations were run by women. Nearly all fish were sold in open-air markets, either fresh, thawed, or smoked. About 50% of fish consumed in the RCI was smoked. The smoking process, which gave the fish a longer shelf life, was carried out by a large number of small entrepreneurs. (Exhibit 3 shows photographs of a typical market in Abidjan.) Prices depended on supply and demand and fluctuated daily. In 1991, the average wholesale price per kg for small mackerel and sardines was 150 FCFA, and the average retail price to the consumer was 175 FCFA. For higher quality fish, equivalent prices were 350 FCFA and 450 FCFA.

Pechazur in RCI

Pechazur began importing frozen fish into the RCI in 1980 to meet a level of consumer demand that was outstripping local supply. However, low prices and competition from other importers that avoided paying import duties forced Pechazur to reduce this activity, and by 1992 less than 10% of Pechazur's sales to the RCI market were of imported fish—the rest being landed by the Sari-Fish subsidiary. The company owned three large freezer-warehouses in Abidjan with a total storage capacity of 400 tons.

By early 1993, stricter RCI government regulations in exacting import duties allowed Pechazur to consider importing frozen fish once again. In addition, Soviet fishing vessels, which accounted for the bulk of imports in the 1980s, no longer represented a reliable source of supply.

N'Dione was planning to purchase three additional vessels in 1993—at a cost of 800 million FCFA—to provide fresh fish to the local Ivorian market. (The Sari-Fish subsidiary had one vessel that did not have on-board freezing capacity and that was already supplying the local market with fresh fish.) The annual catch that each vessel could deliver if operating at capacity was 1,895 tons. Fundamentally different from the original four Sari-Fish vessels, the new vessels would be used exclusively for fishing for fresh fish.

THE WORLD MARKET FOR SHRIMP

In 1990, world shrimp production totaled 2.6 million tons, of which 75% was derived from farm-raised or aquaculture shrimp. Farm-raised shrimp first appeared on the world market in the 1980s, priced on average 50% below traditional wild shrimp. The major sources of farm-raised shrimp were Asia and South America: China supplied 150,000 tons in 1991; Thailand 120,000 tons; South America 150,000 tons, of which Ecuador supplied 50%. Several varieties existed: the "Black Tiger" variety, very popular in Japan, accounted for 46% of farm-raised shrimp volume in 1991, and the "White China" variety for 21%.

Industry experts noted that lower-priced, farm-raised shrimp expanded consumer demand but also increased consumer price sensitivity and led to industry consolidation and restructuring. Many consumers in the West did

---

4 The "Criee" was the daily market located at the port, where wholesalers purchased fish landed by industrial vessels.

Exhibit 3   Photographs of Fish Stalls in a Typical Market in Abidjan

not know the difference between wild and farm-raised shrimp and, therefore, readily substituted the lower-priced, farm-raised product for wild shrimp. However, some experts believed that the superior taste of wild shrimp insured that a niche market would always exist for it.

The world shrimp market was dominated by three regions of consumption: Japan, the United States, and Western Europe. (Table B summarizes consumption and import data for these three markets.)

The Japanese Market

Although Japan represented the largest market for shrimp, all products were sourced from within Asia and it was thought to be very difficult to penetrate this market. The Japanese market was an important influence on prices and product quality standards for the rest of the world.

The U.S. Market

Consumption of shrimp in the United States increased throughout the 1980s to reach 1.2 kg per capita in 1991. The early 1990s, however, saw a decline in consumption, due in part to the economic recession. Away-from-home consumption through restaurants accounted for 75% of U.S. shrimp volume. Although distribution was highly fragmented among 450 importers, a trend towards consolidation was evident. Prices varied substantially according to product type and stock levels. In 1992, shrimp retailed anywhere between $2.99/lb. and 5.99/lb. In early 1993, importers and supermarket chain buyers were increasingly seeking stable, long-term supply agreements, while large, vertically integrated companies such as Aquastar, involved in farm-raising, distribution, and retail branding, were capturing an increasing share of the market.

The domestic shrimp industry consisted of 25,000 independent shrimp fishermen, located principally in Louisiana, who harvested 70,000 tons of wild shrimp in 1992. The quality of their catch was at risk from melanosis, which resulted when the time between capture and freezing of the shrimp was too long. This had created a negative quality image for wild shrimp in the United States. Supermarket buyers preferred farm-raised shrimp for several reasons: higher perceived quality, due to a freezing process that took place immediately following harvest; a cleaner product resulting from the starving of the shrimp prior to harvest; regular, stable supplies; and lower prices.

The U.S. shrimp retail market was dominated by products that increased the ease of preparation; shelled, headless, and cooked shrimp were the norm. In addition, lower-priced, smaller-sized shrimp (40 to 60 units per kg) were more popular. Approximately 70% of retail sales were made through the seafood counter, where shrimp were presented unbranded, loose on ice. The remaining 30% of sales were of cartons or plastic bags from the freezer case where brands such as Neptune, Bumble Bee, and Northern King were dominant.

Table B Characteristics of the Major Shrimp Markets, 1991

	Japan			United States			Western Europe		
Consumption in tons	384,000			300,000			240,000		
Consumption per capita	3.1 kg			1.2 kg			0.8 kg average		
Volume of imports in tons	283,000			227,500			170,000		
Origin of imports	Indonesia	=	20%	Ecuador	=	20%	Africa	=	26%
	China	=	18%	Thailand	=	19%	Ecuador	=	14%
	Thailand	=	18%	China	=	15%	Indonesia	=	12%
	India	=	15%	India	=	7%	Thailand	=	8%
	Others	=	29%	Mexico	=	7%	China	=	6%
				Panama	=	3%	India	=	4%
				Others	=	29%	Others	=	30%

The European Market

In 1991, imports of shrimp into the 12-country European Economic Community (EEC) totaled 170,000 tons, of which 30% went to the Spanish market, and 22% went to both the French and British markets. Per capita consumption in 1992 varied widely among the member countries, from 0.3 kg in Germany to 2.5 kg in Denmark. Consumers in southern European countries such as Spain, Italy, and Portugal, tended to consume pink or tropical shrimp, while consumers in northern European countries preferred grey shrimp (fished in the North Sea). Imports from many African countries, including the RCI and Benin, did not pay import duties into the EEC, due to a trade agreement between the EEC and former colonies of the member states.

Spain dominated the European fish and seafood industry as a result of high per capita consumption and a large, modern fishing fleet that supplied much of the EEC's needs. Due to overfishing in EEC waters and increased levels of pollution, Spanish fishing vessels obtained agreements to fish throughout the West African coast. Large, vertically integrated companies such as Pescanova, involved in shipbuilding to the production of fish-based, ready-to-eat meals, increasingly dominated the market.

THE FRENCH MARKET

Shrimp represented the second-largest category of seafood product imported into France. Imports in 1991 amounted to 37,400 tons, valued at FF 1.4 billion. The majority of imported product was purchased in U.S dollars so changes in the FF/$ exchange rate often impacted demand.[5]

Consumption

Shrimp consumption in France increased by 7.5% from 1990 to 1991. In 1991, 38.5% of French households consumed an average of 1.2 kg of shrimp at home, compared with 37.8% of households consuming an average of 1.1 kg in 1990. Retail prices increased by only 1% during this period; purchases of shrimp were believed to be price sensitive, and stable prices were thought to result in increased consumption. (Exhibit 4 summarizes data on the seasonality of consumption and prices. Exhibit 5 reports market shares by type of shrimp products, and Exhibit 6 shows differences in shrimp consumption by region.)

Exhibit 4   French Retail Shrimp Sales and Prices by Month, 1991

Period	Volume (ton)	Price (FF/kg)
1 (January)	729	99.01
2	545	95.08
3	706	99.31
4	635	97.52
5	529	97.05
6	617	93.10
7	567	94.14
8	433	107.74
9	489	90.18
10	679	95.28
11	783	89.82
12	762	87.41
13 (December)	1,388	87.02

Exhibit 5   French Volume Market Shares by Type of Shrimp, 1991

	Market Shares by Type of Shrimp	
	1990	1991
Grey Shrimp:		
Cooked	23%	18%
Raw	4	5
Pink Shrimp:		
Cooked	35	43
Raw	8	7
Unspecified	30	27

The French retail shrimp market in 1991 totaled 43,000 tons, comprising 11,000 tons of grey shrimp and 32,000 tons of pink shrimp, of which 30% was captured wild and 70% was farm-raised. At-home consumption accounted for 25,800 tons, or 60% of this volume, and away-from-home consumption accounted for 17,200 tons, or 40%. Shrimp were consumed at home mainly on

---

5 1US$ = 5.6 FF in 1992.

Exhibit 6

Exhibit 6 — Differences in Shrimp Consumption by Region, France 1991

Region	Percentage of Volume	Consumption Index[a]
North	12.5	129
East	5.3	56
Paris	29.8	153
West	19.3	102
West-Central	6.2	79
East-Central	7.7	55
South-West	7.4	83
South-East	11.8	101

[a]Based on average consumption per capita.

special occasions, and because they were bought infrequently, consumers often valued the advice of a specialist fishmonger when making a purchase.

Distribution and Retailing

Attracted by an expanding market, more than 60 firms imported shrimp into France in 1992, compared with 12 in 1988. This increasing fragmentation fueled a price war and added to the power of distributors. Successful distributors balanced in-stock availability to ensure rapid customer service with lowering costs through operating with minimum stocks. Other important factors were product quality and consistent availability of supply. Distribution of shrimp in France was highly fragmented and complex. (Exhibit 7 describes the roles of the main players.) As the retail market for shrimp expanded, some supermarket and hypermarket chains were backward integrating to assume the role of wholesaler/distributor for their own retail outlets. In 1992, 69% of retail shrimp sales were accounted for by hypermarkets and supermarkets which had captured market share from traditional fishmongers. (Exhibit 8 shows the share of retail sales by type of outlet in 1990 and 1991, and average retail prices in 1991.)

Most supermarkets and hypermarkets had specialty fish departments staffed by fishmongers. A high-quality fish department was thought to be a source of competitive differentiation. An estimated 70% of shrimp were sold loose and unbranded on ice. A further 10% were processed for use in value-added products such as cocktail mixes and breaded shrimp, while the remaining 20% were sold frozen in the freezer case. The latter were generally packaged in 1 kg plastic bags and carried the brand names of importers or wholesalers such as Surgele des Mer, Sofimar, Adripeche, and Table Plus. (Exhibit 9 summarizes the range of products and prices of shrimp found in the freezer department of a large French hypermarket in January 1993.) Increasingly, smaller package sizes (0.5 kg, 0.2 kg, and 0.1 kg) were being marketed to stimulate impulse purchases.

The French Fish Fillet Market

At-home consumption of fish fillets was estimated at 32,933 tons in 1991—a 2% increase in volume over 1990; 42% of this volume was frozen. Consumption of breaded fish products was estimated at 31,856 tons in 1992—a 5% decline compared to 1990—while whole fish consumption at 14,956 tons registered a 19% growth over 1990. Of the fillets, 34% were cod, 19% pollack, 18% mackerel, and 29% other. More exotic fillets, such as tropical sole and red mullets, were only just starting to appear as stand-alone, frozen products in 1992.

Major brands such as Findus, Vivagel, Captain Iglo, and Servifrais dominated the market for frozen fish. Distributor brands accounted for 22% of retail frozen fish sales. Companies such as Findus were broadening their product lines with various value-added and gourmet products, and packaging of these products was becoming more sophisticated and eye-catching.

PECHAZUR'S OPERATIONS

Production

In 1992, Pechazur sourced 60% of its shrimp from 2,000 Ivorian fishermen, organized into eight cooperatives, all except one of which were located within 10 km of the processing plant. These traditional fishermen used "pirogues," similar to dug-out canoes, to fish by hand with nets in the lagoons, or large saltwater lakes near Abidjan. Shrimp migrated to these lakes from the sea in order to reproduce; consequently, shrimp caught in the lagoons tended to be smaller than those caught at sea. The lagoon shrimp catch was highest between January and August. Pechazur owned and operated refrigerated pick-up vans that collected, weighed, and recorded the volume of shrimp supplied by each fishing cooperative. Pickups took place several times a day to ensure product freshness. Prices were agreed upon for two- to three-month periods and the fishermen were paid by weight, irrespective of shrimp size.

Exhibit 7   Distribution of Shrimp in France—Main Channels and Players

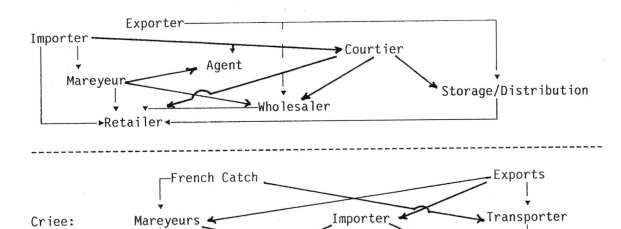

Criee   The main marketplace where the individual fishermen and fishing fleets sell their catch on a bidding basis straight off their boats. Boats returning to port announce their catch to the Criee 24 hours before arriving.

Mareyeurs   They bid for fish at the Criee, either as independents or on behalf of larger, more integrated players. They also prepare and clean the fish and play an important financing role, paying suppliers daily while allowing customers 30-day payment terms.

Wholesalers/Courtiers/Agents   They put together extended product lines and supply their customers on a daily basis.

Platforms   They exist for logistical efficiencies. They are large storage areas where products can be sorted and regrouped to improve the efficiency of transportation to the retail outlets.

Distributors   They typically distribute fish and other fresh produce to the retail outlets.

Source: FIOM.

Exhibit 8　　Share of Shrimp Retail Sales by Type of Outlet and Average Retail Prices of Shrimp, France 1991

Retail Outlet	Percentage of Retail Sales		Average Prices (FF/kg 1991)
	1990	1991	
Hypermarkets	30	35	80.30
Supermarkets	17	18	83.15
Superettes	1	1	75.94
Fishmongers	26	21	107.18
Markets	20	20	102.14
Direct sales	3	3	85.73
Other	3	3	72.07

Exhibit 9　　Range of Shrimp Products and Retail Prices in the Freezer Department of Auchun, a Large Supermarket in France, January 1993

Brand Name	Packaging	Size	Characteristics	Price/kg
Surgele des Mers	1 kg plastic bag	#1	Raw, not shelled	137.38 FF
Camarones	1 kg plastic bag	#2	Raw, not shelled	149.92 FF
Adripeche	1 kg plastic bag	#3	Cooked, not shelled	105.90 FF
Table Plus	1 kg plastic bag	#4	Cooked, not shelled	93.80 FF
Table Plus	0.5 kg plastic bag	#5	Cooked, not shelled	63.50 FF
Sofimar	1 kg plastic bag	#7	Raw, not shelled	59.50 FF
Surgele des Mers	0.2 kg basket	#7	Cooked, and shelled	78.90 FF
SDTP	1 kg plastic bag	#8	Cooked, not shelled	64.98 FF

Pechazur had helped the fishermen form cooperatives and had initially helped supply them with fishing nets. N'Dione believed that Pechazur had managed to establish a stable, long-term relationship with the fishermen, a "moral contract" that effectively prevented potential competitors from being able to source lagoon shrimp in the RCI. A French competitor had attempted to establish a shrimp-processing operation in 1990 but had been unable to obtain a sufficient supply of shrimp to do so.

Sari-Fish, Pechazur's fishing subsidiary, supplied the remaining 40% of shrimp, as well as all the fish destined to be processed into fillets and exported. The Sari-Fish fleet consisted of five vessels, four with on-board freezing equipment and frozen-storage capacity of 30 tons each. Sari-Fish was the only company fishing shrimp out of Abidjan that had the capacity to freeze on board. The vessels fished for 30 days at a time, with 5 days' port maintenance between trips. The average catch was 150 kg of shrimp per vessel each day.

On average, the nets were cast six times a day and shrimp were fished at between 12 and 40 meters depth, three to four miles off the coast. The vessels were not assigned to specific areas; each captain decided where to fish based on experience, and Pechazur captains shared information to help each other's productivity. As soon as the shrimp were brought aboard, they were treated with citric acid to prevent melanosis (which blackened the product), sorted by size into two-kilogram cartons, weighed, frozen for three hours at -40°C, and stored in the freezer until the vessel returned to port. At this point the smaller-sized shrimp, representing 40% of the catch on average, were transported to the processing factory, while the larger shrimp, accounting for roughly 60% of the catch, were exported directly. These larger shrimp accounted for 25% of all Pechazur's shrimp exports. Product quality, particularly the prevention of melanosis, was highly dependent on the immediacy and precision of the freezing process on board the fishing vessels and at the processing plant. Pechazur paid particular attention to ensuring that the product was always kept on ice or frozen.

Although maximizing the shrimp catch was the goal of Pechazur's captains, the nets in fact yielded 80% fish and 20% shrimp by volume. All the fish caught in the process were frozen on board and stored. Some species such as mullet were transferred to the Dabou plant to be processed into fillets for export, but most of the fish were sold locally.

Processing

The Dabou plant could process six tons of raw shrimp a day. It employed 150 women to wash, cook, shell, fillet, freeze, sort, and package the products. Hygiene checks and sanitary precautions were stringent; workers were checked for cuts, wore masks when handling the product, and had to disinfect both hands and feet before entering the factory. In addition, personal hygiene messages were aired frequently over the plant's audio system. Pechazur had successfully met all EEC sanitation regulations. The plant technology was simple, with an emphasis on manual labor. Worker turnover was very low, two-thirds of the workers having been employed since the start of operations. Shelling and sorting were done in groups of twelve workers and one supervisor/worker around aluminum tables. The factory had backup water supply and electric generators so the plant could run autonomously if necessary. Due to shrimp migration patterns, when the lagoon catch was high, the sea catch was lower, and vice versa; this helped level operating capacity.

Lagoon shrimp arrived at the factory during the night and early morning, loose in plastic trays. When the factory began operations in the morning, the shrimp were washed and chemically treated to prevent blackening. Eighty percent of all shrimp passing through the factory were then cooked in boiling water, resulting in a product weight loss of about 13%. Pechazur shrimp cooked to a natural pink and did not require artificial coloring as did competitive Asian products. Following cooking, the shrimp were dipped into a frozen salt and sugar solution for two minutes, lowering their temperature to 2°C. This gave the shrimp a slight sheen and kept them fresh. Approximately 25% to 30% of the cooked shrimp were then shelled. The

shelling process, which resulted in a further 34% weight loss, was an entirely manual process applied to those cooked shrimp that appeared slightly damaged. In addition to the cooked shrimp, 3%-4% of the raw shrimp passing through the factory were also shelled to meet the needs of certain customers.

Following cooking and shelling, the shrimp were manually sorted by size. Shrimp of similar size were packaged into two-kilogram cartons, and the weight of each packaged carton was double-checked. (Exhibit 10 depicts the sorting process at the Dabou factory.) Packaging costs averaged 55 FCFA per kg, and Exhibit 11 shows some of the packaging cartons used by Pechazur. All packaging carried the Pechazur name, a brief product description, and a sell-by date. The cartons were subsequently placed into freezers for four hours at -40°C and later stocked at -18°C in larger storage freezers. Fish fillets followed a similar cleaning process and all filleting was done manually. The freezing process for these products, however, lasted only two hours and each fillet was individually wrapped. The total frozen storage capacity of the plant was 40 tons, and Pechazur also owned additional storage capacity of 150 tons just a few miles away. Four or five containers, each holding 10 tons of product, left the factory each month for shipment by freighter directly to Europe.

Pechazur was planning to enter into an agreement to supply a local Nestle plant with shrimp flour, produced from the by-products of shrimp shells and heads, for use in the production of bouillon cubes.

Product Line

In 1992, 63% of Pechazur's sales by volume and 30% by value were made in the RCI. Ninety percent of these sales were of fish landed by the Sari-Fish fleet and 10% were of frozen fish imports. Exports represented 37% of Pechazur's sales by volume and 70% by value; of exports, 70% were sold in France.

Two-thirds of Pechazur's export sales by volume and 80% by value comprised wild shrimp of various sizes at various stages of processing. (Exhibit 12 depicts seven different sizes of shrimp to scale and the percentage of Pechazur's sales by volume accounted for by each size.) In 1992, of the 434 tons of frozen shrimp exported, 25% were large raw shrimp that had been frozen on board; 72% were cooked, of which 20% were also shelled; and 3% were raw and shelled.

The remaining third of Pechazur's export sales by volume and 20% by value comprised sole, red mullet, cuttle

Exhibit 10   The Sorting Process at Pechazur's Dabou Processing Plant

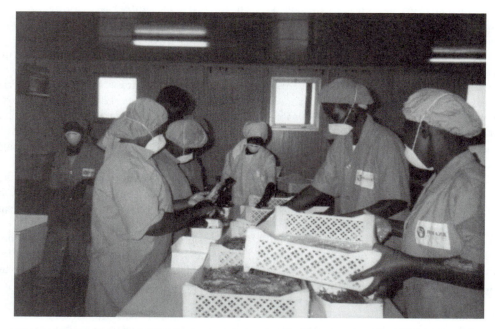

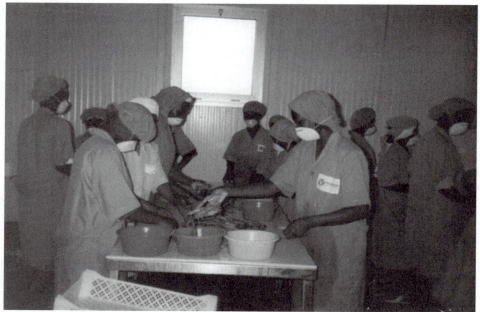

Exhibit 11   Pechazur's Packaging Cartons for Export Shrimp, January 1993

fish, and octopus fillets. (Exhibit 13 itemizes Pechazur's export product line in 1992.) Products were shipped to France in special containers, taking 15 days to reach Marseille, and transport costs were estimated at 1.6 FF/kg, paid for by the importer.

Exports

Pechazur had been exporting wild shrimp to France for 10 years but had experienced growing competition in the late 1980s from farm-raised shrimp, priced 50% below wild shrimp. By 1992, farm-raised shrimp had captured 70% of the French market. Wild shrimp suppliers had to drop their prices by 25% to try to hold market share. Average retail prices in France in September 1992 were 80FF/kg for farm-raised shrimp and 110FF/kg for wild shrimp. (Table C summarizes Pechazur's volume and value exports to France between 1985 and 1992.)

ICA (Societe Internationale de Commerce Agro-Alimentaire) was Pechazur's distribution and marketing subsidiary in France. Established in 1989, it initially distributed both Pechazur and competitor products from Senegal. In 1990, N'Dione purchased a controlling interest in ICA. As he explained:

Pechazur needed credibility and continuity in the French market. We had to have a local operation to protect

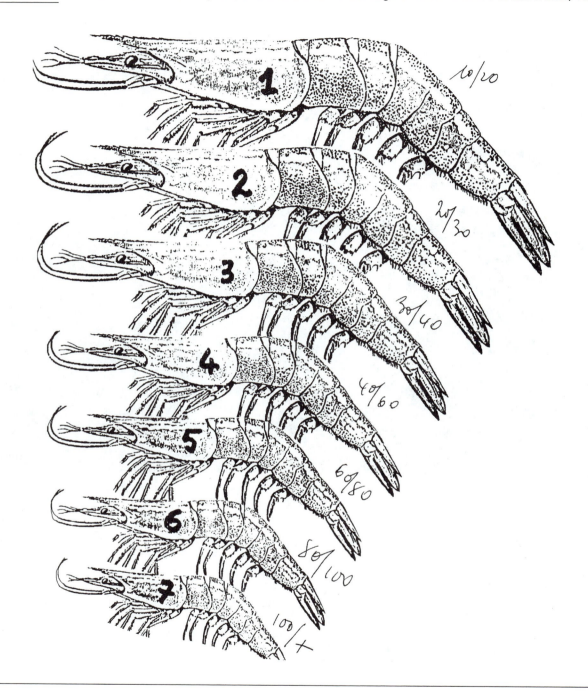

Exhibit 13   Pechazur Export Product Line: January 1993

Whole raw shrimp/frozen abroad:
Boxes = 2 kg - Master carton = 18 kg
   Sizes: #1 (10/20 units per kg)
          #2 (20/30 units per kg)
          #3 (30/40 units per kg)
          #4 (40/60 units per kg)
          #5 (60/80 units per kg)
          #6 (80/100 units per kg)
          #7 (100/120 units per kg)

Shelled raw shrimp:
Boxes = 2 kg - Master carton = 12kg
   Sizes: SSS (40/60 units per kg)
          SS (60/100 units per kg)
          S (100/140 units per kg)
          G (140/190 units per kg)

Whole raw shrimp/day frozen:
Boxes = 2 kg - Master carton = 18 kg
   Sizes: #5 (60/80 units per kg)
          #6 (80/100 units per kg)
          #7 (100/120 units per kg)

Whole cooked shrimp:
Boxes = 2 kg - Master carton = 12kg
   Sizes: SX (10/20 units per kg)
          SL (20/30 units per kg)
          S (30/40 units per kg)
          EE(40/60 units per kg)
          E (60/80 units per kg)
          G (80/100 units per kg)
          M (100/120 units per kg)
          MG (120/140 units per kg)
          ZZ (200/250 units per kg)

Shelled cooked shrimp:
Boxes = 2 kg - Master carton = 20kg
   Sizes: DS 00 (-/100 units per kg)
          DS 0 (100/150 units per kg)
          DS 1(150/250 units per kg)
          DS 2(250/400 units per kg)
          DS 3 (400/700 units per kg)
          DS 4(700/800 units per kg)

Cooked shrimp tails:
Boxes = 3 kg - Master carton = 18 kg
   Sizes: E (-/90 units per kg)
          G (90/150 units per kg)
          M (150/250 units per kg)
          P (250/350 units per kg)

Fillets of tropical sole:
Boxes = 2 kg - Master carton = 16 kg
   Sizes: Large
          Standard

Tropical sole:
IQF (individual quick frozen)
- Loose - Master carton = 16 kg
   Sizes: 0.15/0.2 kg per unit.
          0.02/0.25 kg per unit.

Rockling fillets:
Boxes = 2 kg - Master carton = 16 kg

Rockling medallions:
Boxes = 2 kg - Master carton = 16 kg

Whole red mullet:
Loose - Master carton = 18 kg
   Sizes: #1 (4/6 units per kg)
          #2 (6/8 units per kg)
          #3 (8/12 units per kg)
          #4 (12/16 units per kg)
          #5 (16/+ units per kg)

Fillets of red mullet:
Boxes = 2 kg - Master carton = 16 kg

Cuttlefish whites:
IQF - Loose - Master carton = 20 kg
   Sizes: G (2/3 units per kg)
          M (4/6 units per kg)
          P (6/9 units per kg)
          PP (9/15 units per kg)
          X (4/7 units per kg)

Cuttlefish head and legs:
Boxes = 3 kg - Master carton = 20 kg

Strips of cuttlefish:
Blocks = 1 kg - Master carton = 20 kg

Whole Squid:
Loose - Master carton = 20 kg

Year	Shrimp Volume (tons)	Process Fished Volume (tons)	Shrimp (FCFA millions)	Processed Fish (FCFA millions)
1985	45	N/A	124	N/A
1986	177	19	N/A	N/A
1987	320	212	N/A	N/A
1988	430	98	N/A	N/A
1989	398	97	1,213	130
1990	406	108	1,221	130
1991	352	124	1,075	181
1992	302	156	881	225

us from unethical pressures from wholesalers. For example, wholesalers sometimes complained about the quality of our product arriving in France and demanded price reductions, knowing full well that we could not take the product back. With French employees representing Pechazur in France, such pressures were less likely.

After 1990, ICA distributed only Pechazur products, and N'Dione made all major operating decisions. ICA regularly reported French market prices to Pechazur which could, in response, adjust its production mix at the Dabou factory and press for better raw material prices in the RCI.

In 1992, 40% of Pechazur's export sales were made through ICA; a further 40% was distributed through SOCOPA, a large diversified food distribution group, while the remaining 20% reached the Spanish, British, and German markets through a variety of importers.

When ships transporting Pechazur products arrived in Marseille, the containers were unloaded and transferred to a refrigerated warehouse owned by an independent company called Somatref. ICA rented warehouse space from Somatref, and the ICA warehouse stock averaged 60 tons. Warehouse costs averaged 1.5 FF/kg. ICA organized delivery of the product, but recently some customers, particularly large supermarket chains, elected to collect their purchases directly from the warehouse to reduce storage costs and streamline operations. ICA sold to a stable customer base of wholesalers and distributors, who invariably repackaged and branded Pechazur's products under their own brand

names with the result that the Pechazur brand was unknown to the end consumer. Sales were made throughout France with a focus on the south of the country. According to ICA, Pechazur had established a reputation among French distributors for consistent, high-quality products.

ICA aimed to minimize storage costs while maintaining sufficient inventory to meet customer needs. M. Agazzi, ICA marketing manager, noted: "Our goal is to sell our products in large quantities." In 1992, typical order sizes ranged from 500 kg to 5 tons. ICA was one of only a few importers with a single supplier, which, according to M. Agazzi, resulted in a predictable supply flow and consistently high product quality. The majority of ICA's competitors paid for imported shrimp in U.S. dollars, while ICA paid Pechazur in French francs. As a result, exchange rate fluctuations between the U.S. dollar and the French franc could strongly impact the relative competitiveness of Pechazur products in France.

Pricing and Margins

Costs, selling prices, and average margins for Pechazur products are given in Table D. Since prices fluctuated frequently, these figures represent yearly averages. Larger shrimp commanded higher margins than smaller shrimp, but as the captain of one of Sari-Fish's fishing vessels put it, "Unfortunately, large shrimp do not self-select themselves to be caught. We have to take the small with the large."

Exhibit 14 also details Pechazur export product prices FOB.[6] Prices in France fluctuated weekly; Pechazur had to

---

6 FOB prices did not include transportation costs.

Exhibit 14   Pechazur Export Product Prices FOB to France, January 1993

Whole raw shrimp/frozen aboard≈

#1 (10/20 units per kg)	90FF
#2 (20/30 units per kg)	72FF
#3 (30/40 units per kg)	58FF
#4 (40/60 units per kg)	45FF
#5 (60/80 units per kg)	35FF
#6 (80/100 units per kg)	28FF
#7 (100/120 units per kg)	22FF

Whole cooked shrimp:

SX (10/20 units per kg)	100FF
SL (20/30 units per kg)	88FF
S (30/40 units per kg)	70FF
EE (40/60 units per kg)	58FF
E (60/80 units per kg)	46FF
G (80/100 units per kg)	34FF
M (100/120 units per kg)	29FF
MG (120/140 units per kg)	26FF
Z (140/180 units per kg)	23FF
ZZ (200/250 units per kg)	20FF

Shelled cooked shrimp:

DS00 (-/100 units per kg)	48FF
DS 0 (100/150 units per kg)	46FF
DS 1 (150/250 units per kg)	42FF
DS 2 (250/400 units per kg)	28FF
DS 3 (400/700 units per kg)	22FF

Fillets of tropical sole:

F/S1 0.07kg - 0.1kg	32FF
F/S2 0.07kg	29FF
Tropical sole:	
0.15/0.2 kg per unit	21FF
0.2/0.25 kg per unit	21FF

Cuttlefish whites:

G (2/3 units per kg)	24FF
M (4/6 units per kg)	23FF
P (6/9 units per kg)	21FF

Red mullet:

Fillet/kg	32FF
Whole/kg	9FF

Table D — Costs, Prices, and Margins for Pechazur's Main Product Lines

	Raw Material Cost (FCFA/kg)	Processing (FCFA/kg)	Selling Price (FCFA/kg)	Margin (FCFA/kg)[a]	Percentage Margin
Shelled, cooked lagoon shrimp	1,163	520	2,153	470	28
Shelled, raw sea shrimp	1,992	520	2,950	438	18
Whole, cooked lagoon shrimp	1,072	460	1,890	358	23
Whole, cooked sea shrimp	1,926	400	2,893	567	24
Whole, raw sea shrimp (frozen-on-board)	1,540	103	2,176	533	32
Fish fillets	350	564	1,140	226	25
Whole fish for the local market[b]	300	0	380	80	22

[a]Margins before packaging costs.

[b]Product margins for sales to the local market were 20% of selling price for fresh fish, 11% for imported frozen fish, and 23% for frozen fish.

meet market prices to achieve sales and maintain the existing customer base. ICA's margins averaged 8% in 1992. The margins obtained by the different intermediaries and retailers typically resulted in a final retail market price of two times the ICA sales price. For example, large-sized shrimp, priced at 75FF/kg by ICA, could retail for 150FF/kg in a supermarket. Recently, channel margins had come under pressure due to the consolidation and rising power of the major supermarket chains, who were backward integrating and thereby competing increasingly with seafood distributors.

The Benin Plant

Benin, with a population of 4.8 million, had traditionally been an important transit and trading center for the neighboring countries of Nigeria and Togo. Following a coup d'etat in 1972, a Marxist government had maintained power until 1989. In 1993, the country was plagued with an illiquid banking system, large bankrupt state companies, and high levels of internal and external debt. As part of a structural adjustment program initiated by the World Bank, the IFC was searching for opportunities to promote private enterprise. The majority of entrepreneurs in Benin were, however, involved in trade with neighboring countries (fueled, in part, by the overvalued FCFA and large price discrepancies between Benin and Nigeria) and were not interested in investing in productive assets. Due to Pechazur's recognized success in the RCI, the IFC proposed to N'Dione that he establish a shrimp-processing plant in Benin to be 20% financed by the IFC.

As export prices on shrimp dropped, N'Dione had been looking for ways to decrease Pechazur's production costs in order to remain competitive with farm-raised shrimp. Benin appeared to be a favorable location due to its large source of lagoon shrimp and lower labor and energy costs. Total product costs would be 15% to 20% below those for identical products processed in the RCI.

SOBEP (Societe Beninoise de Peche) was founded in 1992, with N'Dione holding 79% of the shares, the IFC 20%, and a local lawyer, also a personal friend of N'Dione's and a deputy in the National Assembly, 1%. The processing plant, located in the port of Cotonou, was similar to the Dabou plant in the RCI and was expected to be fully operational by February 1993. It could process up to four tons of raw product a day and would source lagoon shrimp from local fishermen as well as sea shrimp and fish from Nigerian vessels with on-board freezing facilities. Expected annual production levels were 520 tons of shrimp, of which 75% would be sourced from lagoon fishermen, and 240 tons of fish fillets, sourced entirely from the Nigerian vessels. The SOBEP plant had a frozen storage capacity of 400 tons.

Five pickup vans would collect the output of 1,000 fishermen, located around a large lagoon, several times a day. The fishermen were not as yet organized into cooperatives but the director of SOBEP explained how this would eventually happen:

> It's all a question of confidence. First we must work at creating a habit, once the fishermen get used to the way we work and see that we pay fairly and regularly, we will be able to help them form cooperatives and ensure a regular and stable supply of lagoon shrimp.

Adjacent to the SOBEP plant, a large frozen warehouse with a storage capacity of 500 tons was being built in 1993 and N'Dione planned to import frozen fish to supply the local Benin market. Consumption levels and distribution channels for fish in Benin were very similar to those in the RCI. In the longer term, N'Dione was considering acquiring a fishing fleet that would operate out of Cotonou in much the same way as Sari-Fish.

OPTIONS FOR GROWTH

N'Dione reflected on the different challenges facing Pechazur and the company's opportunities for further expansion. He wanted to develop a coherent strategy that would address the balance between export and local sales; the relative importance of fish versus shrimp sales; the balance between supply generation and demand management activities; and the further development of the product line.

The Export-Local Sales Balance
N'Dione believed that maintaining a balance between export and local sales was a sensible diversification move that would not result in a lack of focus. The RCI and Benin were both large markets where fish were a major component of the daily diet. However, the local economies of both countries were depressed, and individual purchasing power had declined substantially over the past decade, resulting in increased pressures on prices and profitability. On the other hand, Pechazur was facing substantial competition from farm-raised shrimp in export markets which had caused the company's average revenues per kg of shrimp to decline.

N'Dione perceived the export of fish fillets as "necessary, simply because they are caught along with the shrimp." Fish fillets were useful as a capacity filler in processing, shipping, and export marketing, but the fish fillet market in Europe was dominated by large, well-established brands against which it seemed difficult to compete effectively.

Supply Activities
Pechazur could expand its current supply-side activities by enlarging its fishing fleet and/or constructing additional processing plants, either in RCI or neighboring countries. However, N'Dione believed that expanding supply activities could be justified only if the demand for the output was sufficiently high and if the resulting sales were profitable.

N'Dione had evaluated the possibility of starting a shrimp aquaculture farm. However, not only were the capital requirements high, but an existing aquaculture farm in Abidjan, operated by a local division of Unilever, was experiencing serious productivity and quality control problems.

Demand and Marketing Activities
With the SOBEP factory coming on-line in early 1993, Pechazur needed to expand its sales to the French market and/or attempt to penetrate other geographic markets. N'Dione believed that improving access to export markets was one of Pechazur's key challenges. He was concerned about the perceived quality of African products in Western markets and wondered how best to build Pechazur's credibility.

France Pechazur was known as a quality shrimp supplier in France and could continue to sell through ICA and other importers. On the other hand, due to the changing nature of the distribution structure in France, N'Dione was increasingly interested in striking a private label agreement with one or more supermarket chains. This, however, would place Pechazur in direct competition with its existing client base. Further penetration of the institutional or restaurant market was also appealing but it was highly fragmented and could be accessed only via wholesalers and distributors.

Other export markets These included other European countries and the United States, Japan being perceived as too difficult a market in terms of both competition and logistics. N'Dione wanted to initiate sales to the U.S. market but wondered what the best way of achieving this might be. He explained, "My dream would be to find a U.S. partner committed to developing Pechazur sales and sharing the risks and profit potential with us."

Product Line
Although Pechazur could not change its product mix in terms of shrimp sizes, the company could choose the

proportion of shrimp that were cooked and/or shelled. To date, the volume of cooked and shelled shrimp had largely been determined by customer requirements. N'Dione wondered if Pechazur should attempt to specialize in two products: raw sea shrimp frozen on board; and shelled, cooked lagoon shrimp.

N'Dione pondered whether the long-term success of Pechazur resided in developing consumer brand recognition and applying the Pechazur brand to value-added products sold at retail, such as frozen ready-to-eat meals in which shrimp was at the "center of the plate."

Milkpak Limited—International Joint Venture

On January 25, 1987, Syed Babar Ali, chairman, and Syed Yawar Ali,[1] managing director of Milkpak Limited, prepared for a meeting with a high-level team from Nestle, a multinational food company based in Switzerland. Milkpak Limited, incorporated in 1979, was a pioneer in developing a Pakistani industry for ultra-high temperature (UHT) milk, a sterilized milk that did not require refrigeration when specially packaged. The increasing popularity of UHT milk caused company sales to increase from 96 million rupees in 1982—Milkpak's first full year of production—to 340 million rupees in 1986. The company was increasingly interested in producing value-added products and was exploring a joint venture with a foreign company.[2]

COMPANY BACKGROUND

Milkpak was part of a family group of businesses—the Ali Group—that spanned a number of interests. Considered one of Pakistan's leading industrial families, the Ali Group was involved in razor blade and textile manufacture in addition to having holdings in the insurance industry. The group had major investments in the vegetable oil and soap industries and also managed Ford's auto assembly plant prior to 1973, when the government nationalized all of these businesses.

Milkpak was founded to create a market for packaging materials produced by Packages Limited, a leading company in the Ali Group. Packages Limited was established in Lahore, Pakistan, in 1956, in collaboration with AB Akerlund & Rausing of Sweden, to convert paper and board into packaging. Packages later integrated backwards into pulp and paper manufacturing. The company supplied packaging materials to a variety of industries and also provided technical assistance to packaging plants in Africa and the Middle East. Packages manufactured its own line of facial tissues and other consumer products. In 1986, Packages' total sales were approximately Rs. 633 million.

Milkpak was established following a 1976 review of the use of Packages' equipment. The Tetra Laminator, a machine designed for making packaging material for long-life milk, was used very infrequently. Packages purchased the Tetra Laminator machine in 1967 from Tetra Pak of Sweden, a company affiliated with Akerlund & Rausing. The Tetra Pak aseptic system[3] was developed to package UHT milk. The UHT process heated milk at temperatures of 130–150 degrees centigrade for 2–3 seconds. Milk thus sterilized had a shelf life of up to three months without refrigeration when packaged in Tetra Pak containers. The Tetra Pak system had special advantages for developing countries that lacked extensive refrigeration and distribution systems. Some of the packages were in the shape of tetrahedrons (a four-faced pyramid); rectangular packages that required heavier and more expensive paper were also available.

Packages found that there was one milk plant in Pakistan, at the time inoperative, designed to produce sterilized milk. The company leased the plant, with a capacity of 17,500 liters of milk per day, as a pilot project to test the market for UHT milk. Packages hoped that a successful pilot project would encourage entrepreneurs to produce UHT milk, thereby increasing the demand for Tetra Pak packaging. To implement the project, a number of challenges were surmounted, including developing a low-cost, locally produced paper for packaging and securing reliable sources of milk supply. The pilot project was deemed

This case was prepared by Professor John A. Quelch with the assistance of Afroze A. Mohammed.

Copyright © 1993 by the President and Fellows of Harvard College. Harvard Business School case 9-593-113.

[1] Yawar Ali was Babar Ali's nephew.
[2] Exhange rate in 1986: Rs. 16.65 = $1.00.
[3] An aseptic system is free from pathogenic organisms.

a success in 1978 when, with limited promotional efforts, sales reached plant capacity.

Milkpak was incorporated in January 1979 after Packages decided to invest in a 150,000 liters/day UHT milk plant, at a cost of Rs. 90 million. Financing for the new company was obtained from Tetra Pak; Danish Turnkey Dairies, the equipment supplier; and several development agencies, including the International Finance Corporation and the German Development Institute. (Exhibit 1 summarizes Milkpak's ownership structure.)

Milkpak started commercial production of UHT milk in its new plant in November 1981. (Exhibit 2 provides Milkpak's yearly sales and profit and loss statements from 1981 to 1986.) By 1987, Milkpak's product line had expanded from UHT milk to include fruit juices and other dairy products, though UHT milk still accounted for an estimated 85% of company sales. In 1984, Milkpak started marketing the Frost line of fruit juices, introduced a few years earlier by Packages. Frost juices were premixed, in contrast to existing juices on the market that were available in concentrate form. Milkpak bought the Frost brand name and equipment from Packages, and in 1986 fruit juices accounted for 9% of Milkpak's sales. Additional products included butter, introduced in 1985. In 1986, the company launched a sterilized cream product, "balai," and also a cooking oil, "Desi Ghee." These products were sold under the brand name Milkpak.

PAKISTAN

Pakistan was founded in 1947, when British India was partitioned into two nation states. Pakistan, established as a Muslim country, initially had two geographically separate sections on either side of India. In 1971, the eastern wing of Pakistan separated to form Bangladesh. The western section, which remained Pakistan, had Urdu as its national language, with English widely spoken. By 1986, Pakistan had a population of over 90 million. Pakistan's GNP per capita was $380, although the country had large income disparities. (Exhibit 3 provides basic social and economic data about Pakistan.)[4]

In the 1980s, Pakistan had political and economic policies that promoted the role of private enterprise in the country's economy. This climate was in contrast to that prevailing from 1972 to 1977 when the government was concerned about the high concentration of industrial ownership and nationalized a number of businesses. In the mid-1980s, the rate of growth of manufacturing output was 9.1% per year, while agricultural output grew at 4.6% per year; from 1972 to 1977, these sectors had grown each year at only 5.2% and 2%, respectively.[5] Policy initiatives made in the 1980s offered safeguards against nationalization and sought to ensure the safety of investments.

While the overall climate for private investment was favorable, businesses had to obtain a variety of government licenses and approvals before undertaking or expanding projects. These approvals differed according to a project's source of funds and specific characteristics. The government's permission for a project would address issues such as the amount of investment allowed, procedures governing repatriation of capital and profits, the amount of raw materials that could be imported, and the location of the industrial establishment. In practice, obtaining these approvals could result in project delays, although the Pakistani government was making efforts to facilitate the process.

Exhibit 1   Ownership Shares of Milkpak

Investor Share	Ownership
Ali family	15.7%
Packages Limited	7.1
IGI[a]	5.7
International Finance Corporation	5.7
Tetra Pak[b]	8.6
DEG[c]	5.7
DTD[d]	2.9
IFU[e]	2.9
Public shareholders	45.7%

Source: Company records.

[a]International General Insurance Company, 99% owned by the Ali family.
[b]The Swedish manufacturer of the equipment used to make materials for the nonrefrigerated milk containers.
[c]The German Development Institute, a foreign aid and development institution.
[d]Danish Turnkey Dairies, Limited, Milkpak's equipment supplier and the provider of Milkpak's specialized extension services to Pakistani dairy farmers.
[e]Industrial Fund for Developing Countries, Denmark.

---

[4] Background information in this section is from *Pakistan and the World Bank: Partners in Progress* (Washington, D.C.: The World Bank, 1986).
[5] Shahid Javed Burki, *Pakistan: A Nation in the Making* (Boulder: Westview Press, 1986), p. 115.

Exhibit 2   Milkpak Profit-and-Loss Statements: 1981–1986

	1986	1985	1984	1983	1982	1981 (2 months)
Net Sales	340,343,535	251,835,221	214,662,630	137,310,716	96,129,181	9,409,358
Cost of goods sold	296,417,357	223,485,654	185,175,145	114,742,655	85,894,230	9,986,726
Trading profit	43,926,178	28,349,567	29,487,485	22,568,061	10,234,951	(577,368)
Selling, administrative, and general expenses	30,294,796	17,980,055	14,959,910	10,723,215	8,731,245	1,413,890
Operating profit(loss)[a]	13,631,382	10,369,512	14,527,575	11,844,846	1,503,706	(1,991,258)
Other income	1,043,295	970,458	773,190	342,738	342,021	1,194,391
	14,674,677	11,339,970	15,300,765	12,187,584	1,845,727	(796,867)
Financial charges	7,495,788	5,258,607	5,828,054	5,713,972	6,868,285	900,448
Workers' participation fund	361,500	355,970	546,389	414,430	--	--
	7,857,288	5,614,577	6,374,443	6,128,402	6,868,285	900,448
Profit before taxation	6,817,389	5,725,393	8,926,322	6,059,182	(5,022,558)	(1,697,315)
Provision for taxation	3,045,000	1,603,000	4,535,000	--	--	--
	3,772,389	4,122,393	4,391,322	6,059,182	(5,022,558)	(1,697,315)

Source: Company records.

[a]The decline in operating profit as a percentage of net sales in 1985 and 1986 was primarily due to switching to an aluminum foil packaging paper that improved the shelf life of Milkpak brand milk, starting a new fruit juice plant, and increases in sales promotion expenses.

Exhibit 3   Pakistan: Basic Country Data

Area	803,940 sq. km.
Agricultural land (1983):	254,900 sq. km.
GNP per capita (1984):	$380
Energy consumption per capita (1983):	179 kg. of oil equivalent
Population (1984):	93.3 million
Urban population (percentage of total):	30.1
Protected population in 2000:	143 million
Population density (1984):	116.0 per sq. km.
Population density of agricultural land (1984):	366.0 per sq. km.
Population growth rate (1970-84):	3.1%
Urban population growth rate (1970-84):	4.6%
Crude birthrate (1984):	41 per thousand
Crude death rate (1984):	11 per thousand
Life expectancy at birth (1984):	50.6 years
Infant mortality (1984):	116.2 per thousand
Access to safe water (1981):	346% of population
Urban:	72.0
Rural:	20.0
Population per physician (1981):	3,190
Average size of household (1979):	6.7
Secondary school enrollment (1983):	15%
Adult literacy (1979):	24%
Labor force (1984):	26.4 million
Labor participation rate (1983):	28.3%
Percentage of income received by	
highest 5% of households (1970):	17.8
highest 20% of households (1970):	41.8
lowest 20% of households (1970):	8
lowest 40% of households (1970):	20.2
Estimated absolute poverty income level[a] (1979)	
Urban:	$176.0 per capita
Rural:	$122.0 per capita
Estimated relative poverty income level[b] (1979)	
Urban:	$88.0 per capita
Rural:	$58.0 per capita
Estimated population below absolute poverty income level[c]	
Urban:	32.0%
Rural:	29.0%

Source: Adapted from *Pakistan and the World Bank, Partners in Progress* (1986).

[a]Absolute poverty income level is the level below which a minimal nutritionally adequate diet plus essential nonfood requirements is not affordable.

[b]Rural relative poverty income level is one-third of average per capita personal income of the country. Urban level is derived from the rural level with adjustment for higher cost of living in urban areas.

[c]Percentage of population (urban and rural) who are the "absolute poor."

THE PAKISTANI DAIRY INDUSTRY

Fresh milk was traditionally supplied to urban consumers directly from farms on a daily basis.[6] Consumers obtained milk (1) directly from farmers or dairy colonies (these sources were sometimes referred to as peri-urban producers) that kept buffalos in or near the towns, and (2) from milkmen who purchased milk from farmers. Milkmen would travel the countryside by bicycle, collect milk in 40-liter cans, and then sell it to contractors, who put ice in the milk and then transported it into the city. The milk was then sold to consumers at their homes and through retail milk shops, which did not have refrigeration facilities. The entire process, from milking the buffalos to selling the milk in the city, took place each morning. While the system delivered fresh milk to consumers each day, it had drawbacks. In particular, adulteration of milk with impure water occurred at various stages in the distribution chain. In addition, the absence of a refrigerated distribution infrastructure led to milk spoilage and waste.

The problems of transporting and distributing milk resulted in shortages in major urban centers—Milkpak's target market. Shortages were exacerbated by the marked seasonality in production and consumption of milk. Milk consumption peaked during the summer. In contrast, milk production was highest during the winter months of December-March, called the "flush" season, and lowest during the "lean" season from May to August. Lower production during the summer was caused by hot weather and decreased availability of fodder. As a result of both of these factors, the Pakistani government adopted liberal policies towards the import of milk products. (Exhibit 4 provides data on Pakistani milk production and dairy imports.)

Milk powder was a particularly important dairy import. Milk powder, mixed with water to make fluid milk, had an established place in the Pakistani market, especially in Karachi, where fresh milk supplies were insufficient to meet demand as a result of increases in population. In 1986, about 30% of the demand for fluid milk supplies in Karachi was met by milk powder. Demand for milk powder was met primarily by imports, which averaged 20,000–30,000 tons annually. Powder was imported both as a branded product, in tins, and also in bulk (25 kilogram bags). Bulk supplies were repackaged by retailers in 1 1/2 kg[7] plastic bags. Branded milk powders were typically bought by higher-income consumers while the repackaged bulk supplies were purchased by lower- and middle- income consumers.

Exhibit 4   Milk Production and Dairy Imports, 1975–1976 to 1985–1986

Year	Estimated Milk Production (000 tons)	Dairy Imports Value (million Rs.)	Dairy Imports Milk Equivalent (000 tons)	Imports/Production (percent)
1975–76	8,348	313.0	329.2	3.94
1976–77	8,524	251.0	165.8	1.94
1977–78	8,704	391.1	448.5	5.15
1978–79	8,888	321.6	237.0	2.67
1979–80	9,075	481.9	420.4	4.63
1980–81	9,267	552.3	352.8	3.81
1981–82	9,462	522.6	275.8	2.91
1982–83	9,662	736.8	357.4	3.70
1983–84	10,242	802.1	397.4	3.88
1984–85	10,856	712.0	315.6	2.91
1985–86	11,508	779.2	282.4	2.45

Source: Pakistan Economic Survey Data; imports data from Federal Bureau of Statistics. Adapted from Table 4.2 in *Pakistan's Dairy Industry: Issues and Policy Alternatives.*

---

6 Background information in this case about the Pakistani dairy industry, including the UHT industry, is from *Pakistan's Dairy Industry: Issues and Policy Alternatives* (Islamabad: The Directorate of Agricultural Policy and Chemonics International Consulting Division, 1989).

7 There are 1,000 kilograms in a metric ton.

Efforts had also been made to establish an indigenous local milk processing industry. Packages' decision to invest in Milkpak was made in spite of a history of failed investments in the milk processing industry. During the 1960s and 1970s, Pakistani entrepreneurs established 23 plants in the dairy processing field, including several plants for milk pasteurization. The failure of at least 15 of this "first generation" of dairy processing plants was attributed to poor management, difficulties in obtaining fresh milk supplies, and the lack of an extensive refrigerated distribution infrastructure.

Milk Collection

To ensure a reliable and high-quality supply of milk, especially during the lean season, Milkpak focused attention on developing a system for milk collection and agricultural extension. Milk collection centers were established in areas considered rich in milk production. The company taught farmers scientific techniques of livestock care and breeding, provided veterinary services, and made available high-yielding fodder seed and cattle feed. Milk was supplied to the company by traditional milk contractors who bought milk from farmers. In addition, Milkpak helped establish village cooperatives and, through them, received milk directly from farmers.

During the flush season, Milkpak often had to refuse milk supplies. Milkpak's management visited dairies in India, including Nestle's plant, to gain an understanding of how other dairies in a similar environment addressed problems of seasonality.

UHT Milk Processing

Processed milk was required by law to contain 3.5% butterfat and 8.9% solids not fat (SNF). Fresh milk usually had a higher fat content and a lower level of solids than required. As a result, before being heated to 130–150 degrees centigrade, the milk was decreamed to reduce the fat content. To raise the SNF level, skimmed milk powder and water were added. When there was a shortage of fresh milk, milk powder could be added to increase milk production volumes, although, at prevailing prices for imported milk powder, it was rarely economical to do so. The technology for manufacturing UHT milk was considered expensive, with processing costs accounting for about 25% of total product costs. (Exhibit 5 reports estimates of UHT processing costs, obtained from different manufacturers in the industry.)

Packaging materials, which were heavily taxed, accounted for another 26% of Milkpak's production cost.[8]

UHT Milk Marketing

Positioning. A major challenge facing the company was to introduce urban consumers to the idea of long-life milk. Consumers were concerned that sterilized milk contained preservatives or was somehow not genuine because, unlike fresh milk, the Milkpak brand contained no cream. In one early promotional campaign, households were given two samples of Milkpak, one for immediate consumption and the other to be consumed four days later; the goal was to demonstrate that while the milk remained packaged it did not require refrigeration. Milkpak was positioned as a pure dairy product, processed in a scientific, hygienic way, and consistent in quality throughout the year. (Exhibit 6 and Exhibit 7 show print advertisements for Milkpak brand UHT milk and butter. Sales promotion and advertising expenses for Milkpak are summarized in Exhibit 8.)

Milkpak's heavy users were "modern housewives," who were concerned about both convenience and product quality. Another target market was lower-income consumers, who were often sold relatively cheap adulterated milk by the traditional milkmen; Milkpak provided a higher-quality milk than they had purchased before. (Exhibit 9 presents the results of a consumer survey sponsored by Milkpak.)

Packaging. Milkpak brand UHT milk was initially sold in tetrahedron shaped containers, in sizes of 1/2 liter and 1/5 liter. In 1984, a one-liter rectangular-shaped "brickpak" was introduced. The more conventionally shaped brickpak eliminated the need for special crates required to store tetra paks, but used more packaging material. In 1986, a quarter-liter brickpak was introduced.

Pricing. Table A shows the 1986 retail prices for Milkpak and other types of milk in two major cities in Pakistan. Milkpak competed with the traditional milk distribution system that supplied fresh, or "raw," milk to consumers each day. Milk powder competed with Milkpak as a convenience product.

Distribution A key success factor in Milkpak's rapid growth was the expansion of its distribution network. In 1981, there were an estimated 1,000 retail outlets selling Milkpak; by 1986, the number had grown to 13,000. Milkpak was sold in grocery stores, bakeries, general stores, and supermarkets. The company had sales offices in Karachi, Lahore, and Islamabad, and had a nationwide

---

8 *Pakistan's Dairy Industry*, p. 16.

Exhibit 5   UHT Milk Production Costs

Cost Item	Rs./Liter
Raw milk[a]	2.66
Value of cream separated[b]	(0.45)
Net cost of raw milk	2.21
Conversion to 1 liter volume at 3.5% butter fat	2.28
Skimmed milk powder[c]	0.72
Processing cost[d]	1.72
Packaging cost	1.77
Transportation cost	0.08
Market returns/replacement[e]	0.20
Subtotal	6.77
Processor's margin	0.04
Distributor's margin	0.19
Retailer's margin	0.50
Subtotal	0.73
Retail price[f]	7.50

Source: International Consulting Division, Chemonics. Adapted from Table 2.4 in *Pakistan's Dairy Industry: Issues and Policy Alternatives* (1989).
[a]Price of milk at 5% butterfat and 7% solid not fats.
[b]Cream (50% fat) valued at Rs. 15 per kilogram.
[c]Adding 19 grams of skimmed milk powder @ Rs. 38/kg.
[d]Includes depreciation and financial charges.
[e]Market returns are assumed to be 3%.
[f]Retail UHT milk price in Lahore zone. The price in other areas was Rs. 8/liter.

Table A   Comparative Retail Prices of UHT Milk, Raw Milk, and Dried Milk Powder in Different Cities in Pakistan (rupees per liter)

City	Raw Milk		Whole Milk Powder[b]		UHT Milk
	Peri-Urban Producer	Milk Shop[a]	Tinned	Polythene Bags	
Lahore	5.00–6.00	4.50–5.50	7.50	6.00	7.50
Karachi	5.50–7.00	5.00–6.50	6.88	5.50	8.00

Source: Adapted from Table 2.5 in *Pakistan's Dairy Industry: Issues and Policy Alternatives* (1986).
[a]In general, the quality of milk sold by milk shops was poorer than that sold by peri-urban producers.
[b]In liquid milk equivalent terms, assuming a dried milk to liquid milk convertion ratio of 1:8.

Exhibit 6   Print Advertisement for Milkpak Brand UHT Milk

Translation
Top Lines: Fresh, pure Milkpak milk——the best for the whole family.
Bottom Line: A product of Milkpak dairy. Pure, delicious, and fresh.

Exhibit 7   Print Advertisement for Milkpak Brand Butter

Translation

Top Lines: Prepared from fresh and pure milk. Milkpak butter——the best for the whole family.

Bottom Line: A product of Milkpak dairy. Pure, delicious, and fresh.

Exhibit 8   Milkpak Sales Promotion and Advertising Expenses

1981	778,540[a]	8.2% of sales
1982	1,517,576	1.6
1983	1,158,329	0.8
1984	900,204	0.4
1985	1,728,077	0.7
1986	8,283,452[b]	2.4

Source: Company records.

[a]Sales promotion and advertising expenses of Rs. 778,540 were incurred in 1981, but were written off in three equal yearly installments in 1982, 1983, and 1984.

[b]Increase in sales promotion expenses was required to launch new products and sustain market share.

Exhibit 9   Results of 1986 Milkpak Survey of Middle/High Income Urban Consumers on UHT Milk and Milk Powder

- 65% of respondents used more than one source of milk (e.g., UHT milk, fresh milk, powdered milk).

- In Karachi, 9% of respondents bought UHT milk; in Lahore, 25% bought UHT milk.

- 40% of respondents had no brand preference in purchasing UHT milk, while 35% preferred Milkpak.

- Respondents' prompted recall of the Milkpak brand name was 86%. Unprompted recall was 29%.

- 56% of UHT milk purchasers bought it in general stores, 25% in bakeries, and 16% in shops that were combined general stores/bakeries.

- 58% of respondents purchased UHT milk on a daily basis; 11% bought it three times a week; 18% purchased it twice a week; 13% purchased it less frequently.

- Respondents who did not purchase UHT milk cited the following reasons: it was too expensive (18%); they thought chemicals were added to the milk (12%); they were used to fresh milk (11%); UHT milk contained no cream (10%).

- Consumers purchased family milk powder for several reasons: to feed children (40%); to make the following foods: tea (16%), desserts (11%), yoghurt (11%), drinks made from milk (10%); and for drinking (11%).

- Respondents purchased milk powder from general stores (60%), combined general/medical stores (24%), and bakeries (10%).

- 74% of respondents purchased milk powder once a month; 23% bought it twice a month; only 3% purchased powdered milk weekly.

Source: Company records.

network of distributors in all the major cities and towns. For Milkpak brand milk, the margin to the distributor was between .2 and .25 rupees per liter, depending on the shipping distance. The retail margin was .52 rupees per liter. The UHT business was viewed as similar to the soft drink business, with high turnover and low margins, requiring flexibility and fast decision making.

Evolution of the UHT Milk Industry

Milkpak's success in developing a market for UHT milk spurred the entry of several other companies. By the end of 1986, eight plants owned by different companies could manufacture UHT milk. Total sales of UHT milk grew from 11.25 million liters in 1981 to approximately 80 million in 1986.[9] In 1986, Milkpak estimated that its share of the market was over 50%. Milkpak had a reputation for consistent, high quality, both with consumers and the trade.

Some of Milkpak's early competitors were short-lived. Milkpure and Purabrand, which entered the market in 1983, competed with Milkpak by offering consumer and trade promotions such as free tea bags and raffles for free air tickets. Milkpak did not offer similar promotions in response; management felt that profit margins on UHT milk did not allow such marketing investments. Both companies had financial problems and went out of business by the end of 1985.

Other more stable competitors included Milko, the UHT plant originally leased by Packages to test the market for UHT milk. Milko returned to its original owners after Milkpak's founding. By 1986, Milko had an estimated 10% share of the market. Pakistan Dairies, the country's first producer of cheese, started manufacturing UHT milk in 1983. Because of its other dairy products, Pakistan Dairies had an extensive and effective system for milk collection and was regarded as a high- quality producer. In 1986, the company's share of the market was approximately 18%–20%. A new competitor, Chaudhuri Dairies, entered the market in June 1986 and captured a share of 15% by year end. Chaudhuri introduced its brand Haleeb in rectangular brickpak packaging, which was more convenient to store and was considered a competitive advantage.

While the sales of UHT milk grew rapidly, they still constituted a relatively small share of total consumption. It was estimated that by 1987, UHT accounted for approximately 2% of the milk consumed in Pakistan's urban areas.

The emergence of an industry to process UHT milk was fostered by government policy, notably duty exemptions on the import of machinery for dairy plants and the provision of low cost financing by government agencies. The government had sanctioned a number of additional plants that would be brought on line in coming years, and there was, therefore, concern that the industry would have substantial overcapacity.[10]

STRATEGIC OPTIONS FOR GROWTH

As Milkpak reviewed its growth options, management increasingly saw the development of a milk powder plant as a necessity. First, a powder plant would help smooth the seasonal mismatch between the supply of and demand for milk. During the summer (the time of peak demand), milk powder would be combined with liquid milk to extend the supplies of UHT milk. The growth potential for UHT milk had been limited by seasonality; Milkpak's marketing managers were reluctant to promote UHT milk heavily during the flush season because they felt they were creating demand that could not be satisfied in the lean season. While Milkpak's managers were very committed to increasing UHT milk sales, they knew that the UHT business was inherently a high volume, low margin business. As a result, the company wanted to explore the possibility of producing other value-added foods, such as milk powder, cereal, and infant formula, among other products.

In addition to using milk powder as an ingredient in UHT milk, Milkpak could sell milk powder, which competed with UHT milk, as a convenience product. In 1986, 25,002 tons of milk powder, with a value of Rs. 406 million, were imported. Only two domestic companies manufactured milk powder, one of which produced solely for the military. The other company, Noon Ltd., established with the technical assistance of Cow & Gate, a U.K company, had an output of 600 tons/year. The Pakistan Dairy Association, chaired by Yawar Ali, argued that the government's low tariffs on milk powder imports (which historically had been subsidized by European producers) impeded the development of a domestic dairy industry. In 1986, the government imposed a 16% tax on imports of milk powder, which improved the viability of domestic production.

About 20% of milk powder imports were branded. The major brands, with estimated market shares, were

9 *Pakistan's Dairy Industry*, p. 12.
10 *Pakistan's Dairy Industry*, p. 19.

NIDO, produced by Nestle (24% market share); Red Cow, manufactured by Cow & Gate (25% of market); and Safety, manufactured by Friesland—of the Netherlands—(24% market share). NIDO's prices were the highest (Rs. 107 per 1800 gram tin), followed by Red Cow (Rs. 92–102/tin) and Safety (Rs. 93–97/tin). The demand for branded milk powder was forecast to increase to 18,000 tons/year by 1996.

Milkpak's management had to decide whether to acquire foreign technology and management assistance to develop its own plant. Alternatively, Milkpak considered the possibility of finding a foreign joint venture partner.

Independent Study

Milkpak prepared a feasibility study for a milk powder plant. Exhibit 10 provides a summary of the project costs, financing sources, and projected profits. Milkpak estimated that by the third year of operation the plant would produce 2,400 tons of milk powder. A locally manufactured product could be competitively priced relative to imports. In addition, a Milkpak plant would use buffalo milk, a familiar taste for local consumers. A study of the milk powder market commissioned by Milkpak recommended that Milkpak produce a branded product to capitalize on Milkpak's name and reputation. In addition to producing milk powder, the plant would also manufacture infant formula, butter oil, and butter.

Milkpak expected to hire an experienced expatriate production manager. While Milkpak executives thought it was feasible for the company to develop a powder plant without a joint venture partner, they were concerned about the technical difficulties of doing so. For example, they felt that producing products such as infant formula required technical knowledge and expertise that the company did not have.

Joint Venture Partners

A joint venture partner could provide both the necessary technology and a reputable brand name that could be attached to locally manufactured, value-added products. Milkpak's managers debated the advantages and drawbacks of conducting a joint venture. Some thought Milkpak should seek out a joint venture partner that currently exported branded products to Pakistan and already had some brand recognition in Pakistan. Others were concerned that a company with established brands would expect high

royalties that would leave too little profit for Milkpak to warrant the investment risk.

Another concern was that a large multinational joint venture partner might dominate Milkpak. Chairman Babar Ali, however, felt very comfortable with the prospect of a joint venture; Packages Limited, where he had worked for much of his career, was itself a joint venture.

A major challenge was to identify appropriate joint venture partners and find ways to approach them. Danish Turnkey Dairies and Tetra Pak, companies Milkpak and Packages already had ties with, could help in identifying and providing introductions to potential joint venture partners. As a result, Friesland and Nestle emerged as particularly interesting prospects for a joint venture partnership.

Friesland Friesland, established in 1913 as the "Cooperative Condensed Milkfactory Friesland," was founded by farmers in the Friesland province of Holland. Over 12,000 Dutch farmers supplied milk for the production of a variety of dairy products, including condensed and powdered milk and infant foods. In 1986, Friesland's net sales were 1,807 million guilders.[11]

Friesland's products were sold in 130 countries, primarily through exports. Friesland exported Safety brand milk powder and Omela brand condensed milk to Pakistan. The company also operated some manufacturing facilities and dairies overseas, usually in partnership with a local company. These included manufacturing plants in Guam, Indonesia, Lebanon, Malaysia, Nigeria, Taiwan, Thailand, Saudi Arabia, and Yemen. Friesland provided technical assistance to its affiliated companies as well as management assistance on a contract basis.

Nestle S.A. Nestle was founded in 1867 by Henri Nestle, a chemist who developed the first milk-based food for babies. In 1905, the company merged with the Anglo-Swiss Condensed Milk Company, a former competitor. From a base in dairy products, Nestle's product line grew to encompass chocolate and confectionery, instant and roasted coffee, culinary products, frozen foods, and instant drinks. By 1986, Nestle's consolidated sales were 38,050 million francs.[12]

Early in its development, Nestle established production facilities outside of Switzerland. By 1986, Nestle had plants in 60 countries. In determining whether to set up production facilities in a particular country, the company considered several factors, including the availability of raw

---

11 Exchange rate in 1986: 2.45 Guilders = $1.00.
12 Exchange rate in 1986: 1.80 Swiss Francs = $1.00.

	Rs. '000
1. Cost of Project and Sources of Finance	
1.1 Cost of Project	
Building	2,640
Plant and machinery (including construction)	37,245
Trial run cost and interest during construction	3,100
Contingencies	4,515
	47,500
Working capital	7,500
	55,000

	Foreign Currency	Local Currency	Total
1.2 Sources of Finance			
Issue of preferential shares (one for every three			
shares)	--	11,667	11,667
Loan sanctioned by Agricultural Development			
Bank of Pakistan	16,000	2,000	18,000
New loan required	15,000	5,000	20,000
Bank overdraft	--	5,333	5,333
	31,000	24,000	55,000

	First Year	Second Year	Third Year
2. Profit and Loss Projections			
Sales 67,357	104,703	137,860	
Cost of sales	57,928	86,798	111,407
Operating profit	9,429	17,905	26,453
Financial cost/tax etc.	6,259	6,024	12,140
Net Profit	3,170	11,881	14,313
3. Payback period is three years and two months.			
4. Additional sales of UHT milk from increased availability of			
milk supplies as a result of project.	2,985	3,506	4,298

Source: Company records.

materials, the overall economic climate, and consumer tastes and purchasing power. Nestle's approach to foreign operations was summarized as follows: "The Company is guided in this respect by long-term goals and not by short-term objectives. It is essential for Nestle that an industrial operation be in the reciprocal and lasting interests of both the Company and the host country."[13]

A hallmark of Nestle was decentralization, which enabled the group's overseas subsidiaries to develop their own identity and the flexibility to respond to local market

13 Nestle, S.A., Nestle, *The Story of an International Company* (Vevey: Nestle, S.A., 1991), p. 10.

conditions. At the same time, Nestle provided research, development, and technical assistance to these subsidiaries. This assistance could be used, for example, to develop products suited to local tastes and to improve the productivity of land and livestock.

Nestle in Pakistan Since 1974, Nestle products had been imported and sold by the Burque Corporation, a small Pakistani distributor. In 1975, Burque decided to introduce Nestle's NIDO brand of powdered milk, which accounted for an increasing share of Nestle sales in Pakistan. Nestle products were supported by an intensive distribution network and were also heavily advertised on television.

In 1983, Nestle stationed a marketing advisor, Erwin Wermelinger, in Pakistan. Wermelinger's role was to investigate investment opportunities in addition to providing assistance to Nestle's distributor. During the mid-1980s, Nestle staff conducted a tour of the Punjab region of Pakistan to assess the potential for collecting milk to be used in local production of Nestle products.

JOINT VENTURE NEGOTIATIONS

Discussions with Nestle

Milkpak's management was aware of Nestle's growing interest in the Pakistani market, as indicated by Wermelinger's presence in Pakistan. One of Milkpak's managers, formerly with Packages, knew Wermelinger from an earlier posting in Tanzania. As a result, there was an informal channel of communication between the two companies, which Milkpak viewed as a means of keeping Nestle apprised of Milkpak's progress.

Milkpak approached Nestle's senior management in 1986, when Babar Ali visited Nestle's headquarters in Switzerland. During these conversations, Ali received the impression that Nestle would want majority ownership in a joint venture and might also require sizable royalties and technical fees. In addition, Ali was concerned that Nestle's attitude toward Milkpak seemed overbearing.

Discussions with Friesland

Milkpak first approached Friesland in November 1985, through a mutual contact. Several factors made Friesland an attractive candidate for a joint venture, including extensive experience in the dairy industry and an established position in the Pakistani milk powder market. Milkpak's management also felt that a company of Friesland's size would be more responsive to Milkpak's concerns than a larger multinational.

An initial meeting between Babar Ali and a Friesland marketing director was followed by the visit of a three-member Friesland team to Pakistan in March 1986. The team included representatives from the marketing, finance, and technical areas. They spent two weeks studying both Milkpak and the Pakistani market. After the team's visit, Friesland made several requests for additional information. Company representatives next met in October 1986, when both Babar Ali and Yawar Ali visited the Friesland headquarters in Holland to meet the company's chairman and directors and tour the corporate plant and R&D facilities. Milkpak's executives were not shown the milk powder factory.

Friesland planned to follow the October meeting by sending a team to prepare a detailed feasibility study that would consider the milk powder project and other possible product introductions, such as cheese and ice cream. Friesland's tentative plans were to buy 25% of Milkpak's shares, obtain technical fees and royalties for their brands, and increase equity to 49% over a five-year period. Friesland targeted the end of March 1987 as the date for making a final decision about the proposed joint venture.

A number of issues remained to be resolved. Milkpak needed to determine what government policies were with respect to technical fees and royalties on consumer products, assuming that Friesland made an initial equity investment of 25%. Friesland wanted to obtain royalties on its products in the range of 3%–5%. In addition, for Friesland to be able to increase share holdings beyond 25%, changes in the ownership structure of Milkpak could be required, such as the divestment of some of the existing foreign shareholders.

While Friesland was an attractive candidate for a joint venture, Milkpak had some reservations. Milkpak's executives were concerned that Friesland had not let them tour Friesland's milk powder factory on two separate occasions, which suggested that Friesland might be withholding certain information. Milkpak attributed Friesland's many requests to Milkpak for information to Friesland's relatively limited experience in establishing production facilities overseas. The time period within which Friesland expected to obtain a return on its investment was uncertain. Some managers at Milkpak also felt that, in light of Friesland's history as a dairy cooperative, the company would always be more interested in finding markets for products produced in Holland than in developing the Pakistani dairy industry.

Rudolf Tschan's Visit

In January 1987, Babar Ali was apprised of the forthcoming visit of Rudolf Tschan, Nestle's new executive vice president for Asia Zone II, to Pakistan. According to Erwin Wermelinger, Nestle's marketing representative in Pakistan, Tschan wanted to come to Lahore to meet Ali, tour Milkpak's Sheikhupura factory, and visit the company's milk collection centers.

On January 25, Yawar Ali led Rudolf Tschan and the Nestle team on a tour of Milkpak's plant and milk collection areas. Ali was struck by Tschan's quick assessment of the surroundings: "This side looks a lot like the other side [Indian Punjab], but your buffalo are better and your land is more fertile." As Tschan toured the milk plant, he noted that "we will have one milk powder plant here and one there [India]."

When Yawar Ali briefed Babar Ali about the Nestle team's tour, he noted Tschan's evident interest in the Milkpak operation. Later in the day, top executives from Milkpak and Packages were scheduled to meet with Tschan and Wermelinger to discuss the prospect of Nestle and Milkpak working together. As Milkpak's team prepared for the meeting with Nestle, they considered the major issues that would arise. In addition, they considered the benefits to each company of working together.

Assessing a Nestle Joint Venture

For Milkpak, the possibility of a joint venture with Nestle was appealing. The fact that Nestle had a successful manufacturing operation, including a milk powder plant 80 miles across the border in Moga, India, gave Milkpak confidence that Nestle knew how to operate in a very similar environment. Milkpak's management also believed that Nestle typically took a long-term approach toward developing its operating companies. In addition, Milkpak might benefit from Nestle training for its staff and from increased sales by other companies in the Ali Group. For example, Nestle products could use packaging made by the group's companies.

At the same time, management felt that Milkpak offered a number of advantages as a joint venture partner. Milkpak knew that its extensive milk collection infrastructure provided access to a key raw material for Nestle products. Milkpak's government contacts would facilitate obtaining the requisite licenses for establishing new production facilities. The Ali Group had a successful history of implementing other joint ventures. Through a joint venture with Milkpak, Nestle would eliminate a potential future competitor that knew the Pakistani market. The fact that Tschan had come to Pakistan to see Milkpak's operations indicated that Nestle already had a favorable impression of the company's capabilities.

Retaining majority ownership was important to Milkpak's management because Milkpak executives wanted to ensure that any joint venture partner paid attention to their ideas about the business. Babar Ali's earlier meeting with Nestle management suggested that coming to mutually agreeable terms on topics such as majority ownership could present a challenge. However, Tschan seemed to be more flexible.

In addition to the question of ownership, both companies were likely to be concerned about management control of the operation. For example, Nestle might want to appoint the milk powder plant manager. In addition, Nestle already had an effective existing system for distributing its products in Pakistan, which would need to be integrated with Milkpak's marketing system.

Another agenda item concerned the products to be produced and sold by the joint venture and the location of their manufacture. Some Nestle products currently imported could be manufactured locally in the new plant; others would continue to be imported. The new plant might also permit local manufacture of other Nestle products not currently exported to Pakistan. Finally, there existed the possibility of introducing new products tailored more precisely to the consumption preferences of Pakistani consumers.

CONCLUSION

As Milkpak's management approached the meeting with Rudolf Tschan, they contemplated the key issues that would be addressed. Milkpak's objective was to increase its penetration of and success in the Pakistani market. The company was already involved in an extended negotiation with Friesland, a fact they would tell Nestle, and one that gave Milkpak some additional leverage. At the same time, they needed to carefully evaluate what terms would make a joint venture with Nestle more appealing than one with Friesland. The Milkpak executives had to decide what negotiating positions to adopt. Milkpak's executives were aware that, should they conduct a joint venture with Nestle, today's meeting would set the foundation for a relationship that was likely to change and evolve over time.

MasterCard and World Championship Soccer

One of our goals was to underscore MasterCard's transformation from a U.S. oriented credit card company to a truly global brand and payment services organization.

C. Alexander McKeveny, VP Global Promotions, MasterCard International

On July 17, 1994, Brazil won its fourth World Soccer Cup trophy in the Pasadena, California, Rose Bowl stadium. The four-week final round, played in the United States, was the culmination of hundreds of qualifying matches played between 1992 and 1994, and had been a resounding success. MasterCard International, one of the world's leading global payments franchises, had been one of the 11 worldwide sponsors of the event.

While the Brazilians enjoyed a national holiday honoring their team's success, the group which had orchestrated MasterCard's first global sponsorship gathered to reflect on its impact and lessons. At this stage, the team had to assess what the 1994 World Cup sponsorship had achieved for MasterCard and its member financial institutions. They needed to decide if and how the effort should be repeated. The proposal to sign on as a sponsor for the 1998 World Cup, with the final rounds to be played in France, was already on the table.

MASTERCARD INTERNATIONAL

New York-based MasterCard was a global payments franchise comprising nearly 22,000 member financial institutions. It operated as a not-for-profit association. MasterCard did not issue cards, set annual fees on cards, or determine annual percentage rates (APRs).[1] It did not solicit merchants to accept cards or set their discount rates.[2] Financial institutions managed the relationships with consumers and merchants. MasterCard's mission was "to be the world's best payment franchise by enabling member banks to provide superior value and satisfaction to their customers, thereby building member profitability."

MasterCard fulfilled this mission in three ways. First, it managed a global family of brands (MasterCard, Cirrus and Maestro)[3] and related products, including travelers cheques. Like a franchiser, MasterCard developed new products and services, set and enforced policies governing the use of its brands, and created umbrella marketing programs to support them. The logos of all three brands were based on MasterCard's familiar interlocking circles. Second, MasterCard established procedures for accepting and settling transactions between MasterCard and its members on a global basis. Third, MasterCard provided a communications network for electronic authorization and subsequent clearing[4] of credit and debit card transactions, monitored member banks' compliance with interchange rules, and worked with government authorities to track and combat credit card fraud. MasterCard was funded

---

1 The *annual percentage rate* (APR) was the yearly interest charge applicable to outstanding credit card balances.

2 The *discount* rate was the fee a merchant paid a member bank to process a purchase charged to a MasterCard card. The *acquirer* was a licensed MasterCard member that had an agreement to process the data from merchant transactions involving the card. The *issuer* was an institution that entered into a contractual agreement with MasterCard to issue its cards. *Interchange* referred to the exchange of transactions between acquirers and issuers. At MasterCard, a *principal* member had a direct participation in the interchange system. An *association* member was a member that was controlled by, and formed to service, one or more financial institutions, and that processed credit card transactions on behalf of the group. An *associate* member participated indirectly in interchange via a principal or association member.

3 *Cirrus* was a wholly owned MasterCard subsidiary that operated an international automatic teller machine (ATM) sharing network. *Maestro* was a global, on-line point-of-sale debit program. Transaction amounts were immediately debited against the cardholder's bank deposit account.

through quarterly assessments on members for their use of the MasterCard mark and from operational service fees. The annually set assessments varied from region to region and reflected each issuer's and acquirer's volume of MasterCard sales. Each region had to be self-funding. Operational service fees were charged on a per-transaction basis for services, including card authorizations, settlements of monthly cardholder accounts, and listings of revoked or restricted cards.

MasterCard's Development

The Franklin National Bank (New York) introduced the first modern bank credit card in 1951. California-based Bank of America extended the idea throughout the country by introducing the BankAmericard (now Visa) in 1960. It franchised a single bank in each major city as a local affiliate responsible for enrolling cardholders and signing contracts with merchants to accept cards as payment. In 1966, a group of bankers who were not "franchisees" of BankAmericard created its own network, the Interbank Card Association (ICA), which became MasterCard International.

Unlike BankAmericard, ICA was not dominated by a single bank, but was run by member committees. In 1968, ICA formed an association with the Mexican bank Banamex, with Eurocard International in Europe (later Europay International),[5] and with several Japanese members. The Bank of Montreal joined in 1969. That year ICA acquired for its member banks the rights to the Master Charge name and the interlocking circle logo. Use of the Master Charge logo on the full face of the card became mandatory in 1970. In 1973, a computerized international authorization system was set up. In 1974, the magnetic strip became a standard feature and Access Ltd., a subsidiary of the U.K.'s National Westminster Bank, signed on. In 1975, the Bank of South Africa became the first African member and, in 1979, the first Australian member joined. That year ICA became MasterCard International and its trademark was changed from Master Charge to MasterCard to reflect the association's expansion beyond charge card services.

Throughout the 1980s, MasterCard developed new products and services, including credit products, debit services, point-of-sale processing for merchants, remote banking, and cardholder services. It introduced travelers cheques in 1981 and pioneered market segmentation with its Gold MasterCard card aimed at upscale consumers. In 1983, MasterCard was the first to introduce the laser hologram on its card as an anti-counterfeiting measure. In 1984, MasterCard launched the Banknet global transaction network to authorize MasterCard transactions. By this time, the MasterCard mark had been established, and the size of its logo on the card could be reduced. Card issuers were assigned 60% of the card face for their own identification, compared with 25% in the early stages of brand development. As a result, an issuer's logo and name could appear more prominently. In 1987, card issuers were assigned 80% of the card surface which included a hologram that was two-and-half times larger than its predecessor.

In 1988, MasterCard acquired Cirrus Systems, Inc., owner of the U.S.-Canadian ATM network, which was founded in 1982, and acquired 15% of Eurocard International. MasterCard launched MasterCard Debit,[6] followed one year later by the global MasterCard ATM network. In 1990, MasterCard updated its logo, and let issuers use 85% of the card surface. The global hologram had to appear in the same place on every MasterCard card, with the MasterCard logo directly above or below it. No other local acceptance mark on the card could be larger than the MasterCard logo. In 1990, MasterCard became the official card of the 1990 World Cup, and launched MasterValues, a point-of-sale discount program and the largest bank card retail promotion in the United States. MasterValues coupons offered cardholders instant savings at national and regional merchants.

MasterCard continued to enhance its interchange and clearing systems and perfected its co-branding initiatives which facilitated the entry of major industrial corporations (such as General Motors, AT&T and General Electric) into the credit card business.[7] In 1991, MasterCard entered a worldwide alliance with the Thomas Cook travel group, enabling MasterCard to offer a range of cardholder services

---

4 *Clearing* involved the exchange of financial transaction details between an acquirer and an issuer to facilitate posting of a cardholder's account and reconciliation of a customer's settlement position.

5 *Europay International* resulted from a merger of Eurocard International, Eurocheque International, and European Payment Systems Services (EPSS).

6 *MasterCard Debit* enhanced members' proprietary ATM cards by guaranteeing acceptance at retail and cash-access locations that accepted MasterCard cards. Instead of using a line of credit, MasterCard debit transactions were withdrawn from a deposit account much like conventional checks.

7 A *co-branded* card was a customized card produced for a specific retailer or service provider.

at Thomas Cook locations. The 1994 World Cup sponsorship was agreed to. In 1992, Maestro completed the first-ever U.S. coast-to-coast national on-line POS debit transaction[8] and Maestro International was formed. The familiar interlocking circles were incorporated into the logos of Cirrus and Maestro. At the end of 1993, gross dollar transaction volume was US$ 320.6 billion, cards in circulation reached 210.3 million, and acceptance locations worldwide grew to 12 million locations in more than 220 countries and territories. Maestro debit cards numbered 110.5 million, and the MasterCard/Cirrus ATM Network had grown to 162,000 ATMs in 55 countries. Exhibit 1 summarizes MasterCard's business by product and by region.

MasterCard's Organizational Structure

The president and CEO of MasterCard International was responsible for the entire MasterCard organization and its subsidiaries worldwide. Direct reports included Global Marketing, which developed and managed MasterCard products, promotions, product enhancements, and services worldwide. Its responsibilities included the World Cup sponsorship and global advertising campaign development.

Governed by a global board of directors, elected annually and representing its member financial institutions, MasterCard operations were organized into six regions: Asia/Pacific (21.9% of MasterCard's 1993 total gross dollar volume and 18.8% of all MasterCard cards in circulation worldwide), Canada (4.3% and 4.6%), Europe (24.2% and 15%[9]), Latin America (5% and 5.8%), Middle East/Africa (1.3% and 0.6%), and the United States (43.4% and 53.3%). The U.S. region shared office space with MasterCard headquarters in New York. Historically, MasterCard's operations had been decentralized and there had been limited contact between the United States and other regions. Except in Europe, where licensing and marketing activities were handled by Europay, regional boards reviewed and approved regional marketing plans. MasterCard headquarters also organized a network of marketing and operations committees including members from all regions. Ad hoc advisory committees were sometimes formed on an as-needed basis to provide guidance on specific projects.

THE PAYMENT SERVICES INDUSTRY

At the end of 1993, there were more than 650 million general-purpose cards in circulation worldwide (including MasterCard, Visa, Discover, American Express, Japan Credit Bureau and Diners Club cards). The value of transactions on these cards in 1993 exceeded $1 trillion. The use of debit cards as well as ATM cash access was also rising dramatically. Several types of payment cards and services existed. The two types of general-purpose cards were bank cards (such as the MasterCard and Visa cards), issued by banks and financial institutions, and charge cards referred to as travel and entertainment (T&E) cards which did not come with a line of credit (such as the American Express green cards and Diners Club cards). Cardholders had to pay their total monthly bills upon receipt. In contrast, proprietary credit cards, issued by stores and oil companies, could be used for purchases from the outlets of the issuer. Credit cards offered a consumer installment and/or a revolving line of credit up to a limit set by the issuer. Interest was charged on the outstanding unpaid balance. A debit card was tied directly to a consumer's demand deposit account and functioned as a paperless checking account. MasterCard members offered both credit and debit cards.

Competition varied at a regional level but four players remained constant worldwide: MasterCard, Visa, American Express, and Diners Club. Exhibit 2 presents data on the United States and worldwide performance of these four competitors. At the end of 1993, Visa had the largest card base worldwide, with 335.1 million cards in circulation and access to more than 164,000 ATMs in 69 countries. Gross dollar volume, including travelers cheques, was US$542 billion, generated at more than 11 million acceptance locations. Unlike MasterCard, Visa was a non-stock, for-profit corporation owned by member banks. Like MasterCard, Visa did not issue cards and had no direct payment relationship with cardholders. Visa was also evolving into a payments company, offering a range of on-line and off-line debit products in the United States, and providing travelers cheques and global ATM access to its cardholders worldwide. Visa and MasterCard products from one bank were virtually indistinguishable from those of another. Duality, or the handling of both

---

8 At the point of sale, the merchant swiped the Master Card and the cardholder using a Maestro Card would input his/her personal identification number (PIN). Authorization took a few seconds and the transaction would be deducted from the cardholder's associated bank account. In addition to a POS receipt, the cardholder could see a detailed listing of all transactions on his/her associated deposit account statement.

9 Including ATMs.

Exhibit 1

Exhibit 1   MasterCard Data by Product and by Region, 1993

	Cards in Circulation (in millions) 1993		Gross Dollar Volume (in billions)[b] 1993		Acceptance Locations (in millions) 1993		Acceptance ATMs (in thousands) 1993		Maestro Cards (in millions) 1993
Asia/Pacific	39.5	(12.1)	70.1	(67.8)	4.1	(15.4)	2.9	(193.2)	13.0
Canada	9.6	(11.8)	13.9	(9.6)	0.5	(1.1)	2.5	(1.1)	2.5
Europe	31.5	(8.8)[a]	77.5	(13.4)	2.9	(10)	77.8	(62.3)	70.0
Latin America	12.3	(-5.2)	15.9	(20.1)	1.3	(27.8)	4.8	(119.5)	5.0
Middle East/Africa	1.2	(6.7)	4.1	(23.1)	0.2	(16.1)	1.1	(12.9)	2.0
United States	116.3	(15.5)	139.6	(23.4)	3.0	(3.1)	73.5	(6.1)	18.0
Worldwide	210.3[a]		320.6	(28.1)	12.0	(11.3)	162.6	(31.3)	110.5

Source: MasterCard 1993 Annual report
Note: Numbers in parentheses indicate percentage changes from preceding year.
[a]Includes ATMs.
[b]All volumes are reported in U.S. dollars. Regional growth rates other than in Latin America are adjusted for currency fluctuations.

Exhibit 2   Data for MasterCard, Visa, American Express: 1993

	MasterCard 1993	Visa 1993	American Express 1993	Total 1993
U.S. cards (millions)	116.2	168.6	24.7	309.5
Cards worldwide (millions)	215.8	335.1	35.4	586.3
U.S. volume ($ billions)	139.1	227.0	89.8	455.9
Worldwide volume ($ billions)	320.6	527.9	124.1	972.6
U.S. Merchant locations (millions)	2.9	2.8	N/A	N/A
Non-U.S. merchant locations (millions)	8.6	8.2	N/A	N/A
Total merchant locations (millions)	11.5	11.0	3.6	N/A

Sources: Adapted from company records and Faulkner & Gray's *Credit Industry Directory* (1994 Edition)

MasterCard and Visa International transactions (issuing, acquiring, or both) by a single institution, was common in the United States, but less prevalent in other regions. Exhibit 3 shows a sample credit card application for either a Citibank Visa or MasterCard.

Diners Club introduced the first T&E card in 1950. In 1960, it was the first card issued in Japan. In 1993, Diners Club generated $7.9 billion in worldwide charge volume off a base of 1.5 million cardholders. The world's largest issuer of T&E cards was American Express (AmEx), which introduced its green card in 1958. AmEx had almost five times as many cards as Diners Club and 30% more than the Japan-based JCB card.[10] In 1993, Amex worldwide gross dollar volume was US$124.1 billion, with 35.4 million cards in circulation and 3.6 million merchant locations. Unlike MasterCard and Visa, Amex issued its own cards and maintained a direct relationship with its cardmembers and merchants. This gave the company access to specific consumer information that could be used to segment its cardholder base and offer targeted promotional and customer service programs. To compete more directly with MasterCard and Visa, AmEx introduced in 1987 the Optima Card with revolving credit. Optima remained a small portion of the AmEx portfolio. The Amex gold and platinum cards, targeted at higher income consumers, also came with credit lines.

The Competitive Challenge in the United States

With a return on assets of 2%, credit cards remained retail banking's single most profitable product in the United States from the 1960s to the 1990s.[11] By then, the U.S. region was approaching saturation. The results were heavy competition among credit card issuers, increased market segmentation, waivers of annual fees, reduced APRs, and costly value-added card features.[12] Increases in the number of cardholders now had to come at the expense of other issuers rather than through market growth. Increases in volume required penetration into merchant segments where payments were largely made by cash and/or checks. ATM access was extremely widespread and served as the forerunner of POS debit, the industry's newest battlefield. In the on- and off-line arenas, MasterMoney and Visa Check offered global acceptance at all their merchants' locations, and MasterCard's Maestro competed directly with Visa's Interlink. Finally, bank mergers in the early 1990s increased the power of top member banks by linking huge card portfolios. The five largest MasterCard and Visa issuers accounted for 50% of 1991 cards in circulation in the United States, compared with 30% in 1986.

In addition, new forms of competition emerged in the mid-1980s. The Sears-owned Discover card entered the U.S. credit card market in 1986, was accepted in 1993 at more than 1.8 million U.S. merchant locations, charged no

---

10 In fiscal year 1992, JCB, established by Sanwa Bank in 1961, had 27.5 million cards in circulation and US$30.9 billion in worldwide volume. It was accepted in more than 2.9 million outlets in 139 countries worldwide, and offered access to more than 160,000 ATMs in 47 countries.

11 Wanda Cantrell, "Is there any gold left in credit cards?," *United States Banker* (April 1994), pp. 22-30.

12 Examples of value-added cards : affinity cards, co-branded cards like the General Motors card that offered rebates on product purchases or frequent flyer miles, and cards tied to a retirement annuity or college tuition.

Exhibit 3   Citibank Visa and MasterCard Card Application, 1994

Citibank Visa. Citibank MasterCard.

Some people think all MasterCard® and Visa® cards are the same. The truth is no one else puts more behind their cards than Citibank.

With Citibank Classic MasterCard and Visa, you get the kind of service only the world's largest issuer of MasterCard and Visa cards can offer.

- **Citibank Photocard**
  For added security, you can have your picture and signature digitally imprinted on the front of your Citibank Classic card.*

- **The Lowest Price On Most Card Purchases**
  With Citibank Price Protection, if you find the item advertised in print at a lower price within 60 days of your purchase, Citibank will refund the difference — up to $150!**

- **Round-The-Clock Customer Service**
  Toll-free, 24-hour customer service is available 7 days a week. When you have a billing question, usually all it takes is one call. And if your card is lost or stolen, call us to receive a new one, usually within 24 hours.

- **Extra Coverage For What You Buy**
  Buyers Security℠ covers most anything you charge on your Citibank Classic card against fire, theft or accidental damage for 90 days from the date of the purchase. Also, Extended Warranty doubles the original manufacturer's U.S. warranty period for up to one additional year on most Citibank Classic card purchases.**

  If we were to tell you all the benefits our cards offer, we wouldn't have room for an application. So complete, sign and return the attached application today.

CITIBANK

* Please do not send a photo at this time. Details will be provided once you become a cardmember.
** Certain conditions and exclusions apply. Details will be provided once you become a cardmember.
The Buyers Security and Extended Warranty programs are underwritten by Zurich International (UK) Ltd.

PLEASE DETACH ALONG DOTTED LINE, FOLD, SEAL AND MAIL.

[Application form]

1 YES! I want my Citibank Classic card. Select One: □ Citibank MasterCard® □ Citibank Visa®   SECTIONS 1 THRU 7 MUST BE COMPLETED

PLEASE TELL US ABOUT YOURSELF

2 Please Print Your Full Name As You Wish It To Appear On The Card (First, Middle, Last) | Your Home Address, Number And Street | Apt. #

City Or Town | State | Zip Code | Years At Address | □ Own Home □ Own Condo/Co-op | □ Rent □ Live w/ Parents | □ Other | Social Security Number

Date Of Birth (Month/Day/Year) | Mother's Maiden Name | Home Phone Number And Area Code | Name Home Phone Is Listed Under | Are You A Permanent U.S. Resident? □ Yes □ No

Previous Home Address, Number And Street | City Or Town | State | Zip Code | Years There

ADDITIONAL STUDENT INFORMATION (Only Current College Or Graduate Students Complete This Section)

2A College Or Graduate School Name (Do Not Abbreviate) | Your Mailing Address At School | Apt. # | City Or Town

State | Zip Code | Your Phone Number And Area Code At School | Official School Zip Code | Name Your Phone Is Listed Under

Your Class: □ Fresh □ Soph □ Junior □ Senior □ Graduate □ Faculty/Staff □ Other | Graduation Date mo./yr. | Send Card And Billing Statement To: □ Home □ School

IMPORTANT You must enclose in an envelope with this application a complete legible copy of your validated ID from a college/university (or paid tuition bill) for the current semester.

PLEASE TELL US ABOUT YOUR JOB (Current Students: Job Not Required)

3 Business Name Or Employer At Current Job | Position | Years At Job | Employer Phone Number And Area Code

Check Here If You Are: □ Retired □ Self-Employed | If Retired Or Self-Employed, Enter Bank Name | Bank Phone Number And Area Code | Bank Account Number

ABOUT YOUR INCOME

4 You need not include your spouse's income, alimony, child support or maintenance payments paid to you if you are not relying on them to establish creditworthiness. Your total yearly income from all sources must be at least $8,000 to be considered for cardmembership. (No student minimum.)

Your Total Personal **Yearly** Income $ | Other **Yearly** Household Income $

Other **Yearly** Income Sources

IMPORTANT ACCOUNT INFORMATION

5 Please Check Those That Apply. Be Sure To Specify Institution/Bank Name.

□ Money Market/NOW Account | Institution Name:

□ Checking Account | Institution Name:

□ Savings Account | Institution Name:

□ Visa/MasterCard □ Dept. Store/Sears | □ Diners Club □ Gasoline | □ American Express □ Other

WOULD YOU LIKE AN ADDITIONAL CARD AT NO CHARGE?

6 If Yes, Print The Full Name Of The User (First, Middle, Last) (Students: Does Not Apply)

PLEASE SIGN THIS AUTHORIZATION   REV 7/94

7 I certify that I meet/agree to all Citibank credit terms and conditions of offer on other side. Please allow 30 days to process this application.

X _____ Applicant's Signature _____ Date

1B8WF 3149Y C7185 0000   1CBBI 31499 85088 88YO

[Vertical text at left margin:] Have you included your □ Social Security Number □ Phone Numbers □ Signature?   FOLD, MOISTEN HERE, SEAL AND MAIL.

---

annual fee, and rebated up to 1% on cardholder purchases. It competed directly with MasterCard for the value-conscious consumer segment by offering a cash-back rebate based on charge volume. Discover also introduced tiered pricing based on spending patterns rather than payment patterns. Major banks responded only after the 1990 launch of AT&T's low-rate, no-fee Universal Card, which, three years later, claimed 20 million cardholders. Also, "non-banks," card-issuing banks owned by corporations such as General Electric, increased their share of the general purpose card market from 19.3% to 25.2% in the two-year period ending January 1993.[13]

In 1990, MasterCard's market share had sunk to an all-time low of 26.6% of all Visa, MasterCard, Discover and Amex charges in the United States, compared with 30.6% in 1987. The brand had targeted the mass market and been described as "unfocused."[14] By 1993, MasterCard led the industry in growth for the second consecutive year. MasterCard attributed its turnaround to a new positioning emphasis on value and usefulness, replacing the prior emphasis on using the card in the pursuit of pleasure. This value positioning was adopted for all payments products in the franchise and fit with MasterCard's aggressive pursuit of co-branding whereby MasterCard, its member financial institutions and major corporations, such as American Airlines, AT&T, General Motors and Shell Oil, partnered to create credit card products with a unique and valued consumer benefit. By 1993, these "affinity" or "co-branded" cards accounted for one-third of U.S. MasterCard credit cards. Furthermore, MasterCard's aggressive effort to persuade supermarkets, government agencies, and healthcare organizations to accept the credit card in transactions further expanded its usefulness. The advertising campaign of the late 1980s—"MasterCard. Master the possibilities"—was replaced with the slogan, "MasterCard. It's more than a credit card. It's smart money," which served as an umbrella for all products and services.

Success in the U.S. card business hinged on persuading member banks to issue one's card, on getting customers to adopt and use it regularly, and on convincing retailers to accept it. This prompted the use not only of price promotions such as low APRs and no or low annual fees, but also of non-price added-value features such as merchandise protection, ease of use, reliable and speedy approval and clearing of transactions, fraud control, and attractive merchant discount rates.

The cost of acquiring a new account was estimated at $70 to $100. Voluntary cardholder attrition was 10% to 15% until 1993 when it fell below 10%. Retention and usage frequency were key to ensuring that each cardholder was profitable. "Top-of-the-wallet" positioning was crucial with most customers carrying three or more credit cards from various issuers. As competition for the share of customer transactions increased, credit card companies stepped up advertising and promotional efforts. In 1992, AmEx's worldwide communications budget topped $1 billion, $200 million more than in 1990.[15] Television advertising represented one-third of communications spending. Direct mail campaigns and frequent user programs were gaining in importance. Promotion moved to direct comparisons, away from themes stressing the freedom and prestige the cards offered to users.

Growth in International Markets

Slowing market growth and declining profitability[16] at home focused the attention of U.S.-based payments services companies on growing international markets. Non-U.S. charges at both Visa and MasterCard overtook U.S. volume in 1990. Exhibit 4 summarizes MasterCard and Visa shares per geographic region. The use of payment

Exhibit 4	MasterCard and Visa Relative Shares by Region, 1993 (in percent)	

	MasterCard	Visa
Asia/Pacific	47	53
Canada	31	69
Europe and Middle East/Africa	31	69
Latin America	45	55
United States	38	62
Worldwide	37	63

Source: Company records

---

13 The *Directory of the Card Industry* (1994 Edition), pp. 17-20, was a significant source for this section.

14 See Peter Lucas, "The Master Plan at MasterCard," *Credit Card Management* (February 1993), pp. 41-44.

15 *Business Marketing* (October 1993), p. 73.

16 Bank card profitability as measured by return on assets (outstanding balances) declined from 2.3% in 1990 to 1.87% in 1992. [Source: Faulkner & Grey's *Card Industry Directory* (1994 Edition), p. 18.]

cards differed from country to country, depending on local banking regulations and market conditions, including economic factors such as inflation and credit costs.

After the United States, **Canada** was one of the world's most developed credit card markets. Customers rarely switched banks. Duality was non-existent. Visa led MasterCard in terms of market share, thanks to a five-year head start. The **Asia/Pacific** region's very diverse 41 countries included the well-developed Australian market, export-oriented economies such as Korea, Hong Kong, Singapore and Taiwan, as well as the Indian and Chinese cash-based markets. Banking infrastructure and consumer banking behavior were as diverse as the 900 languages spoken in the region. Duality was common, which meant that many financial institutions issued both MasterCard and Visa credit cards. MasterCard and Visa were tied in terms of gross dollar volume. Diners Club and JCB were also well-established. In 1990, Japan ranked fifth among countries in gross dollar volume of credit card transactions and second in cards in circulation. Japan accounted for 60% of all MasterCard cards in the region.

Western Europe, with a population of 320 million, a GDP twice that of Japan, and low payment card penetration, was particularly attractive to global payment franchises. While Americans held an average of 3.9 credit cards per person in the early 1990s, only 21% of Western Europeans held a single credit card. Where available, credit cards tended to have high APRs. Revolving credit cards, however, were common in the United Kingdom and Scandinavia, and the "pay later" phenomenon was gaining ground throughout Europe. Most European payment cards were debit cards, delayed debit cards, or charge cards tied to checking accounts. The majority of Europeans had access to overdraft lines of credit directly from their banks at much more favorable rates. The Eurocheque card was Europe's leading personal debit payment system. Around 52 million cards served as check guarantees for Eurocheques and were accepted by over 5 million merchants in 25 countries. Whether used locally, in another European country, or in North Africa, the Eurocheque functioned like an ordinary check, enabling cardholders to make purchases in local currency. In the early 1990s, European financial institutions were enhancing their cards by joining on-line global

debit programs such as Maestro. By the end of 1993, more than 50 million cards and 254,000 terminals were involved in the program in Europe. The first on-line intercontinental POS debit transactions were completed in July 1993. Eastern and Central Europe were thought to offer new growth opportunities.

In the early 1990s, household payment card penetration in Europe was in the 40% to 50% range. Visa's penetration averaged 20% while Eurocard/MasterCard's penetration averaged 12% but varied more by country. Eurocard/MasterCard household penetration ranged from 28% in Switzerland to 1% in Spain, compared with 17% and 21% respectively for Visa. Exhibit 5 provides data on payment card ownership and household penetration by brand and country in Europe. MasterCard's European partner, Europay, offered a Europackage with a full range of Pay Before, Pay Now, and Pay Later products. MasterCard's travelers checks (co-branded with Thomas Cook and euro travelers cheque) held a 40% share of the European market. Its Pay Now products included the eurocheque, the European Debit Card, Maestro, and EC-ATM, which offered cash access at nearly 78,000 ATMs in Europe and more than 162,000 ATMs worldwide. Europay surpassed Visa with a 71% share of the European debit market segment. In the Pay Later category, Europay offered co-branded Eurocard/MasterCard cards that targeted higher income consumers and competed with AmEx. AmEx had a much smaller merchant base than MasterCard but was better recognized by a large percentage of Europeans. The Eurocard/MasterCard was long perceived as a T&E card in Germany. In the United Kingdom, the Access MasterCard card was seen as a credit card. The card was referred to as Carta Si MasterCard in Italy and as Etnocard MasterCard in Greece.

Latin America encompassed a range of economies at different stages of development. In the 1990s, many nations passed reforms to counter hyperinflation and embarked on ambitious privatization and economic liberalization programs. Increased foreign investment fueled economic activity and greater consumer spending. MasterCard was the leading bank card in many markets in the region. On the debit side, capitalizing on a strong merchant network and extensive ATM network, Maestro had committed several key institutions in the

	Ownership of any Payment Card	Visa: Penetration of Households	Eurocard/MasterCard: Penetration of Households	American Express Penetration of Households
Austria	47%	8%	13%	1%
Belgium	70	23	11	4
France	61	25	9	2
Germany	33	6	15	5
Italy	11	8	1	2
The Netherlands	31	4	19	3
Scandinavia	45	20	9	2
Spain	42	21	1	1
Switzerland	48	17	28	10
United Kingdom	63	42	26	2

Source: Adapted from *PSI 1991 European Study Report*

region's most important markets. Amex was making inroads in the upscale and tourist markets, mostly at the expense of Diners Club. Visa had over 200 co-branded programs in Latin America, 53 in Mexico alone, but most only netted 5,000 to 10,000 cardholders. The **Middle East/Africa** region was characterized primarily as a destination market (i.e., most card usage was generated by visiting businesspeople and tourists) except for the well-developed South Africa market. MasterCard, Visa, and Amex had all built strong merchant networks. Both MasterCard and Visa issuers offered local-currency-only cards in a few countries due to exchange controls. Many banks in the early 1990s expressed an interest in on-line POS debit services since these products did not depend on the creditworthiness of the population.

WORLD CHAMPIONSHIP SOCCER, 1991–1994

As MasterCard International expanded its products and global presence, creating and maintaining a unified worldwide image became increasingly important. MasterCard also needed to communicate its evolution

from a "U.S. credit card company" to an international payments system. MasterCard executives believed that, as a global payments company, MasterCard should sponsor an appropriate global "property." Soccer, the world's most widely followed sport, was an option.

The Rise of Event Sponsorships and Lifestyle Marketing

Sports sponsorships were by no means new to American corporations. Gillette continued to devote 65% of its advertising and promotional budgets to sports 80 years after having initiated baseball sponsorship in 1910. Coca-Cola was already sponsoring the Olympic Games in 1928. Sports had been popular with sponsors because of their competitive nature, huge consumer interest and awareness, strong emotional appeal and television coverage, and perhaps most important, the fact that sports fans spread across the full range of demographic and psychographic types. Sports crossed national frontiers and cultural barriers, and could involve an individual, a team, or an event. Event sponsorship was most popular with large corporations because, as Mark McCormack, a pioneer in the field of sports sponsoring,[17] once

---

17 McCormack was the founder of IMG, one of the most powerful agencies in the marketing of sporting event rights with a 1993 turnover estimated at US$800 million.

remarked, an event "[did] not break a leg, sprain an ankle, fail a drug test or lose six-love, six-love."

In 1991, for the first time in 30 years, advertising spending in the United States decreased by 1.5%.[18] In contrast, *Special Events Report* estimated that corporate sponsorship in the United States for sports, arts, and cause-related events reached $1.4 billion in 1989 and topped $1.8 billion in 1991. Worldwide spending on sponsorship rights was estimated at $2.5 billion. This figure included only the sponsorship rights. Marketing and promotion-related expenses that usually accompanied sponsorships typically doubled or trebled the investment in sponsorship rights.

The Olympic Games and the World Cup were the only two truly global sporting events. The Olympics were popular with some sponsors because of its strong association with patriotism, its high standards, and the product positioning platform it offered. Visa had been an Olympic sponsor since 1988. An "Olympic product" was positioned as the "best" product of its type. The Olympics' attractiveness as a sponsorship vehicle had been impaired by what was perceived as excessive commercial exploitation and by instances of "ambush marketing," whereby competitors "ambushed" official sponsors by associating themselves with an event indirectly.[19]

The World Cup grew out of the Olympic Movement. Fourteen nations sent a soccer team to the 1920 Antwerp Olympics. In 1928, the Federation Internationale de Football (FIFA) decided to run its own competition and the first World Cup was held in 1930. By the 1980s, it was the single biggest sporting event in the world and the World Cup trophy was the most coveted sports trophy. Originally fixed at 16 teams, the tournament was expanded to include 24 teams in 1982 and would include 32 teams in 1998. The cumulative television audience for the 1990 games was estimated at 26 billion in over 160 countries. More than 31 billion people were expected to watch the matches leading up to and including the final rounds of World Cup '94.

What the World Cup might have lacked in imagery, it made up by offering comparative advantages to potential marketing sponsors. Qualifying matches were held over four years around the world with the four-week finale held in multiple locations in a single country. The Olympics lasted two weeks in a single location once every two years (The Summer and Winter Olympics were held every four years on an alternating cycle.) The 1992 Summer Olympics, for which Visa had been an official sponsor, had a cumulative TV audience of 16.6 billion. No advertising in the form of perimeter signage was allowed at the Olympics, in contrast to the World Cup. Market research data indicated that on-screen visibility of sponsor identities during World Cup telecasts increased brand awareness among match viewers.

The World Cup '94 Sponsorship Decision

ISL, a privately held major sports marketing company headquartered in Switzerland with annual sales around $100 million, owned the marketing rights to the World Cup and the Olympics. ISL approached MasterCard in 1989 with the opportunity to participate as an official product in Italia '90. As "Official Card," MasterCard received no perimeter signage around the soccer fields since this was reserved for "Official Sponsors," but it could use the event as a platform for public relations, advertising, and promotions. This experience led MasterCard to expand its soccer sponsorship efforts. For a reported $15 million, MasterCard became one of the eleven worldwide[20] sponsors of World Cup '94.[21] In April 1992, MasterCard signed on soccer legend Pelé as the exclusive MasterCard World Cup Spokesperson for an estimated $2 million. Pelé, who had led Brazil to three World Cup titles, would be featured on posters and in television commercials and made available to member banks for promotional appearances around the world. Separately, MasterCard signed category-exclusive sponsorship agreements for the United States National Team (which would compete in the World Cup as host nation) and for "gold level" sponsorship of U.S. television broadcasts of World Cup matches.

The MasterCard sponsorship program, internally referred to as "World Championship Soccer" (WCS), guaranteed MasterCard a presence at 269 matches to be played at 16 major international soccer events between 1991 to 1994. MasterCard had exclusivity in the payments systems

---

18 *Marketing News 1992.*

19 A hypothetical example of ambush marketing would be: Coca-Cola sponsors an event and Pepsi buys many of the television advertising spots that run while the event is aired.

20 The 11 worldwide sponsors were Canon, Coca-Cola (*), Energizer, Fuji, General Motors (*), Gillette, JVC, M&M/Mars (*), MasterCard (*), McDonald's (*), and Philips. The Gold Sponsors, who received priority on U.S. prime television commercial time, are marked with an asterisk.

21 The 16 U.S. team sponsors were Adidas, American Airlines, Anheuser-Busch, Chiquita, Coca-Cola, Fuji Film, Gatorade, JVC, M&M/Mars, MasterCard, Procter & Gamble, Sheraton, Sprint, Toys 'R' Us, Transitions Optical, and Upper Deck.

category.[22] Exhibit 6 details the WCS events, and Exhibit 7 summarizes MasterCard's sponsorship rights. Prominent among these was MasterCard's right to have two display boards on the perimeters of the soccer pitches in all 269 matches. These boards would, of course, be picked up on television coverage of the matches. The 1994 World Cup's final 52 games were played from June 17 to July 17, 1994, in nine U.S. cities: Boston, Chicago, Dallas, Detroit, Los Angeles, New York, Orlando, San Francisco, and Washington, D.C. In the United States, ABC broadcast 11 games and ESPN broadcast the other 41 games without interruptions, due to the continuous nature of soccer play. Commercials aired pre-game (1:30-second spot), at half-time (2:30) and post-game (1:30). As a "gold" sponsor, Mastercard received four 30-second ads in all U.S. telecasts, as well as an additional 30-second spot on ABC's "Wide World of Sports" vignettes. The MasterCard logo was superimposed over the game clock on the television screen for a total of 172 minutes per game. In the case of injury/official time-outs and expanded post-games, each gold sponsor received additional exposure on a rotation basis. This format minimized the risk of ambush marketing.

Sharing the Sponsorship Expenses

MasterCard headquarters decided to cover 50% of the estimated $15 million cost of the sponsorship rights and allocate the rest across its regions. An event's commercial impact depended largely on the amount of regional or national media exposure it received. The participation of a country's national team in the final World Cup round increased the media coverage of the final matches in that particular country and increased the member banks' opportunities to exploit the sponsorship. The share of the cost allocated to each region was therefore based on the number of teams from a particular region that participated in the final round. The 30,000 tickets MasterCard was entitled to purchase were allocated to the regions in proportion to their shares of the funding.[23]

Exhibit 6   MasterCard World Cup Sponsorship Rights

World Championship Soccer 1991-1994 Events[a]

Event	1991	1992	1993	1994
European Cup Winners' Cup Final	The Netherlands	Portugal	England	Denmark
European Champion Clubs' Cup Final	Italy	England	Germany	Greece
European Championship (Euro '92)		Sweden		
Under-17 World Championship for the FIFA/JVC Cup	Italy		Japan	
World Youth Championship for the FIFA/Coca-Cola Cup	Portugal		Australia	
FIFA Women's World Championship for the M&M's Cup	China			
FIFA World Indoor Championship		Hong Kong		
World Cup '94				United States
Projected Television Audience	1.9 billion	4.7 billion	1.2 billion	31.2 billion

[a]Represent 269 matches in total.

---

22 Exclusivity in the payment systems category included: credit cards, debit cards, T&E cards, debit cards, check guarantee cards, ATM/ATM networks, travelers cheques, and non-bank wired transfers. Thus, Maestro was the official on-line point-of-sale debit card, and Cirrus was the official ATM network of the World Cup '94.
23 The World Cup '94 finalists represented Argentina, Belgium, Bolivia, Brazil, Bulgaria, Cameroon, Colombia, Germany, Greece, Ireland, Italy, Mexico, Morocco, the Netherlands, Nigeria, Norway, Romania, Russia, Saudi Arabia, Spain, South Korea, Sweden, Switzerland, and the United States.

Exhibit 7   MasterCard World Cup Sponsorship Rights

Introduction

The introduction of the World Championship Soccer sponsorship rests on the rights granted to MasterCard International and our members through our worldwide sponsorship agreement. MasterCard encourages all members to capitalize on the sponsorship opportunities discussed herein to achieve their individual business objectives.

It is very important that all members understand the rights and obligations outlined in this section. All sponsorship-related promotion programs must be linked to MasterCard products and services, and approved in advance by MasterCard International. It is critical to note that your World Championship Soccer marketing programs may not be used with other services offered by your organization, whether or not they compete with MasterCard.

Sponsorship Rights

MasterCard and, as appropriate, its members are granted the rights outlined below on a worldwide basis:

A. Product category exclusivity
B. Official status designations
C. Use of Official marks and emblems
D. Stadium advertising
E. Tickets
F. Display and franchise facilities
G. Program advertisements
H. Use of official music
I. Commercial broadcast time options
J. Use of marks on premium items
K. Use of marks on marketing, advertising, promotion and public relations materials

These rights extend to all 16 international soccer events that are part of the sponsorship package (see Appendix 1, World Championship Soccer Overview, for descriptions of the individual events). World Championship Soccer events include:

World Cup '94 1994
European Championship (Euro '92) 1992
European Cup Winners' Cup Final (The European Cup Final) 1991, 1992, 1993 and 1994
Under-17 World Championship for the FIFA/JVC Cup 1991 and 1993
FIFA/Coca-Cola World Youth Championship 1991 and 1993
FIFA Women's World Championship for the M&M's Cup 1991
FIFA World Indoor Championship 1992

Please note that a number of additional soccer events are scheduled to take place in Africa, Latin America and Asia. The MasterCard sponsorship does not include right to these events (e.g. African Nations' Cup, Copa America and Asian Cup) nor to the qualifying matches for World Cup '94.

Exhibit 7 MasterCard World Cup Sponsorship Rights (continued)

A. Product Category Exclusivity

MasterCard is the exclusive worldwide sponsor in the product category of payment systems, which includes, without limitation:

- Credit cards
- Charge cards
- Check guarantee cards
- Travel and entertainment cards
- On-line and off-line point-of-sale debit cards
- ATMs and ATM access cards
- ATM networks
- Travelers cheques
- Nonbank-branded wire transfers

The term of this exclusivity extends through the World Cup in 1994. However, the term for special cards issued by members which use the official marks extends through 1995.

B. Official Status Designations

MasterCard has obtained the exclusive right to use the designations "Official Sponsor" and "Official Card" in all marketing, advertising, promotion and public relations materials in conjunction with the MasterCard logo.

When the MasterCard mark is used with World Championship Soccer marks—without member of affiliated local acceptance brand identification—examples of designations are:

- "Official Sponsor of World Cup '94"
- "Official Sponsor of Euro '92"

When affiliated local acceptance brands or member identification are used in conjunction with the World Championship Soccer and MasterCard marks, examples of designations are:

- "Official Card of World Cup '94"
- "Official Card of Euro '92"

The designations **"Official Sponsor"** and **"Official Card"** extend to all World Championship Soccer events. Per our agreement, only MasterCard can refer to itself as "Official Sponsor" of a World Championship Soccer Event. Members may call themselves the "Official Card" of such events, upon approval from MasterCard.

Exhibit 7   MasterCard World Cup Sponsorship Rights (continued)

C. Use of Official Marks and Emblems

MasterCard has secured the rights to use the following marks on MasterCard payment systems products, services, promotional materials, advertising and company communications:

- Official Emblem and Mascot of World Cup '94
- Official Emblem and Mascot of the European Championship (Euro '92)
- Official UEFA Promotional Emblem
- Official Emblem and Mascot of the Under-17 World Championship for the FIFA/JVC Cup
- Official Emblem and Mascot of the World Youth Championship for the FIFA/Coca-Cola Cup
- Official Emblem and Mascot of the FIFA Women's World Championship for the M&M's Cup
- Official Emblem of the FIFA World Indoor Championship

Members may use official marks and emblems only in connection with the promotion of MasterCard brand products and services, and must follow the guidelines provided in Chapter III, Use of Marks and Approvals, and the graphics standards outlined in Appendix 4.

World Championship Soccer marks may be used only by members and may not be used by affiliated merchants. Merchants may only display materials provided by MasterCard or its members.

Proposed use of emblems and marks must be submitted to MasterCard for prior approval. Please refer to the procedures outlined in Chapter II, in the section on Obtaining Approvals.

D. Stadium Advertising

MasterCard will have perimeter advertising boards at all of the matches comprising the MasterCard World Championship Soccer program. A total of 169 events will display highly visible, strategically placed boards.

E. Tickets

MasterCard is provided with a limited number of complimentary tickets to each event, and may be able to assist you in purchasing additional tickets. As there will be a great demand for these tickets, we suggest that you plan your needs early and inform your MasterCard regional representative or MasterCard Global Promotions so that we may do our best to accommodate you.

F. Display Facilities

At all events, MasterCard has the right to use space for the display of MasterCard products and services on-site within the stadium area. As space may be limited, we request that members in event host countries who are interested in presenting displays forward their requests to MasterCard International as soon as possible

G. Program Advertisements

MasterCard will be featured in a full-page advertisement in official programs and various other official communications published by the governing bodies of soccer, FIFA (Federation of International Football Associations) and UEFA (Union of European Football Associations).

Exhibit 7   MasterCard World Cup Sponsorship Rights (continued)

H. Use of Official Music

MasterCard has the exclusive use, within its product category, of the official music that will be composed for World Cup '94. This music may be used in conjunction with member advertising and promotion of MasterCard products and services.

I. Commercial Broadcast Time Option

In certain territories, MasterCard members may have the first option to buy advertising time on World Championship Soccer television broadcasts. However, because our rights to such options differ from event to event, we recommend that interested members contact their regional MasterCard representative or MasterCard Global Promotions as soon as possible in order to be informed about the availability of such rights.

In all cases, the right of first option is limited by the following three conditions: (1) if the network permits advertising, (2) if the network already has a conflicting advertising commitment, and (3) if MasterCard or its members are willing to make the minimum advertising purchase required by the broadcaster to obtain product category exclusivity.

For information concerning the availability of television advertising or telecase sponsorship in various markets, see Appendix 2, World Championship Soccer Television Summaries. Members can contact the broadcaster directly to determine the availability of time and the minimum advertising buy required. For information on MasterCard plans for television advertising in your market, contact your regional MasterCard representative or MasterCard Global Promotions.

J. Use of Marks on Premium Items

A premium item is a sponsor's promotional item that is either given away or sold at a subsidized price for advertising or promotional purposes. MasterCard and its members have the right to use the Official Emblem and Mascot of World Championship Soccer events in conjunction with the MasterCard mark on premium items to support marketing, advertising, promotional and public relations activities. Any item that is designed for use as a free giveaway or for sale may use the marks, with prior approval by MasterCard. If the premium item displays member identification, it must also indicate prominently that MasterCard is the Official Card of the particular World Championship Soccer event. Premiums bearing the Official Emblems or Mascots may not be sold for profit.

Specifics on the approval process are outlined in Chapter III, Use of Marks and Approvals. MasterCard is preparing a worldwide premium program to make MasterCard branded World Cup premiums available to members. Information on this premium program will be sent to members in 1992. Preliminary information is provided in Chapter III, in the section on Sourcing of Premium Items, and in Appendix 3, World Championship Soccer Premium Program.

K. Use of Marks on Advertising and Promotion Materials

Under the MasterCard World Championship Soccer sponsorship agreement, members have the right to produce advertising, marketing, promotion and public relations materials using the official marks. All uses of the marks must conform to the guidelines in Chapter III and Appendix 4, MasterCard Graphics Standards, and must be approved in advance by MasterCard. All uses of the marks must be in connection with MasterCard brand products and services only.

Although the funding of local promotions was the responsibility of the member banks, MasterCard provided seed money at the regional level to encourage member participation. For example, MasterCard's $1 million in seed money for World Cup-related projects in Europe stimulated a further $19 million in promotional expenditures by member banks in the region. The same ripple effect occurred in Latin America.

Cultivating the Global Sponsorship Property

Historically, many sponsors had viewed the World Cup as a good media buy primarily because of the brand exposure "embedded" in telecasts of the games, and they had therefore developed only limited World Cup-related promotions. In contrast, MasterCard viewed its sponsorship not just as an advertising opportunity, but rather as the basis for a total marketing program designed to

- *Build brand awareness* through the events' television reach and a brand exposure of 7.5 minutes per 90-minute broadcast, an advertising cost estimated at $0.40 per thousand viewers reached. "Pre" and "post" consumer research showed that average recall of World Cup sponsoring brands increased 40%, even though some long-time sponsors already enjoyed very high awareness.
- *Stimulate card usage and acquisition* by exploiting the global appeal of the World Cup. Members worldwide would have the opportunity to implement customized marketing programs targeted at specific usage, activation, and acquisition objectives. These programs would, it was hoped, increase cardholder interest in member products and services.
- *Provide business opportunities for members* through in-branch programs to build traffic, cross-sell other member products, such as Maestro and MasterCard Travelers Cheques, increase ATM usage, and execute merchant-driven promotions to increase acceptance and preference for MasterCard products.
- *Enhance the perception of MasterCard as a global brand and payment system* by associating for the long-term MasterCard with the world's leading sport. It was hoped that this would enhance consumers' perceptions of the global utility of MasterCard products and services, position MasterCard as the industry leader, and bring together members, merchants, and consumers.

To achieve these objectives MasterCard headquarters had three tasks : obtain buy-in for the sponsorship concept; define, create and sell a multi-dimensional, equity-building

marketing platform that could be used to achieve local, regional, and global marketing objectives; and, help regions and members with implementation. The first step was to communicate the sponsorship program and opportunities to regional organizations and member banks. Then MasterCard Global Promotions prepared a worldwide marketing bulletin, a sponsorship manual, newsletters, a premium merchandise program, perimeter and outdoor advertising, and event-specific plans with each region. To minimize ambush marketing, which was expected to occur in the form of signage, premiums, customer service centers, or sponsorship of venue-specific events, MasterCard decided that "the best defense is a good offense." First, MasterCard secured sponsorship of the U.S. national team and secured advertising rights on Univision, the principal Spanish-language television network. Second, MasterCard's public relations agency secured the broadest possible press coverage of the sponsorship. Third, MasterCard planned to maintain high on-site visibility during matches. Fourth, MasterCard positioned itself as a conduit to other sponsors' goods and services. Finally, MasterCard strongly encouraged member banks to focus any World Cup-related promotions on reinforcing the benefits of MasterCard products and to exercise the option of sponsoring broadcasts of World Cup matches on commercial television networks in their markets.

MASTERCARD'S GLOBAL WORLD CUP '94 MARKETING PROGRAM

At the international level, MasterCard's objectives were also to build brand awareness, stimulate card acquisition and usage, provide business opportunities for members, and enhance the perception of MasterCard as a global brand and payment system. Regions and member banks had the opportunity to sponsor national teams, a first option on the purchase of television commercial time during the matches, access to card usage and acquisition programs including statement inserts, hospitality events and free tickets, and the ability to develop and use a variety of advertising media (print, outdoor, branch, and point-of-sale) around the World Cup theme.

Global Marketing developed a World Cup advertising campaign as well as a marketing kit for member banks. The television commercial for the campaign, featuring Pelé and the first commercial use of Leonard Bernstein's "America" score, was seen in more than 40 countries. Exhibit 8 presents a storyboard of the Pelé television commercial. Global

Promotions also commissioned artwork to be included in all cardholder communications internationally and domestically. The Global Promotions Promotional Action Plan included Official Merchandise Offers, Decal Sweepstakes, MasterValues Program and Point-of-Sales materials. For most communications tools, customization was available but legal approval from MasterCard headquarters and ISL was required.

Global Promotions provided resources as well as promotion ideas. For example, because Europay lacked personnel experienced in event marketing, MasterCard assigned one of its top Global Promotions executives to Europay to exploit Euro '92 and lay the groundwork for 1994. Subsequently, a Global World Cup Project Team was formed to exploit the sponsorship, promote knowledge transfer across regions and members, and provide guidance to MasterCard regions. The senior officer for every region nominated a team member. Quarterly meetings were held in New York and other United States and international locations. The type of effort required from MasterCard headquarters and the Global Team differed from region to region. Some regions understood the sponsorship concept but lacked the resources to fully exploit it. Others were well-resourced and required relatively low levels of hands-on assistance.

Furthermore, members and regions could receive newsletters, promotion execution guides, sponsorship manuals, a promotional video, Pelé photos, Global Marketing bulletins, as well as corporate hospitality invitations and welcome kits. Pelé was very popular with international members. He made 76 appearances in 20 countries and was featured in 22 television commercials and print ads.

The marketing effort behind the sponsorship varied by country. It proved harder to persuade member banks to participate when the national team did not qualify or when regions had no local events to tie into,[24] when national interest in soccer was low, or when the image of soccer as a mass sport did not fit MasterCard's upscale positioning in certain underdeveloped credit card markets. For some members, limited funds, staff and experience, and a low priority assigned to the marketing of the World Cup sponsorship were further challenges. Some members, unaccustomed to proactive financial services marketing, felt uncomfortable about marketing logoed merchandise.

MasterCard's World Cup sweepstakes programs could not be used in some markets because of regulatory restrictions. The need for language translation and local customization caused delays. Any item bearing a World Cup logo had to be approved by MasterCard's legal department and by ISL. Premiums shipped from the United States and some non-U.S. member banks had to pay customs fees.

Initial feedback also revealed that the sponsorship was exploited to different degrees in different regions. The Latin America region bought the rights to the Copa America and fully benefited from the region's passion for soccer. Member banks in the region spent $6 million on marketing the sponsorship.[25] Translated MasterValues coupons were sent to cardholders for travel in the United States. In Canada, where interest in soccer was modest, the sponsorship was sold to members as a means of differentiation, but member bank investment was low. The Middle East/Africa region had bought the rights to the 7th Pan Arab Games/6th Arab Cup and placed a World Cup commercial on airline flights within the region. Seven large member banks ran promotions with free trips to the World Cup finals. The biggest impact in the Asia/Pacific region, which had chosen to sponsor the Asia Cup, World Cup qualifying rounds as well as the Under-17 World Championship, was in Japan, where, as Alexander McKeveny, Vice President Global Promotions, pointed out:

> We used Pelé to solve a specific problem in an important market. Japanese marketing is heavily dependent on celebrity endorsements, so we developed television commercials featuring Pelé paying with his MasterCard in a Japanese restaurant and sporting goods store. Our brand awareness ratings tripled and we minimized the impact of the Japanese economic recession on MasterCard purchase volume.

Also, 14 out of 16 card-issuing Japanese member banks used statement inserts, cardholder magazines and brand posters to support World Cup promotions. In contrast, World Cup promotions were not so common in Singapore where many cardholders, especially women, had little interest in soccer, and in Australia, where banks sponsored the more popular sport of rugby football.

In Europe, 26 member banks in 18 countries, including World Cup non-qualifying countries such as France, implemented programs. Total member expenditures on World Cup-related marketing programs[26] reached $19 million.

---

24 For example, regional championships such as Copa America in Latin America or Euro '92 in Europe at which World Cup qualifying matches were played.
25,26 This figure does not include the region's share of the cost of the sponsorship.

Exhibit 8   Storyboard for Television Commercial

"WORLD CHAMPIONSHIP SOCCER"

MUSIC THROUGHOUT: "AMERICA"

  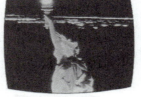 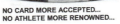 

NO CARD MORE ACCEPTED...
NO ATHLETE MORE RENOWNED...

JOIN MASTERCARD

AND THE LEGENDARY PELE
IN CELEBRATING THE PASSION,
EXCITEMENT AND DRAMA

OF THE WORLD'S MOST SPECTACULAR
SPORTING EVENT.
THE 1994 WORLD CUP.

(FINAL FRAME IF TAGGING COMMERCIAL
WITH YOUR LOGO OR MESSAGE.)

The World Cup sponsorship proved to be an important marketing catalyst for Eurocard/MasterCard in Europe since combined audiences of 7.8 billion Europeans watched the 52 final round matches.

The extent to which the sponsorship property was embraced varied from market to market. In France, the soccer sponsorship became a cornerstone of Europay France's marketing and advertising efforts which included sponsorship of the French national team and World Cup television broadcasts. In Germany, where only 1% of adults held credit cards, MasterCard's licensee was GZS, owned by a consortium of German banks. GZS marketed the Eurocard MasterCard and had an agreed-upon joint logo policy with MasterCard. However, the MasterCard brand rarely appeared in GZS advertising for Eurocard which was budgeted at $20 million in 1994. The Eurocard brand enjoyed 84% aided brand awareness versus 17% for MasterCard. GZS cherrypicked those programs from MasterCard's World Cup communications portfolio that did not depend on mass marketing. These are listed in Exhibit 9. GZS invested $800,000 in World Cup related promotions and insisted

Exhibit 9 Summary of the GZS German World Cup Program, 1993–1994

Event	Impact	Comments	Timeframe
Press conference with Pelé	Conference attended by 50 sports journalists in the GZS headquarters Follow up cocktail	The conference received wide press coverage all over Germany.	October 1993
Promotion with member credit institutions (for their clients and employees)	Mailing to 4,000 credit institutions, 1,500 credit institutions ordered 11,000 packages	Enabled clients to purchase merchandise with World Cup logo and thereby enter lottery	November 1993
Mailing: Description of World Cup program in newsletter (circulation 10,000)	Reached 9,000 credit institutions		January 1994
Point-of-sale display with possibility to win premiums or tickets	100 displays sold reached approximately 1 million clients of credit institutions	400,000 entries returned for two programs	January through March 1994
Statement inserts describing MasterCard/Eurocard World Cup involvement and possibility to win premiums or tickets	3 million statement inserts	Prizes included a trip to the World Cup Final.	
Television commercial featuring Pelé with a Eurocard in hand ran during final rounds (did not choose to dub headquarters-made ad) Print ads featuring Pelé/Eurocard	Message: "you win with the one"	Ad developed in collaboration with Austria and Switzerland and used in three countries	May 1994
Product placement: Pelé columns in weekly sports-magazine *Kicker* (circulation 2.3 million)	Four columns about soccer and his role as ambassador for MasterCard		Spring 1994
Tickets: GZS purchased 650 tickets from MasterCard and sold to credit institutions	Used by credit institutions according to marketing priorities		Spring 1994

Source: Casewriter interview with Gesellschaft fuer Zahlungssysteme.

on Eurocard perimeter signage at all the European soccer matches (including the Euro '92 championship) that were part of the World Cup '94 sponsorship package.

Because the sponsorship's objectives had been to involve members, merchants and consumers, MasterCard's evaluation covered all these groups and included consumer interviews (in the United States, Brazil, Germany, Russia), spectator surveys (for the first and final U.S. match), brand awareness tracking studies in 12 countries, merchant participation and card acquisition/usage reports, as well as an estimate of "free" press/brand exposure. ISL provided a report on MasterCard's comparative aided share of mind (in the payment card categories). The sponsorship's positive internal impact on the MasterCard organization was already clear: improved relations with members, increased dialogue, greater cooperation and idea transfer across regions, cross-functional cooperation at headquarters, as well as improved employee morale at MasterCard and member banks. Exhibit 10 summarizes some of the success measures MasterCard used.

MasterCard also tracked the efforts of its fellow worldwide sponsors. M&M/Mars had launched a special edition Mars Bar featuring flags of the World Cup countries and soccer trivia on the packaging. McDonald's had hosted week-long McSoccer clinics across the U.S and had signed spokesman Andres Cantor as the "Voice of the World Cup" for Univision, the Spanish language TV network. General Motors had chosen to highlight a particular brand in each region rather than mount a global campaign (e.g., GMC trucks sponsored U.S. activities while GM's Opel Division sponsored European activities). GM had also produced a Soccer Instructional Video and distributed World Cup Sponsor Coupons for Value books in showrooms and via direct mail.

U.S. Marketing Program

Starting in mid-1992, the U.S. Promotions Department, with Advantage International, a marketing and special events agency retained throughout the entire project, prepared a full scale marketing campaign and promotion plan tied to the World Cup. Mava Heffler, vice president, U.S. Promotions, set out to "leverage the World Cup as a business-building opportunity incorporating usage and acquisition elements" through a consistent, visible, and comprehensive marketing program. It subsequently had to support MasterCard's new "smart money" positioning, introduced in early 1993, by providing value-added benefits; clearly establish MasterCard

as World Cup host and preferred payment system; integrate within and through all MasterCard divisions and disciplines; maximize MasterCard's impact in the nine U.S. host cities; and finish "big."

The first challenge was to overcome the U.S. region's initial lukewarm response to the sponsorship. In the United States, soccer was considered an insignificant sport. Expected television audiences were one-ninth those achieved during the Olympics. To sell the sponsorship internally, executives highlighted survey results showing that 80% of Americans had seen highlights of World Cup '90 and 50% had expressed an interest in watching World Cup '94 matches after learning that it would be held in the United States. The sponsorship would give MasterCard especially good access to suburban and ethnic markets. Over 16 million Americans played soccer, 79% of them lived in suburbs, and 29% lived in households with disposable incomes over $50,000. Finally, one-third of the U.S. population lived in, or close to, the nine World Cup host cities.

Then, outside partners and the three disciplines of promotions, public relations, and advertising had to be integrated into a comprehensive marketing program designed to reach three target audiences: potential and existing members, cardholders, and merchants. The buy-in of merchants and members required extensive education and communications. Participants within MasterCard included Member Relations, Global Marketing, U.S. Acceptance, Cirrus, and Maestro. Outside "players" included advertising and design agencies as well as the host cities, the U.S. national team, and Pelé. The rallying cry became "maximum integration for maximum leverage." Heffler recalled the process that led to the establishment of a multidepartment task force:

> In event sponsorship, two things matter: what you have and what you do with it. What we had was the world's most important sporting event. It was hosted in MasterCard's most important market. However, it was not the highest impact event given soccer's limited popularity in the United States. This meant that we could not treat soccer as an emotion, as the rest of the world could. It probably helped that I'm not a soccer fan and that my past experience was in packaged goods marketing. Soccer became a platform for solid, comprehensive, value-added business-building programs. MasterCard became the means by which our merchants could get a fair share of the $4 billion projected economic impact of the World

I. *Leveraging of sponsorship by members/regions*

- Number of decals
- Number of point-of-sale packages ordered
- Number of global World Cup television commercials ordered/media value of ad schedule
- Number/dollar value of premiums ordered
- Number of Pelé appearances/impressions
- Card usage increases—World Cup programs
- Card acquisitions—World Cup programs
- Number of members participating in programs
- Member marketing dollar investment in leveraging the sponsorship property ("velocity spend")
- Number of merchants participating in programs
- Number of statement inserts/number of impressions/approximate media value

II. *Brand exposure*

- Cumulative television viewership
- Media value of brand identity exposure on television broadcasts of matches
- Impressions/media value of ad schedule
- Impressions on-site
- Impressions from public relations programs

III. *Qualitative indicators*

- Leveraging across the MasterCard organization: Maestro, CIRRUS, regions, departments, etc.
- Integration of regions, departments, etc., working together on business-building programs
- Members' reactions and perceptions of MasterCard and its sponsorship program
- Consumer perceptions and brand imagery

Source: Company records.

Cup. For other sponsors we became the unifier, or host of the event. Finally, we channeled the rights to our member banks. We did not just put together a few posters and premiums and call that a marketing plan. Our plan was a constellation of national and host city programs.

Exhibits 11 and 12 summarize the main U.S. programs and their timing during 1993 and 1994. The World Cup sponsorship was integrated in the $40 million MasterCard communications budget planned for 1994 with little additional investment. In 1994, 65% of these expenses were devoted to advertising, 25% to consumer promotions, 7% to merchant programs, and 3% to public relations.

PROGRAM RESULTS

When the results were in, television coverage of the 1994 World Cup amounted to 16,000 hours in 188 countries and achieved a cumulative worldwide television audience of 31.2 billion. The average number of matches watched per viewer varied widely from 7.3 in the United States, to 12.4 in Germany, and 15.7 in Brazil.

MasterCard brand perimeter signage exposure on television broadcasts averaged 8 minutes 16 seconds over the 52 matches (versus 7 minutes 30 seconds projected). MasterCard brand exposure during the final match was 12 minutes 8 seconds. Executives estimated that MasterCard would have had to have purchased media

Exhibit 11   MasterCard World Cup USA '94 Program and Timeline, 1993–1994

National Programs

MasterCard's modular programming enabled members to accomplish individual objectives and profit priorities through the use of official World Cup marks and designations and officially logoed premium items, as well as the association with MasterCard's sponsorship/affiliation with Pelé and the U.S. national team. Point-of-sale materials were ordered through a 1-800 number and displayed in approximately 200,000 storefronts. To encourage display, the Decal Program included a sweepstakes entry for a free trip to one of the 24 qualifying nations. The nationwide **World Cup MasterValues** program was designed to increase awareness and usage. MasterCard also enlisted retailers such as Macy's and W.H. Smith bookstores in specific promotions, e.g., a free MasterCard/World Cup poster for a purchase using a MasterCard card.

Through the **World Cup Soccer '94 Collection** MasterCard invited its members to participate in a revenue-generating statement insert program offering cardholders a variety of licensed World Cup merchandise and apparel, including commemorative coins and medallions, for purchase with their MasterCard Card. A Frequent Buyer Sweepstakes was available. The U.S. mint manufactured commemorative coins, and members marketed them through their own marketing plans. The **Mastering the Game of Soccer with Pelé Video** was the first Pelé instructional video produced in 15 years and could be used to create programs for acquisition, usage and retention. It brought the sponsorship into homes. Video orders by member banks exceeded 50,000.

SoccerBlast USA—Legends of Soccer Tour was a 36-city family soccer festival, including clinics and exhibits, in co-sponsorship with Procter & Gamble, Sprint, le Coq Sportif and members. It created additional awareness and visibility for MasterCard in supermarkets in Sunday free-standing inserts through mid '94, as well as advertising inclusion equal to over 200 gross rating points[a] in each market. At each event, 90% of all attendees (2,300 on average per event) passed through the MasterCard booth and 230 card applications were collected. Along the same lines, the uniformed MasterCard team's **Team Up with MasterCard** appearances received an estimated $500,000 in free local radio coverage. The **Ambassadors Cup** honored 24 winners of a nationwide search for individuals who brought the love of soccer to the U.S. The **Kick'in for Kids TV Special** involved the production of a 40-minute "show-within-a-show" in a tie-in sponsorship with the Children's Miracle Network, reaching 197 markets and 98% of U.S. households. A Watch-n-Win World Cup Ticket giveaway was held and 55% of all card pledges were made on MasterCard cards. Representatives of 40 member banks appeared on air in their local markets.

Host City Programs

Nine **MasterCard Welcoming the World Seminars**, organized in collaboration with local World Cup organizing committees and visitors bureaus, were attended by over 7,500 merchants, over 2,000 of whom requested follow-up materials; 61% of the requests were for additional information on current Merchant Acceptance programs. The seminars sought to help merchants leverage the World Cup as business opportunity. An estimated 36 million media impressions were created through local press coverage. A showcase **Main Street USA** area received over 3.6 million people over 52 matches.

Forty-two MasterCard/Coca-Cola **Welcome Centers** were strategically located in high traffic areas around match venues or at airports and provided a total of 10,000 hours of assistance to over 1 million people. Visitors sampled Coke products and received World Cup MasterValues booklets as well as a city information World Cup Value Guide which highlighted MasterValues merchants, Thomas Cook and key member locations. From May to July 1994, the **1-800-MC CUP 94** offered round the clock assistance to over 25,000 callers in five languages. **Thomas Cook** also expanded its services to MasterCard cardholders, including commission-free MasterCard Travelers Cheques, currency exchange, lost and stolen reporting, emergency card replacements and cash advances.

---

[a] **Gross rating points** represent the percentage of a target market reached by advertising in a specified period multiplied by the average number of advertising exposures.

Through **World Cup MasterValues** MasterCard launched its largest marketing initiative to date, in the form of nine city specific programs, involving more than 80 merchant partners and supported by 50 million statement inserts and free standing inserts (FSI). MasterCard provided the umbrella marketing program, the merchant and member point-of-sales materials, the inserts and training videos. **MasterCard at the Mall Programs** were conducted in 19 shopping malls. Consumer purchases with MasterCard cards were rewarded with World Cup premium items and a chance to have a picture taken with Pelé or members of the U.S. national team. Over 2,000 stores displayed MasterCard World Cup point-of-sale materials, over 4,000 applications for MasterCard cards were collected. Ten member banks co-sponsored local events.

Tailored **brand awareness programs** focused on creating a non-preemptable MasterCard presence in host cities during matches and positioning MasterCard as the global preferred payment system with visitors, residents, merchants, press and media. For example, in Chicago, New York and Los Angeles the **MasterCard Hot Air Balloon** garnered an estimated 500,000 impressions. MasterCard and its members were also present at city-specific events such as The Embarcadero Festival in San Francisco, Amerifest in Dallas, and South Street Seaport in New York City. The world's largest soccer theme park, an interactive family festival called SoccerFest, was set up in the Los Angeles Convention Center.

Hospitality programs included free tickets, travel packages, and corporate events hosted by senior MasterCard management. The programs, organized and hosted by the Global Promotions division, were an opportunity to thank members for their support and demonstrate MasterCard's belief in global partnerships. Most of the free 30,000 tickets were used by MasterCard, regions and member banks for promotional and member relations purposes. The final week coincided with meetings of MasterCard's boards.

advertising valued at $493 million to achieve the same number of exposures delivered by perimeter signage. Even if a perimeter signage exposure achieved only 10% of the impact of a 30-second commercial, the media equivalent value of MasterCard's perimeter signage exposure was $49 million.

In the United States, MasterCard estimated that, in addition to the impressions generated by perimeter signage and media advertising, a further 8.5 billion impressions were created by out-of-home media including street banners, billboards, painted buses, telephone kiosks, traincar and bus shelter ads. Media and public relations initiatives, which ranged from appearances and magazine articles by Pelé to personalized services for the media at the matches, also yielded substantial press and media coverage amounting to over one billion impressions.

More than 450 MasterCard members (including 75% of the top 100 card issuers) participated in one or more aspects of the global promotion. Together, they invested $38 million in sponsorship-related marketing. Some 87% of members stated that the sponsorship added value to their own marketing programs. The premium program was used by members in 59 countries. Some 42 million statement inserts for the MasterValues program were distributed by over half the MasterCard members in the United States and Latin America.

McKeveny and his colleagues tracked both consumer and member responses to MasterCard's World Cup '94 sponsorship. MasterCard objectives were achieved to varying degrees from one region and country to another, as indicated in Exhibit 13.

THE 1998 WORLD CUP

The 1998 World Cup would be held in France. Japan seemed a likely candidate for the 2002 World Cup. Both Japan and France were important markets for MasterCard, where brand awareness had historically been below desired levels.

Exhibit 14 summarizes the events included in the World Cup 1998 sponsorship package. The 1996 European Championship would include 16 national teams (versus 8 in 1992). Cumulative television viewership of 6.9 billion was forecast, 8% above 1992, of which

Exhibit 12   MasterCard World Cup USA '94 Promotional Summary

Promotion	Benefits	Communications Tools	Suggested Execution Dates
MasterCard/World Cup USA '94 *Official Merchandise Offers* (Issuer Promotion)	• Promotes usage • Offers high perceived value • Generates revenue • Builds brand preference • Offers flexibility for member customization	Statement Insert(s) 1. Cardholder collectibles insert 2. Members' choice insert	1st quarter 94 – 3rd quarter 94
MasterCard/World Cup USA '94 *Decal Sweepstakes* (Acquirer Promotion)	• Builds brand awareness • Enhances merchant relations • Promotes brand preference	• Decal • Decal folder with sweepstakes rules	1st quarter 94 – 2nd quarter 94
MasterCard/World Cup USA '94 *MasterValues Program* (Issuer Promotion)	• Associates MasterCard card with value • Encourages usage • Reinforces global acceptance • Differentiates MasterCard from competitive payment methods	Statement insert	Early 2nd quarter 94
MasterCard/World Cup USA '94 *Point-of-sale materials* (Acquirer/Issuer Program)	• Associates member with World Cup USA '94 • Builds brand awareness • Communicates excitement of World Cup • Offers flexibility for member customization	• Posters • Print ads • Counter card • Tent card • Postcard	1st quarter 94 – early 3rd quarter 94

Source: This fact sheet was enclosed in the MasterCard Promotional Action Plan folder sent to member banks.

45% would be outside Europe. The 1998 World Cup would include 32 national teams (versus 24 in 1994). A cumulative television audience of 37 billion was projected, 19% higher than in 1994.

Early indications were that the World Cup 1998 sponsorship might cost MasterCard $23 million. McKeveny estimated MasterCard and its members might need to spend around $60 million over four years to fully exploit the calendar of events.

A 1998 World Cup sponsorship raised a number of questions for McKeveny:

1. Should MasterCard renew its World Cup sponsorship?
2. What did it mean for MasterCard's strategy and organization that the final rounds would be held in France? How might the existence of two intermediaries between MasterCard and its member banks (i.e., Europay International and Europay France) influence MasterCard's approach?
3. How might the characteristics of the host country impact the theme and execution of the promotion in France and around the world? How could maximum exploitation of the sponsorship property be guaranteed?
4. How would MasterCard and Europay deal with the limited resources and experience of both Europay and its member banks? Should one or more executives be sent from the United States to transfer know-how? Should a permanent World Cup marketing team be created?
5. Could the formula for sharing the cost of the sponsorship be improved? How should money be raised for local promotions? Could a Global Marketing Fund or World Cup Fund be set up?
6. Should the sponsorship focus only on the MasterCard brand or highlight other global (e.g., Cirrus, Maestro) or

Exhibit 13   Evaluation of Sponsorship Impact Against Objectives

	Japan	France	Germany	UK	Argentina	Brazil	Mexico	U.S.
CONSUMER OBJECTIVES								
Build Brand Awareness								
Brand awareness increased	+	+	+	+	+	+	±0	±0
Closed gap against Visa	±0	+	+	++	±0	±0	±0	±0
Sponsorship awareness increased	+	+	++	+	++	+	+	+
Sponsorship higher than or equal to Visa Olympics	±0	+	++	+	++	±0	±0	NA
Enhance Worldwide Imagery								
Worldwide imagery improved	±0	+	±0	±0	-	±0	±0	NA
Closed gap against Visa	±0	±0	±0	++	-	±0	+	NA
Enhanced opinion of brand due to sponsorship	+	±0	+	±0	++	++	++	+

	Asia/Pacific	Canada	Europe	Latin America	Middle East/Africa	U.S.
MEMBER OBJECTIVES						
Provide Membership with Business Building Opportunities						
Found Sponsorship Valuable	+	-	+	++	++	+
Sponsorship Enhanced Brand Awareness	++	+	++	++	+	++
Sponsorship Enhanced Global Imagery	+	+	+	++	++	++
Sponsorship Offered New Business Opportunities	+	+	+	++	+	+
Stimulated Acquisition and Usage						
Sponsorship Increased Card Usage	+	++	++	++	++	+
Sponsorship Increased Acquisition Efforts	+	+	+	++	++	+
Other						
Enhanced Image as a Strong Marketing Organization	++	++	++	++	++	++

Source: Company records.

Note: ++: very positive; +: positive; ±0: same; -: negative.

Exhibit 14 World Championship Soccer 1995–1998 Events

Event	1995	1996	1997	1998
European Championship		England		
Under-17 World Championship	Ecuador		Egypt	
World Youth Championship	Qatar		Malaysia	
Women's World Championship	Sweden			
World Indoor Championship		Spain		
World Cup '98				France
African Cup		South Africa		TBA

regional/national brands (e.g., Eurocard)? Should a single worldwide spokesperson or several regional spokespersons be retained?

7. How could MasterCard improve its evaluation of the sponsorship?

It was unclear whether MasterCard could—or should—replicate the scope and thrust of the 1994 U.S. region promotions in France in 1998. Since the U.S. national team was not guaranteed a spot among the final 32 in France, some MasterCard executives wondered what value sponsorship of the 1998 World Cup would bring to U.S. members and how it might help to consolidate MasterCard's recent market share gains in the United States. On a broader scale, if MasterCard committed to sponsor the 1998 World Cup and the "World Championship Soccer" package of international championships, a major challenge would be to continue the momentum built up in 1994. Finally, recognizing the significant financial and managerial resources required to plan and execute a worldwide integrated sponsorship marketing program, the viability and merits of alternative approaches to global brand-building needed to be addressed.

WWF

The brand is like the tip of the iceberg. In isolation of the mission and product it makes no sense. Your mission determines what your brand stands for, not the other way around.

Claude Martin, Director General, WWF International

On September 23, 2002, Paul Steele, chief operating officer of WWF International, sat at his desk in Gland, Switzerland, and reviewed the details of three potential corporate partnerships. Over the past few years, WWF had entered into a range of partnership and licensing agreements with various businesses, and Steele now had to decide whether WWF should actively pursue additional corporate partnerships and, if so, with which company or companies.

WORLDWIDE FUND FOR NATURE (WWF)

Founded in 1961, WWF was by 2002 one of the largest independent, nonprofit organizations dedicated to the conservation of nature in the world. It operated in around 100 countries and was supported by nearly 5 million people worldwide. Initially focused mainly on protecting threatened species and spaces, WWF activities had broadened to include tackling pollution and looking for new and sustainable ways of using the planet's natural resources.

In 2002, WWF employed over 3,800 people, 90% of whom were scientists, and invested some $280 million per annum. WWF carried out 700 international projects per annum in addition to the thousands initiated at a local level by WWF's national offices around the world. At the international headquarters in Gland, 35 different nationalities were represented. The WWF Web site summarized the scope of the organization as follows: "Our reach is global yet local, combining localized, practical actions and field projects with broader initiatives to influence environmental decision making and industrial practices."

WWF was a factual, science-based organization with clear objectives and goals. In 2002, it focused on six global priorities: forests, fresh water, oceans and coastal ecosystems, threatened species, toxic pollution, and climate change. (See Exhibit 1 for WWF global conservation targets.) In addition, WWF's approach was one of ecoregional-based conservation, meaning large-scale programs at the biosphere level combining on-the-ground project work with the necessary policy and advocacy frameworks. In 2002, WWF had identified over 200 regions most representative of the world's biological diversity, called the Global 200, and was working in 77 of these areas.[1] WWF's Living Planet report was an example of the organization's scientific approach and focus on quantifying results. The report used an algorithm called the ecological footprint to measure humanity's use of renewable natural resources. (See Exhibit 2 for an excerpt from the Living Planet report.)

WWF's international campaigns and advocacy work spotlighted key issues and influenced national and international policy decisions. In 2002, campaigns included promoting sustainable forestry practices, advocating for a reduction in greenhouse gas emissions, eliminating toxic chemicals, lobbying to halt the depletion of fisheries, and working to ensure fresh water was available for people and nature. To encourage corporations and governments to act, WWF had developed a tool called the Gift to the Earth, an award to recognize specific actions and commitments. The organization's advocacy successes included the international moratorium on the ivory trade in 1990, the

This case was prepared by Professor John A. Quelch with the assistance of Nathalie Laidler.
Copyright © 2003 by the President and Fellows of Harvard College. Harvard Business School case 9-503-113.

[1] WWF's Global Conservation Programme 2001/2002.

Exhibit 1 WWF Global Conservation Targets, 2002

Global Issues	Conservation Targets
Forests	By 2010, the establishment and maintenance of viable, representative networks of protected areas in the world's threatened and most biologically significant forest regions
	By 2005, 100 million hectares of certified forests, distributed in a balanced manner among regions, forest types, and land tenure regimes
	By 2005, at least 20 forest landscape restoration initiatives under way in the world's threatened deforested or degraded forest regions to enhance ecological integrity and human well-being
Freshwater Ecosystems	By 2010, 250 million hectares of high-priority freshwater ecosystems worldwide protected and/or sustainably managed
	By 2010, ecological processes maintained or restored in at least 50 large catchment areas of high biodiversity importance
	By 2010, private-sector practices and related governmental policies concerning key water-using sectors established and/or changed in order to sustain the integrity of the freshwater ecosystem on which they depend and/or impact
Oceans and Coasts	By 2020, the establishment and implementation of a network of effectively managed, ecologically representative marine protected areas covering at least 10% of the world's seas
	Maintain the status of all fish stocks that are currently exploited sustainably and by 2020 halve the number of fish stocks that are overexploited or depleted as currently categorized by FAO
Species	By 2010, populations of key species of global concern stabilized or increased and their critical habitats safeguarded
	By 2010, at least 10 species of global concern no longer endangered by overexploitation
Toxic Chemicals	By 2007, elimination or reduction of at least 30 of the most hazardous industrial chemicals and pesticides with special emphasis on persistent organic pollutants (POPs) and endocrine disrupting chemicals
	By 2007, scientific, educational, and regulatory initiatives firmly in place, enabling decision makers (government, industry, consumers) to make informed choices about toxic chemicals and their alternatives

Exhibit 1   WWF Global Conservation Targets, 2002 (continued)

Global Issues	Conservation Targets
Climate Change	By 2010, a 10% reduction below 1990 emissions in industrialized country carbon dioxide emissions
	By 2010, initiatives under way in 30 developing countries to implement solutions leading to a significant reduction in carbon intensity, in particular from the combustion of fossil fuels
	By 2010, 50 countries implementing adaptation strategies in key ecoregions/biomes and sectors of their economies on the basis of national plans for the reduction of vulnerability to climate change

Source: WWF's Global Conservation Programme 2001/2002.

international moratorium on whaling established in 1985, and the introduction of the Forest Stewardship Council (FSC).

Partnerships with governments, local communities, international agencies, and business and industry were considered central to WWF, which believed that dialogue was key for long-term success and an important conduit for creating awareness and spreading ideas.

In 2001, WWF total annual operating income was $329 million, with 49% coming directly from individual donations. (See Exhibit 3 for WWF network financial statements.)

History

In the early 1960s, Sir Julian Huxley, the first director of UNESCO and cofounder of The World Conservation Union (IUCN), raised public awareness in Britain with a series of articles highlighting the destruction of the East African habitat. He, Max Nicholson, director general of Britain's Nature Conservancy, and others established an international organization, based in Switzerland, to raise funds for conservation. The international organization set up offices in different countries and launched national appeals that would send two-thirds of the funds to WWF International, keeping the remainder to spend on conservation projects of its own choice. During this time, Chi-Chi the panda arrived at the London Zoo, creating a wave of international attention, and the new organization decided to make the animal its logo based upon a design drawn by Sir Peter Scott.

The first national appeal, with the Duke of Edinburgh as president, was launched in the United Kingdom in November 1961, followed by appeals in the United States and Switzerland in December of the same year. In 2002, national appeals were known as national organizations, 28 of which were affiliated with WWF International and four of which operated under a different name and were associated with WWF.

During the 1960s, the majority of funds raised were from individual donations, but in 1970 His Royal Highness Prince Bernhard of the Netherlands, then president of WWF International, launched an initiative that would provide WWF with a solid, independent financial base. The organization set up a $10 million fund, known as the 1001, to which 1,001 individuals each contributed $10,000. Since then, WWF International had used the interest from the 1001 trust to meet basic administration costs.

In 1980, WWF collaborated with IUCN and the United Nations Environment Programme (UNEP) on the publication of a joint world conservation strategy that was endorsed by the United Nations secretary general and launched simultaneously in 34 world capitals. WWF continued to build its popular base, and in 1981 the organization had over 1 million regular supporters worldwide. In 1983, in collaboration with Groth AG, WWF worked with postal authorities in more than 200 countries to select threatened species to feature on official postage stamps. In 2002, the Conservation Stamp Collection program had raised over $13 million.

Exhibit 2	Excerpt from the Living Planet Report, 2002

THE ECOLOGICAL FOOTPRINT

The ecological footprint compares renewable natural resource consumption with nature's biologically productive capacity. A country's footprint is the total area required to produce the food and fibres that country consumes, sustain its energy consumption, and give space for its infrastructure. People consume resources from all over the world, so their footprint can be thought of as the sum of these areas, wherever they are on the planet.

The global ecological footprint covered 13.7 billion hectares in 1999, or 2.3 global hectares per person (a global hectare is 1 hectare of average biological productivity).

This demand on nature can be compared with the Earth's productive capacity. About 11.4 billion hectares, slightly less than a quarter of the Earth's surface, are biologically productive, harbouring the bulk of the planet's biomass production. The remaining three-quarters, including deserts, ice caps, and deep oceans, support comparatively low concentrations of bioproductivity. The productive quarter of the biosphere corresponded to an average 1.9 global hectares per person in 1999. Therefore human consumption of natural resources that year overshot the Earth's biological capacity by about 20 per cent.

The global ecological footprint changes with population size, average consumption per person, and the kinds of production systems, or technologies, in use. The Earth's biological capacity changes with the size of the biologically productive area, and its average productivity per hectare. Hence changes in population, consumption, and technology can narrow or widen the gap between humanity's footprint and the available biological capacity. It is apparent that, since the 1980s, humanity has been running an ecological deficit with the Earth (see Figure 2).

Figure 6: The ecological footprint per person for all countries with populations over 1 million.

Figure 7: Humanity's ecological footprint grew at an average rate of 1.6 per cent per year from 1961 to 1999. (World population grew slightly faster at 1.8 per cent per year.)

Figure 8: The ecological footprints of seven regions of the world in 1999. The footprint per person of high income countries was on average over six times that of low income countries, and over three times greater than the Earth's biological capacity.

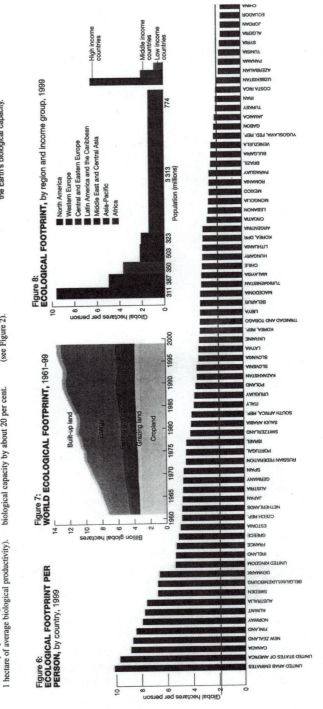

Figure 6:
ECOLOGICAL FOOTPRINT PER PERSON, by country, 1999

Figure 7:
WORLD ECOLOGICAL FOOTPRINT, 1961–99

Figure 8:
ECOLOGICAL FOOTPRINT, by region and income group, 1999

Source: "Building a Sustainable World," A First Report on our Economic, Social and Environmental Performance, 2001, WWF.

Exhibit 3   WWF Network Income and Expenditure, 2000 and 2001

	2000 (CHF 000)	2001 (CHF 000)	2001 (US$ 000)
Operating Income			
Individuals[a]	251,242	275,742	159,879
Legacies	66,171	68,139	39,508
Corporations[b]	23,688	19,877	11,525
Trusts and Foundations	28,811	32,274	18,713
Government and Aid Agencies	113,483	125,621	72,837
Royalties[c]	34,058	29,652	17,193
Financial Income (net)[d]	44,538	7,762	4,500
Other	8,804	8,090	4,691
TOTAL	**570,795**	**567,157**	**328,846**
Operating Expenditure			
National Conservation			
Conservation[e]	89,723	89,329	51,794
Conservation Policy, Education and Awareness[f]	109,845	120,705	69,987
International Conservation			
Conservation[g]	231,956	237,588	137,757
Conservation Policy, Education and Awareness[h]	23,819	23,771	13,783
Fund-raising	80,223	88,786	51,479
Finance and Administration	42,312	45,104	26,152
TOTAL	**577,878**	**605,283**	**350,952**
Surplus (deficit to support current and future projects)	(7,084)	(38,126)	(22,106)

Source: WWF Annual Report 2001.

Note: Exchange rate, CHF 1.798 = US$1, as of June 30, 2001.

[a]Monies received from WWF individual supporters including regular dues and fund-raising activities.

[b]Donations from corporations excluding royalties and licensing and sponsoring fees.

[c]Monies received from royalties, licensing, sponsorship fees, and sale of WWF products via WWF catalogues and retail outlets.

[d]Net results of dividends, bank interest, exchange differences, gains/losses on marketable securities.

[e]Costs of conservation activities of WWF national organizations within their own territory.

[f]Thirteen percent = policy, 44% = education, and 43% = awareness.

[g]Costs of the WWF International Conservation Programme.

[h]Sixty-four percent = policy, 3% = education, and 33% = awareness.

In 1986, as part of its 25th anniversary celebrations, WWF invited leaders from the world's five main religions to attend a retreat in Assisi, Italy. Following the retreat, the leaders issued declarations that conservation was a fundamental element in their respective faiths, and since then an international network consisting of eight religious groups and WWF has worked to achieve common aims.

The 1990s began with the launch of a revised mission and strategy that reiterated WWF's commitment to nature conservation. In 1991, WWF once again joined forces with IUCN and UNEP to publish "Caring for the Earth—A Strategy for Sustainable Living," which was launched in 60 countries and listed 132 actions that people at all social and political levels could take to safeguard or improve their environment. (See Exhibit 4 for a description of key WWF projects and achievements over time.)

Initially established to channel funds, WWF quickly established its own field projects and by 1990 started balancing field and advocacy work. In September 2002, Martin summarized WWF's history as follows:

> WWF is part of environmental history and has always had a broad environmental mission, focusing on developing harmony between man and nature. In the 1960s WWF was largely project oriented, and impact was achieved through specific field projects. In the 1970s, organizations like WWF realized that unless they changed the fundamentals, they could not impact sustainable change. The UN Conference on the Human Environment held in Stockholm in 1972 was instrumental in this shift. In the 1980s, several forces led to an environmental globalization, which preceded economic globalization by a decade: global warming, the Chernobyl disaster, concern about the ozone hole, the disappearance of rain forest. . . . In response, WWF adopted a global mission, which translated into three broad priorities: forests, fresh water, and marine. In the 1990s, following the Earth Summit in Rio, WWF started focusing on specific goals and key targets and, in 1997, WWF played a key role in the creation of the Kyoto protocol. For an NGO [nongovernmental organization], focus is even more important than for a business. Focus requires that you define clearly the few things you want to stand for and want to influence. The impact of this focus, of establishing goals and targets in combination with the strength of the WWF brand, has been formidable. For example, in 2002, through ARPA [Amazon Protection Plan], Brazil established 12% of its rain forest under permanent protection, in no small measure thanks to the 10% goal established by WWF five years ago.

In 2001, WWF's stated mission was to stop, and eventually reverse, the degradation of the planet's natural environment and to build a future in which humans live in harmony with nature.

Organizational Structure

In 2002, WWF comprised an international secretariat (WWF International), 28 national organizations, 24 program offices, including two specialist offices (based in Brussels and Washington, which worked to influence the policies and activities of the European Union and institutions that dealt with global economic issues), and four associate organizations. Each national organization was a separate legal entity, responsible to its own board and accountable to its donors and bound to WWF International by a contract that covered the WWF name and mission. WWF International was accountable to the national organizations, donors, and the Swiss authorities. Most of the members of WWF International's board were drawn from the boards and CEOs of the national organizations. The 24 program offices were linked directly to WWF International as subsidiaries and were responsible for field program implementation and management.

WWF International's role was to identify and monitor emerging conservation concerns and guide the development of WWF's position on international issues as well as coordinate campaign, communications, and fund-raising activities. In addition, WWF International managed the international conservation programs and policy work and built global partnerships.

One of the national organizations' main roles was fund-raising. Additional activities ranged from practical field projects and scientific research to advising on environmental policy, promoting environmental education, and raising public awareness and understanding. A levy was applied to the national organizations by WWF International to cover common activities such as communications, trademark protection, and marketing and to ensure funds to the program offices for the implementation of field programs. National organizations could not start their own field projects abroad and had to operate within the international programs. In 2002, the expectation was that national organizations would spend the majority (two-thirds) of their funds on these international programs, although this depended on the size and maturity of each national organization. (See Exhibit 5 for details on national organization income and expenditures for fiscal year 2002.) "The field programs," Martin explained, "need to excite the national organizations so that they will give a large amount of the funds they raise for field programs." Overall, relationships between WWF International and the national organizations were based on consensus building and influence.

Throughout the 1980s the number of national organizations remained steady. However, in the 1990s WWF added six additional national organizations (including in Brazil, the Philippines, Turkey, and Indonesia) and a number of program offices. Over the next few years, WWF planned on adding at least two additional national organizations, in Hungary and Russia.

Exhibit 4   WWF Key Projects and Achievements

Date	Project/Achievement
1964	WWF works to protect the last 25 Javan rhinos in Ujung Kulon, western Java. In 2002 there were about 60 animals in the reserve.
1969	WWF helps establish the Donana nature reserve in Spain—a haven for the last few Iberian lynx.
1970s	WWF is instrumental in setting up CITES to protect plants and animals threatened by international trade.
1971	WWF participates in the creation of the Ramsar Convention to safeguard wetlands worldwide.
1972	WWF launches "Operation Tiger" to raise funds to protect the last 1,800 Bengal tigers left in the wild. In 2002, there were 2,500 to 3,750 tigers in India and 5,000 to 7,000 in the world.
1973	The World Organization of the Scout Movement and WWF launch the "World Conservation Badge," which is adopted by scouts in 30 countries.
1973	WWF and IUCN persuade the five Arctic nations to sign the International Polar Bear Convention to help protect the species.
1975	WWF raises the funds to establish protected areas in Central and West Africa, Southeast Asia, and Latin America.
1976	WWF and IUCN launch TRAFFIC (Trade Records Analysis of Flora and Fauna in Commerce) to monitor trade in wild animals, plants, and wildlife products.
1980	WWF is the first international environmental organization to be invited into China to help save the giant panda.
1980s	WWF pioneers "debt-for-nature" swaps in countries such as Madagascar, Ecuador, the Philippines, and Zambia, where a portion of the nation's debt is converted into funds for conservation.
1982	Ten Arabian oryx are released on the Jiddat plateau in central Oman—the result of the captive-breeding program that WWF helped set up in 1962.
1986	WWF brings together representatives from Buddhism, Christianity, Islam, and Judaism to forge an alliance between religion and conservation.
1987	WWF and IUCN launch the "Botanical Gardens Conservation Strategy," which guides a network of 600 botanic gardens working for plant conservation in 120 countries.
1988	The WWF-supported Communal Area Management Programme for Indigenous Resources (CAMPFIRE) in Zimbabwe helps villagers see wildlife as a source of income rather than as crop-destroying pests.
1990s	Three new species of large mammal are discovered in Vietnam thanks to WWF-sponsored surveys: the Truong Son muntjac, the giant muntjac, and the Sao la.
1992	WWF plays a critical role in establishing the Convention on Biological Diversity (CBD), which sets the basis for long-term biodiversity conservation around the world.
1993	WWF pioneers the Forest Stewardship Council (FSC) to oversee the independent certification of wood and wood products that come from well-managed forests.
1994	WWF's vigorous lobbying culminates in the Southern Ocean being declared a whale sanctuary.
1996	WWF instigates "Gifts to the Earth"—public celebrations of conservation actions by governments, companies, or individuals.
1996	WWF and Unilever launch the Marine Stewardship Council (MSC), setting global ecostandards for certifying and labeling seafood products.
1997	WWF plays a significant role in protecting the Antarctic from mining and drilling by pushing for a stronger Antarctic Treaty.
1997	WWF acts as the key force in the creation and subsequent improvement of the Kyoto Protocol—the international agreement to fight global warming.
1997	WWF and the World Bank join forces to conserve the world's forests.

Exhibit 4   WWF Key Projects and Achievements (continued)

Date	Project/Achievement
1999	WWF brings together the governments of six central African countries to sign the "Yaounde Declaration" on forest conservation.
2000	WWF Living Planet report shows that in just 30 years the world has lost one-third of its natural resources.
2000	Black rhinos in Africa increase to 2,700, and the Siberian tiger numbers 500 (up from 30 in the 1940s).
2001	The 1,000th golden lion tamarin is born in the wild thanks to WWF's captive-breeding programs.
2001	WWF plays a major role in finalizing the Stockholm Convention to eliminate a number of toxic chemicals.

Source: WWF Annual Report 2001.

Fund-raising and Membership

In 2002, nearly 5 million supporters contributed to WWF on an annual basis. In comparison, Greenpeace had 2.5 million members (although the organization had had 5 million members in 1990) and the Red Cross had 50 million members. Typical WWF members gave to six or seven different NGOs and were quite ready to shift loyalties. Mario Fetz, director of fund-raising and marketing, expanded on this willingness to shift: "In previous years, WWF would publish a member's newsletter that gave members a sense of exclusivity, but with the advent of the Internet, information is readily available and people tend to move in and out of causes. They no longer want to belong to a club." According to an International Research Associates (INRA) survey conducted in Europe in 2000, 11% of Europeans supported WWF because WWF protects nature (44.7%), saves animals (43%), is a good cause (19.9%), saves the rain forests (13.6%), fights pollution (13.4%), improves industry's behavior (5.2%), and influences governments (4.7%).

WWF's total membership levels had been fairly constant since 1990 but varied considerably by country; in the Netherlands it was as high as 6% of the total population due to the heavy use of TV advertising and the association with Prince Bernhard. In Switzerland it was also very high (around 4% of the total population) and was built on strong youth programs and the use by teachers of WWF materials. (See Exhibit 6 for membership levels by major national organization.) Annual attrition rates of members throughout the WWF network averaged 25% but also varied quite widely by country. In Italy, for example, they were higher, and in the United Kingdom and

the United States they were much lower due in part to a direct debit system for collecting membership dues.

Membership income had been declining for many organizations, and the fund-raising environment had become increasingly difficult. As Fetz put it, "In the 1980s you could raise money and get away with a thank you letter. Today donors want to know what WWF is doing with the funds we raise. In the 1980s a cold mailing would result in about a 3% response rate; in 2002 a response rate of 0.5% is considered good." (See Exhibit 7 for details on revenues by national organization.) In addition, the total number of NGOs had increased dramatically over the last few decades and was estimated at over 2,500 in the northern hemisphere alone.[2] These NGOs could be broadly divided into two main groups: large global organizations and fragmented, single-issue groups, the latter often struggling just to survive. The term NGO was increasingly being applied, sometimes to the detriment of established NGOs, to any activist organization, including some extremist groups. "This clutter and confusion makes having a strong brand even more important," declared Fetz.

In 2001, the number of WWF members declined slightly, but overall membership revenues had increased because WWF had been successful in "upgrading" some members to higher membership dues levels. However, the tougher fund-raising environment for WWF in 2002 had raised the pressure to look at other areas for sources of funding.

In 2002, it was also becoming more difficult to raise unrestricted funds that were not earmarked for specific projects. In 2001, 24% of external funds raised were

---

[2] Marc Lindenberg and Coralie Bryant, *Going Global: Transforming Relief and Development NGOs* (Bloomfield: Kumarian Press, 2001).

National Organizations	Gross Income	National Programs as a % of Expenditures	Administration and Fund-raising as a % of Expenditures	International Conservation as a % of Expenditures
Australia	9,331	42%	39%	19%
Austria	10,085	16%	51%	33%
Belgium	7,251	12%	44%	44%
Brazil	7,643	0%	24%	76%
Canada	16,070	52%	26%	22%
Denmark	8,602	4%	32%	64%
Finland	3,437	31%	40%	29%
France	7,820	55%	40%	5%
Germany	30,097	23%	39%	37%
Greece	3,014	59%	34%	7%
Hong Kong	4,228	6%	48%	45%
India	5,762	64%	24%	13%
Indonesia	8,163	77%	23%	0%
Italy	28,416	52%	42%	6%
Japan	7,523	24%	63%	13%
Malaysia	4,472	32%	17%	51%
Netherlands	69,902	3%	37%	60%
New Zealand	1,395	37%	57%	7%
Norway	2,403	15%	25%	60%
Pakistan	3,245	5%	32%	63%
Philippines	3,130	51%	11%	39%
South Africa	9,719	47%	32%	21%
Spain	5,289	38%	39%	23%
Sweden	19,113	22%	31%	46%
Turkey	321	0%	73%	27%
Switzerland	39,964	14%	64%	22%
United Kingdom	74,049	9%	47%	44%
United States	146,767	3%	37%	60%
TOTAL National Organizations	**537,211**	**16%**	**40%**	**44%**
International Nonconsolidated	104,109	0%	15%	85%
Program offices	21,300	0%	10%	91%
Other adjustments	(117,487)	0%	2%	98%
TOTAL NETWORK	**545,133**	**16%**	**40%**	**44%**

Source: WWF.

Exhibit 6 — WWF Membership Levels: Rank Order of National Organizations

National Organizations

United States	Canada
Netherlands	Denmark
Germany	Spain
Switzerland	South Africa
United Kingdom	Japan
Italy	Australia
Austria	Hong Kong
Sweden	Greece
France	Brazil
India	New Zealand
Pakistan	Malaysia
Finland	Norway
Belgium	Indonesia

Source: WWF.

Note: The five countries with the most members—the United States, the Netherlands, Germany, Switzerland, and the United Kingdom—accounted for 71% of WWF's 4.6 million members worldwide and 45% of WWF's 8,630 corporate supporters.

restricted, and in recent years WWF had also experienced a growth in restricted funds from aid agencies. This was in part because certain projects had a particular emotional appeal, particularly those that focused on saving a species such as the Siberian tigers. (See Exhibit 8 for an example of a fund-raising mailer.) "Our membership gets attached to particular species or issues," remarked Fetz, "and this has worked well in the past from a fund-raising perspective." However, species conservation accounted for only a fraction of WWF projects in 2002, and there was some concern that the use of a species conservation message for fund-raising purposes did not reflect the organization's current broader range of activities.

In September 2002, the WWF International Web site was receiving 300,000 hits a week, and the organization was just starting to build a base of international members at a rate of 10 members per week for a total of 1,600 international members in September 2002. During the fiscal-year 2002, WWF International members donated an average of about 309 Swiss francs ($172) per gift. This included special appeals, unsolicited donations, and membership dues. In addition, WWF had an online tool called the Panda Passport, with 30,000 registered passport holders, that encouraged individuals to participate in WWF's advocacy work through online campaigning.

Competition

Competition for funds from all sectors, private and public, was increasing, and by 2002, the search for funding had never been more difficult for WWF. Steele noted, "The environment is becoming increasingly competitive with many more NGOs competing for money in a world economy where people are less willing to give funds. We compete against all NGOs for funding, but there is so much NGO clutter you really need to push your brand. We have no idea how to calculate market share and frankly we're not sure how meaningful it would be."

WWF differed from the other main nature conservation NGOs in that it was active in both field programs and advocacy work. (See Exhibit 9 for an overview of the major nature conservancy players.) "Our competitive advantage is that we maintain the difficult balance between advocacy and field work," explained Martin. "Size is also a competitive factor since we are global and have the organizational capacity to deliver on target." Steele expanded, "WWF also has unique experience in establishing partnerships with the private sector. We have the same language as the private sector and focus on establishing shared vocabulary when we start a partnership." By comparison, Greenpeace had a policy of not accepting any funding from companies, and its approach was to "force" a company to sign an agreement. For example, in the 1990s, Greenpeace had publicly criticized Coca-Cola's use of refrigeration systems that emitted chlorofluorocarbons (CFCs) and had managed to get Coca-Cola to replace these systems through public pressure rather than through dialogue and partnership.

BUILDING THE WWF BRAND

By 1986, WWF realized that its original name, World Wildlife Fund, no longer reflected the scope of its activities, and the organization commissioned its first branding exercise. In order to publicize its expanded mandate, the organization's name was changed to the Worldwide Fund for Nature (with the exception of the United States and Canada, which both retained the old name), and the panda logo was modified to look a little fiercer. (See Exhibit 10 for an evolution of the logo over time.) In 2002, the organization's brand consisted of the acronym WWF and the famous panda logo.

Exhibit 7 2002 Revenues by National organization (CHF 000)

National Organizations	Individuals % Gross Income	Corporations % Gross Income	Trusts and Foundations % Gross Income	Government and Aid Agencies % Gross Income	WWF Network % Gross Income	Earned % Gross Income	Gross Income Total
Australia	26	0	3	34	16	19	9,331
Austria	61	0	0	11	14	13	10,085
Belgium	42	0	0	48	0	10	7,251
Brazil	2	2	3	12	69	10	7,643
Canada	54	7	18	9	3	10	16,070
Denmark	32	0	5	52	1	10	8,602
Finland	37	2	2	25	6	29	3,437
France	67	12	0	16	4	0	7,820
Germany	62	7	2	14	2	7	30,097
Greece	13	0	86	2	0	(1)	3,014
Hong Kong	43	21	6	24	0	3	4,228
India	1	0	0	71	13	10	5,762
Indonesia	1	1	8	45	44	(0)	8,163
Italy	36	0	1	53	0	6	28,416
Japan	48	12	2	5	3	29	7,523
Malaysia	2	4	2	29	57	5	4,472
Netherlands	97	1	0	0	0	1	69,902
New Zealand	57	17	2	2	11	6	1,395
Norway	12	16	11	48	11	2	2,403
Pakistan	10	2	0	34	38	6	3,245
Philippines	1	18	14	14	47	5	3,130
South Africa	9	26	8	4	6	42	9,719
Spain	12	0	11	11	6	24	5,289
Sweden	45	21	4	24	1	5	19,113
Turkey	9	25	14	0	26	20	321
Switzerland	88	1	2	1	0	8	39,964
United Kingdom	77	6	2	10	0	3	74,049
United States	60	4	9	21	10	(3)	146,767
Total NOs	60	5	5	17	7	4	537,208
International	3	3	6	18	64	5	104,109
Nonconsolidated Program Offices		0	0	29	64	0	21,300
Adjustments[a]		0	0	0	100	0	(117,487)
TOTAL NETWORK	60	5	6	22	0	5	545,130

Source: WWF.

[a]Adjustments = to avoid double counting, income has been adjusted to exclude income transfers among WWF entities.

Exhibit 8 — Examples of the Fund-raising Mailer, 2000

From World Wildlife Fund
Exciting news about how you can help us...

SAVE THE TIGER!

Dear Friend:

Please let me quickly explain why I'm sending you the enclosed set of Tiger Post Cards:

You see, they are yours, as a small introductory gift, because quite frankly, I hope they will encourage you...

....to help us save the tiger — and other endangered large cats.

Perhaps you can use one of these Tiger Post Cards to send a quick message to a loved one or a special friend.

Please notice that one post card features the awesome Siberian tiger — the largest of all living cats. This is the only tiger that makes its home in temperate forests.

Regrettably, only about 400-500 Siberian tigers may survive in the wild today, most of them in the Russian Far East...

...where a poacher can earn as much as $10,000 for the fur, head, bones, claws, and teeth of one single tiger!

The second post card features the Bengal Tiger, and even though perhaps 4,000 of these tigers still exist — poaching and habitat loss continue to thin their numbers.

And so — in plain English: We must save the tigers!

And here at World Wildlife Fund, we urgently need new friends like you to join with us in this endeavor. Will you?

Time is running out!

For example, today scientists are warning us that fewer

(over, please)

WWF
World Wildlife Fund
1250 Twenty-Fourth Street, NW   Washington, DC 20037-7787
www.worldwildlife.org

Printed on recycled paper

BENGAL TIGER
(Panthera tigris tigris).
Once roamed widely across India and Southeast Asia. Now threatened by poachers. Needs protection.

© Gary Ellis

To learn more about endangered wildlife like the Bengal Tiger, go to www.worldwildlife.org
WWF

SIBERIAN TIGER
(Panthera tigris altaica)
Largest of all living cats. Only about 200 still survive in the wild. Poachers sell fur, bones, claws, teeth and other body parts. Urgently needs protection.

© Bruce Wünning

To learn more about endangered wildlife like the Siberian Tiger, go to www.worldwildlife.org
WWF

WF0626.1

Source: WWF.

Exhibit 9   Overview of the Major Environmental Organizations in 2002

Organization	2001 Operating Budget (US$ million)	Number of Members	Focus
Worldwide Fund for Nature (WWF)	$329	5 million	Global conservation through field projects and advocacy work
Nature Conservancy	$546		Land conservation through land purchase
Greenpeace	103 (euros)	2.8 million	Focused on advocacy work
BirdLife International	$263	2.6 million	Field projects with focus on bird life and their habitats
Conservation International	$56		"Heavily funded but without a clear idea of priorities," field focus
Sierra Club		700,000	Advocacy organization
World Resources Institute (WRI)			Research and think tank
Friends of the Earth	$1.1		Federation of national environmental organizations focused on advocacy
Earthwatch			
Botanic Gardens Conservation International (BGCI)			

Source: Annual reports.

In March 2000, WWF commissioned a study by INRA to evaluate the WWF brand across Europe and test the general public's attitude to business partnerships. The poll, based on 9,000 face-to-face interviews conducted in nine countries, found that the WWF logo was "well liked and trusted by the large majority of people interviewed." Major findings included the following:

1. Europeans' greatest concerns, in order of importance, were violence, unemployment, health problems, poverty, and environmental disasters/damage to nature. There was a faint decline in people's perceptions of environmental quality, and views for the future were pessimistic.
2. Two-thirds of respondents could, unaided, name at least one environmental organization.
3. WWF's share of voice was about half that of Greenpeace (77% of respondents spontaneously named Greenpeace and 46% spontaneously named WWF). Friends of the Earth and other organizations were rated at 16% or below. (The only notable exception to this ranking was in Italy, where recognition was 84% for WWF and 31% for Greenpeace.)

Exhibit 10   Evolution of the Panda Logo Over Time

Evolution of a symbol

When some of the world's scientists and conservationists met in 1961 to plan how to publicise the threat to wildlife and wild places and to raise funds to support conservation projects, they decided to launch the World Wildlife Fund (WWF), known outside Canada and the United States today as the World Wide Fund For Nature. They needed a symbol, and at the time Chi Chi, the only giant panda in the Western world, had won the hearts of all that saw her at the London Zoo in the United Kingdom. She was a rare animal, like her wild panda cousins in China, and her form and colour were the ideal basis for an attractive symbol. Scottish naturalist Gerald Watterson made some preliminary sketches, from which Sir Peter Scott, world-renowned wildlife conservationist and painter, designed the WWF's giant panda logo. The design of the logo has evolved over the past four decades, but the giant panda's distinctive features remain an integral part of WWF's treasured and unmistakable symbol. For years, the giant panda has been thought of by many Chinese as an unofficial national symbol, too. Today, WWF's trademark is recognized not only in China but also in most countries as a universal symbol for the conservation movement itself.

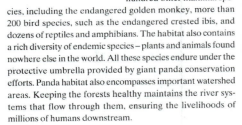

This recognition stems from the understanding that protecting a "flagship" species such as the giant panda benefits more than the single species itself. Conservation of this animal and its habitat provides protection for the whole community of wildlife that coexists with pandas, thus maintaining their entire ecosystem. The mountain forests where the last giant pandas survive shelter over a hundred other mammal species, including the endangered golden monkey, more than 200 bird species, such as the endangered crested ibis, and dozens of reptiles and amphibians. The habitat also contains a rich diversity of endemic species – plants and animals found nowhere else in the world. All these species endure under the protective umbrella provided by giant panda conservation efforts. Panda habitat also encompasses important watershed areas. Keeping the forests healthy maintains the river systems that flow through them, ensuring the livelihoods of millions of humans downstream.

1961

1978

1986

Sketches by naturalist George Watterson (in left column) which Sir Peter Scott used as the basis for his design of WWF's famous logo, which has evolved over the years.

Source: WWF.

4. Prompted awareness of the WWF logo ("Have you seen this logo before?") was at 68%, and 67.3% knew that the logo stood for WWF. Country variations, however, were considerable.

5. Sixty-four percent of respondents agreed that WWF should be partly supported by private companies, and 62% agreed that the WWF logo added value to a consumer product.

6. Sixty-three percent agreed that an association with WWF added value to a company and provided the competitive advantage of "more commitment to the environment (61%), more responsible (43.5%), and more credible/trustworthy (39.1% and 37.9%, respectively)."

7. The majority of respondents thought that it was acceptable for WWF to form a partnership in the following sectors: food industry, energy sector, household goods, telecoms and electronics, and banking. The oil companies and car industry were thought to be unacceptable sectors by the majority (43% to 36%).

(Other INRA findings relating to WWF's image versus that of competitors and reactions to the panda logo are detailed in Exhibits 11 and 12.)

In general, top executives were very happy with recognition of the WWF brand and logo. A study conducted by Edelman Public Relations in 2001 described WWF as a "superbrand" in both Europe and the United States, where WWF came in as the highest-ranked NGO and in fourth place overall, just behind Nike.[3]

However, the organization had a spectrum of constituents, including the general public, the media, WWF membership, staff, business and corporate partners, foundations, government agencies, other NGOs, and the communities impacted by the organization's work. These constituents all had different informational needs and perceptions, and WWF's message, image, and positioning might be slightly different for each. In addition, the WWF brand stood for different objectives in the minds of the general public in different countries. In some countries, particularly where WWF was less well known, the brand stood for species conservation. In countries where WWF was very well known, people recognized that the organization stood for the environment. (In Switzerland in the 1970s, for example, the panda logo was also recognized as a symbol for the antinuclear movement.)

Traditionally, the brand had been focused on WWF's membership audience and stood for species conservation, but this stakeholder group might have been fading in relative importance. The difficulty in communicating the brand revolved around species conservation versus broader environmental conservation. Children in particular latched on to animal emblems such as the panda, but

---

Exhibit 11   WWF Image versus that of Competitors

Image[a]	WWF	Greenpeace	Friends of the Earth
Will be a key player in 10 years	7.98	8.18	7.35
Has a good reputation	7.94	7.34	7.11
Is committed	7.84	8.29	7.34
Is the leader worldwide	7.72	7.62	6.46
Is honest	7.65	7.35	6.98
Is competent	7.61	7.66	6.99
Keeps its promises	7.57	7.65	7.07
Is independent	7.28	7.47	5.89
Is dynamic	7.21	7.94	6.84
Is aggressive	4.51	7.35	5.50

Source: INRA 2000.

[a]Scale of 1 to 10 where 1 = strongly disagree and 10 = strongly agree.

---

[3] Edelman Publc Relations presentations.

Exhibit 12   Perception of the Panda Logo

The Panda Logo is...	% of Respondents Who Agree
Likeable	79
Represents WWF well	71
Trustworthy	70
Successful	62
Gives a feeling of commitment	62
Modern	62
Dynamic	55

Source: INRA 2000.

WWF's activities focused also on global warming and the reduction of carbon dioxide emissions. The key challenge was communicating the link between the two. Martin concluded, "Our focus and perceived focus on wildlife is both a strength and a challenge because many donors, including government agencies, think that we do not address broader issues. However, species conservation is like an icon, closely linked to environmental conservation, that provides identity when fund-raising."

CORPORATE PARTNERSHIPS

The Role of Business
In 2002, WWF believed that, in the future, business would play an increasingly key role in environmental issues and that partnerships with major corporations would be essential both to further conservation goals and generate funds to support conservation.

In 1999, of the world's 100 largest economies, 49 were nations and 51 were corporations,[4] and influences on corporations were becoming increasingly complex. As demonstrated by the increase in the popularity of ecofunds, particularly in Japan, Eastern Europe, and South America, and the increasing recognition of the Dow Jones Sustainability Index, many investors were looking to invest in corporations that demonstrated a commitment to environmental and social development. In 1995, the World Business Council for Sustainable Development (WBCSD)

was formed, and by 2002 it included 160 international companies in 30 countries, representing 20 major industrial sectors. The WBCSD's mission was to "provide business leadership as a catalyst for change towards sustainable development, and to promote the role of eco-efficiency, innovation and corporate social responsibility."

In September 2000, *The Financial Times* published interviews with the CEOs of BP, Coca-Cola, Ikea, and Ford. All emphasized their companies' environmental commitment.[5] For BP, this was reflected in its "Beyond Petroleum" marketing campaigns, and for Coke this implied "becoming more deeply involved in issues of water availability and purity." Ikea worked with both Greenpeace and WWF to address problems of deforestation, and Ford had developed close relationships with environmental groups to work on emission levels and recycling.

Many global companies were recognizing stakeholder groups beyond shareholders and were attempting to become more socially and environmentally responsible. "We really noticed it at the World Summit on Sustainable Development in Johannesburg this year," concluded Steele. "Global corporations are gaining power and becoming increasingly involved. However, these corporations are not always clear on what they want to achieve." In August 2002, an online survey of 212 business leaders across 50 countries on the issue of sustainable development (SD) was conducted by Environics International. Key findings were as follows:

- Nine in 10 business leaders said that SD is accepted as a desirable goal in their companies.
- Six in 10 business leaders strongly agreed that the benefits of being proactive around SD outweighed the costs.
- Three in four business leaders strongly agreed that there needs to be better cooperation between government aid and private investment to ensure that SD takes place in developing countries.
- One in two business leaders strongly agreed that the benefits of environmental and social reporting outweighed the costs.

WWF's Existing Partnerships
In September 2002, WWF's corporate partnerships ranged from in-depth conservation partnerships, to purely fundraising initiatives, to licensing of the panda logo, to

---

4 Institute for Policy Studies, 1999.
5 *The Financial Times* business enterprises article, September 2000.

corporate clubs. (See Exhibit 13 for a list of corporate partnerships.) Steele summarized the benefits that WWF derived from these partnerships in terms of the three currencies (or three Cs): conservation, cash, and communications. The conservation component referred to actions taken by partner companies in support of WWF's conservation goals. These included sustainable use of natural resources, reductions in emissions and toxic chemical use, and recycling efforts. The cash component referred to the donations received from corporations that covered WWF's project and management costs associated with the relationship as well as donations to help fund WWF's different projects. The communications component related to the degree to which the company would go to communicate about the relationship with WWF and, importantly, how the WWF logo would be used in such communications. "No two deals are the same," explained Steele, "because the balance of the three currencies will vary depending on the company. Sometimes no money ever changes hands and the effort is purely one of conservation. In other cases the relationship is one that only furthers the communication and cash components. The value to WWF of our five main corporate partnerships ranges from $12 million to $250,000 per year."

WWF also widely licensed the panda logo. In 2001 royalties from licensing accounted for $16.5 million, or 4% of total 2001 operating income. In 2002, licensing agreements existed with affinity credit cards, a soft-toy manufacturer, clothing companies, and even a fresh-bread manufacturer, complete with an edible WWF logo. Generally, WWF received a percentage of the wholesale price of the product carrying the panda logo, and these licensing agreements provided both a cash and communication component. While some executives worried that the breadth of these licensing agreements might dilute the WWF brand and logo, others argued that the revenues generated were important and that the use of the panda logo on licensed products helped WWF maintain its right to the logo in certain countries. The majority of licensing agreements were negotiated at the national organization level.

Lafarge In September 2002, WWF's most important partnership was with Lafarge, the world's leading cement producer, with 2001 sales of $13.7 billion. Initial discussions had started in 1998 when WWF France representatives had contacted the company expressing concern about a river valley in France from which Lafarge was removing gravel. Discussions extended to forest restoration around quarries, and a partnership evolved to address this issue. In March 2000, a five-year partnership was established with three objectives: restoration of Lafarge's quarries, reinforcement of Lafarge's environmental policy, and financial support of WWF's "Forest Reborn" program. Since 2000, these objectives had been expanded to also include agreements on energy use, a reduction in CO_2 emissions of 10% below 1990 levels by 2010, and discussions about the reduction of toxic chemical use. In 2001, Lafarge published a sustainability report to be used with the investment community. (See Exhibit 14 for an excerpt of Lafarge's sustainability report.) In 2001, the WBCSD published its "cement report," largely based on WWF's work with Lafarge.

Exhibit 13   WWF's Corporate Partnerships in 2002

Company	Description of Partnership
HSBC	Major funding of freshwater projects and some discussion of environmental policies.
Lafarge	Partnership to help reinforce environmental policies and practices and establish. quantitative targets for waste reduction, recycling, energy consumption, environmental audits, and CO2 emissions. Financial support for WWF's "Forest Reborn" program.
Canon	Three-year partnership to raise environmental awareness through joint promotional and marketing activities targeted at young people.
Delverde Pasta	Partnership where the association with WWF reinforces the product message of natural ingredients while WWF benefits from in-store promotions of WWF's work.
Ogilvy & Mather	Free advertisements and placements worth $5 million.

Source: Company interviews.

Note: Value of relationships ranked between $250,000 per annum to $12 million per annum.

Exhibit 14   Excerpt from Lafarge Annual Report

Message from Bertrand Collomb

In the report entitled "Our Common Future", submitted to the United Nations in 1987 by the Brundtland Commission, sustainable development was defined as "development that meets the needs of the present without compromising the ability of future generations to meet their own needs".

When applied to an industrial group like ours, this concept translates into the need to measure the value created by the company according to a "triple bottom line" which aims to combine economic prosperity, environmental quality and social responsibility. Only if we can succeed in all three aspects will we ensure the company's prosperity and that of the world in which it is developing.

For more than 160 years, Lafarge has been producing construction materials that are vital for the development of human society, and therefore extracting non-renewable, abundant natural resources from the Earth's crust. The very nature of this activity, which necessitated the establishment of a firm local foothold, means that Lafarge has historically worked at integrating all three dimensions of sustainable development into its strategy and corporate culture. For example, our *Principles of Action*, published for the first time in 1977, highlight the central role of individuals, inside and outside the company, as well as the importance of cultural diversity, transparency and respect for the public interest. By the same token, *Lafarge's Environmental Policy* adopted in 1995 formalized the commitments to enable us to turn the environment into a competitive advantage and a source of fresh opportunities instead of a mere constraint.

Lafarge is proud of its achievements regarding sustainability as well as of its corporate culture that has contributed so much in this respect. Our progress is recognized by many, including the financial sector - Lafarge is for example a constituent of the Dow Jones Sustainability Index. Nevertheless, we want to take this approach further; on the one hand by pressing ahead with our analysis of what sustainability really means to our businesses, and on the other hand by committing ourselves more strongly than before to a progressive approach.

While it is key to Lafarge's continued prosperity, our current international development also confronts us with fresh challenges, linked to the difficult socio-economic situation in the countries of the Third World and to our responsibility as a global company to face up to world-wide problems like global warming. These heightened responsibilities are just some of the growing expectations of us from our stakeholders. We must meet these expectations.

Therefore, we intend to make headway by engaging in dialogue and exchanging ideas with all our stake-

Delverde From initial discussions between WWF Italy and Delverde, centered on the use of water by one of Delverde's pasta plants located within a national park, a communication partnership evolved with Delverde using the WWF brand in point-of-sale advertising and developing an organic pasta product line.

HSBC In March 2002, HSBC created a five-year, $50 million ecopartnership called Investing in Nature to fund conservation projects around the world and made donations to three NGOs: WWF, Botanic Gardens Conservation International, and Earthwatch. In addition, WWF committed to work with HSBC on environmental policies. "HSBC originally just wanted to donate to support freshwater conservation," explained Steele, "but we've developed a dialogue and relationship where we not only receive funding for our work but get to influence their environmental policies, too."

Other WWF partnerships involved Canon, which maximized the communication component of a partnership with the shared use of photography and the digitization of all wildlife photographs (followed up by recent discussions concerning recycling of photocopiers and use of solar panels), and Ogilvy & Mather, which contributed free advertisements and placements. In both of these cases, initial discussions had been initiated with WWF International. "These were global partnerships that led to local activities, both within the WWF network and within the partners' network, and presented some challenges for both HQs," Steele commented. "We were surprised to find out that other organizations faced the same sorts of local versus HQ office issues that we face."

In 2002, national organizations could make partnership deals at the national level, but any that had global scope had to be referred to WWF International, which played a role both in taking local initiatives global and global initiatives local. Steele summarized:

> We try to assess the impact of a specific partnership on the whole network, and it's up to the international group to demonstrate value added to our national organizations. The difficulty is that no two deals are the same in terms of what they bring to WWF in the way of conservation, cash, and communication. In Europe, though, most prospective corporate partners are operating in more than one country, so, by default, many of the local partnerships become international.

It was the corporate fund-raising team's role to shape the global strategy for corporate partnerships and identify future partner candidates. The team provided leadership and support to the national organizations and helped take some partnerships from local to global. Account managers within the group were responsible for developing partnership opportunities both within specific geographic areas and with targeted large accounts. They managed the partnerships internally, throughout the WWF network, and externally by being the key contact people within WWF. Steele explained:

> It is key to have one person on each side of any partnership who coordinates internally and communicates externally. It is important to have a clear understanding of where, within each organization, the first port of call is. At Lafarge and HSBC, for example, the owner of the relationship is the vice president of external affairs. However, in other more decentralized organizations such as Shell or Unilever, the person with this title sitting in corporate headquarters may not have enough clout.

In 2002, WWF International employed five full-time account managers. Many major partnerships, particularly those involving an intensive communication component, required a full-time account manager. The Lafarge partnership, for example, was managed by a single account manager, based at WWF International, and paid for out of the partnership funds. In the case of the HSBC relationship, which had originated in the United Kingdom and focused primarily on the United Kingdom, the United States, China, and Brazil, a total of four account managers, working out of the U.K. WWF office, managed the relationship and were once again paid for out of the partnership funds.

Risks and Benefits

> Partnering with global companies can help us advance our conservation aims and obtain new sources of funding. However, we need some up-front rules of engagement and need to establish safeguards and standards in approaching industry. We want to further our conservation goals and assist companies in sustainability programs, but we need to adhere to the right to criticize them as well.
>
> Paul Steele

One of the main objectives of establishing corporate partnerships was to further WWF's conservation goals by developing relationships that would bring about change in the way companies operated. "By changing the internal practices of these companies, we can move towards our goals," explained Steele. "The danger, of course, is that we risk being accused of greenwashing." Steele believed that 10 years ago the environment was not on the agenda for most companies, but by 2002, many were keen to address sustainable development but did not know how. He expanded, "There are real dangers in our partnering with corporations, and we need to demonstrate concrete results whilst maintaining our right to criticize the companies we are working with." Although WWF had been working closely with Lafarge since 2000, WWF strongly criticized a specific Lafarge project in Scotland. "I think Lafarge works with us because we don't pull any stunts," explained Steele, "but we still maintain our right to criticize them." Some NGOs sneered at WWF as the "corporate NGO," but few of them made the same demands for internal change with the companies with which they partnered.

Steele was also determined to continue not to use the WWF brand as a certification or validation tool. WWF had been instrumental in the 1990s in establishing both the Forest Stewardship Council and the Marine Stewardship Council, independent bodies with certification standards and a labeling scheme for sustainable forestry and seafood products, respectively. In addition, Steele was reluctant to place the panda logo on consumer products and was concerned about the possible dilution of the WWF brand. "There are a lot of abuses of the WWF logo around the world," he explained, "but we want to put our money into conservation projects rather than policing efforts."

Moving Forward

From the INRA study, Steele knew that Europeans seemed to be generally in favor of the relationships that WWF was developing with business. (Sixty percent of consumers polled said they thought association with WWF would add value to a company, and two in three thought that WWF should be partly supported by private companies.) However, he was concerned that, until now, WWF had pursued a reactive, opportunistic approach to developing corporate partnerships, and he believed that such a piecemeal approach could jeopardize WWF's reputation. Each national organization had had, until 2002, the independence to implement its own local country partnerships. Steele wondered if this policy should continue and how best to manage any change that might be necessary. In addition, given WWF's brand value, Steele wondered if it made sense for any WWF organization to partner with these smaller national and local companies.

"We need three or four more Lafarges under our belt," said Steele, "and we need to make the case that a partnership with WWF can result in financial benefits as well as competitive advantages. We need to make sure that we are also adding value to the partner." In 2002, for example, the global availability of freshwater resources was an emerging issue. Major food companies were starting to realize that freshwater resources were finite and threatened and that continued access could not be taken for granted. Steele explained, "Companies can see that they benefit, that there is an economic rationale for doing something about fresh water, and as a result, we can progress the agendas of both WWF and the company." In addition, WWF wanted to avoid industry or category exclusivity agreements; for example, WWF wanted to leverage its experience with Lafarge to partnerships with other cement manufacturers.

Steele had developed a proactive, coordinated approach to assessing future corporate partnerships within the business and industry unit and had engaged WWF executives to identify target-industry sectors and corporations within these sectors. (See Exhibit 15 for an overview of WWF's business and industry approach.) This process had identified three major corporations from three different industry sectors. Steele set out to assess the pros and cons of each potential corporate partnership:

Company A was a British multinational consumer products group offering a potential partnership package worth $50 million. The partnership consisted of three components:

1. Changes in the group's internal operating practices around raw materials utilization and decreases in energy consumption and CO_2 emissions, with measurable milestones for each and accounting for 25% of the partnership package
2. A contribution to a WWF global conservation program, in this case, a freshwater conservation project, representing 40% of the package
3. A communications program with promotions involving the use of the WWF logo, representing 25% of the package but only to be implemented after the company proved its ability to meet targets specified in the first component

The remaining 10% of funds were reserved for managing the relationship, including salaries and benefits, for a WWF dedicated account team. Benefits of this potential partnership included the group's broad consumer reach and global stature, the access to substantial funds for

Exhibit 15   WWF Business and Industry Approach

Essential Elements of B&I Relationships

* **Pro-Active, Co-ordinated Approach**

* **Clear Objectives**
    - Conservation and/or Funding?

* **Clear Rules of Engagement**
    - What's Expected of Both Parties
    - Contract / MOU in Place
        * WWF Right to Publicly Criticise
        * Use of "Panda" Logo etc.
        * Communications Plan

* **Clear "Ownership" of the Relationship**
    - TDP, NO, PO, International?

* **Sound "Account Management" in Place**
    - How to "Maximise" the Relationship

What The B&I Unit Will Do

* **Assist in the Sector Identification & Targetting Process**

* **Identify "Non-Critical" Sectors to Programme Objectives**
    - Fertile for Fundraising

* **Maintain a B&I Database - Links to Existing Knowledge**

* **Facilitate Setting Integrated Objectives**

* **Facilitate the Network Screening Process**

* **Carry Out or Facilitate the Due Diligence Process**

* **Assist or Facilitiate Direct Engagement With Companies**

* **Manage "Accounts" Where This Makes Sense For The Network**

Source: WWF.
Note: MOU = Memorandum of Understanding, TDP = Target Driven Program, NO = National organization, PO = Program Office.

conservation projects, and the ability to change the group's operating practices and impact on sustainable development. Possible downsides, on the other hand, included the risk of "greenwash," with the group paying lip service to sustainable development rather than being truly committed to it, and the potential for misuse of the WWF brand and logo (for example, the use of the panda logo on a detergent product). "The agreement has to be totally transparent," explained Steele. "WWF has to be able to explain convincingly the benefits of the relationship and prove that we're not just being bought off."

Company B was an American financial services company. The potential partnership centered on a direct financial investment by the company and would be similar in structure and magnitude to the existing partnership with HSBC. The relationship would also include agreed restrictions on lending policies, precluding loans for projects such as forest exploitation, oil exploration, and dam building. "One of the goals we would like to see in this type of partnership," said Steele, "is the development, in collaboration with the partner, of written guidelines for lending procedures. We want to ensure that the right questions are being asked by the company of its prospective loan recipients and the right criteria are being used to assess them."

The benefits of this potential partnership included the fairly straightforward nature of the potential agreement and the relatively low risk to the WWF brand and reputation. The drawbacks included the risk of "greenwash" and the challenge of insuring that any changes in guidelines were actually implemented.

Company C was a South African mining corporation that had contacted WWF with a proposal to provide funding of $5 million per year over the next five years for a species conservation program. Although the funding was attractive, Steele wondered how he could structure an agreement that would make WWF comfortable. One option would be to accept a donation from the corporation's charitable foundation arm rather than directly from the corporation; in the past, WWF had accepted donations from the Ford Foundation and the Shell Foundation.

Another option would be to structure an agreement that required the corporation to make a major commitment not to go into protected areas. The International Union for Conservancy (IUC) had categorized protected areas into six categories, and Steele was tempted to ask the corporation not to develop any activities in the first four categories. Such a request, if accepted, would have a substantially positive impact on WWF conservation goals, in addition to the financial contribution. However, the risk of associating the WWF brand with what many considered traditionally to be the "enemy" was considerable.

All three potential partnerships would be constructed as three- to five-year agreements with quarterly or biannual reviews. In each case, Steele believed that CEO buy-in was key to achieving commitment throughout the corporate partner's organization.

CONCLUSION

In assessing the potential partnership options before him, Steele weighed the pros and cons in each case and wondered which would provide WWF with the greatest benefits for the least risks. Although Steele was sure that building strong global corporate partnerships was the best way forward for WWF, not least from a sustainable development perspective as highlighted at the World Summit on Sustainable Development in Johannesburg, he had recently seen a letter that a member had written to Martin, complaining that WWF was "selling out" and becoming the "NGO of the corporate establishment." Steele was also aware that this sentiment was shared at times by some WWF employees and members but was convinced that these concerns could be effectively addressed.

Part VI

Organizing and Managing Global Marketing Operations

Earlier in the book, we observed companies facing a diverse range of environmental forces and competitive pressures that were creating new strategic imperatives for them. Although sensing, analyzing, and developing appropriate responses to these complex and often contradictory new demands is difficult, it is not where most global marketing programs fail. Far more frequently, companies develop a clear understanding of what they need to do, but struggle to understand how to do it. The greatest challenge usually comes in developing the organizational capabilities and managerial competencies to implement a clearly defined strategic intent.

GLOBAL VERSUS MULTINATIONAL ORGANIZATIONS

The tension between the powerful yet often competing forces shaping a company's global strategy—outlined in the introduction to Part I—has its analogy in equally animated debates about whether a company should be organized around its products, its markets, or its customers. Like the arguments about the need for centralization versus decentralization, such polarization of the options misses the point. To build multiple sources of competitive advantage—global-scale efficiencies, locally responsive flexibility, and above all, an ability to develop and diffuse innovation—a company must build an organization that is multidimensional in its capabilities and flexible in its application of them.

Such an organization is difficult to build on the foundation of a decentralized federation of independent subsidiaries that often characterized the structure of older multinationals such as Philips, Unilever, or ITT. But it is equally difficult to construct this organization on the centralized hub framework that has been favored by many comparatively newer global companies, such as Toyota, Boeing, or Matsushita. As they develop layers of competitive advantage, the subsidiaries in both these classic organization forms find that they can no longer relate only to the corporate center on the basis of either dependence or independence. To implement the multiple strategic capabilities in a flexible manner, they must be linked to the parent company and each other in an interdependent network of specialized operations.

In such an organization, resources are neither centralized in the home country nor spread evenly around subsidiaries. Instead, they are allocated to the part of the organization where they offer greatest strategic advantage. Key strategic competencies are similarly built in the organization wherever the critical scarce knowledge and expertise exists. Thus, a subsidiary with a highly efficient plant might be designated the regional or global source for a certain line or business, another with an extremely creative development group might be named the company's center of excellence for a particular product or technology, and the unit with the most developed marketing capabilities may well become the lead company for the rollout of new product market strategies that are then leveraged worldwide.

Unilever has taken this approach as it adapts its decentralized federation structure into an integrated network. It developed its product market strategy for the fabric softener "Snuggle" in Germany, it led the worldwide rollout of the shampoo "Timotei" from Sweden, and its South African subsidiary developed a whole new category of product called body perfume, later transferring its new product "Impulse" to other subsidiaries worldwide.

MULTIPLE MANAGEMENT PERSPECTIVES

On top of this networked infrastructure, companies must create organizations in which the voices representing the multiple strategic imperatives can not only be heard but have influence on the key decisions. In the various worldwide markets, such organizations need strong geographic managers—whether at the country or regional level—who understand local consumer needs, national market structures, and host government requirements, and are able to represent them in the company. They also need strong global product or business managers who can look across these local needs and interests and recognize the opportunities to capture economies of scale or develop coordinated competitive action. Finally, they need strong functional managers—technical directors, finance managers, human resource professionals, and information officers—who can act as the repositories of the company's scarce financial, human, and knowledge resources and as the facilitators of their movement and application worldwide.

The reason ITT lost its dominant position in the world telecommunications industry was not through strategic blindness or technological incompetence, but simply because it was unable to develop the multidimensional management perspectives and capabilities it took to respond to the multilayered and fast-changing demands in that industry. Dominated by the all-powerful heads of the national companies around the world, ITT was never able to develop equally powerful global business and technology managers who could stop the parochial localization of their potentially powerful System 12 digital switch. After years of trying—and failing—to get all voices represented at the table, ITT sold its telecommunications business to Alcatel.

DIFFERENTIATED ROLES AND RESPONSIBILITIES

As a model, it is appealing to visualize a company as an integrated network of specialized, interdependent operations run by managers representing multiple diverse perspectives and capabilities. But how do companies translate that idealized model into practical reality? What are the specific roles and responsibilities, and how are they allocated?

This is the most complicated and often the most sensitive part of developing a truly transnational organization because it typically involves reallocating power long held by one group or another. To understand the shifts required, we can follow the way in which Unilever, the U.K.-Dutch packaged-goods giant, adapted an organization that had operated for more than half a century on a foundation of autonomous, self-sufficient subsidiaries.

Historically, this organizational structure gave them an exceptional ability to be responsive to local market differences but not a strong capability in cross-market coordination (Figure 6.1[a]). During the 1980s, however, the company recognized that although the packaged food business (margarine, ice cream, frozen foods, mayonnaise, soups) was well served by the nationally responsive, country-based structures, forces driving for cross-market integration required that they manage their commodity chemicals business in a much more centralized manner and that they coordinate many more of the activities in their detergent business (Figure 6.1[b]).

As Unilever's management analyzed what aspects of the detergent business could benefit from greater cross-market coordination, it was clear that research needed to be done on a global basis while sales continued to be a very local responsibility. In between these clear extremes, they decided that development capabilities in overseas countries could be specialized and integrated, as could production facilities. Marketing also needed to be more coordinated, but with some ability to respond simultaneously to local market needs (Figure 6.1[c]).

The particular detergent marketing responsibilities that had to be most nationally differentiated were local promotions decisions. However, the corporate product group wanted to keep clear control over basic product characteristics, market positioning, and other key aspects of product policy. Issues such as advertising and pricing were recognized as requiring

Figure 6.1

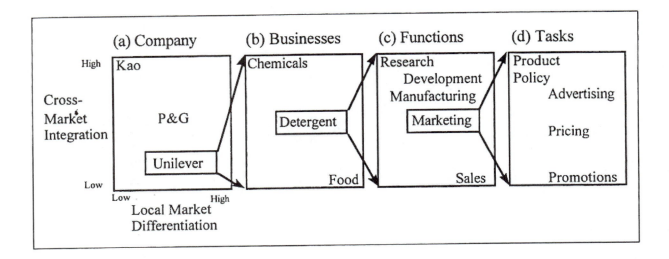

cross-market coordination and local flexibility, and these issues were coordinated by product manager–chaired teams with representatives from local subsidiaries (Figure 6.1[d]).

Such a portfolio of differentiated roles—often managed through cross-border teams and task forces—is a long way from the simple choices between centralized versus decentralized or product versus geography structures. But, as Percy Barnevik, CEO of ABB, said, "An organization that adapts to the new global reality will itself become a durable source of competitive advantage precisely because competitors will find it hard to match."

McKinsey & Company: Managing Knowledge and Learning

In April 1996, halfway through his first three-year term as managing director of McKinsey & Company, Rajat Gupta was feeling quite proud as he flew out of Bermuda, site of the firm's second annual Practice Olympics. He had just listened to twenty teams outlining innovative new ideas they had developed out of recent project work, and, like his fellow senior partner judges, Gupta had come away impressed by the intelligence and creativity of the firm's next generation of consultants.

But there was another thought that kept coming back to the 47-year-old leader of this highly successful $1.8 billion consulting firm. (See Exhibit 1 for a twenty-year growth history.) If this represented the tip of McKinsey's knowledge and expertise iceberg, how well was the firm doing in developing, capturing, and leveraging this asset in service of its clients worldwide? Although the Practice Olympics was only one of several initiatives he had championed, Gupta wondered if it was enough, particularly in light of his often stated belief that "knowledge is the lifeblood of McKinsey."

THE FOUNDERS' LEGACY[1]

Founded in 1926 by University of Chicago professor James ("Mac") McKinsey, the firm of "accounting and engineering advisors" that bore his name grew rapidly. Soon Mac began recruiting experienced executives, and training them in the integrated approach he called his General Survey outline. In Saturday morning sessions he would lead consultants through an "undeviating sequence" of analysis—goals, strategy, policies, organization, facilities,

This case was prepared by Professor Christopher A. Bartlett.

Copyright © 1996 by the President and Fellows of Harvard College. Harvard Business School case 9-396-357.

procedures, and personnel—while still encouraging them to synthesize data and think for themselves.

In 1932, Mac recruited Marvin Bower, a bright young lawyer with a Harvard MBA, and within two years asked him to become manager of the recently opened New York office. Convinced that he had to upgrade the firm's image in an industry typically regarded as "efficiency experts" or "business doctors," Bower undertook to imbue in his associates the sense of professionalism he had experienced in his time in a law partnership. In a 1937 memo, he outlined his vision for the firm as one focused on issues of importance to top-level management, adhering to the highest standards of integrity, professional ethics, and technical excellence, able to attract and develop young men of outstanding qualifications, and committed to continually raising its stature and influence. Above all, it was to be a firm dedicated to the mission of serving its clients superbly well.

Over the next decade, Bower worked tirelessly to influence his partners and associates to share his vision. As new offices opened, he became a strong advocate of the One Firm policy that required all consultants to be recruited and advanced on a firm-wide basis, clients to be treated as McKinsey & Company responsibilities, and profits to be shared from a firm pool, not an office pool. And through dinner seminars, he began upgrading the size and quality of McKinsey's clients. In the 1945 New Engagement Guide, he articulated a policy that every assignment should bring the firm something more than revenue—experience or prestige, for example.

Elected managing partner in 1950, Bower led his ten partners and 74 associates to initiate a series of major changes that turned McKinsey into an elite consulting firm unable to meet the demand for its services. Each client's problems were seen as unique, but Bower and his

---

[1] The Founders' Legacy section draws on Amar V. Bhide, "Building the Professional Firm: McKinsey & Co., 1939-1968," HBS Working Paper 95-010.

Exhibit 1   McKinsey & Company: 20-Year Growth Indicators

Year	# Office Locations	# Active Engagements	Number of CSS[a]	Number of MGMs[b]
1975	24	661	529	NA
1980	31	771	744	NA
1985	36	1823	1248	NA
1990	47	2789	2465	348
1991	51	2875	2653	395
1992	55	2917	2875	399
1993	60	3142	3122	422
1994	64	3398	3334	440
1995	69	3559	3817	472

Source: Internal McKinsey & Company documents
[a]CSS = Client Service Staff (All professional consulting staff)
[b]MGM = Management Group Members (Partners and directors)

colleagues firmly believed that well trained, highly intelligent generalists could quickly grasp the issue, and through disciplined analysis find its solution. The firm's extraordinary domestic growth through the 1950s provided a basis for international expansion that accelerated the rate of growth in the 1960s. Following the opening of the London Office in 1959, offices in Geneva, Amsterdam, Düsseldorf, and Paris followed quickly. By the time Bower stepped down as managing director in 1967, McKinsey was a well established and highly respected presence in Europe and North America.

A DECADE OF DOUBT

Although leadership succession was well planned and executed, within a few years McKinsey's growth engine seemed to stall. The economic turmoil of the oil crisis, the slowing of the divisionalization process that had fueled the European expansion, the growing sophistication of client management, and the appearance of new focused competitors like Boston Consulting Group (BCG) all contributed to the problem. Almost overnight, McKinsey's enormous reservoir of internal self-confidence and even self-satisfaction began to turn to self-doubt and self-criticism.

Commission on Firm Aims and Goals

Concerned that the slowing growth in Europe and the U.S. was more than just a cyclical market downturn, the firm's partners assigned a committee of their most respected peers to study the problem and make recommendations. In April 1971, the Commission on Firm Aims and Goals concluded that the firm has been growing too fast. The authors bluntly reported, "Our preoccupation with the geographic expansion and new practice possibilities has caused us to neglect the development of our technical and professional skills." The report concluded that McKinsey had been too willing to accept routine assignments from marginal clients, that the quality of work done was uneven, and that while its consultants were excellent generalist problem solvers, they often lacked the deep industry knowledge or the substantive specialized expertise that clients were demanding.

One of the Commission's central proposals was that the firm had to recommit itself to the continuous development of its members. This meant that growth would have to be slowed and that the associate to MGM ratio be reduced from 7 to 1 back to 5 or 6 to 1. It further proposed that emphasis be placed on the development of what it termed "T-Shaped" consultants—those who supplemented a broad generalist perspective with an in-depth industry or functional specialty.

Practice Development Initiative

When Ron Daniel was elected managing director (MD) in 1976—the fourth to hold the position since Bower had stepped down nine years earlier—McKinsey was still struggling to meet the challenges laid out in the Commission's report. As the head of the New York office since 1970, Daniel had experienced firsthand the rising expectations of increasingly sophisticated clients and the aggressive challenges of new competitors like BCG. In contrast to McKinsey's local office-based model of "client relationship" consulting, BCG began competing on the basis of "thought leadership" from a highly concentrated resource base in Boston. Using some simple but powerful tools, such as the experience curve and the growth-share matrix, BCG began to make strong inroads into the strategy consulting market. As McKinsey began losing both clients and recruits to BCG, Daniel became convinced that his firm could no longer succeed pursuing its generalist model.

One of his first moves was to appoint one of the firm's most respected and productive senior partners as McKinsey's first full-time director of training. As an expanded commitment to developing consultants' skills and expertise became the norm, the executive committee began debating the need to formally updating the firm's long-standing mission to reflect the firm's core commitment not only to serving its clients but also to developing its consultant (Exhibit 2).

But Daniel also believed some structural changes were necessary. Building on an initiative he and his colleagues had already implemented in the New York office, he created industry-based Clientele Sectors in consumer products, banking, industrial goods, insurance, and so on, cutting across the geographic offices that remained the primary organizational entity. He also encouraged more formal development of the firm's functional expertise in areas like strategy, organization and operations where knowledge and experience were widely diffused and minimally codified. However, many—including Marvin Bower—expressed concern that any move toward a product driven approach could damage McKinsey's distinctive advantage of its local office presence which gave partners strong connections with the business community, allowed teams to work on site with clients and facilitated implementation. It was an approach that they felt contrasted sharply with the "fly in, fly out" model of expert-based consulting that BCG ran from its Boston hub.

Nonetheless, Daniel pressed ahead. Having established industry sectors, the MD next turned his attention to leveraging the firm's functional expertise. He assembled working groups to develop knowledge in two areas that were at the heart of McKinsey's practice—strategy and organization. To

head up the first group, he named Fred Gluck, a director in the New York office who had been outspoken in urging the firm to modify its traditional generalist approach. In June 1977, Gluck invited a "Super Group" of younger partners with strategy expertise to a three-day meeting to share ideas and develop an agenda for the strategy practice. One described the meeting:

> We had three days of unmitigated chaos. Someone from New York would stand up and present a four-box matrix. A partner from London would present a nine-box matrix. A German would present a 47-box matrix. It was chaos... but at the end of the third day some strands of thought were coming together.

At the same time, Daniel asked Bob Waterman who had been working on a Siemens-sponsored study of "excellent companies" and Jim Bennett, a respected senior partner to assemble a group that could articulate the firm's existing knowledge in the organization arena. One of their first recruits was an innovative young Ph.D. in organizational theory named Tom Peters.

REVIVAL AND RENEWAL

By the early 1980s, with growth resuming, a cautious optimism returned to McKinsey for the first time in almost a decade.

Centers of Competence

Recognizing that the activities of the two practice development projects could not just be a one-time effort, in 1980 Daniel asked Gluck to join the central small group that comprised the Firm Office and focus on the knowledge building agenda that had become his passion. Ever since his arrival at the firm from Bell Labs in 1967, Gluck had wanted to bring an equally stimulating intellectual environment to McKinsey. Against some strong internal resistance, he set out to convert his partners to his strongly held beliefs—that knowledge development had to be a core, not a peripheral firm activity; that it needed to be ongoing and institutionalized, not temporary and project based; and that it had to be the responsibility of everyone, not just a few.

To complement the growing number of Clientele Industry Sectors, he created 15 Centers of Competence (virtual centers, not locations) built around existing areas of management expertise like strategy, organization, marketing, change management, and systems. In a

Exhibit 2   McKinsey's Mission and Guiding Principles (1996)

McKinsey Mission

To help our clients make positive, lasting, and substantial improvements in their performance and to build a great Firm that is able to attract, develop, excite, and retain exceptional people.

Guiding Principles

SERVING CLIENTS	Adhere to professional standards
	Follow the top management approach
	Assist the client in implementation and capability building
	Perform consulting in a cost effective manner
BUILDING THE FIRM	Operate as one Firm
	Maintain a meritocracy
	Show a genuine concern for our people
	Foster an open and nonhierarchical working atmosphere
	Manage the Firm's resources responsibly
BEING A MEMBER OF THE PROFESSIONAL STAFF	Demonstrate commitment to client service
	Strive continuously for superior quality
	Advance the state of the art management
	Contribute a spirit of partnership through teamwork and collaboration
	Profit from the freedom and assume the responsibility associated with self-governance
	Uphold the obligation to dissent

1982 memo to all partners, he described the role of these centers as two-fold: to help develop consultants and to ensure the continued renewal of the firm's intellectual resources. For each Center, Gluck identified one or two highly motivated, recognized experts in the particular field and named them practice leaders. The expectation was that these leaders would assemble from around the firm, a core group of partners who were active in the practice area and interested in contributing to its development. (See Exhibit 3 for the 15 Centers and 11 Sectors in 1983.)

To help build a shared body of knowledge, the leadership of each of the 15 Centers of Competence began to initiate activities primarily involving the core group and, less frequently, the members of the practice network. A partner commented on Gluck's commitment to the centers:

Unlike industry sectors, the centers of competence did not have a natural, stable client base, and Fred had to work hard to get them going. . . . He basically told the practice leaders, "Spend whatever you can — the cost is almost irrelevant compared to the payoff." There was no

Centers of Competence	Clientele Sectors
Building Institutional Skills	Automotive
Business Management Unit	Banking
Change Management	Chemicals
Corporate Leadership	Communications and Information
Corporate Finance	Consumer Products
Diagnostic Scan	Electronics
International Management	Energy
Integrated Logistics	Health Care
Manufacturing	Industrial Goods
Marketing	Insurance
Microeconomics	Steel
Sourcing	
Strategic Management	
Systems	
Technology	

attempt to filter or manage the process, and the effect was "to let a thousand flowers bloom."

Gluck also spent a huge amount of time trying to change an internal status hierarchy based largely on the size and importance of one's client base. Arguing that practice development ("snowball making" as it became known internally) was not less "macho" than client development ("snowball throwing"), he tried to convince his colleagues that everyone had to become snowball makers *and* snowball throwers. In endless discussions, he would provoke his colleagues with barbed pronouncements and personal challenges: "Knowing what you're talking about is not necessarily a client service handicap" or "Would you want your brain surgery done by a general practitioner?"

Building a Knowledge Infrastructure
As the firm's new emphasis on individual consultant training took hold and the Clientele Sectors and Centers of Competence began to generate new insights, many began to feel the need to capture and leverage the learning.

Although big ideas had occasionally been written up as articles for publication in newspapers, magazines or journals like *Harvard Business Review*, there was still a deep-seated suspicion of anything that smacked of packaging ideas or creating proprietary concepts or standard solutions. Such reluctance to document concepts had long constrained the internal transfer of ideas and the vast majority of internally developed knowledge was never captured.

This began to change with the launching of the McKinsey Staff Paper series in 1978, and by the early 1980s the firm was actively encouraging its consultants to publish their key findings. The initiative got a major boost with the publication in 1982 of two major bestsellers, Peters and Waterman's *In Search of Excellence* and Kenichi Ohmae's *The Mind of the Strategist*. But books, articles, and staff papers required major time investments, and only a small minority of consultants made the effort to write them. Believing that the firm had to lower the barrier to internal knowledge communication, Gluck introduced the idea of Practice Bulletins, two-page summaries of important new ideas that identified the experts who could provide more detail. A partner elaborated:

> The Bulletins were essentially internal advertisements for ideas and the people who had developed them. We tried to convince people that they would help build their personal networks and internal reputations. . . . Fred was not at all concerned that the quality was mixed, and had a strong philosophy of letting the internal market sort out what were the really big ideas.

Believing that the firm's organizational infrastructure needed major overhaul, in 1987 Gluck launched a Knowledge Management Project. After five months of study, the team made three recommendations. First, the firm had to make a major commitment to build a common database of knowledge accumulated from client work and developed in the practice areas. Second, to ensure that the databases were maintained and used, they proposed that each practice area (Clientele Sector and Competence Center) hire a full-time practice coordinator who could act as an "intelligent switch" responsible for monitoring the quality of the data and for helping consultants access the relevant information. And finally, they suggested that the firm expand its hiring practices and promotion policies to create a career path for deep functional specialists whose narrow expertise would make them more I-shaped than the normal profile of a T-shaped consultant.

The task of implementing these recommendations fell to a team led by Bill Matassoni, the firm's director of communications and Brook Manville, a newly recruited Yale Ph.D. with experience with electronic publishing. Focusing first on the Firm Practice Information System (FPIS), a computerized database of client engagements, they installed new systems and procedures to make the data more complete, accurate, and timely so that it could be accessed as a reliable information resource, not just an archival record. More difficult was the task of capturing the knowledge that had accumulated in the practice areas because much of it had not been formalized and none of it had been prioritized or integrated. To create a computer based Practice Development Network (PDNet), Matassoni and Manville put huge energy into begging, cajoling and challenging each practice to develop and submit documents that represented its core knowledge. After months of work, they had collected the 2,000 documents that they believed provided the critical mass to launch PDNet.

At the last minute, Matassoni and his team also developed another information resource that had not been part of the study team's recommendations. They assembled a listing of all firm experts and key document titles by practice area and published it in a small book, compact enough to fit in any consultant's briefcase. The Knowledge Resource Directory (KRD) became the McKinsey Yellow Pages and found immediate and widespread use firm-wide. Although the computerized data bases were slow to be widely adopted, the KRD found almost immediate enthusiastic acceptance.

Making the new practice coordinator's position effective proved more challenging. Initially, these roles were seen as little more than glorified librarians. It took several years before the new roles were filled by individuals (often ex-consultants) who were sufficiently respected that they could not only act as consultants to those seeking information about their area of expertise, but also were able to impose the discipline necessary to maintain and build the practice's databases.

Perhaps the most difficult task was to legitimize the role of a new class of I-shaped consultants — the specialist. The basic concept was that a professional could make a career in McKinsey by emphasizing specialized knowledge development rather than the broad-based problem solving skills and client development orientation that were deeply embedded in the firm's value system. While several consultants with deep technical expertise in specialties like market research, finance or steel making were recruited, most found it hard to assimilate into the mainstream. The firm seemed uncomfortable about how to evaluate, compensate or promote these individuals, and many either became isolated or disaffected. Nonetheless, the partnership continued to support the notion of a specialist promotion track and continued to struggle with how to make it work.

Matassoni reflected on the changes:

> The objective of the infrastructure changes was not so much to create a new McKinsey as to keep the old "one firm" concept functioning as we grew… Despite all the talk of computerized data bases, the knowledge management process still relied heavily on personal networks, old practices like cross-office transfers, and strong "One Firm" norms like helping other consultants when they called. And at promotion time, nobody reviewed your PD documents. They looked at how you used your internal networks to have your ideas make an impact on clients.

MANAGING SUCCESS

By the late 1980s, the firm was expanding rapidly again. In 1988, the same year Fred Gluck was elected managing director, new offices were opened in Rome, Helsinki, Sao Paulo, and Minneapolis, bringing the total to 41. The growing view amongst the partners, however, was that enhancing McKinsey's reputation as a thought leader was at least as important as attracting new business.

Refining Knowledge Management

After being elected MD, Gluck delegated the practice development role he had played since 1980 to a newly constituted Clientele and Professional Development Committee (CPDC). When Ted Hall took over leadership of this committee in late 1991, he felt there was a need to adjust the firm's knowledge development focus. He commented:

> By the early 1990s, too many people were seeing practice development as the creation of experts and the generation of documents in order to build our reputation. But knowledge is only valuable when it is between the ears of consultants and applied to clients' problems. Because it is less effectively developed through the disciplined work of a few than through the spontaneous interaction of many, we had to change the more structured

"discover-codify-disseminate" model to a looser and more inclusive "engage-explore-apply-share" approach. In other words, we shifted our focus from developing knowledge to building individual and team capability.

Over the years, Gluck's philosophy "to let 1,000 flowers bloom" had resulted in the original group of 11 sectors and 15 centers expanding to become what Hall called "72 islands of activity" (Sectors, Centers, Working Groups, and Special Projects), many of which were perceived as fiefdoms dominated by one or two established experts. In Hall's view, the garden of 1,000 flowers needed weeding, a task requiring a larger group of mostly different gardeners. The CPDC began integrating the diverse groups into seven sectors and seven functional capability groups. (See Exhibit 4.) These sectors and groups were led by teams of five to seven partners (typically younger directors and principals) with the objective of replacing the leader-driven knowledge creation and dissemination process with a "stewardship model" of self-governing practices focused on competence building.

Client Impact

With responsibility for knowledge management delegated to the CPDC, Gluck began to focus on a new theme—client impact. On being elected managing director, he made this a central theme in his early speeches, memos, and his first All Partners Conference. He also created a Client Impact Committee, and asked it to explore the ways in which the firm could ensure that the expertise it was developing created positive measurable results in each client engagement.

One of the most important initiatives of the new committee was to persuade the partners to redefine the firm's key consulting unit from the engagement team (ET) to the client service team (CST). The traditional ET, assembled to deliver a three- or four-month assignment for a client was a highly efficient and flexible unit, but it tended to focus on the immediate task rather than on the client's long-term need. The CST concept was that the firm could add long-term value and increase the effectiveness of individual engagements if it could unite a core of individuals (particularly at the partner level) who were linked across multiple ETs, and commit them to working with the client over an extended period. The impact was to broaden the classic model of a single partner "owning" a client to a group of partners with shared commitment to each client.

Exhibit 4   Group Framework for Sectors and Centers

Functional Capability Groups	Clientele Industry Sectors

Functional Capability Groups

Corporate Governance and Leadership
- Corporate organization
- Corporate management processes
- Corporate strategy development
- Corporate relationship design and management
- Corporate finance
- Post-merger management

Organization (OPP/MOVE)
- Corporate transformation design and leadership
- Energizing approaches
- Organization design and development
- Leadership and teams
- Engaging teams

Information Technology/Systems
- To be determined

Marketing
- Market research
- Sales force management
- Channel management
- Global marketing
- Pricing
- Process and sector support

Operations Effectiveness
- Integrated logistics
- Manufacturing
- Purchasing and supply management

Strategy
- Strategy
- Microeconomics
- Business dynamics
- Business planning processes

Cross Functional Management
- Innovation
- Customer satisfaction
- Product/technology development and commercialization
- Core process redesign

Clientele Industry Sectors

Financial Institutions
- Banking
- Insurance
- Health care payor/provider

Consumer
- Retailing
- Consumer industries
- Media
- Pharmaceuticals

Energy
- Electrical utilities
- Petroleum
- Natural gas
- Other energy

Basic Materials
- Steel
- Pulp and paper
- Chemicals
- Other basic materials

Aerospace, Electronics, and Telecom
- Telecom
- Electronics
- Aerospace

Transportation

Automotive, Assembly, and Machinery
- Automotive
- Assembly

Source: Internal McKinsey & Company document

In response to concerns within the partnership about a gradual decline in associates' involvement in intellectual capital development, the CPDC began to emphasize the need for CSTs to play a central role in the intellectual life of McKinsey. (See Exhibit 5 for a CPDC conceptualization.) Believing that the CSTs (by 1993 about 200 firmwide) represented the real learning laboratories, the CPDC sent memos to the new industry sector and capability group leaders advising them that their practices would be evaluated by their coverage of the firm's CSTs. They also wrote to all consultants emphasizing the importance of the firm's intellectual development and their own professional development, for which they had primary responsibility. Finally, they assembled data on the amount of time consultants were spending on practice and professional development by office, distributing the widely divergent results to partners in offices worldwide.

Developing Multiple Career Paths

Despite (or perhaps because of) all these changes, the specialist consultant model continued to struggle. Over the years, the evaluation criteria for the specialist career path had gradually converged with the mainstream generalist promotion criteria. For example, the specialist's old promotion standard of "world-class expertise" in a particular field had given way to a more pragmatic emphasis on client impact; the notion of a legitimate role as a consultant to teams had evolved to a need for specialists to be "engagement director capable"; and the less pressured evaluation standard of "grow or go" was replaced by the normal associate's more demanding "up or out" requirement, albeit within a slightly more flexible timeframe.

Although these changes had reduced the earlier role dissonance—specialists became more T-shaped—it also diluted the original objective. While legitimizing the two

---

Exhibit 5   CPDC Proposed Organizational Relationships

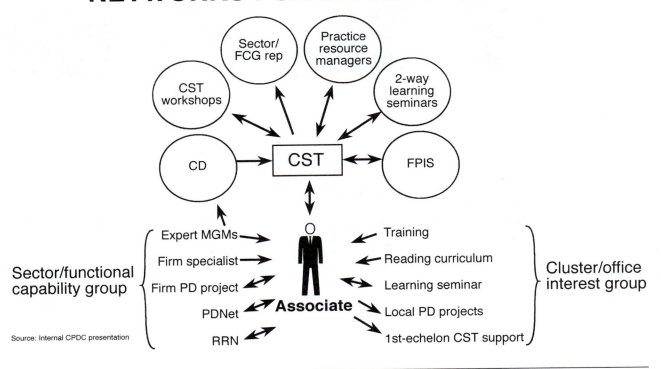

Source: Internal CPDC presentation

client service staff tracks, in late 1992 the Professional Personnel Committee decided to create two career paths for client service support and administrative staff. The first reaffirmed a path to partnership for practice-dedicated specialists who built credibility with clients and CSTs through their specialized knowledge and its expert application. Their skills would have them in high demand as consultants to teams (CDs) rather than as engagement directors (EDs). The second new option was the practice management track designed to provide a career progression for practice coordinators, who had a key role in transferring knowledge and in helping practice leaders manage increasingly complex networks. Valuable administrators could also be promoted on this track. (See Exhibit 6 for an overview.)

Yet, despite the announcement of the new criteria and promotion processes, amongst associates and specialists alike, there was still some residual confusion and even skepticism about the viability of the specialist track to partnership. As he dealt with this issue, Gluck kept returning to his long-term theme that, "it's all about people," even suggesting people development was the company's primary purpose:

There are two ways to look at McKinsey. The most common way is that we are a client service firm whose primary purpose is to serve the companies seeking our help. That is legitimate. But I believe there is an even more powerful way for us to see ourselves. We should begin to view our primary purpose as building a great

---

Exhibit 6   Alternative Career Path Focus and Criteria

CSS[1] Paths   # CSSA[2] Paths

Career Paths/Roles	General Consulting	Specialized Consulting	Practice Expertise	Practice Management Administration
Focus	Perform general problem solving and lead implementation Develop client relationships	Apply in-depth practice knowledge to studies Develop client relationships Build external reputation	Leverage practice knowledge across studies Create new knowledge	Codify and transfer knowedge Help administer practice

(1) Client Service Staff

(2) Client Service Support and Administration

Source: Internal McKinsley & Company presentation

institution that becomes an engine for producing highly motivated world class people who in turn will serve our clients extraordinarily well.

KNOWLEDGE MANAGEMENT ON THE FRONT

To see how McKinsey's evolving knowledge management processes were being felt by those on the firm's front lines, we will follow the activities of three consultants working in three diverse locations and focused on three different agendas.

Jeff Peters and the Sydney Office Assignment

John Stuckey, a director in McKinsey's Sydney office, felt great satisfaction at being invited to bid for a financial services growth strategy study for one of Australia's most respected companies. Yet the opportunity also created some challenges. As in most small or medium sized offices, most consultants in Sydney were generalists. Almost all with financial industry expertise had been "conflicted out" of the project due to work they had done for competing financial institutions in Australia.

Stuckey immediately began using his personal network to find how he might tap into McKinsey's worldwide resources for someone who could lead this first engagement for an important new client. After numerous phone calls and some lobbying at a directors' conference he identified Jeff Peters, a Boston-based senior engagement manager and veteran of more than 20 studies for financial institutions. The only problem was that Peters had two ongoing commitments that would make him unavailable for at least the first six weeks of the Australian assignment.

Meanwhile, Stuckey and Ken Gibson, his engagement director on the project, were working with the Sydney office staffing coordinator to identify qualified, available and nonconflicted associates to complete the team. Balancing assignments of over 80 consultants to 25 ongoing teams was a complex process that involved matching the needs of the engagement and the individual consultants' development requirements. A constant flow of consultants across offices helped buffer constraints, and also contributed to the transfer of knowledge. At any one time 15 to 25 Australian consultants were on short- or long-term assignments abroad, while another 10 to 15 consultants from other offices were working in Australia. (Firm-wide, nearly 20% of work was performed by consultants on inter-office loans.)

They identified a three-person team to work with Peters. John Peacocke was a New Zealand army engineer with an MBA in finance from Wharton and two years of experience in McKinsey. Although he had served on a four-month study for a retail bank client in Cleveland, since returning to Australia he had worked mostly for oil and gas clients. Patty Akopiantz was a one-year associate who had worked in investment banking before earning an MBA at Harvard. Her primary interest and her developing expertise was in consumer marketing. The business analyst was Jonathan Liew, previously an actuary who was embarking on his first McKinsey assignment.

With Peters' help, Stuckey and Gibson also began assembling a group of internal specialists and experts who could act as consulting directors (CDs) to the team. James Gorman, a personal financial services expert in New York agreed to visit Sydney for a week and to be available for weekly conference calls; Majid Arab, an insurance industry specialist committed to a two-week visit and a similar "on-call" availability; Andrew Doman, a London-based financial industry expert also signed on as a CD. Within the Sydney office, Charles Conn, a leader in the firm's growth strategies practice, agreed to lend his expertise, as did Clem Doherty, a firm leader in the impact of technology.

With Gibson acting more as an engagement manager than an engagement director, the team began scanning the Knowledge Resource Directory, the FPIS and the PDNet for leads. (Firm-wide, the use of PDNet documents had boomed in the eight years since its introduction. By early 1996, there were almost 12,000 documents on PDNet, with over 2,000 being requested each month.) In all, they tracked down 179 relevant PD documents and tapped into the advice and experience of over 60 firm members worldwide. Team member Patty Akopiantz explained:

> Ken was acting as engagement manager, but he was not really an expert in financial services, so we were even more reliant than usual on the internal network. Some of the ideas we got off PDNet were helpful, but the trail of contacts was much more valuable . . . Being on a completely different time zone had great advantages. If you hit a wall at the end of the day, you could drop messages in a dozen voicemail boxes in Europe and the United States. Because the firm norm is that you respond to requests by colleagues, by morning you would have seven or eight new suggestions, data sources, or leads.

At the end of the first phase, the team convened an internal workshop designed to keep client management informed, involved, and committed to the emerging conclusions. Out of this meeting, the team was focused on seven core beliefs and four viable options that provided its agenda for the next phase of the project. It was at this point that Peters was able to join the team:

> By the time I arrived, most of the hard analysis had been done and they had been able to narrow the focus from the universe to four core options in just over a month. It was very impressive how they had been able to do that with limited team-based expertise and a demanding client. ... With things going so well, my main priority was to focus the team on the end product. Once we got a clear logical outline, I assigned tasks and got out of the way. Most of my time I spent working on the client relationship... It was great learning for John and Patty, and both of them were ready to take on a management role in their next engagements.

In November, the team presented its conclusions to the board, and after some tough questioning and challenging, they accepted the recommendations and began an implementation process. The client's managing director reflected on the outcome:

> We're a tough client, but I would rate their work as very good. Their value added was in their access to knowledge, the intellectual rigor they bring, and their ability to build understanding and consensus among a diverse management group . . . If things don't go ahead now, it's our own fault.

John Stuckey had a little different post-engagement view of the result:

> Overall, I think we did pretty good work, but I was a bit disappointed we didn't come up with a radical breakthrough. . . . We leveraged the firm's knowledge base effectively, but I worry that we rely so much on our internal expertise. We have to beware of the trap that many large successful companies have fallen into by becoming too introverted, too satisfied with their own view of the world.

Warwick Bray and European Telecoms

After earning his MBA at Melbourne University, Warwick Bray joined McKinsey's Melbourne office in 1989. A computer science major, he had worked as a systems engineer at Hewlett Packard and wanted to leverage his technological experience. For two of his first three years, he worked on engagements related to the impact of deregulation on the Asia-Pacific telecommunications industry. In early 1992, Bray advised his group development leader (his assigned mentor and adviser) that he would be interested in spending a year in London. After several phone discussions the transfer was arranged, and in March the young Australian found himself on his first European team.

From his experience on the Australian telecom projects, Bray had written a PD document, "Negotiating Interconnect" which he presented at the firm's annual worldwide telecom conference. Recognizing this developing "knowledge spike," Michael Patsalos-Fox, telecom practice leader in London, invited Bray to work with him on a study. Soon he was being called in as a deregulation expert to make presentations to various client executives. "In McKinsey you have to earn that right," said Bray. "For me it was immensely satisfying to be recognized as an expert."

Under the leadership of Patsalos-Fox, the telecom practice had grown rapidly in the United Kingdom. With deregulation spreading across the continent in the 1990s, however, he was becoming overwhelmed by the demands for his help. Beginning in the late 1980s, Patsalos-Fox decided to stop acting as the sole repository for and exporter of European telecom information and expertise, and start developing a more interdependent network. To help in this task, he appointed Sulu Soderstrom, a Stanford MBA with a strong technology background, as full-time practice coordinator. Over the next few years she played a key role in creating the administrative glue that bonded together telecom practice groups in offices throughout Europe. Said Patsalos-Fox:

> She wrote proposals, became the expert on information sources, organized European conferences, helped with cross-office staffing, located expertise and supported and participated in our practice development work. Gradually she helped us move from an "export"-based hub and spokes model of information sharing to a true federalist-based network.

In this growth environment and supported by the stronger infrastructure, the practice opportunities exploded during the 1990s. To move the knowledge creation beyond what he described as "incremental synthesis of past experience," Patsalos-Fox launched a series of practice-sponsored studies. Staffed by some of the practice's best consultants, they focused on big topics like "The Industry Structure in 2005," or "The Telephone Company of the Future." But most of the practice's knowledge base was built by the informal initiatives of individual associates who would step back after several engagements and write a paper on their new insights. For example, Bray wrote several well-received PD documents and was enhancing his internal reputation as an expert in deregulation and multimedia. Increasingly he was invited to consult to or even join teams in other parts of Europe. Said Patsalos-Fox:

> *He was flying around making presentations and helping teams. Although the internal audience is the toughest, he was getting invited back. When it came time for him to come up for election, the London office nominated him but the strength of his support came from his colleagues in the European telecom network.*

In 1996, Patsalos-Fox felt it was time for a new generation of practice leadership. He asked his young Australian protégé and two other partners—one in Brussels, one in Paris—if they would take on a co-leadership role. Bray reflected on two challenges he and his co-leaders faced. The first was to make telecom a really exciting and interesting practice so it could attract the best associates. "That meant taking on the most interesting work, and running our engagements so that people felt they were developing and having fun," he said.

The second key challenge was how to develop the largely informal links among the fast-growing European telecom practices. Despite the excellent job that Soderstrom had done as the practice's repository of knowledge and channel of communication, it was clear that there were limits to her ability to act as the sole "intelligent switch." As a result, the group had initiated a practice-specific intranet link designed to allow members direct access to the practice's knowledge base (PD documents, conference proceedings, CVs, etc.), its members' capabilities (via home pages for each practice member), client base (CST home pages, links to client web sites), and external knowledge resources (MIT's Multimedia Lab, Theseus Institute, etc.). More open yet more focused than existing firm-wide systems like PDNet, the Telecom Intranet was expected to accelerate the "engage-explore-apply-share" knowledge cycle.

There were some, however, who worried that this would be another step away from "one firm" toward compartmentalization, and from focus on building idea-driven personal networks toward creating data-based electronic transactions. In particular, the concern was that functional capability groups would be less able to transfer their knowledge into increasingly strong and self-contained industry-based practices. Warwick Bray recognized the problem, acknowledging that linkages between European telecom and most functional practices "could be better":

> *The problem is we rarely feel the need to draw on those groups. For example, I know the firm's pricing practice has world-class expertise in industrial pricing, but we haven't yet learned how to apply it to telecom. We mostly call on the pricing experts within our practice. We probably should reach out more.*

Stephen Dull and the Business Marketing Competence Center

After completing his MBA at the University of Michigan in 1983, Stephen Dull spent the next five years in various consumer marketing jobs at Pillsbury. In 1988, he was contacted by an executive search firm that had been retained by McKinsey to recruit potential consultants in consumer marketing. Joining the Atlanta office, Dull soon discovered that there was no structured development program. Like the eight experienced consumer marketing recruits in other offices, he was expected to create his own agenda.

Working on various studies, Dull found his interests shifting from consumer to industrial marketing issues. As he focused on building his own expertise, however, Dull acknowledged that he did not pay enough attention to developing strong client relations. "And around here, serving clients is what really counts," he said. So, in late 1994—a time when he might be discussing his election to principal—he had a long counseling session with his group development leader about his career. The GDL confirmed that he was not well positioned for election, but proposed another option. He suggested that Dull talk to Rob Rosiello, a principal in the New York office who had just launched a business-to-business marketing initiative within the marketing practice. Said Dull:

> *Like most new initiatives, "B to B" was struggling to get established without full-time resources, so Rob was pleased to see me. I was enjoying my business marketing work, so the initiative sounded like a great opportunity. . . . Together, we wrote a proposal to make me the firm's first business marketing specialist.*

The decision to pursue this strategy was not an easy one for Dull. Like most of his colleagues, he felt that specialists were regarded as second-class citizens—"overhead being supported by real consultants who serve clients," Dull suggested. But his GDL told him that recent directors meetings had reaffirmed the importance of building functional expertise, and some had even suggested that 15%-20% of the firm's partners should be functional experts within the next five to seven years. (As of 1995, over 300 associates were specialists, but only 15 of the 500 partners.) In April 1995, Dull and Rosiello took their proposal to Andrew Parsons and David Court, two leaders of the Marketing practice. The directors suggested a mutual trial of the concept until the end of the year and offered to provide Dull the support to commit full time to developing the B to B initiative.

Dull's first priority was to collect the various concepts, frameworks and case studies that existed within the firm, consolidating and synthesizing them in several PD documents. In the process, he and Rosiello began assembling a core team of interested contributors. Together, they developed an agenda of half a dozen cutting-edge issues in business marketing—segmentation, multi-buyer decision making and marketing partnerships, for example—and launched a number of study initiatives around them. Beyond an expanded series of PD documents, the outcome was an emerging set of core beliefs, and a new framework for business marketing.

The activity also attracted the interest of Mark Leiter, a specialist in the Marketing Science Center of Competence. This center, which had developed largely around a group of a dozen or so specialists, was in many ways a model of what Dull hoped the B to B initiative could become, and having a second committed specialist certainly helped.

In November, another major step to that goal occurred when the B to B initiative was declared a Center of Competence. At that time, the core group decided they would test their colleagues' interest and their own credibility by arranging an internal conference at which they would present their ideas. When over 50 people showed up, including partners and directors from four continents, Dull felt that prospects for the center looked good.

Through the cumulative impact of the PD documents, the conference and word of mouth recommendations, by early 1996 Dull and his colleagues were getting more calls than the small center could handle. They were proud when the March listing of PDNet "Best Sellers" listed B to B documents at numbers 2, 4 and 9. (See Exhibit 7.) For Dull, the resulting process was enlightening:

We decided that when we got calls we would swarm all over them and show our colleagues we could really add

value for their clients. . . . This may sound strange—even corny—but I now really understand why this is a profession and not a business. If I help a partner serve his client better, he will call me back. It's all about relationships, forming personal bonds, helping each other.

While Dull was pleased with the way the new center was gaining credibility and having impact, he was still very uncertain about his promotion prospects. As he considered his future, he began to give serious thought to writing a book on business to business marketing to enhance his internal credibility and external visibility.

A NEW MD, A NEW FOCUS

In 1994, after six years of leadership in which firm revenue had doubled to an estimated $1.5 billion annually, Fred Gluck stepped down as MD. His successor was 45-year-old Rajat Gupta, a 20-year McKinsey veteran committed to continuing the emphasis on knowledge development. After listening to the continuing debates about which knowledge development approach was most effective, Gupta came to the conclusion that the discussions were consuming energy that should have been directed toward the activity itself. "The firm did not have to make a choice," he said. "We had to pursue *all* the options." With that conclusion, Gupta launched a four-pronged attack.

First, he wanted to capitalize on the firm's long-term investment in practice development driven by Clientele Industry Sectors and Functional Capability Groups and supported by the knowledge infrastructure of PDNet and FPIS. But he also wanted to create some new channels, forums, and mechanisms for knowledge development and organizational learning.

Then, building on an experiment begun by the German office, Gupta embraced a grass-roots knowledge-development approach called Practice Olympics. Two- to six-person teams from offices around the world were encouraged to develop ideas that grew out of recent client engagements and formalize them for presentation at a regional competition with senior partners and clients as judges. The twenty best regional teams then competed at a firm-wide event. Gupta was proud that in its second year, the event had attracted over 150 teams and involved 15% of the associate body.

Next, in late 1995 the new MD initiated six special initiatives—multi-year internal assignments led by senior partners that focused on emerging issues that were of importance to CEOs. The initiatives tapped both internal

Exhibit 7   PDNet "Best Sellers": March and Year-to-Date, 1996

Number Requested	Title, Author(s), Date, PDNet #	Functional Capability Group/Sector
21	*Developing a Distinctive Consumer Marketing Organization* Nora Aufreiter, Theresa Austerberry, Steve Carlotti, Mike George, Liz Lempres (1/96, #13240)	*Consumer Industries/ Packaged Goods; Marketing*
19	*VIP: Value Improvement Program to Enhance Customer Value in Business to Business Marketing* Dirk Berensmann, Marc Fischer, Heiner Frankemölle, Lutz-Peter Pape, Wolf-Dieter Voss (10/95, #13340)	*Marketing; Steel*
16	*Handbook For Sales Force Effectiveness—1991 Edition* (5/91, #6670)	*Marketing*
15	*Understanding and Influencing Customer Purchase Decisions in Business to Business Markets* Mark Leiter (3/95, #12525)	*Marketing*
15	*Channel Management Handbook* Christine Bucklin, Stephen DeFalco, John DeVincentis, John Levis (1/95, #11876)	*Marketing*
15	*Platforms for Growth in Personal Financial Services (PFS201)* Christopher Leech, Ronald O'Hanley, Eric Lambrecht, Kristin Morse (11/95, #12995)	*Personal Financial Services*
14	*Developing Successful Acquisition Programs To Support Long-Term Growth Strategies* Steve Coley, Dan Goodwin (11/92, #9150)	*Corporate Finance*
14	*Understanding Value-Based Segmentation* John Forsyth, Linda Middleton (11/95, #11730)	*Consumer Industries/ Packaged Goods; Marketing*
14	*The Dual Perspective Customer Map for Business to Business Marketing* (3/95, #12526)	*Marketing*
13	*Growth Strategy—Platforms, Staircases and Franchises* Charles Conn, Rob McLean, David White (8/94, #11400)	*Strategy*

March 1996

Number Requested	Title, Author(s), Date, PDNet #	Functional Capability Group/Sector
54	*Introduction to CRM (Continuous Relationship Marketing)—Leveraging CRM to Build PFS Franchise Value (PFS221)* Margo Geogiadis, Milt Gillespie, Tim Gokey, Mike Sherman, Marc Singer (11/95, #12999)	*Personal Financial Services*
45	*Platforms for Growth in Personal Financial Services (PFS201)* Christopher Leech, Ronald O'Hanley, Eric Lambrecht, Kristin Morse (11/95, #12995)	*Personal Financial Services*
40	*Launching a CRM Effort (PFS222)* Nick Brown, Margo Georgiadis (10/95, #12940)	*Marketing*
38	*Building Value Through Continuous Relationship Marketing (CRM)* Nich Brown, Mike Wright (10/95, #13126)	*Banking and Securities*
36	*Combining Art and Science to Optimize Brand Portfolios* Richard Benson-Armer, David Court, John Forsyth (10/95, #12916)	*Marketing; Consumer Industries/Packaged Goods*
35	*Consumer Payments and the Future of Retail Banks (PA202)* John Stephenson, Peter Sands (11/95, #13008)	*Payments and Operating Products*
34	*CRM (Continuous Relationship Marketing) Case Examples Overview* Howie Hayes, David Putts (9/95, #12931)	*Marketing*
32	*Straightforward Approaches to Building Management Talent* Parke Boneysteele, Bill Meehan, Kristin Morse, Pete Sidebottom (9/95, #12843)	*Organization*
32	*Reconfiguring and Reenergizing Personal Selling Channels (PFS213)* Patrick Wetzel, Amy Zinsser (11/95, #12997)	*Personal Financial Services*
31	*From Traditional Home Banking to On-Line PFS (PFS211)* Gaurang Desai, Brian Johnson, Kai Lahmann, Gottfried Leibbrandt, Paal Weberg (11/95, #12998)	*Personal Financial Services*

Cumulative Index (January – March)

Source: *Month By Month* (McKinsey's internal staff magazine)

and external expertise to develop "state-of-the-art" formulations of each key issue. For example, one focused on the shape and function of the corporation of the future, another on creating and managing strategic growth, and a third on capturing global opportunities. Gupta saw these initiatives as reasserting the importance of the firm's functional knowledge yet providing a means to do longer term, bigger commitment, cross-functional development.

Finally, he planned to expand on the model of the McKinsey Global Institute, a firm-sponsored research center established in 1991 to study implications of changes in the global economy on business. The proposal was to create other pools of dedicated resources protected from daily pressures and client demands, and focused on long-term research agendas. A Change Center was established in 1995 and an Operations Center was being planned. Gupta saw these institutes as a way in which McKinsey could recruit more research-oriented people and link more effectively into the academic arena.

Most of these initiatives were new and their impact had not yet been felt within the firm. Yet Gupta was convinced the direction was right:

> We have easily doubled our investment in knowledge over these past couple of years. There are lots more people involved in many more initiatives. If that means we do 5-10% less client work today, we are willing to pay that price to invest in the future. Since Marvin Bower, every leadership group has had a commitment to leave the firm stronger than it found it. It's a fundamental value of McKinsey to invest for the future of the firm.

Future Directions

Against this background, the McKinsey partnership was engaged in spirited debate about the firm's future directions and priorities. The following is a sampling of their opinions:

> I am concerned that our growth may stretch the fabric of the place. We can't keep on disaggregating our units to create niches for everyone because we have exhausted the capability of our integrating mechanisms. I believe our future is in developing around CSTs and integrating across them around common knowledge agendas.

> *Historically, I was a supporter of slower growth, but now I'm convinced we must grow faster. That is the key to creating opportunity and excitement for people, and that generates innovation and drives knowledge development. … Technology is vital not only in supporting knowledge transfer, but also in allowing partners to mentor more young associates. We have to be much more aggressive in using it.*

> There is a dark side to technology—what I call technopoly. It can drive out communication and people start believing that e-mailing someone is the same thing as talking to them. If teams stop meeting as often or if practice conferences evolve into discussion forums on Lotus Notes, the technology that has supported our growth may begin to erode our culture based on personal networks.

> *I worry that we are losing our sense of village as we compartmentalize our activities and divide into specialties. And the power of IT has sometimes led to information overload. The risks is that the more we spend searching out the right PD document, the ideal framework, or the best expert, the less time we spend thinking creatively about the problem. I worry that as we increase the science, we might lose the craft of what we do.*

These were among the scores of opinions that Rajat Gupta heard since becoming MD. His job was to sort through them and set a direction that would "leave the firm stronger than he found it."

P&G Japan: The SK-II Globalization Project

In November 1999, Paolo de Cesare was preparing for a meeting with the Global Leadership Team (GLT) of P&G's Beauty Care Global Business Unit (GBU) to present his analysis of whether SK-II, a prestigious skin care line from Japan, should become a global P&G brand. As president of Max Factor Japan, the hub of P&G's fast-growing cosmetics business in Asia, and previous head of its European skin care business, de Cesare had considerable credibility with the GLT. Yet, as he readily acknowledged, there were significant risks in his proposal to expand SK-II into China and Europe.

Chairing the GLT meeting was Alan ("A. G.") Lafley, head of P&G's Beauty Care GBU, to which de Cesare reported. In the end, it was his organization—and his budget—that would support such a global expansion. Although he had been an early champion of SK-II in Japan, Lafley would need strong evidence to support P&G's first-ever proposal to expand a Japanese brand worldwide. After all, SK-II's success had been achieved in a culture where the consumers, distribution channels, and competitors were vastly different from those in most other countries.

Another constraint facing de Cesare was that P&G's global organization was in the midst of the bold but disruptive Organization 2005 restructuring program. As GBUs took over profit responsibility historically held by P&G's country-based organizations, management was still trying to negotiate their new working relationships. In this context, de Cesare, Lafley, and other GLT members struggled to answer some key questions: Did SK-II have the potential to develop into a major global brand? If so, which markets were the most important to enter now? And how should this be implemented in P&G's newly reorganized global operations?

This case was prepared by Professor Christopher A. Bartlett.

Copyright © 2003 by the President and Fellows of Harvard College. Harvard Business School case 9-303-003.

P&G'S INTERNATIONALIZATION: ENGINE OF GROWTH

De Cesare's expansion plans for a Japanese product was just the latest step in a process of internationalization that had begun three-quarters of a century earlier. But it was the creation of the Overseas Division in 1948 that drove three decades of rapid expansion. Growing first in Europe, then Latin America and Asia, by 1980 P&G's operations in 27 overseas countries accounted for over 25% of its $11 billion worldwide sales. (Exhibit 1 summarizes P&G's international expansion.)

Local Adaptiveness Meets Cross-Market Integration

Throughout its early expansion, the company adhered to a set of principles set down by Walter Lingle, the first vice president of overseas operations. "We must tailor our products to meet consumer demands in each nation," he said. "But we must create local country subsidiaries whose structure, policies, and practices are as exact a replica of the U.S. Procter & Gamble organization as it is possible to create." Under the Lingle principles, the company soon built a portfolio of self- sufficient subsidiaries run by country general managers (GMs) who grew their companies by adapting P&G technology and marketing expertise to their knowledge of their local markets.

Yet, by the 1980s, two problems emerged. First, the cost of running all the local product development labs and manufacturing plants was limiting profits, and second, the ferocious autonomy of national subsidiaries was preventing the global rollout of new products and technology improvements. Local GMs often resisted such initiatives due to the negative impact they had on local profits, for which the country subsidiaries were held accountable. As a result, new products could take a decade or more to be introduced worldwide.

Year	Markets Entered
1837–1930	United States and Canada
1930–1940	United Kingdom, Philippines
1940–1950	Puerto Rico, Venezuela, Mexico
1950–1960	Switzerland, France, Belgium, Italy, Peru, Saudi Arabia, Morocco
1960–1970	Germany, Greece, Spain, Netherlands, Sweden, Austria, Indonesia, Malaysia, Hong Kong, Singapore, Japan
1970–1980	Ireland
1980–1990	Colombia, Chile, Caribbean, Guatemala, Kenya, Egypt, Thailand, Australia, New Zealand, India, Taiwan, South Korea, Pakistan, Turkey, Brazil, El Salvador
1990–2000	Russia, China, Czech Republic, Hungary, Poland, Slovak Republic, Bulgaria, Belarus, Latvia, Estonia, Romania, Lithuania, Kazakhstan, Yugoslavia, Croatia, Uzbekistan, Ukraine, Slovenia, Nigeria, South Africa, Denmark, Portugal, Norway, Argentina, Yemen, Sri Lanka, Vietnam, Bangladesh, Costa Rica, Turkmenistan

Source: Company records.

Consequently, during the 1980s, P&G's historically "hands-off" regional headquarters became more active. In Europe, for example, Euro Technical Teams were formed to eliminate needless country-by-country product differences, reduce duplicated development efforts, and gain consensus on new-technology diffusion. Subsequently, regionwide coordination spread to purchasing, finance, and even marketing. In particular, the formation of Euro Brand Teams became an effective forum for marketing managers to coordinate regionwide product strategy and new product rollouts.

By the mid-1980s, these overlaid coordinating processes were formalized when each of the three European regional vice presidents was also given coordinative responsibility for a product category. While these individuals clearly had organizational influence, profit responsibility remained with the country subsidiary GMs. (See Exhibit 2 for the 1986 European organization.)

Birth of Global Management

In 1986, P&G's seven divisions in the U.S. organization were broken into 26 product categories, each with its own product development, product supply, and sales and marketing capabilities. Given the parallel development of a European category management structure, it was not a big leap to appoint the first global category executives in 1989. These new roles were given significant responsibility for developing global strategy, managing the technology program, and qualifying expansion markets—but not profit responsibility, which still rested with the country subsidiary GMs.

Then, building on the success of the strong regional organization in Europe, P&G replaced its International Division with four regional entities—for North America, Europe, Latin America, and Asia—each assuming primary responsibility for profitability. (See Exhibit 3 for P&G's structure in 1990.) A significant boost in the company's

Exhibit 2   P&G's European Organization, 1996

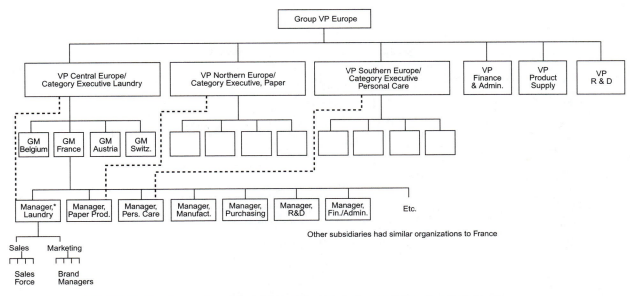

Other subsidiaries had similar organizations to France

* Managers of Laundry Products in all subsidiaries had a similar dotted line relationship to the European Category Executive for Laundry.

Source: Company records.

overseas growth followed, particularly in opening the untapped markets of Eastern Europe and China.

By the mid-1990s, with operations in over 75 countries, major new expansion opportunities were shrinking and growth was slowing. Furthermore, while global category management had improved cross-market coordination, innovative new products such as two-in-one shampoo and compact detergent were still being developed very slowly – particularly if they originated overseas. And even when they did, they were taking years to roll out worldwide. To many in the organization, the matrix structure seemed an impediment to entrepreneurship and flexibility.

P&G JAPAN: DIFFICULT CHILDHOOD, STRUGGLING ADOLESCENCE

Up to the mid-1980s, P&G Japan had been a minor contributor to P&G's international growth. Indeed, the start-up had been so difficult that, in 1984, 12 years after entering the Japan market, P&G's board reviewed the

accumulated losses of $200 million, the ongoing negative operating margins of 75%, and the eroding sales base—decreasing from 44 billion yen (¥) in 1979 to ¥26 billion in 1984—and wondered if it was time to exit this market. But CEO Ed Artzt convinced the board that Japan was strategically important, that the organization had learned from its mistakes—and that Durk Jager, the energetic new country GM, could turn things around.

The Turnaround

In 1985, as the first step in developing a program he called "Ichidai Hiyaku" ("The Great Flying Leap"), Jager analyzed the causes of P&G's spectacular failure in Japan. One of his key findings was that the company had not recognized the distinctive needs and habits of the very demanding Japanese consumer. (For instance, P&G Japan had built its laundry-detergent business around All Temperature Cheer, a product that ignored the Japanese practice of doing the laundry in tap water, not a range of water temperatures.) Furthermore, he found

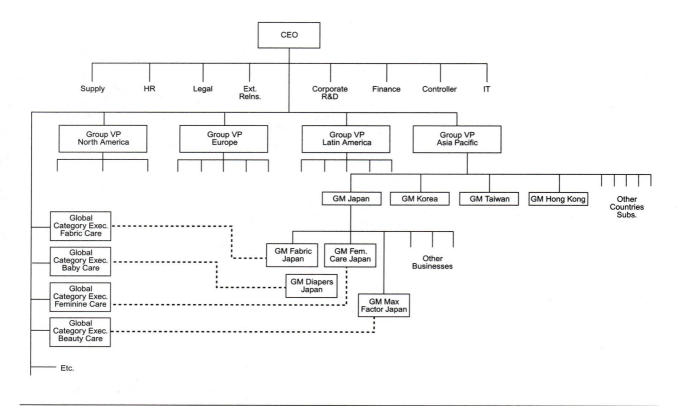

Source: Company records.

that the company had not respected the innovative capability of Japanese companies such as Kao and Lion, which turned out to be among the world's toughest competitors. (After creating the market for disposable diapers in Japan, for example, P&G Japan watched Pampers' market share drop from 100% in 1979 to 8% in 1985 as local competitors introduced similar products with major improvements.) And Jager concluded that P&G Japan had not adapted to the complex Japanese distribution system. (For instance, after realizing that its 3,000 wholesalers were providing little promotional support for its products, the company resorted to aggressive discounting that triggered several years of distributor disengagement and competitive price wars.)

Jager argued that without a major in-country product development capability, P&G could never respond to the demanding Japanese consumer and the tough, technology-driven local competitors. Envisioning a technology center that would support product development throughout Asia and even take a worldwide leadership role, he persuaded his superiors to grow P&G's 60-person research and development (R&D) team into an organization that could compete with competitor Kao's 2,000-strong R&D operation.

Over the next four years, radical change in market research, advertising, and distribution resulted in a 270% increase in sales that, in turn, reduced unit production costs by 62%. In 1988, with laundry detergents again profitable and Pampers and Whisper (the Japanese version of P&G's Always feminine napkin) achieving market leadership, Jager began to emphasize expansion. In particular, he promoted more product introductions and a bold expansion into the beauty products category. When P&G implemented its new region-based reorganization in 1990, Jager became the logical candidate to assume the newly created position of group vice president for Asia, a position he held until 1991, when he left to run the huge U.S. business.

The Relapse
In the early 1990s, however, P&G Japan's strong performance began eroding. The problems began when Japan's "bubble economy" burst in 1991. More troubling, however, was the fact that, even within this stagnating market, P&G was losing share. Between 1992 and 1996 its yen sales fell 3% to 4% annually for a cumulative 20% total decline, while in the same period competitor Unicharm's annual growth was 13% and Kao's was 3%.

Even P&G's entry into the new category of beauty care worsened rather than improved the situation. The parent company's 1991 acquisition of Max Factor gave P&G Japan a foothold in the $10 billion Japanese cosmetics market. But in Japan, sales of only $300 million made it a distant number-five competitor, its 3% market share dwarfed by Shiseido's 20% plus. Then, in 1992 P&G's global beauty care category executive announced the global launch of Max Factor Blue, a top-end, self-select color cosmetic line to be sold through general merchandise and drug stores. But in Japan, over 80% of the market was sold by trained beauty counselors in specialty stores or department store cosmetics counters. The new self-select strategy, coupled with a decision to cut costs in the expensive beauty-counselor distribution channel, led to a 15% decline in sales in the Japanese cosmetics business. The previous break-even performance became a negative operating margin of 10% in 1993. Things became even worse the following year, with losses running at $1 million per week.

In 1994, the Japanese beauty care business lost $50 million on sales of less than $300 million. Among the scores of businesses in the 15 countries reporting to him, A. G. Lafley, the newly arrived vice president of the Asian region, quickly zeroed in on Max Factor Japan as a priority problem area. "We first had to clean up the Max Factor Blue mass-market mess then review our basic strategy," he said. Over the next three years, the local organization worked hard to make Max Factor Japan profitable. Its product line was rationalized from 1,400 SKUs (or stock-keeping units) to 500, distribution support was focused on 4,000 sales outlets as opposed to the previous

10,000, and sales and marketing staff was cut from 600 to 150. It was a trying time for Max Factor Japan.

ORGANIZATION 2005: BLUEPRINT FOR GLOBAL GROWTH

In 1996 Jager, now promoted to chief operating officer under CEO John Pepper, signaled that he saw the development of new products as the key to P&G's future growth. While supporting Pepper's emphasis on expanding into emerging markets, he voiced concern that the company would "start running out of white space towards the end of the decade." To emphasize the importance of creating new businesses, he became the champion of a Leadership Innovation Team to identify and support major companywide innovations.

When he succeeded Pepper as CEO in January 1999, Jager continued his mission. Citing P&G breakthroughs such as the first synthetic detergent in the 1930s, the introduction of fluoride toothpaste in the 1950s, and the development of the first disposable diaper in the 1960s, he said, "Almost without exception, we've won biggest on the strength of superior product technology. . . . But frankly, we've come nowhere near exploiting its full potential." Backing this belief, in 1999 he increased the budget for R&D by 12% while cutting marketing expenditures by 9%.

If P&G's growth would now depend on its ability to develop new products and roll them out rapidly worldwide, Jager believed his new strategic thrust had to be implemented through a radically different organization. Since early 1998 he and Pepper had been planning Organization 2005, an initiative he felt represented "the most dramatic change to P&G's structure, processes, and culture in the company's history." Implementing O2005, as it came to be called, he promised would bring 13% to 15% annual earnings growth and would result in $900 million in annual savings starting in 2004. Implementation would be painful, he warned; in the first five years, it called for the closing of 10 plants and the loss of 15,000 jobs—13% of the worldwide workforce. The cost of the restructuring was estimated at $1.9 billion, with $1 billion of that total forecast for 1999 and 2000.

Changing the Culture
During the three months prior to assuming the CEO role, Jager toured company facilities worldwide. He concluded that P&G's sluggish 2% annual volume growth and its loss of global market share was due to a culture he saw as

slow, conformist, and risk averse. (See Exhibit 4 for P&G's financial performance.) In his view, employees were wasting half their time on "non-value-added work" such as memo writing, form filling, or chart preparation, slowing down decisions and making the company vulnerable to more nimble competition. (One observer described P&G's product development model as "ready, aim, aim, aim, aim, fire.") He concluded that any organizational change would have to be built on a cultural revolution.

With "stretch, innovation, and speed" as his watchwords, Jager signaled his intent to shake up norms and practices that had shaped generations of highly disciplined, intensely loyal managers often referred to within the industry as "Proctoids." "Great ideas come from conflict and dissatisfaction with the status quo," he said. "I'd like an organization where there are rebels." To signal the importance of risk taking and speed, Jager gave a green light to the Leadership Innovation Team to implement a global rollout of two radically new products: Dryel, a home dry-cleaning kit; and Swiffer, an electrostatically charged dust mop. Just 18 months after entering their first test market, they were on sale in the United States, Europe, Latin America, and Asia. Jager promised 20 more new products over the next 18 months. "And if you are worried about oversight," he said, "I am the portfolio manager."

Changing the Processes

Reinforcing the new culture were some major changes to P&G's traditional systems and processes. To emphasize the need for greater risk taking, Jager leveraged the performance-based component of compensation so that, for example, the variability of a vice president's annual pay package increased from a traditional range of 20% (10% up or down) to 80% (40% up or down). And to motivate people and align them with the overall success of the company, he extended the reach of the stock option plan from senior management to virtually all employees. Even outsiders were involved, and P&G's advertising agencies soon found their compensation linked to sales increases per dollar spent.

Another major systems shift occurred in the area of budgets. Jager felt that the annual ritual of preparing, negotiating, and revising line item sales and expenses by product and country was enormously time wasting and energy sapping. In the future, they would be encouraged to propose ambitious stretch objectives. And going forward, Jager also argued to replace the episodic nature of separate marketing,

payroll, and initiative budgets with an integrated business planning process where all budget elements of the operating plan could be reviewed and approved together.

Changing the Structure

In perhaps the most drastic change introduced in O2005, primary profit responsibility shifted from P&G's four regional organizations to seven global business units (GBUs) that would now manage product development, manufacturing, and marketing of their respective categories worldwide. The old regional organizations were reconstituted into seven market development organizations (MDOs) that assumed responsibility for local implementation of the GBUs' global strategies.[1] Transactional activities such as accounting, human resources, payroll, and much of IT were coordinated through a global business service unit (GBS). (See Exhibit 5 for a representation of the new structure.)

Beyond their clear responsibility for developing and rolling out new products, the GBUs were also charged with the task of increasing efficiency by standardizing manufacturing processes, simplifying brand portfolios, and coordinating marketing activities. For example, by reducing the company's 12 different diaper-manufacturing processes to one standard production model, Jager believed that P&G could not only reap economies but might also remove a major barrier to rapid new-product rollouts. And by axing some of its 300 brands and evaluating the core group with global potential, he felt the company could exploit its resources more efficiently.

The restructuring also aimed to eliminate bureaucracy and increase accountability. Overall, six management layers were stripped out, reducing the levels between the chairman and the front line from 13 to 7. Furthermore, numerous committee responsibilities were transferred to individuals. For example, the final sign-off on new advertising copy was given to individual executives, not approval boards, cutting the time it took to get out ads from months to days.

NEW CORPORATE PRIORITIES MEET OLD JAPANESE PROBLEMS

The seeds of Jager's strategic and organizational initiatives began sprouting long before he assumed the CEO role in January 1999. For years, he had been pushing his belief in growth through innovation, urging businesses to invest

---

[1] In an exception to the shift of profit responsibility to the GBUs, the MDOs responsible for developing countries were treated as profit centers.

Exhibit 4   P&G Select Financial Performance Data, 1980–1999

Annual Income Statement ($ millions)	June 1999	June 1998	June 1997	June 1996	June 1995	June 1990	June 1985	June 1980
Sales	38,125	37,154	35,764	35,284	33,434	24,081	13,552	10,772
Cost of Goods Sold	18,615	19,466	18,829	19,404	18,370	14,658	9,099	7,471
Gross Profit	19,510	17,688	16,935	15,880	15,064	9,423	4,453	3,301
Selling, General, and Administrative Expense	10,628	10,035	9,960	9,707	9,632	6,262	3,099	1,977
of which:								
Research and Development Expense	1,726	1,546	1,469	1,399	1,148	693	400	228
Advertising Expense	3,538	3,704	3,466	3,254	3,284	2,059	1,105	621
Depreciation, Depletion, and Amortization	2,148	1,598	1,487	1,358	1,253	859	378	196
Operating Profit	6,734	6,055	5,488	4,815	4,179	2,302	976	1,128
Interest Expense	650	548	457	493	511	395	165	97
Non-Operating Income/Expense	235	201	218	272	409	561	193	51
Special Items	-481	0	0	75	-77	0	0	0
Total Income Taxes	2,075	1,928	1,834	1,623	1,355	914	369	440
Net Income	3,763	3,780	3,415	3,046	2,645	1,554	635	642
Geographic Breakdown: Net Sales								
Americas	58.4%	54.7%	53.8%	52.9%	55.1%	62.5%		
United States							75.4%	80.9%
Europe, Middle East, and Africa	31.9%	35.1%	35.3%	35.2%	32.9%	39.9%		
International							22.3%	22.4%
Asia	9.7%	10.2%	10.9%	11.9%	10.8%			
Corporate					1.2%	-2.1%	2.3%	-3.3%
Number of Employees	110,000	110,000	106,000	103,000	99,200	94,000	62,000	59,000

Abbreviated Balance Sheet ($ millions)	June 1999	June 1998	June 1997	June 1996	June 1995	June 1990	June 1985	June 1980
ASSETS								
Total Current Assets	11,358	10,577	10,786	10,807	10,842	7,644	3,816	3,007
Plant, Property & Equipment, net	12,626	12,180	11,376	11,118	11,026	7,436	5,292	3,237
Other Assets	8,129	8,209	5,382	5,805	6,257	3,407	575	309
TOTAL ASSETS	32,113	30,966	27,544	27,730	28,125	18,487	9,683	6,553
LIABILITIES								
Total Current Liabilities	10,761	9,250	7,798	7,825	8,648	5,417	2,589	1,670
Long-Term Debt	6,231	5,765	4,143	4,670	5,161	3,588	877	835
Deferred Taxes	362	428	559	638	531	1,258	945	445
Other Liabilities	2,701	3,287	2,998	2,875	3,196	706	0	0
TOTAL LIABILITIES	20,055	18,730	15,498	16,008	17,536	10,969	4,411	2,950
TOTAL EQUITY	12,058	12,236	12,046	11,722	10,589	7,518	5,272	3,603
TOTAL LIABILITIES & EQUITY	32,113	30,966	27,544	27,730	28,125	18,487	9,683	6,553

Source: SEC filings, Standard & Poor's Research Insight.

Exhibit 5 P&G Organization, 1999 (Post O2005 Implementation)

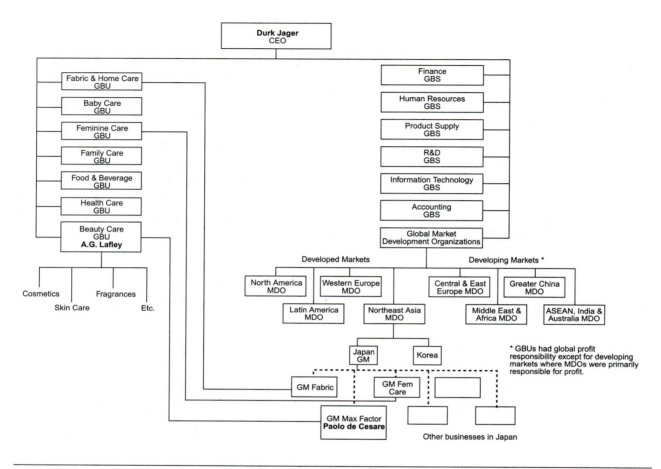

Source: Company records.

in new products and technologies. Even the organizational review that resulted in the O2005 blueprint had begun a year before he took over. These winds of change blew through all parts of the company, including the long-suffering Japanese company's beauty care business, which was finally emerging from years of problems.

Building the Base: From Mass to Class
By 1997 the Japanese cosmetics business had broken even. With guidance and support from Lafley, the vice president for the Asian region, the Japanese team had focused its advertising investment on just two brands—Max Factor Color, and a prestige skin care brand called SK-II.[2] "Poring through the Japanese business, we found this little jewel called SK-II," recalled Lafley. "To those of us familiar with rich Western facial creams and lotions, this clear, unperfumed liquid with a distinctive odor seemed very different. But the discriminating Japanese consumer loved it, and it became the cornerstone of our new focus on the prestige beauty-counselor segment."

---

2 SK-II was an obscure skin care product that had not even been recognized, much less evaluated, in the Max Factor acquisition. Containing Pitera, a secret yeast-based ingredient supposedly developed by a Japanese monk who noticed how the hands of workers in sake breweries kept young looking, SK-II had a small but extremely loyal following. Priced at ¥15,000 ($120) or more per bottle, it clearly was at the top of the skin care range.

Max Factor Japan began rebuilding its beauty-counselor channels, which involved significant investments in training as well as counter design and installation (see Exhibits 6 and 7). And because SK-II was such a high margin item, management launched a bold experiment in TV advertising featuring a well-respected Japanese actress in her late 30s. In three years SK-II's awareness ratings rose from around 20% to over 70%, while sales in the same period more than doubled.

Building on this success, management adapted the ad campaign for Hong Kong and Taiwan, where SK-II had quietly built a loyal following among the many women who took their fashion cues from Tokyo. In both markets, sales rocketed, and by 1997, export sales of $68 million represented about 30% of the brand's total sales. More important, SK-II was now generating significant operating profits. Yet within P&G, this high-end product had little visibility outside Japan. Paolo de Cesare, general manager of P&G's European skin care business in the mid-1990s, felt that, because the company's skin care experience came from the highly successful mass-market Olay brand, few outside Japan understood SK-II. "I remember some people saying that SK-II was like Olay for Japan," he recalled. "People outside Japan just didn't know what to make of it."

Responding to the Innovation Push

Meanwhile, Jager had begun his push for more innovation. Given his firmly held belief that Japan's demanding consumers and tough competitors made it an important source of leading-edge ideas, it was not surprising that more innovative ideas and initiatives from Japan began finding their way through the company. For example, an electrostatically charged cleaning cloth developed by a Japanese competitor became the genesis of P&G's global rollout of Swiffer dry mops; rising Japanese sensitivity to hygiene and sanitation spawned worldwide application in products such as Ariel Pure Clean ("beyond whiteness, it washes away germs"); and dozens of other ideas from Japan—from a waterless car-washing cloth to a disposable stain-removing pad to a washing machine-based dry-cleaning product—were all put into P&G's product development pipeline.

Because Japanese women had by far the highest use of beauty care products in the world, it was natural that the

---

Exhibit 6	Beauty Counselor Work Flow

Skin Care Counseling

Skin Diagnosis

↓

Skin Care Regimen Recommendation

↓

Product Demonstration
Plus
Skin Care Service (i.e., facial/massage)

↓

Make-up Service

↓

Record Consumer's Purchase

Make-up Counseling

Color Counseling
(Consumer Color-tone Analysis)

↓

Product Demonstration

↓

Make-up Service

↓

Record Consumer's Purchase

Source: Company documents.

Exhibit 7   In-Store SK-II Counter Space

Source: Company documents.

global beauty care category management started to regard Max Factor Japan as a potential source of innovation. One of the first worldwide development projects on which Japan played a key role was Lipfinity, a long-lasting lipstick that was felt to have global potential.

In the mid-1990s, the impressive but short-lived success of long-lasting lipsticks introduced in Japan by Shiseido and Kenebo reinforced P&G's own consumer research, which had long indicated the potential for such a product. Working with R&D labs in Cincinnati and the United Kingdom, several Japanese technologists participated on a global team that developed a new product involving a durable color base and a renewable moisturizing second coat. Recognizing that this two-stage application would result in a more expensive product that involved basic habit changes, the global cosmetics category executive asked Max Factor Japan to be the new brand's global lead market.

Viewing their task as "translating the breakthrough technology invention into a market-sensitive product innovation," the Japanese product management team developed the marketing approach—concept, packaging, positioning, communications strategy, and so on—that led to the new brand, Lipfinity, becoming Japan's best-selling lipstick. The Japanese innovations were then transferred worldwide, as Lipfinity rolled out in Europe and the United States within six months of the Japanese launch.

O2005 Rolls Out

Soon after O2005 was first announced in September 1998, massive management changes began. By the time of its formal implementation in July 1999, half the top 30 managers and a third of the top 300 were new to their jobs. For example, Lafley, who had just returned from Asia to head the North American region, was asked to prepare to hand off that role and take over as head of the Beauty Care GBU. "It was a crazy year," recalled Lafley. "There was so much to build, but beyond the grand design, we were not clear about how it should operate."

In another of the hundreds of O2005 senior management changes, de Cesare, head of P&G's European skin care business, was promoted to vice president and asked to move to Osaka and head up Max Factor Japan. Under the new structure he would report directly to Lafley's Beauty Care GBU and on a dotted-line basis to the head of the MDO for Northeast Asia.

In addition to adjusting to this new complexity where responsibilities and relationships were still being defined, de Cesare found himself in a new global role. As president of Max Factor Japan he became a member of the Beauty Care Global Leadership Team (GLT), a group comprised of the business GMs from three key MDOs, representatives from key functions such as R&D, consumer research, product supply, HR, and finance, and chaired by Lafley as GBU head. These meetings became vital forums for implementing Lafley's charge "to review P&G's huge beauty care portfolio and focus investment on the top brands with the potential to become global assets." The question took on new importance for de Cesare when he was named global franchise leader for SK-II and asked to explore its potential as a global brand.

A New Global Product Development Process

Soon after arriving in Japan, de Cesare discovered that the Japanese Max Factor organization was increasingly involved in new global product development activities following its successful Lipfinity role. This process began under the leadership of the Beauty Care GLT when consumer research identified an unmet consumer need worldwide. A lead research center then developed a technical model of how P&G could respond to the need. Next, the GLT process brought in marketing expertise from lead markets to expand that technology "chassis" to a holistic new-product concept. Finally, contributing technologists and marketers were designated to work on the variations in ingredients or aesthetics necessary to adapt the core technology or product concept to local markets.

This global product development process was set in motion when consumer researchers found that, despite regional differences, there was a worldwide opportunity in facial cleansing. The research showed that, although U.S. women were satisfied with the clean feeling they got using bar soaps, it left their skin tight and dry; in Europe, women applied a cleansing milk with a cotton pad that left their skin moisturized and conditioned but not as clean as they wanted; and in Japan, the habit of using foaming facial cleansers left women satisfied with skin conditioning but not with moisturizing. Globally, however, the unmet need was to achieve soft, moisturized, clean-feeling skin, and herein the GBU saw the product opportunity—and the technological challenge.

A technology team was assembled at an R&D facility in Cincinnati, drawing on the most qualified technologists from its P&G's labs worldwide. For example, because the average Japanese woman spent 4.5 minutes on her face-cleansing regime compared with 1.7 minutes for the typical American woman, Japanese technologists were sought for their refined expertise in the cleansing processes and their particular understanding of how to develop a product with the rich, creamy lather.

Working with a woven substrate technology developed by P&G's paper business, the core technology team found that a 10-micron fiber, when woven into a mesh, was effective in trapping and absorbing dirt and impurities. By impregnating this substrate with a dry-sprayed formula of cleansers and moisturizers activated at different times in the cleansing process, team members felt they could develop a disposable cleansing cloth that would respond to the identified consumer need. After this technology "chassis" had been developed, a technology team in Japan adapted it to allow the cloth to be impregnated with a different cleanser formulation that included the SK-II ingredient, Pitera. (See Exhibit 8 for an overview of the development process.)

A U.S.-based marketing team took on the task of developing the Olay version. Identifying its consumers' view of a multistep salon facial as the ultimate cleansing experience, this team came up with the concept of a one-step routine that offered the benefits of cleansing, conditioning, and toning—"just like a daily facial." Meanwhile, another team had the same assignment in Japan, which became the lead market for the SK-II version. Because

Exhibit 8   Representation of Global Cleansing Cloth Development Program

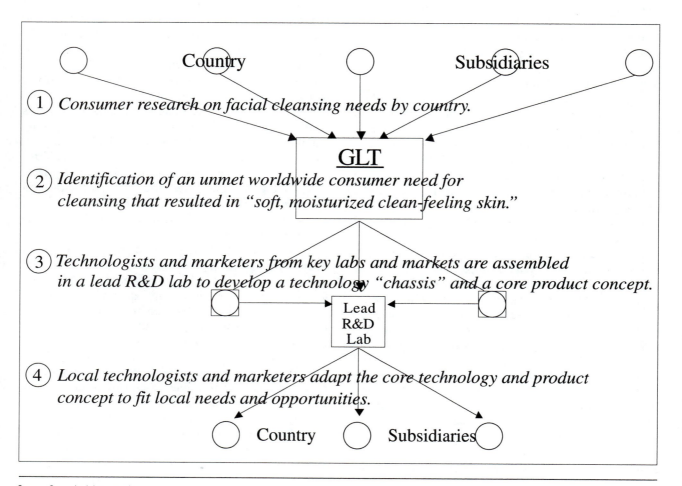

Source: Casewriter's interpretation.

women already had a five- or six-step cleansing routine, the SK-II version was positioned not as a "daily facial" but as a "foaming massage cloth" that built on the ritual experience of increasing skin circulation through a massage while boosting skin clarity due to the microfibers' ability to clean pores and trap dirt. (See Exhibit 9 for illustration of the Foaming Massage Cloth with other core SK-II products.)

Because of its premium pricing strategy, the SK-II Foaming Massage Cloth was packaged in a much more elegant dispensing box and was priced at ¥6,000 ($50), compared to $7 for the Olay Facial Cloth in the United States. And Japan assigned several technologists to the task of developing detailed product performance data that Japanese beauty magazines required for the much more scientific product reviews they published compared to their Western counterparts. In the end, each market ended up with a distinct product built on a common technology platform. Marketing expertise was also

pitera soak

FACIAL TREATMENT ESSENCE
Skin Balancing Essence

The heart of the SK-II range, the revolutionary **Facial Treatment Essence** is the second point in your Ritual. This unique Pitera-rich product helps boost moisture levels to improve texture and clarity for a more beautiful, glowing complexion.

Women are so passionate about **Facial Treatment Essence** that they describe it as their 'holy' water. It contains the most concentrated amount of Pitera of all our skincare products — around 90% pure SK-II Pitera. It absorbs easily and leaves your skin looking radiant, with a supple, smooth feel.

FOAMING MASSAGE CLOTH
Purifying Cleansing Cloth

These innovative **Foaming Massage Cloths** leave your skin feeling smooth and velvety. A single sheet offers the outstanding effects of a cleanser, facial wash and massage. It gently washes away impurities, excess oil and non-waterproof eye make-up, leaving your skin clean, pure and refreshed.

FACIAL TREATMENT CLEAR LOTION
Clear Purifying Lotion

For a perfectly conditioned and ultra-fresh skin, use the **Facial Treatment Clear Lotion** morning and evening after cleansing your face and neck. The final part of your cleansing process, this Lotion helps remove residual impurities and dead skin cells.

Source: Company brochure.

---

shared—some Japanese performance analysis and data were also relevant for the Olay version and were used in Europe, for example—allowing the organization to leverage its local learning.

THE SK-II DECISION: A GLOBAL BRAND?

After barely six months in Japan, de Cesare recognized that he now had three different roles in the new organization. As president of Max Factor Japan, he was impressed by the turnaround this local company had pulled off and was optimistic about its ability to grow significantly in the large Japanese beauty market. As GLT member on the Beauty Care GBU, he was proud of his organization's contribution to the GBU-sponsored global new-product innovation process and was convinced that Japan could continue to contribute to and learn from P&G's impressive technology base. And now as global franchise leader for SK-II, he was excited by the opportunity to explore whether the brand could break into the $9 billion worldwide prestige skin care market. (See Exhibit 10 for prestige market data.)

When he arrived in Japan, de Cesare found that SK-II's success in Taiwan and Hong Kong (by 1999, 45% of total SK-II sales) had already encouraged management to

Exhibit 10

Exhibit 10   Global Prestige Market: Size and Geographic Split

- Global Prestige Market: 1999
  (Fragrances, Cosmetics, Skin) = $15 billion at retail level
  (of which approximately 60% is skin care)

United States	26%
Canada	2
Asia/Pacific[a]	25
United Kingdom	5
France	5
Germany	5
Rest of Europe	16
Rest of World	16

Source: Company data.

[a]Japan represented over 80% of the Asia/Pacific total.

begin expansion into three other regional markets—Singapore, Malaysia, and South Korea. But these were relatively small markets, and as he reviewed data on the global skin care and prestige beauty markets, he wondered if the time was right to make a bold entry into one or more major markets. (See Exhibits 11 and 12 for global skin-care market and consumer data.)

As he reviewed the opportunities, three alternatives presented themselves. First, the beauty care management team for Greater China was interested in expanding on SK-II's success in Taiwan and Hong Kong by introducing the brand into mainland China. Next, at GLT meetings de Cesare had discussed with the head of beauty care in Europe the possibilities of bringing SK-II into that large Western market. His third possibility—really his first option, he realized—was to build on the brand's success in SK-II's rich and proven home Japanese market.

The Japanese Opportunity

Japanese women were among the most sophisticated users of beauty products in the world, and per capita they were the world's leading consumers of these products. Despite its improved performance in recent years, Max Factor Japan claimed less than a 3% share of this $10 billion beauty product market. "It's huge," boasted one local manager. "Larger than the U.S. laundry market."

Although SK-II had sales of more than $150 million in Japan in 1999, de Cesare was also aware that in recent years its home market growth had slowed. This was something the new manager felt he could change by tapping into P&G's extensive technological resources. The successful experience of the foaming massage cloth convinced him that there was a significant opportunity to expand sales by extending the SK-II line beyond its traditional product offerings. For example, he could see an immediate opportunity to move into new segments by adding anti-aging and skin-whitening products to the SK-II range. Although this would take a considerable amount of time and effort, it would exploit internal capabilities and external brand image. Compared to the new-market entry options, investment would be quite low.

An exciting development that would support this home market thrust emerged when he discovered that his SK-II technology and marketing teams had come together to develop an innovative beauty imaging system (BIS). Using the Japanese technicians' skills in miniaturization and software development, they were working to create a simplified version of scientific equipment used by P&G lab technicians to qualify new skin care products by measuring improvements in skin condition. The plan was to install the modified BIS at SK-II counters and have beauty consultants use it to boost the accuracy and credibility of their skin diagnosis. The project fit perfectly with de Cesare's vision for SK-II to become the brand that solved individual skin care problems. He felt it could build significant loyalty in the analytically inclined Japanese consumer.

With the company's having such a small share of such a rich market, de Cesare felt that a strategy of product innovation and superior in-store service had the potential to accelerate a growth rate that had slowed to 5% per annum over the past three years. Although Shiseido could be expected to put up a good fight, he felt SK-II should double sales in Japan over the next six or seven years. In short, de Cesare was extremely excited about SK-II's potential for growth in its home market. He said: "It's a fabulous opportunity. One loyal SK-II customer in Japan already spends about $1,000 a year on the brand. Even a regular consumer of all P&G's other products—from toothpaste and deodorant to shampoo and detergent—all together spends nowhere near that amount annually."

The Chinese Puzzle

A very different opportunity existed in China, where P&G had been operating only since 1988. Because of the

Exhibit 11   Global Skin Care Market Size: 1999

Skin Care (Main market and prestige)

Region/Country	Retail Sales ($ million)	Two-Year Growth Rate
Western Europe	8,736	7%
France	2,019	7
Germany	1,839	14
United Kingdom	1,052	17
North America	6,059	18
United States	5,603	18
Asia/Pacific	11,220	2
China	1,022	28
Japan	6,869	6
South Korea	1,895	9
Taiwan	532	18
Hong Kong	266	6

Source: Company data.

Exhibit 12   Skin Care and Cosmetics Habits and Practices: Selected Countries

Product Usage (% Past 7 Days)	United States[a]	Japan[a]	China[b]	United Kingdom[a]
Facial Moisturizer—Lotion	45%	95%	26%	37%
Facial Moisturizer—Cream	25	28	52	45
Facial Cleansers (excluding Family Bar Soap)	51	90	57	41
Foundation	70	85	35	57
Lipstick	84	97	75	85
Mascara	76	27	13	75

Source: Company data.
[a]Based on broad, representative sample of consumers.
[b]Based on upper-income consumers in Beijing City.

extraordinarily low prices of Chinese laundry products, the company had uncharacteristically led with beauty products when it entered this huge market. Olay was launched in 1989 and, after early problems, eventually became highly successful by adopting a nontraditional marketing strategy. To justify its price premium—its price was 20 to 30 times the price of local skin care products—Shivesh Ram, the entrepreneurial beauty care manager in China, decided to add a service component to Olay's superior product formulation. Borrowing from the Max Factor Japan model, he began selling through counters in the state-owned department stores staffed by beauty counselors. By 1999, Olay had almost 1,000 such counters in China and was a huge success.

As the Chinese market opened to international retailers, department stores from Taiwan, Hong Kong, and Singapore began opening in Beijing and Shanghai. Familiar with Olay as a mass-market brand, they questioned allocating it scarce beauty counter space alongside Estee Lauder, Lancôme, Shiseido, and other premium brands that had already claimed the prime locations critical to success in this business. It was at this point that Ram began exploring the possibility of introducing SK-II, allowing Olay to move more deeply into second-tier department stores, stores in smaller cities, and to "second-floor" cosmetics locations in large stores. "China is widely predicted to become the second-largest market in the world," said Ram. "The prestige beauty segment is growing at 30 to 40% a year, and virtually every major competitor in that space is already here."

Counterbalancing Ram's enthusiastic proposals, de Cesare also heard voices of concern. Beyond the potential impact on a successful Olay market position, some were worried that SK-II would be a distraction to P&G's strategy of becoming a mainstream Chinese company and to its competitive goal of entering 600 Chinese cities ahead of Unilever, Kao, and other global players. They argued that targeting an elite consumer group with a niche product was not in keeping with the objective of reaching the 1.2 billion population with laundry, hair care, oral care, diapers, and other basics. After all, even with SK-II's basic four-step regimen, a three-month supply could cost more than one month's salary for the average woman working in a major Chinese city.

Furthermore, the skeptics wondered if the Chinese consumer was ready for SK-II. Olay had succeeded only by the company's educating its customers to move from a one-step skin care process—washing with bar soap and water—to a three-step cleansing and moisturizing process. SK-II relied on women developing at least a four- to six-step regimen, something the doubters felt was unrealistic. But as Ram and others argued, within the target market, skin care practices were quite developed, and penetration of skin care products was higher than in many developed markets.

Finally, the Chinese market presented numerous other risks, from the widespread existence of counterfeit prestige products to the bureaucracy attached to a one-year import-registration process. But the biggest concern was the likelihood that SK-II would attract import duties of 35% to 40%. This meant that even if P&G squeezed its margin in China, SK-II would have to be priced significantly above the retail level in other markets. Still, the China team calculated that because of the lower cost of beauty consultants, the product could still be profitable. (See Exhibit 13 for cost estimates.)

Despite the critics, Ram was eager to try, and he responded to their concerns: "There are three Chinas—rural China, low-income urban China, and sophisticated, wealthy China concentrated in Shanghai, Beijing, and Guangzhou. The third group is as big a target consumer group as in many developed markets. If we don't move soon, the battle for that elite will be lost to the global beauty care powerhouses that have been here for three years or more."

Ram was strongly supported by his regional beauty care manager and by the Greater China MDO president. Together, they were willing to experiment with a few

Exhibit 13   Global SK-II Cost Structure (% of net sales)[a]

FY1999/2000	Japan	Taiwan/ Hong Kong	PR China Expected	United Kingdom Expected
Net sales	100%	100%	100%	100%
Cost of products sold	22	26	45	29
Marketing, research, and selling/ administrative expense	67	58	44	63
Operating income	11	16	11	8

Source: Company estimates.
[a]Data disguised.

counters in Shanghai, and if successful, to expand to more counters in other major cities. Over the first three years, they expected to generate $10 million to $15 million in sales, by which time they expected the brand to break even. They estimated the initial investment to build counters, train beauty consultants, and support the introduction would probably mean losses of about 10% of sales over that three-year period.

The European Question

As he explored global opportunities for SK-II, de Cesare's mind kept returning to the European market he knew so well. Unlike China, Europe had a relatively large and sophisticated group of beauty-conscious consumers who already practiced a multistep regimen using various specialized skin care products. What he was unsure of was whether there was a significant group willing to adopt the disciplined six- to eight-step ritual that the most devoted Japanese SK-II users followed.

The bigger challenge, in his view, would be introducing a totally new brand into an already crowded field of high-profile, well-respected competitors including Estée Lauder, Clinique, Lancôme, Chanel, and Dior. While TV advertising had proven highly effective in raising SK-II's awareness and sales in Japan, Taiwan, and Hong Kong, the cost of television—or even print—ads in Europe made such an approach there prohibitive. And without any real brand awareness or heritage, he wondered if SK-II's mystique would transfer to a Western market.

As he thought through these issues, de Cesare spoke with his old boss, Mike Thompson, the head of P&G's beauty business in Europe. Because the Max Faxtor sales force sold primarily to mass-distribution outlets, Thompson did not think it provided SK-II the appropriate access to the European market. However, he explained that the fine-fragrance business was beginning to do quite well. In the United Kingdom, for example, its 25-person sales force was on track in 1999 to book $1 million in after-tax profit on sales of $12 million. Because it sold brands such as Hugo Boss, Giorgio, and Beverly Hills to department stores and Boots, the major pharmacy chain, its sales approach and trade relationship was different from the SK-II model in Japan. Nevertheless, Thompson felt it was a major asset that could be exploited.

Furthermore, Thompson told de Cesare that his wife was a loyal SK-II user and reasoned that since she was a critical judge of products, other women would discover the same

benefits in the product she did. He believed that SK-II provided the fine-fragrance business a way to extend its line in the few department stores that dominated U.K. distribution in the prestige business. He thought they would be willing to give SK-II a try. (He was less optimistic about countries such as France and Germany, however, where prestige products were sold through thousands of perfumeries, making it impossible to justify the SK-II consultants who would be vital to the sales model.)

Initial consumer research in the United Kingdom had provided mixed results. But de Cesare felt that while this kind of blind testing could provide useful data on detergents, it was less helpful in this case. The consumers tested the product blind for one week, then were interviewed about their impressions. But because they lacked the beauty counselors' analysis and advice and had not practiced the full skin care regimen, he felt the results did not adequately predict SK-II's potential.

In discussions with Thompson, de Cesare concluded that he could hope to achieve sales of $10 million by the fourth year in the U.K. market. Given the intense competition, he recognized that he would have to absorb losses of $1 million to $2 million annually over that period as the start-up investment.

The Organizational Constraint

While the strategic opportunities were clear, de Cesare also recognized that his decision needed to comply with the organizational reality in which it would be implemented. While GBU head Lafley was an early champion and continuing supporter of SK-II, his boss, Jager, was less committed. Jager was among those in P&G who openly questioned how well some of the products in the beauty care business—particularly some of the acquired brands—fit in the P&G portfolio. While he was comfortable with high-volume products like shampoo, he was more skeptical of the upper end of the line, particularly fine fragrances. In his view, the fashion-linked and promotion-driven sales models of luxury products neither played well to P&G's "stack it high, sell it cheap" marketing skills, nor leveraged its superior technologies.

The other organizational reality was that the implementation of O2005 was causing a good deal of organizational disruption and management distraction. This was particularly true in Europe, as Thompson explained:

We swung the pendulum 180 degrees, from a local to a global focus. Marketing plans and budgets had previously been developed locally, strongly debated with European managers, then rolled up. Now they were developed globally—or at least regionally—by new people who often did not understand the competitive and trade differences across markets. We began to standardize and centralize our policies and practices out of Geneva. Not surprisingly, a lot of our best local managers left the company.

One result of the O2005 change was that country subsidiary GMs now focused more on maximizing sales volume than profits, and this had put the beauty care business under significant budget pressure. Thompson explained the situation in Europe in 1999:

One thing became clear very quickly: It was a lot easier to sell cases of Ariel [detergent] or Pampers [diapers] than cases of cosmetics, so guess where the sales force effort went? At the same time, the new-product pipeline was resulting in almost a "launch of the month," and

with the introduction of new products like Swiffer and Febreze, it was hard for the MDOs to manage all of these corporate priorities. . . . Finally, because cosmetics sales required more time and effort from local sales forces, more local costs were assigned to that business, and that has added to profit pressures.

Framing the Proposal

It was in this context that de Cesare was framing his proposal based on the global potential of SK-II as a brand and his plans to exploit the opportunities he saw. But he knew Lafley's long ties and positive feelings towards SK-II would not be sufficient to convince him. The GBU head was committed to focusing beauty care on the core brands that could be developed as a global franchise, and his questions would likely zero in on whether de Cesare could build SK-II into such a brand.

Silvio Napoli at Schindler India (A)

"Monsieur Napoli, si vous vous plantez ici vous êtes fini! Mais si vous réussissez, vous aurez une très bonne carrière." (Translation: "Mr. Napoli, if you fall on your face here you are finished! But if you succeed, you will have a very nice career.") The words echoed off the walls of Silvio Napoli's empty living room and disappeared down the darkened hallway like startled ghosts. The parquet was still wet from the five inches of water that had flooded the first floor of the Napoli home in suburban New Delhi several days before, during one of the sewer system's periodic backups. Standing in the empty room were Napoli and Luc Bonnard, vice chairman, board of directors of Schindler Holdings Ltd., the respected Swiss-based manufacturer of elevators and escalators. It was November 1998, and Bonnard was visiting New Delhi for the first time to review progress on the start-up of the company's Indian subsidiary, which Napoli had been dispatched to run eight months earlier. Things were not going according to plan.

Napoli, a 33-year-old Italian former semiprofessional rugby player, had arrived in March with his pregnant wife and two young children and had quickly set about creating an entirely new organization from scratch. Since March, he had established offices in New Delhi and Mumbai, hired five Indian top managers, and begun to implement the aggressive business plan he had written the previous year while head of corporate planning in Switzerland. The plan called for a $10 million investment and hinged on selling "core, standardized products," with no allowance for customization. To keep costs down and avoid India's high import tariffs, the plan also proposed that all manufacturing and logistics activities be outsourced to local suppliers.

Shortly before Bonnard's visit, however, Napoli was confronted with three challenges to his plan. First, he learned that for the second time in two months, his Indian managers had approved an order for a nonstandard product—calling for a glass rear wall in one of the supposedly standard elevators. At the same time, his business plan had come under intense cost pressures, first from a large increase in customs duties on imported elevator components, then from an unanticipated rise in transfer prices for the "low-cost" product lines imported from Schindler's European factories. Finally, as Napoli began accelerating his strategy of developing local sources for elevator components, he found that his requests for parts lists, design specifications, and engineering support were not forthcoming from Schindler's European plants.

As the implementation of his business plan stalled, Napoli wondered what he should do. Eight months in India and he still had not installed a single elevator, while his plan showed first-year sales of 50 units. And now Bonnard was visiting. Should he seek his help, propose a revised plan, or try to sort out the challenges himself? These were the thoughts running through Napoli's head as the vice chairman asked him, "So, how are things going so far, Mr. Napoli?"

SCHINDLER'S INDIA EXPLORATIONS

Schindler had a long and rather disjointed history with the Indian market. Although its first elevator in India was installed in 1925, the company did not have a local market presence until it appointed a local distributor in the late 1950s. Almost 40 years later, Schindler decided it was time to take an even bolder step and enter the market through its own wholly owned subsidiary.

The Growing Commitment

Established in 1874 in Switzerland by Robert Schindler, the company began manufacturing elevators in 1889. Almost a century later, the 37-year-old Alfred N. Schindler became the fourth generation of the family to

This case was prepared by Professors Christopher A. Bartlett and Michael Y. Yashino with the assistance of Perry L. Fagan.

lead the company, in 1987. Over the next decade, he sought to transform the company's culture from that of an engineering-based manufacturing company to one of a customer-oriented service company.

By 1998, Schindler had worldwide revenues of 6.6 billion Swiss francs (US$4 billion) and was widely perceived as the technology leader in elevators. It was also the number one producer of escalators in the world. The company employed over 38,000 people in 97 subsidiaries but did not yet have its own operations in India, a market Alfred Schindler felt had great potential.

Although the first Schindler elevator in India was installed in 1925, it was not until 1958 that the company entered into a long-term distribution agreement with ECE, an Indian company. In 1985, Schindler terminated that agreement and entered into a technical collaboration with Mumbai-based Bharat Bijlee Ltd. (BBL) to manufacture, market, and sell its elevators. After acquiring a 12% equity stake in BBL, Schindler supported the local company as it became the number two player in the Indian elevator market, with a 10%–15% share a decade later.

On assuming the role of chairman in 1995, Alfred Schindler decided to take a six-month "sabbatical" during which he wanted to step back and review the long-term strategy of Schindler. As part of that process, he undertook to travel through several markets—China, Japan, and several other Far Eastern markets—that he felt were important to the company's growth. He spent several weeks in India, traveling over 3,000 kilometers in a small Ford rental car. "After his trip Mr. Schindler saw India as a second China," said a manager in Switzerland. "He saw huge growth potential. And once he targets something, he's like a hawk."

With the objective of raising its involvement, Schindler proposed to BBL that a separate joint venture be created for the elevator business, with Schindler taking management control. But negotiations proved difficult and eventually collapsed. In late 1996, collaboration with BBL ended, and the company began considering options to establish its own operation in India.

Silvio Napoli's Role

Meanwhile, after graduating from the MBA program at Harvard Business School, Silvio Napoli had joined Schindler in September 1994. He accepted a position at the company's headquarters in Ebikon, Switzerland, reporting directly to the CEO as head of corporate planning.

With its 120 years of history, Schindler was a formal Swiss company where the hierarchy was clear, politeness important, and first names rarely used. Napoli's office was on the top floor of the seven-story headquarters building, a floor reserved for the three members of the company's executive committee and the legal counsel. (For profiles of top management, see Exhibit 1.) "As soon as I arrived, I was aware that people were very responsive to my requests," said Napoli. "Just by my physical location, I had generated fearful respect, and I realized I would have to manage my situation very carefully." A 20-year Schindler veteran recalled his reaction to Napoli's arrival: "He was the assistant to Mr. Schindler, so I knew I'd better be nice to him."

As head of corporate planning, Napoli was responsible for coordinating the annual strategic review process and undertaking external benchmarking and competitor analysis. But his most visible role was as staff to the corporate executive committee, the Verwaltungsrat Ausschuss (VRA)—which was composed of Alfred Schindler, Luc Bonnard, and Alfred Spöerri, the chief financial officer. As the only nonmember to attend VRA meetings, Napoli was responsible for taking meeting minutes and for following up on action items and special projects defined by the VRA.

The Swatch Project

In 1995, Napoli took on the Swatch Project, a major assignment that grew out of a concern by VRA members that margins on new-product sales were eroding as each competitor strove to expand its installed base of elevators. Since such sales were a vital source of profitable long-term maintenance and service contracts, the project's imperative goal was to develop a standardized elevator at a dramatically lower cost than the existing broad line of more customized products.

It was a project that involved the young newcomer in sensitive discussions with Schindler's plants in Switzerland, France, and Spain to discuss design, determine costs, and explore sourcing alternatives. Napoli described the process and outcome of the Swatch Project:

> As you might imagine, I was viewed with some suspicion and concern. Here was this young MBA talking about getting costs down or outsourcing core tasks that the plants felt they owned. . . . In the end, we developed the S001, an elevator that could not be customized, used many parts obtained from outside suppliers, and incorporated processes

Exhibit 1   Schindler Top Management Profiles

Name:	ALFRED N. SCHINDLER	LUC BONNARD	ALFRED SPÖERRI
Position:	Chairman and Chief Executive Officer	Vice Chairman of the Board and Member of the Executive Committee	Member of the Board of Directors Member of the Executive Committee
Date of Birth:	March 21, 1949	October 8, 1946	August 22, 1938
Education:	1976–1978: MBA, Wharton, USA 1974–1976: Certified Public Accountant School, Bern 1969–1974: University of Basel–Law School (lic. jur.), Abschluss:lic.iur.	1971: Diploma in Electrical Engineering at ETH (Technical University), Zurich	
Experience:	Since 1995: Chairman of the Board and Chief Executive Officer 1985–1995: Chairman of the Corporate Executive (CEO) 1984–1985: Member of Corporate Management 1982–1984: Head of Corporate Planning 1978–1979: Deputy Head of Corporate Planning	1996: Vice Chairman 1991–1996: Member of the Executive Committee 1986–1990: COO Elevators and Escalators, Member Corporate Executive Committee 1985–1986: Member, Executive Committee 1983–1985: Group Management Member, North Europe 1973: Management, Schindler, in France	1991–1998: Member, Executive Committee 1997–1998: Chief Financial Officer 1979–1988: Corporate Controller—Treasurer 1975–1979: COO of Mexico 1971–1974: Area Controller, Latin America 1968–1974: Financial Officer of Mexico 1968: Joined Schindler Group

Source: Schindler India.

never before seen in the group. All of this was unthinkable in the past. We redesigned the entire supply chain and halved the industry's standard 20- to 30-week cycle time.

The Indian Entry Project

Meanwhile, as negotiations with BBL broke down in India, the VRA decided to engage Boston Consulting Group (BCG) to identify and evaluate alternative local partners with whom Schindler might build a more significant business in India. As the company's point man on the project, Napoli worked with the consultants to narrow the list of 34 potential partners to eight candidates for review by the VRA.

As the team pursued the final choices, however, they found that there was no ideal partner. When it was determined that it was now legally and practically feasible to start up a 100% wholly owned company in India, the VRA asked Napoli and the head of Schindler's mergers and acquisitions department to explore that option.

Napoli contacted experts in India who helped him expand his understanding of the situation. Through discussions with market experts and studies by local consultants, Napoli spent nine months developing a detailed analysis of the market size, legal environment, and competitive situation in the Indian elevator market. He integrated this into a business plan for Schindler's market entry and submitted it to the VRA. The plan was approved in October. Soon after, Napoli was offered the job of creating the Indian subsidiary. Napoli recalled his reaction:

> I realized that the future manager of the new company would be key to the success of the business plan I had been working on. Deep down, I knew I could do it and was conscious that my early involvement made me an ideal candidate. So when the offer came, I was not surprised. More surprising was the reaction of my headquarters' colleagues, who thought I was crazy to take such a high-risk career move that involved dragging my family to a developing country.

Bonnard explained the choice of Napoli:

> There are two possible profiles in a country like India. The first is a young guy [who] knows the company, people, and products; the second is someone who is 55 years old with grown kids looking for a new challenge. . . .
>
> Silvio knew lots of people. He was open to go new ways. We needed someone who could handle different cultures,

who was young and flexible. We needed to trust the person we sent, and we trusted Mr. Napoli 100%. And we needed a generalist, not a pure specialist. We needed someone who had courage. Finally, I believe that the people who make the business plan should have to realize it. Of course, we also needed to have someone who was willing to go.

In November Napoli and his wife Fabienne, a French-German dual national, made their first trip to India. "We went on a 'look and see' visit, starting in Mumbai," Napoli recounted. "When we arrived in Delhi my wife looked around and said she would be more comfortable living here. After reaching an agreement on the relocation package back in Switzerland, I accepted the job."

Over the next several months, Napoli made three more trips to India to lay the groundwork for the move. In one key move, he engaged the executive search firm Egon Zehnder to identify candidates for his top management team. Although he had to await government approval to start the new company, when he moved to India, he wanted to have key managers in place.

FORMING SCHINDLER INDIA

As vice president for South Asia, Napoli was responsible for India and a few nearby export markets in Schindler's elevators and escalators division (see Exhibit 2). In March, Napoli relocated to India and began the task of building the company that would implement his business plan.

New Culture, New Challenges

On his first day in the Delhi office, Napoli got stuck in one of BBL's elevators. It proved to be an omen of things to come. He recalled:

> On our first morning in Delhi, six hours after the family had landed, my 2-year-old daughter opened her forehead falling in the hotel room. The deep wound required hospitalization and stitching under total anesthesia. Two weeks later, Fabienne got infectious food poisoning, which required one-week hospitalization, threatening a miscarriage. The day she came back from hospital, my 3-year-old son fell in the hotel bathroom and broke his front tooth. Rushing to an emergency dentist in a hotel car, I really wondered, for the only time in my life, whether I could stand this much longer.

Although Napoli and his family were in New Delhi, where he had opened a marketing and service office, he

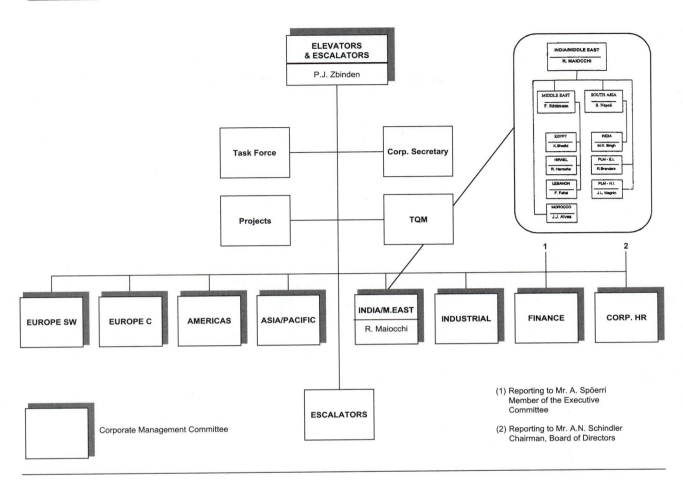

Source: Schindler Management Ltd.

spent most of a typical week at the company's headquarters in Mumbai. "The first two months were really a hard-fought battle between family relocation and company start-up," he recalled. "Weeks were consumed shuttling between Delhi and Mumbai, hunting for office space, filing government registrations, and completing legal paperwork. On the family front, I had to get them started in a totally different system: housing, schools, doctors, grocery shopping . . . all things which are totally different in India."

In the process, Napoli found he had to adapt his management approach. "For example," he recalled, "all types of characters started to approach me offering their services. They had heard that I was representing a Swiss firm about to invest in India. I soon learned to be careful in trusting anybody."

Recruiting the Team

Meanwhile, Egon Zehnder had identified several promising candidates for top positions in the new company. Mehar Karan ("M.K.") Singh, 42, was tapped for the role of managing director, a position that reported to Napoli but was viewed as a stepping stone to heading the subsidiary. (For profiles of key Indian managers, see Exhibit 3.) "At some point in your career you will report to someone younger than yourself," said Singh. "I decided that Schindler was an exciting opportunity to test this scenario."

Exhibit 3   Schindler India: Key Managers' Profiles

Name:	SILVIO NAPOLI	MEHAR KARAN SINGH	T.A.K. MATTHEWS	RONNIE DANTE	JUJUDHAN JENA
Position:	Vice President, Schindler South Asia	Managing Director	Vice President—Field Operations	General Manager—Engineering	Chief Financial Officer
Date of Birth:	August 23, 1965	April 12, 1955	March 12, 1964	November 3, 1959	March 3, 1967
Education:	1992–1994: MBA, Harvard University Graduate School of Business Administration, Boston, Massachusetts 1984–1989: Graduate degree in Materials Science Engineering, Swiss Federal Institute of Technology (EPFL), Lausanne, Switzerland; Lausanne University rugby captain (1987) 1983–1984: Ranked among top 20% foreign students admitted to EPFL, one-year compulsory selection program, Swiss Federal Institute of Technology (EPFL), Cours de Mathematiques Special, Lausanne, Switzerland	1977: B.E.—Mechanical Engineering: ranked top of his class in Indian Institute of Technology, Delhi, India 1979: MBA, Indian Institute of Management, Ahmedabad, India (Awarded President of India's Gold Medal)	1986: B.Sc.—Civil Engineering, University of Dar-E-Salaam, Tanzania 1989: MBA, Birla Institute of Technology, Ranchi, India	1977: HSC, D.G. Ruparel College, Mumbai, India	1990: Chartered Accountant, Institute of Chartered Accountancy, India

Exhibit 3   Schindler India: Key Managers' Profiles (continued)

Name:	SILVIO NAPOLI	MEHAR KARAN SINGH	T.A.K. MATTHEWS	RONNIE DANTE	JUJUDHAN JENA
Experience:	*Since 1998:* Vice President, South Asia, Schindler Management Ltd.	*Since 1998:* Managing Director, Schindler India Pvt. Ltd., Mumbai, India	*Since 1998:* Vice President—Field Operations, Schindler India Pvt. Ltd., Mumbai	*Since 1998:* General Manager—Engineering, Schindler India Pvt. Ltd., Mumbai	*Since 1998:* Chief Financial Officer, Schindler India Pvt. Ltd., Mumbai
	1994–1997: Vice President, Head of Corporate Planning, Schindler, Switzerland	*1979–1998:* Head of Projects and Development Group, Taj Group of Hotels, India (setting up hotels in India and abroad; joint ventures with state governments, local authorities, and international investors, including the Singapore Airlines, Gulf Co-operation Council Institutional investors. Responsible for financial restructuring of the international operations after the Gulf War, culminating with the successful 1995 GDR offering).	*1998:* Modernization Manager, Otis Elevator Company, Mumbai	*1995–1998:* National Field Engineering Manager, Otis Elevator, Mumbai	*1997–1998:* Financial Controller, Kellogg India Ltd., Mumbai
	1991–1992: Technical Market Development Specialist, Dow Europe, Rheinmuenster, Germany		*1989–1998:* Otis Elevator Company, New Delhi	*1991–1995:* National Field Auditor, Otis Elevator, Mumbai	*1996–1997:* Group Manager, Procter & Gamble India Ltd., Mumbai
	1989–1991: Technical Service & Development Engineer, Dow Deutscheland, Rheinmuenster, Germany		• Service & Service Sales Manager	*1989–1991:* Supervisor, Otis Elevator	*1995–1996:* Treasury Manager, Procter & Gamble India Ltd.
	1989–1992: French Semi-Pro Rugby League (Strasbourg)		• Construction Manager	*1984–1989:* Commissioning of New Products, Otis Elevator, Singapore, Malaysia, and Mumbai	*1990–1995:* Financial Analyst, Procter & Gamble India Ltd.
			• Assistant Construction Manager	*1982–1984:* Commissioning Engineer, Otis Elevator Company, Gujarat	
			• Management Trainee	*1977–1982:* Apprentice, Otis Elevator Company, Maharashtra	
			1986–1987: Civil Engineer, Construction Companies, Tanzania		

Napoli explained the choice of Singh: "Having led construction projects for some of India's largest hotels, M.K. had firsthand experience in building an organization from scratch. But most of all, he had been on our customers' side. He would know how to make a difference in service." In addition, being 10 years older and having grown up in India, Singh brought valuable experience and a different perspective. He was also more sensitive to organizational power and relationships, as Napoli soon recognized:

> The first question M.K. asked me after joining the company was, "Who are your friends inside the company? Who doesn't like you?" I never thought about it this way. And I said to him: "Listen, you have to come out with a sense of that yourself. As far as I know, probably people are a little bit cautious of me because they know I used to work for the big bosses at headquarters."

To head field operations (sales, installation, and maintenance) Napoli hired T.A.K. Matthews, 35, who had worked for nine years at Otis India. Matthews recalled: "I had been approached before by elevator people, but after hearing a bit about Schindler's plans, I realized that you don't have a chance to get involved with a start-up every day." For Napoli, Matthews brought the business expertise he needed: "With M.K. and I as generalists, I absolutely needed someone with direct elevator experience to complement our management team. T.A.K. came across as a dynamic and ambitious hands-on manager waiting for the chance to exploit his potential."

Next, Napoli hired Ronnie Dante, 39, as his general manager for engineering. Dante had 24 years of experience at Otis. "Even with T.A.K., we missed a real hardcore elevator engineer capable of standing his ground in front of his European counterparts," said Napoli. "Such people are the authentic depositories of an unpublished science, and they are really very hard to find. Honestly, nobody in the group expected us to find and recruit someone like Ronnie. He is truly one of the best."

Hired to head the company's human resources department, Pankaj Sinha, 32, recalled his interview: "Mr. Napoli and Mr. Singh interviewed me together. There was a clarity in terms of what they were thinking that was very impressive." Napoli offered his assessment of Sinha: "Mr. Schindler had convinced me that the company really needed a front-line HR manager who was capable of developing a first-class organization. But I certainly did not want a traditional Indian ivory tower personnel director. Pankaj

convinced us to hire him through his sheer determination to care about our employees."

Finally, he recruited Jujudhan Jena, 33, as his chief financial officer. (See Exhibit 4 for an organization chart.) Napoli explained his approach to hiring: "You try to see whether the character of the person is compatible with yours, whether you have a common set of values, which in our case range from high ethical standards, integrity, assiduousness to work, and drive. Mostly we were looking for people with the right attitude and energy, not just for elevator people."

Developing the Relationships

As soon as the senior managers were on board, Napoli began working to develop them into an effective team. He recalled the early meetings with his new hires:

> Because some of them were still finishing up their previous jobs, the first Schindler India staff meetings were held at night, in the Delhi Hotel lounge. I'll never forget working together on our first elevator project offer, late after holding a series of interviews for the first employees who would report to the top team. But most of those "undercover" sessions were dedicated to educating the new team about their new company and building consensus around our business plan. . . . The team was really forged through days of late work, fueled by the common motivation to see our project succeed.

In the team-forming process, the different management styles and personal characteristics of Schindler India's new leaders became clear. Even before he was assigned to India, Napoli was recognized as a "strongheaded and single-minded manager," as one manager at Swiss headquarters described him. "There couldn't have been a better environment to send Silvio than India," said another Swiss colleague. "He wants everything done yesterday. And in India, things don't get done yesterday."

Napoli acknowledged the personal challenge. "To survive in India you have to be half monk and half warrior," he said. "I was certainly more inclined to the warrior side, and when I left Switzerland, Mr. Bonnard told me, 'You will have to work on your monk part.'"

Napoli's Indian staff and colleagues described him as "driving very hard," "impulsive," "impatient," and at times "overcommunicative." "Mr. Napoli gets angry when deadlines are not met," added a member of his New Delhi staff. "He's a pretty hard taskmaster." The HR director, Sinha, was more circumspect: "Silvio has a lot

Exhibit 4   Schindler India Organization Chart

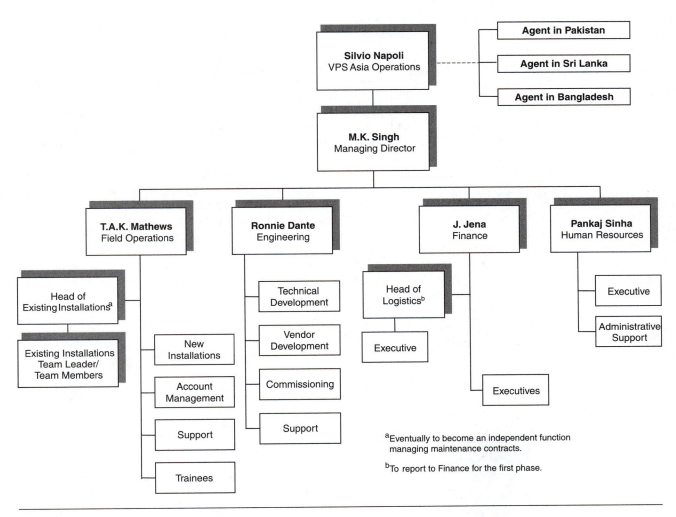

Source: Schindler India.

of energy. When he focuses on an issue he manages to get everybody else's focus in that direction."

Descriptions of Napoli contrasted sharply with those of Singh, whom one manager saw as "friendly and easygoing." Another described him as "much more patient, but he can also be tough." Jena, the finance director, reflected on his first encounter with the two company leaders: "During the interview Silvio came across banging on the table, but I don't think that concerned me. Still, I remember wondering during the interview how two guys as different as M.K. and Silvio would fit

together in a start-up." Matthews, the field operations manager, added another perspective:

It's true that if you look at Silvio, M.K., and myself we are very different. At first we had sessions where the discussion would get pulled in every direction, but I think at the end of the day, it did bring about a balance. I would put it this way. Silvio came to India from Switzerland. But things here are very different: You can't set your watch by the Indian trains. M.K. came from the hotel industry where even if you say "no," it's always made to sound like "yes."

"Silvio was the driver and clearly was the boss," said an Indian executive. "M.K. was great in helping Silvio understand the Indian environment. Having worked in the hotel industry he had a very good network. He had been on the customer side. But he had to learn the elevator business."

Out of this interaction emerged a company culture that employees described as "informal," "open," "responsive," and "proactive." It was also a lean, efficient organization. For example, furniture and office space were rented, and there were only two secretaries in the company—one for the Delhi office and one for Mumbai. "Everyone must do their own administrative work or they won't survive," said Singh.

THE INDIA BUSINESS PLAN

As soon as his team was in place, Napoli worked to gain their commitment to his business plan. At its core were two basic elements: the need to sell a focused line of standard products, and the ability to outsource key manufacturing and logistics functions. This plan had been built on an analysis of the Indian market and competitive environment that Napoli also communicated to his team. (See Exhibits 5 and 6 for data from the plan.)

The Indian Elevator Market in 1998

Economic liberalization in India in the early 1990s had revived the construction industry, and along with it, the fortunes of the elevator industry. Roughly 50% of demand was for low-tech manual elevators, typically fitted with unsafe manual doors (see Exhibit 5). A ban on collapsible gate elevators had been approved by the Indian Standards Institute, and, at the urging of the Indian government, individual states were making the ban legally enforceable. The low end of the market was characterized by intense competition among local companies. The ban, when fully implemented, was expected to make this market segment more interesting to major international players.

The middle segment of the market was promising due to India's rapid urbanization. The resulting shortage of space in Mumbai and fast-growing cities such as Bangalore, Pune, and Madras was leading to the development of low- and

---

Exhibit 5 Indian Elevator Market, Structure, and Product Segmentation

Indian Market Structure

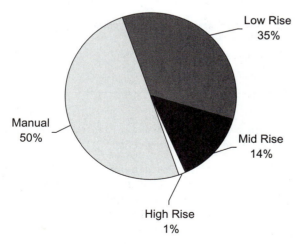

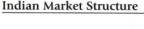
■ Low Rise ■ Mid Rise □ High Rise □ Manual

Segment	Stops	Speeds MPS	Schindler Products
Manual	2–8	0.5–0.7	NIL
Low rise	2–15	0.6–1.5	S001
Mid rise	16–25	1.5	S300P
High rise	>25	>1.5	S300P

Source: Schindler India.

Exhibit 6   Market Research on Indian Elevator Market, 1996

Unprompted Recall of Elevator Brands—Builders

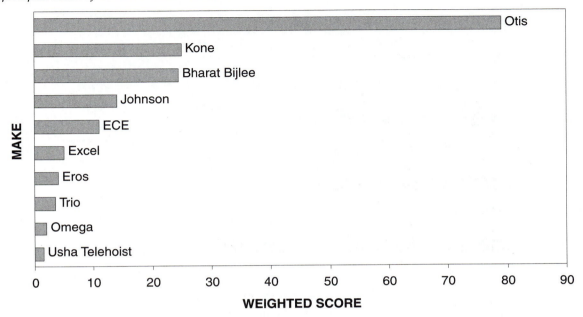

Factors Influencing Elevator Purchase—Unprompted Listing—Builders

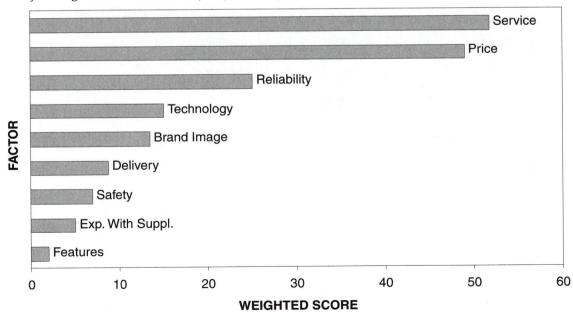

Exhibit 6   Market Research on Indian Elevator Market, 1996 (continued)

Comparative Rating of Elevator Makes—Builders

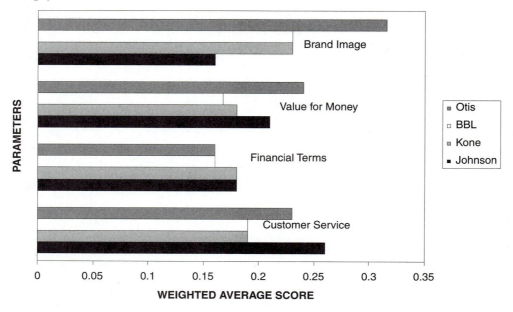

Preferred Communication Channels—Builders

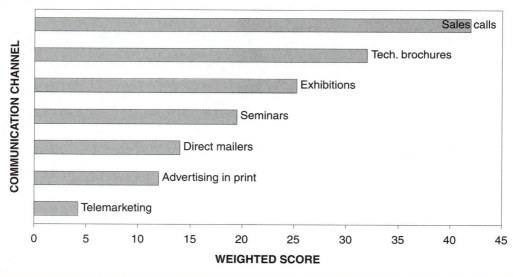

Source: Schindler India.

mid-rise buildings. Concurrently, traditional builders were becoming more sophisticated and professionalized, leading to an emphasis on better services and facilities and on higher quality, safer, and more technologically advanced elevators.

At the top end of the market, demand was growing for top-quality, high-rise office premises and housing facilities, particularly from multinational companies. Tourism was also expanding, greatly aiding the domestic hotel industry, a major buyer of top-line elevators. Although the top-end segment was small, the average value per elevator was five to six times that in the low end.

At the end of 1997, the installed base of elevators in India was 40,000, with an estimated 5,600 units sold during the year. Although this installed base was small compared with those of China (140,000 units) and Japan (400,000 units), India's growth potential was significant. The rapidly expanding residential segment accounted for 70% of the Indian market, followed by the commercial segment (office buildings and shopping centers) with a 20% share. The balance was accounted for by hotels (4%) and others (6%). Total revenues for the industry were US$125 million, including service income. For the first half of the decade, the market grew at a compound annual rate of 17% in units and 27% by value, but in 1996, a slump in the real estate market slowed unit growth to 10%. The unit growth forecast for 1998 was 5% but was expected to rise to 8%–12% in subsequent years. Together, Mumbai and New Delhi represented 60% of the total Indian elevator market.

In India, most sales were of single-speed elevators (65%), followed by two-speed (20%), variable frequency (13%), and hydraulic (2%). Sales of single-speed elevators dominated the residential market, while variable frequency was most commonly used in higher-end commercial applications. Although the Indian market was biased toward the simplest products, it was expected to shift gradually toward two-speed or higher technology in the future.

Competition

Napoli's business plan also documented that four major players accounted for more than three-quarters of the Indian market value: Otis (50%), BBL (8.6%), Finland's Kone (8.8%), and ECE (8.4%). Mitsubishi had recently begun importing premium elevators for hotels and commercial developments, and Hyundai Elevators had entered into a joint venture to manufacture high-end elevators in India. At this stage, however, they accounted for only 1% of

sales. With the exception of Mitsubishi, all multinational players relied on local manufacturing for the majority of their components. The remaining 23% of the market—mostly the price-sensitive low end—was controlled by 25 regional players characterized by a lack of technical expertise and limited access to funds.

Otis India had an installed base of 26,000 elevators, 16,000 of which were under maintenance contracts. It manufactured its own components, spare parts, and fixtures at an aging plant in Mumbai and a new state-of-the-art manufacturing plant near Bangalore. The company staffed 70 service centers, including a national service center in Mumbai, and held an estimated 85% of the high-end hotels and commercial segment. ("You couldn't name any building over 15 floors that did not have an Otis elevator," said ex-Otis employee Matthews. "Otis, Otis, Otis. Any special equipment, it goes Otis. Any fast elevator goes Otis.") Otis was reportedly one of the most profitable industrial companies in India, and its 3,500 employees had an average tenure of 20 years.

The Indian market was highly price sensitive, and there was agreement among industry analysts that elevators were becoming commodity products and that price pressures would increase. However, surveys indicated that service was also key to the builder's buying decision, as were the supplier's financial terms (Exhibit 6).

The elevator life cycle had seven distinct phases: engineering, production, installation, service, repair, modernization, and replacement. Over the 30-year life cycle of an elevator, the first three stages accounted for about one-third of the labor content but only 20% of the profits. In contrast, the latter four accounted for two-thirds of labor content but 80% of profits. As a result, annual maintenance contracts covering routine maintenance and breakdown service were vital. (High-margin spare parts were billed separately.) Service response time varied across segments. Most five-star hotels with multiple installations had a technician on call or on-site; for important commercial buildings and hospitals, the response time was usually within two hours, but many residential and some commercial customers reported an average response time of between six and eight hours.

The Standard Product Strategy

Napoli's analysis of the Indian environment coupled with his work on the Swatch Project led him to conclude that the most effective way for Schindler to enter this market would be to focus on a narrow product line of simple, standardized elevators. Although this was a radically different approach from that of his key competitors, he felt that Schindler could not compete just by matching what others did. It had to find its own unique source of advantage.

He proposed building the business around the Schindler 001 (S001)—the product developed in the Swatch Project—and the Schindler 300P (S300P), a more sophisticated model being manufactured in southeast Asia. The plan was to use the S001 to win share in the low-rise segment as a primary target, then pick up whatever sales the company could in the mid-rise and high-rise segments with the S300P.

Both products could be adapted to meet Indian requirements with only minor modifications (e.g., adding a ventilator, a fire rescue controller function, a stop button, and different guide rails). Equally important, both products could be priced appropriately for the local market as long as the company stuck to the principle of no customization. The plan called for Schindler India to sell 50 units in the first year and to win a 20% share of the target segments in five years. It aimed to break even after four years and eventually to generate double-digit margins.

After communicating this strategy to his management team, Napoli was pleased when they came back with an innovative approach to selling the standard line. If the product was standardized, they argued, the sales and service should be differentiated. Singh's experience with hotel construction led him to conclude that projects were more effectively managed when one individual was responsible for designing, planning, contracting, and implementing. Yet, as Matthews knew, the traditional sales structure in the elevator industry had different specialists dedicated to sales, technical, and installation, each of whom handed the project off to the next person. Together, these managers proposed to Napoli that Schindler organize around an account-management concept designed to give the customer a single "hassle-free" point of contact.

The Outsourcing Strategy

India's high import duties had forced most foreign elevator companies to manufacture locally. But again, Napoli chose a different approach. To keep overheads low, his business plan proposed a radical sourcing concept for the S001 that was expected to account for 75% of sales: Schindler India would have no in-house manufacturing, no centralized assembly, no logistics infrastructure.

Instead, the production of most components for the dominant S001 model would be outsourced to approved local suppliers. (The S300P would be wholly imported from southeast Asia.) Schindler would manufacture only safety-related components (the safety gear and speed governor, together representing 10% of the value), which would be imported from Europe. In addition, the entire logistics function would be outsourced to an internationally reputed logistics service provider. Some basic installation work—part of the on-site assembly of the drive, controller, car, doors, rails, and counterweight—would also be outsourced. However, maintenance contracts resulting from new sales would stay with Schindler.

Inspired by the local automotive industry—Mercedes outsourced most components of its Indian vehicles—Napoli believed he could set up a local manufacturing network that would preserve Schindler's quality reputation. To ensure this, localization of each component would follow the same "product-creation process" criteria used by Schindler worldwide. Furthermore, before the first pre-series batch could be released, it would face an additional hurdle of testing and approval by experts from Schindler's European factories and competence centers.

FROM ANALYSIS TO ACTION: IMPLEMENTING THE PLAN

By June, Napoli's management team members had settled into their roles, and the newly hired sales force was in the field. Almost immediately, however, the young expatriate leader began to experience questions, challenges, and impediments to his carefully prepared business plan.

Business Challenges

From the outset, several of Napoli's managers had questioned him on the feasibility of his plan. In particular, those from the elevator industry wondered how the company would survive selling only standard elevators. They also worried about the outsourcing strategy, because no other company in the industry worked this way. "Some of the doubts were expressed as questions," said Napoli. "Many more were unspoken, and my guess is they thought, 'We'll soon convince this crazy guy from Europe that we have to do something a bit less unusual.'"

In August, Napoli traveled to Italy to be with his wife when she gave birth to their third child. On one of his daily telephone calls to key managers in India, he discovered that the company had accepted an order for an expensive glass pod elevator that was to be imported from Europe. "I was at first just surprised, then pretty angry, since it clearly was a violation of the strategy we had all agreed on," said Napoli. "The project was committed, and it was too late to stop it. But I had a long talk with M.K. and followed it up with an e-mail reminding him and the others of our strategy."

After his return to India, Napoli was delighted when he heard that the company had won another order for four S001 elevators for a government building in Mumbai. It was only in later conversations with a field salesperson that he discovered that there was a possibility of a significant modification to the standard specification—once again involving a glass wall. Although the managers insisted that this was really a minor modification to an otherwise standard product, Napoli believed that installing it would be much more difficult than they expected.

The next challenge to his plan came when the first order for elevators was placed to Schindler's plants in Europe. Napoli was shocked when he saw the order confirmation listing transfer prices on the basic S001 30% above the costs he had used to prepare his plans. "When I called to complain, they told me that my calculations had been correct six months ago, but costs had increased, a new transfer costing system had been introduced subsequently," recalled Napoli.

The impact of the transfer price increase was made worse by the new budget the Indian government had passed during the summer. It included increased import duties on specific "noncore goods" including elevators, whose rates increased from 22% to 56%. Napoli recalled the impact:

> This was devastating to our planned break-even objectives. The first thing I did was to accelerate our plans to outsource the S001 as soon as possible. We immediately started working with the European plants to get design details, production specifications, and so on. Unfortunately, the plants were not quick to respond, and we were becoming frustrated at our inability to get their assistance in setting up alternative local sources.

Reflections of a Middle Manager

As darkness enveloped the neighborhood surrounding his townhouse, Napoli sat in his living room reflecting on his job. Outside, the night was filled with the sounds of barking dogs and the piercing whistles of the estate's security patrol. "Each family here has its own security guard," he explained. "But because guards fall asleep at their posts, our neighborhood association hired a man who patrols the neighborhood blowing his whistle at each guard post and waiting for a whistle in response. But now the whistling has gotten so bad that some families have begun paying this man not to whistle in front of their houses. Incredible, isn't it?"

Thinking back on his nine months in his new job, Napoli described the multiple demands. On one hand, he had to resolve the challenges he faced in India. On the other, he had to maintain contact with the European organization to ensure he received the support he needed. And on top of both these demands was an additional expectation that the company's top management had of this venture. Napoli explained:

> When we were discussing the business plan with Mr. Schindler, he said, "India will be our Formula One racing track." In the auto industry, 90% of all innovations are developed for and tested on Formula One cars and then reproduced on a much larger scale and adapted for the mass market. We are testing things in India—in isolation and on a fast track—that probably could not be done anywhere else in the company. The expectation is that what we prove can be adapted to the rest of the group.

While the viability of the Formula One concept was still unclear, Alfred Schindler commented on Napoli's experience:

> This job requires high energy and courage. It's a battlefield experience. This is the old economy, where you have to get involved in the nitty-gritty. We don't pay the big bucks or give stock options. We offer the pain, surprises, and challenges of implementation. The emotions start when you have to build what you have written. Mr. Napoli is feeling what it means to be in a hostile environment where nothing works as it should.

Napoli reflected, "You know the expression, 'It's lonely at the top?' Well, I'm not at the top, but I feel lonely in the middle. . . . I have to somehow swim my way through this ocean. Meanwhile, we have yet to install a single elevator and have no maintenance portfolio." At this point, Napoli's reflections were interrupted by the question of visiting vice chairman Luc Bonnard, "So, how are things going so far, Mr. Napoli?"

Samsung Electronics Company: Global Marketing Operations

In August 2003, Eric Kim, executive vice president for Global Marketing Operations at Samsung Electronics Company (SEC), was delighted about Samsung's latest position in *BusinessWeek's* annual ranking of the world's most valuable brands. "We are number 25 this year with an estimated valuation of $10.8 billion, up 31% from number 34 and $8.3 billion last year. We are the only Korean brand on the top 100 list, we were the fastest-growing of all 100 brands in 2002, and we're closing in on Sony, which is ranked at 20 this year with a $13.2 billion valuation compared to 21 and $13.9 billion last year."

When Kim became the head of marketing in 2000, Samsung was not even ranked. "Ten years ago, Samsung was a third-tier commodity brand with very little product differentiation," noted Kim. "Now, we're knocking on the door of the premier league, earlier than I ever thought possible." Kim and the top management of Samsung would be meeting soon to discuss how Samsung could reach the top 10 by 2005, completing the company's transformation from an also-ran into a blockbuster brand. Kim's job was to lead Samsung's global marketing and brand building efforts in order to achieve this goal. As Kim explained: "Achieving a high level of awareness is the first step. We have done this. But becoming a truly preferred brand is a whole different challenge."[1]

COMPANY BACKGROUND AND STRATEGY

The Samsung conglomerate's roots dated back to 1938 when the company produced agricultural products. In the 1970s, the company focused on shipbuilding, chemicals and textiles.

Samsung Electronics Company (SEC)[2] was founded in 1969, primarily as a low-cost manufacturer of black-and-white televisions. In the 1970s, Samsung acquired a semiconductor business, thereby setting the stage for future growth in electronics. Throughout the 1980s, SEC supplied global markets with massive quantities of commodity products like televisions, VCRs and microwave ovens. The company sold its products to original equipment manufacturers (OEM), who resold them under their own, better-known brand names. During this time, the company's mission increasingly emphasized manufacturing quality and technical leadership, especially leadership among consumer electronics companies. Profits from these activities were reinvested in research and development and in state-of-the-art manufacturing and supply chain activities.

In 1997, in the wake of the Asian financial crisis, SEC sales were $16 billion with negative net profits. At this time, the very survival of the company seemed in jeopardy, prompting major restructuring efforts. Samsung's debt of $15 billion in 1997 had been dramatically reduced to $4.6 billion by 2002. In this period, net margins rose from - 3% to 13%.

In fact, the Asian financial crisis provided the impetus necessary for change, forcing company executives to dismiss 29,000 workers and to sell off $2 billion worth of corporate assets. As Kim explained, "The economic crisis, in my view, impressed upon people the need for a system that could create a resilient and enduring value proposition unique to Samsung — products that would distinguish us from our competitors."[3]

In 2002, Samsung recorded net profits of $5.9 billion on sales of $44.6 billion compared to $2.8 billion and

---

1 "Samsung Electronics Marketing Special: Brand Reloaded—analyzing the world's fastest growing brand," CLSA Emerging Markets, May 2003.
2 All references to Samsung or SEC refer to Samsung Electronics Company, and not to other affiliate companies or the Samsung conglomerate.
3 "Samsung Electronics Marketing Special: Brand Reloaded—analyzing the world's fastest growing brand," CLSA Emerging Markets, May 2003.

$28 billion in 1999. Exhibit 1 shows the growth in revenues and profits between 1997 and 2002.

By 2003, Samsung was the most widely held stock among all emerging market companies due in part to relatively transparent disclosure practices. Over half of Samsung shares were held outside Korea and the stock price had increased tenfold between 1997 and 2002. The company had a market capitalization of $41 billion in 2002, making it the largest Asian electronics company by this measure.

Samsung Electronics' chairman, Kun Hee Lee, led the transformation. In 1993, Mr. Lee launched the "New Management Initiative" which set out to remake Samsung as a global business leader. It was the changes that followed from this initiative that saved the company during the Asian financial crisis and streamlined the company into a profitable enterprise. Throughout the 1990s, Lee demanded the rethinking of key fundamentals and set the stage for long-term commitment to investment in innovative, premium products and brand value. Following the chairman's new management initiative and the appointment of Yun Jong Yong as vice chairman in 1997, the company pursued a bold combination of strategies, many of which seemingly contradicted conventional wisdom.

Vertical Integration
Instead of outsourcing production to external suppliers and thereby transferring the capital investment and inventory

risk, Samsung remained committed to manufacturing as a core competence. "If we get out of manufacturing, we will lose," Yun stated. "Everyone can get the same technology now. But that doesn't mean they can make an advanced product."[4]

Between 1998 and 2003, Samsung invested $19 billion in new chip factories. In June 2003, the company unveiled plans to invest $17 billion in manufacturing facilities for TFT-LCDs (used in products like flat-screen TVs and computer screens) over the next 10 years. Samsung ensured that its plants remained competitive by forcing them to compete with outside companies for internal business. For example, an internal manufacturing group competed with Sumitomo Chemical Company of Japan to supply the company with its color filters.

Samsung was also flexible in its choice of plant locations. For example, to keep costs low, the company operated 12 manufacturing plants in China by 2003. Similarly, research and development facilities were set up in India to take advantage of the country's abundance of relatively low-cost human capital, especially in the technology sector.

Commoditization and downward pressure on prices and margins argued against vertical integration. To avoid the commoditization trap, Samsung customized as much production as possible. For example, over half of its memory chips were special orders for Dell, Microsoft and even Nokia. As a result of customization and reliable,

---

Exhibit 1   Samsung Revenue and Profit Growth, 1997–2002

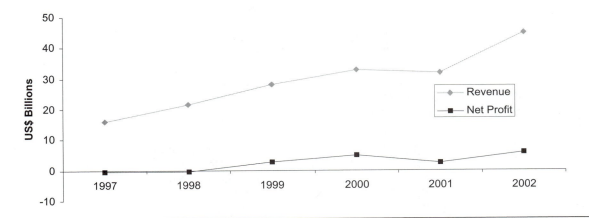

Source: Samsung company records.

---

4 Quoted in: "The Samsung Way," Cliff Edwards et al., *BusinessWeek*, June 16, 2003, pp. 56–64.

timely supply of chips, Samsung's average prices were 17% above industry levels. The mobile telephone market was another category in which Samsung prices were higher than the industry average.

Samsung viewed vertical integration and the investment in manufacturing facilities and research and development, not as a fixed cost, but rather as a source of flexibility and control over the entire production process. While the typical model was to outsource manufacturing and focus on core competencies, Samsung emphasized manufacturing as a core competency in its own right.

Hardware Focus

Unlike rivals such as Sony and Apple, Samsung decided not to develop proprietary software and content like music, movies, and video games. Industry experts contended that, because hardware life cycles were becoming even shorter, content offered higher margins. Samsung's strategy, however, was to focus on hardware and devices and to collaborate with content providers when appropriate. Samsung executives argued that this "open architecture" approach resulted in customers being able to access more software through its devices than was possible with its competitors' products. In addition, they pointed to the increasing challenges associated with protecting proprietary content from piracy.

By 2000, Samsung's top executives contended that they wanted to be as "strong" as Sony by 2005. Software was becoming an increasing part of Sony's overall business, differentiating it from Samsung. Kim commented on Sony's strategy as follows:

> Sony has had twenty years more than Samsung to build its global brand, and spends three times as much as us on advertising each year. But, make no mistake, they have done a great job. We all remember the Sony Trinitron TV and the Sony Walkman as great, consumer-driven innovations. At Samsung, we see no reason why we can't have as strong a brand as Sony's. We're more diversified technologically than Sony, which gives us a better chance to exploit digital convergence. Sony makes as many of its products in China as Samsung does. On the other hand we have not invested in software and entertainment content, and we are not involved in computer games, which, through PlayStation, represent one of Sony's most profitable categories. Perhaps as a result, Sony

has more of a hip image than Samsung, and a stronger appeal to the youth market.

Product Breadth

Samsung's product diversification differentiated the company from its competitors, many of which focused on a single category. Nokia, for example, specialized in cell phones and was the worldwide share leader. Sony was known best for consumer electronics, and Intel focused on chip production. By contrast, Samsung R&D and manufacturing spanned multiple categories, as indicated by the breakdown of sales and profits in Table A.

| Table A | Breakdown of Samsung Sales and Operating Profits, 2002 |

	Sales	Operating Profits
Semiconductors	$ 11 B	$ 3.1 B
Telecommunications	$ 11 B	$ 2.5 B
Digital Media	$ 13.9 B	$ 0.6 B
Digital Appliances	$ 3.8 B	$ 0.2 B
Other	$ 4.8 B	$ 0.4 B

Source: Samsung Electronics Company

The company had come a long way from the mid-1980s when it made cheap home appliances including televisions, microwaves, and VCRs. Following SEC Chairman Mr. Lee's 1993 "New Management Initiative," Yun refocused the company on innovation of higher quality products across all categories in 1997. This paid off. By 2003, the company was associated with the latest products like LCD televisions and video cell phones. In 2002, the company received five awards for industrial design excellence, tying for first place in a number of awards. In all of its major product categories, Samsung was one of the top three brands by market share. (See Table B.)

Samsung was the number one global manufacturer of DRAM (the semiconductor chips primarily used in PCs), SRAM (used in cell phones and handhelds), and NAND flash chips (used in products like digital cameras and MP3 players). This diversity enabled Samsung to

Table B — Samsung Market Position by Category

Category	Global Market Share	Samsung Rank	Key Competitors
Big Screen TVs	32%	1	Sony (25%), Mitsubishi (25%),
Cell Phones	10%	3	Nokia (36%), Motorola (15%)
Flash Memory	14%	2	Intel (27%), Toshiba (11%), Advanced Micro (10%)
LCD Displays	18%	1	LG Philips (17%)
MP3 Players	13%	3	Sonicblue (18%), Apple (17%), Creative (12%)
DRAM Chips	32%	1	Micron (19%)
DVD Players	11%	3	Toshiba (15%), Sony (14%), Panasonic (10%)
Microwave Ovens	25%	1	LG (22%), Galanz (19%)

Source: Adapted from "The Samsung Way," *BusinessWeek*, June 2003, pp. 56-64.

ride out chip cycles. NAND chips produced by Samsung were increasingly preferred over the NOR chips produced by Intel because they could store three times the information for the same price. Samsung already controlled over half of the NAND market which was projected to reach sales of $7 billion by 2005. Due to the increasing popularity of NAND technology, Samsung was closing in on Intel in terms of flash chip revenues. (See Exhibit 2.)

Exhibit 2 — Revenue in the Flash Market

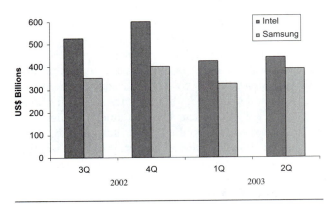

Source: Adapted from "Samsung Closes Flash-Chip Gap on Intel," Don Clark, *The Wall Street Journal*, 9/11/2003, p. B6.

In the telecommunications arena, Samsung was the leading provider of the newest CDMA[5] digital phones and of thin-film LCD displays preferred for PCs, cell phones and televisions. As a result, Samsung became the preferred provider of cell phones to Sprint. In 1997, Sprint began selling SEC phones carrying the Samsung brand name like the SCH-3500, an extremely popular, silver clamshell model.

In the $60 billion cellular phone industry, Samsung was a strong number three, closing in on Motorola at number two. Samsung held 10% of the global market in 2002 (versus 2.7% in 1999). Unlike other major cell phone manufacturers, Samsung was growing rapidly despite its higher prices. Samsung produced only mid-range and high-end cell phones, enabling the company to command higher-than-average prices (approximately 20% higher) than either of the top two players, Nokia and Motorola. Samsung was the first to introduce color screen phones into the United States in 2002. While Samsung sales grew 51% in 2002, Motorola's grew a meager 4% and Nokia's sales flat-lined. Furthermore, while Samsung was number three in terms of handsets sold, it recently surpassed Motorola in terms of revenue. Mobile phones accounted for an increasing share of Samsung's overall sales.

Samsung had been a long-standing leader in liquid crystal display (LCD) televisions due to its ability to mass-produce them at low-cost. In 2003, Sony, the global share leader in televisions for decades, entered into a joint venture with Samsung to produce LCDs to avoid the extra

---

5 Code Division Multiple Access (CDMA) was the leading digital, wireless technology offered for cell phones in the U.S., South Korea, Japan and China. CDMA technology offered users several advantages including clearer voice communication and more traffic on the network at higher speeds. Estimates indicated that over 100 million customers worldwide already used CDMA technology on mobile devices.

capital outlays needed to do its own LCD manufacturing. As Exhibit 3 demonstrates, high-end LCD televisions were a growth category, and Samsung was reaping the benefits of its decision to mass-produce them. In 2003, Samsung unveiled a groundbreaking 57-inch LCD television, a size previously untouched by this technology.

Digital Product Innovation

Under the guidance of the chairman, Mr. Lee, SEC management decided in the late 1990s that the expected transition from analog to digital technology gave Samsung a once-in-a-lifetime chance to catch its better-known rivals. He and his colleagues all but bet the company on digital technology. Six years later, this resulted in a relentless flow of new, digital products from the 17,000 scientists, engineers, and designers who worked in Samsung's R&D centers, an effort which cost $2.45 billion annually. The investment in digital technologies through attracting and retaining top scientific talent paved the way for Samsung's focus on premium products.

The most promising four or five new products in any year were designated pillar products and received incremental marketing support. There were usually around twenty candidates for pillar product status.

Developing a pillar product was a badge of honor for Samsung designers and engineers. According to Lee, "In the past year alone, Samsung has brought to market a dazzling array of products that represent 'world-firsts' in their respective industries. In addition to leading the way technologically, Samsung products are also setting new standards for quality performance and award-winning design."[6]

Thanks to the multiple technology capabilities of its many designers and engineers, speedier decision-making processes and fewer levels of organizational bureaucracy, Samsung could move a concept from drawing board to commercialization in five months (compared to fourteen months five years earlier), twice as fast as its Japanese rivals. As a result, Samsung could refresh its product line twice as often. Product lifecycles shortened, and prices quickly fell as competitive products caught up with the innovator. Yun labeled this the "Sashimi theory" likening new technology products to fish; they sell at high prices on the first day when they are fresh, but prices decline dramatically thereafter.[7]

Yun explained: "In the analog era, it was hard enough for the latecomer to catch up." Now in the digital era, "If you are two months late, you're dead. So speed and intelligence are what matter. The jury is still out as to who the winners in the digital era will be."[8]

Digital Convergence

Due to its focus on digital products across multiple categories, Samsung stood poised to become a leader in the era of digital convergence.

The concept of digital convergence referred to two trends: the merging of different technologies into one major product and multiple technologies linked by one major network. Examples of the former included the Palm OS-based Smart Phone, combining features of a cellular telephone and palm pilot, the "Dick Tracy" Watch Phone, and the SPH-i700 Camera Phone. Camera phones were projected to reach 14% of the global cellular phone market by year-end 2003. The wireless handset was thus becoming much more than a phone and Samsung envisioned countless applications. In front of the television, the device could function as a remote control and be used for programming. Outside the home, the device could be used as a roadmap.

Exhibit 3	LCD's Increasing Share of Television Market

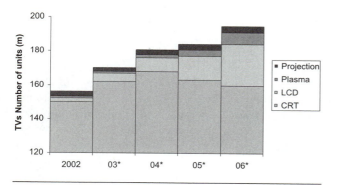

Source: Adapted from "Converging on the living room: digital technology's rise breaks down barriers between PC's and consumer electronics," Richard Waters, *The Financial Times*, 10/3/2003 p. 11.

---

6 Samsung Annual Report 2002.

7 "Samsung's 'Sashimi Theory' of Success", Pete Engardio and Moon Ihlwan, *BusinessWeek*, June 11, 2003.

8 Quoted in "The Samsung Way," Cliff Edwards et al., *BusinessWeek*, June 16, 2003, 56–64.

By 2003, Samsung had already brought a degree of convergence to many of its products, providing groundbreaking innovations in many areas. The Wireless Home AV centre allowed consumers to surf the web from their television screens. The "Systems-in-Package" semiconductor combined a mobile CPU, NAND flash memory and SDRAM for use in mobile products. A Samsung presentation on how digital convergence could impact consumers' lives is reproduced in Exhibit 4.

On a broader scale, Samsung envisioned a future where a single device could control all the electronic devices in a household. To this end, Seoul's Tower Place apartment complex was created to demonstrate the possibilities of the digital household of the future. "We're making the Jetsons a reality,"[9] boasted Kim. Among many electronic amenities, the digital apartment complex offered touch-pad recognition screens instead of keys and a remote control Home PAD operating all electronic devices within the home.

Samsung envisioned that digital devices would themselves converge, as networks and services had done. Single devices integrating multiple services would replace multiple devices. In addition, digital convergence would lead to increasing connectivity of devices through wired and wireless networks such as broadband. As a result, the number of services available to each user and, consequently, potential revenue streams would both expand.

Exhibit 4 Digital Convergence Impacts Consumer Lives

SAMSUNG DigitAll: Making digital convergence come alive

"The Samsung SPH-A600 isn't just for talking—it's for seeing!"

SPH-i700   SGH-E700   SPH-A600   SAMSUNG

Source: Samsung company records.

---

9 Quoted in "Samsung is Aiming to Make the Jetsons' World a Reality—Electronics Maker's Big Push in Home-Networking Market is a Bold Gamble to Beat Rivals," Hae Won Choi, *The Wall Street Journal*, September 16, 2003, B1.

As Yun stated:

> Digital convergence will lead to the ubiquitous network. Computing power will be transplanted into devices we use personally and be applied to virtually everything we encounter in our day-to-day lives. Samsung is uniquely positioned to exploit the potential synergy that comes from being a leader in memory and displays, components and wireless and consumer electronics. We intend to be squarely at the center of this future society.

At this time, Samsung believed it was in a crucial race to capture the digital home.

Nevertheless, several challenges existed before digital convergence could become a reality, including product standardization and simplification as well as customer education on the benefits of convergence. Additionally, digital convergence might render obsolete many existing Samsung products, while others might well be cannibalized.

MARKETING AT SAMSUNG

Historically, Samsung had been a product-driven company that focused on manufacturing existing products at lower cost than competitors and thereby built market share through scale economies. In the early 1990s, the Samsung brand was not widely known outside of Korea; the company sold its products primarily to original equipment manufacturers (OEM) rather than to end consumers. At this time, there was only nominal interest in developing the Samsung brand image globally. Around the world, Samsung's brand message was fragmented and its logo and presentation were inconsistent. Marketing budgets, controlled by product managers, tended to be allocated to "below-the-line" price promotions designed to meet short-term sales targets, rather than to long-term "above-the-line" brand building.

This changed with the 1993 "New Management Initiative" issued by the chairman, Mr. Lee. To transform Samsung from a 'cheap OEM' to a 'high value-added products provider', Samsung had to develop strong brand power. Once costs were brought under control and new products began to flow out of Samsung's research and development pipeline, it became evident that Samsung could extract higher margins by going-to-market under its own brand name, just as Sony had done. After his appointment in 1997, Vice Chairman Yun led the company-wide effort to convert the company's product line from an emphasis on low-end commodities to high-end premium goods.

To be recognized as a premium brand required repositioning through an increased emphasis on marketing. In 1999, Yun therefore recruited an accomplished Korean-born general manager, Eric Kim, as executive vice president of global marketing. Kim was born in Korea but had pursued a successful business career in the United States in the technology sector, most recently as CEO of Pilot Software.

Kim's mission was to build the corporate brand image across 200 country markets and SEC's 17 product-focused business units worldwide. Kim stressed the importance of viewing the brand as a core strategic asset, "one that needs to be thought of strategically and built over time." The objective was to create a global brand; the Korean origin of the brand was not emphasized.

Top executives' support for brand building was critical to Kim's success. Kim stated: "There was a clear conviction, from the very top, that the brand was one of the most important assets in the company and that they were prepared to support someone like me to make it grow."[10]

Nevertheless, Kim faced major internal challenges. Despite prior efforts to emphasize the importance of branding, the true value of marketing was not widely appreciated at Samsung when Kim arrived. Kim realized that internal education about marketing would be fundamental to achieving change.

> Our managers believed that good products sell themselves, that marketing was nothing more than selling, and that selling was only needed when you had a me-too or weak product. I have worked hard for four years to educate our divisional managers on the role of marketing, and the value of developing and communicating superior solutions for our target customers.

> We have made progress, but many Samsung managers responded initially with a "show me" attitude. Not only have we had to develop marketing planning and budgeting processes from scratch for both new and existing products, for headquarters and field operations; we have had to show the divisions that following these new approaches impacts the effectiveness of their marketing expenditures especially because, as manufacturing costs have gone down, marketing has become, next to R&D, the largest expense on their books.

---

10 "From microwaves to The Matrix," Maija Pesola, *The Financial Times*, September 11, 2003, p. 8.

At the same time, we have had to elevate the perceived professional stature of marketing within Samsung, and develop a marketing career path to attract, train and retain top quality marketers who can make the case for marketing expenditures to our general managers, many of whom still remain skeptical.

Kim believed that everyone inside the organization had to understand the essence of the Samsung brand name before it could be sensibly promoted externally. Translating internal education into a communicable message was in part captured by the use of three words: "wow," "simple," and "inclusive." "Wow" referred to groundbreaking innovations that intrigued consumers. They represented key features of any pillar product. There were, in fact, targets for the number of wow products each business unit had to launch each year. "Simple" and "inclusive" referred to the ease-of-use and accessibility along with ubiquity, availability and affordability of Samsung's products to the consumer. Samsung designers emphasized visual simplicity as well as functional performance in arriving at new product designs.

Marketing Organization

Kim headed the corporate Global Marketing Operations (GMO) unit, established in 1999 and based at world headquarters in Seoul. Comprising around 90 staff, the GMO coordinated Samsung's marketing efforts and was responsible for developing the corporate marketing program for the Samsung brand outside Korea (a separate group was responsible for brand building in Samsung's home market). There were three major teams in the GMO, the Marketing Strategy Team, the Regional Strategy Team and the Product Strategy Team, each with different responsibilities.

Marketing Strategy Team

- Developed global marketing strategy
- Controlled the GMO budget
- Controlled the global brand campaign, in coordination with Samsung's in-house agency (Cheil) and its outside advertising agency (Foote, Cone & Belding)
- Controlled the Samsung.com website, and developed internet-related partnerships with service providers and other corporations
- Oversaw global CRM (customer relationship management) strategies, and shared marketing best practices across subsidiaries

Regional Strategy Team

- Planned strategic direction for regional markets
- Interfaced with line managers to set the marketing budgets by region

Product Strategy Team

- Conducted market research, and gathered and analyzed information on competitors
- Planned corporate marketing exhibits at trade shows
- Conceived and implemented strategic marketing alliances and "killer" new product concepts

In 2001, under Kim's leadership, the GMO implemented the initiative to consolidate SEC advertising with a single agency to deliver a consistent brand message worldwide. Previously, various units of SEC were using more than 55 advertising agencies worldwide, and Samsung products were advertised using 20 different slogans. Kim explained:

We consolidated our advertising with a single global agency, Foote, Cone & Belding (FCB). We developed worldwide guidelines for our logo and for its presentation in all SEC communications from letterheads to product packaging to billboards. FCB also developed a unique brand essence for Samsung to differentiate us in the marketplace and boost internal morale. Consolidating agencies has also helped us to gradually strip away sub-brands, which had distracted management and diverted resources.

Allocation of Marketing Resources

In addition to improving marketing education and organization, the GMO changed the way marketing budgets were set. As of 2003, marketing funds were available from the GMO (around $400 million in 2003) and from each of SEC's seventeen worldwide business units (around $600 million). GMO funds could only be used for advertising and other brand franchise building activities. Business unit funds were mainly used for temporary price promotions directed at consumers and the trade. The GMO recommended to SEC's regional headquarters how to prioritize and allocate its funds and those of the business units by country and by product category. Under Kim, the GMO allocated 70 percent of its funds in this fashion, reserving 30 percent to support opportunities as they emerged during the year.

Historically, marketing budgets at Samsung were set as a percentage of current sales rather than in relationship to growth potential. Kim accomplished substantial budget reallocations by deploying a computer program, M-Net, to help determine where funds could reap the highest returns. Eighteen months were spent gathering data on Samsung sales, margins, market shares and marketing expenditures by country and by product category into a central database. The M-Net program analyzed the results of past marketing plans to recommend where marketing dollars should be spent by country and by category. Pricing adjustments were also recommended.

Kim explained the value of the program:

> It was clear from our analyses that we could no longer allocate marketing resources the way we had in the past. We needed a more systematic approach to ensure that our marketing investments were targeted at the highest return opportunities. The entire, approximately $1 billion budget may sound like a lot of money, but it's spread across multiple countries and products.

The M-Net program revealed three opportunities for improvement:

1. SEC was overspending in regions like North America and Russia that did not have a high growth potential. While 45% of the current budget was spent in these areas, spending should have been closer to 35%.
2. Some regions with high-growth potential were correspondingly receiving less investment than appropriate. In particular, Europe and China were receiving 31% of the marketing budget but should have been allocated more like 42%.
3. Similar misallocations existed at the product level: Mobile phones, vacuum cleaners and air-conditioners were receiving more than their share of the marketing budget while camcorders, DVD players, televisions, PC monitors and refrigerators were not getting enough.

These changes recommended by M-Net — if followed in their entirety — amounted to a $150 million dollar reallocation in the marketing budget. M-Net allowed GMO staff to analyze different scenarios for marketing budget allocation; see Exhibit 5 for an example.[11]

Despite initial resistance from regional and product managers to major changes in the allocation of marketing funds, the positive results achieved on measures such as brand preference, market share, and operating profit showed that marketing dollars could be spent better. To complement the new system, Kim also backed changes in management incentives to ensure that line managers were rewarded in part for global performance rather than just their own region-specific or product-specific results.

Market Driven Change

Kim's marketing initiatives complemented a sweeping set of company-wide changes collectively referred to as market driven change (MDC). MDC helped Samsung managers view marketing as an important business function rather than as a series of one-off advertising campaigns and promotions. Kim commented:

> MDC is injecting a much greater focus on customer insight into the new product development process. Rather than merely initiating competitive products or going with an engineer's gut feel, we set out to identify customer segments that are willing to pay higher prices for particular functional or aesthetic innovations. For example, in 2001, we launched the world's first dual screen folder handset. It was designed to be very compact and targeted the female/fashion-oriented segment of the cell phone market. We sold $750 million worth in nine months.

Research for the MDC initiative revealed that the Samsung brand lacked stature, and that the brand image lacked emotion and a human face. With FCB's help, a new umbrella campaign was launched in 2002 and backed by a new emphasis on the use of "DigitAll—Everyone's Invited" in brand campaigns. Kim explained:

> Samsung is generating tremendous brand visibility worldwide with its DigitAll campaign. The rationale behind "DigitAll" is simple: it says that Samsung is uniquely positioned to bring together communication, entertainment and information in easy-to-use digital devices. Through digital convergence and simple practical design, Samsung products can empower people from all walks of life to enjoy a better experience.[12]

Exhibit 6 shows examples of co-operative advertisements with Samsung customers for the DigitAll campaign. See Exhibit 7 for product-specific advertisements under the DigitAll umbrella. Exhibit 8 summarizes the reactions from consumer focus groups of "mobile professionals" and "Generation Y" (in their 20s) consumers to the DigitAll campaign.

---

11 "Optimal Marketing" by Marcel Corstjens and Jefffrey Merrihue. *Harvard Business Review.* October, 2003. For full discussion of M-Net and related changes, see this article.
12 Samsung Annual Report 2002.

Exhibit 5 M-Net Analysis

Bubble Size: Client Potential Profit

Opportunities above this line merit an increased share of marketing budget.

Ideal Allocation to Opportunity

Current Allocation to Opportunity

Italy–Product 1
Spain–Product 1
Russia–Product 1
Mexico–Product 1
S. Africa–Product 1
USA–Product 1
Argentina–Product 1
Singapore–Product 1
Portugal–Product 1
UK–Product 1
Hong Kong–Product 1
Canada–Product 1
Netherlands–Product 1

Misallocations Revealed: Samsung's M-Net system produces graphical depictions of the company's allocation challenges. In this chart, we see the total marketing budget for "Product 1." The horizontal axis shows how Samsung had planned to divide its investment in that product category across the countries in which it is sold. For example, 15% was to be devoted to marketing in Italy. The vertical axis represents M-Net's recommendations— for instance, that 22% of these dollars should go to the Italian market. (Bubble size reflects M-Net calculations of a market's relative profit potential.) Every bubble above the dotted line, like the one for Italy, represents an area where Samsung should devote more resources than it planned to. Opportunities below the line should have their budgets cut. Charts like this one helped Samsung identify misallocations and convince affected managers to accept change.

Source: "Optimal Marketing" by Marcel Corstjens and Jeffrey Merrihue, *Harvard Business Review*, October 2003, p. 117.

Source: Samsung company records.

Exhibit 7 DigitAll Ad Campaign: Product-Specific Advertisements

Source: Samsung company records.

<u>DigitAll Concept:</u>

- "I think it's a great name. I think it really encompasses what they are trying to do, which is combining different tech gadgets into one piece of equipment."
- "It means All-digital. Digital to everybody and All-digital, I think it has these two meanings."
- "To me it means whatever the product is, we can make it digital, we can make it compact, we can advance the technology, we are a company you can trust — so one day when you can afford the product, we are the company to turn to."
- "Everybody is included, you know from the poor to the richer. All products are digital."
- "It all comes together in one place, both on a level of the technology itself, but in another way it is quite clever, the way that even in my mind, as cynical as I am, it all comes under one roof— Samsung's roof."

<u>Everyone's Invited Campaign:</u>

- "I'm usually intimidated by technology, but when I see different people using it, I think it may be easier to use. And the fact that they admit there is confusion, they make it easier. I thought that was appealing."
- "It's available to everybody, it is easy to get. Diverse products for diverse people. There is sort of an international feel about it…you can see that it is from the East and trying to marry the East and West together—it's a fast moving thing."
- "Hi-tech with ordinary people."
- "Everyone is equal, in a digital world, everyone is equal."
- "Fusion, integration, convenience and well-being. Integration means state-of-the-art, but they have to deliver."
- "Puts Samsung in a new light – lively, high-tech, in the top league."
- It's telling you that you just wanted simple things, simple improvements in life from technology, but it got so complex that now you're sitting in your chair and don't know which way to turn, and Samsung is gonna make it so simple that people all over the world with very different cultures can benefit."

Source: FCB Future Focus Consumer Interviews for Samsung, 2002.

After the successful launch of the DigitAll campaign, Samsung took its branding activities to the next level by launching a co-marketing campaign with the Warner Brothers blockbuster movie *The Matrix Reloaded*, a science fiction thriller that opened in May 2003. A Samsung phone played a key role in the movie as the gateway between the physical and virtual worlds.[13] Samsung arranged to produce the phone designed by the Wachowski Brothers for *The Matrix* sequel and sold the phone from the movie in limited quantities in selected markets. Several other new Samsung products were promoted in a billboard and print advertising campaign as depicted in Exhibit 9. Featured products included a flat-screen computer monitor, a digital camcorder, a flat-screen TV, and a rotating camera phone. This sponsorship was designed to promote the Samsung brand among the 20- to 30-year-old-segment who were important consumers of new electronic products and whose brand preferences were not yet solidified. The campaign video game, *Enter the Matrix*, included over 200 impressions of the

---

13 A Nokia cell phone was featured in the original Matrix movie.

Exhibit 9   Matrix Ad Campaign

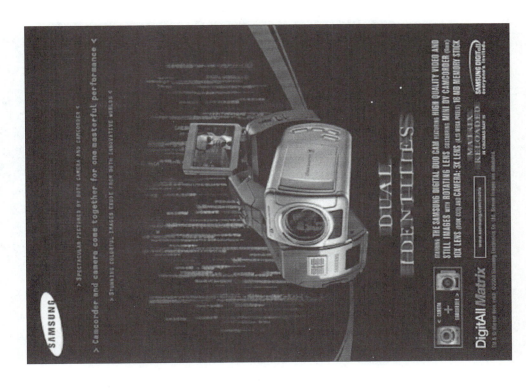

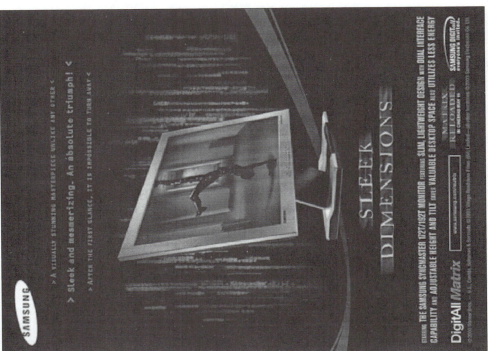

Exhibit 9   Matrix Ad Campaign (continued)

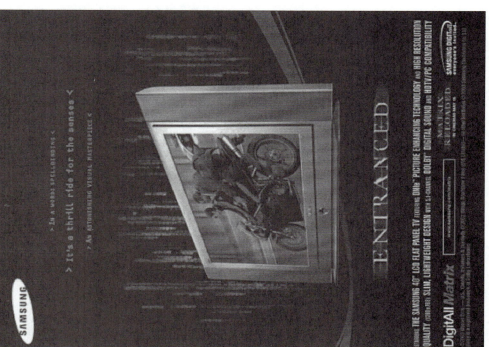

Source: Samsung company records.

Samsung brand. Samsung's Matrix micro-site increased traffic to the Samsung.com website by 65%.

In addition, Samsung signed an agreement with the International Olympic Committee (IOC) in 1997 to be a worldwide Olympic sponsor in the wireless equipment category. Samsung was an official Olympic sponsor for the 2000 Sydney Olympic Games and leveraged this sponsorship internally as well, inviting senior executives from its operating units and key distributors from around the world. Sponsorship of the 2002 Winter Olympic Games in Salt Lake City continued the effort. The company had already agreed to sponsor the 2004 Summer Games in Athens, the 2006 Winter Games in Torino, and the 2008 Summer Games in Beijing.

SAMSUNG'S MARKET POSITION

Domestic Market Dominance

Samsung dominated the South Korean market with over 50% share in almost all its product-markets and complementary repeat purchase rates. Although only 15% of total Samsung sales were in South Korea, the country offered two special advantages as a launch market for new products. First, as a mountainous country, South Korea presented a tough challenge for cell phone usage, forcing development of more sensitive wireless technology. Second, partly because almost three-quarters of South Koreans lived in urban areas, 70% of South Korean households were already wired for broadband by 2003 (compared to 15% of households in the United States and 8% in Europe).

The brand was almost 40 years old in Korea and was well-known, thanks to its widespread presence on home appliances. In this respect, it was comparable to the GE brand in the United States.

Samsung's market penetration in Korea permitted it to launch sub-brands for specific segments of the domestic market. In other markets where the Samsung brand was less developed, a focus on the corporate brand image was deemed paramount. As Kim explained: "Given our high market share in Korea, we have to address all age-groups, so we implement a multi-brand, multi-segment strategy. We've been able to launch sub-brands without compromising the master brand."

International Expansion

Kim recognized that the Samsung brand was at different stages of development in different country markets.

Managers disagreed, however, about how much local adaptation of marketing and brand building communications strategies and tactics was necessary. All agreed, however, that country markets could be grouped into three categories (see Exhibit 10 for more details):

1. *Accelerator:* Markets where the main objective was to build Samsung brand awareness, both aided and unaided.
2. *Turning Point:* Markets where awareness was good, generating significant demand in some product categories, but where the brand image had to be reinforced to improve repeat purchase probabilities.
3. *Advanced:* Markets where Samsung's unaided brand awareness and brand reputation were strong across all categories, and where loyalty needed to be reinforced further.

Kim described the position of the Samsung brand in various country markets as follows:

> In the USA, the Samsung brand is at the Turning Point stage. We've made good progress but our unaided awareness and brand loyalty are still below those of first tier brands like Sony. We have added new partnerships with chains like Best Buy and Circuit City to supplement our earlier relationships with Wal-Mart and Target. Although we are still seen by many consumers as a value brand, we're increasingly viewed by consumers and trade partners alike as reliable, up-and-coming and credible, given the breadth of our product line and our flow of new products. We're working heavily in the USA on customer relationship management to strengthen our partnerships with the channel leaders, especially since the top ten chains account for 60 percent of consumer electronics sales nationwide.

> In Europe, the Samsung brand is stronger in the southern countries like Spain and Italy than in northern Europe. Consumers in these countries don't have such entrenched brand preferences as they do in northern Europe. The Germans in particular are fiercely loyal to German brands, and the fragmentation of retail distribution makes it harder for us to enter with sufficient sales volume to make the market attractive.

The Samsung brand was stronger in emerging than in developed markets. In Russia, for example, Samsung had

Exhibit 10 Country Market Clusters and Marketing Communications

	ACCELERATOR	TURNING	ADVANCED
	BRAND ELEVATION / DEMAND GENERATION / CRM	BRAND ELEVATION / DEMAND GENERATION / CRM	CRM / DEMAND GENERATION / BRAND ELEVATION
Communication Goals	Awareness via high reach frequency & impact	Build reach vs. frequency	Build loyalty via one to one communications
Communication Mix	Primarily broad reach vehicles plus BTL support	Equal mix of above and below the line vehicles	Heavy CRM with some targeted programming
	Anthem		Pillar

Source: Samsung Company Records.

been voted the "people's brand" several years in a row. Kim explained:

> Our success stems from the late 1980s and early 1990s when we continued to supply Russia from warehouses in Finland with value-priced products, which weren't the most technologically advanced but which matched the market's needs at the time and consumers' ability to pay. Samsung is now moving beyond the Turning Point stage. We need to upgrade our image and be recognized for product leadership and innovation. That's why we've just opened a showcase retail outlet on Red Square.

The Samsung brand had made even more progress in China, which was transitioning from the Turning Point stage to the Advanced stage.

> We cannot make any profit at the low end in China, but between a quarter and a third of the Chinese market (in value terms) is available to us. Chinese consumers value quality brands and purchasing power at our end of the market is concentrated conveniently in major cities. We have a national marketing coordinator in Beijing with regional sales and marketing teams in Beijing, Guangzhou and Shanghai.

In China, an estimated 5 million new customers signed up for cellular telephone service each month in 2002. In Latin America, mobile Internet usage was projected to increase to include 47 million people by 2005. India represented another major market opportunity, as Kim explained: "In India, we found that value-added resellers are very important in putting together personal computer packages for consumers. India is an increasingly sophisticated and fast-growing information technology market. Samsung has become a major supplier of computer peripherals and our brand recognition is actually greater than that of Intel or Microsoft."

CONSUMER RESEARCH

FCB began working with SEC in 1999 to understand the company's brand image. To this end, FCB had developed a proprietary model, the Relationship Monitor, which identified: (a) thirteen relational dimensions through which customers connected, to a greater or lesser extent, with a brand; and (b) seven relationship styles which described, in summary form, different types of customer brand relationships (which each implied different levels of brand loyalty). The dimensions and associated styles are summarized in

Exhibits 11A through 11C. The Relationship Monitor study involved asking consumers to rate one or more brands on a battery of attitude and opinion statements associated with each of the 13 dimensions.

In 2000, FCB examined consumers' relationships with Samsung and key competitive brands in six country markets: Brazil, China, Germany, Hong Kong, the United Kingdom, and the United States. In China, Hong Kong, and the United States, Samsung cell phones were rated separately, in addition to the Samsung brand as a whole. The index scores for each of the six country markets (see Exhibits 12A through 12C) show Samsung's relationship profile versus the all-brand average.

The results indicated that the Samsung brand was at different degrees of development in different countries. In China, for example, the Samsung brand was strong on "Delights Me" but not on "Perfect Fit," except in the case of cell phones. In contrast, in the United States, the overall brand was more "Price-Based" though, once again, Samsung cell phones had developed a stronger position, for example, in the "Delights Me" category.

FCB executives advised that Samsung should focus in weaker markets on establishing the brand's leadership credentials through new product development, since perceived category leadership gave consumers a reason to buy into the franchise. In stronger Samsung markets, where the customer base was already significant, the focus of marketing communications should be, it was argued, on moving more consumers into the "Delights Me" and "Perfect Fit" relationship categories. However, questions lingered about the communications strategies which could move consumers from one stage to another on the relationship style ladder.

In addition to country comparisons, the FCB analysis also compared Samsung to its major competitors. Exhibit 13 summarizes consumer perceptions of the brand personalities of five companies along with the implications for Samsung's strategy. Furthermore, competing companies were compared on the basis of the seven relationship styles used in the country analysis. (See Exhibits 14A through 14D.) The strong performance of Samsung cell phones gave the brand a promising starting point from which to build brand leadership.

Taking the analysis a step further, Samsung executives were determined that the brand image be shaped in light of future consumer trends rather than merely respond to those that were currently in vogue. They wanted Samsung to be the brand of choice among "Vanguard Consumers," young opinion leaders around the world. A 2002 series of

Exhibit 11   Design of FCB Relationship Monitor Survey

Exhibit 11A: Thirteen Dimensions that Build Stronger Consumer Relationships

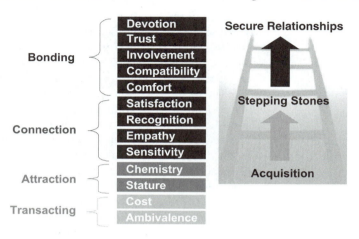

Exhibit 11B: Example of Detailed Opinion Statements for Each Dimension

interviews with industry experts in eleven countries identified the following six consumer trends:

- living on demand and in control
- from consumers to "experiences"
- technology has gone from "wow" to "oh"
- living the converged life
- milking the moment
- moving by instinct

Exhibit 15 details each of these trends and the implications for Samsung's future efforts to build its brand image. For example, "living on demand and in control" implied tailoring services to meet personal preferences, perhaps through a personal preference chip or code to transfer voice and data between devices. This further implied a higher degree of customer segmentation to accommodate variations in consumer preferences than Samsung had

Exhibit 11   Design of FCB Relationship Monitor Survey (continued)

Exhibit 11C: Seven Relationship Styles Derived From Thirteen Dimensions

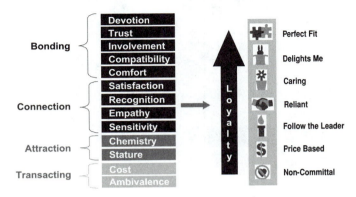

Source: Samsung Relationship Monitor, 2000.

been used to in the past. Meanwhile, the shift in technology from "wow" to "oh" emphasized that digital devices should not become mundane but had to retain their "delight factor," while also fitting into everyday life.

CONCLUSION

Kim was encouraged by positive consumer response to the global DigitAll advertising campaign. He planned to run this campaign through the end of 2004, but he wondered whether it would be enough to propel Samsung into the premier league of global brands. He recalled some of the comments he had heard from Samsung line managers in his travels during 2003:

- "There is no substitute for a constant stream of bigger and better new products. Money spent on R&D is always a better investment than money spent on advertising."
- "Samsung's consumers in my country are pretty mainstream, satisfied and ready to repurchase. Too much emphasis on youth and creativity is inappropriate."
- "Let's not overspend on advertising and promotion just for the sake of beating Sony in some *BusinessWeek* ranking. The brand will gain consumer credibility naturally, at its own pace. You can't force it."

- "The global image campaign is only useful if it helps move products at retail next Monday morning. I'm not convinced that it does."
- "Even if we have the best product, say in LCD televisions, the shelf space is so cluttered with options that we need the strong brand to break through."

In addition to pondering these views, Kim worried about whether Samsung needed to embrace a more complex customer segmentation in its marketing planning. Samsung had, up to this point, used a "one size fits all" approach, advertising broadly to "the sensible brand buyer." But market research pointed towards increasing demand for personalized, customized devices and, therefore, for more segmentation. This might call for new subbrands beyond the Samsung name targeted at premium value segments in one or more categories, and for segmented advertising campaigns. However, such initiatives would be hard to justify if they reduced the cost-efficiency of current marketing expenditures.

Kim had a week to consolidate his thoughts before presenting to Samsung's top management his plan for how Samsung could become a blockbuster brand by 2005. He mused: "To be number one, it's not enough just to be known, you have to be loved."[14]

---

14 "From microwaves to The Matrix" by Maija Pesola, *The Financial Times* September 11, 2003, p. 8.

Exhibit 12   Results of FCB Relationship Monitor Study

Exhibit 12A: Percent of Consumers Exhibiting Each Relational Style by Country

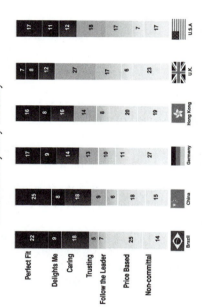

Cell Phones

Exhibit 12C: Representation of Each Relational Style Among Samsung Cell Phone Consumers, Indexed to the Country Average

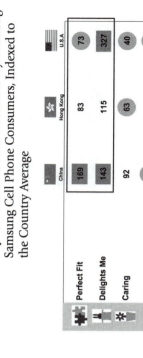

Exhibit 12B: Representation of Each Relational Style Among Samsung Consumers, Indexed to the Country Average

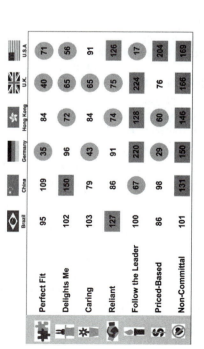

Note: Over 100 means Samsung representation is high relative to the country norm.
Source: Samsung Relationship Monitor, 2000.

Exhibit 13   Brand Profiles And Implications For Samsung

Nokia

Personality:
Curious
Classic
Down-to-earth
Trustworthy
Simple
Straightforward
Colorful
Competitive

Product/Co.:
Innovative
Easy to use
Specialized
Asian

Sony

Personality:
Visionary
Popular
Mature
Confident
Sleek/Style
Trend setter
Adorable
Smart
Fashionable
Cool
Determined
Friendly
Up-to-date
Affluent
Chic
Aggressive

Product/Co.:
Breadth of line
Quality
Good functionality
Leader
Forward-thinking
Dependable
Cutting edge
Resources
Japanese

Samsung

Personality:
Fashionable
Not flashy
Arrogant, off-putting
Sophisticated
Friendly
Not afraid
Exciting
Inventive
Quiet
Loner

Product/Co.:
Not visible, no exposure
New
High/pure tech
Innovative
Low profile
Difficult to use
Good design
Quality inside is unknown or cheap
Can't relate to it, no image

Panasonic

Personality:
Popular
Older
Wiser
Reserved but capable
Comfortable

Product/Co.:
Stable
Reliable
TV's & stereos
Imitating
Not consistent

Motorola

Personality:
Boring
Well-known
Popular
Sophisticated
Cultured
Strong

Product/Co.:
Star Tac
Good design
Good technology
Huge, clunky phones

- **Samsung Implications**
  - **Has the beginnings of a technology and design story**
    - However it is more cold and aloof than human and personal
  - **Doesn't have as much personality or image**
    - Not always perceived as a serious player
  - **Needs to tell its story in a compelling (emotional/personal) way to entice consumers to bring Samsung into their family**
    - More than what you say about quality, digital, technology…it's about how you behave in the marketplace
      - As a personal companion
      - As a brand that understands life facilitation
      - As a brand that supports innovation and style
    - Samsung's vision must differentiate it from the competition

Source: Samsung Vanguard Consumers Study.

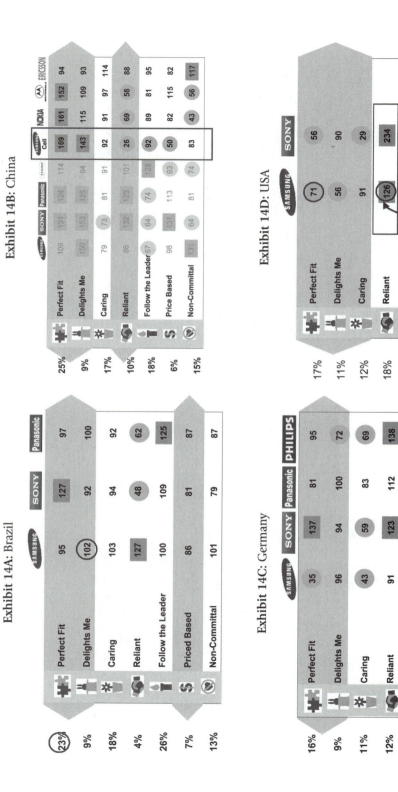

Exhibit 14   Samsung Relational Style By Country Compared to Selected Competitors

Note: Numbers in left column of each chart reproduce data from Exhibit 12A.
Source: Samsung Relationship Monitor, 2000.

Exhibit 15   Key Findings of FCB Study on Samsung's Future Focus

2002 Key Findings: Samsung's Future Focus

Living On Demand and In Control

- Consumers want everything on their terms
  - Focus on controlling and managing the increased amount of available information and data due to technology
    - The magic of the "off" button
    - Self-programming of media
    - Filters and synthesizers of information
    - Cliff notes learning
    - Quality shortcuts
    - "I want what I want when I want it."

2002 Key Findings: Samsung's Future Focus

From Consumers to "Experiencers"

- Consumers have become acquirers of experiences or "experiencers"
  - The acquisition of experiences is as important as the acquisition of things
- Experiences come in a variety of forms
  - Virtual or real, owned or borrowed, created or purchased
  - Always non-routine (using a mobile phone is routine, using a mobile phone to send a video is non-routine…for awhile)
  - Simulated experience is expected to provide the exact same benefit as real
    - Invites you in and involves you
    - Is embedded in emotion and senses

2002 Key Findings: Samsung's Future Focus

Living On Demand and In Control

- Speeding up to slow down
  - New life balance based on feeling that what I want to do is okay

- DIY/DMW (Do-it-yourself and Do-it-My-Way) mentality in all areas of life
  - No waiting, do it now
  - Feel a sense of accomplishment and pride
  - All about creating their own reality/space on their own timetable

- Consumers continue to segment into smaller target niches due to plethora of options in manufacturers and retail outlets
  - Preference for aligning themselves with what they want when they want it, not for following the masses

2002 Key Findings: Samsung's Future Focus

From Consumers to "Experiencers"

- Owning a brand or product is considered an experience if it resonates with your life
  - Provides an emotional response/feeling or visceral benefit
  - Is a manifestation of expertise or knowledge
  - Helps to define or convey your personality, image or lifestyle

- Consumers don't buy technology they buy experiences
  - Technology behind the experience has been eclipsed by the experience
  - The brand point of view becomes a key point of differentiation

2002 Key Findings: Samsung's Future Focus

Living On Demand and In Control

SAMSUNG IMPLICATION

- Development of personal "preference" chips/cards that move between devices and screen "my" world for "my" information and communication

- Incorporate DIY/DMW design/programming opportunities

- Communicate a personal vision of technology that simplifies rather than overwhelms, and clarifies rather than confuses

2002 Key Findings: Samsung's Future Focus

From Consumers to "Experiencers"

SAMSUNG IMPLICATION

- Differentiate the brand with the Samsung experience of technology
  - Create a Samsung "flavor" with a fully developed personality, attitude, and vision
  - Create a lifestyle community, e.g., Harley Davidson, Apple
- Leverage all parts of the purchase and usage cycle where you can develop a Samsung brand experience, e.g.,
  - Augment usage of product
  - Create retail centers of experience
  - Develop branded experience experts
  - Create a no-regrets experience

2002 Key Findings: Samsung's Future Focus

> **Technology Has Gone From "Wow" to "Oh"**

- The "wow" is gone
  - "Wow" is about features and everyone has them
  - Push a button and it works
  - Not interested in how it works

- Digital technology is not innovative
  - It's not what consumers expect innovation to look/feel like…it's like an appliance
  - Gone from contributing to my life to woven into my life…seamlessly integrated and wireless

- Constant, consistent innovation fuels a personal technology evolution and expectation
  - Consumers expect personal technology to change little by little
  - Only medical science technology may see revolutionary change

2002 Key Findings: Samsung's Future Focus

> **Technology Has Gone From "Wow" to "Oh"**

- Technological parity results in "me-too" market saturation
  - Digital is a cost of entry, a non-differentiator
  - Plentitude of options, in many different bundles, is causing some consumer confusion and dissatisfaction
    - "Power" users want all options in one device…seems as if one key feature is always missing
    - Most (mass) users want to know they have all the options
    - Some say they want to build their own options bundle
    - A few on the fringe say they want a no-frills choice…but probably really just want something easy to operate

2002 Key Findings: Samsung's Future Focus

> **Technology Has Gone From "Wow" to "Oh"**

- Consumers seek the "delight factor" in what digital technology brings to their lives
  - Design and style
    - Consumers increasingly focus on design and aesthetics, devices must fit a decorating scheme, style becomes a deciding factor for the mass market
  - Image and attention
    - Consumers delight in expressing themselves with mobile devices and in getting attention from others for what they carry
  - Experiences
    - Consumers expect to be delighted by how the total brand experience enhances their lives

2002 Key Findings: Samsung's Future Focus

> **Technology Has Gone From "Wow" to "Oh"**

SAMSUNG IMPLICATION

- Incumbent that the brand carry the delight since technology cannot deliver the "wow" and that the the brand stays relevant in the "oh" environment
  - Place less focus on the details of the technology inside and more on what the technology produces on the outside…the experience
  - Entice a consumer's "want" versus try to fill a need

- Develop and communicate a brand personality and vision as way of enriching the technology experience
  - Evolve from high-tech to personal-tech

2002 Key Findings: Samsung's Future Focus

> **Technology Has Gone From "Wow" to "Oh"**

SAMSUNG IMPLICATION

- Continue focus on style and ergonomics
  - Integrate more personality than pure-technology into design and aesthetics

- In essence: think like the automotive industry
  - Devices that transport differentiate themselves based on a branded integration of performance, design, image and lifestyle…based on perceptions and experience

2002 Key Findings: Samsung's Future Focus

Living the Converged Life

- Convergence means blended life experiences not combined product features/services
  - It's about what I do with it not what options or features it has
  - If it's not seamless in operation it's not converged

CONVERGENCE IS:	CONVERGENCE IS NOT:
Enjoying the movie theater experience in home	Integration of surround sound with HDTV with flat panel monitor
Suspending belief in reality	Compatibility of DVD player with latest Dolby or dts standard
Being in two places at one time when something cool happens by sharing images	Taking a picture on a camera with my mobile phone and sending it to someone
Being an original music video producer	Downloading, infared beeping, editing, compatibility and distribution
Making social commentary	Sending photos and movies of international travel to friends imbedded in email

2002 Key Findings: Samsung's Future Focus

Living the Converged Life

- A converged life requires reconfigured personal "spaces"
  - Consumers actively rearranging personal "space" to:
    - Support their multi-tasking and multiple roles
    - Support their mobility
    - Support their desire to "be" in multiple places at one time, e.g., movie theater at home, on vacation and at home
    - Deliver real emotional benefits

2002 Key Findings: Samsung's Future Focus

Living the Converged Life

SAMSUNG IMPLICATION

- Facilitate and enable the converged life experience via:
  - Development and marketing of the first personal experience mobile device
    - A data transmission and sharing device that carries voice versus a voice transmission device that also carries data
    - Docking stations in stationary spaces: cars, homes, office, etc.
    - Multiple preference chips/cards for customization

Offer customizing features/services that will put a unique personal brand on the blended life experience

2002 Key Findings: Samsung's Future Focus

Milking the Moment

- Consumers live in the moment
  - Instantaneous life…short attention span
  - Seek maximization of every moment

- Consumers live on a moment's notice due to technology
  - Instant gratification expectation
  - Less long-term planning, increased value in spontaneity

- Efficient mobility maximizes the moments
  - Increased pressure to keep on the move and up to date
  - Increased focus on working smarter not harder via technology
  - Desire for never-fail memory and battery charge

2002 Key Findings: Samsung's Future Focus

Milking the Moment

- Moments and experiences are increasingly created virtually
  - More virtual connections create a desire for more real connections…natural law of paradoxes
  - Consumers desire visceral and tactile experiences, seeking intimacy and reality
  - Virtual reality experiences expected to deliver real stimulation and emotions

- Technology, especially the personal mobile device, is a vital lifeline
  - Seeking relief from more of the "need to do" events in life so there are more moments for the "want to do"
  - Push towards pervasive wireless connection

2002 Key Findings: Samsung's Future Focus

Milking the Moment

SAMSUNG IMPLICATION

- Fuel this living in the moment lifestyle by providing products and features that deliver intensified moments
  - Multi-sensory experiences
  - Multi-location experiences
  - Increased quantity opportunities, e.g., communicating with IM, SMS, and land line concurrently
  - Tailored programming, e.g., make it as loud or scary as you want

- Facilitate intimate and instantaneous connections with mobile personal device experiences
  - Capture, store and share life's moments in real time

2002 Key Findings: Samsung's Future Focus

Moving by Instinct

- Consumers move without thinking, rely on second nature to get through the day
  - Intuiting patterns
  - Interacting with machines with ease
  - Facilitating their style/personality with design

- Technology drives this second nature
  - New languages and interfaces developed
  - Quality short cuts employed

2002 Key Findings: Samsung's Future Focus

Moving by Instinct

- They develop loyalty to brand protocols, patterns and designs
  - One time only learning curving; easy adoption by following accepted or known protocol
  - Feeling of expertise and comfort developed with a specific "system"
  - Specific design/style expresses personal style

- Technology must keep up with consumer second nature versus consumers keeping up with technology
  - Technology taking cues from the consumer…senses how the consumer thinks, operates…and then adapts itself
    - Smarter AI
  - Second nature includes integration of voice commands into technology

2002 Key Findings: Samsung's Future Focus

Moving by Instinct

SAMSUNG IMPLICATION

- Develop Samsung brand protocol that facilitates adoption, while simplifing and differentiating the experience
  - Consider this part of the Samsung "flavor" or brand experience

- Opportunities with consumer/device interaction using voice recognition

Source: FCB Future Focus Study, 2002.

Bausch & Lomb: Regional Organization

Daniel Gill, chairman and chief executive officer of Bausch & Lomb (B&L), a diversified multinational with sales of over $1.7 billion in 1992, believed that a change in organization structure was necessary to guide the further growth of B&L's international business. Despite a compound annual revenue growth rate of 17% since 1986 and an average return on sales of almost 10% over the same period, several internal problems had arisen that Gill attributed in large part to B&L's current organizational structure. The challenge was to manage B&L's rapid growth through an organization structure that would respect the company's core values of autonomy and decentralization.

In 1992, Gill was considering creating an international organization structure based on three geographic regions: Europe; Asia/Pacific; and the Western Hemisphere. However, he wanted to be sure that the organizational change would resolve the problems that had arisen, add value to customers, and enable the company to sustain a compound annual growth rate of at least 15%.

COMPANY BACKGROUND

In 1853, John Jacob Bausch, a German immigrant, opened a small optical goods store in Rochester, New York, and discovered a hard rubber called Vulcanite that could be used to make spectacle frames more durable and at lower cost than the metal and horn-rim frames then currently in use. By 1903 the company had added microscopes, binoculars, and telescopes to its eyeglass business and expanded its sales network and manufacturing capabilities. In the 1920s, B&L was asked by the U.S. government to develop an absorptive

This case was prepared by Professor John A. Quelch with the assistance of Nathalie Laidler.
Copyright © 1993 by the President and Fellows of Harvard College. Harvard Business School case 9-594-056.

glass to help pilots overcome harsh glare conditions; the result—Ray-Ban sunglasses—quickly became a profitable business. Over the following three decades the company went public and developed several breakthrough optical products such as the Oscar-winning Cinemascope lens. Diversification via small company acquisitions expanded the product range to include scientific and industrial instruments such as spectrometers and spectrophotometers[1] which boosted sales to over $100 million by 1966.

In 1966, B&L purchased the rights to a contact lens made of hydrophilic material.[2] After five years of intensive product development, B&L received approval from the Food and Drug Administration (FDA) to launch the "soft contact lens." Acquisitions and new investments reinforced B&L's dominant market shares in contact lens and lens care products (including cleaning units and solutions). By 1981, when Gill was promoted to president and chief executive operating officer, the company's more traditional markets were experiencing increasing difficulty. Gill decided to exit the eyeglass business in 1981 and the industrial instrumentation business in 1984. In 1984, Gill also orchestrated a major organizational change resulting in the creation of an International Division (ID).

THE INTERNATIONAL DIVISION

In 1983, B&L, with sales of $477 million,[3] had subsidiaries in 23 countries. Operations were organized into four worldwide product divisions: professional eye care products (contact lenses); personal products (contact lens solutions and accessories); consumer products (sunglasses and sports optics); and instruments. (Exhibit 1 depicts the organizational structure in 1983.) The four Rochester-based divisions had full functional capabilities and bottom-line accountability for their respective product lines. The

---

1 A spectrophotometer measures the relative intensities of the light in different parts of a spectrum.

2 "Hydrophilic material" is a substance or material that has a strong affinity for water.

3 Restated for 1984 writeoffs and discontinued lines.

Exhibit 1   Bausch & Lomb Organization: 1983

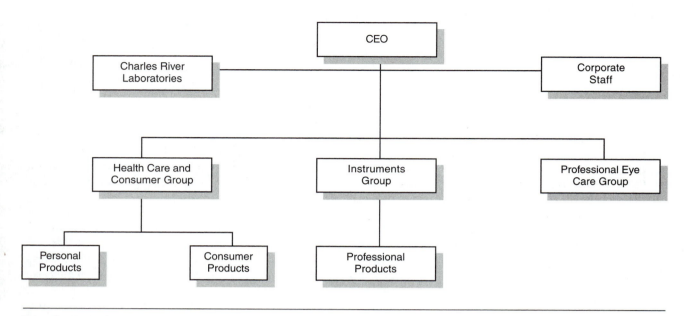

Source: Company records.

technology resided in the U.S. companies, which were each responsible for procurement, manufacturing, and R&D for the rest of the world.

In 1984, international sales accounted for 25% of the professional eye care division, 20% of the personal products division, 31% of the consumer products division, and 34% of the instruments division. International operations varied in size and sophistication, ranging from fully developed subsidiaries with product-specialized sales forces to distributor subsidiaries in which a handful of sales managers coordinated third-party distribution efforts. In the United States, eye care and eye wear products were sold through seven different channels, whereas in most other countries opticians remained the dominant retail channel for both contact lenses and sunglasses.

The Drivers of Organizational Change

Headed by a country manager, each country subsidiary typically had a product manager and sales organization for each product line, resulting in duplication of selling effort and administrative inefficiencies. In 1984, for example, the French subsidiary was made up of three $10 million businesses, none of which had the critical mass of sales or

earnings to retain quality management. Each product manager within a country reported to the worldwide product division manager at headquarters in addition to his or her country manager. Consequently, the country managers' decision-making power was low. B&L executives explained: "The problem was that no one had the authority to set priorities in a particular country and decide which business was more important."

By 1984, country managers started to complain that the Rochester-based division headquarters were not responding to their requests for specific products and/or were sending them products they did not want. On the other hand, Rochester-based product division managers, more focused on the demands of the U.S. market, protested that they could not customize their programs for each of 23 country managers. In addition, by 1984, some international subsidiaries had become larger than the smallest of B&L's seven U.S. businesses, but had to go through two levels of decision making at headquarters to have their programs approved. In effect, the headquarters staff was slowing down the company's growth. Gill noted: "It was becoming increasingly apparent that B&L needed a better focus on its international business."

B&L asked the consulting group of Booz-Allen & Hamilton (BAH) to define organizational alternatives to resolve these increasing conflicts. Following interviews with both Rochester-based and international staff, BAH proposed the creation of a new International Division (ID) with full functional capabilities. The ID was organized into regions encompassing a number of country subsidiaries, each run by a single country manager responsible for all B&L business in the country. (Exhibit 2 shows the new organizational structure.)

The shift to the ID was driven in part by a desire to achieve larger operating units in each country. The resulting benefits included a reduction in headcount and the emergence of a stronger country manager. The ID could now plan with each country manager how much emphasis should be placed on each product line and establish market-specific goals such as obtaining regulatory approval for lens care products. The achievement of these and other goals determined a country manager's bonuses.

Results of ID Structure

By 1992, international sales accounted for almost 50% of B&L's revenues, having grown, on average, by 25% a year since 1987. B&L's international success was reflected by the market shares held by its major products. Outside the United States, B&L held over 25% of the contact lens market, over 40% of the market for high-quality sunglasses, and almost 25% of the lens solution market.

B&L believed that this growth was driven largely by the entrepreneurship of local country managers. B&L executives explained: "Prior to 1985, we were a U.S. business with what we regarded as sales affiliates in international markets. After the creation of the ID, we recognized the importance of our international subsidiaries and chose a single country manager who could lead and develop each subsidiary."

Selecting country managers proved difficult; it was hard to find managers equally excited about the challenge and competent enough to market fashion-intensive products such as Ray-Bans and technology-intensive lens

---

Exhibit 2   Bausch & Lomb Reorganization with International Division: August 1984

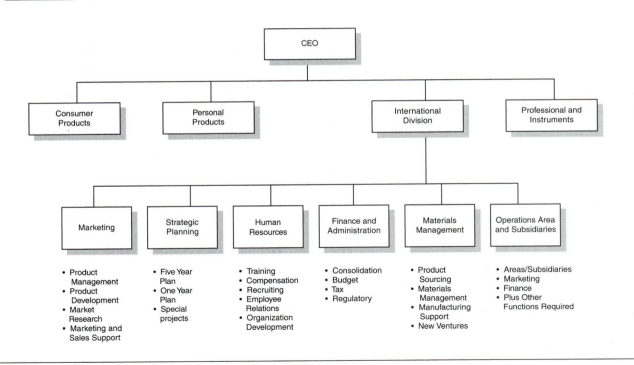

Source: Company records.

care products. Most candidates had emerged from the lens care business but, by 1992, fewer than 50% of the country managers who predated the ID were still in place. Gill was determined to find skilled, entrepreneurial country managers who could put into practice B&L's philosophy of "making every decision as close to the customer as possible."

The benefits of the ID included an expansion of international production facilities, faster response to local country and new capacity needs, and increased market shares and penetration in overseas markets. One B&L executive noted: "Prior to the ID, if a product division manager at headquarters had difficulty getting into a country market, due to tariff restrictions, that particular country would have been ignored. Had the organization not changed, countries such as China, India, and Mexico would never have been developed by B&L."

THE SITUATION IN 1992

During the 1980s, B&L exited certain cyclical industrial product businesses and acquired growing, high-margin businesses with strong brand names (such as Interplak, a line of plaque-removing instruments). By 1992, B&L was focused on two business areas: Healthcare and Optics. Healthcare products, accounting for 60% of 1992 sales, included personal health products (lens care, oral care, eye care, and medications), medical products (contact lenses, prescription pharmaceuticals, and hearing care) and biomedical products. Optics, accounting for 40% of sales in 1992, included sunglasses, sports optics (binoculars and telescopes), and optical thin-film coatings that improved light performance in medically related markets such as operating rooms. (Exhibit 3 lists the main products in each line and their sales volumes in 1992.)

B&L's major international product lines fell into two business segments: the Eyewear business, comprising mainly sunglasses; and the Vision Care business, comprising contact lenses and lens care products (contact lens solutions).

Eyewear In 1992, sunglasses represented 75% of B&L's total Optics sales. B&L Ray-Ban sunglasses, making up over 98% of all B&L sunglasses sales, were considered global in appeal and availability; similar benefits were valued by consumers throughout the world regardless of the stage of economic development of the geographic market. In the early 1980s, B&L sunglasses were sold predominantly through opticians in the United States. However,

by 1992, sunglasses were no longer merely functional products but also fashion products, sold through a broad range of outlets including department stores and duty-free shops. B&L believed that this trend would also subsequently occur outside the United States, where sunglasses continued to be sold mainly through opticians.

In 1992, U.S. manufacturing supplied 70% of Ray-Ban's worldwide unit sales and 40% of international unit sales. Production facilities outside the United States included Waterford, Ireland, where plastic sunglasses were manufactured and all sunglasses could be assembled; Pforzheim, Germany, where metal parts were manufactured for European products; and Hong Kong, where there was an assembly plant. The B&L sunglasses product line comprised 350 stockkeeping units (SKUs)— a figure that had been constant for the past three to four years. Approximately 100 SKUs were replaced each year; it was estimated that, in 1993, 15% of sales would be derived from these new products. Headquarters R&D served all Ray-Ban markets.

Vision Care Worldwide sales of contact lenses approached $300 million in 1992 and major brands included B&L traditional soft contact lenses; SeeQuence disposable soft lenses, designed to be discarded after being worn for one or two weeks; Medalist planned replacement soft lenses, designed to be changed every one to six months; Quantum, rigid gas permeable lenses; and Boston Envision, rigid gas permeable lenses. B&L held 25% of the world market for contact lenses and planned to grow through new product development and geographical expansion. The SeeQuence line was strong in the United States, and B&L hoped to develop the Japanese and selected European markets. The Quantum line was strong in Europe and Asia, and the Boston Envision line had, in 1992, been heavily promoted in Latin America.

In 1992, lens care products worldwide sales were over $350 million, of which 67% came from North America, 16% from both Europe and Asia, and 1% from Latin America. B&L's ReNu multipurpose solution was the world's most advanced product for the care of soft contact lenses, and worldwide sales had risen from $57 million in 1988 to $152 million in 1992. The Boston line of solutions were used with rigid gas permeable lenses, and 1992 worldwide sales reached $66 million. B&L believed that the lens care market had become more technology driven and that more marketing and educational programs needed to be directed at eye care professionals.

	1992 Sales ($ millions)	Percentage Non-U.S.
HEALTHCARE		
Personal:	$540	33%
Lens care products		
Oral care products		
Eye care products		
OTC medications		
Medical:	341	47
Contact lenses		
Prescription pharmaceuticals		
Hearing care		
Biomedical (Charles River Labs)	155	NA
OPTICS		
Sunglasses	500	53
Sports optics	100	35
Optical thin films	25	50

Source: Company records.

B&L supplied eye care professionals with care kits for new contact lens wearers and estimated that more than 80% of patients who started out using a B&L kit became loyal, long-term buyers of B&L lens care products. B&L intended to continue to streamline and simplify lens care regimens. Lens care sales depended highly on the volume of contact lens sales, and the marketing synergies between the two product lines were recognized and exploited.

Vision Care products were manufactured in Germany, Ireland, Italy, and the United States. B&L planned to open manufacturing facilities for soft contact lenses and lens care products in both India and China.

B&L Strengths

Gill described the company's strengths in 1992: "B&L has superior technology that results in quality products. Eighty-five percent of our sales are in product categories where B&L is the world leader. During the 1980s, investments were made to upgrade manufacturing facilities so now B&L is the low-cost producer in the main categories we compete in."

B&L executives described the company as highly goal-oriented and decentralized, unique in its managers' willingness to challenge the status quo and to do whatever it took to get a job done. Gill was seen as a catalyst for change; he communicated to employees that change was a way of life at B&L. Key managers were promoted through a variety of roles, broadening them beyond their areas of functional expertise and developing a top management team of seasoned generalists.

The main company driver was technology and the ability to narrow the time between conceptualization and commercialization of products. Future success depended on developing better products, faster. R&D and productivity issues were expected to remain critical to B&L's success.

In marketing its products to consumers, B&L placed more emphasis on gaining the support of professional intermediaries such as opticians than on advertising. One B&L executive explained: "We are not a typical consumer marketing company. We emphasize push rather than pull marketing. For example, we focus on educating dental professionals to recommend our Interplak product line and we still rely heavily on opticians to recommend Ray-Bans even though they are now also sold through department stores."

Problems with the ID Structure

By 1990, a growing number of internal challenges had arisen. The U.S. domestic divisions and ID made separate marketing and manufacturing decisions. As a result, brands such as Ray-Ban sunglasses and B&L contact lenses could not be managed globally. Pricing disparities raised important diversion problems. For example, a typical pair of Ray-Ban sunglasses that sold to the trade for $25 in the United States were sold for $60 to the trade by B&L France. A pair of contact lenses that sold to the trade for $6.70 in the United States would be sold in Japan for over $30. Due to the high value-to-bulk-ratio of these products, some distributors reshipped product bought in the United States to other countries for resale at below B&L's suggested prices, often through unauthorized channels. It was estimated that as much as 30% of U.S. Ray-Ban sunglass sales were diverted in this way.

Tensions between the ID and U.S. domestic divisions increased as the latter were criticized for shortchanging the ID of R&D and manufacturing resources. In addition, manufacturing plants tended to set production schedules without sufficient concern for the optimal allocation of global capacity. As the ID expanded, it gained increasing influence relative to the domestic U.S. divisions which, by 1990, were affected by a downturn in the U.S. economy.

Gill described the impact of these problems:

> Some competitors were fighting us globally but we were only responding to them as local competitors. The lack of communication between the ID and U.S. divisions meant that we did not see that Johnson & Johnson was attacking us in the disposable lens business worldwide, not just in the domestic market. Incentive plans were geographically based so, for example, the Irish plant manager would not cut production on items that could be manufactured more cheaply in the United States, because this would have caused negative manufacturing variances and lowered his bonus. The culture at B&L has always been very profit driven.

Country managers from France, Italy, and Spain complained that decisions were made too far away and too slowly. Optimizing manufacturing capacity worldwide and standardizing product quality requirements proved hard to achieve. Some B&L executives believed that the successful growth of the ID had resulted in an increasing central bureaucracy in Rochester that was not responsive to local subsidiaries.

Gill's inclination was to push decision making down the organization and increase the autonomy of B&L's international subsidiaries. He believed that an organizational change was inevitable given the rapid growth of international operations. However, it was clear that certain issues, such as global pricing, would require increased cross-border coordination in tandem with decentralization.

REGIONALIZATION

In January 1991, a task force was established to generate and review alternative organizational structures that would help resolve the conflicts and allow B&L to continue its international expansion. The B&L task force, working with McKinsey consultants, set three parameters for its work: speed of results; process to be driven by B&L executives; and input from as many B&L employees as possible. Some B&L executives were skeptical about the need for change, remarking that, in its international businesses, B&L had achieved a 25% compound annual growth rate (CAGR) and margins between 15% and 20% in the early 1990s. They argued: "If it ain't broke, why fix it?"

The Task Force

Six key B&L employees were assigned to the task force. They included the VP of Marketing from the Polymer Technology Division; the VP of Business Development from the Eyewear Division; the VP of International Marketing from the ID; the U.S. Controller from the Personal Products Division; the Staff VP of Financial Planning and Analysis from corporate HQ; and a senior executive who had just completed a Harvard Business School senior executive program, who became chair of the task force. The project comprised three phases: information gathering via over 20 workshops and 150 interviews with B&L employees worldwide; further in-depth interviews on issues raised in the first phase, and the development of a list of organizational options; and a further refinement of the most attractive options. The team reported periodically to an Advisory Committee of corporate officers and eventually prepared final recommendations for the Management Executive Committee. The whole process was completed within seven months.

The project team concluded that the current organizational structure was no longer appropriate, given B&L's

growing international revenues. The team considered several organizational options. These were, in order of the degree of change involved, fine-tuning of the current organization structure; a regional structure; a product-region matrix; and a global product structure. (These options are depicted in Exhibit 4.)

The Proposed Organizational Change

The Advisory Committee rejected the fine-tuning option: although it would be easy to implement (low risk and low cost), it did not improve the focus on specific businesses within the international division. The matrix organization offered a balance between a geographic and a business focus while resulting in little structural change at the subsidiary level. However, it was felt to be contrary to B&L's cultural emphasis on clear decision-making responsibility and, as a result, potentially confusing and difficult to implement. The regional and global product organizational structures were considered more favorably. (The pros and cons of each are summarized in Table A.)

The regional structure was eventually selected because it helped achieve B&L's strategic objectives and resolved key issues. In addition, it was thought to be flexible enough to accommodate subsequent revision if necessary.

Exhibit 4   Bausch & Lomb Organization Options Considered by the Task Force: 1992

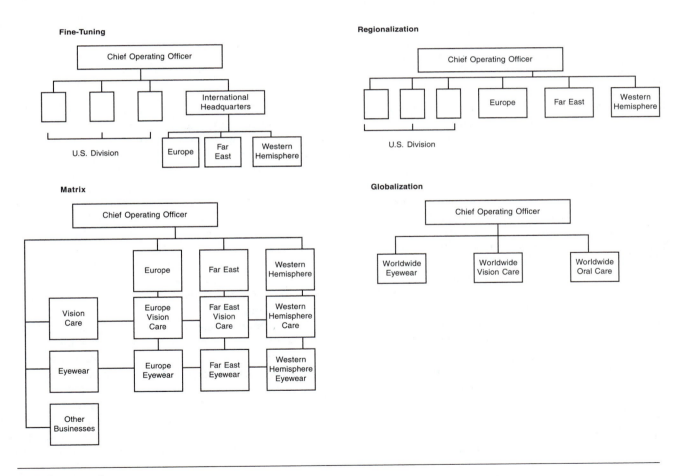

Source: Company records.

Table A — Pros and Cons of the Regionalization and Globalization Options

	Pros	Cons
Globalization	• Improves coordination • Captures U.S. lens/lens care synergies • Provides individual business focus • Develops global managers • Fosters global-oriented decision making	• Reduces responsibilities of regions and countries • Risk of decision making being driven by the United States • Difficult to capture synergies between international eyewear and vision care sales forces[a]
Regionalization	• Improves coordination • Moderate structural change • Elevates role of region presidents, increasing focus on non -U.S. operations • Provides opportunity to develop global thinking • Decision making pushed closer to markets	• Lack of product line focus • No cross-regional integration of functions • Wide COO span of control • Dual role of regional presidents as corporate executives and champions of their respective regions

[a] In many international markets, eyewear and vision care product lines were marketed through the same distribution channels by different sales forces.

In effect, the ID would be eliminated and replaced by three autonomous, self-contained regional headquarters: Europe, Middle East and Africa; Asia-Pacific; and Western Hemisphere. The three regional presidents were expected to ensure that their countries' new product ideas and needs were developed quickly and that an integrated strategy was developed for each business line in the countries in their respective regions, approved by corporate headquarters.

Of the 160 people currently employed by the ID, it was expected that 50% would be reassigned to one of the three regional headquarters, 25% to corporate headquarters in MIS and finance positions, and 25% to the various U.S. divisions. Several B&L companies including Charles River Laboratories ($155 million in annual sales), Sports Optics Division ($100 million) and Thin Film Technology ($25 million) would maintain separate responsibility for their operations outside the United States. The organization of U.S. operations would remain unchanged and structured around product lines. Almost all B&L's R&D would remain in the United States.

Committees and Networks

To coordinate decision making between the regions and U.S. operations, Business Management Committees (BMCs) and Global Business Networks (GBNs) were

conceived. Three BMCs would meet the need for high-level worldwide strategic coordination for B&L's three core product lines: Eyewear (sunglasses), Oral Care, and Vision Care (contact lenses and solutions). These BMCs would maintain communication of the individual division's strategic imperatives; identify strategic issues of global importance, such as Ray-Ban sunglass and contact lens pricing; and coordinate initiatives and resolve conflicts with a common global perspective. The members of BMCs would include the U.S. Division presidents, the regional presidents, and B&L's president and COO. The latter's role would be to ensure that as many decisions as possible were made at the BMC level rather than in the Executive Committee.

Five GBNs were conceived, covering marketing and operations functions: Oral Care Marketing and Operations; Eyewear Operations; Eyewear Marketing; Vision Care Operations; and Vision Care Marketing. The purpose of the GBNs would be to facilitate communication across functions and to identify and coordinate decision making on issues of global importance. As indicated in Exhibit 5, network participants would be senior middle managers with specific functional responsibilities drawn from both the U.S. divisions and the regional headquarters. For example, GBN participants might include the

Exhibit 5   Network Members

Eyewear Operations Network

VP-Operations, Western Hemisphere
   (Chairman)
VP-Manufacturing, Eyewear Division
Director-Materials, Eyewear Division
VP-RD&E, Eyewear Division
VP-Quality, Eyewear Division
VP-Operations, Asia-Pacific Division
General Manager, B&L Ireland Sunglass

Eyewear Marketing Network

VP-Marketing, Eyewear Division
VP-Eyewear Marketing, Western
   Hemisphere Division
Director, Consumer Products, B&L Japan
VP-Eyewear Marketing, Europe Division
VP-Sales, Eyewear Division
VP-Worldwide New Product Marketing,
   Eyewear Division
Marketing Director, East Asia Region,
   Asia-Pacific Division
Market Research & Services Manager,
   Eyewear Division

Vision Care Operations Network

VP-Operations, Personal Products Division
   (Chairman)
VP-Operations, Contact Lens Division
Director-Manufacturing Operations, Polymer
   Technology Corporation
VP-Operations, Europe Division
VP-Operations, Asia-Pacific Division
VP-Operations, Western Hemisphere
   Division

Vision Care Marketing Network

VP & GM, Contact Lens Division
   (Chairman)
VP-Vision Care Marketing, Western
   Hemisphere Division
VP-Vision Care Marketing, Europe Division
VP-U.S. & Int'l Operations, Polymer
   Technology Corporation
Director-Marketing, Asia-Pacific Division
Marketing Product Manager-Contact
   Lenses, B&L Japan

Oral Care Network

VP-International Oral Care (Chairman)
VP-Operations, Oral Care Division
Division Director, Oral Care Division,
   B&L Canada
VP-Operations, Asia-Pacific
VP-Marketing, Oral Care Division

VP-Oral Care Marketing, Europe Division
Director Engineering/
   Development-Oral Care Division
Director-Oral Care Business, B&L Japan
Manager-Oral Care, B&L Netherlands
Director-International Oral Care

VP of operations from the Western Hemisphere Division, the VP of marketing from the Eyewear Division, and the VP of marketing from the European Division. The responsibility for chairing each GBN would rotate every 18 months among the network members. GBNs would meet at least three times a year in addition to frequent tele-conferencing and video-conferencing. (Exhibit 6 outlines a sample agenda for an Eyewear Marketing Network meeting.)

The BMCs and GBNs were regarded as critical to the new organizational structure. B&L executives sought to ensure that participation on these committees would be seen as an honor and that participation should be included in job

Exhibit 6   Sample Agenda for an Eyewear Marketing Network Meeting

- Role of Marketing Network
  - Communication
  - Coordination

- Key Projects
  - Coordination of market research
  - Quality standards
  - Bench-marking
  - Pricing
  - Warranty/returns
  - Strategic plan volumes
  - UV Issue[a]

- Secondary Projects
  - Opinion leaders of the 1990s

- Core principles

- New products

- Review of financial results by region

- Competition

[a]The U.V. (ultraviolet) issue concerns the holographic markings that could be used to identify the distributor source of product and reduce product diversion.

descriptions and evaluation criteria. Some executives questioned how many GBNs should be set up and what issues they should address. On the one hand, B&L wanted to avoid too many networks since this might result in confusion and second-guessing and waste management time. At the same time, executives in charge of functions such as quality control and regulatory compliance also wanted the status of having GBNs that would address their issues.

Gill believed that the effectiveness of the BMCs and GBNs would depend largely on each chairperson's leadership capabilities and coordination abilities, and that different product lines would benefit to varying degrees from the increased coordination. For example, lens solutions were subject to local regulations and there appeared to be a limited opportunity for cross-regional or country transfer. On the other hand, contact lens solutions in the United States had moved from prescription status to widespread over-the-counter (OTC) distribution. This transition was thought likely to occur in other countries, and B&L executives believed that substantial information and

expertise could be transferred from the United States to other countries to prepare for these market developments. In the case of sunglasses, the worldwide introductions of new product lines appropriately adapted to different markets would require considerable coordination.

The designated chairperson of the vision care marketing network did not anticipate any coordination problems within the network. He explained: "There are no really contentious issues. The minor issues that may come up will be resolved pretty quickly. My guess is that the network will be highly cooperative. One reason is that, in the past, there have been no strong disagreements on marketing strategy in the vision care field."

The prospective chairperson of the eyewear marketing network had a different view. He stated:

One of the main issues at B&L is the relationship between the U.S. and ID concerning Ray-Ban sunglasses. It will take some time before network members start communicating, given the current level of distrust. Eventually the network will be able to add value because we will be able to create a common agenda and a clear set of goals. Achieving this, however, will take time and effort.

Benefits and Challenges

Regionalization was expected, first, to empower regional and country managers and encourage entrepreneurship in country subsidiaries. The transfer of marketing, product planning, and operational support functions to the regions would enhance B&L's capabilities in the field. Support functions would be closer to the customer, enabling subsidiaries to respond quickly to local customer needs. Second, the increased emphasis placed by B&L on international experience would enable the company to create a pool of global managers to become future leaders in the company. Third, the BMCs and GBNs would stimulate communication within the company, facilitate worldwide strategic planning, and transfer the best ideas and practices to markets everywhere. Finally, it was expected that regionalization would encourage further sales growth in international markets because regional managers would be more likely than the ID to focus on untapped country markets within their regions.

Gill believed that the key to growth and success lay with B&L's country general managers. The 27 subsidiary managers had been increasingly frustrated by the slow decision making of the Rochester-based ID. Regionalization would enable them to have decisions discussed and approved more quickly.

At the same time, there was concern that regionalization would not resolve the fundamental challenges facing B&L in 1992. First, it was not clear that the necessary coordination between U.S. product divisions and international operations would be achieved through the BMCs and GBNs. Under the current ID structure, a special staff liaised between the country organizations and the Rochester-based product managers. Under regionalization, each region would deal directly with U.S.-based product divisions, possibly adding to the complexity of coordination. In addition, the B&L culture, based on decentralization, entrepreneurship, and accountability, did not obviously mesh with the coordination culture required to make the BMCs and GBNs work effectively. Several B&L executives believed that the success of regionalization would depend on the success of the BMCs and GBNs and that, therefore, clarifying their terms of reference, membership obligations, and ability to implement decisions was critical.

Second, as the country subsidiaries continued to grow, the regional headquarters, particularly in Europe, could become an obstacle to speedy decision making just as the ID had become. As subsidiaries grew both in volume and product-line complexity, country general managers would have less time to oversee each particular product line. The same span of control problem might be true of regional presidents who would have to manage a growing number of ever-expanding country subsidiaries.

From the consumer perspective, potential benefits of the reorganization included products that would be locally adapted, higher service levels, more consistent positioning, and more new products brought to market faster. B&L intended to discontinue the traditional approach of rolling out a new product one market at a time in favor of simultaneous introductions in several countries across all regions.

REGIONAL ORGANIZATION AND MARKETING EFFECTIVENESS

The impact of the regional organization on the marketing function was expected to vary by region. In Europe, it was expected that there would be three Marketing VPs covering Oral Care, Vision Care, and Eyewear. Asia was thought to be behind Europe on the development curve, and, due to greater diversity of markets, a standard regional marketing approach seemed less likely; the regional marketing staff might specialize geographically, with some executives focusing on more- developed markets like Japan and others focusing on emerging markets like China, Malaysia, the Philippines, and Taiwan. In GBNs, such as the Vision Care Marketing Network, it seemed likely that more than one marketing manager from Asia would have to be included. At the same time, there appeared to be more hitherto unexploited marketing coordination opportunities in the Asia/Pacific region than in Europe.

There was concern that the Western Hemisphere region would lack the critical mass to warrant a regional marketing organization. Canada, although included in the region, had frequent contact with U.S. operations because of geographical proximity and market similarity. For example, the contact lens solutions business in Canada was OTC driven (the only other country apart from the United States where this was true). While Canada's role in the new Western Hemisphere remained unclear, Latin America had been a "lost continent" under the ID structure and was expected to benefit from the visibility that regionalization would provide. Marketing in Latin American subsidiaries focused more on the basics of sales and distribution whereas strategic marketing issues were perhaps more important in the European subsidiaries.

In 1992, 27 subsidiaries, 6 joint-ventures (China, Indonesia, Korea, Hong Kong, India, and Japan), and many national distributors sold B&L products around the world. Additional export operations existed in Geneva for Africa and the Middle East; in Miami for smaller Latin American countries; and in Hong Kong for East Asia. (Exhibit 7 lists the subsidiaries and joint ventures by region.)

Product Development

Prior to regionalization, all new product development decisions on which technologies and fashion trends to pursue were made in Rochester. ID Headquarters developed the products and marketing programs that were launched around the world. Under regionalization, each region would have its own product development team and be able to develop unique products for its own markets if this made economic sense. If a product manager in France had a new product idea which the French country manager endorsed, its regional and worldwide potential would then be evaluated at European headquarters. If the idea was deemed to have worldwide potential, the VP of Marketing for Europe would present the idea to the relevant GBN. The U.S.-based development group, also represented on the GBN, would give priority to those ideas that promised to generate the most profits worldwide. Ideas specific to a single, small market would receive the lowest priority. The development group would then prepare production plans and decide where the product would be manufactured.

R&D groups in Rochester handled the various B&L product lines. If a subsidiary wished to develop, at its own expense, a local packaging variation that had no medical or regulatory implications, it would be able to do so under regionalization. If, however, the desired variation held implications for product stability (as, for example, in a switch from polyethylene to clear plastic containers for contact lens solutions), R&D groups in Rochester would have to be involved.

Market Research and Advertising

Under the ID structure, B&L's eyewear businesses outside the United States had sought out an advertising agency that not only could implement a global campaign but also be a global strategic partner. Young and Rubicam was selected as the Eyewear agency of record for all international subsidiaries and subsequently improved the coordination of advertising strategy around the world. A pool of print executions and television commercials with voiceovers was available to subsidiaries; they could also shoot commercials locally at their own expense subject to ID approval. The process of formulating advertising strategy was not expected to change very much under regionalization although it was expected that the European region, in concert with Young and Rubicam, would play a leadership role in copy development and that the other regions would follow suit. Some B&L executives believed that this would not result in consistent global advertising. Subsidiaries would still be able to use local advertising developed at their expense subject to regional headquarters approval.

There were no market research studies carried out in a consistent manner worldwide. It was hoped that the GBNs would be able to establish standardized market research tracking studies for each product line. Increasingly, product managers wanted to understand consumer trends in other geographical markets beyond their own and believed that market information gathered in a consistent way around the world would help. Recent market research, used to develop advertising copy strategies for sunglasses, had shown that very similar consumer drivers were at work in both France and the United States.

The B&L logo and most brand names were not expected to change. Some brand name variation across country markets might be rationalized. For example, the U.S. contact lens ReNu solution was marketed as ReNew in France, and as Multipurpose in four other European countries.

Pricing

In 1992, the U.S. Eyewear Division's sales of sunglasses and its manufacturing capacity utilization were being boosted by substantial product diversion. Distributors buying product in the United States could profitably resell a portion of their purchases in overseas markets where B&L factory prices were often higher than in the United States. U.S. Eyewear executives believed that to control diversion, they might have to discontinue about 15 U.S. distributors, resulting in a loss in revenues of approximately $30 million for the U.S. Division. It was hoped that the BMCs, with the help of the COO, would be able to coordinate pricing strategies and worldwide distribution to minimize product diversion. For example,

Exhibit 7   B&L Subsidiaries by Operational Activity: 1984–1992

	Manufacturing		Marketing	
	1984	1992[a]	1984	1992[a]
United States	21	25	0	5
Bermuda	0	0	0	3 W.O.
Brazil	0	2 W.O.	0	2 W.O.
Canada	1	1 W.O.	2	2 W.O.
Colombia	0	0	0	1 W.O.
Mexico	0	1 MIN	0	1 MIN
Puerto Rico	0	0	1	1 W.O.
Venezuela	0	0	0	1 W.O.
Austria	0	0	1	1 W.O.
Belgium	0	1 MAJ	0	0
Czechoslovakia	0	1 W.O.	0	0
Denmark	0	0	1	1 W.O.
Finland	0	0	1	1 W.O.
France	1	2 W.O./MAJ	1	1 W.O.
Germany	0	8 W.O.	0	1 W.O.
Great Britain	1	3 W.O.	1	3 W.O.
Greece	0	0	0	1 BRC (W.O.)
Hungary	0	1 W.O.	0	0
Ireland[b]	1	1	0	0 BRC (W.O.)
Italy	2	2 W.O./MAJ	2	2 W.O., BRC (W.O.)
Netherlands	0	0 W.O.	0	1 W.O.
Norway	0	1	1	1 W.O.
Portugal	0	0	0	1
Spain	0	2 MAJ/W.O.	1	1 W.O.
Sweden	0	0	1	1 W.O.
Switzerland	0	1 W.O.	2	2 W.O.
Australia	0	0	1	1 W.O.
Hong Kong	1	1 W.O.	1	0
India	0	1 MIN	0	1[c]
Indonesia	0	1 MAJ	0	1 MAJ
Japan	2	2 MIN/W.O.	1	1[c]
Malaysia	0	1 W.O.	0	0
New Zealand	0	0	0	1 W.O.
P.R. of China	0	1 MAJ	0	0
Philippines	0	0	1	0
Singapore	0	0	1	1 W.O.
South Korea	0	1 MAJ	0	0
Taiwan	1	2 MAJ/W.O.	1	0
Turkey	0	0	0	1 W.O.

[a]Type of subsidiary (1992): W.O.—wholly owned; MAJ—joint venture with majority ownership; MIN—joint venture with minority ownership; BRC (W.O.)—branch, wholly owned; DIS—distributor.
[b]Bausch & Lomb Ireland was a branch of Bausch & Lomb (Bermuda) Limited.
[c]Planned for start-up in 1992.

to discourage diversion by permitting identification of the distributor source of product, each product could be marked with an invisible holographic marking that became clear under ultraviolet light.

IMPACT ON THE EYEWEAR AND VISION CARE BUSINESSES

Eyewear

B&L's Ray-Ban brand had benefited from the ID organization. Worldwide sales of Ray-Ban had skyrocketed from $60 million to over $500 million between 1985 and 1992, corresponding to a 30% compound annual growth rate. Under the ID's auspices, Ray-Ban sunglasses with fittings adapted to Oriental faces had been developed for the Asian market. In addition, a new product development group had recently been established to determine where new products should be made and to help manufacturing plants reduce product start-up costs. Product development times had been reduced from 12 to 5 months and ideas for changes in product design were solicited from B&L marketing executives worldwide. R&D and design were gradually becoming more customer driven. Consumer dissatisfaction with lenses that scratched had resulted in R&D developing a diamond-hard, nonscratchable lens. Development objectives for 1993 included a line for women aged over 30 years, based on a brief from marketing.

B&L Eyewear executives in Rochester believed Ray-Ban was a global brand that required global coordination of pricing and advertising strategies. Consequently, they felt that a worldwide product division headquartered in the United States was preferable to a regional organization which would encourage the regional presidents to build independent fiefdoms with their own manufacturing plants, design teams, and other functions. Despite being recognized throughout the world, there was no worldwide positioning or advertising strategy for the Ray-Ban brand. Under regionalization, this was likely to continue. There was also skepticism that regionalization would help resolve the pricing and diversion problems. Some executives feared that the GBNs such as the Eyewear Marketing Network might focus on old problems rather than new ways to share information and leverage good ideas. Under the ID structure, there were two decision-making entities—the United States and the ID—both located in Rochester. With regionalization, there would be four decision-making entities in different locations, adding to the complexity of communication and coordination.

Vision Care

Country markets varied in both preference and regulations governing the different kinds of lenses and chemical specifications of lens care solutions. Contact lenses in particular had to be adapted to meet specific country regulations. Lens care products also had specific packaging and labeling requirements depending upon the country. Neither product line could, in 1992, be described as global. Vision Care executives believed that regionalization would substantially benefit the business. However, some B&L executives argued that country specific differences were still important, reflecting varying stages of market development, and that most markets would likely follow product trends set in the United States.

IMPACT ON THE EUROPEAN REGION

Regionalization would aid independent and faster decision making in Europe, the largest region. Money would be saved through the consolidation of certain back room functions at the regional office and through regional sourcing of standard data processing and other equipment to be used in the country offices in the region. In addition, regionalization promised that new product initiatives could be pursued and launched in Europe even if the United States was not interested. The regional marketing manager would coordinate the development of pan-European strategies and marketing programs where consistency was considered appropriate and/or saved money. For example, common European product catalogs could be developed.

The European regional headquarters was expected to grow from 16 to 35 people. Most of the new positions would be in accounting and finance since the European headquarters would consolidate results for the region before forwarding them to Rochester. Eight people would work in Marketing, including three vice presidents—each overseeing one of B&L's main product lines—and a vice president of business development.

Following regionalization, the marketing manager of a country subsidiary such as France would participate in shaping regional marketing strategies and setting new product development priorities in conjunction with the European regional headquarters in London. The French marketing manager would report to a country general manager, as before, who in turn would report to the vice president of field operations of B&L Europe. Product managers for all the country subsidiaries in a region would meet three or four times a year in addition to a formal annual regional meeting. Sales and brand contribution in their own markets would remain the basis for their compensation while, at the country manager level, 25% of the annual bonus would be based on pan-European performance to encourage coordination and communication.

Ray-Ban sunglasses had a similar brand image throughout Europe and a dominant market share of the premium sunglasses market in most European countries. In 1992, sales growth was derived from expansion into new distribution channels (such as airport duty-free shops) and new product development. The ability to influence new product development was considered by B&L executives in Europe to be critical to future growth. Contact lens solutions were also believed to represent an important growth opportunity in Europe; idea transfers from the United States through the GBNs were expected to be useful, particularly for the ReNew product.

CONCLUSION

The principal issue for senior B&L executives was how to manage the company's international growth. Under the seven-year period of the ID, the subsidiaries' average annual revenues had grown from $20 million to $55 million, but some executives believed that the subsidiaries could have grown even faster had they been able to take more initiative in generating and developing their own marketing ideas. These executives hoped that the three regional headquarters would push more decision-making responsibility down to the subsidiaries.

PART VII

Social Enterprise and Global Marketing

In the text and in the cases presented in the first six parts of this book, we have focused on the marketing-based strategies, concepts, and tools used by multinational companies (MNCs) to help define their relationships and exchanges with their customers and consumers in markets around the world. But in a world in which—according to the World Bank's 2003 Development Report—a quarter of the population exists on less than $1 per day, 1 billion people suffer from malnutrition, and 10 million children die annually from preventable diseases, it is clear that the principal agents in providing goods and services cannot always be MNCs, and that the exchanges cannot always be defined in commercial terms.

Yet this does not mean that companies cannot or should not be involved in dealing with such problems, or even that marketing concepts are irrelevant. In this final part of *Global Marketing Management*, we consider global marketing's role in what we describe as "social enterprise." In doing so, we examine a group of organizations and a set of activities operating in an international business environment characterized not only by the huge opportunities we have emphasized thus far, but also by major social, political, and economic problems that cannot be ignored by those who benefit from the opportunities.

We use the term "social enterprise" to describe two quite different types of global entities: MNCs acting not only in response to their normal profit maximization motive, but also through a sense of corporate social responsibility; and nonprofit organizations that operate in a global environment to provide goods and services in response to unmet humanitarian or social needs.

MARKETING AND GLOBAL CORPORATE SOCIAL RESPONSIBILITY

Whereas some companies define their purpose and manage their operations with a tight focus on the single objective of maximizing returns to shareholders, many others define their roles more broadly. For example, Johnson & Johnson's famous credo acknowledges the company's responsibility to provide a fair return to its shareholders, but only *after* meeting its obligations and commitments to doctors and patients, to its suppliers and distributors, to its employees, and to the communities in which it operates.

Particularly in the global business environment of the early twenty-first century, MNCs are being pressured to recognize that they cannot expand into a new country and treat it solely as a market for their goods and services. Governments, activists, and, increasingly, consumers require them to recognize that with the significant power that comes through operating across national boundaries comes an equal responsibility for MNCs to be sensitive and responsive to the needs of the countries in which they operate. Those companies that ignore—or worse, exploit—local community vulnerabilities and social disadvantages often find themselves the object of actions that can put at risk their commercial operations around the world.

Examples abound. In the 1970s, activist groups mounted worldwide consumer action against Nestle in protest of the way it was promoting its baby formula in developing countries; in the 1980s, as a means of bringing about change to apartheid policies, shareholder pressure was brought to bear on companies not to invest in South Africa; in the 1990s, Nike suffered a tarnished image and significant sales losses as the result of a worldwide campaign to protest the company's employment practices and the working conditions of its suppliers in developing countries; and in recent years, the widespread condemnation of a dozen large pharmaceutical companies for their refusal to make AIDS drugs available to poor African nations devastated by the pandemic eventually led the companies to back off their rigid defense of their intellectual property rights in the world's poorest and most vulnerable countries.

Although such pressure has sometimes been necessary to force MNCs to withdraw products, modify designs, reduce prices, or withhold distribution, in many more cases companies have recognized that they can and should take these actions of their own volition. Whether their motivation is to avoid protest action, to promote favorable public relations, to engender a sense of pride among employees, or simply that it is "the right thing to do," a large number of MNCs have begun to view their worldwide product development, distribution, and selling activities not only through the light of competitive strategy, but also through the prism of corporate responsibility.

In a world in which these companies operate largely outside the regulatory control of any one single government, farsighted and responsible management recognizes that with the power and independence that is part of operating in a global context comes a similar responsibility to exercise that power judiciously. The examples of Genzyme and IBM in the cases that follow illustrate companies that try to balance that responsibility with an equally demanding responsibility to be commercially viable.

Operating in a responsible manner does not mean that the concepts, models, and tools of global marketing are irrelevant, however. Indeed, the challenges of developing products that are sensitive to market differences, positioning them in ways that are appropriate to local cultural norms, and pricing and distributing them in a manner that is responsive to local needs becomes a task that requires a delicate and sensitive application of all the marketing concepts in a manager's tool kit. The task is made even more complex by the reality that products (and increasingly, services) flow rapidly across national boundaries, and that concessions made in one market for socially responsible reasons may quickly flow into another and undermine commercial or competitive positions.

NONPROFIT ORGANIZATIONS AND GLOBAL MARKETING

The only management challenge greater than running a multinational company across the barriers of distance, language, time, and culture may be the enormous difficulty of managing a global humanitarian organization. Not only do these so-called "nongovernmental organizations" (NGOs) operate in the same complex global environment, but they do so in environments in which MNCs seldom tread.

Organizations such as CARE, Oxfam, Save the Children, and others typically find themselves in war-torn countries or famine-ravaged regions where infrastructure is usually poor, government is often unstable, and the needs are huge and urgent. Thrust into these environments on a moment's notice, such NGOs rarely have the time to build the sophisticated structures, systems, and processes that an MNC manager takes for granted. Then, into that hostile environment, they may send a bright 30-year-old with enormous commitment but very limited operating experience and tell him or her to "deal with the crisis." Clearly, these are management challenges that few professional MNC executives will ever see.

Defining their role as "operating in the unserved spaces between governments and companies," the mission of many global NGOs has been evolving over the past few decades. Seeking more sustainable solutions to the difficult problems they tackle, many have expanded from providing short-term humanitarian relief to facilitating long-term community development, and eventually to assuming advocacy roles to pressure others to bring about desired changes.

It is in this process of mission change that many NGOs have begun to interact more directly with MNCs—sometimes in partnership, and sometimes as adversaries. Recall our earlier discussion of Nestle, Nike, and the pharmaceutical companies. In each case, pressure on those companies came largely through the actions of globally organized social advocacy groups. But NGOs can also act as powerful allies and partners of MNCs, teaming up with them in ways that meet the needs of both organizations to deal collaboratively with important social or developmental problems.

In this process of interaction between organizations from the corporate and the nonprofit sectors, both have found ways to learn from each other. In a classic *Harvard Business Review* article titled "What Business Can Learn From Nonprofits," Peter Drucker highlighted three of the key lessons for the corporate world: the power that results from building an organization around a mission, the important trustee role a board must play in governance, and the ability to engage the commitment and dedication of employees.

On the nonprofit side, many of the global NGOs are recognizing that they can take many lessons from the corporate playbook. In particular, they are learning to translate their broad and powerful missions into more tightly defined strategies. More specifically, they are beginning to articulate more explicitly how they "add value" in the work they do.

In this value-added analysis, many NGOs are coming to the central conclusion that one of the most valuable assets they control is their brand. Recent research has shown that brands such as Habitat for Humanity, CARE, and UNICEF have enormous value that needs to be managed with all the care of brands such as Mercedes, Coca Cola, or Sony. They are also learning from the corporate world the importance of communicating effectively with both of their audiences—their donor base as well as their clients. Today, the challenge of fund-raising makes the marketing programs of many of the leading NGOs as sophisticated as some of the most experienced global marketing organizations.

Genzyme's Gaucher Initiative:
Global Risk and Responsibility

In May 2001, Tomye Tierney faced a big decision on an important initiative she had helped create almost three years earlier. Since 1998, Genzyme Corporation's Gaucher Initiative had been providing the company's life-saving drug Cerezyme®[1] to sufferers of Gaucher disease worldwide, regardless of their ability to pay. But now Tierney faced a decision that would determine the future of the bold experiment. Established as a partnership with the respected humanitarian organization Project HOPE, the Gaucher Initiative had been very effective in locating and treating Gaucher patients in many less-developed countries and had built a particularly strong program in Egypt. However, Genzyme's sales organization was becoming increasingly concerned that the fast-growing free distribution program in Egypt represented a barrier to its commercial objectives.

Although the company had grown rapidly in recent years, the high-risk biotech business required that it manage its resources carefully. (Exhibits 1 and 2 summarize Genzyme's financial history.) From the outset, therefore, Genzyme CEO Henri Termeer had told Tierney that the company's commitment to universal provision could not undermine its commercial viability. Specifically, he emphasized that the Gaucher Initiative was not to be viewed as a permanent solution to providing care in any country. Recognizing this, Tierney wondered if the time had come to transfer the care of these patients to the government of Egypt. What if it refused to accept the responsibility? What if Project HOPE was unwilling to scale back its activities? In short, how exactly could the company balance the strong

humanitarian and commercial principles it had built into its culture and values?

BIRTH OF A COMPANY

In contrast to other biotechnology firms that burst on the scene with impressive science-based, discovery-driven business models, Genzyme began by focusing on supplying raw materials—enzymes, fine chemicals, and reagents—to large research labs and pharmaceutical companies. Company co-founder Henry Blair had worked at the New England Enzyme Center of Tufts University School of Medicine and had many contacts in the research community. He founded the company in 1981 on the conservative belief that it should use revenues generated by selling reagents to generate cash flow and to create a track record that would allow it to fund further growth.

With a small pilot plant and office in a loft in Boston's Chinatown, Blair began searching for larger facilities to manufacture enzyme factors and reagents on a large scale. Within a year, he had located a company in the United Kingdom that was producing enzymes, substrates, and intermediates. Dissatisfied with the plant's efficiency and quality, Blair personally relocated to England to improve processes and increase yields. Within a few months the plant was profitable, and Genzyme was generating a positive cash flow. Sales in the first year were $2.2 million.

Laying the Foundation

Among all of Genzyme's early supply agreements, one had particular importance. Building on a long-term relationship he had with the National Institutes of Health (NIH), Blair obtained a contract to manufacture and supply the enzyme glucocerebrosidase (GCR) being used by Dr. Roscoe Brady in research on Gaucher (pronounced GO-shay) disease. Gaucher disease is an extremely rare and deadly condition

This case was prepared by Professor Christopher A. Bartlett with the assistance of Andrew N. McLean.

Exhibit 1   Genzyme Corp. Selected Consolidated Balance Sheets ($000s)

Year ending December 31,	2000	1999	1998	1997	1996	1991	1986	1981[a]
Assets:								
Current assets								
Cash and equivalents	$236,213	$130,156	$118,612	$102,406	$93,132	$29,031	$2,309	$828
Short-term investments	104,586	255,846	175,453	51,259	56,608	78,147	19,496	-
Accounts receivable	205,094	166,803	163,042	118,277	116,833	31,838	2,728	-
Inventories	170,341	117,269	109,833	139,681	125,265	16,329	4,243	-
Prepaid expenses & other	37,681	18,918	31,467	17,361	100,287	3,688	299	-
Deferred tax assets – current	46,836	41,195	41,195	27,601	17,493	-	-	-
Non-current assets								
Net property, plant & equipment	504,412	383,181	382,619	385,348	393,839	32,057	4,020	-
Long-term investments	298,841	266,988	281,664	92,676	38,215	172,529	-	-
Notes receivable – related party	10,350	-	-	2,019	-	4,000	-	-
Net intangibles	1,539,782	253,153	279,516	271,275	247,745	13,362	-	-
Deferred tax assets – non-current	-	18,631	24,277	29,479	42,221	4,186	-	-
Investments in equity securities	121,251	97,859	51,977	30,047	-	-	-	-
Other non-current assets	42,713	37,283	30,669	28,024	38,870	5,371	2,098	-
TOTAL ASSETS	$3,318,100	$1,787,282	$1,690,324	$1,295,453	$1,270,508	$390,538	$33,095	$2,926
Liabilities and stockholders' equity:								
Current liabilities								
Accounts payable	$26,165	$27,853	$27,604	$19,787	$22,271	$4,584	$1,004	-
Accrued expenses	139,683	73,359	72,370	72,103	70,124	10,964	548	-
Payable to joint venture	-	-	1,181	-	-	-	-	-
Income taxes payable	46,745	27,946	16,543	11,168	17,926	4,305	-	-
Deferred revenue	8,609	3,700	2,731	1,800	2,693	1,987	-	-
Current LT debt and lease obligations	19,897	5,080	100,568	905	999	1,484	225	-
Non-current liabilities								
Long-term debt and lease obligations	391,560	18,000	3,087	140,978	241,998	101,044	162	$382
Convertible notes and debentures	273,680	272,622	284,138	29,298	-	-	-	476
Deferred tax liability	230,384	-	8,078	-	-	-	176	-
Other non-current liabilities	6,236	2,330	-	7,364	12,188	6,298	-	1,924
TOTAL LIABILITIES	$1,142,959	$430,890	$516,300	$283,403	$368,199	$130,666	$2,115	$2,782
Stockholders' equity	2,175,141	1,356,392	1,172,554	1,012,050	902,309	259,872	30,979	180
	$3,318,100	$1,787,282	$1,688,854	$1,295,453	$1,270,508	$390,538	$33,094	$2,962

Source: Adapted by casewriters from Genzyme Corp. Annual Reports.

[a] 1981 results cover the period from company inception on June 8, 1981. (Source: Genzyme 1986 IPO Prospectus.)

Exhibit 2 Genzyme Corp. Selected Consolidated Income Statement ($000s)

Year ending December 31,	2000	1999	1998	1997	1996	1991	1986	1981[a]
Revenues:								
Product sales	$811,897	$683,482	$613,685	$529,927	$424,483	$72,019	$9,770	$2,167
Service sales	84,482	79,448	74,791	67,158	68,950	21,503	-	-
Revenue from R&D contracts	6,941	9,358	20,859	11,756	25,321	28,394	2,366	-
TOTAL REVENUES	$903,320	$772,288	$709,335	$608,841	$518,754	$121,916	$12,136	$2,167
Expenses:								
Cost of products sold	$232,383	$182,337	$211,076	$206,028	$155,930	$33,164	$5,421	$936
Cost of services sold	50,177	49,444	48,586	47,289	54,082	14,169	-	-
Selling, admin. & general	264,551	242,797	215,203	200,476	162,264	39,118	5,084	838
Research and development	169,478	150,516	119,005	89,558	80,849	27,232	2,285	57
Purchase of in-process R&D	200,191	5,436	-	7,000	130,639	-	-	-
Charge for impaired asset	4,321	-	-	-	-	-	-	-
Amortization of intangibles	22,974	24,674	24,334	17,245	8,849	-	-	-
TOTAL EXPENSES	$944,075	$655,204	$618,204	$567,596	$592,613	$113,683	$12,790	$1,831
Income (loss) before unusual items	($40,755)	$117,084	$91,131	$41,245	($73,859)	$8,233	($654)	$336
Investment income	$45,593	$36,158	$25,055	$11,409	$15,341	$12,371	$889	-
Interest expense	(15,710)	(21,771)	(22,593)	(12,667)	(6,990)	(2,088)	(194)	(92)
Equity in net loss of unconsolidated affiliates	(44,965)	(42,696)	(29,006)	(12,258)	(5,373)	-	-	-
Affiliate sale of stock	22,689	6,683	2,369	-	1,013	-	-	-
Sale of equity securities	15,873	(3,749)	(6)	-	1,711	-	-	-
Minority interest	4,625	3,674	4,285	-	-	-	-	-
Sale of product line	-	8,018	31,202	-	-	-	-	-
Sale of Gene-Trak	-	-	-	-	-	4,065	-	-
Credit from operating loss carryforward	-	-	-	-	-	8,387	-	-
Other revenue (expense)	5,188	14,527	-	(2,000)	(1,465)	2,726	-	-
Income (loss) before income taxes	($7,462)	$117,928	$102,437	$25,729	($69,622)	$33,694	$41	$244
Provision for income taxes	(55,478)	(46,947)	(39,870)	(12,100)	(3,195)	(12,848)	0	(165)
NET INCOME (LOSS)	($62,940)	$70,981	$62,567	$13,629	($72,817)	$20,846	$41	$79

Source: Adapted by casewriters from Genzyme Corp. Annual Reports.
[a] 1981 results cover the period from company inception on June 8, 1981. (Source: Genzyme 1986 IPO Prospectus.)

caused by the body's inability to manufacture the GCR enzyme. Cells of the spleen, liver, lymph nodes, and bone marrow need GCR to break down and dispose of fatty residues from red blood cells' normal deterioration processes. Without this enzyme, fats collect and cause pain, fatigue, bone deterioration, fractures, and swelling of the affected organs.

Current estimates are that one in 400 of the general population carries the genetic mutations that cause Gaucher disease, but because both parents must pass on the mutation for a person to develop the disease, fewer than six of every one million people worldwide are predicted to have Gaucher disease. Of those 20,000 to 30,000 people, only about a quarter were thought to be ill enough to require treatment. (Populations with more intermarriage report a higher incidence of the disease. For example, among Jewish people of Eastern European ancestry, one in every 450 children is affected.) At the time of Brady's research, the treatment of choice was bone marrow transplantation, an extremely costly procedure with a 10% mortality rate.[2]

Throughout most of the 1970s, Brady's efforts to develop an enzyme replacement therapy had been unsuccessful, but in 1978, some members of his research team began suggesting that the large GCR molecule could better enter affected cells if the carbohydrate portion was modified, or "pruned." However, to put this idea into human trials involved expensive and risky protocols, and other team members expressed serious doubt that the modified molecule would work. After years of divisive internal debate, the NIH team put the "pruned molecule" hypothesis to the test in 1983. In its support role, Genzyme developed a production process for the enzyme required for the trials.

New Management, New Priorities
Meanwhile, Genzyme's top management was in transition. While Blair had been cleaning up the U.K. production processes, company co-founder Sheridan (Sherry) Snyder had been managing the financial and administrative side of the start-up. Although he had a background in the packaging business, Snyder was an entrepreneur and investor more than a professional manager, and the board decided the young company needed to engage a president to support him.

A search firm recommended Henri Termeer, a 36-year-old executive running a business making therapeutic products to treat hemophiliacs at medical products giant Baxter International. Termeer had joined Baxter in 1974 after completing his MBA and had built his reputation as an effective country manager of the company's German subsidiary. The search firm believed that his impressive management record, his broad industry knowledge, and his particular knowledge of blood-derived therapeutic treatment of genetic diseases made him an ideally qualified candidate.

Immediately upon joining Genzyme in October 1983, Termeer initiated a series of weekend discussions involving top management, members of the company's scientific advisory board of MIT and Harvard faculty, key investors, and a few outside advisors. Over several months they developed a few broad strategic principles that would guide Genzyme's future activities. First, Genzyme would be committed to building a diversified portfolio of targeted products and well-defined markets, with a particular focus on niches where needs were largely unmet. Equally important was its determination to remain independent by generating revenues from the start, by integrating vertically across the whole value chain, and by funding new development with internally generated funds or nonequity financial mechanisms.

Termeer also confronted several operating problems. Although he was aware that internal controls were all but nonexistent, the new president was still surprised to discover that one of the U.K. plants listed as an asset a particularly unsuccessful racehorse named Genzyme Gene. At that point he realized he had quite a job ahead in building a professional team and a sound management structure.

While working on the strategic and operational issues, Termeer also began to articulate the values he hoped to build in Genzyme. Over and over, he emphasized the centrality of the patient and the need for everyone to link what they were doing to those whose lives they could affect. Setting the tone himself, Termeer preferred to visit patients rather than just studying their diseases or trying to master the science behind the therapies being developed. He explained that patient contact gave him the emotional energy to work toward finding a cure, a feeling and commitment he wanted to convey to his entire organization.

Betting the Ranch
Meanwhile, Brady's new "pruned molecule" NIH trials were progressing. The results were disappointing yet

---

2 Estimates of prevalence were gathered from National Gaucher Foundation Web site, <http://www.gaucherdisease.org/prev.htm>, accessed July 18, 2002; and from "Genzyme Corp. Strategic Challenges with Ceredase," HBS Case No. 793-120 (Boston: Harvard Business School Publishing, 1994), pp. 7–8.

tantalizing: only one patient out of the seven in the trial showed any response to the therapy, but his symptoms were dramatically reversed. The blind trial protocols masked the identity of the study participants, and critics of the modified enzyme in Brady's lab blocked the supporters' proposal to investigate the reason for the widely differing outcomes.

When the results of the trial became known, most within Genzyme were pessimistic about the prospects for this therapy. But Termeer was not ready to give up. After learning that the identity of the one patient who was in dramatic recovery was Ben Bryant, a 4-year-old boy from the Washington, D.C., area, he called the family.[a] Over the following months, he visited Ben and his family regularly and was very impressed that treatment resulted in a total reversal of symptoms, but when the injections stopped, Ben relapsed. Yet while Termeer became convinced the therapy could work, Genzyme's scientific advisory board was much less optimistic. For one whole day the scientists debated the issue with management, trying to answer three questions: Does it work? Is it safe? And could it be made profitable?

On the first question, the scientific advisors were doubtful, arguing that there was no strong indicator that this one case could have general implications. While agreeing with Termeer that Ben's recovery was impressive, they did not share his belief that this was no aberration. The debate about safety was equally troubling. The enzyme used in the trial was extracted from the rare proteins found in human placentas collected from maternity wards in four large Boston hospitals. Growing publicity about risks of HIV and hepatitis C had led to widespread public concern about products derived from human tissue, leading the advisory board to suggest it would be more prudent to wait until biotechnology could create a recombinant version. Finally, there were questions about whether a business could be created. Some raised concerns about accessing enough placentas, while others focused on the huge investment required to develop this product. Blair, conservative by nature, was worried it could bankrupt the company. Snyder also argued against the proposal.

Despite these many concerns, Termeer decided that it was unacceptable that product development should not proceed with a therapy potentially able to reverse this terrible disease. At this time, the company's best guess was that 2,000 patients worldwide could eventually use the product, with the potential of generating profits on a projected $100 million in annual sales—*if* further trials proved successful and *if* the product could qualify for "orphan drug" status, which would raise high entry barriers to any competing therapy for seven years. (Genzyme faced no patent barriers or licensing costs, since the government had decided not to patent the discovery of the modified GCR molecule to encourage further research.)

Throughout this process, Termeer and Blair had been talking to Scott Furbish, one member of the NIH team advocating the pruned molecule treatment. Frustrated by the infighting, Furbish was ready to quit NIH. They convinced him to join Genzyme and head up the research that would take his NIH work to fruition. But Termeer also took his scientific advisors' recommendation seriously and initiated parallel research on a recombinant form of the GCR enzyme.

Furbish and his team soon hypothesized that it was Ben Bryant's small size that allowed the therapy to succeed. By increasing the dosage to adult patients, they believed further clinical trials would show it was equally effective on them. Recalling all the uncertainties of 1985 as Genzyme made a new-drug application for Ceredase® enzyme under the Orphan Drug Act, Furbish said, "I would like to ask Henri how he had the guts to make that decision."

Going Public

By 1985, Termeer had tightened Genzyme's operations, set its broad strategic direction, strengthened its ongoing businesses, and committed to several important new research initiatives, of which the Gaucher therapies were the boldest. With sales of 32 research reagents, diagnostic intermediaries, and fine chemicals generating almost $10 million in revenues, the company was approaching the financial break-even point. Termeer felt it was now time to take Genzyme public.

With the board's full support, he became CEO in late 1985 (Snyder had left the company) and soon after began planning an IPO for 1986. (See Exhibit 3 for excerpts from the prospectus.) Recognizing that most of the $27.4 million IPO cash infusion would be needed to finance the growth of existing operations, Termeer began exploring other means of funding product development. Unlike most other biotech companies, which financed research and development (R&D) by raising equity or

---

[a] Patient's name disguised.

The Company

- Genzyme develops, manufactures, and markets a variety of biological products used in human health care applications.

- Genzyme has additional human health care products under development. . . . [It] believes its practical experience in the production and sale of biological products will enhance its ability to manufacture and commercialize new products.

- As of March 1980, the company had 169 employees, of whom 39 are engaged in R&D.

Risk Factors

- Short operating history and losses . . . during each of its last few years.

- Regulation by government agencies . . . no assurance that . . approvals will be granted.

- Uncertainty of product development.

- Patents with proprietary technology.

- Engaged in a segment of health care which is extremely competitive.

- Product liability.

Genzyme's principal products and process development programs, 1986

Products and Processes	Applications	Status
Therapeutics		
Hyaluronic acid	Ophthalmic surgery	Development stage
	Soft-tissue implants	Development stage
	Surgical trauma	Research stage
	Joint disorders	Research stage
	Drug delivery	Research stage
Glycoprotein remodeling	Therapeutic glycoproteins	Research stage
Glucocerebrosidase	Treatment of Gaucher disease	NIH clinical trials
Ceramide trihexosidse	Treatment of Fabry disease	NIH development stage
Bulk pharmaceuticals	Active ingredients in branded and generic pharmaceuticals	Product sales
Diagnostics and reagents		
Diagnostic enzymes and substrates	Manufacture of diagnostic kits	Product sales
Research reagents	Lymphokine and glycoprotein research	Product sales
Fine Chemicals		
Chiral compounds	Production of single isomer drugs	Development stage
Organic chemicals	Bioprocess compounds	Product sales

Source: Adapted by casewriters from Genzyme Corp. 1986 IPO Prospectus.

entering into partnerships with large pharmaceutical companies, Genzyme elected to do so by creating a limited research partnership. Sales of the partnership units in 1987 raised a crucial $10 million to continue Ceredase development, splitting the risk and rewards of R&D but leaving Genzyme the option to buy back successful developments at a preset price.

GENZYME IN LIFTOFF

By 1989 Ceredase approval seemed only a few years away, but public concern about the transmission of HIV from human-derived factors was growing. Recognizing that Genzyme could not develop a genetically engineered version of GCR quickly enough in-house, Termeer jumped at the opportunity to merge with Integrated Genetics (IG), a Massachusetts-based biotech firm with expertise in recombinant genetic engineering but an empty development pipeline following a patent-suit loss to Amgen.

Pursuing its strategy of diversification, Genzyme continued product development on multiple fronts— researching enzyme replacement for Fabry disease, developing genetic-screening tests, and working on therapies for cystic fibrosis, for example. With a continuing need for funding, a second limited research partnership in 1989 raised $36.7 million, followed by a second public stock offering for $39.1 million. In 1990 a special-purpose, publicly traded research company was created, raising an additional $47.3 million for targeted genetic research, including promising work on cystic fibrosis. But the real excitement at Genzyme focused on bringing Ceredase to market.

Building a Product Pipeline

As the Ceredase trials continued, the company worked to ensure product supply. First-stage processing was contracted to the French Institute Merieux in Lyon, where rare proteins—among them GCR—were extracted from placentas shipped from the United States and all over Europe. (A year's supply of Ceredase for the average patient contained enzyme extracted and purified from 20,000 human placentas, or 27 tons of material.) Back in Boston, Genzyme modified the GCR enzyme then processed it to ensure its safety, purity, and concentration.

The U.S. Food and Drug Administration (FDA) finally approved Ceredase for marketing in the United States in 1991, giving Genzyme the momentum for another $143 million stock offering. As approved, Ceredase had the distinction of being the most expensive therapy on the market. The complex extraction process, the limited availability of raw material, and the small number of patients combined to make production extremely costly. (Even when it was collecting 35% of all the placentas in the United States and over 70% of those in Europe, Genzyme could effectively supply Ceredase to only 1,000 to 1,500 patients.) Over one-third of this cost was attributable to acquiring and processing raw material, compared with raw material costs of 5% to 10% in typical drug manufacturing processes. (See Exhibit 4 for cost estimates.) Protocols called for patients with the severe form of the disease to initially receive 50 units of Ceredase per kilo of body weight every two weeks. At $3.70 per unit, the first year's treatment could cost over $300,000, and although maintenance therapy could drop to roughly two-thirds of the initial dosage, the cost was high enough to attract the attention of regulators and politicians. (See Exhibit 5 for dosage calculations and costs.)

Meanwhile, a team of biochemists from Genzyme and IG spliced the human gene responsible for producing GCR into cells cultured from Chinese hamster ovaries, producing recombinant GCR. Others worked on scaling up production from the two-and-a-half grams of product made in a one-liter container for the trials to a new proposed production facility with four bioreactors of 2,000 liters each. In 1992, well before the production process was fully developed and more than a year before Genzyme would be ready to file the new-drug application for the product to be called Cerezyme, construction began on the new plant. To help finance the $180 million investment, a dramatic structure on the Charles River that stamped Genzyme's presence on Boston's skyline, Genzyme raised $100 million in debt. When commissioned, the plant's round-the-clock, 365-day-a-year production capacity would be six kilos of medicine annually—an output that would fit in a six-pack cooler but still sufficient for the 2,000 patients Genzyme hoped to treat worldwide.

Responding to Regulatory Pressures

The political environment in which Ceredase was launched was a difficult one for pharmaceutical and biotech companies. The emphasis on health-care reform in President Clinton's first term turned the spotlight on high-priced therapies, and along with a few other products such

Exhibit 4

Ceredase Cost and Profit Estimate, 1994

	$	$	%
Per patient annual price		$150,000	100%
Less Cost of Goods			
Material	$47,900		
Mfg. Labor, overhead	5,300	$53,200	35
Gross Profit		$96,800	65
Less Operating Expenses			
Selling/reimbursement expense	$12,200		
Distribution	10,500		
R&D amortization	4,500		
Mfg. development amortization	2,000		
Corporate/admin. expenses	12,600		
Bad-debt provision	4,900		
Medicaid allowance	2,800		
Free goods	1,500	$51,000	34
Pretax Operating Profit		$45,800	31
Less state/federal taxes		14,600	10
Net Income		$31,300	21

Source: Adapted by casewriters from Elyse Tanouye, "What Ails Us—What's Fair?" *The Wall Street Journal*, May 20, 1994, p. R11. (Source of data in the article given as Genzyme figures.)

Note: Estimated average per patient revenue includes pediatric and adult patients on initial and maintenance treatments.

Exhibit 5

Dosage Annual Cost Calculations for Ceredase and Cerezyme

Regimen and Patient Weight	Annual Cost
Initial Treatment of 50 units/kg.	
165 lbs. (75 kg.)	$360,750
110 lbs. (50 kg.)	240,500
33 lbs. (15 kg.)	72,150
Maintenance Treatment of 35 units/kg.	
165 lbs. (75 kg.)	$252,525
110 lbs. (50 kg.)	168,350
33 lbs. (15 kg.)	50,505

Source: Prepared by casewriters with information supplied by Genzyme Corp.

Note: Assumes biweekly infusions at $3.70 per unit medicine cost.

Annual cost = price x dosage x weight x annual number of infusions.

as Burroughs Welcome's AZT treatment for AIDS, Ceredase was singled out as an example of a drug that was seeking protection by exploiting the Orphan Drug Act.[3] Termeer's response was immediate and strong. (See Exhibit 6 for an editorial expressing his views.) He went to Washington and asked members of Congress and the regulatory authorities what they wanted to know. He recalled: "I invited them to visit our operations and offered to open our books so they could see what it cost to develop and produce the product. I asked them for their suggestions—to tell me if we had done anything wrong. We would listen. Our approach was to be completely open and transparent. We were proud of what we had done and had nothing to hide."

In addition to showing his visitors the facilities and giving the Congressional Office of Technology Assessment (OTA) access to the books, Termeer also explained the company's philosophy: "Since the beginning, I have told this organization that our first responsibility is to treat patients with the disease, not to maximize financial returns. Regardless of where those people are or

---

[3] Larry Thompson, "The high cost of rare diseases: When patients can't afford to buy lifesaving drugs," *The Washington Post*, June 25, 1991, p. Z10; David Stipp, "Genzyme counters criticism over high cost of drug," *The Wall Street Journal*, June 23, 1992, p. B4; John Carey, "How many times must a patient pay?" *Business Week*, February 1, 1993, p. 30.

The Cost of Miracles

By Henri A. Termeer

As part of his continuing attack on the pharmaceutical industry, President Clinton has proposed establishing a federal committee to review the prices of "breakthrough" drugs, including those developed by the biotechnology industry. The Senate's Special Committee on Aging is scheduled to hold hearings today on the subject. Its chairman, Sen. David Pryor (D., Ark.), says the purpose of the hearings is to determine whether market forces are adequate to restrain prices.

The real danger, however, is not that the prices of new drugs will be too high, but that government controls, whether direct or indirect, will discourage investors from taking risks on biotechnology companies that develop new drugs.

The truth is that breakthrough drugs already face an onerous review: It's called the marketplace. Today, companies such as mine that develop breakthrough drugs can expect to have meaningful market exclusivity for only a few years. While a company's patent, or the special protection it can claim for its so-called orphan drugs, may preclude competitors from selling an identical product, it does not preclude others from designing and selling substantially similar products.

My own company's product, Ceredase, is an example of how market forces work. In the early 1980s, Genzyme was the only company working on a treatment for Gaucher's disease, a rare, inherited enzyme deficiency that causes crippling, and sometimes fatal, bone and organ deterioration. The CEO of another major biotechnology company had considered and rejected the idea of developing a treatment for such a rare disease because he could not imagine how his company could get an adequate return on a product intended for a few thousand patients.

Success Breeds Competition

Since Genzyme developed Ceredase, however, other companies have jumped into Gaucher's disease research. We are now competing with a company working on a variation of our drug, and two others are competing with us to develop gene-therapy approaches. There could be as many as four or five treatments for Gaucher's disease on the market within the next four years. If we hadn't taken the first step, there would be no market and no additional research on the disease.

My point is this: When an innovator company proves that its product works, and that a sufficient market exists to earn a return, it encourages other companies to develop similar products that enable them to compete for a share of that market. Given the breathtaking pace of biotechnology progress, it takes a relatively short time for other companies to develop substantially similar drugs. These will succeed, of course, only if they offer either price or therapeutic advantages over the innovator product.

Market forces are thus already creating price competition among pharmaceutical companies. A number of companies are implementing such programs as customer rebates and money-back guarantees. No government regulatory mechanism was necessary to induce this result.

In this respect, it is ironic that the same commentators who complain about pharmaceutical companies developing "me too" drugs (new versions of existing drugs) often fail to recognize that, at the very least, the introduction of such drugs helps constrain the prices of similar products, especially under a managed competition system in which insurance companies provide physicians with a greater incentive to consider the cost-effectiveness of the products they prescribe.

Congress should be less concerned about the possibility that a company might someday charge a high price for its AIDS vaccine for the two or three years before a competing product is available than about that company's ability to obtain the research-and-development funds needed to develop the vaccine in the first place. It is imperative that Congress and the administration consider the following question: If we alter market mechanisms by imposing price controls on breakthrough drugs, will we continue to get breakthrough drugs?

Congress and the administration must ask the following question: If we impose price controls on breakthrough drugs, will we continue to get breakthrough drugs?

A breakthrough drug committee is not needed to ensure that drugs are priced reasonably. If a drug's benefit is not commensurate with its cost, physicians won't prescribe it, particularly under a managed competition system. From the patient's perspective, a committee's refusing to provide Medicare coverage for "excessively priced" drugs would substitute a bureaucrat's judgment for a physician's. It would also result in second-class medical care for aging Americans: Medicare patients would be denied access to drugs that are covered for the privately insured.

A breakthrough drug committee as proposed by Mr. Clinton is not only unnecessary, it is counterproductive. It will discourage investors from seeing the development of breakthrough drugs as an investment capable of reaping returns that are commensurate with the risks. Another Clinton proposal would allow the secretary of health and human services to negotiate prices for new drugs, under threat of excluding them from Medicare. Taken together, these proposals would constitute a price-control system that discriminates against biotechnology and other innovating pharmaceutical companies by threatening to blacklist their products unless government bureaucrats concur with company pricing decisions.

These Clinton proposals do little more than constrain our ability to develop breakthrough medicines. In the first eight months of this year, biotechnology stocks declined by 30%; and through initial public offerings and other investor appeals companies were able to raise only about 25% of the amount they spent during this period. Obviously, this is not sustainable for an industry that lost $3.6 billion last year.

My own company raised $100 million two years ago to fund its research and development of a treatment for cystic fibrosis, a common fatal genetic disease that kills the average patient at the age of 29. Even though we recently performed the first successful clinical trial of a gene-therapy treatment for cystic fibrosis, Genzyme would be hard-pressed to raise half that amount in today's investment environment. We will need to make a total investment of more than $400 million to bring this product to market. If we succeed, we will be able to treat successfully 30,000 Americans who, in the severe phase of the disease, now receive annual medical care costing up to $50,000.

Proposals that discourage breakthrough drug development may be smart politics. But they are bad medicine and an ineffective means of cost control.

Japan, which has a single-payer system in which the government sets reimbursement rates for all health care products and services, uses government regulation of drug prices as a form of industrial policy to reward breakthrough drug development with a pricing premium. It is typical for the Japanese government to set prices for biotechnology drugs and other breakthrough pharmaceutical products at two to three times U.S. market prices, reflecting such a premium. On the other hand, the Japanese government cuts the prices of older pharmaceuticals annually according to a formula. The message to Japanese industry is clear: Innovate or die.

No Price Abuse

Sen. Pryor and the White House propose precisely the opposite—that breakthrough drugs be subject to government policies aimed at preventing "excessive" prices while old drugs continue to escalate in price at the general inflation rate.

In citing Japanese policy, I do not intend to suggest that the U.S. should adopt that system. To the contrary, I think that the relatively higher prices that the Japanese government willingly pays for breakthrough drugs are compelling evidence that American companies are not abusing the pricing freedom they enjoy in a system like ours.

Finally, let me note that the Japanese government has targeted biotechnology as an industry Japan wants to dominate by the year 2000. The U.S. will only forfeit its leadership position to Japan if its government encourages the development of breakthrough drugs and our own does not. The Japanese threat to our industry is not nearly as great as the threat from our own government.

Mr. Termeer is CEO of Genzyme Corp. in Cambridge, Mass.

the financial circumstances they find themselves in, we take it as our responsibility to see they are treated."

To implement this "universal provision" philosophy, Genzyme created the Ceredase Assistance Program (CAP) even before Ceredase was approved to market. A CAP committee reviewed cases of extreme need—patients who had lost insurance coverage, for example—and where there was no alternative, provided Ceredase free. But they always continued working with the patients to try to secure an ongoing supportive, paying party. In addition to Termeer, the CAP review committee consisted of medical, legal, and caseworker professionals.

After a detailed examination, the October 1992 OTA report concluded that, while the benefits of NIH research and the Orphan Drug Act did reduce its risk, Genzyme had also invested significantly in R&D and production facilities. It found Genzyme's pretax profit margin on the drug to be in line with industry norms. (OTA's calculation excluded any R&D unrelated to Ceredase, bad debt, and free goods expenses.) Furthermore, OTA found that insurers were reimbursing the cost of the therapy because it was less expensive than surgery or extensive hospitalization.[4]

Going to Market

Meanwhile, the company had been tackling the formidable task of bringing to market an extremely expensive therapy for a rare, poorly understood, and seldom-diagnosed disease. Termeer knew that once again he would have to attract different kinds of people to take on the challenge: "Recruiting the right people has been a key part of Genzyme's success. . . . I look for people with a passion to tackle things that seem impossible to solve. Practical dreamers who have a sense of compassion but believe they can change things. . . . And we attract people who see what we are doing as a worthwhile fight. There has to be a real personal involvement."

Drawing on the pool of biotech sales veterans in the Boston area, the company recruited an eight-person pioneering sales force with good industry knowledge whose members fit Termeer's "passionate practical dreamer" profile. In contrast to the traditional pharmaceutical model of making sales calls to doctors, pharmacies, and hospital purchasing agents, the Ceredase team focused on patients. After working to identify who they were, they educated them about the disease, organized them in support groups, and found treatment for them. They

also educated physicians and reassured them about reimbursement.

Very quickly, the field sales force found the need for a support staff of caseworkers—typically, trained nurses and social workers—who advocated for patients with insurance companies. The caseworkers explained the therapy to the insurance representatives, provided supporting research materials, and handled the huge administrative demands for each submission. Said one of the early sales force members: "Because of insurance, it was a patient-oriented approach. Then, as the patient got better, the physician became motivated. We worked patient by patient, physician by physician. . . . This company is really about caring for our patients and doing the right thing for them. When a patient calls, you respond—it's the culture here."

Patient profiles were prominent in Genzyme's annual reports, photos of patients were pinned on cubicle walls in the offices, and company employees spoke passionately about how patients motivated them. Alison Lawton from regulatory affairs was typical: "Two months after I joined Genzyme, I went to a Gaucher patient meeting in Israel. . . . I cried my eyes out just seeing the patients and hearing them basically begging the Ministry to get them the therapy. . . . I remember thinking, 'I'm really going to make a difference if I can get this product registered here.'"

Yet some in the R&D labs claimed to be unmoved by Termeer's regular attempts to link their work to real patients' stories, believing their scientific training forced a more disciplined attitude. "If you are immersed in the science, you become intrigued by trying to figure out the problems," said one. "You're not inspired by stories of human tragedies or a picture of a kid on the wall." But others were. Furbish felt that most Genzyme scientists were different from others in the industry:

> There are clear philosophical divides in the biotech world. Technology looks down on sales and marketing, and Ph.D.s are trained to sneer at profit. But that doesn't hold at Genzyme. The patient focus builds from Henri down. His commitment is real and it affects everyone— even the Ph.D.s. Yet he also sets very aggressive business goals, and we come to appreciate that this is paying the bills as well as helping patients.

The same attitude had spread to plant engineers and technicians. For Blair Okita, vice president of Therapeutics

---

4 "Federal and Private Roles in the Development and Provision of Alglucerase Therapy for Gaucher Disease," Office of Technology Assessment, Washington, D.C.: Government Printing Office (1992).

Manufacturing and Development, Genzyme was much different from earlier experiences at SmithKline Beecham and Merck: "Here we are motivated by a patient focus—right down to the technician level. For example, before doing their first run of the new Pompe product, our staff in the fill and finish area had a family with a child with Pompe's disease talk to them. . . . Each one of us is providing a life-saving therapy to a patient. That is a powerful motivating force."

As the network of educated patients and aware physicians expanded, sales of Ceredase grew rapidly. In 1993, after three years on the market, 1,000 patients were being treated, and cumulative sales were almost $250 million. Regulatory applications for Ceredase were pending in many international markets, and Cerezyme, the recombinant version of the therapy, was due for FDA approval in the United States in 1994. Genzyme's future looked promising indeed.

OPENING FOREIGN MARKETS

Even before Ceredase was launched, Genzyme had been approached by companies wanting to cross-license or distribute the product abroad. True to his principle of controlling his business both upstream and downstream, Termeer refused. "International markets were an exciting opportunity," he said. "Besides, we were committed to seeking out and responding to Gaucher patients."

Pioneering Initiatives

In late 1990, Termeer called Tomye Tierney, an ex-colleague at Baxter, and convinced her to lead Genzyme's thrust into Europe. With her experience marketing Baxter's hemophilia products in many markets around the globe, Tierney had strong skills in building relationships with patients, physicians, and government officials. Said Termeer, "Tomye is one of those unusual people you can send into an impossible country where there are all kinds of roadblocks, and she can find a way."

Joining at the same time Genzyme was recruiting its U.S. sales force, Tierney had no sales model to build on. "Henri told me I would have to develop the international strategy," she recalled. "And when I asked him how long I had, he told me, 'Two weeks.'" She headed straight to Europe and within two months she had contacted her old physician friends, been referred to the few specialists working on

Gaucher disease, located known patients in the United Kingdom, France, and the Netherlands, and begun connecting the network. Winning "investigational new drug" use approval, she made the first sales by December 1990.

Having set up the basic network, in September 1991 Tierney called another old Baxter colleague, Jan van Heek, and told him about Genzyme's European plans. Van Heek had just been offered a promotion at Baxter so he was not very interested. "But I went to a patient and physician meeting and was astonished how much Genzyme meant to those people," he recalled. "There was an enormous sense of optimism and hope in the company, and I decided on the spot to join." By year's end, he had established Genzyme's temporary European headquarters—a rented house with a phone and a fax—and had hired the five entrepreneurial individuals who would develop the European market.

As the company pursued the long, complicated process of registration and approval in each of Europe's national health care systems, the high cost of Ceredase inevitably led to equally long and complex negotiations over price. But Genzyme's response was always simple, straightforward, and unwavering. The company had a universal global pricing policy. Termeer explained:

> We have only two prices—the commercial price or free. By taking an absolutely transparent position, the discussion finishes quickly. We have not exploited our position by increasing prices—we have remained basically the same over that whole period. As our margin has gone up, we have taken on more responsibility to support patients around the world.

A Mobile Missionary

With van Heek running Europe, Termeer asked Tierney to become vice president and general manager of emerging markets and develop opportunities in the rest of the world. Although she began initiatives in many markets, including Canada, Latin America, and Australia, it was the Middle East that captured much of her time and attention. Due to its high concentration of Gaucher patients, Israel was a priority and in 1993 became the first country outside the United States to approve Ceredase. Another market that seemed to offer potential was Egypt, and since 1990 Tierney had been in contact with Dr. Khalifa, a physician with an interest in Gaucher disease.

After four years, Tierney had built her widespread portfolio of markets into a $16 million business. In 1996, Termeer asked her to relocate to Asia, a market previously thought to have limited potential. Setting up her base in Singapore, she continued her missionary work. By that time, she had established a clear step-by-step approach to entering new markets. She explained:

The key is to hire a smart local person to manage the process. For example, in Korea I found a pharmacist who had worked for the German drug company Boehringher. I connected him to a physician who we felt could be a local thought leader. She was treating a Gaucher patient willing to pay for his own treatment. This gave us the base to create a forum for patients and help them channel their frustration at not having access to therapy toward the government. Our local manager then worked with the patients, physicians, and government to enact orphan drug legislation and approve Cerezyme for reimbursement. It's a lot of work, but the Genzyme credo is "you've got to find a way."

As she opened markets in Japan, South Korea, Taiwan, Hong Kong, and other developed Asian countries, Tierney was increasingly aware that there were other, less developed economies—China, India, and Vietnam, for example—that simply could not afford this therapy. It was an issue that had become a growing concern for Termeer as well. For several years, patients from countries without access to Cerezyme had been coming to Boston to request free product from the CAP committee. (See Exhibit 7 for one well-publicized example.) This presented Termeer with a real dilemma: "We were having families moving to the United States asking to get free drug and treatment here forever. The real solution had to be to get treatment in their home country. It's less disruptive for the family and also educates the country about the therapy so more patients can be treated."

To the critics, however, the requirement to return home seemed to be a hard-hearted and even manipulative tactic designed to use patient needs to develop new market opportunities. It was a charge Termeer strongly refuted:

What I will never tolerate is to create a blackmail situation where the patient is in the middle. There can be no circumstance where a patient on therapy is taken off therapy to create leverage. Or where a patient that needs therapy is denied it to create leverage. We have to make sure there is a critical need, then we must respond to the need.

But we cannot take on the responsibility forever and we need to make people aware of the role they must play to help. . . . In the Peruvian family's case, we asked them to move back, then worked very hard with the government and got reimbursement in Peru. In the end we were able to help other Peruvian patients get the treatment also.

THE GAUCHER INITIATIVE

As Termeer thought about how to address the question of providing treatment to Gaucher sufferers in less developed countries, he decided this would be an ideal project for Tierney. But Tierney was not so sure. After nine months of persuasion and negotiation, she returned to Boston in June 1998 with a mandate to develop a humanitarian program for emerging markets—but without jeopardizing the company's existing or future commercial opportunities.

Setting Up the Program

As soon as Tierney returned, she scheduled a meeting with Termeer to review the parameters of her new assignment. She found he was deeply involved in the issues, and the meeting turned into the first of many brainstorming sessions she had with Termeer and Sandy Smith, the vice president of International, to whom she reported. The first issue Termeer addressed with Tierney was the charter of what they began calling the Gaucher Initiative. He recalled the guidelines clearly: "It was really just a continuation of the philosophy we had implemented through CAP. Where there is a critical need, we will respond. But we cannot take on the responsibility forever. Our goal must be to create a situation in which the country itself will eventually take responsibility for the treatment. That's where we need to get to."

Implementation of this philosophy was complicated by the conjunction of the company's humanitarian commitment to universal provision and its commercial objective of a universal price. Recognizing that the humanitarian provision needed to be insulated from the commercial operations, Tierney and Termeer concluded they would need to work with an independent agency that had the infrastructure to distribute Cerezyme around the world. To ensure Genzyme's efforts would be both direct and discrete yet would not involve the company in decisions about who would receive treatment, they would also need an independent, medically qualified

Exhibit 7 *The Boston Sunday Globe Article,* April 11, 1993, p. 1

A father, a drug and an ailing son

By Philip Bennett
GLOBE STAFF

Justo Ascarza knows the logic of big business, of borders, of probable endings. But he lives by the logic of a parent whose child is dying, which is something else entirely.

"To struggle for the life of a child, for the life of a son, is to put yourself above rules, and even above laws," he said in a waiting room at Massachusetts General Hospital, impatient for his son to get better.

It was thinking like this that led Ascarza, without money, influence, or an understanding of English, across the globe to Boston to persuade doctors, hospitals, and Genzyme Corp. to save his son for free with one of the world's most costly drugs.

For a few months, Ascarza, a grade-school principal from Peru, made the system work for him. But, perhaps not surprisingly, it hasn't lasted. He says now that he is being made to work for the system, with the health of his son, Amaru, as leverage.

Ascarza and Genzyme are at odds over how long Amaru, 13, will receive free doses of Ceredase, the Cambridge biotechnology firm's premier drug, which the company says costs patients an average of $140,000 annually. Genzyme says the boy's next free dose, on Thursday, will be his last unless the Ascarzas return to Peru, where they would receive three more free months for introducing Ceredase to the country. The company then expects the government of Peru to pay for Amaru's treatment.

While the scheme might open a new South American market for Genzyme, Ascarza fears it may also result in suffering and death for his son. Peru is a country with shortages of medical resources and a surplus of tragedies. Ascarza, whose school salary is about $90 a month, asserts the government there will not pay for the drug, a claim supported even by the Lima physician Genzyme obtained for the family.

While the case is unusual, its issues are at the core of the health care debate, involving responsibility for care and its enormous expense and conflict over treatment that is costly to institutions but priceless for individuals and their families.

Because the Ascarzas are Peruvian, their case raises another, increasingly common question: should foreigners or unnaturalized immigrants living in the United States have the same rights to emergency care—some of it unavailable anywhere else—as U.S. citizens?

What nobody disputes is that Amaru Ascarza is very sick. He has Gaucher's disease, a rare genetic illness. Its symptoms include severe enlargement of the liver and spleen, excessive bleeding, and erosion of bones until they may start breaking. The disease can be fatal if untreated.

At 13, Amaru is 4 feet tall and weights 68 pounds. His abdomen is swollen grotesquely. His gums bleed. Struck with headaches, he presses his palms against his skull as if to hold the bone in place. His hands are delicate and tiny. He plays the flute and is a talented cartoonist.

He is a thoughtful and self-conscious teen-ager, usually quiet. His father says that prior to receiving Ceredase Amaru would often be prostrated by pain, wailing helplessly.

An effective treatment

Ceredase replaces an enzyme missing in Gaucher's victims, in many cases reversing the disease. Such has been the case with Amaru, who during three months of treatment has improved "miraculously," his father says, "inside and out."

"The medicine makes me feel better," Amaru said. "I go outside, do more things. When it wears off I feel sick again."

Since Ceredase was approved in the United States two years ago, it has been a bonanza for Genzyme. The company says that fewer than 6,000 of an estimated 20,000 Gaucher's patients worldwide can benefit from treatment with the drug, but its extraordinary cost has made it Genzyme's sales leader, generating $100 million last year.

The company currently has a monopoly on Ceredase under the Orphan Drug Law, which gives economic incentives to companies to develop drugs for rare diseases. And the drug attracts faithful customers: like insulin for diabetics, it is usually taken regularly for life.

Genzyme has been criticized for the cost of Ceredase, which can exceed $200,000 a year for patients. Executives say the drug is fairly priced. In addition, they say, no Gaucher's patient has been deprived of Ceredase for inability to pay, and they point by way of example to the day Justo Ascarza came to the door.

Ascarza, originally from a provincial town in the Andes, is an elementary school principal in a poor urban neighborhood in Lima. He speaks no English. He and his wife, Gladys, who joined him here recently, worry about their two other children, who remain in Peru. Yet with a relentlessness that can be breathtaking, he has made his case to any physician, attorney, government official, executive, or journalist who will listen.

His efforts have probably saved his son. In Peru, where no cases of Gaucher's had been previously noted, Amaru's condition went undiagnosed for five years. The Ascarzas were told their son might have leukemia until physicians correctly identified the illness and put the Ascarzas in touch with the National Institutes of Health, near Washington.

Company could benefit

Physicians studying Gaucher's disease invited the family to NIH last November. The Ascarzas persuaded American Airlines to donate airfare. A doctor there who examined him found him seriously ill. But because he was not affected neurologically, he did not qualify for an NIH study that would have resulted in free treatment and was discharged.

It was then, with airfare donated by an NIH physician, that the Ascarzas with the help of a distant relative living in Cambridge, turned to Genzyme. They were accepted into a program of free treatment, "conditioned on the full cooperation of the parents and the patient," said Henri Termeer, Genzyme's chairman and chief executive.

In the Ascarzas' case, those conditions require them to return to Peru by the end of April in order to receive three more months of the drug for free. After that, the family must find financing, presumably from the government of Peru, to pay Genzyme an estimated $82,000 a year.

If the Ascarzas were to succeed in Peru, the benefits for Genzyme would be clear. Ceredase would presumably receive expedited approval for use. Publicity about the case would bring forward patients with Gaucher's disease who are currently undiagnosed. And, as in countries such as Brazil and Argentina, where Ceredase is now subsidized, the company would have a government guarantee of payment.

But Ascarza said he appealed to the wife of Peru's president, Alberto Fujimori, for aid and was turned down. Ceredase would be a great expense in a country where nurses at public hospitals earn less than $100 a month and tens of thousands of children die each year of dehydration caused by diarrhea because the government cannot afford to provide even the most basic care.

Question of responsibility

Genzyme executives, for their part, point out that they cannot solve the problems of health care in Peru and that the company is not a charity.

"We never give up on attempts to make the patient part of a safety net," said Termeer. But, he said, "We cannot do this in a way that we lose total leverage on the system. We cannot allow ourselves to be used in a way that takes everybody off the hook."

Genzyme has assured the Ascarzas that the company has arranged care from a respected Lima hematologist, Dr. Jose Galvez, and is ready to ship the Ceredase. Yet, in a telephone interview last week, Galvez was hardly reassuring.

"I don't know anything really," Galvez said. "His physician called me last week and told me about the patient and that they'd send me something in the mail. I'm just waiting. I just don't know anything else."

Asked whether he believed the Peruvian government would pay for the treatment, Galvez said: "I don't think so. I have to be honest with you. We have a lot of problems here and this is not a priority. Things are not good here."

Meanwhile, Ascarza said that he has been rebuffed only once for seeking free care for his son in the United States. Ironically, he said it came from a Peruvian doctor practicing here.

But the issue is more widespread.

"It's a horrible problem," said Dr. Norman Barton, who examined Amaru at the NIH. "To what extent do we as a society have the responsibility to provide advanced technologies to countries that have no means to pay for them?"

"I don't know, Ascarza said. "Maybe what I am doing is wrong. But it is my responsibility to guarantee that Amaru doesn't die because he didn't have the luck to be born in a developed country."

committee of experts to make case-by-case diagnoses and decisions about the relative needs of candidates for treatment.

As she developed the program design, Tierney worked with a corporate philanthropy consultant and shared development ideas with the program director for the Mectizan Donation Program, Merck's initiative to combat river blindness.[5] In October, after carefully screening several partner candidates suggested by the outside consultant, Tierney selected Project HOPE for its worldwide distribution network, long track record, emphasis on health education, and sterling reputation. Additionally, the organization had a strong presence in China and Egypt, markets which Tierney knew had a recognized need for this therapy. Project HOPE's emphasis on health-care development within a country, rather than ongoing charitable health-care provision, was also consistent with Genzyme's long-term commercial goals.

For its part, however, Project HOPE took some convincing. It wanted assurances th at it would not be mixing a commercial agenda with its humanitarian mission and that the program would be run independently of Genzyme. Finally, an agreement was reached, and Tierney worked feverishly to get the program up and running by January 1, 1999. (See Exhibit 8 for contract highlights.)

Implementing the Program

Tierney's first task was to work to establish a secretariat with a full-time program manager and an independent case review board. She then won Termeer's agreement to supplement the in-kind donation of Cerezyme with a yearly budget to support the program manager and secretariat and provide training, travel, and office peripherals for local treatment centers. Eager to begin shipment of the drug to Egypt and China, Tierney appealed to the quality control personnel at Genzyme to inspect and approve Project HOPE's delivery system immediately. With excitement about the new program running high at Genzyme (Termeer and Tierney had widely communicated the company's commitment to the Gaucher Initiative), plant personnel helped to bypass a two-month backlog, and the first product was shipped ahead of Tierney's year-end target date.

Working with Project HOPE, Tierney convened the independent six-member medical review board that would meet three times a year to establish patient-intake procedures, qualify new cases, and decide to terminate treatment for patients who did not respond to the therapy. The board consisted of three leading experts in Gaucher disease, Genzyme's chief medical officer, a Project HOPE staff member, and a medical ethicist, who quickly tested the board's independence.

As Project HOPE spread the word in Egypt and China, local doctors made case-by-case requests to the local Project HOPE office. Applications were forwarded to Genzyme, which coordinated a case docket for the medical advisory board. After medical advisory board approval, Genzyme prepared patient and dosage lists for distribution to Project HOPE, which then shipped the drug overseas in coolers. At its destination it was carried by truck—or sometimes by hand—to local hospitals, where it was reconstituted and prepared for infusion. Project HOPE qualified local doctors to administer the therapy and participate in the program. In its first year, the Gaucher Initiative treated 60 patients worldwide (37 in Egypt and 23 in China); by 2001 the number was 140.

The Humanitarian/Commercial Tension

To the employees at Genzyme, the commitment to the Gaucher Initiative was another confirmation of the values they had heard Termeer espouse since the company's earliest days. Yet within the commercial organization, some voices of concern were emerging, particularly from those responsible for less developed markets. "We have a person who covers most of our Eastern European markets who was really concerned that if people began to understand we would give product away, it would be impossible to sell," Tierney recalled.

Christi van Heek, president of Genzyme's therapeutics division, reinforced the view that reimbursement could easily be lost if health-care providers felt they could obtain free product. She described how she had visited a physician in the Czech Republic who explained that his hospital lacked the money to buy Tylenol. Yet he eventually had six children on Cerezyme therapy. "He got reimbursement through the system," she said. "He had to fight for it, but this drug really works."

However, as the product penetration in developed nations approached saturation—sales growth increased only 6% between 2000 and 2001—the opportunities in markets outside the most developed economies began to attract more attention. (See Exhibit 9 for sales and patient growth.) Furthermore, Ceredase had come off orphan drug

---

5 Peter Wehrwein, "Pharmaco-Philanthropy," *Harvard Public Health Review*, Summer 1999, pp. 32–39.

| Exhibit 8 | Highlights of Gaucher Initiative Agreement |

Program Objectives

- "To establish Expert Committee to provide technical, ethical and programmatic guidance."
- "To coordinate and facilitate training of eight physicians on the treatments of Gaucher disease."
- "To organize and carry out the timely shipment and delivery of Ceredase/Cerezyme to identified locations in the People's Republic of China and Egypt."
- "To provide treatment to approximately 60 patients" annually.

Project HOPE Responsibilities

- "Establish a Secretariat . . . to direct and manage the day-to-day activities and administration."
- Identify Project HOPE field staff to assist with implementation from the local level.
- "Establish an Expert Committee, which will meet bi-annually . . . to provide technical, ethical and program-matic guidance to the Gaucher Initiative. Provide a voting member to the Expert Committee."
- Coordinate and facilitate the training of four physicians from China, two from Egypt, and two from Project HOPE.
- "Arrange for the timely shipment and delivery of appropriate quantities of Ceredase/Cerezyme."
- "Provide liaison with participating hospitals and medical institutions, physicians and medical personnel, and the patients selected for participation in the Gaucher Initiative."
- "Collaborate with appointed Genzyme representatives to . . . publicize the Gaucher Initiative."
- "Submit to Genzyme quarterly financial and narrative reports on progress."

Genzyme Responsibilities

- "Identify patients . . . for selection by the Expert Committee for inclusion in the program."
- "Assist in the creation of the Expert Committee. Provide a voting member."
- "Donate to Project HOPE appropriate quantities of Ceredase/Cerezyme."
- "Facilitate the training of eight physicians . . . at the Gaucher workshop held at Genzyme."
- "Provide Project HOPE with technical assistance in the training aspects and treatment of Gaucher disease."
- "Collaborate with Project HOPE . . . to publicize the Gaucher Initiative."
- "Genzyme shall be responsible for funding the Gaucher Initiative."

Resolution of Disputes

- In the event of a dispute, "the parties shall first attempt to resolve the dispute through friendly discussions." After 14 days "the parties may mutually select a third party" for "non-binding mediation." After another 14 days "either party may refer the dispute to arbitration and withdraw from the Program" with 30 days' written notice.

Liability

- "Project HOPE will be responsible for obtaining liability insurance to protect the Expert Committee from any suits resulting from decisions concerning patient selection and program guidance."
- "Any liability associated with the products Ceredase/Cerezyme will be the responsibility of Genzyme."
- "Local liability concerning the treatment of patients will be the responsibility of the local physician."

Duration, Extension, and Termination

- Duration: five years.
- Extended by "mutual agreement and the signing of a letter defining the length of the extension."
- The agreement may be terminated "without cause upon giving 90 days' written notice."

Source: Adapted by casewriters from memorandum of understanding between Project HOPE and Genzyme Corp., effective January 1, 1999.

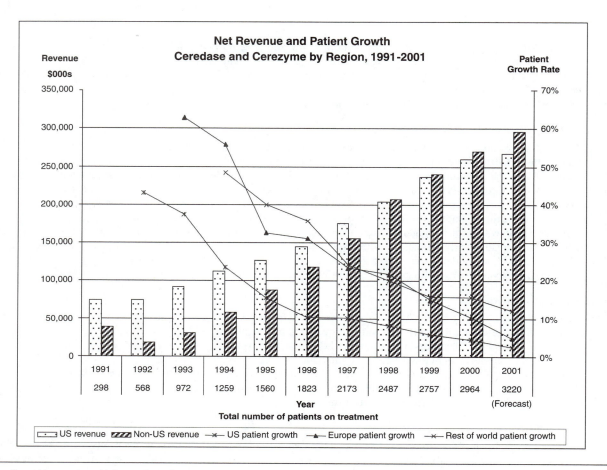

Net Revenue and Patient Growth
Ceredase and Cerezyme by Region, 1991-2001

Legend: US revenue — Non-US revenue — US patient growth — Europe patient growth — Rest of world patient growth

Total number of patients on treatment: 1991: 298, 1992: 568, 1993: 972, 1994: 1259, 1995: 1560, 1996: 1823, 1997: 2173, 1998: 2487, 1999: 2757, 2000: 2964, 2001: 3220 (Forecast)

Source: Prepared by casewriters with data supplied by Genzyme Corp.

Note: Patient growth figures are year-to-year growth percentages averaged over three years.

protection in 1998, and Cerezyme's would expire in 2001. Already competitors had applied for marketing approval for different therapies. Although Genzyme analysis cast doubts on their safety and effectiveness, it was a clear signal that this larger-than-expected market was attractive to competitors. "The interesting question will be what the entry of competitors will do to this responsibility we have taken on," said Termeer. "Will it be a burden for us alone, or will it be a joint responsibility? We have not begun to sort that one out."

THE EGYPTIAN DILEMMA

Even after she moved to Singapore, Tierney had kept her eye on the nascent opportunity in Egypt. It was a responsibility that would absorb much time and energy in coming years.

Building a Presence, Having an Impact

In late 1996, Khalifa had informed her that he had obtained funding to treat a child with Gaucher disease.

On a "named-patient basis," he also had obtained permission to import Cerezyme on humanitarian grounds even though it was not registered for sale in Egypt. However, several months later, when Tierney was visiting Egypt, she found that the funding was insufficient to cover the required treatment, and the patient was not responding to the low dosage provided. She immediately offered to request Genzyme's CAP program to sponsor a matching dose. Under this partial reimbursement arrangement, over the next two years Khalifa and Dr. Khaled, another physician now involved, had expanded treatment to a dozen patients, mostly children who were reimbursed under the government's Student Fund.

But now, with Tierney leading the Gaucher Initiative, responsibility for the Egyptian market was transferred to the general manager of Genzyme's Israel subsidiary, Zev Zelig. As a way of handing off her commercial responsibilities, Tierney introduced the Jordanian sales associate hired to cover Arab markets to her key physician and health insurance contacts. She also introduced him to the Project HOPE staff in Egypt. "The HOPE people were a little uncomfortable that we were actually making money on some of these patients," she explained. "They wanted a clear separation."

New Demands, New Expectations

In Project HOPE's first year in Egypt, the number of patients grew from 12 to 37, many of them infants, since children under five were not covered by the government-financed Student Fund. Sales through the partial reimbursement program were also up, increasing from $82,200 in 1998 to $146,500 in 1999. But the growing number of "named patients" attracted the attention of regulatory authorities, and in early 2000 Zelig was told that Genzyme would have to register Cerezyme. Zelig asked one of the company's regulatory staff to help him assess the task, but after talking to the Egyptian authorities, they concluded that registration would be too expensive to be justified.

After the first quarter of 2000, sales stopped. Almost immediately, Tierney began to feel pressure from Zelig to scale back her program in Egypt. She recalled: "At our strategic planning meeting, Zev kept saying, 'I can't do it

because she's giving away free drug.' And I'd come back, 'You need to hire an Egyptian sales associate and register in Egypt.' We went back and forth for almost a year."

Meanwhile, Project HOPE had just appointed Dr. John Howe as its new CEO. A well-respected cardiologist from Texas, Howe joined the organization with much energy and an ambition to expand its operations. "He told me he wanted to grow Project HOPE at least 50%," said Tierney. "And he was particularly interested in expanding the relationship with Genzyme."

Facing the Problem

In early 2001, the tension between the commercial and humanitarian agendas in Egypt was still unresolved. While sales had stopped for a year, by May 2001 the Gaucher Initiative had expanded to 41 patients, with 5 more approvals about to start treatment. When Mike Heslop, Genzyme's vice president for global marketing, hired Tarek Ebrahim, an Egyptian physician, he made "sorting out the Egyptian issue" one of the newcomer's first assignments.

On May 25, Smith, Genzyme's vice president of International, convened a meeting to which he invited Heslop, Ebrahim, Zelig, and Tierney. Tierney recalled the discussion:

> The others were all from the commercial side and had been talking to Zev. So they were sitting there telling me to put a lid on the free drug program. Zev took the lead and said we had to get the word out that Project HOPE was not taking any more patients. I told them that the solution was to register the drug and get a local presence in Egypt. Then we could manage the transition. I told them I could not stop the program.

The meeting broke up with the proposal that Ebrahim go to Egypt, evaluate the situation, and return with his analysis and recommendation. Tierney liked and respected her new Egyptian marketing colleague but wondered how the situation could be resolved. How could she think through the problem? If Termeer were to be involved, what kind of recommendation could she make to him? And how could she and her colleagues implement the necessary changes?

Year	Significant Events
1981	Genzyme founded by Henry Blair and Sherry Snyder, begins to supply NIH with GCR under contract.
1983	Genzyme hires Henri Termeer as president; becomes CEO, 1985.
	NIH launches first GCR enzyme-replacement trial.
1985	FDA designates Ceredase an orphan drug.
	Scientific advisory board (BIA) recommends against development of Ceredase.
1986	Genzyme IPO, June, raises $27.4 million cash for a company valuation of over $83 million.
1987	Forms R&D limited partnership, raising $10 million to develop Ceredase.
1989	Ceredase approved for seriously ill patients prior to marketing approval.
	Raises $39.1 million through public stock offering and $36.7 million through Genzyme Development Partners.
	Acquires Integrated Genetics (founded in 1981).
1990	Ceredase available outside United States on a named-patient basis.
	Forms Neozyme I, raises $47.3 million to fund R&D.
1991	Ceredase approved and receives orphan drug status.
	Raises $100 million in 10-year 6% debt, and raises $143 million in public stock offering.
1992	Begins work on gene therapy to treat cystic fibrosis.
	Congressional OTA report issued on the development of Ceredase.
	Forms Neozyme II, raises $85 million; purchases four research programs from Neozyme I for $49 million.
1993	New-drug application to FDA for Cerezyme.
1994	Cerezyme approved in United States, Germany, France, Holland, Australia, United Kingdom.
	Break-even on Ceredase.
1995	Ceredase sales approved in Portugal, Italy, New Zealand, Sweden, Spain.
	Genzyme General public offering raises $141 million.
1996	Japan approves Cerezyme.
1998	Genzyme General places $250 million 5.25% seven-year debt.
1999	Launches Gaucher Initiative.

Source: Adapted by casewriters from Genzyme Corp. sources.

IBM On Demand Community

On November 24, 2003, at 90 locations worldwide, IBM launched a new initiative to encourage and sustain corporate philanthropy through volunteerism. The On Demand Community (ODC) initiative armed IBM's employees with 140 technology tools designed to assist nonprofit community organizations and schools. IBM employees could access these tools online and share them with the organizations for which they volunteered. In addition, IBM committed to increased levels of in-kind technology support and cash awards to eligible organizations when IBM employees utilized the new on-demand tools.

The ODC was conceived by IBM's new chairman and chief executive officer, Sam Palmisano, in conjunction with Stanley S. Litow, vice president of IBM Corporate Community Relations. According to Litow: "The size and scale of this corporate employee volunteer program sets it apart. The ODC enables us to involve all IBM employees worldwide and give them technology resources that will transform the schools and community organizations where they donate their time. We're taking community service to a whole new level." ODC was an extension of Palmisano's spearheading of the IBM values initiative.

IBM Strategy

During the 1990s, Louis Gerstner transformed IBM from a product-centered company to a market-centered company that generated more revenues and profits from the sale of software, services and consultancy than computer hardware. IBM revenues of $88 billion in 2002, generated by 315,000 employees worldwide, were derived as follows:

34%—Hardware (mainframes to notebooks)
16%—Software (operating systems, databases, collaboration tools, organized into 12 industry groups)

45%—Global Services (the delivery system, 180,000 employees including 60,000 consultants)
4%—Global Financing
1%—Enterprise Investment

Revenues from Global Services had almost tripled since 1991. When Sam Palmisano became chairman and chief executive in 2002, he reaffirmed Gerstner's strategy. IBM would continue its technology focus—it had been the world leader in patents registered for 10 years, including 3,400 in 2002 alone. However, Palmisano saw differentiation through technology alone as insufficient:

> "Differentiation is going to come from the interpretation of technology into the core elements of your business. You'll get the competitive edge at the intersection of business process and technology."

In most corporations, a variety of computer systems served different divisions or performed different tasks and could not easily "talk to each other," let alone interface with the computer systems of suppliers and customers. Palmisano saw tremendous opportunities for IBM to improve transaction speed and productivity and save money for large organizations through improving business process integration. Describing it as "a big bet but not a risky bet," Palmisano named his new approach E-Business On Demand. He announced it in October 2002, along with a $10 billion investment program to develop the simple, more automated and more cost-effective software and hardware needed to connect the internal processes of an enterprise and extend out to its business partners. Steve Mills, head of IBM's software division, commented:

> "On Demand is a statement of flexibility. It doesn't start with technology, it starts with business operations. The aim is to achieve smoothness of processing, from demand to delivery."

Thise case was prepared by Professor John A. Quelch.

Copyright © 2004 by the President and Fellows of Harvard College. Harvard Business School case N9-504-103.

To underscore IBM's new commitment to consulting services that could connect business processes to technology solutions, Palmisano purchased PricewaterhouseCoopers' consulting business in 2002 for $3.5 billion; 30,000 PWC employees joined IBM as a result. The company committed to spending $700 million to advertise and explain the "e-business on demand" concept. IBM's competitors soon followed. Hewlett-Packard, for example, launched its "Adaptive Enterprise" strategy in May 2003. HP emphasized partnerships with other vendors to address each customer's needs. This contrasted with IBM's approach, which was to be the single source of supply for a total customer solution. To this end, IBM set about improving its outreach to software developers around the world in order to enlist as many as possible to work on solutions for its clients.

The marketplace responded favorably to the IBM strategy. For example, American Express signed a $4 billion contract in 2002 to have IBM handle all its information technology operations. Procter & Gamble signed a $400 million contract in 2003 to have IBM handle its business process outsourcing. Concerns that customers would not accept IBM consultants recommending IBM hardware and software solutions proved to be largely unfounded. Many customers, who had been burned in the 1990s by making heavy investments in information technology that proved incompatible and unproductive, welcomed the opportunity to outsource the complexities of information technology management to a single supplier of the stature of IBM.

IBM and Strategic Philanthropy

IBM's commitment to giving back to the communities in which it operated was pioneered by IBM's founder Thomas J. Watson Sr. As early as 1914, he urged employees "to get involved in the communities where you live and work." Throughout its history, IBM was an example of good corporate citizenship, leading the way in sound labor practices, commitment to diversity and a family-friendly workplace, and environmental consciousness.

Between 1983 and 2001, IBM contributed over $2 billion. At its peak, IBM contributed $187 million in 1986 and, even during the tough financial crunch of the early 1990s, IBM continued to donate over $100 million per year. By 2002, IBM contributed $127 million, 72% of which was in technology services and 77% of which was given to support K–12 and higher education, the areas

of greatest interest to its employees and shareholders. In addition, through IBM's matching grant program, a further $56 million was donated to charities supported by IBM employees through employee giving and matching grants. IBM employees in the United States alone also contributed 4 million hours of volunteer time, one quarter of which was spent in the education sector; these hours were not time off from work, that required the permission of a local manager. Approximately 30% of contributions were made outside the United States; foreign markets accounted for over 50% of IBM sales by 2002.

During the 1990s, under the leadership of Louis Gerstner, IBM decided to focus its philanthropy worldwide on "Reinventing Education." Previously, as chief executive of RJR Nabisco, Gerstner had launched the "Next Century Schools Program." Now, he aimed to apply IBM's technology and expertise and its "solutions for a small planet" philosophy to improve the way teachers teach, engage parents, raise student achievement and bridge the digital divide between rich and poor, all to improve skills and competitiveness in the new knowledge economy. Working with individual schools and school districts, 25 demonstration projects were funded in the United States alone. IBM contributions were part cash, part technology hardware, and part services that involved researchers from the IBM labs plus short-term consulting by IBM employees or long-term secondments of IBM personnel to projects overseen by Litow's group. Through such contributions, IBM built long-term partnerships not only in the United States but around the world with many national Ministries of Education in both emerging and developed economics. IBM also contributed to unique high profile collaborations with important cultural institutions such as the Cairo Museum in Egypt and the Hermitage Museum in Russia. These contributions were held at arm's length from IBM's commercial activities; relevant IBM account managers typically did not attend meetings at which IBM philanthropic projects were discussed, though once projects were completed, commercial opportunities were presented.

Throughout the 1990s, IBM's strategic philanthropy initiatives were managed by Stanley S. Litow. A former deputy chancellor of the New York City public school system, Litow was appointed by Gerstner in 1993 to spearhead the "Reinventing Education" initiative.

Gerstner and Litow both wanted to make IBM's philanthropic efforts more focused and strategic and to measure results. Litow commented on the early challenges:

"When I arrived, IBM's business was still weak, people were being laid off yet we were still donating over $100 million a year due to prior commitments and pledges. That posed a significant internal communications challenge. Another challenge was Lou's conviction that philanthropy was only of benefit to the IBM shareholders if it was strategic and delivered results. To some, IBM had been a soft touch with many not-for-profits able to get the local IBM manager to write a check. My mission was to transform IBM's philanthropy from reactive to proactive and obtain significant returns.

Traditionally, grant officers at big companies behaved like those at foundations. They read the proposals that came in and made recommendations to a board of directors. We decided to change this model and proactively search out potential collaborators whom we thought deserved funding and would do something innovative and exciting with it, using our creative technology solutions.

The shift to collaboration from check writing meant that grants of technology and talent assumed more prominence in IBM's philanthropic budgeting. We were no longer simply a cash machine."

Litow also commented on the decision to concentrate on a single big challenge like Reinvesting Education:

"By announcing a focus on education, we insured that a lot of high quality proposals reached us. We also made it easier for line managers around the world to say 'no' to ad hoc requests for donations that didn't fit with the new strategy in favor of more ambitious, longer-term philanthropic partnerships that yielded measurable returns.

Some argue that corporations shouldn't engage in philanthropy and should pass the money through to shareholders to give away as they see fit. The problem is that very few individuals are able to put up significant money to tackle the big problems on which the future of the market economy depends."

Throughout the 1990s, Gerstner and Litow spearheaded educational reform in the United States. In 1996 they organized the National Education Summit at IBM headquarters, which brought together business and government leaders to discuss standards in public education; in the years following this summit, the number of states using academic student tests across public schools increased from 14 to 49. Follow-up summits were held in 1999 and 2001.

During the 1990s, Litow and his colleagues developed a range of innovative programs in the education arena. These included:

- *MentorPlace.* Over 8,000 IBM employees mentored K-12 students on-line in 2003.
- *Exite* (Exploring Interests in Technology and Engineering). Summer camps targeting middle and high school girls with IBM employees following up as e-mentors.
- *KidSmart.* Software programs targeting preschool children, their teachers and parents.
- *TryScience.* Interactive presentations to promote student learning in the sciences, drawn from 450 science museums worldwide.
- *Teaming for Technology.* This program delivered personal computers and IT training to 18 communities in North America in 2003.

By 2003, major multinational companies frequently sought Litow's advice on how to design and organize strategic philanthropy programs. Litow's team included 60 people, 20 based at headquarters and 40 working in the field, principally in corporate community relations (CCR). Down significantly from 1993, two-thirds of Litow's team were long-time IBM employees, former line managers respected by their colleagues; the other third were appointed from the outside. The CCR executives, who oversaw the Reinventing Education and other programs at the school district and community level, had reported previously to local IBM line managers; under Litow, they reported to him with a dotted line relationship to local management.

Global Reach

Outreach programs developed in the United States were extended internationally. The Reinventing Education program, for example, spawned education summits in Latin America and Europe. One-third of MentorPlace participants were working outside the United States. The strategic priorities of line managers overseeing IBM's regional divisions often determined which countries received the most focus from Litow's group. Program success depended heavily on the line managers' commitment—not just financial but emotional—and their continuity in their positions.

Robin Willner, director of corporate community relations, described how a Reinventing Education program had had a major impact in Vietnam:

"First, we had a keen and committed country manager. Second, Vietnamese public education is very structured, standardized, and centrally controlled, with the result that we could scale up our solution very fast once we discovered what to do and had won the trust of our government partners. Third, President Clinton was scheduled to visit Vietnam to sign a trade agreement in 1999 and this galvanized all of us to move fast on project design and implementation."

The Vietnam Reinventing Education project involved introducing personal computers into classroom teaching of mathematics and science, designing information technology courses for teacher training candidates and enabling qualified teachers to observe classrooms where IT was being used. An IBM consultant was granted a full-time secondment from his regular job to serve as project manager for a year. Documented results from the Vietnam project later helped to persuade Chinese education officials to partner with IBM on several large-scale projects in China.

Reinventing Education projects across Europe engaged head teachers in a virtual network. In the United Kingdom and Italy, it focused on IT training for teachers. It used personal computers to link the parents in an Irish school district into a virtual school community, sharing ideas and concerns about their children's education.

Virtually every IBM education initiative was also implemented internationally. For example, 2,000 IBM employees who served as MentorPlace volunteers lived outside the United States. And the KidSmart program that introduced PCs to young children and trained teachers how to use them in class, had, for example, over 1,000 installations in preschools around Lima, Peru. KidSmart software used in Peru was localized as well as translated. In Western Europe, IT played an insignificant role in nursery education except in France. In other European countries, free play was still the norm, but this was being increasingly questioned by education specialists who saw value in the program incentive that KidSmart software could provide. A recent European Union conference for minorities of education across Europe highlighted the effectiveness of KidSmart.

ODC Planning and Launch

In 2003, Gerstner retired after almost ten years at the helm, during which IBM's stock market capitalization increased eight-fold. An insider, Sam Palmisano, succeeded him as chairman and chief executive officer.

Palmisano's appointment gave Litow an opportunity to reflect on accomplishments to date and to fashion, with Palmisano's guidance, a new umbrella strategy for all IBM's philanthropy efforts. While the Reinventing Education initiative had been effective, its impacts were concentrated and focused in a few communities rather than spread evenly throughout the IBM world. Palmisano and Litow decided, while it would continue, IBM needed a strategic philanthropy program that would also recognize IBMers' commitment to volunteerism and reinforce Palmisano's "on-demand" strategy. With these objectives in mind, Litow and Palmisano conceived of the IBM "on-demand community," which would fuse the concepts of on-demand computing and volunteer effort, allowing individual IBMers to "live" the IBM brand in countries worldwide. Litow appointed a planning team to develop the concept further.

In the spring of 2003, Litow established within his organization an ODC planning team of eight members with international representation and an advisory committee of country general managers and senior executives. He asked the team to develop a plan to launch ODC later that year.

The ODC planning team identified four target groups, two primary and two secondary:

Primary: (1) Potential volunteers who had not volunteered before through IBM but had donated already to not-for-profit organizations.

(2) Current high commitment (over eight hours per month) volunteers through IBM programs.

Secondary: (1) IBM executives responsible for communicating the benefits of volunteering, internally and externally.

(2) IBM corporate community relations volunteer coordinators who organized major events (including any ODC launch events).

ODC therefore aimed to attract not only existing volunteers to register under the new ODC umbrella, but also new volunteers. Thirty percent of IBMers had been employed by IBM fewer than five years; many of these younger employees were unfamiliar with IBM's volunteer philosophy and options, but they were used to accessing information through the web. To attract the second group, the ODC web site would have to include information on why volunteering was important and on how to become a successful IBM volunteer. Based on focus group research, the ODC planning team concluded that IBMers' awareness of and ability to participate in existing volunteer programs were both limited, especially outside the United States. The team described the attitudes they wanted to inculcate among visitors to the ODC web site as follows:

"Any time I can spare for volunteering will really help IBM make a difference as well as giving me a positive feeling from helping those in need."

"IBM supports my volunteer efforts 100% and is seeking to provide resources both to enable the community and myself to benefit."

The ODC planning team had to decide which of many alternative software tools and solutions to include on the site when it was launched. Other applications could be implemented later. The planning team decided that the site should, in the first instance, enable visitors to do the following:

- Discover IBM's Commitment to Volunteering
- Learn How to be an IBM Volunteer
- Find Solutions
- Volunteer for Solutions/Register
- Learn Materials
- Prepare for Volunteer Work
- Submit Volunteer Hours (receive recognition)
- Submit Feedback Form
- Ask a Question, Get Advice

Exhibit 1 lists the important modules (incorporating 140 distinct technology tools) that the ODC planning team decided would be included on the launch web site.

Exhibit 1   ODC Launch Web Site Content

Volunteering
- Managing Your Volunteer Commitment
- Introduction to K12 Education for Volunteers
- Introduction to Nonprofits for Volunteers
- Becoming an Effective Nonprofit Board Member
- On Demand Volunteer Recognition Program
- Executive and Employee Training
- Technology Planning 101
- Rewards & Recognition—Employee Partnership Programs
- Nonprofit Technology Pricing

Content Tools
- Mentor Place
- TryScience Experiment Toolkit
- Web Adaptation Technology
- KidSmart
- Open Source Education
- Reinventing Education Change Toolkit
- Professional Development for Teachers
- School Visits to Promote Math, Science and Engineering

Source: Company records

Five modules dealt with volunteering and how to help not-for-profit organizations. Ten content modules brought information about all of IBM's existing education outreach programs under one roof. Based on research with IBMers in the target groups, some of the existing solutions had to be adapted for ease-of-use by individual employees. Efforts were also made to ensure that the content of each module was applicable across international boundaries. All modules would be available in eight languages by January 2004. In addition, the software had to be adjusted to take account of privacy legislation in European Union countries.

At a later date, the team planned to add features such as nominating an IBM volunteer for a recognition award, voting for the best volunteer and community service stories, finding local events and enabling registration by IBM's 170,000 retirees worldwide.

In the next phase, the ODC planning team also hoped to match more precisely prospective volunteers with volunteer opportunities according to their interests, prior experience, location and time available. In the first phase, the site simply listed opportunities, as illustrated in Exhibit 2.

On November 24, 2003, at the time of the annual Thanksgiving holiday in the United States, ODC was launched at 90 IBM sites, half in the United States, half international. Each launch event attracted 200-300 employees, was led by a senior local IBM executive, and was reported extensively by local media.[1]

At the time of the launch, Sam Palmisano posted a letter to employees on the IBM web site in which he described the ODC initiative as "a concrete vehicle to give our values of success, innovation and personal responsibility added, real-world meaning" (Exhibit 3).

The well-designed ODC web site described ODC as "a new model for employee volunteerism" (Exhibit 4). The ODC program included a greater emphasis on "dollars for doers" community grants to local service organizations; IBM volunteers seeking such grants had to have volunteered for an average of eight hours per month over a five-month period to qualify (Exhibit 5). An exception was support for IBM MentorPlace volunteers; if they committed to the program for the full school year, IBM would make donations after six months of participation. ODC grants were also available to not-for-profit organizations where IBM volunteers did not use

ODC solutions but grant levels were lower that when they did.

Having perfected programs and tools such as TryScience and KidSmart during the 1990s, IBM felt comfortable making these available through community grants to a broader audience without the level of oversight that would have been necessary a few years earlier (Exhibit 6).

Measurement

Litow and his team had, for many years, been refining input and output measures to justify IBM's investments in strategic philanthropy. For example, evaluations of MentorPlace tracked the number of IBM employees signing up as volunteer mentors and the length of time they continued in this role. These input measures were complemented with output measures of student attitudes, attendance and test scores. In addition, IBM proudly tracked the number of employees it had serving on community and not-for-profit boards; indeed, regionally based community relations managers worked to ensure that senior IBM executives served as thought leaders and solutions providers on important community boards including, for example, the United Way.

As for the ODC web site, the planning team expected to capture two types of user data:

Implicit data derived from user behavior would include click-throughs, page views, time on site, path through site, submissions, referring and destination URL, search results clicked, welcome e-mails sent, downloads, and link popularity.

Explicit data submitted by the user would include registration, login, feedback on each tool used, ability to report success stories and submit pictures, hours volunteered, opt-ins and opt-outs, survey responses, search terms, popular forum on each tool used threads.

The planning team recognized that there were innumerable metrics on which data could be collected. They therefore set out to choose metrics that were aligned with measures of success that related to IBM business objectives and business drivers. This approach is illustrated in Exhibit 7.

Initial reactions to the ODC launch were encouraging, but some prospective volunteers questioned the likely level of backup and support. Sample comments included:

- "ODC is a terrific effort. It's more a treasure chest than a tool kit." (*IBM sales manager, Charlotte*)

---

[1] Normally, more than one-quarter of IBM media mentions related to IBM's community relations activities and those of its employees.

on demand ∴ community

IBM Corporate Community Relations
Volunteer Opportunities - Massachusetts

**The following opportunities are available for Massachusetts IBM employees and retirees.
Please go to the On Demand Community website (w3.ibm.com/ondemandcommunity) to register for
On Demand Community activities and for additional information.**

Volunteer Activity	Description
MentorPlace Program New Hampshire - Openings available for January 2004 Tech Boston Academy - Openings available for January 2004	Middle-school-aged boys and girls from the Kennedy- Longfellow School in Cambridge, Candia, New Hampshire, and girls who have participated in the Cambridge EXITE camp are matched with an IBM employee who corresponds with them throughout the academic year via email. In addition, IBM employees can be matched with high school students enrolled in the TechBoston Academy. Each year a formal training is held at the beginning of the program. Occasional face to face meetings are held on site and at the participating school(s). Typically, specific projects are assigned to students requiring input from their adult volunteer. Examples including writing the IBMers biography, getting proofreading assistance on writing assignments, and help with specific research projects. Information on the academic projects are provided to provide suggestions to volunteers in how can help their student with the assignment. The time commitment is 15-20 minutes every week with 2-4 face to face meetings two hours in duration. For more information on IBM's larger initiative, go to www.mentorplace.org.
Holiday Gift Collection Volunteers Needed December 2003	During the month of December many IBM sites organize location-specific collection of items to be donated to people in need. Recent examples include book collections, toy collections, and collections where employees may select a star and purchase an item for a particular person. Volunteers are needed to provide publicity for the collection, to staff the table for employees to select stars, and to assist in the collection and delivery of items collected. Cambridge, North Reading, Westford, Lexington, and Waltham locations have participated.
Help in Schools - TechCorp Volunteers Needed	TechCorp places technical volunteers in short term projects in public school districts in eastern Massachusetts including Boston, Framingham, Littleton, Mansfield, Maynard, Nashoba, Plainville, and Worcester. Volunteers can select from a variety of projects and contribute according to their interest, skill level, schedule, and time availability. For more information go to www.techcorps.org.
Join a Board of Directors - United Way's Board Bank Volunteers Needed	The United Way of Massachusetts Bay's BoardBank provides a service to 150+ nonprofit agencies to help match you to agencies in need of board members. For more information go to http://www.uwmb.org/howtohelp/boardbank.htm

**For more information, employees can go to w3.ibm.com/ondemandcommunity or contact Cathleen Finn via email or
SameTime at cathleen_finn@us.ibm.com or by phone at 617-693-0623 or tie line 693-0623 odc_volunteer_opportunities_nov_2003.doc**

Source: IBM web site

Exhibit 3   CEO Launch Letter On ODC Web Site

Dear IBMer,

As your outpouring of responses to last week's publication of "Our Values at Work" demonstrates, IBMers are already being energized and inspired by the values you yourselves have shaped. And among the more eloquent comments I've read were those touching on IBM's work in society at large, addressing the needs of the communities where IBMers live and work.

So I'm especially pleased to announce On Demand Community, an important new initiative that underlines our support for volunteerism around the world. A global program with a local focus, On Demand Community facilitates IBMers' own volunteer efforts – and provides a concrete vehicle to give our values of success, innovation and personal responsibility added, real-world meaning.

Specifically, this initiative focuses on the contribution that not-for-profit community organizations and schools have told us they value most – the skills and expertise of IBMers. (It's not, surprisingly, IBM's financial support – though they certainly need that, too.) On Demand Community gets its name by applying the concepts of an on demand business to the needs of volunteers and the organizations they assist – anytime, anywhere. The new On Demand Community site on w3 offers information and tools to support your volunteer work, as well as volunteer opportunities and an extensive library of resources to make volunteering easier. It builds on existing programs, such as Reinventing Education, and introduces entirely new resources, such as tools to help develop a technology plan or ways to open the power of the Web to community organizations, for example.

I encourage you to take a moment to register on the On Demand Community site, even if you are not ready to begin volunteering today. By registering now you will be able to access its resources and be immediately prepared once you are able to share your skills and time in the future.

If you're already among the many IBMers spending time and energy on behalf of a worthy cause, I want to thank you. I know you'll want to explore this program more fully so you can put its many resources to work for the people and communities needing our help – and show, in yet another context, that IBM and IBMers are led, first and foremost, by our values.

Sam Palmisano
Chairman and Chief Executive Officer

Source: Web site, <http://w3.ibm.com/ondemandcommunity/Gateway?jadeAction=HOMEPAGE_ SHOW_ACTION> accessed December 12, 2003.

- "It's so exiting that I'm worried about demand being too high. I can't afford to have too many of my employees sidetracked." (*IBM business manager, Sao Paolo, Brasil*)
- "I want to use the ODC tools to help my local church. But I'm afraid there won't be as much IBM backup if you're not volunteering through an IBM program like MentorPlace." (*IBM office manager, Dallas*)
- "In France, the state takes care of a lot more citizen needs than in the USA. There isn't the same spirit of philanthropy. But many IBM employees want to give back to their communities. Until now, it hasn't been obvious how to leverage IBM's resources to do it. The ODC initiative is a big step forward." (*IBM regional marketing director, Paris*)

Conclusion

Stan Litow and the ODC planning team were uncertain how many IBMers would register and take advantage of the opportunities the ODC web site presented. They had projected 25,000 registered employees out of 315,000 worldwide during the first two years following launch. Every ODC participant had to sign a disclaimer stating that (s)he was volunteering for his or her chosen community organization as a private individual rather than as an IBM employee. But Litow and his team were keen to ensure that the firm's reputation was not merely protected but enhanced by the efforts of ODC volunteers. Litow wondered how he would answer the question, which Palmisano was sure to ask: "By 2005, what will define success for the IBM ODC?"

Exhibit 4   ODC Program Summary

IBM Corporate Community Relations

IBM On Demand Community: A new model for employee volunteerism

IBM On Demand Community is a new global initiative that gives employees access to an extensive array of tools and resources to facilitate personalized volunteer efforts in not-for-profit organizations and schools

"No company can mandate volunteerism. The decision and self-sacrifice comes from within the individual. What we can do is encourage and support this distinctive aspect of our culture by providing education, technology, funding and recognition to tens of thousands of IBM colleagues who enrich their communities with their expertise and caring."

Sam Palmisano
Chairman and CEO
IBM Corporation

24/7 access to technology and resources for IBM volunteers

For more than 85 years, a unique combination of IBM technology, resources and employee community involvement has set an unmatched standard for corporate citizenship. Now, a revolutionary initiative—designed to meet the needs of today's workers, including mobile and work-at-home employees—sets a new standard for corporate volunteerism. It's called IBM On Demand Community

Through the On Demand Community Web site, volunteers can register to gain "on demand" access to training materials and information for personalized volunteer projects. They will also be recognized for their contributions to the community. In addition, discounted prices on selected IBM products for qualified schools and not-for-profit organizations help support and extend these employee volunteer efforts.

on demand ❖ community

w3.**ibm.com**/ondemandcommunity

"Our research shows that as much as communities appreciate donations of money and equipment, local agencies and schools are most interested in receiving volunteers who can share their skills and intellectual capital," said Stanley Litow, vice president of IBM Corporate Community Relations.

"IBM On Demand Community gives our employees an unprecedented opportunity to leverage their skills and to be recognized for their volunteer activities."

A comprehensive set of materials for volunteers

There are dozens of state-of-the art online presentations, videos, Web site reference links, software solutions and documents to assist IBM volunteers in not-for-profit organizations and educational settings. The materials are designed to allow employees maximum flexibility in engaging in short-term or more involved volunteer projects.

Topics on the IBM On Demand Community Web site include: "School Visits," "Mentor a Student," "Help Teachers with Technology," and

"Technology Planning for the Not-for-Profit."

A question of values: IBM On Demand Community

IBM On Demand Community combines the strengths and skills of our employees with the power of innovative technologies and solutions. The immediate concern is to drive significant and measurable change within agencies and organizations that would have never had access to this level of volunteer support.

This important work also reinforces the belief that IBM and IBMers can and should make a difference in the world. "I can think of no stronger statement of IBM's leadership as a global business than sharing our technology solutions and employees to address societal issues," said Litow. "IBM On Demand Community is a huge step forward in leveraging these strengths around the world."

For more information, IBM employees may access the IBM On Demand Community Web site at: w3.**ibm.com**/ondemandcommunity

The IBM On Demand Community Web site is the focal point for a revolutionary new approach to corporate philanthropy which makes volunteer information, support and resources available on demand to employees around the world

> IBM On Demand Community Web site is a new model of corporate volunteerism that delivers a portfolio of proven solutions, tools and strategies to employees for their volunteer projects. Areas of emphasis include:
>
> - **Helping Improve Local Schools** Software and activities that help promote math, science, e-mentoring, learning and other programs.
>
> - **Assisting Local Communities** Technology planning and new program offerings for not-for-profit agencies and teachers to expand and enhance their activities.
>
> - **Discounts and Grants** Grants of IBM equipment and technology discounts for qualified not-for-profit organizations, agencies and schools where IBMers volunteer.
>
> The On Demand Community Web site also provides background on IBM's rich heritage of community service. All Web site materials are designed to be shared with not-for-profit agencies and schools at no charge.
>
> *IBM volunteers participating in On Demand Community activities are sharing their personal time and are not representing IBM in any way.*

Source: IBM web site

Exhibit 5   ODC Community Grants

IBM Corporate Community Relations

IBM Community Grants: Supporting IBMers while adding value to community agencies

IBM Community Grants is a new program that increases grant award limits for employees and retirees who regularly volunteer with not-for-profit organizations and utilize IBM On Demand Community solutions.

"Through IBM On Demand Community, the time and expertise of our employee volunteers provide real value to the community. By adding technology and cash awards through IBM Community Grants, we greatly increase their impact and maximize the value."

Stanley S. Litow
Vice President
IBM Corporate Community Relations

Community grants: A key aspect of IBM On Demand Community

Imagine what thousands of IBM employees can accomplish worldwide when they're given the tools to be effective volunteers, and they can access them online—anytime, anywhere. That's IBM On Demand Community.

Now imagine how much more valuable the volunteers can be to schools and other organizations when they also have access to IBM equipment grants, reduced prices for selected hardware and software, and cash awards for the organizations where they donate their time.

This extraordinary combination of IBM employee expertise and innovative technology distinguishes IBM On Demand Community from all other corporate philanthropy initiatives.

"This is a powerful combination that stands to make an unprecedented impact on schools and community organizations worldwide," said Stanley S. Litow, vice president of IBM Corporate Community Relations. "We've dramatically increased the range of IBM equipment available to agencies where our employees volunteer, with

on demand community

w3.**ibm.com**/ondemandcommunity

Through the IBM Community Grants program, groups of IBMers or retirees may request up to $7500 in IBM equipment grants for eligible schools and not-for-profit organizations when using On Demand Community solutions. Individual IBM employees are eligible for up to $3,500 in technology grants or $1000 in cash awards a year for organizations where they regularly volunteer.

even more incentives for those who use our on demand tools in their volunteer work."

Eligibility requirements for community grants

IBM volunteers must be working with an eligible community service organization for an average of eight hours per month for five consecutive months to be eligible for either a cash or equipment grant. The one exception is requests for grant support for IBM MentorPlace. Volunteers must commit to the program for the full school year with donations made after six months of successful program participation.

IBM volunteers may request grants for schools and not-for-profits organizations not utilizing IBM On Demand Community solutions. However, grant limits are lower.

"Our new Community Grants program strengthens IBM On Demand Community by leveraging the full strength of IBM innovation and technology," Litow continued. "We fully expect that the volunteer efforts of our employees, combined with IBM Community Grants, has the potential to make a lasting impact on organizations that provide some of society's most important services."

For more information on eligibility for IBM Community Grants or information on IBM On Demand Community, please access:
w3.**ibm.com**/ondemandcommunity

Among the range of organizations that IBM Community Grants has assisted are:

- K-12 schools
- Preschools/Childcare Centers
- Adult and Youth Literacy Programs
- Community and family service agencies
- Job training programs
- Organizations that aid the elderly and disabled
- Museums, libraries and other cultural organizations
- Substance abuse programs

Building on IBM Community volunteer support:

- Employees are eligible for higher grant awards when using On Demand Community Solutions.
- Organizations are now eligible to receive an IBM Community Grant once every calendar year.
- Employees are eligible to apply for grants after only five months of consecutive service (average eight hours of volunteerism per month)

Source: IBM web site

Exhibit 6   ODC Fact Sheet for Not-For-Profits and Schools

on demand community
Fact sheet for not-for-profits & schools

What is IBM's On Demand Community?

On Demand Community is a global program to promote the spirit of volunteerism across IBM's world-class workforce—over 315,000 employees in more than 160 countries. IBM has a long tradition of investing in the communities where we work and live, and this guides our efforts to find the most valuable ways to help the schools and not-for-profit agencies upon which we all depend.

IBM is transforming the way it serves customers, to fulfill a vision of technology that is on demand—available as needed and more flexibly than ever. This same strategy underpins On Demand Community, through which IBM equips its people with an array of resources to help them match their talents with the needs of schools and organizations serving our communities.

What does On Demand Community mean for you?

It means that IBM volunteers are sharing with you the skills and talents IBM relies upon to run a world-class company. It means they can offer leading-edge solutions and tools, built upon the same technologies and expertise IBM offers customers of all sizes, in virtually every industry.

Presentations, programs, software, information—every On Demand Community resource is designed to address the specific needs of schools and not-for-profit agencies, based on all we have learned from long-standing IBM Corporate Community Relations programs. Many are successfully used today; here is a small sample of what's available:

- *IBM MentorPlace*, through which thousands of IBMers worldwide mentor students online
- *TryScience* presentations to promote learning and student advancement, drawn from hundreds of science museums around the world
- *School Visits by IBMers* to share their passion for math, science and engineering with students of all ages
- *KidSmart*, a program to introduce technology to pre-school children, their parents and teachers, in ways that enhance early education
- *Reinventing Education*, a Web-based "Change Toolkit" to help education leaders as well as school and district teams accelerate reform and eliminate barriers to student achievement

How does On Demand Community work?

Fundamental to the program is the relationship between our volunteers and your organization. Volunteers require different levels of assistance—you might be asked to provide facilities, schedule activities, or find new participants. Since the goal is always to bring value to your organization and those it serves, you might be asked to provide feedback in order to help us improve the program.

Although IBM encourages its employees to volunteer, please be aware that On Demand Community participants are sharing their personal time and are not representing IBM in any way. For example, they cannot make commitments on IBM's behalf, they are not covered by any IBM insurance, and IBM will not be responsible for their actions in connection with their volunteer work. We ask that you notify volunteers of any insurance coverage or other liability coverage you may provide. We also want you to know that your organization will be responsible for complying with any laws, including any legal obligation to do a background check, in connection with any volunteer.

How can you learn more?

To learn more about On Demand Community or IBM's many other community programs and philanthropic initiatives, visit us online at http://www.ibm.com/ibm/ibmgives/.

on demand community

Source: IBM web site

Exhibit 7   Linking ODC Metrics and Objectives

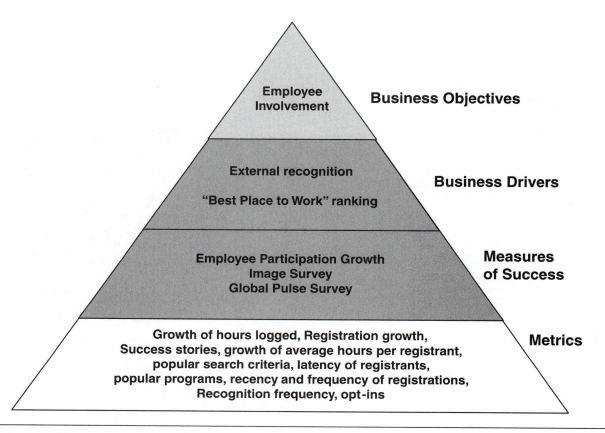

Source: Company records

ACCION International

The challenge we face at ACCION is how to take an organization whose network of microfinance institutions currently serves close to 1 million people, to one that reaches 10, or even 100 million borrowers. Our mission is to use microfinance to make a real difference in addressing world poverty. In order to meet this mission, we now have to take ACCION to the next level and overcome any barriers to our ability to grow.

Maria Otero, CEO, ACCION International

ACCION International was an independent, not-for-profit organization based in Boston and one of the world's premier microfinance organizations. ACCION worked with 27 financial institution partners in 21 countries in Latin America, the Caribbean and Africa, many of which ACCION had helped create and to which ACCION provided technical assistance and training.[1] These institutions offered small individual loans and, for borrowers who lacked collateral, small group loans, in which each client cross-guaranteed the other's share. Between 1992 and 2002, ACCION's network of institutions had reached 2.7 million clients and disbursed $4.6 billion in loans, with a repayment rate of 97.5%. ACCION's own operating budget for 2002 was $10.7 million with 52% of funding coming from private contributions, 19% from U.S. government grants, and the remaining 29% comprising international grants, interest, investment income, and contract and training fees.

History

ACCION International was founded in 1961 by Joseph Blatchford, a law student and amateur tennis player who completed a goodwill tennis tour of 30 Latin American cities in 1960, returning to the U.S. haunted by images of Latin America's urban poor. Determined to help, Blatchford and his law school friends raised $90,000 from private companies to start a community development organization designed to help the poor help themselves. In the summer of 1961, Blatchford and 30 volunteers flew to Venezuela and set to work. Initially greeted with skepticism, the fledgling "ACCIONistas" were soon working closely with local residents to identify the most pressing community needs. Together, volunteers and residents installed electricity and sewer lines, started nutrition programs, and built schools and community centers.

Over the next ten years, ACCION started programs in three additional countries (Brazil, Peru and Colombia), placed over 1,000 volunteers and contributed more than $9 million to development in some of the poorest communities of Latin America. By the early 1970s, ACCION's leaders became increasingly aware that these projects did not address the major cause of urban poverty in Latin America: the lack of economic opportunity. "We began to sense that a school or water system didn't necessarily have long-term impact. We were simply reorganizing the resources that a community already had within it, rather than increasing their resources," said former ACCION director Terry Holcombe.

The employment situation in many of Latin American urban areas in the 1970s was dire. Drawn by the mirage of industrial employment, thousands of rural migrants flocked to the cities each year. Once there, however, few found jobs. Those that were available often did not pay a living wage. Unable to find work, and lacking a social safety net, many of these urban poor survived by starting their own small businesses or "microenterprises." They made shoes, banged out pots or sold household goods or vegetables. Lacking the means to grow their tiny businesses and to buy supplies, they often borrowed from local loan sharks at

This case was prepared by Professor John Quelch with the assistance of Nathalie Laidler.
Copyright © 2003 by the President and Fellows of Harvard College. Harvard Business School case N9-503-106.

1 As of 5/03 Benin, Bolivia, Brazil, Colombia, Ecuador, El Salvador, Guatemala, Haiti, Honduras, Mexico, Mozambique, Nicaragua, Panama, Paraguay, Peru, Tanzania, Trinidad and Tobago, Uganda, United States, Venezuela, and Zimbabwe.

rates as high as 10% a day. Consequently, most of their profits went to interest payments, leaving them locked in a daily struggle for survival.

In 1973, ACCION staff in Recife, Brazil, contended that if the many small-scale entrepreneurs could borrow capital at commercial interest rates, they might be able to lift themselves out of poverty. ACCION coined the term "microenterprise" and began issuing small loans, effectively launching the field of microcredit. The experiment proved successful and, within four years, the organization had provided 885 loans and helped stabilize 1,386 jobs.

Over the next decade, ACCION helped start microlending programs in 14 countries in Latin America. ACCION and its affiliates, the ACCION Network, developed a lending method that met the distinct needs of microenterprises: small, short-term loans that built confidence and a credit record combined with site visits by a loan officer. With a loan repayment rate of close to 99% in those early years, ACCION Network borrowers soon shattered the myth that the poor were bad credit risks. ACCION also found that microlending could pay for itself, with the interest each borrower paid helping cover the cost of lending to another. In the mid-1980s, the demonstrated ability to cover the costs of lending, enhanced by ACCION's new loan guarantee fund, the Bridge Fund, enabled ACCION's affiliates to borrow from the local banking sector and dramatically increase the number of microentrepreneurs they reached. Between 1989 and 1995, the amount of money loaned by ACCION's Latin American Network multiplied more than 20 times. Yet the ACCION Network was reaching fewer than 2% of the microentrepreneurs in need of its services. "In the 1980s," explained Michael Chu, president and CEO of ACCION International from 1994 to 1999, and current board member, "we created nonprofit organizations, gained support of key business leaders and proved that microfinancing worked. Initially, most of our loans were group loans, based on what became known as the solidarity model, but increasingly they have declined relative to individual loans."

ACCION remained convinced that microlending had the potential to transform the economic landscape of Latin America. To do so, however, ACCION knew that microlenders would need access to a much larger pool of capital. In response, ACCION helped create BancoSol, the first commercial bank in the world dedicated solely to microenterprise. Founded in Bolivia in 1992, BancoSol was the bank of the poor: its clients were typically market vendors, sandal makers and seamstresses. By 2002, however, BancoSol offered its 45,000 clients an impressive range of financial services including savings accounts, credit cards and housing loans (products that as late as the mid-1990s were only accessible to Bolivia's upper classes). BancoSol was no longer unique, and in 2002, the majority of ACCION partners in Latin America were regulated financial institutions, with the power to access the financial markets and the potential to reach not just thousands, but millions of the poor. Carlos Castello, senior vice president of international operations/Latin America & Caribbean, explained, "About five years ago, ACCION decided to support and focus on what we call the commercial approach to microfinance. Since then, most of our partner organizations have radically changed and today most of the major players are for-profit financial institutions."

In 1991, concerned about growing income inequality and unemployment in the United Sates, ACCION brought its microlending model home, starting a program in Brooklyn, New York. Over the next five years, ACCION worked to adapt its lending model to the very different social and economic context of the U.S. In 2000, ACCION's U.S. initiative was renamed ACCION USA. In 2002, ACCION USA was the largest microlender in the country, with lending locations in California, Georgia, Illinois, Massachusetts, New Mexico, New York, Rhode Island and Texas. By year-end 2002, the ACCION USA Network had loaned more than $62 million to over 8,000 low-income entrepreneurs.

A nonprofit subsidiary of ACCION International, ACCION USA's goal was to serve microentrepreneurs throughout the United States, regardless of location. In 2001, ACCION USA merged with Working Capital, a New England-based microlender, adding five new lending locations to the ACCION USA Network and, in 2002, ACCION USA was centralizing its loan processing, exploring Internet-based lending and call centers, and opening new lending offices.

In October 2000, ACCION made the strategic decision to begin working in Africa in partnership with microlending organizations in sub-Saharan Africa, marking its first initiative outside the Americas. According to Otero, "ACCION recognized the vital need for microcredit throughout Africa and believed it could fulfill its mission of addressing poverty by reaching increasing numbers of the continent's poor." In 2002, ACCION was providing technical assistance to microlenders in Benin, Mozambique, South Africa, Uganda and Zimbabwe. (See Exhibit 1 for a timeline of the major milestones in ACCION's history).

Exhibit 1   Timeline of ACCION's Major Milestones

Time period	Characteristics and Innovation
1960 – 1972	*ACCION created as a "private peace corps"* Programs in Venezuela, Brazil, Colombia and Peru ACCION deploys volunteers in the field with a major focus on community development.
1973 – 1980	*Microlending Experiment Begins* First microloans made in Recife, Brazil, 1973. Replication efforts in other countries: Ecuador, Colombia Shift from volunteers to professionals with staff of 5 people
1981 – 1985	*Developing a new Technology* ACCION begins to test "Solidarity Group" lending in the late '70s. It is deployed widely by the mid-1980s. Expansion to Dominican Republic, Ecuador, Mexico and Peru in the early 1980s Focus on self-sustainability of microenterprise lending institutions via commercial interest rates and the belief that the poor could pay commercial rates of interest Early successes in reaching much poorer clientele and women Staff of 10
1986 – 1990	*Building a Network* Pro-active expansion with new affiliates in Bolivia, Brazil, Chile, Costa Rica, Guatemala and Honduras Emphasis on increasing scale and outreach and establishment of a formal network Establishment of reporting standards for network affiliates including standard definitions for key ratios ACCION collects data on a monthly basis. ACCION creates the Bridge Fund, a guarantee mechanism that will facilitate access to commercial (bank) funds by network members (active in 1986). Emphasis on institutional development, ACCION launches publication series designed to document its experience and disseminate it to others. Staff of 18
1991 – 1994	*The "Gran Salto" Expanding an Industry* Network commits to lending $1 billion in five years and accomplishes this goal. 1992 inauguration of BancoSol, La Paz, Bolivia, as the first commercial bank specialized in microfinance, after transformation of PRODEM, the microlending NGO ACCION & local business leaders established in 1987 Creation of Centro ACCION Microempresarial, ACCION International's training and technical assistance arm, in Bogata, Colombia Widespread use of Bridge Fund enables rapid program growth in terms of number of loans, new clients and total portfolio. Number of clients grows from 40,000 to 259,000 and portfolio from $13.7 million to $137.3 million. Expansion to Argentina, Nicaragua, and Panama

Exhibit 1 Timeline of ACCION's Major Milestones (continued)

Time period	Characteristics and Innovation
	Design and implementation of ACCION CAMEL. Network establishes standards of financial performance and develops rigor and transparency in this area.
	ACCION plays active role in members' efforts to transform into or create regulated microfinance institutions. Corposol/Finansol in Colombia comes close to bankruptcy due to poor management and flawed governance. ACCION takes the lead in re-capitalizing and managing the institution.
	Launch of U.S. microlending initiative in NYC. Total staff of 40 people
1995 – 1999	*The Commercialization of Microfinance: New Players / New Models*
	Strong emphasis on accessing financial markets through the issuance by microfinance institutions of financial instruments such as bonds and Cds
	New mechanisms for providing equity and loans – ACCION creates the Gateway Fund and is one of the founders of PROFUND, to invest in MFIs in Latin America
	ACCION takes on a significant role in the governance of investee microfinance institutions by participating on the Board of Directors.
	Competition begins, especially in Bolivia
	Expansion to Honduras and Venezuela
	Near collapse of Finansol in Columbia absorbs staff time, loss of funds; teaches ACCION hard lessons about the importance of strong governance and financial transparency. ACCION rebuilds the institution, now Finamérica.
	Lending methodology evolves. New products designed to face increased competition
	US program expands to six sites and model undergoes re-engineering.
	Staff of 65
2000 – 2002	*Current Situation*
	Strong emphasis on performance & commonality of vision results in departure from the Network of several institutions. MFIs in Mexico, Haiti, Ecuador and Brazil join the network.
	27 ACCION partners in 14 countries in Latin America, the Caribbean and five countries in Africa
	Five associated lending programs serving over 30 cities and towns in 5 U.S. states, and direct lending by ACCION USA in five states.
	Creation of ACCION Investments SPC, an investment company capitalized at $18 million by nine investors and managed by ACCION's for profit arm, GAIM.
	Total number of active clients = 798,031
	Active portfolio = $440 million

Source: ACCION Board Members Manual 2002 and interviews

"What has been critical to ACCION's success" explained Chu, "has been the organization's ability to question itself and its lending models, and to adapt to the very environment it has contributed to change."

Mission and Activities

In 2002, ACCION International's mission was to give people the tools they needed to work their way out of poverty. By providing microloans and business training to poor women and men who started their own businesses, ACCION's partner lending organizations helped people work their own way up the economic ladder, with dignity and pride. ACCION strove to bring this opportunity to as many of the world's self-employed poor as possible by developing microfinance institutions that were financially self-sustaining and together, capable of reaching millions of people.

ACCION's Partners Initially, many partners were NGOs (non-governmental organizations); many later became commercial banks. Chu explained:

> At first, microfinance was so new, and so inconceivable to the established financial sector and regulatory bodies, that we had to start with nonprofit organizations. Our objective has always been to make microfinance economically viable, so we developed nonprofits with a business approach. For many years we then worked on transitioning these NGOs to financial institutions, and now ACCION is starting to work with established banks and get them involved in microfinance.

"We currently have four partner models," explained Castello, "NGOs that have transformed into banks or finance companies, boutique microfinance banks, large national or international banks that have created microfinance subsidiaries, and NGOs". See Exhibit 2 for a list of ACCION partners in December 2002.

1. *NGOs that had transformed into banks.* This was the dominant model with eight ACCION partners having gone this route, and two partners currently in transition.

"We have struggled with these transformations," admitted Castello:

> All of our affiliates would agree that these transformations have been time consuming and expensive, and institutions have had difficulties with cultural issues. For example, in most cases, we have found that people with banking backgrounds tend to instinctively implement controls for managing risk, thereby increasing hurdles for clients to obtain credit and pulling the institution up-market. While there are exceptions, we have found that what works best is a president with an NGO background, loan officers who know microfinance, and bankers in the rest of the organization.

Despite the demands of transformation, most of ACCION's affiliates had however, transferred successfully and were reaching their mission objectives while expanding the range of products they offered their clients. "Many other players are now following our lead

in transforming NGOs," explained Castello, "but I believe that this model has run its course in Latin America because nearly all the NGOs capable of transforming have taken this step, and because it is so expensive and cumbersome when compared to other new recently developed models."

2. *Boutique banks.* This model began in the mid-1990s and was represented by two partners in the ACCION network in 2002. Castello explained:

> These organizations started off as for-profit entities, with the backing of social or multi-lateral investors, focused on microfinance. The problem with this model is that it takes time to build up a portfolio and register returns and you need patient, long-term investors. In the case of Banco Solidario in Ecuador, it started with larger loans to facilitate funding while building up a microfinance portfolio, and these larger loans are now being phased out. The advantage of this model is that the organizations don't have to undergo internal reporting changes, and are already regulated, so they don't have to wait to receive a banking license.

In both cases, the bank president had a banking background but the credit area was still staffed with microfinance experts.

3. *Large banks with a microfinance subsidiary.* This was the most recent and promising ACCION model, represented by three partners in 2002. Under this model, ACCION helped to set up a service company as a separate subsidiary of a large bank. The service company originated and managed microloans that were then booked by the bank. The service subsidiary was not a regulated financial institution and was therefore lean and flexible, requiring only minimum operating funds. Typically, the bank would hold 80% of the service organization's shares and ACCION the remaining 20%. "We have found," added Castello,

> that this does not work when the bank views microfinance loans simply as an additional product. There's too much of a culture clash because a bank, which is set up for low-risk and high-profit clients (by original standards), just cannot accommodate microfinance loans. By establishing a separate entity staffed with microfinance experts, one can build up a profitable portfolio that can be maintained separately or gradually integrated into the bank in five or six years.

> The main advantages of this model were that there was no pressure to go up-market since the service organization's

Exhibit 2   ACCION International Partners, 2002

Partner Name	Country	Model	ACCION's Role T.A. Technical Assistance Inv = Investor Brd = Board Member R.A = Resident Advisor
BancoSol – Banco Solidario S.A.	Bolivia	NGO to commercial bank	T.A. / Inv / Brd / R.A
Finamérica - Financiera América S.A.	Colombia	NGO to finance company	T.A. / Inv / Brd / R.A
Cooperativa Emprender	Colombia	Cooperative (regulated)	T.A. / Inv / Brd
Fundación Mario Santo Domingo	Colombia	NGO	
FED – Fundación Ecuatoriana de Desarrollo	Ecuador	NGO	
Banco Solidario S.A.	Ecuador	Boutique bank	T.A. / Inv / Brd / R.A
Génesis – BancaSol	Guatemala	NGO to commercial bank (in-process)	T.A. / Inv / Brd / R.A
FINSOL – Financiera Solidaria S.A.	Honduras	NGO to finance company	T.A/ R.A
ADMIC - ADMIC Nacional A.C.	Mexico	NGO	T.A / R.A
Compartamos – Financiera Compartamos	Mexico	NGO to finance company	T.A. / Inv / Brd / R.A
CREDIFE	Ecuador	Service co. of a major bank	T.A. / Inv / R.A
FAMA – Fundacion para el Apoyo a la Microempresa	Nicaragua	NGO	T.A. / R.A
Multicredit Bank	Panama	Commercial bank	
Fundación Paraguaya	Paraguay	NGO to finance company (in-process)	T.A. / R.A
BanGente - El Banco de la Gente Emprendedora	Venezuela	Boutique bank	T.A. / Inv / Brd
Integral – Apoyo Intergral S.A.	El Salvador	NGO to finance company	T.A. / Inv / Brd / R.A
SogeSol – Societe Generale de Solidarite	Haiti	Service co. of major bank	T.A. / Inv / Brd / R.A
El Comercio – El Comercio Financiero SAECA	Paraguay	Finance company	T.A. / R.A
CML – Caribbean Microfinance Limited	Trinidad and Tobago	Commercial bank	T.A.
MicroKing – MicroKing Finance	Zimbabwe	Subsidiary of major bank	T.A. / Brd / R/A
Nkwe – Nkwe Enterprise Finance *	South Africa	NGO	T.A.
Padme – Association pour la Promotion et l'Appui au Developpement de MicroEntreprises	Benin	NGO	T.A. / R.A
Tchuma	Mozambique	Credit Union	T.A. / Brd / R.A
UMU – Uganda Microfinance Union	Uganda	NGO to finance company	T.A. / R.A
Mibanco	Peru	NGO to commercial bank	Inv / Brd
Réal Microcrédito	Brazil	Service co. of a major bank	T.A. / Inv / Brd / 2 R.A

Source: ACCION International

* ACCION withdraws in early 2003 due to very poor performance and Nkwe's lack of funds to grow the institution.

major shareholder, the bank, was already competing in that segment. In addition, the infrastructure of the existing bank could be leveraged to allow relatively low-cost and very fast expansion of lending.

SogeSol in Haiti Valerie Kindt, director, international operations, had been a resident advisor to Sogebank, the leading national Haitian bank for over two years, helping establish SogeSol, a direct subsidiary of the bank, focused on microloans. She explained the challenges she had encountered:

> Haiti has a population of around 8 million, an ineffective government with no legislation or restrictions on interest rates, and a thriving informal economy. The Haitian microfinance industry is well developed and competitive, with the majority of institutions being NGOs and rural cooperatives. To date, five major banks have entered into microfinance. The first, Banque Union Haitienne (BUH) incorporated microloans as an additional bank product and did not establish a subsidiary. Unibank, with the help of IPC, a German consulting firm, established a subsidiary called MCN (Micro-Crédit National), which offers slightly larger loans than SogeSol who was the third player to enter the market. Since then, two additional players have entered what is an increasingly competitive market place.

Kindt believed that much of SogeSol's success stemmed from the fact that ACCION focused on technical assistance and training of local management, rather than running the project itself. Pierre Marie Boisson, president of SogeSol, Sogebank's chief economist and Harvard graduate, was committed to the project from the outset, and had secured the funding required to implement the methodology, technology and systems required. Challenges had included the in-class training time required for loan officers (five weeks compared to an average of two weeks in other countries) and overcoming the perception that it was 'dirty work'. "Haiti has a strong hierarchical society," explained Kindt, "and one of the challenges has been overcoming Sogebank staff perceptions of SogeSol." She expanded on the resulting problems that this caused for SogeSol:

> One of the main problems is that SogeSol customers must come into Sogebank branches to make their loan payments. These customers are often treated very rudely by the bank tellers, who believe that they are their social superiors. They might refuse to take small change as part of a loan payment for example, resulting in the customer defaulting on his or her loan. Although we provide very fast, efficient service at SogeSol, it is difficult to control behavior at Sogebank. The result is that our customers often feel more comfortable with a really good NGO competitor such as ACME. We are working on ways to resolve this issue.

Boisson expanded on the challenges SogeSol faced. "This is still a young industry," he explained, "with significant competition and virtually no regulation. SogeSol is also still a young organization and we need to continue to grow and manage our client base." Boisson was particularly concerned about keeping delinquency rates low and client retention rates high. He expanded on the two issues:

> Our current 30-day delinquency rates are 3.7%, which, compared to our competitors, is pretty good. The concern I have, however, is that the judicial system in Haiti is so slow that lawyers used by SogeSol can take up to a year to collect collaterals of delinquent clients. This means that SogeSol may be wrongly presenting an image of tolerance towards bad clients, encouraging other clients to become delinquent, therefore reducing overall portfolio quality. Our client retention is currently around 80%, which is a little lower than I would like. However, this is also influenced by the fact that we are unlikely to renew a client who misses payments and we tend to encourage clients to be more conservative.

4. **NGOs.** NGOs comprised the fourth group of ACCION partners. In 2002, there were six such partners in the Latin American Network. Castello explained, "Many successful NGOs operate just as efficiently as commercial organizations and, as long as they don't have financing constraints, they may not need to become commercial entities." This had been ACCION's initial partner model and, in some countries, particularly in Africa, remained a viable option.

In Latin America, ACCION provided all of its partners with technical assistance services and financing, and held minority shareholder positions (between 6% and 24%), giving ACCION board representation. ACCION professionals worked with local partner management, as resident advisors, often with line responsibility, to build lending operations capable of reaching hundreds of thousands of microentrepreneurs. In December 2002, out of 18 resident advisors in Latin America, nine held temporary line positions within partner organizations. Additional services ranged from business planning to staff training and new product development. By strengthening partners, ACCION hoped to help them become a permanent part of the financial fabric of the countries where they operated. See Exhibit 3 for an overview of ACCION requirements of its partners. "Because ACCION does not own its partners," explained Kindt, "influence is based on bringing solutions. ACCION has to stay relevant and continue to ask the question; what is the best way forward to achieve our mission."

ACCIONs Lending Model ACCION's loan methodology was designed to both meet the needs of microentrepreneurs and ensure that their microfinance partners were financially sustainable. ACCION considered microentrepreneurs skilled business people, not objects of charity. Like traditional banks, ACCION partners evaluated potential borrowers using measurements such as: business assets; amount and cost of goods sold; cost of raw materials; and household expenses. Unlike traditional banks, loan officers would meet potential borrowers at their places of business, where they would also weigh intangibles like references from customers and neighbors, and the loan officer's own "gut feeling" about the microentrepreneur's drive to succeed. This character-based lending allowed ACCION to go "beyond the numbers" and develop a more complete picture of a potential borrower than could be obtained from a traditional credit score.

Loan officers themselves varied from individuals with university degrees and a sense of social mission to individuals with less formal education. Most worked on an incentive system based on the number of active clients they managed and portfolio quality. "A loan officer's background is less important than his or her personality," explained Castello, "they need to be people-people, with sales skills, an ability to work in the field and adaptable in nature." Boisson expanded, "Loan officers cannot be traditional bankers," he explained, "they need to be close to the social groups they serve in order to be accepted by them, but also need to be highly competent. The best loan officers are young, outgoing commercial types for whom this is often their first job."

The focus on financial sustainability had enabled ACCION's partner programs to increase the number of active borrowers from 13,000 in 1988 to nearly 800,000 in 2002. ACCION's experience over 30 years had demonstrated that microlending could both help the poor and be profitable. In Mexico, for example, ACCION's partner Financiera Compartamos served 143,000 poor and low-income entrepreneurs by year-end 2002, and turned a substantial profit. Financial viability enabled microlenders to break free from the limitations of donor funds because they could attract private investment, and had the potential to access billions of dollars in the international financial markets to help the very people that traditional banking systems had excluded.

ACCION Clients In 2002, an estimated 3 billion people lived on less than $2 a day, and 40% to 60% of people working in the developing world were self-employed. ACCION's borrowers were self-employed women and men who relied on microenterprise as their main source of income. They included the very poor and those who had some assets but remained marginalized from the mainstream economy and society. ACCION's Latin American, Caribbean and African borrowers were among the region's poorest people at the time of their first loan. They usually had no collateral, might not read or write, and sometimes did not even have enough capital to open for business every day. Sixty-five percent of them were women. (See Exhibit 4 for details on ACCION's borrowers and loans). According to the IDB (Inter-American Development Bank) in 2001, there were more than 50 million microenterprises, providing jobs to over 150 million people, in Latin America alone. Microlending in Latin America had a 30-year track record and studies from the 1980s clearly demonstrated microlending's positive effect on business income and family welfare.

Exhibit 3   ACCION Requirements of its Partners

1. Private and independent.

2. Specialized in the provision of financial services to the poor households.

3. Understand the markets they serve and commit to improving services to these markets.

4. Have strong board leadership drawn from the private sector.

5. Have the objective of achieving massive reach in their operations.

6. Strive toward financial sustainability or have achieved economic viability.

7. Access the financial markets as their main source of capital.

8. Do not depend on, or provide, subsidized credit.

Source: ACCION International

	ACCION Latin American Network	ACCION African Partners	ACCION USA	Totals
Active clients at year-end	740,321	57,710	3,807	801,838
Total amount disbursed	$785.3 million	$34 million	$18.1 million	$837.4 million
Active portfolio at year-end	$420 million	$18.4 million	$20.4 million	$458.8 million
Average loan	$581	$317	$5,976	

Source: ACCION web-site

Services and Products

ACCION had helped to found, build and strengthen some of the most successful microlending institutions in the world. Over half the partners in Latin America, including all the regulated institutions, with the exception of BanGente in troubled Venezuela, earned a profit in 2002. ACCION had pioneered many of the best practices and standards in the industry including: individual and solidarity group lending methodologies; the CAMEL diagnostic system to assess and compare microfinance institutions' performance; and guarantees and equity funds for microfinance institutions. About 30% of ACCION's operating costs were paid for directly by partners, either from their profits or from funds made available by multi-lateral or bilateral institutions specifically for technical assistance or product development.

ACCION CAMEL™ This was a diagnostic and management tool that measured the capital adequacy, asset quality, management capability, earnings and liquidity of microfinance institutions. (See Exhibit 5 for details of the ACCION CAMEL tool.) Designed to help managers assess an organization's financial health and overall performance, and initially developed by the U.S. Federal Reserve to evaluate the solvency of U.S. banks, ACCION adapted CAMEL in 1993 to the field of microfinance. Since then, ACCION had performed more than 40 CAMEL evaluations, and CAMEL had been adopted by government regulators, such as the Bolivian bank superintendency as the evaluation tool for all microfinance institutions in the country. It was also being implemented as a due diligence tool for Banco Centro Americano de Integracion Economica based in Honduras, by the SIDBI Foundation for Microcredit in India, and for training staff from supervisory entities from eight African countries.

Deborah Drake, vice president, policy and analysis division, expanded on the importance of the CAMEL tool. "The analysis is similar to that carried out of traditional financial institutions," she explained. "The CAMEL reviews the same areas and indicators, but the relative weightings and ranges that we use for microfinance institutions are different. For example, it is much more expensive to manage a microfinance institution and operating expenses are more likely to amount to 20% instead of the less than 5% of average loan portfolio, recorded by traditional banks." Although the ACCION CAMEL issues a rating, the primary purpose of the ACCION CAMEL has been to provide a diagnostic tool for ACCION network members. Drake explained further, "It is really a working tool. A CAMEL team, composed of ACCION staff, will go to a partner institution and carry out an in-depth, on-site assessment, that can take up to two weeks. The ACCION Camel team provides a presentation of initial findings to the institution's senior management and board of directors, followed by a comprehensive written report. Not only is the process quite time consuming," added Drake, "but it is also fairly expensive, with a full evaluation costing around $25,000 to complete."

Given widespread demand for this type of analysis, other organizations had begun to offer their own evaluations and ratings. Drake expanded, "Until last year, we did not offer CAMEL outside our own network, but, as a result, we missed an opportunity to shape the industry by implementing more widely what many consider to be the best tool in the industry, and we let a number of competitor products, some less expensive, gain a foothold." Drake was currently looking at developing versions of the ACCION CAMEL that would focus on specific target audiences such as investors. She explained:

> *Our strong point is assessing the strengths and weaknesses of an institution and their impact on financial*

Exhibit 5   Details of ACCION CAMEL, 2002[2]

The CAMEL methodology was originally adopted by North American bank regulators to evaluate the financial and managerial soundness of U.S. commercial lending institutions. The CAMEL reviews and rates five areas of financial and managerial performance: Capital Adequacy, Asset Quality, Management, Earnings, and Liquidity Management. As microfinance institutions (MFIs) increasingly reach out to formal financial markets to access capital, there is a need for a similar tool to gather and evaluate data on the performance of MFIs.

Based on the conceptual framework of the original CAMEL, ACCION developed its own instrument. Although the ACCION CAMEL reviews the same five areas, the indicators and ratings used by ACCION reflect the unique challenges and conditions facing the microfinance industry. The ACCION CAMEL analyzes and rates 21 key indicators, with each indicator given an individual weighting. Eight quantitative indicators account for 47% of the rating, and 13 qualitative indicators make up the remaining 53%. The final Camel composite rating is a number on a scale of zero to five, with five as the measure of excellence. This numerical rating in turn, corresponds to an alphabetical rating (AAA, AA, A; BBB, BB, B; C;D; and not rated).

CAMEL Information and Adjustments

The MFI is required to gather the following information for a CAMEL examination: 1. Financial statements, 2. Budgets and cash flow projections; 3. Portfolio aging schedules; 4. Funding sources; 5. Information about the board of directors; operations/staffing; and macroeconomic information. Financial statements form the basis of the CAMELS' quantitative analysis, and MFIs are required to present audited financial statements from the last three years and interim statements for the most recent 12-month period. The other required materials provide programmatic information and show the evolution of the institution. These documents demonstrate to CAMEL analysts the level and structure of loan operations and the quality of the MFIs infrastructure and staffing.

Once the financial statements have been compiled, adjustments need to be made. These serve two purposes: they place the MFIs current financial performance in the context of a financial intermediary; and they enable comparisons among the different institutions in the industry. The CAMEL performs six adjustments, for the scope of the microfinance activity, loan loss provision, loan write-offs, explicit and implicit subsidies, effects of inflation, and accrued interest income.

CAMEL Scoring

Based on the results of the adjusted financial statements and interviews with the MFIs management and staff, a rating of one to five is assigned to each of the CAMEL's 21 indicators and weighted accordingly.

Capital Adequacy. The objective of the capital adequacy analysis is to measure the financial solvency of an MFI by determining whether the risks it has incurred are adequately offset with capital and reserves to absorb potential losses. One indicator is *leverage*, which illustrates the relationship between the risk-weighted assets of the MFI and its equity. Another indicator, *ability to raise equity*, is a qualitative assessment of an MFI's ability to respond to a need to replenish or increase equity at any given time. A third indicator, *adequacy of reserves*, is a quantitative measure of the MFI's loan loss reserve and the degree to which the institution can absorb potential loan losses.

Asset Quality. The analysis of asset quality is divided into three components: portfolio quality, portfolio classification system, and fixed assets. Portfolio quality includes two quantitative indicators: *portfolio at risk*, which measures the portfolio past due over 30 days; and *write-offs/write-off policy*, which measures the MFIs adjusted write-offs based on CAMEL criteria. Portfolio classification system entails reviewing the portfolio's aging schedules and assessing the institution's policies associated with assessing portfolio risk. Under fixed assets, one indicator is the *productivity of long-term assets*, which evaluates the MFIs policies for investing in fixed assets. The other indicator concerns the institution's *infrastructure*, which is evaluated to determine whether it meets the needs of both staff and clients.

Management. Five qualitative indicators make up this area of analysis: governance; human resources; processes, controls, and audit; information technology system; and strategic planning and budgeting. *Governance* focuses on how well the institution's board of directors functions, including the diversity of its technical expertise, its independence from management, and its ability to make decisions flexibly and effectively. The second indicator, *human resources*, evaluates whether the department of human resources provides clear guidance and support to operations staff, including recruitment and training of new personnel, incentive systems for personnel, and performance evaluation systems. The third indicator, *processes, controls, and audit*, focuses on the degree to which the MFI has formalized key processes and the effectiveness with which it controls risk throughout the organization, as measured by its control environment and the quality of its internal and external audit. The fourth indicator, *information technology system*, assesses whether computerized information systems are operating effectively and efficiently, and are generating reports for management purposes in a timely and accurate manner. This analysis reviews the information technology environment and the extent and quality of the specific information

---

2 Source: Adapted from Sonia Saltzman and Darcy Salinger "The ACCION CAMEL" Technical Note, September 1998.

Exhibit 5   Details of ACCION CAMEL, 2002 (continued)

technology controls. The fifth indicator, *strategic planning and budgeting*, looks at whether the institution undertakes a comprehensive and participatory process for generating short- and long-term financial projections and whether the plan is updated as needed and used in the decision making process.

Earnings. The ACCION CAMEL chooses three quantitative and one qualitative indicator to measure the profitability of MFIs: adjusted return on equity, operational efficiency, adjusted return on assets, and interest rate policy. *Adjusted return on equity (ROE)* measure the ability of the institution to maintain and increase its net worth through earnings from operations. *Operational efficiency* measures the efficiency of the institution and monitors its progress towards achieving a cost structure that is closer to the level achieved by formal financial institutions. *Adjusted return on assets (ROA)* measures how well the MFI's assets are utilized, or the institution's ability to generate earnings with a given asset base. CAMEL analysts also study the *MFI's interest rate policy* to assess the degree to which management analyzes and adjusts the institution's interest rates on microenterprise loans, based on the costs of funds, profitability targets, and macroeconomic environment.

Liquidity Management. This area evaluates the MFI's ability to accommodate decreases in funding sources and increases in assets and to pay expenses at a reasonable cost. Indicators in this area are liability structure, availability of funds to meet credit demand, cash flow projections, and productivity of other assets. Under *liability structure*, CAMEL analysts review the composition of the institution's liabilities, including their tenor, interest rate, payment terms, and sensitivity to changes in the macroeconomic environment. The types of guarantees required on credit facilities, sources of credit available to the MFI, and the extent of resource diversification are analyzed as well. This indicator also focuses on the MFIs relationship with banks in terms of leverage achieved based on guarantees, the level of credibility the institution has with regard to the banking sector, and the ease with which the institution can obtain funds when required. *Availability of funds to meet credit demands* measured the degree to which the institution had delivered credit in a timely and agile manner. *Cash flow projections* evaluate the degree to which the institution is successful in projecting its cash flow requirements. The analysis looks at current and past cash flow projections prepared by the MFI to determine whether they have been prepared with sufficient detail and analytical rigor, and whether past projections have accurately predicted cash inflows and outflows. *Productivity of other assets* focuses on the management of current assets other than the loan portfolio, primarily cash and short-term investments. The MFI is rated on the extent to which it maximizes the use of its cash, bank accounts, and short-term investments by investing in a timely fashion and at the highest returns, commensurate with its liquidity needs.

---

performance. We don't want to become a rating agency. We are designing a shorter, less expensive CAMEL that will be piloted in 2003, with modules that can be added onto the CAMEL evaluation as needed. For example, there is a specific module when the CAMEL is being used for investor due diligence. We have also developed a CAMEL update product that can be used by institutions that have already been through the full analysis and there may be other possibilities that we have not yet fully explored."

Other products included training programs for partner staff and microentrepreneurs, credit scoring, market research and product development tools, and automation technology. See Exhibit 6 for details of selected products.

Financing for Partners ACCION's Capital Markets Department helped partners obtain equity financing, debt financing and other commercial funding. By enabling partners to link directly with investors and commercial banks, ACCION helped them become independent of donor funds and develop as commercial financial institutions. Equity financing options included:

- ACCION's Latin America Bridge Fund was established in 1984 and was the first loan guarantee fund for microfinance institutions. By providing standby letters of credit, the Bridge Fund enabled ACCION's partners to borrow from local banks. Capitalized at over $7 million in 2002, with loans from socially responsible investors, the fund had provided guarantees averaging $5 million per year and enabled 27 institutions in 12 countries to access local commercial funding.

- The Gateway Fund LLC, ACCION's wholly owned equity fund, made equity, quasi-equity and debt investments in its affiliate microfinance institutions with a proven track record in Latin America and the Caribbean. The Fund was capitalized at $7 million in 2002 and was managed by Gateway ACCION International Manager Inc (GAIM), a wholly-owned, for-profit subsidiary of ACCION international.

- The IDB/MIF Fund, a $2.5 million investment fund, administered by GAIM for the Multilateral Investment Fund of the Inter-American Development Bank

Exhibit 6   Details of Selected ACCION Products

ACCION's Dialágo de Gestiones (Client Training Program) Was a training program designed to help microentrepreneurs to better manage their small businesses. Created by Centro ACCION in Bogota, Colombia, with support from the Mulitlateral Investment Fund of the IDB, and launched in 1999, Diálogo is based on feedback from microentrepreneurs that revealed that traditional lecture-based courses were not as effective for learning as participatory workshops. Encompassing interactive role-plays, games and discussions, Diálogo's 40 modules taught business basics: pricing, quality control, marketing, customer service, dealing with competition, in an accessible and practical way. Since its launch, more than 230,000 microentrepreneurs, 62% of them women, had participated in the training program,which charged a fee for service established by each Diálogo licensee. The program was licensed to 28 partners in 14 countries, some of them microfinance affiliates of ACCION, and others entities specially dedicated to training. Licensees all received ACCION training of their own trainers, assistance in marketing the program, promotional materials, and monitoring visits. ACCION had trained 650 trainers for its licensees and additionally had brought them together as a network to conduct impact evaluations of the business training. Based on such feedback, ACCION had developed new training modules and materials. Through 2002, sales of workbooks to licensees yielded over $100,000 in royalty fees for ACCION.

Credit Scoring for Microenterprise Was a credit-scoring model that provided partners with an easy-to-use tool to rate prospective borrowers and calculate the risk of extending credit to them. The model was developed in partnership with LISIM, a professional credit scoring firm based in Bogota, Colombia. In 2002, the model was in use at BancoSol in Bolivia, Banco Solidario in Ecuador, FINAMERICA in Colombia and Mibanco in Peru.

Market Research and New Product Development ACCION had developed a range of tools to help partners attract and retain clients. These tools included: qualitative market research, such as focus groups and interviews, and quantitative surveys on specific issues such as brand image in the market place. The results helped partners understand their client's needs in order to provide them with appropriate products and services. Building on the market research, ACCION helped a partner improve existing products and develop new ones. In 2002, ACCION was developing and testing a number of new products including: home improvement loans, rural lending, remittances from relatives in developed countries, and savings plans.

PortaCredit Was a microloan processing software for personal digital assistants (PDAs), developed by ACCION to reduce the time required to make a microloan and to reduce operating costs. Using hand-held computers equipped with the software, loan officers could record the necessary data and upload to the microfinance institutions' centralized database, thereby standardizing and streamlining the credit process. Initially implemented in Mexico City in 1999, PortaCredit was now being used in ACCION partner programs in Bolivia, Colombia, Ecuador and Venezuela.

Source: ACCION International

(IDB/MIF). The fund invested in equity, quasi-equity and debt of microfinance institutions in Latin America and the Caribbean. Investment objectives were to leverage private investment in microfinance institutions while generating long-term gains.

- ProFund, a $21 million equity fund for small and micro-enterprise lenders in Latin America and the Caribbean, was created in 1994. ACCION was one of four founding members. Over the next eight years, ProFund invested in, or made quasi-equity available to, 11 microfinance institutions in the region. ACCION held a board seat and was a member of its investment committee.

- The AfriCap Microfinance Fund was an investment fund created by ACCION and Calmeadow, a Canadian foundation. The fund was dedicated to financing commercial microfinance institutions in Africa, in which ACCION was a founding investor and board chair. AfriCap aimed to underwrite Africa's emerging microfinance sector by investing in selected microlending institutions and financing technical assistance to those institutions. With capital of $13.8 million, the fund made its first investments in 2003.

- ACCION created ACCION Investments in Microfinance SPC in March 2003. A worldwide investment company for microfinance capitalized at $18 million, it was initially funded by nine investors, including both multi- and bi-lateral governmental entities, private investors from the United States and Europe, and ACCION. The company was managed by ACCION's for-profit arm, GAIM, and had a board comprised of its investors. ACCION Investments would allow ACCION to take on the new responsibility of managing funds on behalf of other investors, such as the IFC (International Finance Corporation, a part of the World Bank) and the IDB (Inter-American Development Bank). Otero noted that GAIM's management of ACCION Investments would impact on ACCION's investment approach to new microfinance institutions and would have an influence on ACCION's operations. She also believed that ACCION could leverage ACCION Investments to attract new investors and commercial partners. See Exhibit 7 for the New York Times announcement.

Castello summarized ACCION's partnership role as follows:

> Today we provide our partners with three things: investment and financing; technical assistance, including training, new product development, and technology; and management advice. As the markets in Latin America evolve, ACCION will take on more of an investor (through GAIM) and governance role, with technical assistance providing our point of entry to other areas of the world. I also see ACCION adding value by connecting investors and technology providers, and by matchmaking strategic alliances. Because ACCION aims to establish long-term and intense partnerships, this precludes us from having more than one or two partners in any county, given the issues of competition. So in order to achieve our mission, we have to play a role in leading the industry, establishing and sharing best practices."

Exhibit 7   *New York Times* Announcement on ACCION Investments, March 2003.

This announcement appears as a matter of record only.

ACCION Investments in Microfinance, SPC

A company investing in microfinance institutions in Latin America, the Caribbean and Africa has been formed with a capital of

$18,023,000

was the sponsor

Investors are:
Inter-American Development Bank (IDB)
Kreditanstalt für Wiederaufbau (KfW)
International Finance Corporation (IFC)
ACCION International
Netherlands Development Finance Company (FMO)
Belgian Investment Company for Developing Countries (BIO)
The Finnish Fund for Industrial Cooperation Ltd. (FINNFUND)
Andromeda Fund
Arthur Rock 2000 Trust

Source: ACCION International

Boisson described how ACCION had helped him establish SogeSol as follows:

> Microfinance is a very specialized business and you need the right business model to succeed. When I first presented the idea of getting into microfinance to my board in 1998, the fact that ACCION would provide technical assistance was critical. In practice, ACCION helped in four key areas: client selection, speed of implementation, establishing procedures and systems, and human resource selection and training. In terms of client targeting for example, we had originally thought about going after existing bank clients who were microentrepreneurs and had savings accounts. ACCION suggested doing a market survey of potential clients branch by branch to segment the market and divide each area per credit officer. This enabled us to access a large number of clients quickly and gain the economies of scale that are so critical in this business. ACCION's experience helped us define the roles and responsibilities of the credit officers and implement time management processes that were key to productivity. The only area we are still having trouble with is the information systems which we have had to adapt, but these were not supplied by ACCION.

Organizational Structure and Funding

In December 2002, ACCION implemented a new organizational structure in which ACCION International, ACCION USA, and GAIM were managed separately. ACCION International's staff included: a team of microfinance and investment specialists in the U.S. (located in Boston and Washington); Centro ACCION, a nonprofit Colombian NGO that served as ACCION's technical assistance arm for Latin America; and 19 resident advisors working with local partners. ACCION's key competitive strength lay in the extensive microfinance experience of its staff.

- 20 technical specialists
- 19 resident advisors
- 4 technology/MIS specialists
- 4 CAMEL specialists
- 3 business-training specialists
- 4 investment experts.

The new International Operations division had two pillars: Latin America / Caribbean and Africa, with functional specialists in research and development reporting into the two regional senior vice presidents to improve ACCION's ability to respond to the field. The CAMEL team reported into the Policy and Analysis department, and the Financial Services department oversaw ACCION's direct investments and governance work. (See Exhibit 8 for ACCION's most recent organization chart).

Over 50% of ACCION International's revenues in 2001 came from private contributions including individuals, corporations and foundations. (See Exhibit 9 for ACCION International's consolidated statement of revenues and expenses over time.) Roy Jacobowitz, vice president, resource development, expected this trend to continue in the future. "ACCION's income has doubled in size in the last eight years," explained Jacobowitz, "This is largely due to an increased recognition of the power of microfinancing. Over the same period we have reduced the percent of our funding from public sources from 60% to 25%, and our funding from private sources has risen from 20% to 55%."

Otero expanded on this increasing role of private sector funding, "Accessing resources to sustain our future growth is a challenge," she said. "Although public funds come in large dollar amounts, an organization can become dependent on a public donor and beholden to it. Private funds are more labor intensive and expensive to bring in, but ultimately give an organization more freedom to act. Also, if we really want to grow, we need to tap into the private sector more efficiently." Exhibit 10 shows ACCION's communication and fundraising budgets over time. Otero believed however, that ACCION's main funding achievement was that by 2002, ACCION partners had managed to grow their combined lending portfolio to $440 million, nearly all funded from capital markets sources. "Although ACCION's operating budget is only $10 million," she explained, "ACCION's real impact comes from helping our partners access commercial sources of funding and operate independently of subsidies. This is the kind of leverage we want to continue to achieve."

Branding

Although the ACCION brand was very well known in the worlds of microfinance and international development, it lacked broader public awareness. Robin Ratcliffe, vice president of communications expanded, "To date, high recognition and awareness for our brand has been limited to players in microfinance, multi-lateral and governmental development agencies. This has been sufficient in the past, but is not so going forward." A focus group of a dozen direct mail donors who contribute to international relief organizations, conducted in the U.S. in October 1998, revealed the following: no one had heard of ACCION International and no one knew about the concept of microfinancing. However, once the group was shown a short

Exhibit 8   ACCION International Organizational Chart, December 2002

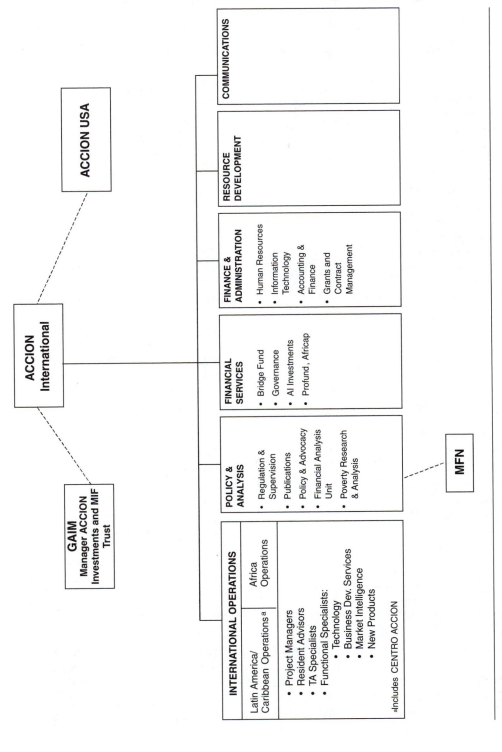

Source: ACCION International

Note: GAIM (for profit), ACCION USA, and CENTRO ACCION are separate wholly owned institutions. GAIM is the company manager of ACCION Investments, which is not a subsidiary of ACCION International. GAIM also manages the MIF Trust.

ACCION International is the host organization for MFN (MicroFinance Network), global network of microfinance institutions.

Exhibit 9   ACCION International Consolidated Statements of Activities

$000	1990	1995	2002
REVENUES			
Private contributions	1,033	2,463	6,306
United states government grants	1,866	1,828	1,908
International grants	0	1,645	808
Investment and fee income	224	914	949
Contracts and training fees	0	437	2,246
TOTAL	3,123	7,287	12,217
FUNCTIONAL EXPENSES			
Program Services			
Latin America and Caribbean microenterprise	1,936	1,448	3,619
Africa microenterprise	N/A	N/A	681
Unites States microenterprise*	61	836	2,281
Capital markets	227	741	1,062
Research, development and policy	180	266	1,020
Communications	84	134	597
TOTAL	2,488	3,426	9,260
Supporting Services			
General and administrative	302	767	1,641
Fundraising	109	443	901
TOTAL	411	1,210	2,542
Total functional expense	2,899	4,636	11,804
Net increase in assets from operations	223	2,651	413
Equity in BancoSol net income	N/A	N/A	60
Change in accounting principles	N/A	1,416	N/A
Currency translation loss	0	0	(116)
Loss on Investments in Affiliates			(33)
Total increase in net assets	223	4,067	324
Board-designated for liquidity reserve			250
Net assets, beginning of year	258	1,400	19,456
Net assets at 31 December	481	5,467	19,781

Source: ACCION International Annual Reports

* ACCION USA line item of $2.5 million includes the lending staff, not just technical assistance, as is the case in LA and Africa.

videotape, and given a number of hand-outs, response to ACCION and its mission was overwhelmingly positive. Specifically, the emotional appeal of case studies combined with ACCIONs pragmatic approach to alleviating poverty was considered very powerful. (See Exhibit 11 for an example of an ACCION print ad). Some confusion, however, was evident around whether ACCION was more a bank or a charity. Otero commented:

> We need to be known by our target market but we probably don't need to become a household name. The interesting

Exhibit 10 ACCION Communications and Fundraising Budgets

$'000	2000	2001	2002	2003 (budget)
COMMUNICATIONS				
Salaries	136	203	262	225
Professional services	44	76	104	116
Travel and conferences	15	24	90	25
Office and occupancy	100	108	126	130
Depreciation and amortization	6	7	7	4
Total Functional Expenses	301	418	592	500
FUNDRAISING				
Salaries	314	440	515	454
Professional services	49	185	65	103
Travel and conferences	46	58	23	141
Office and occupancy	176	264	233	235
Awards and grants	2	14	2	N/A
Interest and fees	3	4	3	5
Depreciation and amortization	8	14	12	5
Miscellaneous	1	9	3	0
Total Functional Expenses	599	988	856	973

Source: ACCION International

thing about ACCION is that although we work in the field, through our partners, with over 800,000 clients, all of whom have wonderful stories to tell, our partners don't carry the ACCION brand name. Consequently, when a media story is run on one of our Latin American or African partners and their clients, the ACCION name hardly ever appears. In the U.S. however, all ACCION programs are branded as ACCION and we are gaining some brand awareness for our activities in the United States. One question we ask ourselves is whether it is feasible or even desirable to attempt to ask all our partners to carry the ACCION brand name.

ACCION's tagline was "ACCION – More than hope, success" and the brand promise was "Facilitating permanent access to financial services for poor households by building locally-run, sustainable microfinance institutions together capable of reaching millions of people." Key brand attributes were derived as part of an internal strategic examination of the ACCION brand that began in 2000. They are summarized in the brand map on Exhibit 12. Ratcliffe expanded:

Members of ACCION's Communications department, along with the pro-bono counsel of a marketing executive

from American Express, created a list of key attributes we felt were essential to ACCION. This list was a compilation of thoughts from the management, fundraising, and communications teams. The list was then honed and combined to form an initial "Brand Map" which aimed to express ACCION's unique value proposition, backed up by these key attributes. In 2002, in conjunction with an analysis of ACCION's competitors in the marketing and PR areas, the Brand Map was fine-tuned to crystallize those attributes that most set ACCION apart from the competition. This resulted in a new, more comprehensive map, with more definitive language.

Chu believed that branding was particularly important as a means of differentiating ACCION from its competitors. He explained, "We need to build the ACCION brand and position it properly. In order to be true to our mission, we need donors to accept that we do things a bit ahead of when it's rational to do them. That's what makes advances in this field happen."

Otero added,

We need to communicate clearly and simply our model and achievements. In the private sector, a company's success

Exhibit 11   Example of ACCION Print Ad, 2002

The loan, she'll pay back.
Her dignity, she'll keep.

SHE MAY BE POOR, but she doesn't want
charity. She just wants to grow her tiny business and make enough
to feed her family. Thanks to ACCION, there's hope. For over
25 years we've provided business loans as small as $100 to
hardworking people like her. But we can't do it without your help.
Please call (617) 625-7080 or visit www.accion.org today.

More than hope, success.

ACCION International, 56 Roland Street, Suite 300, Boston, MA 02129 USA
617-625-7080 • www.accion.org

Source: ACCION International

is determined by its bottom line; measures for success are clear and quantifiable. In the not-for-profit world, there is often a disconnect between flow of funds and results in the field, and as long as you can present what you do in an appealing way, you can raise funds even if you are not particularly effective. That is why branding ACCION and clearly differentiating ACCION from its competitors are so important for us.

Exhibit 12   ACCION International Brand Map, 2003

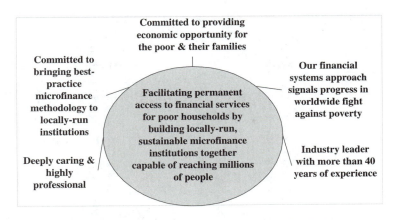

Tone: Professional, Successful, Progressive, Knowledgable, Yet Caring
and Sensitive with a Local, Community Focus

Source: ACCION International

Competition[3]

In 2002, ACCION shared the spotlight with five major competitors in the field of microfinance: Grameen Bank/Grameen Foundation, Opportunity International, FINCA, Freedom from Hunger, and IPC. (See Exhibit 13 for an overview of ACCION's major competitors).

Grameen Bank A nonprofit NGO established in 1976 by Muhammad Yunus, Grameen Bank was the best-known microfinance organization in the world. Their lending model was known as the "village banking method" or "Grameen method" and they focused on the poor women in rural Bangladesh. In 2002, Grameen bank employed 11,770 staff and worked in over 41,000 villages, providing US$292 million in loans. The average loan size was just under $110, 95% of the bank's customers were women, and loan recovery rates stood at 98%. Grameen bank claimed to outperform all other banks in Bangladesh and most banks around the world. In November 2001, a negative *Wall Street Journal* article claimed that "Grameen's performance in recent years hasn't lived up to the bank's own hype." Specifically, the article claimed that repayment rates were misrepresented by Grameen and were in fact considerably lower than the organization claimed due to the rescheduling of bad loans.

In the early 1990s, Grameen partnered with Results Educational Fund, a U.S. based lobbying organization with close to 40,000 volunteers who sought to create the political will to end hunger and used Grameen as a model, thereby putting Grameen on the map. Building on its strong brand name, in 1999 Grameen created the Grameen Foundation USA, based in Washington DC. It served as Grameen's fundraising arm in the U.S. with the objective of replicate the Grameen model in other countries.

Otero believed that Grameen's model was dated and had not evolved over time. She explained:

> Grameen demonstrated that it's possible to reach the poor with credit in massive numbers. This was very important. But Grameen did not build sustainability into its model, depending on decades for subsidies and yet it does a very good job of marketing itself. In the US, Grameen Foundation is serious competitors when it comes to fund-raising. They have offices in Washington DC, Dallas and Seattle, and whomever we call on they have already been there. They have a different business model from ours and their fund-raising strength is based in large part on the charisma of Dr. Yunus. I just met with people from the UNDP and the first organization they think of when you say microfinance is Grameen.

---

3 This section based largely on web-site information for each organization in December 2002.

Exhibit 13   Overview of ACCION and Competitors 2002

	ACCION International	Grameen Bank	Opportunity International	FINCA	Freedom from Hunger
Tagline	More than hope, success	Banking for the poor	Giving the poor a working chance	Small loans, big changes	Health, self-reliance. Dignity
Target	Microentrepreneurs /poor households	Rural poor	Family	Family (credit as a human right)	Women, building healthy lives
Number of countries	21	1	27	20	16
Geographical focus	Latin America, Caribbean and Africa	Bangladesh	Africa, Asia, Eastern Europe and Latin America	Latin America, Africa, former Soviet Union	Latin America and Africa
Number of active clients at year end 2002	798,031	2.4 million	397,489	189,587	240,000
Total number of clients served over last 10 years	2.7 million	N/A	800,000	N/A	N/A
% Women clients	60%	95%	86%	N/A	100%
Loans outstanding year end 2002	$440 million	$263 million	$64 million	$40 million	$18 million (estimated)
Total loaned in 2002	$820 million	$292 million	$127 million	$98 million	N/A
Average loan	$575	$110	$237	$518	$75
Payback rate	97.5%	98%	98%	97%	N/A

Source: ACCION International, web-sites and interviews.

Opportunity International A nonprofit humanitarian organization founded in 1971 by Al Whittaker, president of Bristol-Myers International Corporation, Opportunity International aimed to help poor families transform their lives, emotionally, spiritually and materially, with loans and basic business training. Opportunity International's commitment was religious in nature and "motivated by Jesus Christ's call to serve the poor." Forty-two autonomous but affiliated partners delivered the loan program in 27 countries in Africa, Asia, Eastern Europe and Latin America. In 2002, Opportunity International served 397,489 clients (86% of them women) and loaned $127 million, with a 98% repayment rate.

FINCA A nonprofit NGO established in 1984 by American economist John Hatch, FINCA (Foundation for International Community Assistance) saw its role as creating employment, raising family incomes and reducing poverty worldwide. The emphasis was on building hope for the future and promoting financial independence. FINCA used similar models and terminology to Grameen and also emphasized access to credit as a "human right." FINCA's vision was to tap into community spirit, enabling one family to help another family escape poverty. In 2002, FINCA served 189,587 clients and had outstanding loans of $40 million, administered through 20 partner programs in Latin America, Africa and the former Soviet Union, and arrears estimated at 3 percent.

Both FINCA and Opportunity International stated in 2002 that they were focused on commercialization, transforming NGOs (non-governmental organizations) and village banks into regulated institutions and that they were following the "financial systems" approach of ACCION. Both presented models like ACCION's but claimed to reach even poorer segments of the population. "Both organizations are following the transformation model which we started over 10 years ago," commented Otero, "they are beginning to experience the demands of converting. In a way." She added, "By following the path we have opened, they are validating what we have done at ACCION and underscoring our model. As colleagues, we interact in a variety of settings. But from a business model perspective, we have very little to learn from these competitors and this may make us seem a little arrogant."

Freedom From Hunger Was a nonprofit NGO established in 1946 as Meals for Millions, which provided Multi-Purpose Food, a high-protein powdered food supplement. The organization shifted its focus in 1970 to the implementation of applied nutrition programs, focusing almost exclusively on the health and nutrition of mothers and children. In 1988, Freedom from Hunger developed an integrated microcredit/health and nutrition education program. By 2002, Freedom From Hunger was an international development organization, focused on supporting women with innovative and self-sustaining solutions to poverty and chronic hunger. FFH stressed the importance of empowering the poor through nutrition information. In 2002, according to its web-site, the organization worked in 16 countries through 20 local partners serving 240,000 families. Average loan size was $75 and outstanding loans were estimated at over $18 million.

IPC (Internationale Projekt Consult GmbH) was a for-profit German consulting company founded in 1981 to improve the opportunities for micro and small enterprises to access formal financial services, and bank loans in particular. IPC's objective was to reduce the degree to which micro and small enterprises were dependent on informal providers of credit. IPC's services covered three areas:

1. *Consulting services:* IPC helped central banks, banking supervision bodies, private commercial banks and development banks in areas such as: organizational development; product development; the regulation of financial institutions (especially microfinance institutions); and the definition of coherent policies in the field of micro, small and medium enterprise development.

2. *Project management:* IPC had a track record of long-term collaborations with commercial banks in microlending projects included Russia, Ukraine, Kazakhstan, Armenia and Paraguay.

3. *Bank management services:* By 2002, IPC had management services agreements with 15 target microfinance oriented institutions in Eastern and Southeastern Europe, South America, Africa and Asia. Under these agreements, IPC staff occupied key positions at the financial institutions (General Manager, Credit Manager and Finance Manager). IPC often took an investment stake in those institutions with which it had management services agreements. IPC was respected for its technical excellence, and had received substantial funds from multilateral and bilateral donors. "They are our main competitor in the field," said Elisabeth Rhyne, a leading microfinance expert and Harvard PhD, "they take a similar approach to ACCION, in terms of technical assistance and governance, and in many countries our partners are in direct competition with theirs." Otero added, "IPC is more hands-on and directive; they own and manage most of their partner institutions. We do however, share a commitment to commercial

microfinance and its integration into the financial system, and we can learn from IPC's innovative and coherent strategy."

FUTURE CHALLENGES AND OPPORTUNITIES

Changing Client Base and Industry Dynamics

Several microfinance markets in Latin America were becoming increasingly competitive. In a few countries, particularly Bolivia and Nicaragua, market penetration was approaching saturation. With increased competition, attracting and retaining clients was becoming more important. However, in some countries, client over-borrowing and increased delinquency were causing concern. Growth expectations were lowered as markets reached saturation, and the prospect of mergers and consolidation in the microfinance industry was on the horizon. This resulted in pressure, particularly in Bolivia, to move up-market, providing larger loans to established or new clients, or to impose restrictions on access to the remaining poorest clients. The latter approach could risk compromising ACCION's mission. "It's difficult to measure market saturation," explained Castello, "but there are two main indicators in microfinance that saturation is starting to occur. First, you see a deterioration of portfolio quality over time and among multiple institutions. For example, in Bolivia, arrears have risen to 7% to 9%, as opposed to just 2% a few years ago. Second, as competition increases, interest rates drop. In this way, market saturation actually empowers the small entrepreneur." Recent analysis of BancoSol clients however, showed that the majority of first time loans continued to be below $500.

In Haiti, Boisson was interested in expanding SogeSol's customer base to include what he called small loans rather than microloans, the former being loans between $300 and $3,000 and the latter being loans from $500 to $5,000. He explained his rationale, "We have found that small loans perform even better than microloans and we would like to go beyond ACCION's traditional focus on microloans to include these types of clients."

Within the microfinance industry there was also a growing division between those institutions that used a commercial approach, including ACCION's partners, and those that did not, the latter characterizing themselves as more poverty-focused. The trend toward microfinance services being delivered via licensed, regulated financial institutions continued in Latin America and was beginning in Africa. Commercially oriented microfinance institutions increasingly needed equity capital to grow, consolidate, and launch new operations. In 2002, equity capital was available primarily from specialized equity funds as well as from multilateral and bilateral agencies and socially responsible financial institutions. Equity in microfinance was receiving a lot more attention and additional sources of equity could include: regional investors, foundations, universities, pension funds, individual socially-responsible investors, and potentially, international and local commercial investors. In 2003, ACCION sponsored the creation of the Council of Microfinance Equity Funds, which brought together 12 private equity funds to examine equity investment issues and provide guidance in this area.

Regulators

As the number of licensed microfinance institutions grew, government agencies such as banking superintendecies, became more involved in assessing and regulating the industry, although they lacked knowledge and experience of the sector. In 2002, regulations for microfinance were being revised and devised in countries throughout Latin America and Africa, sometimes to the industry's benefit, sometimes not. Otero expanded, "ACCION can help by educating regulators on the differences between traditional banking and microfinance lending. The interest and knowledge level of central bankers varies widely from country to country."

Otero noted that regulatory bodies for financial institutions protected the public and kept the financial systems of their countries solvent. She continued, "The existing global banking standards are not applicable to microfinance, and regulators must develop norms and regulations that ensure proper supervision of microfinance institutions. This is difficult to achieve because in many countries, microfinance is not a priority since it represents such as small proportion of the financial system. However, if the necessary frameworks are not in place, it will hinder the development of the microfinance industry." ACCION had established an internal policy department to work with regulatory bodies. Otero wondered whether ACCION should be devoting more resources to this area.

Drake believed that the ACCION CAMEL tool could be adapted to help regulators. "We can either impact regulatory bodies at the legislative level, but that's really more a role for the World Bank," she explained, "or we can work with central banks and train key individuals using an instrument that has been tried and tested for over 10 years."

Geographic or Product Expansion?

Otero had championed the recent expansion into Africa. She viewed the move as essential for ACCION to maintain its leadership. "Microfinance is an industry," she asserted, "whose leaders must be global in their perspective. If you are not global, you cannot be a leader and we want ACCION to continue to be a leader."

Africa During the 1990s, microfinance was growing not only in Latin America but in Africa, Eastern Europe and Southern Asia. Funding was increasingly available for microfinance in these regions, and ACCION's main competitors, with the exception of Grameen, were international in scope. "Our mission is to reach as many people as possible," explained Otero, "and we felt that, at ACCION, we had learned a lot that we could contribute to other areas of the world. In addition, it could be a competitive weakness to focus on just one geographical area."

In May 2000, Otero drafted a proposal to the board for initiating work outside the Americas and suggesting an initiative in Africa. She believed that ACCION should focus on a single region beyond Latin America and that a focus on Africa might be preferable to Asia or Eastern Europe: First, ACCION's learning curve would be faster in Africa because sub-regions would vary less in context and culture; second, ACCION's technical assistance capabilities would add greater value to institutions addressing issues of institution building; and third, donor funding, especially from international aid organizations, was readily available for initiatives in Africa and would not take away from ACCION's donor support for Latin America. "Africa was the natural next step," explained Otero. "In Asia there were already several well established microfinance organizations. In Africa there was great need, the opportunity for high potential impact, and a funding base different from that for our work in Latin America."

Otero proposed building on the work of a Canadian foundation called Calmeadow (whose founder had been on ACCION's board), that had initiated microfinancing in several African countries in 1996. Working with a South African for-profit consulting firm called Vulindlela, in a joint-venture agreement, Calmeadow had secured four projects to provide technical assistance to microfinance institutions in Benin, Zimbabwe and South Africa. In 2000, the majority of Calmeadow funding came the Canadian International Development Agency (CIDA) and the organization had been looking to spin off its Africa program in order to concentrate its efforts on developing a an equity fund for microfinance for Africa.

Otero proposed a phased approach to ACCION assuming responsibility for Calmeadow's Africa program, and recruited Elisabeth Rhyne, a leading microfinance expert and Harvard PhD, to both head up the Africa initiative and direct ACCION's Research and Development department. Although the Calmeadow strategy enabled ACCION to expand its geographical reach quickly and with relatively low risk and cost, Otero recognized the challenges and suggested a two-year learning period for ACCION. Some of the challenges when comparing Latin America and Africa included: much lower per capita incomes; higher proportion of rural populations; less developed financial sectors; high HIV infection rates; and political instability. In addition to these market differences, many of ACCION's microfinance experts spoke only Spanish and ACCION's manuals and documentation were mainly in Spanish as well.

ACCION found that Africa differed from Latin America in a number of ways. For example, microentrepreneurs in Africa had lower incomes than their counterparts in Latin America, resulting in the need for smaller loans. In addition, since the financial systems in many African countries were less developed, ACCION believed that it had a key role to play in influencing government policies and regulations. (See Exhibit 14 for targets for ACCION partners in Africa).

A key challenge for ACCION moving forward was the choice of partners in Africa. "ACCION does not yet have the history or depth of knowledge in Africa that it does in Latin America," explained Rhyne. "We have a choice between partnering with existing organizations or starting new organizations. Most competitors in Africa have used the village-banking model so ACCION's greater focus on individual loans can be a competitive advantage, especially in urban areas."

The Uganda Experience Victoria White, senior director, international operations, had been living and working in Uganda since early 2002. In December 2002, she was deeply involved in providing technical assistance to an ACCION partner, Uganda Microfinance Union (UMU), an NGO, which was transforming into a regulated financial institution and hoped to become licensed under the new legislation covering microfinance institutions in May 2003. She expanded on the environment in Uganda and the challenges facing UMU:

> *Uganda, with a population of 25 million, is still largely rural. The lengthy civil war destroyed many aspects of civil society, including the financial sector, which has a history of bank failures. Currently, about 15 major banks, including a number of international banks such as Citibank and*

Barclays, are present in Uganda, but they target the upper income segments of the population and corporate clients. Microfinance has been very vibrant in Uganda, appearing in the early 1990s and currently reaching 500,000 borrowers. The most popular model has been a modified village-banking model, based on lending groups providing guarantees for individual loans. In December 2002, legislation was passed establishing a legal structure for microfinance institutions. Currently, there are a dozen strong players providing financial services (including both UMU and FINCA), but, under the new legislation only 3 to 5 organizations will become licensed, regulated microfinance institutions.

In December 2002, UMU served over 32,000 clients, of which 16,000 were borrowers, and was in the process of becoming a for-profit financial institution with an initial capital base of between $3 million and $4 million. "We are looking for five or six initial investors," explained White, "and enough capital to support our aggressive growth plans. For this we will be relying on help from ACCION's financial services group." Much of the transformation work involved the implementation of MIS and management systems, as well as training of staff in financial and treasury management skills. "To date," explained White, "we have fully automated two branches. It has gone very smoothly and productivity levels have increased significantly."

"Now that there is legislation," explained White, "ACCION can play a key role in training bank supervisors, using a modified CAMEL tool. In Africa we are still working with NGOs who need more basic financial management skills. In addition, most of the organizations we are dealing with in Africa have been up and running for a while and our approach needs to be more collaborative."

New Products In several countries—Bolivia, Chile, Paraguay, Ecuador, El Salvador, Nicaragua, and Guatemala—urban microfinance markets were becoming increasingly competitive. To stimulate growth, ACCION was considering helping partners expand their range of products to include: home improvement finance, rural lending, savings and remittances.

However, ACCION's area of competence was on business credit. ACCION had little expertise in areas such as remittances. In addition, some ACCION executives wondered if this shift to other products would compromise ACCION's mission of providing access to credit for the poor. Several of ACCION's partners were moving toward becoming full-service banks, developing additional products and services without ACCION assistance or approval. Chu expanded on the dilemma:

> *It's good business to hold onto one's existing customers and provide them with products and services they want. We cannot forget that new credit customers represent a feeder into the system, and that our mission is to reach the greatest number of poor people and provide them with access to whatever financial tools help them out of poverty. I believe that we need to constantly redefine the best way to serve the poor, and extend our notion beyond microloans to other services that can be profitable, for example by providing health insurance. But not all ACCION professionals necessarily agree.*

Boisson expanded on ACCION's future role, "ACCION can continue to help SogeSol and other partners by providing: new products and access to new clients, helping us grow and improve our technical management, and improving management information systems dedicated to microfinance. ACCION has tremendous strength in its network," he continued, "and can leverage this to help partners."

ACCION's three-year strategic plan addressed some of the challenges and opportunities outlined above, and reiterated the organizations' commitment to achieving its social mission through the commercialization of microfinance via the three current models and the strengthening of its investment activities. (See Exhibit 15 for a summary of the main points of the strategic plan and Exhibit 16 for the associated financial forecast.) As part of this strategic plan, ACCION

(Exhibit 14)   Targets for ACCION Partners in Africa 2002 to 2005

	2001	2002 projection	2003 projection	2004 projection	2005 projection
Active Clients	35,000	57,000	85,000	112,000	137,000
Active portfolio	$11 million	$19 million	$29 million	$40 million	$52 million

Source: ACCION Strategic Plan

defined four new products in which it would concentrate its efforts: rural lending; home improvement financing; remittances; and savings products.

Barriers to Growth

Chu believed that the main barrier to ACCION's growth and expansion involved the ability of its affiliates to demonstrate sustained, reliable profitability over the long term. He explained further:

> *BancoSol's profitability, for example, has been erratic. Its success spawned an industry, drawing in competitors, and resulting in client over-indebtedness and lower repayment rates. In addition, the economic turmoil in Latin America requires nimble management that can navigate the ups and downs to achieve consistent returns. I believe that ACCION's strengths today lie in technical assistance but we need to ensure that the knowledge we transfer is up-to-date as the reality we operate in changes. We need to become better at helping our partners develop business strategies and we also need staff members who can manage the capital markets side of our business. In addition, we need to leverage our minority positions in the governance of our partner institutions.*

CONCLUSION

Keeping in mind ACCION's overall objective to dramatically increase the number of borrowers and impact world poverty, Otero prepared for a strategic retreat with her key managers and identified three issues that she especially wanted her team to address:

1. Was ACCION poised for a shift in both its activities and priorities? If so, what were the key changes Otero and her staff would have implement to take the organization into the next phase of its development?
2. Should ACCION remain focused on business credit and continue to expand geographically or should it broaden its technical assistance to cover a wider variety of banking services, responding to the needs of its existing partners in Latin America? Could the organization do both and were these parallel ways of evolving compatible?
3. How should ACCION promote its brand, particularly in the light of the growing proportion of funds coming from private donors? In the current challenging fundraising environment, which strategy would maximize private donations?

Exhibit 15 Summary of ACCION Strategic Plan 2002–2005

ACCION's medium-term strategic plan stated that the organization would continue to serve as clients, the poor, and people previously excluded from the financial system, with a focus on the microentrepreneur and his or her family, and with an emphasis on extending the boundaries of the financial system to include those excluded from it.

Although ACCION has established the goal of reaching 1 million borrowers by 2005, it would in fact, exceed this goal by the end of 2003. ACCION was dedicated to the integration of microfinance into the mainstream financial system and the commercialization of microfinance services. Support for microfinance institutions would continue via long-term partnerships and would include technical assistance, investment, and governance.

With the exception of CAMEL, products would not be made available on a one-off basis. ACCION would remain a mission-driven NGO, operating in a business-like manner on commercial principles and the organization would continue to grow in a way that combined the agility of a small organization with the productivity and resources of a larger one.

Channels ACCION would continue for the period of the strategic plan to balance its efforts across the three main approaches to microfinance commercialization: transformation of NGOs into financial institutions; establishment of specialized financial institutions; and launching of microfinancial services by existing commercial banks.

Products The plan called for ACCION to continue providing microfinance institutions with both technical assistance, on the one hand, and debt and equity instruments on the other. In line with this, was the additional goal of contributing to the development of the microfinance industry through policy advocacy and research and the use of the CAMEL assessment tool.

Source: ACCION Strategic Plan

Exhibit 16   ACCION International Financial Plan Summary 2002 – 2005

$'000	2003 projected	2004 projected	2005 projected
REVENUE			
Private grants and Donations	6,294	9,122	9,902
Public grants	3,087	3,050	2,600
Interest and fees	1,038	1,047	1,107
Contracts, fees, public and Other	2,721	3,228	3,993
Total	13,140	16,447	17,602
EXPENSES			
Program services			
USA (includes network support)	3,325	4,156	4,511
Latin America operations	2,225	2,493	2,771
Africa operations	1,230	1,591	1,822
Technical teams	1,205	1,419	1,490
Financial services	823	1,671	1,813
Policy and financial Assessment	747	618	648
GAIM	501	N/A	N/A
Communications	500	514	566
TOTAL	10,555	12,462	13,621
Supporting Services			
USA supporting services		622	639
Resource development	972	1,026	1,077
General and administrative	1,150	1,425	1,496
TOTAL	2,122	3,073	3,212
Total	12,880	15,535	16,833
Revenue less operating expenses	463	912	769
Additions to liquidity reserve	250	336	365
Investments	154	550	400
NET REVENUE	10	26	4

Source: ACCION Strategic Plan
Note: Does not include ACCION USA

Amnesty International

In January 2003, Irene Khan, secretary general of Amnesty International, reflected on the organization's expanding mission, recent organizational changes, and increased competition. "We are starting to take a serious look at brand management," she said. "We need to clearly define who we are and then communicate this through the Amnesty brand."

Amnesty International (AI) was a worldwide campaigning movement that worked to promote internationally recognized human rights. It was impartial and independent of any government, political persuasion, or religious creed and, in 2002, had close to 1.5 million members and supporters in over 140 countries and total gross income of over £90 million.[1] Activities were largely funded through public subscriptions and donations. An International Secretariat was based in London and employed over 350 staff members and 100 volunteers from over 50 countries around the world.

History

AI was founded in 1961 by British lawyer Peter Benenson. Upon learning about a group of students in Portugal who were arrested for raising a toast to "freedom" in a public restaurant, Benenson launched a one-year campaign called Appeal for Amnesty in the *London Observer*. The Appeal for Amnesty called for the release of all people imprisoned because of the peaceful expression of their beliefs, politics, race, religion, color, or national origin. Benenson's plan was to encourage people to write letters to government officials in countries that held prisoners of conscience[2], calling for their release. The campaign grew and spread to other countries, and within a year AI was formed.

AI's mandate was based on the United Nations Universal Declaration of Human Rights (UDHR) established in 1948, which underscored the principle that people have fundamental rights that transcend national, cultural, religious, or ideological boundaries. Early activities by members organized into prisoner-adoption groups focused on letter writing on behalf of specific prisoners of conscience. Members often developed a bond with individual prisoners, whose names, cases, and families they grew to know. In this way, AI focused on individuals, not countries or political systems.

During the 1960s, AI members became more active at the local level in publicity, fund-raising, and educational activities. In the late 1960s, in order to maintain impartiality and protect human rights activists themselves, AI adopted the rule that people in the organization were to work only on cases outside their own countries. In the mid-1980s, a number of musicians and artists adopted AI as a special cause, giving concerts and tours, the profits from which they donated back to the organization. This brought tremendous growth and visibility to AI, whose budget increased dramatically. In 1997, AI was awarded the Nobel Peace Prize.

Throughout the 1970s and 1980s, AI developed its research capability at the International Secretariat and devoted resources to obtaining accurate information about prisoners of conscience. Khan expanded on AI's evolution:

> In the 1960s, AI was just a social movement, but in the 1970s and 1980s, a bureaucracy started to evolve with the International Secretariat at its center, and the organization expanded its capabilities and resources. As it grew, institutions and rules were developed concerning policy, activities, decision making, and funding, with great emphasis being placed on internal democracy. By the early 1990s, AI's internal structure was marked by several large country sections, a centralized International Secretariat, and a large number of

1 $1US = £0.65 on average in 2002.

2 Prisoners of conscience are defined by AI as people imprisoned solely because of their political or religious beliefs, gender, or racial or ethnic origin who have neither used nor advocated violence.

smaller sections and structures, primarily in the global South, creating different power dynamics within AI. Several of the larger sections had significant capacity and resources and were eager for greater freedom to carry out their activities. They were getting frustrated with the inability of the International Secretariat to meet their demands as speedily and effectively as they wished. Demands for internal change were matched by enormous changes in the human rights world around AI. Prior to 1990, AI focused on governments and prisoners of conscience, but as the political world changed, AI started to expand its activities both in terms of the kinds of people suffering from human rights abuses and the entities responsible for these human rights transgressions.

Turning 40—AI's Mid-Life Crisis[3]

In August 2001, AI drafted an internal document called the State of the Movement 2001 Report that concluded:

> *On its 40th anniversary, AI finds itself at a critical juncture. The international political, economic, and social landscape has significantly changed. The focus of the global human rights movement has expanded from civil and political rights (CPR) to also encompass violations of economic, social, and cultural rights (ESCR), and whereas AI was among the first human rights organizations in 1961, there has been an explosion in the number, strength, and diversity of NGOs (nongovernmental organizations) addressing human rights issues. While AI's reputation as a leading international human rights organization remains intact, the overall relevance and effectiveness of the organization have become increasingly questioned. AI is going through a critical transition period.*

Pierre Sané, AI's then-secretary general, believed that AI's vision and mandate had to be clarified and that the "mid-life crisis" that the organization was experiencing would enable AI to reassess priorities and develop a more relevant purpose and vision.

A changing global environment The end of the Cold War, the declining role of the nation state, the increase in conflicts, and the multiple effects of globalization had created a new context for AI. There had been, during the 1990s, an increase in the influence of violent nonstate actors perpetrating human rights violations, and the focus of the human rights community had expanded from political and civil rights to economic, social, and cultural rights.

The number of NGOs focusing on human rights had proliferated yet, in many countries, the relationships between NGOs and states had evolved from being confrontational to cooperative. Collaboration among NGOs was also on the rise. Competition for resources, members, and public support had also escalated. The communications revolution and the growth of the Internet had dramatically changed the way human rights activists mobilized support, collected and disseminated information, and launched protests.

AI's key challenges in 2001 A key question was whether AI was still a leading agent of change in the human rights movement. Many people within the organization and outside it felt that, since the 1990s, AI had lost its edge and failed to respond quickly enough.

1. *Shift in mandate* In the early 1990s, the international human rights movement began to embrace economic, social, and cultural rights (ESCR) in addition to the traditional civil and political rights (CPR). AI, however, continued to focus primarily on CPR. While some members criticized the organization for responding only to one group of rights, arguing that this restricted AI's collaboration with local NGOs and made the organization appear less relevant, other members believed that AI's strength lay in the organization's focus on a core area of rights and that such focus resulted in greater coherence and effectiveness.

2. *Work on own country* By 2001, the restriction on members against working on cases within their own country had become a point of great contention. Some members argued that the restriction was no longer relevant and prevented the organization from being perceived as relevant locally; others believed that it maintained AI's impartiality and international solidarity.

One of AI's most criticized actions had been to campaign for better conditions for imprisoned members of the Baader-Meinhoff Gang, a left-wing political terrorist group active in Germany in the 1970s. German AI members became deeply involved and pressed the International Secretariat to investigate charges of torture and human rights abuses against members of the Baader-Meinhoff Gang. Jonathan Power, author and journalist, concluded:

> *Amnesty came dangerously near to being used by a group that had no sympathy for the values Amnesty stood*

---

[3] Much of this section is based on the 25th International Council Meeting Circular 36, July 2001.

for and which sought to overthrow the kind of Western European democracy that allowed Amnesty to flourish. Looking back, the Baader-Meinhoff effort was not the organization's finest hour. Against the better judgment of some of its members, Amnesty allowed the German national group to involve it more deeply than the case deserved.[4]

3. ***Adapting research and campaigning*** During the 1990s, AI had increased its participation in local and regional human rights networking and collective campaigning. Meanwhile, changes in communication had made it easier to launch global campaigns and promote electronic debate. Some members, however, were concerned that, although AI was known for the quality of its information, it did not always disseminate it quickly enough. In addition, AI's centralized campaigning approach was believed by some to limit the flexibility of individual national sections, and the campaigns themselves, always developed through consensus, were thought to be sometimes vague and lacking in impact.

4. ***Streamlining decision making*** Given the democratic nature of AI (described in detail below), the organization recognized that its slow decision-making processes, involving broad participation and consensus building, were costly in terms of organizational effectiveness.

5. ***Membership development*** In 2001, AI's membership was heavily skewed, with almost a million members in Western Europe, a little under 400,000 in North America, and only a small proportion in the global South and East. Many of the smaller national sections felt that they needed additional support, training, and capacity building. Others pointed out that many of the smaller national sections, which were dependent on international funding, were required to submit regular reports, but the larger self-sufficient sections were not. As a result, no standardized information was available on the entire organization. Yet others worried that the number of national sections depending on funding from the International Secretariat was increasing and that AI had not managed to raise many funds in countries where other NGOs had apparently succeeded. Finally, there was a general concern that AI should strive to promote a more consistent and universal brand, although there was, as yet, no clear definition of what the AI brand represented.

Mission and Objectives

In August 2001, AI's International Council amended its statute to include a new vision statement, mission statement, and set of core values.

- *AI's vision* was of a world in which "every person enjoys all of the human rights enshrined in the Universal Declaration of Human Rights and other international human rights standards."
- *AI's mission* was to "undertake research and action focused on preventing and ending grave abuses of the rights to physical and mental integrity, promote freedom of conscience and expression, and uphold freedom from discrimination."
- *AI's core values* included the principles of international solidarity, effective action for the individual victim, universality and indivisibility of human rights, impartiality and independence, and democracy and mutual respect.

Khan explained:

> *The essence of the Amnesty brand lies in its core values. The notion of international solidarity stems from the fact that AI is all about people in one part of the world working on behalf of other people in the world. Shining the light on individual cases has been our trademark, and we want to keep it that way. We work hard to maintain impartiality—for example, in the Middle East conflict we report on human rights abuses on both sides—and our organizational structure is highly democratic.*

AI's stated objectives were to address governments, intergovernmental organizations, armed political groups, companies, and other nonstate players. It sought to disclose human rights abuses accurately and quickly, and it systematically and impartially researched the facts of individual cases and patterns of human rights abuses. The findings were publicized, and members, supporters, and staff mobilized public pressure to stop the abuses. AI urged all governments to observe the rule of law and ratify and implement human rights standards and carried out a wide range of educational activities.

Activities

AI cooperated with other NGOs, the United Nations, and regional intergovernmental organizations to address human rights abuses. AI had developed a core strength in researching abuses, and in 2002, AI delegates visited dozen

---

4 This section based on the book by Jonathan Power, *Like Water on Stone* (New York: Penguin Press, 2001).

of countries to meet victims of human rights violations, observe trials, and interview local human rights activists and officials. The organization then communicated the results of its research, organized human rights education and awareness-raising programs, and sought to mobilize public opinion through specific campaigns.

AI was often cited, by journalists and third parties, as a credible source of information on issues of human rights abuses. In most cases this publicity was beneficial to AI's goal of raising awareness, but in specific situations, AI had had to request that a third party not reference the organization's work. In 1990, for example, during his efforts to build a coalition against Saddam Hussein prior to the Gulf War, President George Bush quoted AI reports on Iraq. At the same time, U.S. authorities ignored AI's critique of the role of the CIA in torture in Guatemala or the use of capital punishment in the United States. AI felt that its brand name was being used in a one-sided, high-profile diplomatic war that threatened international human rights efforts and requested that U.S. officials stop quoting from the organization's reports.[5]

AI members, supporters, and staff around the world mobilized public opinion to pressure governments and other players with influence to stop human rights abuses. Activities ranged from public demonstrations to letter writing, from human education programs to fund-raising concerts, from approaches to local authorities to lobbying intergovernmental organizations, and from targeted appeals on behalf of a single individual to global campaigns on a specific country or issue. "Letter writing has been our core strength in the past," explained Khan, "and our commonest form of action. Over the years, AI members have written millions of letters on behalf of more than 44,000 prisoners of conscience; about 50% of the cases were eventually resolved. This is changing now," she added, "and we are shifting to e-campaigning, where text messages are easy to access on our Web site and can be sent on via e-mail." In addition, Khan believed that members were increasingly looking for more visible ways to campaign. "Younger members want to express their views more forcefully," explained Khan. "In Poland for example, Amnesty organized a human chain going from the Israeli Embassy to the Palestine Mission."

Each year, AI members around the world joined forces on one global campaign to achieve change. In 2002, this was the Campaign Against Torture, which fought against torture and ill-treatment of women, children, ethnic minorities, and lesbians, gays, bisexual, and transgender (LGBT) people. During 2002, four countries ratified the U.N. Convention against Torture, and a number of government leaders and officials made commitments to adopt legislation to prevent torture in their countries. (See Exhibit 1 for an excerpt from AI's "Justice for Torture Victims" briefing, a publication that appeared in April 2002.)

In 2002, AI worked on behalf of 2,813 named victims of human rights violations. AI's Urgent Action Network, made up of 80,000 volunteers in 85 countries, initiated 408 actions on behalf of people in 81 countries who were either at risk or had suffered human rights violations including torture, disappearance, the death penalty, death in custody, or forcible return to countries where they would be in danger of human rights abuses. Of these urgent actions, 117 resulted in good news about the case. (See Exhibit 2 for a direct-mail piece from Amnesty International USA describing the Urgent Action Network.)

AI's Web site contained over 20,000 files and was visited by 10,000 people a day from all over the world. It featured a library of reports, press releases, and information on the latest campaigns, appeals for action, and online petitions. In 2002, more than 120,000 e-mails were sent to various governments as part of AI's Campaign Against Torture. AI also worked through a number of specialist networks to further its objectives. (See Exhibit 3 for a description of AI's specialist networks.)

Expanding the scope of activities Throughout the 1990s, AI had slowly expanded the scope of its activities from prisoners of conscience to include human rights abuses against refugees, women, children, ethnic minorities, and LGBT people. In addition, the organization broadened its target audience from governments to include intergovernmental organizations, armed political groups, companies, and other nonstate players. In 2001, AI also voted to expand its focus from human rights, narrowly defined, to include a whole spectrum of economic, social, cultural, and educational rights.

Organizational Structure

In addition to the International Secretariat, the AI movement consisted of 56 national sections, pre-section coordination units in an additional 24 countries, and 7,800 local, youth, specialist, and professional groups in over 100 countries.

AI was a democratic movement, self-governed by a nine-member Internal Executive Committee (IEC), whose

---

5 Anecdote based on the book by Power, *Like Water on Stone* (New York: Penguin Press, 2001).

Justice for torture victims

What you can do

● **You can help the people featured in this briefing:**
Please write appealing for:
- their cases to be impartially investigated;
- for them to be given prompt reparations from the state including financial compensation, medical care and rehabilitation; and
- for those responsible to be prosecuted and given a fair trial in proceedings which exclude the death penalty.

● **You can challenge your government to ensure that torture is not committed with impunity in your country:**
- torture should be expressly defined as a crime in national criminal law;
- all reports of torture should be promptly, independently, impartially and thoroughly investigated;
- decisions on whether to prosecute should be made by an independent prosecutor or investigating judge, not a political official;

- people suspected of torture should be brought to justice in fair trials;
- the rights of victims to an effective remedy against torture should be recognized in national law;
- victims of torture, witnesses and relatives should be protected before, during and after trials;
- victims of torture and their dependants should be entitled to reparation from the state including compensation and medical care.

● **You can challenge your government to ensure that your country is not a safe haven for torturers from other countries:**
- your country should ratify and implement the 1984 UN Convention against Torture, if it has not done so;
- your country should ratify and implement the 1998 Rome Statute of the International Criminal Court, if it has not done so;
- your country's legal system should allow the courts in your country to exercise universal jurisdiction over

alleged torturers (they should have the right to try cases no matter where the torture took place, and the nationality of the people involved);
- your country's legal system should allow people suspected of torture to be brought to justice in fair trials, or extradited to another country able and willing to prosecute them.

● **You can take a step to stamp out torture:**
- join Amnesty International's campaign against torture and impunity;
- join Amnesty International and other local and international human rights organizations which fight torture and impunity;
- make a donation to support Amnesty International's work;
- tell friends and family about the campaign and ask them to join too;
- register to take action against torture at *www.stoptorture.org* and campaign online. Visitors to the website will be able to appeal on behalf of individuals at risk of torture.

Around the world, AI members and other human rights activists campaign against torture and impunity. Among their activities, they press the authorities in their countries to declare Torture Free Zones. One of the many ways of attracting attention is to wrap public buildings, former detention centres and other places of symbolic significance with Torture Free Zone tape
Photos: © AI

© Amnesty International Publications 2001
Original language: English.
All rights reserved.
Printed by Lynx Offset Ltd.

Amnesty International,
International Secretariat,
Peter Benenson House,
1 Easton Street,
London WC1X 0DW,
United Kingdom

www.amnesty.org

AI Index: ACT 40/022/2001

ISBN: 0-86210-309-6

ISBN 0-86210-309-6

9 780862 103095

Source: Amnesty International.

Dear Friend,

I regret to inform you that we are faced with a severe crisis here at Amnesty International.

In plain English:

Our lifesaving Urgent Action Network to help prisoners of conscience and others threatened with torture or death is literally staggering under the weight of new emergencies.

However, you are not being asked to picket a prison in a foreign country, or attend a freedom demonstration, or in any way put yourself in jeopardy. Instead ...

... you can help us, quietly but effectively, right there in your own home.

And you can begin with the simple act of signing your name to the "Message of Hope" card that I'm enclosing with this letter.

Then mail it back to me, and I'll see that it is forwarded to a prisoner who is facing torture, or is being held in isolation for a political reason, or perhaps even faces the very real possibility of being executed.

For example, please listen to just one voice of the more than 45,000 individual prisoners whose cases were resolved with Amnesty International's help.

His name is Constantino, and for years he was held in a tiny cell; his only human contact was with his torturers. He said:

> "I did not experience a human face or see a green leaf, and my only company was cockroaches and mice.

> "The only daylight that entered my cell was through a small opening at the top of one wall. For eight months I had my hands and feet tied.

> "On Christmas Eve the door to my cell opened and the guard tossed in a crumpled piece of paper. I moved as best I could to pick it up.

> "It said simply, 'Constantino, do not be discouraged; we know you are alive.' It was signed 'Monica' and had the Amnesty International candle on it.

> "These words saved my life and my sanity. Eight months later, I was set free."

What happened here was the result of Amnesty's extraordinary programs, such as the Urgent Action Network.

AMNESTY INTERNATIONAL USA • 322 EIGHTH AVENUE • NEW YORK, NY 10001
(212) 807-8400 • www.amnestyusa.org

- 2 -

In the case of Constantino, we received reliable information, verified by our skilled researchers. The facts were fed into our massive worldwide network. And then, volunteers responded by sending urgent appeals, telegrams and telex letters to those responsible for detaining Constantino.

You see, our Urgent Action Network strips away the mask of secrecy that many governments hide behind.

We force them to ask the burning question: "Is this particular prisoner worth all of this negative publicity?"

Or: "Can we afford to further damage our domestic and international image?"

Sometimes prisoners do not know we are working on their behalf. Yet it can make a difference. Christine Anyanwu, a journalist long-imprisoned in Nigeria for reporting views in opposition to the ruling party, wrote to us upon her release:

> **"It has indeed been most reassuring to know that someone cares enough to hold one in his thoughts even for a second. I thank those friends who, undeterred by my silence, have continued to send messages of encouragement: 'We know you are there,' 'Hold on!' 'Stay strong.' Kindly convey my profound appreciation to the Amnesty International U.S. branch for its hard work and great effectiveness."**

A short message can give prisoners the needed courage to survive during the remaining days of their torture, because they know that they are not alone and that their captors are under pressure to release them.

Regrettably, other prisoners are not as fortunate.

Some die from torture, mistreatment or execution. But when that happens, we do everything possible to get the facts of that story told to the world.

The guilty must not have anywhere to hide!

We've exposed the shocking truth about the gouging out of a child's eyes in front of his or her parents, or mock execution by firing squad, or being buried alive, or spending weeks blindfolded and isolated and then the blindfold being removed and the prisoner forced to watch a family member being raped.

And we expose acts of torture, such as the case of one woman prisoner, who was taunted by the guards, saying, "We are God in here," ... while they applied electrical shocks to her body as she lay handcuffed to the springs of a metal bed.

Thank goodness many of us do not have to fear the kinds of atrocities described above, although serious violations do happen right here in the U.S.

But if you lived in certain other parts of the world ... your life might be far different, especially if you were a person who exercised the voice of your conscience and opposed an immoral and repressive government.

- 3 -

Frankly, I'm sure that you yourself have a strong sense of right and wrong. And even though an injustice thousands of miles away from your home does not affect you physically – it does make you feel angry and frustrated. <u>And this is where Amnesty International comes in.</u> <u>We can help you express your moral indignation – and do something about it.</u>

But please understand. We seek the release of activists, civilians and others held because of their beliefs or identity. We do not take a stand on issues of political ideology. And frankly, that's what makes us so unique and effective ...

... <u>We demand that all prisoners of conscience be set free immediately and unconditionally</u> ...

... <u>We demand that political prisoners receive a fair trial within a reasonable time</u> ...

... <u>We demand that all forms of torture and ill-treatment stop at once and that the death penalty be abolished in all cases</u> ...

... <u>We demand that death squads which carry out extrajudicial executions be disbanded</u> ...

... <u>We demand that "disappearances," a form of state kidnapping, cease</u>

Naturally, we have our critics. <u>Some say we are too stern and unbending in our demands.</u>

But we look back to the year 1961 when Amnesty International was launched by a British lawyer named Peter Benenson, who published a newspaper appeal entitled: "The Forgotten Prisoners."

His appeal resulted in individuals in many countries offering to support the idea for an international campaign to protect human rights.

<u>And today?</u> <u>We are spreading the word faster and farther than ever.</u> <u>We have fax machines.</u> <u>We have satellite communications.</u> <u>We have e-mail and the World Wide Web.</u>

We have 1.1 million members in 162 countries and territories, including more than 80,000 Urgent Action Network volunteers in over 80 countries who are ready to go into action hundreds of times a year with letters, faxes, telegrams and phone calls appealing for justice and mercy.

And as a result, thousands of prisoners have been freed. Torture chambers have been closed, and executions have been stopped.

We deeply believe that: "The free must remember the forgotten."

<u>However</u>, in spite of our growth and our effectiveness, torture and political imprisonment and "disappearances" go on – seemingly at an accelerated rate.

<u>And our Urgent Action Network and other programs cannot keep up with demands.</u> <u>This is our dilemma.</u>

This is why I am writing you today, in the hope that you will sign your name to the enclosed card so it can be forwarded to a prisoner of conscience who needs your help. If you prefer not to sign the card, I will understand.

- 4 -

But I trust you will still support our lifesaving mission ...

... and send a gift of $10, $15, $25 or even $50 so that Amnesty can respond to the growing number of urgent requests. Of course, if you wish to join with those who send $100, please do so. Any amount you are able to contribute will be deeply appreciated.

And, as a member of Amnesty, you will receive our informative quarterly newsmagazine, *Amnesty Now*.

Some of the stories you will read in this publication may shock you. Some stories will make you feel outrage. Some will break your heart. And some will give you a feeling of intense satisfaction.

You will realize that you are doing your share to help us stand up and fight back against those ruthless powers that throw people in jail, torture them and execute them for "crimes" such as simply criticizing the government.

Basic human rights are being violated right now – this very day. It is up to you to remember that important changes in the world often hinge on the actions of ordinary people. And Amnesty International is made up of ordinary people from across the political spectrum working with extraordinary levels of courage and commitment. Many display the decal I've enclosed for you.

You can share in this movement. I hope that you will.

Sincerely,

William F. Schulz
Executive Director

P.S.   Please let me repeat just two things.

First, if you'll sign your name to the enclosed "Message of Hope" card, I'll do my best to see that it gets to a prisoner of conscience who is being tortured, or detained or possibly facing death.

(And even if the card never actually reaches the prisoner, when the jailers or those responsible are deluged with a flood of these cards, they are going to realize that they are no longer operating in secrecy. The word is out. Their prisoner is in the public eye. This could result in freedom or better conditions for the prisoner.)

And second, if you can send a gift of $10, $15, $25 or perhaps even $50, please do so right now.

As I said, our Urgent Action Network is sagging under the pressure of an extraordinary volume of requests. Never before in our history have we even considered the possibility that we could not honor these requests and could not go to the aid of a prisoner.

Help us keep this much-needed tradition alive.

Source: Amnesty International USA.

Exhibit 3	AI Specialist Networks in 2003

- The Lawyers Network worked as a member of the Coalition for an International Criminal Court, campaigning for states to sign and ratify the Rome Statute of the International Criminal Court (ICC). By 2002, more than 60 countries had ratified the Rome Statute, triggering the establishment of the International Criminal Court on February 5, 2002.
- The Military Security and Police (MSP) Network campaigned for effective controls on the transfer of arms and security assistance in order to prevent these being used for human rights abuses. In 2001, for example, the network campaigned for the suspension of electro-shock weapons.
- The Company Approaches Network worked with other NGOs to campaign for controls on the international diamond trade. Profits from the diamond trade were used to purchase weapons, which contributed to human rights abuses in Angola, the Democratic Republic of Congo, and Sierra Leone. In 2002, governments had made progress towards an international diamond certification system. In addition, the network worked with companies to help them develop policies which incorporated human rights standards.
- The Children's Network lobbied states to ratify the Optional Protocol to the UN Children's Convention on the involvement of children in armed conflict. This protocol entered into force in February 2002.
- The Women's Network and LGBT Network campaigned around two major reports: "Broken bodies, shattered minds: Torture and ill-treatment of women," and "Crimes of hate, conspiracy of silence: Torture and ill-treatment based on sexual identity."
- The Medical Network, which consisted of doctors, nurses, psychologists and other health professionals in over 30 countries, acted on behalf of sick prisoners denied access to medical care or health professionals who had been harassed by the authorities for providing treatment to opponents of the government. In 2001, the network acted on over 50 actions.

Source: AI Web site.

members were elected every two years by an International Council (IC) representing the country sections. The IC's role was to set the organization's vision, mission, and core values and to discuss and approve AI's integrated strategic plan. The IEC's role was to provide leadership and stewardship for the organization as a whole. The day-to-day management of the organization was the responsibility of the International Secretariat.

The IC comprised 500 delegates from the different sections, with larger sections having a proportionally greater number of representatives. It met every two years, for 12 days, to debate and vote on resolutions. All major decisions concerning AI's human rights activities and the organization's internal operations were made by the IC. In 2001, 49 resolutions were put forward by various sections and voted on. They ranged from decisions concerning standardized financial reports to organizational development projects, the decision to take on the rights of internally displaced persons, and the resolution to develop a corporate brand identity. In 2003, however, the roles of the IC, the IEC, and the International Secretariat were changing. Khan expanded on these changes:

AI's mandate has grown over the years as sections or the IEC proposed resolutions, which were then debated and adopted by the IC. Over 40 years, this has led to an incremental expansion of the mandate, which lacked a clear overall vision. Furthermore, it was very rigid because changes to the mandate could only be made through the democratic decision-making process involving all 56 sections. At the 2001 IC meeting, AI decided to move away from detailed development of its mandate through such a cumbersome decision-making process. The IC replaced AI's mandate with a "mission," defined in general terms and covering civil and political rights as well as economic, social, and cultural rights. The IC also agreed to adopt an integrated strategic plan which would focus on a broad set of themes and goals for a period of six years. Sections and the International Secretariat are expected to develop two- to three-year operational plans within the broad framework of the strategic plan. This gives us much greater flexibility and allows us to select issues strategically and to respond more quickly and effectively to the changes in the external world.

An AI section could be established in any country with the consent of the IEC. To be recognized, a section needed to demonstrate its ability to organize and maintain basic AI activities, consist of not fewer than two groups and 20 members, submit its statute to the IEC for approval, pay an annual fee, and be registered with the International Secretariat. Sections had to act in accordance with AI's core values and methods, strategic plans, working rules, and guidelines. Sections varied in size and culture. In some sections, members played a very strong role, for example in the United Kingdom and the United States. In other countries, sections were essentially staff run. "Sections play a critical role," added Khan. "They campaign, raise funds, educate, and represent our members." Kerry Hutchinson, AI's U.K. director of marketing, expanded, "Sections raise all the money and are responsible for delivering the majority of our communications."

Evolving role of the International Secretariat In 2002, the International Secretariat's budget was just under £21 million and was spent as follows: 24% for research and action (campaigning action), 17% for administration costs, 15% for membership support, 14% for research and action support, 13% for publications and translations, 10% for campaigning activities, and 7% for deconcentrated offices.[6]

Traditionally, the International Secretariat was responsible for all human rights abuse research, government relations, and coordination with the United Nations and international media. In addition to taking a more active role in developing strategies and campaigns, the International Secretariat was becoming active in fund-raising and section development. Khan explained, "Fund-raising is traditionally a role managed by the sections. However, traditional national boundaries are crumbling. For example, media is truly international, and online fund-raising is increasing in importance." "The International Secretariat used to be a service organization that supported the decisions taken by the sections," added Mark Hengstler, director of international fund-raising. "Today that role is changing, and the secretariat is starting to play a greater role in the management of resources among and between sections." Poland, a new section established in 2001, derived most of its funding from the section development fund, managed by the International Secretariat. In 2002, the Danish AI section began training the Polish AI section in fund-raising techniques. AI UK was partnered with AI Benin to provide similar training. "The International Secretariat," concluded Hengstler, "is moving from a service role to an advisory role and, increasingly, towards a guiding role for the whole organization."

Balancing democracy and effectiveness Although the democratic process by which AI developed strategies and took decisions was one of the organization's core values, some executives questioned its effectiveness, particularly as the organization continued to grow and expand its mission. Khan explained, "AI has always operated according to democratic principles, but the world at large functions on market principles, and this creates an inherent tension." In addition, many sections were managed and staffed by volunteers. The lack of professional staff, particularly in areas such as fund-raising, was believed by some to result in less than effective section organizations.

Differences among sections Within AI there were two main groups of members: older members who had joined the organization in the 1970s and 1980s, and newer and younger members in their 20s and 30s. These two groups were often reflected at the section level. Khan expanded:

> *Canada, for example, has a high proportion of youth members. Australia has a number of board members who are in their 20s. This contrasts with the French section, for example, where the average age of board members is above 65. The age difference is reflected in the positions each section takes. Older members tend to focus on AI's traditional roles such as prisoners of conscience and the elimination of torture, and they would like to see AI continue to focus on these issues. Younger members see human rights as covering a broader spectrum of human rights, including economic, social, and cultural rights. This creates a huge debate within the Amnesty movement not only on how much the organization should change, but also how fast it should change. In 2001, AI decided to expand its focus and address economic, social, and cultural rights, so one could say that the younger members are winning out. Another difference across sections is their interest in fund-raising. Some sections with a greater number of older members tend to reject modern methods of fund-raising as being overly aggressive.*

A number of sections, such as those in Belgium and Switzerland, aware of the issue, were consciously trying to bring in new, younger members to their organizations.

---

6 Deconcentrated offices played a coordination role similar to that of the International Secretariat but for specific geographic regions. There was a deconcentrated office, for example, in Kampala.

BRAND MANAGEMENT

Brand Trust

In a study conducted by Edelman PR in January 2003, Amnesty International ranked number one in terms of public trust among brands in Europe, above all other NGOs and major corporations such as Microsoft, Coca-Cola, Nike, and McDonald's. In the United States, the Amnesty brand ranked 10th in brand trust, behind the major U.S. corporations and the World Wildlife Fund and just behind Nike.

"The issue for the AI brand," said Sean Barrett, senior director of communications and campaigning at the International Secretariat, "is that while the International Secretariat is at the hub of the organization's wheel, it does not control how the AI brand is expressed in different countries." Different sections had distinct personalities and even used different logos. In 2002, for example, Amnesty International Israel used a logo depicting interlocking hands, and Amnesty International France used the symbol of a dove. "While the AI brand has great recall and is very powerful," added Barrett, "it has been modified around the world, and the challenge now is whether and how to standardize both the brand and the logo."

Despite the recently adopted vision and mission statements, no organization-wide brand identity existed. "We don't actively manage our brand," commented Hengstler, "but perhaps as a result, we do have a very strong brand reputation and recognition."

Funding

No funds were sought or accepted from governments. All funds were contributed by AI's members, the public, and organizations such as trusts and foundations. Funds were only accepted from companies deemed ethical, and AI accepted no more than 10% of total funds from any one donor, with the exception of legacies. "It makes sense that the bulk of our funding should come from individuals," explained Khan, "because of our commitment to the individual." Increasingly, however, corporate funding and fee-for-service schemes were being developed. "In some sections," Khan explained, "for example Norway, AI provides companies with advice and training and charges consulting fees. Other sections, such as Germany, won't even talk to companies."

Corporate fund-raising In 2003, AI UK put forward a resolution, to be discussed at the International Council, calling for a review of AI's corporate fund-raising strategy. AI UK members in particular believed it was important to understand the current and future levels of corporate fund-raising and its impact on AI's brand and reputation for impartiality. The desired outcome would be a transparent organization-wide corporate fund-raising policy. Corporate fund-raising included payments and funds from corporate entities, including donations, licensing arrangements, sponsorships, discounted services, gifts in kind, and consultancy fees. In 2002, guidelines for corporate fund-raising existed but required time-consuming and expensive screening of companies, and these guidelines were interpreted and implemented inconsistently throughout the AI movement.

AI had long maintained the principled position of not accepting funds or financial support from governments in order to preserve impartiality and credibility. Many believed this was still one of AI's most distinctive features. Some members believed that it would be unrealistic to refuse all involvement with corporations, while others believed that the principle of refusing all government funding should be applied to corporate funding as well. The latter argued that AI needed to remain financially independent of the targets of its campaigning, including corporations, and be able to withstand any conflict of interest spotlight as a result of a relationship with a corporation.

Amnesty International UK AI sections provided the International Secretariat with between 22% and 44% of the funds they raised in 2002. AI UK, for example, transferred 40% of its income to the International Secretariat, and the 10 top sections accounted for over 90% of AI's total revenues. AI UK's marketing income had risen over time, from £7.9 million in 1996 to £14.4 million in 2002, and was projected to reach £19 million in 2006. Expenditures over the same period had risen from £2 million to £4.5 million and were projected to reach £5.6 million by 2006. (See Exhibit 4 for details of AI UK's forecasted marketing income and expenditures.)

AI UK's marketing strategy was primarily based on the recruitment and development of individual supporters. Using a variety of recruitment techniques, the section aimed to grow its supporter base as the key driver to increasing income. Supporters were recruited to committed-giving programs (paying by direct debit), and in 2002 over 80% of AI UK's entire supporter base participated in these programs, providing a valuable and reliable platform on which to plan and build. These committed-giving programs and other membership payments accounted for 60% of AI UK's annual income.

Most fund-raising activities were holding steady or improving, with the exception of telefund-raising.

Exhibit 4   AI UK's Marketing Budget—Five-Year Forecast

£'000	2002	2003	2004	2005	2006
INCOME					
Section[a]					
Fund-raising	1,734	1,410	1,500	1,600	1,700
Scotland	137	123	175	190	190
Appeals and PIF[c]	910	818	830	850	870
New Member Acquisition	1,012	676	678	678	678
Existing Individual Members	5,446	6,448	6,837	6,957	7,023
Shops	275	298	350	441	536
Trading	73	85	84	88	92
Corporate and Affinity	214	189	150	160	165
Welcome Members[d]	0	44	50	50	50
Total Section	9,801	10,090	10,653	11,013	11,304
Trust[b]					
Legacies	0	1,000	1,000	1,100	1,200
Committed Giving	0	1,483	2,651	3,516	4,293
Major Donor	0	376	450	490	670
Other Trust	0	1,021	1,175	1,389	1,576
Total Trust	4,645	3,880	5,276	6,495	7,740
Total Income	14,446	13,970	15,929	17,508	19,043
EXPENDITURES					
Fund-raising	795	784	814	883	1,032
Scotland	55	57	87	92	91
Trust	496	1,372	1,372	1,372	1,372
Trust Upgrade		35	35	35	35
Appeals and PIF	215	259	260	275	285
New Member Acquisition	2,209	1,548	1,610	1,674	1,741
Membership	179	263	271	279	287
Shops	167	199	252	298	320
Trading	52	14	25	27	28
Major Donor	8	17	94	115	171
Director	326	150	158	165	174
Welcome Members[d]	54	65	68	71	75
Total Expenditures	4,555	4,763	5,044	5,285	5,611
Net Income	9,891	9,207	10,885	12,224	13,433

Source: AI UK.

[a]Section referred to the main AI UK organization.

[b]Trust was a separate fund established by AI UK that benefited from earning gift aid on donations.

[c]PIF = Partners in Freedom, high-value supporter product. To be a PIF required an annual donation of £100. PIFs received specialized information about AI.

[d]Welcome members are new members who have not made a regular gift (direct debit) at the point of recruitment. They are sent a welcome pack introducing them to AI and two months later receive a telephone call asking them to convert to direct debit.

Telefund-raising involved telephoning around 30,000 supporters to ask them to participate in a door-to-door collection program. This form of fund-raising had, in the past, generated annual net income for AI UK of around £200,000. In 2002, however, this had dropped to £40,000 against expenditures of £235,000. Hutchinson believed that this reflected a trend throughout the United Kingdom and was due in part to the higher costs of telefund-raising and in part to the declining audience receptiveness to this type of activity. In 2002, AI UK was exploring new methods of fund-raising including major donor development and community fund-raising and events. In addition, AI UK was planning on switching 50% of future recruitment activity to its trust fund. The trust enabled AI UK to claim back inland revenue taxes of 28% through a scheme known as gift aid on behalf of willing supporters for their donations to the trust. AI UK also needed to use the trust for legal and administrative reasons to implement two new recruitment programs, house-to-house recruitment and direct-response TV. (Exhibit 5 projects the size of the supporter base and associated income for both AI UK and the trust over time.)

Building section fund-raising capability As noted in the membership development section of the 2001 key challenges, an increasing number of smaller, newer national sections depended on funding from the International Secretariat. Competitive research carried out in 2002, and outlined in detail below, suggested that in certain countries, AI had not managed to raise funds even though other NGOs had been successful in doing so. In 2002, the International Secretariat established a Fund-raising Investment Fund (FIF) with the aim of boosting certain dependent sections' own fund-raising capabilities over time, with the result of creating financially independent sections that would also contribute to the International Secretariat's expenses. (The expected resulting cash flow is outlined in Exhibit 6.)

Membership

AI's integrated strategic plan called for an increase of 1 million members over a 10-year period and a doubling in global gross income. One complication, however, was that different sections measured membership differently. Although AI had over 1.6 million members in 2002, an estimated 50% paid monthly dues and the rest were active letter writers. The International Secretariat's future fund-raising efforts would focus on committed or sustainable giving. "We don't want to have one-off donors," explained Hengstler. "We want to bring in long-term members who pay monthly dues over a number of years." AI's International Secretariat was urging sections to increase the proportion of sustainable or committed-giving programs through automatic credit card and electronic transfers. Studies indicated that donors who gave through credit cards

---

<table>
<tr><td>**Exhibit 5**</td><td colspan="5">AI UK Projected Supporters and Related Income</td></tr>
<tr><td></td><td>2002</td><td>2003</td><td>2004</td><td>2005</td><td>2006</td></tr>
<tr><td>**Membership**</td><td></td><td></td><td></td><td></td><td></td></tr>
<tr><td>Supporter base</td><td>164,000</td><td>167,000</td><td>173,000</td><td>174,000</td><td>174,000</td></tr>
<tr><td>Income[a]</td><td>£5.4m</td><td>£6.6m</td><td>£6.8m</td><td>£6.9m</td><td>£7m</td></tr>
<tr><td>**Trust Givers**</td><td></td><td></td><td></td><td></td><td></td></tr>
<tr><td>Supporter base</td><td>18,000</td><td>38,000</td><td>53,000</td><td>67,000</td><td>78,000</td></tr>
<tr><td>Income[a]</td><td>£1.5m</td><td>£1.4m</td><td>£2.6m</td><td>£3.5m</td><td>£4.3m</td></tr>
<tr><td>Gift Aid[b]</td><td>£0.4m</td><td>£0.4m</td><td>£0.5m</td><td>£0.7m</td><td>£0.8m</td></tr>
<tr><td>Total Income</td><td>£1.9m</td><td>£1.8m</td><td>£3.1m</td><td>£4.2m</td><td>£5.1m</td></tr>
<tr><td>**Total**</td><td></td><td></td><td></td><td></td><td></td></tr>
<tr><td>Supporter base</td><td>182,000</td><td>205,000</td><td>226,000</td><td>241,000</td><td>252,000</td></tr>
<tr><td>Income</td><td>£7.3m</td><td>£8.4m</td><td>£9.9m</td><td>£11.1m</td><td>£12.1m</td></tr>
</table>

Source: AI UK.

[a]Corresponds to income from "Existing Individual Members" line and "Committed Giving" line in Exhibit 4.

[b]Gift Aid donations qualified for U.K. tax deductions.

Exhibit 6

Exhibit 6   Fund-raising Investment Fund—Cash Flow Over Time

£'000	2001	2002	2003	2004	2005	2006	2007	2008	2009	2010
Loans to sections	(1,000)	(1,000)	(1,000)	(1,000)	(1,000)	(1,000)	(1,000)	(1,000)	(1,000)	(1,000)
Repayments from sections	0	300	550	800	1,000	1,000	1,000	1,000	1,000	1,000
Increased assessment from sections	0	0	0	700	1,309	1,849	2,328	2,752	3,128	3,461
Net inflow (outflow) for the year	(1,000)	(700)	(450)	500	1,309	1,849	2,328	2,752	3,128	3,461
Cumulative net inflow (outflow)	(1,000)	(1,700)	(2,150)	(1,650)	(341)	1,508	3,836	6,588	9,716	13,177

Source: AI International Secretariat.

remained active for on average three years, those who gave through electronic funds transfer remained active seven years, and those who gave one-time gifts remained active for only 12 months. Across the entire AI membership, an estimated 45% of donors gave through sustainable giving programs.

Supporter recruitment was also central to AI UK's income strategy. AI UK projected to grow the number of supporters from 182,000 in 2002 to 252,000 in 2007. The number of members was projected to grow from 164,000 to 174,000, and the number of trust and committed givers was expected to increase from 18,000 to 78,000. (See Exhibit 5 for a forecast of AI UK supporter numbers over time.) Costs of recruiting new supporters were on the rise: in 2001 the average cost per recruit for AI UK was £48; in 2002, it was £60. "The majority of our members live in large urban areas such as London and Manchester," explained Hutchinson, "and they are roughly 50% male, which is different from the competition, whose supporter base is predominantly female."

Hutchinson believed that, in the United Kingdom, several trends were affecting supporter recruitment. First, the overall costs of recruitment were increasing. Second, direct-dialogue recruits (those supporters recruited through a face-to-face interaction, principally on the street) formed the largest segment of AI UK's membership base (25%) but were not responsive to AI's traditional fund-raising approaches such as direct mail, telefund-raising, or raffles.

Direct-dialogue recruits were very good value because they were recruited directly into a committed-giving program and generated, on average, £70 over four years. Hutchinson summarized, "While the new supporters we recruit are highly valuable, they are not receptive to our current range of offers, and we need to develop a tailored plan for them." AI UK was also planning to test a new recruitment program in January 2003 called Caring Together, a house-to-house, committed-giving recruitment program that Hutchinson hoped had the potential to recruit supporters in the same volumes as direct dialogue used to.

Competition

In 2002, AI commissioned research to understand the organization's global positioning, particularly in the world's 39 most important economies,[7] in relation to Greenpeace, the World Wide Fund for Nature (WWF), CARE, and Save the Children Fund. Although AI had the greatest number of offices, 38 sections out of 39 countries, it lagged both WWF and Greenpeace in terms of number of supporters. (See Exhibit 7 for a competitive comparison.) In terms of number of supporters per country office, AI averaged just below 50,000, far behind WWF at 200,000, Greenpeace at nearly 100,000, and CARE and Save the Children at 60,000 and 70,000, respectively. In terms of income per supporter, CARE excelled, with the average supporter contributing £100 a year. Save the Children followed close behind with the average supporter contributing £90, and AI, WWF, and Greenpeace followed at £55, £50, and £35, respectively.

---

7 Countries included Argentina, Australia, Austria, Belgium, Brazil, Canada, Chile, the Czech Republic, Denmark, Finland, France, Germany, Greece, Hong Kong, Hungary, Iceland, Ireland, Israel, Italy, Japan, Korea, Luxembourg, Mexico, the Netherlands, New Zealand, Norway, Peru, Poland, Portugal, Russia, Slovakia, Slovenia, Spain, Sweden, Switzerland, Taiwan, Turkey, the United Kingdom, and the United States.

AI believed that competition from many local NGOs had increased in the prior decade but that its only main global competitors in 2002 were Human Rights Watch and Greenpeace.

Human Rights Watch (HRW) HRW was an independent NGO founded in 1988 that investigated and exposed human rights violations and held abusers accountable. With operating revenues in fiscal-year 2002 of $19.5 million and close to 200 professional staff, HRW tracked developments in over 70 countries, published findings in dozens of books and reports every year, and sought to generate extensive coverage in local and international media. HRW met with government officials to urge changes in policy and practice and, in moments of crisis, provided up-to-the-minute information about conflicts to help shape the response of the international community.

HRW had a very small membership base; its main advocacy strategy was to shame offenders by generating press attention and enlisting influential governments and institutions to exert political and economic pressure. Initially focused on civil and political rights, HRW had increasingly addressed economic, social, and cultural rights as well. Similarly to AI, HRW prided itself on its impartiality and the accuracy of its reporting and accepted no government funding. Past campaigns had included prohibiting the use of child soldiers, banning the use of land mines, and documenting abuses in Kosovo and Rwanda. "Human Rights Watch is taking away our media exposure," explained Hengstler. "They are a young, dynamic organization and are much quicker at getting out a press release or condemning specific human rights abuses. AI might take two months to put out a report by the time it goes through our policy, legal, and media departments, but Human Rights Watch can get a similar report out in two weeks. In addition, they don't function along a democratic process so can react more swiftly than we can." Although AI had lost a number of senior staff to HRW, HRW was perceived as U.S. focused and not as global in its reach as AI.

Greenpeace Greenpeace was an independent nonprofit organization that relied on contributions from individuals and foundation grants. It focused on threats to the planet's biodiversity and environment and campaigned to stop climate change, protect forests, save the oceans, stop whaling, limit genetic engineering, stop nuclear threats, and eliminate toxic chemicals. Started in 1971 when a small boat of volunteers sailed into Amchitka, an area north of Alaska where the U.S. government was conducting underground

nuclear tests, Greenpeace advocated bearing witness as a core component of the organization.

In 2002, Greenpeace had 2.8 million supporters and a total income of around $140 million. Headquartered in Amsterdam, the organization had 41 national offices worldwide. "As a campaigning organization, Greenpeace tends to be top of mind for many people because they are in the news a lot," explained Hutchinson. In some respects, Greenpeace and AI were similar; both were membership organizations based on bearing witness and campaigning, and they had collaborated on a number of occasions in campaigning and advertising.

Market Research

In February 2000, AI USA conducted brand audit research, based on internal and external interviews and focus groups, in order to create a brand vision for the AI USA organization. During 2002, AI UK undertook a series of market research studies with the objective of understanding consumer awareness and perceptions in order to develop a marketing and communication strategy for the organization.

Brand awareness and recognition In February 2000, external interviews and focus groups conducted in the United States revealed that people viewed the issue of human rights as being closely linked to the U.S. Constitution, particularly freedom of speech, but did not include human rights in their "charity preference list." There was little recognition of the Amnesty International brand name or logo, although more people recognized the AI USA acronym. Even those focus group participants who recognized AI knew what the organization stood for but not what it did and could not recall any successes that AI USA had had. Most respondents were motivated by AI's mandate but unsure what membership involved. Those respondents who knew AI fairly well complained that "AI USA seems to have lost focus and is entering into areas that are related but fall outside their mandate." Or that "Amnesty is spreading themselves too thin." Others still worried that AI USA failed to take credit for success or take advantage of its worldwide membership base.

In April 2002, Haslam Callow and Partners was retained to conduct six two-hour focus groups in the United Kingdom designed to explore current perceptions of AI and reactions toward a range of advertising approaches. It found that, for the majority, there was a lack of awareness and uncertainty about AI and the work it did, with some people describing the organization as remote and impersonal.

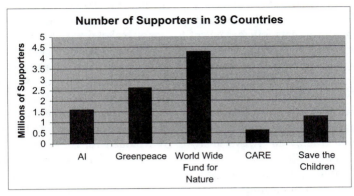

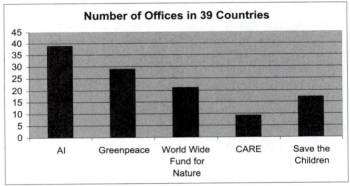

Source: Amnesty International.

"The focus groups show that AI is not very accessible," commented Hutchinson, "and that we have an overly intellectual image."

Those consumers who did know AI recognized the organization's focus on human rights and described it as independent and centered on individuals and specific groups. The researchers also felt that older consumers were more knowledgeable and interested in human rights issues and AI than the younger focus group participants. "In the United Kingdom," expanded Hutchinson, "we have some young members in school or at university, but there's a gap between them and another group of members in their 40s. In the U.K., most people in their 20s and 30s are not really engaged in politics." The researchers also recommended that AI communicate on human rights issues that involved innocent victims; were outside the arena of war; did not conflict with the values, laws, or religion of

another society; and involved obvious abuse. Issues surrounding refugees and asylum seekers as well as the death penalty were seen by many as borderline and emotive.

In October 2002, nfp Synergy was retained to conduct a telephone poll of over 1,000 adults. It found that AI's spontaneous awareness stood at 5%, behind the Red Cross at 11% and Oxfam at 26%. Semiprompted awareness, as defined by the question "Which charities or NGOs have you heard of who work on human rights, international issues and overseas development?" stood at 27% for AI versus 55% for the Red Cross and 64% for Oxfam, and total aided-awareness figures were 78% for AI, 99% for the Red Cross, and 99% for Oxfam. "The AI brand has great potential and credibility," added Hutchinson. "People don't necessarily know what we do, but they think we're good."

Sixty-six percent of respondents could recall an advertisement for a charitable organization that they had seen in the last three months. Television ads and appeals, as well as letters, were the dominant form of communication. (See Exhibit 8 for details of what people recalled.) "There is a sense," said Hutchinson, "that our media presence was greater in the past, but according to our records, AI's media exposure has actually increased." Seventy-four percent of respondents claimed to have given money to charity in the last three months, and 19% claimed to have volunteered their time. When asked, "Do you ever think you'd like to volunteer but don't know who to approach or where to go?" 81% responded no. When asked if there were any charity activities that they found annoying, 50% responded no, while the remainder were spread fairly evenly over many fund-raising activities (outlined in Exhibit 9).

Communicating the brand "We have learned," explained Hutchinson, "that communicating about a specific campaign is easy, but talking about AI as an organization is difficult. Because of the democratic nature of our organization, many people at AI UK expressed their own views about how best to communicate what AI stands for. We needed help channeling and condensing these opinions." In December 2002, Shaw Research Planning was retained to conduct focus groups with both AI members

and staff and nonmembers to determine a communication platform that would attract new members to AI UK. First, the researchers found that throughout the focus groups, members had been drawn to AI by their belief in the importance of fairness and justice. Second, the researchers tested the appeal of five positioning boards designed to present AI in various ways: as a global force, as the world's eyes and ears, as relentless campaigners, as a people's movement, and as defiant for justice. (See Exhibit 10 for a description of the concept areas.)

The global force concept was found to describe a manner of working but lacked emotional appeal and did not differentiate AI. The world's eyes and ears concept seemed to be a comfortable restatement of where the organization currently stood and made members feel like "insiders." It inspired respect and admiration but implied distance. The relentless campaigners concept provoked an image of martyrdom, depressed members, and contained no benefit for nonmembers. The people's movement concept had a potent "feel" to it, but members felt that they did not seek to "belong," and nonmembers felt it was vague, albeit interesting. The defiant for justice concept was by far the most appreciated and was seen by members as the spirit that had

---

Exhibit 8   Recalled Sources of Information About Charitable Organizations, AI UK 2002

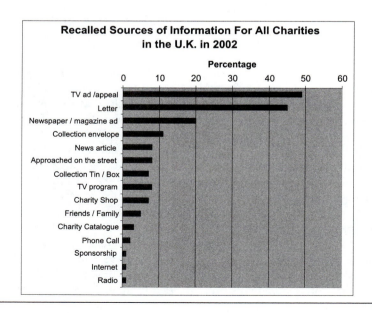

Source: nfp Synergy.

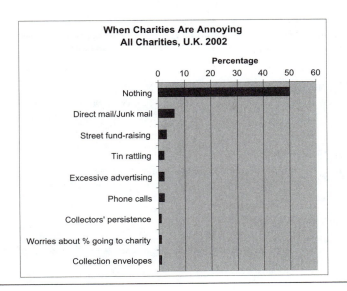

Source: nfp Synergy.

sustained AI for 40 years. For a few, however, it was too strident, and for others it suggested an intense level of commitment that was off-putting. Hutchinson summarized as follows:

> *Although AI has an intellectual image, we elicit an emotional response, and so our communications have to reach people at the emotional level. We are also asking people to make a leap of faith. We don't build wells or vaccinate children, we are more values based. In a way, it's a state of mind. If you believe in justice and fairness, AI is attractive. Historically, AI has not been good at claiming success. We want the governments to claim success so that they enter a virtuous cycle of improving human rights in their countries. At the same time, it makes it difficult to promote the organization if we can't portray our effectiveness.*

During internal interviews conducted in 2000 at AI USA, AI's main strengths were considered to be the ability to mobilize large groups of individuals to action, the deep network across the globe, and the integrity in research and calls to action. Weaknesses included the bureaucratic nature of the organization, too many meetings and different opinions, and a resulting slow decision-making process. In addition, AI was felt to be divorced from the world of

"regular folks." Recommendations from external interviews and focus groups in the United States included communicating exactly what AI USA does and stands for and how to become a member. Positive communications focusing on achievements at the individual level were considered important, as were the use of the logo and the full Amnesty International brand name everywhere possible.

Khan concluded, "You need lofty goals to energize people but concrete examples of success."

Future Brand Management

"People in NGOs are often uncomfortable and suspicious when you start talking about branding," said Barrett. "Brand management at AI must start with an education and discussion process. People need to build an appreciation that our brand is a considerable asset and that we have common ownership of the brand as well as a common duty to protect the brand and its value." Barrett also believed that the AI brand was strongly associated with the organization's history: "AI is on the cusp of entering new areas such as economic and social rights, and there is a very real danger that this will confuse the public, undermine the AI brand, and erode existing value." Barrett also believed that moving into new areas could give AI the opportunity

GLOBAL FORCE

In today's global village, Amnesty International is the world's largest network of human rights campaigners. Amnesty believes that to make the world a safer place for all of us and achieve change on a global scale, international cooperation, international action, and international solutions are the only way.

THE WORLD'S EYES AND EARS

In a world of spin, bias, and superficial reporting, Amnesty International is a research-based organization that provides thorough and trusted reporting of human rights abuses. As it does not take money from governments or unethical companies, it is uniquely placed to provide impartial reporting and unbiased solutions.

THE RELENTLESS CAMPAIGNERS

In a complex world where problems can't be resolved overnight, Amnesty International refuses to accept that the way things are, is the way they will always be. So even though fighting for change and protecting human rights can be a struggle, Amnesty and its members will never give up hope.

A PEOPLE MOVEMENT NOT A CHARITY

In a world where individuals feel more and more powerless, Amnesty International demonstrates the power of many. Ordinary people—ready to stand shoulder to shoulder for their own rights and the rights of other ordinary people. Each individual part of a bigger community able to change the world together in a way they can't alone.

DEFIANT FOR JUSTICE

In a world where some people still do not have basic human rights, Amnesty International believes in justice for all without exception. This can mean standing firm or even confrontation. But Amnesty believes in doing what's right rather than what's easy, and if that means taking on the establishment, governments or the powerful, so be it.

Source: Shaw Research Planning.

to gain new supporters and members but that the key would be to communicate consistently and not allow a vacuum to develop into which the AI brand could fall.

In addition, the AI brand did not have a common global perception and awareness. While in the developed countries, or "North," it was an established, well-known brand in its mid-life, in the developing world, or "South," it was a very young, fairly unknown brand. "We are still perceived as a Western or Northern NGO," added Khan, "which is ironic because we have been the most active in the South and East." AI also had aspirations to grow its membership base in the South, and Barrett wondered how best to position the brand to achieve this as well.

CONCLUSION

Khan reflected on how to develop and manage a new global AI brand and how a new brand positioning would enable AI to achieve its membership and revenue growth goals.

First, she wondered how to maintain the brand's value in developing countries while communicating the organization's new mandate, particularly to new and prospective members throughout the world.

Second, she was concerned that the AI brand be strongly positioned relative to competition and that market research findings be incorporated in both the development and the communication of the new brand.

Third, Khan realized that, given the democratic nature of AI and the diversity within the movement's network, she would have to be creative and persuasive in her implementation of a global AI brand positioning.

World Vision International's AIDS Initiative: Challenging a Global Partnership

On January 19, 2002, Ken Casey, director of World Vision International's HIV/AIDS Hope Initiative, walked into a safari lodge in South Africa to present the final session of a conference attended by 40 senior staff from 17 countries with the highest prevalence of HIV and AIDS in Africa and nearly 20 senior executives from worldwide support offices. As he stretched his back, he felt a sharp pain from wounds he had received during a vicious attack by a baboon on the hotel's patio the day before the conference began. Badly cut and bruised, Casey had staggered to the conference center where he had been wrapped in towels and rushed to a hospital. It had required 135 stitches and 27 staples to close the wounds.

Determined to proceed with the conference which he saw as a potential turning point in his year-long struggle to get the Hope Initiative off the ground, Casey had returned the next day. Largely driven by the senior leaders of World Vision International, the initiative was an ambitious attempt to implement common goals and strategies in fund-raising, programming, and advocacy across the 48 independent members of the World Vision Partnership. But its future was unclear. Not only did its focus on HIV/AIDS represent a major shift in World Vision's programming, but in many ways, the initiative's top-down implementation challenged the federated organization model the Partnership had pursued throughout the 1990s. As he addressed the conference, Casey worried that if it did not go well, the Hope Initiative might well be dead in the water.

BIRTH OF WORLD VISION INTERNATIONAL

World Vision International was a Christian relief and development partnership linking 48 national members in a

This case was prepared by Professor Christopher A. Bartlett with the assistance of Daniel F. Curran.

global federation. Together, the partnership raised over $732 million in cash and nearly $300 million in commodities in 2002. (See Exhibit 1 for representative World Vision Partnership financial data.) Almost 50% of World Vision's funding flowed from private sources, mostly through child sponsorship. Governments and multilateral agencies provided the other 50%.

A Visionary Founder: 'Faith in Action'

Founded in the United States in August 1950 by Bob Pierce, a Christian evangelist who was moved by the suffering he witnessed in Korea, World Vision was funded by North American Christians whom Pierce connected to individual Korean orphans through photographs and personal correspondence. Through this innovative sponsorship program, he successfully translated the massive needs he saw in Asia into personal terms in America. In 1952, the organization's first statement of purpose read: "World Vision is a missionary service organization meeting emergency needs in crisis areas of the world through existing evangelical agencies."

Although Pierce cultivated a small, dedicated staff, he called the shots in his young organization. He challenged his team by telling them, "Cut through the reasons why things can't be done. Don't fail to do something just because you can't do everything."[1] With this entrepreneurial attitude, Pierce soon extended World Vision's work into Hong Kong, Indonesia, Taiwan, India, and Japan.

By the 1960s, World Vision offices were opening in other countries. In 1961, it incorporated an affiliate office in Canada as a separate national entity, and in 1966 a separate national entity was also established in Australia. During this period, it also refined its "child sponsorship" model and, by the mid-1960s, was supporting 15,000 children in Southeast Asia. Responding to church film screenings, radio advertising and direct mail appeals, Christians in the United States, Canada, and Australia were promised a loving

---

[1] Irvine, Graeme, (1996) *Best Things in the Worst Times: An Insider's View of World Vision*. Wilsonville, Oregon: World Vision International, p. 18.

Exhibit 1   World Vision International FY2002 Financial Data

PARTNERSHIP INCOME FY2002

(Offices receiving $200,000 or more in thousands of U.S. dollars)*

National Offices	Contributions	Gifts-in-Kind	Total
Armenia	$ 360	$	$ 360
Australia	78,543	$ 14,844	93,387
Austria	2,121	543	2,664
Brazil	2,786		2,786
Burundi	205		205
Canada	105,656	38,924	144,580
Chad	339		339
Chile	265		265
Colombia	1,041		1,041
Costa Rica	274		274
Finland	1,407	-	1,407
Germany	34,370	2,987	37,357
Haiti	331		331
Hong Kong	25,885	1,237	27,122
India	1,214		1,214
Indonesia	219		219
Ireland	4,538		4,538
Japan	12,055	2,294	14,349
Korea	20,802	1,282	22,084
Malaysia	918		918
Mexico	1,410		1,410
Myanmar	213		213
Netherlands	3,973	372	4,345
New Zealand	13,459	21	13,480
Philippines	505		505
Sierra Leone	1,287		1,287
Singapore	2,615	-	2,615
South Africa	507		507
Switzerland	12,599	704	13,303
Taiwan	31,221	75	31,296
Tanzania	722		722
Thailand	3,707		3,707
United Kingdom	46,529	1,199	47,728
United States	317,744	235,086	552,830
Zambia	1,030		1,030
Other Offices	1,185		1,185
Total Partnership Income	$ 732,035	$ 299,568	$ 1,031,603

*In approximate U.S. dollars. Exact amounts depend on time currency exchange is calculated

Source: World Vision 2002 Annual Report.

Use of Resources FY2002
(In cash and gifts-in-kind in millions of U.S. dollars)

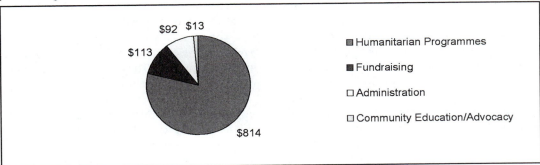

■ Humanitarian Programmes

■ Fundraising

□ Administration

□ Community Education/Advocacy

What World Vision's resources accomplish:

Humanitarian Programmes provide for emergency relief in natural and man-made disasters and for development work in food, education, health care, sanitation, income generation and other community needs. Also included are the costs of supporting such programmes in the field.

Fundraising supports humanitarian programmes by soliciting contributions through media and direct marketing appeals. Included are costs of marketing, creative services and publishing materials.

Administration includes donor relations, computer technology, finance, accounting, human resources and managerial oversight.

Community Education/Advocacy promotes awareness of poverty and justice issues through media campaigns, forums, speaking engagements, and public advocacy.

Ministry Support & Programmes by Region FY2002
(In cash and gifts-in-kind in millions of U.S. dollars)

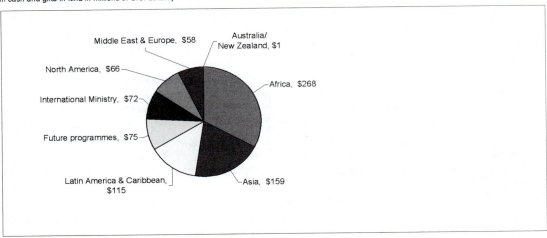

Source: World Vision International 2002 Annual Report.

connection to a poor child in the developing world for a monthly contribution of around $10. Full-time staff and hundreds of volunteers coordinated the delivery of photos and letters between children and sponsors while more than a dozen marketers created appeals to attract more donors. It was a successful process requiring a great deal of administrative support.

By 1969, World Vision managed $5.1 million in funding of which 80% was delivered to 32,600 children in 388 projects. The remaining 20% supported fund-raising and administrative costs. All funding and most support services flowed through the headquarters offices in Monrovia, California. As the war in Vietnam began absorbing the organization's energy, significant changes in approach occurred. Instead of working through existing orphanages and ministries, World Vision staff opened refugee schools, recruited and trained local teachers, and built houses for the displaced.

A New Leader, A New Approach: The Evolving Mission

Toward the end of the 1960s, World Vision began to run into some trouble. A senior executive described the emerging problems: "Anyone looking at World Vision would see an organization that reflected Bob Pierce himself: action-oriented, strongly evangelical, innovative and progressive. But we had no long-range planning or adequate mechanisms for administration." But Pierce resisted the changes that many felt were needed. As money became short, tensions grew between him and his board. Finally, in 1967, Pierce resigned.

Pierce's successor, Stan Mooneyham, was another action-oriented risk-taker. With the fall of South Vietnam and Laos and the rise of the Khmer Rouge in Cambodia, World Vision lost contact with much of its program staff in those countries. More importantly, nearly 30,000 sponsors lost contact with their sponsored children. But the four core fund-raising offices—the United States, Canada, Australia, and New Zealand—found that most of their donors were willing to transfer their assistance to children elsewhere. The organization shifted its focus to Latin America, establishing offices and sponsorship programs in Brazil, Columbia, Ecuador, Guatemala and Mexico.

At the same time, some in the organization began questioning the sustainability of World Vision's traditional model of selecting and supporting children. At a conference

in 1971, Gene Daniels, WV director in Indonesia, proposed a new model of rural community development. Undeterred by the lukewarm reception his ideas received, for the next two years Daniels quietly experimented with his approach. As he began to succeed, others voiced an interest in a new approach. Graeme Irvine, president of World Vision-Australia, described a need to shift to longer-term commitments rather than "dump and run" emergency relief. He stated, "Development is not something you do for people. Those who wish to help may walk alongside, but not take over."[2]

Influenced by these voices, in 1972, Mooneyham promised that World Vision would build a Christian Children's Hospital in Phnom Penh. He presented a proposal to the International Board, but was disappointed to be turned down. Then the presidents of World Vision Australia and World Vision New Zealand offered to organize staff and fund the program themselves. Six months later, when World Vision opened the hospital in Phnom Penh, Mooneyham wrote, "The Cambodia medical program was an example of World Vision's emerging international partnership at work. It illustrated our principle of looking for alternative solutions to major problems."[3]

In 1973, following a series of consultations, the World Vision Board made a commitment to establishing relief and development as new lines of action in World Vision's mission. But the consensus over becoming a "transform" rather than "transfer" organization meant significant changes to the structure and governance. "What you are doing in development is according people the dignity of voice and self determination," stated Irvine. "But a big organization like World Vision has all kinds of baggage—bureaucracy, systems, reports, layers of authority, policies and many committees—that got in the way of development. How would we work as a partnership?"[4]

Moving Toward Partnership: Forming WVI

Until the early 1970s, World Vision's U.S. organization, as the founding country and by far the largest contributor, had made most of the significant programming decisions. Under its guidance, the organization had expanded beyond Asia and Latin America into Africa and the Middle East. Typically, each initiative had arisen from special circumstances or through initiatives led by interested groups, churches or individuals.

2 Irvine, p. 71.
3 Irvine, p. 45.
4 Irvine, p. 72.

Increasingly, however, the presidents of Canada, Australia, and New Zealand—the other key "support" offices—wanted to move beyond just providing funds to "field" offices. They wanted to participate with the U.S. office in policy and strategy decisions. "This was not so much a desire for control as it was a need for accountability to donors," explained a past executive at World Vision-NZ. In 1973, Mooneyham responded by forming an Internationalization Study Committee to recommend a basis for "a true partnership among all national entities: a partnership of both structure and spirit."

Over the next few years, the committee met to define the issues and consider the options. "At the core we saw it not as structure or even as process but an attitude toward each other that did not view one partner as superior to any other," stated one committee member.[5] Finally, in April 1976, the International Board unanimously decided to form a new distinct entity, World Vision International (WVI), as the common program delivery arm of World Vision's four main fund-raising "support" offices—United States, Canada, New Zealand, and Australia. The directors of each sat on the International Board. (World Vision-US maintained the World Vision name and trademark, but gave its WVI partners the right to use them.) World Vision national entities in developing countries (the "field" offices) became members of WVI's Council, but did not have equal partner status with the four board members. The Council agreed on WVI's mission and in May 1978, adopted a formal Declaration of Internationalization.

BUILDING THE WORLD VISION PARTNERSHIP: DEFINING A FEDERATION

To provide coordinated management of the global field operations funded by the core support offices, WVI's Council created a central International Office, co-located with the World Vision U.S. office in Los Angeles. However, rather than functioning as a servant to the four council member organizations, it soon became a separate power base. A WVI manager at the time recalled:

> Mooneyham brought all of the bright and creative folks with him to the International Office and this had two unintended consequences. First, the program delivery mechanism became the dominant force in the organization, so the fund-raising team left in the WV/US office

was not seen as particularly important or valuable. Second, this organization separated marketing from production, and each group developed its own culture.

The separation lasted for almost a decade, during which time the national directors of the largest support offices, feeling frustrated at just delivering the funds they raised to the International Office, started to demand more of a say in strategy. Said one senior WVI manager, "Our core competitive advantage—what we do particularly well—is clearly our child sponsorship mechanism. It is the most sustainable form of fund-raising and we are one of the best in the world at doing it. But, at that time, we did not recognize it. No wonder they were frustrated."

Challenging Central Control

When Tom Houston became the new president of WVI in 1984, his attention was drawn to the devastating drought in Ethiopia. The global response from donors was staggering. Under agreements with the U.S. government and UN agencies, WVI's Ethiopia response budget grew from $2.3 million in 1984 to $43.4 million in 1986. To manage the funding, World Vision's staff in Ethiopia grew from 100 to 3,650. In the following year, WVI launched 11 large development projects in six other African nations. Because of the need for coordination, all logistics and program functions were managed from the International Office giving even more power to this fast growing group.

By 1987, World Vision had survived and grown through a decade of expansion. But there was discontent within the organization, and Houston discovered that the unhappy support office directors were meeting together informally to share their frustrations. "Tom was abrupt and frank and did not like the notion of a dominant person pushing the little guys around," said one executive. "So he turned our culture upside down." To bring the support office directors into the fold, he asked several of them to sit on the International Planning Committee, the president's primary consultative group on partnership decisions. In addition, he shook up the management of the International Office by requiring that all regional vice presidents came from their regions.

But frustration reached a boiling point in August 1987 when national directors responsible for the work in over 60 countries gathered at a Director's Conference in Sierra Madre, California. When, as was the norm at these events,

---

5 Irvine, p. 136.

executives from the International Office began to deliver presentations on strategy and operations, three new regional VPs from Brazil, Nigeria, and Egypt stood together. "If this is a director's conference, why are we working on your agenda?" they asked. The directors of the main support offices joined the "revolt." Recognizing the legitimacy of the challenge, Houston surrendered the agenda. Following the conference, 30 senior executives spent a year studying how to redefine the relationship between field and support offices and the International Office.

Creating Area Development Programs

Meanwhile, the 11 large-scale development programs World Vision had launched in 1985 were struggling. Each had a budget of more than $1 million, a time span of more than three years, and a geographic scope greater than a single community. The causes of the problems were diagnosed as unrealistic initial expectations, lack of local management and technical expertise, and a top-down planning and control system.

A study commissioned to propose solutions to these problems recommended a new approach that sought to retain the benefits of scale while engaging more local involvement in community-level transformational development. Through the 1990s, a new way to work, referred to as the Area Development Program (ADP), became the dominant means of program delivery for World Vision. In Africa, for example, over 300 ADPs were defined, each aiding 50,000 to 200,000 persons. Wilfred Mlay, African regional vice president, explained their operation:

> Each ADP is managed by a coordinator from that country who understands the local language and customs. He or she negotiates an agreement with the community for a 10 to 15 year multi-sectoral engagement; then they sign a contract promising to work together. . . Before, communities tended to consider the local projects—a bore hole, a school, a health center—as World Vision projects. If something went wrong, they said, "Come and fix your pump. Come and fix your vehicle." There was no ownership…Now we don't just dig wells and provide clean water; we partner with each ADP area to identify root causes of their problems, then we work with them to provide a long-term program that will address the needs they identify. The strength of the approach is in finding local solutions to local problems.

Engaging Federalism

When Houston resigned in 1988, Graeme Irvine, former head of World Vision Australia, became acting president. On his appointment, Irvine made a commitment to make WVI "a professional, enlightened, efficient and humane organization [that] will nurture a climate of creativity in which people feel free to contribute."[6] He then launched a process to reexamine the organization's values, mission, and structure, all of which were to be open to challenge and change.

A working group developed a set of core values (see Exhibit 2) that was adopted by the board of World Vision International in 1990. Next, after 24 drafts, in 1992 the board adopted a new mission. Finally, Irvine led the creation of a Covenant of Partnership (see Exhibit 3) that was signed by all members of the newly defined World Vision Partnership. "We want to be held together by shared agreements, values and commitments rather than legal contracts or a controlling center," said Irvine. "The Covenant is a statement of accountability to each other, setting out the privileges and responsibilities of national member-entities of the World Vision family."

By 1995, with over a million sponsored children in its care—up from 70,000 fifteen years earlier—the World Vision Partnership decided to build its formal organizational architecture on a "federal" model. Recognizing that that simple decentralization would mean losing economies of scale, the goal of the new structure was to try to make all partners as self-sufficient as possible, but to maintain a strong core of common language, systems and operations. Bryant Myers, senior vice president of Operations explained the philosophy:

> We wanted to combine the strength of the central organization with centers of expertise and action that existed around the partnership, balancing the contributions and needs of each. That should result in centralizing some things because they can be done better and cheaper that way and decentralizing others things that can be managed more effectively on the front lines. . . . We learned that the biggest misreading of federalism is to call it decentralization. The key to federalism is to ensure the right of intervention held by the leader at the center.

Designing the Structure and Governance

Under the federal structure that emerged, membership in the WVI Partnership required commitment to its core

---

6 Irvine, p. 134.

WE ARE CHRISTIAN. We acknowledge one God; Father, Son and Holy Spirit. In Jesus Christ the love, mercy and grace of God are made known to us and all people…We seek to follow him—in his identification with the poor, the powerless, the afflicted, the oppressed, the marginalized; in his special concern for children; in his respect for the dignity bestowed by God on women equally with men; in his challenge to unjust attitudes and systems; in his call to share resources with each other; in his love for all people without discrimination or conditions; in his offer of new life through faith in him…

WE ARE COMMITTED TO THE POOR. We are called to serve the neediest people of the earth; to relieve their suffering and to promote the transformation of their condition of life…We respect the poor as active participants, not passive recipients, in this relationship…

WE VALUE PEOPLE. We regard all people as created and loved by God. We give priority to people before money, structure, systems and other institutional machinery… We celebrate the richness of diversity in human personality, culture and contribution…We practice a participative, open, enabling style in working relationships. We encourage the professional, personal and spiritual development of our staff.

WE ARE STEWARDS. The resources at our disposal are not our own. They are a sacred trust from God through donors on behalf of the poor. We are faithful to the purpose for which those resources are given and manage them in a manner that brings maximum benefit to the poor…We demand of ourselves high standards of professional competence and accept the need to be accountable through appropriate structures for achieving these standards. We share our experience and knowledge with others where it can assist them.

WE ARE PARTNERS. We are members of an international World Vision Partnership that transcends legal, structural and cultural boundaries. We accept the obligations of joint participation, shared goals and mutual accountability that true partnership requires. We affirm our inter-dependence and our willingness to yield autonomy as necessary for the common good. We commit ourselves to know, understand and love each other… We maintain a co-operative stance and a spirit of openness towards other humanitarian organizations. We are willing to receive and consider honest opinions from others about our work.

WE ARE RESPONSIVE. We are responsive to life-threatening emergencies where our involvement is needed and appropriate. We are willing to take intelligent risks and act quickly. We do this from a foundation of experience and sensitivity to what the situation requires. We also recognize that even in the midst of crisis, the destitute have a contribution to make from their experience…We are responsive to new and unusual opportunities. We encourage innovation, creativity and flexibility. We maintain an attitude of learning, reflection and discovery in order to grow in understanding and skill.

OUR COMMITMENT. We recognize that values cannot be legislated; they must be lived. No document can substitute for the attitudes, decisions and actions that make up the fabric of our life and work. Therefore, we covenant with each other, before God, to do our utmost individually and as corporate entities within the World Vision Partnership to uphold these Core Values, to honor them in our decisions, to express them in our relationships and to act consistently with them wherever World Vision is at work.

Source: World Vision International internal documents.

Exhibit 3   Extracts from World Vision's Covenant of Partnership

THE COVENANT (EXTRACTS)

Regarding World Vision as a partnership of interdependent national entities, we, as a properly constituted national World Vision Board (or Advisory Council), do covenant with other World Vision Boards (or Advisory Councils) to:

A. UPHOLD THE FOLLOWING STATEMENTS OF WORLD VISION IDENTITY AND PURPOSE;

The Statement of Faith, the Mission Statement, and the Core Values.

B. CONTRIBUTE TO THE ENRICHMENT OF PARTNERSHIP LIFE AND UNITY BY;

Sharing in strategic decision-making and policy formulation through consultation and mechanisms that offer all members an appropriate voice in Partnership affairs…

Accepting the leadership and organizational structures established by the WVI Council and Board for the operation of the Partnership…

Fostering an open spirit of exchange for ideas, proposals, vision and concern within the Partnership…

C. WORK WITHIN THE ACCOUNTABILITY STRUCTURES BY WHICH THE PARTNERSHIP FUNCTIONS, by;

Affirming the principle of mutual accountability and transparency between all entities…

Accepting Partnership policies and decisions established by WVI Board consultative processes.

Honoring commitments to adopted budgets to the utmost extent possible…

Executing an agreement with World Vision International to protect the trademark, name and symbols of World Vision worldwide…

D. OBSERVE AGREED FINANCIAL PRINCIPLES AND PROCEDURES, especially;

Using funds raised under the auspices of World Vision exclusively in World Vision approved ministries.

Keeping overhead and fund-raising expenses to a minimum to ensure a substantial majority of the funds raised are responsibly utilized in ministry among the poor.

Accepting Financial Planning and Budgeting Principles adopted by the WVI Board.

Ensuring that funds or commodities accepted from governments or multi-lateral agencies do not compromise World Vision's mission or core values, and that such resources do not become the major ongoing source of support.

E. PRESENT CONSISTENT COMMUNICATIONS MESSAGES, that;

Reflect our Christian identity in appropriate ways.

Include words, images, and statistics that are consistent with ministry realities.

Avoid paternalism and cultural insensitivity.

Are free from demeaning and degrading images.

Build openness, confidence, knowledge and trust within the Partnership.

In signing the Covenant, we are mindful of the rich heritage of Christian service represented by World Vision and of the privilege which is ours to join with others of like mind in the work of the Kingdom of God throughout the world. We therefore recognize that consistent failure to honour this Covenant of Partnership may provide cause for review of our status as a member of the Partnership by the Board of World Vision International.

Signed in behalf of (NAME OF NATIONAL ENTITY)

by resolution carried at a meeting of the [Board] (or Advisory Council) on

---

Chair of [Board] (or Advisory Council)

Source: World Vision International internal documents.

documents (Mission Statement, Statement of Faith, Core Values, and Covenant of Partnership), WVI ministry policies, and the WVI Trademark Agreement. Organizationally, the Partnership was governed through a set of linked structures (see Exhibit 4).

By 2002, there were 48 national Partners, each with one vote on the **International Council**, the partnership's highest authority. Held once every three years, Council meetings were attended by the International Board members, the chairs of the National Boards or Advisory Councils, National Office directors, and elected delegates from all Partner offices. The Council reviewed the objectives of World Vision International, assessed the accomplishment of previous goals, and made recommendations to the Board in relation to global strategies and policies.

World Vision's **International Board** was composed of the International President and 23 directors selected from the governing bodies of WVI's National Offices. It oversaw the partnership, meeting twice a year to appoint WVI's senior officers, approve strategic plans and budgets, and set international policy.

Seven **Regional Forums** were composed of representatives from the National Boards or Advisory Councils of each National Office in each region. They shared experiences on regional programs and strategies and nominated representatives to the WVI Board.

The **Partnership Office** (previously the International Office) located in Monrovia, California, was WVI's executive group. Headed by an International President, four regional and six functional vice presidents, its staff of around 160 supported the day-to-day operations of the Partnership. Several other Partnership Support Offices in cities such as Geneva, Los Angeles, and Vienna represented WVI in the international arena through lobbying and advocacy work.

Four **Regional Offices** in Costa Rica, Cyprus, Nairobi and Bangkok each oversaw the program operations of the National Offices in its respective region. Regional Offices reported directly to the Partnership Office.

Most of WVI's 48 **National Offices** were either primarily support (fund-raising) offices or field (program delivery) offices, but a few did both. Each National Office had equal

---

Exhibit 4   The Elements of the WVI Partnership

The World Vision Partnership refers to the entire World Vision family throughout the world. Any expression of the World Vision ministry is in some way connected to the Partnership. The word "Partnership" is used in this document in a broad, informal sense, rather than a legal sense.

World Vision National Entities comprise the membership of the Partnership. The conditions and categories of membership are described in the By-Laws of World Vision International. All function with the guidance and advice of a National Board or Advisory Council.

World Vision International (WVI) is the registered legal entity which, through its Council and Board of Directors, provides the formal international structure for the Partnership.

The WVI Council provides the membership structure for the Partnership. It meets every three years to review the purpose and objectives of World Vision, assess the extent to which they have been accomplished and make recommendations to the WVI Board in relation to policy. All member-entities are represented on the Council.

The WVI Board of Directors is the governing body of World Vision International as outlined in the By-Laws. The membership of the Board is broadly representative of the Partnership and is appointed by a process determined by the Partnership.

The International Office is the functional unit of World Vision International, housing most of the central elements of WVI. It operates under the authority of the WVI Board of Directors.

Source: World Vision International internal documents.

Exhibit 5   World Vision International Organizational Structure

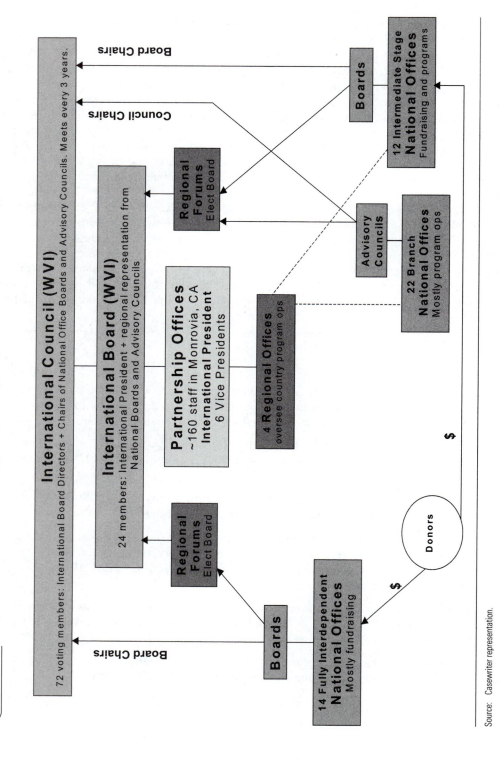

Source: Casewriter representation.

direct representation on the International Council and also took part in the election of regional representatives to the International Board through its Regional Forum. Local governance and independence from the International Office was determined by the National Office's stage of development category:

- WVI's 22 **Branch** Offices were governed by national Advisory Committees, but WVI maintained legal responsibility and strong management control over their budgetary and personnel decisions through its Regional Offices.
- The 12 **Intermediate Stage** Offices were governed by local boards composed of business, church and social service leaders. They voluntarily agreed to seek approval from WVI for critical management decisions such as appointment or termination of a national director or national board member, budgets, and off-budget expenditures.
- The 14 **Fully Interdependent** Offices were nationally registered nonprofit organizations with their own local boards of directors. Although they did not need WVI approval for decisions except for certain items specified in the Covenant of Partnership, they were expected to voluntarily coordinate with Partnership Office. (Branch and Intermediate offices were considered to be in transition toward full interdependence. The process involved peer reviews, WVI consultation, and interaction with the international board.)

In 1996, Dean Hirsch became the sixth president of World Vision International following two decades in which he had helped establish World Vision national programs in Rwanda, Zaire, Tanzania, Mali, Ghana and Malawi, then managed major donor marketing for WV/US. He described his role in the emerging federated partnership:

> My job is to cast a vision, to make sure that we have alignment between our mission and operations, and to ensure we stay strategic. Because of our dispersed governance, we must operate with trust. The best thing I can do is help to build relationships. So I am the biggest cheerleader in the world…but as President of WVI, I also hold a seat on every World Vision board in the world. Either one of my representatives or I attend all meetings. It provides an immediate means of keeping alignment. And I can intervene at any time if one of partners drifts from our mission or core values.

FUND-RAISING IN THE PARTNERSHIP: WORLD VISION U.S.

Within the evolving World Vision global partnership, most national entities were adjusting to the more complex structure within which they had to operate. In the United States, for example, the WV/US board began to look for a new president to strengthen its fund-raising activity. In June 1998, it offered the job to Richard Stearns, an experienced manager who had spent 23 years in strategic and marketing roles in Gillette Company and Parker Brothers Games, and as CEO of Lenox, the well-known tableware and gift company. As WV/US president, Stearns was responsible for all WV/US operations, which included fund-raising, advocacy, and international program development, each run by one of the five senior VPs reporting to him.

Revitalizing WV/US: Marketing, Metrics, and Money

Over the years, WV/US had remained the largest financial contributor to the partnership providing almost 50% of global revenues by 1998. "But the organization was missing opportunities and faltering in its operations," said Stearns. "In particular, our appeals had become costly and we were inefficient. I was given two key goals: increase revenues and lower overhead ratios." This ratio was the cash income raised divided by the cost of fund-raising. In 1998, it stood at around 3 to 1.

In 2000, Stearns hired Atul Tandon as Senior VP of Marketing. Like Stearns, he had come from the corporate sector, serving for over 20 years with Citibank in marketing. In WV/US, Tandon saw his primary objectives to build the brand and improve customer satisfaction. "I soon realized that I was in a fundamentally different world," he said. "When I asked, 'What is our bottom line? To whom are we accountable?' no one could answer." Furthermore, staff members were unable to describe their outputs and measures. "There were no profit and loss statements and people were unaware of our spending and the returns we were getting."

Tandon and Stearns reorganized the WV/US office, laying off a number of staff, and elevating innovators to senior positions. They replaced the traditional Direct Response Marketing Department with integrated Product and Channel Marketing Teams who worked with new Communications and Creative Teams to focus on the "key drivers" of marketing effectiveness: cost of donor acquisition, costs and methods of donor retention, and long-term donor value. They challenged these new teams to concentrate on growth through partnering, brand building, and new channels of recruiting and retaining donors. They found that child sponsorship, particularly the flagship $26 monthly program linking donors and sponsored children through regular two-way updates and letters, was the most effective means of raising funds. They also found that while donors were difficult to recruit, if they were properly cultivated, they were relatively easy to keep.

Marketing teams were now expected to be "research-driven" in defining what appealed to donors. They then worked with three new channel-specific sales teams to design products specifically for church groups, major donors, and Internet sales. Believing strongly in "learning to listen to the customer," Tandon allocated nearly 75% of the $50 million marketing budget to donor recruitment, retention, and communications. With no increases in marketing and communications allocations over a four-year period, Tandon and his team devoted themselves to increasing revenues while holding expenses flat. "We call it widening the jaws," said Tandon.

The results came quickly: double-digit growth every year for four years with an unchanged marketing budget. "Over those four years, we increased our cash income to fund-raising cost ratio from 3 to 1, first to 3.4 to 1, then to 4.1 to 1, and finally to 5.5 to 1," Tandon reported. Additionally, donor satisfaction increases as did name awareness in the core target markets – from 49% to 76% over three years. To evaluate WV/US's efforts more effectively, Stearns introduced a balanced scorecard measurement system. (See Exhibit 6 for copy of scorecard.) Tandon volunteered to make his marketing group as the guinea pig for the new system, explaining:

> We identified specific numbers-driven goals and a few subjective goals. Most revolved around measuring brand strength, brand awareness, and customer satisfaction. But I believe the most important driver is the customer satisfaction number. Ours is measured twice yearly by survey. We have increased satisfaction levels from 84% to 92% over the last thee years. We don't have a good benchmark in the nonprofit world, but, in the corporate sector, Amazon's customer satisfaction is the highest at 88%. So we are in the right ballpark.

Managing in the Partnership: All in the Family
In addition to running the operations at WV/US, Stearns sat on the Strategy Working Group (SWG), the key executive

decision-making body of the World Vision Partnership. Chaired by WVI president, Dean Hirsch, the SWG included 16 senior executives from throughout the Partnership. At first, working in WVI was not easy for Stearns. "I was bewildered by the lack of any real authority structure in the World Vision Partnership," he said. "I kept wondering who was in charge." He also reflected on the governance structure. "The International Board is truly representative. The U.S. appoints two of its 24 members and has a founder's chair. The other 21 are from other nations. Although we have financial influence by representing 50% of overall revenues, we hold only 12% of the political influence. This would be unthinkable in the corporate world."

Over time, Stearns recognized that the Partnership traded control and efficiency for richness of perspective and strength in local programming and fund-raising. "We are able to make our own decisions and set our own priorities. President Hirsch has no line authority over me . . . . He does not participate in my performance review and he issues no directives to me or any other CEO. But, through the SWG, we make joint decisions that benefit the global organization and our mission better than if any one of us acted alone."

PROGRAMMING IN THE PARTNERSHIP: THE AIDS HOPE INITIATIVE

By the late 1990s, the World Vision partnership was beginning to feel more stable. The ADP concept had made program delivery more effective, the child sponsorship fund-raising model had been refined, and the federal organization framework was helping to integrate the global network of World Vision entities. Yet while World Vision had been struggling to refine its internal operations, the impact of HIV/AIDS was changing the needs of those it served externally. The global pandemic had reached crisis levels in many parts of the world, but nowhere more than sub-Saharan Africa.

Recognizing the Need: Lessons for a Latecomer
Two months after joining World Vision, Rich Stearns went on a field trip to Uganda. Visiting a household of three boys, aged 11 to 13, who lived alone after being orphaned by AIDS, Stearns learned that an estimated 10 million African children were living in similar circumstances. When he asked what World Vision was doing about it, the

Exhibit 6 Balanced Scorecard for WV-US Marketing Department

Marketing & Communications
Level 1 Scorecard

Atul Tandon

Reporting Period: Q4 of FY03 (Jul, Aug, Sep)   Quarterly

Measure	Actual	Target	Variance (%)	Variance Flag	FY03--Q1 FY03 Actuals	FY03--Q1 FY02 Actuals	FY03--Q2 FY03 Actuals	FY03--Q2 FY02 Actuals	FY03--Q3 FY03 Actual	FY03--Q3 FY02 Actuals	FY03--Q4 FY03 Actual	FY03--Q4 FY02 Actuals
CHANGE HEARTS												
1 Media Impressions (in millions)	4,515	2,280	98%	●	625	570	2,717	1,880	3,230	2,815	4,515	3,445
INCREASE INVOLVEMENT												
2 Gross Sponsorship Assignments	144,613	182,941	-21%	■	43,139	44,751	82,473	89,921	116,700	129,514	144,613	169,028
3 Matrix Income ($1,000s)*	$8,797	$6,950	27%	●	$2,923	$3,514	$4,157	$4,507	$6,612	$6,070	$8,797	$6,795
4 Income ($1,000s)*	$229,007	$230,103	0%	◆	$60,054	$56,487	$114,404	$104,455	$171,997	$155,705	$229,161	$208,553
5 Sponsorship File Size	612,815	625,381	-2%	◆	594,216	555,325	601,842	564,575	610,636	574,131	612,815	581,874
6 Donor Involvement - Avg. Annual Giving	$296	$296	0%	●	$278	$271	$285	$276	$277	$276	$296	$280
INCREASE EFFECTIVENESS												
7 Expenses ($1,000s)*	$52,304	$53,975	3%	●	$14,920	$13,460	$28,912	$25,801	$40,453	$37,477	$52,304	$49,431
8 Sponsor Attrition Rate	16.2%	16.5%	2%	●	17.4%	19.5%	17.0%	18.5%	16.4%	17.7%	16.2%	17.4%
9 Donor Satisfaction	90.8%	N/A	N/A		N/A	N/A	90.3%	N/A	90.8%	N/A	90.8%	89.4%

Variance Thresholds

● Meets Goal
◆ <5% Adverse
■ >5% Adverse

* MAC Yield to Ministry (Revenues less Expenses) was better than previous year by $19.5 million (11.7%) and better than budget by $2.4 million

Metric:	Definition:
CHANGE HEARTS	
1 Media Impressions (in millions)	Number of Christian & Secular Media impressions through publication or broadcast story
INCREASE INVOLVEMENT	
2 Gross Sponsorship Assignments	Cum total gross sponsorship acquisitions (all channels except RM)
3 Matrix Income ($1,000s)	Income motivated by Marketing & Communications, but booked to other areas - Major Donor + Ethnic Mktg + Corp Partnership
4 Income ($1,000s)	Income generated by Marketing & Communications from all sources
5 Sponsorship File Size	# of Money Sponsorships Ending last period + Acquisitions - Cancels
6a Donor Involvement - Avg. Annual Giving	Rolling 12 mos giving / # donors (cash only for now, GIK to be added later)
INCREASE EFFECTIVENESS	
7 Expenses ($1,000s)	YTD Total Marketing & Communications Expenses
8 Sponsor Attrition Rate	# of money sponsorships that have not made a payment in the last 6 months/total money sponsorships 6 months prior
9 Donor Satisfaction	Donor Satisfaction Rating (Sponsorship Only)

Source: World Vision International Internal Documents

answer was, "Very little." Although he was new to the agency, he felt he had to speak out:

> When I was at Parker Brothers, we failed to realize that games were moving from the parlor table to the video screen. When new competitors came out with fast and interesting computer games, they stole 90% of the market from under our noses. This was what was happening to us with HIV/AIDS. We had developed top-notch skills at rural community organization, water systems, health, childcare, and economic regeneration and responded well to hurricanes, disasters, wars and other emergencies. But while all of this was exemplary, we were not prepared to face the unprecedented scale of devastation wrought by the AIDS pandemic.

With 58,000 people in Africa dying from AIDS each week—equal to the entire loss of American lives in Vietnam—Stearns felt there was a real chance that decades of progress by the development community would be rolled back. He began to speak more forcefully, telling his colleagues that they were building beautiful sand castles on the beach while an 80-foot high tidal wave was just off-shore. "I kept saying it for over two years, fully mindful that I did not know what specifically I was proposing to do about it," he recounted. He was supported by Bruce Wilkinson, senior vice president of his International Programs Group. But while other members of the partnership listened, Stearns felt that, to them, it was "just another woe to add to the list."

Then, in July 2000, Wilfred Mlay, African regional vice president gave a powerful presentation to the SWG. "AIDS is killing our people," he said. "It is devastating our work, our families, our staff. I really need your help." A few months later, when *Time* ran a cover story on the 10 million to 12 million estimated orphans in Africa caused by AIDS, Stearns circulated a memo to senior executives of the partnership asking, "Why, as a child-focused organization, are we not addressing the AIDS crisis?"

Mlay's appeal and Stearn's prodding prompted the SWG to appoint Bryant Myers, vice president for International Programs Strategy, to study WVI's commitment to the crisis. After speaking with a number of people throughout the partnership, he wrote a draft document suggesting that HIV/AIDS needed to be a priority for World Vision for the five reasons: It cared about children and was particularly concerned about the over 40 million children projected to lose one or both parents to HIV/AIDS by 2010; it had over 900,000 sponsored children in the 30 worst hit countries and nearly 2 million sponsored children at risk worldwide; it was investing almost $200 million a year in the 30 worst hit countries; its worldwide staff was at risk and many members were personally affected by HIV/AIDS in their own extended families; and as a Christian organization, it had a unique opportunity to share the hope of Christ to those affected by HIV/AIDS.

Launching the AIDS Hope Initiative

On World AIDS Day in December 2000, Dean Hirsch preempted a formal decision on the strategy by announcing that World Vision would launch a $30 million initiative to address AIDS. Believing that the moment was right and that some members were already moving forward, Hirsch pushed the Partnership into action. Over the following months, Myers prepared a plan entitled "The AIDS Hope Initiative." The plan outlined the need, identified the scope of the problem, and discussed its challenge to the efficacy of World Vision's work. It also categorized a series of programming approaches for high prevalence countries, medium prevalence countries, and the rest of World Vision's country programs.

Just before presenting the plan to the SWG at a meeting in Costa Rica in February 2001, Hirsch approached Ken Casey and asked him if he would lead the initiative. "I was surprised by the request," recalled Casey. "It was an entirely new and different task for me. I had spent six years as a senior line manager in operations for the U.S. organization. Now I would be taking on a key strategic role within the international office." For most of his eight years with WV-US, Casey had served as Senior Vice President for Fundraising and Programs. But, in 1999, Stearns' reorganization had left him a senior executive without a portfolio. "For about a year, I worked on special projects. They were rewarding and I was within the senior management team, but I was considering moving on."

As he thought about it, Casey decided that the project represented an interesting and worthwhile challenge. In March 2001, he assumed his new role as director of the AIDS Hope Initiative. He would report directly to Hirsch but continue to work out of the WV-US office in Seattle.

Assessing the Challenge

Casey returned to Seattle with an approved operating budget of approximately $750,000 but no staff. As he reviewed the existing document, he recognized the difficulty of his task:

> I began working off of the document that Bryant had prepared. Although it was good work, it had been devised almost entirely at the headquarters office. Essentially, I was being asked to implement an unprecedented worldwide program effort on perhaps the most controversial issue imaginable that would require new levels of coordination that we had never previously achieved. Yet there was no ownership or buy-in from the Regional VPs.

Casey understood that, within the partnership, the four Regional VPs (for Africa, Asia, Pacific, and Middle East/Eastern Europe) held a great deal of power over programs and operations. Not only did all of the National Directors report to them, they also provided strategy and leadership for their regions. In recent years, however, the National Offices had been pushed by the International Board to become more independent in their strategies and programs. Casey stated: "In our efforts to devolve autonomy to the national offices, we had worked for 10 years to develop viable governing boards for each one. But we also wanted them to be responsive to WVI's priorities through their link to the regional VPs. Because national directors were answerable to two masters, this could cause problems."

To build support, Casey began a six-month process of travel and discussion with the regional VPs and national directors to come up with a working model for the Hope Initiative. He wanted to make sure that the Initiative would remain true to its ideal, but also wanted to ensure that the ambitious fund-raising and programmatic objectives were realistic.

Resistance from Donors

Casey knew that funding such a big initiative would be a challenge, and hoped to implement a joint marketing effort across the Partnership offices, hopefully reaching out to new donors in the process. He also wanted the marketing effort to be well connected to the programs in the field. But almost from the outset, he encountered resistance from the marketing departments in the major partnership support offices. Stearns remembered:

> Our WV/US marketing people were very skeptical. They told us that any work with HIV/AIDS would never sell with our donors. Our top people in brand building told us that we have a very wholesome, child-focused image.

> People equate us helping children and families in need. If we start talking about AIDS, prostitutes, drug users, long-haul truckers, and sexuality, it will hurt our image.

WV-US commissioned a market survey among evangelical Christians and loyal donors in the United States. "It was devastating news," stated Casey. "We asked them if they would be willing to give to a respectable Christian organization to help children who lost both parents to AIDS. Only 7% said that they would definitely help while over 50% said probably not or definitely not. Surveys in Canada and Australia found the same thing. "It was stark and clear that our donors felt that AIDS sufferers somehow deserved their fate."

Beyond donor reaction, Casey dug deeper to understand the marketing organization's challenge. "Their incentives and targets for the year were based on the efficiency of their appeals," he said. "But by its very nature, this was going to be a costly appeal." Instead of returning a usual 4:1 or 5:1 ratio of revenues to expenses, the marketers felt that, in the beginning, any AIDS appeal would return something closer to 1:1. When Casey asked the heads of the Partnership Offices to adjust the targets for HIV/AIDS programs for their marketing teams, response was mixed. While Stearns convinced his board to remove the HIV/AIDS appeals from the normal cost ratio calculations for U.S. appeal, Canada, the United Kingdom, and several other key fund-raising countries were less willing to do so.

Resistance from the Field

As he focused on program implications, Casey's natural ally was Wilfred Mlay. As regional vice president for Africa, Mlay reported to Hirsch at WVI and was responsible for 25 national country offices with over 8,000 staff and a budget of $500 million. "My role is to help coordinate all programs, identify priorities in each country, develop strategy and articulate it to the Partnership," he said. To manage his domain, Mlay had divided Africa into three subregions, each headed by a director (based in Johannesburg, Dakar, and Nairobi) responsible for eight or nine countries.

The African Regional Office maintained a large number of technical specialists in programming areas such as micro-enterprise, health, child protection, and Christian ministry. "I have structured the African region differently from any of other regions. For example, in Asia, all the senior leaders share one office in Bangkok. But because it is difficult to travel and communicate, my senior leadership and technical teams are dispersed. And I want them to be where the action is happening."

Although he managed the African Region as he saw fit, Mlay also made use of services in the Partnership. "I am in charge, but have access to resources when needed. For example, we have some sophisticated protocols for emergency operations. If I put out the call for help, we will have a conference call within 5 hours. And I have access to a global rapid response team that can allocate $1 million within 72 hours, so I can promise that WV will be present at a crisis within 24 hours."

Mlay worked with the boards and advisory councils in his 26 national offices to implement WVI priorities. But while he held regular meetings with national directors and hosted conferences and forums to determine how to allocate his technical resources, he had only limited ability to determine the strategy of national programs. "The advisory councils and boards help us to connect to the local community and society," he said. "But I have a reserved seat on every board in Africa so World Vision management and local boards share the governance of our work." Managing the boards was a time-consuming task for Mlay who sometimes had to take action if a board went in a direction that WVI disapproved. "For example, we discovered that the head of one of our boards had a set of values that conflicted with those of the organization. We intervened and asked him to step down. Most of the board was against us, but we prevailed. There is a fine line between granting autonomy and maintaining standards."

Despite his ability to intervene when necessary, Mlay had long encouraged his national directors to determine their own goals and strategies through the ADP system. But now that he wanted to push AIDS/HIV programs, there was resistance. "There is a culture of silence around the issue," he said. "In Tanzania, entire families and villages are being wiped out by AIDS. We have grandmothers caring for ten and twelve children. The ADPs are strong, but people are ashamed to speak about it. This is especially true of church leaders."

Casey also reflected on the "phenomenon of denial" he encountered. On an early trip to Capetown, he spoke to a taxi driver who told him that his awareness of HIV/AIDS had not changed his lifestyle because it would not get him. "A few minutes later, he was describing how the trucking company for whom his sister worked had just adopted a new HR policy stating that employees could not attend more than three funerals per month," recalled Casey. "It was uncanny how he could hold both thoughts in his head and not make a connection. In the face of such clear evidence, even intelligent people did not want to recognize the crisis."

Casey described the response to his first six months in the field: "Program officers were working flat out on existing projects and we came in telling them that, while those are important, we want you to change your whole focus. In addition, most program officers were skilled in technical sectors such as water, education, and economic development. Few knew about HIV/AIDS work. Their practical response was, 'What can we really do about this?'"

Casey hired two teams of HIV/AIDS specialists, one in Uganda and one in Zambia, to create a "Models of Learning" program. He also hired a research associate to work out of the International Office (see Exhibit 7). Hoping to build an active learning tool for the rest of the field, they prepared models of programming that they hoped to make available to others. But early response from a number of national offices was muted. "In the face of the overwhelming need and workload, many felt that this was just the emphasis of the day," Casey explained. After all, it was not the first time that field offices had been asked to implement cross-organizational strategies as Myers recalled:

> In the mid-1990s, we embarked on a long and expensive process of rebranding. Many national offices plunged time and resources into the effort, but got little value out of it. And a subsequent initiative to move relief activities from the center out into the National Offices ran into difficulty trying to mix the cowboy culture of the relief teams with the slower culture of the development teams on the front lines. Not surprisingly, some national offices are wary of any new top-down initiative.

THE SOUTH AFRICAN CONFERENCE

In December of 2001, Casey released a first draft of the Hope Initiative matrix (see Exhibit 8 for a subsequent version), which had been developed over months of dialogue and meetings with key personnel from across the Partnership. It laid out the goals, beneficiaries, values, and key design principles for each of the three HIV/AIDS program areas: prevention, care, and advocacy. An

Exhibit 7   HOPE Initiative 2001 Organizational Structure

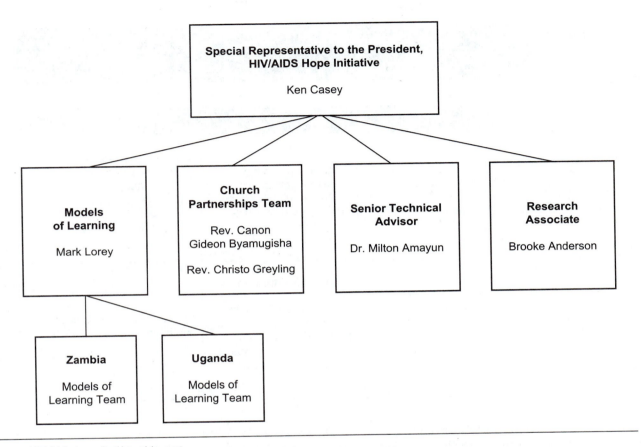

Source: World Vision International internal document.

accompanying document outlined actions that would seek to meet several goals. First, it would aim to prevent new cases of HIV/AIDS by contributing to the reduction of national incidence rates, especially among children, high-risk groups, and pregnant and lactating mothers. Second, it would aim to provide measurable improvements in the quality of care for children affected by HIV/AIDS, including those orphaned by AIDS, living with HIV-positive parents, and in households fostering AIDS orphans. Finally, it would advocate the adoption of public policy and programs that would minimize the spread of the disease and provide care for those living with or affected by HIV/AIDS.

On January 12, 2002, the real roll-out for the Hope Initiative was about to begin at a week-long High Prevalence Country Workshop held at a safari lodge in South Africa. Casey's goal was to bring together the national directors, senior program officers, and area development managers from the 17 African countries hardest hit by the crisis. He planned to ask them to tackle the HIV/AIDS problem with the same energy that they worked to bring communities clean water, education, and health care, food security, and economic development. "It was a make or break time for the initiative," said Casey. "Without their energy and buy-in, the initiative would only exist on paper."

Exhibit 8   HIV/AIDS Hope Initiative Program Matrix

	Prevention	Care	Advocacy
Overall Goal	The overall goal of the HIV/AIDS Hope Initiative is to reduce the global impact of HIV/AIDS through the enhancement and expansion of the World Vision programs and collaborations focused on HIV/AIDS prevention, care and advocacy.		
Track Goals	Make a significant contribution to the reduction of national HIV/AIDS prevalence rates	Achieve measurable improvements in the quality of life of children affected by HIV/AIDS	Encourage the adoption of policy and programs that minimize the spread of HIV/AIDS and maximize care for those living with or affected by HIV/AIDS
Target Groups	• Children, aged 5-15 years old • High risk population groups • Pregnant and lactating mothers	**Vulnerable Children** (living with, affected by and orphaned by HIV/AIDS, including parents and care-givers of vulnerable children)	Policy Makers (local, national, and international)
Values	Bring a Christian response to HIV/AIDS, one that reflects God's unconditional, compassionate love for all people and affirms each individual's dignity and worth.		
Key Program Design Principles	• Clear and measurable impact indicators • Integrated with key agencies and organizations in the country • Multi-sectoral in approach • Scaleable—the ability to impact a large number of people • Empower, engage, and equip the local church as a primary partner, as well as other faith-based organizations • Integrated with WV national office program strategies		

Source: World Vision International internal documents.